# Nineteenth-Century Literature Criticism

# Guide to Gale Literary Criticism Series

| For criticism on | You need these Gale series |
|---|---|
| Authors now living or who died after December 31, 1959 | *CONTEMPORARY LITERARY CRITICISM (CLC)* |
| Authors who died between 1900 and 1959 | *TWENTIETH-CENTURY LITERARY CRITICISM (TCLC)* |
| Authors who died between 1800 and 1899 | *NINETEENTH-CENTURY LITERATURE CRITICISM (NCLC)* |
| Authors who died between 1400 and 1799 | *LITERATURE CRITICISM FROM 1400 TO 1800 (LC)* <br><br> *SHAKESPEAREAN CRITICISM (SC)* |
| Authors who died before 1400 | *CLASSICAL AND MEDIEVAL LITERATURE CRITICISM (CMLC)* |
| Authors of books for children and young adults | *CHILDREN'S LITERATURE REVIEW (CLR)* |
| Black writers of the past two hundred years | *BLACK LITERATURE CRITICISM (BLC)* |
| Short story writers | *SHORT STORY CRITICISM (SSC)* |
| Poets | *POETRY CRITICISM (PC)* |
| Dramatists | *DRAMA CRITICISM (DC)* |
| Major authors from the Renaissance to the present | *WORLD LITERATURE CRITICISM, 1500 TO THE PRESENT (WLC)* |

*For criticism on visual artists since 1850, see*
**MODERN ARTS CRITICISM (MAC)**

ISSN 0732-1864

Volume 39

# Nineteenth-Century Literature Criticism

Excerpts from Criticism of the
Works of Novelists, Poets, Playwrights,
Short Story Writers, Philosophers, and Other
Creative Writers Who Died between 1800
and 1899, from the First Published Critical
Appraisals to Current Evaluations

**Joann Cerrito**
Editor

**Judith Galens**
**Tina Grant**
**Alan Hedblad**
**Jelena O. Krstović**
**Elisabeth Morrison**
**Lawrence J. Trudeau**
Associate Editors

**Gale Research Inc.** • DETROIT • WASHINGTON, D.C. • LONDON

## STAFF

Joann Cerrito, *Editor*

James P. Draper, Judith Galens, Tina Grant, Alan Hedblad, Jelena O. Krstović, Elisabeth Morrison, Joseph C. Tardiff, *Associate Editors*

Meggin M. Condino, James A. Edwards, Kathryn Horste, Anna J. Sheets, Brian J. St. Germain, *Assistant Editors*

Jeanne A. Gough, *Permissions & Production Manager*
Linda M. Pugliese, *Production Supervisor*
Donna Craft, Paul Lewon, Maureen Puhl, Camille Robinson, Jennifer VanSickle, Sheila Walencewicz, *Editorial Associates*

Sandra C. Davis, *Permissions Supervisor (Text)*
Maria L. Franklin, Josephine M. Keene, Michele Lonoconus, Denise Singleton, Kimberly F. Smilay, *Permissions Associates*
Jennifer A. Arnold, Brandy C. Merritt, Shalice Shah, *Permissions Assistants*

Margaret A. Chamberlain, *Permissions Supervisor (Pictures)*
Pamela A. Hayes, Keith Reed, *Permissions Associates*
Arlene Johnson, Barbara Wallace, *Permissions Assistants*

Victoria B. Cariappa, *Research Manager*
Maureen Richards, *Research Supervisor*
Robert S. Lazich, Mary Beth McElmeel, Tamara C. Nott, *Editorial Associates*
Kelly Hill, Donna Melnychenko, *Editorial Assistants*

Mary Beth Trimper, *Production Manager*
Catherine Kemp, *Production Assistant*

Cynthia Baldwin, *Art Director*
Nicholas Jakubiak, C. J. Jonik, Yolanda Y. Latham, *Desktop Publishers/Typesetters*

Library of Congress Catalog Card Number 84-643008
ISBN 0-8103-7978-3
ISSN 0732-1864

Printed in the United States of America
Published simultaneously in the United Kingdom
by Gale Research International Limited
(An affiliated company of Gale Research Inc.)
10 9 8 7 6 5 4 3 2 1

The trademark **ITP** is used under license.

# Contents

Preface  vii

Acknowledgments  xi

# Preface

Since its inception in 1981, *Nineteenth-Century Literature Criticism* has been a valuable resource for students and librarians seeking critical commentary on writers of this transitional period in world history. Designated an "Outstanding Reference Source" by the American Library Association with the publication of its first volume, *NCLC* has since been purchased by over 6,000 school, public, and university libraries. The series has covered more than 300 authors representing 26 nationalities and over 15,000 titles. No other reference source has surveyed the critical reaction to nineteenth-century authors and literature as thoroughly as *NCLC*.

## Scope of the Series

*NCLC* is designed to serve as introduction for students and advanced readers to the authors of the nineteenth century, and to the most significant interpretations of these authors' works. The great poets, novelists, short story writers, dramatists, and philosophers of this period are frequently studied in high school and college literature courses. By organizing and reprinting the enormous amount of commentary written on these authors, *NCLC* helps students develop valuable insight into literary history, promotes a better understanding of the texts, and sparks ideas for papers and assignments. Each entry in *NCLC* presents a comprehensive survey of an author's career or an individual work of literature and provides the user with a multiplicity of interpretations and assessments. Such variety allows students to pursue their own interests; furthermore, it fosters an awareness that literature is dynamic and responsive to many different opinions.

Every fourth volume of *NCLC* is devoted to literary topics that cannot be covered under the author approach used in the rest of the series. Such topics include literary movements, prominent themes in nineteenth-century literature, literary reaction to political and historical events, significant eras in literary history, prominent literary anniversaries, and the literatures of cultures that are often overlooked by English-speaking readers.

*NCLC* continues the survey of criticism of world literature begun by Gale's *Contemporary Literary Criticism (CLC)* and *Twentieth-Century Literary Criticism (TCLC),* both of which excerpt and reprint commentary on authors of the twentieth century. For additional information about *TCLC, CLC,* and Gale's other criticism series, users should consult the Guide to Gale Literary Criticism Series preceding the title page in this volume.

## Coverage

Each volume of *NCLC* is carefully compiled to present:

- criticism of authors, or literary topics, representing a variety of genres and nationalities
- both major and lesser-known writers and literary works of the period
- 7-10 authors or 4-6 topics per volume
- individual entries that survey critical response to each author's work or each topic in literary history, including early criticism to reflect initial reactions; later criticism to represent any rise or decline in reputation; and current retrospective analyses.

# Organization

An author entry consists of the following elements: author heading, biographical and critical introduction, list of principal works, excerpts of criticism (each preceded by an annotation and followed by a bibliographic citation), and a bibliography of further reading.

■ The **author heading** consists of the name under which the author most commonly wrote, followed by birth and death dates. If an author wrote consistently under a pseudonym, the pseudonym will be listed in the author heading and the real name given in parentheses on the first line of the biographical and critical introduction. Also located at the beginning of the introduction to the author entry are any name variations under which an author wrote, including transliterated forms for authors whose languages use nonroman alphabets.

■ The **biographical and critical introduction** outlines the author's life and career, as well as the critical issues surrounding his or her work. References are provided to past volumes of *NCLC*.

■ Most *NCLC* entries include **portraits** of the author. Many entries also contain reproductions of materials pertinent to an author's career, including manuscript pages, title pages, dust jackets, letters, and drawings, as well as photographs of important people, places, and events in an author's life.

■ The list of **principal works** is chronological by date of first book publication and identifies the genre of each work. In the case of foreign authors with both foreign-language publications and English translations, the title and date of the first English-language edition are given in brackets. Unless otherwise indicated, dramas are dated by first performance, not first publication.

■ **Criticism** is arranged chronologically in each author entry to provide a perspective on changes in critical evaluation over the years. All titles of works by the author featured in the entry are printed in boldface type to enable the user to easily locate discussion of particular works. Also for purposes of easier identification, the critic's name and the publication date of the essay are given at the beginning of each piece of criticism. Unsigned criticism is preceded by the title of the journal in which it appeared. Publication information (such as publisher names and book prices) and parenthetical numerical references (such as footnotes or page and line references to specific editions of works) have been deleted at the editors' discretion to provide smoother reading of the text.

■ Critical excerpts are prefaced by **annotations** providing the reader with information about both the critic and the criticism that follows. Included are the critic's reputation, individual approach to literary criticism, and particular expertise in an author's works. Also noted are the relative importance of a work of criticism, the scope of the excerpt, and the growth of critical controversy or changes in critical trends regarding an author. In some cases, these annotations cross-reference excerpts by critics who discuss each other's commentary.

■ A complete **bibliographic citation** designed to facilitate location of the original essay or book follows each piece of criticism.

■ An annotated list of **further reading** appearing at the end of each author entry suggests secondary sources on the author. In some cases it includes essays for which the editors could not obtain reprint rights.

# Cumulative Indexes

■ Each volume of *NCLC* contains a cumulative **author index** listing all authors who have appeared in Gale's Literary Criticism Series, along with cross-references to such biographical series as

*Contemporary Authors* and *Dictionary of Literary Biography*.  Useful for locating authors within the various series, this index is particularly valuable for those authors who are identified with a certain period but who, because of their death dates, are placed in another, or for those authors whose careers span two periods.  For example, Fyodor Dostoevsky is found in *NCLC,* yet Leo Tolstoy, another major nineteenth-century Russian novelist, is found in *TCLC* because he died after 1899.

- Each *NCLC* volume includes a cumulative **nationality index** which lists all authors who have appeared in *NCLC*, arranged alphabetically under their respective nationalities, as well as Topics volume entries devoted to particular national literatures.

- Each new volume in Gale's Literary Criticism Series includes a cumulative **topic index**, which lists all literary topics treated in *NCLC, TCLC, LC 1400-1800*, and the *CLC* Yearbook.

- Each new volume of *NCLC*, with the exception of the Topics volumes, contains a **title index** listing the titles of all literary works discussed in the volume.  In response to numerous suggestions from librarians, Gale has also produced a **special paperbound edition** of the *NCLC* title index.  This annual cumulation lists all titles discussed in the series since its inception and is issued with the first volume of *NCLC* published each year.  Additional copies of the index are available on request.  Librarians and patrons have welcomed this separate index: it saves shelf space, is easy to use, and is recyclable upon receipt of the following year's cumulation.  Titles discussed in the Topics volume entries are not included in the *NCLC* cumulative index.

## Citing *Nineteenth-Century Literature Criticism*

When writing papers, students who quote directly from any volume in Gale's Literary Criticism Series may use the following general forms to footnote reprinted criticism. The first example pertains to material drawn from periodicals, the second to material reprinted from books:

[1]T.S. Eliot, "John Donne," *The Nation and Athenaeum*, 33 (9 June 1923), 321-32; excerpted and reprinted in *Literature Criticism from 1400-1800,* Vol. 10, ed. James E. Person, Jr. (Detroit: Gale Research, 1989), pp. 28-9.

[2]Clara G. Stillman, *Samuel Butler: A Mid-Victorian Modern* (Viking Press, 1932); excerpted and reprinted in *Twentieth-Century Literary Criticism,* Vol. 33, ed. Paula Kepos (Detroit: Gale Research, 1989), pp. 43-5.

## Suggestions Are Welcome

In response to suggestions, several features have been added to *NCLC* since the series began, including annotations to excerpted criticism, a cumulative index to authors in all Gale literary criticism series, entries devoted to criticism on a single work by a major author, more extensive illustrations, and a title index listing all literary works discussed in the series.

Readers who wish to suggest authors or topics to appear in future volumes, or who have other suggestions, are cordially invited to write the editors.

# Acknowledgments

The editors wish to thank the copyright holders of the excerpted criticism included in this volume, the permissions managers of many book and magazine publishing companies for assisting us in securing reprint rights, and Anthony Bogucki for assistance with copyright research. We are also grateful to the staffs of the Detroit Library, the Library of Congress, the University of Detroit Library, Wayne State University Purdy/Kresge Library Complex, and the University of Michigan Libraries for making their resources available to us. Following is a list of the copyright holders who have granted us permission to reprint material in this volume of *NCLC*. Every effort has been made to trace copyright, but if omissions have been made, please let us know.

**COPYRIGHTED EXCERPTS IN *NCLC*, VOLUME 39, WERE REPRINTED FROM THE FOLLOWING PERIODICALS:**

*Ball State University,* v. XIX, Winter, 1978. © 1978 Ball State University. Reprinted by permission of the publisher.—*Bulletin of Hispanic Studies,* v. XL, 1963. © copyright 1963 Liverpool University Press. Reprinted by permission of the publisher.—*ELH,* v. 48, Spring, 1981. Copyright © 1981 by The Johns Hopkins University Press. All rights reserved, Reprinted by permission of the publisher.—*Encounter,* v. LXVI, January, 1986. © 1968 by Encounter Ltd.—*ESQ: A Journal of the American Renaissance,* v. 19, 1973 for "Point of View in 'The House of the Seven Gables' " by Sheldon W. Liebman. Reprinted by permission of the publisher and the author.—*Essays by Divers Hands,* n.s. v. XXXIV, 1966 for "Disraeli the Novelist" by Robert Blake. © Robert Blake 1966. Reprinted by permission of the author.—*I & L,* v. IV, September-October, 1983. Copyright © 1983, Institute for the Study of Ideologies and Literature. Reprinted by permission of the publisher.—*The Journal of English and Germanic Philology,* v. LXXIX, April, 1980 for "Schiller's Concept of the Sublime and Its Pertinence to 'Don Carlos' and 'Maria Stuart' " by Ellis Finger; v. 86, April, 1982 for "The Faces of Power in the Poetry of Friedrich Schiller" by Margaret T. Peischl. © 1980, 1982 by the Board of Trustees of the University of Illinois. Both reprinted by permission of the publisher and the respective authors.—*Journal of Popular Culture,* v. 19, Winter, 1985. Copyright © 1985 by Ray Browne. Reprinted by permission of the publisher.—*Modern Language Forum,* v. XX, September, 1965.—*Modern Philology,* v. 56, February, 1959 for "The Function of Dance in the Melodramas of Guilbert de Pixerécourt" by O. G. Brockett. © 1959, renewed 1987 by The University of Chicago. Reprinted by permission of the University of Chicago Press and the author.—*PMLA,* v. LXXXII, December, 1967. Copyright © 1967 by the Modern Language Association of America. Reprinted by permission of the Modern Language Association of America.—*Prairie Schooner,* v. XXXVIII, Summer, 1964. © 1964 by University of Nebraska Press. Reprinted from *Prairie Schooner* by permission of the University of Nebraska Press.—*Romance Notes,* v. XVIII, Winter, 1977. Reprinted by permission of the publisher.—*South Atlantic Quarterly,* v. LII, October, 1953. Copyright 1953, renewed 1981 by Duke University Press, Durham, NC. Reprinted with permission of the publisher.—*Studies in Romanticism,* v. 11, Spring, 1972. Copyright © 1972 by the Trustees of Boston University. Reprinted by permission of the publisher.—*The Times Literary Supplement,* n. 3671, December 8, 1972. © The Times Supplements Limited 1972. Reproduced from *The Times Literary Supplement* by permission.

**COPYRIGHTED EXCERPTS IN *NCLC*, VOLUME 39, WERE REPRINTED FROM THE FOLLOWING BOOKS:**

Ahmad, Aijaz. From an introduction to *Ghazals of Ghalib: Versions from the Urdu.* By Aijaz Ahmad and others, edited by Aijaz Ahmad. Columbia University Press, 1971. Copyright © 1971 Columbia University Press, New York. Reprinted with the permission of the publisher.—Ali, Ahmed. From an introduction to *Ghalib: Two Essays.* By Ahmed Ali and Alessandro Bausani. Istituto Italiano Per il Medio ed Estremo Oriente, 1969. All rights reserved. Reprinted by permission of the publisher.—Bausani, Alessandro. From "Ghālib's Persian Poetry," in *Ghalib the Poet and His Age.* Edited by Ralph Russell. George Allen & Unwin, 1972. © George Allen & Unwin, 1972. All

# Benjamin Disraeli

## 1804-1881

English novelist and essayist.

For further discussion of Disraeli's works, see *NCLC,* volume 2.

### INTRODUCTION

Acknowledged as the originator of the political novel genre, Disraeli was also a unique and remarkable figure of Victorian England. In spite of numerous obstacles, including prevalent anti-Semitism and a bias on the part of aristocrats against members of the middle class, Disraeli ascended to the highest social and political circles in a career that culminated with his election to Prime Minister in 1868. As a literary figure, Disraeli is best known for his political trilogy of the 1840s, comprising the novels *Coningsby, Sybil,* and *Tancred.* The trilogy celebrates England's aristocracy while also recounting the social ills brought about by the Industrial Revolution.

Disraeli was born to Maria and Isaac D'Israeli in a middle-class London neighborhood. Although the family was Jewish, Disraeli's father broke from Judaism and had his children baptized as Anglicans; throughout his life Disraeli maintained an interest in all religions, finding his Jewish heritage in particular to be a source of spiritual value. He grew up in a home filled with literary activity—the family library was extensive and his father was a respected and well-liked author and critic. Disraeli's formal education was brief: he went to private schools for a time, but then his father decided to instruct him at home, hoping to prepare him for a career in law. Although he developed political aspirations at an early age, Disraeli disliked legal pursuits, preferring instead to further his interest in literature. As a young man, he invested in several ambitious projects designed to endow him with fame and fortune but which instead resulted in the accumulation of enormous debts that plagued him for years. In an attempt to alleviate these debts, Disraeli wrote his first novel, *Vivian Grey,* which portrays the manners and mores of upper-class English society. Published anonymously, the work caused an immediate sensation and was quite popular. When it was discovered that the author was not actually a member of the aristocracy, but a middle-class Jewish citizen, Disraeli became the object of bitter attacks from London literary figures. After the *Vivian Grey* controversy, Disraeli was befriended by fellow novelist Edward Bulwer-Lytton, who helped him gain entrance to the fashionable society that had previously despised him. Disraeli, operating under the maxim that "affectation is better than wit," earned a reputation as a dandy with his unusual behavior and flamboyant appearance. While his eccentricity proved entertaining in London's social circles, it did not assist him in realizing

his political ambitions, and he soon began to modify his conduct.

In 1837 Disraeli was elected to Parliament and soon thereafter assumed leadership of the Young England movement. This group, which advocated a new direction for the conservative Tory party, espoused the preservation of the monarchy and the privileged class, compassion for the poor, and a return to the religious devotion of ages past. During the next decade, Disraeli fictionalized these tenets in *Coningsby, Sybil,* and *Tancred.* In 1847 he was chosen as leader of the Tory party in the House of Commons, a position he retained for over twenty years. He served as Prime Minister for a short time in 1868, and was elected to that position again in 1874. For most of this time, Disraeli devoted himself solely to politics, publishing no fiction after the Young England trilogy until *Lothair* in 1870. He retired from public life in 1880 and published his last novel, *Endymion,* that same year. He had only completed a few chapters of a novel that parodied the life of his political nemesis, William Gladstone, when he died in 1881.

Disraeli began writing fiction at a time when England was experiencing increased social mobility; an influx of money and the acquisition of land was helping middle-class citizens become landed gentry. Living amidst these developments, Disraeli experimented with a fashionable literary genre known as the "silver fork" novel, which featured highly romantic depictions of aristocratic life and which served as social guidebooks for parvenus. Frequently these novels, like Disrael's *Vivian Grey* and *The Young Duke,* contained character sketches of well-known public figures and required keys to decipher the characters' real-life counterparts. Disraeli also experimented with a number of other genres, including poetry and drama. Robert Blake, an eminent Disraeli biographer, has succinctly and pointedly assessed the author's achievement in these literary fields: Disraeli "produced an epic poem, unbelievably bad, and a five-act blank verse tragedy, if possible worse."

With *Coningsby,* Disraeli infused the novel genre with political sensibility, espousing the belief that England's future as a world power depended not on the complacent old guard, but on youthful, idealistic politicians. This novel was followed by *Sybil,* which was less idealistic than *Coningsby* in its examination of the vast economic and social disparity between the privileged and working classes. Completing Disraeli's political novel trilogy was *Tancred,* in which the author advocated the restoration of the Anglican church to a position of spiritual preeminence in England. Disraeli rounded out his literary career with *Lothair* and *Endymion,* the former a novel of political life and a commentary on the Roman Catholic Church and the latter a concluding statement of his economic and political policies.

Although critics have acknowledged that romantic elements can be found in all of Disraeli's works, his early novels particularly reflect that influence. Daniel Schwarz has suggested that "as an outsider, as a man who savoured his own feelings and sought unusual sensations, the youthful Disraeli saw himself as an heir to Byron and Shelley." The young heroes of his novels frequently travel to mysterious lands in search of adventure and romance, and they often consult an older man whose wisdom is of a prophetic, even mystical nature. Commentators have also discussed how Disraeli's political philosophy heavily influenced the fictional events in his novels, observing that while the early works reflect a youthful idealism, the later ones show evidence of a more mature humanitarian concern. The cumulative effect of these insights, critics have maintained, make Disraeli's novels exceptionally valuable both as highly original works of art and as important reflections of the changes that took place during the Victorian age.

Commentators have also argued that stylistically Disraeli's prose reveals a sparkling wit and colorful imagination, as well as a skillful use of irony, deft psychological analysis, and the creative depiction of aristocratic mores and fashions. However, supporters and detractors alike have acknowledged that certain stylistic flaws cannot be ignored. They cite clumsy prose and poorly constructed plots as particularly weak elements of Disraeli's novels, as well as his failure to convey emotions sincerely and to describe working-class life and poverty convincingly. Furthermore, Disraeli has been censured for what some consider the unwieldy, rambling nature of his novels, but Sch-

warz has defended the author by asserting that "reading Disraeli's novels . . . is more like moving from room to room in a large museum than studying a single painting for hours."

## PRINCIPAL WORKS

*Vivian Grey*   (novel)  1826
*The Voyage of Captain Popanilla*   (satire)  1828
*The Young Duke*   (novel)  1831
*Contarini Fleming: A Psychological Autobiography* (novel)  1832
*The Wondrous Tale of Alroy. The Rise of Iskander* (novel and short story)  1832
*The Revolutionary Epick*   (poem)  1834
*A Year at Hartlebury; or, The Election*  [published with his sister Sarah, under the pseudonyms Cherry and Fair Star]   (novel)  1834
*Henrietta Temple: A Love Story*   (novel)  1836
*Venetia; or, The Poet's Daughter*   (novel)  1837
*The Tragedy of Count Alarcos*   (drama)  1839
*Coningsby; or, The New Generation*   (novel)  1844
*Sybil; or, The Two Nations*   (novel)  1845
*Tancred; or, The New Crusade*   (novel)  1847
*Lothair*   (novel)  1870
*Endymion*   (novel)  1880
*Whigs and Whiggism: Political Writings*   (essays)  1913

---

### Benjamin Disraeli   (essay date 1849)

[*Here, in the preface to the fifth edition of* Coningsby, *Disraeli explains his political and religious motivations for writing the first novel of his Young England political trilogy.*]

**Coningsby** was published in the year 1844. The main purpose of its writer was to vindicate the just claims of the Tory party to be the popular political confederation of the country; a purpose which he had, more or less, pursued from a very early period of life. The occasion was favourable to the attempt. The youthful mind of England had just recovered from the inebriation of the great Conservative triumph of 1841, and was beginning to inquire what, after all, they had conquered to preserve. It was opportune, therefore, to show that Toryism was not a phrase, but a fact; and that our political institutions were the embodiment of our popular necessities. This the writer endeavoured to do without prejudice, and to treat of events and characters of which he had some personal experience, not altogether without the impartiality of the future.

It was not originally the intention of the writer to adopt the form of fiction as the instrument to scatter his suggestions, but, after reflection, he resolved to avail himself of a method which, in the temper of the times, offered the best chance of influencing opinion.

In considering the Tory scheme, the author recognised in the CHURCH the most powerful agent in the previous development of England, and the most efficient means of that renovation of the national spirit at which he aimed. The Church is a sacred corporation for the promulgation and maintenance in Europe of certain Asian principles, which, although local in their birth, are of divine origin, and of universal and eternal application.

In asserting the paramount character of the ecclesiastical polity and the majesty of the theocratic principle, it became necessary to ascend to the origin of the Christian Church, and to meet in a spirit worthy of a critical and comparatively enlightened age, the position of the descendants of that race who were the founders of Christianity. The modern Jews had long laboured under the odium and stigma of mediæval malevolence. In the dark ages, when history was unknown, the passions of societies, undisturbed by traditionary experience, were strong, and their convictions, unmitigated by criticism, were necessarily fanatical. The Jews were looked upon in the middle ages as an accursed race, the enemies of God and man, the especial foes of Christianity. No one in those days paused to reflect that Christianity was founded by the Jews; that its Divine Author, in his human capacity, was a descendant of King David; that his doctrines avowedly were the completion, not the change, of Judaism; that the Apostles and the Evangelists, whose names men daily invoked, and whose volumes they embraced with reverence, were all Jews; that the infallible throne of Rome itself was established by a Jew; and that a Jew was the founder of the Christian Churches of Asia.

The European nations, relatively speaking, were then only recently converted to a belief in Moses and in Christ; and, as it were, still ashamed of the wild deities whom they had deserted, they thought they atoned for their past idolatry by wreaking their vengeance on a race to whom, and to whom alone, they were indebted for the Gospel they adored.

In vindicating the sovereign right of the Church of Christ to be the perpetual regenerator of man, the writer thought the time had arrived when some attempt should be made to do justice to the race which had founded Christianity.

The writer has developed in another work (*Tancred*) the views respecting the great house of Israel which he first intimated in *Coningsby.* No one has attempted to refute them, nor is refutation possible; since all he has done is to examine certain facts in the truth of which all agree, and to draw from them irresistible conclusions which prejudice for a moment may shrink from, but which reason cannot refuse to admit. (pp. vii-ix)

> *Benjamin Disraeli, in a preface to his* Coningsby, or the New Generation, *fifth edition, Longmans, Green, and Co., 1849, pp. vii-ix.*

## George Saintsbury   (essay date 1886)

[*Saintsbury has been called the most influential English literary historian and critic of the late nineteenth and early twentieth centuries. As a critic of novels, he maintained that "the novel has nothing to do with any beliefs, with any convictions, with any thoughts in the strict sense, except as mere garnishings. Its substance must al-ways be life not thought, conduct not belief, the passions not the intellect, manners and morals not creeds and theories. . . . The novel is . . . mainly and firstly a criticism of life." In the following excerpt from an essay originally published in* The Magazine of Art *in 1886, Saintsbury discusses Disraeli's career both as novelist and as statesman. With regard to Disraeli's novels, he suggests that in each work the individual parts exceed the whole in terms of quality and interest.*]

[Disraeli] had little or no history out of politics and literature, and the first being here in a manner 'taboo,' and only to be dealt with indirectly and in the way of general remarks on his character, his literary work may justly receive some particular attention. It is unfortunate that, while that work in fiction has been collected in an accessible and satisfactory manner, some of his political and miscellaneous writings have never been reprinted at all; while none are accessible except in fragmentary and uncoordinated form. The reproach ought to be removed, and the addition of some half-dozen volumes to the Hughenden edition of the novels would remove it. We should then have a uniform collection of literary work quite unique in character. It has been frequently objected to the authors of the present century that they are 'not quotable'; that the jewels five words long, which they contain, from the point of view of thought, as well as from that of style, are conspicuously few as compared with those of former ages, when the intense mass of the production, both of the whole period and of separate authors, is considered. This reproach may be true: there is, at any rate, some truth in it. But it is not true of Mr. Disraeli. The excellence of his separate phrases, of his epigrams, of his maxims of life, perhaps contrasts, and certainly has for the most part been thought to contrast, with the inequality and disappointingness of his works as wholes. Again, there is some truth in this. Except *The Infernal Marriage* I do not know any work of Lord Beaconsfield's which is entirely *par sibi.* In that respect even *Ixion* is inferior; and if the author had done more work of this kind he would have equalled (as it is, he has very nearly equalled in *The Infernal Marriage*) the author of the incomparable volume which begins with *Babouc,* and ends with *Le Taureau Blanc.* In a very different way, I think, *Henrietta Temple* may be called a masterpiece, though it is a masterpiece, of course, in a conventional style, and played upon few strings; in fact, upon only one. Of all the others, from *Vivian Grey* to *Endymion,* a critic, that is to say a person who does not indulge in indiscriminate superlatives, must speak with certain allowances. *Vivian Grey* itself is a marvel of youthful brilliancy, but the brilliancy is decidedly youthful. *The Young Duke* contains one scene, the gambling party, which is not inferior to anything of the kind in fiction; but the author's apology for it as 'a picture rather of fleeting manners than of perennial character' is its best description as a whole. *Contarini Fleming* is, no doubt, a book of great power, and I know critics, whom I respect, who rank it first of all the novels. But I suspect that, to rank thus, it ought to be read in youth; and by an accident I happen never to have read it myself till middle age, though I had long known all the others. *Alroy,* good of its kind, belongs to a kind which must be better than good to be first-rate. *Popanilla* is inferior to *The Infernal Marriage* and *Ixion.* For *Venetia,* I have myself a peculiar affection, and it seems to me (contrary, I believe, to the general opinion) a very happy instance of the peculiar faculty which Mr. Disraeli had in common with all the great writers who have woven real characters into the characters of novels—the faculty of giving a certain original twist to the borrowed personality. Of the trilogy, I prefer *Sybil* to *Coningsby* and *Tancred,* despite the unmatched political portraits of the second and the picturesque imagination of the third. I should call *Sybil* Mr. Disraeli's best novel, a judgment which is not incompatible with the judgment above given, that *Henrietta Temple* is a masterpiece; and finally, running contrary to the general judgment once more, I should prefer *Endymion* to *Lothair.* But in all these books (except *Henrietta Temple,* and not excepting *Sybil* ) the parts surpass the whole, and even make the reader lose sight of the whole. The inimitable social and personal judgments, the admirable epigrams, the detached phrases and scenes that bring their individual subjects before the eye as by a flash of lightning, dwarf or obscure the total impression. No doubt the author had definite purposes in writing all, or at least most of them, but the purpose is not the chief thing that impresses itself, nor are the characters, still less the plot, or what does duty for a plot, which those characters combine (*tant bien que mal,* and it must be confessed quite as often *mal* as *bien*) to work out.

For the present purpose, however, the chief thing is to see what light these books and their author's other writings give us on his character, and on that career. Undoubtedly the light which they give is not small. Perhaps the most remarkable illumination of all is that thrown by their combination of Voltairean wit with a singular imaginativeness, political and other, a considerable tendency to sentiment, and a distinct belief in ideals. Voltaire himself never wrote anything in his own peculiar style much superior to the description of the Elysians; but a Voltaire who could write *Tancred* or *Henrietta Temple* would have been (if Mr. Disraeli had not shown it in fact) an inconceivable thing. So, again, there is the other odd mixture (not the same by any means, though also to be illustrated from Voltaire) of a proneness to foppery of various kinds, combined with the keenest and most cynical delight in satirizing the foppery of others. If there is one thing more noteworthy than Lord Beaconsfield's famous inclination to 'upholstery,' it is the certainty that Lord Beaconsfield must have known and laughed at this tendency himself.

One of the most interesting subjects of the whole life is Mr. Disraeli's connection with the Young England movement. The famous speech at the Manchester Athenæum, with *Sybil* and other documents, has naturally caused him—indeed, did naturally cause him at the time—to be regarded as a leader, if not the leader, of the whole movement. Yet it is no secret that the invention, not merely of the name (that required no very great ability after Young Ireland and Young France) but of the thing, is attributed, by many people who ought to know, to Monckton Milnes. A year or two ago I wrote something in one of the magazines on Young England—a something which did not pretend to any esoteric knowledge, and merely dealt with the generally known facts. The next time that I met Lord Houghton he said to me, 'I wish you had told me that you were

going to write that. I could have set you right on a great many things which nobody knows now except Lord John Manners.' I pointed out to him that he could give the information at first hand a great deal better than I could possibly do at second, and that he ought to give it. 'Well,' he said, 'I did think of writing something, but I am too old, and it is too much trouble.' Let it be hoped that his literary executors will find that his first thoughts bore some fruit. The only point in the rest of the conversation which has relevance here was the remark, 'He (Disraeli) knew nothing at all about it at first: he came in afterwards'; which, indeed, was already pretty generally known. It hardly detracts from Mr. Disraeli's genius that he did come in afterwards, and that, despite that drawback, he gave the school by far the most important literary and historical monuments that it is likely to have. As concerns Mr. Disraeli himself, the Young England matter, interesting as it is, is chiefly noteworthy as illustrating the rapidity and success with which he would grasp any contemporary movement that showed signs of contributing to the general tendency which he strove to impress on the nation. His whole life, his whole work, is full of such indications. The anonymous *Wit and Wisdom of Lord Beaconsfield* (which, though no one who reads it must fancy that he has exhausted the subject, is both a very useful introduction to that subject and a very convenient bird's-eye view of it to one who has quartered it over) will show how admirably he carried out the system. It will show, also, what a master of both wit and wisdom was lost in him. The spirit of epigramatizing occasionally led him, like all masters of epigram, into odd places. I never met any man of brains who was prepared to endorse the matter of all Mr. Disraeli's propositions. But, then, I never met any man of brains who could produce an even appreciable number of propositions which he could endorse from some of Mr. Disraeli's rivals. And the great charm of the book, which may be taken as a fair representation of the man, is that it is never *bête*. Of how many statesmen of our days can we say the same?

There remains, of course, the stale calumny, which must be noticed here, because it forms part of all hostile and most neutral criticisms of our subject, that Lord Beaconsfield was 'an adventurer.' The more intelligent persons who speak about the political adventures of Lord Beaconsfield are, naturally, not touched by the contempt which must fall on the precious phrase which has been briefed to them. They are convinced that Lord Beaconsfield was an adventurer, exactly to the same extent as Mr. Serjeant Buzfuz was convinced that Mr. Pickwick was a Lothario and a scoundrel. But the dupes, the platform orators, the rag and tag of the believers in the adventurer theory, what is to be said of them?

Lord Beaconsfield was an adventurer in politics in very nearly the same sense Mr. Gladstone is an adventurer, and as Canning was. He was not nearly so much of an adventurer as Burke, and he was not very much more of one than Mr. Pitt. That is to say, Mr. Disraeli was not cradled and rocked and dandled into legislatorhood; he had no political sponsors in English politics, and he did not belong to any of the great houses which have governed Great Britain, on the whole for Great Britain's good, during the last few hundred years. On the other hand, he was so little of an adventurer that he entirely lacked, and never attempted to gain, the adventitious aids to political success which all the four distinguished persons above-mentioned possessed. He did not come into public life as a nominee of a great man like Mr. Gladstone and Canning, or as a useful 'devil' like Burke, or as a freelance, subsidized by party hatred to a great minister, like Pitt. There is no Duke of Newcastle, there is no Marquess of Rockingham, there is no Duchess of Marlborough, in Lord Beaconsfield's career. He fought the fight with a barely sufficient independence of property, and with a great deal more than sufficient independence of character. It is a subject of some amusement to the critics of his detractors that these detractors, at the very moment that they decry Mr. Disraeli as an adventurer, quote with pride and joy the heartburnings of great Tory magnates over his friendship with their sons, and the flings of Tory members of Parliament at the gradual progress of this astonishing *autarkes.* What I wish to point out is that in English, we don't call that kind of success the success of an adventurer; we call it the success of a genius.

Let us, to conclude, sum up the simple facts of what this adventurer did. Without great fortune, without patronage, without popular agitation, without the popular subscription of money which two of his famous contemporaries, Cobden and O'Connell, did not disdain, he raised himself from a very ordinary, though not mean, station to the Prime Ministership of England, and to something which has been mistaken by men not altogether fools for the arbitership of Europe. I do not mention his earldom, because that has been attained by quite otherguess sort of persons, and because it has been suspected that at least one part of Mr. Disraeli's reasons for accepting it was good-humoured delight in feeling that the fact of his acceptance made a similar acceptance by other people, who would really have liked it much more, a political impossibility. As to what he did for England, we get once again into contested matter. Let it only be said what the men before referred to, some of whom have not been deemed fools, *thought* he did for England. They thought—and it would appear have not ceased to think after seven twelvemonths and a day—that he raised the country once more to its proper position among European nations, after a generation of backsliding; that he put it in a state to maintain, if it chose, that position; that he ranked as a kind of pacific Wellington, as a bloodless Marlborough, as a restorer of English honour after a long eclipse. Very likely they were wrong: on that point it would be improper to offer the least opinion here. But who else that can be mentioned has ever spread such an opinion of himself and his actions not among the thirty millions 'mostly fools,' but among the thousands or hundreds, some, at least, of whom are most certainly not foolish?

I was walking not long ago with a friend of mine from whose society I find it difficult to cut myself off, despite the extraordinary and most provoking difficulty of finding out exactly what he means. The subject of *Judenhetze* had somehow or other turned up, and I remarked, perhaps rashly, 'After all they have given us the greatest poet of this century.' 'Yes,' he said, 'and they have given us the greatest statesman too. Anybody with ordinary talents can

direct a development. It is not everybody that can arrest a decay.' I daresay we were both talking nonsense: yet there are moments when I doubt it. (pp. 176-82)

> *George Saintsbury, "Disraeli: A Portrait," in his* A Saintsbury Miscellany: Selections from His Essays and Scrap Books, *Oxford University Press, Inc., 1947, pp. 175-82.*

---

**Leslie Stephen assessing Disraeli's works:**

[His novels] have the faults of juvenile performances: they are too gaudy; the author has been tempted to turn aside too frequently in search of some brilliant epigram; he has mistaken bombast for eloquence, and mere flowery brilliance for warmth of emotion. But we might hope that longer experience and more earnest purpose might correct such defects. Alas! in the year of their publication, Mr Disraeli first entered Parliament. His next works comprised the trilogy, where the artistic aim has become subordinate to the political or biological; and some thirty years of parliamentary labours led to **Lothair,** of which it is easiest to assume that it is a practical joke on a large scale, or a prolonged burlesque upon Mr Disraeli's own youthful performances. May one not lament the degradation of a promising novelist into a Prime Minister?

*Leslie Stephen, in his* Hours in a Library, *Smith, Elder & Co., 1876.*

---

## Louis Cazamian    (essay date 1903)

[*A noted French literary scholar, Cazamian has published histories of English and French literature. In the following excerpt taken from* Le roman social en Angleterre, *which was first published in French in 1903 and translated into English in 1973, Cazamian presents a pioneering study of Disraeli's political and literary career. The critic concludes that the novels of Disraeli's Young England trilogy—*Coningsby, Sybil, *and* Tancred—*possess value not only as literary works, but also as historical documents that convey the political, social, and religious attitudes and concerns of mid-nineteenth-century England.*]

Disraeli's social novels have a distinctive representative value. The subject matter of the books gives them historical interest, as does their influence, which appears in their association with a powerful intellectual movement. In keeping with their author's personality, they are highly individual. The mental process which led him to social Toryism offers no illustration of the ordinary Englishman's crisis of conscience. With that reservation, it is legitimate to look at the books as representative examples of reactionary interventionism. From our point of view, Disraeli's tremendous political subtlety is less important than the assimilative skills by which he discovered and revived some of the public's deepest convictions, and the intuitive intelligence which enabled him to comprehend and formulate the new needs of the age.

Were his convictions sincerely held? And was his sympathy for the poor genuine? These questions are difficult, and may be unanswerable. One thing seems clear: unlike Bulwer, whose utilitarianism was a passing phase, Disraeli's whole being was bound up with social Toryism. His conception of the grandiose ideas which were to bring him personal success and his country civil peace and foreign greatness owed as much to the natural bent of his temperament as to any calculation of his own interests. He put his own spontaneous leanings into his imaginative theory of government: his profound belief in the weakness of ideas and the power of instincts to shape a nation's overseas power and domestic tranquillity. (p. 175)

The new Tory message came under three heads: political, social, and religious, set out in *Coningsby, Sybil,* and *Tancred* respectively. *Sybil* is the most interesting from our point of view, but our survey would be incomplete without a quick examination of *Coningsby* and *Tancred.* The author's ideas changed from novel to novel, so that it is best to consider them chronologically.

In *Coningsby, or The New Generation* Disraeli . . . takes the Reform Act as a vantage point from which to survey political conditions. The book concerns itself entirely with the ruling classes, so that the struggle for mastership of England rules out any real consideration of the proletarian struggle for justice. The new bourgeoisie is shown challenging the old aristocracy; the existence of an urban proletariat is glossed over, and the agricultural workers, romantically called 'the peasantry', are made to stand for the entire populace. Peasants and workers, it is suggested, comprise a unique historical class which was contented with feudal government, as it is naturally adapted to medieval forms. The danger to the nation lies in the rivalry of factory and manor-house. Public order has been seriously disturbed by the Reform Act. New upsets are feared, and the prevalent political theories do nothing but intensify the existing antagonism between the old ruling class and the new bourgeoisie. The problem is to reconcile the traditional rights of the one with the just expectations of the other. And the new Toryism puts forward a formula for just such a peaceful reconciliation. Of course it will restore the people's ancient rights as part of the procedure for settling society. And the order of barons, enlarged and enriched by the admission of the new aristocracy of industrialists, will dedicate itself to fostering the well-being of its vassals. The Church, recalled to its duty by the Oxford Movement, will dispense charity in the countryside. But above all, the expanding nation must be given a unifying moral vision: this will be the task of the 'new generation'.

*Coningsby* comes before *Sybil* logically as well as chronologically. Even its plot is dated earlier, running from the eve of the Reform Act of 1832 to the Tory electoral victory of 1841. The political vicissitudes of these nine years are examined exhaustively, while the depression, which reached its climax in 1842, is barely touched on. Chartism is left in the background. *Sybil* is quite different, opening as it does in 1837, and carrying the reader down to 1844.

The dedication of *Coningsby* to Henry Hope, a leading member of the Young England party, includes these words: 'In these pages I have endeavoured to picture something of that development of the new and, as I believe, better mind of England, that has often been the subject of our converse and speculation.' The leaders of the movement appear under different names. Coningsby, the hero of the book, is none other than George Smythe, and Lord John Manners is recognisable in his friend Henry Sydney. We follow a group of young men, all brilliant and ambitious, and nearly all of noble birth, from Eton, where their characters are formed and they become friends, to the threshold of their political careers and public lives. In the process we see them at university, where their studies have made them mature already, and in the metropolitan palaces or sumptuous country houses which are their family homes. The interest is focused on the hero's career. He is the orphaned scion of a rich, ancient family. By turns he is the favourite and the victim of the caprice of his grandfather, the Marquis of Monmouth. His early initiation into life's difficulties gives him the energy appropriate to a future party leader; and his exposure to the most generous side of the nobility, as well as its corruption, shows him both the advantages and disadvantages of oligarchy. A boyhood friendship, a journey to Manchester, and a romance with the daughter of Millbank the industrialist all serve to point out to him the existence, and inevitable future importance, of the industrial bourgeoisie. As he witnesses the merciless struggle between Monmouth, the typical old aristocrat, and Millbank, the representative of industrial greatness, Coningsby searches his heart and mind, and scrutinises history, to try and discover principles which will satisfy his personal and patriotic ambitions. His friends are troubled by the same uncertainties, and they arrive at the same conclusion as he does: the new Toryism appeals to the generous instincts of youth. It should also prove acceptable to men of superior intelligence when they have thought it over.

Meanwhile the mysterious Jew, Sidonia, whose birth, tastes, and enormous wealth all serve to keep him out of the centre of the world of affairs, has been helping the intellectual growth of Young England with his advice, his epigrams, and his profound and original ideas. This unique character unites the genius of a Disraeli with the wealth of a Rothschild. He is the outstanding figure, wherever he goes. He is the equal of kings, whom he supports or opposes with his personal diplomacy, and maintains on their thrones with his gold. He is the embodiment of modern high finance. Under a skilful yet transparent disguise, the author himself is represented in Sidonia in his unofficial role among the chiefs of the new Toryism.

'Young' England was dominated by the memory of olden days; the 'new' Toryism put itself forward as a return to the party's old, traditional principles. Not even Disraeli's art could enliven the political dissertations which make up a good part of the book. The arguments of the *Vindication of the English Constitution* appear again, though less rigorously and continuously put. After the Reformation, according to Disraeli, when the Church's property had been distributed among Henry VIII's favourites, a class of parvenus arose. These were the Whig nobility, and it was in their interest to destroy the monarch's absolute power, the equality of all faithful subjects before the throne, the prosperity of the nation, which had been ensured by wise paternalistic government, and the Church's welfare work.

They strove for these dismal and unpatriotic objectives until the Revolution of 1688 brought them to power.

> The great object of the Whig leaders in England from the first movement under Hampden to the last most successful one in 1688, was to establish in England a high aristocratic republic on the model of the Venetian, then the study and admiration of all speculative politicians. . . . And they at length succeeded. . . . They brought in a new family on their own terms. George I. was a Doge; George II. was a Doge; . . . George III. tried not to be a Doge. . . . And a Venetian constitution did govern England from the accession of the House of Hanover until 1832.

Bolingbroke, Pitt, and Shelburne, in the eighteenth century, and Huskisson and Canning in the first years of the Liverpool administration had all tried to throw off the yoke of oligarchy. But their work had no lasting results, and the Reform Act enshrined the Whig triumph. The king had already been excluded from the cabinet, and the 'Seven Year Bill' emancipated Parliament. Now the reform of the electorate destroyed the internal balance of power in Parliament in favour of the Commons. Every source of division and discord in the nation—among which Disraeli even listed protective tariffs—was blamed onto the Whigs: 'The Whigs introduced sectarian religion, sectarian religion led to political exclusion, and political exclusion was soon accompanied by commercial restraint.' By contrast, the Tory party was national, and stood for the instinctive aspirations of the whole people. In the past it had based the people's freedom and the nation's prosperity on the absolute power of the Crown:

> Confidence in the loyalty of the nation, testified by munificent grants of rights and franchises, and favour to an expansive system of traffic, were distinctive qualities of the English sovereignty, until the House of Commons usurped the better part of its prerogatives.

Since then the party had degenerated, and in the hands of its present leadership its policy of loyalty to the Crown had become little more than a doctrine of self-denial. But the value of the old formula was not defunct: a return to the 'Pitt system' would restore England to health. The Tory ministers of Liverpool's Government were the only people who could have brought to a satisfactory conclusion the conflict which had been settled in so dangerous and revolutionary a manner by the Reform Act.

> They might have adjusted the rights and properties of our national industries in a manner which would have prevented that fierce and fatal rivalry that is now disturbing every hearth of the United Kingdom.

Thus the political doctrine Disraeli wanted to introduce to England was a long way from the merely reflex Toryism of 1832. He put the character of Lord Fitz-Booby into *Coningsby* to represent 'stupid' Toryism. But 'conservatism', the new form of resistance to social change which had come into being after the Reform Act, was no more appealing to him. He realised that Peel and his partisans constituted a dangerous rival for Young England. So although he spared his chief personally, and even flattered

him, he had not a good word to say for his policies. There was no such thing, he said, as conservatism. It was simply a new name for Liverpool's negative programme. Peel's attempt to broaden the base of Toryism had failed miserably. 'The Tamworth Manifesto of 1834 was an attempt to construct a party without principles.' 'What will you conserve?' asked Disraeli. There was, according to him, only one alternative to Young England Toryism: namely radicalism, which was at least logical, however much it might disgust popular sentiment. Bentham and Mill had succeeded in constructing a theoretical system of government with their utilitarianism. But their theory would collapse if it turned out that self-interest was not the normal motive force behind human action. Moreover, the greatest good of everyone was peculiarly the sovereign's concern: 'The only power that has no class sympathy is the Sovereign.' Like Carlyle and Dickens, Disraeli perceived that the sociological phenomenon of the expansion of industry and the aggrandisement of the bourgeoisie was connected with the psychological phenomenon of increasing moral severity and doctrinaire utilitarianism. He also attacked all forms of individualism. He saw a whole sequence of contemporary phenomena as being indissolubly connected: middle-class materialism; the weakening of artistic and aesthetic values; the rigours of the new Poor Law; mental prosiness; radical politics; and utilitarian philosophy. The covert relation between temperament and opinion was apparent to him: Lord Everingham, the representative of Whiggism, is described as 'a clear-headed, cold-blooded man'. By contrast the young heroes, who set themselves the task of bringing about a regeneration of national life, are zealous, sensitive missionaries, full of enthusiastic imagination. Like Coningsby, they feel that England needs 'something sound and deep, fervent and well defined,' and that the priests of this new faith must be sought in the 'New Generation'. Their leader pronounces Benthamism's epitaph.

> 'The Utilitarian system is dead,' said Coningsby. 'It has passed through the heaven of philosophy like a hail-storm, cold, noisy, sharp, and peppering, and it has melted away.'

Imagination alone wins and holds empires:

> A cause is a great abstraction, and fit only for students; embodied in a party, it stirs men to action; but place at the head of that party a leader who can inspire enthusiasm, he commands the world.

For this reason, the rational doctrine of radicalism is weak, and the future belongs to social Toryism: 'Man is only truly great when he acts from the passions; never irresistible but when he appeals to the imagination. Even Mormon counts more votaries than Bentham.'

How was the imperfectly-settled conflict of 1832 to be resolved? The Whig aristocracy would be powerless without the support of the industrial bourgeoisie: the Reform Act, and all the other measures which had overthrown the old order, would never have come about without the presence of this new class. Degenerate Toryism had tried to refuse them a place in society. Rejuvenated Toryism would offer the bourgeoisie its proper place in the State, and thus do away with the *raison d'être* for the alliance of Whiggism and radicalism. Like Carlyle, Disraeli perceived the future importance of industry. ' "The Age of Ruins is past," says Sidonia. "Have you seen Manchester?" ' And on the advice of his wise old friend, Coningsby visits the 'Metropolis of labour'. There he sees all the attractive, expansive, honest, hardworking side of heavy industry, with its magnificent enterprise, clear determination, productive energy, and humane care for the hands in its employ. Mr Millbank is the representative good employer. He is 'a well-proportioned, comely man, with a fair face inclining to ruddiness, a quick, glancing, hazel eye, the whitest teeth, and short, curly, chestnut hair, here and there slightly tinged with grey. It was a visage of energy and determination.' His factory has been built 'by a capitalist as anxious to raise a monument of the skill and power of his order, as to obtain a return for the great investment.' His house is built along classical lines and furnished tastefully. There he graciously entertains his son's friend, Coningsby, with gentlemanly hospitality. He is educated, enlightened, and a good conversationalist. The only foibles apparent to his observant guest are entirely excusable: he has a tendency to be obstinate and dogmatic, and takes considerable pride in his profession. An employee tells Coningsby, in heartfelt tones, of his master's charitable and philanthropic activities:

> He detailed to Coningsby the plans which Mr. Millbank had pursued, both for the moral and physical well-being of his people; how he had built churches, and schools, and institutes; houses and cottages on a new system of ventilation; how he had allotted gardens; established singing classes.

In this honest and pleasant household Coningsby comes across a girl he has loved even before knowing her. Her charms have won him over in advance, and he is willing to be convinced, and astonished, by Millbank's political arguments. The industrial classes have their rights; their wealth and energy are the strongest guarantees of national prosperity. They must be accorded their proper place in society and government. But this particular industrialist voices the familiar radical demands without their normal utilitarian asperity: he makes a gentler case, involved with the justifiable protest of the national spirit against foreign domination. For by an imaginative master-stroke, Disraeli makes a bold assumption which links Millbank's radicalism with Young England's nationalism. The industrial classes, he argues, are none other than the old Saxon races, submerged since the Norman conquest. In nobility and antiquity they are the equals of the Normans. The political conflict is 'Saxon industry competing successfully with Norman manners'. And so Millbank's nationalist radicalism can easily be reconciled with Coningsby's social Toryism. The industrialist bears the cost of the reconciliation: converted by his young friend, he not only stands down in his favour, but gives him the hand in marriage of his daughter 'Edith; a Saxon name, for she is the daughter of a Saxon.' Their union is symbolic: once benevolent monarchical despotism has reorganised society and restored peace and prosperity, the hostility between the Saxon aristocracy of the mills and the Norman aristocracy of the manor-houses will be ended, for they will be equally obedi-

ent before the monarch, and equally privileged above the rest of society.

Disraeli, however, could not completely disregard the sufferings of the people. He knew that the problem posed by the Reform Act had been complicated considerably by the rise of Chartism. Although he did not name or describe the Chartists precisely, he allowed social problems to be discernible behind the political question.

They were to be resolved in the same way. The misery of the 'peasantry' was yet another outcome of Whig misdeeds, which the feeble Toryism of 1815 to 1830 had done nothing to counter. 'Now commenced that Condition-of-England Question of which our generation hears so much.' The phrase is Carlyle's: Disraeli had read *Chartism*. Some aristocratic throwaway remarks give us a brief glimpse of the squalid horrors surrounding the nobility's country-houses: ' "Theresa brings me terrible accounts of the sufferings of the poor about us," said the Duke, shaking his head.' The new Poor Law is not only cruel and unjust; it violates the historical rights of the 'order of peasantry'. When Lord Everingham, the Whig, coolly cites reports and statistics in favour of the new Law, Coningsby's friend, young Henry Sydney, takes the same weapons as Dickens and Carlyle to attack his logic. He argues from his heart and, more particularly, from his historical imagination, which he draws upon for the social theory of Young England:

> He assured his father that it would never be well for England until this order of the peasantry was restored to its pristine condition; not merely in physical comfort, for that must vary according to the economical circumstances of the time; but to its condition in all those moral attributes which make a recognised rank in a nation.

Moral sufferings are worse than material hardship: 'there is no error so vulgar as to believe that revolutions are occasioned by economical causes.' The rising of 1640 was first and foremost a religious movement: 'The imagination of England rose against the government.'

Thus the Tory social programme Young England put forward was as idealistic as anything in Dickens, but under the reactionary influence of the aristocracy it took a feudal, authoritarian form. The nobility were to mix with the people, join in their amusements, gain their confidence, and recover the moral leadership they had forfeited. They were to be generous alms-givers, and quick to heal class enmity with sympathetic words and friendly familiarity.

As if intending to realise Lord John Manners's fantasies in every detail, Disraeli takes us to the Christmas celebrations at the home of a Catholic gentleman, Eustace Lyle, who fervently supports the new ideas. 'All classes are mingled in the joyous equality that becomes the season.' Local people push past each other to the master's buttery, while a procession of the gentry slowly follows the boar's-head into the dining hall, singing a medieval Latin hymn. The fact that Lyle is a Catholic is significant: the ecclesiastical bias of *Coningsby* is unobtrusively, but consistently, towards the Oxford Movement. St Geneviève, Lyle's manor, is built in the neo-gothic style; its chapel is a wonder of colour, ornament and splendour. Twice a week villagers come from the surrounding district, to the sound of the chapel bell, to receive alms from the owner. The Church does not play a major role in this book, as it was to do in *Sybil*. But Disraeli associates Lyle's mystical and poetic piety with the charity which was essential to social Toryism.

Such is the substance of *Coningsby*. Feeling it was a little heavy, Disraeli did his best to lighten it with stylistic brilliance and animated narrative. Thus he wrote a hybrid, but original book: a political treatise which was also a fashionable novel. In spite of its disjointed plot the book still has some appeal, and it must have had still more when well-known individuals could be detected under each character. *Coningsby* is a lively political satire, as well as a serious manifesto, and it offers a picturesque account of fashionable life. The manners of aristocratic circles at the time of the Reform Act are described by a writer better informed than Dickens, who is also more indulgent towards his subject. Disraeli does not disguise the corruption of Lord Monmouth's world, where French fashions cloak elegant dissipation, and scepticism fends off philosophical inquiry. But he knows how to spare his illustrious readers' feelings. He is not interested in parading his own virtue, and easily associates himself with their amiable hedonism. Coningsby meets the cream of civilised refinement in London, at Lord Monmouth's mansion; in Paris, where he goes to complete his social education; and at Beaumanoir, the magnificent country house where Henry Sydney's family lives. He also meets the caricatured politicians Rigby, Tadpole, and Taper. The author's wit is given free play in these merciless character-sketches, as it is in the less attractive aristocrats, distinguished though their manners may be.

None of Disraeli's other novels had such an immediate success. Three editions came out in three months, and 15,000 copies were sold in America. Several 'keys', and a three-volume parody (*Anti-Coningsby*, 1844), bore witness to its popularity. The new Toryism had captured the public's attention. But was it winning over opinion? It hardly seemed so. The ladies who were particularly fond of the book doted on it for everything *except* the arguments. And although it was interesting, it was not really persuasive. Its paradoxical arguments were not backed up by enough evidence. *Sybil*, on the other hand, was to be full of eloquent details which would make a deeper impression on the reader's mind.

Only a year separates *Coningsby* from *Sybil*, but the social settings of the two differ vastly. We are no longer concerned with two classes above and beyond the people, contending for power: now there are two nations restively confronting one another, prepared for war and growing increasingly irritated. The demarcation line falls between the rich and the poor. The movement from *Coningsby* to *Sybil*, with the new conflict of interests developing alongside the old, is a perfect illustration of the changing current of English history between 1840 and 1850.

Why did Disraeli develop the interventionist element in Toryism in this book? He seems to have been following a preconceived plan: he says, in the last pages of *Sybil*,

> A year ago, I presumed to offer to the public some volumes that aimed at calling their attention to the state of our political parties. . . . The present work advances another step in the same emprise. From the state of Parties it now would draw public thought to the state of the People whom those parties for two centuries have governed.

Thus, Disraeli was carrying out a programme to educate the public. But so attentive an observer of public feeling would never have risked the outspokenness of *Sybil* unless he thought the time ripe for it. . . . [The] middle-class crisis of conscience was at its keenest around 1845: the new philanthropy was at work, and social conscience was in the air. Was Disraeli, then, prepared to describe the conditions of the people? The year before when he told his sister, 'Manchester has invited me to take the chair at their literary meeting' [*Correspondence of Lord Beaconsfield with his Sister*, letter of 30 August 1844], he seized the opportunity to travel through the surrounding countryside and see the workings of industry for himself. He went on to Yorkshire with Smythe and Manners, visiting factories and benevolent institutions and making speeches from time to time to promote the cause. Furthermore his political work had made him familiar with Blue books and, by a friend's assistance, he had been able to read correspondence that had passed between O'Connor and the other Chartist leaders. These sources were enough to give him a firm grasp of the facts. If his acquaintance with the industrial proletariat on familiar terms was as limited as Dickens's, he did hold a compensatory picture in his clear and excellent brain of the way in which society worked economically. *Sybil* tells us everything about working-class life that one would expect a highly intelligent and politically well-informed tourist to bring away from a quick survey of the situation. It is a picture in which the most shocking instances of misery are tactfully softened: Disraeli never forgot that he was writing for the ruling classes, and even the dialogue he puts into the mouths of his working-class characters does not compel him to disregard his own association with marchionesses and duchesses. His Preface explains that such idealisation was necessary, and puts forward a defence against the charge of exaggeration. The writer, he says,

> thinks it . . . due to himself to state that the descriptions, generally, are written from his own observation; but while he hopes he has alleged nothing which is not true, he has found the absolute necessity of suppressing much that is genuine. For so little do we know of the state of our own country, that the air of improbability which the whole truth would inevitably throw over these pages, might deter some from their perusal.

The action and political argument of *Sybil* follow the same pattern as *Coningsby*. The main plot is the same: a highly aristocratic young man is prompted by his own dissatisfaction, and the encouragement of mature thinkers, to arrive at the doctrine of the new Toryism. He is disgusted by the foppish indolence with which his peers waste their lives, and by the self-interest concealed under the mimic contest of political parties: the search for sympathy and understanding leads him to the best of his contemporaries. He resolves to forestall the dangers threatening the country, and goes to meet the underprivileged classes in a spirit of sincere goodwill. He chooses a wife from among the enemies of his hereditary caste, and by this marriage becomes leader of a group we recognise as Young England.

Egremont, the younger brother of Lord Marney, has all the charm and talent of Coningsby. But he is portrayed as a rather more mature character, with more decided opinions, as becomes a hero who represents Disraeli himself in his public and official capacity. Lord Milford, Alfred Mountchesney, and Lord Fitzheron parade their bored and gilded youth from clubs and *salons* to the racecourse; the Derby concerns them more than the nation's destiny. But Egremont, with 'a generous spirit and a tender heart', is driven by a need for a more serious life, nobler interests, and more productive activities. He travels alone through the different districts where various social conditions are to be seen, and weighs them up. He perceives the degeneracy of monarchical power, the wickedness of the Whigs and conservatives, and the necessity of a return to the old Toryism. Thus he gradually arrives at the policy of reuniting the different classes of society under the benevolent authority of an absolute monarch. Egremont's progress to conversion is the same as Coningsby's, and so are his objections to the existing parties. We need only note the comic relief Disraeli gets from the character of Lord Marney. He is better than Lord Everingham as a representative of the policies of social inaction and self-interest. As a Whig and a political economist, he is a firm supporter of the new Poor Law; as a great landowner, however, he is also a resolute supporter of the Corn Laws. There is something of the Dickensian villain about him:

> The countenance of Lord Marney bespoke the character of his mind; cynical, devoid of sentiment, arrogant, literal, hard. He had no imagination, had exhausted his slight native feeling; but he was acute, disputatious, and firm even to obstinacy. . . . He had formed his mind by Helvetius, whose system he deemed irrefutable, and in whom alone he had faith. Armed with the principles of his great master, he believed he could pass through existence in adamantine armour, and always gave you in the business of life the idea of a man who was conscious you were trying to take him in, and rather respected you for it, but the working of whose cold unkind eye defied you.

Disraeli, like Dickens, followed the popular instinct of the times by linking intellectual sociology with the outward signs of an inner moral sterility.

Coningsby married Millbank the industrialist's daughter. Egremont marries Gerard the foreman's daughter, and this contrast epitomises the difference between the two novels. The hero of *Sybil* goes to the people: the nation of the poor. Disraeli is at pains throughout to soften the extravagant boldness of his marriage: Gerard is not a common worker, but an overseer; his manners and culture are those of a man from a higher class; and in the end it turns out that he is of aristocratic descent. He has always been known to have come from a family distinguished before the Norman Conquest, and so to be of 'noble' Saxon birth. But Disraeli also felt it necessary to provide him with a more definite escutcheon: he proves to be the descendant of an aristocratic family whose property was seized at the Reformation. His daughter, Sybil, inherits the fortune and manor of the lords of Mowbray, thus bringing Egremont the gift he needs if he is to lead the new Toryism.

At her side, in spite of all difficulties, Egremont espouses the cause of the people; for it transpires that the manors and parks of *Coningsby* are surrounded by a huge proletariat, as by a sea. And the people are Saxons, with the prestige of racial antiquity, so that their naked subjugation and poverty are unnatural. This farrago of imaginary history does not stop that poverty from being described: the reader is taken among and alongside the workers, and a great deal of the novel is given over to scenes of industrial life. And so the social message of Young England is developed alongside its political theory.

The monarchy should be restored to its primacy of authority; the aristocracy should show some concern for their dependants. And in the same way the bourgeoisie and the clergy have a part to play in the organisation of charity. Trafford, the model employer, is a second Millbank:

> With gentle blood in his veins, and old English feelings, he imbibed, at an early period of his career, a correct conception of the relations which should subsist between the employer and the employed. He felt that between them there should be other ties than the payment and the receipt of wages.

The chimneys of his house are Elizabethan; the church he has built is neo-gothic. He has also put up schools, hospitals, and sanitary cottages. He pays his workers at the factory itself, and not, as was then common, at an alehouse. His experience as a philanthropist has been encouraging.

> 'I should find an ample reward in the moral tone and material happiness of this community; but really viewing it in a pecuniary point of view, the investment of capital has been one of the most profitable I ever made.'

But it is the Church whose role is especially illuminated by *Sybil*. Mr St Lys, the priest, is the finished portrait for which Eustace Lyle was the sketch. Instead of a pious gentleman, we now have a cleric to consider. Like all Disraeli's heroic characters, he is the offspring of an old family, and he has dedicated himself to personal social work among the poor of Mowbray. But although he brings fervent generosity to his alms-giving, he has a nobler concept of his mission. The clergy are the body of men traditionally charged with bringing enlightenment to deprived souls. By their sympathy and the poetry of their ritual, they must appease, console, and improve the poor. In the Middle Ages the Church accepted this role and carried it out. By renouncing it, the Church has contributed to the ills of society:

> 'For all that has occurred, or may occur,' said Mr. St. Lys to Egremont, 'I blame only the church. The church deserted the people; and from that moment the church has been in danger, and the people degraded.'

This aesthetic and historical Christian philosophy is inseparable from the Oxford Movement. St Lys is a keen supporter of church restoration, and has himself restored Mowbray's famous old cathedral with loving care. He believes in the efficacy of forms and ceremonies: 'What you call forms and ceremonies represent the divinest instincts of our nature.' Such ideas and leanings tend towards Catholicism, and Disraeli makes no secret of his sympathy for the Church of Rome. Gerard and Sybil, both Catholics, are moved by the sight of ruined abbeys torn down by Renaissance iconoclasts; they regret the passing of the monasteries, which were havens of peace and charity. Sybil loves to make retreat with the nuns of Mowbray, and whenever we catch glimpses of nuns, they are prestigiously shrouded in romantic charm. When we consider the controversies surrounding the Oxford Movement, the imminence of Newman's conversion, and the strength of outraged Protestant feeling, Disraeli's audacity seems astonishing. But he was careful to take all necessary precautions. Egremont puts the vital question to St Lys: are ceremonies necessary? And has not 'their revival in our service at the present day a tendency to restore the Romish system in this country?' The ritualist clergyman has a ready answer: his enormous respect for the Roman Church does not impel him towards Rome. Rome has tradition, antiquity, ritual, and the apostolic link with the Saviour. But Judaism has all this and more. Disraeli anticipates the theme of *Tancred,* and claims for Judaism the veneration which is its due as the cradle of Christianity. Says St Lys,

> I do not bow to the necessity of a visible head in a defined locality; but were I to seek for such, it would not be at Rome. . . . The prophets were not Romans; the apostles were not Romans; she who was blessed above all women, I never heard she was a Roman maiden.

In *Coningsby* the alternatives to the new Toryism were utilitarian radicalism and Peelite conservatism. Now, in *Sybil,* the changed social basis leads to a different set of erroneous doctrines. Chartism and socialism are revolutionary answers to the problems which Young England hopes to resolve peacefully. The author's attitude to Chartism is exactly the same as it was in 1839—and he takes good care to draw attention to his own steadfastness of opinion: Egremont is the parliamentary speaker whose stirring speech on the people's behalf is read by an enthusiastic Sybil.

Highly dramatic scenes from the activities of the labour movement are described, as the narrative moves swiftly from 1837 to 1839: the National Convention is organised to confront Parliament; groups of workers in the provinces are arming, and preparing for the coming disturbances with a boycott of dutiable goods. Gerard stirs up a belligerent crowd at a torchlit midnight meeting on a piece of waste land:

> His tall form seemed colossal in the uncertain and flickering light, his rich and powerful voice reached almost to the limit of his vast audience, now still with expectation and silent with excitement. Their fixed and eager glance, the mouth compressed with fierce resolution or distended by novel sympathy, as they listened to the expo-

sition of their wrongs, and the vindication of the sacred rights of labour; the shouts and waving of the torches as some bright or bold phrase touched them to the quick; the cause, the hour, the scene, all combined to render the assemblage in a high degree exciting.

We see the Chartist leaders visiting Members of Parliament whom they hope to win over to their cause, and time after time we see the Members refusing to spare them any time. We hear the Chartists outline the five points of their national petition. While the politicians in their clubs are deaf to the rumblings of popular discontent, we are astonished by the July riots in Birmingham. In the end, we see a secret meeting of the Chartist leaders, driven to extremes, plotting a general strike and civil war. It is a sombre, powerful scene, which Disraeli has rendered lifelike by the use of a good deal of accurate information: the arrest of Gerard and his friends, and his eighteen-month prison sentence, palpably parallel to the historical fate of Vincent and Lovett. And the sight of this dismal upset, which halted the progress of Chartism for three years, leads us to the same conclusion as Sybil. She staunchly supports the people's cause, even refusing Egremont's love because she believes the gulf between rich and poor to be impassable, until she sees the helpless quarrels of the divided people's assemblies. Then her social aspirations are daunted as she faces the harsh and complex nature of reality:

> She had seen enough to suspect that the world was a more complicated system than she had preconceived. There was not that strong and rude simplicity in its organisation which she had supposed. The characters were more various, the motives more mixed, the classes more blended, the elements of each more subtle and diversified, than she had imagined. The people, she found, was not that pure embodiment of unity of feeling, of interest, and of purpose, which she had pictured in her abstractions. The people had enemies among the people: their own passions; which made them often sympathise, often combine, with the privileged.

Failure, prison, and misfortune leave Gerard a wiser man too, and he renounces 'moral force' as well as 'physical force'. He comes to mistrust his own class, and turns respectfully towards the generous noblemen who offer him a helping hand from above. He agrees with Egremont's words: 'They are the natural leaders of the People, Sybil; believe me they are the only ones.'

Socialism is less sparingly criticised, and Disraeli did not really know very much about Owenism. Stephen Morley is the character through whom it is expounded and exposed. He is Gerard's friend, but absolutely different from him. He is an intellectual; an educated worker with a determined, reflective temperament, and modern tastes and opinions. He belongs to a temperance society, and follows a vegetarian diet. He is opposed to physical force, and looks forward to the advent of communism with all the longing of a rationalist propagandist. Co-operation is his social ideal, and he describes the principle of association thus to a group of miners:

> 'Suppose, instead of sticking out and playing, fifty of your families were to live under one roof. You would live better than you live now; you would feed more fully, and be lodged and clothed more comfortably, and you might save half the amount of your wages; you would become capitalists; you might yourselves hire your mines and pits from the owners, and pay them a better rent than they now obtain, and yet yourselves gain more and work less.'

As he anticipates this economic transformation, he takes little account of good employers, and his concept of organically changing society means that he has little confidence in the efficacy of individual great men who, for Disraeli as for Carlyle, represent the hope of the century. In contrast with Young England, his theory of progress looks to the future. He can spare little more than a passing sigh for the historic memories that inspire Gerard and Sybil. He wants the people to win their own enfranchisement, and instinctively hates the aristocratic Egremont. His democratic spirit and hostility to the feudal programme make him the most dangerous rival of the new Toryism. Disraeli has also tried to make his character antipathetic. He is, as a man, less elevated than his ideas; indeed, intellectualism has made him as morally degraded as his worst enemy, Lord Marney. He is clear-sighted, and sees the weaknesses of Chartism, whose failure he predicts, yet from motives of self-interest he acts as if he believed in it. He is Egremont's jealous rival for Sybil's affections, and tries to assassinate him. He is a traitor to his class, and betrays the secret meeting where Gerard is arrested. Personal ambitions motivate him to lead a riot off course, to the castle of the Lords of Mowbray, where he hopes to steal the papers proving their title. When he is struck down by soldiers under Egremont's command he dies confessing his defeat, and the reader is expected to conclude that his ideas have failed with him.

The idea is interesting, but the execution is marred by the author's obvious bias against the character. Morley is sacrificed to Egremont; socialism to Young England. Disraeli does not do justice to the heroic courage of Owen's supporters amongst the Chartists. He purports to see a clear connection between Morley's private moral failings and the doctrines he expounds, and judges the latter in the light of the former. Sybil has no love for Morley, whom she sees as the cause of the people's sufferings: ' "We have merited this," said Sybil, "who have taken an infidel to our hearts." ' And indeed Morley is a freethinker, like most of Owen's followers. Disraeli uses the same arguments against the Owenites that he used against radical utilitarians; he saw socialism and classical economics as similar in spirit, no matter how different their conclusions might be. They shared the vice of rationalism, and they were both materialistic, valuing nothing more highly than tangible goods and satisfactions. Gerard says of Morley, 'Englishmen want none of his joint-stock felicity.' Here again Disraeli turns out to be attacking the psychological corollaries of certain beliefs rather than the beliefs themselves.

The most interesting parts of *Sybil* are those which give us a picture of the people's conditions. Disraeli's methodical review of the various aspects of working-class life be-

trays by its order the influence of Blue books. To begin with, there is the agricultural proletariat. Egremont personally witnesses the distress which has overtaken the descendants of the 'yeomanry' at the hands of his brother, Lord Marney. The little country town of Marney is delightfully situated, 'In a spreading dale, contiguous to the margin of a clear and lively stream, surrounded by meadows and gardens, and backed by lofty hills, undulating and richly wooded.' But the illusion vanishes as one draws nearer. Apart from an inn, a market, and a few houses for the well-to-do, there is nothing to be seen but wretched tumble-down cottages.

> The gaping chinks admitted every blast; the leaning chimneys had lost half their original height; the rotten rafters were evidently misplaced; while in many instances the thatch, yawning in some parts to admit the wind and wet, and in all utterly unfit for its original purpose of giving protection from the weather, looked more like the top of a dunghill than a cottage. Before the doors of these dwellings, and often surrounding them, ran open drains full of animal and vegetable refuse, decomposing into disease, or sometimes in their imperfect course filling foul pits or spreading into stagnant pools, while a concentrated solution of every species of dissolving filth was allowed to soak through, and thoroughly impregnate, the walls and ground adjoining.

There are rarely more than two rooms in these dwellings, in one of which an entire family may have to sleep: a father with typhus might be lying here, on his pallet, alongside his wife and children.

Why is there all this squalor and degradation? For fifty years now landed proprietors have been tearing down the cottages on their estates to avoid paying poor-rates, and now their former tenants have huddled together in these hovels in the town. The Settlement Act prevents them from moving into neighbouring parishes; competition is fierce, and wages have sunk to subsistence level. The Church has done nothing to help matters; here, as elsewhere, it has forgotten its sacred mission. The Game Laws savagely punish the slightest attempts at hunting for food. The same newspaper which reports the prowess of Lord Marney and his friends in bagging 730 head of game in four hours, notes the conviction of 'Thomas Hind' for poaching, and his sentence of two months imprisonment. The noble lord, however, like Bounderby in *Hard Times*, has nothing but ridicule for any suggestion that relief is needed:

> 'I say that a family can live well on seven shillings a-week, and on eight shillings very well indeed. The poor are well off, at least the agricultural poor, very well off indeed. Their incomes are certain, that is a great point, and they have no cares, no anxieties; they always have a resource, they always have the House.'

And so, when Egremont arrives to stay with his brother, there is unusual excitement afoot in the little town: 'The torch of the incendiary had for the first time been introduced into the parish of Marney; and last night the prim-

*A sketch of Disraeli with Queen Victoria, 1877.*

est stacks of the Abbey farm had blazed, a beacon to the agitated neighbourhood.'

The industrial proletariat figures more largely in the book, as is only right and proper. Gerard and Sybil live near the industrial town of Mowbray, which is evidently one of the Lancashire industrial centres. Disraeli shows us the tall, barrack-like factories, and takes us through the noisy suburbs where the weavers and their families are crowded together. Here is one of the typical scenes of urban life: marketing on Saturday.

> It was Saturday night; the streets were thronged; an infinite population kept swarming to and from the close courts and pestilential cul-de-sacs that continually communicated with the streets by narrow archways, like the entrance of hives, so low that you were obliged to stoop for admission: while, ascending to these same streets from their dank and dismal dwellings by narrow flights of steps, the subterraneous nation of the cellars poured forth to enjoy the coolness of the summer night, and market for the day of rest. The bright and lively shops were crowded; and groups of purchasers were gathered round the stalls, that, by the aid of glaring lamps and flaunting lanterns, displayed their wares.

Here we meet Mrs Carey, a street-trader, with her usual clientele: Dandy Mick, the Don Juan of the factories—a

precocious scamp of sixteen—and some working girls, notably Julia and Caroline, who are well aware of their own charms: 'They were gaily dressed, a light handkerchief tied under the chin, their hair scrupulously arranged; they wore coral necklaces and earrings of gold.' They chat among themselves, exchanging the latest news and gossip, and to finish the evening Dandy Mick takes them to the 'Temple of the Muses', a sort of concert hall with refreshments, where the workers enjoy the performances of professional entertainers. Here Disraeli draws our attention to the naïvety of their taste, and the careful deportment with which they attempt to ape middle-class manners. In fact he is aiming for a picturesque and comic effect; the tone is humorous rather than didactic. We are more struck by the topsy-turvy society in which children of fifteen set up house together as husband and wife than by the dismal side of working-class life. True, we hear complaints about 'Shuffle and Screw', the bad employers; we learn about their shameful system of squeezing back the workers' wages through fines, and we hear complaints about having to clean machinery during meal-breaks.

The gaiety comes to an end with the great depression of 1842. The Temple of the Muses is closed down; Mrs Carey declares that she has never heard tell of such hard times; Dandy Mick becomes a Chartist, and is determined to march under a banner bearing the famous slogan, 'A fair day's wage for a fair day's work'. But these events are restrained, and the writing is marked by wit and humour. Disraeli used these episodes for light relief among the highly pathetic scenes filling the novel.

These last deal with notorious aspects of industrial poverty and questions which had particularly attracted public attention. The lot of the hand-loom weavers . . . comes under this head, and in a few pages Disraeli summarises an entire Blue book. At daybreak on a winter's morning Warner the weaver sits at his loom in the wretched garret where his wife and three children lie asleep without any covering, and while he plies his shuttle he gives himself up to thought. He utters a highly artificial soliloquy, in which verisimilitude and life are crushed by the sheer weight of economic information. But of course the general public might learn from it details of Government Reports that had not been put before them.

> 'Twelve hours of daily labour, at the rate of one penny each hour; and even this labour is mortgaged! How is this to end? Is it rather not ended? . . . Then why am I here? Why am I, and six hundred thousand subjects of the Queen, honest, loyal, and industrious, why are we, after manfully struggling for years, and each year sinking lower in the scale, why are we driven from our innocent and happy homes, our country cottages that we loved, first to bide in close towns without comforts, and gradually to crouch in cellars, or find a squalid lair like this, without even the common necessaries of existence; first the ordinary conveniences of life, then raiment, and at length food, vanishing from us.

> 'It is that the Capitalist has found a slave that has supplanted the labour and ingenuity of man. Once he was an artisan: at best, he now only watches machines; and even that occupation slips from his grasp to the woman and the child. The capitalist flourishes, he amasses immense wealth; we sink, lower and lower; lower than the beasts of burden; for they are fed better than we are, cared for more. And it is just, for according to the present system they are more precious. And yet they tell us that the interests of Capital and Labour are identical.'

A little later the physical and moral degradation of coal miners wrings a genuinely sympathetic tone from Disraeli:

> Naked to the waist, an iron chain fastened to a belt of leather runs between their legs clad in canvas trousers, while on hands and feet an English girl, for twelve, sometimes for sixteen hours a day, hauls and hurries tubs of coals up subterranean roads, dark, precipitous, and plashy; circumstances that seem to have escaped the notice of the Society for the Abolition of Negro Slavery.

Sir Joshua Reynolds, a painter of genius, once portrayed the same child's charming face in various attitudes on the same canvas, and called the composition 'guardian angels'. Disraeli wonders whether Landseer or Etty would dare to do the same with today's 'trappers'—five- or six-year-old children who work alone in the darkness of the mines?

The truck system, as we have said, oppressed the miners in particular, and so we hear a group of these slow-witted, coarse men giving their naïve opinions. They ponder heavily over the ideas that slowly penetrate their consciousness, and are almost brutishly slow and sluggish. They are sitting in an alehouse after leaving the pits.

> 'The fact is, we are tommied to death.'

> 'You never spoke a truer word, Master Nixon,' said one of his companions.

> 'It's gospel, every word of it,' said another.

> 'And the point is,' continued Master Nixon, 'what are we for to do?'

> 'Ay, surely,' said a collier, 'that's the marrow.'

> 'Ay, ay,' agreed several; 'there it is.'

> 'The question is,' said Nixon, looking round with a magisterial air, 'what *is* wages? I say, 'tayn't sugar, 'tayn't tea, 'tayn't bacon. I don't think 'tis candles; but of this I be sure, 'tayn't waistcoats.'

And we witness the payment of these peculiar wages. Diggs the shopkeeper and his son Joseph satisfy their crude lust for power on the crowd flocking to the tommy-shop. They impudently double their prices, and fine protesters; threaten to kick out workers who demand payment in cash; and distribute foodstuffs to suit their own interests or whims. And the haggard, worried women, tired out by their long morning's journey, hardly dare to whisper among themselves how much they resent the shopkeeper's short weights, chalky flour, and mouldy tea.

The Report of 1842 on the employment of children in factories contained one chapter that was more sensational than all the rest. R. H. Horne, as sub-commissioner in the Midlands, uncovered an extra-ordinary town in the middle of Staffordshire where metal-working had been expanding for some years without being reached by Christianity, law, or civilisation. The population of Willenhall were half-barbarian, and their strange way of life caught Disraeli's imagination. He described 'the town of the locksmiths' under the name of 'Wodgate' or 'Wogate', and drew upon the official Report to produce two of the strangest chapters in social literature. The workers of Wodgate are famed all over England for their skill, but no offer can tempt them to leave their native district,

> that squatters' seat which soon assumed the form of a large village, and then in turn soon expanded into a town, and at the present moment numbers its population by swarming thousands, lodged in the most miserable tenements in the most hideous burgh in the ugliest country in the world.

There is no local authority, no school, and no church in Wodgate. Factories and big industrial works are unknown there: Wodgate industry has stuck to the old methods which have died out everywhere else.

The business of Wodgate is carried on by master workmen in their own houses, each of whom possesses an unlimited number of what they call apprentices, by whom their affairs are principally conducted, and whom they treat as the Mamlouks treated the Egyptians.

The masters constitute an exclusive tyranny of violence. They punish their apprentices brutally, beating them with locks and hammers so that they injure, and even kill them. Apprentices are often put up for sale. They are fed on rotten food and housed in garrets, and yet they feel a sort of savage attachment to their masters. People work on four days of the week in Wodgate; the other three they are dead drunk. They cannot be described as ignorant or immoral; they are a gang of insensate animals, ruled only by the grossest instincts: 'Ask them the name of their sovereign, and they will stare; ask them the name of their religion, and they will laugh: who rules them on earth, or who can save them in heaven, are alike mysteries to them.' Morley the socialist visits Wodgate, where he finds unprecedented hardship. He stops two deformed, rickety creatures—a boy and girl, working with files at the threshold of a hovel—to ask his way. The boy has a terrible scar on his forehead. Morley questions him:

'An accident?'

'Very like. An accident that often happened. I should like to have a crown for every time he has cut my head open. He cut it open once with a key, and twice with a lock. He knocked the corner of a lock into my head twice, once with a bolt, and once with a shut; you know what that is; the thing what runs into the staple.'

And with a sort of ferocious grin, 'Tummas'—to give the lad the only name he owns to—tells how he married his companion. Their master joined them in matrimony; he is the most famous, brutal, and terrible master in Wodgate. People nickname him the 'Bishop' as a piece of heavy irony. 'So he sprinkled some slat over a gridiron, read "Our Father" backwards, and wrote our name in a book: and we were spliced.' Tummas is a good Christian, too: as his wife says, he believes in 'our Lord and Saviour Pontius Pilate, who was crucified to save our sins; and in Moses, Goliath, and the rest of the Apostles.'

Thus the evidence showed how low humanity could sink in the industrial classes without the vigilant intervention of public opinion, laws, and local authorities to check and reverse the inevitable effects of competition and industrial anarchy. Willenhall was a scandal: a social plague-spot in the very heart of England. But Disraeli wanted to appeal to his readers' consciences with still more pressing arguments; he wanted to show the imminence of revolution and the threat to the very existence of society. He appealed to the instinct of self-preservation, the ultimate powerful motive of human action. Several episodes cast a vivid light directly on the danger of catastrophe. The character who stands for the most dangerous hostility to the established order is named 'Devilsdust'. He has survived an infancy which killed off his contemporaries in their hundreds. He was born in the street, and handed over to be looked after by an old woman who nursed him on laudanum and treacle. He has been brought up in hunger, vice, and neglect,

and if he has survived, it has been in the teeth of society's manifest preference for his death. One day his anonymous existence was absorbed into factory life. Now we see him as a patient, obstinate, adult worker. He reads the working-class papers which expose the crimes of capital and the enslavement of labour. He is earnest and strong-willed, and like Morley, looks to the workers' physical courage to provide ammunition for strife. Class hatred is instinctive in him, and it has been intensified by experience and reflection. He is prepared for hand-to-hand fighting or carefully calculated acts of violence. He is an active member of the Mowbray trade union.

The trade union movement . . . was not long past its revolutionary phase, and what Disraeli describes is still a secret society with an initiation ceremony surrounded by superstitious terrors. Dandy Mick, prompted by Devilsdust, dares to face introduction as a neophyte. We see him at dead of night in a deserted warehouse: two masked figures bearing torches appear, blindfold him, and lead him to the presence of 'the Seven'. This robed and masked tribunal sit on a dais with a skeleton behind them, and men with drawn swords on either hand. Two men with battle-axes stand by the supplicant, and men with white robes and masks are ranged around the room, with torches in their hands. A sacred book is open on the table, and Mick pronounces the solemn oath, by which he undertakes to obey any orders for 'the chastisement of Nobs, the assassination of oppressive and tyrannical masters, or the demolition of all mills, works and shops that shall be deemed by us incorrigible.' One point is very important: the meeting condemns 'any member who shall be known to boast of his superior ability, as to either the quantity or quality of work he can do, either in public or private company.' Clearly, Disraeli sees the union as an instrument of oppression, holding down wages and skills, regardless of individual excellence.

The last chapters of **Sybil** are given over to a dramatic account of the great strikes and riots of 1842. Mowbray is alarmed: the 'hell-cats' of Wodgate, led by their 'Bishop', are advancing over the surrounding countryside, closing down factories, and pillaging and burning any that resist. They bring a spirit of brutal violence to the peaceful labour troubles of Lancashire. They set fire to Diggs's tommy-shop, and his son dies in the flames. Their leader, the 'Liberator of the People', represents the worst elements of popular revolution: he is a dull, stupid drunkard—a caricature of O'Connor. The armed band trailing behind him ransacks Mowbray Castle, and after a violent, drunken orgy the hell-cats perish in the flames they have lighted. Disraeli feels nothing but hatred and contempt for them: his tone is that of a prophet who dreads his own visions. It is as though he is warning England of the fate awaiting the country if it fails to accept the new Toryism to safeguard society.

This open exposition of his opinions was blunt enough to cause immediate offence. **Sybil** was less successful than **Coningsby;** if some readers loved it, other detested it. It was embarrassing to politicians: it purported to favour the new Toryism and aristocratic philanthropy, yet it could not be accepted without reserve by its friends. On the other hand, its social conscience was so powerful that Whigs and radicals could not decently treat its plea for collective charity with too much severity. And so both sides seem to have tried to say as little as possible about it. The *Westminster Review* was alone among the serious journals in giving it a full notice: W. R. Greg predicted [in the *Westminster Review* XLIV] that it would be less successful than its predecessor. It is also noteworthy that *Coningsby* and *Tancred* both figure in the many lampoons *Punch* directed against Disraeli at this time, but *Sybil* never does. None the less the book was widely read. Writing from France, Disraeli noted that on 'Our first walk in Boulogne, we found *Sybil* "affiched" in a large placard, "Disraeli's new novel", in every window' [*Correspondence of Lord Beaconsfield with his Sister,* letter of 17 September 1845]. And in the long run it made its influence felt: the passage of the Ten Hours Bill in 1847 owed something to it.

*Sybil* is one of the masterpieces of English social fiction. It has its blemishes: the working-class protagonists—Morley, Warner, Gerard, even Sybil herself—are artificial; Disraeli's attempt to use intuition in the absence of knowledge of working-class life was more daring than successful; and there is something stagy about the book as a whole. But for all that it is serious and sparkling. The style is nearly always lively and colourful; the narrative and descriptive passages are forceful and well imagined; upperclass characters, from the world the author knew, are convincing; and finally, the satirical wit has lost none of its sting after a century. The book has permanent social documentary value for the extensive and more or less accurate descriptions of conditions it gives, while the ideas of Disraeli's it puts forward are equally important historically. A comparison with the source material shows that a minimum of artistic distortion went into the boldest parts of *Sybil,* which are an effective popularisation of facts which were generally overlooked, or too little known. Certain vehement passages echoing Carlyle may have done much to soften the conscience of society: consider the following:

> If a spirit of rapacious covetousness, desecrating all the humanities of life, has been the besetting sin of England for the last century and a half, since the passing of the Reform Act the altar of Mammon has blazed with triple worship. To acquire, to accumulate, to plunder each other by virtue of philosophic phrases, to propose a Utopia to consist only of Wealth and Toil, this has been the breathless business of enfranchised England for the last twelve years, until we are startled from our voracious strife by the wail of intolerable serfage.

But in general, the tone of the book is cool and ironic; the author's views did not carry within themselves the faculty of arousing proselytising zeal. And in this respect Disraeli contrasts sharply with Dickens: his achievement was not psychological or emotional. Instead he impressed on his readers a recognition of existing conditions, for he understood the inadequacies of industrial society, even if he could not understand its spirit.

*Tancred, or The New Crusade* (1847) was intended to illustrate the religious element in social Toryism. But the two years which had elapsed since the publication of *Sybil* had apparently changed some of Disraeli's ideas. The repeal of the Corn Laws in 1846 had tied him more closely to the landed aristocratic interest, and his open break with Peel had made him the effective leader of the opposition. Now that power was nearly in his grasp, he was more acutely aware of the chimeric nature of some of Young England's plans, and he saw that compromise would be necessary, even if it meant pruning his more ambitious schemes. Furthermore, the tone of this third novel is different. It is both mystical and self-mocking, and it openly uses implausible events and situations. Serious ideas are concealed under a mass of symbolism; scepticism peeps out of the most impassioned flights of declared faith. On the other hand, the union between industrialists and the nobility which *Coningsby* had proposed is no longer viewed as possible or even desirable. Disraeli is, at bottom, putting in a blow for reactionary politics in their bitter war with liberalism. He castigates the men and ideas of bourgeois civilisation immoderately, hurling diatribes at them which are as unremittingly violent and final as biblical curses.

As a matter of fact, an oriental flavour runs through the whole book. *Tancred* is first and foremost a plea for the Jewish race and spirit. Disraeli has moved away from the oppression of English working men to the persecution of his own race. The Victorian religious and sentimental reaction becomes the signal for a return to the Asiatic origins of Christianity. The divine element in human regeneration can no longer be represented adequately in the social role of the clergy or the philanthropic work of pious Catholic gentlemen. It will take a great mystical vision from the heart of Asia to revive decadent European society.

The French Revolution was a great Aryan apostasy. 'Half a century ago, Europe made a violent and apparently successful effort to disembarrass itself of its Asian faith.' From this sprang the monstrous growth of industrial civilisation, and the secret evils endured by its victims. 'Enlightened Europe is not happy. Its existence is a fever, which it calls progress. Progress to what?' Now impious doctrines denying the creation have been devised; philosophers question man's divine origin, and suggest that he evolved from an animal. ' "I do not believe I ever was a fish," said Tancred.' Only the reversal of all this, a revival of faith, will be of any help to the world. But where is salvation to come from? Catholicism cannot engender such a rebirth; it is itself derivative. Only the Holy Land can expect a new revelation; the God of Moses will speak from a second Sinai. The doctrine of 'theocratic equality' must come from Jerusalem, and then, when England has absorbed this ideal, it will find the faith and determination to carry out the grandiose schemes of social Toryism. But first, justice must be done to the persecuted children of the chosen race. England must recognise her inestimable debt to the descendants of the apostles, venerate the true cradle of Christianity, and take Jews all over the world under her protection.

The action begins in 1845. Tancred, son of the great Duke of Bellamont, belongs, yet again, to the highest nobility. But the promptings of his restless heart do not lead him directly to social work: several years of solitary meditation have made him the apostle of a new crusade. To destroy scepticism and materialism he must re-establish contact with God by visiting the holy places. The heroes of the two previous novels appear, and recognise a kindred spirit in him, while intellectuals, egoists, Whigs, and gilded youths see him as a dreamer. Sidonia encourages him, and promises his all-powerful financial support. Coningsby and Egremont sympathise with him, giving unity to the three novels.

Tancred, the passionate pilgrim, prostrates himself before the Holy Sepulchre. A daughter of Israel, Eva, becomes his guide and inspiration. He becomes involved in warlike adventures with the Maronites and Druses, and performs feats of valour in the desert. He is captured by Arabs who treat him courteously. He climbs to the top of Mount Sinai, and prays for inspiration from heaven:

> 'Faith fades and duty dies. A profound melancholy has fallen on the spirit of man. The priest doubts, the monarch cannot rule, the multitude moans and toils, and calls in its frenzy upon unknown gods.'

And, as is only just, he does see a vision in which the divine message is delivered to him:

> 'The equality of man can only be accomplished by the sovereignty of God. The longing for fraternity can never be satisfied but under the sway of a common father. . . . Announce the sublime and solacing doctrine of theocratic equality.'

And Tancred comes back down to earth, where failure, deception, gnawing doubts, and the slow decay of his cherished hopes await him. The book ends on a melancholy note:

> 'Of all the strange incidents and feelings that we have been talking over this day,' said Eva, 'there seems to me but one result; and that is, sadness. . . .
>
> 'Perhaps, all this time, we have been dreaming over an unattainable end, and the only source of deception is our own imagination.'

The confession was unnecessary. *Tancred* is more of a brilliant fantasy than a social novel. The Eastern Question commanded a good deal of attention at this time, and the Jews had suffered persecution in Rhodes and Damascus around 1840. This was the origin of this remarkable novel, which opens in the only-too-real uncertainties of London during this difficult period, and then moves to a background of legend and dream in Palestine. The book's strength lies more in its defence of the Jewish people than in any exposition of practical philosophy. The Church of England is brought face to face with its own origins and doctrines, and effectively convicts itself of inconsistency. Its indifference to the cult of the Holy Sepulchre cannot be justified; it must recognise the chasm between medieval faith and modern disbelief. 'Persecute us!' cries Eva: 'Why, if you believed what you profess, you should kneel to us!'

On the other hand, the plans for social reorganisation proposed in *Sybil* could have been damaged by their proximi-

ty to the extravagance of *Tancred.* But for Disraeli, serious ideas and imaginative dreams really were linked. The mystical basis of social Toryism was, as far as he was concerned, an experienced fact; only faith would bring about the alliance of Church, Crown, and People. In the most romantic pages of *Tancred* there is a sort of sincerity. The oriental themes, which seem to combine so strangely with the projects for feudal socialism, actually answer to logical and historical experience. At this point in time, the reaction against the eighteenth century associated itself with the spirit of national expansion. Utilitarian radicalism was, of its very nature, cosmopolitan. Historicism, in Britain as in Germany, was nationalist. Here again we find the seeds of imperialism. Fakredeen, a volatile young sheikh to whom Tancred has confided his beliefs, outlines a plan for British control over Asia:

> 'Let the Queen of the English collect a great fleet, let her stow away all her treasure, bullion, gold plate, and precious arms; be accompanied by all her court and chief people, and transfer the seat of her empire from London to Delhi.'

Twenty-seven years later, Lord Beaconsfield had Queen Victoria proclaimed Empress of India.

We should like to leave Disraeli on this note. For the rest of his career his words and deeds were in harmony; he was able to be more straightforward once he had gained power. When he became Prime Minister he was able to implement a large part of the social programme outlined in *Sybil,* and it was through no fault of his own that he could not carry out still more. As we take leave of this great man, whose abilities compel our admiration, however much he lacked charm, it is only fair to recall the fact that social Toryism really did do something for the people. But these belated fruits of the novelist's work are not our concern here. When we look at *Coningsby, Sybil,* and *Tancred* in the context of their own decade, they take on the worth of extremely valuable historical documents. They demonstrate the diffusion of certain attitudes and feelings throughout a particular section of society; attitudes which found expression in social Toryism. (pp. 183-210)

> *Louis Cazamian, "Disraeli: Social Toryism,"
> in his* The Social Novel in England, 1830-
> 1850: Dickens, Disraeli, Mrs Gaskell, Kingsley, *translated by Martin Fido, Routledge &
> Kegan Paul, 1973, pp. 175-210.*

## Morris Edmund Speare   (essay date 1924)

[*In the following excerpt, Speare examines Disraeli's literary significance, describing him as a spirited, eccentric individualist who deserves credit for establishing the political novel as a genre.*]

The "Primrose Sphinx" of English politics has left something of his mystery to the history of English letters. Himself a fascinating figure in his time, product of a peculiar race who combined in a curious manner the stirring influences of his own age, Disraeli perfected a new form and launched it upon the literary world. The Political Novel, as Disraeli conceived it, is as fascinating and various a production, when measured by the side of the novel-forms of the time, as its author was unique among Victorian statesmen.

It is especially true of Disraeli that *le style est l'homme même.* All his characteristic intensity flames in his written word; his great strength struggles for utterance. The novel-forms of his day were incapable of embracing the stretch of his ideas, of enduring the speculative intrepidity of his mind. They offered no vehicle for the development of 'programs,' for launching manifestoes, for the destruction of adversaries, for exposing plans that would rejuvenate England. He chose to present a form of his own. The path out of the main highway upon which he, more than any other, trod, has since his day been widened, paved, and used by many travellers. The course of time has made the journey a familiar one. The life of politics, particularly to people like our own—active participants in a thoroughly popular government—is now a well-known story. But to the masses of people, in the days of Disraeli's novels, when England was passing from behind the shadows of rule by close corporation to the dawn of a new day of democracy, the inner life of politics was not familiar. Even less so was it to Americans: by that fact they showed the greater curiosity. The spectacle of a Prime Minister presumably revealing, in the form of romance, what 'made the wheels go around' in the English government, encouraged many to buy his novels—at one time at the rate of 1000 copies a day, 80,000 in a few months. Disraeli, however, far from desiring to make any such revelation, whether as minister or member of the Commons, perceived only a world of men, women, and customs which had never before been adequately portrayed in the novel. More intimately familiar with that world than any other writer of his time, he resolved therefore to present it. He was not disturbed by fixed artistic principles which govern every form of creative work. He was probably not conscious of their existence. He simply accepted certain facts: that the novel is capable of holding and shaping real experience of any kind, as it affects the lives of men and women; that it is, in literature, the most adaptable of forms; and that no man has a right to set limits to its range. So he rode audaciously across the impediments which the very nature of his material would have made into stumbling-blocks for a more conscious artist, a better educated writer than he, and his very audacity landed him safe on the other side. For not only in England, but in America and upon the continent Disraeli has had a great reading public.

Disraeli was a pioneer in English letters. The definitive biography of him which has been completed, and which reveals now and for the first time that this highly imaginative and romantic character had, from early manhood, laid out a course from which he never deviated, that he possessed the qualities which went to form a great statesman, obliges us also to give more importance than we have given heretofore to his place in our literature. In his own time friendly contemporaries who had perceived the difficulties he encountered gave voice to an appreciation of his accomplishment. He had taken—so they declared—the barren field of politics and had founded upon it a new school of novel writing. He had breathed a soul into dead bones, genius into facts, power into mechanics! Here, they said, is a man who by means of the novel has established what are the principles of power; by what method the English people may sustain their realm; by what social and political measures the nation may assure future happiness; how the individual, by a visit to the founts of Christianity, may, in an age of doubt and perplexity, come back to a broader and nobler faith. Some of his admirers, particularly those of the Young England group, believed that for what he did for his party, Disraeli was as truly an elemental force in English politics as Lord Byron had been in English poetry. Upon the very classes whom he had chosen to lead he poured satire, lampoon, and ridicule; he showed off their self-contentment, their superciliousness and frivolity, their self-indulgence, their aversion to originality and genius, their disinclination to self-sacrifice; he did all this until he aroused them out of their languors and stung them into action. Though he succeeded only at first in earning their hostility, he eventually educated these proud men up to his own level, and forced them to accept him as their leader! The man who could transpose the first three letters of his own name, and use them to begin that of an intellectual Messiah leading Coningsby to a Promised land, himself became a sort of 'Sidonia' to the English nobility. Of all men of his time Disraeli was least under the sway of current influences, though he shows that he was familiar enough with them. Less than most of his contemporaries was Disraeli enslaved by the authority of accepted opinion. He dared to be eccentric, individual, audacious.

Something of the same spirit is what he brought into literature. Here, too, he was self-reliant, surprising, unconventional. Less than others did he depend upon the forms of the past; less than others did he follow the established methods of his contemporaries. His descriptions of certain types of national character have not been equalled by any other English writer. He was the first to give us the satire of politics in a novel. His pictures of social and political England undergoing democratic transformation must remain a permanent and moving record of historical phenomena. Much of what he gave us is unique in Victorian literature, because there was none other, at the same time a novelist, who was so conversant with the machinery of public affairs. The same hand that signed Exchequer accounts and executive orders of the First Minister in Downing Street, busied itself at Hughenden Manor with the most glowing kind of political romance. In that political romance Disraeli was one of the first of the nineteenth century to defend the right of women to rank as intellectual beings. He was one of the first to appraise the rôle they may play, through their charm and their sympathy, in the lives of great men—particularly men of public affairs. There are few writers who have had as great an affection for youth as he, and who show that the world is for the young. To him "youth were the trustees of posterity." His heroes are almost always young men of power, filled with energy, resolution, adventure, and high idealism. With the single exception of Endymion, they are youth trying to emancipate themselves from the tyranny of custom, from the conventional, from the accepted, and they are usually either permanently or temporarily conquerors in their struggles. His young women are always charming, sweet, and gracious, and though in his portrayal of them he seems to follow the 18th century conventions, still they are never the colorless, flabby persons one associates with that period of 'heroines,' but are always creatures of ardent affection, lively imagination, and independent spirit. Toward them the author is supremely courteous,—gallant, almost, to the point of adoration.

These are a few of many things upon which one likes to pause and comment as one recalls what it is that Disraeli has incorporated into his novels. The whole, however, is greater than its parts. In their own day these materials out of which Disraeli compounded his political novels, achieved a remarkable result. By the side of *Don Quixote*, which is said to have annihilated Chivalry, and *Tartuffe*, which dealt a powerful blow to the Church; *Vanity Fair*, which relieved us of much snobbery, and *Bleak House*, which gave an impulse to law reform; beside works like these Frederic Harrison would place **Coningsby** and **Sybil.** These created a 'new political party' and thus directly achieved an effect upon English history.

His style is a reflection of his fascinating personality. It is invariably lively, ardent, colorful. Usually it is a pageantry of rhetoric, a verbal orchestration of thought. Much has already been said of Disraeli's riotous imagination, of his oriental tastes; how he surrounds his schemes of power and sets off his vistas of genius with fabulous wealth, elegant patrician life, Babylonian terrace and ideal cathedrals, alabaster tombs and ropes of pearls. The society to which he sometimes introduces us appears to have stepped out of an Aladdin's cave, laden with the spoils of centuries. The worst of these descriptions are so extravagant as to be altogether unreal. Some of the best of them—such as the famous passage recounting the accession of Queen Victoria, the description of Jerusalem, the mountain scene during Tancred's prayer—have become part of every biography written of Disraeli. Not so well known are passages in his novels which, for swiftness of narration, rival the work of Sterne. Still more surprising in Disraeli, and unfortunately never quoted, are descriptions in every one of his novels that are filled with the beauty of nature and characterized by the highest simplicity of art. Where, for example, can one find in the range of nineteenth century English literature a more natural, a more simple pastoral picture than this, in which Disraeli is presenting the effect of a summer shower?

> The oppressive atmosphere had evaporated; the grey, sullen tint had disappeared; a soft breeze came dancing up the stream; a glowing light fell upon the woods and waters; the perfume of trees and flowers and herbs floated around. There was a carolling of birds; a hum of happy insects in the air; freshness and stir, and a sense of joyous life, pervaded all things; it seemed that the heart of all creation opened.
>
> [*Coningsby*]

The man's airiness of invention, his shimmer of wit, the hundred and one resources of his fresh and frolicsome genius, never show themselves to better advantage than in the short, epigrammatic descriptions of persons and scenes with which his novels abound, the sparkling, vivacious dialogue of his clubs, lobbies, and drawing-rooms,

and his phrase-making. There are none in the comedies of Congreve and Sheridan better than Taper and Tadpole, the young and romantic Lady Bertie and Belair, Count Mirabel, Mrs. Guy Flouncey, Leander the French chef, Lady Firebrace, Lord St. Aldegonde. "Nature had intended Lucian Gay for a scholar and a wit: necessity had made him a scribbler and a buffoon." From the same novel, *Coningsby,* we choose a description of a noblewoman. Lady Gaverstock's "mother having been divorced, she ever fancied she was paying a kind of homage to her parent, by visiting those who might some day be in the same predicament." Here is one of a nobleman from *Lothair.* "Every day when he looked in a glass, and gave the last touch to his consummate toilet, he offered his grateful thanks to Providence that his family was not unworthy of him." Of a lesser character in Parliament: "Bertie Tremaine was one of those who always walked home with the member who had made the speech of the evening," and welcomed at his table "every one except absolute assassins." Of the Utilitarians: "Their dogma is—rules are general, feelings are general, therefore property should be general." Of his political enemy, Peel: "Peel caught the Whigs bathing and walked off with their clothes." "Peel's precedents are tea-kettle precedents: he traces the steam-engine always back to the tea-kettle." There were politicians who were "Forcible feebles," "Tory men and Whig measures," "Patricians in a panic." He once defined the Austrians as "the Chinese of Europe," and diplomatists as "the Hebrews of Politics."

These imaginative works of a peculiarly subtle character, whom a contemporary once described as able to "maintain the mingled gravity of Oedipus with the *insouciance* and *diablerie* of Robert Macaire," show unfortunately much unevenness of writing, and certain organic defects. They should, perhaps, be explained as due to a novelist whose active life was devoted primarily to the lists of party strife, and to the busy affairs of state; only occasionally could he find that repose, that retirement, which could sustain even short periods of contemplation so necessary for an artist. Disraeli too often irritates the reader by his complete detachment from the class of society of which, in active life, he desired and did become both philosopher and leader. He lampoons out of all reason the stock whose children he idealizes, making a separation in his novels between the older nobility and the younger generation that violates every natural and historical law. How can one believe, in novel after novel, that the same atmosphere of England, the same sun, produces such dissimilar fruits? What means can perform such a miracle in a single generation? Take another example. There is not, in all of Disraeli's political novels, a single portrait of a statesman, or of a minor public character, in whom love of country and desire to give service to the state is the sole and moving passion. Disraeli was too much the cynic in his worst moments, and too much the actor at his best, to be able to speak feelingly of the statesman of great integrity, or to analyze ambition which thinks only of serving the nation. Surely, in Victorian England, there must have been such men in active public life! When we turn to examine closely his occasional defects in English composition we must believe that many a sentence was placed upon a page "as hot and as hurried as ever was penned." Again and again he fails to command the English idiom, and sometimes he employs constructions that are so bad that his statements are quite ridiculous. Of some of these, the less said the better.

Historically, the place of Disraeli in English literature is assured. Time alone will fix his permanence and convince men of his importance. He smashed through the traditions of English literary forms, broadly interpreted laws or altogether ignored them, and established a *genre* in modern literature. He did so by widening the technique of the novels already in existence, and by employing it to absorb a new kind of material. Preceding him there is but one exception: the novel *De Vere* by Robert Plumer Ward. Strictly speaking, however, Plumer Ward is only a forerunner of the master: *De Vere* was but a link between *the novel with a purpose* of the 18th century and the political novel as Disraeli firmly established it in *Coningsby* and *Sybil*. Disraeli, therefore, poured new wine into old bottles. He did that for the novel which Ibsen, in more recent days and in another fashion, has done for the drama: for Ibsen broke through the technique of the so-called "well-made play" and thus enlarged the scope of the drama for all future playwrights. The publication of *Coningsby* was an event of no less importance to the history of the novel than the appearance of *The Doll's House* was to modern dramatic literature. Disraeli has not, like Ibsen, founded a school. Still, the writers in both England and America who have used the *genre* that he established have been persons of prominence and great influence. Taken all together they make a very respectable showing . . . [When an] analysis has been made it will be found that the great political novel has yet to be written. So has the great problem play. Neither fact, however, can lessen the historical significance which both Disraeli and Ibsen hold in their respective fields of literature, nor can it undervalue the contribution which their establishment of special forms has made for the creative artist of to-morrow. (pp. 176-84)

> *Morris Edmund Speare, "The Literary Significance of Benjamin Disraeli," in his* The Political Novel: Its Development in England and

---

**Anthony Trollope on Disraeli's prose style:**

To me [Disraeli's novels] have all had the same flavour of paint and unreality. In whatever he has written he has affected something which has been intended to strike his readers as uncommon and therefore grand. Because he has been bright and a man of genius, he has carried his object as regards the young. He has struck them with astonishment and aroused in their imagination ideas of a world more glorious, more rich, more witty, more enterprising, than their own. But the glory has been the glory of pasteboard, and the wealth has been a wealth of tinsel. The wit has been the wit of hairdressers, and the enterprise has been the enterprise of mountebanks.

> *Anthony Trollope, in his* Autobiography, *Harper & Brothers, 1883, reprinted by Oxford University Press, 1923.*

---

in America, *Oxford University Press, Inc., 1924, pp. 143-84.*

**Muriel Masefield   (essay date 1953)**

[*In the following excerpt, Masefield discusses Disraeli's novels in terms of their social and historical value, concluding that despite certain stylistic weaknesses, his works contain exuberant and colorful portrayals of the English aristocracy.*]

In the year 1826 a novel called *Vivian Grey* was published anonymously. The manuscript had been submitted to the publisher Colburn by a Mrs. Austen, a charming lady in whose judgment he had considerable confidence, on behalf of a protégé whose anonymity she protected by copying the entire book in her own handwriting. Colburn, realising that here was a piquant specimen of the novel of fashionable life for which Plumer Ward's *Tremaine or a Man of Refinement* had just whetted the appetite of a wide public, made shrewd use of the mystery. The book was advertised as a society novel with characters drawn from contemporary social and public life, and it was implied that the author was well qualified to indulge in his satirical portraits, but naturally did not wish to disclose his name. The publisher himself was content to take the book on trust at first—perhaps he even preferred not to know the truth which, indeed, had no prestige value, since *Vivian Grey* was the first impact upon the world at large of an unknown young man of twenty-one, saddled with debt and bearing a name which had no affinity with the English aristocracy—Benjamin Disraeli.

*Vivian Grey* took London by storm. Keys professing to identify the characters were passed round in society; the lovely Mrs. Norton (Sheridan's granddaughter) learned pages of it by heart, and only one reviewer, Jerdan of the *Literary Gazette,* was perspicacious enough to write that "the class of the author was a little betrayed by his frequent recurrence to topics about which the mere man of fashion knows nothing and cares less". A nemesis awaited the young Disraeli when his presumption was at last unmasked, but for the moment he basked deliciously in anonymous fame.

*Vivian Grey* was the first of eleven full-length novels in which we may pass in review a pageant of English life and manners from 1826 to 1880. Dukes and Marquesses, fine ladies, politicians, wire-pullers, Chartists, labourers and even mill-girls crowd the stories which flowed from Disraeli's prolific pen. In the earlier books we find the traditions of Regency elegance, now a little over-blown, still a force in high society. Although Beau Brummell was now only a memory, dandies still lounged and postured at assemblies and balls, and in *Henrietta Temple* Disraeli gives us an enchanting picture of the very High Priest of the cult, Count D'Orsay, an artist in more than dress, whose gaiety and wit sparkle from the pages as freshly as they did when Disraeli himself enjoyed them at Gore House, presided over by Lady Blessington. The gilded youth of society, their manners, talk and pursuits, live for us again in these novels, and we may accompany them to the racecourse, the gaming-table, the spunging-house, the duel and on the Grand Tour of Europe. The splendid town houses and the stately country homes of the nobility, with the hierarchy of servants and that typical figure of the time, the toady, are drawn in all their real magnificence, and perhaps a little more. Disraeli loved splendour for its own sake; at this time the peacock—few of his country houses are without their peacocks—with the gorgeous plumage of its oriental ancestry, was in the ascendant in his nature, the young writer had still far to go before the English primrose could be accepted as his sign and symbol. Even now, however, his admiration was not slavish, the grandeur must be superb in its kind to please him and already the irony which was to become one of his greatest gifts acted upon his imagination as an astringent.

The young Disraeli had, in fact, a splendid society to describe; it was a period of which Mrs. Gore (a fashionable novelist) could write with some truth: "Throughout Europe it was holiday-time for people intent on promoting the greatest happiness of the smallest number." Nevertheless, beneath the surface the currents of reform and democracy, to which Disraeli himself was one day to make his contribution, were already gathering force under popular leaders of a new type. In the same year that *Vivian Grey* was published Cobbett set out on the last of the journeys described in his *Rural Rides,* in which he attacked rotten boroughs and other abuses with vitriolic gusto. Robert Owen's model factory at New Lanark was attracting more than national attention and he had already fathered the co-operative movement; it was in the magazine founded by the London Co-operative Society in this very year (1826) that he coined the significant new word "socialist". Meanwhile Francis Place, the radical tailor of Westminster, assiduously coached the factory hands brought up to town from the industrial north, whose witness enabled Joseph Hume to induce Parliament to repeal the Combination Laws, and so prepare the way for the rise of strong, legitimate trade unions. In Parliament itself reform was "in the air". The days were numbered when a Duke who regarded a Parliamentary borough as his personal property could be outraged when the electors presumed to vote against his nominee, and exclaim passionately in the House of Lords: "What! May I not do what I will with my own?"

These portents, however, barely ruffled the surface of aristocratic society when Disraeli wrote *Vivian Grey;* the gilded youths still looked down on lesser breeds from pinnacles of glory, and few would have quarrelled with the sentiment in his second novel: "Oh, to be a Duke, and to be young, it is too much!" The English "Milord" had, in fact, every excuse for regarding himself as the cream of mankind; after the defeat of Napoleon his country's prestige stood higher than that of any other in Europe, and when he travelled it was as "a proud citizen of the proudest of lands" (*Lothair*), a representative of "the wealth and authority of the richest of nations" (*Tancred*). He had behind him the august aura of Downing Street, which Disraeli could fairly describe as that "happy spot where they draw up constitutions for Syria and treaties for China with the same self-complacency and the same success!" (*Tancred*). In the charmed circle of the aristocracy values were still stable and the objects of ambition for a young man of

family clear and unchallenged. High-born youths eager to prove their talents "panted for the Senate" (*Vivian Grey*); others accepted a seat in the House of Commons, representing a family borough, as part of the natural order of life, following Eton and the university or a tour of Europe. Speaking wistfully of pre-Reform Bill days, a member of a select London club could say, "I remember when there were only ten men in the House of Commons who were not either members of Brooks' or this place" (*Coningsby*). Lady Montfort (*Endymion*) was expressing a truism of her circle when she exclaimed: "Not go into Parliament? Why, what are men made for except to go into Parliament? I am indeed astounded." Disraeli also noted with sly relish that the House of Commons, conferring immunity from arrest, could be a blessed alternative to a debtors' prison. Stapylton Toad (*Vivian Grey*) admitted that he had accepted the Chiltern Hundreds "to make room for Augustus Clay, Ernest Clay's brother, who was so involved that the only way to keep him out of the House of Correction was to get him into the House of Commons". In such circles the only perplexity was that of the younger son who was unable to command a seat in Parliament, refused the Church and could not afford the Guards.

A presage of coming change to which Disraeli gave full value in his first novel was the rise of the New Rich, when mere wealth, more widely diffused as industrial magnates made fortunes, began to encroach upon the preserves of rank. He was no sycophant of the aristocracy when he described the arrival of Mrs. Million at Château Désir, the country home of the Marquess of Carabas. Her entrance was spectacular, in crimson silk, pelisse, hat and feathers, diamond ear-rings and a rope of gold round her neck, and she was followed by a large train of toad-eaters, physicians and secretaries: "All fell back. Gartered peers and starred ambassadors, baronets with blood older than creation, and squires, to the antiquity of whose veins chaos was a novelty; all retreated, with eyes that scarcely dared to leave the ground; even Sir Plantagenet Pure, whose family had refused a peerage regularly in every century, now, for the first time in his life, seemed cowed."

Mrs. Million is not the only representative of the New Rich in the book; travelling on the Continent Vivian Grey meets the Fitzloom family:

> This family is one of those whose existence astounds the Continent much more than any of your mighty Dukes and Earls, whose fortunes, though colossal, can be conceived, and whose rank is understood. Mr. Fitzloom is a very different personage, for thirty years ago he was a journeyman cotton spinner. Some miraculous invention in machinery entitled him to a patent, which has made him one of the great proprietors of England. He has lately been returned a member for a manufacturing town, and he intends to get over the first two years of his Parliamentary career by successively monopolising the accommodation of the principal cities of France, Germany, Switzerland and Italy, and by raising the price of provisions and post-horses through a track of five thousand miles.

It was, indeed, the rise of such families as the Millions and the Fitzlooms that accounted largely for the popularity of the novel of fashionable life in the eighteen-twenties and thirties. For the most part the chief ambitions of the New Rich were to share the privileges of the aristocracy and ape their manners. They seized upon Ward's *Tremaine,* Disraeli's ***Vivian Grey*** and Edward Bulwer's *Pelham* as manuals of initiation, and soon silver fork fiction, as it came to be called, even superseded the tales of mystery and horror of which Mrs. Radcliffe had been the arch-priestess. Thackeray parodied silver fork fiction in a delightful Burlesque under the heading: "LORDS AND LIVERIES. By the Authoress of *Dukes and Déjeuners, Hearts and Diamonds, Marchionesses and Milliners etc.*" Few found fault with the limited personnel of such novels; Miss Edgeworth was a pioneer when she introduced scenes of Irish peasant life into her books, and so inspired Scott to look for characters amongst the lowly-born of his own country. Scott was, in fact, the only giant in the fiction of the eighteen-twenties.

***Vivian Grey*** is, however, something more than an example of silver fork fiction in that parts of it are romanticised autobiography. Disraeli's second novel, ***The Young Duke,*** he himself described as half fashion and half passion, but the fashion, overgorgeous as it is in places, is its chief interest. In ***Contarini Fleming,*** which followed it a year later, we can trace much of the mental and spiritual ferment of Disraeli's own youth; he called it a psychological romance and claimed that its theme was the development of the poetic character. After this he produced ***The Wondrous Tale of Alroy,*** the heroic story of a Jewish Prince of the Captivity in the twelfth century, which gave him a congenial chance to revel in scenes of splendour and romance, with high-flown prose to match. The next book, ***Henrietta Temple,*** was the fruit of a happy infatuation for a delightful mistress of his own world and was intended to be primarily a love-story, but its best features are gay and witty portraits of well-known society characters and realistic scenes at Crockford's and in a spunging-house. ***Venetia*** was published in the same year, owing to the fact that Disraeli was virtually a prisoner in his room at Bradenham, which he dare not leave in case he should be "nabbed" for his debts. The chief distinction of this novel is a life-like portrait of Byron as the hero, under the name of Lord Cadurcis.

After this group of early novels, written between the ages of twenty-one and thirty-three, there was a gap of seven years during which Disraeli established his position as a member of Parliament and married Mrs. Wyndham Lewis. By 1844, when he turned to writing again, Queen Victoria's court had brought a new influence to bear on morals and manners; extravagance in behaviour, dress and character were beginning to give place to dignity, modesty and sobriety. Parliament had been reformed by the Act of 1832, which gave the country a first instalment of democracy and was followed by various progressive measures, and now England had to learn that it was not everything for a country to become the workshop of the world at the expense of being unable to feed its people on its own produce. The "hungry 'forties" had begun.

Disraeli had revelled in the colourful extravagance of the pre-Victorian period. As a young man he recorded with satisfaction how one of his spectacular costumes had startled Regent Street: "The people", he wrote complacently, "quite made way for me as I passed. It was like the opening of the Red Sea, which I now perfectly believe from experience. Even well-dressed people stopped to look at me." His failure in his maiden speech in Parliament was no doubt partly due to the antagonism caused by his jet-black curls, bottle-green coat and white waistcoat covered with gold chains. Even his friend Bulwer (known later as Bulwer Lytton), himself a notable dandy, rallied him gaily on his magnificence—"Why so many gold chains, Dizzy?"—and asked him if he thought of becoming a Lord Mayor. Ten years earlier, perhaps, a man who wore rings outside his gloves might have set a fashion. Now he was suspect; the reformed House of Commons preferred young Mr. Gladstone's dark suits and serious manner. Disraeli himself commented ironically on this in his last novel (***Endymion***), in which he looked back on the eighteen-thirties with detachment: "An insular country, subject to fogs, and with a powerful middle class, requires grave statesmen."

Despite his natural affinity with a more colourful and romantic age, Disraeli did not live in the past, and he had from the first a genuine sympathy with the under-dog and a passionate faith in the individual's right to make the best of himself. At the age of twenty-eight, when he contested the seat of High Wycombe before the Reform Bill, he promised that he would "seek the amelioration of the condition of the poor", at that time an unusual bait to offer to the limited electorate (actually thirty-two voted), all of whom must of necessity be "substantial" men. He was expressing a life-long conviction when, in a famous speech at the opening of the Manchester Athenæum, he declared: "Every individual is entitled to aspire to that position which he believes his faculties qualify him to occupy."

Disraeli's seventh novel—***Coningsby or The New Generation***—represents a change of outlook. The self-interest and ambition of Vivian Grey and the introspection of Contarini Fleming give place in Harry Coningsby to a real concern for the condition of the English people, and this book gives us a picture of the Young England group, formed of idealistic young members of Parliament who adopted Disraeli as their elder brother and leader. They saw their mission as the regeneration of the monarchy, church and aristocracy in a benevolent partnership to abolish "class legislation" and serve the welfare of the whole people. They had no faith in immediate manhood suffrage, which would only lead to "a government carried on by a neglected democracy who, for three centuries, have received no education" (*Coningsby*).

***Coningsby*** was a new phenomenon in fiction, the political novel. It was also the first of a trilogy of novels, published between 1844 and 1847, in which Disraeli set himself to diagnose the sickness of contemporary society and prescribe threefold remedies—political, social and religious. The second of these novels, ***Sybil or The Two Nations,*** followed ***Coningsby*** within a year. The best commentary on the title is a dialogue between the book's aristocratic hero,

Egremont, and a young working-man who aspires to be a leader of the people:

> "Well, society may be in its infancy," said Egremont, slightly smiling, "but, say what you like, our Queen reigns over the greatest nation that ever existed."
>
> "Which nation?" asked the younger stranger, "for she reigns over two."
>
> The stranger paused; Egremont was silent, but looked enquiringly.
>
> "Yes," resumed the younger stranger after a moment's interval. "Two nations; between whom there is no intercourse and no sympathy; who are as ignorant of each other's habits, thoughts and feelings, as if they were dwellers in different zones, or inhabitants of different planets; who are formed by a different breeding, are fed by a different food, are ordered by different manners, and are not governed by the same laws."
>
> "You speak of—" said Egremont, hesitatingly.
>
> "THE RICH AND THE POOR."

It is interesting that Mrs. Gaskell struck the same note when writing of this period (in *Mary Barton*). After saying that the working people needed a Dante to record their sufferings—"And yet even his words would fall short of the awful truth"—she states that "the most deplorable and enduring evil that arose out of these years of commercial depression was the feeling of alienation between the different classes of society". Disraeli may have given her a lead, but Mrs. Gaskell wrote from personal knowledge of poor homes in Manchester and her corroboration of his theme is valuable.

Dickens was before Disraeli in using the novel to expose social evils; while Disraeli spoke more than once in the House of Commons against the harsh pressure of the new Poor Law of 1834, Dickens pilloried it in *Oliver Twist*. Nevertheless, *Sybil* was the first complete example of a new type of book which came to be described as the condition-of-England novel, and it is a mine of social history. In particular it throws much light on the Chartist movement, which Disraeli took pains to study, staying in the north of England for the purpose. He soon realised that, although the chief articles of the Chartist faith were manhood suffrage and the secret ballot, Chartism was fundamentally a "knife and fork" agitation, a revolt against empty fireplaces and bare cupboards, and in *Sybil* he gives us some realistic and touching scenes from the life of working-people in the industrial north. Disraeli had broken new ground, but he was soon followed into this field by Mrs. Gaskell, with *Mary Barton,* and Charles Kingsley, with *Alton Locke,* who both gave their books a Chartist background.

The third novel of the trilogy—*Tancred or The New Crusade*—represents a different approach to the ills from which Europe, as well as England, was suffering. The young crusader, described by a Bishop as a visionary, posed to himself many of the same questions as the votaries of Young England, but he could not see salvation in the regeneration of national institutions or the operations of "that fatal drollery called a representative government". He came to the conclusion that the supreme need of the age was "to restore and renovate our communications with the Most High". He was irresistibly drawn to the Holy Land, where alone God had vouchsafed direct revelation to man. He would kneel at his Redeemer's tomb in vigil, as a crusading ancestor had done six centuries before, and there he would lift his voice to Heaven and ask: "What is duty, and what is faith? What ought I to DO, and what ought I to BELIEVE?" Tancred, however, had not allowed for the vagaries of the human heart, which betrayed him into uncertainty and delay; this part of the book has its full quota of Disraelian wit. The second part of Tancred's story has a vivid eastern setting, based on Disraeli's own travels.

*Tancred* illustrates the duality of Disraeli's own nature— the vein of oriental mysticism (or at least fantasy) and the shrewd prescience and skill of the great statesman. To many of his contemporaries the novelist seemed to belie the man of action, they deplored such lapses into extravagant fiction on the part of one who aspired to be a leader in the House of Commons. In fact, as Carlyle said, it was perhaps as well for Disraeli that many of his colleagues in the Tory party never read anything.

After this trilogy Disraeli was absorbed in a life of action and there were no more novels for twenty-three years. He was sixty-six when he published *Lothair* (1870), and his last book, *Endymion,* only appeared the year before he died, aged seventy-seven. In these books the elder statesman is no longer driven by urgent political theories or crusading against social injustice. He once said, "When I want to read a novel I write one", and in *Lothair* he seems at last to be writing to entertain himself without any ulterior or motive. The main theme is the conflict between the Roman Catholic and Anglican churches for a young man's soul, but there is a characteristic diversion in which a woman of almost mystic magnetism, and of course great beauty, involves Lothair in one of Garibaldi's campaigns for the liberation of Italy. This novel, too, has its great country house and a galaxy of witty, exotic or exquisitely bored characters.

By the time *Endymion* was written Disraeli the statesman had lived to translate some of the ideas of the author of *Coningsby* and *Sybil* into Acts of Parliament. As *Sybil* had been a condition-of-England novel, so Disraeli's ministry of 1874-80 was a condition-of-England government. A Public Health Act and an Artisans' Dwellings Act provided for improvements in the care of national health and made possible the clearance of slums; a Trade Union "Charter" placed the workman on an equality with the employer in bargaining, hours of labour were limited to fifty-six a week, with a free half-day on Saturday, and various useful sanitary measures were passed. It was Disraeli, too, who, in spite of the views of *Coningsby* in 1844, gave the vote to town householders—and also originated the phrase "we must educate our masters". The young fop who had exulted in holding up pedestrians in Regent Street to stare at him had travelled far.

Disraeli had compared Gladstone's out-going ministry to a row of exhausted volcanoes; he himself in his last novel has lost his volcanic quality, but, still gently smoking, he looks back on the political and social scene of the 'thirties and 'forties with a detachment at once benign and ironic. **Vivian Grey, Contarini Fleming, Coningsby, Tancred,** and even **Alroy,** had embodied some of the agonies and ecstasies of his own youth, in **Endymion** he sees the period of his early manhood down the perspective of years with a more temperate eye.

In all Disraeli's novels the incidentals are more striking than the theme or story, and scattered about them are thinly disguised sketches of well-known people of the day. In some cases they are life-like, in others the originals have been used as little more than suggestions for characters. Through his eyes we can see and hear some famous men as they actually moved and spoke. There is this vignette of the Duke of Wellington speaking in the House of Lords, for instance:

> "In the Lords, I admire the Duke. The readiness with which he has adopted the air of a debater shows the man of genius. There is a gruff, husky sort of a downright Montaignish naïveté about him, which is quaint, unusual, and tells. You plainly perceive that he is determined to be a civilian; and he is as offended if you drop a hint that he occasionally wears a uniform, as a servant on a holiday, if you mention the word *livery*" (**The Young Duke**).

There is, in fact, far too much in each of the novels, including language which is anything but simple and direct by the standards of today, although even in the most florid passages he often gives us the *mot juste,* and epigrams stand out of the verbiage with pointed finish. Scenes, characters and incidents crowd upon one another, digressions and soliloquies add to the indigestible mixture, and yet the books are full of life. G. K. Chesterton, in a Preface to a juvenile work of Jane Austen's, wrote: "Her power came, as all power comes, from the control and direction of exuberance. But there is the presence and pressure of that vitality behind her thousand trivialities; she could have been extravagant if she chose." Disraeli's exuberance is fully apparent in his early novels, and he never lost it, but it is only spasmodically brought under control, he too often chose to be extravagant.

A recent biographer (Hesketh Pearson in *Dizzy,* 1951) while disparaging Disraeli as a creative artist, reminds us that "though none of his novels is a work of genius, nearly all of them are works of a genius". Certainly the ironic wit which was so effective in the House of Commons runs through them like an electric current. Disraeli may have lacked the gift of fusing characters and story into the convincing unity that makes a really great book, but many of his faults (such as lengthy digressions) are those common to writers of his period. (pp. 11-21)

> *Muriel Masefield, in his* Peacocks and Primroses: A Survey of Disraeli's Novels, *Geoffrey Bles, 1953, 319 p.*

## John Holloway   (essay date 1953)

[*Holloway is an English educator and poet. In the essay below, he suggests that Disraeli successfully integrated his political ideology with a lighthearted treatment of high society to create well-balanced and engaging novels.*]

Exotic fantasies like **The Rise of Iskander** or **Alroy,** the fantastic 'Wanderjahr' politics and adventures of **Vivian Grey** or **Contarini Fleming,** the dandiacal politics of **The Young Duke,** high-life romances like **Henrietta Temple** or **Venetia,** politics and society in **Coningsby** or **Sybil,** religion, travel and speculation in **Tancred** or **Lothair,** and the objective and subtly felt panorama of **Endymion**—all these together make Disraeli one of the liveliest and most versatile novelists of his period. He could scarcely seem more different from Carlyle. Indeed, it is not at first clear that Disraeli wrote much, or indeed anything, which gives expression to a point of view not merely political, but genuinely speculative or philosophical. And just as Carlyle would not have concerned this enquiry had he been merely an opponent of Free Trade and Parliamentary elections, so Disraeli would not, had he been merely a romancer or merely a protagonist of the Tory party.

But there is usually more to his work than this; as there must be, perhaps, in any serious political writer and as indeed there was in the novelists of the 'dandy' and the 'silver-fork' schools even before Disraeli, exploiting their materials, did a good deal to deepen their impact. An outlook that is more than political, and is proved to be more than political because it finds as natural an expression in the German forests, on the Italian sea-shore, or among the Arabs or Syrians, as it does at home in England, runs through all his work—except, strangely enough, the quite untendentious **Endymion.** It is not, to be sure, there alone; Disraeli lacks the insistence of Carlyle. He has not Carlyle's singleness and earnestness of purpose. The line of his polemical interest runs waveringly athwart his work, and often it is hidden by Disraeli the romancer or Disraeli the more narrow politician. But for all that it is there: and although it must be disentangled from other elements and then seen in the context of them, its intermittent nature results in a colourful, irresponsible brilliance that is not without its relevance, as we shall see.

Disraeli's novels, one after another (though some much more clearly than others), contain a pattern of enquiry typical of the moralist or seer raising 'ultimate' questions; and one must see how it is to these ultimate questions that his novels suggest an answer, not only to more circumscribed political issues. The elements of the pattern are those traced already in Carlyle: Disraeli creates the same sense of perplexity, the same unsureness about fundamentals, and the same dissatisfaction with conventional answers on the ground that they are shallow. Sooner or later his heroes tend to find themselves confronted with questions about ultimates. Tancred says: 'It is time to . . . renovate our communications with the Most High . . . I . . . would lift up my voice to heaven, and ask, what is DUTY, and what is FAITH? What ought I to DO, and what ought I to BELIEVE?' [In **Sybil**] Charles Egremont, disappointed in love, begins to detect his illusions, to stop and think, 'to observe, to enquire, and to reflect . . . he discovered that, when he imagined his education was completed, it had in fact not commenced'. For the young Coningsby, 'What were his powers? What should be his aim? were often . . . questions infinitely perplexing . . . '; he 'loved to pursue every question to the centre'; he had 'a mind predisposed to enquiry and prone to meditation'.

Through his characters, Disraeli not only suggests these problems, but also indicates what frame of mind can hope to solve them. His view here is, once again, typical of the 'prophet'. Coningsby, 'sustained by a profound, however vague, conviction, that there are still great truths, if we could but work them out', pursues his questions to the centre 'not in a spirit of scepticism . . . on the contrary, it was the spirit of faith'. He 'found that he was born in an age of infidelity in all things . . . he needed that deep and enduring conviction that the heart and the intellect, feeling and reason united, can alone supply'. Tancred also unites these qualities; and 'life is stranger than I deemed' is the epitome of what is essentially his religious education. Lothair, though intellectually complacent at first, is really 'of a nature profound and inquisitive, though with a great fund of reverence'; he says (with an air of distress) 'We live in dark times'; and the novel of which he is hero portrays a quest for something that will remove his perplexity. What he seeks is a religion, a 'Life-Philosophy'— this is still true, even though he chiefly makes his enquiries among the women he falls in love with.

There is thus no doubt that at least these four novels present the prophet's familiar, basic problem, although they do so in novel form, and of course do much else too. The doctrine advanced by Disraeli in answer to this problem is revealing. It illuminates with particular vividness the contrast between abstractly stating a view of life, and something which will really evoke it in the reader's imagination. For, put in its baldest terms, Disraeli's central premiss about the human situation is only that human society as a whole is like a live thing. Its essential qualities are *continuity* and *vitality*. From this all the rest would follow logically, if logic were relevant. Disraeli makes this point explicitly in the *Vindication of the English Constitution*. The individual's character, he says, produces a salutary consistency of conduct without 'that organized philosophy which we style *system* . . . the blended influences of nature and fortune form his character; 'tis the same with nations'. Wise nations from time to time reflect on the sources of institutions that flourish in them, and 'in this great national review, duly and wisely separating the essential character of their history from that which is purely adventitious, they discover certain principles of ancestral conduct . . . and . . . resolve that these principles shall be their guides and their instructors . . . '. But the nearest that he ever gets to this in his novels is, once only, to draw for an explanation on a more limited and only half-explicit version of the principle. In a speculative discussion between the two philosopher-poets of *Venetia,* Cadurcis and Herbert, he makes the latter say: 'All the inventive arts maintain a sympathetic connection between each other, for, after all, they are only various expressions of one internal power, modified by different circumstances either of the individual or of society'. Here, for once, the key principle shows itself in the relatively plain form beyond which such cryptic generalizations can never go. What makes this the key principle, however, is not that it is proved or

reiterated, but that the whole quality and texture of Disraeli's work mediates it to the reader.

Like Carlyle, and like Newman or George Eliot too, though more expressly than any of them, Disraeli insists upon the barrenness of abstractions, and the rich wisdom inherent in practice. 'Eschew abstractions' he argues in the *Vindication*: 'remember instead how entirely the result of a principle depends upon its method of application'. Characters, in the novels, serve as mouthpieces for the same opinions. Vivian Grey belittles 'the progress of liberal principles . . . your philosophy, your philanthropy, and your competition', by arguing that a simple fall in stocks can sweep them all away. Contarini Fleming, at the very beginning of his life-history, writes, 'when I turn over the pages of the metaphysician, I perceive a science that deals in words instead of facts . . . imaginary principles establish systems that contradict the common sense of mankind'. Incidents bring this to life: in *Vivian Grey* idealist metaphysicians fall victim to a crafty and satirical Nature which makes them desert their principles and admit materiality by eating 'kalte schale'. The false outlook can be dramatized as easily as the true: in *The Young Duke,* the odious Mr. Duncan Macmorrah, stupid, aggressive, self-opinionated, and after all sychophantic—'an acute utilitarian', in short—orates in praise of first principles in the not altogether appropriate environment of an early morning coach to London. We are shown Disraeli's hero, the Duke himself, winning the argument merely by calm replies and well-bred smiles. In *Sybil* Stephen Morley, champion of Moral Force and the principle of association, is a consistently ineffective figure until he abandons his theories, and Sybil herself who also theorizes and idealizes in the beginning, has after a time 'seen enough to suspect that the world was a more complicated system than she had preconceived . . . found to her surprise that great thoughts have very little to do with the business of the world'.

Tancred, on the other hand, is significantly less intellectualist than Sybil. Though he is insistent for truth, he is accommodating about abstractions:

> 'You are going into first principles,' said the Duke, much surprised.
>
> 'Give me then second principles,' replied his son; 'give me any.'

This distaste for dogmatic generalizations shows itself sometimes even unexpectedly. *Lothair* is the story of a youth for whom at first 'one conclusion . . . was indubitable: life must be religion'—'life should be entirely religious'. But after some experience he 'now felt that he had started in life with an extravagant appreciation of the influence of the religious principle on the conduct of human affairs'. Coningsby, we are left to hope, will at the end of all his experiences 'denounce to a perplexed and disheartened world the frigid theories of a generalizing age that have destroyed the individuality of man'. The characters, the incidents, the author's explanations display everywhere that excogitated rationalisms are artificial, naïve, crude, something that experience and maturity necessarily correct.

On the other hand, traditional continuity as a guide in life is exalted throughout Disraeli's work both directly and indirectly. 'It is useless to argue the question abstractedly. The phrase "the people" is sheer nonsense. It is not a political term. It is a phrase of natural history. A people is a species; a civilized community is a nation. Now, a nation is a work of art and a work of time. A nation is gradually created by a variety of influences . . . ' [*Vindication of the English Constitution*]. Many scenes and incidents in the novels bring this creed to life. Tancred's vision in the desert (nothing less, I fear, than a gigantic angel slowly waving a palm-tree sceptre) utters the same message: 'the eternal principle that controlled barbarian vigour can alone cope with morbid civilization'. Tradition accounts also for all that is best in Tancred's own ancestral town of Montacute, set in a fertile clearing in its age-old north-country forest, a neat, stone-built town with an ancient church, a modern one in the best traditional style (modern readers may be sceptical of this), a bridge provided by a munificent ancestor of the present Duke, a charter, with 'under the old system' a representative stake in Parliament, and the towers of the ducal castle rising high over the whole scene before the forest begins again. Westminster Abbey has similar associations; its instructiveness, indeed, is made explicit [in *Sybil*]. Pen Bronnock, the Duke of St. James's great isolated country residence, standing in its antiquated park by the sea, once the scene of a Royal Council, exerts the same influence [in *The Young Duke*]: 'am I not standing here among my hereditary rocks', its owner meditates, 'and sighing . . . to be virtuous!' Chateau Desir with its prominent muniment room, family arms in the gateway spandrils, mixture of Gothic and Italianate architecture (traditional and exotic), and setting of ancient forest trees, is the scene of Vivian Grey's early political manœuvres. Coningsby's house Hellingsley is 'one of those true old English Halls . . . during many generations vigilantly and tastefully preserved by its proprietors'. No scene could recall 'happier images of English nature, and better recollections of English manners'. Sometimes the significance of these scenes is given point (rather stiltedly) in conversation:

> 'There are few things more pleasing to me than an ancient place,' said Mr. Temple.
>
> 'Doubly pleasing when in the possession of an ancient family,' added his daughter.
> [*Henrietta Temple*]

Sometimes, as in the Duke of Bellamont's henchman Colonel Bruce, who has all the functions and understanding of a great landowner's assistant, and thinks the Duke and Duchess the best people in the world, Disraeli portrays a character who both incarnates and sets a true value on these various traditional activities and virtues.

But the traditional position of the great landed noble is not admired as merely picturesque or conventionally proper. It has more significant qualities: it is, or at least can be, grand and patriarchal. These qualities may appear also in other settings, but for Disraeli, wherever they appear, they are always praiseworthy. That these are the real grounds of his admiration will become plainer from seeing how Disraeli shapes the movement of entire novels, one after

another. But also he emphasizes it by details. The great landowner is a great public servant. Tancred 'long pondered' his 'duties as a great proprietor of the soil'; with regard to 'a great estate, no doubt it brings great cares'; among Mr. Dacre's distresses on account of his entailed property was the thought of the numerous tenantry 'who looked up to' him 'with the confiding eye that the most liberal parvenu cannot attract' [*The Young Duke*]. There is also a good deal of cottage visiting in the novels. The Duke of St. James goes with May Dacre when she visits her cottagers as Lady Bountiful, Ferdinand accompanies Henrietta Temple on the same errand, Vivian Grey relieves the cottager's distresses single-handed, Egremont visits the cottage children with Sybil, 'their queen'. When Tancred comes of age there is a great festival, the country people foregather from miles around, pavilions are erected in the ducal gardens for their dinner, each parish by itself, with its flag and band—'an immense but well-ordered fair'— there are village sports and games, cricket matches, morris dancing, and a complimentary visit by the mayor and councillors of Montacute. Other examples must be reserved for later on. All in all, the great house and its occupants are the focus of a vigorous patriarchal society.

If there is any doubt that the aristocratic society of the great estate was for Disraeli typical of society at its best, it is dispelled by an explicit comparison that he draws in the *Vindication:* the great statesmen of English history, he says here, 'looked upon the nation as a family, and upon the country as a landed inheritance. Generation after generation were to succeed to it, with all its convenient buildings and all its choice cultivation, its parks and gardens, as well as its fields and meads, its libraries and its collections of art, all its wealth, but all its encumbrances.' The significant metaphor of the treatise simply becomes a significant example in the novels; seeing its point is for Disraeli the basis of rightly ordering human society. To complete the parallel with this analogy between good society and family, Disraeli has in *Tancred* a portrait, full of interest, of the Baroni family of musicians and performers. They live a humble nomadic life in a caravan, but when the great merchant and financier Sidonia visits them, father Baroni says, 'I rule and regulate my house like a ship'; the children honour their parents, the family lives by an ordered system of invariable rules, and all pursue those arts which are their traditional mode of livelihood.

In this visit to humble compatriots (for the acrobat and the financier are both Jews) Sidonia too is a patriarch: and it is he also who encourages Tancred to visit Palestine and the Levant as the traditional land of wisdom. Moreover, he represents another tradition, that of the great London merchants, an aristocracy of its own, builders of mansions, Disraeli says, even more than the landowners; and Sidonia's own noble house, though indeed 'agitated with the most urgent interests of the current hour', has an elegance, dignity and peace that give it 'something of the classic repose of a college'. After he arrived in the East, Tancred finds that tradition and the patriarch can take still other forms. He visits the 'superb Saracenic castle' of Fakredeen, Emir of Canobia ('This is the first gentleman's seat I have seen since I left England' his man-servant significantly observes). The young Emir, elsewhere quite puerile and unreliable, here lives up to his great position: he is 'brilliant, sumptuous, and hospitable, always doing something kind . . . ' and all the Emirs and Sheikhs ride in to pay him their respects. There is a great hunting party, conducted with elaborate and hieratic orderliness, and afterwards a grand banquet. Preparations for this illustrate both the decorum and the kindly condescension of a patriarchal society. Disraeli's account is too colourful, too characteristic, and too pointed, not to quote in full: 'the huntsmen were the cooks, but the greatest order was preserved; and though the Emirs and the great Sheikhs, heads of houses, retiring again to their divans, occupied themselves with their nargillies, many a mookatadgi mixed with the servants and the slaves, and delighted in preparing this patriarchal banquet, which indeed befitted a castle and a forest'.

But the tradition to which Disraeli finds himself attracted is not one of unvarying institutions, or a rigid and immutable class hierarchy. It is a tradition of energy, insight and adaptability, and its aristocratic or patriarchal virtues could find expression in new forms and institutions as easily as in old. It is so far from being hostile to popular movements, that it is exactly what they make essential. In the eighteenth century, when the common people could be safely ignored (so the argument runs), an oligarchy without either talent or ideals might survive. 'But we live in a different age: there are popular sympathies, however imperfect, to appeal to; we must recur to the high primeval practice, and address nations now as the heroes, and prophets, and legislators of antiquity' [**Tancred**]. A popular and democratic age must find its own aristocrats.

Of these, Millbank in **Coningsby** is an example. His seat, of residence as of operations, lies in a parkland in Lancashire where 'a clear and powerful stream flows through a broad meadow land'. Here, among the traditional setting of ancient elms, rises 'a vast deep red brick pile . . . not without a certain beauty of proportion and an artist-like finish'. But over the 'principal entrance'—'a lofty portal of bold and beautiful design'—stands a statue of Commerce: for this is not Mr. Millbank's ancestral home, but his principal factory. Disraeli, portraying his ideal for the new industrialized world, still adopts the patriarchal pattern of society, though he modifies its form. Salubriously away from the factories (there were three in all) stands the new village, its architecture neat and 'even picturesque', with gay gardens everywhere, a 'sunny knoll', a church, rectory and school 'in the best style of Christian architecture' and—the new and old again organically fused—what would now be called a community centre. 'The mansion of the millowner' completes the plan; and this, with its situation 'on an agreeable and well-wooded elevation', its beautiful meadows, its variety of gardens and conservatories, is—though 'in the villa style'—the typical home of an improving landlord.

Disraeli emphasizes this aspect of the millowner: Coningsby is taken round the factory by a Mr. Benson, whose conversation is chiefly of how its owner builds churches, schools and houses ('on a new system of ventilation') for his work-people; and the factory itself is not simply a means of making money, but an emblem of the new indus-

trial aristocracy. 'The building had been fitted up by a capitalist as anxious to raise a monument of the skill and power of his order, as to obtain a return for the great investment.' And over a glass of claret, after a dinner 'perfect of its kind', Millbank explains to Coningsby the theory that lies behind this picture: he asserts that the country requires not a nominal aristocracy of meaningless titles, nor an 'artificial equality', but a genuine aristocracy of virtue, ability and power—of this, Millbank himself in his whole setting is an example, and his sincere and powerful personality lends support to the special sense of 'aristocracy' which the discussion puts forward.

That the aristocracy which Disraeli admires is one of quality, not lineage, is clear also in **Sybil.** Here the present landed aristocracy is portrayed in one of its failures. Lord Marney is a harsh and inconsiderate landowner, the town of Marney (so different from Montacute) is neglected, squalid and abjectly poor, the agricultural labourers are sullen and burn the ricks. His brother and a stranger, among the ruins of Marney Abbey, recall how the monks of an earlier time, before their expropriation, were kindly, altruistic, improving landlords, and in addition were patrons of the arts and great architects. They formed a genuine aristocracy; and that most of the mitred abbots were 'sons of the people' seems even an advantage, for it contributed something to 'the principle of the society'. At length this conversation advances the words 'association' and 'gregariousness' as names for the good and the bad patterns of society; and it is clear that for Disraeli an aristocracy is something of value not for snobbery, but for its patriarchal and integrating functions.

In **Henrietta Temple,** Disraeli (it is one of his lighter moments) can even trace the aristocratic virtues in a money-lender. Mr. Levison is one of the rich boors of his profession. He neglects his fine old city house, 'in that gloomy quarter called Golden Square . . . a noble yet now dingy mansion'—jumbles his portraits and *genre* paintings, crowds his rooms with ugly furniture and his furniture with ponderous ornaments, juxtaposes a faded Turkey carpet and a handscreen with a view of Margate. In person he is the same—a little stout, a little bald, garish clothes, too many rings, too big a gold chain, too keen an interest in selling coal. Mr. Bond Sharpe, with his meticulously cared-for residence in Cleveland Row, pursues the same profession in the other and proper style. His footman is impeccable, his exquisite dinners (the knives and forks have Dresden china handles!) are famous, his gold plate, though rarely on display, is elegant and superb—furniture, flowers, gardens, everything is the perfection of refined opulence, and so is Mr. Bond Sharpe. 'His figure was slight but compact. His dress plain, but a model in its fashion. He was habited entirely in black, and his only ornaments were his studs. . . . ' He lends the hard-pressed Ferdinand fifteen hundred pounds in the coolest possible manner, and invites him to dinner into the bargain. Although Bond Sharpe is making his fortune, started life as a prize-fighter, and lends money generously so as to get into good society, Disraeli portrays him in an entirely amiable light. He is good because he knows how to live and act in the grand manner: he has taste, respects good society, seeks the public responsibilities of wealth (he will be in the next Parliament), and for Disraeli is an admirable example of how a new but genuine aristocracy can be conceived and born from nothing.

But one element in the portrait of Mr. Bond Sharpe has so far been ignored; and although less tangible than the others, it is of crucial importance, for it takes us beyond an external survey of the forms and institutions which Disraeli admired, to their inner and essential quality. We advance from the mechanisms to the 'feel' of things. This new element is the freshness, the brilliance, the life and colour and movement that Disraeli lends his whole portrait. The cabriolet that brings Ferdinand to Bond Sharpe's house goes dashing and twisting and whirling through the streets; it draws up with beautiful ease before the door; the staircase is perfumed with flowers, the gold plate glitters with gems; in one room they are busy preparing for dinner, in another the table is covered with papers. This quality of animation is sustained by Disraeli's choice of words in the most trivial places: 'The chairs had been *rifled* from a Venetian palace; the couches were part of the *spoils* of the French revolution'. Even more important for Disraeli's view of things than the formal outlines, is this vivid animation filling them through and through.

That Disraeli sees this life and energy not opposed to long-rooted tradition, but an essential aspect of it, is something quite distinctive in his outlook. It is unmistakable in his account in **Coningsby** of the great house of Lord Monmouth. This the reader sees first with 'the beautiful light of summer' shining over it . . . 'there was not a point which was not as fresh as if it had been renovated but yesterday'. It was a Tudor house, a medley of architecture 'with a wild dash of the fantastic in addition'. The surrounding countryside is 'sparkling with cultivation'. Coningsby himself wanders out into the gardens in a beautiful, calm evening, but 'the mitigating hour that softens the heart made his spirit brave'. When the moon rises, it is 'a pale and then gleaming tint . . . and soon a glittering light flooded the lawns and glades'. The chapter ends as Coningsby reaches 'a rushing river, foaming in the moonlight, and wafting on its blue breast the shadow of a thousand stars'. There are no ancestral slumbers here.

Lothair's visit to his country seat, Muriel Towers, has the same brilliant colour and animation. 'Muriel Towers', the chapter begins, 'crowned a wooded steep, part of a wild and winding and sylvan valley at the bottom of which rushed a foaming stream' and 'the park, too, was full of life', with deer and fierce white cattle roaming among the glens and dells and savage woods, or by the glittering lake. Lothair arrives in his barouche: the postilions dash through the park, the startled deer scud away across the grass. There is a 'sinuous' lake with green islands and golden gondolas, the principal gateway was once 'the boast of a celebrated convent on the Danube'. Later that day, as he wanders over the castle, 'What charmed Lothair most . . . were the number of courts and quadrangles . . . all of bright and fantastic architecture, and each of which was a garden, glowing with brilliant colours, and gay with the voice of fountains or the forms of gorgeous birds'. On another day, he and his friends explore the place together. They go everywhere in the interior, but all is so novel and

beautiful that no one is tired; and no one, he repeats, is tired that afternoon, when they drive for hours in the park. The gardens 'had been formed in a sylvan valley enclosed with gilded gates . . . the contrast between the parterres blazing with colour and the sylvan background, the undulating paths over romantic heights, the fanes and the fountains, the glittering statues, and the Babylonian terraces, formed a whole much of which was beautiful, and all of which was striking and singular'. Some of this, of course, is nonsense, but Disraeli's nonsense, as we shall see, has a certain method in it.

This love of what is brilliant and colourful does not find expression only in the scenes of aristocratic traditionalism. It pervades the novels, is perhaps their most striking quality, and produces innumerable descriptions, incidents and conversations, all with this distinctive bias. It is supported by Disraeli's swift, vigorous, staccato style. It lies behind the extraordinarily large number of fine mornings in these books—it is a fine morning when Ferdinand Armine [in **Henrietta Temple**] surveys his ancestral park after coming home at last ('the tall trees rising and flinging their taller shadows over the bright and dewy turf '), when the Duke of St. James sets off to give his maiden speech in the House of Lords [in **The Young Duke**], when Tancred leaves Jerusalem, when Lothair first sees it, and each time it is the glitter and gusto and life of the morning that Disraeli wants to secure. He pursues these same qualities in describing, for example, the rivers of Damascus:

> They gleam amid their groves of fruit, wind through their vivid meads, sparkle among perpetual flowers, gush from the walls, bubble in the courtyards, dance and carol in the streets: everywhere their joyous voices, everywhere their glancing forms, filling the whole world around with freshness, and brilliancy, and fragrance, and life.

—and, as so often, he goes straight on to indicate how this scene provokes meditation and gives it a certain bias:

> One might fancy, as we track them in their dazzling course, or suddenly making their appearance in every spot and in every scene, that they were the guardian spirits of the city.
>
> [**Tancred**]

Because of the contrast it offers with other novelists, Disraeli's description of an early morning coach ride [in **Henrietta Temple**] is illuminating:

> Away whirled the dashing Dart over the rich plains of our merry midland; a quick and dazzling vision of golden cornfields and lawny pasture land; farmhouses embowered in orchards and hamlets shaded by the straggling members of some vast and ancient forest. Then rose in the distance the dim blue towers, or the graceful spire, of some old cathedral, and soon the spreading causeways announce their approach to some provincial capital. The coachman flanks his leaders, who break into a gallop; the guard sounds his triumphant bugle; the coach bounds over the noble bridge that spans a stream covered with craft; public buildings, guildhalls, and county gaols rise on each side. Rattling through

many an inferior way they at length emerged into the High Street, the observed of all observers, and mine host of the Red Lion, or the White Hart, followed by all his waiters, advances from his portal with a smile to receive the 'gentlemen passengers'.

'The coach stops here half an hour, gentlemen: dinner is quite ready!'

'Tis a delightful sound. And what a dinner! What a profusion of substantial delicacies! What mighty and iris-tinted rounds of beef! What vast and marble-veined ribs! What gelatinous veal pies! What colossal hams! Those are evidently prize cheeses! And how invigorating is the perfume of those various and variegated pickles! Then the bustle emulating the plenty; the ringing of bells, the clash of thoroughfare, the summoning of ubiquitous waiters, and the all-pervading feeling of omnipotence, from the guests, who order what they please, to the landlord, who can produce and execute everything they can desire. 'Tis a wondrous sight.

George Eliot used coaches to introduce quite a different picture of life . . . ; and so did Dickens, for he catches the same richness and plenitude as Disraeli, but adds to it the humane and whimsical geniality of a mood that is quite different.

Another way of seeing how carefully selective Disraeli's situations are usually, is to examine chapter 66 of *Lothair;* for here, in a grand Catholic procession and service at Rome, he has exactly the sort of opportunity he seizes so often with gusto, but it so happens that this time he wishes to present the scene unsympathetically. Despite all the lavish colour and excited movement, the touches that secure this effect are easily seen. The cardinal's coaches were 'brilliant equipages', but this time it was because they had had to be recently replaced, Garibaldi having burnt the traditional ones; a phrase here and there—'monsignori and prelates without end'—suggests that the procession is grandiose rather than grand; the congregation in church flutter their fans, eat sugar plums, take snuff; Lothair's escort is clearly a schemer; the marshals are 'experienced' and business-like; the cardinals' trainbearers are 'exhibiting with the skill of artists the splendour of their violet robes'. All that seems achieved by the brilliant ceremony is that this long service 'could not be said to be wearisome'. The whole incident is important because here Disraeli refuses to find the qualities of life that he finds so often, and this exceptional case throws the usual case into sharp relief.

Sometimes Disraeli, or one of his characters, expresses this view of things explicitly. 'Life is adventurous. Events are perpetually occurring, even in the calmness of domestic existence, which change in an instant the whole train and tenor of our thoughts and feelings', he writes [in *Henrietta Temple*]; or 'how full of adventure is life! It is monotonous only to the monotonous' [*Tancred*]. 'The sense of existence' alone is the charm of life to Sidonia. Lord Monmouth finds the world 'a masquerade; a motley sparkling multitude, in which you may mark all forms and colours, and listen to all sentiments and opinions' [*Conings-*

*by*]; for him, the driving force behind this is only a desire for plunder, but in adding this he ceases to speak for the author. Perhaps the clearest passage of this kind is in *Venetia,* when the two poets indulge in philosophical remarks as—one early morning—they sit together on the Italian coast and look out over the sea:

> '. . . The great secret, we cannot penetrate that with all our philosophy, my dear Herbert. . . . And yet what a grand world it is! Look at this bay, these blue waters, the mountains, and these chestnuts, devilish fine! The fact is, truth is veiled, but like the Shekinah over the tabernacle, the veil is of dazzling light.'

> 'Life is the great wonder,' said Herbert, 'into which all that is strange and startling resolves itself. The mist of familiarity obscures from us the miracle of our being. Mankind are constantly starting at the events which they consider extraordinary. But a philosopher acknowledges only one miracle, and that is life . . . '

Herbert (he is in part a portrait of Shelley) then leads the conversation on further, to life in the biologist's sense; but it is clear that for a moment the two men's conversation has been moulded so as to express the author's own view; and the word 'miracle', applied to life as a whole, shows by itself how much, at this point, Disraeli has in common with Carlyle—and with Newman.

It is on this exuberance, this almost boisterous zest for life, that one must rely in order to meet an obvious criticism of Disraeli as a novelist with any considered view of the world; for in many of his books there are remarks or incidents that seem thoroughly melodramatic and irresponsible—seem nonsense, in fact, like the fanes and glittering statues and Babylonian terraces of Muriel Towers. Coningsby first met Sidonia, for example, after a tramp in the forest that was interrupted by a thunderstorm: the wildfowl and deer were in panic, the forest trees roared and shrieked, 'the passion of the ash was heard in moans of thrilling anguish'. Coningsby, under a sky black as ebony, took refuge in a forest farmhouse. There, as he stood at the window, 'a flash of lightning illumined the whole country, and a horseman at full speed, followed by his groom, galloped up to the door'—Sidonia has arrived. Sybil, sitting on a bench in St. James's Park (it was a beautiful summer morning, with shining clouds, glittering waters, and prismatic wild-fowl), reads Egremont's moving speech in the House of Lords. There were tears in her eyes; she looked up 'as it were for relief', and 'before her stood the orator himself'. Earlier in the same novel Egremont, Morley and Gerard converse among the ruins of Marney Abbey. One of them enunciates the doctrine of The Two Nations. A sudden flush of rosy light suffuses the grey ruins, the twilight star glitters through a vacant arch, a lovely voice is heard singing the evening hymn to the Virgin. It proves to be Gerard's daughter; no one can take all this very seriously.

One is tempted by their humour, presumably half-conscious, to quote other instances. Tancred and Fakredeen go to visit the Queen of the Ansarey: both dress in their best, one is a blaze of shawls and jewelled arms, and Tancred 'retained on this, as he had done on every other occasion, the European dress, though in the present instance it assumed a somewhat more brilliant shape than ordinary, in the dark green regimentals, the rich embroidery, and the flowing plume of the Bellamont yeomanry cavalry'. Vivian Grey, at seventeen, 'a young and tender plant in a moral hothouse . . . paced his chamber in an agitated spirit, and panted for the senate'. Glastonbury, in **Henrietta Temple,** wanders on foot as a young man through Switzerland and Italy; we are told that he is probably driven by an unconscious desire to discover the ideal: what he brings back, after three years, is several thousand sketches, and a complete Alpine Hortus Siccus. When Ferdinand is under arrest for three thousand pounds, he is offered the money by the girl he thinks has abandoned him for another man, is sent it by the girl whom he has abandoned himself, and receives the following note from the elegant and imperturbable Count Mirabel, who went gambling the previous evening in an effort to win something to lend him:

Berkeley Square, half-past 7, morning

Mon ami. Best joke in the world! I broke Crocky's bank three times. Of course; I told you so. I win 15,000 1. Directly I am awake I will send you the three thousand, and I will lend you the rest until your marriage. . . .

—the marriage is to the richest heiress in England. These are a few examples of a quality that really runs through the novels; many passages quoted earlier in other contexts resemble them; and many readers are likely to feel that as a result, Disraeli's novels are to some degree in the realm of farce or fantasy. If this is where they belong, they can hardly also mediate a serious view of the world—or at the very least, these rollicking irresponsibilities must surely detract from their power to do so.

But on reflection, the problem seems more complex: for while it is clear that these incidents cannot be taken seriously *in isolation,* as specimens of what life is like, it is less clear that, in an unexpected and indirect way, they do not encourage the reader to accept the whole tenor of the novels in which they occur. This may appear paradoxical; but less so, if we bear in mind the rather distinctive view of things to which Disraeli wanted to give expression. He was an optimist about both the quality of life, and its ultimate results: he saw the world as an exciting, exhilarating place, and a place that characteristically supplied happy endings. A twofold cheerfulness of this kind, however, is extremely likely to put readers out of sympathy: they can too readily call exceptions to mind, or they are too familiar with people who advance these controversial opinions with a complacent pomposity that is revolting. Disraeli's farcical and fantastic touches are a kind of safety-valve; they provide for scepticism because they do not have to be taken in full seriousness; they invite us to suspend disbelief for the sake of fairy-story pleasures, and so they provide for a margin of disagreement within the frame of a general agreement. And they also modify the reader's impression, not of the world, but of the author: it is so obvious in these passages that Disraeli is enjoying himself, and his attitude to the world is infectious through a direct contact with his sanguine personality. In other words, these intrinsically flippant touches in the novels help to control Disraeli's tone: and thereby they adjust both the general character of his work, and our sense of himself.

What this general character is, however, has still not quite been identified, for Disraeli's thoroughgoing optimism has another significant result. It means that he need not make depicting the world as it is, and suggesting to his readers how they ought to behave in it, two distinct tasks. Probably he had a less detailed interest in the moral implications of his view of things; but for an optimist the 'painful right' of George Eliot does not exist; there is no inescapable contrast between what is and what should be, and in depicting the former an optimistic author tends to depict the latter. The two coalesce. Coningsby is sometimes an example of this process: meditating on the spectacle of King's Chapel, Cambridge, by moonlight, he says: 'Where is the spirit that raised these walls? . . . Is it indeed extinct? . . . But I cannot believe it. Man that is made in the image of the Creator, is made for God-like deeds. Come what may, I will cling to the heroic principle. It can alone satisfy my soul.' But only a few pages before this, we read that Coningsby had 'the heroic feeling', 'born in the heart'. In a sense, then, he already is the noble figure that he strives to become. This ambivalency between the normative and the descriptive runs through the novels, and qualifies Disraeli's extravaganzas in another way: when his work cannot be accepted as describing the world as it is, one accepts it as having shifted for a moment to describing the world as it should be. Like any optimist, Disraeli often finds the transition from one to the other imperceptible; and very often his work carries conviction because we are brought to see it as somehow a portrait of what is, and of what should be, all in one.

This is reinforced by the general pattern of the novels (for in this respect they have a remarkable—indeed a revealing—sameness), and in their basic selection of material. Every one of Disraeli's novels is centred upon a young man's growing to maturity, forming his views on the world, and finding his right place in it (**Sybil** is different only in that this happens to both the hero and the heroine). As, each time, this takes place, Disraeli's sense of the brilliance and variety and colour of the world finds expression not only in the details of incidents, but also in their juxtaposition. All the novels involve a considerable variety of scene—a sharp contrast to the rigidly circumscribed locale of the typical George Eliot novel. The large majority of them are novels of travel; and (except for **Vivian Grey,** set in England and Germany) it is travel always in the same direction, to Paris, Rome, Greece and the Levant. But their variety comes from changes in mode of life, as well as in scene: the great country house, the London season, high life in Paris, aristocratic business and industrial society, cottage scenes, industrial slums as in **Sybil,** the world of servants (**Tancred** opens with a delightful scene from the private life of Leander, the celebrated cook), inns and coaching scenes (**The Young Duke**), a Dickensian spunging-house (**Henrietta Temple**), a drunken carouse among German barons (**Vivian Grey**), fishermen, artists, an Italian patriot army (**Lothair**)—in every novel, Disraeli exploits the varieties of place and class to make his panorama as changeful and colourful as he can.

But it is not a systematic changefulness: Disraeli does not explore how the elements of society are interrelated. Even *Sybil* has a good deal of the picaresque in its form. The novels rarely develop through any internal logic: they turn on casual events, on delightful, exhilarating operations of chance. The Duke of St. James is rescued, at the nadir of his fortunes, by lucky financial accidents, the unexpected ability to make a brilliant speech on Catholic Emancipation, and a rise in the price of coal; the deadlock in *Venetia* evanesces because Lord Herbert is reconciled to his wife though everything has made this seem impossible; Coningsby's problems are solved by the opportune death of his grandfather, and his quite unexpected ability to become a future Lord Chancellor, apparently at no trouble to himself; Ferdinand, in *Henrietta Temple,* escapes ruin through a chance introduction to his munificent money-lender, and then another to the wonderful Count Mirabel; *Lothair* turns upon a moonlight vision in the Coliseum at Rome, *Endymion* on an opportune loan of twenty thousand pounds; Egremont's life is transformed by a chance meeting in the ruined abbey; *Vivian Grey, Contarini Fleming* and—very differently—*Tancred,* are picaresque fantasies from beginning to end. But although Disraeli's situations do not develop through any inner necessity, they mediate a definite view of things nevertheless. The world may be largely one of chance, but it is one of chance that is exhilarating, colourful and benign—of Chance fit for heroes to live on.

Disraeli's view of the world is conveyed through what he omits as well as what he presents. In some of the novels, one finds the seclusion, rich with tradition, of the remote country house; but there is never any drabness—even in *Sybil* the working-classes are fierce and colourful. And there is really no badness either. Mrs. Felix Lorraine in *Vivian Grey,* Sir Lucius Grafton in *The Young Duke,* Joseph Diggs in *Sybil,* are all quite secondary and not perhaps wholly serious figures; and they all come to bad ends in just the same casual, chance way that the good characters come to good ends. The Young Duke's gambling bout, Ferdinand's disappointments in love, even the angry scenes in *Sybil,* are incidentals that are cancelled out by the whole trend of the novels in which they appear. Disraeli does not explore that part of human experience which comprises sin, guilt, depravity or misfortune; they are not primary data in the view of life which his work conveys.

Disraeli's polemical interest is often somewhat fitful; his high spirits and optimism and brilliance often serve the needs only of a happy romantic *Wanderjahr* or love-story. But nearly all his novels sooner or later concentrate on that self-renewing traditionalism that he regarded as key to the good life. That this is true, in various ways, of the *Young England* trilogy needs no proof; but the other novels are polemical in this respect also. The essential line of their plots recommends their author's scheme of values. The Young Duke abandons his thoughtless extravagance for an interest in politics and the life of a territorial magnate. Cadurcis and Venetia settle down as country nobility and repair their ancestral home. Ferdinand Armine becomes an improving landlord, and his successes in public affairs seem likely to revive the family barony. Lothair

*A portrait of Disraeli in 1852.*

finds a solution to his perplexities in the duties of a great landowner, and the traditional anglicanism that goes with them. *Vivian Grey* is no exception: the upshot of all Vivian's German experiences is that whatever was good in the traditionalism of the petty princes can be transferred without loss to the greater princes. Even *Endymion* has something of it, for the hero, rising from poverty to become Prime Minister, is only restoring the tradition of his father; while the great industrialist, Job Thornbury, becomes a landed patriarch and is jokingly called 'Squire' by his sons. One novel after another bears witness, in its whole contour, to the view that life is colourful and kindly, and that the right ordering of it lies in an active and adaptable traditionalism.

But this is to say that Disraeli's fiction has a much more genuine integration than is sometimes allowed. It does not break into two unrelated halves, empty political generalities on the one hand, and irresponsible though picturesque frivolities on the other. Disraeli's respect for tradition is inseparable from his zest for what is colourful and lively, because it is the latter which interprets the former. For him, this light-hearted brilliance is the world's enduring and traditional quality. The serious and the rollicking parts of his work unite; and this fact enables one to see two things, first that a more or less serious expression of his outlook is diffused quite widely through the novels, and second that Disraeli's qualities as a light entertainer, so far from destroying the more overtly serious and considered of his works, do something to clarify, and even I think to deepen their meaning. Moreover, they do this not merely in a quite abstract way. It is these qualities which largely control the tone in which Disraeli expresses his message, and the frame of mind of the reader approaching that message. The lighter side of Disraeli's work both interprets, and makes more sympathetic, the side which is more in earnest. (pp. 86-110)

> John Holloway, "Disraeli," in his The Victorian Sage: Studies in Argument, 1953. Reprint by Archon Books, 1962, pp. 86-110.

## Christopher Hollis (lecture date 1954)

[*Hollis was an English author, journalist, and statesman. In the lecture below, which was delivered at Oxford University in commemoration of the sesquicentenary of Disraeli's birth, he summarizes Disraeli's political career and surveys his major novels.*]

It has always been the tradition of this country—more, I think, than in the tradition of any other parliamentary country—that we expect writers to play their part in political life; in the records of the House of Commons a long list of distinguished writers have been Members of Parliament at one time or another. A very long list also of politicians have written books at one time or another.

A large number of Prime Ministers have written books but a rather smaller number of Prime Ministers have written good books; and there are many Prime Ministers who will not be primarily remembered as the writers of great prose. I do not imagine that it will be thus that Mr. Attlee will be primarily remembered in history. And almost without exception, it has been possible to say of any individual that he was primarily a writer and secondarily a politician or primarily a politician and secondarily a writer. For instance, if we take the record of the great writers who have sat in the House of Commons, most of them have doubtless added to the dignity and wisdom of the House of Commons by sitting there, but have not played a very large part in the actual life of Parliament. At the beginning of the eighteenth century Addison did not make a speech in the House of Commons until he was made Secretary of State, and at the end of the century Gibbon never made a speech at all. In the nineteenth century three of our greatest historians sat in the House of Commons: Macaulay, Leckie and Lord Acton. Of them, Macaulay recorded that to be a Member of Parliament was the highest honour known to man; Leckie said that most of the duties of a Member of Parliament would be better performed by a fairly intelligent poodle dog; and Lord Acton sat through three Parliaments and made no observations whatsoever.

In that record Disraeli holds very nearly a unique position. I think I would not be challenged in saying that there are only two men in British parliamentary history who have risen to the first rank, of whom it can be even a matter of opinion whether their literary contribution was not almost as important as their political contribution. The one is, of course, the present Prime Minister [Winston Churchill], and the other is Disraeli. Though I do not think anyone would seek to put Disraeli absolutely in the very first rank of English writers—if we merely consider

his style, there were clearly certain impurities which would make anyone hesitate—nevertheless, even if he had had nothing to do with politics in all his life, his position in English literary history would have been extremely important. It would have been important because he really was the inventor of a new form of art, to which he himself made most notable contributions and in which he inspired others after him. The form of the political novel was an invention of Disraeli, an invention which was afterwards very carefully copied throughout all his political novels by no less a man than Trollope, who owed a very great debt to Disraeli; it was also most carefully copied by George Meredith in *Beauchamp's Career* and by H. G. Wells in *The New Machiavelli*. Disraeli also had a very faithful disciple in the United States in an author whom I used to read years ago but whom I do not hear talked about today nearly as much as I would like—the American novelist, Winston Churchill. So there is no question that Disraeli's place in English literature is a considerable one; it is our task . . . to try and estimate it in more detail.

Disraeli's career as a political novelist divides itself very clearly into three periods: the period before he had arrived, the period when he was arriving and the period after he had arrived. That is to say, the first batch of his political writings was written before he had gone into Parliament at all, the second batch when he was already a politician but not yet of the first rank, and the final writings when he was a politician of the very first rank. We will take the first stage first.

Disraeli was born . . . in 1804, exactly one hundred and fifty years ago. Unlike myself, he did not come to [Oxford] University, and therefore he had to occupy the period of his life when he would otherwise have been an undergraduate by writing a novel, and the first novel of this first period was **Vivian Grey,** which appeared in 1825 when he was twenty-one years old. Of course, in criticising **Vivian Grey** it is always important to remember that fact, that it really was the work of an undergraduate; it was a book that had strange merits but also, as Disraeli himself freely confessed in later life, strange faults. It is a political novel, and a political novel—up to a point—of the type with which we were to be made familiar throughout the rest of Disraeli's career; his stories always tended to run to a kind of formula. They were nearly always what might be called double autobiographies. There were two main characters, both of which were Disraeli thinly disguised. On the one hand, there is always a young man who dreams dreams and worries about the world, and falls under the influence sometimes of males, sometimes of females, and is trying to find what the world is all about. That is obviously Disraeli in one form. Then there is apt to be, at the end of the novel, some mysterious stranger from the East who hints at certain impenetrable wisdoms in which lie hid all the secrets of the universe—though it is sometimes not quite clear what those secrets are—and that is also obviously a second sort of Disraeli, in a way acting as a mentor to the first sort of Disraeli.

Now this first novel **Vivian Grey** starts off according to the formula, in the sense that there is a young man who is facing the world and going to see what he can make out of the great adventure of politics. He goes into political life, he joins a political combination that is forming at that time under a man called the Marquess of Carabas, and they have a lot of not very edifying and indeed sometimes rather absurd adventures in order to try to carve out Vivian Grey's political career. But the obvious fact about *Vivian Grey,* in contrast to Disraeli's later novels, is that there is no hint there whatsoever that political life is anything but a purely personal adventure. There is no beginning of a hint that the Party formed under the Marquess of Carabas is going to do anything good, or that it has any purpose to serve; indeed it is an exercise in pure careerism that we are given in *Vivian Grey,* and without as much moral disapproval of such a career as doubtless we would have found if the book had been written by him a little later in his life. Indeed, I think the simplest way to understand *Vivian Grey* is to remember that Oscar Wilde stole one half of his title when seventy-five years later he wrote *Dorian Gray.* That is to say, Wilde's idea was that the one Gray should use the aesthetic life as a mere platform to adventure in the way that the other Grey had used the political life. I think that as fair a summary and as just a criticism of *Vivian Grey* as one can find comes from a source whence you would perhaps not expect a fair criticism of an early and vulnerable work of Disraeli. On March 20, 1874 (that is to say, almost fifty years afterwards), having nothing better to do after dinner, Mr. Gladstone records in his diary that for the first time in his life he read *Vivian Grey,* and he writes: "Finished *Vivian Grey.* The first quarter extremely clever, the rest trash."

We come from *Vivian Grey* to the next of these early political novels, *Contarini Fleming. Contarini Fleming,* if we were engaged on purely literary criticism, is a book about which one might say a good deal, but I think all that we need for our particular purpose at the moment is to notice here for the first time another motif that is present throughout all Disraeli's life. Contarini Fleming, the hero of that book, is, of course, as you would guess from his name, an Italian; and one of the points in his adventure in English life that he is continually stressing is how he feels himself an alien and the contrast between himself with his dark features and the big blond English schoolboys among whom he has to live. There is no doubt that in *Contarini Fleming* Disraeli gives expression to his feeling that as a Jew he was something of an alien and different, and certainly in his early years he had to some extent to fight his way in face of prejudice in the more narrowminded English society of his day.

Then we come to the third of these early novels, *The Young Duke,* and here we are again back in that rather naïve atmosphere of *Vivian Grey,* of politics as purely personal adventure; there is a little more morality than in *Vivian Grey,* but morality still of a rather crude type. Slightly and unfairly parodying it, the story of *The Young Duke* is that the hero is a young nobleman of great wealth and great possessions who in all the early chapters of the book is proving unworthy of his privileges and living a life of mere luxury and debauchery. Then he is suddenly converted, becomes a proper and good citizen, and is able to offer himself to the lady of his choice and to marry and live happily ever after. A quite edifying story as far as it

goes, but the method in which he shows this conversion to the good life is somewhat comically naïve: it is to go down to the House of Lords and take his seat. The moment that he does that his fiancée thinks it is all right and she can have him at last, whereas she would never have dreamed of accepting him until he took his seat in the House of Lords. Then he gets up and makes one speech, and having made one speech in the House of Lords has apparently proved himself for ever after to be a worthy citizen, deserving of his high privileges and of his great wealth. Almost as in a penny novelette, Disraeli ends the book: "His life is passed in the agreeable discharge of all the important duties of his exalted station and his present career is by far a better answer to the lucubrations of young Duncan Macmorrogh than all the abstract arguments that ever yet were offered in favour of the existence of an Aristocracy. Parliament and in a degree society invite the Duke and Duchess each year to the Metropolis." With that comparatively easy way of saving his soul, the Young Duke apparently passes to his reward.

Next, Disraeli broke in on this first series of novels which he was writing throughout the late 1820s with three books of a somewhat different kind which he wrote in the early 1830s and which are, I think, all well worth reading. He turned from the straightforward novel to imitations of either the classical Lucan or, if you prefer, of Swift. These tales in which he satirised, most brilliantly, the principles of the time are: *Ixion in Heaven, The Infernal Marriage* and *The Voyage of Captain "Popanilla".* The last is very well worth reading to this day. It is a kind of parody of *Gulliver's Travels;* to some extent, in form, it is based on *Gulliver's Travels,* and in critical spirit on Voltaire's *Candide.* As you doubtless remember, in *Candide* Voltaire takes what seemed to him the absurdly superficial formula that everything was for the best in the best of all possible worlds, and makes *Candide* suffer various appalling calamities in order to show that the world is by no means as easy and rosy a place as such a formula pretended; in *Popanilla* Disraeli does the same thing by taking the formula of what it was then fashionable to call the natural or the economic man. Just as the French Encyclopaedists in the previous century had tried to raise a laugh, and sometimes succeeded, by showing the absurdities in which people landed themselves by paying too much attention to convention and tradition, so Disraeli turns it round and shows the absurdities in which people land themselves by paying too little attention. He shows what ridiculous consequences follow if a man does really go through life seriously pretending that there is nothing whatsoever that he has to do except, on all occasions, to buy in the cheapest markets and sell in the dearest. He creates, as a satire on the Benthamite philosophers, the character of Mr. Flummery Flum. He is the imaginary economist, who gets into absurd scrapes through following out in a blind, wooden and ridiculous way his economic principles, in neglect of the traditions of the society in which he lives. Of course there you get the first beginnings of the shaping of what was, throughout the rest of his life, to be one of the most important points in Disraeli's philosophy—that any system that neglects tradition and history and is not wise enough to try and build the institutions of the present and the future out of the institutions of the past, is a system which is bound to come to calamity. His reverence for tradition was one of the most important parts of Disraeli's teaching. That brings us to the end of this first period of Disraeli's literary career, before he had in any way made for himself a position in the political world.

Then we pass on to the next period. In 1832 he stood for Parliament for the first time and in 1835 he was elected. The Whig Government under Melbourne was then in power and continued in power—it tried to get out of power over the Bedchamber question in 1839 but did not succeed—until 1841 when Peel came in. Disraeli had high hopes that he would receive office from Sir Robert Peel and indeed, as it subsequently turned out, had written in not very dignified fashion to Peel to ask for office, though subsequently he pretended that he did not do so. Anyway, he did not receive office, so in the Conservative Government he was a backbencher. It looked quite probable, to begin with, that he would have no further political career at all, because Peel seemed in a strong position and had also taken a very strong dislike to Disraeli. However, as the years went by, it became increasingly obvious that Peel was likely to turn from the traditional policy of the Tory Party and repeal the Corn Laws, which indeed he did in 1845. There followed a revolt of the Party—the greater number of the members of the Tory Party opposing their own leader, Peel. He was able to carry repeal only by the aid of Whig votes, and the Tory Party was split. This gave the opportunity to Disraeli to make his name in opposition and denunciation of Peel, whereas it would have been difficult for him to make his name as long as Peel succeeded in keeping the Party united. Of course, one of the great controversies . . . is to what extent Disraeli was sincere or insincere in pretending this passionate devotion to the Corn Laws.

Anyway, through a happy or unhappy accident, it was thus that he was able to find for himself a position where he could subsequently have a political career of the first eminence. We are not concerned with that career in itself, but we might just remember that amount of political history in order to understand the setting in which he now wrote the three great central political novels of his career: *Coningsby*, published in 1844, *Sybil* in 1845, and *Tancred* in 1847. It is enormously important, to understand those novels, to remember that *Coningsby* was written in 1844 just before he quarrelled with Peel, while *Sybil* was written, I suppose, just before the Corn Laws came up and published just afterwards.

Both were written at a time when Disraeli was a discontented member of Sir Robert Peel's party, thinking that he would soon have occasion to split with him, and *Tancred* was written just afterwards. He felt himself under a particular obligation to say something positive, to try and sketch a positive political philosophy, because he wanted at that time to come out as a critic of Peel; so he put before the world in these three novels what is sometimes called the 'Doctrine of Young England'. He appealed to the 'Young England' group, a group of people younger than himself, of better birth than himself for the most part, who also were beginning to be discontented with the line of Peel's policy which they thought was simply the policy of the

Liberals supported by the votes of the Conservatives. Against that 'Flummery Flumism', as he would have called it, he pretended to find his inspiration in the past, in the gospels of Bolingbroke and Burke, and preached essentially the two doctrines of 'One Nation' and of Tradition. The central of these three novels I am speaking of at the moment—*Sybil*—had as its secondary title **The Two Nations.** The doctrine of the One Nation, as indeed we are reminded in these times in pamphlets, was that it was the duty of a Tory to oppose all disruptive doctrines which seek to set class against class.

Coningsby goes out to the East, as Disraeli's characters so often do, and comes under the influence of an almost Messianic figure, the great and mysterious Jew, Sidonia, the first three letters of whose name are the first three letters of 'Disraeli' the other way round. Sidonia preaches to him about the great Asian mystery, without an understanding of which it is impossible to understand any problem in the ultimate analysis at all; but at the same time, as I have said is rather apt to happen, he does not make it clear exactly what this great Asian mystery is. That is the positive side of *Coningsby,* but at any rate to some of the more irreverent among us the easiest pages to read in *Coningsby* are the negative or satirical ones. In these, in contrast to Coningsby himself searching with difficulty after the truth, we are shown the absurdity and contemptible nature of the hack politicians who are running the show. The great buffoon of the book is a man he calls Rigby, who was modelled on Croker, the diarist of those days; he, justly or unjustly, was unfortunate enough to incur the very great dislike both of Macaulay and of Disraeli—a formidable pair of enemies to make—and therefore has never cut much of a figure in history.

Below Rigby are the immortal figures of Tadpole and Taper, the symbols of people who take no interest whatsoever in politics except in mere jobbery, and who are held up to ridicule and contempt throughout. There are some exquisite conversations and descriptions of Tadpole and Taper. There is one which, with very slight emendation of a detail of figure, I think might be considered by some people to have a strange topicality today. Disraeli writes of Tadpole and Taper and such people: "It is a peculiar class that. Twelve hundred pounds per annum, paid quarterly, is their idea of political science and human nature; to receive £1,200 per annum is government; to try to receive £1,200 per annum is opposition; to wish to receive £1,200 per annum is ambition; if a man wants to get into Parliament and does not want to get £1,200 per annum, they look upon him as daft and a benighted being. They stare in each others' face and ask, 'what can Dash want to get into Parliament for?' ". And then the question comes up in the novel of the dissolution of Parliament.

> "Ah! Tadpole," said Mr. Taper, getting a little maudlin; "I often think, if the time should ever come, when you and I should be joint Secretaries of the Treasury."
>
> "We shall see, we shall see. All we have to do is to get into Parliament, work well together, and keep other men down."

"We will do our best," said Taper. "A dissolution you hold inevitable?"

"How are you and I to get into Parliament if there be not one? We must make it inevitable. I tell you what, Taper, the lists must prove a dissolution inevitable. You understand me? If the present Parliament goes on, where shall we be? We shall have new men cropping up every session."

"True, terribly true," said Mr. Taper. "That we should ever live to see a Tory government again! We have reason to be very thankful."

"Hush!" said Mr. Tadpole. "The time has gone by for Tory governments; what the country requires is a sound Conservative government."

"A sound Conservative government," said Mr. Taper, musingly. "I understand: Tory men and Whig measures."

Well, as I say, we have to remember the circumstances and the date when that was written; rightly or wrongly—it is not our business . . . to go into whether he was right or wrong—Disraeli was very critical of Sir Robert Peel on the grounds that in order to keep office Peel was betraying Tory principles in repealing the Corn Laws. Those particular political circumstances, in detail, are obviously irrelevant to our problems today. But of course it is the test of a great political satire that it must, inevitably and in the nature of things, be about something that is ephemeral; obviously the vast bulk of political satire ceases to be in the least interesting when it ceases to be topical. But there are in literary history the examples of a few great political satirists, the test of whose greatness is that though particular issues about which they are writing are purely ephemeral, and in after years people do not greatly care about them, yet the writing itself is such that out of this ephemeral issue they have been able to wrest some eternal principles which make the writing live long after the conditions which have ceased to be interesting. I suppose the greatest example of that is the greatest of all Tory political satirists—Dryden. Who cares today about the personalities of the very dim and corrupt politicians of Charles II's reign who fought about the Exclusion Bill? Yet though he does not care and has to look to the footnotes to know who the men are who are being written about and what precisely they did, anyone who appreciates good writing is anxious to read *Absolom and Achitophel*. A great many people will read *Gulliver's Travels* who are quite indifferent to the issues of the War of the Spanish Succession out of which *Gulliver's Travels* arose. A great many people, if they could read Greek, would read Aristophanes who were not particularly interested in the Peloponnesian War. I think it is a task in which we can say Disraeli succeeded—in wresting something eternal in satire out of a purely temporary and ephemeral situation.

We turn from *Coningsby* to *Sybil* which is the social, rather than the purely political, criticism which *Coningsby* had been. It was a challenge which the critic inevitably raised after the publication of *Coningsby,* to say, "You show us there how everything was wrong and corrupt and feeble, but you do not show what is right". *Sybil* was an

answer to that, an answer coming through the claim that we cannot solve these problems in the political and parliamentary sphere alone, but must study social conditions as opposed to the mere theory of the *laissez-faire* economists; we must examine the actual industrial conditions out of which this situation has arisen. Sybil, the heroine of the book, is almost a symbol of the new workers of the industrial classes, who somehow had to be welded into the spirit of the nation if England was going to survive as a great nation under the new industrial conditions. There again you see the contrast both among the manufacturers and among the aristocrats between the two types—the aristocrat or the industrialist who is solely concerned to retain his privileges, and who is therefore to be condemned, and the other who realises that no privileges are justifiable unless they are used to enable one to serve the general welfare.

Here again, side by side with this high seriousness, Disraeli's irrepressible taste for political satire does break out; just as the best passages in *Coningsby* are the passages about Tadpole and Taper, the best passages in *Sybil* from that point of view are the passages about Mr. Hoaxem, who is the P. P. S. to the Prime Minister. There is some most excellent fooling when the Prime Minister is coaching Mr. Hoaxem about two deputations which he is to receive, one from industrialists and one from farmers, about the new Free Trade legislation which the Government is proposing to put through. The Prime Minister, who is a thinly disguised Sir Robert Peel, tells Mr. Hoaxem how he is first to go to the industrialists and explain that the beauty of this legislation is that prices will be less, because corn will be cheaper when the foreign corn comes in; and then to go afterwards to the farmers and explain that there is no question of any foreign corn coming in, so it cannot possibly make any difference to the prices. Then, if he gets into difficulties, says the Prime Minister, "ring the changes on great measures and great experiments until it is time to go down and make a House. Your official duties, of course, must not be interfered with. They will take the hint. I have no doubt you will get through the business very well, Mr. Hoaxem, particularly if you will be frank and explicit. That is the right line to take when you wish to conceal your own mind and confuse the mind of others. Good morning."

Then we come on from *Sybil* to *Tancred,* where Disraeli goes one stage further and argues that these problems cannot indeed be solved on the merely political level, but nor can they be solved on the merely social level. The issues are in the last analysis religious issues. So Tancred, too, goes out to the East, falling under the influence of three people: a Syrian lady called Eva, whom he meets at Bethany, and a Greco-Syrian lady named Astarte who puts rather more pagan philosophies side by side with the Christian philosophy of Eva; then there is another mysterious Asiatic stranger, Sidonia re-incarnated and called Fakredeen, who preaches to him two things. First that the gospel of Christianity is a predominantly oriental gospel. It is in Tancred that you find that splendidly insolent phrase in Fakredeen's mouth, where he speaks of 'that intellectual colony of Arabia called Christendom'. It was the argument of Disraeli throughout his life—whether he said it just to annoy or whether he believed it, or a bit of both, I don't know—that Christianity was essentially an oriental religion and that Europeans intellectually and spiritually were colonists of the Arabians. On the one hand Fakredeen preaches this religious gospel and on the other hand he also introduces what was quite a novelty at that time and in Disraeli's own thinking—though it was to play so large a part in his thinking in later life—the new gospel of imperialism. Fakredeen comes to Tancred and tells him that Englishmen must form a Portuguese scheme on a grand scale:

> quit a petty and exhausted position for a vast and prolific empire. Let the Queen of the English collect a great fleet, let her stow away all her treasure, bullion, gold plate, and precious gems; be accompanied by all her court and chief people, and transfer the seat of her empire from London to Delhi. There she will find an immense empire ready made, a first rate army, and a large revenue. . . . I will take care of Syria and Asia Minor. The only way to manage the Afghans is by Persia and by the Arabs. We will acknowledge the Empress of India as our suzerain, and secure for her the Levantine coast. If she likes, she shall have Alexandria as she now has Malta: it could be arranged. Your Queen is young; she has an *avenir*. Aberdeen and Sir Peel will never give her this advice; their habits are formed. They are too old, too *rusés*. But, you see, the greatest empire that ever existed; besides which she gets rid of the embarrassment of her Chambers! And quite practicable; for the only difficult part, the conquest of India, which baffled Alexander, is all done!

Now that is enormously important; though such talk, although with a very great difference which I will refer to in a minute, became fairly familiar towards the end of the nineteenth century, it was of course entirely unfamiliar in the middle of the century. All the Victorians before Disraeli who considered themselves to be Imperialists were not in the least interested in colonies. Having a strong foreign policy, being a patriotic Englishman in the middle of the century, meant thinking that the country should play a very large part in European politics, but there was very little interest in the world outside Europe itself. Even such a man as Palmerston, you will remember, said to the clerk in the Colonial Office, "Come upstairs after dinner and show me where these damned places are on the map!" Though he was the arch-example of a man who believed in a strong policy, Palmerston's interests were entirely centred on Europe. It was in fact a quite new thing when Disraeli, with whatever degree of sincerity or insincerity, burst upon the world with the notion that the future of England lay in its relations with people outside Europe altogether. I will come back to that in a minute if I may, but that really brings us to the end of this second phase in the 1840s, with Disraeli writing novels—doubtless, as people do, because he liked writing novels—but also using them as weapons in his political career.

Then of course, the Peelites and the Protectionist Party split permanently. The Peelites ceased to be Tories. The new Protectionist Party was formed with George Bentinck, to begin with, as leader in the House of Commons.

He died comparatively soon, in 1848, and that left the Protectionist Party under Lord Derby as leader, with Disraeli as leader in the House of Commons. By this chapter of accidents he had at one step risen from being nobody to being leader of the Opposition and then, when Derby came into Office, Chancellor of the Exchequer. He never held any lower position in office than that of Chancellor of the Exchequer. That meant, of course, that throughout the 1850s and 1860s he was busy as an active politician and therefore he wrote no more. However, at the end of his life he begins the third phase. With whatever motives, he starts writing again. In 1868 he became Prime Minister when Derby retired and died. He became Prime Minister for the first time for just a few months, he had no majority and out he went; he was Leader of the Opposition from 1868 to 1874 and then Prime Minister from 1874 to 1880.

During this last period of his life he wrote one novel, *Lothair,* in 1870. It is important to remember that he wrote when he was Leader of the Opposition. After he had ceased to be Prime Minister, after he had left the House of Commons for the Lords and, as I think he must have known, when he was a dying man with his political career finished, he wrote what is known as *The Unfinished Novel* [*Falconet*] (1880) and *Endymion* (1881).

In *Lothair* again, there is the rich young man, in this case immensely rich—Lothair apparently could finance revolutions and wars without turning a hair—who again, according to the Disraeli formula, is under various influences which are fighting, as it were, for his soul in order to lead him to Truth. Of the three influences in this case, three female influences, one is Clare Arundel who represents the Catholic reaction, the second is Theodora Campian who represents the spirit of world revolution, and the third is Lady Corisande who represents traditional and respectable society and does eventually marry him.

The date, as you will remember, was 1870, when all the world was filled with arguments about the Italian Risorgimento; and this novel, in some ways a rather fantastic novel, very largely turns, in the first half, on the adventures of Lothair when he goes and fights in the republican army for the recapture of Rome under Garibaldi. The tug for his soul, as I say, is between the revolutionary spirit of Theodora Campian and the Catholic spirit of Clare Arundel, both of whom are clearly disapproved of by the author as extremists. So eventually Clare Arundel becomes a nun and Theodora Campian dies, and Lady Corisande is left as the odd woman out and is able to get Lothair, which is presented as a highly satisfactory conclusion. Again, he goes off to the East and meets a mysterious Asian stranger, on this occasion called Paraclete, a Syrian Christian prophet, who tells him that the best thing he can do is to go back to England and live his life soberly in the state of society to which he has been born.

It is not a point on which to take sides here or to develop, but it is an interesting point that has often been raised—why Disraeli's apparent attitude towards the Roman Catholic church in *Lothair* is so very different from the attitude in the earlier novels twenty years before, when all the Catholic characters (such as Eustace Lyle in *Coningsby* and Trafford in *Sybil*) had been extremely sympathetic characters. I think there are two lines of answer and people can take their choice between them. The cynic and the critic say, of course, that from the point of view of political advantage, Disraeli had been rather too favourable to Catholics in the early novels to please all the electors of a Protestant country, and that therefore it was as well to say something on the other side. Nobody would pretend that Disraeli was the sort of man to whom motives of that sort were wholly impossible. But I think there is another line of explanation which is more creditable.

Disraeli liked traditional institutions; as a traditionalist it was therefore not illogical that he should like the Mediæval Catholic Church and disapprove very strongly of the Reformation, which he considered as a revolutionary movement that had upset the traditional rhythm of English life. But the new Catholics are of the sort of Cardinal Manning, whom he satirises pretty unsympathetically as Cardinal Grandison, and Monsignor Catesby, who cuts an even worse figure in *Lothair;* and what he thought of this new aggression of the mid-nineteenth century was quite a different thing. Rightly or wrongly, the Church of England was England's Church, and he did not like any attack upon an established state of affairs. Therefore he shows not merely the intriguing Catholics at the Vatican but also has another strange scene where Lothair falls into a meeting of the Irish Fenians down in the Mile End Road; we have held up for us the picture of the Catholics as a revolutionary enemy to established English society, only perhaps slightly less dangerous than the direct revolutionary force represented by Theodora Campian, the disciple of Mazzini. Anyway, the lesson of *Lothair* is quite clearly that between these two extremes it is most important that sane and sober Englishmen should follow the *via media* of maintaining their own traditions.

*Lothair* was written in 1870. In 1874 Disraeli became Prime Minister and was naturally fully occupied until 1880. Then in 1880, as Lord Beaconsfield, no longer Prime Minister, and two years before his death, he settled down to a rather peculiar task which, for better or worse, he never finished. That was to write a satirical novel about Mr. Gladstone, then Prime Minister and his great opponent. Mr. Gladstone's career was to be satirised under the name of Joseph Toplady Falconet. He states the beginning of it as he intended it to be.

> Joseph Toplady Falconet had been a child of singular precocity. His power of acquisition was remarkable and as he advanced in youth his talents were not merely those which ripen before their time. He was a grave boy and scarcely ever known to smile, and this not so much from a want of sympathy for those among whom he was born and bred, for he seemed far from being incapable of domestic affection, but rather from a complete deficiency in the sense of humour from which he seemed quite debarred. His memory was vigorous, ready and retentive but his chief peculiarity was his disputatious temper and the flow of language which even as a child was ever at command to express his arguments. In person with a commanding brow, his countenance was an exaggeration of that of his father, austere even to harshness and grave even to melancholy.

Eventually the young Mr. Falconet gets launched on his political career.

> And so it came about that Mr. Falconet and his son were invited to spend the Whitsun week at the great house and a public meeting in the borough on the revival of the slave trade in the Red Sea having been arranged, Mr. Joseph Toplady Falconet had the opportunity of making a speech which literally electrified the audience. The speech, indeed, became not only famous in the place where it was delivered but it was reported in the London papers, and leading articles were written attesting its commanding eloquence and announcing the advent of a new and powerful candidate for the honours of public life. True it was that it subsequently appeared that there had been no revival of the slave trade in the Red Sea but the misapprehension had occurred from a mistake in the telegraph manipulated by a functionary suffering from a *coup de soleil* or *delirium tremens.* But this did not signify and made no difference whatever in the eloquence of Joseph Toplady Falconet or the result which that eloquence was to accomplish.

Whether that was in very good taste or not, being written by the Leader of the Opposition, about the Prime Minister, or whether it was altogether fair, is perhaps a matter for debate. But if you are going to satirise young Mr. Gladstone, that that was a very brilliant way to satirise him is surely beyond debate; because it is quite clear, as Labouchère said from the other side of the House, that the peculiar characteristic of Mr. Gladstone was his capacity to find great moral issues in actions which were really wholly to his advantage. Labouchère said, "I do not object to our revered leader always having the ace of trumps up his sleeve, but I do object to his assumption that it was the Almighty that put it there." Incidentally, it was also an additional piece of malice that the Gladstone family did owe its early fortune very largely to the slave trade, not indeed with the Red Sea, but with the West Indies. Disraeli never finished this satire and it was not published until well after his death, in 1903. Perhaps, on balance, he thought it better not to finish it. He turned instead to what was to prove the last of his novels, *Endymion,* written in 1881 and in a different and rather interesting mood. *Endymion* is clearly the reverie of an old man.

It is a political novel, but a novel whose scene is cast not in the time at which Disraeli was writing, but fifty years before in 1829, in the premiership of the Duke of Wellington. Here again is the young man who falls under this tugging female influence, first of his sister Myra who, in rather a strange career, marries a French nobleman and eventually ends up as Queen of France. Then there is Lady Montfort, whom he is able to marry through the fact that Lord Montfort rather conveniently dies at a crucial point in the book. And in the course of the book Disraeli takes the opportunity to do a thing which is of course comparatively easy if you are writing sixty years afterwards: to take two young and at that time unknown men who were as a matter of historical fact in England, and to paint their portraits. It so happened that at that time Bismarck was an Attaché in London, and the man who was afterwards Napoleon III was living in exile in London. So Disraeli put Bismarck into the book as the Count of Ferrol and Napoleon III into the book as Prince Florestan and made them say what they think of one another with pregnant remarks that would of course have been extraordinarily prophetic if they had really been made at the time, but were not so difficult to make up afterwards if you knew what was going to happen. But he also brings back to life another historical character, of less interest in itself but of great interest as a character in the book from the literary point of view. He brings back, under the name of Baron Sergius, a man called Baron Bruno who was, in point of fact, a Russian Military Attaché at that time in London, and he makes Baron Bruno the vehicle for a number of reflections upon the value and also upon the vanity of public life in general.

> "I should like to be a public man", said Endymion.
>
> "Why?" asked the baron.
>
> "Well, I should like to have power," said Endymion, blushing.
>
> "The most powerful men are not public men", said the baron.
>
> "A public man is responsible, and a responsible man is a slave. It is private life that governs the world. You will find this out some day. The world talks much of powerful sovereigns and great ministers; and if being talked about made one powerful, they would be irresistible. But the fact is, the more you are talked about the less powerful you are."

And then Endymion gives three examples of three men whom he alleges are apparently powerful in the world of that day and one is a King, and the second is an Emperor and the other is a Prince. Baron Bruno answers about the King, that he is governed by his doctor, and the Emperor is governed by his mistress, and the Prince is governed by an altogether obscure individual who may, at this moment, 'like ourselves', be drinking a cup of coffee in a hired lodging.

Well, of course, it is interesting that a man who has scaled the summits of practical success should indulge in such reveries at the end of his life. The question is how much we are to make of it. I think it is fairly obvious how much and how little we are to make of it. The dreamer who has enjoyed great position must inevitably have his moments in which he meditates on the difference between the appearance of power and its reality. He meditates, but that does not say that, if he had his life again, he would live it differently.

What is the lesson to be learnt from his novels? To begin with, the first and basic gospel of Disraeli was the gospel of the One Nation as opposed to the formulæ of the Utilitarians, the *laissez-faire* mongers and also, of course, the power that came into force towards the end of his life—the Socialists from the other side.

We are often told to admire Dickens because of his sympathy with and his understanding of the poor: but I think it

is a very true thing that George Orwell said in his essay on Dickens, that when you come to read Dickens you find that he is never in the least interested in anybody working. Nobody ever works in Dickens: he never describes how they work, and he never had any idea how factories were managed or had any curiosity to find out. All Dickens was interested in was people of odd character—Sam Weller floats through life—but getting down to any work, knowing how factories are managed, is a thing that interested Dickens very little.

On the other hand, if you read first the record in Monypenny of how Disraeli prepared himself to write *Sybil* and then read *Sybil* itself, you will discover that he has a most remarkable knowledge—a knowledge incomparably superior to that of Dickens—of how the poor did in fact live in England. I think we can fairly say that there was at that day neither to be found another politician, nor was there to be found another novelist, who knew the actual facts of industrial life as Disraeli knew them. So I think we can say that is his gospel. There was criticism of him in his own time, perhaps repeated afterwards, that this was really negative, this was all phrases, that he was jeering at Utilitarians and Liberals; but whenever he came to any positive programme—so went the argument of criticism—what he was after was extremely vague. Perhaps the greatest exponent of that line was Carlyle, who called him a "superlative Hebrew juggler", and asked in *Latter day Reflections,* "How long will John Bull permit this absurd monkey to dance upon its stomach?"; he argued that whatever verbal praise there might be of English traditions in Disraeli's work, in point of fact Disraeli was essentially an adventurer, an entirely unEnglish force, and it was absurd to take the things that he said seriously.

That he was what Ernest Raymond called 'an alien patriot', and something very different from an Englishman, is indeed profoundly true. But I think it is enormously important to understand the nature of Disraeli's imperialism. As I argued just now, I think he was profoundly original in being an imperialist at that date. By 'imperialist' I mean that he was interested in the fundamental problem of the relations of this country with peoples outside Europe altogether. He was original in being an imperialist, but also, and almost more important, his imperialism was quite different from the later imperialism of Joseph Chamberlain or Kipling. Whereas the later imperialism was essentially the imperialism of the 'white man's burden'—the gospel that the Englishman had something to teach to the Oriental—Disraeli's imperialism was just the opposite: it was essentially the Oriental who had something to teach the Englishman.

Incomprehensible as they may seem, the observations of Fakredeen are really more profound than the observations of Gunga Din. This is perhaps not quite fair to Kipling, but still his best Oriental is of the type of Gunga Din, and the question is for the white man to say how he has performed his duty to him: but that he has something to learn from him is, of course, a reflection not often present to Kipling and not present at all to Joseph Chamberlain. Yet that was essentially Disraeli's view.

Essentially he was an alien patriot, a patriot who came to

England from outside; he also was, in a good and in a bad sense of the word, an adventurer. Of all the careers in English political history his was incomparably the most improbable. As a general rule the sort of people who get jobs in England—probably in most other countries—are those who from their social origins you would expect to get them. That was true with hardly an exception in nineteenth century England: but this one extraordinary adventurer from nowhere in particular, with every prejudice against him, succeeded not only in getting into and making himself a leader of the most exclusive society in the world but also—what is odder still—making himself the actual champion and symbol of the most conservative elements of that society. It was a very extraordinary feat, and that he did enjoy the mere accomplishment of that feat, in a whimiscal and meditative way, is beyond question. You will remember the story at the Congress of Berlin, where Bismarck had laid on the Countess Radetzki to try to fascinate Disraeli. The whole Congress had been completed, success reached, and a great ball was held in celebration at the end. Disraeli came slightly late to the ball and stood at the door watching the people dancing and saying nothing. The Countess went up to him and said, "What are you thinking of?"; and he replied "I am not thinking. I am enjoying myself". There was no doubt at all that there was present in his mind the amazing achievement that he had carried through in imposing himself upon this Christian world.

You may remember, too, the story at the beginning of his life when, in the oddest of meetings the old *roué,* rather debauched, very tired Lord Melbourne, who was then Prime Minister, was introduced to the young Disraeli and said to him, "What do you want to be?" Disraeli answered, "I want to be Prime Minister". To Melbourne, of course, there was a double insanity in such a thing: first, the idea that such an extraordinary figure should imagine by any conceivable possibility that he could be Prime Minister, and, secondly—almost as amazing to Melbourne— that he should *want* to be Prime Minister if he did not have to be. To Melbourne, the last weary relic of the eighteenth century, intolerably bored with the whole business, the great ambition of this young Jew from nowhere did seem very extraordinary. Naturally enough, I do not suppose it ever occurred to Melbourne that there was the smallest possibility that this ambition would ever be satisfied. The amazing thing about Disraeli's history is that it was satisfied.

There is a number of stories of the death-bed scene of this man, one of the most remarkable and colourful men in English history. But the story which is, whether true or not, at any rate artistically the most appropriate is, I think, this: that in his last moments, when all had given him up, he was heard muttering to himself, and they bent over to hear what he was saying. What he was saying was "Eli, Eli, Adonai Eli", the old Hebrew words, "There is one Lord, there is one Lord, and the Lord is Lord"—the last triumph of the alien patriot over the people whom he had loved, in a way despised and laughed at, and also saved. (pp. 98-117)

*Christopher Hollis, "Disraeli's Political Novels," in* Tradition and Change: Nine Oxford Lectures *by R. A. Butler and others, Conservative Political Centre, 1954, pp. 98-117.*

### Arthur H. Frietzsche   (essay date 1961)

[*In the excerpt below, Frietzsche examines the shifting role of religion in Disraeli's novels, concluding that* Lothair *contains the clearest expression of his religious beliefs and that it could be considered Disraeli's spiritual autobiography.*]

It is . . . only when the religious aspects of each of [Disraeli's] novels are discussed in turn that the increasing political application and the slow Protestant drift of Disraeli's religious thought become apparent. It is tempting to say that Disraeli wrote "a Jewish novel" (**Alroy**), "a Catholic novel" (**Contarini Fleming**), "a mystic novel" (**Tancred**), and "an Anglican novel" (**Lothair**). However, the actual case is much more complicated. **Lothair,** for instance, is based upon a three-cornered battle between Roman Catholicism, free-thinking, and Anglicanism, and, though Anglicanism wins, it is by elimination rather than simple virtue.

Neither Disraeli's first novel, **Vivian Grey** (1826), nor its separately printed second part (also called "the Sequel," 1827) has any significant religious bias in evidence. The twin emphases are politics and melodrama, and, although there may be instances in which comments on or descriptions of church or doctrine might be in order, religion is simply ignored. The brief satire **Popanilla** (1828) is largely devoted to an attack upon the practicality of Utilitarianism, but it also makes some pungent comments upon the Anglican Church and the workings of the English constitution. The chapter dealing with the character "Fruit" is, as Froude says [in his *The Life of the Earl of Beaconsfield,* 1914], "a humorously correct sketch of the Anglican Church," but its aim is merely to point up an inadequate sense of mission; the comments are negative.

With **The Young Duke** (1830) we come for the first time to a literary work in which religion has some notable place. The heroine, May Dacre, is a Roman Catholic, and Disraeli uses this fact obliquely in the plot. Speare explains the situation [in *The Political Novel,* 1924]:

> . . . the young duke determines once for all to redeem his heritage. How does he do this? He steals secretly down to the House of Lords, he takes his rightful place once for all in that distinguished Assembly, and, it being then the occasion for the discussion of certain grave injustices perpetrated upon religious beliefs in portions of England, the youth is fired and makes the great speech of the evening! Then, and then only, does he return to win the heroine for his reward and (as the author would imply in the last paragraphs of the novel) to win also his own self-respect.

It is notable that the differing beliefs of hero and heroine form no barrier to their marriage. The question never arises; apparently it never entered the author's mind. We can agree with Monypenny [in *The Life of Benjamin Disraeli, Earl of Beaconsfield,* W. F. Monypenny and

G. E. Buckle, 6 vols., 1910-20] when he speaks of Disraeli as being, in 1829, clearly an enthusiastic believer in Catholic Emancipation, but there is no indication that his feeling for or understanding of Roman Catholicism ran any deeper. May's father, the unimaginatively named Dacre Dacre, is one of a long line of characters in these novels whose function it is to advise the hero. A surprising number of these men, all of them shown in the best possible light, are of religions other than Anglicanism—Adrian Glastonbury, the Catholic lay-priest in *Henrietta Temple;* Sidonia, the omniscient Jew in *Coningsby* and *Tancred;* Paraclete, the Syrian Christian in *Lothair;* and several others. Since the first of this line, Horace Grey in *Vivian Grey,* was patently modelled on Disraeli's father, such a situation, otherwise unaccountable, might be traced to Isaac D'Israeli.

The highly rhapsodic *Contarini Fleming* (1832) offers what the author called "a development of my poetic character" and "a secret history of my feelings." It is the tale of the childhood and adolescence of a "Venetian temperament" nurtured in a northern (Scandinavian?) climate, and is complicated in that the hero, an idealized version of the author himself, is a budding poet cast from the Byronic mold. Religion is not a topic for discussion, but is considered as an aspect of the hero's emotionalism. See, for instance, Contarini's "conversion" to Catholicism. . . . It is the objects of religious observance and the emotions which they arouse in him which are of interest to Contarini—and that rarely. Clearly the problems of religion and doubt had made no impression as yet upon the author. Disraeli was avowedly attracted by the surface glitter of Roman Catholic practice, but he had neither knowledge nor interest in the theology and belief which lay behind it.

*Alroy* (1833) appeared less than a year after *Contarini Fleming* and was apparently written at the same time, at least in part. The diary quoted above refers to it as an exposition of the author's "ideal ambition," a statement not to be taken literally. At 28, Benjamin Disraeli most certainly had no serious intention of leading the Jews out of captivity, much less turning Tamburlaine. Monypenny furnishes an apt discussion on this point ascribing the novel, no doubt correctly, to "genuine racial sentiment." In the depiction of David Alroy, a racial bond blocks the author's vision, and there is a ridiculous imposition of self upon a supposedly historical figure. Roth quotes [in his *Benjamin Disraeli, Earl of Beaconsfield,* 1952] a statement attributed to Disraeli in his old age that "*Alroy* is a legend," but the young Disraeli neither believed this nor wrote as if he did. More important, as Monypenny says,

> . . . *Alroy* is saturated with the language and spirit of the Old Testament; and more than any other of Disraeli's works, even more than *Tancred,* it reveals the Hebraic aspect of his many-sided nature.

This is certainly true. But the principal attraction clearly is racial. In their finest aspects, *Alroy*'s literary qualities do owe a debt to the Old Testament, but it is notable that the author does not treat Judaism as a religion.

With *Alroy* appeared the short *The Rise of Iskander,* a kind of parallel to *Alroy* in which the hero who leads his people to freedom is a Christian. It is indeed fortunate that Disraeli tells us this, for the best summary which could be given is Pearson's witty one [in *Dizzy: The Life and Personality of Benjamin Disraeli, Earl of Beaconsfield,* 1951]—"the Cross beats the Crescent by double-crossing it." Christians need feel no outrage, however. The two-dimensional figures are carefully labelled "good" or "bad," "Christian" or "Moslem," but there is neither thought nor belief to trouble these thin straws.

*Henrietta Temple* (1836) and *Venetia* (1837) were simply potboilers, written for the purpose of procuring money at a time when their author needed it desperately. Because they lack the pretension and Byronism of the earlier works (and some, at least, of the later ones) and because experience had taught Disraeli something about novel-writing, both are more enjoyable to the modern reader than are some of this author's better-known novels. . . . [*Henrietta Temple*] is actually a rewriting of *The Young Duke* in which the hero instead of the heroine is a Roman Catholic but the religious emphasis of the climax is replaced by a secular one.

Adrian Glastonbury, the lay-priest, is portrayed with considerable affection. As in *The Young Duke,* the differing religions of hero and heroine are cause for neither concern nor comment. In short, religion is in *Henrietta Temple* once again a matter of feeling rather than of belief.

*Venetia,* published soon afterward, contains the first exposition of the idea that the Church is a great Conservative force, an idea which became very important in Disraeli's political philosophy. Dr. Masham, who represents the Church of England, is something of a split personality, although his development may reflect the changes which the author hoped to bring about in the National Church. When we first meet Dr. Masham, he is a typical eighteenth-century rural parson, almost a caricature, "dreading the Pope, and hating the Presbyterians." But when he appears later in the work he is a highly sophisticated bishop seated in the Lords, and we are left wondering whether he or the young Lord Cadurcis has completed the most thorough process of "growing up." It is as a bishop that he escorts Cadurcis into the House. . . . If we take the Young Duke's speech on Catholic Emancipation to have only accidental relevance, the incident described in *Venetia* marks the first time that Disraeli actually *used* religion in his novels for any serious purpose.

Disraeli's trilogy (*Coningsby,* 1844; *Sybil,* 1845; and *Tancred,* 1847) was planned as the explanation-by-example of the abortive "Young England" group. We might reasonably expect, then, that the place of religion in English life would be discussed and the place of religion in Disraeli's thought would be revealed. To a large extent, this is so, although little of it appears in *Coningsby.* One of the three people who influence the political and social thinking of young Coningsby is Sidonia, who is "of that faith which the Apostles professed before they followed their Master." Immensely wealthy, brilliant, and powerful, Sidonia yet remains an incompletely motivated figure. And certainly he is not the guiding spirit of Coningsby, as some commentators would have him. In the rare instances when

Coningsby takes his advice on some action, there is no effect on the workings of the plot. It is as an intellectual stimulus and as the mouthpiece of Disraeli's ideas that he is valuable. True, he lauds Jewish Emancipation, but Sidonia is more god than man, and his religion actually has little bearing on his position in the novel.

The relation of Church and aristocracy is clarified in this novel, however, during the scenes at the Catholic estate, St. Geneviève. The description of the Catholic chapel is more restrained than that in *Contarini Fleming,* although this is a matter of degree. Eustace Lyle, as a Catholic, has reason to be a Whig-hater, but he finds the Tories unaware of the need to recognize and foster the traditional, conservative elements of English society. "I have revived the monastic customs at St. Geneviéve. There is almsgiving twice a week," says Lyle, while blushing. And he is answered by a Tory duke, "I am sure I wish I could see the laboring classes happy." Note that in his search for traditional values, Disraeli turned to the most traditional of Western Christian churches, and not to the Church of England. He did so merely to lend force to his example; there is no indication that he desired or would welcome a return to the "Old Faith," as he calls it. When the sense of political urgency replaced that of social enlightenment, it was the Church of England to which he turned.

*Sybil* also retains this Catholic bias. Egremont's first sight of the Roman Catholic Sybil Gerard has an emotional impact rivalling that of Contarini Fleming's vision of the Magdalene. Significantly, it takes place in the Lady Chapel of a medieval abbey ruined when the Catholic Church fell in Britain; the meeting place of the "old aristocracy" and the best elements of the "new aristocracy" is a hallowed ruin which represents the tradition and reach into the past upon which the religious aspects of Disraeli's "Tory principles" are grounded. It is no accident, however, that the activities of the Catholic Eustace Lyle in *Coningsby* are practiced and even expanded in this novel by the Anglican Aubrey St. Lys. St. Lys shows how the Anglican Church can carry forward the traditional services in social and spiritual affairs which it inherited from its predecessor and which Disraeli considered to be among its most important functions. Disraeli's religious views retain some of their romantic fervor in *Sybil,* but religion was now clearly assuming the place in his political thinking which it was to occupy for so long.

*Sybil* was followed by two novels of especial interest to the student of Disraeli's religious attitudes, *Tancred* (1847) and *Lothair,* which did not appear for nearly another quarter-century. Despite the long hiatus between them, these novels have distinct resemblances in plot and characterization and contain the fullest treatments which Disraeli was to give religion. Because of this emphasis, both novels demand extensive discussion here.

In *Tancred,* especially, religion is central to the novel, but most of the religious attributes displayed are nebulous. And although *Tancred* was planned to demonstrate the duties of the Church of England in carrying out the "Young England" scheme, it does nothing of the sort. By 1847 the political motivation had faded (along with the idealistic little splinter-party); the sections dealing with

the Church of England have a half-hearted air about them. The major point which Disraeli makes in *Tancred* about the Anglican Church is that it should lay more stress upon its Hebrew origin and less upon its medieval tradition. Since he had previously, beginning with *Contarini Fleming* and continuing through the recently published *Sybil,* lauded the Roman Catholic Church for the splendid panoply of its medieval heritage, and had urged the Anglican Church to foster this neglected tradition, the *volte-face* comes as a sudden surprise. Certainly it shows a sudden Protestant coloring in Disraeli's religious thought; since this work was published two years before the "Papal Aggression," Newman's defection must be the cause. The Jew and the Catholic in Disraeli find themselves at war in *Tancred,* and apparently the Jew is winning out.

The Jewish racial theories first broached by Sidonia in *Coningsby . . .* are at the heart of *Tancred,* and Sidonia again appears to proclaim them. And Tancred himself is, like his author, overwhelmed by mysticism once the Holy Land is reached; in fact, as Tancred stands (finally) upon Mt. Sinai a divine message is presented to him—"perhaps the boldest flight of imagination that occurs in the writings of Disraeli" [Robert Arnot, in his *Critical Introduction to the Works of Benjamin Disraeli, Earl of Beaconsfield,* 1904]. A contrast is made with the Hellenistic strains of Western culture with Tancred's journey to the realm of Astarte, a pagan, "Aryan" (Disraeli's word) queen in Syria. But in the end it is Judah which holds sway over Tancred, Judah in the shapely form of Eva, for (as we shall see in *Lothair*) Disraeli was a great believer in feminine influence and often presents various abstract forces personified by women.

Although Judaism apparently governs the second half of the novel, the first half concerns itself with the religious aspects of Toryism, with the necessary alliance of Crown, Church, and People. In such an alliance, the decadent Church of the day was useless.

> A spiritual renaissance was necessary for England; a new crusade had to be undertaken, the Asian mystery had to again be discovered before English character, chastened and made intelligent by a visit to the Holy Land, might rear a great empire. This program, wedded to the stirring desire of Disraeli to vindicate once for all before England the glories and rights of the Jewish race, . . . [had a] supreme religious motive.
> [*The Political Novel*]

Tancred, Lord Montacute, is a typical young heir of a noble house until he is overwhelmed by such questions as (to quote his words) "What is DUTY, and what is FAITH? What am I to DO, and what ought I to BELIEVE?" The answers escape him, and he decides to go to the Holy Sepulchre to find them (the symbolism is obvious but worth noting). The amusing attempts to dissuade him fail, despite the blandishments of numerous young women and the arguments of the worldly bishop already mentioned. Sidonia proves of great help in his preparations, manages to restate the views on Judaism with which we have already associated him, and furnishes a fearless companion-servant named Baroni, who later proves to be Jewish also. Tancred reaches the Holy Land, and the second half of the novel is concerned with his physical and spiritual adventures as he roams the Near East under the divergent influences of the Jewish Eva and the pagan Astarte.

The book abounds with a myriad of religious sidelights. Perhaps the best and certainly the most humorous scene in the book is a typical Oriental divan, furnished with an assortment of Oriental types. The scene, which reads like a parody of *Nathan der Weise,* has many implications on religion, both the religion of the speakers and that of the English, who are under discussion—after all, they say, the idea that a modern Englishman would go on a pilgrimage and pray at the Holy Sepulchre is absurd, but if Tancred's visit is merely a prelude to military conquest perhaps it will bring a trade in crucifixes! Chief among the debaters is the scheming Fakredeen, soon to become Tancred's companion and rival, who makes an interesting foil to the young Englishman. Both young men suffer religious and political "prostration"; neither has found "paramount religious truth." "If truth is in the established church of their respective countries, why, they ask, does the government support dissent? . . . In nothing . . . do they find Faith paramount over Mammon" [*The Political Novel*].

Tancred is offered "paramount religious truth"; his problem is to understand it. Atop Mt Sinai (rather than at the Sepulchre) he is confronted by the "Angel of Arabia," who in "a couple of pages of fluent journalese" (Monypenny's delicious phrase) proclaims the "sublime and solacing doctrine of theocratic equality." This scene is the culmination of the line of mystic revelations which was begun in *Alroy.* And like *Alroy, Tancred* is concerned with what the author calls "mystery"—in Sidonia's words, "It appears to me that what you want is to penetrate the great Asian mystery." Since the principal characters of Charles Kingsley's *Yeast* (1848) were to go off at the conclusion of the work to seek the "Asian mystery," it may be surmised that at least some members of Disraeli's audience saw nothing ridiculous in this point. But what about Tancred's relation to the "mystery?" Is the reader to assume that this "mystery" is exposed by the angel's message of "theocratic equality?" Such an assumption seems unjustified, for Tancred receives this message before the novel is half over. Is the reader, then, like Speare, to assume that the "mystery" has "something to do with Eva," though it is not certain what this something is? Monypenny records Disraeli's response to a clergyman who wrote to him for fuller explanation of this "mystery;" the best answer that he could give was to recommend continued rereading. Any serious spiritual message which *Tancred* may communicate will likely be found in the first half of the book; thereafter the novel becomes an exotic adventure story, scarcely differing except in color from several of the earlier works. Bluntly, the serious reader will have doubts about the sincerity of *Tancred.*

Such doubts were expressed by many readers even in Disraeli's time, and the novel contributed to J. K. Stephen's puzzles over Disraeli's "mysticism" and Carlyle's well-known decision that the author was "a Hebrew conjuror." Brandes was depressed by the "narrow spirit" in which Disraeli treated "the scholastic problems," but, by comparing his ideas with some of Gladstone, Brandes is able

to "perceive that, within the prescribed limits, for a Tory he is almost an advocate of religious Radicalism." And, to be fair, Astarte and the "Greeks" are presented as profound in faith, although they have scant chance against the overwhelming mind of Sidonia and the ethnic wisdom and powerful special pleading of Eva on behalf of the Semitic stem and its most fruitful branch, the Jews.

Less pressing and perhaps less important than the puzzle over the "great Asian mystery" is the puzzle over the spiritual ambition of Tancred himself. Alroy's ambitions, tied to his race, were achieved and then perverted; Contarini Fleming's ambitions similarly were diverted from spiritual to worldy ends. Tancred's ambitions at the beginning of the novel are vague but completely sincere, and of great intensity. But when we last see him in a Jerusalem garden, with Eva's head sinking upon his shoulder, what are we to judge? Is Eva the physical embodiment of "the great Asian mystery," of Disraeli's favorite "Semitic principle"? And what is Tancred's true feeling toward her? The novel is simply cut off before any answer can be given; indeed, it is difficult to see what Disraeli could have done to end the novel properly.

One last problem of *Tancred* is its autobiographical content. All of Disraeli's heroes are in a large sense Disraeli, several of them avowedly so. One view is expressed by Speare: "Mysticism and a love for the exotic and the Oriental turn together in *Tancred,* a novel which is Disraeli's spiritual autobiography." And Monypenny makes a similar estimate:

> As in *Vivian Grey* and *Contarini Fleming,* he has let his thoughts run; and the true completion of *Tancred,* as of them, is to be found in his own career. In the deepest sense, it stands with these two as the most autobiographical of his novels.

At the risk of dispute with two of Disraeli's most able critics, it must be pointed out that if any one of the novels has a claim to be labelled "Disraeli's spiritual autobiography," that work is *Lothair* (1870). It deals with the usual semi-autobiographical hero, but this time he is cast as the prize in a battle between three separate religious philosophies, all of which have their attractions for him. *Lothair* has the advantage, too, of having been written late in Disraeli's life, when his religious attitudes were as settled as they ever would be, and his religious commitments had been made irretrievably. It reflects the spiritual struggles which many had suffered in the England of the 1850's and 1860's, and, significantly enough, Lothair's reluctant decision was also Disraeli's.

Mid-century in Victoria's England had witnessed a deadly struggle between the growing forces of mechanistic science (of which evolution was only one representative) and the forces of religious faith. But the latter forces were divided; indeed, many persons in England saw Roman Catholicism as a more dangerous enemy than scientific thought. In *Lothair,* the young, wealthy, titled hero is a pawn in the struggle between these forces, each of which is personified as a woman. The combination of Anglican Church and English Aristocracy (that is, Disraeli's "Tory principle") is represented by the correct, affectionate, but bland Lady Corisande, who is leading candidate for the young nobleman's hand before he sets off on his adventures and who eventually wins him by default, as it were. The Roman Catholic Church and romantic tradition are represented by the devoted and devout Clare Arundel, who is in effect cheated of her rightful victory by the manipulations of other Catholics and ends her days in a convent. And the forces of free-thinking and popular democracy are represented by the dashing Theodora Campion, wife of an American adventurer and supporter of Garibaldi, whose hold on Lothair is scarcely weakened by her death in battle in the cause of freedom.

Strikingly enough, Disraeli's respect for all of these forces is shown in his treatment of the three women. Lady Corisande is dutiful, conventional, and decent, like the Tory cause which she represents; she lacks originality and force, but such qualities are not always sought in women (or religions, although this is not the author's point). Although the Roman Catholic Church is subjected to scathing treatment in *Lothair,* all of the ire is reserved for the higher ranks of the priesthood; Clare's integrity is never compromised, and her final taking of the veil is viewed as fulfillment—for her. And, surprisingly, Theodora is presented with such fervor and appreciation that the reader is left wondering if the author had to kill his character in order to free Lothair from her direct influence.

Of all the religious aspects of the novel, the one most likely to stand out on first reading is Disraeli's attitude toward the Roman Catholic Church. As Masefield says of *Lothair* [in *Peacocks and Primroses: A Study of Disraeli's Novels,* 1953], "it is difficult to assess from it his true attitude toward Roman Catholicism"; we may judge with surety, however, that it was a complex of many reactions, from attraction to thorough distrust. *Lothair* contains full acknowledgement of the tremendous attraction which the traditional and emotional aspects of Catholicism held for the author even in 1870. Lothair at a Tenebrae service may well be compared with the young Contarini Fleming at the chapel. In *Lothair,* however, the author holds back the curtain and shows us the fascination of the ritual being fostered and deliberately manipulated by the higher clergy to lure the susceptible Lothair into their fold. The life-long attraction of the Catholic ritual remained for Disraeli, but *Lothair* displays another side of the coin for the first time, and the savagery with which it is laid bare shows us Disraeli's final if reluctant personal rejection of Catholicism. Cardinal Grandison and Msgr. Catesby are the only major villains in *Lothair;* their schemes and subtleties are untouched by scruple. They are surrounded by a band of priests, most of whom are devout and honest, but we see this latter group simply as the unwitting tools of the schemers, for whom "ends justify means."

Lothair's final enlightenment takes place after the Battle of Mentana, in which he is wounded while battling for Garibaldi. He is taken to Rome, unconscious, to be nursed by Clare. News is published that he had fallen while fighting for the Pope, and when he protests he is airily informed by the Cardinal that his revolutionary adventures were merely the illusions of a disturbed mind. A near-captive, Lothair is trapped into a number of incidents to make it look as though he were preparing to join the Church of Rome; it is published that Clare Arundel had been led to him on the battlefield by a miracle. The time even comes when he finds that it has been announced that he is to be received into the Church by the Pope himself, and Lothair is saved only by physical collapse and by an eventual lucky escape.

Why this fierce bitterness? Why, after a lifetime of chaste, if occasionally passionate flirtation, does Disraeli reject the lure of Catholicism so decisively and angrily? Roth suggests that this anti-Catholicism springs from his Marrano background, although this explanation seems to ignore the obvious attractions which Catholicism had held, and continued to hold, for Disraeli. Even his remarks in the General Preface of 1870 about "mediaeval superstitions which are generally only the embodiments of pagan ceremonies and creeds" (as opposed, of course, to the true "Semitic principle") do not offer a satisfactory explanation. The obvious explanation seems to have been discounted by most commentators except Buckle: Prime Minister Disraeli's dealings with the Catholic Church during the Irish Church Disestablishment Controversy of 1868. This occurred, it will be recalled, only in the year *Lothair* was written; during its course the Catholic hierarchy in Britain withdrew support from Disraeli when Gladstone made what seemed a better offer.

> It was not unnatural that Disraeli should have felt that he had been treated shabbily by the representatives of the Roman Catholics, and especially by Manning. He said on more than one occasion to Roman Catholic friends that he had been stabbed in the back. [Monypenny and Buckle]

Since it was the Irish Church question more than any other which caused the downfall of Disraeli's 1868 Government, and since Disraeli more than once vented his spleen on political enemies in his novels (*vide* Croker as "Rigby" in *Coningsby,* Thackeray as "St. Barbe" in *Endymion,* Gladstone as the hero in *Falconet,* etc.), the reasons for his bitterness against the Catholic hierarchy are apparent. Buckle treats this question thoroughly and well in his fifth volume.

Theodora Campion's free-thinking is associated with the revolutionary societies stirring on the Continent at this time. Yet Theodora, though not a sectarian, is what many will concede to be a religious person. As she herself remarks early in *Lothair* to the Oxford Professor, she has religion—the religion of "God in her conscience." This is in itself an improvement over the puzzled emotionalism in which Lothair had been struggling; her influence upon him is vital to the process of finding himself. Actually, Lothair never rejects her ideology; he merely assimilates it into the broader, more satisfying view at which he finally arrives.

Naturally he finds that view in Palestine; as Pearson wittily comments, ". . . Lothair would not have been Disraeli if he had not set sail for the Holy Land." By the Sea of Galilee he meets a "fourth force," in the person of a young Syrian Christian named Paraclete. The message which he receives from this master is that there is for man a higher possible unity, of far greater and more venerable antiquity than even that of the Roman Catholic faith. As Speare notes, "Lothair finds happiness and satisfaction in a broad Christian belief." Is there significance to the fact that each of the three lesser influences is exemplified by a woman, but that this fourth, the greatest, is exemplified by a man? When Lothair realizes that the time has come to return to the world of action (and Lady Corisande), it is to the Church of England that he turns, for it alone is fitted for such a broad view. In fact, this broad view, closely related to Disraeli's "Semitic principle," holds the spirit of regeneration which Disraeli so desired the Anglican Church to learn.

*Lothair* is the clearest statement of religious possibility and choice which Disraeli ever made, and may, therefore, be considered as in a sense his spiritual autobiography. The obvious attractions of Roman Catholicism do not counterbalance its limitations and the lack of scruple among its leadership. Humanitarianism is needed, but it is not enough. The Church of England, too, is found lacking, but, regenerated by true Christian principles, for which it should return to the Holy Land instead of to the Middle Ages, it will be able to regain its place as partner to Crown and People.

Disraeli's last novel, *Endymion* (1880), and the fragment left at his death, *Falconet* (1881), may be dismissed as a charitable act, for both are lacking in mental energy and force. The sister of the "prudent and plastic" Endymion is received into the Roman Catholic communion so that she may marry the King of France, but neither author nor characters have any comment to make on the event. Very early in the book there is a drawingroom discussion of religion which does NOT recall the divan scene of *Tancred.* Later, in a calm, almost objective representation of the "Papal Aggression" of thirty years before, there appears a juster and more attractive view of Cardinal Manning than that found in *Lothair.* In the fragment, *Falconet,* the hero is presented as champion of the Church; other than the obvious parallel of his attitudes and career with that of Gladstone, we have no inkling as to where Falconet's spiritual inclinations might lead him. All in all, the cry of the young Vivian Grey, Disraeli's first literary hero of more than half-a-century before, echoes through these works: "The springiness of my mind is gone!" *Lothair* remains as Disraeli's culminating treatment in novel form of the problems of religion. Viewed alone, it is a comprehensive statement; viewed as the last important member of a series of novels which show in unguarded fashion Disraeli's changing attitudes toward religion, it has an even deeper significance. (pp. 29-42)

*Arthur H. Frietzsche, in his* Disraeli's Religion: The Treatment of Religion in Disraeli's Novels, *Utah State University Press, 1961, 46 p.*

## Robert Blake   (lecture date 1966)

[*Blake is an English political historian and the author of several book-length studies of Disraeli, including* Disraeli and Gladstone *(1970) and* Disraeli's Grand Tour: Benjamin Disraeli and the Holy Land, 1830-31 *(1982).*

*His acclaimed biography* Disraeli *(1967) has been praised for its depth and scholarship as well as its lucidity. In the lecture below, which was originally given to the Royal Society of Literature in 1966, Blake presents an overview of Disraeli's fiction, assessing the works and placing them within the context of both the author's political career and nineteenth-century English literature.*]

Benjamin Disraeli's career as a statesman is famous and he would of course live in history if he had never written a work of fiction in his life. But I would like to suggest that he would have a place in history, though not such a great one, if he had never held office at all. His novels are probably not much read today, and many of them are undeniably not worth reading. Yet he did write three or four which will never be forgotten, and his names and phrases have become a part of the language of politics used by many who do not realize where they come from. It is this aspect of his career on which I am going to speak. . . .

His novel writing was spread over a long period. He published his first complete novel in 1826 when he was 21. He published his last in 1880 when he was 75 and had been twice Prime Minister. Between *Vivian Grey,* the first, and *Endymion,* the last, he wrote eleven other novels. He also produced an epic poem, unbelievably bad, and a five-act blank verse tragedy, if possible worse. Further he wrote a discourse on political theory, and a political biography, the *Life of Lord George Bentinck,* which is excellent, and, considering how soon after its hero's death it came out, remarkably fair and accurate.

Disraeli's writings were not spread at all evenly over his long career. Eight of his thirteen novels appeared in the eleven years 1826-37. Then he got into Parliament, married a rich wife, and concentrated on politics. But he was balked by Peel's—very understandable—refusal to give him office in 1841 when the Conservatives regained power. He became an anti-Establishment figure, and chose the novel as the form through which he would express his criticism of English politics and English society. Hence the three novels by which he is perhaps known best, the political novels of the 1840's: *Coningsby* (1844), *Sybil* (1845), and *Tancred* (1847). They were the last that he was to write for many years. In 1849 he became Leader of his party in the House of Commons, and, apart from the life of Bentinck in 1852 undertaken as a work of *pietas* towards a friend, ally, and benefactor, he published nothing for twenty-one years until 1870. *Lothair,* which appeared that year, caused a sensation, as one might expect of a novel from an ex-Prime Minister. Then ten years later came *Endymion.* Nor should we forget *Falconet,* his unfinished novel which he began after *Endymion.*

Disraeli, then, began life as a writer and ended it as a writer. It was natural that he should have thus begun. His father Isaac was a distinguished man of letters, a friend of Byron, Southey, Samuel Rogers, Moore, and the greatest publisher of the age, John Murray the Second. As a boy he heard talk about literature at his father's table and he was given the run of his father's large and ever-expanding library. Isaac intended his son to be a solicitor and had fixed up a partnership in a prosperous city firm. For a time Benjamin was an articled clerk—incongruous though the role may seem. But he was intensely ambitious. He longed to cut a dash, create a sensation, to be *someone*. The law was far too humdrum. For fame he needed fortune—and needed it quickly. He decided to make it on the Stock Exchange by speculating in the boom in South American mining shares. Indeed his first venture in writing was not a novel but a trio of pamphlets puffing the merits of some of the dubious concerns in which he and his friends had invested. They were as much works of fiction as any novel.

At the same time that he tried to make his fortune on the Stock Exchange he was also engaged in founding along with John Murray a new daily paper, *The Representative,* intended to be a rival to *The Times.* Disraeli agreed to put up a quarter of the capital though he had none at all. He acted as intermediary in negotiations to get J. G. Lockhart as editor, hurried up to Scotland, stayed at Chiefswood, met Sir Walter Scott at Abbotsford. Back in London he arranged for printing presses, new buildings, foreign correspondents, etc. There was a collapse on the Stock Exchange, mining shares became worthless, Disraeli was unable to produce his share of the capital and dropped out of *The Representative,* which was a disastrous failure and ceased publication in the summer of 1826, having cost John Murray £26,000.

Disraeli was barely 21 when the collapse occurred. Nothing daunted, he resolved to recoup himself by writing. Hence **Vivian Grey,** written at high pressure early in 1826. Or rather I should say the first part of **Vivian Grey,** the first two volumes in the first edition. The second part in three volumes appearing later in the year has little connexion with it and is of little interest. **Vivian Grey** is of course, like most novels written by young men, largely autobiographical. It is an extraordinary compound of reckless satire, youthful worldliness, cynical observation, grandiloquent sentiment, sheer fun, and impudence. In point of form and construction it could hardly be worse but its vigour and vitality make it wonderfully readable even to-day.

The story is the story of Murray, Lockhart, and *The Representative* transposed from journalism into politics, Vivian himself being Disraeli.

> And now . . . this stripling who was going to begin his education had all the experience of a matured mind—of an experienced man; was already a cunning reader of human hearts; and felt conscious from experience that his was a tongue which was born to guide human beings. The idea of Oxford to such an individual was an insult. . . . THE BAR—pooh! law and bad jokes till we are forty; and then with the most brilliant success the prospect of gout and a coronet. . . .

So Vivian decides to make his way by becoming the *éminence grise* to some 'magnifico'. His choice is the Marquess of Carabas who holds a grand political sinecure but has lost any real political influence. One of his friends is 'Lord Beaconsfield—a damned fool'. Lord Carabas, who is a prosy bore, wishes to become Prime Minister but he needs a leader of the House of Commons. Vivian persuades a former politician, Cleveland, who after a short but brilliant career in Parliament has forsaken the world for the pleasures of a *cottage orné* in Wales, to play the part. Just

when all seems set for success, and Vivian is discoursing on 'political gastronomy' to the Marquess, Mrs. Lorraine, the Marquess's sister-in-law, whose amorous advances have been repulsed by Vivian, ruins the plot by poisoning the minds of the chief plotters against him. They repudiate their allegiance. The Marquess rounds on Vivian. He departs to take vengeance on Mrs. Lorraine, falsely telling her that he has defeated her machinations and is about to enter Parliament. The result is gratifying:

> When he ended she sprang from the sofa, and, looking up, and extending her arms with unmeaning wildness, she gave one loud shriek, and dropped like a bird shot on the wing—she had burst a blood vessel.

Vivian has a duel with Cleveland whom he kills, and retires to bed with the then equivalent of a nervous breakdown. The early editions conclude with a tongue-in-the-cheek passage later expurgated:

> I fear me much that Vivian Grey is a lost man; but I am sure that every sweet and gentle spirit, who has read this sad story of his fortunes will breathe a holy prayer this night, for his restoration to society and to himself.

The question of expurgation is important. In 1853 Disraeli brought out a collected edition of his novels. He was by then an ex-Chancellor of the Exchequer, and the tone of society and literature had greatly changed in the intervening quarter of a century. He drastically cut his early novels, omitting whole scenes and chapters which seemed embarrassing, exuberant, in bad taste, or libellous. Nearly all modern collected editions are based on the 1853 text, and, although this does not matter as far as the famous trilogy of the forties is concerned—**Coningsby, Sybil, Tancred**—for he left them unchanged, it does affect **Vivian Grey, The Young Duke, Henrietta Temple,** and others. The earlier versions are not easy to secure. I am lucky enough to possess a first edition of **Vivian Grey,** which, it so happens, has in it the book-plate of Lord Birkenhead's father. Lucien Wolf, an eminent Disraeli scholar, began to issue a 'centenary edition' in 1904 reprinting the original texts and indicating the changes. But only two, **Vivian Grey** and **The Young Duke,** appeared, and the project lapsed.

This is to be regretted, for the full flavour of the early novels can only be appreciated from the pre-1853 version. Nor can one otherwise appreciate the offence which Disraeli gave to living persons. For **Vivian Grey** is highly personal. The Marquess of Carabas is obviously John Murray, and in the original edition he is presented quite unwarrantably as a tipsy nincompoop. If I may quote from the scene after dinner at Château Désir where the new party is being formed:

> Here the bottle passed, and the Marquess took a bumper. 'My Lords and Gentlemen, when I take into consideration the nature of the various interests of which the body politic of this great empire is regulated; (Lord Courtown, the bottle stops with you) when I observe, I repeat, this, I naturally ask myself what right, what claims, what, what what—I repeat what right these governing interests have to the influence which they possess? (Vivian, my boy, you'll find champagne

on the waiter behind you.) Yes gentlemen it is in this temper (the corkscrew's by Sir Berdmore), it is, I repeat, in this temper, and actuated by these views, that we meet together this day.'

Later we are told that the worthy Marquess 'reeled and retired'. Naturally this infuriated Murray. The portrait of Cleveland equally enraged Lockhart. There were many other recognizable figures. Moreover, the early editions contained absurdities, locutions, *naïvetés,* which at times almost remind one of *The Young Visiters.* 'The Marquess dashed off a tumbler of Burgundy'—'The *cuisine* of Mr. Grey was *superbe*'—'Her Ladyship was now *passata,* although with the aid of cachemeres diamonds and turbans, her *tout ensemble* was still very striking.' These and many other solecisms and *gaffes* were cut out in 1853.

*Vivian Grey* is in part a political novel, perhaps the first of that genre. It is, however, more obviously what has come to be called a 'silver fork' novel, or a novel of high society. This was all the rage in the 1820's: Theodore Hook, Mrs. Gore, Plumer Ward who wrote *Tremaine or the Man of Refinement* and whom Isaac D'Israeli knew well, and Bulwer Lytton whose *Pelham* was avowedly inspired by *Vivian Grey.* Novels which purported to describe the *beau monde* were at a premium in an age of ostentation, extravagance, and social fluidity. The outsiders wanted to read about the insiders, and the insiders, of course, then as ever since, loved to read about themselves. *Vivian Grey* was published anonymously, and Colburn, the publisher, contrived to give the impression that the author was a man of fashion. For a time the reviewers were cautious but when they discovered that it was written by a middle-class Jewish solicitor's clerk of 21, they let themselves go in no uncertain fashion. *The Monthly Magazine* wrote:

> We shall probably never have to mention his name again, . . . he is evidently incapable of anything better, and his only chance of escaping perpetual burlesque is to content himself with 'wearing his violet coloured slippers', 'slobbering his Italian greyhound' [both phrases were cut out in 1853] and sinking suddenly and finally into total oblivion.

This was a premature judgement.

I have dwelt on *Vivian Grey* because it sums up the quintessential Disraeli. It is a bad novel in form. The language is extravagant and often absurd. But this was true to the end. One can find expressions in *Lothair* forty-five years later which are not so very different. Yet in spite of all its defects it is gay, sparkling, very amusing, and highly entertaining.

We can move quickly over Disraeli's next few novels. *Popanilla* (1828), though admired oddly enough by John Bright, is too much of an imitation of *Gulliver's Travels* to be at all convincing. *The Young Duke* published in 1831 is an avowed potboiler, a frank attempt to exploit silver forkery. 'I am confident of its success, and that it will complete the corruption of the public taste', Disraeli cheerfully wrote to a friend. 'What does Ben know of dukes?' his father is said to have asked. Not much, is the answer. The Duke of St. James is more like the Duke in *Zuleika Dob-*

*son* than any other in fact or fiction, but the book, though Disraeli became even more ashamed of it than of *Vivian Grey,* has a vitality which still makes it worth reading. *Contarini Fleming* (1832) has great interest as a piece of autobiography, especially the early chapters, but it never caught on either at the time or since. Of *Alroy* (1833), an historical romance written in a sort of poetic prose, Disraeli himself admitted that the first chapter made just as good sense if it was read backwards, and *The Rise of Iskander* which came out with it is scarcely more meritorious.

There followed a pause while Disraeli was deeply involved in a love affair and his epic poem. At the end of 1836 when both had collapsed he published *Henrietta Temple,* the one book of his in which the authentic note of passion sounds. He had been living for three years with the real Henrietta, wife of a baronet, Sir Francis Sykes. In 1836 she left Disraeli for the artist Maclise. The first half of the novel, which he began when their affair began, reflects his genuine love; the second half written after Henrietta's departure is an urbane comedy of manners with a delightful portrait of his friend Count d'Orsay. The novel is highly autobiographical. It is also easier to read than any since *The Young Duke.* He followed it with *Venetia* (May 1837), a strange quasi-historical romance based on the lives of Shelley and Byron but set in the period of the American War of Independence. Chronologically it is as if in recent times someone had written a novel about T. E. Lawrence or Rupert Brooke and set it in the Crimean War. One would not expect it to come off—and *Venetia* did not. Nor is the story improved by the names chosen. Lord Cadurcis for Byron is clumsy enough, but Marmion Herbert for Shelley is too much to bear.

So far Disraeli had not really achieved much in terms of literature. But when he resumed his pen in 1843 five years later, he began the famous trilogy by which he must stand or fall as a novelist. Before we consider it, I ought to make plain my view about Disraeli's general position. Too much should not be claimed for him. He was not a great novelist, like Scott, Dickens, Thackeray, or George Eliot, nor even a very good novelist like Trollope. Yet though he is not in the top class he is not exactly in the second either. He is not, for example, a Wilkie Collins. Examiners in the Oxford final schools when puzzled by a candidate who has touches of brilliance mingled with incongruous errors and follies used sometimes to award the mark of alpha/gamma. This fits Disraeli. He was the alpha/gamma novelist of the day. And his alpha element is not to be disregarded. In *Coningsby* he produced the first and most brilliant of English political novels, a genre which he may be said to have invented; and in *Sybil* he produced one of the first and one of the most famous social novels. He would be remembered for them if he had written nothing else, and had never entered the Cabinet.

The eighteen-forties were the years of the novel-with-a-purpose, the *roman à thèse:* Mrs. Gaskell's *Mary Barton* (1848), Kingsley's *Yeast* (1848), Newman's *Loss and Gain* (1848), Froude's *Nemesis of Faith* (1849). It was an era of religious and social heart-searching: the position of the Church, Tractarians against Evangelicals; the Condition

*Disraeli's country home, Hughenden Manor.*

of England question. Carlyle and Newman were the key figures. The novel-with-a-purpose could be carried rather far, for example Mrs. Frewin's off-putting title, *The Inheritance of Evil, or the Consequences of Marrying a Deceased Wife's Sister* (1849). And a reviewer seeking a 'purpose' in *Wuthering Heights* decided that its moral must be to 'show what Satan could do with the law of Entail'. Disraeli's object when he wrote *Coningsby* was set out many years later in his General Preface to the collected edition of 1870:

> The derivation and character of political parties; the condition of the people which had been the consequence of them; the duties of the Church as a main remedial agency in our present state; were the principal topics which I had intended to treat, but I found they were too vast for the space that I had allotted to myself.

So *Coningsby or the New Generation* while adumbrating all three themes only dealt fully with the first—political parties. *Sybil or the Two Nations* dealt with the second, the condition of the people. *Tancred, or the New Crusade* is concerned with the third, the question of the Church. Both in its ideology and literary merit, *Tancred* is the least satisfactory of the three, and I do not intend to say much about it. The first third of it—Volume I in the original three-decker edition—is very amusing, but it trails off into an oriental phantasmagoria when once Tancred arrives in

the Holy Land. Sidonia—that strange amalgam of Rothschild and Disraeli himself, his revenge for Fagin—observes early in the book, 'It is no longer difficult to reach Jerusalem; the real difficulty is the one experienced by the crusaders, to know what to do when you get there.' Moreover, the point of the book was intended to be a great religious experience for its hero. This was something Disraeli had never known himself. Not surprisingly his effort to convey it ends in bathos. The book would make a splendid film scenario. Indeed, all three would do this, especially *Sybil* with its lurid ending, and it is surprising that the attempt has never been made. But, although Disraeli liked *Tancred* best of his novels, and, although it does throw much interesting light on his own religious, racial, and other beliefs, it must be pronounced markedly inferior to *Coningsby* and *Sybil.*

In these he is putting across his Tory 'philosophy' based on the notions of that curious little group in Parliament which he headed—Young England. The leading members were Lord John Manners, and George Smythe who is in fact Coningsby. I do not propose to discuss this 'philosophy'. If we take it seriously, we must admit that it was basically romantic, escapist, unhistorical, illiberal, and reactionary in the true sense of the word, hostile to 'progress', 'reason', and the Parliamentary system (not that the three are synonymous). It was a counterblast to the Whig theories of history. It was not more foolish or erroneous than some of those, but this is perhaps no great praise. It is not necessary to analyse all this for our purposes today.

What of the merits of the novels as such. We need not share the views of the author of a *roman à thèse* in order to enjoy the novel. We can appreciate Disraeli's novels without believing that Shelburne dominated the mind of Pitt or that Charles I was 'the holocaust of direct taxation'. *Coningsby, Sybil,* and indeed all Disraeli's later novels are totally different from any other novels in the nineteenth century. For that matter there is nothing quite like them in the twentieth century either, though one might perhaps detect a faint echo in the early Evelyn Waugh.

Lord David Cecil goes so far as to say, 'Disraeli's novels, for all their brilliance, are not strictly speaking novels. They are not, that is, meant to be realistic pictures of life, but discussions on political and religious questions put into fictional form.' To discuss this criticism would entail a long digression. If Disraeli's novels have any parallel at all in contemporary literature, perhaps those of Peacock come nearest. No doubt the same point can be made about them too, but, if neither Disraeli nor Peacock wrote novels in the usual sense of the word, what they wrote was more like the novel than anything else. Large sections of Disraeli's books are, indeed, conversation pieces uttered by persons who are 'humours' rather than individualized characters, for example the immortal Tadpole and Taper. But in *Coningsby* he succeeded in creating—or anyway describing—two unforgettable personalities, Lord Monmouth and Rigby; and in *Sybil* he gave a highly realistic picture of life in the grim northern manufacturing towns which formed the breeding ground of Chartism, a picture based partly on his own observations; partly on the correspondence of Feargus O'Connor obtained for him by his friend Thomas Duncombe, a radical M. P.; and very largely upon Part II of the Appendix to the Second Report of the Children's Employment Commission of 1842. His novels were not devoid of realism or of characters.

And if it is true that they are to a considerable extent conversation pieces, the severest critic must concede that the conversation is excellent even as Disraeli's own was—witty, ironical, epigrammatic. He caught wonderfully the hard rattle of society drawing rooms, or the languid affectation of the *jeunesse dorée,* like Alfred Mountchesney and Lord Eugène de Vere in *Sybil* who 'had exhausted life in their 'teens, and all that remained for them was to mourn, amid the ruins of their reminiscences, over the extinction of excitement'. There is indeed an Oscar Wilde-like quality in the famous scene on the eve of Derby Day at Crockford's, with which *Sybil* opens:

> 'Nothing does me any good', said Alfred throwing away his almost untasted peach. 'I should be quite content if something could do me harm. . . .'
>
> 'Well for my part', said Mr. Berners, 'I do not like your suburban dinners. You always get something you can't eat, and cursed bad wine.'
>
> 'I rather like bad wine', said Mr. Mountchesney, 'One gets so bored with good wine.'

It was not for nothing that Oscar Wilde gave one of his best-known works a title that is but a slight variant on *Vivian Grey.* Yet there is a great gulf between the two writers. Disraeli's heroes, to quote Mrs. Tillotson, 'all think—perhaps ineffectually, ignorantly, fitfully, but in their puzzled or impulsive way they do think about their social rights and responsibilities'. Oscar Wilde's world was the apolitical world of a revived silver forkery from the eighteen-twenties. Disraeli's was one of social stress and political bewilderment. This is what gives the novels their perennial interest, for the problems that vexed Coningsby and Egremont and Tancred are with us still in essence. Only the form has changed. Conservatives are still wondering what they should conserve. Many in recent times must have felt that only a slight variation was needed on Mr. Taper's immortal words, 'a sound Conservative government, I understand: Tory men and Whig measures' to fit their own situation. And in 1966 members of the Labour party may well be thinking that an inverted version would describe theirs too. In portraying, as he does in *Coningsby,* the conflict between political compromise and political principle Disraeli portrays the eternal dilemma of politics. And if he does not solve it, no one else has done so either. As for *Sybil,* it is true that the two nations in our Britain are not the same or divided by the same gulf as in Disraeli's, but although the extremes of wealth and poverty no longer exist within Britain they exist in the world as a whole and constitute one of its gravest problems. And are not Gerard's words which make the famous ending to Book II highly relevant today if moved from a national to a global setting?

> I speak of the annual arrival of more than three hundred thousand strangers in this island. How will you feed them? How will you clothe them? How will you house them? They have given up butcher's meat; must they give up bread? . . . Why, go to your history—you're a scholar—and see the fall of the great Roman Empire—what was that? . . . What are your invasions of the barbarous nations, your Goths and Visigoths, your Lombards and Huns, to our Population Returns?

In spite of—perhaps because of—the materialism of the 1840's there arose a group, largely from generous youth, who reacted against it, seeking an ideal, a cause, something to which they could dedicate themselves and which would give a purpose to their lives. Disraeli was no longer young but one of his most attractive traits was the sympathy with youth, which he felt to the end of his career. Life to him, despite the cynicism and world-weary air which he sometimes affected, always remained the endless adventure that it was to Vivian Grey.

In many ways *Coningsby* is the better of the two novels. The plot is rather more convincing, though it is not very convincing in either novel. Lord Monmouth and Rigby are characters who have no equals in *Sybil.* Rigby is supposed to be Croker against whom Disraeli undoubtedly had a grudge. There is in fact no likeness at all but it does not matter that the portrait is a libel on someone who seems to have been worthy and honourable if rather narrow-minded. Rigby exists in his own right as the epitome of the bustling toady, the busy know-all, the efficient tool of a selfish grandee; yet not despicable if only because he is so formidable, an enemy worthy to be fought.

Monmouth is drawn from the same original as Thackeray's Lord Steyne in Vanity Fair, the profligate, heartless, ambitious, fabulously rich Marquess of Hertford, and is far more convincing. Lord Steyne is a mere stage villain cut out of cardboard. Lord Monmouth is seen in the round. He may be larger than life but he lives intensely and vividly, the very quintessence of the old aristocratic order that was passing away, the arrogant grandee with his palaces, his mistresses, his minions; unscrupulous in his determination to secure a dukedom, despite the loss of his rotten boroughs; hard and relentless in his fearful family feuds; but a man of polish, charm, and breeding who could fascinate when he chose and who would do anything to avoid a scene. He is more real than the New Generation, more real even than Coningsby himself who is George Smythe, and far more real than the rest.

Disraeli was better than any other Victorian novelist at portraying the aristocracy. To say this is not to disparage such creations as Sir Lester Dedlock or the two dukes of Omnium. But neither Dickens, nor Thackeray, nor Trollope could quite shed a sort of middle-class uneasiness towards the nobility. It was not that they were ignorant of the grand world. The idea that Dickens could not write about it because he 'was not a gentleman' and had never met such people is quite untrue. But it is true that none of them knew it as well as Disraeli, true too that none of them accepted it as Disraeli did; Disraeli could visit his contempt on individuals like Lord Marney whose cold-hearted selfishness discredits his order, or Lord de Mowbray whose bogus pedigree conceals his descent from a club waiter. But he felt none of the moral disapprobation which the world of the Athenaeum felt for the world of White's. He never doubted that there ought to be an aristocracy, and in spite of social origins no less *bourgeois* than those of most other Victorian literary men, regarded himself as meeting the aristocracy on equal if not superior terms—a by-product of his eccentric theories about Jewry and his erroneous belief in his own descent from its most aristocratic branch.

Moreover, by the time he came to write *Coningsby* Disraeli knew the life of the London salons and the country-houses intimately. Politics and dandyism were more effective passports to those circles than literature. Disraeli had yet to stay at the grandest houses of all, but he had early been the protégé of the heir of Stowe. He and his wife were regular guests at Deepdene, the seat of the millionaire Henry Hope, where much of *Coningsby* was written. In London they attended the receptions given by the great political hostesses whom Disraeli lightly and delightfully satirizes in *Sybil.* Disraeli is always good on women young or old. In his novels as in life he understood them better than men, and apart from Sybil herself who never comes alive he rarely deviates into those portraits of virtuous insipidity which mar so many of his contemporary novelists. But with regard to both sexes in the upper class he knew what he was talking about, and, when allowance is made for epigrammatic rhetorical prose that he puts in their mouths and the romantic extravagance with which he in-

vests their background, his picture is probably the most authentic that we have.

The same applies to politics. Admirers of Trollope will challenge the statement but surely in *Coningsby, Sybil,* and to a lesser degree *Endymion* Disraeli puts across the drama and excitement of parliamentary life—not to mention the comedy—in a way that no one else has quite achieved: the intrigues, the manœuvres, the calculations, the rumours, the fluctuations of fortune, the agony of being out, the triumph of being in. Politics was the very fibre of his being. He loved it for its own sake and he had a wonderful eye for the amusing as well as the serious side of it. The conversation of those admirable twin political hacks, Tadpole and Taper, names that have passed into the English language, constitutes some of the most entertaining passages in all fiction. It does not matter in the least whether they are accurate portraits of Bonham or other forgotten wire-pullers whom Disraeli disliked. They are the vehicles of his wit and Disraeli was one of the wittiest men that ever lived.

Trollope's novels are not political at all in the sense that Disraeli's are. For one thing Trollope was not a politician. He tried and failed to get into Parliament as a Liberal and was bitterly disillusioned in the process. His profession was that of civil servant, and through his novels one constantly detects just below the surface that contempt, or if this is too strong a word, that bewilderment, which civil servants so often feel at the conduct of their ostensible masters. Trollope was concerned more with the social background of politicians than with politics as an end in itself. This does not detract from his novels. In many ways he was a far superior writer to Disraeli. But it does mean that he misses the thrills and the suspense of that strange closed world which inhabits the great gothic Palace of Westminster, the absorption with victory or defeat which could make Disraeli in the fifties describe some now long-forgotten division on a matter of fleeting significance as 'an affair of Inkerman'.

It is in no way surprising that Trollope detested Disraeli and Disraeli's novels. In a well-known passage in his *Autobiography* he says:

> In whatever he has written he has affected something which has been intended to strike his readers as uncommon and therefore grand. Because he has been bright and a man of genius he has carried his object as regards the young. He has struck them with astonishment and aroused in their imagination ideas of a world more glorious, more rich, more witty, more enterprising than their own. But the glory has been the glory of pasteboard and the wealth has been the wealth of tinsel. The wit has been the wit of hairdressers, and the enterprise the enterprise of mountebanks.

It is a stock criticism that Disraeli created an artificial world. But do not all novelists do this to some degree? The world of high society and of politics was and is in many ways a highly artificial world. Disraeli's novels would not sparkle as they do if all his diamonds had been paste. Trollope and Milnes missed the point, and for all the shrewdness of their criticisms they never understood what it was that gives the novels their gaiety and vitality.

*Coningsby* is set exclusively in a background of politics and the *beau monde*. It must be admitted that Disraeli was less sure of himself in *Sybil* where he tries to draw the contrast between the classes and the masses. Although 'the two nations' became a household word, the novel did not have the impact of Mrs. Gaskell's *Mary Barton,* and not simply because of Disraeli's reputation as a society novelist or his esoteric political ideas. One never doubts that the details are correct but he could not project himself into the lives of the poor as Mrs. Gaskell did. The dialogue is too stilted and implausible. The characters are sociological case-studies rather than individuals. If the descriptions of squalor are memorable it is largely because those in the Blue Books from which Disraeli lifted them are memorable too. On quite a different level the same uncertainty in an unfamiliar field is discernible in the Eton scenes of *Coningsby.* Here again the details are correct. Disraeli had had himself carefully coached by the Revd. W. G. Cookesley, a well-known Eton master. Nor had he forgotten what it was like to be a boy. The famous passage beginning 'At school friendship is a passion . . . ' has a very authentic ring. Nor is the trouble to be found merely in his rococo language, odd though it often is. Who else could have referred to a boy who ate too many sweets as 'the irreclaimable and hopeless votary of Lollipop, the opium eater of schoolboys'? The real difficulty is the same as in *Sybil,* an inability to enter into the unfamiliar. Sir William Fraser is surely right in saying that no Eton boys ever talked like the boys in *Coningsby.*

The truth is that Disraeli lacked imagination. This may sound paradoxical. He praises the value of imagination so much that we tend to assume that he had a great deal of it himself. But imagination is not the same as fantasy or day-dreaming. The capacity to invent characters, to get inside them and present their development, the power to put oneself into unfamiliar scenes and situations, everything that is meant by creative imagination, was not Disraeli's *forte.* Of course he possessed it to some degree, or he could not have written novels at all. But compare him with Dickens, Scott, Jane Austen—or even Trollope—and one sees the difference. It comes out too in his creation of characters. Disraeli's were largely based on living models. He began his literary career as author of a *roman à clef,* and never quite got away from this literary genre. Even his seemingly most fantastic inventions like Sir Vavasour Firebrace in *Sybil,* the man who sought to revive the non-existent rights of baronets to sit in Parliament, were copied from life. There really was a man, Sir Richard Broun, author of *Broun's Baronetage,* who pursued this unpromising cause. He also wrote a book with the intriguing title, *The Precedency of Honourable Baronetesses.*

It is easy to list Disraeli's defects. His descriptions are conventional and unperceptive. This was largely because he was extremely short-sighted, and vanity forbade him to use anything but an inadequate eyeglass. His novels are hastily written, ill constructed, a series of scenes rather than a story, and what plot there is is often implausible, sometimes impossible. His range was limited, and he

> **[Disraeli's novels] are great fun, they deal with real problems, if not always with real people, and their vitality is attested by the fact that so many of their expressions have passed into the very language of politics, and that they are still read with pleasure long after most of their contemporaries have vanished into oblivion. Their flavour is unique. There has been nothing like them before or since, and there probably never will be.**
>
> **—Robert Blake**

sounds hollow and unconvincing whenever he tries to touch the deeper feelings. He could descend to astonishing bathos and, to the end, could commit errors of taste almost as bad as those in *Vivian Grey.*

Yet in spite of all this he lives. His prose may have been careless, indeed at times ungrammatical, and with its echo of Burke and Bolingbroke was old-fashioned perhaps for its day, but it is extremely effective. Walter Allen writes in his shrewd introduction to *Coningsby* in the Chiltern Library series:

> It admits of no hesitations, no half-lights; it is completely sure, completely dogmatic. It is the prose of a superb lawyer presenting a case, seemingly holding nothing back, addressing the bemused inarticulate jury as one man of the world to a dozen others, flattering them by his assumption that they are men of equal sophistication and worldly wisdom, wheedling them with his wit. For above everything else Disraeli is a wit. The very structure of his sentences is witty and his epigrams invite the reader into his confidence.

Disraeli was all of a piece. This was the same technique that he used in Parliament. His novels are part of his politics and his politics at times seem to be an emanation of his novels.

Just as Disraeli was at heart an optimist who enjoyed life, so his novels at their best have a gaiety, a sparkle, a cheerful vivacity which carries one over their improbabilities and occasional absurdities. In *Coningsby, Sybil,* and the first third of *Tancred* there is not a dull page. They are essentially the product of an extrovert, splendid novels to read for anyone who is feeling out of sorts. They may not be very profound, they do not touch the inner depths of human character and emotions, they are often careless, but they are great fun, they deal with real problems, if not always with real people, and their vitality is attested by the fact that so many of their expressions have passed into the very language of politics, and that they are still read with pleasure long after most of their contemporaries have vanished into oblivion. Their flavour is unique. There has been nothing like them before or since, and there probably never will be.

Before I discuss very briefly *Lothair* and *Endymion,* I would like to say something about the more material aspect of Disraeli's writings. Two points are of interest. First, he never attempted to produce his books in monthly numbers as Dickens and Thackeray did. He published them in the ordinary 'three-decker form' (*Vivian Grey* was an exception, the first part being in two volumes). The 'three-decker' sold for a guinea and a half. Disraeli did not make a great deal of money out of his novels until the end of his life. *Vivian Grey* part I brought him in £200, part II £500. *The Young Duke* sold for the same, *Contarini Fleming* was a complete flop. *Coningsby* and *Sybil* did better, selling about 3,000 copies and bringing in about £1,000 in each case. *Tancred* sold 2,250 and brought in £750. Disraeli was read by society and parliament, but he never touched the hearts of the great middle class. He was too cynical, too fanciful, too artificial. Incidentally, he had little use for his fellow authors. I doubt if he read them, apart from Bulwer, or anything much since Walter Scott. Dickens to him is 'Gushy' mentioned in *Endymion,* and Thackeray is savagely satirized as St. Barbe in the same novel.

We must now jump nearly a quarter of a century. The Disraeli who was the leader of romantic anti-Peelite protest in his early forties has, after a long career of extraordinary political vicissitudes, 'climbed to the top of the greasy pole' in 1868—only to go slithering down it to a crushing defeat ten months later. Prime Minister for a brief period he is now in the political doldrums. The party is in confusion. Gladstone is triumphant. Disraeli's political position totters in the balance. Instead of rushing around with ephemeral programmes and policies written by equally ephemeral bright young men, he settles down to writing a novel. *Lothair* appeared in 1870. It is an extraordinary performance, one of the best—perhaps *the* best—of his novels. The theme is the struggle for the soul of a young heir to vast estates (really Lord Bute whose conversion to Rome was one of the sensations of the day). Is he to become a Papist, or a radical republican, or will he marry a reputable Anglican heiress and settle down? After many adventures he marries and settles down.

It is in some respects the best of his novels. It is not only full of brilliant Disraeliana, it is in a subtle and not too obvious sense a critique of the glittering world in which Disraeli moved as a sardonic, half-sceptical, half-admiring inhabitant. And he got his own back on a host of enemies, Cardinal Manning, Bishop Wilberforce, Professor Goldwin Smith. The satire is not crude or obvious. One could read it—and many did—as a gaudy romance of the peerage. There is much more to it than that. Carelessly written, abounding even at this stage in his life with extravagant and absurd locutions, it is wonderfully entertaining and yet, if carefully considered, a profoundly sceptical commentary upon the age.

It was financially a great success, and made some £7,500. True, Disraeli's political colleagues were not very enthusiastic. Letters of congratulation are notably absent from his surviving papers. Politically it probably did him more harm than good. But luckily politics do not depend on this sort of thing. The tide turned. The electorate became weary of Gladstone's strenuous moral energy. In 1874 Disraeli was back in office. For six years he governed England, and in 1878 at Berlin he became an international figure.

But he had not abandoned novel writing. As soon as *Lothair* was finished he began a new book, *Endymion.* Its precise dating is not quite clear (I have attempted to clarify the matter in a rather dry piece of speculative detective work appearing in the May 1966 number of the *Review of English Studies*). A large part was written before 1874, but some of it was certainly written while he was Prime Minister. In 1880 the pendulum swung again, and Disraeli was out. He repaired to Hughenden and finished *Endymion,* which was published in November. He received for it the biggest advance that anyone up to that time had received for any novel. Longmans without even seeing it offered £10,000. Later, when they seemed to be losing, Disraeli offered a refund—a characteristic piece of generosity. Longmans, equally creditably, refused to consider the matter, and—a happy outcome—they made a profit in the end.

*Endymion* is set in the past. It is in a sense an historical novel, beginning with the death of Canning in 1827 and ending in the early eighteen-fifties. Unlike *Lothair* it is a political novel, but it is very different from the trilogy of the forties. It lacks the ironic ambiguity of those works, and it has a langour and tiredness which are absent from them and from *Lothair.* Endymion himself is a bit of a stick, and his whole career from the son of a ruined Tory politician *manqué* to becoming Prime Minister is unconvincing. Yet the story has charm, and, for all its fantasies, is highly readable. Disraeli surveys the past, the people he had known, the houses where he was a guest, through rose-coloured spectacles—though once again he paid off some old scores, notably Thackeray. By and large it is, in keeping with its title, a landscape by the light of the moon, the full harvest moon on a warm night softening all that is harsh and familiar, lending magic to the ordinary, poetry to the humdrum.

This was not the end of Disraeli's career as a novelist. No sooner was *Endymion* out, than he began a new book. It was palpably designed as a lampoon on Gladstone, but the G. O. M. never saw it. Its nine short chapters first appeared in *The Times* in 1905. The hero, Joseph Toplady Falconet son of Mr. Wilberforce Falconet, an Evangelical merchant living on Clapham Common, is 'arrogant and peremptory' and as a boy 'scarcely ever known to smile'. The Christian names are not accidental. Joseph is supposed to refer to Joseph Surface, the immortal hypocrite in *The School for Scandal,* and Toplady was the cleric who wrote 'Rock of Ages' which Gladstone in 1839 had translated into Latin. Falconet begins his political career seeking to win a pocket borough under the patronage of Lord Bartram—a portrait of Palmerston. He attacks the revival of the slave trade in the Red Sea. 'True it subsequently appeared that there had been no revival of the slave trade in the Red Sea, but that the misapprehension had occurred from a mistake in the telegraph manipulated by a functionary suffering from *coup de soleil* or *delirium tremens.* But this did not signify. . . .' At a dinner at the Falconets to celebrate victory Lord Bartram is against pursuing the matter. ' "I think I would leave the Red Sea alone," said the Earl. "It was a miracle that saved us being drowned in it before." Mrs. Falconet looked grave and her husband quickly turned the conversation.' The book shows no sign of failing powers, and parts of it are very funny. One can only regret that he never finished it.

There is something absurd, undignified, disreputable—yet infinitely engaging in Disraeli thus setting about his old rival in his own old age. It is as if Sir Winston Churchill in 1945, instead of writing his memoirs, had produced a belated successor to *Savrola,* in which he satirized Lord Attlee. But there is a sense in which, for all his sophistication, worldliness, and grandeur, Disraeli never grew up—or perhaps one should say—never grew old. 'What happened to Vivian Grey?' a friend asked him late in life. 'There was no inquest', replied the Earl of Beaconsfield, 'they say he still lives.' (pp. 1-18)

> Robert Blake, "Disraeli the Novelist," in Essays by Divers Hands, *n.s. Vol. XXXIV, 1966, pp. 1-18.*

## Bertha Keveson Hertz   (essay date 1978)

[*In the essay below, Hertz explores Disraeli's satirical writings in the period from 1824 to 1837, maintaining that it is in these works, and not the autobiographical early novels, that Disraeli reveals the most about himself.*]

Benjamin Disraeli's early thought can be understood through four clever satires which reflect a changing view of himself and of society in his pre-parliamentary period. During this time (1824-1837) of great literary activity and of political gestation, the ambitious Disraeli probed the turbulence in his nature through ironic literature. The early novels (*Vivian Grey, The Young Duke, Contarini Fleming, Henrietta Temple,* and *Venetia*) all feature multiple-faceted young men. They may be said to represent the Bildungsromans of pre-Victorian England. While it is not difficult to identify Disraeli with the pronouncements of the male protagonists in these works, I believe that it is rather in his lesser-known satires that the true revelation of self exists. The conflicts expressed in the satires regarding literature, politics, and society are also clues to the chameleon-like character of their author.

Disraeli was considered an alien by many despite his Christian baptism in 1817. The degree of humiliation he experienced varied from unintentional slur to ugly invective. But he was determined to gain recognition from the powerful arbiters of his time, to overcome all obstacles in his way. These early satires (three of them fantasies) pose the problem: Shall fame come from the pursuit of literature or from activity in the political arena? **"The Dunciad of Today,"** in 1826, *The Voyage of Captain Popanilla* in 1828, *Ixion in Heaven* in 1832-33, and *The Infernal Marriage* in 1834, all attest to his absorption with success. They also contain enduring elements of his complex nature, his penetrating intelligence, and his imagination.

Historical currents of change surrounded Disraeli's experience in what might be described both as an age of progress and of reaction. This transition from the eighteenth to nineteenth century perhaps explains Disraeli's equal regard for aspects of the old and of the new throughout his life. In the early period, contradictions between the Byronic revolutionary and the Gifford conservative coexist in his views. Napoleonic enthusiasm for reform and American experimentation with federalism also find booking next to admiration for Bolingbroke's patriot-king and Burkean traditionalism. Like the Romantic poets whom he so much emulated, Disraeli simultaneously entertained notions on the baroque and the Puritanical, on the heroic and the puny, on the classical and the extravagant. His *souplesse* gave rise to criticism. But despite his eclecticism, Disraeli appears to me to have been partisan to each cause which he espoused. This discursiveness has many implications: his detractors call it lack of principle; less negative interpreters regard this as lack of bias. I believe that the *souplesse* indicated a dualism in his nature as he ponders which route to take. He has left sufficient documentary material of himself in the romans à clef. But it seems to me that his brooding self-interest is more significant in the satires, underneath the various personae which he assumes. Beneath the wit, humor, and repartee is serious reflection, the personal crises of an extraordinary young man.

The verse satire remained unacknowledged, and Disraeli later dismissed the three fantasies as "ambitious nonsense." In his Preface to *Lothair* (his famous apologia in 1870) he disparaged these "youthful indiscretions." *Lothair* was written after Disraeli had been a parliamentarian for thirty years, and when he was in temporary retirement. In his maturity, he regretted the rich clues he had left in the satires which explained his arrogance and disdain as well as his generosity and gallantry. It is precisely this self-reproof (expressed in 1870) which is adumbrated in these satires and which serves to correct the ego-centered qualities of the hero/author. The interchange between inner and outer self demonstrates Disraeli's efforts to mold the literary to the political life. The satires bind the interior imaginative life to the exterior practical man. These early efforts seem devised also to protect the divided sensibility of the "monstrous clever young man."

In **"The Dunciad of Today,"** the objective critic of literary pretensions at the beginning of the poem gives way to the artist as self-critic at the end. In his critique of contemporaries, Disraeli follows the *Dunciad* tradition by attacking minor imitators of the classics, the eclogue fanciers, the lady bards, the journalists, and the dramatists. The general themes that come under suspicion are false taste, mediocrity, and dullness. Like Pope, he satirizes the poor writing of the moderns. Unlike Pope, Disraeli avoids quarreling with dispensers of disputatious knowledge, although he scrutinizes frivolous speculation and pedantry.

**"The Dunciad of Today"** has no allegorical or theological apparatus as does its eminent Popean predecessor. Instead of philosophical dialectics, Disraeli engages us in jog-trot mockery. He cannot compete with Pope's superior intellectualism (to which he pays homage in the opening lines), and he never achieves the metaphysical verbal flights that Pope does. Partly, this is due to the difference in physical and religious temperament. It is also due to a different view of life. Pope sought consummate polish in his verse while Disraeli sought distinction through action. To the ambitious Disraeli, verse satire was just one avenue to follow to another, more powerful level of experience. In the hands of Pope, the morphology of satire achieves architectonic significance. For Disraeli, it is a means for probing his own sensibility. He did not see himself as an autocratic arbiter of taste: he had been troubled with persecution of this type too much to impose it on others. His **"Dunciad"** has a viability and humanity which is absent in the neo-classicist Pope.

The anonymous five-hundred verse satire which had appeared in 1826 in two instalments of a short-lived weekly journal, *The Star Chamber,* is much closer to the Romantics than it is to Pope as regards taste and sense of history. Many characters are borrowed from Byron's *English Bards and Scotch Reviewers* either in direct emulation of Disraeli's romantic hero or as extension of Byron's criticism. The note of wasted genius at the end of **"The Dunciad of Today,"** the genuine self-doubt show Disraeli's empathy with the lost heroes epitomized by Keats. There is a touching tribute at the end of the poem which is both to the unsung, fallen poet and to his philosophy of "negative capability." Disraeli interprets this as the right to be in doubt without having to resolve uncertainty; yet he himself cannot fully accept doubt. He is left in despair.

The protagonist of the poem is Disraeli himself first as the satirist, then as the Shelleyan elegiast. In this verse satire, we may share with him the burden of self-evaluation, a process to which he was constantly subjecting himself. But we may also view the other side of the clever word magician, the witty portraitist, and the parodist. As the poem moves from its early vigorous satire to later melancholy and uncertainty, it becomes a spiritual autobiography. Objective perspicuity at the beginning changes to painful introspection at the end of the poem as the artist's feeling for defeated, buried genius leads to recognition of his own predicament. He says: "Sad was his lot, now slow the tear that greets / Thy blighted triumph, young Endymion Keats." The poem ends on a note of perplexity not only about fame but also about the route which the author should take. Eight years later, in 1834, Disraeli had definitely decided to throw his talents into politics.

Analysts of satirists point out that this type "makes a career of commenting on contradictions" [Leonard Feinberg, in his *The Satirist,* 1963]. This might indicate that the satirist tends to be hypercritical. In *The Voyage of Captain Popanilla,* where the total framework is criticism, Disraeli's efforts become self-modulating. With several views on every topic under consideration, he is able to traverse inner to outer criticism by use of satire. Aiming broadsides at politicians, theoreticians, social ameliorationists, snobs, he does not propagandise for any single position. Instead of a serious polemic, the work is a humorous exposé of the foibles of all classes of English society. Yet if Disraeli does not petition for any specific position, this is not because he lacked convictions. It is rather that he recognized the contradictory nature of his own postures. In fact, he appears to have exploited his divergent

outlooks. The mysterious and the paradoxical become dramatized aspects of the self. Sometimes enigmatic, sometimes explicit, he yet seeks to understand each "self" so that his next image may be an advancement of his ambition. Kaleidoscopic in perspective yet quite specific in motivation is his manipulation of the satiric mode in order to balance the ambivalence of his views.

Modelled after Lucian, Swift, and Voltaire, *The Voyage of Captain Popanilla* is a spoof on Utopianism. Of particular interest to historians here is young Disraeli's anti-protectionist and anti-imperialist stands, which he dramatically revamped during the later parliamentary period. For this reason, Disraeli attempted to suppress the tale: its anti-establishment flavor proved an embarassment to the future Prime Minister of England. The original manuscript is not in the archives at Hughenden Manor with the rest of Disraeliana; it is in the Pierpont Morgan Museum in New York City.

In this fantasy, Disraeli looks at early nineteenth-century English society through special, inverted lenses. He assails abstract political, religious, social, and economic theoreticians. His criticism is based on the observation that theories cannot be arbitrarily applied to man/society. Imposition of universalist doctrines result in a disjunction between man and nature. Utopian notions are charted on assumptions of probable cause and effect, but Disraeli finds that only the improbable is predictable. Hence, his burlesque of Whig principles of the 1820's deliberately emphasizes the negative aspect of positivist presumption. This spirit of inversion animates the satire in *The Voyage.* The author early cautions the reader:

> Indeed, this book is so constructed that if you
> were even, according to custom, to commence
> its perusal by reading the last page, you would
> not gain the slightest assistance in finding out
> how the story ends.

A great deal of the criticism in the tale is directed against the commercial philosophers epitomized by Hobbes and Ricardo, although there are also quick forays against Adam Smith and Malthus. The major assault, however, is reserved for Jeremy Bentham, whose utilitarian philosophy Disraeli felt had been usurped by the new commercial classes. The gospel of "the greatest happiness for the greatest number" stressed a secularized materialism which Disraeli always deplored as a crass intrusion into politics. He had the Romanticist's distrust of scientific systems applied to society as well as the satirist's traditional impatience with the disparity between verbal idealism and actual performance.

Like Candide and Gulliver before him, Popanilla's search for the ideal state remains incomplete. Although he continues his quest for Utopia, he has been tempered by experience. He has learned to discriminate between the natural good and the artificial in theories of perfectibility. The machinery of civilization is encroaching on the good, and Popanilla sees that he had allowed himself to be deceived by "goods" that were misleading. Disraeli's statement is that Popanilla has mistaken information for knowledge. For to Disraeli, experience must give birth to ideas and not the other way round. There is hope for Popanilla, however, who is open to newer experiences in the newer ideas. He is courageous enough to prefer innovation to ignorance. Most important, at the end of the fantasy (which Disraeli promised to continue) Popanilla has recognized that survival depends on judicious use of imaginative expediency. This was to be the guiding principle in Disraeli's life.

The close relationship between the author and Popanilla is noticeable throughout his work, in the gentle mockery of Popanilla as well as of the author himself. The ironic disparagement, however, is deliberately deceptive. Disraeli's point is that "innocence" is reproof; that it is lack of insight, that it is ignorance. The author's inversions seem at times to be betrayals of Popanilla who always has to face reversals of his expectations. But this is the author's intention: to question the probable. Only the unpredictable, Disraeli ironically contends, is human. Deterministic policies are absurd. Only the self is knowable.

Mythology fascinated Disraeli, as many of his titles, diary entries, and letters show. He was particularly fond of tales and myths with the theme of wit over force, like "Jack the Giant Killer," he told Sir William Fraser! Certainly, Disraeli's credo seems to have been that individual intelligence and wit could overcome most opposition. Although less whimsical than Jack the Giant Killer, Ixion performs the super-human feat of defying the nineteenth-century giants, the English arbiters of social and literary tastes in England. From several authorial incursions in *The Voyage of Captain Popanilla,* we know that Disraeli had experienced personal chafing with these supercilious types. He says, with some bitterness: "To witness excellence without emotion and to listen to genius without animation, the heart of the insensible may as often be influenced by Envy as inspired by Fashion." His own genius, the author felt, had not been recognized. The satirization of the "insensible" social structure in *Ixion in Heaven* undercuts considerably the nonchalance of upper-class superiority.

Disraeli brought the myth up to date by characterizing Ixion as a determined interloper into high society. To win entrance to Olympus was difficult enough, but to retain that shaky status, it would be necessary to neutralize the smothering superciliousness of the gods. Ixion, however, who wants more than mere acceptance, uses the dual methods of flattery and/or defiance for gaining a foothold on Olympus/Mayfair. In this respect, Disraeli's interpretation of the Ixion myth is very much a reflection of his own methods and personal goals. It is his emphasis on the use of defiance which demonstrates that it is the author himself contemplating his prospects for success. He seriously characterized this elsewhere [in *Contarini Fleming*] as "my absorbing selfism." In Ixion the projection of self is revealed through satire and irony as he attempts to knock over barriers in the way of the gifted man.

His main theme is that the talented individual has mobile social rights inherent in his birthright, a revolutionary notion in nineteenth-century English society. At first, Ixion is tolerated when he arrives on Olympus. The gods are amused by him. He is a maverick, he is a diversion (they are so bored!), he is different. But when he claims his place next to them as their social equal, the Olympians react quickly; they denounce him for treason. Failing to ostra-

cize him, they decide to destroy him by sentencing him to eternal banishment in hell, the form of symbolic expulsion that Disraeli had long known. But unlike the mythological Ixion, doomed to circling (and going nowhere) on his wheel in hell, Disraeli's hero fights the sentence. He counters the gods' prejudiced decision with a spirited speech on free will. Ixion insists that there are personal rights in his national rights, an early enunciation of Disraeli's famous principle that the "Individual Character" as leader may indeed emerge from the "National Character." Leadership, Ixion proclaims to Jove, has to be earned and demonstrated rather than merely inherited. Disraeli's characterization of Jove as an uxorious husband is particularly amusing. The greatest of the gods is here portrayed a domesticated, senile dolt. The other gods and goddesses, when active, are malevolent, envious, belligerent; when not occupied in self-admiration, they are lazy and vacuous. The Olympians, Disraeli shows, are unimaginative and uninspired.

In addition to the sharp wit and humor, there is a sober confessional irony in the work. This serious quality resides in reflections on personal ambition, debts, literary opinions, and disenchantment with women. While these topics hardly concern the mythological Ixion, they were very much a preoccupation with Benjamin Disraeli at this time. He seemed, however, to have been singularly effective in masking these real problems with froth and frivolity. But I believe that Disraeli's version of the myth, particularly the ending, represents a turning point in his career. In Disraeli's version of the ending, Jove orders Apollo to bring a wheel from his sun chariot and to bind Ixion to it with the girdle of Venus. Hercules then holds Ixion aloft, and the myth ends, before the punishment is carried out. We do not witness Ixion's fall. There is only the unpleasant sight of Ixion in the grip of Hercules. It is at this point that Ixion turns back the justice of the gods. It is he who determines what his fate will be as he challenges the whole Olympian system by reviling the judgment of eternal punishment. It is unacceptable to him. "I defy the immortal ingenuity of thy cruelty," he tells them.

Ixion, we see, is someone of considerable gifts, frequently honored by his superiors but also frequently disdained. In defiance of the Olympians, Ixion/Disraeli makes important assertions regarding the individual's right to free choice, and the self-divined privileges for non-Olympians. In the course of its development, *Ixion in Heaven* becomes a Bill of Rights for parvenus.

In the other mythologically derived satire, *The Infernal Marriage,* set in Hades, the author is concerned with political and artistic conflict. This satire may be the most reliable documentary, although it may be unintentional, that we have of Disraeli's shift from Radical to Tory, especially if we view the terms as symbols of life as well as of political positions. By 1834, Disraeli appears to have decided that sentiment must give way to reality. Yet his satirization of his expedient decision to become a political missionary for Toryism is tinged with cynicism and (I believe) with regret. The Proserpine myth, therefore, symbolizes his own infernal marriage. It marks also his definitive move into practical politics: the creation of a newly revealed self for a new political vehicle.

Through the thinly-disguised personalized myth of Proserpine, Disraeli presents an ironic account of the most controversial subject of his time, reform. Using various mythological personae, he introduces the ancillary issues of free will/predestination and expediency as a political creed. The personae engage in discussions which express, at different times, their independent as well as their hostile responses to political ideas which constitute Disraeli's dilemma. Reform or reaction? Revolutionary or royalist? Radical or Tory? Together the personae (Proserpine, Pluto, Tiresias) represent the expediency of his choice to leave Romantic ideas and to become a practical politician. Yet unlike *Ixion,* the notion of freedom is ironically limited, in this work, by the determinism of his political ambition. The Proserpine myth, is therefore also a metaphor for his transformation. Many years later, in 1878, he was to observe: "I am dead. Dead, but in the Elysian fields" [quoted in Cecil Roth's *Benjamin Disraeli, Earl of Beaconsfield,* 1952]. While the earlier fantasy, *Ixion in Heaven,* ended on a note of defiance, *The Infernal Marriage* finishes with the mocking of Disraeli's concept of accommodation. The myth's demography charts his satiric arrival into practical politics, metamorphosed and ready for his next role. He soon adapted his old Radical tag to the reformation of the Tory party in the emergence of Radical Toryism, a political union of expediency.

Despite this amalgam of Radical Tory, one should not look for lasting fusion in Disraeli's ideas. He is, like his heroes, quite multiple-faceted, and he remains undeceived about himself. In the novel of this same period, *Contarini Fleming,* which Disraeli himself dubbed his "psychological autobiography," he says:

> I never labour to delude myself; and never gloss over my faults. I exaggerate them; for I can afford to face truth, because I feel capable of improvement.

It is in these satiric pieces, nonetheless, rather than in the novels, that the syndrome of self-improvement, the ability to evaluate himself, prepares him for potential criticism. He shows himself to be aware of his own defects before anyone else is. The satiric voice is the interacting medium between his self and the outer world. In this way, the various personae are his means of balancing his contradictory ideas rather than of fusing them. This is part of his heritage from his Romanticism: the freedom to change, to outrage, to upset, but also to adapt.

Through the various roles, moreover, Disraeli mediates also between his self and his audience. In **"The Dunciad of Today"** his liberated selfness is celebrated in the poet manqué; in *Popanilla,* he is the free-roving picaro/ingenue; in *The Infernal Marriage,* he is the political missionary. As for *Ixion in Heaven,* Disraeli poignantly proclaims his elevation from eternal punishment in hell to emancipator in heaven. The verse satire, the travelogue, the myths, are used to keep his individualism inviolate. The audience is recognized as the special recipient that views the artist's self and is expected to be as analytical as the artist is. The audience is also kept alerted to the con-

stantly-shifting positions by the author himself. In one particularly amusing "meet-the-author" sequence in *The Voyage of Captain Popanilla,* both the author and the reader peer through the mirror at themselves. Deflections of the selves tend to stabilize, to equalize the contradictions between the principals. The result is art as conscious experience. Disraeli described his method [in *Contarini Fleming*]:

> I construed characters on philosophical principles and mused over a chain of action which should develop the system of our existence.

It is my opinion that this "system of our existence" (described in the novel which he called "psychological") can be called Disraeli's paradox and inconsistency, but the "chain of action" is effected by use of multiple satiric voices. The objective appears to be to emphasize the differences and then to dramatize the self-modulatory capacity of the author. Disraeli's shifts and changes thus become dynamic aspects of the self. There are, therefore, no "endings" to these four satires: always another stage is ahead in the struggle to attain recognition.

He had found that one of the many obstacles to fame was the "alien" label that was early attached to his personality, his ideas, and his background. Characteristically, instead of abdicating from the appellation, he deliberately incorporated it into his ethic: first, by emphasizing his exoticism, then by exalting what he called the national character—a mystical notion that elevated the British character. He became more patriotic than non-alien Britishers, passionately anxious to become part of the structure that seemed determined to separate him from it. In many other ways a modern spirit, he fought the "ancient heritage" attacks not by apologizing but by extolling them. This baptized Jew adorned himself with interpretations of Judaism that the Bible never intended. As a result, he suffered estrangement from both sides. To protect himself, he often distanced himself from his audience through satiric personae. He was even able to chide his readers for their lack of judgment. In *The Voyage of Captain Popanilla,* he is sarcastic about capricious material he has used: "This is claptrap, and I have no doubt will sell the book." Taking a philosophical tack, he muses: "It cannot be expected that ancient prejudice can, in a moment, be eradicated, and new modes of conduct instanteously substituted and established." He is too proud to solicit overt sympathy.

The survivalist quality of Disraeli's life view is action. Illness, failure, scorn—all served to refuel his deflated hopes. Instead of withdrawing from the world (even when seriously ill) he designed new strategies for conquering it. The satires are his rehearsals for that action. The author says:

> Popanilla consoled himself for neglect by the indefinite sensation that he should some day or other turn out that little being called a great man.

In the same way, through constant revaluation, Disraeli reshuffles and discards ideas which have not promoted him. He creates a self which will better serve him. With sheer force of will, he redistributes his new beliefs. Like Ixion, his own disappointments inspire him to daring new assertions. Each time, he emerges from a setback with re-inforced vigor. He experiments with new forms in literature, in politics, and in society. His psychological double, Contarini Fleming, is explicit: "I puzzled them, and no one offered a prediction as to my future career." He wrily concedes that he must be "a remarkable compound of originality and dulness."

His self-assessment is accurate in *Contarini Fleming,* but there is little "dulness" in the satires. They are alert, seemingly spontaneous (they were actually carefully planned), and safety valves for his intermittent depression. Popanilla/Disraeli, the mock-crusader, has ideals that only the sane can worship in a world where probability has become a farce. Disraeli/Ixion punctures the Olympians and their caste system. And Disraeli/Proserpine arranges his own metamorphoses in the symbolic marriage to Pluto, whose other name, we know, is Dis.

A modern critic has said of twentieth century fiction that the hero has become a nowhere man and his locale is a nowhere land, where he makes all the nowhere plans for nobody [Stephen Koch in "Fiction and Film: A Search for New Sources," *The Saturday Review,* 27 September 1969]. For Disraeli, this would have been unthinkable. The force, the struggle ultimately resulted in high office and honors. But they were no higher than he had prophesied. With oracular prescience, often brilliantly self-disparaging, he had announced his plans. He could satirize himself because he was always his own best subject. (pp. 2-10)

> *Bertha Keveson Hertz, "Satire as Self-Revelation," in* Ball State University Forum, *Vol. XIX, No. 1, Winter, 1978, pp. 2-10.*

## Daniel R. Schwarz    (essay date 1979)

[*Schwarz is an American educator and critic who specializes in literature of the late nineteenth and early twentieth centuries. In the excerpt below, he describes* Sybil *as Disraeli's finest novel and a major work of the nineteenth century, asserting that it is the fictional embodiment of Disraeli's political philosophy.*]

Disraeli returned to fiction [in the 1840s] with the specific purpose of arguing the political viewpoint of Young England. He wanted the ideas of Young England, the group which recognised him as its leader after years as an outsider, to have impact upon the governing class. Disraeli wished to use *Sybil* not only to explain but to justify his political philosophy; to do this, he needed to expose the condition of England. He believed that as a potential leader he had to be identified with clearly defined theoretical positions: 'My conception of a great statesman is of one who represents a great idea—an idea which may lead him to power; an idea with which he might identify himself; an idea he may develop; an idea which he may and can impress upon the nation.' In the 1849 preface to the fifth edition of *Coningsby,* he recalled his realisation that he could 'adopt the form of fiction as the instrument to scatter his suggestions . . . [and] avail himself of a method which, in the temper of the times, offered the best chance of influencing opinion'. Published in 1845, *Sybil: or the Two Nations* was one of the most inclusive novels of English life

to have been written since *Tom Jones* (1749). *Sybil's* space is co-extensive with England, its time is England's history, and its subject is the political and social circumstances of English life. Although conceived as the middle volume of the Young England trilogy of which *Coningsby* (1844) and *Tancred* (1847) are the other novels, *Sybil* is the superior work of art. Avoiding the bizarre subjectivity of *Tancred* or the drawing-room claustrophobia of *Coningsby,* *Sybil* revolves around the exposure of social conditions and the indictment of a complacent aristocracy that neglects them. Once we understand the kind of novel Disraeli wrote, we shall then understand that *Sybil* deserves to stand among the major novels of the nineteenth century.

Steeped in the tradition of Austen and Eliot, critics of the English novel feel most comfortable discussing the novel of manners and morals, with its emphasis on linear character development, its equation of social and moral maturity, and its exploration of the psychological and moral conflicts within the minds of major characters. Yet an aesthetic that stresses the novel as a prose poem and, as its ultimate standard, measures the structural relationship of every incident to the protagonist's personal history is not appropriate to a kind of fiction that presents a panorama of representative social and economic episodes as its major ingredient. The historical vision of the epic novel in English (for example, *Tom Jones, Vanity Fair* and *Ulysses* ) is secondary to the acute observation of characters' actions and decisions in situations requiring a moral response. But in novels informed by a political and/or historical thesis, characters are rendered both as unique human beings and as representatives of social and economic circumstances that shape their destinies. Of course, Stendhal, Balzac and Tolstoy wrote such novels, but it may be that most Anglo-American criticism has tried to fit similar novels like *Sybil* (and, I would argue, *The Secret Agent, Nostromo* and *The Plumed Serpent* ) into traditions which do not quite accommodate them. It follows that the critic of these novels should consider as *aesthetic issues* the inclusiveness of the novel's vision of the imagined *Zeitgeist* and the plausibility and complexity of the insight into political tensions and economic forces. For in polemical novels such as *Sybil* the author often seeks to convey a grammar of historical cause and effect rather than a grammar of motive, and how well he does it is one valid criterion by which to judge the novel. Historical verisimilitude depends upon the author's understanding of the social and economic circumstances in which events might hypothetically take place.

In such novels, the author seeks plausibility in terms not only of character psychology, but in terms of historical explanation. Since the imagined world is a detailed, if partial, factual model, an informed reader will require a knowledge of the original historical world both to understand how the writer is transmuting fact into fiction and to see what kind of order the novelist is imposing on reality. The novelist becomes historian and the historian becomes novelist, and the two roles are inseparable. *Sybil's* status as a neglected masterpiece depends in part on its insight into the causes of Chartism and its analysis of its shortcomings, on its dissection of party politics in the 1832-44 period, and on its compelling presentation of the life of the common people.

In no other Disraeli novel are character and event so subordinated to theme. The plot of *Sybil* is organised around Charles Egremont's gradual development, but no recapitulation of the plot can do justice to the novel's cross-section of English life from 1832 through 1844. The novel opens with chapters that show bored aristocrats living a dissipated idle life. The major figure, Charles Egremont, a younger son of a family that had gradually risen in prominence subsequent to Henry VIII's seizure of the monasteries, is among the bored aristocrats. Although he is a warm, generous and impulsive character, 'Enjoyment, not ambition seemed the principle of his existence'. Yet he is a man of enormous potential, highly intelligent and observant. His widowed mother persuades him to run for Parliament. On the understanding that he has the financial support of his brother, Lord Marney, he makes the race and wins. But Marney, an example of the benighted, selfish aristocracy which is oblivious to the needs of the common people and which has no sense of an organic community, refuses to help Egremont pay his election debts. After courting the woman who ultimately marries his brother rather than himself, because he lacks an appropriate fortune, Egremont is disgusted with the 'arrogant and frigid' aristocratic life which his brother exemplifies. To solve his financial plight Lord Marney wants his brother to marry into the Mowbray family, but Egremont is not interested.

Walking near the ruins of Marney Abbey, Egremont discovers Morley, Walter Gerard and Gerard's daughter Sybil who is planning to become a nun. The Gerards, an old Catholic family, have a legitimate claim to the Mowbray estate. But Gerard is also a worker who identifies with the people and becomes one of the leaders of the Chartist movement until he is arrested. Morley is a journalist and later a theoretician of the Chartist movement; he is attracted to Sybil and thinks of Egremont as a rival for her. He helps Gerard recover his estates by discovering a man named Hatton who is expert in such affairs. Under the identity of Franklin, Egremont goes to live near the Gerards and becomes close friends with them. After Sybil and her father go to London and lobby on behalf of the Chartist petition, she learns that Egremont is an aristocrat and becomes temporarily disaffected until he arranges for her release after she and her father are seized. Gradually Egremont learns that the people of England are divided into those that are materially comfortable and those that are not. As Egremont is educated about the real condition of England, he learns about the rural poor on his brother's estates and the urban poor created by the industrial revolution. He comes to understand that aristocratic and political life ignores the needs of a discontented and miserable population. He upholds the rights of labour in Parliament. Gerard intervenes during the riotous national strike to save the Trafford factory, which has been presented as a model of the benevolent community that industry can create; this represents to Disraeli the possibility of a union between people and property. With Hatton's help, Morley uses these riots as an occasion to locate the document sustaining Gerard's claim. Marney and Morley conveniently die in these riots, and Egremont becomes heir to Marney's estate and marries Sybil.

At the outset we should review the crucial premises that inform *Sybil*. Disraeli believed that the so-called Glorious Revolution had been the occasion for the Whigs' installing an oligarchical political system which he called the Venetian Constitution. By this he meant consultation among a group of self-interested aristocrats had replaced the monarchy in substance if not form. Disraeli believed in the possibility of great men transfiguring the imagination of the people. The myth of the political messiah recurs in each of the Young England novels. In *The Political Novel* Morris Speare notes the parallel between Disraeli and Carlyle:

> [Disraeli], like Carlyle, castigated the Nobility for their weaknesses, their dilettantism, their grotesque and time-consuming habits, the effeminacies of their 'dandies,' and the hollow and superficial knowledge of their great landowners and their womenfolk about public affairs, and the phantom and mockery of their sense of responsibility to the body politic. He went farther even than Carlyle in satirizing these foibles. With Carlyle, whose *Chartism* shows a direct influence upon *Sybil,* he saw the danger in the rise of the Chartists, and preached with him the doctrine that to the landed proprietors of his day there must return that grave sense of paternal duty, that profound authority based upon personal excellence, that willingness to undertake the leadership in the solution of grave public problems, which characterized the chiefs of the great estates, and the abbots over their countrysides in the days of the Past, when men lived under a purely paternal government.

Disraeli's belief that a man could not fulfil himself in private life, but rather required a position with defined responsibilities to give life meaning, is contrary to the emphasis on private fulfilment through love or communion with nature that pervades nineteenth-century literature. As Robert Langbaum has written [in his *The Modern Spirit: Essays on the Continuity of Nineteenth and Twentieth Century Literature,* 1970], 'The real man, the romanticist felt, was not to be got at through his social relations—his actions, his manners—there he was superficial, he was playing a role. The real man was to be got at when he was alone, in nature, when he was "musing"—thinking, that is, by free association—or when he was having visions or dreams'. Egremont fulfils himself as a public man. Although not possessing the heroic potential or personal magnetism of Coningsby or Tancred, he is a more successful representative of the aristocratic resurgence for which Disraeli hoped, because he continually demonstrates his integrity, sympathy and judgment.

Within *Sybil,* we feel a narrowing of the distance between Egremont and the narrator, as Egremont develops into the kind of man the narrator admires. Egremont is at first an aristocratic spectator observing Sybil's world, a world from which he is excluded by virtue of class and sympathy. In the first stage of Egremont's metamorphosis after he assumes the identity of Franklin, he is rather like a Wordsworthian stereotype when he responds to the sublimity of rural life. But after his self-enforced rustication, he sympathises with the physical conditions and psychological lives of others and does not, like Coningsby at times and Tancred always, seek refuge in vague abstractions. He develops a concept of self-responsibility that places service to the people before gratification of personal desires.

After he has earned the stature of a responsible leader, Egremont's own words carry substantial weight:

> The People are not strong; the People can never be strong. Their attempts at self-vindication will end only in their suffering and confusion. It is civilization that has effected, that is effecting, this change. It is that increased knowledge of themselves that teaches the educated their social duties. There is a dayspring in the history of this nation, which perhaps those only who are on the mountain tops can as yet recognise. . . . The new generation of the aristocracy of England are not tyrants, not oppressors. . . . Their intelligence, better than that, their hearts, are open to the responsibility of their position. . . . They are the natural leaders of the People.

Later, he explains that the present problem is the balance of political parties; but when that ceases, 'You will witness a development of the new mind of England which will make up by its rapid progress for its retarded action. . . . The future principle of English politics will not be a levelling principle: not a principle adverse to privileges, but favourable to their extension. It will seek to ensure equality, not by levelling the Few, but, by elevating the Many'. Egremont becomes a spokesman for what Marx and Engels, speaking of Young England [in *The Communist Manifesto*, 1849], dismissed as the 'spectacle' of 'feudal Socialism': 'half lamentation, half lampoon; half echo of the past, half menace of the future; at times, by its bitter, witty and incisive criticism, striking the bourgeoisie to the very heart's core, but always ludicrous in its effect, through total incapacity to comprehend the march of modern history'.

In *Sybil,* the novel's narrator is continually present, arguing for the possibility of the heroic mind, demonstrating the effects such minds can have on their followers, and indicating the preferability of leadership by extraordinary men to more representative forms of government. The persona is something of a vatic figure, the visionary artist whose concern is *res publica.* The narrator speaks as if his consciousness is identical with the nation's collective conscience. In the historical chapters, we feel the personal urgency of a man who identifies his own well-being with the health of his nation, which is presently undermined by 'a mortgaged aristocracy, a gambling foreign commerce, a home trade founded on a morbid competition'. The speaker presents himself as one motivated by the desire that he should ultimately contribute to the welfare of the British people by means of showing them that their true interest does not lie either with the Whigs or the present Tories, who under the leadership of Peel have departed from the great Tory principles and tradition. Within his consciousness is a historical perspective stretching back beyond Henry VIII to the Norman invasion. On the last pages, the narrator emphasises that while narrating the plot of *Sybil,* he has corrected and re-interpreted Whig historiography:

> In an age of political infidelity, of mean passions, and petty thoughts, I would have impressed upon the rising race not to despair, but to seek in a right understanding of the history of their country and in the energies of heroic youth, the elements of national welfare. . . . The written history of our country for the last ten reigns has been a mere phantasma; giving to the origin and consequence of public transactions a character and colour in every respect dissimilar to their natural form and hue. In this mighty mystery all thoughts and things have assumed an aspect and title contrary to their real quality and style: Oligarchy has been called Liberty; an exclusive Priesthood has been christened a National Church; Sovereignty has been the title of something that has had no dominion, while absolute power has been wielded by those who profess themselves the servants of the People.

*Sybil* represents a substantial development in Disraeli's artistry. In it, Disraeli uses the novel form to discover the potential within extant institutions and to posit their revival as a conservative alternative not only to the present condition of the Church, the monarchy and the political parties but also to the anarchy and disruption of Chartism. The Chartists wished to extend the vote to the working class (but not women). They sought to elect their own representatives to a convention in London which, as Halevy writes [in his *The Triumph of Reform, 1830-1841,* 1950], 'in contrast to the members of Parliament returned by a restricted franchise, would be the genuine representatives of the people'. But the Chartists also flirted with armed rebellion and roused fears of an English version of the French Revolution. From Disraeli's perspective the Chartists were the inevitable result of the failure of the Whigs' middle-class government and utilitarian philosophy to serve the common people.

The relationship between Egremont and Sybil is explored for its historical implications. For example in one crucial scene, Egremont visits Westminster Abbey and discovers Sybil there. Sybil's presence gives meaning and vitality to the church, as she had done before at Marney Abbey, and implies to Egremont that the present degradation of the Anglo-Catholic Church need only be temporary. She replaces within the Abbey the 'noisy vergers [who] sat like ticket-porters' and 'the boards and the spikes' which made the Abbey seem 'as if [it] were in a state of seige'. Because Charles's consciousness is synonymous with the narrator's retrospective understanding, Sybil becomes an *emblem,* within the novel's dialectic, for the potential of the Church:

> The sounds, those mystical and thrilling sounds that at once exalt the soul and touch the heart, ceased; the chanting of the service recommenced; the motionless form moved; and as she moved Egremont came forth from the choir, and his eye was at once caught by the symmetry of her shape and the picturesque position which she gracefully occupied; still gazing through that grate, while the light, pouring through the western window, suffused the body of the church with a soft radiance, just touching the head of the unknown with a kind of halo.

Ministering charity and providing spiritual encouragement, the Catholic Sybil and the Anglican vicar of Mowbray, St. Lys, demonstrate the potential of England's true religious traditions working in unison. The convent and the Mowbray Cathedral are remnants of the tradition of mercy and charity represented by Marney Abbey before the monasteries were seized by Henry VIII. (As we have seen, until the 1850s, Disraeli was sympathetic to Catholics because they too had been an ostracised minority until 1828.) By implying that the Anglican Church is not fundamentally different from the Catholic Church particularly at a time when several members of the Oxford Movement had made the journey to Rome, Disraeli was taking a controversial position. One reviewer of *Sybil* chidingly commented, the 'extinct worship of the Catholic saints is regretted'. Perhaps because Disraeli in *Sybil* seemed to endorse the Tractarians, he went out of his way to dramatise Tancred's religious epiphany as a private Protestant experience. In *Tancred,* moreover, he attempted to move beyond contemporary religious politics by broadening his ecumenical spirit to include Judaism.

The Oxford Movement stood for tradition and wished to introduce rituals into the Anglican Church which were part of the Catholic service prior to the Reformation. In 1841, the members of the Movement had published the ninetieth of *Tracts for the Times.* Newman tried to show how an Anglican Protestant could subscribe to the Thirty-nine Articles of the Book of Common Prayer, but did so in terms that made clear that the rubric of that Book was not being observed by non-Tractarians as scrupulously as it should be. In writing to strengthen the waverers among the Tractarians, Newman seemed to be arguing that the Prayer Book was essentially Catholic. The result was a ferocious attack on Newman. The subsequent decline of the Oxford Movement's influence was accelerated when W. G. Ward published *The Ideal of a Christian Church* in 1844. In his *The Oxford Movement,* R. W. Church summarises Ward's arguments: 'only the Roman Church satisfies the conditions of what a Church ought to be, and [he argued] in detail that the English Church, in spite of its professions, utterly and absolutely fails to fulfil them'. Edward Pusey, Regius Professor of Hebrew, had been suspended from preaching for two years in 1843, and Newman's long rumoured conversion was soon to take place on 9 October 1845.

The Oxford Movement had parallels to Young England not only in its desire to revive the medieval church but in its nostalgia for the medieval world and its love of ceremony. As Blake has noted [in his *Disraeli*, 1966], 'Young England was the Oxford movement translated by Cambridge from religion into politics. Both stemmed from the same origin—an emotional revulsion against the liberal utilitarian spirit of the time'. Disraeli's conception of the proper role of the Anglican Church was influenced by the Oxford Movement which like Young England was a revolt against rationalism and the Enlightenment. What A. C. Chadwick has written of the Oxford Movement [in his introduction to *The Mind of the Oxford Movement,* 1960] is equally true of Young England: both wanted 'to find a place and value for historical tradition, against the irrelevant or sacriligious hands of critical revolutionaries

for whom no antiquity was sacred. They suspected the reason of common sense as shallow. They wanted to justify order and authority in Church as well as State'. Moreover, both movements thought of Charles I as a martyr and discarded the epithet 'Glorious' to describe the revolution of 1688.

At the beginning of Book V, Sybil apprehends Egremont's value when she reads his speech expressing 'immortal truths' and upholding 'the popular cause': '[He] had pronounced his conviction that the rights of labour were as sacred as those of property; that if a difference were to be established, the interests of the living wealth ought to be preferred; [he] had declared that the social happiness of the millions should be the first object of a statesman, and that, if this were not achieved, thrones and dominions, the pomp and power of the courts and empires, were alike worthless'. While it is easy to smile at the unintended bathos when she looks up from the journal she is reading in St. James Park and finds Egremont standing before her, this is to ignore the novel's polemic aesthetic. Disraeli does show how Egremont's response to Sybil combines sexual attraction and religious adoration. The 'portrait of a saint' that he selects from his mother's collection because it suggests Sybil seems more sexual than iconographic: 'The face of a beautiful young girl, radiant and yet solemn, with rich tresses of golden brown hair, and large eyes dark as night, fringed with ebony lashes that hung upon the glowing cheek'.

By dramatising how Egremont discovers Sybil's spiritual potential and how she discovers his political insight, Disraeli suggests that their possible union is significant and desirable in far more than personal terms. Because he wishes Sybil to represent the spiritual values that England requires, it is not surprising that she does not emerge as a distinct personality. It might be objected that Sybil's soul-searching about whether she should take the veil never becomes vivid, but Sybil's conflict is peripheral to Disraeli's concerns.

At times a major flaw in Disraeli's prior fiction is his unintentionally bathetic change in voice which has the effect of trivialising both the thrust of his satire and the reader's engagement with the intellectual and emotional lives of his characters. But in *Sybil* rapid changes in tone are often rhetorically effective; they accompany shifts in place and do contribute to the contrast between the neglected and the over-indulged—and within the latter group, between those like Egremont who recognise their responsibility to the deprived and those like his brother and the residents of Mowbray castle who do not. By presenting a panorama of people from every class and rapidly sweeping across the geography of England, Disraeli creates an elaborate canvas where the meaning of each episode depends upon its relation to the whole. Disraeli's principal mode of rhetorical argument is the rapid juxtaposition of contrasting scenes not only from chapter to chapter, but even from paragraph to paragraph within a chapter. An example of the latter takes place in the second chapter of Book II. After establishing the beautiful landscape that might be seen approaching the rural town of Marney, the narrator readjusts the perspective of the potential visitors (and the readers) and discovers a scene of deprivation and filth. In the very next paragraph he further arouses the reader's sense of outrage by suddenly revealing that within one of these 'wretched tenements' of two rooms live three generations of a family, including a pregnant woman and a father stricken by typhoid. Later, Gerard explains to Egremont why these 'wretched tenements' exist: how Henry VIII's seizure of the monasteries permanently affected the quality of rural life; how those owning estates had destroyed rural cottages; and how absentee landlords had exploited the land for revenue.

The aristocracy's stupidity, boredom and enervation contrast both with the vitality and energy of the common people and with Egremont's developing self-awareness and understanding about his country. Egremont's opposite, his brother Lord Marney, disdains the needs of the people and represents the model that Egremont must renounce. He places self before family, family before party, and party before class. Until the last chapter's *deus ex machina* when the poor are either miraculously restored to their former position or elevated to a higher economic situation, the gradual decline of the Mowbray poor is contrasted with the stasis and ennui of aristocrats. Disraeli exposes the aristocrats' abdication of responsibility by juxtaposing the conversation of the downtrodden Londoners who congregate outside Deloraine House with that of the people attending the party inside. How can the Chartist frustration be condemned when the Members of Parliament to whom Gerard and Morley take their petition are not only uninformed but arrogant and disdainful? The names of such MPs as Wriggle and Thorough Base are self-indicting, and their conduct verifies their names. Kremlin, another MP, informs Gerard and Morley that he is uninterested in 'domestic policy' and that 'forms of government were of no consequence'. Only Lord Valentine receives them intelligently and courteously, even if with condescension. But unlike Egremont, Valentine has not experienced the condition of the common people firsthand and cannot comprehend the depth of their feeling.

A brief look at the first eight chapters of Book III shows Disraeli's artistry. He deftly organised his chapters so that we necessarily perceive Egremont's personal life not simply in its private moments, but also in the context of the moral and economic conditions to which it is his duty to respond. Book III oscillates rapidly from poverty to wealth, beginning with the juxtaposition of life in the mines (ch. i) to the aristocratic pretence of the Marneys (ch. ii). Both Digg's Tommy Shop (ch. iii) and Wodgate (chs. iv and vii) parody the heartless tyranny of Lord Marney as if to imply that a cynical and indifferent aristocracy inevitably affects the quality of civilisation for the entire population. While misery and degradation swirl around him, Egremont seems to have neither the means nor the desire to redress social and economic blight. For, as we have seen, he has temporarily withdrawn to an idyllic life where, under the pseudonym of Franklin, he has developed his friendship with Gerard and Sybil (chs. v and vi). Chapter vii switches back to the Bishop of Wodgate as if to emphasise the alternative leadership that is developing while Egremont eschews his responsibility. Trafford's factory (ch. viii), an example of enlightened aristo-

cratic behaviour, explicitly suggests the need for Egremont, who has been elected a Member of Parliament, to assume his public responsibilities.

In the opening chapter of Book III, the narrator conveys his outrage and indignation as he recalls the degradation of children working in the mines:

> . . . troops of youth, alas! of both sexes, though neither their raiment nor their language indicates the difference; all are clad in male attire; and oaths that men might shudder at, issue from lips born to breathe words of sweetness. Yet these are to be, some are, the mothers of England! But can we wonder at the hideous coarseness of their language, when we remember the savage rudeness of their lives? Naked to the waist, an iron chain fastened to a belt of leather runs between their legs clad in canvas trousers, while on hands and feet an English girl, for twelve, sometimes for sixteen hours a day, hauls and hurries tubs of coals up subterranean roads, dark precipitous, and plashy; circumstances that seem to have escaped the notice of the Society for the Abolition of Negro Slavery. Those worthy gentlemen too appear to have been singularly unconscious of the sufferings of the little trappers, which was remarkable, as many of them were in their own employ.

Disraeli has turned his talents for elaborate description and ironic observation to graphic rendering of social evil. He has learned to use a single sentence, such as the last one in the prior passage, to point out swiftly and surely a grim social incongruity—in this case, the neglect of their own employees by those professing worthy motives and subscribing to noble causes. When the narrator in the next chapter elegises the close of an 'agreeable party' at Mowbray castle, conditions such as those depicted in the above quotation ironically undercut his prior narcissistic pose:

> The sudden cessation of all those sources of excitement which pervade a gay and well-arranged mansion in the country unstrings the nervous system. For a week or so, we have done nothing which was not agreeable, and heard nothing which was not pleasant. Our self-love has been respected; there has been a total cessation of petty cares; all the enjoyment of an establishment without any of its solicitude. We have beheld civilisation only in its favoured aspect, and tasted only the sunny side of the fruit.

Disraeli's ventriloquism here has intentionally made the reader momentarily complicit in Lord Marney's selfish and infantile self-absorption. But Disraeli wants us to realise that any attempt to lyricise Marney's sense of loss becomes reductive and trivial:

> But sometimes it is not in our power; sometimes, for instance, we must return to our household gods in the shape of a nursery; and though this was not the form assumed by the penates of Lord Marney, his presence, the presence of an individual so important and so indefatigable, was still required. His lordship has passed his time at Mowbray to his satisfaction. He had had his own way in everything. His selfishness had not received a single shock. He had laid down the law

and it had not been questioned. He had dogmatised and impugned, and his assertions had passed current, and his doctrines had been accepted as orthodox.

The entire social and political system at Wodgate—from its mock theocracy to the high-handed ruthlessness with which the 'aristocrats' treat their subjects—is an indictment of the English Church and Government which should provide moral, political and religious leadership. The savage master of the lock manufacturing enterprise is called the Bishop, and he rules not only his shop but Wodgate himself. As the brutalised youth explains to Morley, 'That's his name and authority; for he's the governor here over all of us. And it has always been so that Wodgate has been governed by a bishop; because, as we have no church, we will have as good. And by this token that his day se'nnight, the day my time was up, he married me to this here young lady'. If Disraeli seemed to be calling for a new feudal relationship between man and master, between worker and factory owner, between tenant and landowner, between common man and aristocrat, he felt no reason to be apologetic. He once said, 'The principle of the feudal system . . . was the noblest principle, the grandest, the most magnificent that was ever conceived by patriot'. His basic premise was that the ownership of property conferred moral and economic responsibilities in regard to the poor and unfortunate.

Because even uneducated barbarians have a natural need to 'adore and obey', the Bishop and his fellow master workmen fill a vacuum in the lives of their followers which is created by the abnegation of responsibility by the aristocracy, government, and clergy: '[The Wodgate aristocracy] is distinguished from the main body not merely by name. It is the most knowing class at Wodgate; it possesses indeed in its way complete knowledge; and it imparts in its manner a certain quantity of it to those whom it guides. Thus it is an aristocracy that leads, and therefore a fact'. As Bishop Hatton marches at the head of the Hell-cats during the Chartist uprising, the procession is bathetically compared with 'the Pilgrimage of Grace'. By viewing his procession in terms of such a historically significant religious event as the 'conversion of Constantine', Disraeli stresses the ironic disjunction between past and present—in this case, between the former dignity of the monarchy and the church and those who now 'preach' and 'control'.

Arthur Frietzsche has commented [in his *Disraeli's Religion,* 1961] that Disraeli's compassion for the working class 'was never lifted above aristocratic paternalism'. (At times Disraeli does tend to associate complacent vulgarity and insolence with the quality of life led by the working class, as if this were prima-facie evidence for placing faith in the leadership of a revived aristocracy.) But in *Sybil,* vitality, intelligence and resourcefulness give the working class characters such as Bishop Hatton, Dandy Mick and Devilsdust the kind of energy and substance that we associate with the minor personae of Shakespeare and Dickens. Disraeli's challenge as an artist was to render the minor characters as the inevitable results of social and economic conditions that had to be changed, while simultaneously dramatising the vitality, the individuality and the essential humanity of what he regarded as England's ne-

glected resource—the downtrodden common people. Describing the unique manners and personality of the minor characters proves less difficult for Disraeli's artistry than presenting a character as representative of a crystallising social situation. Yet he can be extremely effective in the latter, as in the case of the poor weaver, Warner, whose bewilderment and estrangement are the result of his being rendered obsolete by machinery:

> It is not vice that has brought me to this, nor indolence, nor imprudence. I was born to labour, and I was ready to labour. I loved my loom, and my loom loved me. It gave me a cottage in my native village, surrounded by a garden, of whose claims on my solicitude it was not jealous. There was time for both. It gave me for a wife the maiden that I had ever loved; and it gathered my children round my hearth with plenteousness and peace. I was content: I sought no other lot. It is not adversity that makes me look back upon the past with tenderness.
>
> Then why am I here? Why am I, and six hundred thousand subjects of the Queen, honest, loyal, and industrious, why are we, after manfully struggling for years, and each year sinking lower in the scale, why are we driven from our innocent and happy homes, our country cottages that we loved, first to bide in close towns without comforts, and gradually to crouch into cellars, or find a squalid lair like this, without even the common necessaries of existence; first the ordinary conveniences of life, then raiment, and at length food, vanishing from us.

If we were to read the above remarks as a psychic gesture of Warner's inner life they would seem artificial and stylised. The movement from 'I' to 'we' obviously stresses that Warner typifies an economic situation for which he is the novel's spokesman. But Warner's set speech is part of the evolving indictment of a society which neglects its working poor. Within the novel's polemic, the speech is an implicit comment on a conversation in the previous chapter between Lord Marney and St. Lys. As is his custom, Marney takes refuge in theories and abstractions that confirm his prejudices and justify his stinginess: 'I have generally found the higher the wages the worse the workman. They only spend their money in the beer-shops. *They* are the curse of this country' (emphasis Disraeli's).

More consistently than in his prior novels, wit and paradox are an intrinsic part of the novel's themes. For example, speaking of two aristocratic brothers, Disraeli has his narrator remark: 'Both had exhausted life in their teens, and all that remained for them was to mourn, amid the ruins of their reminiscences, over the extinction of excitement'. Disraeli never wrote an opening that approached the brilliance of the opening chapters of *Sybil.* The scene in a 'golden saloon' prior to a major horse race captures the prodigality, the misplaced spasms of energy alternating with boredom, and the dissipation of lives and resources wasted in the pursuit of narcissistic pleasure that characterises aristocratic life. The participants are oblivious to the Chartist storm of dissatisfaction and protest gathering over their heads. The race becomes a metaphor for the political struggle between two parties that lack any purpose or principle other than their own survival. The horse race is depicted in language that would be more appropriate to a major historical event; the incongruity between the language and the object of description stresses how far the aristocracy has strayed from its historic heritage;

> A few minutes, only a few minutes, and the event that for twelve months has been the pivot of so much calculation, of such subtle combinations, of such deep conspiracies, round which the thought and passion of the sporting world have hung like eagles, will be recorded in the fleeting tablets of the past. . . . Finer still, the inspired mariner who has just discovered a new world; the sage who has revealed a new planet; and yet the 'Before' and 'After' of a first-rate English race, in the degree of its excitement, and sometimes in the tragic emotions of its close, may vie even with these.

Like the aristocrats in Pope's *The Rape of the Lock,* these men have confused trivial with important matters.

It is a curiosity of **Sybil** that the basic theme, the division between the wealthy and the poor, is articulated by Morley—Egremont's amoral, agnostic and paranoid rival who foresees the decline of family: 'Two nations; between whom there is no intercourse and no sympathy; who are as ignorant of each other's habits, thoughts, and feelings, as if they were dwellers in different zones, or inhabitants of different planets; who are formed by a different breeding, are fed by a different food, are ordered by different manners, and are not governed by the same laws'. It is part of the novel's subtlety to show that perspicacity is not the province of the well-meaning characters alone. If at first Morley seems to be Disraeli's spokesman, we should remember that (i) his rational analysis provides no solution; (ii) he lacks imagination, sympathy and manners; (iii) his abstractions are often not sustained by the action; (iv) his disregard for the past is contradictory to Disraeli's beliefs; and (v) Morley's attempt to murder his rival and implicitly to barter his father's safety for Sybil's declaration of love for him completely discredits him. Ultimately, by showing the possibilities of bridging the schism between rich and poor by the merger of Sybil and Egremont, Disraeli refutes Morley's view that the division could not be breached. (Yet how much more effective the novel's resolution would have been—and how shocking to Disraeli's Victorian audience—if Sybil did not have an aristocratic heritage!)

Disraeli gradually changes the reader's mind about Morley. While Egremont grows in knowledge, feeling and judgment, Morley contracts in stature when he is shown to be motivated by venomous class hatred. Disraeli has learned to show how a character learns from experience. While in past novels, characters have a kind of conversion experience following a major event (the Young Duke's riotous night of gambling, Vivian's killing a man in a duel, the death of Contarini's wife), in this novel an accretion of important events gradually changes Egremont. This kind of character development, used only by Austen in the English novel prior to Disraeli, is a cornerstone of the later nineteenth-century realistic novel and its successor, the twentieth-century psychological novel.

The narrator re-educates the reader to understand that Morley's reductive view of the irrevocable division between the privileged and the people derives from paranoid class hatred. Even if no permanent solution to economic disparity is dramatised within the novel, Trafford's benevolent capitalism, as well as Egremont's ever-expanding perspicacity and willingness to speak in Parliament for the poor, is meant to refute Morley's view that the schism between rich and poor is inevitable. Morley's faith in progress is a parody of the material determinism of Robert Owens and of the Victorian cliché (which Disraeli rejected) that new and better institutions will continue to evolve:

> The domestic principle has fulfilled its purpose. The irresistible law of progress demands that another should be developed. It will come; you may advance or retard, you cannot prevent it. It will work out like the development of organic nature. In the present state of civilisation, and with the scientific means of happiness at our command, the notion of home should be obsolete. Home is a barbarous idea; the method of a rude age: Home is isolation; therefore antisocial. What we want is Community.

Disraeli would have expected his Victorian audience to recognise that there is something fundamentally wrong with a character who questions that most sacrosanct cornerstone of Victorian life, the family. Disraeli effectively undermines Morley when he has Gerard rather touchingly respond, 'but I like stretching my feet on my own hearth'. In the Victorian period, the family was equated with home which was, as Houghton has written [in his *The Victorian Frame of Mind,* 1957], 'both a shelter *from* the anxieties of modern life, a place of peace where the longings of the soul might be realized (if not in fact, in imagination), and a shelter *for* those moral and spiritual values which the commercial spirit and the critical spirit were threatening to destroy, therefore also a sacred place, a temple' (emphases Houghton's). The agnostic Morley is revealed as a fundamentally amoral character who would aid Gerald only if *paid* with Sybil's affections. Admiringly, he tells Baptist Hatton, a man whose ruthlessness and expediency resemble his own: 'You have a clear brain and a bold spirit; you have no scruples, which indeed are generally the creatures of perplexity rather than of principle'. As if to emphasise the mechanistic nature of the utilitarian Morley, Disraeli has him assault Egremont with his 'iron grasp' and 'hand of steel'. Morley's motive is sexual jealousy rather than fanatical commitment to any social values. At Morley's death, Disraeli stresses the ironic discrepancy between Morley's apparent idealism and actual behaviour; his narrator relates how, with the name of Sybil on his lips, 'the votary of Moral Power and the Apostle of Community ceased to exist'.

Yet *Sybil* ends not with a prediction but with a prayer:

> That we may live to see England once more possess a free Monarchy, and a privileged and prosperous People is my prayer; and that these great consequences can only be brought about by the

energy and devotion of our Youth is my persuasion. We live in an age when to be young and to
be indifferent can no longer be synonymous. We
must prepare for the coming hour. The claims
of the Future are represented by suffering millions: and the Youth of a Nation are the trustees
of Posterity.

The narrator has the perspicacity to analyse England's
problems. But he suggests no programme for ameliorating
the spiritual and moral condition of England, because neither Disraeli nor Young England had a coherent political
programme. The novel's conclusion does not eradicate the
intense analysis of the effects of industrialisation, mediocre government or irresponsible landlords. The deaths of
Morley and Bishop Hatton do not solve England's underlying problems. Yet, if the novel does not dramatise a revival of ceremony and form, a restoration of the position
of the Church, or the ascent to power of an enlightened
aristocracy, it does show the potential within England of
creative sympathy among the classes, the desire of the people for strong charismatic leadership, and a feudal alternative to a centralised government that imposes its laws from
London. Because the conclusion lacks the intensity of the
chapters at Wodgate and at the mines, one suspects that
the 'three good harvests' that follow the resolution of the
plot are nothing more than a temporary cycle in the *economic* plight of the miners and the agrarian poor not so
fortunate to have Egremont as their landlord. (Earlier, the
narrator obliquely had expressed Disraeli's continuing
concern that economic prosperity might damage the
moral and spiritual condition of the people: '[The system
of Dutch Finance] has so overstimulated the energies of
the population to maintain the material engagements of
the state, and of society at large, that the moral condition
of the people has been entirely lost sight of '.

Certainly too much has been made of Disraeli's optimism.
For example, in *The Victorian Sage,* John Holloway
writes:

> [Disraeli] was an optimist about both the quality
> of life, and its ultimate results: he saw the world
> as an exciting, exhilarating place, and a place
> that characteristically supplied happy end-
> ings. . . . There is no inescapable contrast be-
> tween what is and what should be. . . . Disraeli
> does not explore that part of human experience
> which comprises sin, guilt, depravity, or misfor-
> tune; they are not primary data in the view of life
> which his work conveys.

This view does not do justice to the implications of Disraeli's art in *Sybil.* Like *Bleak House, Sybil* does not con-
strain or ameliorate the malevolent social forces that
blight the quality of English life. Even more than *Bleak
House, Sybil* opens up the dark side of Victorian England,
the side revealed in the Blue Books. Whereas in *Bleak
House* the omniscient narrator's panorama of disease, injustice and grinding poverty alternates with Esther's private journal of personal development and fulfilment, in
*Sybil* the historical and sociological perspective pushes relentlessly forward as it satirises aristocratic pretensions
and exposes the discrepancy between those who labour to
survive and those who live an idle, luxurious life. Disraeli

the novelist is more honest than Disraeli the theoretician
of Young England. Hence the novel ends with a tentative
conclusion rather than rhetorical optimism. Disturbing
facts of economic life and troubling aspects of aristocratic
life are not resolved by Egremont's marriage to Sybil. The
novel leaves the polemic of the early chapters behind. The
power and specificity of the women and children working
in the mine; of the gradual decline in working class prosperity in Mowbray, as evidenced by 'The Temple of the
Muses' and Mrs Carey; of the misery in the Warner household; of the turbulence created by rural and urban poverty; and of the desperation of the Chartist petition—all
these undermine Disraeli's more parochial political diatribes, particularly such partisan oversimplifications as
'Whiggism was putrescent in the nostrils of the nation'.

Georg Lukács' praise of the great nineteenth-century realists, Balzac and Tolstoy, is appropriate to Disraeli's artistry in *Sybil:*

> If, therefore, in the process of creation their con-
> scious world-view comes into conflict with the
> world seen in their vision, what really emerges
> is that their true conception of the world is only
> superficially formulated in the consciously held
> world-view and the real depth of their *Weltan-
> schauung,* their deep ties with the great issues of
> their time, their sympathy with the sufferings of
> the people can find adequate expression only in
> the being and fate of their characters. [*Studies in
> European Realism,* 1964]

The marriage between Egremont and Sybil—after seemingly impossible obstacles are overcome by an unlikely
plot—is not the apocalypse that Disraeli seems to have intended, because the lives of Egremont and Sybil remain
peripheral to and are transcended by Disraeli's moving
presentation of the exploitation in the mines, the degradation of Wodgate, and the recurring threat of rural and
urban deprivation. (pp. 105-24)

> *Daniel R. Schwarz, in his* Disraeli's Fiction,
> *Barnes & Noble, 1979, 167 p.*

---

**Edmund Gosse on Disraeli's literary legacy:**

[His] books have not merely survived their innumerable fellows, but they have come to represent to us the form and
character of a whole school; nay, more, they have come to
take the place in our memories of a school which but for
them would have utterly passed away and been forgotten.
Disraeli, accordingly, is unique, not merely because his are
the only fashionable novels of the pre-Victorian period
which anyone ever reads nowadays, but because in his person that ineffable manner of the "thirties" reaches an isolated sublimity, and finds a permanent place in literature. But
if we take a still wider view of the literary career of Disraeli,
we are bound to perceive that the real source of the interest
which his brilliant books continue to possess is the evidence
their pages reveal of the astonishing personal genius of the
man.

> *Edmund Gosse, in the foreword to* Vivian
> Grey: A Romance of Youth, *Dunne, 1904.*

**Donald D. Stone    (essay date 1980)**

[*Stone is an American educator and critic whose works include several studies of late-Victorian literature. In the following essay, he explores the influence of Romanticism on Disraeli's fiction, from the youthful self-absorption evident in his early works to the humanitarian elements of his later novels.*]

Historians have long recognized the Romantic element in Disraeli's political beliefs, and their view of his place in history has been considerably influenced by their attitudes toward those Romantic traits. Disraeli viewed a political career as a Romantic mission, as a vehicle for his Romantic artistry: in public service a Shelleyan devotion to the welfare of others could be united to a Byronic display of will and a Keatsian display of imagination. As one of the earliest English statesmen to capitalize on what Walter Bagehot called the public readiness to be governed by appeals to their imagination, Disraeli had many detractors who were disturbed by the ways in which he, in creating a myth of his own role and person for public consumption, occasionally disregarded humble matters of truth. The hero of Trollope's series of political novels, Plantagenet Palliser, was conceived, in large part, in protest against the manner in which Disraeli had risen to eminence. Everything about Palliser's political ideals and performance is at variance with Disraeli's:

> He was not a brilliant man, and understood well that such was the case. He was now listened to in the House, as the phrase goes; but he was listened to as a laborious man, who was in earnest in what he did, who got up his facts with accuracy, and who, dull though he be, was worthy of confidence. And he was very dull. He rather prided himself on being dull, and on conquering in spite of his dulness. He never allowed himself a joke in his speeches, nor attempted even the smallest flourish of rhetoric. He was very careful in his language, labouring night and day to learn to express himself with accuracy, with no needless repetition of words, perspicuously with regard to the special object he might have in view. He had taught himself to believe that oratory, as oratory, was a sin against that honesty in politics by which he strove to guide himself. [*Can You Forgive Her?*]

Palliser's dullness and honesty lead him to only a limited success, as head of the sort of coalition government that, Disraeli noted, England did not love. Disraeli, by contrast, took advantage of his resources of imagination and language to become one of the most popular, if also one of the most mistrusted, of Victorian British leaders. The Romantic state of mind that he brought to politics is candidly and often engagingly revealed in his novels, and the connection between Disraeli's Romantic politics and his literary endeavors provides an intriguing perspective on the allure and dangers of the Romantic impulse.

Where Trollope sought to conceal or discipline his Romantic sensibility, Disraeli delighted in exposing and

making use of his. Although he was, like his friend Edward Bulwer Lytton, a second-generation Romantic, Disraeli gave his assent to many of the cardinal Romantic tenets, such as faith in the supremacy of the will as controller of one's destiny and in the primacy of the imagination as arbiter of reality and redeemer of mankind. However, he also gave the impression, on occasion, that he was taking advantage of these beliefs and of the credulity of his audience in order to create an effect. In this respect, his championing of the rights of the imagination, for example, might be compared with the claims of his predecessors. The Romantic poets' refusal "to submit the poetic spirit" to what Wordsworth called "the chains of fact and real circumstance" is well known: in Blake's case, for example, "the things imagination saw were as much realities as were gross and tangible facts." One of the most extreme instances involving a Romantic poet's disregard for historical accuracy occurs in Keats's "On First Looking into Chapman's Homer," where Cortez is substituted for Balboa as the discoverer of the Pacific Ocean. However accidental the original slip may have been, once Keats's imagination had conjured up Cortez he was obliged to leave the line as it stood: "Or like stout Cortez when with eagle eyes / He star'd at the Pacific." Keats's claim for the "truth of the imagination" is well known. "What the imagination seizes as Beauty must be truth—whether it existed before or not," he says in a famous letter. The imagination, as far as a Romantic poet is concerned, *creates* truth, rather than reflects something that for a scientist or explorer is merely real. "The Imagination may be compared to Adam's dream—he awoke and found it truth."

Keats's words help to clarify a major theme in Disraeli's political life and in his fiction: the supreme importance of the imagination as an instrument of redemptive power and the consequent irrelevance of facts. It is this faith in the imagination (and in what Keats calls "the holiness of the Heart's affections") that prompts the words of Sidonia in Disraeli's best-known novel, *Coningsby:* "Man is only truly great when he acts from the passions; never irresistible but when he appeals to the imagination. Even Mormon counts more votaries than Bentham." The heroes of Disraeli's novels aspire to be leaders in a thoroughly Romantic fashion: by influencing their constituents through the magnetic force of their brilliantly endowed imaginations. Disraeli's popularity as a statesman was based on this realization; he claimed that his motive in writing the trilogy of *Coningsby, Sybil,* and *Tancred* was to recognize "imagination in the government of nations as a quality not less important than reason." But it was his resultant lack of interest in the factual details so dear to Utilitarian philosophers and realistic novelists that won him so many enemies as a statesman and a writer. "The intellectuals detested him almost to a man," as Robert Blake notes [in *Disraeli,* 1966]. Trollope's denunciation of the novels as having only the "flavour of paint and unreality" is the classic statement showing why the then Prime Minister and his novels should both be consigned to the dust bin:

> In whatever he has written he has affected something which has been intended to strike his readers as uncommon and therefore grand. Because he has been bright and a man of genius, he has

carried his object as regards the young. He has struck them with astonishment and aroused in their imagination ideas of a world more glorious, more rich, more witty, more enterprising than their own. But the glory has ever been the glory of pasteboard, and the wealth has been a wealth of tinsel. The wit has been the wit of hairdressers and the enterprise has been the enterprise of mountebanks. [*An Autobiography,* 1950]

An answer to this line of attack (though not made in response to Disraeli) is to be found in Oscar Wilde's "The Decay of Lying," a defense of the creative power of the imagination and the need to divert from reality in the name of something better—which brings us back to Keats's premise quoted earlier. What to a Romantic-minded author is poetic license, to a realist is lying. When a Tory member of Parliament chooses to embellish the truth or discard it altogether, as Disraeli did on a number of occasions, he faces the resistance of opponents who are uninterested in whether he is speaking on behalf of what to him appears a larger and grander objective. "I like a lie sometimes," one of his fictional characters admits, "but then it must be a good one" [*Henrietta Temple*].

The second major component of Disraeli's Romanticism was his faith in the transforming power of the human will. If his associates in the Young England group [as described in *Disraeli* ] "sought to revive a Toryism not the less potent for having never existed outside their imagination," Disraeli, with a mixture of idealism, ambition, and pragmatism, was uniquely able to transform some of their political fancies into concrete policy and action. The key Romantic personality for Disraeli (as for George Smythe, the leading figure in Young England and the model for Coningsby) was Byron, whose assertion of will in his life and whose celebration of will in much of his work were seen by repentant first-generation Romantics like Coleridge and Southey as a Satanic predilection: the liberated imagination and will finding expression in egoistic fantasies and questionable behavior. The Romantics were willing to admire heroes, as Carl Woodring notes [in *Politics in English Romantic Poetry,* 1970], because "they lived in an atmosphere where will was ascendant . . . In the actuality around them, reason subsided under the growing supremacy of will. The old Renaissance belief in man's freedom, immortality, and reason became less prudently belief in man's freedom, creative imagination, and illimitable power of will." In Disraeli's case, however, the dangerous potential of the will was neutralized by his boyish faith in romance. No setback encountered by the future Prime Minister and his literary protagonists could make them abandon their sense of being ordained to occupy a dominating position. [In a review of *Coningsby* reprinted in *Contributions to the "Morning Chronicle,"* 1955] Thackeray spoke with admiration and mockery of Disraeli's "strong faith" in his heroes' ambitious fantasies: the reader "can't help fancying (we speak for ourselves), after perusing the volumes, that he too is a regenerator of the world, and that he has we don't know how many thousands a year." But if an individual has sufficient faith in his will power, Disraeli repeatedly proclaimed, he will not go unrewarded: the prerogative of the romance hero—to come into good fortune "without any effort or exertion of

your own"—accompanies the ambition of the Byronic hero.

Disraeli's huge political success—achieved in spite of the handicaps of his non-Christian birth and his nonaristocratic background—is a tribute to the possibilities of romance as well as to the hold that romance and Romantic values had on the Victorians. A reaction against the excesses of Romanticism is characteristic of what we think of as Victorianism: Victorian writers replaced the Romantic glorification of the individual will with an emphasis on communal and domestic values. "Close thy Byron, open thy Goethe" was Carlyle's shorthand way of arguing that English society would collapse if men and women saw themselves as superior to the world they lived in. The call for self-renunciation and a redirection of one's individual energies into social causes is the theme of that great work to which all Victorian fiction aspires, *Middlemarch.* But while Disraeli did open his Carlyle he never closed his Byron, and it was with reference to George Eliot that he tartly observed that when he wanted to read a novel, he wrote one. Unlike many of his contemporaries who worshiped Byron in the early nineteenth century but regarded him as one of the sins of their youth when they and the century reached middle age, Disraeli never lost his enthusiasm for the figure whom he once claimed to be "greater even as a man than as a writer." There is a suggestion in Disraeli's first novel, *Vivian Grey* (1827), that if Byron had only lived longer and returned to England he might have become a political force to reckon with. (Byron himself had toyed with the idea of achieving fame in a political and military, as well as literary, capacity. After his eloquent speech in the House of Lords defending the rights of the people during the Frame-Work Bill debate, Byron noted that "Ld. H[olland] tells me I shall beat them all if I persevere." In later years, however, he denied being "made for what you call a politician, and should never have adhered to any party." The "intrigues" and "contests for power" that Disraeli delighted in Byron professed disgust for.) The hero of Disraeli's second novel, *The Young Duke* (1831), distinguishes himself politically by speaking in the House of Lords in favor of Catholic Emancipation, the subject of Byron's own speech in the same House in 1812. Disraeli's efforts on behalf of Jewish rights were an extension of Byron's pro-Catholic efforts, just as Disraeli's continuing and deliberately provoking references to "the sacred and romantic people from whom I derive my blood and name" were in line with Byron's great pride in his own ancestry.

Byron's hold on the public resembled Napoleon's: theirs seemed the triumph of men of destiny whose egotism was bold and splendid enough to speak for and direct the hidden wishes of the multitude. Disraeli associated himself with the assertive Byron, although in times of dejection he also identified with the thwarted Byron, the melancholy figure bumping his head against social convention and cosmic fate. Unlike Bulwer Lytton, however, and greatly to his own advantage as novelist and statesman, Disraeli was able to adopt the role of the self-mocking Byron as well. Disraeli was later to identify himself with another Romantic statesman, Napoleon III, and just as Byron's rise to literary power provides the plot for his early novel *Venetia*

(1837), Louis Napoleon's rise to political eminence is celebrated in his last novel, **Endymion** (1880). In both cases, Disraeli was fascinated by the spectacle of a man of strong will attaining influence over others. Louis Napoleon's determination to link "the rights of the people and the principles of authority" is similar to Disraeli's romantic Tory conviction that the aristocracy is the natural ally of the people; and where Louis Napoleon confidently invoked his uncle's name and his own "Star" as proof that he was "fated" to lead France, Disraeli interpreted his ambitions in a similarly romantic manner. Both leaders were hugely popular with multitudes hungry for a grand myth, and both were assailed as charlatans.

Disraeli gained greater prominence as a statesman than as a writer, but as a young man he hoped to win for himself the literary power that Byron had wielded and also to wield political power over others as a result of following the Byronic formula. To know oneself thoroughly, as Byron had known himself, meant to be aware of the passions that animate mankind. "Self-knowledge," as he notes of successful orators in **The Young Duke,** "is the property of that man whose passions have their play, but who ponders over their results. Such a man sympathises by inspiration with his kind. He has a key to every heart. He can divine, in the flash of a single thought, all that they require, all that they wish." "It is the personal that interests mankind," he writes in **Coningsby,** "that fires their imagination, and wins their hearts. A cause is a great abstraction, and fit only for students; embodied in a party, it stirs men to action; but place at the head of that party a leader who can inspire enthusiasm, he commands the world." It was Disraeli's fantasy to become the acknowledged and the unacknowledged legislator of the world: Shelley's famous line from "A Defence of Poetry" is quoted in the novel **Venetia,** which appeared just as Disraeli was finally preparing to enter Parliament. The Shelleyan echo should remind us that Disraeli's Romanticism was ultimately directed toward a goal of public service, not selfish gratification. In recent years the Byronic clinging to a position of "self-assertion in an alien universe" has been interpreted as an existential triumph, a heroic model of "humanistic self-reliance"; but the Byronic conquest of self-will, as displayed in his campaign for Greek independence, was hailed by many Victorians as an example of humanistic self-denial. By linking the Byronic will with the Shelleyan sympathetic imagination, Disraeli attempted to show that Romantic convictions could be made to serve the public interest. In his political speeches and his novels alike, Disraeli increasingly held up Romantic values as bulwarks against the anti-Romantic, socially corrosive forces of materialism, Utilitarianism, and nihilism.

In a diary entry for 1833, Disraeli, who had recently been twice defeated in bids for a Parliamentary seat, noted how difficult it would be to overcome the obstacles and prejudices lying in the way of the political success he craved. For the moment, he acknowledged, writing was "the safety-valve of [his] passions," but he panted "to act what" he wrote about. He then described three of his novels as "the secret history of [his] feelings." "In **Vivian Grey** I have portrayed my active and real ambition. In **Alroy** my ideal ambition. **The Psychological Romance** [**Contarini**

**Fleming** ] is a development of my poetic character" [quoted in *The Life of Benjamin Disraeli,* 1929, by W. F. Monypenny and G. E. Buckle]. Despite differences in the books' backgrounds and subject matter, the theme in the trilogy is the same: the determination to achieve power in one form or another. There is a passage or two in each book in which the hero thinks of exerting power for humanitarian or libertarian ends, but this is only incidental to the grand ambition itself.

"Superior power, exercised by a superior mind," is the professed goal of Vivian Grey while yet a schoolboy; but this Byronic audacity gives way to Byronic melancholy when Vivian's schemes for political power are thwarted. In the second part of the novel, Vivian switches from an active to a passive role: he looks on while, in a memorable episode, a German minister, Beckendorff, achieves the very sort of power he has desired. Beckendorff himself sounds for the first time in Disraeli's writings the belief in the power of the will to achieve what it wishes. "If, in fact, you wish to succeed," he tells Vivian, "success . . . is at your command." In **The Wondrous Tale of Alroy** (1833), which was inspired partly by Disraeli's trip to the Middle East in 1831, partly by his fascination with a minor Jewish prince of the twelfth century who had declared himself the Messiah and achieved a brief success, Disraeli advanced the claim that his Jewish ancestry entitled him to be considered as worthy a claimant for English office as any nobleman. His hero, Alroy, describes himself as "the descendant of sacred kings, and with a soul that pants for empire"; and the escapades of the original princeling are blown up into the heroics of one who is a cross between Napoleon and Moses. Although the heroism comes to nothing, Disraeli protests that "a great career, although baulked of its end, is still a landmark of human energy."

Whether fantasying himself as a Metternichian minister of state in **Vivian Grey,** a Jewish Napoleon in **Alroy,** or a great writer in **Contarini Fleming** (1832), Disraeli's obsession in the trilogy is with power. Like Vivian Grey, Contarini Fleming spends his childhood dreaming that "life must be intolerable unless I were the greatest of men. It seemed that I felt within me the power that could influence my kind." In the course of the novel, Contarini indulges in a number of power games: in his schoolmates he sees "only beings whom I was determined to control" through the force of his eloquence; the creatures his youthful poetic imagination invents he sees as an army which will "go forth to the world to delight and to conquer"; even his beloved he regards with a possessive eye, and despite an operatic flourish of grief after her death, he consoles himself with the thought "that at the moment of departure her last thought was for me." By his father, who has achieved a political prominence not unlike that of Beckendorff in Disraeli's first novel, Contarini is advised to model himself upon "really great men; that is to say, men of great energies and violent volition, who look upon their fellow-creatures as mere tools, with which they can build up a pedestal for their solitary statue." An admirer of Napoleon, the elder Fleming represents the cynical extreme to which Disraeli's Byronic fancies might have led him. Looking upon people as brutes who can easily be manipulated, Fleming believes "all to depend upon the influence of individual character." The son rejects the political career his father has directed him toward, but he uses the same methods when he becomes a Shelleyan poet, determined to "exercise an illimitable power over the passions of his kind."

In no other Disraeli novel are the author's ambitions and self-conceit so profusely illustrated as in *Contarini Fleming.* It might be said that if Narcissus had been a novelist, this is the book he would have written. Everyone Contarini meets he longs to dominate, and everything he sees becomes a subjective correlative of his own feelings. Having crossed the Swiss Alps and visually absorbed the geographical and meteorological props so dear to a Romantic poet, he exults in the new images he can use to overwhelm his readers. Creativity is reduced to the status of a martial art. Contarini's exploits form a pattern-book of romantic behavior—a boyish version of Bulwer Lytton's Maltrevers novels. At one point, for example, he persuades his schoolmates to follow in the footsteps of Schiller's robbers. (They balk, however, at his proposal that they become Byronic pirates.) Contarini defends his egotistical adventures as sentimental heroics in an "age of reality." The fictionalized Byron in Disraeli's novel *Venetia* similarly sees himself as having a "chivalric genius" in a "mechanical age." But while Contarini lusts after power, Disraeli has neglected to grant him conspicuous talents other than the audacity that demands to have whatever it wishes. When the young hero confesses his desire to be a poet to a successful artist whom he has just met, he is told, "when a mind like yours thinks often of a thing, it will happen." This artist figure, Peter Winter, is presented as a foil to Contarini's father; but while Contarini chooses the poet's career over the politician's, he still honors the advice his father has given him: "with words we govern men."

Disraeli's own dazzling career was established at the fortuitous moment when the protectionist wing of the Tory party lacked an articulate spokesman to argue its cause. Disraeli's desire to achieve success as a poet is evidenced in the poem he began about this time, *The Revolutionary Epick* (1834), which aimed at presenting Shelleyan principles in Miltonic form, and in the verse play *The Tragedy of Count Alarcos* (1839), which he undertook, as he claimed, in competition with Shakespeare. (The subject of both works is the attainment of power. In the poem the spirits of Burkean "Feudalism" and Shelleyan "Federalism" contend, but the narrative breaks off just as "that predestined Man [Napoleon], / Upon whose crest the fortunes of the world / Shall hover,'" arises—with perhaps the aim, like Disraeli's, of reconciling the claims of tradition and liberty. The protagonist of *Alarcos,* on the other hand, discovers that the price of political power is murder.) No reader of these turgid outpourings would wish that Disraeli had pursued a poetical career at the expense of his political goals; but perhaps the fairest way to interpret *Contarini Fleming* is in light of the political and personal frustrations its author was experiencing at the time. The colossal egotism of Contarini is a mask for Disraeli's insecurity. At one point dejectedly believing himself "the object of an omnipotent Destiny, over which I had no control," Contarini later consoles himself with the thought that "Destiny is our will, and our will is our nature." The

boyish romance of an outsider who triumphs over everyone and everything was indeed a "safety-valve" for the energies of one who saw himself as an innately gifted individual in an age that lacked heroic grandeur. "I am only truly great in action," he confided to his diary in an effort at self-hypnotism. "If ever I am placed in a truly eminent position I shall prove this," he added prophetically; "I could rule the House of Commons, although there would be a great prejudice against me at first."

During the same decade in which Disraeli composed his autobiographical trilogy, he wrote three other novels with no higher aim in mind than making money to pay off his debts. But although *The Young Duke, Henrietta Temple,* and *Venetia* were initiated as hack works, they are a good deal more fun to read than Disraeli's serious novels of the period. They also express aspects of his active, ideal, and poetic ambition, but without the egotistical bombast and with a certain amount of mockery directed at his own high pretensions. The willingness to satirize his ambitions and posings is one of the most endearing of Disraeli's Byronic traits. In each of the books a young woman is the moral agent who converts a selfish young man to a sense of domestic or social responsibility. One might almost say that under the romantic trappings of these books a Victorian conscience is struggling to be heard. (*Henrietta Temple* and *Venetia* were published in 1837, the year Victoria ascended the throne.)

The hero of *The Young Duke* is an immensely wealthy young lord who spends his money lavishly and then converts to a serious sense of his duties as an aristocrat. The novel contains marvelous and witty set pieces of fashionable life—no less effective for being almost entirely the concoctions of Disraeli's imagination—and a description of a gambling den in which all the aristocratic forms are thrown off to reveal "hideous demons" lurking underneath. In the Romantic tradition, Disraeli saw Utilitarians rather than aristocrats as major threats to the moral and social well-being of the age. His animus against Utilitarian philosophers is humorously expressed in the description of the Benthamite writer whose hatred of aristocrats extends to a hatred of mountains: "Rivers he rather patronised; but flowers he quite pulled to pieces, and proved them to be the most useless of existences. Duncan Macmorrogh informed us that we were quite wrong in supposing ourselves to be the miracle of Creation. On the contrary, he avowed that already there were various pieces of machinery of far more importance than man; and he had no doubt, in time, that a superior race would arise, got by a steam-engine on a spinning-jenny." Disraeli's answer to the Utilitarian theories is the figure of the young duke at the end of the novel, whose feudal determination to take care of a people imaginatively enthralled by him is seen to be more effective in the long run than any Benthamite legislation.

Whether Disraeli himself could achieve political prominence is a matter for doubt in these books. Despite the will to be great, the heroes of Disraeli's early novels do not always achieve their objective or enjoy it for long. Those who do succeed, moreover, do so with the help, or at the will, of others. Disraeli interrupts the narrative of *The*

*Young Duke* at one point to express his anguish that the most "supernatural" of energies—such as those of Byron or Napoleon—have been known to "die away without creating their miracles." A sense of personal insecurity is especially evident in *Henrietta Temple.* His hero, Ferdinand Armine, possesses "the power and the will" of his chivalric ancestors: as the "near descendant of that bold man who passed his whole life in the voluptuous indulgence of his unrestrained volition," Armine decides that he need only be willful himself for all to yield "to determination." Moreover, Armine possesses the requisite Romantic imagination: "His imagination created fantasies and his impetuous passions struggled to realise them." In the end, however, he attains his desires in large part because of Disraeli's own strong need for a fantasy of "acceptance" at this stage in his career. Armine achieves his goal because others are eager and determined to thrust greatness on him: "The most gifted individuals in the land emulated each other in proving which entertained for him the most sincere affection." The Romantic faith in will is overshadowed by the romancer's reliance on wish-fulfillment.

The twin heroes of *Venetia* are no less than Byron and Shelley, whom Disraeli renames Plantagenet Cadurcis and Marmion Herbert. Disraeli's defense of his Romantic idols is tempered, however, by his recognition that the same imaginative energies that produce great poetry can also find expression in questionable conduct. As a young radical poet and philosopher, Herbert has "celebrated that fond world of his imagination, which he wished to teach men to love." But despite intense idealism, Herbert's disbelief in conventional morality, his atheism, and his revolutionary politics wreck his marriage and exile him from England. It is intriguing to contemplate Matthew Arnold's "beautiful and ineffectual angel" becoming a general and fighting in the American Revolution against his native land; Disraeli sets his novel far enough in the past that his Shelley-figure can achieve that fate. However, the sight of his daughter Venetia and his wife Lady Annabel, from whom he has separated under conditions that echo Byron's separation from Lady Byron (Herbert's defense of American freedom is similarly reminiscent of Byron's crusade for Greek independence), is enough to make him cast off his past beliefs and sigh instead for "domestic repose" and "domestic bliss." "The age of his illusions had long passed"; in middle age Herbert cautions his poetic and political disciple Cadurcis that it is more important for a poet to "sympathise" with his fellowmen than to express his scorn for or exert his will upon them: "It is sympathy that makes you a poet. It is your desire that the airy children of your brain should be born anew within another's, that makes you create; therefore, a misanthropical poet is a contradiction in terms." Disraeli illustrates in Herbert's career the waste of an idealistic imagination and in Cadurcis's case the misuse of imaginative energies.

Despite his Romantic sympathies, Disraeli by 1837 had come to see, as Coleridge had earlier, that imagination and will have negative possibilities: by stressing Ferdinand Armine's passivity in *Henrietta Temple,* Disraeli disengaged his hero from any misexpenditure of will. (Scott had employed a similar strategy in the Waverley novels.) In Cadurcis, Disraeli embodies what to young Victorians ap-

peared to be the quintessentially Byronic man of imagination and will. "If ever there existed a being who was his own master, who might mould his destiny at his will, it seemed to be Cadurcis." Yet Venetia's mother, quite rightly from a Victorian point of view, rejects Cadurcis's appeal for her daughter's hand on the basis of his "genius." "Spirits like him," Lady Annabel says, are swayed by a dangerous impulse: "It is imagination; it is vanity; it is self, disguised with glittering qualities that dazzle our weak senses, but selfishness, the most entire, the most concentrated." When Cadurcis insists to his friend Masham (modeled after Bishop Wilberforce) that he must have Venetia, the Bishop replies that Cadurcis only really wants what his imagination has seized upon for momentary gratification. Once he had married Venetia, he "would probably part from her in a year, as her father parted from Lady Annabel." "Impossible!" replies Cadurcis, "for my imagination could not conceive of anything more exquisite than she is." "Then it would conceive something less exquisite," says the Bishop. "It is a restless quality, and is ever creative, either of good or of evil." The portrait of Cadurcis is the culmination of Disraeli's lifelong Byron-mania: we see Cadurcis evolve from a moody and willful child, whose mother is every bit as eccentric as Lady Gordon, to a young man of strange habits (including the famous diet of biscuits and soda water), misanthropic moods, and extraordinary literary success.

Disraeli collected information about Byron and Shelley from a variety of published and unpublished sources: among others, Thomas Moore's *Life of Byron,* Thomas Medwin's remembrances of Byron and Shelley, and anecdotes related by Edward Trelawny, Lady Blessington, and Byron's former manservant, Tita, whom Disraeli had acquired as a human souvenir during his trip to the East in 1831. But a recognition of Byron's genius did not prevent Disraeli from seeing an incompatibility between imaginative ambition and domestic virtues: if Medwin, Trelawny, and Moore were not sufficient witnesses to the improprieties of genius, his father Isaac D'Israeli's *The Literary Character, or The History of Men of Genius* was a treasure-trove of biographical episodes proving that men like Byron could not be "tamed" to fit the hopes of a character like Venetia. In the end, Disraeli was obliged to drown both his Byron and Shelley figures, despite their abrupt conversion away from their willful early lives, their Shelleyan unorthodoxy and Byronic "selfism." Although Disraeli himself was now in the process of toning down his Romantic rhetoric and posture in the hope of attaining recognition in the House of Commons, he was not about to show his poetic idols selling out. *Venetia* seems intended, as Disraeli's biographer [Robert Blake] observes, as a "last tribute to the Byronic myth . . . a final protest against the respectable world with which he now had to come to terms." But if Romantic flamboyance was no longer serviceable to Disraeli, the Romantic tradition of humanitarianism could now be turned to account.

The great trilogy of the 1830s represent Disraeli's major claim to be taken seriously as a novelist. In these works, for the first time, his heroes have a mission; they want not only power, like the early heroes, but something to direct that power toward. They want to see England governed by a real aristocracy, composed of talented and earnest young men who inspire others by their creative abilities. Noting a debt to Carlyle's idea of "Hero Worship" in *Coningsby,* Thackeray smiled at the "pining" of "Young England . . . for the restoration of the heroic sentiment, and the appearance of the heroic man" [*Contributions to the "Morning Chronicle"*]. Indeed, the spirit of Carlyle and Scott had been joined to the spirit of Byron and Shelley, and the result—in *Coningsby* and *Sybil* at least—is the sort of work to please novel-readers who would perhaps rather be reading political tracts. Yet a Romantic quality permeates even these books. The appeal is to the imagination, but the imagination speaks not only the "language of power" (in Hazlitt's phrase) but the language of sympathy. A Byronic magnetic figure is still required to fire the passions of the public, but this figure also needs Shelley's humanitarian imagination. In defending the moral force of poetry, Shelley maintains, "A man, to be greatly good, must imagine intensely and comprehensively; he must put himself in the place of another and of many others; the pains and pleasures of his species must become his own. The great instrument of moral good is the imagination; and poetry administers to the effect by acting upon the cause" ["A Defence of Poetry," in *Works,* 1930]. In *Coningsby, or The New Generation* (1844), Disraeli treats the political hero as Shelley regarded the poet: a great man, like a great book, produces "a magnetic influence blending with our sympathising intelligence, that directs and inspires it."

Coningsby himself exerts over his schoolmates "the ascendant power, which is the destiny of genius"; and he is granted a heroic will so that he and his friends can satisfy the English people's craving for great leaders to lead them in a time of crisis. "Surely of all 'rights of man,' " as Carlyle declares, somewhat less attractively, in *Chartism,* "this right of the ignorant man to be guided by the wiser, to be, gently or forcibly, held in the true course by him, is the indisputablest." For leadership, according to Carlyle and Disraeli, not only satisfies an instinctive need of the multitude—it also keeps the multitude from satisfying their passions in socially destructive ways. When Coningsby asks Sidonia, Disraeli's portrait of a wealthy Jewish Tiresias-figure who knows everything and everyone, whether "Imagination," which "once subdued the state . . . may not save it," Sidonia replies, "Man is made to adore and to obey: but if you will not command him, if you give him nothing to worship, he will fashion his own divinities and find a chieftain in his own passions."

In *Sybil, or The Two Nations* (1845), Disraeli shows to what a state the abdication of leadership by the aristocracy and the church has brought modern England. In that novel "a spirit of rapacious covetousness, desecrating all the humanities of life," has been spread by the newly powerful middle class. Their goal, as Disraeli sees it, is "to acquire, to accumulate, to plunder each other by virtue of philosophic [that is, Utilitarian, laissez-faire] phrases, to propose a Utopia to consist only of WEALTH and TOIL." Deserted by their natural allies, the upper classes, and exploited by the middle classes, the workers have been left totally degraded and at the mercy of Chartist slogans, which promise relief but lead only to destructive acts. It

is precisely at such a time, as Sidonia urges, that great men are called for—not to follow the spirit of the age but to change it, to advocate reverence for heroic values in place of materialism, and to protect the poor who cannot defend themselves. Ten years earlier Disraeli had contended that "The Monarchy of the Tories is more democratic than the Republic of the Whigs. It appeals with a keener sympathy to the passions of the millions; it studies their interests with a more comprehensive solicitude" [*Whigs and Whiggism: Political Writings by Benjamin Disraeli,* 1913]. A political career for Harry Coningsby or Charles Egremont (the hero of *Sybil* ) is seen as a romantic crusade, a chivalric adventure in which the successful hero slays Whig (or factitious Tory) dragons and ends up in Parliament making speeches in favor of the "rights of labour." The creator of these heroes draws at least as much from *Arabian Nights* fantasies of wish-fulfillment as from his observations of the actual political process. "Life was a pantomime," as Coningsby discovers; "the wand was waved, and it seemed that the schoolfellows had of a sudden become elements of power, springs of the great machine."

*Tancred, or The New Crusade* (1847) brings Disraeli's political trilogy to a brilliant, if also perplexing, climax. It is much less earnest in tone, though no less serious in purpose, than *Coningsby* and *Sybil,* and the seriousness is not deflected by Disraeli's many witty, and sometimes perverse, digressions. Tancred himself is an extremely earnest young nobleman, the descendant of crusaders, who wants "to see an angel at Manchester" and who does in fact see an angel on Mount Sinai. For Tancred, another Disraeli hero possessed of "indomitable will and an iron resolution," the achievement of political power is meaningless without a secure national religious faith to prop it up. "It is time to restore and renovate our communications with the Most High," he tells his astonished father. "What ought I to DO, and what ought I to BELIEVE?" To Coningsby and his friends, Tancred complains that without a magnetic religious influence directing human behavior, "Individuality is dead; there is a want of inward and personal energy in man; and that is what people feel and mean when they go about complaining there is no faith." Luckily for Tancred, Sidonia appears in time to encourage him to find the answer to his dilemma by penetrating "the great Asian mystery"—that is, by traveling to Palestine to discover why God chose to speak to mankind from there and not from Manchester.

Tancred's adventures in the Middle East are an odd sort of reverie to be coming from a member of Parliament who was about to assume the mantle of Tory leader Robert Peel. Yet the brilliant political invective Disraeli was using in his campaign against Peel and against the repeal of the Corn Laws at about this time was a product of the same imagination that created Tancred's "new crusade" to bring back religious principles to England and, at the same time, created the intrigues of the Arab prince Fakredeen to attain power for himself by any means possible. (Fakredeen's alliance of Arab princes, for example, may be a parody of Disraeli's own Young England Party.) Disraeli's gift for romantic image-making was matched by his brilliant ability to expose the sham underneath. If principle and opportunism appear almost inextricably connected in Disraeli's personality—as do the polar Romantic attitudes of reverential obeisance and heroic self-assertion—the novelist personifies and travesties this dualism in the contrasting characters of Tancred and Fakredeen.

Tancred's pilgrimage seems serious enough until he meets Fakredeen—this "Syrian Vivian Grey," as Leslie Stephen calls him [in *Hours in a Library,* 2nd ser., 1928]—who parodies Tancred's earnestness and utters many of Disraeli's sentiments. Fakredeen is ambitious, vain, and unscrupulous; but he is given many of the author's favorite ideas, including the maxim "everything comes if a man will only wait." While Tancred seeks to convert the world—as soon as he can find a principle of religious certainty for himself—Fakredeen wants only to conquer it. The two men join forces for a time in a preposterous plan to "conquer the world, with angels at our head," as Tancred explains, "in order that we may establish the happiness of man by a divine dominion." He settles in the end for domestic bliss, an angel in the house taking the place of the Angel of Arabia. (There is possibly an allusion to Keats's *Endymion* here: Tancred's beloved supplants the angel he has sought, while Endymion's Indian maid is the physical incarnation of Cynthia, goddess of the Moon.) Eva, his Jewish bride-to-be, comforts Tancred for the loss of some of his illusions. "Perhaps," she suggests, "all this time we have been dreaming over an unattainable end, and the only source of deception is our own imagination." The novel ends in confusion with Tancred still wanting to believe—and Disraeli wanting Tancred to want to believe—but with what to believe in still a matter for doubt.

What ultimately redeems the book is not its message (although Disraeli considered this his most important book) but its wit, seen in the political intrigues of Fakredeen, which mock the pretensions of many a Disraeli hero and the young Disraeli himself; in the epigrams, such as "Christianity is Judaism for the multitude"; and above all in the mockery directed against an English society that has lost all reverence for spiritual values. The parody of Robert Chambers's *Vestiges of the Natural History of Creation,* which had recently appeared and which offered in popular form an evolutionist's theory of history, is one of the great set pieces of Disraeli's comic spirit. Lady Constance hands Tancred a copy of " 'The Revelations of Chaos,' a startling book just published, and of which a rumour had reached him." "It is one of those books one must read," Lady Constance blithely declares. "It explains everything, and is written in a very agreeable style."

> "It explains everything!" said Tancred; "it must, indeed, be a very remarkable book!"
>
> "I think it will just suit you," said Lady Constance. "Do you know, I thought so several times while I was reading it."
>
> "To judge from the title, the subject is rather obscure," said Tancred.
>
> "No longer so," said Lady Constance. "It is treated scientifically; everything is explained by geology and astronomy, and in that way. It shows you exactly how a star is formed; nothing can be so pretty! A cluster of vapour, the cream of the milky way, a sort of celestial cheese,

> churned into light, you must read it, 'tis charming."
>
> "Nobody ever saw a star formed," said Tancred.
>
> "Perhaps not. You must read the 'Revelations;' it is all explained. But what is most interesting, is the way in which man has been developed. You know, all is development. The principle is perpetually going on. First, there was nothing, then there was something; then, I forget the next, I think there were shells, then fishes; then we came, let me see, did we come next? Never mind that; we came at last. And the next change there will be something very superior to us, something with wings. Ah! that's it: we were fishes, and I believe we shall be crows. But you must read it."
>
> "I do not believe I ever was a fish," said Tancred.

This famous passage should remind us that Disraeli was perfectly serious when, speaking at Oxford in 1864, he declared himself on the side of the angels, protesting that "instead of believing that the age of faith has passed, I hold that the characteristic of the present age is a craving credulity." Evolution, like Utilitarianism, deprived man of his power of volition; yet for Disraeli, as for Newman and Tennyson, the will to believe was a proof that there was something to believe in, something that affirmed the power of the will after all.

Like Keats in his substitution of Cortez for Balboa, Disraeli knew that the scientists' discoveries could not be discounted; in terms of the requirements of the imagination and the will to believe, however, such facts were irrelevant. "Craving credulity" is both the theme of and the danger in two of Disraeli's last three fictional works: *Lothair* (1870) and the unfinished *Falconet.* The doubts and fears of the 1870s and 1880s find vivid expression in these books. Lothair, a young nobleman who like Tancred is searching for religious certitude, is characterized in terms of passivity rather than willfulness. "I often think . . . that I have neither powers nor talents," he laments at one point, "but am drifting without an orbit." He finds himself at the mercy of several opposing religious and political doctrines, all of which Disraeli treats with a certain amount of sympathy. The most troublesome temptation comes from Cardinal Grandison, whose endorsement of Roman Catholicism is an invitation for Lothair to resign his will altogether. The cardinal expresses Disraeli's fear that the rise of science has aided materialism and atheism. "The world is devoted to physical science," he charges, "because it believes these discoveries will increase its capacity of luxury and self-indulgence. But the pursuit of science leads only to the insoluble." For the cardinal, as for Sidonia, "all the poetry and passion and sentiment of human nature are taking refuge in religion." "Religion is civilisation," he argues later in the novel; "the highest: it is the reclamation of man from savageness by the Almighty. What the world calls civilisation, as distinguished from religion, is a retrograde movement, and will ultimately lead us back to the barbarism from which we have escaped." Like Dostoevsky, at about the same time, Disraeli is warning that when God is not believed to exist all things become permissible.

Lothair's susceptibility to Roman Catholicism does not lead to conversion only because he is even more susceptible to a strong-minded woman, Theodora, who wins him over to the cause of Italian freedom, and because Disraeli sees Jerusalem, not Rome, as the real fountainhead of religious truth. Action becomes the antidote for Lothair's morbid introspection; his romantic activity as a soldier in the cause of Italian unification is described as an "easy distraction from self-criticism." He is not the first troubled Romantic to come to that conclusion. "A region of Doubt . . . hovers forever in the background," Carlyle declared in 1831; "in Action alone can we have certainty" ["Characteristics," in *Works,* 1898-1901]. "The only tolerable thing in life is action," especially youthful action, as Theodora's friend the Princess of Tivoli says to Lothair. "You have many, many scrapes awaiting you . . . You may look forward to at least ten years of blunders: that is, illusions; that is, happiness. Fortunate young man!" It is the princess who later sounds the theme of the romance of the will in opposition to the cardinal's doctrine of renunciation. "The power of the passions, the force of the will, the creative energy of the imagination," she proclaims, "these make life, and reveal to us a world of which the million are entirely ignorant." In the opposition between the romance of the will and the need for obedience and reverence, Lothair takes one side and then another, settling finally, like Tancred, for domestic bliss in a world of unresolved and unresolvable questionings.

There is no way of knowing what the outcome of *Falconet* would have been: before his death Disraeli had completed fewer than ten chapters of this novel, in which all values seem to be dissolving and only self-righteous hypocrites like Falconet (modeled after the Liberal leader Gladstone, whom Disraeli regarded as the "Arch Villain") or nihilistic philosophies seem to be thriving. England seems exhausted of her energies, and no youthful heroes have yet appeared when the manuscript breaks off to indicate how the visitors from the East and Germany, who turn up in the novel to preach a doctrine of "Destruction in every form," are to be thwarted—if they are to be thwarted. In one of the last scenes we are shown one of the invaders recommending a book by "a friend of Schopenhauer," a book that presumably offers Schopenhauer's message of the sublimation of the will.

Yet despite the sense that his was "an age of dissolving creeds" (*Falconet*) and threats to civil order—or perhaps because of the realization that he himself had risen to power by seizing the initiative in a time of social instability—Disraeli's last completed novel, *Endymion* (1880), is the most romantic and optimistic of all his works. "It is a privilege to live in this age of rapid and brilliant events," he had exulted in 1864. "What an error to consider it an utilitarian age! It is one of infinite romance. Thrones tumble down and are offered, like a fairy tale, and the most powerful people in the world, male and female, a few years back were adventurers, exiles and demireps" [quoted in Blake's *Disraeli* ]. Disraeli may have been describing the rise to power of men like Louis Napoleon, but he was also contemplating his own success, the fulfillment of the unrealistic ambition stated in the 1833 diary. By 1875 he was not only prime minister but Lord Beaconsfield. There is

no mention of dissolving creeds in *Endymion:* indeed, Nigel Penruddock's rise to the position of Roman Catholic cardinal is celebrated here—though it would have been deplored in *Lothair*—because it is an assumption of power. All ways to eminence are to be admired, whether in the figure of Endymion, who becomes prime minister of the Whig, not the Tory, party; Vigo, who as a railway magnate is linked with what to the Victorians was the most visible symbol of material progress; or Prince Florestan, who is Disraeli's version of Napoleon III with touches added from the wondrous career of Alroy. "All you have got to do is to make up your mind that you will be in the next parliament, and you will succeed," Lady Montfort tells Endymion; "for everything in this world depends upon will." "I think everything in this world depends upon women," replies Endymion; to which Lady Montfort retorts, "It is the same thing."

*Endymion* expresses Disraeli's Romantic view of history, in which heroes triumph by the force of their will, buttressed by the spirit of romance, in which wishing for something to happen is enough to make it happen. Endymion rises from poverty to political power without having to engage in any of the intrigues and subterfuges necessary for climbing the "greasy pole." His only conspicuous qualities are youth, tact, and "the power and melody of

*A caricature of Disraeli appearing in* Vanity Fair, *1869.*

his voice." Yet he is awarded the highest honors partly because of his intense desire for them and largely through the agency of a set of fairy godsisters. "If we cannot shape your destiny," his sister Myra contends of the power of women, "there is no such thing as witchcraft." Myra devotes her will, which Endymion recognizes to be "more powerful than his," to the great aim of making her brother prime minister. "I have brought myself, by long meditation, to the conviction that a human being with a settled purpose must accomplish it," she claims, "and that nothing can resist a will that will stake even existence for its fulfillment." In the end, all men and women of indomitable will have assumed power: Myra herself becomes the Queen of France, the bride of King Florestan. How little Disraeli decided to rely on reality in concocting *Endymion*—how much he chose to present a Keatsian set of imaginative values instead—can be seen in the way he used as prototype for Florestan's hugely successful career an emperor who in historical fact had been driven from power a decade earlier.

One might be tempted to dismiss *Endymion* as an exuberant piece of wish-fulfillment if not for the disconcerting links between the improbabilities of its plot and the historical improbabilities that saw the rise of so many self-proclaimed men of destiny in the nineteenth century. Despite the revulsion of Victorian intellectuals—many of them searching for an authentic principle of authority to replace the fallen gods of their ancestors, and in no mood to hail the exploits of a survivor from the Romantic period—Disraeli had discovered that his Romantic views were shared by many of his countrymen. By no means an original thinker, as Bagehot recognized, he was able to rise to power by demonstrating a force of personality and by "*applying* a literary genius, in itself limited, to the practical purpose of public life" [*Bagehot's Historical Essays*, 1965]. His success indicates that in an age of disbelief people will follow a leader who believes in his own star and who is able to exert power over others with the right image and rhetoric. The power of words and images was a central Disraelian concern, as both a fictional and a national theme: "He thought in symbols," as Louis Cazamian noted [in his 1973 work *The Social Novel in England: 1830-1850*], "and was acutely alive to the power of images over human thought and conduct, for he recognized it in himself." When Gladstone defeated Disraeli in 1880, he exulted that "the downfall of Beaconsfieldism is like the vanishing of some vast magnificent castle of Italian romance" [Philip Magnus, *Gladstone*, 1964]; yet there occurred in the 1880s a revival of the romantic spirit, whether in the form of the fiction of Robert Louis Stevenson and H. Rider Haggard or in the form of imperial adventurism, which the Victorians had never really exorcised.

The adventurist and merely rhetorical aspects of Disraeli's Romanticism—the qualities that Trollope, for example, found so offensive—cannot be defended; but a more positive strain of Romanticism dominates his mature views. The negative aspect of his Romantic impulse is readily seen in the early novels, where his youthful narcissism and Byronic egoism are ingenuously revealed. In subsequent novels, however, he exhibited the humanitarian and reverential side of Romanticism; and in this respect, his devel-

opment from self-preoccupation to concern for society may be said to parallel the development within Romanticism itself. The Romantic celebration of the powers of heroic will and sovereign imagination was transformed into a recognition of the need for responsible leadership and a sympathetic, morally attuned imagination. In the end, the country's political, economic, and spiritual interests and the imaginative desires of Coningsby, Egremont, and Tancred—and Disraeli himself—are seen to be synonymous. To Disraeli's credit, while he translated into political and fictional terms the romance of the will, his Byronic sense of self-mockery forbade his ever taking himself and the idea of leadership unduly seriously, and thereby insulated him from Carlylean delusions of grandeur.

A perennially boyish element in Disraeli accounted for his persistence in regarding life as a romance in which, like Aladdin, he had only to will things for them to happen. But this sense of wonder was related for Disraeli, as it was for Coleridge and Newman, to a belief in spiritual forces in the universe with which modern man seemed increasingly to be losing touch. Coleridge's Biblical reminder that "WHERE NO VISION IS, THE PEOPLE PERISHETH" is close to Disraeli's insistence on the role of imagination in the nation's life. Against the Utilitarian appeal to a self-interested populace in a materialistic universe, he offered a Romantic dream of human potentiality in a world of mutual respect. In the unfinished *Falconet,* moreover, he seemed to be warning of a triumph of nihilism in a world that has lost faith in the Romantic values that sustain spiritual belief and that produce altruistic heroes. Uncharacteristic though it appears in theme and tone when compared with his other novels, *Falconet* betrays the sense of anxiety that underlies the euphoric fantasy of *Endymion.* Far more fearsome, as Disraeli realized, than the famous "leap in the dark" by which he had acted in 1867 to enfranchise members of the English working class, was the leap into darkness that might result from modern man's disenfranchisement from the visionary imagination. (pp. 74-98)

Donald D. Stone, "Benjamin Disraeli and the Romance of the Will," in his *The Romantic Impulse in Victorian Fiction, Cambridge, Mass.: Harvard University Press, 1980, pp. 74-98.*

### Charles Mosley    (essay date 1986)

[*In the following essay, Mosley examines the political novel tradition in England from the early nineteenth century to the present, naming Disraeli as the founder of, and the principal influence on, the genre.*]

What is a political novel? Leaving aside fables such as More's *Utopia, Gulliver's Travels,* Benjamin Disraeli's *Popanilla,* and futuristic exercises such as *1984* and Zamyatin's *We* (all, perhaps significantly, by authors not, or not at that time, professionally involved in politics), one might say that in the English tradition it tends to feature ministerial and parliamentary life, or at any rate the struggle to get into Parliament and possibly, having got there, to gain office. Naturally the focus varies according to whether the author is a practising politician, as Disraeli was from quite early on, or an MP *manqué* like Trollope.

It was Guizot who principally drew attention to Disraeli as the first political novelist, and he was certainly the English founder of that art form, although in a European context Stendhal, with *Le Rouge et le noir* (1830) and *Lucien Leuwen* (1894), runs him close. Disraeli's early novels, written when he was just as unsuccessful on the hustings as Trollope, are obviously less concerned with specifically administrative problems than his later ones. But even the latter are astonishingly unconcerned with the actual mechanism of government.

What Disraeli does provide in abundance is ideas. In this he is an exception. Kathleen Tillotson has observed [in her *Novels of the Eighteen-Forties,* 1954] that his heroes Coningsby, Egremont, and Tancred all think—though perhaps fitfully. This passage was misleadingly cited by Lord Blake in his *Disraeli* (1966) as if it applied to all Disraeli's heroes. Actually, one can ascribe ratiocinative powers to a wider selection of Disraeli's characters than do either Mrs Tillotson or Lord Blake. Even Disraeli's figures of fun like Sir Vavasour Firebrace have a programme, however dotty the erection of baronets into an order of *equites aurati* may be. As for the celebrated passages in *Coningsby* (1844) and *Sybil* (1845) urging the revival of paternalistic monarchy and excoriating the Whigs' "Venetian Oligarchy", they are surely unique, in Disraeli's day or after, in that they plant a manifesto into a work of fiction—and do it very neatly too. There are novelistic parallels in the dialogue of Peacock's novels and W. H. Mallock's *New Republic* (1877). But the latter makes no proper attempt at being a novel, and the sole excursions of Peacock into anything more politically solid than table talk are the slapstick irruption of the *jacquerie* into Chainmail Hall at the end of *Crotchet Castle* (1831) and the hilarious rottenborough election of the orang-outan Sir Oran Haut-ton, Bart., in *Melincourt* (1817).

Disraeli, for all his carelessness, does at his best achieve a temporary synthesis of political ideas and plot. Unfortunately, the notions he advances are mostly so absurd as to border on high camp, and the trappings he caparisons his characters with scarcely help. For example, there can be no English novelist so given to resurrecting the names of the high medieval nobility: Scrope, de Vere, Mowbray, Mountchesney, Bohun, Montacute, and Montfort. Given contemporary yearnings after a make-believe Gothicism, superimposed on his native romanticism, Disraeli was bound to indulge. Still, his vision of the Middle Ages— flower of chivalry, that sort of thing—was sufficiently rooted in his own time to be a Tory one rather than full of the collectivist tendencies William Morris looked back to. (Morris was much influenced by More's *Utopia.*) Unfortunately this meant that Disraeli could not develop a very coherent political philosophy. It was based on such a selective reading of history.

All the same, Disraeli's eccentric line on the Middle Ages had its strengths. In *Sybil,* Walter Gerard defends the monasteries' charitable role. Given that it is put in secular terms it is as good a case as anything that Thomas More might have made along the same lines. And Gerard's tren-

chant attack on the game laws has seldom been expressed more forcefully and economically. Think how Cobbett goes on about the spoliation of the peasantry. (Curiously enough, an excellent and succinct demolition of the Corn Laws occurs in *Popanilla.* Disraeli was lucky not to have it cast in his teeth after he broke with Peel in 1846.)

Perhaps the most important instance of Disraeli's putting his medieval obsessions to good use is Eustace Lyle's revived Christian paternalism in *Coningsby.* Though described with the author's customary tendency to stick his tongue in his cheek, it helps illustrate a practical working of that Tory paternalism which, along with all paternalism, has been too promptly ridiculed and for which Disraeli's novels are the nearest to an intellectual justification. Disraeli's social legislation in the 1870s may not amount to much as a conscious programme of amelioration prosecuted according to a rigorously planned paternalistic ideology. What government's actions do follow neatly a predetermined programme? But it was carried out by a government whose leader had written feelingly about poverty and had invested responsibility by the upper classes with glowing, if slightly absurd, hues.

Although we nowadays think of the politician novelist as a rather rare creature, nimbly combining onerous official duties with flights of creativity, the blend of statesmanship and imaginative literature in one person is as old as the novel itself. Petronius was not just a crony of Nero and leader of the first-century fashion, but a successful governor and consul. (It is true that the *Satyricon*—at any rate in the truncated form we possess today—eschews politics, unless one counts Eumolpus's bitter castigation of the venality of Senate and people in his lines on the Civil War.) In the 16th century Sir Philip Sidney, one of the earliest English novelists, not only practised politics but introduced the subject into his fiction. As well as representing Elizabeth I on diplomatic missions, he stood high in her circle of domestic counsellors and was also an MP. (Sidney briefly visited Ireland, but only to see his father, who was Lord Deputy there; had he succeeded his father in the post, as was briefly mooted, his *curriculum vitae* would have borne an even closer resemblance to that of our contemporary statesman/novelist Douglas Hurd, until recently Secretary of State for Northern Ireland.)

Sidney's *Arcadia* contains two or three passages of political exposition. It preaches a paternalistic monarchism very like that which Disraeli so endearingly but unconvincingly recommends in *Coningsby.* And not only does Disraeli borrow Sidney's name for his character Lord Henry Sydney (based on Lord John Manners), but that of the historic Sidney's friend Sir Thomas Coningsby for his hero. (George Smythe, usually recognised as the principal model for Coningsby, was collaterally descended from Sir Philip Sidney.) Moreover, Disraeli refers to Sidney outright in *Endymion* (1880). (Endymion was the forename of the third Viscount Strangford, whose father was Sir Philip Sidney's great-nephew: this Endymion was also great-great-grandfather of George Smythe.) Not only Disraeli's fanciful names for his characters but his love of a Near Eastern or Greek setting and his frequently florid and hyperbolic language have their harbingers in Sidney's

*Arcadia*. So Disraeli, although the real founder of a genre, did not stand entirely apart from a certain tradition.

Disraeli's novels reflect his personality more obviously than most writers'. Perhaps nobody has flouted more wantonly Flaubert's dictum that the novelist should be everywhere but, like God, unseen. *Vivian Grey* (1826), *Contarini Fleming* (1832), and *Henrietta Temple* (1836) are the most overtly autobiographical, but all bear their author's peculiar impress. This makes for an interesting rift between Disraeli's tales of high life and the political realities in his professional career. Disraeli had a broadminded, cosmopolitan, cultivated, and aristocratically inclined character which in social terms consorted better with what one thinks of as the typical Whig magnifico than with the narrower country squires who in practice formed the backbone of the Tory Party.

In this respect Disraeli's case is a curiously complementary contrast with his younger contemporary Trollope's. Although Trollope supported the Liberals he was by background from the old Tory squirearchy. (It is often forgotten, so great is the emphasis on Trollope senior's improvidence in Trollope's autobiography, that he came of an ancient family, well established as landowners centuries before they became baronets.) In his attitude towards the Greshams and the Fletchers and the Whartons in his novels it is easy to see where Trollope's visceral sympathies lay. Disraeli is exactly the opposite. He was more at home in houses such as Stowe or Deepdene, yet was the political leader of Victorian England's Whartons, Fletchers and Greshams, squires of impressive lineage but threatened rent-rolls, provincial ascendancy but metropolitan insignificance.

A unique element in Disraeli's novels is the theatrical one. He was himself a highly theatrical man, although the fact may have been obscured from contemporaries by his tendency—at any rate after a flamboyant youth—to underplay. (The Victorian age preferred ranters, like Edmund Kean in his melodramas or Henry Irving in virtually anything: Disraeli became famous for his impassivity.) In nearly every novel there is a play, whether publicly or privately performed. Now, it is a commonplace that politicians have many similarities to actors, as both have with barristers. And it has been suggested that MPs' theatrical, even buffoonish antics in the House of Commons ritualise and therefore soften the acerbity of opposition. In the days of a narrowly restricted franchise it would be almost true to say things were the other way round: elections ritualised violence. They were often highly dramatic, being conducted under conditions of near-carnival, saturnalian exuberance, with broken heads and windows, hurled brickbats, broached hogsheads, etc. Since universal suffrage, elections have become comparatively tame affairs.

Naturally Disraeli was not the only writer of his time to deal with elections. Indeed the literature of such contests would make a little anthology: Dickens with Eatanswill in *Pickwick Papers* (1837), for instance, and Surtees with Jorrocks's contest against the Marquess of Bray in *Hillingdon Hall* (1845)—over Corn Law repeal too. Trollope is good on elections, especially over Frank Tregear's canvassing at Polpenno in *The Duke's Children* (1880), where, for all

the massive prestige attaching to Tregear's friend and supporter Lord Silverbridge, the author makes it clear that victory is attributable to the diligence of a local tailor. But only Disraeli could devote a whole novel to a local contest, as he did in partnership with his sister, albeit pseudonymously, in *A Year at Hartlebury, or The Election* by "Cheri and Fair Starr" (republished in 1983, in which year its true authorship was publicly proclaimed).

Related to the dramatic aspect of politics is clearly a fantasy side of sorts, and Disraeli is particularly given to an almost fantasy idealism. For example, although the politician must be shrewd in assessing what is and what is not possible, he also lives by making unfulfillable promises. This element of wishful thinking may account for many political novels; manifestos are mostly too bland to accommodate even the sheer fantasy of a Karl Marx. (Consider the notion of the withering away of the state: pure moonshine.) It is not surprising that the novels of a politician so fertile in expedient as Disraeli should have a fairy-tale flavour. How much easier it is to manipulate characters of one's own creation than real people! So Vivian Grey, the young man on the make, has all the impudence and skill at bluff of Puss in Boots. (Both worked to advance a Marquess of Carabas, although one cannot see Vivian displaying the cat's selflessness.) There are numerous references to fairy tales in other Disraeli novels. Once it is a comparison with Ricquet of the Tuft (like Puss in Boots a Perrault creation.) Sometimes it is merely a comparison with the fairy-tale atmosphere as such. *Endymion* is a sustained fairy tale: one of the poor orphaned twins becomes Prime Minister, the other a queen. And of course Disraeli was fond of referring to Queen Victoria as "the Faery."

For all Disraeli's nostalgia and love of dreams, he could put some of them into effect. It would not be true to say the political ideas expressed in his novels bear no relation to his actions in office. He was a masterly politician who made some of his fantasies come true. This is more than most people do, whether politicians or otherwise, and it is partly why he is so endearing. The harmlessness of his fantasies is an added attraction. Politicians in the 20th century have had nastier ambitions, and those who have come closest to achieving their dreams have been nuisances at best. But in this general respect Disraeli has affinities with Mussolini, whose own venture into literature, *The Cardinal's Mistress* (1909), contains an interesting sub-Stendhalian treatment of the clergy, foreshadowing the author's adroit Papal Concordat of 1929. The essential point is that dictators go beyond conventional politicians in being prepared to act out their most bizarre fantasies. They are just that much less constrained, not so much by reality (for all too appallingly often they achieve their aims), but by that very British phenomenon of good form.

Though nobody could be more democratic than Disraeli, one does feel that there is much of the fantasy-fulfiller in him. Or perhaps it is his more-than-usually exotic imagination, a feature not especially noticeable in other democratic statesmen. The examples are instructive. Disraeli introduces Lord Beaconsfield into *Vivian Grey*—the pert effusion of his extremist youth—and some fifty years later himself chose to become Lord Beaconsfield. Fakredeen in

*Tancred* (1847) urges the queen to sail away to the east and set up her empire there. Disraeli in 1876 made her Empress of India. (Saki, whose references to Disraeli show him too to be under the master's spell, has the royal family choosing Indian exile when the Germans invade Britain in *When William Came,* published in 1914.) *Sybil* ends with the heroine, an "old" Catholic whose surname is Gerard, regaining her family's barony, now called out of abeyance. In 1875 Disraeli created one Sir Robert Gerard, scion of an ancient landed family of Catholic recusants, a peer. But perhaps the truly astounding fulfilment of an early fantasy is the triumph of Disraeli in reaching the premiership at all, considering his youthful bumptiousness and exhibitionism. The other cases are little matters, but climbing to the top of the greasy pole, as Disraeli himself described it, is for a man of his early reputation rather as if the late Kenneth Tynan had ended in Number Ten Downing Street.

How good are Disraeli's novels? The truth is they are both excruciatingly bad and excitingly good. Some are so atrocious as to be unreadable even by a devotee of 19th-century fiction: the second parts of *Vivian Grey* and *Tancred,* nearly all of *Contarini Fleming* and *Venetia* (1837), much of *Henrietta Temple.* The mythological conceits such as *Ixion in Heaven* (1822-23) and *The Infernal Marriage* (1834) and the fable *Popanilla* (1828) are little to modern tastes, but have their moments. *Coningsby, Sybil, Lothair* (1870), and *Endymion,* on the other hand, are novels which only the great masters need be too proud to have written. (Disraeli, incidentally, must be one of the few novelists to win praise from Goethe, Heine, and F. R. Leavis.) It is a pity they are not better known.

Even a minor work such as *The Young Duke* (1831) can attract. It ought, for instance, to appeal to lovers of Balzac. The allusive witticisms of the dandies, so extraordinarily disembodied from any identifiable speaker as to foreshadow the technical experiments of Sybille Bedford and Claude Mauriac, are indeed rather better than that tediously sparkling dinner to which Raphael is haled in *La Peau de chagrin* (1831), though that is not saying much. The combination of high life and money troubles is as irresistible as in Balzac. Oddly enough, Disraeli had not read him at the time. Yet the two have several features in common: both came to mix in aristocratic circles though originally outsiders; both were hopeless about money; both had worked as lawyer's clerks; both looked to mistresses who were mother figures. I confess I even detect a faint whiff of the Carlos Herrera-Lucien de Rubempré relationship in the way Lord Lyndhurst took Disraeli, the fledgling politician, under his wing. But the parallels are chiefly embodied in the way Balzac locates political intrigue in the salon—a characteristic which, because of Balzac's enormous versatility and fecundity, we think of as more typically Disraelian.

Whatever one may say about Disraeli as a pure novelist, it is his political stories that get most attention. This is perhaps unfair considering that *Lothair,* reckoned by some his best work, is scarcely political at all, but rather a psychological study of a young noble trembling between fascination with the Scarlet Woman (Rome) and love for that personification of republicanism Marianne (Theodora). Disraeli preferred the prestige of politics to the praise heaped on authors, which was not of a very high order in his day. We need not repine on his behalf.

Right from the start Disraeli's will to power is overwhelming, and his novels reek of it. *Vivian Grey* is the work of a young puppy impatient for political influence. Yet even *Vivian Grey* forcefully teaches the precariousness of a mere adventurer's stratagems and the insubstantiality of *Château Désir,* that archetypal castle in Spain. Though Trollope usually conveys failure better than Disraeli, even he never catches the bitterness of Vivian at his sudden downfall. And Vivian is more "whole" than Ferdinand Lopez in *The Prime Minister* (1876), whose City speculations are remarkably like the young Disraeli's: the contrast between Lopez's early gloss and the desperado's shifts of the final scenes is too stark to convince.

*Coningsby* and *Sybil* are the works of a maturer careerist, and by the time *Lothair* and *Endymion* were published Disraeli had held the highest positions. Oddly enough, neither book much reflects this fact. Even *Endymion* is more concerned with the hero's social life than with his problems as Foreign Minister and Prime Minister. Yet there is a far greater feel of ambition about these books than in any other English works of political fiction, including Churchill's (the only such novelist apart from Disraeli to achieve supreme office). The predominant impression after a diet of Disraeli's novels is that the early struggles were what the author found most inspiring. Every single one except *Lothair,* which is notoriously untypical, is set during Disraeli's early life.

The political novel has become a genre in its own right since *Vivian Grey.* But was Disraeli an influence which those who came after him were aware of? Even apart from Trollope, who was born about ten years after Disraeli and survived him by a year, there might seem to be the obvious case of Maurice Edelman, with his quasibiographical works of fiction about Disraeli himself. Actually Edelman's contemporary political novels, which are the truer continuation of that tradition, have more in common with C. P. Snow's, and Snow is predominantly heir to Trollope. But, even when apparently antithetical to the Disraelian style, these two 20th-century writers deal with solid plots of manoeuvre in which people play the game according to the rules, and the backdrop of public life is relatively tranquil. It is a world similar to, though less sumptuous than, Disraeli's: debates in the Commons, crises in the Cabinet, intrigue in country houses.

It may well be that this tradition owes more to the continuity of British politics and its seeming security until fairly recently. It is only from the early 1960s that the ground rules of British politics became radically different. Thriller writers such as Bertie Denham and the Douglas Hurd/Andrew Osmond partnership took over. Impatience with fair play, accepted ways of gaining power, and constitutional methods of promoting change were mounting. If one believes that novels reflect a society with an accuracy that is the more acute for being unconscious, then Hurd and Osmond represent a depressing change. Parliamentary drama fades away to nothing. The action tends to be sited in the executive, rather than in the legislature. Moreover, their villains are ensconced in the most exalted of high places: senior army officers, the sovereign's Private Secretary. (After the Anthony Blunt episode, even that may not be wholly inconceivable.)

Disraeli too could write of insurgency and threats to parliamentary sovereignty, though not actual terrorism. The fact that the 1830s and 1840s in the end saw Chartism fade away should not blind us to the genuine apprehensions of contemporaries, although Disraeli does not convey any very convincing feeling of terror among his aristocrats. This may be a literary failure, or it may be that the British tradition of the stiff upper lip forbade any displays of extreme emotion in real life, and Disraeli was simply being faithful to this when he made his characters lament the coming revolution in too insipid a fashion. That said, such scenes are not very numerous.

Since it appears that the mainstream political novelists of the 20th century owe more to Trollope than to Disraeli, it is pertinent to probe further into what Trollope himself felt about Disraeli. Although ultimately a full-time novelist, Trollope did not write his first political work of fiction till the 1860s. Disraeli was therefore the precedent against which Trollope reacted, whether in admiration or disgust. As it happens, Trollope ill conceals his hostility to the older man, but in a way this serves to underline Disraeli's extraordinary ascendancy. Trollope furnishes a waspish little sketch of his fellow-novelist in Mr Daubeny (or "Dubby" as he is familiarly known), and even when writing about someone wholly different can lapse into curiously Disraelian language: "He says he is as good a Conservative as there is in all Herefordshire, only that he likes to know what is to be conserved", or "A drunkard or a gambler may be weaned from his ways, but not a politician", or "The apostle of Christianity and the infidel can meet without a chance of a quarrel; but it is never safe to bring together two men who differ about a saint or a surplice." The first of these quotations, which is from *The Prime Minister,* appeared thirty years after Coningsby had asked the same question.

If one were so disposed, one could level some of the same charges against Trollope as against Disraeli. "Why will Mr D'Israeli be so fond of dukes?" asked Monckton Milnes in his celebrated (but anonymous) *Edinburgh Review* article [of July 1847] (nominally a review of *Tancred* ) on the novels; and "What does Ben know of dukes?" supposedly enquired Ben's father Isaac. One might put such questions to Trollope, who not only devotes many pages to the political activities of the dukes of Omnium and St Bungay, but takes a very long novel to probe into the minutest detail into Omnium's domestic crises in *The Duke's Children.* Disraeli's *The Young Duke,* though frivolous enough, is at least eminently suitable, coming from a future Chancellor of the Exchequer, in that it conveys in fearful terms the perils of an unbalanced Budget, a lesson which could be digested with advantage by today's politicians. The truth is that in Disraeli's day a political novel without dukes would have been rather like one today without terrorists. Early Victorian Cabinets were a tangle of strawberry leaves, but by the time Trollope was writing

(the 1870s and 1880s) such vegetation had become scantier.

One political novelist who was certainly under Disraeli's spell was Churchill, with *Savrola* (1900). For a start the prose style is in places a pastiche of the master's: "She had arrived at that age in life, when to the attractions of a maiden's beauty are added those of a woman's wit." And who can doubt that Churchill had Disraeli's kind of language in mind when he wrote: "The King of Ethiopia, horrified at the low dresses of the unveiled women and dreading the prospect of eating with odious white people, had taken his departure"? Or this: "The supper was excellent: the champagne was dry and the quails fat". A healthy interest in food is typically Disraelian. Churchill even introduces a Countess of Ferrol, recalling the Count of Ferroll in *Endymion.* The tone of *Savrola* displays more than just the sort of unconscious echo of Disraeli observable in Trollope. The whole plot recalls Prince Florestan's triumphal restoration in *Endymion.* In any case it can plausibly be argued that borrowed tricks of style are more flattering than deliberate acts of *hommage* (as it is nowadays fashionable to call mimicry).

Another writer whose work has reminded some critics of Disraeli's is Evelyn Waugh. Waugh was not a practising politician, but he must at one time have contemplated a parliamentary career, for he mentions the possibility in his diary. (He also sought a consular post in Yugoslavia, though more from a sense of duty to his Balkan co-religionists than because of any inclination to assist British foreign policy as a Civil Servant.) Lord Blake has observed that Waugh's early novels are the only examples one can think of which ring with even a faint echo of Disraeli's. But there is more to it than that.

Waugh makes a direct reference to *Coningsby* in a novel of his middle period, *Put Out More Flags* (1942). He slyly compares the dishevelled Basil Seal with Lord Monmouth, who "never condescended to the artifice of the toilet." And he talks of Ambrose Silk exhibiting the swagger and flash of the young Disraeli. It is Waugh's *Black Mischief* (1932) which is the truly political novel, however. So pertinent does its theme remain that had the late Shah of Iran studied it he might have avoided disaster. Be that as it may, who can read about Basil Seal and his impudent plausibility, his personal ascendancy over the poor booby Seth, and their untutored meddling in affairs of state, without recalling Vivian Grey's management of the Marquess of Carabas?

Then there is Waugh's passion for recusant families, so copiously documented in *Brideshead Revisited* (1945) and the *Sword of Honour* trilogy (1952, 1955, and 1961). Disraeli has him flat beat there. In *The Young Duke* there are the Dacres, in *Henrietta Temple* the Armines and Fr Adrian Glastonbury, in *Sybil* the Gerards and the Traffords, in *Coningsby* the Lyles, and in *Lothair* the families of Mgr Berwick and Lord St Jerome.

One might further contrast the tendency of Waugh, the Catholic, gratuitously to people his novels with Jews, mostly exotic ones, against Disraeli's equally gratuitous habit of introducing high-born Catholics. There can be no doubt that Disraeli had a considerable romantic attachment to the idea of beleaguered adherents of the "Old Faith" in penal and early post-penal times, just as Waugh did. Even though Disraeli quarrelled with O'Connell and in some speeches of his hot youth attacked papists with considerable vigour, it was in language that censured loyalty to a foreign power rather than any doctrinal or disciplinary deviance from Anglicanism. In the 1860s Disraeli flirted with the Roman Catholic voters—surely negligible numerically if one discounts the Irish, a group Disraeli did little to cultivate. Why then bother at all but for predominantly emotional reasons? Even the blackening of Manning in *Lothair* should be seen as a revulsion against ultramontanism (and Manning himself) rather than against Roman Catholicism as such. (Some old recusant families looked askance at Manning, come to that.) In *Endymion,* the product of Disraeli's autumn, the Anglican priest Nigel Penruddock, who "goes over" and is made a cardinal, is a noble being: the description of ritualism creeping over Hurstly after Mrs Job Thornberry's like conversion has a sweetly elegiac tone.

It is not too fanciful to assume that the plight of England's Roman Catholics before emancipation awoke the sympathy of a baptised Jew, for Disraeli's own people suffered civil disabilities as well. Further, the cult of Our Lady is bound to have attracted in compensation a male who felt as estranged from his mother as Disraeli did. Yet even here Disraeli could not resist laughing up his sleeve, for Contarini Fleming venerates Our Lady but confuses her with Mary Magdalene. A still more celebrated example of Disraeli's sardonic/affectionate attitude to Mariolatry is Eva's question to Tancred—is he one of those Franks who worship a Jewess or is he one of those that revile her and break her images? And it is worth comparing *Tancred* with Waugh's *Helena* (1950) where Helena's arrival in the Holy Land and her encounter with the Wandering Jew evoke memories of Tancred's encounter with Eva, though the former is written from a Christian angle rather than Disraeli's obsessional insistence that Jewish racial pride is essentially proto-Christianity. It also happens that *Helena* is Waugh's second most heavily political novel, containing fine descriptions of the dismal palace intrigue endemic to autocracy.

I am not for a moment suggesting that Disraeli approaches Waugh as a novelist, but both his books and his politics do at times reflect private preoccupations of a highly idiosyncratic nature. Moreover Disraeli always manages to be entertaining about the bees infesting his bonnet. Lastly, he makes it plain that to him politics is enormous fun. It is in this not unimportant respect that he heads an exclusive little principality inhabited by Churchill and Waugh. To the rest of the breed—Trollope, Edelman, Snow, even Harold Nicolson—statecraft may be satisfying, even rewarding; but it is not seemly to approach it in lighthearted mood.

If we grant that Disraeli is the originator whom Trollope abhors but cannot ignore and sometimes even emulates, can it be said that the two form different faces of a single coin? Or perhaps that they stand for two types of political novelist—the Parliamentarian and the Civil Servant—

between whom subsequent practitioners of the craft oscillate?

Writers of political novels are by no means all involved in politics in the same way. Some are Civil Servants, such as Stendhal. Trollope was at one time a Civil Servant, then briefly a parliamentary candidate, and eventually a professional writer who had gained manly independence by his pen. Harold Nicolson had resigned from the Foreign Office by the time he brought out *Public Faces* in 1932; he did not become an MP till 1935. Presumably Churchill had developed parliamentary ambitions by the time he wrote *Savrola.*

C. P. Snow, on the other hand, despite serving from 1964 to 1966 as a junior Minister in Harold Wilson's first government, never managed to rid himself of a predominantly Civil Service viewpoint. He certainly did not draw on his experience of office for his novels: Lewis Eliot in *Last Things* (1970) refuses a government job. Snow has been cruelly quoted as looking to Civil Service minutes as models for his prose style, and there is a pathetic little scene in *Last Things* where Eliot's former boss Sir Hector Rose proclaims the functionary's intellectual superiority to mere politicians. It amounts to a panegyric on Snow's own clearly indicated preferences in government: an orderly, intelligent mandarinate.

But let it not be thought Disraeli has no picture of the Civil Service in his novels. There is a vignette in *Endymion* where the hero is introduced to his new clerkship in a public office—the only preferment his once powerful father can procure for him. It stands up well to those marvellous pictures the Russian 19th-century novelists give of the bureaucracy, or the atmosphere of Balzac's *Les Employés* (1837).

In contrast to Disraeli, Snow shows extraordinarily little interest in ideas, far less than a stolid clubman such as Trollope. Even when describing what is presumably an early attempt at unilateral nuclear disarmament in *The Corridors of Power* (1964), he never tells us what precisely the protagonist Roger Quaife has in mind. Disraeli's characters are nearly all either reactionary or conservative according to 20th-century criteria yet are ideologically fecund, whereas Snow's are labelled "progressive" (Francis Getliffe) or "reactionary" (G. S. Clark), and that is that. They never discuss political ideas or have an argument about anything as abstract as strategy. Life appears to consist of endless small manoeuvres to advance oneself with people who count—sweetened, it is true, by a praiseworthy respect for hard work and a *petit-bourgeois* tendency to admire "professional people", as well as a genuine kindness to those less fortunate in life's obstacle race. There is just one preoccupation of Snow's which recalls a Disraeli novel: the excited speculation over who made the Athenaeum this time, whom the Royal Society has elected, who is to be the next Master, and the likely outcome of the passage of so-and-so's Bill through the House (never mind what it proposes). Although a more meritocratic world, it is really no different from Lord Monmouth's, Tadpole's and Taper's.

There is therefore a tenuous but genuine tradition of British political novels, and Disraeli, even though his direct influence has spent itself in Churchill or Waugh, remains head of the stream. Yet it is still possible that modern political novelists follow Disraeli in expressing their aspirations and attitudes to constitutional development. One would certainly expect politicians to write for reasons other than mere gain, if only because it must be something of a handicap for a politician to have written a novel at all. It took decades for Disraeli to live down *Vivian Grey*. Writers then were little revered, it is true. Even today, however much he may affect the *gravitas* necessary to a Cabinet Minister (though his awareness of what terrorists can stoop to may be as useful in his present job as Home Secretary as it was when he was Secretary of State for Northern Ireland), there will surely be many who find Douglas Hurd diminished by his forays into literature. Modern politicians' novels and their non-fiction are often intellectually threadbare, so much so as to suggest the whole struggle is indeed little more than a game. In that case they are just as bad as the worst interpretation put on Disraeli, that of Archbishop Tait, who accused him of appearing to treat politics as a "mere play and gambling." At least Disraeli amuses us while he does so.

It may seem that political novels cannot be both good literature and coherent treatises on statecraft. It would be truer to say that unless a novel is good it is unlikely to furnish a good treatise on statecraft. *Black Mischief* says much that is needful about the folly of over-rapid modernisation in the Third World. (Lord Bauer's economic lucubrations are merely a footnote to Waugh, much as Western philosophy is said to be to Plato.) Disraeli's best novels are those which hit off the combination of political programme and artistry most creditably.

It is a pity that politicians now prefer writing thrillers to conventional stories. Possibly they feel safer because nobody looks for messages in a thriller. Actually, Hurd and Osmond's books do have a message: that our rulers are gravely deficient in imagination and quick reactions, while democracy's enemies are unscrupulous and inventive. In a way this is nothing new. Disraeli's novels did not ignore extra-Parliamentary ferment. *Sybil* features Chartist agitation and no fewer than three cases of arson, the last and grandest, at Mowbray Castle, forming the novel's climax. *Lothair* is drenched with conspiracy: in an early chapter Disraeli describes a Fenian meeting and the secret societies pervade the action. Hurd and Osmond are more distressing; they imply that civilisation is fraying at the edges.

Disraeli believed one could only act upon the opinion of Eastern nations through their imagination. As the West becomes less self-confident and less disciplined, imagination may well have its uses in Europe. Neither rulers nor political novelists have even tried to answer Coningsby's question: "What will you conserve?" Still less has the Conservative Party.

Douglas Hurd could try, perhaps. He may have had the imagination necessary for governing the Irish, and the recent riots in Handsworth are sufficiently reminiscent of the insurrections and agitations dealt with by Disraeli in *Sybil* to suggest scope for the new Home Secretary to exercise imagination on the British mainland. Hurd shows

himself sufficiently enterprising to create genuine wealth with strokes of the pen, even if it is only for his own benefit, rather than the specious prosperity which interventionist politicians claim by their wizardry to be capable of producing. Could not he or some other literate politician give us a sequel to Disraeli's novel of ideas? (pp. 46-53)

*Charles Mosley, "Disraeli's Invention," in* Encounter, *Vol. LXVI, No. 1, January, 1986, pp. 46-53.*

**John Vincent (essay date 1990)**

[*Vincent is an English critic and educator. In the excerpt below, he discusses Disraeli's later novels,* Lothair *and* Endymion, *as works that deal primarily with England's aristocracy.*]

The novels *Lothair* (1870) and *Endymion* (1880) are sometimes seen as entertainments, if only because they entertain. They are relaxed; they glitter with knowledge of the great world; they propose no overt doctrine. True enough: they are poetry, a lyrical celebration of the innocence of wealth enclosed in a stable and confident moral order where all is accustomed, ceremonious. Yet such a display of the aristocratic virtues is itself a point of view, a hidden doctrine. Middle-class critics were little pleased by the comparison in *Lothair* between aristocratic serenity, bourgeois anxiety, and priestly worldliness. It is the aristocrat who rises above the deformities of the world, because his function is to *be* rather than to *do;* and yet, by only being, he performs a vital public office in the national life.

The justification of a social class in terms of a sub-Christian spirituality is a risky business; but if Disraeli's fictional aristocracy had less knowledge of the argument of force than in the 1840s, that was because the social landscape had changed. Bathed in popularity, ruling by consent with skill and enjoyment, with fortunes undiluted by plutocracy and undiminished by agricultural depression, the members of the aristocracy were not aware of the economic euthanasia that awaited them. They ruled the freest, richest, most successful nation the world had ever seen; no other class even wished to replace them. Well might they preside over national energy and social repose with guiltless minds. Guiltless, but not untroubled. The question facing a young man of the 1860s was what to believe. Young Lothair, orphaned at an early age, brought up without schooling or companions by a grim Scottish guardian, is just down from Oxford, the heir to great estates. He is a *tabula rasa* for the ideological tumults of the age.

One guardian was a Scottish Calvinist, but the other was a cardinal, not unlike Manning, who had gone over to Gladstone in 1868. Cardinal Grandison in *Lothair* was Disraeli's revenge: a flattering one. On one level, *Lothair* is a no-popery romance, a *Maria Monk* of the upper classes. But Disraeli says more than that Romanism is wily and prelatical and stops at nothing; he adds a weightier argument. The difference between Anglicanism and Romanism was not theological but social. Church and the social order are intimately linked; for a young noble who joined

Rome prevented himself from being a natural leader of the nation, thus exposing it to government by unnatural ones. Old Roman Catholic families like the St Jeromes are portrayed as pious and aesthetically pleasing, but they cannot stand in the same relation to the nation as Anglicans, and hence their virtues are merely private ones. In choosing Rome, a young landowner is choosing not to exercise his public function.

Disraeli's point was a fair one. Romanism did in fact bring exclusion from public life. Young noblemen were at risk: Lord Bute's spectacular reception into the Roman Church in 1868 served as the model for Lothair. Disraeli had no petty sectarian or theological objections to the Roman faith, but his opposition to acts of abdication by the aristocracy was based on a belief that to separate religion from authority led to barbarism. 'The connexion of religion with the exercise of political authority is one of the main safeguards of the civilisation of man.'

The wiles of Rome were only one theme in *Lothair.* There was also the question of which woman was to guide Lothair's path. Lady Corisande, a tender if insipid English rose and a duke's daughter to boot, is first in the field, and, indeed, wins the race in the last furlong. In between, however, she is mainly conspicuous for her forgetability. The second candidate is the nun-like Catholic of an old family who wants Lothair to build Westminster Cathedral. She inspires slightly more respect; but it is Theodora who steals the show. Theodora is a principled revolutionary. She has more in common with the school of Mazzini than of Marx. She is an Italian dedicated to the liberation of Italy. She is a pure, lofty soul, albeit married to an American colonel—an arrangement which did not impede Lothair's adulation of her, for this is no fleshly tale. In real life Theodora was Mrs Jessie White, an Englishwoman who nursed on the battlefields of Italy with Garibaldi. Theodora is conscience without tradition, conscience unshaped by a moral order. She represents modernity, missionariness, the aspiration to regenerate society, and intensity. Her role is to *do,* not to *be.* She symbolizes, perhaps even heads, the forces of change in Europe. She is revolution placed on a pedestal, and found wanting.

For Disraeli, the attractiveness of the revolutionary is his or her goodness; and it is this goodness that must be guarded against. The seasoned revolutionary general, Captain Bruges, appears in *Lothair* as the perfect gentleman. Disraeli had only contempt for pretenders at revolution; of the Irish, Bruges says: 'No real business in them. Their treason is a fairy tale, and their sedition a child talking in its sleep.' The First International is likewise caricatured as the Standing Committee of the Holy Alliance of Peoples: a pot-house talking-shop relishing the rhetoric of extremism. It is the real revolutionary who is serious and good—and should be opposed, because his seriousness and goodness need to live through action.

Disraeli had several reasons for setting up Theodora in order to knock her down. First, he was the Tory leader; he had boycotted Garibaldi's visit to England. Secondly, his nervous temperament, always delicate, produced an exceptional, if intermittent, need for tranquillity which led him to idealize the rural peace of ducal life, sometimes ab-

surdly. When Lady Corisande and her sisters 'asked their pretty questions and made their sparkling remarks, roses seemed to drop from their lips, and sometimes diamonds.'

Disraeli knew well enough that his novels bowdlerized the life of polite society, as his memoirs and letters show. Nobody knew better the dark under-side of high society, or realized how much could not be mentioned in a Victorian novel. His conclusion is none the less what he really felt: that the harmonious torpor of a great landed estate, symbolized by the festivities at Lothair's coming-of-age, where all classes met on a basis of mutual affection and trust, was morally richer and less ambiguous than anything that exertion or merit could supply. Where there is no action, no whiff of the morally imperative, conflict can hardly arise. The message of *Lothair* is that great Victorian theme, the union of hearts in the context of rural and aristocratic values. Modernity is firmly rejected, even in its most attractive form—Theodora; and social optimism is firmly tied to traditionalism.

The critics could not see this. They could not forgive the absence of an elevated tone, by which they meant liberal high-mindedness. What were the author's principles? None that any liberal could see; worse, did not Disraeli mock the very idea of principle? As the young Henry James said, the critics were 'savagely negative'. At worst, they said, *Lothair* is two novels arbitrarily joined: a social comedy of English high society, switching without apology to Mediterranean melodrama. At best, they said, *Lothair* is valuable for its vignettes. The good things in it are its asides.

Disraeli did indeed make some happy inventions. He invented that Wodehousian figure, the glumly tyrannical head gardener. He invented Tory anti-intellectualism with his portrait of the Oxford professor 'who was not satisfied with a home career', and whose 'restless vanity . . . prevented him from ever observing or thinking of anything but himself'. 'Like sedentary men of extreme opinions, he was a social parasite.' Here Baldwin was to continue what Disraeli had begun. Mr Phoebus (drawn from Lord Leighton) happily embodies the frailties of the artistic poseur. Through him, the Oxford professor, and a gallery of revolutionary types, the inadequacies of art, science, and revolution are successively exposed, and, after a few wise authorial words on race and religion from the oriental sage Paraclete, we are free to return to the redeeming virtues of the English landowner. The vignettes are not just vignettes: they are there to lead us to an irresistible conclusion.

Criticism of Lothair himself is misplaced. To Sir Leslie Stephen, the hero was 'a passive bucket to be poured into . . . he is unpleasantly like a fool'. To which one may reply that an Oxford undergraduate, an orphan brought up in solitude, and not a public-school man, may well enter society in undecided mood. The verdict of Stephen, an agnostic Puritan and morose Alpinist, on *Lothair* was characteristically grim: 'a practical joke on a large scale, or a prolonged burlesque'. This perhaps tells us more about Stephen than about Disraeli; and in the twentieth century, when Alton Towers and Trentham, the homes of Lothair and Lady Corisande, form theme parks for the delight of the masses, it is Stephen's earnestness which has faded, and Disraeli's taste for magnificent settings which commands popular enthusiasm.

Politically, *Lothair* did Disraeli no good. Liberals thought it flash, vulgar, and lacking in seriousness; Tories were uneasily reminded that Disraeli was an alien being who kept losing them elections. Commercially, however, it was his most successful novel to date, reaching eight British editions in 1870. By the end of 1876 he had received £6,000 from *Lothair.* In America, 15,000 copies were sold on the first day. Financially, Disraeli's ship had come home at last.

*Endymion,* published in 1880, after Disraeli had lost office, received a publisher's advance of £10,000, the largest of its time. This was not undeserved. If its mood was serenely autumnal, it was not marked by fading power. Two or three of its best passages have passed into the language. Unlike its two predecessors, *Tancred* and *Lothair,* it was not marred by large areas of silliness. What other ex-Prime Minister (Disraeli was then 75) could have produced so happy a work of imagination just before his death? The tone is youthful. The novel not only ends with wedding bells; they intrude regularly into the narrative. Set in English political society between 1827 and 1855, the novel need not be taken as more than light entertainment.

The hero, Endymion, a youth of gentle birth (and not much else) is more of an author's dummy than Lothair. He does not ascend; he is elevated to fulfil the surrogate ambition of those around him. Forced by reduced circumstances to enter life as a government clerk, he is nevertheless raised to the premiership by the determination of his well-wishers. The chief among these is his twin sister, who first enters the Rothschild household as a companion to their daughter, then marries Palmerston, and then, on his death, marries Napoleon III (all, of course, in fictional guise). If that were not enough, another female well-wisher anonymously sends him £20,000 in order that he should have the means to enter Parliament. Truly, we are in fairyland.

The charm of the book, and it is as charming as it is mellow, lies in its sense of period, its grasp of history, and its vignettes of famous persons. Palmerston, Cobden, Manning, Napoleon III, and Bismarck are charitably portrayed; only Thackeray, seen as the most self-centred of social climbers, is harshly mocked. If little is usually said about *Endymion,* it is because it seems so self-explanatory. To most readers it is a story pure and simple, without a message and untouched by thought. It is a political novel without a political revelation; it is indeed a novel about politicians in which politics plays a minimal part, save for shifting the action from one scene to the next.

There is some casual repetition of earlier ideas. Secret societies still rule Europe; women still rule politics; race is the key to history; will overcomes all difficulties; and the Rothschilds, all-wise, are the spiders at the centre of the web. Such views were nothing new; but in *Endymion* Disraeli does not press or develop them. He had recanted nothing: so much is clear. If he had a new point to make, it was that tact and persuasiveness are the supreme politi-

cal qualities. But *Endymion* is not a political novel; it is a society novel. Even more than *Lothair,* it is a study of London society, in the sense of the 'upper ten thousand'. It is in society, Disraeli asserts, that the alliances are made which determine careers. Parliament, by comparison with society, is a shadowy epiphenomenon. In quiet times it is society which makes up the political nation. Those outside London are outside society, and therefore outside politics. Society is St James's, Mayfair, and perhaps even South Kensington, and the country houses that go therewith. It is true, as Disraeli says, that should 'some event suddenly occur which makes a nation feel or think', then 'the whole thing might vanish like a dream'; but barring that, society goes its own way. The adventurer on the lowest rung of society counts for more, and has more opportunities, than the most notable figure (like Dickens) outside society. Society is the real hero of *Endymion;* of all great forces it is the most neglected by students of politics today or yesterday, because they stand outside it and are unaware of its operations.

*Endymion* is about 'the art of creating a career.' Those who create careers are the women: ambitious, virile, ruthless women who wish to make things happen. Rich, powerful, and underemployed, they fulfil themselves by using groups of friends as instruments for determining the fortunes of the next generation. The group of friends, an artificial extended family, is the unit which determines advancement. Sociology, too used to painting with a broad brush, has been so concerned with the character of ruling classes as a whole that it has paid scant attention to the microsociology of advancement: how do individuals get to the top? To Disraeli this was a question of no small interest. His answer was that the advancement of individuals over a lifetime depends on multiple extreme improbabilities. Many of these improbabilities are social: a weekend matters more than a committee, a dinner more than a speech. Society, remarks Schwarz, is like the City or Parliament: a great self-regulating entity, the guarantor of its own health. In the end, its judgement is just; it does not make mistakes.

To those within society, little outside is visible. Though *Endymion* covers the same period as *Sybil,* the condition of England question is notable by its absence, save for one visit to the North. No social doctrine is suggested. Yet in the end there is a contradiction at the heart of *Endymion.* On the one hand Disraeli states that what matters is the world of those who do not work. This was no doubt as true in the 1870s as in the 1830s. On the other hand, *Endymion* is a 'bourgeois novel about succeeding in an aristocratic world.' Like Samuel Smiles, though in a very different context, Disraeli sings the praises of honest toil; he has embraced Victorian values. Those who work, rise in the world. Lord Roehampton (Palmerston) embodies the aristocratic virtues; but in fact he is a workaholic who dies at his desk in the small hours. Job Thornberry (Cobden) and Nigel Penruddock (Manning) rise from humble origins to national greatness: their secret is application. That arduous toiler, Mrs Guy Flouncey, the great social climber of *Coningsby* and *Tancred,* had once been the exception; now, in 1880, her disciplined approach to social success has become the rule. Even Endymion's own ascent, though forged for him by others, could not have been sustained without dull tenacity on his part. Work may even gain a throne, as with Napoleon III, or an authority exceeding that of mere governments, such as Neuchatel (Rothschild) possesses. In **Endymion** all those who succeed, work (including, not least, the great ladies); and upward mobility is there for all who honestly seek it.

Two eras mingle in **Endymion.** The Disraeli of 1880 dwells fondly on the Disraeli of the 1830s, the pet of great ladies; but his eye also falls on a gallery of eminent Victorians who made their own destiny. Young Endymion, who is Disraeli without the genius, is the toy of a benevolent establishment which open-mindedly looks after whatever it comes to see as its own. (pp. 105-12)

> *John Vincent, in his* Disraeli, *Oxford University Press, Oxford, 1990, 127 p.*

---

## FURTHER READING

### Bibliography

Stewart, R. W. *Benjamin Disraeli: A List of Writings by Him, and Writings about Him, with Notes.* Metuchen, N. J.: The Scarecrow Press, 1972, 278 p.
> Includes a list of earlier bibliographies of Disraeli's work and a chronological compilation of his speeches.

### Biography

Blake, Robert. *Disraeli.* London: Eyre and Spottiswoode, 1966, 819 p.
> Acclaimed biography stressing Disraeli's personality and its influence on his novels.

Braun, Thom. *Disraeli the Novelist.* London: George Allen & Unwin, 1981, 149 p.
> Biographical study of Disraeli tracing the development of his career as a novelist.

Davis, Richard W. *Disraeli.* Boston: Little, Brown and Co., 1976, 231 p.
> Emphasizes the political career of Disraeli, whom the biographer describes as a man with "immense charm, great rhetoric, and an unerring political instinct for the feasible."

Maurois, André. "Disraeli and Victorian England." In *Lives of Today and Yesterday: A Book of Comparative Biography,* edited by Rowena K. Keyes, pp. 158-74. New York: D. Appleton and Co., 1931.
> Presents excerpts from Maurois's *Disraeli, A Picture of the Victorian Age* (1928) chosen by the editor to "emphasize [Disraeli's] oddity and his charm."

Monypenny, William Flavelle, and Buckle, George Earle. *The Life of Benjamin Disraeli, Earl of Beaconsfield.* 6 Vols. New York: Macmillan, 1910-1920.
> Definitive biography of Disraeli.

### Criticism

Bewley, Marius. "Towards Reading Disraeli." *Prose* 4 (1972): 5-23.
> Discusses how Disraeli's political career informed his fiction, defending the author against charges that he lacked a sense of history and that his novels were excessively theatrical.

Bivona, Daniel. "Disraeli's Political Trilogy and the Antinomic Structure of Imperial Desire." *Novel* 22, No. 3 (Spring 1989): 305-25.
> Asserts that Disraeli's political novels—*Coningsby, Sybil,* and *Tancred*—embody the imperial ideology that was fundamental to his career as a statesman.

Bloomfield, Paul. *Disraeli,* rev. ed. Writers and Their Work: No. 138. Published for the British Council by Longman Group, 1970, 44 p.
> Presents a critical overview of Disraeli's life and career.

Bodenheimer, Rosemarie. "Politics and the Recovery of Story." In her *The Politics of Story in Victorian Social Fiction,* pp. 166-230. Ithaca, N. Y.: Cornell University Press, 1988.
> Examines Disraeli's *Sybil* in a study of how "the shape and movement of narrative" in mid-Victorian novels expresses a response to social change.

Brantlinger, Patrick. "Tory-Radicalism and 'The Two Nations' in Disraeli's *Sybil.*" *The Victorian Newsletter,* No. 41 (Spring 1972): 13-17.
> Discusses the weaknesses of Disraeli's *Sybil,* exploring the implications of the title character's aristocratic background.

Clausson, Nils. "English Catholics and Roman Catholicism in Disraeli's Novels." *Nineteenth Century Fiction* 33, No. 4 (March 1979): 454-74.
> Evaluates the ambivalence toward Catholicism in Disraeli's novels.

——. "Disraeli and Carlyle's 'Aristocracy of Talent': The Role of Millbank in *Coningsby* Reconsidered." *The Victorian Newsletter,* No. 70 (Fall 1986): 1-5.
> Disputes critical assessments of *Coningsby*'s Millbank as an example of the "aristocracy of talent" discussed by Thomas Carlyle, arguing that Disraeli instead presents Millbank as a man whose limitations preclude his becoming an effective political leader.

Engel, Elliot, and King, Margaret F. "Benjamin Disraeli." In their *The Victorian Novel before Victoria: British Fiction during the Reign of William IV, 1830-37,* pp. 61-86. London: Macmillan, 1984.
> Asserts that Disraeli's novels of the 1830s were "at best interesting failures" due to the author's "inability to create a realistic structure onto which his Romanticism could be effectively grafted."

Fido, Martin. "The Treatment of Rural Distress in Disraeli's *Sybil.*" *The Yearbook of English Studies* 5 (1975): 153-63.
> Discusses Disraeli's depiction of the plight of the rural working class in *Sybil,* noting in particular the author's indebtedness to Edwin Chadwick's *Report on the Sanitary Condition of the Labouring Population of Great Britain, 1842.*

Graham, Peter W. "Byron and Disraeli." *The Victorian Newsletter,* No. 69 (Spring 1986): 26-30.

Evaluates the extent of Byron's influence on Disraeli's literary style, asserting that Disraeli contracted "a full-scale and feverish case of Byronism."

Handwerk, Gary. "Behind *Sybil's* Veil: Disraeli's Mix of Ideological Messages." *Modern Language Quarterly* 49, No. 4 (December 1988): 321-41.

Analyzes the "multiple, even divergent, aims" of *Sybil.*

Hersey, G. L. "Aryanism in Victorian England." *The Yale Review* LXVI, No. 1 (October 1976): 104-13.

Discusses the philosophy of Aryanism and its effect on Disraeli in a review of two books: Leonée and Richard Ormond's *Lord Leighton* and the Oxford University Press edition of Disraeli's *Lothair.*

Himmelfarb, Gertrude. "Social History and the Moral Imagination." In *Art, Politics, and Will: Essays in Honor of Lionel Trilling,* edited by Quentin Anderson, Stephen Donadio, and Steven Marcus, pp. 28-58. New York: Basic Books, 1977.

Includes a discussion of Disraeli's novels in a larger study that addresses the treatment of class and social structure in nineteenth-century English fiction.

Matthews, John. "Literature and Politics: A Disraelian View." *English Studies in Canada* X, No. 2 (June 1984): 172-87.

Provides an overview of Disraeli's early novels in an examination of the author's view of the political process.

McCabe, Bernard. "Benjamin Disraeli." In *Minor British Novelists,* edited by Charles Alva Hoyt, pp. 79-97. Carbondale and Edwardsville: Southern Illinois University Press, 1967.

Evaluates Disraeli's literary career, acknowledging his achievement in making the novel "something intelligently concerned with the spirit of the age."

McCully, Michael. "Beyond 'The Convent and the Cottage': A Reconsideration of Disraeli's *Sybil.*" *CLA Journal* XXIX, No. 3 (March 1986): 318-35.

Analyzes the development of the title character in *Sybil,* concluding that Disraeli "can be credited with considerable success in bringing his principles to life in her character."

Mitchell, Paul. "The Initiation Motif in Benjamin Disraeli's *Coningsby.*" *The Southern Quarterly* IX, No. 2 (January 1971): 223-30.

Asserts that Coningsby's initiation into adulthood and into the world of politics provides the structure and unity of the novel.

Modder, Montagu Frank. "The Alien Patriot in Disraeli's Novels." *The London Quarterly and Holborn Review* 3, series 6 (July 1934): 363-72.

Explores how Disraeli's novels reflect both his status as a Jewish member of English society and his pride in his heritage.

Nettell, Stephanie. Introduction to *Vivian Grey* by Benjamin Disraeli, edited by Herbert Van Thal, pp. vii-xv. London: Cassell & Co., 1968.

Provides a biographical sketch of Disraeli at the time he wrote *Vivian Grey,* discusses the novel's reception, and characterizes it as an entertaining but flawed work.

O'Kell, Robert. "The Autobiographical Nature of Disraeli's Early Fiction." *Nineteenth Century Fiction* 31, No. 3 (December 1976): 253-84.

Offers a psychoanalytic reading of Disraeli's early novels, asserting that they represent a fictional depiction of the author's fantasies.

————. "Two Nations, or One?: Disraeli's Allegorical Romance." *Victorian Studies* 30, No. 2 (Winter 1987): 211-34.

Contends that *Sybil* differs from *Coningsby* and Disraeli's earlier novels in that it is an allegorical rather than a psychological romance.

Oppenheimer, Franz M. "Survival and Ascendancy." *The American Scholar* 61, No. 3 (Summer 1992): 446-52.

Surveys Disraeli's career, includes excerpts from his private correspondence, and briefly discusses his political trilogy.

Rosa, Matthew Whiting. "Disraeli." In his *The Silver-Fork School: Novels of Fashion Preceding "Vanity Fair,"* pp. 99-115. New York: Columbia University Press, 1936.

Discusses Disraeli's prose works from *Vivian Grey* through *Coningsby* as examples of the fashionable novel.

Stafford, William. "Romantic Elitism in the Thought of Benjamin Disraeli." *Literature and History* 6, No. 1 (Spring 1980): 43-58.

Cites passages from Disraeli's novels to support his assertion that Disraeli's political ideas were informed by Byronic romanticism.

Strachey, Lytton. "Dizzy." *The Woman's Leader* XII, No. 24 (16 July 1920): 543.

Denigrates Disraeli as a vain egotist in a review of W. F. Monypenny and G. E. Buckle's *Life of Benjamin Disraeli, Earl of Beaconsfield* (1920).

Weeks, Richard G., Jr. "Disraeli as Political Egotist: A Literary and Historical Investigation." *Journal of British Studies* 28, No. 4 (October 1989): 387-410.

Contends that Disraeli's novels demonstrate the development of his "peculiar psychology, his consuming sense of ambition, and his romantic Young England vision."

---

Additional coverage of Disraeli's life and career is contained in the following sources published by Gale Research: *Dictionary of Literary Biography,* Vols. 21, 55; *Nineteenth-Century Literature Criticism,* Vol. 2.

# José de Espronceda

## 1808-1842

Spanish poet.

### INTRODUCTION

Espronceda is considered one of the most powerful and original Spanish lyric poets of the nineteenth century. In his best known works, *El estudiante de Salamanca* and *El diablo mundo,* impulsiveness and idealism converge with disillusionment and a dark cynicism, reflecting not only Espronceda's links to European Romanticism, but also the social, political, and philosophical uncertainty of his time.

Born near Almenadrajo de los Barros, Espronceda was educated at the Colegio de San Mateo in Madrid, where his training included courses in Latin, French, Greek, English, and ancient mythology, taught by the noted classical scholars José Gómez Hermosilla and Alberto Lista. In 1823, due to a shift of power in the Spanish government, the Colegio was closed by royal order and Espronceda joined Lista's academy for the humanities, where he became a prominent member of the Academia del Mirto, a movement whose purpose was to restore and foster interest in the national poetry of Spain. Two years later, Espronceda, an ardent Republican, joined a group of conspirators known as "Los Numantinos"; he received a sentence of five years imprisonment in the Franciscan convent of Guadalajara for his protests against Spanish political absolutism. According to some biographers, he escaped after four months. It was there that he began his epic poem entitled *El Pelayo,* which also included several poems contributed by Lista. In 1826 Espronceda left Spain for Portugal, where he met Teresa Mancha, the daughter of a Spanish exile, with whom he had a tumultuous love affair that continued long after her marriage to a Spanish businessman. He followed her to London, where he is said to have studied the works of John Milton, William Shakespeare, and Lord Byron, and to have written the poems "La entrada del invierno en Londres" and "A la patria," among others. In 1829 Teresa left her husband and fled to Paris with Espronceda; there, he fought for the libertarian cause on the Paris barricades in the French Revolution of 1830. Under the amnesty act of 1833, Espronceda returned to Spain and received a commission in the Queen's Guards, but he forfeited it by writing a seditious song for which he underwent a brief imprisonment at Cuéllar. He wrote *Sancho Saldaña,* an historical romance in the manner of Walter Scott, while in prison. After years of violent quarrels, Espronceda and Teresa parted, and, in 1839, she died. Following her death, Espronceda described their relationship in the celebrated stanzas entitled "A Teresa"—widely considered his masterpiece—which form a section of his *El diablo mundo.*

The latter work was never completed because of the poet's sudden death in 1842.

Espronceda's poetry is marked by a development from classicism to Romanticism and, finally, to a dark and grotesque form of Romanticism characteristic of his later and more famous works. His early poems were written under the guidance of Lista, and tend to focus on classical themes, celebrating nature in a conventional manner. Critics suggest that Espronceda's Romantic poetry, including the libertarian "A la patria" and the highly individualistic and rebellious "Cancion del pirata," "El verdugo," and "A Jarifa en una orgía," developed in response to Spanish political absolutism. In these works he manifests a Romantic hostility toward the restrictions of society and aspires to individual freedom, idealizing such figures as the pirate, the hangman, the prostitute, and the rebel, all presented as social outcasts protesting the brutality, selfishness, and injustice of organized society. Critics have suggested that the shift in Espronceda's poetry toward a darker form of Romanticism may have been induced by a sudden loss of faith in God or doubting of the validity of reason. For example, the philosophic "Himno al sol," a poem which earned Espronceda widespread praise, contrasts the mutability of human life with the sun's permanence, questioning the nature of existence in a mood of despair. Espronceda's most famous work, *El estudiante de Salamanca,* is a variation on the Don Juan legend dealing with the adventures of Felix de Montemar, a Romantic hero who, in an environment marked by general disintegration, witnesses his own funeral. Commentators agree that the eerie atmosphere and brilliant imagery of this long poem make it one of the most interesting versions of the Don Juan story. Characteristic of works written in the latter portion of Espronceda's career, the poem is marked by bold shifts in meter and rhyme scheme and graphic violence that often leads to the deformity of people and landscapes, contributing a sense of disorder and hinting at the grotesque and the weird. *El estudiante de Salamanca* reflects the influence of French and English poetic models, especially Lord Byron, whose disillusioned view of life and picturesque mingling of misanthropy and idealism strongly influenced Espronceda's verse. This Byronic mood is also evident in the fragment *El diablo mundo,* which deals with the attempt of Adán, or man, to transform woman into a supernatural or spiritual figure. When the woman falls from grace, Adán succumbs to bitter disappointment and despair, illustrating Espronceda's pessimistic concept of love.

Early critical commentary regarding Espronceda tended to focus almost entirely on his life, but modern criticism centers on his style and craftsmanship, addressing particularly his spiritual, psychological, and political beliefs. Although scholars agree that Espronceda's works exemplify Spanish Romanticism, many have also detected elements of modernism in his poetry. E. Allison Peers and Paul Ilie have found that the grotesque visual imagery and distorted presentation of sounds in his works tend to create a surreal atmosphere. Richard Cardwell has asserted that Espronceda's sense of metaphysical separation and solitude has inspired many of Europe's greatest contemporary works: "His work expresses the sense of life on trial . . . , the sense of existential despair and emptiness that pervades the writings of the great European writers of the modern age."

## PRINCIPAL WORKS

*Poesías*  (poetry)  1840
*\*El diablo mundo*  (poetry)  1852

\*This work was written in 1840-41 and includes "Canto a Teresa."

---

### O. Frederica Dabney  (essay date 1895)

[*In the following excerpt, Dabney comments on several of Espronceda's works, praising his choice of subjects and his poetic style.*]

[Espronceda's **'Pelayo'**] is a succession of wonderful pieces, like a few scattered pearls rescued from a broken necklace, the rest of which have rolled into who knows what dusty, obscure corners. . . .

Pelayo is a fine theme for a Spaniard to select as the basis of a narrative poem,—Pelayo, the Gothic hero who began the great work of restoring Spain to the Spaniards, the work ended centuries later by Ferdinand and Isabella. Whatever they may have done to their poor country since she was restored to them,—and they have not always treated her very well,—no one can help sympathizing with the sons of Spain in that great struggle; no one with any poetry in his composition can help his heart swelling with its picturesque romance and grandeur. . . . In Espronceda's **'Pelayo'** it is all painted for us by a master-hand at word-pictures in a language so beautiful that even the merest rhymer cannot help evoking music from it. (p. 547)

[A spirited battle-piece] is the longest consecutive fragment of the poem, every verse of which is a treasure of harmonious and spirited writing. In another fragment, . . . the smooth-flowing verse describes the beauties of a seraglio; only seven of his octave stanzas, but nothing that could charm the senses fails to appear in them. What a contrast in the next eight! A picture of a famine, the horrors so thick on one another that the reader shudders as he reads, until the final touch of a gaunt famine-stricken creature attacked by a vulture, in which bird and man die in the ghastly struggle, is almost too much.

The rest, though up to the mark of the first in phrase, is very disconnected, and consists of various episodes in the great contest of restoration. Espronceda relates, not as a spectator centuries removed from what he describes, but as if he himself had been an actor in the grand tragedy of his country. (pp. 548-49)

Espronceda began only one more great poem, ***El Diablo Mundo.*** Seven cantos were completed, but its plan, as a critic says, was "elastic without measure." Many Spanish poems have been written on such plans to their own detriment and the weariness of the reader. In the opening stanzas—octaves like those of **'Pelayo'**—he promises us nothing less than a picture of the whole world and human society. His hero was to go through all manner of adventures typical of life as the author had found it in the midst of political strife and private dissipation. It shows more maturity of powers, certainly, than the earlier **'Pelayo,'** but the latter is so full of the generous enthusiasm of youth that it contrasts favorably as pleasant reading with the bitterer and more cynical ***Diablo Mundo.***

One of Espronceda's critics has asserted that he took Byron for a model. Whether he did or no, certain it is that the genius of Byron is very closely allied to the spirit of Spanish poetry, and as a consequence, he is one of our poets best known and most admired in Spain. Espronceda lived some time as a political refugee in London, and while there spent his time in the study of English poetry. It was while there that he wrote the exquisite elegy to his country, beginning,—

> How solitary now the nation where one day
>   The multitudes ne'er ended,
> The nation whose omnipotence of sway
>   From East to West extended!

It breathes throughout a pure, sad love for that country. He was even more patriot than poet,—one of those brave, wild spirits natural to Spain, who love their country not always wisely, but too well for their own lives to turn out anything but wrecks in the long, long battle for liberty and a wider life. (pp. 549-50)

Of [his] short lyrical poems . . . , all are worth reading and re-reading. That one beginning,

> Hail, oh! thou night serenest
> Augustly watching o'er the earth,
> And with thy shadows softening
> A mourner's aching dearth,

breathes a spirit of twilight which recalls Gray's *Elegy* most forcibly, though its metrical form is so different. It is written with the favorite assonant or half-rhyme of Spain; the same one on the vowels *u a* is carried through the whole poem.

Then turn to the wild freedom of the pirate's song. We seem ourselves to be rocked on the waves of the broad ocean as he sings:—

> While the thunder
> Roars profoundly,
> And around the
> Winds do rave,
> I can slumber
> Here securely
> Rocking surely
> On the wave,
> For my ship is all my fortune,
> And my God is liberty;
> Wind is my law and my power,
> And my country the wide, wild sea.

With this we may class the Cossack's song, **'The Beggar,'** and **'The Hangman.'** 'To Jarifa in an Orgy,' is an outcome of the natural consequences of the disorderly private life led by our poet, which, no doubt, led to the rapid decline of his health and his premature death. (pp. 550-51)

> *O. Frederica Dabney, "A Son of Spain: José de Espronceda," in* Poet-Lore, *Vol. VII, No. 11, November, 1895, pp. 546-51.*

## Ernest H. Templin   (essay date 1930)

[*In the following excerpt, Templin investigates the elements of Romantic nostalgia in Espronceda's poetry, suggesting that recollections of past happiness coupled with present discontent create the mood of pervasive emptiness and disillusionment in his works.*]

If Espronceda is the "representative man" of Spanish Romanticism, as he was described by Piñeyro, we should naturally expect him to be impregnated with a certain amount of romantic nostalgia. In some writers this refinement of the imagination assumes the form of an incommensurate longing for a something that is not always too clear in the mind of the sufferer ("the desire of the moth for the star"). Others yield themselves up to despair at the mere recollection of past happiness, which has brought them nothing but emptiness and disillusionment. This feeling of despair is frequently, though not necessarily,

seasoned with at least a hint of fresh hopes and illusions, which in turn, if allowed to attain their full development, will only redouble the poet's (or novelist's) nausea and *taedium vitae*. Romantic nostalgia is, then, in many instances, a sort of endless chain whose alternating links are hope and despair. The nostalgic poet is not, however, content to seek the remedy for his ailment in some future happiness, for bitter experience has taught him that it will be inevitably, i.e., fatally, blighted and converted into disillusionment. If no comfort is afforded him by his emotional escapes, he often turns to woman, who in all probability was the primal cause of his nostalgia, to Nature, or even to religion, as occurs in the case of Pierre Loti. Too often the attempt at communion meets a dismal end, thereby aggravating rather than calming the affliction of the Romanticist.

It goes without saying that the ingredients which make up Romantic nostalgia vary from temperament to temperament, according to the imaginative susceptibility of the individual writer. In the case of Espronceda we shall try to make some sort of a diagnosis of the various elements that contribute to the formation of his nostalgia. He is the most thoroughly steeped representative of the Romantic movement in Spain, and offers abundant testimony of his nostalgic penchants in his shorter compositions, as well as in **El estudiante de Salamanca** and **El diablo mundo.**

If we turn to **"A Jarifa en una orgía"** we find one of the most virulent specimens of nostalgia in all Romantic literature. The poet, whom we discover in the throes of despair, calls for wine and the love of Jarifa so as to carouse away his past illusions of truth, virtue, and purity. As he might have expected, he is immediately overcome with disgust, and launches a violent diatribe against the arts and wiles of women: he aspires to a love and a "*deleite divino*" that are not to be had anywhere. He is tortured by his equally burning and vague desire, as well as by the certainty that behind all these pleasures and love-affairs he will find nothing but revulsion and ennui. His uncurbed imagination seeks happiness but finds only doubt, and the virtue and glory which he pursues so avidly turn out to be *hediondo polvo y deleznable escoria*, while at his touch pure women are converted into *lodo y podredumbre*. His eternal and insatiable desire causes him to hate life and trust no other remedy except death ("sólo en la paz de los sepulcros creo"), for life is a torment and pleasure a deception, without happiness or peace of mind for him. Then, curiously enough, he concludes that such is the punishment God metes out to those who seek to pry into the secrets of truth—a thought that recalls to a certain extent the scene in Scott's *William and Mary* where the latter perishes for not "revering the doom of heaven." The poem ends with a bitter self-plea for a hardened susceptibility, a "*letargo estúpido*" that will narcotize suffering and transform it into painless unreality.

A similar emotional strain runs through the intensely personal **"Canto a Teresa."** In fact, these magnificent octaves are the expression of a torrential nostalgia for a vanished

> ensueño de suavísima ternura . . .
> de amor la llama generosa y pura . . .

Gone are the golden hours of innocent passion, a passion

so centrifugal that it led the poet to embrace the universe itself within his ego. The illusion collapses, and the idealized Teresa forfeits her "purity," like a "fallen angel": Espronceda is left with nothing but rankling memories and the *tumba,* and little it avails him to reflect that love has only been adoring love, and that (with Wordsworth, perhaps) his suffering may be

> Memoria
> acaso triste de un perdido cielo,
> quizá esperanza de futura gloria.

He does find a grain of consolation in the afterthought that Teresa is happier now in death, since death alone can allay her sorrows. The mood shifts to pity, both for her and for himself, and passes through a reproachful despair to the sardonic grimace of the last two stanzas:

> Mi propia pena con mi risa insulto,
> y me divierto en arrancar del pecho
> mi mismo corazón pedazos hecho.
>
> Gocemos, sí; la cristalina esfera
> gira bañada en luz: ¡ bella es la vida!
> ¿ Quién a parar alcanza la carrera
> del mundo hermoso que al placer convida?
> Brilla radiante el sol, la primavera
> los campos pinta en la estación florida:
> truéquese en risa mi dolor profundo . . .
> Que haya un cadáver más, ¡ qué importa al
> mundo!

Albeit the poet would seem to welcome death as the sole panacea for his multiple woes, he really entertains a healthy dread of both death and old age, which itself may be taken as a sort of death in life. An instance of this attitude is found in *El diablo mundo,* when the aged Adam bemoans the happiness and youth that lie behind him, for he realizes that death is slowly but inexorably advancing to claim him as its own. In another part of the poem Espronceda, speaking for himself, laments having reached the age of thirty:

> ¡Malditos treinta años,
> funesta edad de amargos desengaños

and bids farewell to love and youth:

> ¡Ah! para siempre adiós: mi pecho llora
> al deciros adiós: ¡ ilusión vana!
> Mi tierno corazón siempre os adora,
> mas mi cabeza se me vuelve cana.

It is, therefore, only natural that the rejuvenated Adam, the symbol of mankind as viewed by a Romanticist, should taste disillusionment at every turn in his life: the salient example is the love-affair with La Salada, the *manola,* which, incidentally, Espronceda has painted with what may be termed a nostalgic vividness. The stupidity and insensibility of the world of men also contribute to the blasting of Adam's hopeful aspirations, until he could well repeat a passage that occurs earlier in the epic:

> Delirio son engañoso
> sus placeres, sus amores,
> es su ciencia vanidad,
> y mentira son sus goces:
> ¡sólo verdad su impotencia,
> su amargura y sus dolores!

Although this pessimistic nihilism is the logical reaction to the rebuffs of experience, Adam cannot be considered as a perfect victim of nostalgia since his rejuvenation constitutes a violent rupture between the painful recollections of the past (the Adam of Canto I) and the illusions contained in the future (the fledgling youth). The more customary sufferer from nostalgia exhibits simultaneously varying traces of both stages of the "malady."

Passing now to the phase of Espronceda's relations with external Nature that interests us, there would seem to be less communion than in other Romantic poets and novelists. Certain of his lyrics may be profitably read in this connection, such as **"A una estrella,"** which, however, reveals more community of feeling than communion with the star. The poem in which he appears to have established a genuinely "working" communion with Nature is the *romance* entitled **"A la noche."** The opening lines are as follows:

> Salve, o tú, noche serena,
> que el mundo velas augusta,
> y los pesares de un triste
> con tu oscuridad endulzas.

Night falls on a bucolic setting reminiscent of Lamartine, while the shepherd and plowman return home:

> Todos süave reposo
> en tu calma ¡oh noche! buscan,
> y aun las lágrimas tus sueños
> al desventurado enjugan.
>
> ¡ Oh qué silencio! ¡Oh qué grata
> oscuridad y tristura!
> ¡Cómo el alma contemplaros
> en sí recogida gusta!

After a delightful description of the placid moonlight scene, he closes the poem thus:

> ¡ Oh! salve, amiga del triste,
> con blando bálsamo endulza
> los pesares de mi pecho,
> que en ti su consuelo buscan.

More frequently Nature offers a chill rebuff to any attempt at communion on the part of the poet. In the sonnet with which he dedicates his verse he bewails the saddening effect of stern reality upon the creations of his fantasy, and adds these lines:

> Los ojos vuelvo en incesante anhelo,
> y gira en torno indiferente el mundo,
> y en torno gira indiferente el cielo.

The same thought, expressed in almost identical language, occurs in **"El ángel y el poeta":** he infers, however, from the impassibility of Nature that his lamentation is but a part of the eternal torment and agony of the cosmos. He hears every grain of sand, every plant, and every living creature pour forth its grief and bitterness, while

> Las aguas de las fuentes suspiraban,
> las copas de los árboles gemian,
> las olas de la mar se querellaban,
> los aquilones de dolor rugian.

In *El estudiante de Salamanca* a further aspect of this sentiment presents itself, when the impassibility of Nature is mentioned in the same breath with the indifference of humankind, which, as we have already noted, left a trace in *El diablo mundo:*

> Miró sus suspiros llevarlos el viento,
> sus lágrimas tristes perderse en el mar,
> sin nadie que acuda ni entienda su acento,
> insensible el cielo y el mundo a su mal . . .
>
> Y ha visto la luna brillar en el cielo
> serena y en calma mientras él lloró,
> y ha visto los hombres pasar en el suelo,
> y nadie a sus quejas los ojos volvió . . .

An additional variety of Espronceda's nostalgia is the homesickness that plunged him into bitter thoughts, specifically during his sojourn in London. In the elegy **"A la patria,"** the emphasis is not merely on the exile's personal sufferings, but also on the deplorable plight of the Spain that he conjures up in his imagination. Espronceda, the Romantic poet, identifies in a sense his lot with that of his native land, for both have lived their Golden Ages, and both are now rent with reminiscential heartaches. In **"La entrada del invierno en Londres,"** attributed to our poet, the dreary and forbidding London winter leads him into fond memories of home and springtime with its *cantos de amores.* It was there—in far-off Spain—that he "felt the flame of his first love," and celebrated *"la Patria"* and *"la Libertad,"* until hypocrisy and treason drove him into banishment. He bids adieu to his *lares queridos* and adds that nothing remains for him to do except to weep and rue his misfortune, which he feels to be irremediable. His homesickness finds a parallel in the plaint of **"La cautiva,"** who is, likewise, a victim of frustrate love:

> No hallan mis ojos mi patria;
> humo han sido mis amores;
> nadie calma mis dolores,
> y en celos me siento arder.
>
> ¡Adiós, patria! ¡adiós, amores!
> La infeliz Zoraida ahora
> sólo venganzas implora,
> ya condenada a morir.

(pp. 1-6)

*Ernest H. Templin, "The Romantic Nostalgia of José de Espronceda," in* Hispania, *Vol. XIII, No. 1, February, 1930, pp. 1-6.*

## E. Allison Peers   (essay date 1941)

[*In the following excerpt, Peers examines the implied moral and emotional meanings of the imagery of light, color, and darkness in Espronceda's* El estudiante de Salamanca.]

Of the three principal poets who represent the Romantic Movement in Spain, two—Rivas and Zorrilla—make frequent and often effective use of images of colour. The third—Espronceda—though also more of a colourist than is commonly supposed, depends for his effects much more commonly on imagery of light and darkness. . . . [He] was attracted by it at a very early stage in his career, experimented with it in his short poems, and had acquired a mastery of it by the time he began *El Estudiante de Sala-*

*manca* (1839), the work in which he employed it with the greatest skill. Though it occurs also in *El Diablo Mundo,* it is there used . . . with very much less effectiveness. This [essay] attempts only to examine Espronceda's use of light-imagery in *El Estudiante de Salamanca.*

The first "part," or canto, of the poem, has the three-fold object of creating its distinctive atmosphere or emotional tone, of describing the scene of its action and of presenting its two principal characters, Don Félix de Montemar and his unhappy victim, Elvira. The task, which is accomplished with considerable skill, involves the use of two devices to which Espronceda had for some time been applying himself. One of these is metrical variety: the lessons learned through the experiments made in the short poems are now for the first time utilized in a work of substantial length. The other is the handling of imagery of light and darkness.

The atmosphere of a poem was never more effectively conveyed in six short lines than in the opening lines of *El Estudiante de Salamanca.* Darkness (lines 1, 4), mystery (line 3), supernatural influences (lines 5-6) and the impressiveness and glamour of tradition (line 2): each of these suggestions is, in the first place, lightly indicated, and then, as the reader comes increasingly under the author's spell, impressed upon him with greater intensity. Darkness, however, is the predominating element: "lóbrega . . . la tierra"; "las densas tinieblas"; "el cielo . . . sombrío":

> Y allá en el aire, cual negras
> fantasmas, se dibujaban
> las torres de las iglesias,
> y del gótico castillo
> las altísimas almenas.

Then, from amid the shadows, is picked out the form of a man, to be lost again in the shadows almost immediately:

> Y en la sombra
> se perdió.

The scene of the action emerges from the darkness no less uncertainly, but here, for the first time, is introduced the theme of light, and we have the first of the many light-and-darkness pictures, of a purely descriptive kind, which form perhaps the most characteristic artistic feature of the poem. The midnight gloom of the Calle del Ataúd, "siempre oscura,"

> cual si de negro crespón
> lóbrego eterno capuz
> la vistiera,

is lit only by the lamp above an image, the light of which, though it is on the point of expiring, is yet sufficiently strong to glance ("lanzó vivo reflejo") upon the unsheathed sword of the muffled figure as it passes. Then follows one of Espronceda's favourite moon images, introduced boldly but not allowed to disperse the effect of mist and shadow which it is the poet's care to create.

It is against this typically Romantic background that Espronceda, with the utmost vividness, presents his two principal personages. Don Félix de Montemar is outlined sharply, by means of precise diction, a profusion of epithet and another characteristic change of metre, without the aid of any kind of visual imagery. Elvira, on the other hand, portrayed in rather more conventional language, is introduced in a stanza almost entirely compounded of light-images and words suggestive of light:

> Bella y más pura que el azul del cielo,
> con dulces ojos lánguidos y hermosos,
> donde acaso el amor brilló entre el velo
> del pudor que los cubre candorosos;
> tímida estrella que refleja al suelo
> rayos de luz brillantes y dudosos,
> ángel puro de amor que amor inspira,
> fué la inocente y desdichada Elvira.

In the four stanzas which follow, this impression is intensified:

> Su corazón se abría,
> como al rayo del sol rosa temprana. . . .
>
> Del cielo azul al tachonado manto,
> del sol radiante a la inmortal riqueza,
> al aire, al campo, a las fragantes flores,
> ella añade esplendor, vida y colores.
> . . . . . .
> Fueron sus ojos a los ojos de ella
> astros de gloria, manantial de vida.

As a result of this treatment of the characters the clearest impression left upon the sensitive reader is that of the radiant figure of the wronged Elvira standing out against a background of pitch-darkness: the moral significance of this may or may not strike him, but it seems unlikely that, at this point, the author intended it to do so. From a purely artistic standpoint, the effect of the first canto is undoubtedly that of darkness gradually giving place to dawn, and of the sun appearing at first timidly among the clouds and then ("astro de gloria") flooding the whole world with its brilliance. So strong does this impression grow when one has become really familiar with the first canto that I have sometimes wondered if, when Espronceda planned its construction, the desire to create this effect was not uppermost in his mind.

The second canto, unintelligently introduced by a meaningless epigraph from Byron, describes Elvira's decline and death. It makes full use of light-imagery, though also appropriately laying stress upon the theme of virgin whiteness. Those who set store by statistical evidence in matters of this sort will perhaps be surprised to learn that in the 255 lines of the canto, of which 207 are descriptive or reflective, the word *blanco* occurs only five times, and that, except for a single mention of the acacia flower, there are no other references to objects inseparably associated with the colour white. This fact illustrates the unsatisfactoriness of the statistical approach to questions of artistry. But the effect of the few passages just referred to is indescribably enhanced by the constant occurrence of such words as *cándido, trasparente, cristal, gasa, alba, alborada, lava, pureza virginal,* and still more so by the profusion of words and phrases, including five separate references to the moon, suggestive of light. Typical of a large number are: *lucero, naciente luz, cándida mañana, luz del día, argentado río.* No useful result, however, could be attained by cataloguing these. There is no method of measuring the de-

grees of intensity with which light-impressions may be conveyed in words, nor is it possible to assess the effect produced by the grouping of images, by the use of contrast and by the reinforcement of images with phraseology which, though not itself descriptive or even suggestive of light, is given a force of this kind by its context. In this second canto of *El Estudiante de Salamanca* there are many such cases. "Al resplandor de la luna," for example, is a conventional phrase making hardly any visual impression at all. Definition and force are given to it by the addition of words not themselves suggestive of light: "entre franjas de esmeralda." Similarly, the almost meaningless "el arroyuelo de plata" takes life with the addition of an adjective of light, and form with the addition of a noun:

> el arroyuelo,
> fúlgida cinta de plata.

Finally, a composite and striking whole, bathed in light to an extent quite unpredictable by any enumeration of its component elements, is obtained by the fusion of the two partial pictures:

> Deslízase el arroyuelo,
> fúlgida cinta de plata,
> al resplandor de la luna,
> entre franjas de esmeralda.

By the use of these devices, and with a clear impression in his mind, we may be sure, of the effect which he desires to convey, Espronceda succeeds in describing his heroine's sad fate in terms of virginal whiteness and of soft diffused light. The scene is in a moonlit garden, described in eight introductory quatrains, which present a complete and vivid contrast to the opening lines of the preceding canto. In this garden is a white figure ("Blanca silfa solitaria"; "Blanco es su vestido"): it is Elvira, plucking flowers to pieces as she walks along. As visual imagery is reinforced by auditory, description gives place to reflection, and amid a profusion of figures of all kinds—the clouds of dawn, fallen leaves swept along by the wind, land devastated by the eruption of a volcano, and so on for several pages— there emerge two, not only more vivid than the rest, but of especial relevance as relating directly to Elvira. Both are images of light. First, her life is compared to a crystal lantern—"un fanal trasparente de hermosura"; then, to a crystal cup in which are mirrored the "rich colours" of sunlight: each is shattered to pieces by human passion.

Here, since the beauty of both cup and lantern is inherent in their transparency we seem to be glancing at the theme of light once more from a symbolic angle. The same suggestion recurs in the reminiscent stanzas which follow; but, in the final quatrain of the canto, describing Elvira's tomb, we return to the purely picturesque.

In the whole of the third canto, which is in dramatic form, and describes Don Diego's challenge to Don Félix, there occurs only one image of light, but in the fourth and last, which is about as long as the other three put together, light-imagery is utilized to the utmost. We are again in the Calle del Ataúd; Don Félix, having slain Don Diego, is standing over his body; and the flickering lamp of the first scene has at last gone out, leaving the "mysterious street" enveloped in darkness. Wrong, in short, has again triumphed over right, and the fact is expressed symbolically by means of imagery.

Then, with the appearance of the "fatídica figura envuelta en blancas ropas," comes the second of the main contrasts in the poem between light and darkness. But, whereas the first, spread over two cantos, was not immediately apparent, the second is more startling and more intense. Light now appears in the very midst of darkness; good challenges evil, and that unmistakably. A second duel—and a duel to the death—is about to begin—not, this time, in the material sphere, but in the moral.

The apparition, key-note of this fourth canto, is fundamental to this conception of the poem and the author spends much care upon his attempt to make it impressive:

> Flotante y vaga, las espesas nieblas
> ya disipa, y se anima, y va creciendo
> con apagada luz, ya en las tinieblas
> su argentino blancor va apareciendo.

As it recedes, it resembles a point of light, looking to Montemar like a "wandering star revolving in the expanse of the heavens" and making him doubt the testimony of his own sense of sight. As he blasphemes with more than ordinary audacity, the light above the shrine re-kindles itself and reveals the kneeling figure of a woman. It is a woman in white—artistically, we have once more the virginal motif of the second canto—"la blanca dama," clad and veiled in white: "velada en blanco traje . . . cándido lino." Discovered, as she is, kneeling at the shrine, she is to be identified more closely than before with the concept of good. Montemar, impelled by the spirit of evil, seizes the lamp and holds it to her face. But the lamp goes out; the woman rises; and, as she moves away—like the illusion of hope, remarks the poet in a Byronic aside—pure picturesqueness regains the ascendancy, and Espronceda's favourite moon-image is requisitioned once more:

> Su forma gallarda dibuja en las sombras
> el blanco ropaje que ondeante se ve,
> y cual si pisara mullidas alfombras,
> deslízase leve sin ruido su pie.

> Tal vimos al rayo de la luna llena
> fugitiva vela de lejos cruzar,
> que ya la hinche en popa la brisa serena,
> que ya la confunde la espuma del mar.

And now follows the pursuit of light by darkness, of the "blanca figura" by the libertine, which continues until practically the end of the poem. The emotional tone rises from the almost colloquial language of Don Félix' address to the phantom ("Y perdonadme, senora . . . "), to the scene in which the narrative reaches its horrible climax. In the main we have here a display of pure artistry—the enhancement and diversifying of the author's light-effects (of colour there is almost none) with the most varied devices.

The narrative of the pursuit and its sequel divides into two nearly equal parts, separated by a descriptive passage in *octavas.* The first part brings pursued and pursuer to the door of the house of death. The intermediate passage ends with Montemar's address to the phantom ("Diablo, mujer o visión . . . "). The final part, which, except for a *coda*

of three stanzas in *octavas,* concludes the poem, comprises the famous *escala métrica* and describes the ghostly marriage of the libertine and his victim and the libertine's death. Throughout the fourth canto a large part of the artistic effect is derived from its metrical skill, surpassed nowhere in Espronceda and perhaps nowhere in the Spanish Romantics. It is this, in particular, that is primarily responsible for the rapidity and the sureness of touch with which the poem moves to its climax. But the tone and atmosphere are still to a great extent conditioned by the varied use made of the motifs of darkness and light.

During the pursuit, the scene is plunged into darkness: "noche de nieblas"; "noche borrascosa"; "melancólico arenal, sin luz." Ahead, all the time, glides the phosphorescent phantom—"la blanca fantasma":

> La blanca figura su pie resbaló,
> cual mueve sus alas sílfide amorosa
> que apenas las aguas del lago rizó.

> En tanto Don Félix a tientas seguía,
> delante camina la blanca visión,
> triplica su espanto la noche sombría,
> sus hórridos gritos redobla Aquilón.

To diversify this effect of simple contrast between purity and vice and to enhance the impression produced by the rapid narrative and dialogue, Espronceda calls in the horrible and the grotesque: clumsily dancing spectres salute the pursuer; weathercocks incline before him; the echoes of the bells repeat his name. At one point the lightning-flashes which illumine the "negras masas" of the silent buildings disclose new terrors:

> Se remonta ante sus ojos
> en alas del huracán,
> visión sublime, y su frente
> ve fosfórica brillar
> entre lívidos relámpagos
> en la densa oscuridad,
> sierpes de luz, luminosos
> engendros del vendaval.

Then passes the ghostly funeral, a new contrast of light and darkness—the "cien luces" revealing, first, the "enlutados bultos," and next, the "blanca dama" on her knees. To the accompaniment of the same impression the journey recommences:

> Las aves de la noche se juntaron,
> y sus alas crujir sobre él sintió:

> Y en la sombra unos ojos fulgurantes
> vió en el aire vagar que espanto inspiran,
> siempre sobre él saltándose anhelantes:
> ojos de horror que sin cesar le miran.

In the *octavas* which, to the accompaniment of mystery and horror, describe the house of death, light still strives with darkness. The doors, opening in response to a "misterioso impulse" unconnected with human agency, reveal a deserted hall, on the walls of which a "lánguida luz y cárdena" is shed by yellow candles, resembling funeral tapers. Strange shadows, distorted by the flickering candles, lurk around the lofty galleries, and in them are set deep, glowing eyes. We are now plunged into pure Romantic picturesqueness ("todo vago, quimérico y sombrío"); and, though the "blanco manto" of the "blanca misteriosa guía" is always visible, her symbolic value seems to be forgotten, whilst the author's imagination plays with the effect of her draperies against the black marble floors and balustrade. They . . . suggest smoke rising from incense or a moonbeam striking a dark hillock. Down the "eterna espiral" of the winding staircase of black marble Montemar follows the "mágica visión del blanco velo," and neither he nor the reader can be surprised, when they reach the bottom, to discover the "blanca dama" seated at the foot of a "negro solemne monumento." Now that the contrast is losing its symbolic significance, we find that the effect of it, like so many Romantic effects, is becoming rather childish.

But any such impression that one may be forming is at once forgotten with the abrupt change of the metre from *octavas reales* to *quintillas* as the libertine interrogates the "blanca visión," while the succeeding passage—the *escala métrica*—throws the emphasis on rhythmical rather than on pictorial interest. For the first time in the poem, the darkness-and-light motif is cast aside. Why so? One might conjecture that the author was afraid of over-emphasizing his contrast, which had long since been indelibly impressed upon the reader's mind. Or it may be that for him, as probably for most careful readers of the poem, whatever force it had lay in its symbolism, and this, as we have seen, has been fast degenerating into picturesqueness. Or again, as the poem neared a climax the effect of which Espronceda was doing his utmost to accentuate, the introduction of a more startling motif became necessary—and this last view is supported by the nature of the devices which accompany the *crescendo* and the *diminuendo* of the *escala métrica*. The effect of the visual imagery is, as has happened once before in the poem, enhanced by auditory imagery, itself gathering force as it proceeds: complaints of love, sighs of anguish, languid music, the murmurs of memory, sepulchral echoes, raging winds, dashing waves, mountain thunder—all this and much more:

> todo en furiosa armonía,
> todo en frenético estruendo,
> todo en confuso trastorno,
> todo mezclado y diverso.

When this infernal symphony has died, appear a hundred skeleton-like spectres, forming around the libertine as the phantom lady takes his hand. Though she is still "la visión del blanco velo," the imagery now used of her is not so much visual as tactile:

> Y era su tacto de crispante hielo,
> y resistirlo audaz intentó en vano:

> Galvánica, crüel, nerviosa y fría,
> histérica y horrible sensación,
> toda la sangre coagulada envía
> agolpada y helada al corazón. . . .

Throughout the rest of the grisly scene, the author finds such pictorial effect as he needs in the grotesque and the horrible, which indeed well suit his theme. Much of it, nevertheless, is extremely crude, and at one point—the approach of the skeleton to Montemar—even ridiculous. But once more the situation is saved by an abrupt change of metre and we are swept up into the "furioso veloz re-

molino" of the "aérea fantástica danza"—the dance of death—in which, though the grisly element is forgotten, vigour and rhythm set the pace, until, his soul still untamed but his body exhausted, Montemar's life comes to a close. In all the three hundred lines of the *escala métrica*, there occur only three light-images, two of which are scarcely more than conventional. The third, which illumines the final moment of the narrative, recalls the light above the street-shrine which flickered into life and then expired—it is the image of a flame leaping up and dying again in the darkness as the libertine's soul passes away.

To regard *El Estudiante de Salamanca* purely as a study in black and white or in light and darkness would of course be to take a completely one-sided view of it. When one contrasts the poem, however, with other and more substantial versions of the legend upon which it is built, it is impossible to treat it seriously from any standpoint save that of form. It will live, longer in all probability than any of its author's other works, as the most nearly perfect example of the longer narrative poem produced by the Romantic Movement in Spain. Less spontaneous than many, more seriously marred than some by conventionalities, it yields to none, if taken as a whole, in excellence of form. The greater part of it owes its character to nothing so much as its use of the imagery of light and dark.

Whether or no any or all of the reasons suggested for the condonment of this motif in the second half of the last canto be correct, it cannot be doubted that, down to the beginning of the *escala métrica*, Espronceda intended this to be one of its major characteristics. Colour, in experiments with which he dabbled, not too successfully nor, apparently, with any great enthusiasm, both in the earlier short poems and in the later *Diablo Mundo*, he almost entirely rejected in the *Estudiante de Salamanca*, concentrating all the pictorial efforts upon the representation of light and darkness. Those who prefer word-artistry to narratives about libertines will like to think of this as of a unique example of that art in which a master in it reached his highest level. (pp. 199-209)

> *E. Allison Peers, "Light-Imagery in 'El Estudiante de Salamanca',"* in Hispanic Review, *Vol. IX, No. 1, January, 1941, pp. 199-209.*

## Bruce W. Wardropper    (essay date 1963)

[*An American scholar, Wardropper has established himself as an authority on Spanish literature through his extensive studies of the classical Spanish theater and Spanish lyric poetry. He is the author of* Introduction al teatro religioso del Siglo de Oro *(1953) and a contributor of several scholarly articles to periodicals. In the following excerpt, Wardropper analyzes Espronceda's* "Canto a Teresa" *in the context of Spanish literary history, focusing on themes drawn from the elegiac tradition.*]

The modern reader, inured to poetic sensationalism by a century of poetry designed to *épater le bourgeois,* still cannot fail to be shocked by Espronceda's **"Canto a Teresa."** Two things above all are hard to stomach: the gratuitous blasphemy of the final stanzas, and the poet's condescending vituperation of the fallen woman whose plight he did so much to bring about. In these details we see Espronceda cast in his self-appointed role as an iconoclast. But the **"Canto a Teresa,"** if one examines it carefully, is perplexing not because it is intolerant of conventional attitudes but because, being the work of a well-known rebel, it is at the same time so traditional in feeling and execution.

According to Espronceda, this elegy, parenthetically inserted into *El diablo mundo* to form its second canto, is nothing more than 'un desahogo de mi corazón'. The reader is invited to skip it 'sin escrúpulo, pues no está ligado en manera alguna con el poema'. The meaning of this is, clearly enough, that Espronceda wrote the canto for therapeutic reasons, sacrificing his art to his need for spiritual health. Like Lope de Vega and Cadalso before him he decided to reduce his personal chaos to order by means of the discipline that only artistic creation could impose. The effort of resolving conflicting emotions, turbulent thoughts, pity for oneself and grief over another's tragic fate could best be channelled by the composition of a poem. So Espronceda, the rebel in poetry, is obliged to seek in art the solace of what he was rejecting: order, control, tradition. Though he might affect not to believe it, art consists of precisely this effort: the attempt to discover new meaning for the raw material of human life by forcing it into the strict mould of form. The therapeutic by-product ironically turns out to be the iconoclast's masterpiece. Poetic tradition served its despiser well.

Espronceda chose as his mould the dignified *octava real,* the metre in which gentlemen and royalty speak in the Golden Age theatre, and the verse form selected by the epic poets of the Renaissance for their most ambitious works. Into it he poured not just his sobs and groans but also some language of classic excellence, reminiscent of the great lyric tradition of Spain. When he refers to the pleasure he once took in the life of the world—'¡Oh! Cuán süave resonó en mi oído / El bullicio del mundo y su ruido' (verses 1522-23), the poetry of Fray Luis de León echoes, however distorted in meaning, in the mind's ear. The line 'Truéquese en risa mi dolor profundo' (1850) reflects perversely Nemoroso's expression of grief in Garcilaso's First Eclogue. When we read the passage

> y las rosadas
> Tintas sobre la nieve, que envidiaron
> Las de mayo serenas alboradas (1677-79)

we are reminded of Góngora, not simply because of the daring hyperbole, but especially because of the poetic world which it evokes, a world in which beauty is enhanced by the rivalry and envy of its components. At the end of the **"Canto a Teresa"** the opening theme of Góngora's *Primera Soledad* is condensed into the words 'la primavera / Los campos pinta en la estación florida' (1848-49), and the idyllic nature of the Baroque poet is briefly revived before it is shattered with the final dissonant line: 'Que haya un cadáver más, ¡qué importa al mundo!' (1851).

In addition to recalling the language of the poetic past Espronceda does not hesitate to fall back on the *topoi* of earlier poetry. The *carpe diem* theme of the Renaissance suits his love elegy so well that he uses it and alludes to it re-

peatedly. Teresa, in her state of innocence, was 'sobre tallo gentil temprana rosa' (1671). But time wreaks its vengeance on beauty for the Romantic poet just as it did for Garcilaso or Góngora:

> ¡Oh! ¿Quién, impío,
> ¡Ay! agostó la flor de tu pureza? (1692-93)

There is of course a difference. In the Renaissance and the Baroque the destroyer of beauty is old age and death, death which comes so swiftly. 'Hoy comamos y bebamos / que mañana moriremos,' sing the shepherds of Juan del Encina. 'Ayer naciste y morirás mañana,' Góngora (if it was he) begins his sonnet to a rose. For Espronceda the beauty of Teresa is already destroyed some time before death overtakes her. Her fall from grace—the lover's, not God's grace—made her loathsome. Death is merely a rounding off of the spiritual deflowering of Teresa once her purity was lost.

> Las rosas del amor se marchitaron,
> Las flores en abrojos convirtieron,
> Y de afán tanto y tan soñada gloria,
> Sólo quedó una tumba, una memoria (1736-39).

The other great theme of the past which Espronceda exploits is the *Ubi sunt?,* so proper to the elegiac and the macabre traditions. In the fifteenth century Jorge Manrique had transformed this *topos* by bringing it up to date—he asked not with Villon where 'Flora la belle Romaine' was, but where the late King John—and by evoking existential reality with it—'¿Qué se fizieron las damas, / sus tocados, sus vestidos, / sus olores?' Espronceda too would handle the theme with the apparent ease of an innovator. For him time is not, as it was for Jorge Manrique, an exterminator, an agent of death; it is the stuff of life. If the traditional question 'Where are they?' symbolizes the inexorable movement of human time towards death, Espronceda complicates if by equating 'they' with hours, with time itself.

> ¿Dónde volaron ¡ay! aquellas horas
> De juventud, de amor y de ventura . . . ? (1508-
> 09)

He does not ask: where is happiness? He asks: where is the time of happiness? Time, the vehicle of death in the Mediaeval and Baroque interpretations of the *ubi sunt?* theme, is startlingly fused with Renaissance time, the time of youth, joy and life. But it is important to realize that, even while he is renewing the *topos,* Espronceda in the **"Canto a Teresa"** falls back on a venerable tradition from which writers of elegies can hardly escape. (pp. 89-91)

[The **"Canto a Teresa"**] . . . seeks to give relief to an ailing spirit. It laments one of 'los casos . . . de la suerte impía,' insisting rather heavily on the impious nature of death. The *ayes* that proliferate in the poem express the 'gemidos.' The **"Canto"** makes no claim to wit or beauty: the reader is urged to omit this section of *El diablo mundo* written for the satisfaction of the author alone. It is most economical in poetic resources. . . . Espronceda's elegy, far from being dishevelled or tattered, is decently clothed in widow's weeds fashioned by an expert designer.

We have seen . . . how Espronceda, caught in the spider's

web of the elegiac tradition, could not fail to insist in his poem on the problem of human time. From Jorge Manrique and other fifteenth-century elegists he took the *ubi sunt?* theme: the fateful question about the destructiveness of time to which the only possible answer could be silence. From the Renaissance he took the *carpe diem* theme: time seen as a beautiful flower to be plucked and enjoyed while this was yet possible, since the autumn of old age and the winter of death threatened it with withering and decay. But Espronceda, we have seen, used these outworn themes in his own way, to illustrate his peculiar view of life and death. We must now pursue further our inquiry into his peculiarities vis-à-vis the poetic tradition.

Time for Jorge Manrique . . . was a river. Slowly, deliberately it passed on its way to the sea 'que es el morir'. If one stands on the bank of a river each drop of water that passes is irretrievable: 'Pues si vemos lo presente / cómo en un punto se es ido / y acabado . . . ' The only sane view of time relates it to eternity—the philosophical abolition of time—which comprehends and transcends this remorseless flow: 'si juzgamos sabiamente, / daremos lo no venido / por passado'. Time filtered through the memory—past time—acquires human overtones not possessed by the inhuman time of the present ticking clock: 'cómo, a nuestro parescer, / cualquiera tiempo passado / fue mejor'. This analysis of time is Christian and Mediaeval: time is subordinated, in the poet's scale of values, to eternity.

Espronceda too is fond of traditional water imagery. But he uses it for quite different purposes. The poet is a great ship navigating with difficulty across the treacherous sea of life, risking destruction at every turn, but free and partly responsive to the helmsman's control. The forces of nature, irrational and cruel, are the helmsman's constant foe:

> A un tiempo mismo en rápida tormenta,
> Mi alma alborotaban de contino,
> Cual las olas que azota con violenta
> Cólera, impetuoso torbellino (1572-75).

The meaning of this sea of life is diametrically opposed to the meaning of the sea image in Jorge Manrique. The river image is also used differently. In Espronceda we have springs, which are the sources of love; but in a world corrupted by infernal powers, they are swollen by human tears, and soon change from crystalline purity to sombre torrents, which end up as stagnant mire.

> Tú fuiste un tiempo cristalino río,
> Manantial de purísima limpieza;
> Después torrente de color sombrío,
> Rompiendo entre peñascos y maleza,
> Y estanque, en fin, de aguas corrompidas,
> Entre fétido fango detenidas (1694-99).

The water images point to the *engaño* of life and love. False symbols of purity and innocence, they conceal the rottenness of human nature, the inaccessibility of human ideals.

Time, for Espronceda, called for a different kind of image. It was not so much, as it was for Jorge Manrique, an implacable natural phenomenon, something that man had better learn to live with and to evaluate properly. It was a swarm of gadding butterflies or birds, always elusive, ca-priciously flitting through life at vertiginous speeds. Time does not flow; it flies. So too the poet's ship, instead of sailing, flies like a bird (1591). Time is fragmentarized into its component hours, which become the subject of the *ubi sunt?*:

> ¿Dónde volaron ¡ay! aquellas horas
> De juventud, de amor y de ventura . . . ? (1508-09)

This time, still *hours* by the mid-point of the poem—'Y aquellas horas que pasaron / Tan breves ¡ay! como después lloradas' (1680-81)—, passes through the memory of the poet in his elegiac contemplation. As it becomes fixed in the past the hours subtly change to years, and an ¡ay! underlines the pathos of the new vision: 'Los años ¡ay! de la ilusión pasaron' (1732). Finally—in a flashback—the poet himself surrenders to time. He plans, like the hours, to put on wings and ascend with his Teresa to heaven (1794-95), there to enjoy timeless eternity with her:

> Y en un tiempo sin horas y medida
> Ver como un sueño resbalar la vida (1802-03).

But he does not carry out his plan because the sense of time intervenes, because he, a modern man, cannot really believe in eternity. The flying hours, of course, had been identified with love: 'en alas de mi amor' (1794). Time is made memorable by love, and only exists in virtue of it. Eros and Chronos had become one in the personification of the hours. But life lived less rapturously, less intensely—in years, not hours—is a life filled with loveless time. The poet, in his disillusionment, now holds time to be the inexorable flow that Jorge Manrique had said it was. Each drop of water that passed might be a new drop, but it was identical to all the other drops. There was monotony in this diversity. Chronos, unimpassioned by Eros, was profoundly depressing. Espronceda did not share Manrique's faith in an end to time. Just as the macabre was merely gruesome for a faithless man like Cadalso (whereas it had been the touchstone of reality for a believer like Góngora), so time, which reinforced the Mediaeval man's sense of the meaning of life, merely exacerbated Espronceda's awareness of his perplexity.

The essence of the interpretation of time in elegiac poetry is the filtering process it undergoes in the memory. The poet remembers the past, imbues it with an emotional aura, interprets it in a personal way. So the court of Juan II—a part of this past time which to Manrique and the men of his time seemed 'better'—is evoked in terms of 'las justas y los torneos, / paramentos, bordaduras, / y cimeras' and the lovers, poets, musicians, dancers who embellished with their skills this life on earth. Manrique's heart is in this description. 'Tristes recuerdos del placer perdido' (1501), Espronceda begins his poem. *Re-cord-ar*: to restore to the heart a lost pleasure, this is an essential function of the elegy. 'Un recuerdo de amor que nunca muere / Y está en mi corazón' (1780-81). The heart, not the mind, interprets past time: 'y sus ecos sentidos / nacen del corazón, no de la mente,' as Martínez de la Rosa put it. Espronceda's hours, those fragments of intensely lived time which are the very stuff of love, are also his memories. As such they have a proper place in his elegy. 'Es el amor que recordando llora / Las arboledas del Edén divinas' (1632-33). The heart in Espronceda has assumed a much more important role than the soul. The soul remains for the contemplation of an eternity scarcely believed in: it is still the seat of nascent life and departing life, and thus the fit organ to contemplate death. But the heart responds to the warmth of life on earth. For the Mediaeval poet life on earth was but a shadow of eternal life. For Espronceda it is the real thing, because he believes in love and equates life with love. The heart then is ardent (1720), capable of loving and of suffering because of love (1648-50). Deprived of love, it is deprived of its natural object, and ceases to be its true self: 'este desierto corazón herido' (1503), 'mi mismo corazón pedazos hecho' (1843). The heart, therefore, in assuming the loving functions ascribed by the sixteenth-century Neoplatonists to the soul, inevitably converts the elegy into a poem of lost love.

Espronceda's theory of love is essentially Mediaeval in origin, however much he may have misunderstood his sources. The Romantic's mystique of the Middle Ages led him to seize upon, not the robust courtly love of the earliest troubadours, but—screened through his Romantic imagination—what he imagined Jaufre Rudel's *amor de lonh* to have been. Espronceda made things difficult for himself, increased his perplexity, by thinking that the love of woman could be entirely disembodied and spiritualized. The spirit is a breath; breath endowed with meaning is a voice; love, by this reasoning, is therefore to be found not in a body but in a voice.

> Hay una voz secreta, un dulce canto,
> Que el alma sólo recogida entiende,
> Un sentimiento misterioso y santo
> Que del barro al espíritu desprende (1580-83).

Teresa first makes her appearance in the poem as woman, not as a particular woman. The first manifestation of her presence is her voice.

> Oir pensaba el armonioso acento
> De una mujer, al suspirar del viento (1594-95).

As Espronceda in the elegy meditates on the increasing awareness he once had of Teresa he sees a progression from love, the 'voz secreta,' to the voice of a woman, the fantastic pre-Fall Eve of his imagination—'Mujer que amor en su ilusión figura' (1612)—, then on to the real woman, Teresa, whom he nevertheless steadfastly refuses to regard as a woman with physiological needs, to—finally—the fallen woman, whom he rejected so crudely. The trouble was that his love was Narcissistic. He was in love with love: 'Es el amor que al mismo amor adora' (1628). He could not understand that love demanded an object which itself was capable of loving, that this object needed to receive and return his love as much as he needed to give it. Here the break with the past was complete. Neither Thomistic nor Platonic nor any other interpretation of love had dared make the lover so selfish. Espronceda's theory was bound to conflict with his practice. His dreams were very nearly psychotic ones.

These dreams possessed a quasi-religious quality. Though Espronceda cannot have been an orthodox believer he experienced a need for religion in his life. So he debased the religion of believers into an unsatisfying myth. He goes

back to the *donna angelicata* but with no real understanding of her (1596-1619). Teresa, he thought, was 'angélica, purísima y dichosa' (1673). But Teresa was in fact no angel, however much he persisted in seeing her as such. The damsel of the Middle Ages, waiting to be rescued from her tower (1562), symbolized pristine purity for him, a virginal innocence that he was only too ready to demand of all women as *his* right. When the evidence showed beyond the shadow of a doubt that woman was no supernatural or spiritual creature he made the mistake of plunging into the depths of misogyny. A less self-centred man would have revised his theories to make them conform to reality. Espronceda, perversely seeing the storm-tossed ship of his life as a fixed point in the universe, downgraded an individual woman, and with her her whole sex. Teresa was once a 'cristalino río, / Manantial de purísima limpieza' (1694-95). She was this no longer: '¿quién, impío, / ¡Ay! agostó la flor de tu pureza?' (1692-93). He was forced to see her now as a fallen angel.

> ¿Cómo caiste despeñado al suelo,
> Astro de la mañana luminoso?
> Angel de luz, ¿quién te arrojó del cielo
> A este valle de lágrimas odioso? (1700-03)

Indeed he must admit this verdict to be true of all women: 'Mas, ¡ay! que es la mujer ángel caido' (1708). Woman is accordingly demonic:

> Sí, que el demonio en el Edén perdido
> Abrasara con fuego del profundo
> La primera mujer . . . (1712-14)

This dilemma which, obeying the irrational impulses of the heart, Espronceda manoeuvred himself into was the root cause of his perplexity. The rigorous Christian morality of Jorge Manrique enabled him to write an elegy firmly grounded in faith, an affirmation of eternal verities. Even Garcilaso, treating of death in the second part of his first Eclogue, spoke with no sense of doubt about the lovers' reunion in the Elysian fields. Espronceda, proclaiming the liberty of the sensitive man—freedom from reason, from authority, from social restrictions—could not emancipate himself from conventional morality. In the plainest possible terms, he wanted his woman to be a virgin. Since she was not one, he did not know where to turn. His perplexity reveals itself in the unashamed repetition of the normally unpoetic 'tal vez', interspersed with an occasional 'acaso' or 'quizá'.

So Espronceda, faced with death and the loss of a love, composes his elegy on traditional lines. He has a problem. He must try to straighten himself out by using his art to discipline his life. And the elegy he writes reflects the problem, not the answer. In this sense he has failed. Jorge Manrique taught himself, to his own satisfaction and to that of countless readers, the meaning of death and suffering for the Christian believer. Espronceda remained as perplexed when he had finished as before he had begun. The philosophy of death escaped, as it was bound to escape, this incoherent mind of his. But the therapeutic value of the poem was not entirely lost. Even if its composition served merely to vent his spleen, confirm him in his unreasonable prejudices, organize his mistakes, the elegy had at least succeeded in clarifying the issues before him.

Espronceda had in his own way—a way that can hardly be ours—learned to formulate his views on death and to review within the organized framework of artistic form his passion for Teresa. This stocktaking was in itself no small accomplishment. His approach was the culmination of an eighteenth-century one. For the men of reason death was the great cipher because it was not amenable to reason; for Espronceda life itself was irrational, and death part of the same fabric. It would take a new approach—that of Lorca, Alberti and Antonio Machado—to show that death can be transcended in poetry, that life can be projected by means of poetry beyond the frontiers of death, and that death may in this way be vanquished by the living. (pp. 95-100)

> *Bruce W. Wardropper, "Espronceda's 'Canto a Teresa' and the Spanish Elegiac Tradition," in* Bulletin of Hispanic Studies, *Vol. XL, 1963, pp. 89-100.*

---

**Landeira on the evolution of Espronceda's literary style:**

In the totality of his verse production, one of its constants, the sentimental, expresses Espronceda's growing pessimism as years go by and his bitterness resulting from love's disillusionment. From the semihopeful, sweet and nostalgic love song in the early sonnet **"Fresca, lozana, pura y olorosa,"** his muse turns gradually to resentful songs of indifference toward life and damnation of the loved one or erotic object, as in **"A Jarifa en una orgía,"** where Espronceda's own suffering is beyond doubt. This trajectory suggests an increasing realization of the abyss separating what he as a poet is able to fantasize and what he as a man has within reach.

*Ricardo Landeira, in his* José de Espronceda, *Society of Spanish and Spanish-American Studies, 1985.*

---

## Paul Ilie   (essay date 1972)

[*In the following excerpt, Ilie examines the handling of Romantic grotesque in Espronceda's* El diablo mundo *and* El estudiante de Salamanca, *suggesting that their "aesthetics of distortion" is a natural response to the general degradation of the environment.*]

The evolution of the Romantic grotesque in Spain begins with Goya and ends with Bécquer. Between these two figures stands another contributor to the aesthetics of distortion, José de Espronceda, whose works reflect an intermediary phase which recapitulates earlier trends and prefigures later ones. The grotesquerie of *El diablo mundo* and *El estudiante de Salamanca* is somewhat removed from the twisted caricatures that serve Goyaesque social satire, for it hints at the eerie, incongruous supernaturalism that is to come in Bécquer's *leyendas*. Yet Espronceda's practices continue to be influenced by the ethical concerns of an earlier age. His use of typically Romantic diabolical motifs is reminiscent of the Dantesque tradition, but just as the Christian element begins to impose itself, it is dispelled by a larger psychological atmosphere not too different from the modern sensibility. This vacillation is an in-

teresting literary phenomenon, for its mixture of morality and nightmare draws upon categories as diverse as the macabre, the Bacchic, and the dreamstate.

A good summary of Espronceda's theory of the grotesque can be constructed by inference, on the basis of a general statement about neoclassical poetics at the end of *El diablo mundo:*

> ¡Oh, cómo cansa el orden! No hay locura
> igual a la del lógico severo;
> y aquí renegar quiero
> de la literatura
> y de aquellos que buscan proporciones
> en la humana figura
> y miden a compás sus perfecciones.

This rejection of neoclassical order fails to specify what might replace the old aesthetic, but the very concepts repudiated invoke their own antithesis. Several new notes can be heard if we mute such familiar tones as "orden," "proporciones," and "perfecciones." ' Old words like these are sounds of a pre-Romantic concert, and they must be slurred in order to detect the angular rhythms of Espronceda's infernal symphony. In the new score, the important notes are "compás," "humana figura," and "lógico," which become transported into a new key. The grotesque rendition of "compás" is probably the most striking feature of both *El diablo mundo* and *El estudiante de Salamanca,* where cacophonies and broken cadences mark the violent irregularity of their form. Similarly, it is the "humana figura" which is denaturalized and used as the deformed basis for the macabre beings who haunt the magic world of these poems. As for "lógico," its antithesis in the irrational, sometimes absurd perception of reality is fundamental to the poems as a whole, as well as to their grotesque episodes.

Thus Espronceda conspicuously dismisses the aesthetic principles of previous generations even with respect to how the grotesque will be practiced. He goes beyond emphasizing the heterogeneity of forms and the blending of genres ("en varias formas, con diverso estilo, / . . . ora en trivial lenguaje, ora burlando"). These innovations are conventionally Romantic, but they barely touch upon the problems of the grotesque. By challenging the logician's authority in the councils of artistic law, Espronceda calls attention to his own advocacy of disorder. This is his real point, the intention to follow caprice, whim, and haphazard fancy without regard to rules: "conforme esté mi humor, porque a él me ajusto / y allá van versos donde va mi gusto." If the *capricho* is the operative principle for poetic creation in general, then its specific effect on the grotesque is readily grasped. To repudiate the "lógico severo" is to invoke his adversary, the irrationalist, whose unbridled imagination will breed every kind of excess, including disproportion and madness. Such an alternative allows for near-chaotic dementia and liberation, and in the case of one rejuvenated character, release is found "en su agitada fantasía, / volando con locura el pensamiento, / en vaga tropa imágenes sin cuento."

These verses also demonstrate how an exacerbated imagination works. In the light of the first quotation, they add nuances to the concepts of "compás," "humana figura," and "lógico." Rhythm ceases to be measured against some predictable regularity, and acquires convulsive, uncontrollable qualities ("agitada," "volando con locura"). The image of the human figure is replaced by "vaga tropa [de] imágenes," a generic imprecision enabling other creatures besides human beings to be included within the circle of grotesquerie. And instead of logic, the operative faculty is "fantasía." The references cited are surprisingly consistent, despite their random occurrence in the poems, and they tend to confirm each other in their theoretical implications. They are also supported in practice by the general atmosphere of frenzy, noise, and violence among the uncontrolled movements of people and scenes—themselves often deformed. While they may be typical of Romantic spontaneity and inspiration, these elements are also peculiar to the grotesque mode as a conscious aesthetic position. (pp. 94-6)

The theory of grotesque creation begins with Espronceda's view of imagination. He assumes that poets are endowed with the normal creative faculties associated with fantasy, but that due to their yearnings and restlessness, their capacity is somehow impaired. New stimuli are thus required to reactivate the imaginative process. One recourse is to furnish the means for distortion and enchantment:

> Optico vidrio presenta
> en fantástica ilusión
> y al ojo encantado ostenta
> gratas visiones, que aumenta
> rica la imaginación.

The mechanisms normally at work in the imagination are thus newly engaged in two ways. The magical vision of the "ojo encantado" lends its special power, and sense perception is newly focused in order to produce illusionary effects. With this groundwork of sorcery and sensory illusion, a considerable number of grotesque transformations can be effected. . . .

Another aid to the imagination is the dream, which merges its voluntary process with the poet's conscious talents. The dream is not to be considered an internal faculty like the creative imagination, but rather an exterior force whose activity is assimilated by the poet's mind. As depicted by Espronceda, it is a second source of fantastic visions, which is to say, a second imagination. In Adán's dream, for example, the symbolic climb to the mountain peak involves an aspiration beyond the self to increasingly higher flights of fancy. The use of the fiery winged horse characterizes the fulfillment of that goal through an unbridled ascent to the pinnacle of sensory and creative freedom ("siguiendo a mi loca fantasía, / jinete alborozado en mi bridón."

Within the experience of this dream, two psychological events encourage grotesque exploitation. The psychology of the situation is summarized by the couplet "en incesante vértigo y locura, / desvanecida en confusión la mente." The presence of vertigo is one factor in the distorted perception of reality. At the same time, the dizzying state has its source in the poet's drunkenness, a theme whose Dionysian echoes also have implications for the grotesque. The vertiginous aspect is complemented by the

allusion to madness, which indicates a second approach to the concept of imagination. If vertigo involves perceptual relationships, especially space, and inner sensations of a kinesthetic nature, "locura" belongs to a more metaphysical order. It depends on older traditions of inspirational madness on the one hand, and on radical types of derangement on the other. The mental "confusión" that results, therefore, does not refer simply to the endemic emotional instability that ravages much of the Romantic sensibility. It also implies, and leads to, specific forms of disfiguration wrenched from the molds of confused sensory and intellectual categories.

Dreams can thus be understood in a facultative sense, as mechanisms which furnish secondary imaginative structures. Whether dreams are of internal or external origin is less important than how well their fantasy-making apparatus operates. In any case, the problem was of little interest to Espronceda. The coherence of dreams, on the other hand, concerned him a great deal, and he used types that ranged from mild, chimerical dreams to those which produced "figuras mil en su delirio insano."

But beyond the dream state lie still other means of intensifying the Romantic imagination. Espronceda's poetic frenzy bears vestiges of an inspirational theory running parallel to oneiromancy. The central idea here is that creativity feeds on psychic states marked by turbulence and confusion. If the source of this inspiration is external, either divine or diabolic, Espronceda does not acknowledge it. He does place the creative energy within a dreamlike frame of reference, making subject matter rather than psychological mechanisms the focal point. The turbulent vision itself, and especially its fantastic core, is utterly at variance with the real world. Therefore the dream may be enlisted as a metaphor to explain the unreal, impossible, but vividly convincing images that swarm to the surface of the conscious mind. Yet the substance of this metaphor properly belongs to the domain of inspiration and not dream.

Thus we have principles associated with the activity of poetic imagination: emotional violence and imagistic perception divorced from reality. A third principle, already mentioned, is vertigo. This involves both a physiological experience and a perspective toward the world. It is the dizzying sensation that interferes with normal sensory knowledge, while also recoiling upon the subject's internal sense of his physical and psychological conditions. As an active event in the imaginative process, vertigo helps to shape or misshape the configuration of objects and events perceived in the world. It also affects the subject's kinesthetic perception of himself, his sense of the body's balance and behavior. All this is tersely stated in an octet summarizing most of the conditions or faculties mentioned thus far:

> Y como el polvo en nubes que levanta
> en remolinos rápido el viento,
> formas sin forma, en confusión que espanta,
> alza el sueño en su vértigo violento:
> del vano reino el límite quebranta
> vago escuadrón de imágenes sin cuento
> y otros mundos al viejo aparecían . . .

Every activity derives from the distorted dreamstate and

takes place within its elastic framework. "Remolinos" is the metaphor used to embrace several psychological and formal categories. Yet the fact remains that two separate kinds of deformation are taking place. On the one hand there is the mental condition, which is not only confused but is a "confusión que espanta." This means that it is an emotional state compounding severe perceptual inaccuracies with disturbed negative feelings. Moreover, the spasms of fear are quite different from the purely sensory experience of the vision itself, and they convulse the deep-seated emotional core which supplies Espronceda with his material for his mood-building. On the other hand, we have the surface images themselves, with indeterminate shapes that float along regardless of the subject's ability to focus correctly upon them. The independence of these images cannot be overestimated, for they are separate entities in their own right, no matter how unstable or defective the viewer's faculties may also be at the time. Finally, this is a supernatural world, and the poet relies on two different sources or levels of deformation, one stemming from the subject's own condition, and the other from the magic nature of the phenomena. Thus the "vértigo violento" provides one kind of distortion in the perception of things, while the "vago escuadrón de imágenes sin cuento" bears witness to irregularity and confusion among the things themselves. The subjective category penetrates the phenomenal one, and perhaps even influences the final description of events. But the reference to "formas sin forma" suggests that the contents of the whirlwind-dream are imprecise anyway, even though their psychological framework suffers from its own impairment.

The separation and fusion of these two categories, perception and image, is what makes the atmosphere so fantastic. How do the two processes actually work? If we take an episode consisting of a dual sequence, we can easily distinguish the attributes of each type. In part one, another whirlwind analogy is used, but now it is restricted to the objective representation of the vision:

> Como nubes que en negra tormenta
> precipita violento huracán,
> Y en confuso montón apiñadas
> de tropel y siguiéndose van,
> Y visiones y horrendos fantasmas,
> monstruos raros de formas sin fin . . .
> Así, en turbio veloz remolino
> el diabólico ejército huyó.

We are obviously meant to be impressed by the linear imprecision of the images, and by the violence of their movement. Pictorial detail is difficult to find in passages like these, and whatever is vivid from a visual standpoint can be traced to the blending of forms, the smudging of outlines, and the swift motion of changing masses. It is this dynamics of amorphism which is intensified by the element of violence. The torrential sweep of moving images eliminates the need for clarity of line. A sense of space replaces the delineation of forms, and whatever plasticity exists is achieved by describing not specific shapes but the location of masses: their direction and how they are grouped (*precipita, montón, apiñadas, tropel, siguiéndose, remolino*).

When we move past the external account of the scene to its subjective counterpart, we can see how decisive the distinction is between formal and psychological categories. The perspective now assumes the subject's point of view, and the events narrated are the workings of his own faculties as they react to the grotesque phenomena already described.

> Embargada y absorta la mente
> en incierto delirio quedó,
> y abrumada sentí que mi frente
> un torrente de lava quemó.
> Y en mi loca falaz fantasía
> sus clamores y cánticos oí,
> y el tumulto y su inquieta porfía
> encerrado en mí mismo sentí.

Side by side, the two passages could not be more dissimilar in sensibility, even though they deal with the same event. The only carryovers from the first account are the noises of the infernal horde. Otherwise, part two reveals a private experience joined to an analysis of the subject's irrational mind. Most striking is the centrifugal frame of reference. Whereas the first passage bursts outward in every direction, the second one turns inward and down toward a hidden center within the self. The imagery is full of encirclement, restriction, shrinking away (*embargada, absorta, abrumada, encerrado*). The vocabulary reflects introspection rather than observation, as if the sources of events were imaginary and not in the external world. In order to make sense of the monstrous vision, the poet attributes incoherence and madness to his faculties. The "incierto delirio" is supposed to account for the imbalanced perception of the already disordered images. And the "loca falaz fantasía" further explains the insensate vision by declaring the imagination to be out of control and susceptible to the errors of illogic and absurdity.

Nevertheless, a prior deformation exists here. Even before the poet contemplates them, the images are already grotesque. What, then, is the point of attributing a deformative power to the subjective processes of contemplation? The answer lies in the subjectivism of the Romantic vision. It is inconceivable that the subject not be caught up in the object's field of action, or not participate in its mode of being-in-the-world. This participation can mean communion or alienation, pathetic fallacy or objective antipathy, but in either case the subject must be emotionally involved with the object. In the grotesque aesthetic, the subject-object relationship is usually negative, with parallel disfigurations evident on both sides. The subject is deluded, or he suffers from delirium, or else he is victimized by the superior unnatural forces around him. In any event, he is not responsible for initiating the grotesque, even though his psychic reactions offer grotesque structures that correspond to the external forms. We can see, therefore, that Espronceda's concept of imagination plays a role in the grotesque by way of the subject's inner psychological experience. But the concept must be construed narrowly, excluding artistic creativity and inspiration, and referring only to the kinds of perception that the subject may be prone toward. A "loca falaz fantasía" will interfere with the normal apprehension of things and distort them. This makes the problem epistemological, not aesthetic.

Related to the psychology of deformation is another factor

typical of the Romantic movement: Bacchic revelry. If mind submits weakly to the vagaries of imagination, it is just as vulnerable when the senses are intoxicated. Drunkenness is usually exploited for its dramatic interest in episodes of abandon, in carnival scenes, and in witches' sabbaths. However, the Bacchic strain can also be used for grotesque ends. This role is fulfilled intermittently in *El diablo mundo,* beginning with the devils' "tartárea-bacanal" at the start of the work, and ending with the "inmunda orgía" of the macabre tavern near the conclusion. In these cases, intoxication is a theme or a motif. However, it also changes into a technique in *El estudiante de Salamanca,* where the hero's reeling senses magnify the process of disintegration as he sees it in the world around him.

It is the second aspect which requires our attention. While external events are isolated from their impact on the subject, Espronceda allows them to be temporarily replaced by spurious cause-effect relationships, which are suggested as possible explanations for what is happening. For example, Félix sees a sinister figure wavering before him, "tal vez engaño de sus propios ojos, / forma falaz que en su ilusión creó, / o del vino ridículos antojos." But then the interpretation is rejected, "que ya mil veces embriagarse en vano / en frenéticas orgías intentara." Nevertheless, two possible sources of deformation have been indicated, "ilusión" and "vino." Regardless of their actual participation in the present vision, they are singled out as perception-distorting agents. As a hypothesis, the "forma falaz" wrought by the imagination is justifiably considered to be a serious sensory problem, and we have already seen proof of this. Not so, however, for wine. It merely stirs up "ridículos antojos," hardly to be taken seriously when one considers the drunkard's preposterous condition. The reference exploits the foolish aspect of drunken contexts, demeaning the horror inherent in the spectre and rendering its ominousness ambivalent. True, the reader grasps the implications of the menacing apparition, and his terror is reinforced. But for the moment, the explanation based on drunkenness is pushed to the background, and the scene continues:

> La calle parece se mueve y camina,
> faltarle la tierra sintió bajo el pie;
> sus ojos la muerta mirada fascina
> del Cristo, que intensa clavada está en él.
> Y en medio el delirio que embarga su mente,
> y achaca él al vino que al fin le embriagó,
> la lámpara alcanza . . .

Here is a second reference to the influence of wine, and it is not humorous at all. Intoxication can no longer be regarded as a hallucinatory cause, and with this possibility gone, the street-tremors begin their ominous threat.

What actually is happening to Félix? He is in the throes of a "delirio," a concept intended to mark the growing duality of the situation. Independent supernatural forces have been established on one hand, and private confusion on the other, thus complicating the external madness. Moreover, a grotesque note emerges from the confrontation of Dionysiac and Divine principles. It could scarcely be otherwise, since the street is obedient to its own delirium, while the protagonist staggers against the lurching background. The Christ image intrudes upon the scene incongruously with its fixed and presumably sober state. We should note at this point that "delirio" refers to sense perception only, since Félix's mental faculties still permit him to understand events rationally. In fact, his last gesture of self-defense is a rationally conceived stratagem: he will face the weird powers around him with an air of bravado: "Y un báquico cantar tarareando, / cruza aquella quimérica morada / con atrevida indiferencia andando, / mofa en los labios y la vista osada." The levels of grotesquerie now multiply, with the uncanny environment receding before the disparate raucousness of the impious student. His levity clashes with the deadly serious challenge thrown out by those beings pitted against him. And there is further incongruity in the gay but hollow song that dances in the atmosphere, the very air that readers perceive to be laden with certain doom.

Throughout the scene, the role of drunkenness assumes a special character, having little to do with the use of wine to exalt the senses for inspirational purposes, and still less with the pleasure-seeking bacchanals of Romantic exoticism. Inebriation has both a psychological and a moral purpose. It produces a dislocation of the senses that erroneously claims responsibility for the chaos glimpsed in the surrounding reality. And it turns the hero's reckless mockery into an absurd moral stance, given the grave religious retribution that awaits him. Drunkenness as a state of mind offers no method for coping with the hostile environment, and as a mode of behavior it is the most grotesque response that can be made to a desperate situation. The drunken state wavers between perspectives, simulating an epistemological problem while exerting an imbalancing effect upon Félix. At the beginning, he thinks, "O Santanás se chancea, / o no debo estar en mí, / o el Málaga que bebí / En mi cabeza aún humea." And by the end, every possibility except the correct one is mentioned to explain the source of the nightmare around him. Indeed, the fact that he can reason clearly is enough to remove this episode from the usual Romantic category of Bacchic themes and place it instead under a grotesque heading.

So much for the psychological predisposition of the grotesque. Turning to its formal execution, we find three different approaches, which will be the subjects of the next sections. The first makes use of macabre elements, a component which is familiar enough in the Romantic repertoire to require little comment were it not for Espronceda's deliberate distortion. It is one thing to parade skeletons, ghosts, or monsters for the purpose of creating pure emotional states like terror and fear, but it is something else again to invent impure mixtures of indefinable moods that combine laughter, fright, and disgust. The macabre in its nongrotesque form is unadulterated and rarely comic. Its frightening aspects are unmistakably frightening, and whatever is ugly or morally repugnant maintains a purity of character. When horror and suspense are to be emphasized, death is imbued with an air of supernaturalism, and when revulsion or shock are intended, we find devices that play on the physical and moral differences between the living and the dead.

Differences between nongrotesque and grotesque macabre usage can be demonstrated easily by tracing the corpse motif in Espronceda's poems. A traditionally macabre scene shows the following stereotype: "y en una estancia solitaria y triste, / entre dos hachas de amarilla cera, / un fúnebre ataúd, y en él tendida / una joven sin vida / que aun en la muerte interesante era." The triteness of this example illustrates the basic techniques of the conventional macabre as they became derivative Romantic formulas. There is also a suggestion of necrophilia, another staple motif. On the other hand, a new macabre accent appears in the description of another feminine figure, who is compared to a corpse: "de vagos contornos confusa figura, / cual bello cadáver, se alzó una mujer." The reversal of metaphorical terms transforms the entire basis of comparison. Normally, it is the corpse which is the subject described, with its necrophilic appeal linked to certain preserved human qualities. Thus, the usual comparison is to a human being. In this case, however, the subject itself is human and alive, with the corpse acting as the point of reference. The terms of the metaphor are reversed, although the woman is neither a cadaver nor a figure with cadaver-like traits. Despite this, she is likened to a "bello cadáver," a bizarre qualification by any standard of female beauty except a grotesque one. The deformation of the image depends upon the attribution of beauty to a corpse, a fact then used as a standard by which to measure this woman's beauty. Such a standard, gauged by a necrophiliac's taste, can only be termed a perversion. No matter how we turn the phrase "cual bello cadáver," even while admitting that some female corpses are beautiful, there is no contextual indication that the woman is meant to display mortuary qualities. The description is not only macabre, it is grotesquely so.

Another conventional use of the macabre also hints at a new orientation, the blurring of spheres of reality: "Era más de media noche, / antiguas historias cuentan, / cuando en sueño y en silencio / lóbrego envuelta la tierra, / los vivos muertos parecen, / los muertos la tumba dejan." These opening lines of *El estudiante de Salamanca* trail off into commonplace allusions to ghosts and witches, but for a moment they suggest the idea of confused realities where the living and the dead become indistinguishable, at least on the surface. Those who are alive take on the appearance of the dead, and the dead rise up into a state of animation. This macabre reality is then extended to other areas without regard to any descriptive logic. For example, in one simile concerning the earth under the effects of a storm, the macabre image is gratuitous: "Y entre masas espesas de polvo / desaparece la tierra tal vez, / cual gigante cadáver que cubre / vil mortaja de lienzo soez." The corpse motif is converted into an abstract configuration having little to do with its original meaning, and it joins a vocabulary of grotesque allusions whose application does not directly involve normal usage. The words "cadáver" and "mortaja" no longer retain their primary reference to authentic funeral scenes. On the other hand, their very transference to a metaphorical plane shows a refinement in the concept of the macabre. From realistic immediacy in scenes such as the one cited earlier describing the girl in the coffin, there evolves a language that is once-removed from macabre reality. This language, when applied to other subjects, imbues them with the same morbid pallor

of the original, while the incongruity of such usage renders the image grotesque.

The most vivid of Espronceda's macabre effects occur in the area of animation. Playing on hypersensitive fears of being touched, he uses grimacing skeletons in stiff formation to amass a sense of forward motion:

> y al tremendo tartáreo ruido
> cien espectros alzarse miró:
> de sus ojos los huecos fijaron
> y sus dedos enjutos en él . . .
> se acercaron despacio y la seca
> calavera, mostrando temor,
> con inmóvil, irónica mueca
> inclinaron, formando enredor.

The technique is as elementary as the result is frightening. This is why the same elements are often borrowed by later generations, especially the surrealists, to create atmospheres of terror or paranoia. It is not the physical aspect of the skeletons that is significant but rather the sensibility that emerges: encirclement, irony, relentless stares. In contrast, another scene provides a fairly intricate portrait of a skeleton:

> El cariado, lívido esqueleto,
> los fríos, largos y asquerosos brazos
> le enreda en tanto en apretados lazos
> y ávido le acaricia en su ansiedad.
> Y con su boca cavernosa busca
> la boca a Montemar, y a su mejilla
> la árida, descarnada y amarilla
> junta y refriega repugnante faz.

The episode involves the bizarre marriage of Félix to Elvira's ghost, and the graphic diabolism of the entire scene is reflected in the rich details of this excerpt. Once again a taste of necrophilia can be detected, except that now it is the hero, not a dead woman, who is passive and without desire. This reversal of the standard love-death scene makes the situation eerie, although the effect also owes much to the textural qualities of the description. The amorous duet offers the gruesome spectacle of cadaverous lust and human disgust, of a dead body eager for the warmth of living flesh, and for the touch of a young man's cheek. As the skeleton's mouth approaches to complete the half-formed kiss, the grotesquerie of love is fulfilled. The lover is sexless yet full of aggressive desire. With effort, we remember that this figure was once a woman, and that her partner is now a trapped victim stripped of the masculine resources that used to serve him at appropriate times. As the pursued male, he must play a passive role, acting the part of a corpse in an inverted necrophiliac situation. The lover-skeleton grotesquely assumes the necrophile's role, and this is the final irony in the most incongruous Don Juan scene ever written.

The macabre, then, is one of the approaches undertaken in the formal construction of the grotesque. The second basic method involves devices of a sensorial nature. These techniques are acoustic and visual, as might be expected, with a sea of noise finally obliterating whatever linear coherence that might have been gained by pictorial means. Where sounds and shapes blend almost perfectly, as at the beginning of *El diablo mundo*, the strongly imagistic representation is still covered gradually by a flood of different noises:

> Y en medio negra figura / levantada en pie se mece,
> de colosal estatura / y de imponente ademán.
> Sierpes son su cabellera / que sobre su frente silban,
> su boca espantosa y fiera / como el cráter de un volcán.
> De duendes y trasgos / muchedumbre vana
> se agita y se afana / en pos su señor. . . .
> Bullicioso séquito / que vienen y van,
> visiones fosfóricas, / ilusión quizá.
> Trémulas imágenes / sin marcada faz,
> su voz sordo estrépito / que se oye sonar,
> cual zumbido unísono / de mosca tenaz.

Due to the overwhelming spatial confusion, it is easy to overlook the presence of pure grotesque figures here. So too, the overall cacophony can easily blot out the carefully drawn pictorial imagery. For example, the grotesque "negra figura" is of a "colosal estatura" with a head crowned by "sierpes" and followed by a swarm of goblins and elves. And yet this graphic image is rendered imprecise by movements like "se mece," "se agita," and "vienen y van," as well as by a vague spatial-chromatic blur in which the fluidity of shapes and motions merge into a vibrant illusion of forms: "fiera como el cráter de un volcán," "visiones fosfóricas," "trémulas imágenes / sin marcada faz." At the same time, the cacophonous sound grows in prominence, beginning with the controlled noises associated with the "negra figura" ("silban," "boca . . . de un volcán"). Added to the din ("bullicioso") are other noises emitted by the "muchedumbre vana" until the last verses impose a uniform veneer of sense data with their "zumbido unísono." The entire episode is a remarkable harmony of dissonant elements, with grotesque shapes receding before dynamic movements of masses, and with the sharp pictorial impact being counterbalanced by the appeals to sound. Despite the excess and exaggeration, the scene is somehow held in check, and what fills our mind is a masterful *symphonie fantastique* in which the grotesque is but one controlled component among several.

Nevertheless, it is the acoustic factor which ultimately dominates the sensorial aspects of Espronceda's works, and when one leaves his major poems, it is with a head aching with sound rather than dulled by a riot of color. The variety of auditory allusions is enormous, a range that in itself might be considered out of proportion. Yet dissonances become distorted enough to warrant special attention, particularly in the description of actual sound-making. That is, sound is interesting not only as a descriptive trait to color an event, but also as a phenomenon in itself, by virtue of the manner in which it is produced. We see this in the way Espronceda seems to be fascinated by the hollowness of resonance, the emptiness within the shell of sound as contrasted to the wall of vibration itself. In the passage "temerosas voces suenan / informes, en que se escuchan / tácitas pisadas huecas", the emphasis falls on the tenuous outlines of sound rather than on its substance: tone, pitch, volume, etc. The lack of form, a carryover from the ghostly shapes of the imprecise setting, has its acoustic counterpart in muffled tones. Like negative

space in sculpture, a soft echo is the hollow content of silence. In grotesque usage, this device amplifies the doleful insubstantiality of the phenomenon, and even of its source:

> resonando cual lúgubre eco
> levantóse en su cóncavo hueco
> semejante a un aullido una voz
> pavorosa, monótona, informe,
> que pronuncia sin lengua su boca,
> cual la voz que del áspera roca
> en los senos el viento formó.

The eerie howl is disembodied and without form, yet it is described variously with emotion-laden qualifications that surround the central physical fact of its hollow concavity. In another instance, the hollow echo of steps caused by a "maldecida bruja / con ronca voz" raises the dead from their tombs. These two cases use empty resonance to deform the voices present, and then give special counterpoint to their terrifying effect by referring to concurrent sounds made by other agents. When a full cacophony is constructed on the basis of many different noises, it is heard against the uncanny background of a world shattering into pieces:

> Y algazara y gritería,
> crujir de afilados huesos,
> rechinamiento de dientes
> y retemblar los cimientos
> y en pavoroso estallido
> las losas de pavimento
> separando sus junturas.

In short, grotesque sensory perception occurs during the weird or distorted presentation of sounds, either alone or in conjunction with sinister supernatural beings. However, it also depends ultimately on a vision of reality which irrationally decomposes amid the most horrible of shrieks and shapes. The din is terrific, and if most of the auditory references are merely noises heard under amplification, the effect produced in the reader is one of unrelieved dissonance. The act of listening is abolished and everything is reduced to a state of hearing or being heard. It is a condition of the most elementary kind, where sounds assault the ear without any other effort or act of comprehension on the part of the subject. This primitive disjunction is also part of the larger vision of reality, a world which traps human victims in a tangle of unrelated phenomena. Sounds are emitted from unlikely places in response to the general disintegration of the environment, and these emissions are intended to frighten the protagonist and reader, and also to convey the sensory experience most likely to reign during cataclysmic moments.

The third and final approach in the formal construction of the grotesque is the simulation of disturbed dream-states. What we have just seen represents an inferior form of symphonic fantasia composed with the paraphernalia of stock supernaturalism. In the nascent dream-grotesque, the quality of the components as well as of the technical execution is excellent. The high point of creativity is reached in *El estudiante de Salamanca*, where the hero races madly to his death along avenues subjected by an evil sorcery to constant change. The situation is comparable to a nightmare without the sophisticated symbolism that has come to the conscious surface in the twentieth century. As the narrative turns into a frantic state of mind, the dominant feeling is one of psychological disorientation induced by the contradictory information given to Félix's senses as he tries to find his bearings:

> Y cuando duda si duerme,
> si tal vez sueña o está
> loco, si es tanto prodigio,
> tanto delirio verdad,
> otra vez en Salamanca
> súbito vuélvese a hallar . . .
> y en su delirante vértigo
> al vino vuelve a culpar.

With the immediate reality in epistemological doubt, a grotesque representation emerges from the narrative. An ever-changing environment is combined with mental imaginings. Physical and emotional planes transfuse each other with elements flowing freely in both directions. (pp. 97-110)

To sum up, it is useful to think of Espronceda's grotesque as the means for supplementing the creative imagination. His advocacy of disorder begins with whim, follows haphazard fancy, and ends by breeding excess and disproportion. The process results in an interpenetration of subjective and phenomenal categories. In the external world, violence, blurred outlines, and the dynamics of amorphism prevail. In the subjective world, a centrifugal orientation is coupled to an involuntary vertiginous kinesthesia. A sense of encirclement and of retraction becomes the inner response to the "loca falaz fantasía" and the "incierto delirio." Perception-distorting agents, such as wine, make their contribution to the grotesque too. Yet the physical world is also responsible, as demonstrated by the duality apparent in the dislocation of the senses and the supernatural environment. Conventional themes such as the Bacchic, the macabre, and the Dantesque are transformed or adulterated, while Christian motifs provoke morally ambiguous attitudes. The most unusual contribution to the grotesque is Espronceda's inversion of necrophilia to the point where love-making and cadaverous animation are not far apart. The sensory aspects of grotesquerie emphasize space and sound; in addition to cacophony, uncannily hollow sounds are used as the acoustic counterpart of negative space. Finally, there are premonitions of surrealist practice in the paranoid, phantasmagoric vision, and especially in the chronological perception of time. (pp. 111-12)

> *Paul Ilie, "Espronceda and the Romantic Grotesque," in* Studies in Romanticism, *Vol. 11, No. 2, Spring, 1972, pp. 94-112.*

### Donald L. Shaw    (essay date 1972)

[*Shaw is an American journalist, editor, and contributor of articles to several books and journals on sociology. In the following excerpt, he provides a brief overview of Espronceda's works, emphasizing his "growing spiritual and intellectual malaise."*]

There is little in *Pelayo* (written, like Rivas's similar *Florinda,* in stiff *octaves reales*) to suggest Espronceda's future evolution. It is not in fact until Espronceda tried his hand at fiction in a rambling and undistinguished histori-

cal novel, **Sancho Saldaña** 1834), that we perceive signs of his future outlook. The core of Sancho's character is the Romantic formula 'vacío del alma' combined with a deep desire to recover his lost belief in some enduring principle, leading to despair when love fails to provide it. Like Rugiero's in *La conjuración de Venecia,* Sancho's misery is quite arbitrary and unrelated to his actual situation. His repeated exclamations of horror at the prospect of further existence can be interpreted only in terms of Espronceda's own growing spiritual and intellectual malaise.

The growth of this pessimistic insight can be followed in his poetry. Three groups of lyrics stand out. The first is that of the patriotic and libertarian political poems beginning with **'A la patria'** (1829) which like Rivas's more popular 'El desterrado' attacks the prevailing despotism in Spain and bewails the exiles' lot. This was followed by the much more aggressive sonnet on the death of Torrijos, and the lament for Joaquín de Pablo in whose futile *pronunciamiento* Espronceda had taken part in 1830. Finally, in 1835 Espronceda wrote a call to arms against the Carlists, which is simply a rabble-rousing demand for bloodshed and violence:

> ¡Al arma, al arma! ¡Mueran los carlistas!
> Y al mar se lancen con bramido horrendo
> de la infiel sangre caudalosos ríos
> y atónito contemple el Océano
> sus olas combatidas
> con la traidora sangre enrojecidas.

The intemperate and exalted tone of this poem and the 'Dos de Mayo' (1840), at a time when the older Martínez de la Rosa and Rivas were in rapid retreat from their earlier principles, sufficiently marks the gap between the two Romantic generations.

A second group of lyrics includes **'El canto del cosaco'**, **'Canción del pirata'**, **'El mendigo'**, **'El reo de muerte'**, and **'El verdugo'**. These poems in different ways illustrate the Romantics' hostility to social bonds and conventions, and their aspiration to absolute individual liberty. **'El mendigo'** in particular with its rancorous tone of protest marks the beginning of 'social' poetry in Spanish. But the poems of real importance are **'El reo de muerte'** and **'El verdugo'**. In the former we note the absence of any reference to the condemned prisoner's crime or sense of remorse. It is fate, not his own actions, which the prisoner curses, while the end of the poem, with its emphasis on illusion shattered by bitter reality (Espronceda's favourite theme), further emphasises the underlying meaning. We are all in the prison-house of life, condemned by fate to inexorable death: *el reo de la muerte* is Everyman. **'El verdugo'** is more explicitly symbolic. At the climax of the poem the headsman is identified with an eternal force of evil willed into existence by a cruel God against whom man strives in vain.

Closely associated are the poems of the third group which includes **'A Jarifa en una orgía'**, **'A una estrella'**, and most of all the **'Himno al Sol'**. This last occupies a unique place among Espronceda's shorter poems as the only one of them which is exclusively philosophic. In the body of the poem a carefully organised series of contrasts with time's mutability establishes the Sun as a symbol of all that is dependably eternal and enduring. But at the climax this pattern of absolute dependability is brutally shattered:

> ¿Y habrás de ser *eterno,* inextinguible,
> sin que *nunca jamás* tu inmensa hoguera
> pierda su resplandor, *siempre* incansable
> . . . y solo, *eterno, perenal,* sublime
> monarca poderoso, dominando?
> No; . . .

Nothing can be conceived of as eternal: not merely love, glory, and happiness, but even truth and certainty. Ideals and beliefs, the sun-symbol reminds us, have no absolute time-defying existence.

It is superficial in this connection to relate Espronceda's sceptical pessimism simply to his unhappy love-affair with Teresa Mancha. Teresa as a woman of flesh and blood was far less important than what she represented: the attempt to promote human love to fill the gap left by the collapse of faith in religion or reason. Casalduero is right in his assertion:

> No debemos partir de Teresa para llegar al sentimiento de la vida de Espronceda, sino que partiendo del sentimiento que de la vida tiene el poeta debemos llegar a ver la forma que debía adquirir su amor.

*El estudiante de Salamanca,* which appeared, in two parts, in 1836 and 1837, is one of the first and best examples of the *leyenda,* a favourite narrative genre of the Spanish Romantics, who cultivated it both in verse and prose. It tells the story of a corrupt and arrogant young nobleman, Don Félix de Montemar, who, after killing the brother of his abandoned mistress, is drawn by a spectre to a macabre punishment, meeting his own funeral on the way. Hardly longer than some of the *Romances históricos* which Rivas was already writing, it has all their vivacity and suspensefulness, if not their brilliant use of visual effects. It differs from the *Romances,* however, in being completely a work of imagination, in its audacious diversity of metres, and most of all in the characters of Don Félix and Elvira. She illustrates the Romantic conception of love as, at one and the same time, both an illusion and the only vital ideal. Once the illusion is outlived, her hold on life is broken. Like the lovers of Hartzenbusch's *Los amantes de Teruel,* where the symbolism is identical, she simply dies of grief. Don Félix is at first glance anything but a figure of Romantic insight. The element of abstract thought which (in Don Álvaro's soliloquy, for example) occasionally allows the Romantic hero to express the author's deeper vision of life, is conspicuously absent from his makeup. But Espronceda cannot resist turning him, without warning, into a figure of cosmic rebellion:

> . . . alma rebelde que el temor no espanta,
> hollada, sí, pero jamás vencida;
> el hombre, en fin, que en su ansiedad quebranta
> su límite a la cárcel de la vida,
> y a Dios llama ante él a darle cuenta,
> y descubrir su inmensidad intenta.

The victim of the prison-house no longer groans, but rattling the bars of his cell calls his unjust gaoler to account. In contrast, the *gemido* of the phantom in the middle of the poem, largely unconnected with the story, represents an outcry of the poet himself once more against the bitter reality behind the world of appearances, against the irreparable loss of protective illusion:

> ¡Ay! el que descubre por fin la mentira;
> ¡Ay! el que la triste realidad palpó; . . .

These lines might serve as an epigraph for Espronceda's last and most ambitious poem, *El diablo mundo,* which began to be published in 1840 and was unfinished at the time of his death. It is an allegory of existence. In it Adán, who stands for man, is allowed to choose between death and understanding of ultimate truth or eternal life. Inevitably he chooses the latter, and the poem records his discovery of the bitter consequences. Most of the principal elements of Espronceda's final outlook are contained in the prologue to the poem. The chorus of voices expresses his doubts and disillusionment; the Spirit of Man his rebellion against a malign God who is in turn perhaps only a hypothesis. In the body of the poem Adán comes, like man, naked and guileless into the world, only to find himself according to Romantic precept at once immured (literally and figuratively) in the prison-house. Here his bitter introduction to reality begins. As yet, however, he is possessed of the fount of illusion—Youth; and at the touch of love his shackles are broken. So far the poem is worked out in detail. But from here on difficulties of interpretation supervene because of the poem's unfinished state. It is clear that disillusionment follows. Two further phases are incompletely mapped out: Adán's dissatisfaction with the love-ideal and finally his dawning tragic insight. Beside the corpse of Lucía, an innocent child, arbitrarily struck down by Death, Adán suddenly becomes aware of the problems posed by her inexplicably undeserved fate. In the voice and language of the luciferine Spirit of Man in the prologue he questions defiantly:

> El Dios ese . . .
> que inunda a veces de alegría,
> Y otras veces, cruel, con mano impía
> Llena de angustia y de dolor el suelo

and is suddenly aware of 'La perpetua ansiedad que en él se esconde': the Romantic (and modern) quest for a satisfying answer to life's enigma. Here the poem breaks off. But although its climax was never written, we can hardly doubt its nature. It is foreshadowed in the grim warning of the Spirit of Life in Canto I that if Adán ever came to regret his decision, he was to remember that the responsibility for it was his alone.

Espronceda's plays and the articles he contributed to various periodicals are disappointing. He had little ability to present conflict and mistook horrific effects for dramatic ones. Like many creative writers he was a poor critic and only one brief article, the amusing **'El Pastor Clasiquino'** satirising the bucolic Neo-classical tradition of poetry, is nowadays remembered. (pp. 14-18)

*Donald L. Shaw, "Espronceda and Larra," in his* A Literary History of Spain: The Nineteenth Century, *Ernest Benn Limited, 1972, pp. 14-22.*

## Ricardo Landeira    (essay date 1977)

[*In the following excerpt, Landeira focuses on Espronceda's treatment of woman in his love lyrics, noting that the poet finds her to be "a demoniacal figure and source of a love that is damned."*]

Aesthetic distance in Espronceda's poetry is never too significant. This does not imply, however, that all of his poems grow out of a real circumstance nor that those which do are uniformly memorable. Yet it can be said that among the poet's most important compositions, those whose ascendancy derives from daily or the poet's own intimacy, that have a *raison d'être* extrinsic to the strictly literary, are masterpieces. In the totality of his production, one of its constants, the sentimental, expresses Espronceda's growing pessimism as years go by and his bitterness resulting from love's disillusionment. From the semihopeful, sweet and nostalgic love sung in the early sonnet "Fresca, lozana, pura y olorosa," his muse turns gradually to bitter songs of indifference toward life and damnation of the loved one, as in **"A Jarifa en una orgía,"** where Espronceda's own suffering is beyond doubt. This trajectory suggests an increasing realization of the abyss separating what he as poet can fantasize and what he as a man has within reach. He is confronted with a fundamental incongruence between vital posture and artistic manifestation, hence the ascending index of *angst* and rebellion. The awareness of this imbalance—the imaginable versus the attainable—leads Espronceda to despair, first, because he feels incapable of bridging the distance that separates them, and second, because he cannot adjust his desires to the possibilities before him. Herein lies the inherent contradiction of Romanticism, of an art out of true with the poet's experience. By following the course of his lyrical love poetry through four key poems, **"Fresca . . . ," "A una estrella," "Jarifa . . . ,"** and the **"Canto a Teresa,"** I intend to reveal the fascinating dilemma which Espronceda as a Romantic faced, the fundamental dilemma of the skeptic.

Because Romanticism is a system of contradictions amounting to an aesthetic of sentiments, the muse of Romantic poetry is sentimental exaltation. We owe to Teresa Mancha, the *femme fatale* of Espronceda's love life, the inspiration of the most valued category of his verses, the emotional or love lyric. The subject corresponding to this lyric will always be a woman, whom the poet identifies and confuses with love itself.

The sonnet, preferred lyric form of Spanish Renaissance and Baroque literatures, is rarely used by that country's Romantics who shy away from its rigid structure. Its fixed form does not allow a free-flowing rhythm, demanding instead a sober and restrained language. Bécquer wrote only one, not too successfully, while Espronceda produced nine. His first, written before he was twenty, constitutes Espronceda's initial great love poem. Known by its inaugural verse, **"Fresca, lozana, pura y olorosa"**, the composition remains relatively faithful to classical canons, especially if one focuses on its central metaphor, "rosa-ilusión de amor." Nevertheless, it is infused with unusual freeness, with a note of subtle sensuality ideally suited to a young love. The poem contains two united or connected

thoughts: the delight derived from the rose's beauty, and the sorrow at its ephemeral existence, both present in the quatrains. The parallel course followed by love, hope and then the pain of love's loss, is insinuated in the tercets. This sonnet is distinguished from the poet's secondary poems by virtue of a singular lyric lexicon foreshadowing the simplicity and spontaneity of expression characteristic of Espronceda's later verse. Its fundamentally Romantic character can be appreciated in the play of opposites which functions in terms of the metaphor of the rose and the poet's love—freshness-flaccidity, hope-despair—concordant with the bimembrated structure already pointed out. As the initial milestone of the author's sentimental itinerary, this sonnet enunciates the belief that love carries a fateful burden of sadness, even if temporarily alleviated by illusion. As time passes, this initial dose of illusion diminishes progressively while the implied bitterness turns into total despair.

Of a more tranquil nature because of its quietly discursive tone so infrequent in Espronceda, **"A una estrella"** pursues serenely for one hundred and twenty verses the poet's path of love from incipient happiness

> ¡Ay, lucero! yo te vi
> resplandecer en mi frente,
> cuando palpitar senti
> mi corazón dulcemente
> con amante frenesi. (29-33)

through the sadness and grief felt as a result of the loss of the loved one

> Mas ¡ay! que luego el bien y la alegría
> en llanto y desventura se trocó: (21-22)

to end in a glacial apathy as seen in the last strophe

> Yo indiferente sigo mi camino
> A merced de los vientos y la mar,
> y entregado en los brazos del destino,
> ni me importa salvarme o zozobrar. (116-120)

In Romantic poetry, love is typically either impossible or ephemeral. In **"A una estrella"** the second is true. The poem constitutes a dialectical lament for the joy and sorrow shared between the poet and a star. The latter comes to represent the former's hopes, refulgent when the lover feels joyful and dark when he senses himself abandoned, in an obvious pathetic fallacy. Light-happiness then is the central metaphor of the poem, uniting both subjects. The anthropomorphic star projects the poet's nostalgia and grief, so that the "timidez," "tristeza," "juventud" and "melancolía" attributed to it are but an echo of his mood. The poet, withdrawn and hermetic, seeks the company of the star as a mute consolation following his amorous disappointment. The star, visualized as faithful, elevates love to an idealized plane with the perpetuity and radiance of its light. On the other hand, human love fatally suffers the same mortality as those who experience it, rarely achieving the desired perfection. Consequently, incapable of reconciling his dream of love with the reality of man's destiny, the poet retreats from life.

In these first two poems, Espronceda has avoided all sentimental stridency. In **"Fresca, lozana . . ."** with traces of youthful optimism, he harbors the possible hope that a love may exist capable of uplifting man even if the joy derived lasts ever so briefly. The sustained but controlled tone of **"A una estrella"** manifests the growth of the pessimistic concept of love which has begun to grip the poet. The certainty of an irrevocable despair ultimately leading to a *tedium vitae* is the new attitude from which Espronceda henceforth will not stray.

The composed tones of amorous sentiment characterizing the two poems above disappear, to be replaced by the agitation and violence animating **"A Jarifa en una orgía,"** the most bitter of all poems from Espronceda's pen. In it the poet feels cheated by deficient reality, aware that it does not respond to his aspirations, but is conscious that, short of death, he can expect nothing more. Much like the drug addict who comes to loathe his dependency,

> Y aturdan mi revuelta fantasía
> los brindis y el estruendo del festin, (105-106)

the poet finds himself against his will a prisoner of the passions of an imperfect and impure love that ultimately jades his life. Woman, a demoniacal figure and source of a love that is damned, does not fit the poet's dream, as he despairs for having once conceived a pure love. The spiritual passion exists only in his heart. Once externalized, it becomes hopelessly stained. And so the contemplated joy turns to grief, the flower becomes a thorn and all that man cherishes he receives in a distorted image. In the search for a love concordant with his desires, Espronceda falls into the morass of eroticism and suffocating sensuality. Happiness lies beyond the realm of palpable reality. Pleasure and hope are, alas, but chimeras which man cannot avoid despite the grief and disenchantment which surely follow.

---

**The dissatisfaction of a Romantic spirit such as Espronceda's stems from that stance which arbitrarily pretended to reduce all meaning to an extremely subjective and personal vantage point, producing a capricious tedium, a universal skepticism and damnation of the woman beloved.**

**—Ricardo Landeira**

---

The poet, forced to renounce the dreams of his internal world, allows himself to be seduced by ataraxia

> ni el placer ni la tristura
> vuelvan mi pecho a turbar. (95-96)

seeking to assuage the bitterness of his disillusionment. In this manner he avoids the "paz de los sepulcros" (76), his decision amounting to a renunciation of all that which his inner turmoil dictates. The poet withdraws from his defiant stance to seek the company of another being wounded by the same annihilating perception

> Ven, Jarifa; tú has sufrido

> como yo; tú nunca lloras.
> Mas ¡ay, triste! que no ignoras
> cuán amarga es mi aflicción.
> Una misma es nuestra pena,
> en vano el llanto contienes . . .
> Tú también, como yo, tienes
> desgarrado el corazón. (109-116)

The arms of the beloved Jarifa, equally burned by despair and suffering, are the sought-after consolation to his tedium.

Espronceda's despair, so patent in the love-madness of **"Jarifa"** and renewed in the **"Canto a Teresa"** is profoundly rooted in the perennial dichotomy between vital reality and the reality conceived by the poet's imagination or sentiment. The inevitable result of this dilemma is the destruction of idealistic aspirations and the poet's consequent demoralization. The **"Canto a Teresa"** does not represent an attempt to resolve the conflict between a runaway idealism and impure reality, as was the case in **"Jarifa,"** but simply an exposition of that antagonism in terms of personal despair and vilifying cruelty towards the loved one.

The poet, an unlucky and resentful lover, struggles to rid himself of a grief attributable less to the death of Teresa than to the prior loss of love for her due to her fall from the pedestal where Espronceda had placed her. His suffering, therefore, results not from the corporeal death but rather the demise of his love for Teresa when she ceased to exist as beloved because of her inescapable condition as a woman of flesh and blood; her descent from Eve causes her to become the soulless and perverse woman of the poem. The **"Canto a Teresa"** is Espronceda's last elegy. In this type of composition, memory completely absorbs the attention of the poet and his remembrances during the forty-four *octavas reales* of the **"Canto"** are immediate and intimate. The theory of the poem's two different dates of composition is by now well-known and generally accepted. The first writing corresponds to the eighteen inaugural strophes motivated by the separation of the two lovers and the second section to the death of Teresa. This lapse does not diminish the total impact; on the contrary, sentimental content increases with the interval, revealing the vastly different reactions of the poet to the two most painful jolts of his existence. In the first part, Espronceda dwells upon the remembered happiness of a shared love; in the second, he laments the loss of this love and rails against the beloved. The twenty-fifth strophe synthesizes this interpretation thus:

> Tú fuiste un tiempo cristalino río,
> Manantial de purísima limpieza;
> Después torrente de color sombrío,
> Rompiendo entre peñascos y maleza,
> y estanque, en fin, de aguas corrompidas,
> Entre fétido fango detenidas. (1694-1699)

The last division best characterizes the mood of the entire poem even though it appears as a contrast to the initial segment. Whereas in the first section the lover's longings for a pure and eternal love appear, in the final portion the poet's disillusionment and vituperation of the loved one for not possessing at once the qualities of Aphrodite and Madonna are most memorable. Such is the form taken by the reconsideration of the constant struggle between Espronceda's inner self and the outer world. The poet's egotism cannot be overstated. Espronceda weeps more at the impossibility of fulfilling his own desires than for the death of Teresa, dead for him when she ceased to be the ideal woman. He damns her yet is unable to forget her; his heart is wounded but not free of her. He says as much in the first strophe, thus continuing the love-hate antilogy. Espronceda intends thereby to be as cruel with her as he avers she was with him in revealing herself as only human. In his passionate, blind egocentrism the poet subjugates every concept of woman and love to one aspect which allows no modification: the candid and beautiful woman, a celestial creature of pure fantasy, too perfect to be real. Naturally, the imagined beauty will turn to dust when the poet discovers the Edenic caste—poisoned by the apple and the serpent—of his beloved. The sin attributed to her, alluded to in the antepenultimate strophe is, then, not only Eve's own, but the defraudation of the poet: the beloved turns out to be neither god-like nor virginal.

Espronceda tries in many ways to reduce human existence exclusively to the amorous dimension, since in the mind of many Romantics love can redeem man. Zorrilla's don Juan, rescued from the eternal flames by his sincere love for Inés, is a case in point. But Espronceda always found exiguous for his thirst the love within his grasp. He was not satisfied, because he could never satiate his wants with mediocre reality. Love having failed him as a means whereby to rescue his existence from banality, Espronceda abandoned himself to follow cynically and indifferently the course of the world around him. This explains why not only the **"Canto a Teresa"** but other poems including **"A una estrella"** and **"Jarifa"** end on a note of wounded indifference. For the poet, powerless against the world, there remains only the sleep of the sepulchre or drifting with the current like other mortals since all struggle with fate is futile. The climax of such an attitude is the empty defiance of the last verse, "Que haya un cadáver más, ¡qué importa al mundo!" (1851), whose pained sarcasm is all too obvious.

In his poetry Espronceda is unable to reconcile his views of the world. Not only does he know how to orient his own life in order to harmonize his inner world—which nurtures his poetry—with external reality, and so it follows that continuity and intermittence can be jointly observed in his life as well as in his work. He remains unaware of how to adapt himself to the reality in which he must dwell. The resultant shock of the encounter between the two worlds produces an enduring sorrow, making him pessimistic, darkening his verse. His disenchantment with life is thus not surprising. The dissatisfaction of a Romantic spirit such as Espronceda's stems from that stance which arbitrarily pretended to reduce all meaning to an extremely subjective and personal vantage point, producing a capricious tedium, a universal skepticism and damnation of the woman beloved. (pp. 192-99)

*Ricardo Landeira, "The Whore-Madonna in the Poetry of José de Espronceda," in Romance Notes, Vol. XVIII, No. 2, Winter, 1977, pp. 192-99.*

## Richard Cardwell   (essay date 1980)

[*In the following excerpt from his introduction to his edition of* El estudiante de Salamanca, and Other Poems, *Cardwell addresses the general collapse of religious, moral, and rational values in Espronceda's works, placing the poet in the context of Romanticism and finding that his existential solitude and metaphysical separation render him modern.*]

Romanticism as a spiritual and psychological phenomenon and Espronceda's supposed attitudinizing are linked in that they both express views concerning the nature of the world. The word 'Romantic', as D. L. Shaw has argued in a remarkably lucid analysis [in "Spain/Romántico-Romanticismo" in *Romanticism: The History of a Word,* 1972], had two closely related but separate connotations. The first of these was literary and was linked to the fact that the Romantics rejected certain attitudes, forms and standards of judgement that had been current at an earlier period. The second connotation was moral. It arose from the fact that the Romantics were seen by certain critics as subversive, not merely of literary standards and traditions, but also of ideals and beliefs, particularly in the political and religious spheres, on which the stability of society was thought to depend. The hostile reaction to Espronceda can be understood if we recognize that the Romanticism Espronceda exemplifies flies in the face of traditional moral and ideological standards. It questions the basic suppositions and axioms on which society has rested since the earliest civilised times. It opposes the central presumption which underlies the history of Western civilization, that to the central questions about the nature and purpose of men's lives, about morals, about death and the hereafter, true, objective, universal and eternal answers could be found. This was the great foundation of belief which Romanticism attacked and weakened. In the work of the Romantics there runs one major basic notion, held with varying degrees of consciousness and depth, that truth is not an objective structure, independent of those who seek it and eternal in duration. From this comes not only the exaltation of the ego which is echoed in Romantic sonority but the psychological and spiritual distress of the discovery. A change in literary taste may explain Ribbans's strictures; it is a break with the traditional interpretations of belief and value systems which explain much of the hostility to Espronceda and his fellow Romantics. What we are concerned with is a spiritual crisis involving the apparent collapse of previously established absolute values, religious, moral and rational. Because of the heterodoxy of Espronceda's response to this new situation his biographers have tended to adopt a condemnatory tone, to deny his sincerity or, as with Escosura and Cascales Muñoz, to ignore the evidence and recruit him into the Catholic fold. The work of Bonilla, Casalduero and Shaw has underlined this ideological dimension of Espronceda's thought.

In spite of his reputation Espronceda was no atheist. He probably enjoyed periods of belief. What seems clear, however, is that he lacked authentic religious confidence. This, rather than any alleged pose or idealised conception of himself as a Romantic hero, as suggested by Pattison, lies at the root of his personality. The reasons for the modern decline of confidence in absolute criteria, be they religious or rational, are to be found in the history of ideas of the last decades of the eighteenth century. Espronceda's loss of vital certainties is a part of that general collapse. (pp. 17-19)

In 'A la luna', probably written soon after [Espronceda's] arrival in London in early 1828, we find . . . echoes of poems to the moon by Lista, Meléndez Valdés and Jovellanos. This poem shares something of the sentimental melancholy made fashionable in Spain by Young's *Night Thoughts* and the verses of Saint-Lambert. . . . But there is nothing of Meléndez Valdés's contrast of the constancy of the moon and man's impermanence; none of the philosophical consolation drawn from that contrast. . . . Espronceda contrasts two moments in time. The moon reminds the poet of a former time of emotional consummation as he stands beneath the moon in a present characterised by loss and abandonment. Hooting owls have replaced the sound of nightingales and doves. The moon, a companion spirit in separation, will find Endymion again; the poet, separated from Teresa Mancha, who has remained in Portugal, is left to complain alone. The emphasis is again on the self. Espronceda might accept from Lista's 'A la luna' the idea of a *beleño* to melancholy, but his model has no sense of irreparable desolation.

Espronceda's vital attitude is clear. He longs for and, briefly, enjoys the fullness of expectation. But he discovers that the belief in the permanency of *gloria, amor* and *alegría* cannot be squared with personal experience. Indeed, they become mere illusions blown away like the rose petals on the winds of reality. We are now far from the work of his elder contemporaries. The purity and harmony of nature evoked in 'Fresca, lozana' which, in spite of mutability, had confirmed Meléndez Valdés's belief in a divinely-ordered universe fail to convince the young Espronceda. This is confirmed in a comparison of their poems to the night. In Meléndez Valdés's 'De la noche' the poet enjoys the sounds, scents and sights of nightime 'sin sustos ni recelos'. In 'La noche y la soledad' in a more philosophical vein he flees the 'mundo corrompido' to find in the mystery of night 'dulce paz', 'alegría', 'quietas mansiones' and 'favor celestial'. His sensibility allows a perception of the nature of man's destiny: 'el hombre iluminado ve en sí mismo / las señas inmortales.' The 'divina norma' of 'el inmenso Hacedor' is revealed. The moral imperative of the universe illuminates his consciousness in a 'fuego generoso' and he discovers 'virtud', a combination of self-knowledge and knowledge of the designs of his Creator. In 'La noche' Lista experiences a sense of 'amargura' but discovers an 'alivio' in submitting his experience to reasoned examination. In Espronceda's poem, for all the pastoral décor, there is no philosophical comfort. Rather we discover one of the earliest examples of the pathetic fallacy, which the Symbolists were to adopt and refine, where the landscape takes on the emotional attributes of the poet-spectator. There is no explanation for the poet's 'pesar'. There is no mood of spiritual equilibrium and 'religioso miedo'. He cannot exclaim with Meléndez Valdés '¡Oh noche! ¡Oh soledad! en nuestro seno / sólo hallo el bien y en libertad me miro'. The sensibility is quite distinct. It is not of self-examination but of self-

contemplation: '¡Oh, qué silencio! ¡Oh, qué grata / oscuridad y tristura! / ¡Cómo el alma contemplaros / *en sí recogida* gusta.' Delight is found in musing on personal sadness. We are on the threshold of a literary and spiritual reaction which is uniquely modern. The process had begun when Meléndez Valdés expressed the consoling power of nature as a revelation of selfhood and divinity in Art. Espronceda uses Art itself as a mirror and projects his personality upon the world. It is a motif which is to dominate the lyric down the century. It is discovered most tellingly, of course, in the person of the *dandy* figure. For Espronceda the soothing attractions of the world of pastoral, the poetic Arcadia, are conjured as a possibility for happiness. But its enjoyment, even if recalled with nostalgia, belongs to others. It can never be his. Others might enjoy its bliss; he cannot. He erects an invisible but impassable barrier between himself and the cosmos about him. The sense of unity and purpose of Meléndez Valdés's Deistic universe has become the isolated and subjective world of the Romantic ego. Espronceda cannot accept the confident assertion of Meléndez Valdés that 'El justo, firme en su opinión, seguro / de su conciencia, reirá a la suerte. / Miedo, amenaza, inútiles asaltan / su ánimo fuerte' ('A la fortuna'). Nor his 'La virtud adoro y corro / tras su celestial hechizo. / Mi ilusión es su consuelo, / el desengaño un martirio; / mas quiero soñar virtudes / que ver y llorar delitos' ('Mis desengaños'). By contrast Espronceda suggests a world of disharmony. Eve is expelled from Eden in 'A Eva' with no hope of redemption at the hands of an implacable God who rages against his Creation. For Eve 'amargo duelo / sempiterno . . . sin esperar consuelo' is all that remains. Such a vision, like the prophecy of the fall of Troy in 'Vaticinio de Nereo' has all the apocalyptic terror of the paintings of his English contemporary John Martin. Even Espronceda's apparently neo-classic décor belongs, as R. P. Sebold has demonstrated [in 'Contra los mitos antineoclásicos españoles', *Papeles de son Armadans* (1964)], to the process of adaptation by the Romantics of neo-classical precepts. . . . Before the journey into voluntary exile, before the contact with European Romanticism and Byron, the major psychological and spiritual features of Romantic ideology are to be found in Espronceda's work. The revolutionary and libertarian aspects of the Romantic manifestation appear, again in a neo-classical guise, in 'A la patria. Elegía', 'Canción patriótica', 'A la muerte de Don Joaquín de Pablo (Chapalangarra)' and 'La entrada del invierno en Londres'. It is unnecessary to comment on the obvious idealism of these poems save to observe that much of the unhappiness concerning the decline of Spain and the loss of political freedom seems inextricably linked to the poet's own sense of spiritual and emotional insecurity. Spain's 'pesares' in 'A la patria' are underlined by personal deprivation, 'yo, desterrado de la patria mía', in a vein quite unlike poems lamenting Spain's condition by Meléndez Valdés and Rivas (who look to a brighter future) or Quintana and Lista (who rail against moral corruption). The dominant cry is '¡contemplad mi tormento!'. 'La entrada del invierno' deals principally with lost illusions before a backcloth of a winter landscape, pathetic fallacy for spiritual withering. It does not celebrate the liberal ideals learned at Lista's side. Winter brings no distress to *pastor, sabio* or *marinero*. Their contentment, contrasting starkly with the poet's 'quebranto' and 'enlutada alma', is not possible for the poet. Again the contrast of past felicity and present pain: '¡Ay! yo en el suelo de la *Patria* mía / *gocé* también la paz.' The *beatus ille* tradition is employed against itself for the 'dichoso aquel' can no longer apply to the poet as it had in 'La vida del campo'. The burden of emphasis in the elegy to Chapalangarra is on the poet, the defender of liberty now vanquished, standing on a mountain top lamenting his separation from his homeland. Only incidentally does it dwell on the dead guerrilla leader. [Espronceda's] early poetry suggests, then, an underlying sensibility which is negative. It is to this negative attitude rather than to a sense of 'liberation' that many of the accepted manifestations of Romanticism (be it flight into political action, into the bosom of nature, into unfettered emotion or subjectivity) should be related. Genuine Romanticism is not an optimistic leap forward, it is a negative retreat. Liberation loses its meaning if, in the process of its attainment, hope and optimism are lost. (pp. 27-31)

---

**The related themes of soaring flight and upward aspiration, of longing for life and love, of ideals that give wings to the imagination but which are dashed into the pit of the grave are to appear with greater insistency in the last seven years of Espronceda's life. As a consequence of the thirst for the ideal and inevitable failure to attain it, there comes an intense feeling of isolation. . . .**

*—Richard A. Cardwell*

---

If we examine his next group of poems, for the most part written in exile between 1830 and 1832, we discover one of the primary responses to the crisis situation. In Espronceda, as in other sceptical Romantics, there exists an intimate link between the sentiments and emotions expressed and their world view. Shaw's comment that if any proof were wanting of the capital importance of the vital problem to the Romantics, the *metaphysical* context in which their emotional experience took place would supply it is essentially correct. With remarkable regularity in the plays and poetry of this period emotional disillusionment or the forced parting of lovers is translated into terms of metaphysical despair. This reaction suggests that in the Romantic mind there existed some form of interdependence or correlation between emotional fulfilment and metaphysical confidence. That is, the sense of security engendered by the love relationship dictates how successfully the artist is able to confront disillusionment and corrosive ideas. In **'A la luna',** for example, the beloved is described as 'mi vida'. In the poems of this period lovers' final parting is a dominant motif. Since the poet did not break with Teresa until late 1836 these poems express not experiences but comments on life. (p. 32)

[In **'Oscar y Malvina'**] we witness Espronceda's loss of confidence. With the poet, the reader's imagination surges upwards to the plane of idealism—love, courage and duty—and despairs as fate prevents its fulfilment. Nor can we put trust in the idealism of the poem, for it has been condemned to destruction from the outset. With all possibility of love gone Malvina dies. In this poem and **'La despedida del patriota griego'** we find, in addition, the exaltation of the Romantic self. Oscar, in seeking out Cairvar, strives to raise himself in the esteem of his clan, to rise above personal desires and self-interest. H. Ramsden properly argues [in 'A Stylistic Study of José de Espronceda, with Special Reference to His Violation of Norms Established within the Reader's Mind'] that the Romantic hero projects himself in triumph upon the world and refuses to yield to mediocre demands even though it cost him all that from which his sense of self-preservation strives to protect him: effort, suffering, even death. Oscar, unlike the Greek, is not so much in conflict with society as with the basic psychology of the real world: self-adaptation to life and minimal effort to survive. He breaks with the most fundamental norm of all, the instinct of self-preservation. As he breaks with it, the reader participates in that soaring of the human spirit above the common herd. Like the Greek, Oscar rises to an ideal plane of virtue, honour, courage and patriotism. He stands before the dreaded Cairvar and exclaims 'cual hórrida tormenta / eres tú de temer', breaking with the norms of expectation as he cries in defiance 'mas yo no tiemblo'. When he might have remained at Malvina's side or taken Cairvar in sleep he chooses mortal combat. The Greek might have accepted Islam and the Sultan's rule; he might also have had the hand of his *amada*. They refuse the easy compromise for higher ideals. '¡Ah los martirios del infierno nunca / igualaron mi pena y mi agonía!' he exclaims in self-exaltation. Death will come as a happy release where lovers are parted, a country betrayed and unprecedented suffering and ignominy enslave a nation. '¡Quién resistir podrá!' Espronceda's imagination can resist, even in the face of all the instinctive demands that argue for compromise and submission. It is a refusal of reality and a rupture with the norm of self-effacement. The stylistic patterning celebrates the nobility of the Romantic spirit, the refusal of the commonplace and mediocre. But that heroism embodies little confidence. In spite of the subordination of personal desire to greater ideals neither hero achieves his goal. Oscar's death leaves his clan desolated, the Greek's homeland remains enslaved. (pp. 34-5)

**'Al sol'**, one of Espronceda's most patently philosophical poems, embodies a variation of the device of rupture of expected norms. Ramsden has argued that, unlike the natural reaction to fear and death, the image of the sun bids no prior assumptions. The celebration of its magnificence and glory is increasingly associated with childhood innocence, intense idealism and permanence. The vocabulary, syntax, rhythm and reiterated dental and plosive consonants all contribute to establish a universal norm in the reader's mind. The sun, formerly a celestial body among others, now becomes the symbol for all that man desires and all that in which he places his trust. Once more the theme of expectation and craving emerges as we witness the imagination of the poet soar, 'atrevido, ansioso, intrépido, ardoroso, anhelante', towards a central focus which he believes enshrines the life-force itself and embodies the eternal principle of life, surviving the diurnal round, 'siglos sin fin', the rise and fall of empires and the Deluge. The sun is the Prime Mover itself, symbolising eternity and by implication all those ideals, beliefs and absolute values which, like the sun, give light, life and permanence to the world. Thus when the seeker after truth, for such is the poet, puts the question '¡Y habrás de ser eterno?', an interrogation extended over some seven lines, reinforcing in the reader's mind the principle of certainty for which he seeks confirmation—that which is 'eterno, inextinguible, nunca jamás, siempre incansable, inmortal, las edades contemplando, eterno, perenal, sublime, poderoso'—, the expectation is dashed by the simple, but sickening negation: 'No.' We recognise, as the poem once more rehearses the path of grandeur and pomp, of childhood illusions, as each of these expires, that nothing is secure. The poem ends in despair as we are presented with a vision of the universe exploding and the world falling shattered from the hands of God, a God who is powerless to prevent it from falling into eternal darkness and nothingness. (p. 36)

'El reo de muerte', 'El verdugo' and 'El mendigo' have been described [by V. Cerny in *Essai sur le titanisme dans la poésie romantique occidentale entre*, 1935] as 'titanic anarchism', humanitarian concern, an attack on social vices, a critique of the 'morale routinière' of the age. For Marrast they mark the emergence of the dominant aspect of the movement, 'le romantisme social' and Espronceda's break with 'le romantisme historique, chevaleresque et exotique'. Since Espronceda never belonged to the Christian faction of Durán and Böhl von Faber with their identification of Romanticism with Catholicism and monarchical absolutism, we might fault the latter view. The idea of a 'romantisme social' is equally suspect. 'El reo' and 'El verdugo' are concerned with two sides of the same theme: justice and punishment. There can be no argument over Espronceda's obvious affiliation to radical and revolutionary political ideals. It is possible, as some recent critics have attempted to show, to read these poems as a comment on the society of his day.

It must be admitted, however, for all the apparent anger of Espronceda's tone, that there is little that is positive or concrete in them in terms of a possible means to reforming or altering the social ills they illustrate. Indeed, the anger is tinged with cynicism and negative sentiments. They may stand as symbols of the evils of society and Espronceda's pessimistic view of it. On the other hand they could be concerned not so much with specific social ills as with other ills, the ills the Romantic mind had diagnosed as a regrettable and disturbing part of the human condition. There is little genuine social rebellion here, rather a philosophical one. For all the possible models cited by Marrast these poems belong to the age of *romanticismo actual*. The beginning of the poem provides the clue with the familiar reference to 'vez postrera'. The *reo* is young, the epitome of youth and the ideals and aspirations of the poet. The sounds of the worldly pleasures of others mock him in his echoing cell and sleep offers no solace. . . . [The] preterite verbs dash dreams to disillusionment and despair, de-

stroyed in the moment they seemed his, 'la vida / llena de sueños / pasó ya, . . . y oye de amor que suspira / la mujer que *un tiempo amó*'. As he reaches out to consummation he discovers a chilling reality: 'Y gozoso a verla vuela, / y alcanzarla intenta en vano, / que al tender la ansiosa mano / su esperanza a realizar, / su ilusión la desvanece / de repente el sueño impío, / y halla un cuerpo mudo y frío / y un cadalso en su lugar.' The related themes of soaring flight and upward aspiration, of longing for life and love, of ideals that give wings to the imagination but which are dashed into the pit of the grave are to appear with greater insistency in the last seven years of Espronceda's life. As a consequence of the thirst for the ideal and inevitable failure to attain it, there comes an intense feeling of isolation, a feeling which is emphasised since the ideal in **'El reo'** is couched in physical terms. Isolation is a common Romantic and post-Romantic motif. The solitude of the *reo*, underlined by the proximity, yet inaccessibility, of the world outside and by the sleeping confessor, is symbolic. Espronceda expresses his profound despair at the limitations of the scope of individual assertion, an excruciating solitude of metaphysical dimension. The *reo* feels a sense not only of social alienation but of cosmic abandonment and, as such, is a forerunner of Camus's Meursault. Imprisonment is a dramatic and symbolic form of isolation; death its most extreme statement. The prisoner's reflections on the fullness of life that others enjoy and that he might have enjoyed, especially in the contrast of his youth and the celibate priest, 'ya viejo y postrado [que] le habrá de sobrevivir', raise a question of ultimate justice. Where is the justification of a world in which the young and idealistic perish and the infirm live on? The prisoner is not condemned because society is unjust or uncaring. The supposed 'social comment' here is strangely understated. There is no evidence on which we can judge the social justice meted out for the *reo*'s crime; it has been judged in advance by the perspective from which Espronceda presents it. There is a contrast between what the young man ardently craves and believes the world should offer, and what he receives. And what he receives is symbolised in his sense of isolation and the image of the prisonhouse. This last image, along with those of judge, scaffold, noose and executioner, implies the view of a humanity trapped within an existence presided over by a God of wrathful injustice. The *reo* is the victim of that divine malevolence. Moreover, he feels abandoned in the absence of a God of love, guilty for the want of a God of justice. The Church, symbolised in the inattentive confessor, can no longer offer an easy restoration of justice through the balance of crime and punishment. Even individual supplication brings no message of forgiveness, love or pity. With the breakdown of the traditional system of morals, the falling away from religion and the freedom of a subjective and relativistic interpretation of transgression, the prisoner's sense of guilt becomes one of anxiety and fear. Without the confessional his life becomes a continual sense of trial. He is presented as guilty, on trial for a guilt which is unstated, of which he even seems unaware, but which, nonetheless, must exist. This uneasiness again recalls Camus and, more particularly, Kafka and Dürrenmatt. The prisoner's feelings are a mixture of guilt and fear. And yet what is he guilty of ? Is he being punished for wrongs he has not committed? It does seem that any metaphysical reward or consolation that could be offered cannot make up for the sentence of death and the consequent loss of human freedom, experience and love. Why, implies Espronceda, is human deprivation and suffering tolerated by God, and why are the idealistic punished? The *reo*'s captivity is both metaphysical abandonment and imprisonment. His existence *is* imprisonment. Here we return to the theme of fate raised in **'La despedida'**. He rages not at human injustice (which is never mentioned), but at his fate, cosmic injustice. Like Chateaubriand again, he curses the mother who conceived him, the hour in which he was born, 'y maldijo el mundo todo, / maldijo su suerte impía'. In the end we perceive that if any principle is observable in the world it is malign. Death overwhelms all human ideals and endeavour. His rage is not social or political revolt. It is one of the earliest examples of what Camus, in a remarkable restatement of Romantic ideology nearly one hundred and twenty years later [*L'Homme Révolté*], was to call 'la révolte métaphysique'.

**'El verdugo'** further elaborates the theme. The first part of the poem appears to confirm Marrast's contention that the executioner is the scapegoat for society's bad conscience over what amounts to justified murder. That is, like so many of his European contemporaries, Espronceda is commenting on the moral properties of the death penalty: '¿Quién al hombre del hombre hizo juez?' This suggests a relativistic, rather than an absolute, view of justice, questioning the moral right of the state to stand as God's moral minister. It is at this point that the supposed 'social meditation' is expressed in an ambiguous way, for the hangman insists that he is 'de la imagen divina / copia también'. The sadistic and voyeuristic account of the complicit savouring of torment and death by spectator and executioner alike introduces another necessary stage in Espronceda's argument. The hangman is the symbol and the agent of human viciousness, hate and malevolence; but he is also, like the *reo,* guilty without guilt, 'sin delito soy criminal'. He stands as the incarnation not only of human cruelty but of cosmic cruelty. From 'rey de venganzas' he becomes the agent of destiny, the incarnation of evil that will persist through time immemorial, that cruel *fuerza del sino* against which the Greek apostate and the *reo* cry out, and against which man strives in vain. The executioner's position is paradoxical for he alone sees that human injustice and evil are, in reality, the worldly manifestation of divine malevolence. This conviction engenders, arguably, the most pessimistic outburst Espronceda was ever to make. He is faced with the thought that man's striving for ideals and intimations of immortality is a vain pretension. He is forced to such a conclusion in the light of the eternal and unchanging sway of the cosmic evil of God, the executioner. We find here the persistent theme of pride leading to illusion which collides with reality, that is, man's curiosity and idealism are used as a means to bring him to insight and despair. And so he apostrophises the mother of his child to urge nothing less than infanticide. From the initial catalogue of the innocence and unspoiled purity of his child—'puro, gentil', 'gracia de un ángel', 'risa infantil', 'candor', 'inocencia', 'dulce hermosura'—to the sudden contrastive reversal of the norms of human expectation and of parental love in the exhortation '¡Oh! mué-

strate madre piadosa con él, / ¡ahógale, y piensa será así feliz!' the direction of Espronceda's thought is essentially negative. His radical solution of the extermination of the species to break the sway of malign cosmic forces seems to approach something of the temper of the systematic pessimism of his contemporary, Schopenhauer (1788-1860). We notice also a further development in Espronceda's world view. The majority of his sceptical Romantic contemporaries (Larra, Rivas, García Gutiérrez, Pacheco, Hartzenbusch) employ in their *criticista* dramas the device of malignant fate, Rivas' *fuerza del sino*. It is a mark of their protest against the divine ordering of events in this world, and Don Alvaro's suicide may be taken as the supreme response of man's negation of cosmic injustice. Espronceda, here and more explicitly in *El estudiante* and *El diablo mundo,* conceives of a God of anguish, suffering, cruelty and death. For the moment it is a statement of his growing convictions that traditional religious and moral interpretations of life are untenable. Later, as we shall see, his poetic heroes are to find the injustice of the universe unbearable and rather than seek release in suicide or retreat become rebellious and inquisitive.

Marrast has argued that **'El mendigo'** also belongs to a literature of social comment. A careful reading suggests, however, a portrayal of a specific psychological reaction to the world-view expressed in the other two poems of the group and earlier lyrics. Marrast's view that the beggar stirs the conscience of the rich to make them aware of the precarious nature of man's estate, that it is a reflection of the unsettled economy of the 1830s, is arguable. But in the context of the whole poetic canon there remains a more profound comment on human existence. First, the repeated refrain, 'dar limosna es un deber', is a cynical cliché, a tag doubly mocked by the slap-stick evocation of the pungent odours of the beggar's person offending the highborn lady and aristocratic gathering alike. Second, the flat statement that 'no hay placer sin lágrimas, ni pena / que no transpire en medio del placer' suggests a worldweariness and an abandonment of illusion. Third, 'para mí no hay mañana, / ni hay *ayer;* / olvido el bien como el mal, / nada me aflige ni afana' conveys a vision of an anodyne featureless life, a monotony of melancholy without shape or distinction. The levelling of opposites and the equation of difference makes all things ridiculously equal. We are not far from the modern view of absurdity. Last, the beggar is mentally and spiritually exhausted. He cannot even mock that which he has lost. Each moment is lived as it comes. There is no past, for illusions are gone; nor future, for he has no hope. He has become a nothing, a 'cuerpo miserable' who looks forward to nothing but a shallow grave. His derision is not born of social awareness or protest, it is born of insight. His scorn and cynicism are a pose, the pose of a man who once worshipped the ideals and manners he now derides. **'El mendigo'** is an embittered, negative version of an elegy for lost illusions.

The break with Teresa served to give further shape to Espronceda's negative pattern of thought. By 1837 he had begun *El estudiante de Salamanca* and had completed **'A XXX dedicándole estas poesías'**, **'A una estrella'** and **'A Jarifa en una orgía'**. The latter poem is a condensation of virtually all of the major elements of the poet's final preoccupations. There are obvious similarities of theme and expression in this group of poems, forming as they do, along with Espronceda's last, unfinished project, *El diablo mundo,* a clear and unified expression of his mature vital attitude. Increasingly we find an awareness of the growing gulf between the ideals and idealism of the early years and the reality of earthly experience. The ironic parenthesis in **'El verdugo'** to the effect that man's dreams are doomed at the outset, is a mere prelude to the explicit expression of a state of chilling insight which is to destroy Espronceda's confidence in any harmonious interpretation of life. We begin with the executioner's revelation that, 'Y en vano es que el hombre do brota la luz / con viento de orgullo pretenda subir. / ¡Preside el verdugo los siglos aún!'. In the Introduction to *El diablo mundo* the poet recognises that there exists some form of uncontrollable urge engendered of doubt and ardent enquiry which is to become another *verdugo,* a force for disillusionment and *angustia,* spiritual anguish. The direction is essentially negative and sceptical. 'Me erigiste en tu verdugo, / me tributaste temores, / y entre Dios y yo partiste / el imperio de los orbes. / Y yo soy parte de ti, / soy ese espíritu insomne / que te excita y te levanta / de tu nada a otras regiones, / con pensamiento de ángel, / con mezquindades de hombre.' Espronceda is confronted with a question of absolute value and ultimate knowledge in an age that seemed unable to supply them. Man, endowed with reason and imagination, rejecting traditional interpretations of life, seeks some source (truth, virtue, glory, love) from which meaning in life might flow. In essence, he seeks to discover the truth concerning his role and destiny, the purpose of life and its nature here and in the hereafter. All too often ardent idealism and flights of imagination end in disappointment and despair. Man's critical faculty reveals that illusion and the truth he seeks are not coincident, rather the reverse. In **'A XXX'** the 'ricos colores [que] pinta alegre . . . mi fantasía' become 'la triste realidad sombría'. In **'A una estrella'** 'el bien y la alegría', the anticipated goal of 'un ansia eterna / de amor perpetuo y de placer sin fin', 'en llanto y desventura se trocó'. 'Yo me lancé con atrevido vuelo / fuera del mundo en la región etérea,' cries Espronceda in **'A Jarifa',** 'y hallé la duda, y el radiante cielo / vi convertirse en ilusión aérea.' Virtue and glory become filth and dross, love corrupted and vile. But this theme of cruel disillusionment is not simply that of the man who strives beyond the limits of his feeble powers. Rather we return to the theme of ultimate justice. Espronceda confesses in **'A Jarifa'** that he was born with an exuberant and restless imagination, but one which deceived him, a 'falso guía'. In *El diablo mundo* we are reminded of the *reo* whose person is trapped within the walls of his cell and whose mind is confined in the prisonhouse of life itself. But there is an added explicitness of the cosmic dimension of man's *ansia:* '¡es Dios tal vez la inteligencia osada / del hombre siempre en ansias insaciable, / siempre volando y siempre aprisionada / de vil materia en cárcel deleznable?' When the 'espíritu del hombre', man's questing mind, 'remonta su vuelo / a un mundo que desconoce, / cuando osa apartar los rayos / que a Dios misterioso esconden, / y analizarle atrevido / frente a frente se propone', he receives not a revelation of life's mysterious origins and a pattern for moral and spiritual conduct

but a vision of cosmic disintegration, pain, disillusionment and injustice. The Spirit goes on to observe that, 'Tú te agitas como el mar / que alza sus olas enormes, / humanidad, en oleadas, / por quebrantar tus prisiones'. But there follows a series of significant questions: '¡Y en vano será que empujes, / que ondas con ondas agolpes, / y de tu cárcel la linde / con vehemente furia azotes? / ¿Será en vano que tu mente / a otras esferas remontes, / sin que los negros arcanos de vida y muerte ahondes?' The Spirit of Man, increasingly identified with Lucifer and Satan, is torn between the desire to probe the eternal mysteries and a growing recognition that increased knowledge and insight brings increased *angustia.* '¡Cuán terrible condición me aqueja / para llorar y maldecir nacido!' His conclusion, albeit in the form of a rhetorical question, is evidence enough of Espronceda's mature existential position. '¿Es Dios tal vez el Dios de la venganza, / y hierve el rayo en su irritada mano, / y la angustia, el dolor, la muerte lanza, / al inocente que le implora en vano?' For all the noble protest and rebellion here, the corrosive effect of doubt has muted Espronceda's response. The repeated 'tal vez' in this section, seven times in all, may suggest that he was toning down the violence of his outburst to meet the religious susceptibilities of his readers. Yet the series of interrogations and repeated qualifications may suggest that Espronceda held little faith in his cosmic rebellion, that even the 'fatal truth' perceived should be doubted.

The stress in **'Al sol',** in **'A una estrella'** and **'A Jarifa'** on eternal values shifts to an affirmation of the absence of them. Indeed, the man who seeks them (hence the stress on *analizar, razón, recorrer* in the late poems) is punished for his daring curiosity (*osar, locura, atrevido, rebelde, saber*). As he seeks reassurance that his sense of lost directions is a temporary one he learns that his longing for absolute criteria is an offence. He is punished for seeking the law, the guiding principles for life. Thus the anxious '¿por qués?' of **'A Jarifa'** are answered, as in *El estudiante* and *El diablo mundo,* by a mysterious voice: 'Muere, infeliz: la vida es un tormento, / un engaño el placer, no hay en la tierra / para ti, ni dicha, ni contento, / sino eterna ambición y eterna guerra. / Que así castiga Dios el alma osada, / que aspira loca, en su delirio insano, / de la verdad para el mortal velada / a descubrir el insondable arcano.' This is yet another facet of the theme of guilt which we have explored. In the Romantic mind there remains an unanswerable dilemma in that the quest for metaphysical reassurance is always countered by insight, the recognition that any foundation for firm belief or rational conduct is impossible. Be it Byron (the supposed source of much of Espronceda's anguished response), Vigny, Larra or Espronceda, the conclusion is the same. Manfred's statement that 'Sorrow is knowledge, they who the most / Must mourn the deepest o'er the fatal truth, / The tree of knowledge is not that of life' (*Manfred,* I, i), the constant references in this poem and *Cain* to 'the quest of hidden knowledge', to journeys 'to the caves of death, / Searching its cause in its effect', to 'The words of God, [that] tempt us with our own / Dissatisfied and curious thoughts', are all expressions of the Satanic temptation to probe the *arcano,* the eternal mysteries of life. But the Witch tells Manfred that his enquiry concerning the enigmas makes him 'fatal and fated in thy sufferings' (II, ii). The truth, when learned, brings anguish. Byron's conclusions are matched almost exactly in Espronceda's '¡La razón fría! ¡La verdad amarga!' and '¡Ay!, el que descubre por fin la mentira. / ¡Ay!, el que la triste realidad palpó!'. Espronceda's debt to Byron lies less in the list of verbal echoes established by critics than in this central and common ideological statement. The poet, quester for knowledge, is cursed. It is his fate to be thus. Man's adventurous mind finds not paradise but hell on earth. Fated to enquire he is punished by insight, hence his sense of guilt and his spiritual unease. (pp. 37-45)

[The] intimate relationship established between emotional fulfilment and metaphysical confidence suggests that it is not religion, nor virtue-idealism, nor political utopianism, but love that remained the last surviving absolute principle on which the Romantics rested their hold on life. The second part of *El estudiante de Salamanca* bears unequivocal witness to this reaction. In Part I Elvira believes Félix's pretensions of love. But, as always, the desire for eternal love is doomed. Espronceda's 'fingido', 'mentía', 'falaz' and the statement 'Placeres, ¡ay! que duran un instante / que habrán de ser eternos imagina / la triste Elvira en su ilusión divina' underline the potential for tragic insight. Félix becomes Elvira's 'dios que la enamora' just as the beloved in 'Suave es tu sonrisa' becomes a 'divinidad' to whom all those attributes normally reserved for Christian worship are applied. Love, not religion, becomes their last vital support. It is no surprise, therefore, to find a repetition of 'Fresca, lozana, pura,' in the parallel of falling leaves/failing illusions, and the repeated theme of preterite illusion and present anguish as insight supervenes. But now, quite explicitly, the collapse of illusion is the result of conscious rational experience, *análisis.* With the loss of love Elvira loses her hold on life, recognises the vanity of illusion and dies through disillusioned love. Love is the last sustaining ideal she had embraced, 'era el amor de su vivir la fuente'. At the moment of death her delirious mind clears and she expresses, in two lines, the essence of the negative Romantic response we have traced thus far: '¡La razón fría! ¡La verdad amarga! / ¡El bien pasado y el dolor presente! . . .' (pp. 46-7)

In 'A una estrella' and the other poems of the group the passage from illusion to a tragic sense of reality is effected by the collapse of the poet's emotional equilibrium. The poet becomes melancholic, is the victim of spiritual anguish as he surveys the ruins of his existential confidence. At the end of 'A Jarifa', having learned the 'fatal truth' that man is a victim of cosmic injustice, that 'la vida es un tormento, / un engaño el placer', he withdraws from life as an anodyne against its pain. This retreat from life is essentially a negative response, seeking a precarious and temporary peace withdrawing from accepted human feelings of love, compassion, sensibility, pleasure or sadness. This sense of spiritual isolation was soon to be expressed in a more positive way in *El estudiante de Salamanca.*

In this poem we find a contrastive presentation of the dilemma. In many ways Espronceda's *cuento* and the unfinished *El diablo mundo* are clearer statements of the pattern of Espronceda's mature thought than the idealistic and emotional poems we have examined. The earlier work reveals a temperament which oscillates between brief moments of intense joy, passion and a form of conviction and profound emotional torment, despair and spiritual uncertainty. It would be mistaken to assume that Espronceda's intellectual unease was provoked by occasional tragic intuitions. By temperament he was reflective and analytic. (p. 49)

But there is little to prepare the reader for the personality and the vital attitudes of Félix de Montemar, the 'estudiante de Salamanca'. Félix has virtually no illusions of the type we have examined. He begins his journey where the idealist ends in 'A una estrella'. The burden of the mysterious *gemido,* where consoling illusions are revealed as falsehood and 'la triste realidad' the only certainty, provokes no melancholic response. At the first revelation Félix jokes; the second message from across the grave passes virtually unheard since Montemar is 'atento sólo a su aventura'. He remains untouched by emotional problems and attaches no deeper significance to his many erotic adventures other than the gratification of the senses. His curt denial of the Romantic belief in the supremacy of love in Part III (248-51) is only a part of the necessary delineation of Félix's outlook. He does not feel the need for love, glory, beliefs; rather he lives entirely for the moment, outside the value systems and modes of moral conduct of the society in which he lives. Paradoxically, in spite of the abuse and misuse of his obvious qualities—'valor', 'buen talante', 'generosa nobleza', 'hermosura varonil', 'agilidad y bravura'—, in spite of his monstrous antisocial behaviour, 'en su impiedad y altiveza, / pone un sello de grandeza' (I, 137-8). His dominant characteristic is his indomitable will-power, which, coupled with extreme courage and daring, make him a formidable adversary and the very incarnation of the Romantic ego. In six telling adjectives (I, 100-4) he is portrayed and typified as a Don Juan. He remains a mystery until the last line (I, 139) when his name is revealed. In spite of his obvious Romantic qualities he lacks the dimension of melancholy-scepticism so typical of the heroes of Larra, Rivas or Musset. He lacks the element of abstract thought we find in *Sancho Saldaña* which allowed an expression of the author's philosophical viewpoint and 'vacío del alma'. In his physical restlessness he is more akin to the heroes of Byron. Félix's obvious generous and noble qualities have turned sourly destructive. Why? Espronceda does not explain but there are a number of clues. And if we take the poem in the context of the other lyrics of 1836-7, the moment when *El estudiante* was begun along with the Introduction to *El diablo mundo* (where very similar ideas are expressed), we can suppose these previous poetic statements to be Félix's prehistory. Of course, Espronceda has modelled his hero on the Golden Age Don Juan and similar legends and Félix has, perforce, to be a libertine and irreligious. But he is not simply a *burlador* in the mould of Tirso de Molina, he is also a student. Now even though Lisardo, one of Espronceda's models, was a student there are some very obvious differences. The Golden Age stories stressed the immortality of the Don Juan figure, his failure to heed the prescriptions of Church teaching and his lack of spiritual preparedness for the afterlife and Divine Judgement. That is, he places worldly pleasures above spiritual devotion and duty. Espronceda, while preserving many of the elements of his sources (the supernatural, the funeral, the *convidado de piedra* in the shape of Don Diego's ghost, the final confrontation scene), subtly modifies them and emphasises other aspects. First, Félix as a student is less like Lisardo than those other student-figures of his immediate predecessors. He is more like Goethe's Faust and Byron's Manfred than Lisardo. His contemptuous regard for the outrage he causes is less akin to Don Juan, *the burlador,* than to the cynical detachment of El Mendigo or the sentiment expressed in the closing lines of '**A una estrella**'. His amorality is the result of *análisis.* Like Byron's heroes he is 'damned by the demon thought'. Thought and insight, an essentially Romantic combination. Unlike Faust he does not sell his soul, although his desire for increased knowledge is similar. But he has not lost all regard for the idealism he once had. In spite of his rejection of traditional values and codes of conduct, for he no longer attaches meaning or sense to them, he retains a lingering nostalgia for what he has lost. In the fleeting glimpses of the face of the veiled figure (IV, 39-42; 81-8) he is reminded of 'alegres memorias . . . / . . . tiempos mejores que pasaron ya' (IV, 83-4). But these moments recall only the familiar preterite illusions. Now, he is without them. Despair breeds indifference to what once he cherished. And, like Manfred and other Romantic figures, he falls into the temptation to seek out some meaning in life, be it in unbridled hedonism and the breaking of the 'fanal / transparente de hermosura / . . . misterioso cristal' of love, alcohol, rebellion against society and God's universe or the pursuit of a mysterious figure that hints at those sources of consolation and felicity he once enjoyed. He seeks to understand what lies beyond the enigma represented by the ghostly figure in the gloomy street. The atmosphere of mystery and darkness is no mere décor, even though it combines all the clichés of the Romantic nightmare with clanging bells, howling dogs, phantoms, witches, howling wind and inky blackness. Nor is the conjunction of the figure of Christ and the kneeling figure coincidental. Beauty and religion, love and faith, as we have seen, go hand in hand in the art of sceptical Romanticism. If any proof were wanting of this assertion, Acts II and V of *Don Alvaro* or Chateaubriand's *Le Génie du Christianisme* (1802) would supply it. Above all, he is a quester, he is ardently curious. 'Osadía, atrevido, arrogancia, audacia, temerario brío, insolente' are terms consistently applied to Félix. 'Y he de saber', 'Que yo he de cumplir mi anhelo', he exclaims. What does he seek? He is led on in part by bravado (IV, 125-8), by lust (IV, 220-3) and by the thought, given that the future holds no hope or redemption, that with death pleasure comes to an end (IV, 239-46). But he is drawn on less because it reminds him of the pleasures enjoyed momentarily with Elvira than because he senses in the figure a challenge, that of the enigmas beyond the grave, and a source of metaphysical certainty. Félix's primary motivation lies in the fact that he is allowed to glimpse 'la esperanza blanca y vaporosa / . . . / y el alma conmueve con ansia medrosa / mientras la rechaza la adulta razón' (IV, 97-9). This is the meaning he longs for which reason, 'la razón fría', has taught him to be an illusion. At one point the goal is expressed clearly: 'Un término no más tiene la vida / término fijo; un paradero el alma' (IV, 511-12). For all his lack of values and the exer-

cise of reason he still clings to the belief that there *is* some finality even though it be in the realms of the supernatural or beyond the grave. Moreover, since the ghostly figure reminds him of the dead Elvira, he is in reality pursuing, as Manfred had, the secrets that lie beyond death itself (*Manfred,* II, ii). Byron's Don Juan expresses this curiosity exactly: 'What are we? Whence came we? What shall be our ultimate existence?' (*Don Juan* [1819] Canto VI, lxiii). Montemar's curiosity leads him on through experiences which might dement a weaker man until, at the last, he stands before what might be a vision of love, beauty and fulfilment. Given the tone of the other poems and the warning which the *gemido* gives Félix—'el que el esqueleto de este mundo mira, / y sus falsas galas le arrancó . . .'—the outcome is not surprising. In *El burlador de Sevilla* Don Juan is given explicit and increasingly weighty doctrinal warnings against his persistent refusal to repent. Don Félix, by contrast, is given no moral warnings, rather that the search for knowledge is ill-advised. The *gemido* of the phantom is an outcry of the rebellious poet against the final collapse of ideals and illusions that protect and beguile humanity from 'truth'. It is also, at the same moment, a revelation to Montemar of the bitter reality behind the world of appearances. It is here that the two aspects of the poem are fused. The rebellious, flamboyant superman and the sense of total despair expressed by the shadowy figure seem contradictory. Yet such an antithetical cast of outlook was common among Romantic writers; Byron, Lermontov and Musset are obvious examples. In fact the voice is scarcely audible. It affects the heart more than the ear; it is a potent poison for the soul administered in the symbolic shape of a sylphide who lures her lover to destruction. The exchanges between Félix and the phantom are in reality an intimate monologue in the heart of the poet himself where the two sides of his personality come together. He rebels because life no longer holds any meaning for him and all his gestures express his cynicism. He rebels in protest against a meaningless and malevolent universe and in his defiance expresses the only reply man has in the face of such disorder. In so doing it is the first existentialist gesture. And yet, in his heart he knows the 'truth' as it is revealed in explicit form by the ghostly voice. He expresses despair in the grim words and, subsequently, in the vision of the skeleton which lies beneath the veils of the ghostly figure, experiences the chill horror of an empty world where Beauty and Love no longer exist. The end of man's quest in life is not a structure of meaning, harmony, beauty or consoling serenity but the grinning mask of death. The search, expressed clearly in Félix's speech to the figure in the underground chamber (IV, 688ff ), where the promise of love seems to dominate and curiosity abounds ('a descubrirse el rostro la conjura'), ends not in a vision of bliss but on a familiar note: 'Y era / (¡desengaño fatal!, ¡triste verdad!) / una sórdida, horrible calavera, / ¡la blanca dama del gallardo andar! (IV, 846-9). In this recognition of the collapse of all illusions and the nothingness of life in this world and the hereafter the poem repeats, with an increased sense of desolation, the substance of the other lyrics of the late 1830s. It is quite unrelated to the intention that underlies a similar episode between Cipriano and Justina in Calderón's *El mágico prodigioso* where Cipriano is deceived by the promises of the Devil and can only gain *bondad, amor* and *ciencia* by repentance and belief. Félix's questions and quest reveal no benevolent divine structure beyond the diabolic visions he witnesses. But this poem has two additional features. First, Félix is a rebel. His persistent curiosity and his wilfulness, his belief in a 'término', imply that he still conceives that some principle must exist. And it is not Beauty/Love alone, an illusion which was to captivate those poets who follow Espronceda later in the century: Baudelaire, Samain, Darío or Jiménez, among others, and was to be as destructive as for Félix. His rebellion also implies a search for justice, one of the last principles to which he cleaves. This aspect is the least satisfactorily prepared for in the poem. In the Golden Age of Don Juan stories the theme of crime and punishment is clear. Sin brings Divine Retribution. But Félix recognises no sense of sin, stands outside of all accepted codes. He is never judged by them. Besides, while the ghostly figure is the symbol of Heaven's punishment, it is also the ghost of Elvira, a memory of past happiness, an alluring figure of Beauty and sexual pleasure as well as a possible figment of the imagination that draws Montemar into the world of the irrational. Thus the theme of justice is confused with other related aspects because Espronceda uses the one symbolic figure in multiple ways. This must count as one of the weaknesses of the poem. Félix's 'osadía' prepares us for the seeker after the *arcano,* the Byronic Fatal Man. It only prepares us in part for the view that man's existence is a metaphysical prison. It does not properly prepare us for the sudden revolt against God. Félix, we learn, is impious and blasphemous. He wilfully follows the figure in spite of the warnings: the earth shudders (IV, 70, 482); the *gemido* presents a vision of despair, lost illusions and spiritual anguish; he is told of the risks and the offence to heaven (IV, 223-5); he is informed, prophetically, of his death (IV, 230, 473-5); he stares in contest into the face of Christ (IV, 68), snatches the taper from the altar, cries out in the name of Satan repeatedly, and proposes an encounter with God and the Devil (IV, 500-1). Even so, the sudden elevation of the autobiographical hero to the status of Satan, 'alma rebelde', and subsequently as the symbol of man himself is too abrupt. But the theme is familiar: man, endowed with an 'ansia' that gives his imagination wings and his spirit an arrogant pride suddenly feels the confining walls of mortal existence. Espronceda's 'Con pensamiento de ángel, / con mezquindades de hombre' in the Introduction to *El diablo mundo* expresses the theme clearly. Félix's journey into the frightening world of dislocated space, time, of silence and uproar, of shifting perspectives, is a symbol of the questing mind in the galleries of the imagination and of thought. As the alluring enigma passes on so man's *ansia* follows it into the corridors of the mind and, eventually, into the symbolic pit of despair itself. The irregular stresses of the stair episode echo that fall of man. Canto VI and the Spirit of Life episode in Canto I of *El diablo mundo* also contrast the vision of a God 'que inunda a veces de alegría, / y otras veces, cruel, con mano impía / llena de angustia y de dolor el suelo' with Adán's 'perpetua ansiedad que en él se esconde'. Significantly Adán is warned in Canto I that his decision to be re-born, to discover the 'truth' of life, is his responsibility. In the same way the implication of the *gemido* episode is that

Félix, now warned, must bear the anguish and outcome of his own *ansia.* As Espronceda recognised in Canto III man's *ansia* will not allow him to live 'cual sandio mentecato' in 'un continuo tedio'. 'Pero ¿qué hemos de hacer, no examinar?'

Félix's grisly death by crushing and asphyxiation, mirrored in the whirlpool effect of the shrinking verse lines (IV, 914-1008), though reminiscent of the condemnation of Don Juan to the flames of Hell, has none of the eschatology of the Counter-Reformation. While the powerful hand that holds him is reminiscent of the clutch of the *convidado de piedra* in Tirso de Molina's play, there is no charge of mortal sin and a failure of spiritual preparedness. No reminder that '¡Largo plazo me lo fiáis!' is an ill-conceived view of the promise of the Resurrection. Montemar does make statements that echo Don Juan's '¡Tan largo me lo fiáis!' (IV, 234-6), but there is no assertion at the end of the balance of sin and retribution, the necessary purgation of moral turpitude or the ultimate justice of a Christian universe. The accent is on a betrothal, the fulfilment of a pledge, the consummation of a quest for an ideal. But at the end of life there stands not Love or Beauty, not the embrace of a loving God nor the sword of a God of retribution. There stands the foetid, nauseating caress of 'el carïado, lívido esqueleto', symbol of the finality of death and the nothingness beyond the grave, a sentiment further echoed in the monosyllabic final gasp of 'son' (IV, 1008). Man's life has no meaning or purpose other than as the plaything of an unjust God and gaoler. Popular rumour, shaped by traditional Catholic allegiances, has it that the Devil came for Montemar. But there is no Christian context in which he is judged, if indeed he is judged. He is not called to account for his sins. The warnings he receives are against his prying curiosity, his 'ansia'. Like Manfred, he is 'fatal and fated'. He is punished for plumbing the hidden mysteries. He peers into the *arcano* only to discover a 'triste verdad': with death everything comes to an end. Thus life has no significance either. But what can man do if he has lost his faith in life? Espronceda's reply is that man must assert his unique individuality, must move from passive acceptance to active revolt. Camus, in *L'Homme révolté* (1951), was to formulate this attitude into a philosophical principle. Espronceda would have accepted his view that the rebel cannot turn away from the world, cannot resign himself to evil and injustice. The act of revolt draws the rebel artist into combat with the realities of existence, provokes confrontation, imbues his life with a sense of liberation until in the end, in the absence of any coherence, revolt becomes a means of justifying the individual's life and provides him with his only reason for living. (pp. 50-8)

[Espronceda's] work expresses the sense of life on trial that subsequently appears in Dostoevsky, Camus, Kafka and Dürrenmatt, the *humorismo* of Unamuno, Gide and the Surrealists, the sense of absurdity of Valle-Inclán, Ionescu and Genet, the metaphysical rebellion of Malraux and Camus, the sense of existential despair and emptiness that pervades the writings of the great European writers of the modern age. In a comment recorded by his friend Escosura he expresses not only the sense of difference from ordinary men that the authentic Romantics felt, but also that sense of metaphysical separation and existential solitude which is the inspiration of our greatest contemporary European works of art:

> A pesar de todo, Patricio mío, eres más feliz de
> lo que presumes; tienes casa, tienes mujer, tienes
> hijos; estás en las condiciones de todo el
> mundo . . . ¡y yo!
>
> (p. 70)

> *Richard A. Cardwell, in an introduction to* El
> Estudiante de Salamanca and Other Poems *by
> José de Espronceda, edited by Richard A.
> Cardwell, Tamesis Texts Limited, 1980, pp.
> 13-70.*

## Thomas E. Lewis   (essay date 1983)

[*In the following excerpt, Lewis explores Espronceda's
search for social and metaphysical explanations for individual suffering and lack of fulfillment in his poetry.*]

As contradictions developed between those divergent political goals that eventually fragmented Spanish liberals into Moderates and Progressives, Espronceda produced in his poetry two explanatory systems for the crisis of liberal consciousness in the 1830's. In 1835, based on his perception of social obstacles placed in the path of individual fulfillment, he devised in poems such as **"El Mendigo"** and **"El Verdugo"** a *social* explanation for society's failure to realize individual freedoms. Based on his notion of the paradoxical nature of desire, however, he elaborated in such later poems as **"A una estrella"** and **"A Jarifa en una orgía"** a *metaphysical* explanation for individual suffering. Espronceda's poetry as a whole, therefore, presents us with two contradictory visions: one that indicts specific social practices as the source of human misery, and another that suggests that melancholy and suffering constitute inescapable realities of the human condition.

In affirming the existence of these two sequences of poems, however, we do not wish to draw too neat a line of demarcation between them. Often both explanatory systems reveal their presence in the same poem, giving rise to perhaps the most exhilarating quality of Espronceda's work. Indeed, its trajectory tends increasingly to bring these systems together in opposition within the same poem—not so as to integrate them, for that resolution always remained beyond Espronceda's reach—but rather in a manner that causes such systems to effect the metacommentary of the other. We shall ultimately discover that it is precisely the contradiction between these two alternative visions of human unfulfillment that generates and informs the structure of Espronceda's most ambitious work, *El Diablo Mundo.* (p. 11)

Espronceda's poetry reveals . . . the onset of a romantic and politically radical interrogation of abstract liberal ideals, a questioning whose formulation attempts to locate the disjunction between liberal theory and practice, and thereby to heighten liberal ideological consciousness. Indeed, in response to the political events of 1835, we witness in Espronceda the articulation of a poetic system which explains human alienation and the absence of Enlightened freedoms on the basis of a critique of Spanish liberal society itself.

Espronceda's first look at contemporary reality in 1835 betrays an abstract orientation conditioned by the fact that political events . . . had yet to prompt a full awareness of those contradictions between liberal theory and practice which soon became visible. In **"Canción del pirata"**, Espronceda clearly adopts a posture of Enlightened liberalism that projects an optimistic faith in the efficacy of individual liberty. Generally taken to mark the beginning of Espronceda's properly romantic career, this poem engages the pirate in a moment of self-definition. Such a format recurs frequently in his shorter poetry, and its technical dependence upon the lyrical mode achieves larger relevance by positing its speaker as a representatively ideal figure. In this instance, the poem establishes that figure generically as the unfettered individual of personal political liberty and economic free enterprise.

The poet's two-stanza introduction to the pirate's song, for example, spatially inserts the personna within a circumstance of unbounded freedom:

> y ve el capitán pirata,
> cantando alegre en la popa,
> Asia a un lado, al otro Europa,
> y allá a su frente Estambul.

The joyous vigor of this passage never dissipates, for the self courses freely through a world which offers it no resistance: "que ni enemigo navío, / ni tormenta, ni bonanza/ tu rumbo a torcer alcanza,/ ni a sujetar tu valor" (ll. 19-22). On the contrary, all nations acquiesce in admiration to the exercise of the pirate's right to impose himself upon the world by extracting wealth when and where he can (ll. 41-48). The refrain of the poem, moreover, overtly champions the pirate's freedom from national, geographic, or dynastic constraints, and it defines the essence of his character by putting his social activity—and his economic means of livelihood—in direct relationship to the creed of Enlightened liberalism:

> Que es mi barco mi tesoro,
> que es mi dios la libertad,
> mi ley, la fuerza y el viento,
> mi única patria, la mar. (ll. 31-34)

Thus, the pirate stands as a figure authentically committed to an unproblematic liberal ideology of freedom, natural law, and equality; he is one "a quien nadie impuso leyes" (l. 40) and who distributes among his men "lo cogido/ por igual" (ll. 52-53).

Nevertheless, we can detect the abstract quality of the exposition of liberal ideals in **"Canción del pirata"** when we compare it to two poems published the following September. At one level, the speaker in **"El Mendigo"** bears resemblance to the pirate in that each finds himself above the constraints of normal social conventions, each contains elements of "natural man," and each pursues individualistically a marginalized means of living. Whereas the pirate's existential space remains wholly *outside society,* however, **"El Mendigo"** articulates its persona in relation to various social classes. This change represents the most striking of the poem's innovations, for Espronceda's situating of his subject within a social context leads the poem to undertake a fledgling critique of liberal society and its values.

The key to the poem's interpretation lies in the observation, shown especially in the third movement, that the beggar bases his whole enterprise upon the rational calculation that people will give him charity when confronted by a spectacle that fills them with fear in regard to their own well-being. Thus, "le mendiant se fait l'accusateur d'une société qu'il méprise et dont il exploite les faiblesses." Marrast [in his *José de Espronceda et son temps,* 1970] suggestively relates the cynicism with which the beggar affirms that his benefactors act out of their own self-interest to the social fact of the presence in Madrid during the '30's literally of armies of beggars, refugees from rural poverty and unemployment, who could also find no work in the city. . . . Espronceda thus reproves liberal society for having done nothing concretely in the way of addressing the social origins of the economic plight of the lower classes.

We may extend Marrast's reading of the poem, however, and suggest that **"El Mendigo"** employs this indictment of a specific material reality belonging to liberal society in a manner which criticizes the ideological practice of liberalism itself. Society as a whole here consists of an undifferentiated mass whose members are uniformly held captive by a system of false values. The beggar thus remains the only representative of the Enlightened ideals of either individualism or liberty. Nevertheless, in view of the sordid social reality to which the poem alludes, Espronceda unleashes a heavy irony in relationship to the beggar's *apparent* "freedom" and "individualism" that successfully calls into question the historical status of the bourgeois category of "individual liberty" itself:

> Mío es el mundo: como el aire libre
> otros trabajan porque coma yo;
> todos se ablandan si doliente pido
> una limosna por amor de Dios. . . .
>
>    Vivo ajeno
> de memorias:
> de cuidados
> libre estoy.
> Busquen otros
> oro y glorias,
> yo no pienso
> sino en hoy.     (ll. 87-90; 97-104)

By a signal switching of perspectives, the reality of the beggar's individualism compared to the rest of society becomes, at one and the same time, the mark of his oppression. His freedom stands revealed as a metaphorical freedom only; it in no way implies the beggar's opportunity to participate fully and equally in social life. Thus, for Espronceda, liberal society in 1835 has not only failed to remedy basic social ills, but it has also compromised its own ideology—its own resolve to effect social reform—since it allots to the beggar the only social space in which it permits "individualism" and "freedom" to exist. Espronceda employs the beggar as a symbol, therefore, to assert that these values remain the abstract and unrealized fictions of contemporary society.

**"El Verdugo"** pursues this theme a step further. Relying formally on the prototypical speaker we have seen developed, the poem begins by asserting the same proposition adduced in **"El Mendigo"** that the executioner's social status derives from society's ostracization of the individual. Indeed, Espronceda constructs the entire poem around the opposition between the subjective consciousness of the *verdugo* and the objectified activity of society, represented by the use of the impersonal "they." As in **"El Mendigo,"** therefore, individualism manifests itself within a limited sphere which society labels as "other" and which it subsequently invests with a negative valence through a perverse displacement:

> De los hombres lanzado al desprecio
> de su crimen la víctima fui;
> y se evitan de odiarse a sí mismos
> fulminando sus odios en mí. (ll. 1-4)

Instead of acknowledging the *verdugo* to be a human being, moreover, society strips him of his humanity in order to create an ideological illusion masking the awareness that the executioner acts as society's agent, avenging crimes that society itself produces and defines as such. In contrast to **"El Mendigo,"** however, **"El Verdugo"** provides no social space for personal liberty, for here the only representative of individualism constantly discovers that society rebuffs his attempts at self-realization.

The second and third sections of the poem inaugurate a curious double movement whereby the executioner first looks at himself from the inside and then evaluates himself from the objective vantage point of the *pueblo.* In many ways the second section (ll. 41-60) represents a psychological foray into the *verdugo's* personality. Espronceda displays the evident pride that the executioner takes in his work and communicates all the subjective impressions that his senses register in the moment of putting a prisoner to death (ll. 41-52). This section conveys clear overtones of perversity on the part of the *verdugo.* Indeed, its purpose is precisely that of awakening in us the suspicion that perhaps society acts rightly in stigmatizing the executioner.

The third section (ll. 61-80) then subtly modulates the perspective into an objective view of the executioner's personality, seen now through the eyes of the *pueblo.* The verdugo's self-valorization in section two, however, still exercises a residual influence, for this section offers a vision of the executioner elevated above all the strata of society:

> Ya más alto que el grande que altivo
> con sus plantas hollara la ley
> al verdugo los pueblos miraron,
> y mecido en los hombros de un rey;
>   y en el se hartó
> embriagado de gozo aquel día
> cuando expiró. . . . (ll. 61-67)

The exalted identification of the executioner in this passage with the regicide carried out by the French Revolution achieves two ends. It constitutes the initial assertion of the function the *verdugo* performs as a symbol of history itself. More immediately, it attests to a distance established between the *verdugo* and the people based upon the recognition of his role as the ultimate enforcer of state power:

> Que el verdugo
> con su encono
> sobre el trono
> se sentó.
> Y aquel pueblo
> que tan alto le alzara bramando,
> otro rey de venganzas, temblando,
> en el miró. (ll. 73-80)

It is a devastatingly revelatory aspect of this poem that the nature of the crimes committed by the executioner's victims are never specified. Given the sympathy bestowed upon the criminals by the imagery in section one (ll. 28-32), however, every indication points to the fact that Espronceda has political prisoners *foremost* in his mind, and indeed, the only specific crimes referred to in the poem are the political crimes of Louis XVI and the "crimes" of social ostracization committed against the *verdugo* himself. Thus, as this last passage illustrates, the poem considers the objective social significance of the executioner to be that of a repressive state apparatus; no sooner have the *pueblo* constituted themselves as a state power to eradicate the *ancien régime,* then, to their horror, they witness the executioner survive as a component of the newly created state.

Hence, the question of the *verdugo*'s perversity loses its relevancy, for in section four (ll. 81-100) the poem conflates subjective and objective assessments into an overriding symbolism of the historical process itself:

> En mí vive la historia del mundo
> que el destino con sangre escribió,
> y en sus páginas rojas Dios mismo
> mi figura impaciente grabó. (ll. 81-84)

The figure of the *verdugo* thus becomes the nodal point of a massive textual overdetermination. Subjectively, society has rigidly shaped his destiny; objectively, his symbolic status indicts the repressive power of society, and in particular, that of Spanish bourgeois society. Ultimately, the *verdugo*'s message is that still nothing has changed in terms of social freedoms, for every execution he carries out testifies to the continued crimes which humanity generically inflicts upon its members:

> ¡Preside el verdugo los siglos aún!
>   Y cada gota
> que me ensangrienta
> del hombre ostenta
> un crimen más.
> Y yo aún existo
> fiel recuerdo de edades pasadas. . . .(ll. 92-98)

Finally, as the poem dissolves back into the subjective viewpoint of the fifth section (ll. 101-120), Espronceda makes it plain that no real opportunity exists as yet for the realization of personal liberty and individual desire. In a pitiful scene the verdugo addresses his son and wife, even suggesting to her that she might smother her infant child; for he painfully understands that his son *must* grow up to be another verdugo, and that, if he is to have any pleasure in life at all, he will have to seek it in the perverse satisfaction of performing a job well-done.

The sequence of poems written between January and September 1835, therefore, shows that for Espronceda the values informing liberal ideology have lost their abstract appeal and pristine façade. Once Espronceda socially situates his prototypical speaker, the naiveté of the pirate's comfortable espousal of Enlightened creeds, as well as the ease by which he lives by them, vanishes before a vision of the increasingly problematic relation between liberal ideology and social reality. In **"El Mendigo,"** we first detect the presence of fissures breaking apart what in **"Canción del pirata"** the poet assumes as the organic seams uniting liberal theory and practice. **"El Mendigo"**'s cynical irony, set in motion by the accusatory social plight to which the poem refers, paints a dismal picture of the extent to which Spanish liberal society has realized its self-professed ideals. **"El Verdugo"** subsequently mounts an even more damaging indictment of this failure, illustrating with crippling effect the exclusion of the individual and denial of his freedom, as determined by the historical process then at work. In this sense, therefore, we may speak of Espronceda's articulation of a poetic system which responds to the political crisis of liberal consciousness through a criticism of various social practices themselves. The failure, that is, lies with society, with its reneging on its own ideology, and not with some contravening mechanism intrinsic to human experience, as will surface as a possibility in Espronceda's later poetry.

In a poet of the artistic caliber and political consciousness of Espronceda, the leaving behind of his social themes in order to occupy himself almost exclusively for two years with a metaphysical problematic largely without precedent in his earlier work testifies to the onset of a deep personal crisis whose implications, both in his life and his poetry, are ultimately epistemological. It was not just Teresa's abandonment of Espronceda in late 1836 or early 1837 that alone provoked this stunning shift in poetic perspectives, nor is it that his new poetry simply carries on the solipsistic dialog of the poet's persona with his absent lover. Rather, certainly precipitated most immediately by Teresa's departure, this poetry nonetheless has politics itself as one of its determinants, and—in the same way that M. H. Abrams suggests [in "English Romanticism: The Spirit of the Age" in *Romanticism and Consciousness,* 1970] that the themes of joy and despair in the later English romantics have as their absent referent the disillusioning experience of the French Revolution—this poetry continues to allude to the social and political world in which it was born.

What has occurred, however, is that Espronceda has lost his ability to provide answers—that is, material explanations—for the problems he discovers. His poetry thus seeks refuge in metaphysics, which offers at least the descriptive "explanation" vulgarly contained in the *cliché*: "That's the way it is." Nevertheless, the outstanding feature of this period of Espronceda's poetic production remains the fact that ultimately he cannot be satisfied with such an answer. His poetry indeed dramatizes the conflict of a man who has no answers for himself, who feels attracted by the *intellectual certainty* of the metaphysical response, but who fights as tenaciously as he can against having to surrender to that desperate view of human existence. (pp. 12-18)

Espronceda's most important poetry of this period (1837-38), therefore, concerns his creation of that second explanatory system for human unfreedom and unfulfillment that rivals the social code elaborated in 1835. The formal design of the poems that express Espronceda's metaphysical explanation of what now figures in his works as the familiar romantic subject/object dilemma receives an early and, until 1837, almost unique formulation in **"A una dama burlada"** (1833). Here the male speaker taunts bitterly a woman whom he once loved and to whom he remains emotionally attached through feelings of contempt and rejection. The poet highlights two significant features of their past relationship. He characterizes it even at the outset as a kind of prison devised by the female in order to confine the male:

> Dueña de rubios cabellos,
>    tan altiva
> que creéis que basta el vellos
> para que un amante viva
>    preso en ellos
> el tiempo que vos queréis. . . . (ll. 1-6)

Espronceda signals an ultimate inadequacy of the love-object to answering the totalizing demands of the (male) self, furthermore, by representing the *dama* as having only a partial satisfaction to give her three lovers. Each desires her exclusively, but each, with great disdain, discovers her limited resources:

> ¡De cuántas mañas usabas
>    diligentes!
> Ya tu voz al viento dabas,
> ya mirabas dulcemente,
>    o ya hablabas
> de amor, o dabas enojos;
> y en tus engañosos ojos
> a un tiempo los tres galanes,
> sin saberlo tú, leían
>    que mentían
> tus afanes. (ll. 23-33)

This poem remains important for understanding the concerns of the poetry of 1837-38 in that it introduces the notion of the paradoxical nature of desire within a thematic context of a psychology of the sexes. The desiring self is here compelled to seek relationship with an object which attracts it but which eventually thwarts the infinite nature of its demands. That is, subjective desire is *absolute* and *requires* the object world for its satisfaction, but every object with which it attempts to find fulfillment is ontologically limited. Thus, what initially constitutes a free act of libidinal investment, suddenly becomes a suffocating state of fixation from which the self can only be freed, as we shall later see, through a terribly painful process. No matter how painful the process, however, the same impulse to absolute gratification that prompted the self to enter relation in the first place similarly forces it to negate the existing relation and undertake the search for a new one. Although **"A una dama burlada"** broaches this dialectic of self and other in only the most superficial fashion, its significance as a contrast to the later poetry lies both in that this early poem views the problem solely from the perspec-

tive of the subject and that, while not optimistic, it resists asserting despair as the dominant emotional note. Indeed, it stops short with a kind of disdainful brush-off; we have no doubt that the speaker will have a new mistress tomorrow.

Were Espronceda to have been an English poet, then his **"A una estrella"** would have already been classified, along with "Frost at Midnight," "Tintern Abbey," "Mont Blanc," and "To Autumn," as one of the most accomplished examples of what Abrams has called the greater romantic lyric [in "Structure and Style in the Greater Romantic Lyric" in *Romanticism*]. Adapting in a much more sophisticated way the metaphysics of desire and the psychology of the sexes foreseen in **"A una dama burlada,"** this poem evinces that genre's tripartite structure of the poet's initial confrontation with a natural scene, his subjective immersion within the scene itself, and his final withdrawal into a reflexive position where he expresses an emotional conclusion about his own relation to the object world. Interestingly enough, however, **"A una estrella"** operates a formal innovation of outstanding brilliance upon this basic schema. In the stages (one and three) where the poet remains most distant from the object of his discourse, the star functions metaphorically as his double; when in section two he moves emotionally most closely toward it, the star substitutes for his absent lover. Thus, the dialectic of genre between form and content here—that is, the poem's purposeful disruption of pure states of distance and identification—itself contributes to an overriding sense of indeterminacy.

As the poet turns his gaze toward the evening sky, the poem's first movement (ll. 1-28) posits both the ontological mystery that the star represents and simultaneously introduces the star as a metaphorical double:

> ¿Quién eres tú, lucero misterioso,
> tímido y triste entre luceros mil,
> que cuando miro tu esplendor dudoso,
> turbado siento el corazón latir?
>
> ¿Es acaso tu luz recuerdo triste
> de otro antiguo perdido resplandor,
> cuando, engañado como yo, creíste
> eterna tu ventura que pasó? (ll. 1-8)

The suggestion here that the star is at once an unfamiliar object and a mirror-image of the self calls attention to Espronceda's personal disorientation. The "estrella" perhaps has experienced a felicitous past filled with the profound expectation of infinite happiness and the endless satisfaction of desire. Like the poet himself, now abandoned and left only with the shadowy memory of a disillusioning first love, the star has lost all of its former plentitude of being. In the final stanza of this section, therefore, the poet contemplates *himself* in the image of the star, which returns his look echoing the inevitably sour outcome of libidinal relation: "Y ahora melancólico me miras,/ y tu rayo es un dardo del pesar;/ si amor aún al corazón inspiras,/ es un amor sin esperanza ya" (ll. 25-28).

The second phase of the poem (ll. 29-99) pursues a highly complex strategy of metamorphoses in which the star serves at different points as the poet's double, the displaced image of his lover, and as a symbol for an ontological causality that the poet can only vaguely indicate. The first two stanzas continue the identification of poet and star by projecting both back in time and space to the period of each one's fulfilling past. That the star figures as shining brightly upon the poet himself, however, lays the groundwork for its symbolic registering of causality. The next four stanzas inaugurate the most interesting and important sequence of verses in the entire poem:

> ¿Quién aquel brillo radiante
> ¡oh lucero! te robó,
> que oscureció tu semblante,
> y a mi pecho arrebató
> la dicha en aquel instante?
>
> ¿O acaso tú siempre así
> brillaste, y en mi ilusión
> yo aquel resplendor te di,
> que amaba mi corazón,
> lucero, cuando te vi?
>
> Una mujer adoré
> que imaginara yo un cielo;
> mi gloria en ella cifré,
> y de un luminoso velo
> en mi ilusión la adoré.
>
> Y tú fuiste la aureola
> que iluminaba su frente,
> cual los aires arrebola
> el fúlgido sol naciente,
> y el puro azul tornasola. (ll. 39-58)

The first stanza here seems still to resonate with the identification of the poet and the star, but it poses an epistemological question—"what causes the frustration of human desire?"—that, when pursued in the second stanza, reveals that the poet instead interrogates the stars as the displaced image of his former lover. Indeed, he considers an idealist explanation for the star's diminution of brightness (i.e., the loss of its attractive power for the poet) by suggesting that it was he who endowed it with a brilliance it never possessed. The speaker then offers a concrete example of this idealist deception, again confirming that the star in the preceding two stanzas represents his lover, and remarks bitterly that she owed her captivating charms to his projection of an ideal image upon her. The last stanza of this sequence, however, abruptly breaks the identification of star and lover by telling us that the star itself illuminated her face with all its beauty. Nevertheless, this final metamorphosis does not restore the identification of poet and star. Rather, by recalling the star's illumination of the poet's face—"¡Ay, lucero! yo te vi/ resplandecer en mi frente . . ." (ll. 29-30)—it inhibits that operation and in fact posits the star as a metaphysical power which has overseen, and perhaps directed, the whole itinerary of the poet's disillusioning experience: "Y, astro de dichas y amores,/ se deslizaba mi vida/ a la luz de sus fulgores . . ." (ll. 59-61).

The remaining stanzas of section two, however, undo the tentatively idealist assertions and conclusions that have just arisen in the course of the poet's philosophical questioning. Paradoxically enough, any intellectually con-

vinced idealism disappears with the poet's recourse to the "pathetic fallacy:"

> ¡Ah, lucero! tú perdiste
> también tu puro fulgor,
>   y lloraste;
> también como yo sufriste
> y el crudo arpón del dolor
>   ¡ay! probaste.
>
> ¡Infeliz! ¿por qué volví
> de mis sueños de ventura
>   para hallar
> luto y tinieblas en tí,
> y lágrimas de amargura
>   que enjugar?
>
> Pero tú conmigo lloras,
> que eres ángel caído
>   de dolor,
> y piedad llorando imploras,
> y recuerdas tu perdido
>   resplandor.
>
> Lucero, si mi quebranto
> oyes, y sufres cual yo,
>   ¡ay! juntemos
> nuestras quejas, nuestro llanto:
> pues nuestra gloria pasó,
>   juntos lloremos. (ll. 76-99)

As the poet here portrays the suffering of the objective background (the star), it becomes clear that, though *similar*, the cause of their pain and that pain itself are ontologically separate. Each one has his own reasons for suffering, and thus the idealist speculation (ll. 44-48) that the poet projected upon the star its former brilliance is negated by the process of reestablishing the star's function as a double. Indeed, the epistemological questioning ceases in the very moment in which the poet recognizes change, activity, and response in the "other." This same process, moreover, successfully undermines that other epistemological possibility (ll. 54-63)—that the star represents a metaphysical agency of causality set above both poet and lover—for this section ends with an appeal for both poet and star to unite as equal companions in the search for consolation.

In the final section of the poem (ll. 100-119), we subsequently witness the poet's admission of defeat in his quest to explain the material cause of his failure to achieve lasting happiness. His continued inability to give himself over *completely* to a metaphysical view—i.e., that suffering the unfulfillment intrinsically define the human experience—manifests itself again when he grants the star the possibility of a future happiness that he denies himself: "¿Quién sabe? . . . tú recordarás acaso/ otra vez tu pasado resplandor . . ." (ll. 104-105). Significantly, however, such happiness will fall neither to him nor to his contemporaries, for it awaits a future, utopian moment in history: "un oriente más puro que el del sol" (l. 107). The poem culminates, therefore, on a note of despair that, in the context of Espronceda's poetry as a whole, signals a total collapse of confidence in the existential and political values of Enlightened liberalism. In a passage whose agony is rivalled only by the final lines of **"A Jarifa en una orgía"** and **"Canto a Teresa,"** the poet makes a direct and bitterly ironic reference to the vitality, initiative, and creative freedom celebrated in **"Canción del Pirata"**:

> Yo indiferente sigo mi camino
> a merced de los vientos y la mar,
> y entregado en los brazos del destino,
> ni me importa salvarme o zozobrar. (ll. 116-119)

Thus, **"A una estrella"** treads the dark waters of epistemology with a technical excellence that cannot save it either from a philosophical agnosticism or an existential resignation. Its significance lies with the changed aesthetic format in which Espronceda discusses the problem of human unfulfillment. No longer, as in **"El Mendigo"** and **"El Verdugo,"** does he create representatively ideal *personae* whose self-preservation and poetic *mise-en-scène* launch a dialectical interaction between liberal ideology and social reality that is productive of a critical vision of Spanish society. The confessional speaker in **"A una estrella"** becomes instead the naked and radically individual "I" of romantic poetry in general. Unlike the English romantics, however, the eminently solitary speaker here fails to achieve any kind of cultural representativeness. The poetic exploration of the subject/object dilemma that, in varying forms, lends itself to romantics outside Spain as an enormously valuable cognitive model for the "reconstitution of value" remains stillborn in Espronceda. Having abandoned any attempt to explain or to situate his problem socially, Espronceda contorts his way through a topologically complex cosmic landscape ultimately informed by epistemological indeterminacy. What causes human suffering? After much effort to provide an answer, the poet tells us only that people suffer. Thus, while metaphysically asserting the inadequacy of the love-object to subjective desire, this poem resolves nothing in terms of a knowledge of the causes of such a condition; its significance resounds rather in the poet's *emotional* battle against the absence of meaning forced on him by his ignorance and confusion.

That this struggle assumes the form of an exploration of a possible idealist, or metaphysical, causality leads the poem to begin codifying the elements of Espronceda's second explanatory system. The theme of the paradox of desire, for example, operates explicitly here. The poet's libidinal life traces the path from fulfillment to frustration, and yet the compelling drive to relation—the self's necessity for the object world—reappears in the community that the poet establishes between himself and the star (ll. 94-99). Though the psychology of the sexes (as another component of Espronceda's metaphysical problematic) may remain somewhat submerged in **"A una estrella,"** it surfaces with a vengeance in the other outstanding composition in this mode, **"A Jarifa en un orgía."** While reiterating, moreover, the same formulation of epistemological indeterminacy based on the metaphysics of desire, **"A Jarifa"** inaugurates the juxtaposition within one poem of contradictory explanatory systems that *El Diablo Mundo* fully establishes. It does so by overtly casting Espronceda's renewed inquiry into the source of human misery directly in the form of a debate concerning idealist and materialist causality.

The first of **"A Jarifa"**'s three sections establishes a spirit/body dualism that provides the basis for the machi-

nations of the metaphysical paradox of desire. As the poem opens, the poet's soul feels victimized by his own body and its sensuality. Seeking relief by asking Jarifa to place her hand on his feverish forehead, he discovers that her body too performs a violence, not so much against his body, as against his spirit: "Ven y junta con mis labios/ esos labios que me irritan,/ donde aun los besos palpitan/ de tus amantes de ayer" (ll. 5-8). The self, according to this scenario, cannot be content with solipsism; in a perfect illustration of Freud's economy of the libido, the ego falls ill when its libidinal drives are bottled up and corked inside. Nevertheless, in Espronceda's world the objects of possible libidinal relation all prove unsatisfactory. Here his psychology of the sexes intrudes to concretize the paradox of desire: men play the role of subjects possessed by an infinite desire for a totally fulfilling relationship; women both literally and symbolically function as objects of limited capacity whose inevitably disappointing inadequacies are signalled (until we meet Salada in *El Diablo Mundo*) by their infidelity or their career as prostitutes.

In the face of the libidinal disillusionment that Jarifa symbolizes, therefore, the poet briefly considers drunken escapism as a solution (ll. 13-16) but then suddenly shifts his attention to denounce vehemently the spiritual, emotional and physical poverty that the object world represents:

> Huye, mujer, te detesto,
> siento tu mano en la mía,
> y tu mano siento fría,
> y tus besos hielo son.
>
> ¡Siempre igual! Necias mujeres,
> inventad otras caricias,
> otro mundo, otras delicias,
> ¡o maldito sea el placer! (ll. 21-28)

As this last passage reveals, however, the speaker still suffers an overwhelming attraction for the object world, despite his knowledge beforehand that any relation with it will only disappoint him. Desire inescapably defines his essence, inadequacy just as irrevocably defines the world, and so by the end of this first section, he finds himself cornered into an ontological dualism that even turns its back upon the community he tenuously establishes with the star in **"A una estrella"**:

> Yo quiero amor, quiero gloria
> quiero un deleite divino,
> como en mi mente imagino,
> como en el mundo no hay;
> y es la luz de aquel lucero
> que engañó mi fantasía,
> fuego fatuo, falso guía
> que errante y ciego me tray. (ll. 33-40)

The association with the star and its false path—i.e., a possible flight into a metaphysical and transcendent idealism—thus leads in the second section of **"A Jarifa"** (ll. 41-88) to a resurgence of the philosophical question (ll. 41-56) also at the core of **"A una estrella."** Pleasure is illusory, but my suffering is real: why? Fulfillment is a fiction, but this force which drives me to seek it is real: why? I can imagine my happiness, but the world will not correspond to my desire: why? Indeed, the reanimation of this interrogatory process itself testifies both to the persistence of the epistemological indeterminacy of the metaphysical response as well as to the poet's emotional refusal to accept its potential conclusions about the nature of human existence.

He confirms, for example, that his encounter with the star only attenuated his uncertainties and proceeds to chronicle for us the next step in his quest:

> Yo me lancé con atrevido vuelo
> fuera del mundo en la región etérea,
> y hallé la duda, y el radiante cielo
> vi convertirse en ilusión aérea.
>
> Luego en la tierra la virtud, la gloria
> busqué con ansia y delirante amor,
> y hediondo polvo y deleznable escoria
> mi fatigado espíritu encontró. (ll. 61-68)

The return to reality, therefore, proves as unfulfilling as ever, but the poet has here discarded a facile idealist resolution in another unmistakable reference to **"A una estrella"** (ll. 61-64). Furthermore, despite the fact that he finds himself with "mi ilusión desvanecida/ y eterno e insaciable mi deseo" (ll. 73-74), he still searches for a potentially fulfilling pleasure in the real world. We may say, then, that by the end of this section the poet has definitively rejected any form of idealist transcendence, but that he still cannot emotionally accept that reality *is* as he has experienced it. Emitting an anguished question, he receives the damning answer which we have been led to anticipate:

> "Muere, infeliz: la vida es un tormento,
> un engaño el placer: no hay en la tierra
> paz para tí, ni dicha, ni contento,
> sino eterna ambición y eterna guerra.
>
> Que así castiga Dios el alma osada
> que aspira loca, en su delirio insano,
> de la verdad para el mortal velada,
> a descubrir el insondable arcano." (ll. 81-88)

Who is it that answered him? It is, as you would have it, the "Voice of Reality," the "Voice of the Other," or that component of his own subjectivity exhausted and ready to call it quits with experience itself. Triumphantly, material reality announces both its own supremacy over subjective desire (ll. 82-84), as well as its epistemological impenetrability (ll. 85-88); its intractable advice remains that the poet commit suicide. And indeed, the third section of the poem (ll. 89-116) opens with the poet responding to this "acento pavoroso" precisely in the form of a death-wish:

> ¡Oh, cesa! No, yo no quiero
> ver más, ni saber ya nada;
> harta mi alma y postrada,
> sólo anhela descansar.
> En mí muera el sentimiento,
> pues ya murió mi ventura;
> ni el placer ni la tristura
> vuelvan mi pecho a turbar. (ll. 89-96)

This is a death-wish of the self, of course, which echoes the poet's earlier assertion that, "sólo en la paz de los sepulcros creo" (l. 76). Nevertheless, as Espronceda prepares to change stanzaic forms, the last two lines here foreshadow what becomes in the following two stanzas a death-wish directed against reality. The poet now defies

reality and dares all its "mujeres voluptuosas" to tease his desire with every one of their powers. Instead of self-destructively wishing not to "ver más," he hopes rather to neutralize the attractive power of reality itself: "Pasad como visiones vaporosas/ sin conmover ni herir mi corazón" (ll. 103-104). Having rejected a solipsistic transcendence in section two, therefore, and having here turned the gun away from his own temple and aimed it at the reality which frustrates him, we nevertheless still find the poet stuck in a dualistic situation in which either subject or object must give way and initiate a movement of *rapprochement* toward the other.

It is only in this sense, moreover, that we may understand the poem's final two stanzas. The penultimate stanza affirms that the reality he dared to affect him has in fact done so, but that thanks to some sort of functional drunken insulation, he has successfully survived the night with all its sensual temptations and potential frustrations. He has entered again, much to his own surprise, into the morning light. The recourse to the excuse of alcohol, however, as well as his own astonishment at having survived the impulse to suicide and the renewed attack of desire, attest to a fundamental intellectual mystification. That is, those devices, other than connoting a certain deadening of the senses, emphasize the poet's incapacity to formulate intellectually the combination of attitudes and realities which permit him to come out into the bleary light of a new day. Whatever this causality, it does elicit, in the same stanzaic form, an alternative response from the poet to the "Voice of Reality" that counters the suicidal tenor of his initial reply:

> Ven, Jarifa; tú has sufrido
> como yo; tú nunca lloras.
> Más, ¡ay, triste! que no ignoras
> cuan amarga es mi aflicción.
> Una misma es nuestra pena,
> en vano el llanto contienes . . .
> Tú también, como yo, tienes
> desgarrado el corazón. (ll. 109-116)

Such a concluding note, again as in **"A una estrella,"** offers no kind of *intellectual* resolution for the subject/object dilemma, even though the project of the poem as a whole has aimed at none other than the accomplishment of this goal. So it is that Espronceda's only existential recourses are to the gut emotion of refusing to surrender to an impoverished reality, to the continued search for an exit from the epistemological maze in which he wanders. In **"A Jarifa,"** moreover, these two impulses materialize in the poet's sympathetic *rapprochement* toward Jarifa herself: at one and the same time, Espronceda grants to the poem's *symbol of objectivity* a *subjectivity* (i.e., a determinism) of its own. In so doing, he quite tentatively suggests that the only way out of the false dialectic of individual subject vs. objective reality is the constitution of a human community based upon the recognition of a common oppression.

This point represents as far as Espronceda's exploration of the subject/object dilemma and its epistemological implications ever progresses. Indeed, this final scene in **"A Jarifa,"** looks forward to the closing movement in *El Diablo Mundo,* where Adán seems about to embark upon a new path in his attempt to work out a fulfilling relationship to the world. In order to avoid an anachronistic reading of Espronceda, however, we must emphasize that there is nothing politically or consciously collective about this tentative indication of new direction. If Espronceda has intuited that the only manner of freeing oneself from the philosophical binds inherent in the romantic subject/object dualism is to adhere to a dialectical vision which abolishes the category of the *subject* as its systemic center, none of the intellectual implications or social imperatives of such a discovery make their presence felt with any clarity whatsoever. Rather, this second metaphysical explanatory code has as its hallmark that, despite all its emotional resistance to such a conclusion, it ultimately confesses itself powerless to break down the disillusioning force of the metaphysical response. The paradox represented by the metaphysics of desire raises an impenetrable barrier to human cognition.

Thus, in these years the poet's own authorial ideology of radical bourgeois liberalism runs head on into a social reality which defies his desires and understanding; the result is that stalemate figured in an epistemological indeterminacy. But if neither an idealist metaphysics nor a social material determinism eventually gains the battleground, it is at least true that **"A Jarifa"** establishes within itself this debate as the key conflict for deciphering the nature of human experience. While fully elaborating Espronceda's alternative to his social explanatory code of 1835, therefore, this poem moves closer to the conscious juxtaposition of explanatory systems that informs the structure of *El Diablo Mundo.*

As this second phase of his poetic development comes to an end, Espronceda begins to describe in such poems as **"Canto del Cosaco"** (1838), **"El Dos de Mayo"** (1840), and **"A la traslación de las cenizas de Napoleón"** (1840) a new facet of reality which helps him to concretize in *El Diablo Mundo* one of the reasons for which reality repeatedly offers itself in a dissatisfying form. These poems represent Espronceda's ultimate refusal of a purely metaphysical problematic and herald the rebirth of the social explanatory code, though the latter's resurgence never escapes the influence of the metaphysical code, as we shall see in *El Diablo Mundo.*

If the politics of the period 1836-1838 made visible only confused, muddled images of the historical process, at the infrastructural level "invisible" (at the time) forces were at work transforming the basis of Spanish society. In 1837, for example, José de Salamanca began his spectacular career, and in effect, the years 1836-38 witnessed "une lente évolution à laquelle les mésures économiques de Mendizábal ont donné l'élan et qui se manifeste dans divers domaines." The legislative groundwork—the *desamortización,* the abolition of *mayorazgos* and *señoríos,* and the suppression of the guilds—for the capitalization of the Spanish economy was set down. Though Spanish industry as a whole continued in an underdeveloped stage, advances in commerce were sufficient to make evident to the most radical (and most conservative) observers the increasing "commodification" of daily life that capitalism entails. In his poetry of 1840, therefore, Espronceda at-

tacks this replacement of the more personal, though still repressive, relations of feudal economic production. He does so from the standpoint of one who views the triumph of the mercantile spirit as tolling the deathknell of the revolutionary drive toward "liberty, equality, and fraternity."

We may best view this process at work in **"A la traslación de las cenizas de Napoleón."** Here Espronceda launches a frontal attack against modern society:

> Miseria y avidez, dinero y prosa,
> en vil mercado convertido el mundo,
> los arranques del alma generosa
> poniendo a precio inmundo;
> cuando tu suerte y esplandor preside
> un mercader que con su vara mide
> el genio y la virtud, mísera Europa,
> y entre el lienzo vulgar que bordó de oro,
> muerto tu antiguo lustre y tu decoro,
> como a un cadáver fétido te arropa. . . .
> (ll. 1-10)

Cast in other terms, Espronceda witnesses the revolutionary hopes he entertained for Spain and Europe in the early 1830's now turn to dust. The energies which might have carried Western civilization into a new era of freedom and equality now find their outlet in a practice that converts all human endeavor and all objective reality into a degrading, "commodifying" activity: "con prosaico afanar en tu miseria,/ arrastrando en el lodo tu materia,/ sólo abiertos al lucro sus sentidos . . ." (ll. 18-20). Admittedly, Espronceda presents a "humanist" rather than scientific critique of capitalist reality. Yet he raises his voice in disgust not so as to seek refuge in a mythically ideal past. Rather, he rejects the posture of the lamenting poet and vows to throw himself in the midst of life in order to incite people to change the reality which is denying them the full glory of which they are capable. Rhetorically querying if the reader believes that he will become an impotent "segundo" Jeremías," he proclaims:

> No, yo alzaré la voz de los profetas;
> tras mí la alborotada muchedumbre,
> sonarán en mi acento las trompetas
> que derriben la inmensa pesadumbre
> del regio torreón que al vicio esconde,
> y el mundo me oirá en donde
> el precio vil de infame mercancia,
> del agiotista en la podrida boca,
> avaricioso oía. (ll. 37-45)

At this point, therefore, we have laid out all the socio-historical and poetic-thematic raw materials that go into the textual production of *El Diablo Mundo:* a social explanatory system from 1835 which criticizes the disjunction between liberal theory and practice; a philosophical explanatory system (1837-38) which questions inconclusively the metaphysical basis of human suffering through a theme of the paradox of desire; and finally, an indictment of one of the major phenomenological forms of capitalist reality (1840). We may say at the outset of our analysis of *El Diablo Mundo,* moreover, that there exists a certain compatibility between the resurfacing of explanation in the social mode and the persistence of a metaphysical approach to human unhappiness when the object of such inquiry is capitalist reality. (pp. 19-30)

Despite Casalduero's emphasis on the occasionally useful concept of the "fragmento romántico," [in his *Forma y visión de "El Diablo Mundo,"* 1951] *El Diablo Mundo* is above all a narrative poem, and clearly, its narrative thread is the biography of its protagonist, Adán. What critics less often recognize, however, is that the obvious form in which the poet casts this biographical narrative is that of a fictional testing of the Rousseauian hypothesis: namely, that human beings come into the world naturally pure and innocent, and that society, by despoiling this pristine state, becomes the source of human suffering and unhappiness. Cantos I, III, and IV, for example, devote themselves to this fictional project. (p. 31)

Canto IV then pursues this juxtaposition of Adán's healthy and innocent individualism with society's repressive and corrupting power by confronting the problem of the individual's socialization. Thrust in jail among victims of society who nonetheless share society's dominant values, the canto describes the process of "deforming" the original Adán and of "forming" a new one who can successfully be inserted into society's twisted culture:

> Ni leyes sabe, ni conoce el mundo,
> Sólo a su instinto generoso atiende,
> Y un abismo de crímenes inmundo
> Cruza y el crimen por virtud aprende.
> Y aquel pecho que es noble sin segundo
> Y que el valor y el entusiasmo enciende,
> Aplica al crimen la virtud que alienta
> Y puro es si criminal se ostenta.

His indoctrination, of course, covers the gamut from the most minute detail—"fuma aunque no fume"—to the discovery of his first feelings of genital sexuality: "Y cuando ella con amor le mire,/ En la ansiedad vehemente que le aqueja/ Yen ardor violento que le inspira,/ Quiere romper la maldecida reja." Importantly, we may observe here that the beginning of Adán's relationship with Salada signals society's channelling of Adán's original polymorphous libidinal impulses into a more "acceptable" format. We may point out indeed that the society of *El Diablo Mundo* substitutes, for Adán's initial attempt to experience a totalizing satisfaction through an all-encompassing relation to the world, a form of relationship that places all the demands for a totalizing satisfaction upon a single libidinal object. . . .

Similarly, the instruction Adán receives in jail under the tutelage of Salada's uncle augurs poorly for Adán's future. In contrast to Salada's desire to forge a human relationship with Adán, tío Lucas's sermons about the ways of the world serve only to dramatize the fact of division within society. Here the pettiness and avarice of human beings—qualities constantly reinforced and recreated by the determinant position that money occupies—produces a highly atomized society where everyone *must* exist individual*istically:*

> ¿Será del hombre el hombre el enemigo,
> Y, en medio de los hombres solitario,
> El su sola esperanza y solo amigo
> Verá en su hermano su mayor contrario?

Society in this scenario thus rejects Adán's form of liberating individualism which sought to establish relationships with the world and among his fellow humans as equals. Rather, it opts to manufacture that contradictory type of "individual," who is such in ideological designation only, insofar as competition and self-interest force one to live an isolated, unfulfilling life. The social making of individuals under the exigencies of these controlling principles, then, insures the absence within society of any possibility for the pursuit of an authentic individual liberty within the context of a historical community based on a genuine practice of equality.

Thus, even by Canto IV, the case for the Rousseauian hypothesis has already been decided: society *does* corrupt the healthy and innocent drives of the individual toward liberty and self-realization. It would seem, therefore, that there should be no reason to continue the poem, except perhaps to follow Adán's and Salada's careers to the bitter end. Yet formally the poem *must* continue throughout two more cantos—at which point it must then end after having exhausted its themes—for the presence within *El Diablo Mundo* of Espronceda's metaphysical explanatory system complicates the treatment of the Rousseauian theme, as well as its implications. Indeed, the poem initially inscribes itself within a metaphysical space in the "Introducción," where the poet *qua* poet attempts to grasp the meaning of the chaos which surrounds him. Canto II, moreover, again develops the private struggle of the poet to determine an epistemology for human suffering. Interestingly, therefore, we can detect in these two intensely personal sections of *El Diablo Mundo* the still unresolved thematic residue of Espronceda's battle against epistemological indeterminacy during 1837-38. (pp. 33-4)

Once having demonstrated the disjunction between liberal bourgeois theory and social practice, Espronceda could not imagine an efficacious remedy for himself and his society. The subsequent appeal to metaphysics which, if an answer were found, would have alleviated the poet from the responsibility to continue his search for a solution at the social level, proves *intellectually*—not *artistically*—more sterile than his thwarted attempt to discover the correct combination of social ingredients that might furnish hope for a better society. Hence, *El Diablo Mundo* stands as the most elaborate achievement of, and profoundest witness to, Espronceda's life-long effort to account for human misery, social oppression, and the failure of Spain's bourgeois revolution to fulfill its libertarian promises. (p. 44)

*Thomas E. Lewis, "Contradictory Explanatory Systems in Espronceda's Poetry: The Social Genesis and Structure of 'El Diablo Mundo'," in I & L, Vol. IV, No. 17, September-October, 1983, pp. 11-45.*

---

## FURTHER READING

Adams, Nicholson B. "Notes on Espronceda's *Sancho Saldaña.*" *Hispanic Review* V, No. 4 (October 1937): 304-08.

Describes the relationship between Walter Scott's *Waverly* novels and Espronceda's *Sancho Saldaña.*

Bretz, Mary Lee. "Espronceda's *El diablo mundo* and Romantic Irony." *Revista de Estudios Hispanicos* XVI, No. 2 (May 1982): 257-74.

Discusses the development of Romantic irony in Espronceda's *El diablo mundo,* noting the poem's innovative movement beyond the despair of European Romanticism.

Churchman, Philip H. "Byron and Espronceda." *Revue Hispanique* XX (1909):5-210.

Examines Byron's influence on Espronceda's verse.

Dreps, Joseph A. "Was José de Espronceda an Innovator in Metrics?" *Philological Quarterly* XVIII, No. 1 (January 1939): 35-51.

Analysis of the metrical innovations in Espronceda's poetry, concentrating on individual verses and stanza forms.

———. "Carelessness in the Metrics of José de Espronceda." *The Northwest Missouri State College Studies* XIX, No. 1 (June 1955): 73-103.

Metrical study charging Espronceda's poetry with irregularity and careless versification.

Fitzmaurice-Kelly, James. "The Nineteenth Century." In his *A History of Spanish Literature,* pp. 363-82. New York and London: D. Appleton and Company, 1898.

Highly regarded critical overview of Espronceda's life and works.

Hafter, Monroe Z. "*El diablo mundo* in the Light of Carlyle's *Sartor Resartus.*" *Revista Hispánica Moderna: Columbia University Hispanic Studies* XXXVII, Nos. 1-2 (1972-73): 46-55.

Compares Espronceda's *El diablo mundo* with Carlyle's *Sartor Resartus* in terms of composition, structure, and exposition, finding resemblances in their handling of satire and pervasive mood of spiritual dissatisfaction.

Landeira, Ricardo. *José de Espronceda.* Lincoln, Nebr.: Society of Spanish and Spanish-American Studies, 1985, 159 p.

Detailed assessment of Espronceda's life and works which includes a discussion of Romanticism in Spain.

Pattison, Walter T. "On Espronceda's Personality." *Publications of the Modern Language Association of America* LXI, No. 4 (December 1946): 1126-45.

Introduction to Espronceda's life and works, identifying the poet's literary personality.

———. "Sources of Espronceda's 'El mendigo'." In *Filología y Crítica Hispánica,* edited by Alberto Porqueras Mayo and Carlos Rojas, pp. 299-308. Madrid: Ediciones Alcalá, 1969.

Dismisses previously suggested influences on Espronceda's "El mendigo" while recommending those of Izaac Walton and Walter Scott.

Polt, J. H. R. "Espronceda's 'Canto a Teresa' in Its Context." In *Studies in Eighteenth-Century Spanish Literature and Romanticism in Honor of John Clarkson Dowling,* edited by Douglas and Linda Jane Barnette, pp. 167-76. Newark, Del.: Juan de la Cuesta, 1985.

Asserts that the "Canto a Teresa" in *El diablo mundo* fractures the poem's unity, thus contributing to its failure in arriving at any form of resolution.

Samuels, Daniel G. "Some Spanish Romantic Debts of Espronceda." *Hispanic Review* XVI, No. 2 (April 1948): 157-62.

Identifies the influence of Espronceda's Spanish Romantic contemporaries on his "A una estrella," "Amor venga sus agravios," and *El diablo mundo.*

# Ghalib

## 1797-1869

(Pseudonym of Mirza Muhammad Asadullah Beg Khan. Also wrote under pseudonym Asad.) Indian poet, essayist, historian, memoirist, and handbook writer.

### INTRODUCTION

Ghalib is regarded as the most important Urdu-language poet of the nineteenth century. Praised in particular for his artful use of the short lyric form known as the *ghazal,* he also wrote poetry in other forms, numerous volumes of letters, and a compelling account of the Sepoy Rebellion of 1857, an attempt by natives of India to overthrow British Colonial rule.

Ghalib was born into an aristocratic Muslim family in Agra. Orphaned at age five, he was reared with his brother and sister by maternal relatives. Ghalib started writing poetry in both Urdu and Persian as a child. At age thirteen, he married and moved to his wife's home in Delhi, where, except for occasional travel, he resided the rest of his life. In Delhi he made the acquaintance of several prominent and influential poets and wrote both occasional and lyric poetry for patrons at the Mughal court. In 1827, Ghalib made a business trip to Calcutta and met a number of writers and scholars in that city and in Lucknow, gaining him admittance to the literary world outside of Delhi. While in Calcutta, Ghalib observed the material prosperity of British civilization and attributed this wealth to English academic and legal innovations. Thereafter, Ghalib began to challenge Indian institutions, especially the practice of educating Muslims in an Indianized dialect of Persian that varied from the traditional Persian in both vocabulary and grammar; Ghalib argued that Indians should write Persian as native speakers wrote it, and presented his ideas at a symposium held by the university at Calcutta. Ghalib's audience strongly criticized the unfamiliar style of Persian he was espousing, which prompted Ghalib to condemn his opponents in Calcutta newspapers. His challenge to Indian tradition and his outspokenness provoked animosity among many of Ghalib's colleagues and involved him in a lifelong controversy. However, the quarrel also brought Ghalib greater attention and the resulting correspondence with other scholars established his reputation as both an innovative writer and an uncompromising scholar.

In 1841, Ghalib published his collected Urdu poems, *Divan-i-Ghalib.* His next book did not appear until 1849, when he produced *Panj ahang,* a kind of handbook on the writing of letters and poetry interspersed with samples of his own work; throughout the next decade, he published only sporadically. In 1857, Ghalib was forced to reassess his great admiration for Western culture when the British rulers of India responded to the Sepoy Rebellion with violence, martial law, and the forced exile of Delhi's Muslim

and Hindu populations. Eighteen months after the start of the fighting, he published *Dastanbu,* his memoirs of the suffering brought on by the conflict, and sent copies to various British officials, including Queen Victoria, both to plead for moderation in the treatment of Indians and to establish his own innocence in the rebellion. At this time, motivated by the realization that most of his unpublished manuscripts had been destroyed when the rebels and British alike looted the libraries of Delhi, Ghalib attempted to gather his remaining *ghazals* into expanded editions of his *Divan.* In the loneliness caused by the deaths and exile of many of his friends, Ghalib began to write several letters a day for solace; many of these were collected for publication. Despite rapidly failing health in his later years, Ghalib helped edit some of these collections and critiqued poems sent to him by poets all over India. He died in 1869.

Although Ghalib wrote in several genres, his *ghazals* have generally been the best received of his works. *Ghazals* usually consist of five to twelve couplets which are linked by common meters and rhyme schemes, but not necessarily by subject matter or tone. They were common in both Urdu and Persian, although Persian poetry generally brought greater prestige. As a young man, Ghalib preferred to compose in Persian until he noticed a growing taste for Urdu verse among Delhi poets. From the 1820s onward, he composed increasingly in Urdu, and now is remembered chiefly for his Urdu writings. Critics remark that Ghalib expanded the range of themes of the *ghazal* genre and utilized conventional Persian and Urdu poetic devices in new ways. For example, a nightingale singing in a garden for love of a rose was a common metaphor for a poet composing his works through the inspiration of a beloved, but unresponsive, woman. Ghalib used the same allusion to suggest his interest in progress and modernity: "My songs are prompted by delight / In the heat of my ideas; / I am the nightingale / Of the flower garden of the future." By identifying his symbolic beloved as a future age, Ghalib stressed his interest in change. He broke more strongly with established literary practice in his letters. Educated Indian Muslims usually wrote letters, as they did poetry, in Persian rather than in Urdu, while Ghalib wrote increasingly in Urdu. Moreover, in either language, letter writers customarily employed rhyming sentences and addressed their correspondents with flattering epithets. In place of such formality, Ghalib substituted colloquial language and nicknames or terms of endearment like "brother." His letters proved so popular that they were adopted as models by subsequent writers of Urdu.

Highly regarded for his contributions to the development of Urdu poetry, Ghalib was virtually unknown outside of Urdu-speaking communities for decades following his death. His work, however, came to the attention of Western readers as a result of the efforts of Indian and Pakistani scholars in the 1960s, and the centenary of his death in 1969 was marked by several volumes of English translations of his poems, with critical notes and biographical essays. Recent scholars have focused in particular on his handling of *ghazal* stylistic conventions and his contribution to the development of Urdu literature, and they agree that his extraordinary skill as a lyric poet makes him one of the most prominent figures in nineteenth-century Indian literature.

## PRINCIPAL WORKS

*Divan-i-Ghalib* (poetry) 1841; revised editions, 1847, 1861, 1862, 1863
*Panj ahang* (poetry and handbook) 1849
*Dastanbu* (memoirs) 1858
*Kuliyat-i-nasr* (poetry, memoirs, history, and handbook) 1868
*Ud-i-Hindi* (letters) 1868; revised as *Urdu-i-moalla* 1869, 1899
*Makatib-i-Ghalib* (letters) 1937
*Khutut-i-Ghalib* (letters) 1941; revised edition, 1969
*Nadirat-i-Ghalib* (letters) 1949
*Ghalib ka nadir tahirin* (letters) 1961
*Dastanbūy: A Diary of the Indian Revolt of 1857* (memoirs) 1970
*Ghazals of Ghalib* (poetry) 1971
*Urdu Ghazals of Ghalib* (poetry) 1977
*Urdu Letters of Mirza Asadu'llah Khān Ghālib* (letters) 1987

## Sufia Sadullah    (essay date 1964)

[*In the introduction (written in 1964) to her edition of Ghalib's poetry, Sadullah, a Pakistani writer and translator, identifies three phases of Ghalib's career, the major sources of his poetic strategies, and the problems inherent in translating his works.*]

The eighteenth and nineteenth centuries saw the great renaissance of Urdu poetry. The three outstanding poets of this period are Shaikh Muhammad Ibrahim Zauq, Hakim Momin Khan Momin and Ghalib. Although no doubt strongly influenced by the Persian tradition each had his own distinctive style and method. (pp. viii-ix)

Ghalib, according to his own statement, was greatly influenced by three poets, namely, [Mirza] Bedil, Urfi and Zahuri. Ghalib's literary career passed through three distinct phases.

(*i*) a phase in which words counted more than inner significance, and Persian modes of expression were used freely to make the verses ornate and sweet-sounding.

(*ii*) a phase of sobriety when Persian modes and methods were combined with depth and significance.

(*iii*) the final phase, a phase of superb perfection, when language, grammar, rhyme and beauty came unsought, and he could write with effortless abandon and, what is more, with striking originality.

A certain section of Ghalib's admirers hold the view that Ghalib is untranslatable. This opinion may perhaps be justifiable, so far as the question of language is concerned. Every language, has its own rules and regulations and its own characteristic forms of diction; these we cannot and need not violate unless we are attempting a dead-literal translation, which, in any case, will be, all but incomprehensible. To explain my point, I would like to give an instance. In Urdu the phrase "Dard-e-Jigar" is meant to express the heart-aches of love. A literal translation of this will be "Pain in the liver". Such a phrase would not only suggest nothing of the intended meaning to the English reader, but would be completely misleading. Words however apt or beautiful, are merely a medium, and if, in another language, they are inappropriate or inadequate for the purpose of expressing the inner essence of the poet's thoughts and emotions, they must be discarded. . . . Human emotions are always expressible, since they are universal, and as such they are never circumscribed by any language. They remain unchanged and unchangeable from one decade to another; from one end of the world to another.

I do not claim that I have been able to fathom Ghalib's extraordinary genius. Despite the fact that he has definite and clear-cut views on love and sorrow, hope and despair, piety and sin, life and death, it is inevitable that a mind so great and diverse, must be, and will be, interpreted somewhat differently, according to the readers' width or limitations of mind. . . . Ghalib's technique is enchantingly subtle; it clings to the thinking mind and hence one cannot resist the desire to fathom the meanings of his poems.

Of the three great poets of the Urdu renaissance, Ghalib's name is monumental and his talent defies emulation. Ghalib died in Delhi on the 15th February, 1869, leaving behind an immortal name. (pp. ix-x)

*Sufia Sadullah, in an introduction to* Hundred Verses of Mirza Ghalib, *edited by Suraiya Nazar, translated by Sufia Sadullah, revised edition, A. M. Sadullah, 1975, pp. vii-x.*

## R. K. Kuldip  (essay date 1967)

[*In the following excerpt, Indian poet and scholar Kuldip discusses Ghalib's work in relation to Indian philosophy and the* ghazal *genre.*]

Mirza Asad Ullah Beg Khan (alias Mirza Nosha) to which is added Ghalib as his *nom de plume* is the great representative of India's spirit, grace and genius. The Indian national consciousness is the base from which his works grow. Ghalib has absorbed India's cultural heritage, made it his own, enriched it, given it universal scope and significance. Its spiritual directions, its intellectual amplitude, its artistic expression, its political forms and economic arrangements all find utterance in fresh vital, shining phrases. We find in his works at their best, simple dignity of language, precision of phrase, classical taste, cultivated judgement, intense poetic sensibility and fusion of thought and feeling.

In his verse we find pathos, power, beauty and great skill in his mastery of Urdu & Persian and delineation of character. He is at home in royal courts, and on desert plains, in happy homes and humble hermitages. He has a balanced outlook which enables him to deal sympathetically with men of high and low degree, fishermen, courtezans, dancing girls and servants. These great qualities make his work belong to the literature of the world. Humanity recognizes itself in them though they deal with Indian themes. In India, Ghalib is recognised as the greatest poet in Urdu literature. While once the poets were being counted, Ghalib as being the first occupied the last finger since the second to Ghalib has not yet been found.

History associates Ghalib with Akbar Shah and his son Bahadur Shah, the last Moghul Emperor in whose Court Ghalib had an opportunity to both study and appreciate the work of poetical luminaries of the age and match his own skill and accomplishments against theirs. We do not know many details about Ghalib's life. Numerous legends have gathered around his name which have little historical value. From his writings it is clear that he lived in an age of polished elegance and leisure, was greatly attached to the arts of song and dance, wine and women. He travelled widely in India and seems to have been familiar with the geography of the country from the Himalayas to Kanya Kumari. His graphic descriptions of the Himalayan scenes, of the saffron flower, the plant which grows in Kashmir, look like those of one who has personal acquaintance with them. He was sensitive to beauty in nature and human life.

Ghalib had self confidence. In the beginning of his poetic career at Delhi, Ghalib had hoped to carry the audience off its feet at a symposium held at Anglo-Arabic College. He however found a cold and discouraging response. The verse, it was said was without meaning and unintelligible. To which Ghalib retorted.

> "I desire no praise, I wish no award for me.
> If my verse be without meaning, well, so let it be."

This sense of assurance is inconsistent with humility as Ghalib was highly egoistical. In answer to people's criticism of his verse both at Agra and Delhi, he had composed a quatrain which could be paraphrased as

> Oh my heart my verse is difficult
> The masters of verse on hearing it
> Recommend to me to adopt an easy style
> It is difficult for me to say something
> And difficult for me not to say anything.

The master artist suggests by a few touches what others fail to express even by elaborate discourses. Ghalib is famous for his economy of words and naturalness of speech in which sound and sense match. His pen pictures are graceful and perfect. His writings instruct not by direct teaching but by gentle persuasion as by a loving wife. By an aesthetic presentation of great ideals, the artist in the poet leads us to an acceptance of the same.

We live vicariously the life of every character that is set before us and out of it all comes a large measure of understanding of mankind in general. Ghalib projects his rich and growing personality on a great cultural tradition and gives utterance to its ideals of order and love. He expresses the desires, the urges, the hopes, the dreams, the successes and the failures of man in his struggle to make himself at home in the world. India has stood for a whole integrated life and resisted any fragmentation of it. The poet describes the psychological conflicts that divide the soul and helps us to put the whole pattern together.

Ghalib's works preserve for us moments of beauty, incidents of courage, acts of sacrifice and fleeing moods of the human heart. His works will continue to be read for that indefinable illumination about the human predicament which is the work of a great poet. Many of his lines have almost become like proverbs in Urdu.

There is a striking amount of mysticism in Ghalib's verse as also spurts of the realisation of seeming futility of human effort, futility of life and man's unknown destiny. In all these traits, the poet finds joy in contentedness with a view to achieving a measure of equanimity. Says he:

> If thou be sure of God thy prayer to grant
> Then ask for naught but a heart without a want

And

> Both these worlds form but curling lips of despair
> And hope but a house of sand that a child does prepare.

Ghalib 'tis great one's own faults to find

> That helps to discover and master your mind

> Yesterday I found Ghalib huddled far down in
>   the Taverns' nook
> With head on his knees, hands on his head and
>   a heart that no joy did brook.
> Oh God call me not for my sins to account
> For the heart burns of desires unfulfilled I do
>   recount.

The poet's thoughts are essentially spiritual in quality. We are ordinarily imprisoned in the wheel of time, its historicity and so are restricted to the narrow limits of existence. Our aim should be to lift ourselves out of our entanglement to an awareness of the real which is behind and beyond all time and history, that which does not become, that which is absolute, non historical being itself. We cannot think it, enclose it within categories, images and verbal structures. We know more than we can think and express in historical forms. The end of man is to become aware by experience of this absolute reality. Compare the self praise and lamentation of which Ghalib is the master.

> Such mystic thoughts Ghalib
> Such style and word
> Would take ye for a prophet
> If thou not a drunkard wert.

The man of enlightenment reaches the supreme timeless life. The performer of good deeds has heaven for his share, but as we know the real self by the deepest part of our being. Ghalib's reference to the drunkard in the above stanza reduces all his spiritual thoughts to another phenomena of nature which deeply influenced his mind and made him pour out his heart in his verse. These were the beauties of the dawn, the glories of the monsoon and charm and excitement of the days in winter. Vivid pen portraits of these phenomena as experienced by him are drawn both in his Urdu and Persian verse. As human beings we have our roots in nature and participate in its life in many ways. The rhythm of night and day, changes of season suggest man's changing moods, variety and capriciousness. Nature had not become mechanical and impersonal for Ghalib. It had still its enchantment. His works carry a sensitive appreciation of plants and trees, of hills and rivers and a feeling of brotherhood for animals. We see in his writings flowers which bloom, birds which soar and animals which spring. They reveal not only his visions of nature's beauty, but also of understanding human moods and desires. His knowledge of nature was not only accurate but sympathetic. His observation was wedded to imagination. His descriptions of the winter season, of the music of the mighty current of the Jamuna, of the different animals illustrate his human heart and appreciation of natural beauty.

No man can reach his full stature until he realises the dignity and worth of life that is not human. We must develop sympathy with all forms of life. The world is not made only for man.

The love of man and woman attracted Ghalib and he lavished all his rich imagination in the description of the different kinds of love.

He does not suffer from any inhibitions. His women have a greater appeal than his men; for they reveal a timeless universal quality whereas the men are dull and variable. They live on the surface while women suffer from the depths. The competitiveness and self assertion of the men may be useful in the office, factory, or battle field but do not make for refinement, charm and serenity. The women keep the traditions alive with their love for order and harmony.

When Ghalib describes feminine beauty, he adopts the conventional account and falls into the danger of sensuous engrossment and sometimes over elaboration. Very often he gives us a pen picture of a typical dancing girl which may well make a painter envy. Mark the graphic description in the following lines.

> As the cup of wine to her lips she drew
> Each drop of wine stood as on grass the dew
> Stunned with her beauty, sparkling like a pearl
> Each drop in the cup itself into a necklace did
>   hurl.

In the gallery of women Ghalib presents, we have many interesting types. For many of them conventional pretences and defences of society did not work. Their sensitive natures were not adjusted to social expectations. Their conflicts and tensions called for integeration. The men felt certain and were secure. They accepted polygamy as the normal rule. But Ghalib's women had imagination and understanding. So they were victims of doubt and indecision.

Love is deepened by hardships and sufferings borne for the sake of love. It grows a hundred fold in its intensity by obstacles to its realization even as the current of a river blocked on its way by uneven rocks (flows with greater force). Ghalib does not judge the first union of lovers as moral lapse. They are not sinners but they have to grow through suffering. Sex life is not inconsistent with spiritual attainment. Wild life or unrestrained passion is however inconsistent. The goal of life is joy or serenity and not pleasure or happiness. Joy is the fulfillment of one's nature as a human being. We must affirm our being against the whole world, if need be. When Socrates was condemned to death or when Jesus was crucified, they did not take death as defeat but as fulfillment of their ideals. The aim of love is a happy harmony of man and woman, for the woman does not belong to the man but makes a whole with him.

For Ghalib, the path of wisdom lies in the harmonious pursuit of the different aims of life and the development of an integeral personality. He impresses on our mind these ideals by the magic of his poetry, the richness of his imagination, his profound knowledge of human nature and his delicate descriptions of its most tender emotions.

It has been said by many eminent critics of Urdu literature that a study of the *Diwan-E-Ghalib* on the whole leaves on one the impression of Ghalib being a poet of despair and pessimism. While it is true that pessimism seems to reach a new low in some of his couplets and several of them breathe of utter despair and lack of hope, it would be unfair to hold that Ghalib's poetry is primarily a poetry of despair and pessimism. As a famous English poet has put it, our sweetest songs are those which tell us of our saddest thoughts. Notwithstanding the truth of another famous English saying 'laugh and the world laughs with you, weep and you weep alone,' harrowing tales of woe leave a more lasting impression on the human mind than stories of cheer and happiness. As it happens almost every great writer and poet tends to exploit this direct appeal to human heart as best as he can in his work. The mere presence of this element in a work cannot render that work as a product of a man in despair, or one with a pessimistic outlook on life. The real questions to be asked in such a case are: 'What is the object of such expression? And does the writer suggest any way out?" There are only extremely rare people in the world who experience nothing but joy and cheer in their life. For most life happens to be either uneventful or dominated by unfortunate and unhappy occurrences. Art has to portray life on the whole. It cannot afford to ignore reality, howsoever, unpleasant it may be.

Fortunately Ghalib's verse has several pieces which are of great help to a man in woe and despair. He portrays life as it ought to be, brings out its deception and futility, but then offers a bit of paternal advice to sustain a sinking soul and provide it a healthy buoyancy. He exhibits a delightfully unconcerned concern about life. As in one of his couplets:

> The very Heavens move in a cycle day and night,
> Something is bound to happen, why should I
>   take fright?

Or as in another:

> Man unto himself is a world of thought;
> Solitude with me anon into multitude is
>   wrought.

He also gives sound advice to counteract jealousy, vice, pride, and even despair. For instance:

> Woe ceases to be woe,
> If it does man oft hound;
> So many my difficulties, Lo!
> They have their own solution found.

or

> Of your high position in the world,
> Be ye never so proud,
> For, 'a fall from heights,' the wise word,
> 'Fate for man does ever shroud.

He takes the world in one single sweep by declaring:

"The world for me is naught but child's play: With a frivolous show on night and day" and exhibits none of the depressed nature of a pessimist. On the contrary there are not a few of his couplets which would impel a man to action rather than throw him down. And there are several other pieces which enable him to develop a detached outlook and cultivate that rare yet so-essential human quality of having a laugh at himself. It is this quality of Ghalib's verse which takes the sting out of his seemingly pessimistic pieces also. And some of these pieces are mellowed by mystic thought. For instance when he says: "God was my pre-existence; God would be my non-existence; Existence mars my existence. Ah! what lies in non-existence!" or "Tis difficult for any task to be easy. It is not easy. It is not easy even for man to be a Man."

He has wit and humour and loves to enjoy life as best as he can. He knows the good of pious acts but is not inclined that way. Wine has a strong appeal for him and seems to be a source of great inspiration as when he declares in one of his couplets: "Set here the glass, wine and flask: Then watch the flow and spell of talk." And so great is his thirst for wine that he has to say: "I would drink if I see a few barrels of wine: What are these cups, glasses and flasks that you before me line." Even the Almighty does not escape the shafts of joyful wit and humour. Says he: "O' God, call me not for my sins to account: For the heart-burns of desires unfulfilled I do recount." And at another place: "Had I so many a heart-burn to befall my lot: Then O' Lord, you should have given me many a heart." And this couplet of his bespeaks of his confidence and hope which no pessimist can ever have:

> She would have come round one day,
> Had I some days more in life to stay.

But with all his love for life and wine, the ideal he wishes to live by, is to overcome all his wants and yearnings, forgive the sins of others and ignore the wrongs done to him. He wishes to attain that sense of equanimity, that peace of mind which can spring out of only a life fully and well-lived. His advice to the world is:

> If thou be sure of God thy Prayer to grant,
> Then ask for naught but a heart without a
>   want

And also;

> Hear not, if one talks ill of you;
> Speak not, if one does evil too;
> Hold him back that be misled,
> Let forgiveness his wrongs wed;
> Is there one in this world without a want,
> Whose prayer then should one grant?
> Ghalib why complain of anyone
> When the very hope of life be gone.

And after having enjoyed all the worldly things of life he wishes to retire to a corner where he has none except himself to live by. The piece below, interpreted by some as a piece of despair, voices the feelings of one who wants to shake off the fetters of the world and experience the joys and thrills of a completely liberated soul, under obligation to none.

> Lead me now, forever to a place,
> Forever, where there is none of my race;
> None my language to understand,
> None my worries to expand;
> Neither door nor wall to shield
> The house I myself should build;
> None to tend if sick I lie,
> None to mourn if there I die.

Love is the other theme which runs through most of Ghalib's ghazals, Love in fact is the principal theme of a ghazal in Urdu and before Ghalib's time was almost the only theme, Ghalib alone broadened its scope to bring in other subjects. The object of love in Urdu poetry is referred to in masculine form. The reference may be to a real object or it may pertain to the Almighty. Most couplets in Urdu verse are capable of both interpretations.

Love by poets in Asia, as a whole, and in India, in particular, has been conceived as an emotion spelling misery, trouble, and destruction for the lover. The lover is invariably faithful and the beloved faithless. A happy union is an impossibility. There are bound to be rivals in the field and the beloved likely to be more favourably inclined to them than to her true lover. All except the lover are motivated by base sexual urges. His is the only platonic love. A miserable death is the only end of the lover. In fact love makes him experience a constant death in life.

Urdu poetry has no concept of love bringing joy and cheer to the lover except through the pain and misery inflicted on him by the cruel acts of the beloved. The beloved is often a courtesan, or one almost similarly placed, and hence all the mention of her being under the influence of drink and indulging in coquettish acts. The lover cannot dream of dropping his love and taking some other infection to the eye. He must also exercise restraint and care in his overtures to the beloved. In no case must he appear to be bold and impatient. Moans, wails, sighs and patience, must be his qualities. The beloved on the other hand must always be cheerful, happy and lost in pursuit of pleasures of life. She should deliberately keep away from the lover and subject him to innumerable trials and tribulations. She must always devise new ways and means to torture his soul. Only when he is on deathbed or when he has actually passed away, must she come to him and realize the cruelties of her past acts and repent. Till then she should keep him on false hopes and promises.

The above, in brief, is the picture of love presented on the whole in Urdu poetry from its earliest times to the present day. This has been characterised as a morbid, unnatural trait of Urdu verse by several critics. It is against this tradition of some three hundred years of Urdu poetry that Ghalib's work in this field is to be judged. He could not possibly make a complete break with the tradition. All he could do was to introduce a little more of sanity into love and make the lover develop some sense of self-respect, dignity and independence of character. And these are the outstanding features of Ghalib's love lyrics, which distinguish him from the poets of the old school. Ghalib's love is no less tortuous and coy, and he no less faithful and true than lovers in Urdu verse as a rule. But he has a delightfully refreshing concept of love. 'Love' for him "is a fire raging unrestrained, neither by wish begun nor by will contained." Nevertheless he experiences through its media a new-found joy and an exciting thrill when he declares:

> Love to me the very joy of life has brought
> A cure for the pain, a pain without cure,
> all unsought

This is an unusual expression of feeling for most of the Urdu poets, for they see in love nothing but a road to the realm of unending pain, agony and affliction.

Not that Ghalib is not aware of this aspect of love unfulfilled to which [William] Shakespeare makes a mention in the *Romeo-Juliet* saying:

> Love is a smoke rais'd with the fume of sighs;
> Being purg'd, a fire sparkling in lovers' eyes;
> Being vex'd a sea nourish'd with lovers' tears

In fact many of his ghazals deal with this aspect of love and vividly portray the living Hell in life which is the lot of a disappointed lover. But he does not loose hope and has a remarkable tenacity of faith. He is not discouraged by the cruel ways of love for he feels that such is love's course as a rule. He retains his sense of humour and displays his ready wit even in such a situation. In fact he learns to find pleasure in pain and would have himself condemned if he did not do that. He knows "sighs to take effect need an age," and also that "the thing called love is but for madness another word," but he is unmindful of all that and joyously proclaims.

> Mine not love, let it madness be,
> Let my madness bring fame to thee

And sensing the great embarrassment to which the beloved is put by being seen in his company, he whispers with a mischievous twinkle in his eye into his beloved's ear:

> If my company doth bring bad name to thee,
> Then in private, and not in public, let us be

Love for Ghalib is indispensable. It holds him in a tight grip. There is no escape. To use the poet's words "In the very first field of love I have sorely hurt my feet: Nor can I stand there now nor beat a retreat." He has his own plans to get equal with his tormentors. Indeed he is confident of that. Just mark his lines:

> In Heaven I will take full revenge upon these
> sons of fairies fair,
> If by Grace of God I find 'em turn as Houries
> there

Ghalib totally differs from his predecessors in enjoining on the lovers to be platonic in their emotion and restrained in their overtures. He makes bold to say:

> Love is mad and loves a love part;
> Love under restraint is but love hurt.

He gives a chance to his beloved to correct herself: 'Call me back any time you wish to be kind: For I am not time past that is ever left behind,' is his sporting offer. And this not withstanding his unfortunate experience in her company which he narrates in his following couplet:

> I said: 'strangers from our midst should go,'
> The cruel love made me quit, and said: 'you
> wished it so?

But there are moments when he finds himself on the verge of revolt. He is not ever to remain at his beloved's doorstep for he is a man and not a stone. Moreover there are not a few beauties to whom he can turn for solace in place of his cruel love. He becomes conscious of his sense of self-respect and dignity and makes a firm declaration that if his love stands on prestige and sticks to her ways, he too would go his own way. Now he detests making a complaint. For when there is no 'heart left in the side why should one keep a tongue in his cheek.' That is his counsel.

There are also moments when he gives the impression of being utterly down and out. When he does no more have a heart of which he was once proud: when he experiences no emotions and thrills and in fact has no thought of love.

He is then disgusted with his life and makes it known to his love asking her not to remind him that he once called her "my love, my life." But this is a passing mood. He soon recovers his usual cheerful adventurous self and is out in search of new thrills and excitements. He wants to relieve his earlier experience and gives beautiful expression to his inner yearnings and desires in his ghazal opening with the line, "Tis an age I had my love my house to grace." This is in line with human nature. Optimism and not pessimism is the rule of life; although no one can escape moments of utter despair at some time or the other in this world. But man being the most adaptable of all creatures, what appears at first to be wholly intolerable and the very end of life in the course of time looses its sting and becomes after all not so bad. Then Man sees new hope and regains in some measure his earlier courage and ardour. That is what sustains him in life. Difference in degrees of this quality of man, distinguish the strong from the weak. Ghalib displays no mean degree of strength of character in this regard. And that should to a great extent clear him of the charge of being a poet of despair and pessimism. In fact that is what makes him beloved of the masses. He portrays the moods of despair in the life of Man with as real a poignancy and bitterness as are capable of being experienced by one. But his object is not to make him loose hope, but realize the reality of life and attain an enlightened sense of equanimity. He learns not to be vanquished by griefs and troubles, but to overcome them and emerge smiling and cheerful as a Man.

Ghalib constitutes a turning point in the history and development of Urdu verse. No other poet of Urdu verse up to his time seems either to have attempted to present a complete picture of life or succeeded in breaking away from the traditional mode of composition limited by a few selected subjects. Ghalib was neither a philosopher nor a preacher; nor did he ever try to fall into the role of a propagandist. He contented himself with being just a poet. But he was not a mere poet in the accepted sense of the term in those days; concerned with intellectual themes, and poetry of highflown and sometimes far-fetched ideas and imagination. He was a man, almost a complete man, with rich experience of life and profound understanding of his mind. The more he understood himself, the more he tried to overcome his shortcomings, both in his real life and in the sphere of his verse. And this constantly helped him take his life to a higher and still higher plane; finding pleasure in woe; joy in distress; and calm in turbulence and storm. His work throughout scintillates with his characteristic humour, combined with his unique understanding of human mind and experience of the problems of life, which profoundly influences the reader.

For the succeeding generations of Urdu poets over the time also, Ghalib's verse has acted as a guiding star. It has served as a source of great inspiration for them to break new ground in the field in various directions. Urdu verse today is no more concerned with beauty and love alone. It embraces the whole sphere of life and there are not a few pieces of note which deal with the current political, social and economical problems of the world as well. While the spread of western education and ideals has had its due impact on the development of Urdu poetry, it owes

not a small debt to Ghalib for its present growth. It was he who first blazed the trail following which other poets have helped it achieve its present stature and form. But no Urdu poet has so far succeeded in presenting a more understanding and complete picture of human life than Ghalib in his verse. His work still stands as a class by itself. To quote one of his couplets:

> There is many another famous poet in the world,
> But Ghalib, it is said, is different in style and
>     word.

Time has only helped accentuate this difference between him and others.

Like [Johann Wolfgang von] Goethe in Germany, Ghalib in India symbolises the highest development of human thought in verse exercising a profound influence on the culture, education and thinking of the times. There is hardly an aspect of life which remains untouched in his work. His ***Diwan-E-Ghalib*** a slim volume of 100 and odd pages which has established his claim to immortality has greatly enriched the Urdu language by Persian similies and expressions enabling it to become probably the most virile, expressive and honoured language of this subcontinent.

Ghalib is cosmopolitan in his outlook and his lines have a remarkable universality of appeal. . . . Truly, Ghalib has few equals among the literary figures of his age. (pp. 1-23)

> *R. K. Kuldip, in his* Mirzā Ghālib: A Critical Appreciation of Ghalib's Thought & Verse, *Intertrade Publications (I) PVT. Ltd., 1967, 112 p.*

---

**Ghalib on the poet's relation to tradition:**

The rhythmic speech which men call poetry finds a different place in each man's heart and presents a different aspect to each man's eyes. Men who make poetry all pluck the strings with a different touch and from each instrument bring forth a different melody. Pay no heed to what others see and feel, and bend all your efforts to increase your own perception.

*Ghalib, in a letter to Hisam ud Din Haidar Khan, quoted by Russell and Islam in their* Ghalib 1797-1869; Volume I: Life and Letters, *Harvard University Press, 1969.*

---

**Alessandro Bausani    (lecture date 1969)**

[*Bausani is an Italian critic of Persian literature. Here, in an excerpt from a paper originally read at the University of London in 1969, he briefly discusses Persian and Urdu attributes of Ghalib's poetry.*]

Attempts have been made to compare Ghālib's poetry to the metaphysical poetry of English literature, or to Euphuism; I have also suggested certain stylistic resemblances between Ghālib and [Luis de] Góngora [y Argote]. Though all comparisons of this kind are open to obvious criticism, they can nevertheless be useful for a better understanding of certain aspects of Ghalib's art. But those who make them seem to forget that the literary situation of India at the period of Ghalib was perhaps more similar to that of our Middle Ages than to more modern periods of European literary history.

Persian held, in Mughal India, a position somewhat similar to that of Latin in our early Middle Ages. It was not the mother tongue of anybody, and vernaculars like Urdu (to speak only of the Muslim environment) were already alive. 'Indian-style' poets are in a position, *mutatis mutandis,* comparable to that of certain authors of the early Middle Ages studied by [Erich] Auerbach in his stimulating essays. In his 'Latin Prose of the Early Middle Ages', trying to explain the twistedness and difficulty of the style of writers like Cesarius of Arles, Gregory of Tours, and Raterius, he says that they used those specific stylistic forms not because of their inability to write in classical Latin, but simply because 'the objects and the thoughts that had to be expressed, could not be expressed in the stylistic forms of the high classical culture'. The 'mannerism of Raterius' language is certainly not erudite ornamentation but the peculiar form assumed by his new content'. 'He thinks that his obscurity aims at a superior clarity, which, however, reveals itself only to those who make an effort to understand him', speaking *à la* Ghalib, to a *zabāndān:* . . . 'If there is one here who knows the language, bring him to me. This stranger in the city has something to say.' (Similar expressions can be found in Bedil.) Some sentences of Auerbach, in that same essay, could be almost literally applied to the situation of the 'Indian style' of a Bedil, only changing 'Latin' into 'Persian': 'His [he still speaks of Raterius] peculiar quality is due not only to his temperament, but also to the linguistic materials he uses. It is a Latin [read: Persian] that had for a long time no more been enlivened by everyday usage . . . In order to express his own peculiar quality he had no other means than that of adding a sort of expressionistic ornamentation, operating through the disposition of words, etc.' This is why a [Mirza] Bedil, a Qatīl and a Vāqif wrote in what for Ghalib was such a 'bad' Persian. Ghalib felt it his duty to 'reconstruct' the real 'Iranian' Persian, if not that of Firdausī or [Shaikh Muslihu-al-Din Ibrahim] Sa'dī, at least that of Zuhūrī and Nazīrī. But the sixteenth century and the social, spiritual and linguistic conditions of Mughal India of that age were forever gone; this is the reason why the 'better' and simpler Persian of Ghalib seems to us not much more than a literary exercise. His public—still to use Auerbachian concepts—was the extremely restricted literary aristocracy of Delhi, and even they were not always in agreement with him, as it is shown by their criticisms.

Just as he had nothing poetically new to say in Persian poetry—and therefore he could exercise himself in writing in the comparatively simple style of the ancient tradition—so too he could exercise himself in difficult Persian prose, he had no urgent need of being understood by people. Conversely, in Urdu verse he felt he had something new to say, and this new element, stylistically, in the conditions of the Mughal India of his time, could not but be the historical continuation on more modern lines of Bedil's novelty and, therefore—at first sight—difficult.

But in Urdu prose he had a practical need to be understood; hence his famous clarity and simplicity. Of course he was not himself conscious of all this and, as everybody knows, he preferred his Persian verses. . . . In the *'intikhāb'* (selection) of 'pearls at random strung', without too much conscious exercise of style (that is his Urdu *dīvān*), he wrote not for the public but for himself, and therefore he followed his own secret taste. Paradoxically the result was that in the last resort he identified himself with historical reality, whereas the 'public' for which he studied his *rangs* in Persian poetry was the only possible public for Persian in India, the idealized public of the century of Zuhūrī and Nazīrī.

This, I think, is a fairly satisfactory explanation of the contradictions of Ghalib's styles. Ghalib, seen from this point of view, is the last Persian poet of India, and the first 'modern' Urdu poet. But, being a really poetical genius, it is obvious that even in his more artificial Persian 'exercises' he achieves remarkable results of 'pure poetry'.

Ghalib himself felt a clear conscience about being a 'last' representative of classical Mughal India; the outward power and glory of the Mughals is transformed in him into a poetical, spiritual glory: . . . 'The pearl has been taken away from the royal standard of Persia and in exchange a pearl-strewing pen was given to me. The crown has been torn away from the head of the Turks of Pashang, and the flaming Glory of the Kais was transformed, in me, into poetry!

The pearl was taken from the crown and was set in wisdom: what they outwardly took away, was given to me in secret.'

And in a *rubā'ī* he says that 'the broken arrow of my ancestors was transformed into my pen'. . . .

His was not therefore a social or political poetry, but rather an intimate, 'hidden' one. Ghalib was what would be called now a 'formalistic poet'. In his form, in spite of his repeated claims of 'Iranism' he was typically Indian, and it is not an accident that he is presently more celebrated in India than in Pakistan. The subtlety of his poetical analysis of reality is characteristic of Indian style: . . . 'The real seer is the one that, when he analyses the psychological details of love, is able to see in the heart of the stone, the dance of the fire-idols of Āzar!'

To see what is potentially hidden in the given stony reality is the task of the poet; not that of giving more or less social messages. The woof and warp of Ghalib's poetry is a sort of dialectical monism, transposed into poetical forms (and in this too, his Bedilian heritage is evident). It would be a fascinating subject of study—though an extremely difficult one—to retrace possible Indian sources in the stylistic trends of Indian style, of which Ghalib is one of the last examples in Persian. But since my task is to speak of Ghalib's Persian poetry, I can do no more here than mention this possibility. It is certain, however, that some verses of Ghalib seem to call to mind Śankara's monism or even certain aspects of modern dialectic idealism. (pp. 100-04)

*Alessandro Bausani, "Ghālib's Persian Poet-*

*ry," in* Ghalib the Poet and His Age, *edited by Ralph Russell, George Allen & Unwin Ltd., 1972, pp. 70-104.*

**Ralph Russell   (lecture date 1969)**

[*Russell is an American scholar of Muslim civilization. In the following excerpt from a paper originally read at the University of London in 1969, he explains the generic traits of Urdu* ghazals *and places Ghālib's poetry in that context.*]

In considering Ghālib's poetic achievement—and, for that matter, his achievement as a prose-writer too—it is entirely appropriate to look first at his Persian work. It is well-known that he himself took pride above all in his Persian poetry, and even on occasion expressed contempt for his Urdu verse. Thus, in much-quoted lines, he says. . . .

Look at my Persian: there you see the full range
   of my artistry—
And leave aside my Urdu verse, for there is
   nothing there of me.

At the same time, one must be careful not to over-rate the importance of statements such as these. It is undoubtedly true that he regarded his Persian as his great achievement. He lamented the fact that in his day Urdu had ousted Persian from its former place as *the* language of poetry and culture. He knew his Persian verse was little understood and little appreciated, and this pained him. But it is also true that the most forceful of his statements contrasting his Persian and his Urdu to the great disadvantage of the latter, are made in a particular context, in a context where his Urdu verse is under attack, or where he anticipates such an attack, or where his Urdu is being compared unfavourably with that of rival poets such as [Shaikh Ibrahim] Zauq. In such a context it is his standard reaction to represent his Urdu as written under some sort of external compulsion, and not from any desire of his own, and to vaunt his superiority in a field where such slighting comparisons cannot be made. The poem from which I have just quoted itself belongs to just such a context. Later in the same poem he writes: . . .

I tell you truth, for I am one must tell the truth
   when all is done,
The verse on which you pride yourself is verse
   I should feel shame to own.

[Khvajah Altaf Husain] Hālī, with characteristic timidity tells us that these lines are 'generally said to have been addressed to Zauq', but the matter is put beyond all doubt by Ghālib himself in one of his Persian letters in a context where, without mentioning Zauq by name, he makes it perfectly clear that it is Zauq of whom he is speaking in this verse. And this serves to re-emphasize the point I am making. Zauq didn't *write* any Persian verse, and so in this field it is true, in the most literal sense of the words, that there can be no comparison between him and Ghālib. It is true that the sort of judgment which Ghālib here makes is repeated on other occasions, but I believe that it could in every case be shown that these judgments are all given against the sort of background I have described.

I make this point at the outset not because I have any intention of making the reverse assertion. To exalt Ghālib's Urdu at the expense of his Persian, or his Persian at the expense of his Urdu is in my view quite misleading, and does not help one to make a just assessment of his achievement. This notwithstanding the fact that Ghālib himself on different occasions did both these things. One of his *ghazals* ends with the line: . . .

If one should say, 'Can Urdu then, better what
   Persian offers us?'
Read him a line of Ghālib's verse,
   Tell him, 'It can: it does so thus!'

But here too a note of warning is no less necessary. The *ghazal* is the *ghazal,* and exaggeration to the point of hyperbole is one of its familiar conventions. Ghālib is perhaps here doing no more than assert that his Urdu verse too is good verse. And we know that he did think so, and that he was quite right in thinking so.

It is not true—no matter what Ghālib may sometimes have told himself—that it was only under some sort of external pressure that he wrote in Urdu. He began writing in Urdu, as well as in Persian, in his childhood, and by the time he moved to Delhi from Agra in his teens he had already written a substantial amount of Urdu verse and made at any rate some sort of name for himself as an Urdu poet.

It is true that a time came when he turned his attention mainly to Persian, and true again that when in the 1850s he was retained at the Mughal court it was the King's preference for Urdu verse which more or less compelled him to take to the medium of Urdu once more. But what Hālī—Ghālib's friend and biographer—has to say in this connection is just. He writes:

It is important to emphasize here that Ghālib did not regard Urdu poetry as his field. For him it was a diversion; he would write an occasional *ghazal* sometimes because he himself felt like it, sometimes at the request of his friends, and sometimes in fulfilment of the commands of the King or the Heir Apparent. That is why in his Urdu *dīvān* there is no significant number of poems in any form other than the *ghazal* . . . Yet since most of his contemporaries were men of cultivated taste and quick to discern poetic merit, in his Urdu poetry too he was concerned to maintain the same pre-eminence as in Persian, and he gave all his attention and all his efforts to writing it.

And Ghālib's own letters of this period to his friend Nabi Bakhsh Haqir show that during these same years he produced Urdu verse of which he felt proud, even where it was at the King's instance that he wrote. Where he was pleased with the results he praised them with an engaging lack of reserve, and demanded that [Muhammad Taqi] Haqir praise them equally highly; and, indeed, some of his very best *ghazals* are the product of these years. Early in 1851—probably between April and June—he writes:

You should know that when I attend upon the King he usually asks me to bring him Urdu verse. Well, I wouldn't recite any of my old *gha-*

*zals.* I compose a new one and bring that. Today at midday I wrote a *ghazal* which I shall take and recite to him tomorrow or the day after. I'm writing it out, and send it to you too. Judge it truly: if Urdu verse can rise to the height where it can cast a spell or work a miracle, will this, or will this not, be its form?

He then appends not one *ghazal,* but two. The second is still one of his best-loved.

In May or June 1852, he writes, enclosing another, now famous *ghazal:* 'My friend, in God's name, give my *ghazal* its due of praise. If this is Urdu poetry, what was it that [Muhammad Taqi] Mir and Mirza wrote? And if that was Urdu poetry, then what is this?' In other words: 'My verse is in another class from that of Mir and Mirza [the colloquial names for Mir and [Mirza Mohammad Rafi] Sauda, the two greatest Urdu poets of the eighteenth century]— so much so that you cannot call their work and mine by the same name.'

Finally, in the early years after the Revolt of 1857, it is the loss of his *Urdu* verse in the looting of which the British soldiers were guilty to which he alludes with evident distress in his letters to his friends.

We can surely regard it as established, then, that G̲h̲ālib *did* in fact take a pride in his Urdu verse. And having done so let us proceed to see what it has to offer us.

We have just seen that nearly all of G̲h̲ālib's Urdu verse is in the *ghazal* form. In the collection of his verse which has been reprinted innumerable times over the last century, *ghazals* occupy something like eighty per cent of the whole. This means he writes in a *genre* bound by very strict conventions both of form and of theme. In form it is a fairly short poem, rarely of more than a dozen couplets, rhyming AA, BA, CA, DA and so on. Generally, every couplet is a complete and independent entity, commonly (though not obligatorily) differing from its neighbours not only in theme but even in mood. The last couplet must include the poet's *nom de plume*—that is to say in G̲h̲ālib's case, the name [Asad] occurs in the final couplet of every *ghazal.*

The themes too are largely prescribed by convention. The predominant theme of the *ghazal* is love—the poet's love for an earthly mistress, or his love, as a mystic lover, for God, his Divine Beloved. Very many lines can bear either interpretation or both. But provided these themes predominate, he may write also of almost any other theme he chooses. G̲h̲ālib frequently does so, and this is not an innovation on his part; the great *ghazal* poets before him did so too. However, because the standard themes do predominate I must describe them a little more closely, and then say something of how G̲h̲ālib handled them.

First, on the theme of earthly love. I will not repeat in detail what I have had occasion to write elsewhere on this theme. To people previously unfamiliar with any kind of medieval literature, the situations of love which they find portrayed in the *ghazal* come as something of a shock, and even when increasing familiarity at length banishes their surprise, they tend to settle into a state of mind which accepts that the conventions of the *ghazal are* what they clearly are, but assumes that this is a purely conventional picture, largely unrelated to anything in real life. . . . [Despite] a measure of exaggeration quite disconcerting to the modern reader in the west when he first encounters it, the conventional picture of earthly love in the *ghazal* is in fact far less fantastic, and far less removed from reality, than it at first appears. As in the love poetry of medieval Europe, love is generally illicit love—the love of a man for a woman already married or betrothed to another man—and hence a love persecuted by conventional society. The poet's beloved, his mistress is—in real life sometimes, and in the *ghazal* convention nearly always—angered by his love, and the lover thus has to bear not only the cruel persecution of society, but also the even more grievous persecution of the girl whom he loves. True love therefore demands of him almost superhuman courage and fortitude. He must love for its own sake, not only without any expectation of his love being returned, but knowing that his beloved will treat him with unrelenting hostility, and resolving nevertheless to be ever true to her even though his life be forfeit. Once again, in the *ghazal* convention he is in fact put to this supreme test. His mistress's eyebrows are bows which loose the sharp arrows of her eyelashes into his breast. She is his executioner, who has him led out to the execution ground and there strikes him down with the sharp sword of her beauty. And he submits not only uncomplainingly, but gladly.

These are the situations of earthly love which are then taken over bodily, so to speak, and applied to the experience of divine love, or mystic love. A modern audience perhaps understands this aspect of the *ghazal* more readily if it is expressed in non-religious terms. The poet's beloved here stands for the ideals of life in which he passionately believes, for the sake of which he is ready to face every hardship, to withstand every persecution, and in the last resort to sacrifice even his life. In a medieval society—and the *ghazal* is the poetry of a medieval society—such ideals could only be conceived and expressed in religious form. But the essence of the mystic love which the *ghazal* portrays is a self-sacrificing devotion to an ideal which, conceived in modern terms, is not *necessarily* a religious ideal at all, though of course it *may* be that.

The *ghazal* does not spell out in any great detail what these ideals involve for a man's personal and social life, but two features emerge very strongly. First, the *ghazal* poet's ideal is a strongly humanist one. It stresses the greatness of man, and proclaims his almost infinite potentialities, urging his claims even against God himself. Its cardinal religious commandment is to love your fellow men, no matter what their creed and nationality. Hāfiz, the great fourteenth-century Persian poet, proclaimed this commandment in a much-quoted verse which may be translated:

> So that you do not harm your fellow men, do
>   what you will.
> For in *my* Holy Law there is no other sin but
>   this.

And secondly, the *ghazal* poet takes it for granted that to proclaim such an ideal and to act upon it consistently necessarily incurs the wrath of the pillars of society. To take one's stand uncompromisingly on humanist ideals and not to flinch from any of their practical implications means to face persecution throughout one's life and ultimately to suffer death at the hands of the upholders of the established order of things.

I said earlier that among the conventions of the *ghazal* is exaggeration—exaggeration of an order that the modern reader accustoms himself to only with great difficulty. This exaggeration is evident in the depiction of the situations I have briefly described. There are famous Urdu poets who indeed had illicit love affairs and suffered because of them; but none lived out his life as a cruelly persecuted social outcast, either because of such a love affair or because of his dedication to the ideals of the mystic lover. Nor did any of them end his life on the execution ground, on the gallows or the impaling stake. In other words, the *ghazal* picture is a conventional one—a picture through which the poet portrays in terms of the most extreme symbolism his dedication to the ideals of love and of mystic humanism in face of the hostility of the conventional and the worldly-wise who dominate the society in which he lives. One can sometimes go further than this and say of many Urdu poets—though not of the greatest among them—that they present themselves in the *ghazal,* not as they are, but as they would like to be—as they see themselves in fantasy or as they want to be seen by their audience. Approaching the *ghazal* from another angle, one can say that it is the verse form in which the poet/lover expresses his devotion to his beloved, and that in the case of the poet whose real-life experience and real-life emotions and beliefs come closest to those which the *ghazal* convention portrays, the beloved in this context means two things: a real-life woman whom he loves, and the ideals of life to which he dedicates himself even in the face of the most bitter hostility of society at large. (pp. 105-11)

Ghalib was heir to this *ghazal* tradition that I have tried briefly to describe, and he wrote within its conventions. Some modern critics have claimed that he did so reluctantly chafing under the restraints which one of his verses calls . . . 'the narrow straits of the *ghazal*'. But I do not think that any such view can be sustained. The verse in question has a quite restricted reference. Ghalib is writing in praise of one Tajammul Husain Khan, and it is in this context that he feels that the *ghazal,* which is by definition a short poem, does not afford him the scope he needs. Nor does he reject the traditional symbolism of *ghazal* expression. Two much-quoted couplets run: . . .

> One means her airs and graces, but one cannot
> 　talk of them
> Unless one speaks of them as knives and daggers
> 　that she wields.
> One speaks of God's creation, but one cannot
> 　talk of it
> Except in terms of draughts of wine that make
> 　the senses reel.

I do not think it is in any spirit of complaint or frustration that he speaks these lines. Rather he is saying that he is quite content to express what he has to say in terms of the traditional imagery.

At all events, the *ghazal* form is *par excellence* the form of his choice. One could hardly expect it to be otherwise, for he was a man with a great love of the old cultural traditions, and the *ghazal* stands at the centre of these traditions. And there are reasons even more substantial than this of which I shall have occasion to speak presently.

It is perhaps appropriate to say a word at this point about his development as a *ghazal* poet. I have already said that he was heir to a long tradition. True, in Urdu, the north Indian tradition goes back only about a century before him. But this Urdu tradition was itself heir to the whole *ghazal* tradition of Persian poetry, going back 500 years from Ghālib's time, back to [Mohammad Shams al-Din] Hāfiż and beyond him; and Ghālib knew the Persian tradition exceptionally well. His early verse shows especially strongly the influence of Bedil, a leading Persian poet of the late seventeenth century, and he himself writes about this, quoting a *maqta*'—i.e. a concluding couplet—from one of his *ghazals:* . . .

> He writes in Urdu, but in [Mirza Muhammad]
> 　Bedil's style.
> What a man is this Asadullah Khan!

—Asadullah Khan being, of course, Ghālib's real name.

There is a great deal of purely technical virtuosity about much of his early verse, and a straining after originality which produced some verses of quite outlandish obscurity. Hīlī and others have related stories which show how verses of this kind exposed him to a good deal of ridicule: 'I have heard [writes Hālī] that the poets of Delhi would come to *mushairas* where Ghālib was present and recite *ghazals* which sounded very fine and impressive but were really quite meaningless, as though to tell Ghālib in this way that this was the kind of poetry he wrote.'

Others conveyed their criticism more privately. Hālī relates one instance: 'On one occasion *maulvi* Abdul Qādir of Rāmpūr said to Ghālib, "There is one of your Urdu verses which I cannot understand," and there and then made up this verse and recited it to him: . . .

> First take the essence of the rose out of the eggs
> 　of buffaloes—
> And other drugs are there; take those out of the
> 　eggs of buffaloes.

Ghālib was very much taken aback and said, "This verse is certainly not mine, I assure you." But *maulvi* Abdul Qādir kept up the joke and said, "I have read it myself in your *dīvān;* if you have a copy here I can show it you here and now." At length Ghālib realized that this was an indirect way of criticizing him and telling him that verses of this kind could be found in his *dīvān.*'

By and large Ghālib treated attacks on his early verse with the contempt which he thought they deserved. One of his couplets—I do not know whether it belongs to this period, but it expresses his attitude accurately enough—reads: . . .

> I want no praise; I seek no man's reward.
> My verses have no meaning? Be it so.

But the same sort of criticisms were made—no doubt in a more serious manner—by men whom he greatly respected, and when he came to put his *dīvān*—that is, his collection of *ghazals*—in more or less its present form, he discarded a great many of his early verses. He himself wrote of this, with characteristically gross exaggeration, many years later: 'Between the ages of fifteen and twenty-five I wrote on highly fanciful themes, and in these ten years got together a big *dīvān*. But in the end, when I learned discretion, I rejected this *dīvān*—tore it up completely—leaving only some ten to fifteen couplets in my present *dīvān* by way of samples of my former style.

Ḥālī's more sober estimate, that he discarded about two-thirds of his early work at this time, is nearer the truth. So is his statement that even now his *dīvān* is not devoid of examples of this kind. It must be admitted that Ghālib continued to retain even in his later years a fondness for the striking image and the far-fetched conceit that sometimes produced rather hair-raising results, and a wish to test his readers' ingenuity sometimes inspired verses rather like the clues of a difficult crossword puzzle in which the barest indication demands the use of a great deal of ingenuity to fill in the blanks. One example of each kind of verse must suffice. The first is from a *ghazal*—not devoid of a certain charm once you have deciphered its meaning—in which, in verse after verse, he contrasts on the one hand the comfort and serenity in which his mistress spends her days against the misery in which her hopeless lover spends his—a contrast heightened by a certain surface similarity in the two situations. One verse . . . , literally translated, means

> There, kindness had the excuse of the rain to bridle walking.
> Here, from weeping the cotton-wool of the pillow was the foam of the flood.

In other words: 'She said she could not come to me because it was raining, and so on my side the rain of my tears produced a flood.' Or, to move closer to the original: 'The rain provided an excuse to her not to show her professed kindness towards me, for it prevented her from walking to see me. On my side the torrent of my tears produced a flood, on which the white cotton-wool of my pillow was like the white froth on the swirling waters.'

A verse of the other kind is quoted with complacent approval, and then explained, by Ghālib himself in a letter of 1864: . . .

> I do not breathe a word against you, friend, but
> if you meet
> The man you gave my letter to, just give him my
> regards.

This theme calls for something by way of preamble. The poet [lover] needed a messenger [to take a letter to his mistress]. But he was afraid that such a messenger might himself fall in love with her. A friend of the lover brought a man to him and said, "This man is a man of honour, a man whom you can trust. I can guarantee that he won't do any such thing." Well, he was given a letter to take to her. As fate would have it, the lover's misgivings proved well-founded. The messenger looked upon the beloved and at once fell madly in love with her. The letter, the reply—all were forgotten, and in his frenzy he

rent his clothes and made off to the wilderness. And now the lover, after all this has happened, says to his friend, "Only God has knowledge of the unseen. Who knows what is in another's heart? So, my friend, I bear no grudge against you. But if by any chance you meet my messenger, give him my respects and say, 'Well, sir, what now of your tall claims that you would not fall in love?' "

Let me remind you again of the verse from which you are supposed to deduce all this:

> I do not breathe a word against you, friend, but
> if you meet
> The man you gave my letter to, just give him my
> regards.

—not, if Ghālib worshippers will forgive my saying so, a verse of any great poetic merit, but one which affords some consolation to those who sometimes struggle unavailingly to discover Ghālib's meaning. If Ghālib's own friends and contemporaries needed to have such verses explained to them, we twentieth-century Europeans need not feel too distressed if we also need to have explanations supplied us.

But when this kind of extravagance is left aside, a great deal of good poetry remains. I said earlier that Ghālib is quite content to say what he has to say within the *ghazal* form. What *does* he want to say? And how, some of you may wonder, within a form where themes and situations and imagery are prescribed in such detail, *can* a poet say anything new and distinctive at all? Well, firstly, his style is distinctive—just as, to use a rough parallel, a man's handwriting is distinctive even if he writes the identical words that another man has written. Secondly—and this is more important—the limitations of theme are not as severe as one might think. Firstly, the poet may present in a new light what I may call the stock characters of the *ghazal*—the lover, his mistress, his unworthy rivals for her love, and so on—or, in the sphere of religion and mysticism, he may again show in a new light man's relationship with God, his view of God's role in the universe, of the different prophets of Muslim tradition, and so on. Secondly, as I indicated earlier, if themes of love (in both senses) predominate in the *ghazal,* they are not its only themes, and the *ghazals* of the great masters, like Mir in the eighteenth century and Ghālib in the nineteenth, include verses on an almost unrestricted range of themes, and they say in them whatever they want to say.

In a short [essay] like this, one cannot hope to convey more than a very inadequate idea of Ghālib's range. If I were to single out what seem to me to be the most characteristic, distinctive qualities which his Urdu poetry reveals, I would say that they are: firstly, a keen, unsentimental, detached observation of man and God and the universe; secondly, a strong sense of independence and self-respect; thirdly, a conviction of the originality, and of the value to mankind, of what he has to say and a determination to say it, upholding his beliefs to the end, no matter what other men may think of them (it is here above all perhaps that the *ghazal* tradition meets his needs most perfectly); fourthly, an ability to see how limited is the scope for human enjoyment, a power to enjoy to the last drop everything that life brings, and yet to hold aloof, not to be trapped or enslaved by desire for the things he loves; and finally, a dry, irrepressible, unabashed humour which he is capable of bringing to the treatment of any theme, not excluding those on which he feels with the greatest seriousness and intensity. It is this last quality which has especially endeared him to successive generations of his readers.

Some of these qualities emerge clearly in his treatment of the conventional themes of love. The ambiguity or, as I would think it more accurate to call it, the universality of the term 'beloved', serves the *ghazal* poet in good stead. His 'beloved' is someone, or some *thing,* to which his dedication is complete and unshakeable, but the precise identification varies from poet to poet. For Mir, Ghālib's greatest predecessor in this field, the identification with a woman already married to someone else is a valid one. Mir did love such a woman deeply and constantly for years together, and suffered in consequence much of the persecution which such a love incurred. Ghālib, almost equally certainly, never experienced such love. He states his philosophy in a celebrated letter to his friend Hatim Ali Beg Mihr in which he tries to persuade him to banish the sorrow he felt at the recent death of a courtesan who had been his mistress:

> Mirza Ṣāhib, I don't like the way you're going on. I have lived sixty-five years, and for fifty of them have seen all that this transient world of colour and fragrance has to show. In the days of my lusty youth a man of perfect wisdom counselled me, "Abstinence I do not approve: dissoluteness I do not forbid. Eat, drink and be merry. But remember that the wise fly settles on the sugar, and not on the honey." Well, I have always acted on his counsel. You cannot mourn another's death unless you live yourself. And why all these tears and lamentations? Give thanks to God for your freedom, and do not grieve. And if you love your chains so much, then a Munna Jan is as good as a Chunna Jan. When I think of Paradise and consider how if my sins are forgiven me and I am installed in a palace with a houri, to live for ever in the worthy woman's company, I am filled with dismay and fear brings my heart into my mouth. How wearisome to find her always there!—a greater burden than a man could bear. The same old palace, all of emerald made; the same fruit-laden tree to cast its shade. And—God preserve her from all harm—the same old houri on my arm! Come to your senses, brother, and get yourself another.
>
> Take a new woman each returning spring
> For last year's almanac's a useless thing.'

The tone is of course humorous, and is adopted in a particular context which it would take too long to go into here; but I think he is quite serious about the philosophy of life which it expresses, and an entirely serious Persian letter written many years earlier had expressed essentially the same view:

> . . . though grief at a beloved's death tears at the soul and the pain of parting for ever crushes the heart, the truth is that to true men truth brings no pain; and amid this tearing of the soul

and this crushing of the heart we must strive to ponder: Where is the balm than can banish this distress? . . . You who have eyes to see, think upon this: that all the capital of those who venture all for love . . . is this one heart, lost now to the supple waist of their beloved, caught now and fettered in the ringlets of her curling locks. But where has a dead body the suppleness of waist to make the heart leap from its place? And where the curling ringlets to catch the soul in their toils? . . . The nightingale, notorious for love, pours forth his melody for every rose that blooms, and the moth to whose great passion all men point, give his wings to the flame of every candle that makes radiant her face. Truly, the candles radiant in the assembly are many, and roses bloom in the garden abundantly. Why should the moth grieve when one candle dies? When one rose fades and falls why should the nightingale lament? A man should let the world of colour and fragrance win his heart, not bind it in the shackles of one love. Better that in the assembly of desire he draw afresh from within himself the harmonies of happiness, and draw into his embrace some enchanting beauty who may restore his lost heart to its place and once more steal it away.

Ghālib then knew the joys of earthly love, and there are many verses which express it: . . .

> Sleep is for him, pride is for him, the nights for him
> Upon whose arm your tresses all dishevelled lay.

But he neither knew nor perhaps, in practice believed in, the kind of love for a woman in which one devotes one's whole life and one's whole being completely to her. He subscribes to the traditional view that the lot of the lover—even if his love is not returned—is more enviable than that of any other man: . . .

> He who sits in the shade of his beloved's wall
> Is lord and king of all the realm of Hindustan.

But if here we interpret 'beloved' in the more literal sense, it must be admitted that the beloved to whom it was applied might change from year to year. On the other hand, the verse can equally apply to a symbolic beloved, to a high ideal in life, and to the deep spiritual happiness which a man attains by serving it faithfully.

It is not surprising that in the conventional picture of human love, besides many verses distinctive in style rather than in content, there are many in which the rights of the *lover* are stressed as much as or more than the rights of his mistress, and in which the lover's self-respect is asserted.

One of his *ghazals* begins: . . .

> To every word that I utter you answer, 'What are you?'
> *You* tell me, is *this* the way, then, I should be spoken to?

And another begins with a rejoinder to her taunt that what he suffers from is not love, but madness: . . .

> 'It is not love, but madness'? Be it so.

My madness is your reputation though.

—that is, it is my mad love for you that makes *you* famous.

The lover traditionally accepts all that fate has to inflict upon him, and is proud to do so for the sake of his love. Ghālib sometimes takes a different view, and one feels that it is not in any very respectful tone that he addresses his 'friend', as the Urdu *ghazal* calls the beloved (even though the friendly feelings are generally only on the lover's side), when he says: . . .

> A lover needs no more than this to work his ruin
> utterly.
> You are his friend. What need is there for fate
> to be his enemy?

and, in the very next verse of the same *ghazal,* protests against the harsh treatment designed, as she alleges, to test him: . . .

> If this is testing, can you tell me, what would
> persecution be?
> It was to *him* you gave your heart; what do you
> want with testing *me*?

It would not, I think, be true to say that no poet before Ghālib ever spoke of, or to, his beloved in this way, but it is certainly true that in Ghālib this bold, mocking tone occurs a good deal more frequently than in his predecessors.

But if these verses are especially characteristic of Ghālib, there are plenty more that are closer to the main tradition in their handling of the themes of earthly love. To those who have, so to speak, grown up in the company of the *ghazal* I think that perhaps these present no problem. To us in the west, they do. We have seen that Ghālib was not the man to bind himself in the bonds of a single love. Why then does he so often speak as though he were? If one takes the whole range of these verses, I think the answer is three-fold. Firstly, some are there to show that he too can handle these themes just as well as the great masters of the past; and he does indeed show this. Secondly, in some of them he is creating in fantasy the beloved which real life denied him, and pouring out to her all the intensity of feeling which no real woman in his life ever inspired in him. And, stated in these terms, his situation is not an uncommon one in the history of the *ghazal.* I have argued elsewhere that in medieval society the *ghazal* often represented, for poet and audience alike, the release in fantasy of emotion which could not without drastic consequences have been released in real life. In the typical case it is a fear (a very understandable fear) of the social consequences that holds the poet back from the forbidden joys of love: in Ghālib's case it was perhaps rather that no woman ever evoked in him the intense, all-consuming devotion that he would have wished to experience. In a letter written perhaps only a year or two before his death he looks back on his life and quotes a verse of the Persian poet Anwarī as describing his own position: . . .

> Alas! there is no patron who deserves my praise.
> Alas! there is no mistress who inspires my verse.

It is perhaps not too fanciful to read into this something of the situation I have described.

But there is a third explanation which, valid though I think the other two are, has, I feel sure, a much wider relevance. This has to do with what I described earlier as the universality of the *ghazal's* symbolism. If one sketches the character of the lover/hero of the *ghazal,* first with the context of literal earthly love in mind, and then in more generalized terms, one can see its striking relevance to Ghālib's character and personality, and to his expression of what he feels in terms of the *ghazal* tradition. The lover is a man whom the experience of an all-consuming love has completely transformed. Few men in the society in which he lives have ever undergone such an experience, and to one who has not undergone it, it is something that thought and emotion alike can hardly even begin to comprehend. Yet it is this experience which alone gives meaning to the lover's life. All other values, all other standards of conduct, are either discarded or are absorbed into, and given new meaning by, the way of life which is learnt from love, and which love alone can teach. The lover thus lives out among his fellow men a life dedicated to, and directed by, ideals which even the most sensitive and sympathetic among them cannot comprehend; and that great majority which is neither particularly sensitive nor particularly sympathetic, because it cannot comprehend his values, shuns him and fears him; and because it fears him, hates him; and because it hates him, persecutes him. If one condenses this description and expresses it in more general terms one can say that the hero of the *ghazal,* and the *ghazal* poet casting himself in that role, is a man to whom all the things that are most precious in life are the product of a unique, nearly incommunicable experience which is to him all-important, but which isolates him from his fellows and condemns him to live his life among men who cannot understand him, let alone appreciate him, and who cannot really accept him as one of their own community. But if this is true, any man who is a poet and who feels himself to be in this position, can express what he feels by using the *ghazal's* portrayal of the situations of the lover as the symbols of his own experience. Ghālib, both as a poet and as a man, felt himself to be in this position, and used the *ghazal* in this way. His great poetic forebear Mir, whose diction was often of a crystal simplicity, described himself in metaphor as 'speaking a language no-one understood'. Of a great part of his own verse, and more especially of the Persian work which he so prized, Ghālib could say the same even in a literal sense. And in the metaphorical sense it was true even of his Urdu, for his Urdu includes only a small proportion of which it could be argued that it was the obscurity of his style that baffled his audience; for the most part it was the poverty of their emotional and intellectual experience that denied to the verse into which he distilled the essence of himself the appreciation which he justly felt to be its due. Writing to his friend Alai in his sixty-eighth year he says: ' . . . I share your inauspicious stars, and feel your pain. I am a man devoted to one art. Yet by my faith I swear to you, my verse and prose has not won the praise it merited. *I* wrote it, and I alone appreciated it.'

As a man too he often felt that he stood alone. He felt it the more keenly when he reflected on the reason for his position, for he was forced to conclude that he put himself in this position because he lived by the standards which all his fellows professed, but which he was almost alone in practising. He had seen the practical value of their professions in 1847, when he was imprisoned on a charge of gambling and when, of all of his friends in and around Delhi, only Shefta stood by him and fulfilled the obligations of friendship towards him. Nearly fourteen years later he still held to the same position, and, just as the lover accepts that steadfastness in love necessarily makes him the target of persecution, so does Ghalib accept that steadfastness in observing a high standard of personal conduct necessarily brings misfortunes in its train. He writes to his friend Shafaq in 1861: 'You are a prey to grief and sorrow, but . . . to be the target of the world's afflictions is proof of an inherent nobility—proof clear, and argument conclusive.' This was a judgment he was to repeat in the words of one of his Persian verses little more than a year before his death, when he had to witness the spectacle of respectable gentlemen who had been on visiting terms with him, taking the stand in court and testifying against his character in the most insulting and humiliating terms.

When therefore Ghalib depicts himself in his *ghazals* as the true lover of a beautiful woman, gladly suffering all her cruelties, what he is often doing is asserting in traditional symbolism his unshakeable conviction of the soundness of his values and/or of the high quality of his poetry, and declaring that so long as he has breath he will continue to affirm them: . . .

> I filled the blood-stained pages with the story of
> my love
> And went on writing, even though my hands
> were smitten off.

Interpreted in this sense, many of the verses that on first reading seem to be depictions of the love of man for woman are instead (or, perhaps, as well) expressions of emotion and belief which fall within the traditional category of mystic love of God but which, I have suggested, a modern audience understands most readily as dedication to ideals which are not necessarily religious.

Where Ghalib writes more explicitly in the mystic tradition his verses show the same sort of range as those which depict the situations of earthly love. For example, there are verses expressing the same bold, almost impudent attitude to God—his Divine Beloved—as some of those in which he addresses his human mistress. He demands from God treatment consistent with his self-respect. He tells Him: . . .

> I serve You; yet my independent self-respect is
> such
> I shall at once turn back if I should find the
> Ka'ba closed.

And in numbers of verses he makes it clear that he does not always receive such treatment. According to Muslim belief, man's good and evil deeds are written down by recording angels, and it is on their written testimony that his fate is decided on the Day of Judgment. What sort of justice is that? asks Ghalib. You take the evidence for the prosecution, but what about the witnesses for the defence?: . . .

> The angels write, and we are seized. Where is the
> justice there?
> We too had someone present when they wrote
> their record down.

Here, as often, he speaks in some sense as the champion of mankind as a whole. Similarly he does so when, like other poets before him, he accuses God not only of injustice but of simple inconsistency in His treatment of mankind. He refers to the story of how when God created Adam He commanded the angels to bow down before him. All did so except Iblis—and Iblis was punished by eternal banishment from Heaven. If this, then, was the status that God intended for man, how is it that God himself has not continued to uphold it?: . . .

> Today we are abased. Why so? Till yesterday
> You would not brook
> The insolence the angel showed towards our
> majesty.

Elsewhere Ghalib, being Ghalib, speaks not for mankind at large, but specifically for himself in his relationship with God. Here am I, he says in effect, a great poet, and a man of unique understanding, and there are You passing me by and revealing Your secrets to men who cannot sustain them!: . . .

> You should have let your radiance fall on me,
> not on the Mount of Tur
> One pours the wine having regard to what the
> drinker can contain.

The reference is to the story which appears in Christian guise as that of Moses and the burning bush. The Mount of Tur is the place where God revealed his radiance to Musa—the Muslim name to which our 'Moses' corresponds. Ghalib's lines suggest two comparisons. The first is between himself and the mountain—the huge, strong mountain, which for all its strength cannot compete with man—man whose apparent frailty is more than counterbalanced by an awareness and a sensitivity which enables him to accept from God the heavy burden of a trust which even the mountains could not sustain. Secondly, the verse suggests a contrast between Ghalib and Musa. Musa's response to God's radiance was to swoon before it; Ghalib would have had the strength to gaze upon it.

He certainly does not accept either the earlier prophets or the outstanding men of his own day as men who know all that a man needs to know, men in whose guidance he can implicitly trust. Thus he says of Khizr, that somewhat mysterious figure in Muslim legend who found and drank the water of eternal life, who roams the desert places and comes to true Muslims who have lost their way and guides them on to the right path, and who on one occasion explained the mysterious workings of God's benevolence to a perplexed Musa: . . .

> I am not bound to take the path that Khizr indicates.
> I'll think the old man comes to bear me company on my way.

Or, rather less politely, he hints that Khizr is in any case not above some rather sharp practice. Legend has it that he guided Sikandar (Alexander the Great) to look for the water of eternal life and that, in somewhat obscure circumstances, Khizr got it and drank it while Sikandar did not: . . .

> You know how Khizr treated Alexander.
> How then can one make anyone one's guide?

And he states it as his own principle: . . .

> I go some way with every man I see advancing
>     swiftly.
> So far I see no man whom I can take to be my
>     guide.

One is reminded of what he once wrote in a letter to his friend [Munshi Hargopàl] Tufta: 'Don't think that everything men wrote in former ages is correct. There were fools born in those days too.'

But if he sees himself as unique among men, he fully accepts, in line with the whole tradition of the *ghazal,* his oneness with his fellow men, the value of man *as* man, regardless of his formal religious and other allegiances. We have seen one aspect of this belief in his assertion of the rights of man in his relationship with God. He asserts the same values in relationships between man and man. And here he is not simply following a poetic convention. He was a man who had a wide circle of friends in all communities—Muslim, Hindu and British—and he rejected all narrow communal and national prejudices in his dealings with them. In one of his letters to his friend Tufta he wrote: 'My gracious friend, I hold all mankind to be my kin, and look upon all men—Muslim, Hindu, Christian—as my brothers, no matter what others may think.' His verses express this attitude. One of them links it with the central tenet of Muslim belief—belief in the absolute oneness of God: . . .

> My creed is oneness, my belief abandonment of
>     rituals;
> Let all communities dissolve and constitute a
>     single faith.

But like his predecessors he knows how hard it is for men to hold consistently to the principles of humanism, and he expresses this in paradox: . . .

> How difficult an easy task can prove to be!
> Even a man does not attain humanity.

Armed with this sort of philosophical outlook he surveys the whole human drama and the universe in which it is played. He recognizes how limited is the scope that the universe offers, both for joy pure and simple, and for that more complex joy which is inextricably linked with sorrow and sacrifice. And by the same token he recognizes that a man should live intensely, treasuring all that life can bring—not only its pleasures, but its suffering too. Poor Khizr again comes in for a rebuke in this context: . . .

> Khizr, *we* are alive who know the busy world of
>     men
> Not you, who slunk away unseen to steal eternal
>     life.

Ghālib states his own attitude in two successive verses of a *ghazal,* deliberately parallel in their structure, in which he speaks in turn of the cruelty of fair women and the transience of spring, and stresses that without in any way blinding himself to these realities, it is to their beauty that he surrenders himself: . . .

> The fair are cruel. What of it? They are fair.
> Sing of their grace, their swaying symmetry.
> Spring will not last. What of it? It is spring.
> Sing of its breezes, of its greenery.

Or, in a more general statement: . . .

> My heart, this grief and sorrow too is precious;
>     for the day will come
> You will not heave the midnight sigh nor shed
>     your tears at early morn.

Linked with this view of life is a strong feeling for the value of the here and now, and a marked scepticism about even the allegedly certain benefits still to come. It is not that Ghālib lives only for the moment, heedless of the future; to describe his outlook thus would be to cheapen it and do him less than justice. It is rather that he seeks to live every moment to the full, prepared to face what is still to come, but careful to make no optimistic assumptions about it. Verses in which he expresses this sort of feeling even about life after death—usually in a humorous tone—are strikingly frequent. He *knows* the joys that he has tested; as a Muslim he believes in the coming joys of Paradise; and yet . . . after all he has not proved them by experience. Best not assume too much. But anyway, leaving aside the question of whether or not they will prove to be hereafter all that is claimed for them, they are pleasing fancies here and now, and even at this rating they have their value: . . .

> I know the truth, but, be that what it will,
> The thought of Paradise beguiles me still.

The true Muslim is forbidden to drink wine here on earth, but in Paradise God will give him to drink his fill of the wine of purity. Well, Ghālib has broken the prohibition, and has verified here and now that wine is good to drink. So this, at least, is one of the joys of Paradise that he has already proved. In fact, come to think of it, it is perhaps the *only* joy of Paradise that he has proved; and he says: . . .

> For what else should I value Paradise
> If not the rose-red wine, fragrant with musk?

For the rest, he *hopes* that the joys he will know there will match the joys he has already known here in this present world. He tells his mistress: . . .

> All that they say of Paradise is true, and yet
> God grant it be illumined by *your* radiance.

Space does not here permit more than the bare assertion, but in my view the vicissitudes of the historical period in which he lived, the traditions of his immediate ancestors, and the environment in which he passed his boyhood were all forces which led Ghālib to conclude early in life that he must 'settle on the sugar, and not on the honey' and to cultivate the attitudes that these verses express. It is very characteristic of him that, in life and in poetry alike, he shields himself against 'the slings and arrows of outrageous fortune' with an irrepressible, unquenchable humour, and with an ability to get outside himself and look at himself even in the most painful situations with a dry, ironical detachment. In one of his letters he writes to a friend: 'I watch myself from the sidelines, and rejoice at my own distress and degradation'—and many of his verses reflect this attitude. Thus he says to the mistress who spurns his love, even though she knows that he demands nothing of her: . . .

> I grant it you, my dear, Ghālib is nothing.
> But if you get him free then what's the harm?

Or he himself brings about a situation where he makes one of his closest friends a rival for his mistress's love: . . .

> It was *her* beauty I described, and my words that described it—
> And now he is my rival who was once my confidant.

But with this all too inadequate sample I must draw to a close.

Like many great men before him, Ghālib looked to posterity to award him the praise which men of his own times denied him. Two Persian couplets on the theme express his feelings in striking metaphors: . . .

> Today none buys my verse's wine, that it may grow in age
> To make the senses reel in many a drinker yet to come.

---

**Ghalib on his method of composing poetry:**

Persian as we know it is a compound of two languages— Persian and Arabic. In the colloquial, Turkish words are also used, but only to a small extent. I am no scholar of Arabic, but I am not completely ignorant of it either. All I mean is that I have not studied the language deeply. There are points on which I have to consult the scholars, and I have to ask them to quote authorities for various words. In Persian, from the Bounteous Source I received such proficiency that the laws and structure of the language are as deeply imbedded in me as the temper is in steel. Between me and the Persian masters there are two differences: first, that their birthplace was Iran and mine India; and second, that they were born a hundred, two, four, eight hundred, years before me. . . .

It makes me laugh when I see how you think that I am like other poets, who set some master's ghazal or ode before them, or copy out its rhymes and then fit other words to them. God preserve me from such things! Even in my childhood when I began to write Urdu verse, may I be accursed if I ever set an Urdu poem or its rhyme-scheme before me. All I did was look at the metre, the rhyme and the end-rhyme, and then set to write a ghazal or ode on the same pattern. You write that I must have had Naziri's diwan open before me when I wrote my ode . . . I swear to God that until I got your letter I never even knew that Naziri had written an ode in this scheme. . . . My friend, poetry is the creating of meaning, not the matching of rhymes. . . .

*Ghalib, in a letter to Munshi Hargopál Tufta, quoted by Russell and Islam in their* Ghalib 1797-1869; Volume I: Life and Letters, *Harvard University Press, 1969.*

---

> My star rose highest in the firmament before my birth:
> My poetry will win the world's acclaim when I am gone.

When he was gone his verse did indeed begin to win the world's acclaim, until today wherever Urdu is spoken it is known and loved. But for the barrier of language it would, I am convinced, win wider acclaim still. At all events, a stage has been reached when interest in him and his work has spread far beyond the confines of his own homeland, to the U.S.A., the U.S.S.R., and many other countries. (pp. 111-31)

> *Ralph Russell, "Ghālib's Urdu Verse," in* Ghalib: The Poet and His Age, *edited by Ralph Russell, George Allen & Unwin Ltd., 1972, pp. 105-31.*

## Ralph Russell and Khurshidul Islam    (essay date 1969)

[*In this excerpt, Russell and Islam briefly comment on Ghalib's letters as literature.*]

It was during [1829-47] that [Ghalib] first compiled the volume of his selected Urdu verse, discarding much of his earlier work. . . . He also gathered together his Persian verse and prose, and wrote many new Persian ghazals at this time. The Persian prose collection was probably compiled by about 1840 (though it was not printed until 1849), and is in five sections, of which the third and the fifth are the most interesting. In the third section Ghalib quotes selected lines from his Persian verse and instances appropriate contexts where they might be quoted in letter-writing; in the fifth he assembles his Persian letters to his friends. These include letters to many of the most famous names in the literature and scholarship of the nineteenth-century Muslim India, and show how well-established Ghalib's reputation was. It is worth stressing that these letters were written with the most elaborate care—as is clear from some of those already quoted—and Ghalib regarded them as much as any other of his Persian prose writings, as models of literary composition on which he could pride himself. They cover a number of years, and most of them are either undated, or dated with insufficient precision to be placed accurately. Moreover in the published text of Ghalib's collected Persian prose the publishers supplemented them in 1875 with any other Persian letters they could find, without indicating at what point in the text these later additions begin. From internal evidence it is clear that the letters go back at least to the time when he was contemplating his journey to Calcutta, and a number of them were written during that journey. They vary greatly in mood, so that while some are intensely serious, others are equally light-hearted; and though as a general rule Ghalib composes them with the utmost care, he does not sacrifice warmth and spontaneity of feeling. In one he stresses that letter-writing should be like conversation:

> God is my witness that as I write this letter of humble service to you the desire to be with you so wells up within me that it leaves no room for the formal styles and titles of address. For I want to write to you in every way as though I were

talking to you; and this means that many a time my words stray from the point, and I take no thought of what comes first and what comes last, and I write on and on without care for the length at which I write. Lost to myself, I let the reins fall from my hand, and am carried along over the ups and downs as I pass through the valley of conversation.

To another correspondent he writes,

> Praise be to God that I was born a straightforward and a truthful man. My tongue speaks out all that my heart holds. If I have sinned against the religion of love and loyalty, then I deserve the torment of punishment; and if I be thought worthy of forgiveness, then I deserve the good tidings that my fault is pardoned.

He often jokes with his correspondents. One letter is addressed to a man named Alif Beg, to whom a son had been born in his old age, and who had written to Ghalib asking him to suggest a name for the boy. Ghalib's answer plays upon the technicalities of the Urdu alphabet associated with the letter *alif* and the sign *hamza*. *Alif* is a simple vertical line, while *hamza* has a zig-zag shape. Both represent the same phonetic value, and both happen also to be used as personal names. He writes:

> Kind of face and kind in grace, greetings! The tree of hope has borne fruit out of season, that is, a son has been born to you in your old age. Congratulations on so happy and auspicious an event! You wrote . . . to me to name the newborn babe. . . . Know then, I did not have to undertake the toil of thought. A name flashed on my mind; my mind despatched a poem to my tongue; and my tongue entrusts the poem to the pen. May the Lord prosper him whom I name with this auspicious name! And may he be a loyal son to you, and in your lifetime live to be your age, and live for years and years when you are gone! This is the poem:
>
> A child is born to Alif in old age,
> A perfectly entrancing little son.
> I name him Hamza, for, as all men know,
> An Alif bent with age turns into one!
>
> Your old associates speak often of you. Some day you should take the road towards this wilderness too.

He writes to Rae Chajmal Khatri from somewhere on the way to Calcutta:

> Congratulations on becoming the agent of Zeb un Nisa Begam—and may this prove the prelude to further advancements in the future. If only you had told me what salary you were receiving I should have known in what measure to congratulate you.

(pp. 56-8)

*Ralph Russell and Khurshidul Islam, "Delhi, 1829-47," in* Ghalib, 1797-1869: Life and Letters, Vol. I, *edited and translated by Ralph Russell and Khurshidul Islam, Cambridge, Mass.: Harvard University Press, 1969, pp. 51-70.*

## Ahmed Ali   (essay date 1969)

[*Ali is a Pakistani poet, critic, and novelist. In the following excerpt, he analyzes Ghalib's style in relation to his historical context and comments on several key influences on his poetry.*]

The nineteenth century in India was an age of upheavals, doubts and uncertainties, religious controversies, esoteric doctrines, orthodoxy and moral recession, revolts and acceptance, decay and disorder, but also of hope as a new order was emerging like

> Dispersed light in the mirror, a speck of dust
> Caught in the sunlight in the window

to use Ghalib's imagery. With the passing of the care of Urdu and the culture of India to British hands under the treaty of 1765, British ascendancy had been acknowledged. The people still owed allegiance to the Mughal Emperor, but found no glory at the Court which was incapable of inspiring any sense of national pride. Torn between the reality and a future still incomprehensible, they felt helpless if not stunned. Some were exasperated into taking up arms under the banner of religion, and some were lost in the pursuit of pleasures or apathy typical of defeatism. Psychologically it was a difficult period of warring loyalties, instinct demanding attachment to what was national, expediency suggesting alignment with a power that had virtual control of India. Attitudes underwent a change. The main pattern of culture remained oriental, but Western ways were making inroads into the minds of men. Since knowledge of alien manners and customs was superficial, and imitation inherent in the situation, a laxity became visible in life and morals, encouraged by the loosening hold of tradition and failing faith in the stability of a society which could no longer uphold its values by giving its members an assurance of its strength. The divine right which sustained it had collapsed. In poetry, therefore, the fleshly school, developing in a fast degenerating Lucknow, the second seat of culture, decaying before it had become ripe, gained popularity and subsidized a desperate order floundering in a morass of superficies. Some patriotic minds revolted against the rising tide of the West, and preached revolution, like the Vahabis and [Momin Khan] Momin who said:

> O Doomsday, come, shake up the world
> And rend it up and down, about;
> It may be it will come to nought,
> But in revolt there is hope at least.

a sentiment echoed by Ghalib himself:

> Some feeling souls are waiting
> For revolution;
> Make those who have found happiness
> Unhappy again.

But their voices were stilled in death or defeat.

These currents produced sentiments and attitudes difficult to analyze. Ghalib's developed sensibility accepted a variety of thoughts as valid experiences. His peculiar mind amalgamated these experiences into a unity so that the sifting of their elements becomes a hopeless task, the more so as Ghalib had a comprehension of his age, like Baudelaire, while the changing pattern of the age was still incomplete and unknown to his contemporaries. It is still largely unknown, as no serious attempt has been made to find its true form and nature, in the preoccupations of the day, and because of the inadequacy of scholarship to tackle the complex problem. Without full awareness of it any study of the mind and method of Ghalib is bound to remain incomplete. (pp. 1-3)

[Ghalib] started writing verses in Urdu at the early age of ten without ever having become anyone's disciple, contrary to the established practice, and adopted Asad, 'lion', as his pseudonym, but abandoned it later in favour of Ghalib, 'conqueror'. Very early in his poetic career he became the talk of the town, and many spoke of him with sarcasm and ridicule and said, as the University Wits had done of Shakespeare, that an insolent poet had appeared on the scene who took his stand on ways other than those of Shah Naseer[–uddin] and [Sheikh Ibrahim] Zauq (the two most popular poets of the day), who talked of unbeknown and absurd worlds. His art had, however, already reached perfection before he was twenty-three years of age, as the manuscript of his poems known as the Hamidia Manuscript of Bhopal dated 1237 Hijra or 1821 A.D. proves. Nearly half of the 3,776 lines of this manuscript were included in the definitive selections of his Urdu works which he prepared on the insistence of friends who wanted him to delete his more difficult and obscure poems. The Bhopal MS displays all the characteristics and qualities that distinguish his poetry, even though he altered and chiselled many lines in later years.

The years between 1825 and 1833 were spent in a futile attempt at the restoration of his family pension given in lieu of service rendered in the Army but withheld by British authorities. The attempt continued almost until 1844, even though he had lost the case for the pension in 1833. This was a period of vicissitudes and mental strain during which he travelled to Calcutta, visiting Benares and other cities on the way. His admirers and pupils, among them the rulers of Rampur and Lucknow, and the Mughal Emperor himself whose chronicler he became in 1850 and his teacher in 1855 after the death of Zauq, gave him annuities. Most of these, however, ceased after 1857. The Mughal court conferred on him two titles, and the King bestowed other gifts and honours, but they meant no permanent relief, and his life remained one of struggle and financial worries which run to the end of his days like a persistent experience. The two great sorrows of his life seem to have been the death of a woman he loved, perhaps the same woman of his early love affair, and that of Zainul Abedin Khan Arif, his adopted son and nephew, to both of whom he addressed passionate elegies.

A few more facts are recounted by commentators and recorded by him in letters written in the finest prose to many friends in later years, while the rest of his life is obscure like that of many great authors of the Renaissance. The obscurity becomes pronounced in view of his temperament which combined originality with pride in his noble birth, intellect with imagination, truth of observation with philosophical doubt. Unsympathetic criticism and the in-

difference of people left him with a sense of frustration, even bitterness:

> There is no place for me in any heart;
> Melodious is my work, but still unheard.
> As a man bitten by dog dreads water,
> I dread the mirror for I have been bitten by man.

As a result his poetry is full of poignant grief and intense yearning:

> Driven by an unknown hope
> I go, I know not where;
> The path itself is the straight line
> Of grace to me.

This is expressed in many ways, time and again, as emotion recollected in tranquillity, as longing for love and leisure and time past, the regret for lost perfection leading to the search for the ideal, a moving realization of Beauty:

> The lightning heat of heart's anguish filled the cloud
> With terror last night; each whirl of the vortex was molten flame.
> With the lustre of the rose by the water bloomed a garden of lamps,
> But a channel of blood flowed from my eyes bedewed.
> My clamouring head had turned to a wall with lack of sleep,
> But, head on silken pillow, that beauty was rapt in peace.
> Whereas my breath lit the lamp of forgetfulness,
> The splendour of the rose was the extent for the meeting of friends.
> From the earth to the sky was a tumult of colour wave on wave,
> For me this space was only the door of a burning waste.
> Then suddenly the heart, ravished with the joys of pain,
> Began to drip, out of this colour, red tears of blood.
> Enraptured was it with the coming of the storm,
> But a reed to the water's sound the lover's soul.

The search continues throughout his life, now appearing as the past, now as quest for beauty in nature and behind it awareness of a mystical presence:

> The world is full of the effulgence
> Of the one-ness of the well-beloved;
> Where would we be if Beauty
> Did not possess self-love?

leading to a teleological approach to God:

> When nothing here exists without Thee,
> Then wherefore all this tumult, O Lord?

Under his keen and enquiring mind these ideas break up into many forms, aesthetic, material and metaphysical. He disbelieves the evidence of the senses:

> My mad despair is the enemy
> Of the evidence of the world:
> The heavenly sun is only a lamp
> Along the path of the wind.

and advances towards philosophical scepticism:

Be not deceived by life:
However they may say
It is, it does not exist.

He could not accept the established view of things and was sceptical of known beliefs. In fact, he was in revolt against many of them which his rational mind was loath to accept; and though a good deal of his imagery was based on the conventional one, he inverted it to suit his thought, sometimes grotesquely perverting it:

I know the truth of Paradise:
A futile thought, but desirable.

exposing, at the same time, the emptiness of orthodox attitudes:

If Paradise he desires,
None else but Adam is heir to Adam.
The brilliance of the priest's faith
Is dullness of action.

Ghalib saw through hypocrisy:

Deception of the hypocrite,
I'm the illusion of those
Distressed without a cause.

and emphasized action:

Men are put to shame
By false courage. Therefore
Produce tears, Asad,
If the sigh has no effect.

The dialectic of Ghalib's poetry is double-edged. He uses current imagery, but makes new use of it, and shows its hollowness as it has become empty of thought and is inadequate to reflect the reality. His imagination is esemplastic. Perception and thought are continuously fused in his mind, so that he could see creation and the Creator all at once involved in the situation:

Life's leisure is a mirror of the hundred hues
Of self-adoration;
And night and day, the great dismay
Of the onlooker of this scene.

The position is reversed from the accepted belief. Life in its multiple forms is engrossed in itself alone, and the Maker, bound by His own laws, turns a beholder of the scene of night and day he had himself made, sorry at its plight. Life goes on caught in its own vortex, concerned with itself alone; and even God cannot change the pattern and views it with dismay.

Ghalib is both a representative of a culture and in revolt against it. He makes the temporary eternal, and the divine helpless in the face of necessity:

Intelligence Unconcerned
Is caught in the great despair
Of encirclement; and man's
Image remains imprisoned
In the mirror of the world.

God, and He is the Intelligence Unconcerned, is encircled within the laws of the universe and cannot disentangle Himself, hence the great despair, while the world, the house of mirrors, acts as a prison for man's image so that he cannot look beyond it. Even the Creator is bound by the laws of responsibility and change, and cannot help mankind caught in the whirl of life, the prison-house of the perceptual world. Both man and God are held inevitably and cannot get out of the necessity of night and day. A situation more tragic was not visualised even by [John] Milton, and most difficult to find outside of Greek drama!

Ghalib saw life as a moment between two opposites, and wished to escape the gravitational force of either to stand clear of them and be free. He does not make naïve accusations like [Muhammad Taqi] Mir, though valid in the context of Mir's vision and the social reality:

For nothing we, the helpless ones,
Accused of independence are,
For you act as it pleases you,
And yet it's we who get the blame.

Ghalib was aware of the limitations of man:

It has not been given to man to become even
man

and of man's predilection for self-deception:

In the joy of blossoming the rose
Is lost in a sea of colour;
O consciousness, the lure
Of illusion is everywhere!

as well as the imperfection of life:

How can perfection of love
Be found in this defective world?
The thought of maturity
Of mind is futile here.

Ghalib's poetry reflects the movement of thought. It is the product of a civilization standing on the brink of change and conscious of it. The quality it displays is a personal one, and Ghalib's personality was complex. The nature of his experience was, therefore, varied and concentrated. The stamp of his individuality is present in every line he wrote, so that he founded no school nor left an heir to his rich tradition. Only a mind like his could feel and express like him, hammer out plastic images from a piece of steel on the anvil still red hot. People like him are born after an age of Wonder and Romanticism, when the imagination is still active to participate in the whirl of life, but shaped by experiences divergently opposite. They represent a change of something more fundamental than form, the mind itself; and Ghalib's mind is on a different plane from Mir, [Khwaja Mir] Dard, [Mirza Muhammad Rafi] Sauda, and [Vali Muhammad] Nazir.

The poets of the eighteenth century blended other qualities of heart and imagination. They were products of a different social order, one which found its sustenance from the very Indian air they breathed, and wrote in an idiom with which every one was familiar, in spite of the divergences in their approach to life and poetry. Theirs was an age of awakening Romanticism and Renaissance. They were relishing the wonder of the freedom of thought from the bondage of orthodoxy and an order based on authority which the reign of Aurangzeb had stood for. They were also critical of society, its faults and foibles and essential weaknesses, such as Sauda in his satires and Nazir in his odes. If Dard could indulge his fancy in the trained flights of mysticism, Mir's imagination could soar up to the very skies and travel back to pre-existence or forward to post-existence in a unique comprehension of the universe, grieving not for any failure of vision, but the crass casualty of accidental birth. When we come to Ghalib, however, we find that something had happened to the mind of India itself. The genius of Urdu poetry had taken a different turn from the traditional appeal to the emotions towards an intellectual approach. The gap between Ghalib and his predecessors of the eighteenth century was bridged by Nazir and Momin who display, though as yet undemonstrably, the role of the mind in the shaping of emotion. Nazir had known the injustices of a society in which man had degraded man, where poverty and wealth had held either extreme. He possessed a greater consciousness of Time than any other Urdu poet, time that destroys and time that reconciles, time conscious and time remembered, and the mind as conscious of time as it was aware of itself. Momin had known the tribulations of revolt and the incursions of an alien civilization into the established order, the time-old landscape of love and jealousy. All of them were busy rediscovering truth buried under the debris of rigid laws and beliefs. But Ghalib carried the search for truth to a more rational and metaphysical plane, cutting out for himself a path more difficult, at the same time presenting a view of the age as the age itself could hardly understand.

He used the suggestive richness of the language of his predecessors, but made it more precise and sharp, imparting to it a profound quality of their thought, even to the extent of becoming a nihilist. But a good deal of his nihilism had root in the religious controversies and the esoteric doctrines of the nineteenth century which was the sowing time of the rationalism and free thinking of the later decades. A good deal of this never came to any thing, and a good deal was watered down by the hold of orthodox Islamic thought into a laxity of morals and religious beliefs, so that a section of the rising middle class ceased to have more than a superstitious fear of God and the retribution of Hell. This situation was helped by the increasing Western education and the materialistic tendencies advancing in consequence, until today we do not witness more than superficial adherence to the tenets of the faith, and largely find mere lip service paid to religion. The reformistic movement of Shah Valiullah (1703-62) and his son Shah Abdul Aziz (1746-1823) in the second half of the eighteenth century, which had stood for purifying Islam of extraneous practices which had become incorporated in it, gave place to the Vahabi movement for restoring its uncorrupted simplicity, and which was mistaken, with such disastrous consequences for its adherents later in the century, by the British as a militant and subversive move directed against them. Along with its more ecclesiastical successors of the Deoband and its parallel system of the Ahl-e-Hadis (followers of the Tradition), as well as the dissident sectarian doctrines of the non-Vahabis and the non-Muqallids, the opponents of the Ahl-e-Hadis, it had a great influence over the minds of Indian Muslims. The mid-nineteenth century was, in fact, charged with intellectual restlessness in which the middle class and the intellectuals were as passionately involved as the religious leaders themselves, for the border-line between religion and secu-

larism was as narrow as a thread, and discussions on religious matters were as common among Ghalib's friends and associates as exchanges on poetry and life, and Ghalib could hardly escape being involved in the religious ideas of his age. He was accused both of obscurity and difficultness of thought as well as of Shiistic tendencies and atheism. Had he lived in the reign of Aurangzeb his fate would have been anybody's guess; but the boldness of his imagination and the metaphysical depth of his thought stood him in good stead, as they stand witness to his intellectual integrity and honesty of search for truth.

But then, Ghalib expresses an attitude, not an emotion. There is no room for sentiment in his poetry. His approach is through the mind: it is a state of mind. He is a poet not of the past, but of the present. He is not interested in a philosophy, and attempts at finding in him adherence to this mystical belief or that religious doctrine are beside the point. He is primarily concerned with communicating his experience, sensing his thought and turning his ideas into sensations. He is essentially a poet of our civilization, and "poets of our civilization, as it exists at present", as T. S. Eliot says in his essay on the Metaphysical Poets, "must be *difficult*. Our civilization comprehends great variety and complexity, and the variety and complexity, playing upon a refined sensibility, must produce various complex results. The poet must become more and more comprehensive, more allusive, more direct, in order to dislocate, if necessary, language into its meaning".

Ghalib possessed the quality of absolute curiosity, love of comprehension, and a sense of beauty which led to a capacity for acute impressions, heightening of imaginative feeling and perception of beautiful images, even in such social concepts as the home, for it is in the awareness of the presence or absence of an emotion, an object, that beauty resides:

> There is in the desert
> Desolation on desolation,
> Endless, without extent,
> Reminding me of home.

and the opposite state:

> On wall and arch grows green the grass;
> I am in the desert, at home it is Spring.

which speaks of the same mental agony as is felt at the recession of the ideal. His romantic sense of sorrow and regret is really a means of seeking the opposite state of joy. His poetic experience was intentive, or intentional, in Jaques Maritain's phrase, having a tendential existence, presenting an object in the idea of it. Hence the intellect played the substantive part in his poetry which has its source in the preconceptual life of the intellect. The experience presented in words is symbolized; the emotion is raised to the level of the intellect and transcends itself by becoming that which it knows:

> The heat engendered by thought is indescribable;
> I had just thought of despair when the desert went up in flames.

He could, therefore, see both sides of thought at once, the

face and the obverse, the light and the shadow. This is not confined to one facet, but is a characteristic of his mind:

> In my construction lies
> Concealed the form of ruin;
> The lightning's flash that strikes
> The granary
> Is the burning blood
> Of the peasantry.

which was certainly written before the publication of *Das Kapital.* For the same reason he had a dread of conventions:

> Kohkan could not die unaided by the pick;
> Poor man was slave to conventional thought and
>    belief.

This is not a mere façade or sophistication. It is a mental state, a personal realization of things born of a realistic approach and the habit of analysis, which is the basis of Ghalib's contemporaneity and consciousness of movement and change:

> Each change of the mirror
> Of creation
> Brings sorrow in its train:
> The cloud sheds its tears
> At the departure of Autumn.

He is the perfect example of the intellectual poet, a poet not so much of the nineteenth century as of the present one, and in the present of the modern age to which both Eliot and [Charles-Pierre] Baudelaire belong:

> What are the roots that clutch, what branches
>    grow
> Out of this stony rubbish? Son of man,
> You cannot say, or guess, for you known only
> A heap of broken images, where the sun beats,
> And the dead tree gives no shelter, the cricket
>    no relief,
> And the dry stone no sound of water.

But in the positiveness of his vision, the affirmation of faith in humanity, Ghalib stands apart from both Eliot and Baudelaire, his vision and insight penetrating the darkness of the mind:

> Your light is the basis of creation;
> The grain of sand is not formed without
> The glow of the sun.

presenting not the nemesis of an over-ripe civilization, but a message of hope:

> Wearied, desire invents and seeks refuge
> In temple and mosque, mere reflections in
> The mirror, hope's images multiplied.

Helpless and weary, humanity has gone on from faith to faith, accepting one, discarding another. And yet each one has proved illusory, a reflection in the glass, not reality. But out of despair hope is born again, and man multiplies illusions, never to become hopeless and lost. The thought recurs in Ghalib time and again:

> Where is, O Lord, the other foot of hope?
> I found this desert of contingent existence
> A mere foot-print.

This can be understood only through Ghalib's theory of association by which the poet must leave suggestions for the guidance of the intelligent reader. For when this contingent world is like a foot-print, where would the other foot be whose traces are found on the sands of existence? Thus the thought expands into:

> We have only known this shadowy world
> Of contingent existence;
> In what other world of certainty
> Can we repose our trust?

Yet, since the illusion exists, there must also be the reality, for one cannot exist without the other. It is this reality which has been the object of man's search and in which mankind must repose its trust.

Ghalib's poetry demonstrates the difference between the esemplastic imagination and one bound up with tradition however admirable, the esemplastic seeing the opposite in the same breath as the object, the cause and the effect, presenting them as an inseparable entity by a third quality of the mind which singles out each colour of a complex picture and then reassembles them into a complex whole:

> The world is full of the effulgence
> Of the oneness of the well-beloved;
> Where would we be if Beauty
> Did not possess self-love?
> The music of the ebb and flow
> Of life and oblivion are both false;
> Absurd the thought of difference
> Between madness and good sense.
> Despair, like Spring, is only an image
> In the looking-glass of contentment;
> Doubt is but a mirror of the birth
> Of the image of certainty.
> Vain is the boast of wisdom, and
> The gain of worship is—well-known
> Mere dregs of the cup of negligence,
> The world or religion.
> Faith and unbelief are both
> A swell of the remorse of drunkenness,
> Truth and doubt are the curvature
> Of a line from a ruler drawn.
> There's neither longing nor spectacle,
> The sense of wonder nor the eye;
> The mirror of the heart is veiled
> In the amalgam of mercury.

This quality, thus, reflects the whole process of separating the colours of a painting and combining them again in the finished production, and make his poetry difficult. Unless the reader's mind becomes a filter capable of separating and combining the colours, he cannot get into the spirit of the poet and know the tones and shades of his thought and feeling. And unless it is split up, the thought cannot be comprehended. Ghalib's imagination was, thus, panchromatic, sensitive to all the spectrums of thought. It could receive the different shades all at once and separate them too.

This brings us to the problem of Ghalib's style and obscurity which has been the subject of discussion since Ghalib's day and which lies behind a hundred bitter accusations hurled at him:

> We have understood the works of Mir,

And those of Sauda understand;
But what he writes that he alone
Or God can comprehend!

Ghalib was a serious poet conscious of his responsibility, and looked upon poetry as a vocation. He had a definite attitude to his art and believed that the function of poetry was to show a mirror to truth. His intensive mind, analytical and reflective, full of an excess of thought and originality, needed a new diction and grammar, a new imagery, to express itself. The language of poetry to him, therefore, was not the language of every day life, nor was his imagery the same familiar one of the poets of the eighteenth century or that of his day, although he could not altogether avoid the use of old symbols for, as he himself said:

However the talk may be of the observation of
   truth,
We cannot avoid the mention of flask and wine.

The question of technique cannot be divorced from thought; and thoughts represent mental states, new concepts demanding a new attitude to symbols and language. Ghalib often introduces subjects which to the people of the eighteenth century would have seemed unpoetical, and did so to many of his day, and presented them as ideas which, being preconceptual, bewildered the readers, the bewilderment increasing with Ghalib's original use of words, not only in a new order, but often in a new meaning to convey the wide range of his thought and emotion, thus becoming a "counter-romantic" like Baudelaire. He used a diction of his own, more Persian and highly conjuncted; and his difficultness became more pronounced when words were displaced, their position changed and the syntax distorted to form a new grammar. Ghalib employs this method of *ta'qeed,* verbal displacement, justifying its use as an embellishment of style on the precept of the Persian masters who used it to make the sense less direct and more oblique:

To split asunder the breast of the wave
Of the sea of sparkling wine, the saki
Used the ray of light from the eye
Of the slim decanter's needle, and joined
It to the lip of the cup.

Although Ghalib avoided sense-displacement and condemned it as a fault we, nevertheless, find something akin to it in his poetry, or at least feel the displacement of sense, for the meaning eludes our grasp. But that is because Ghalib leaves out words and sentences, the steps in an argument, which alone could have bridged the gulf between thought and thought, and thus leaves the reader groping for the connection and the meaning:

Life is a mirror of the hundred hues
Of self-adoration;
And night and day, the great dismay
Of the onlooker of this scene.
Then wherefore, like the candle, raise
In vain the accusing head?
Where is the claim of permanence?
The flaming rose is born
With a heart for grief and patience.
Lamentation is a blood-stained page,
The rose, the subject of twilight;
The beautifier of the soul
Is the despair of loneliness.

The rose's scent is evil awake,
The garden, a wardrobe of dreams,
Union is the dress of disgrace
On the bliss of eagerness.
From the silence of the heart's garden
Now desolate, the word
Of love speaks of the burnt-up breath
As the secret of the garden.

This method is characteristic of Ghalib, and is the real cause of his difficultness. It demands utmost intelligence and alertness on the part of the reader. The obscurity is, however, relieved by subtle links inherent in the concepts which invariably appear in series of contrasts, such as:

Intelligence Unconcerned
Is caught in the great despair
Of encirclement; and man's
Image remains imprisoned
In the mirror of the world.

where four concepts are advanced: 1) Intelligence Unconcerned, 2) despair of encirclement, 3) man's image imprisoned, and 4) the mirror of the world. The contrary of Intelligence Unconcerned is man involved, and that of encirclement the world of mirrors. Followed further, the opposite of the world is God who is caught in the despair of encirclement by the laws of necessity and change, while man remains confined within the world—his own problems. These links are provided by Ghalib in the suggestions which, he believed, should be provided so that the mind of the reader could easily turn to the eschewed words and sentences and he could, thus, ferret out the meaning, as in the lines already quoted above, or as in:

Where is, O Lord, the other foot of hope?
I found the desert of contingent existence
a mere footprint.

or:

How we press the sky to return, and claim
From it, the pleasures lost and gone,
Taking this captured wealth to be
A debt due from the highwayman.

This suggestiveness is different from the associative quality of European poetry like that of Eliot whose basis is purely personal and accidental, which we also meet in Ghalib though rarely as in:

Of whose gay workmanship
Does the painting complain
That every portrait wears a paper dress?

which has a reference to the ancient Persian custom whereby the plaintiff appeared before the judge wearing dress made of paper. It is not the associative quality of simile or metaphor either. It is rather a quality of thought which leads to a connection between 'foot' and 'footprint', between 'pressing for return' and 'debt'. For without foot there could be no foot-print, and the foot-print leads to the speculation that the foot which has left its print must surely be present somewhere. Similarly, in the other quotation, pressing the sky, as one pesters a borrower, to return the lost, or captured, pleasures, suggests that the sky (time, fate) has captured the wealth from us, and yet we claim it as though it were a debt and the highwayman (the sky) was liable for the return of the usurped property. These divergent mental states have their root in the same though remote associative feeling, and the 'suggestion' leads to the catalyst, the agent which had brought the two together and fused them. The solution lies in Ghalib's careful and studied use of words, heavy with meaning in the context, e.g. *taqaza,* pressing for return, and *qarz,* debt, as well as "sky" and "highwayman". This is another way of finding "verbal equivalent for states of mind and feeling" which we come across in the Metaphysical Poets of England who were as mature and difficult as Ghalib was without the requisite of philosophy.

Thus we find in Ghalib a method similar to that of the Metaphysical Poets, the same multiplied associations and telescoping of images, the same forcing and dislocation of language into the meaning. We have the same use of conceit which presents the flux of the poet's thought but arrests that of the reader. Ghalib's poetry was less lyrical than that of Mir and Momin, and more impersonal, implying intellectual energy and a multiplication of thought, thus enlarging the scope of intelligence. That is why it was less popular and considered difficult, therefore absurd. The average reader demanded, like his counterpart today, literature of wider appeal to the basic primary emotions, such as was found in the poetry of the fleshly school of Lucknow which had a direct appeal to erotic sensations:

> I am a lover of breasts
> Like pomegranates:
> Plant then no other trees
> On my grave but these.
>
> —Nasikh

or:

> May those arms, smooth like sandalwood,
> Be thrown around my neck;
> And may it be my fate to have
> The pleasure of caressing those silken thighs.
>
> —Saba

To such readers, and their name was legion, Ghalib was "man-effacing" wine. They could not catch his nuances nor catch up with the flights of his fancy or the import of his thoughts and words. The more so as he developed, like [John] Donne and [Abraham] Cowley, commonplace comparisons into subtleties of conceit:

> With what joy in front
> Of the executioner I walk
> That from my shadow the head
> Is two steps ahead of my feet.

which recalls Donne's comparison of parted lovers to a pair of compasses. Like them he elaborates conceits to the farthest extreme of ingenuity:

> The wing of the moth was the sail
> Of the boat of wine, perchance;
> For with the warmth of the festive company
> The cups began to go round.

Ghalib makes the seemingly easy more difficult by juxtaposing the intellectual with the physical:

> You wait until the poison of grief
> Permeates the veins and arteries;

> At present it's only the bitterness
> Of love and dreams that is on test.

Subjects of astonishment were many, and Ghalib was conscious of the excess of thought:

> With intense expression of subjects of astonish-
> ment
> Each finger-tip has become the point of a worn-
> out pen.

And rush of ideas demanded a new measure, a new gauge of speed. When they start flowing no flood-gate of speech could contain them:

> The playfulness of words does not endure
> The despair of grief;
> To wring the hands with sorrow is
> A promise of the renewal of desire.

Hence words take on ingenuous tones, stretching the meaning to the farthest extent:

> The pledge of words is to open the door
> Of a mind unawakened:
> For me the charm of the alphabet's lock
> Was hidden in the building of the school.

Not only is the thought intense and packed with passion, the economy is explosive. To express such mental states one has, naturally, to have a new dictionary, for they reveal strange experiences, implying the excitement of discovery, and the integration of the external reality of the senses and the inner world of the mind, making thought an emotion and emotion a thought. They express the unity and multiplication of the perceptual world, the accepted universe. Images hurry, experience assumes the garb of words, and vocabulary is inadequate to express the richness and concentrated fire of thought, the unity in its singleness and division. The verb and substantive come together and are tacked with ellipses which multiply. New words and compounds are manufactured to express the peculiar mental states, and to confine the flood of thoughts within a reasonable space of compressed language, employing old words in new combinations to elaborate new concepts, giving them original tones and symbolical meaning based in his own peculiar experiences. In this manipulation Ghalib uses the Persian conjunctive form to produce a string of compounds which are themselves often conjuncted together with bewildering effect. He is coining new phrases all the time, compounded of noun and adjective, or noun and noun, and noun and verb, such as, "inebriety of custom", "silent fire", "the river of wine", "the snare of desire", "sea familiar", and so on, using the same word at different places to denote a different meaning. As he does not pause to explain, and the reader hurries along with the words, he is left behind with thought which he cannot resuscitate from the inhibitive process of his mind.

In Ghalib's well managed sensibility the scattered images, seemingly unrelated, become an entity, though to a reader whose sensibility is untrained, this looks more of a riddle than a statement, as the central idea breaks up into the colours of the spectrum so that the putting back of the different colours into the pencil of light again, if not impossible, becomes a formidable task, and requires a trained mind and considerable agility. Ghalib's central idea, with all its component elements (for no thought is ever single, and is always a compound of many states), becomes an active metabolical process. As there is an under-current of plasma in the body-organism, there is a continuous under-current of feeling in Ghalib's poetic system which forces us to revert to his poetry all the time. This is a sure test of great poetry as Coleridge pointed out, and even in his obscurest moments there is something in Ghalib which compels us to go back to him. It is this which lies behind his undying appeal, so that in spite of any psychological aversion one may have for this kind of poetry, in spite of the impossibilities of his poetic technique and impenetrable obscurity, one cannot ignore him or put him out of mind. Because what he says is universal, and because it had never been said in the way Ghalib says it, he becomes a classicist in expression, and no one, not even the average reader, can forget his lines. Ghalib's poetry pleases for the same reason as it intrigues, and he remains a living poet. For the thoughtful reader the search for the meaning becomes a stimulating mental exercise, and the casual reader derives enough aesthetic satisfaction from the surface. Even when inscrutable, his expression is so architectonic that he remains like the Sphinx, delightful in its mystery.

Love of poetry was inborn to Ghalib; and his thought remained intricate throughout his life, although he did simplify it in later years, not due to any weakening of intellectual energy or perception, but as a result of constant pruning and perfecting, and as a reconciliation with life when the intellectual situation of the age advanced towards a settlement. Even then the purity of his vision remained, as did the resilience of his thought. In the process he acquired the additional quality of a wider appeal. As in youth so in maturity, he expressed his experiences not because he thought they were unique, but because he was compelled by an inner urge to do so. His whole being was suffused with them so that no distinction between the experience and himself remained, and what was within found expression as poetry:

> Like the mirror's light the eye
> Is familiar with the heart;
> Every tear-drop that falls
> Is suffused with observation.

The wonder is that Ghalib wrote poetry of such high order, for the nineteenth century was a spiritless age, almost hostile to poetry, pushing it to the edge of didacticism as in Zauq, or the very abyss of orgasmic pleasure as in the poetry of the fleshly school. That there was a personal conflict in Ghalib's mind is undoubted; and he presented its essence as truth. And truth as the extract of mental struggle cannot appear as simply as the resolution of spiritual struggle in submission. Ghalib expressed submission not as a consequence of spiritual faith, but as an acceptance of forces beyond his control, over which he could have no control, when he realized that the outcome was pre-determined.

This was largely the cause of the misunderstanding about his personal faith and beliefs. A man with the courage of his convictions, Ghalib stood for no compromise and paid no heed to what others thought. His personal experiences, embedded in the frustrations originating from his deprivation of the family pension, conviction of the justice of his cause, belief in his own genius and superiority as a poet which, however, did not find unqualified acceptance in circles he admired, led to bitterness and a search for a charismatic leader who alone, by virtue of divine authority, could set the wrongs right. The search was intensified by an awareness of the apathy of his countrymen towards political and social degeneration, their hypocrisy and failure to arise from the atmosphere of indifference in which the age was steeped, sung now with sarcasm as in the ghazal beginning:

> In so far as we are full
> Of longing for the beloved,
> We are rivals of the desire
> For seeing the face of love.

now with sadness as in the one beginning:

> I am the lip parched with thirst,
> The holy place of men
> With afflicted breasts.

The feeling of helplessness that runs through his work like a thread, led him to an admiration for Ali, the cousin and son-in-law of the prophet, an intellectual like himself, in whose personal situation Ghalib saw a pale reflection of his own. Time and again, in moments of doubt and distress, Ghalib addressed him, seeking spiritual solace and support, in a spirit not of any schism but confession and appeal, as in the **"Qasida in praise of Ali"**. His attitude of philosophical doubt, rooted in the nature of his experience, was mistaken by superficial readers for atheism. It is highly improbable that a life-long friend of fighters for freedom and purity of religious thought and belief like Momin, the rebel poet, and the orthodox Sunnite Molvi Faz le Haq, should have been a schismatic or an atheist.

What is comprehensible is that the world of perception and shadows stood in the way of the perfect realization of the deity. In Ghalib's view the 'house of mirrors' confused sight and deflected the image of the divinity, Beauty lost in the flaw and impurity of the senses, the amalgam of tin or mercury through which alone reflections reached the eye causing confusion between the Reality and Illusion, resulting in nihilism, the *nity-nity* of Vedanta:

> Be not deceived by life, Asad,
> The world is all a mesh
> Of the web of thought.

Positive affirmation requires a different kind of passion, an experience of identification as that of the Persian mystic Hallaj. In the world of physical phenomena to which Ghalib belonged, the mirage of dried-up sense-perception hides the awful mystery unveiling of which could only lead to annihilation, the dissolution of nothing into nothing, idea into idea. Hence, of necessity, the mystery must be preserved:

> I fear the secret of the beloved
> May become known, otherwise there is
> No mystery in dying.

For this alone opens the door to the secret of life and not-life. Had nothing been, only one of four alternatives would have been possible: 1) It would not have mattered, as there would have been no distinction between being and not-being. Creation has resulted in the bifurcation, the duality of creator and the created. 2) The creator would have been there. 3) The created would have had existence in the creator, the reality in the idea, man in God. 4) That man would have been God. All these possibilities have been summed up by Ghalib in the brief but far-reaching question:

> When there was nothing, there was God,
> Had nothing been, God would have been;
> My being has brought about my fall,
> Had I not been, what would have been?

Sorrow comes of knowledge, of having known the joy and exuberance of life. The tragedy of Adam was enacted because he ate of the fruit of knowledge which gave him consciousness of the reality, the distinction between life and not-life, and resulted in the necessity of change and physical death. Yet change is movement and progression, and Ghalib is a poet of movement and change:

> Ambition is busy weaving dreams
> Of happiness;
> Yet there is death
> Without which dull would be life itself.

That is why his symbols are not just erotic. They are charged with social and political intent:

> The breath cannot but reap
> The harvest of the flame
> When with the effort of checking
> The fire we are aflame.

In spite of the apparent despondency and despair that abound in him, Ghalib was filled with the rapture of life. In fact, life to him was ecstasy:

> Life is the ecstasy of the whirl
> Of rapture. Why
> Should one complain
> About the saki's negligence?

The fear that this ecstatic song will end brings more anguish than the thought of total extinction of being:

> I fear the wheel of joy
> May come full circle. I do not grieve
> For loss everlasting.

And he sought comfort in the lost memories of the human mind, of timelessness when night and day did not exist and time itself was lost in time, the final end indistinguishable from the origin of existence in whose womb it was conceived:

> The month and year are rapt
> In thoughts of eternity,
> The bright day of the night
> Beyond the reach of thought.

And he wanted to be free, free of everything, the world, even love and himself:

> The curls of my beloved's hair
> Lie in ambush to encircle me;
> Enable me, O Lord, to keep
> My intent of remaining free.

These are the facets of his mind and imagination that lift his poetry to a pre-conceptual plane and give it universal appeal.

In the final analysis, therefore, Ghalib was closely bound up with a culture and a tradition, even though he leapt beyond their concepts and scope. The same poet who could turn and twist thought round his little finger, play with conceit and hyperbole as with marbles, could also write with disarming simplicity:

> I wish to go away and live
> In a lonely and forsaken place,
> Where not a soul will talk to me,
> Nor I behold a face.
> And I will build myself a house
> With neither roof nor walls nor doors,
> And not a neighbour nor a friend
> To listen to my woes.
> Where if bad luck would have me ill
> There will be none to care for me;
> And when death lays me low no one
> Will ever care for me.

And yet behind the ideal setting the poem rings with deeper meaning and a sense of eternal peace, for the house he wished to build was not a house of brick and mortar or wood and stone. To escape from the awning of the domeless sky which gives neither shelter nor security from ineluctable fate, he would have rather built another world, a new universe:

> I could have built another scene,
> Another landscape on a height,
> If only my home were far away
> Beyond the empyrean.

It is not given to man, alas, to realize his dreams in the face of mortality and death, for

> All elements of Creation tend to decay.

Like the victims of Dante's *Inferno* he must suffer with the

---

**An excerpt from Adrienne Rich's translation of the *Ghazals of Ghalib***

> I suppose my love for you is a form of madness.
> Why shouldn't that madness play like fire about
>     your name?
>
> Don't let a nullity fall between us:
> if nothing else, we could become good haters.
>
> Our time of awareness is a lightning-flash,
> a blinding interval in which to know and suffer.
>
> My method shall be acquiescence and a humble
>     heart:
> you method may be simply to ignore me.
>
> Don't lose heart in this skirmish of love, Asad:
> though you never meet, you can always dream
>     of the meeting.

*Ghalib, in the* Ghazals of Ghalib, *translated by Adrienne Rich, edited by Aijaz Ahmad, Columbia University Press, 1971.*

keenness of mind and memory heightened by a sense of loss and regret:

> I'm moved to tears, O Ghalib,
> To think of the helplessness of love:
> Where will this all-destructive flood
> Go after me when I am dead?

And he was right. There has been no poet in a hundred years to inherit the wealth and richness of mind he bequeathed to humanity! (pp. 4-28)

> *Ahmed Ali, in an introduction to* Ghalib: Two
> Essays *by Ahmed Ali and Alessandro Bausani,*
> *Istituto Italiano per il Medio ed Estremo Ori-*
> *ente, 1969, pp. 1-28.*

## Khwaja Ahmad Faruqi   (essay date 1970)

[*Faruqi, a scholar of Urdu literature, here examines
Ghalib's* Dastanbu *in the historical context of the Indian rebellion of 1857.*]

During the [Indian revolt of 1857], Ghalib wrote his diary of events called **Dastanbuy** or 'nosegay', in pure Persian with an unwitting admixture of Arabic words and in an oblique style of which he was a master and which the delicate occasion also demanded. This diary . . . covers the events of fifteen months to the first of August, 1858. To a general reader this is a diary, or, better still, a chronicle of events, as they happened mainly in Delhi, but, if studied in the chronological context, it is a fresh attempt to reiterate his earlier claims in respect to his pension and position, so fearlessly pursued since 1828 before the highest British authorities in India and in England. This is an attempt by Ghalib to absolve himself of involvement in the revolt of 1857, which ended in government by gallows, the blowing to bits of helpless multitudes, punishment-parades, the banishment of a whole population, and the hanging of many thousands of citizens 'after travesties of trial or none at all'.

In spite of his protestations to the contrary, which can be explained, as he had to protect himself during those stormy days and get his rightful bread, there is no doubt that Ghalib sided with the Mughal emperor, and presented a versified *sikka* (inscription) on the joyous occasion of Bahadur Shah Zafar's assumption of full authority in 1857. This *sikka,* hitherto unknown, was quoted by Munshi Jiwan Lal in his original diary and left out by [C. T.] Metcalfe in his English translation, and is reproduced below:

> *Bar zari aftab o nuqra-i-mah*
> *Sikka zad dar jahan Bahadur Shah.*
>
> On the gold of the sun and on the silver of the
> moon Bahadur Shah has struck his coins.

Not only this, Ghalib attended the Mughal court frequently and presented a *qasida* [panegyric] to the emperor on the 13th of July, 1857, on the triumphant occasion of the fall of Agra to the Indians. He again presented a *qasida* to the emperor on the eleventh of August, 1857 and received a *khil'at* or a robe of honour from him.

The revolt of 1857 was not an isolated event or an accident of history. It was the result of accumulated discontent among the Indian people, who had suffered politically and culturally from the British conquest. As early as 1817, Sir Thomas Munro, after pointing out the advantages of British rule, wrote to the governor-general, Lord [Warren] Hastings, 'but these advantages are dearly bought. They are purchased by the sacrifice of independence, of national character, and of whatever renders a people respectable . . . The consequences, therefore, of the conquest of India by the British arms would be, in place of raising, to debase a whole people. There is perhaps no example of any conquest in which the natives have been so completely excluded from all share of the government of their country as in British India.' In the same Minutes he wrote 'none has treated them (the natives) with so much scorn as we; none has stigmatized the whole people as unworthy of trust, as incapable of honesty, and as fit to be employed only where we cannot do without them. It seems to be not only ungenerous, but impolitic, to debase the character of a people fallen under our dominion.'

And the British dominion was relentlessly extending all the time: the Panjab was occupied in 1849 'by extensive treachery', Avadh was annexed in 1856 'in open infraction of acknowledged treaties', Dalip [Ranjit] Singh was converted to Christianity, exiled to England and the properties of the Lahore Darbar were auctioned. Lord [James Andrew Broun] Dalhousie, conscious of the white man's burden and convinced of the superiority of British rule, annexed eight states, abolished two sovereignties and gave notice to the Mughal emperor at Delhi, still the greatest living influence in India, that his title would lapse at his death.

On the eve of the revolt, the British dominions extended from coast to coast and from the Himalayas to the Indian Ocean. As far as the eye could travel the British banner fluttered in contempt over the Indian lands. An entirely alien rule, alien in language, culture and tradition based upon economic exploitation after the loss of the American colonies, with no sensitivity towards Indian sentiment and no respect for her age-old traditions and culture, was established to the utter distaste and dismay of all classes, soldiers, scholars, theologians, princes and landlords. The learned became illiterate overnight since they did not know English. The scholars, poets, divines, artisans and craftsmen were left without patronage and were reduced to beggary. Nearly all classes of people in north and central India rose in rebellion as discontent and unrest were widely prevalent among the civil population and at several places the people rose before the soldiers actually mutinied. The insurrection also brought forth leaders of outstanding ability, stolid courage and endurance, who did not surrender but continued their arduous guerilla warfare in the hills and jungles. The social forces of the old society were 'vanquished in their final attempt at rehabilitating their power in 1857' and the British secured for themselves the hegemony of the world through their Indian empire, with its enormous resources.

Ghalib's **Dastanbuy** is important as it describes the story of the planned revolt, the ebb and flow of changing fortunes, of alternating hope and gloom as it affected a Delhi citizen—the throbbings of a sensitive soul and the reactions of a poet to an important historical situation—a story hitherto untold. This story has remained untold as it was impossible for Indians to tell it during those days of drumhead courts-martial, indiscriminate shootings and summary hangings. In the words of Vincent Smith [in the *Oxford History of India*], 'The story has been chronicled from one side only, and from one set of documents; or from no documents at all.' Ghalib was writing under tremendous limitations. A slight suspicion would have cost him his life. Therefore, he has suggested the story rather than described it and has enhanced the effect of concealment by employing an oblique and formalized style and using obsolete words of pure Persian. But if one reads, between the lines, there is in *Dastanbuy* an abundance of human kindness and sensitivity, and a faithful expression of his attitudes towards society. He has expressed his sympathies with the afflicted and the tormented—and it is impossible to punish sympathies. This treatise contains sentences of rare and unaffected beauty and passages of moving excellence. Similes and metaphors are woven into the fabric of his ideas and make his thoughts compact and concise and his words apt and impressive.

As Ghalib's *Dastanbuy* is a product of an overgrown formalism, it is a question whether *Dastanbuy* unlocks his heart. It does. A compromise there was, but hardly a spiritual surrender.

Ghalib's *Dastanbuy* is frequently adorned with the noblest sentiments, though it must be confessed that at times the author displays a sort of Machiavellian realism and a regard for expediency, dictated by that unique situation and not uncommon in those days. Ghalib was vitally concerned with the wrong done to him in the matter of his family pension on which depended all his living, all his pride and honour.

Therefore, in *Dastanbuy,* intended for the highest officials, honour and tradition are mixed with realism and operate with double impetus.

True to his Central Asian descent and Turkish seed, Ghalib was always vacillating between tearful piety and excessive pride, between mysticism and materialism, between convention and liberalism, between despondency and hope. With his conception of courtesy, he could not dispense with his extreme formalism of Turko-Persian origin, already cooled into set responses and prescribed attitudes. This formalism was motivated by a semi-conscious urge for preservation of artistic solidarity with his ancestral world with which he had lost direct touch. Moreover, in those feudal days all emotions required a rigid form, for without such form passion would have made havoc of life. The contradictions and paradoxes had to be wrapped up in veils of fancy in order to exalt and refine them and thereby to obscure the cruel reality.

Delhi fell to the British after one of the bravest battles in her history. On its capture, the whole population of Delhi was driven out by the British and a general massacre of the inhabitants was openly proclaimed. The Muslims were long denied any employment around Delhi. 'A Mahomedan was another word for a rebel' There were serious pro-

posals to level the whole city to the ground, to demolish the Jami Masjid, to convert the Fatehpuri mosque into military barracks and the Zinatul Masajid into a bakery. The royal palace was to be used as quarters for the British garrison and the Hall of Public Audience as a hospital. The exquisite buildings south of the Diwan-i-Khas were to be utilized for troops and sanction was given for the tearing down of all buildings within a radius of 448 yards from the Fort walls. The palace proper and the whole of the haram courts 'were swept off the face of the earth . . . without preserving any record of the most splendid palace in the world.'

In the words of Ghalib, 'Five armies, one after the other, invaded the city: first was the army of rebels which robbed the citizens of their reputation; second was the army of *khakis* (British) who plundered life, property, honour, home, sky, earth and every remnant of life; third was the army of famine at the hands of which thousands perished; even those who were fed were struck down by the fourth army of cholera; the fifth was the army of fever which sapped the endurance and strength of the people.

In Delhi, a reign of terror prevailed: Trembling old men were cut down, harmless citizens were shot, clasping their hands for mercy or blown to bits by guns. Tens of thousands of men and women and children were hounded out of Delhi to wander homeless over the country in mournful processions. Ghalib, however, stayed in the city and waded through this ocean of blood. He was reduced to poverty—without money, without clothing, without pension, without a record of his poems. His insane brother was shot dead by the British soldiers, a fact which he has concealed in his diary. Muinuddin Hasan has a different story to tell: 'Mirza Eusuf Khan, brother of Mirza Asadulla Khan, who had long been out of his mind, attracted by the noise of the firing, wandered out into the street to see what was going on; he was killed.' The treasures and belongings of Ghalib were ransacked and looted. He was questioned, suspected of high treason and of being in league with the rebels and accused of composing a versified *sikka* for the Mughal emperor. His pension was stopped, which was not only a question of right and reputation, but of bread.

India was prostrate before the might of the foreigner, alien in religion, language and culture. And Delhi was a mere small appendage of the Panjab. In this situation Ghalib was less than a piece of straw, without either pension or patronage. He made every effort to regain these, thereby indirectly disproving the charges made against him during the revolt of 1857. In making these efforts, Ghalib naturally used only those methods he was familiar with. Along with *Dastanbuy,* his diary, he wrote a *qasida,* or panegyric, for the queen of England; and *qasida,* in the orient, was an age-old ceremonial instrument employed by the poets with all the dignity of a ritual and attended by loud and pompous formalities to gain riches from the powerful and the wealthy, 'and their adulations, more often than not, were blatantly hypocritical.'

In *Dastanbuy* Ghalib has used a conventionalized style of archaic and elegant diction which has the virtue of dignity and reputability and commands attention and respect as being the accredited method of communication under his scheme of life. In Mughal India, as in Renaissance Italy, France and England, the artist was lavishly patronized by kings and nobles, and the poet, in turn, praised these patrons in language of ceremony and extreme formality. Hyperbole and honorific address were considered indispensable for this kind of communication. It was quite customary to compare these dignitaries in superlative terms to gods, philosophers, conquerors and wise men. It was not necessary that divinity or courage or wisdom should actually be an attribute of their objects of veneration and praise. This, did not mean, however, that the artist or poet was in any way insincere. He was merely following the literary custom of the day. What appears to be insincere flattery to an unceremonious age such as ours was to Renaissance society or Mughal India a gracious way of life. Ghalib was no exception. He followed the practices of his age. He could not do otherwise. Sometimes he was more concerned with the office than with the person and sometimes he changed the title of a *qasida* and endorsed it in the name of another patron.

Ghalib, as a true-bred nobleman of his times, saw the world from the point of view of personal relationships, and sought to systematize behaviour on this basis. Nationalism as it is understood today was then unknown even in Europe. But there is no doubt that Ghalib sympathised with the tormented, irrespective of their race or religion. His diary is animated by compassion. It shows how the old world society to which Ghalib belonged, broke down under the impact of new forces. The letters of Ghalib, read with his **Dastanbuy,** are the best lament on old Delhi and the passing away of an age. (pp. 16-18)

> *Khwaja Ahmad Faruqi, in an introduction to* Dastanbūy: A Diary of the Indian Revolt of 1857 *by Mirza Asadullah Khan Ghalib, translated by Khwaja Ahmad Faruqi, Asia Publishing House, 1970, pp. 1-22.*

## Ali Sardar Jafri  (essay date 1970)

[*Jafri is an Urdu poet. In the following excerpt, he traces Ghalib's development as a thinker and artist and explains his significance for contemporary Indian culture.*]

Ghalib was endowed with a rare intellect, transcendental vision and an outstanding and ingenious artistry. His genial nature and inherent courtesy overshadowed the egocentric traits of his character. Ghalib began writing poetry at a very early age. Before he was twenty-five he had already composed some of his finest *ghazals* (lyrics) and *qasidas* (odes). By the age of thirty-two he had become the literary rage from Delhi to Calcutta. Details of his education have not yet come to light, but we do know that Ghalib had full command of the branches of knowledge studied during his time. He had a deep knowledge of Persian language and literature. His study of life was vast. He writes: "By the time I had reached the age of seventy, apart from the jostling crowds of commoners, a cavalcade of seventy thousand men of consequence had passed before my weary eyes. Therefore, I can call myself a fairly shrewd judge of human beings." His personal friends included kings and tavern-keepers, Muslim scholars and English officials, noblemen as well as ordinary people. He often commented wistfully on the gaieties and frivolities of his younger days when he heartily enjoyed drinking bouts, visited courtesans and gambled. But while still in his mid-twenties, he was suddenly disenchanted with this kind of life, and turned to mysticism.

Of an astonishingly catholic bent of mind, Ghalib did not differentiate between Hindus, Muslims, Christians and Jews. He never said his prayers, did not fast during the month of Ramzan, and continued his love for drinking to the end of his days. He called himself a sinner and had an implicit faith in God, in the Prophet and in the religion of Islam. His appetite for the good things of life was enormous. He hungered after knowledge and also yearned for social position and worldly status. He loved good food, good wine, good music and pretty faces. Whenever he was in possession of some of these things he fancied himself to be happier than kings.

Some events in Ghalib's troubled life stand out as important landmarks and had a deep influence on his mind and art. His orphaned childhood; his stay in Delhi; and a fairly long visit made to Calcutta. The erratic and capricious vagaries of his youth were reflected in his early obtuse poetry. Ghalib had lost his father at the age of five. He had been denied a proper upbringing and was required to launch out in life entirely under his own steam. In an unsheltered life of this kind recklessness and a sense of adventure take the upper hand. Life's trials and tribulations thus become the only guide and preceptor. [Mir Taqi] Mir, on seeing Ghalib's early work remarked: "A good mentor would turn this lad into a fine poet, otherwise he may end up writing nonsense." Apart from Mulla Abdul Samad, the Iranian, whose existence is not yet fully proved, Ghalib learned only in the school of life. Though his early, extremely ambiguous and involved poetry was ridiculed in Agra, the young Ghalib with characteristic swagger brushed aside all adverse criticism. After his marriage he left Agra and settled in Delhi. In the Mughal capital he met renowned scholars and master poets and could not ignore their opinions. Before he was twenty-five he found himself concentrating on sound balanced verse.

His journey to Calcutta in 1827 came as another turning point in his life. He went there to sort out the affairs of the pension given to him by the government of the East India Company for the military services rendered by his father and uncle. There was also a property matter to be settled. In Calcutta Ghalib not only saw glimpses of the modern age, he also bitterly realized the failure of his own life. Ghalib had imbibed the last flowering of Mughal culture. He was now greatly affected by the industrial civilization introduced by the conquering British. But the greatest single factor to influence his life was perpetual destitution. This kept him in anguish to the very last day of his life.

The worldly glories of Ghalib's ancestors (who proudly traced their descent from the ancient kings of Iran) had departed long ago. The academic traditions of Avicenna had also vanished in preceding centuries. Therefore, Ghalib turned his pen into his personal heraldic banner. "The broken spears of the ancestors were transferred into a fiery quill." His pen illumined the wasteland of his life. His courageous spirit led him by still waters and green pastures. This magnificent sweep of his creativeness enriched Urdu literature for all time.

The important question now arises whether Ghalib possessed a world-view and a philosophy of life. He is certainly not the founder of a new school of thought, and it would be futile to look for an integrated or disciplined point of view or a message in his poetry. But the philosophical content and the high seriousness of his work cannot be overlooked. Despite the poetic contradictions created by *ghazal*'s conventional theme and imagery, a philosophical preoccupation with man and his universe remains dominant in his verse.

Ghalib was deeply influenced by medieval mystic traditions which, apart from his own studies, he had inherited from Persian and Urdu poetry. He once said: "Mysticism does not behove a poet." And yet he sought the help of sufi thought to understand life and to avoid the hypocricies of formal religion. Mysticism also disciplined his unfettered and unconventional nature.

Ghalib believed in pantheism. In a Persian *masnavi* (narrative poem), he calls the cosmos "the mirror of knowing whose reflections of the Eternal Beauty fascinate the inner eye of the beholder. Wherever man turns his face he finds Him, and whichever side man turns is His own side."

In one of his prose writings in Persian he says: "The existence of an atom is naught beyond its I-ness. All emanates from Truth. The river flows everywhere, its waves and whirlpools rise on the surface. Everything is God."

Since existence is Unity and the Absolute is everlasting, the universe cannot be transient. Ghalib has not explicitly expressed this view anywhere, but in his Persian work *Mehri-Nimroze* (Midday Sun) he expresses the belief that the world has no exterior existence. Divine Being is the only Reality, the attributes are also Reality; the idea of independent existence of attributes is merely an illusion and a dream. "Though one may say it is, it is not." And so the question of permanence and transience, of renewal and decay does not arise. God's attributes or manifestations in the form of matter are identical with His Reality and Absolute Being, just as the rays of the sun are not exterior to the sun itself. A new Adam shall be born on the Day of Reckoning; Adam shall follow Adam and the world shall continue for evermore. (Hindu cyclic concept of time.)

This gives rise to a second query. If the world is a reflection of the Absolute, what, then is the origin of evil? Whence come sorrow, pain and affliction? How can the contradictions be explained? The traditional reply to the query is that the reflection collects dross and is polluted as it moves away from the Source. But the weakness of this logic is self-evident, for the distance of the reflection becomes a thing separate from the Absolute, and thus negates the view that all is God.

Ghalib raised this question but could not arrive at a satisfactory conclusion. This is reasonable. A poet should not be expected to solve an enigma which has baffled great mystics and philosophers of all ages. However, in the opening hymn of his Persian *masnavi* he could say: "the contradictions arise at a certain point of Ultimate Perfection." But this attractive turn of phrase is merely an elucidation of the doctrine of pantheism, and does not answer the fundamental question. A more poetic and reasonable answer is found in the first Persian ode in which Ghalib addresses God in these words:

> Expressing thyself as non-self has caused chaotic discord.
> Thou uttereth the Word and is lost in its illusion.

This distinction between God and His world, the duality between the Creator and the Creation, between Self and non-Self is such that the beholder and the Object appear to be two separate entities despite being one and the same. "They are separated by the curtain of customary worship although Unity cannot contain duality." Later, the poet reveals certain esoteric secrets and says: "Pain and sorrow emerge from the Source, so that the pleasure of experiencing happiness may increase. . . . Trials and tribulations are a test which distinguish friend from foe. Life welcomes its tired guests on a carpet of thorns. They enjoy the comforts when they have overcome their weariness." The distinction between Self and non-Self results in a paradox which makes life what it is. This is the essence of non-duality. On this point Evil becomes a part of Good and the difference between Perfect and Imperfect comes to an end. Spirit and matter, life and death are equated, and the belief of formal religion appears like a mirage. The act of rejecting the barriers of race and religion turns into an integral part of true faith that unites all humanity. The difference between joy and sorrow becomes meaningless, and spring and autumn are attuned to each other.

In one of his verses Ghalib employs the colourful imagery of the tavern . . . A prismatic wine-glass is forever in circulation, the seasons of decay and renewal being its different colours. Night and day are chasing one another . . . a whirling movement of Divine ecstacy, a swiftly revolving point in its frenzied flight turns itself into a dancing flame. Beyond the concepts of pleasure and pain, life is the exuberant, dynamic manifestation of the non-duality of all existence . . . "The drowning man was slapped by the wave. The thirsty quelled his thirst at the river's bank. The river neither wished to drown one, nor did it wish to slake the thirst of the other." The river is absorbed in itself. Action and reaction are its waves which turn time present into time future and also time future into time present.

This pantheistic vision of Ghalib embraces the Vedanta as well as neo-Platonism. His philosophy of the Absolute includes renunciation and negation of Attributes. At the same time he adorns the Person of the Qualified Absolute with gorgeous similes. In Ghalib's poetry we find a fascinating harmony of Persian and Tartar paganism and Hedonistic sensuousness. It depends on one's strength and capacity either to renounce worldly life on reaching a certain stage in one's spiritual evolution, or to pick up this colourful, musical toy called the world of senses.

Ghalib has certainly assumed an optimistic attitude through this belief and this optimism becomes the lifeblood of his poetry. Sorrow is the basis of all joy. To avoid sorrow is to deny life. Playing with sorrow gives true meaning to existence. Death itself enhances the joy of living and bestows the courage to enjoy action. Man needs his various baptisms of fire which life amply provides. In his Persian *qasida* he says: "If the fire is strong I fan it more. I fight with death. I hurl myself on unsheathed swords. I play with daggers and shower kisses on arrows."

This defiance and courage makes Ghalib's melancholy a thing of enchantment. This glorious ecstasy of pain is not to be found in any other poet of Urdu. Iqbal is closer to Ghalib in this respect but the philosophical aspect of his poetry overshadows his zest for life.

It is impossible to separate the concord of joy and sorrow in Ghalib's poems. Therefore, it would be wrong to call him the poet of melancholy or the singer of joy. Ghalib sings of the joyous splendour of agony.

After this brief survey of his philosophy of life, it is not difficult to understand the place of man in Ghalib's universe. Man too, like other creatures, is a reflection of the Absolute. But he differs from other beings because of his capacity of hope, longing and ambition. Man's conscience is a tempest of agitation and turmoil, "just as the water in life's ocean has its quality of wetness and silk within the cocoon contains its silkiness." Moreover, man possesses reason and intellect. "His hands and mind combine together to create his character." His spirit and intelligence give him the power of expression. His mind, though limited, is yet a part of the Infinite Supreme Intelligence. In his **Mughanni Nama (The Singer and the Song)** Ghalib calls human wisdom "the decorator of the world, the dawn-light of the mystics and the lamp that illumined the marble halls of the ancient Greeks." The wondrous spectacle and the gaiety of the world is primarily due to man and his endeavours. Man is the very pivot of a universe which was solely created for him. . . . 'Round the point of my being revolves the compass of seven spheres.'

This troublesome, energetic, zealous creature, made of humble clay, nevertheless, attempts to understand what it is all about. He wants to remain an inquisitive spectator at all times and in all conditions. In order to reach the heart of mysteries he sometimes goes through fiery ordeals. If he cannot comprehend the content, he contemplates the form and ultimately reaches the beatific vision. As long as one possesses the wealth of imagination, fancy and desire, one arrives at the goal. . . . "Whatever the coffer of life contains, is mine."

The traditional theme of renunciation has no place in Ghalib's poetry. As a gloriously happy pagan and an Epicurean aesthete, Ghalib wishes to imbibe beauty with such intensity that his eyes are a barrier between himself and the object of his desire. Mere sight does not suffice and his heart longs for fulfilment. Sight disturbs oneness by keeping the illusion of duality alive. He drinks straight from the wine-pitcher. When he starts sinning "the river of ingenuity dries up in no time." He wants to change the very laws of pre-determination and free-will through the circulation of the wine-cup. He thinks *absurd* zest is as important as rebellious fortitude, to achieve one's ambitions. And this carries him to the stage of a refined and delightful

sensuality. Perhaps his libertine and rakish youth had taught him that a reckless life may lead to ruin but it also sharpened one's mind and bestowed maturity.

The measures Ghalib creates for assessing his sensuality are in terms of his uncommitted sins and unfulfilled desires. With his tears he fathoms his defeats and failures. The entire wilderness cannot measure his fatigue. For, "when desert after desert overflows with his weariness," his "footsteps begin floating like bubbles on the sandy waves of his frenzied trail." The known world cannot satisfy his urge, "The Sahara of possibilities" is merely "a step in his eternal search." His poetry is a heady quest for the next step, a quest which is constant restiveness, pain, heart-burn and movement like a river overflowing its banks.

*Relish* is his favourite word, along with *desire* and yearning. Madness, which is the last stage of longing, always spurs him on to greater madness. This dizziness which is the outcome of zest, "keeps a man aloft even when he is in the depth of abject misery." It gives "a speck of sand the immensity of a desert and turns a drop into a stormy river." He remains unsatiated throughout his magnificent pursuit. For him journeying has greater pleasure than arrival. "When I visualize Paradise and consider that if my sins are forgiven I'll be granted a Pearly Palace together with a Houri, I find the thought depressing. To live with one single hour till all eternity is an alarming thought indeed. Wouldn't that poor paragon of virtues get on my nerves? Imagine having only one emerald castle, under a solitary bough of Paradise. . . ." (in a letter).

Ghalib's early life had taught him to taste a little sugar but never to settle on honey like a bee . . . else the power of flight would be sapped. And so he became the poet of the uphill trek, not of destination, of non-fulfillment rather than consummation. The urge of the unattainable introduces one to the pleasures of lonely highways. This has enriched his poetry with a sense of movement, a concept expressed through a profusion of such images as the waves, storm, flame, mercury, lightning and flight. Movement has become a part of Ghalib's aesthetics. His beloved in his poetry is also swift and mercurial like flame and lightning. These highly dynamic word-pictures are the perfection of imagist poetry. The printed word dances under the spell of his novel metaphors and similes. Characters become fluid; abstract thought turns into a figure of life and colour. Arid waste-lands steam up under the frenzy of his wanderings. The wilderness begins to run ahead of the wayfarer. Unsculptured idols begin to dance within the heart of the stone. Mirrors dissolve into eyes. The lines of the palm become throbbing veins in the hand of the cup-bearing saqi. Cypresses follow the beloved like her shadow. Attracted by the perfect height of the fair one, the boughs languidly yawn, rise and carry the flowers to her headdress. Time ambles on the road of restlessness. Years are not measured by the orbit of the sun, but by the flash of lightning. The true visionary sees the road ahead not as a mere track but as the throbbing vein of life.

Ghalib's poetic fancy is entirely an expression of his inner restiveness. He leaves much unsaid. This makes a poem difficult but more beautiful and profound.

Ghalib has turned his gay melancholy and hopeful agony into an imagery of dancing movement as a result of his own temperament and the healthier traditions of mystical poetry.

While analysing his emotional and psychological make-up, the background of the poet's social environment cannot be ignored. When Ghalib says that it is sinful to breathe outside "the company of dreams" he does not reveal a longing for mundane riches and a few kisses. It is his desire for "the garden yet uncreated," whose ecstatic vision has compelled him to sing. To think that this is his subjective dream is to belittle his greatness as a visionary. The 'still uncreated garden' is an indication of his social awareness, for, this 19th century Urdu poet did possess a reasonably sound concept of social evolution and progress.

It is difficult to propound the real meaning of a *ghazal* because the motif is usually hidden behind an intricately wrought facade of stereo-typed imagery. Still a poet who called the world 'the mirror of knowing' could not be oblivious of his environment and remain content with the subjective romanticism of his 'bleeding heart.'

In his letters after 1857, he wrote painful elegies of the destruction of Delhi, often quoting his own verse and suddenly revealing the social content of his poetry.

Long before 1857 he had realized that the flickering candles of Mughal culture and society were about to blow out for ever. Although he greatly loved the values of his own ancient civilization, yet he knew that its superstructure was fast decaying. The foundations had shaken and the roots had become rotten, ready to crumble before a gust of wind. His own life resembled the falling ruins of his culture. His personal melancholy was attuned to this collective melancholy pervading Delhi and Agra, and had saddened and disillusioned him in his young manhood. At the same time, as has been pointed out earlier, he had seen a glimpse of the new order based on scientific and industrial progress. He could not grasp the significance and the extent of the new economic exploitation of the country by a Western colonial power (if he did, we do not find its proof in any of his works). Nevertheless, he was greatly impressed by the science and industry introduced by the British. Many years before the Mutiny of 1857, Sir Syed Ahmad Khan annotated Abul Fazl's *Ain-i-Akbari* and asked Mirza Ghalib to write a commentary on the historic work, the poet waived his old-world courtesy and frankly told the young scholar:

"Look at the Sahibs of England. . . . They have gone far ahead of our oriental forebears. Wind and wave they have rendered useless. They are sailing their ships under fire and steam. They are creating music without the help of the *mizrab* (plucker). With their magic words fly through the air like birds. Air has been set on fire. . . . Cities are being lighted without oil-lamps. This new law makes all other laws obsolete. Why must you pick up straws out of old, time-swept barns while a treasure-trove of pearls lies at your feet?"

The conclusion drawn by Ghalib is significant: the worth of *Ain-i-Akbari* can certainly not be doubted. But God is ever bountiful. Since goodness knows no end, good things become better and the betterment of the world continues from epoch to epoch. Therefore worshipping the dead in this way cannot be called a sound habit of mind. (Persian *masnavi* 10.)

Ghalib with his social consciousness preferred modern industrial order to the laws and decrees of Akbar's period and was in favour of giving scientific inventions and concepts an honoured place in poetry. (**Letters.**) It was difficult for him to understand the economic relationships of the new social setup. He did not know the inherent destructiveness of the new socio-economic structure. Still one of his couplets is astonishing in this context:

> Beauty and innocence are ravished by what else brings
> virgin rose-buds from the garden to the market place.

Ghazal is the epitome of subjective, lyrical poetry. Therefore it is hard to draw a line of demarcation between personal emotions and expressions of social discontent and protest. Still, it is easy to ascertain that Ghalib was not most dejected about his own times. This despair, born out of his personal misfortunes and historical events, becomes strangely moving in his verses. (pp. 4-14)

It pained him that his qualities of broadmindedness, self-sacrifice and generosity were not appreciated. "It is not possible for the whole world to be well-fed and prosperous. But at least in the town where I lived, I wished that no one went hungry nor wore rags. Condemned by God and man, old, weak, ill, poverty stricken, I, who cannot bear to see others begging from door to door, must myself beg . . . that is I . . ." (in a letter).

This, then, is Ghalib's picture of man, for whom he weeps and can do nothing.

In another work he says: "God merely kindled the flame of faith. Man embellishes cities and lights up civilizations. He cried out to God complaining of injustices. But his grief for human suffering turned into sharp satire when he took up his own weapon. He raised his anguish from the level of emotion to the plane of intellect.

Ghalib laughed in the face of extreme hardships. His countless jokes and humourous anecdotes and most of all his letters tell us how bravely and cheerfully he faced hunger, disgrace and finally, death. A satirist becomes bitter when he has suffered intensely. His personal pride makes his slings poisonous, although superficially his light-hearted vein may appear to be mere joviality. Ghalib used his pungent wit as an armour against a very cruel world. His subtle irony and banter was mingled with his tears. His sharp satire also enabled him to laughingly receive his wounds. This ability to laugh contained the secret of his pride and individuality which an unkind world had turned into ego and conceit.

Ghalib's ego was a shield without which the world could not be confronted. He did not bow before his fellow beings, and did not give in to romantic gloom, self-pity or world-weariness. He was not enamoured of Majnun or Farhad the legendary tragic lovers, nor was he impressed by Alexander the Conquerer or Khizr the prophet who guided lost travellers. He was not interested in unfaithful beloveds. Even in his obedience to God, Ghalib remained as free and as self-contemplating as he was while adoring God's fickle creatures. He retained the same personal dignity in his *odes* (qaseedas) though they are the weakest aspect of his creative life and art. Compelled by circumstances, he begged favours of the mighty. At the same time he remained miserably conscious of this degrading servility. ("I hate myself more than those who hate me.") In his preface to his Persian poems he regrets that half his life has been wasted praising fools. For this reason the purely adulatory parts of the odes are the weakest while the poetic prologues are always powerful. Ghalib was keenly aware of his own superiority to the subject of his ode and often slyly found a way to put in a few, oblique words in his own indirect praise.

Ghalib's last refuge was his own imagination and inspiration, for, "the poor depend for their life on their imagination." (*Letters.*) In the world of fancy a pauper can rule the world and make up for the wants of his actual life. No temporal king, only the maker of dreams can reign in these fantasy-realms where "potentates appear in the form of jaguars," and "poets become prophets." Gabriel sings here as the camel-driver of the Muse's caravan. In this world of dreams cruelty is replaced by kindness, regrets give way to the joys of success. The drinker moulds his own exquisite wine-cup and creates his own special saqi. The river itself comes to the thirsty. Adversity engenders the determination to live. Bitter pills of sorrow create their own glow on the sufferer's face. Imagination goes flower-picking in virgin arbours and pours forth rhapsodies of spring. This fantasy-land, again, has vibrance, rhythm and airiness. 'So that I have naught to do with Echoes.'

This spiritual fortitude gives a new dimension to the idea of love, a dimension hitherto unknown in Urdu poetry. In the face of utterly un-Platonic, devastating, down-to-earth physical attraction, despite his desperate surrender, Ghalib remains haughty and dignified as ever. He believes that a repressed sigh would turn into a painful heart-burn. Therefore "patience and restrain should be replaced by passionate anger." "If the beloved does not yield to one's pleas, she should be faced belligerently." *Ghazal's* symbolism implies that not only the beloved, but any ideal, even the desire for a better life, should be taken up like a challenge. Perhaps for this reason Ghalib calls himself 'a rebel, irreverent to the polite rules of ghazal-writing.'

This non-conformist poet appeared on the literary scene as a novel and unique personality, whose fiery assertion of self was tinged with a strange rebellion which expressed itself through scepticism, satire and romantic fancy. Ghalib's contemporaries could not understand this new mood which made the poet laugh through his tears and which gave a new grandeur and meaning to the human condition. None before Ghalib had poked fun at God and satirized the sacrosanct beloved with such haughty impatience. No other poet had turned "the sword of injustice into a sweeping wave" of his own "inner torment." No one before him had added such deep philosophical import to the sentiments of ghazal. Ghalib removed the difference

between the language of *ghazal* and *qasida* and paved the way for modern Urdu poetry (nazm).

Ghalib's popularity in the late 19th and early 20th century was mainly due to the fact that apart from other qualities, his poetic mood and temper was that of a modern man. This new emotion is also in harmony with the mood and character of a new, emergent India which is proud of its past splendours, is sorrowful of its present and is seeking greater glories of Tomorrow.

Ghalib did not write political poetry, but he represented the spirit of the modern age. And so, when India's freedom fighters, visionaries and new poets came to the fore, they derived their inspiration and strength from him.

It is not accidental that [Khwaja Altaf Hussain] Hali, who protested against the conventional and stylized Urdu poetry, was a disciple of Ghalib. Sir Syed [Ahmed Khan], the educationist, had heard Ghalib praise the new technological civilization long before 1857 which is the great watershed of Indian history. Similarly, Maulana Shibli's patriotic poems have echoes from Ghalib. Iqbal's philosophy and art bear an imprint of the great master. The Urdu poets of succeeding generations including the modern and the very modern, have all been influenced by Ghalib in varying degrees, and tones. Countless lines from 'Uncle Ghalib,' as he is affectionately called, have become proverbs in Northern India. Hardly an Urdu-speaking household is without its copy of the immortal ***Diwan.*** After Independence Ghalib has become a bestseller in Hindi.

Today Ghalib's poetry has come down to us as an interpreter of the past as well as a pointer to the present. It possesses the pleasing hangover of a bygone era and the exhilirating intoxication of present times. It conveys to us the agony of the night that has fled and the joyful light of the sun that is newly risen.

Ghalib's greatness lies in the fact that he not only encompassed the inner turmoil of his age, he also created new urges, inner agitations and demands. Breaking through the bonds of time, his poetry reaches out into the past and the future. To use the language of Eastern metaphor, Ghalib tested his personal experiences, born out of an exceedingly refined aesthetic sense, on the touchstone of human psychology and translated them into pure poetry. This gave him a universal voice, making him a poet who celebrated each individual moment of human life. He knew the varied states of the human soul. Extreme happiness or despair, conditions of religious doubt or miracle-making faith, profound metaphysics or utter trivialities, sensations of love-making and the pleasure of loving and being loved . . . Ghalib's poetry accompanies the reader through all stages of human experience. Lesser poets can adopt one of his attitudes as their personal philosophy, but Ghalib captivates us with his over-powering, comprehensive, larger-than-life genius.

To enjoy his poems it is not enough to know superficial meanings. When read again and again, the words emerge as kaleidoscopic pictures. They become familiar like human faces and gradually reveal their personalities. The inner rhythm of their meanings emerges after the ears have got used to their outer music. Then from the meaning of words you reach their poetic significance. You enter a world where *fidelity* is perfumed like the beloved's hair; where candle-lit cypresses dance, where love is a state of the human soul, an exquisite, passion filled action, a majestic deed and an aesthetic taste. In this special domain of Ghalib the loved one's beauty merges into the loveliness of the world at large, and the grandeur of the scimitar and the allure of charmers is dramatic and electric. As you continue to read the pang of separation would turn into rapturous, gladsome longing, and union with the beloved would be like the bliss of unfulfilled desire. Zest for life would appear as the all-powerful urge of creation. Madness would turn into a quest that is obstructed by prison chains and the high walls of the temple and the Kaaba. The reader would then see that these walls are decorated by utter werines of the seeker.

Then, Ghalib's tavern would emerge before the readers' eyes as the destination of perfect humanism and complete freedom. And it is then that the pages of the **Diwan** would light up with Ghalib's thrilling creatures of imagination. His beloved would smile through the words and the world would become more beautiful and man would command greater respect. (pp. 14-19)

> *Sardar Jafri, "Ghalib," in* Ghalib and His Poetry *by Sardar Jafri, translated into English by Qurratulain Hyder, Popular Prakashan, 1970, pp. 1-19.*

---

**Husain on Ghalib's *ghazals*:**

Ghalib is a master of the ghazal, which though apparently lacking in unity of theme has its own organic form, pulsating with creative imagination which imparts an underlying unity. Ordinarily each verse of the ghazal is complete in itself although at times it may be connected with other couplets through continuity of thought and feeling. Ghalib has also written odes (qasidas) and quatrains (rubaiyat) but he has excelled in his ghazals. In this form he has no equal. In this medium his poetic sensibility has found its full expression.

*Yusuf Husain, in his* Urdu Ghazals of Ghalib, *translated and edited by Yusuf Husain, Ghalib Institute, 1977.*

---

## Aijaz Ahmad    (essay date 1971)

[*In this excerpt, the Urdu writer and critic Ahmad addresses the difficulties of translating Ghalib's poetry.*]

The seven decades of Ghalib's life (1797-1869) were not a very auspicious time for the writing of poetry for anyone who lived in the city of Delhi. The British conquest of India was completed during those decades, the fabric of the entire civilization came loose, and the city of Delhi became a major focal point for countless traumatic crises. Ghalib was not, in the modern sense, a political poet—not political, in other words, in the sense of a commitment to strategies of resistance. Yet, surrounded by constant carnage, Ghalib wrote a poetry primarily of losses and conse-

quent grief; a poetry also of what was, what could have been possible, but was no longer. In sensibility, it is a poetry somewhat like Wallace Stevens': meditative, full of reverberations, couched in a language at once sparkling and fastidious, and testifying to a sensibility whose primary virtue was endurance in a world that was growing for him, as for many others of his time and civilization, increasingly unbearable. The journey from nothingness to a totally human affirmation which is the essential growth of a poet of that tradition—beyond time, beyond the merely spatial relations—was achieved in his case with a necessary and austere urgency related, finally, to the experience of having been possessed. He is a tragic poet. (p. vii)

In order to place Ghalib in his true context, one should perhaps first speak briefly of his language and tradition. In the initial stages of its growth, Urdu represents an amalgam of the medieval languages of Northern India— Bhasha, Khari Boli, and others—and languages of the Middle East, mainly Persian, which the Muslims brought with them. Thus, it is written in the Persianized form of the Arabic script, is syntactically based on a combination of Persian and Prakrit grammatical structures, and draws its highly flexible and assimilative vocabulary from a variety of Indo-European languages. The Persian element, however, has been dominant, to the extent that the entire body of traditional Urdu poetics—prosody, poetic forms, concepts relating to poetic diction and subject—have been almost wholly Persian. We can safely say that, from its beginnings in the fifteenth century until the latter half of the nineteenth, it was part of the larger Persian-Indic tradition. It is only in the closing decades of the nineteenth century that Urdu begins to assimilate Western forms and concepts through the growing influence of English throughout the subcontinent.

Like Persian, Urdu is also very much a language of abstractions. In this sense, it is very difficult to translate from Urdu into English. The movement in Urdu poetry is always *away* from concreteness. Meaning is not expressed or stated; it is signified. Urdu has only the shoddiest tradition of dramatic or descriptive poetry. The main tradition is one of highly condensed, reflective verse, with abundance and variety of lyrical effects, verbal complexity, and metaphorical abstraction. And this preference for abstractions is not, as should be obvious, merely a characteristic of language, but is also a way of thinking—of reflecting on man's place in the universe and his relations with the world, with others, with God, with his own interiority. Thus, although always a poetry of love, Urdu poetry, in its classical phase, never contemplates the experience of love in terms of a specific love relation. Specification and personality are kept rigorously out of the poetic substance.

The metaphysics of Urdu poetry, and of Ghalib in particular, can be approached in terms of three questions: What is the nature of the universe and man's place in it? What is God? What is love? For the Urdu poet, as for the Persian, these questions are interdependent. There is no question of clarifying man's place in the universe without first contemplating the nature of God, or of love. Similarly, there can be no poetry of love unless love is understood, first, as a human reflection of a divine possibility and, second, as a definition of man's place in his moral universe. Ghalib does not offer a celebration of love, or longing, or ecstasy, as mystic poets do. Except in some places, his is not normally a poetry of mystic disciplines; rather, it is a poetry of contemplation, making subtle, and if possible, precise distinctions between one experience and another, and various shades of each. Thus love is defined not once or twice but over and over again, so that a whole collection of couplets may signify the complexity involved.

As we have already said, the main body of Urdu poetics has been borrowed from the Persian. At the center of these poetics is the form of the ghazal, the basic poetic form in Urdu from the beginnings of the language to the middle of this century. The ghazal is a poem made up of couplets, each couplet wholly independent of any other in meaning and complete in itself as a unit of thought, emotion, and communication. No two couplets have to be related to each other in any way whatever except formally (one may be about love, the next about the coming of a season; one about politics, the next about spring), and yet they can be parts of a single poem. The *only* link is in terms of prosodic structure and rhymes. All the lines in a ghazal have to be of equal metrical length. The first is a rhymed couplet, and the second line of each succeeding couplet must rhyme with the opening couplet. The unit of rhyme repeated at the end of each couplet may be as short as a single syllable or as long as a phrase of half a line. The convention is that a ghazal should have at least five couplets. Otherwise it is considered a fragment. There is no maximum length.

It should be obvious that this form, based on two lines of equal length as a self-sufficient unit of poetry, is the product of the abstract nature of the language itself, and in turn reinforces the same character. Only when a unit of poetry is meant to communicate a single thought or emotion, and only when the poet sets out to deal with just the essence rather than the many particulars of an experience, can one have so small a unit and dispense with the idea of continuity. Within these expectations, the ghazal functions with an easily identifiable and almost repetitious pattern of imagery—the rose, the tulip, the nightingale, the seasons, a handful of descriptions of this or that, human or extra-human states—as does Japanese poetry, in which a certain flower, a certain time of day, even the plunge of a stone, can signify something other than itself.

Good poetic translations, like good poetry itself, are very much a matter of luck: talent, skill, and labor have all to be blessed with the divine spark. The problem is, of course, one of revealing the *whole* of the original mind by transferring to another language not only what it is saying, but also how it is saying whatever it says. Success can only be relative; the translator is in an impossible situation and translations of poetry can be not only rarely but also relatively good.

The problem of translating poetry from an Asian language is that the best translators of an age are its poets, but there is hardly a major poet in America today who knows even one of the languages of Asia well enough to translate from it without substantial, even decisive assistance from a native speaker of the language. This problem is further complicated by the contradictions within the environment in which translations from Asian languages are usually undertaken. I believe that the present is—next perhaps only to the Elizabethan—a great age of translation in the English language, particularly by the American poets. Yet something has clearly gone wrong: there are too many *academic* translations. A labor which needs to be, and rarely is, a labor of love is being undertaken on a vast scale and being accomplished with deadening efficiency. (pp. xv-xviii)

The Urdu poet, and his Persian counterpart even more, has suffered not only from neglect but also from the wrong kind of attention. By the time the British settled down in their colonies and areas of influence securely enough to start dabbling with the native literary traditions, the nineteenth century was well on its way. This tradition of translation has suffered fatally from the fact that the first conspicuous translations were done by people who came in contact with Urdu and Persian because of their involvement with matters and consequence of the Empire; by people who were not poets themselves, nor, with the exception of [Edward] Fitzgerald, even men of imagination. They knew very little about poetry and worked with a poetic ideal derived from a post-Romantic, Tennysonized jargon in which, as [Ezra] Pound once noted, the same adjectives were used for women and sunsets. For these gentlemen of the Empire, poetry was essentially a substitute for daydreams and candy: twilit, sumptuous, escapist, and, finally, trivial. It was the pedants' attempt to turn out something sweet. Soon enough, even worse happened. With the British take-over of the educational system, Indians were themselves alienated from their own language and were brought up on huge chunks of Tennyson, [Charles Algernon] Swinburne, [Thomas Babington] Macaulay, [Walter] Pater, and others. By the beginning of this century there were numerous Indians who considered Ghalib both the greatest poet of Urdu that ever lived and a sort of native Tennyson. The complex, the apocalyptic, and the moral were carefully sifted out in favor of a post-Romantic grief that fed upon itself, a synthetic nostalgia that had nothing whatever to do with the concrete stresses of public and private history that Ghalib suffered. If he wasn't already a Victorian Romanticist, he had to be made into one; if the tradition of Urdu poetry wasn't already minor or trivial, the design of the Empire demanded that triviality be imposed upon it. For decades major Urdu poets were being read according to standards set by minor English ones.

Out of all this bungling, there has emerged an image of the Persian and Urdu poets which is hard to undo: that of an amoral, epicurean poet eternally sitting under a tree with his woman, his loaf of bread, and his jug of wine. It is characteristic that Omar Khayyam, rather than [Abu ol-Qasem Mansur] Firdausi or [Jalal al-Din] Rumi or [Mohammad Shams al-Din] Hafiz, should be the best-known Persian poet in the West; it is characteristic that Khayyam's own reputation should be based on a translation which is Victorian and in fact very much an English poem of the Victorian temper; and, finally, it is characteristic that Robert Graves, the only major English poet who has so far addressed himself to Persian poetry, should return to the well-known *Rubaiyat* and not to much greater Persian poets, like Hafiz and Rumi, whose work lies buried under uninspired and unreadable translations. I give these illustrations from Persian because Persian poetry has been more widely—if not better—translated into English, and because Classical Persian and Classical Urdu are related to each other in the same way as Old English and modern English are related; and Hafiz is to Ghalib roughly what [Geoffrey] Chaucer is to [William] Shakespeare. Good translations should now aim at a revaluation which will finally show that, far from being epicurean or, as has often been said, a "poetry of roses and nightingales," the tradition of poetry that reaches its first greatness with Hafiz and Rumi in Persia and ends its Classical phase with Ghalib in Delhi is, at its best and in its own altogether different terms, as complex and moral as, for instance, the tradition of poetry from Chaucer to [John] Berryman in English. (pp. xix-xxi)

Ghalib lived at a time in the history of the subcontinent . . . [when] a whole civilization seemed to be breaking up and nothing of equal strength was taking its place. Worse still, what replaced the older civilization ran altogether counter to what Ghalib stood for. For a Muslim poet-intellectual who lived within the older order, life was difficult but intrinsically intelligible, being supported by a tradition within which he could confront and contain experience: there was a religion which he might or might not have observed in external detail and ritual but which certainly gave him a sense of contact with his God and the universe God had created; there were shared experiences, and shared concepts of love, anxiety, friendship, and all the other emotions that define man's place in society; there was, in short, much suffering in that society but also a sense of relation and, finally, a sense that the poet lived in essential harmony with, not opposition to, his society. By the beginning of the nineteenth century, however, this sense of order was already going and the civilization was in serious doubt about its own validity: the British trader had assured that the old order was simply not worth preserving. It was at this moment of almost cosmic self-doubt in the subcontinental consciousness that Ghalib grew up and started writing. The seventy or so years of his life are the years when these self-doubts about civilization grew into final despair. There is in Ghalib a moral grandeur, as in Hafiz, but also an intense moral loneliness, a longing for relations which were no longer possible, and a sense of utter waste. To illustrate, I quote here the following four couplets, from four different ghazals, translated . . . by Adrienne Rich:

> I am neither the loosening of song nor the close-
>     drawn tent of music;
> I'm the sound, simply, of my own breaking.

and:

> Our time of awareness is a lightning-flash
> a blinding interval in which to know and suffer.

and:

> The dew has polished the sheen of the flowering
>     branch.
> The nights of spring are finished, nightingale.

and, finally:

> I'm too old for an inner wildness, Ghalib,
>     when the violence of the world is all around me.

In addition to this despair, there is, of course, a sense of tradition as well, a great longing for it and for a human contact possible only for a man who decides to live at all costs within human community. Take, for instance, the following couplets from a ghazal translated by William Stafford:

> Held behind lips, lament burdens the heart; the
>     drop
> held to itself fails the river and is sucked into
>     dust.
>
> If you live aloof in the world's whole story,
> the plot of your life drones on, a mere romance.
>
> Either one enters the drift, part and whole as
>     one,
> or life is a mere game: Be, or be lost.

All these themes, and many more, come together with an interplay of wonderfully concise images in a freer translation by W. S. Merwin of a ghazal that I quote in part:

> The heart is burnt out
> but its sufferings were nothing to yours
>     oh my cry
>
>     charred dove
>     nightingale still burning
>
> Worse than any fire fed by what was
> was the fire of longing for what was not
>     nothing was left of the spirit
>     but the heart's suffering
>
> Love holds him
> prisoner he says
> and something has him sealed
>     like a great rock on his hand
>
> Sun who turn everything into day
> shine here too
>
>     a strange time
>     has come upon us like a shadow

This is a poetry of intense moral privacies; and of love—not *about* love, but *of* love. Love is the great, over-arching metaphor because love is conceived as the basic human relation and all life is lived in terms of this relation—even when those terms are terms of failure. And, finally, it is a poetry of reflections, in every sense of that term. Like a mirror within a mirror, each couplet is related to every other, and each reflects a situation that has been lived and reflected upon.

The Western poet most similar to Ghalib is perhaps Wallace Stevens. All the poems taken together create a single, intense impression of a life lived in fact and in mutual relations of facts, in the mind as much as in the imagination; and everything that enters the life also enters, in one way or another, into the poetry of that life. The chronology of the poems—what poem was written when, under what impulse—is far less important than the inner relations. For a poet like Ghalib—and for all the great Urdu poets, really—time does not happen in sequences, but in a sort of circular motion: immediate grief becomes a part of total grief, the poem written at sixteen enters into the poem written at sixty, all poems become parts of a single poem which, in turn, signifies the morality of a single mind.

As I have said, it is a poetry of moral privacies: moral and private. Everything that happens to the poet, either personally or to the times in which he lives, is deeply related to his poetry, but the immediate event is kept scrupulously out of that poetry. The response is immediate and moral, but the urgency is assimilated within privacy, and the response, as it is expressed in poetry, is not so much to the event as to the consequences of that event, to the way it has altered the poet, the experience of the poet. Ghalib undercuts the whole debate which proceeds from an assumption that the particular and the universal are, in some way, in opposition. For Ghalib, the particular *is* the universal: a man's history is the history of his intelligence, *plus* his emotions, *plus* his times. The image of man Ghalib posits is very much a matter of what man makes of his emotions. Again, this too is like the work of Wallace Stevens, where the Romantic and the rational are in a hard, terrifying, victorious embrace.

Like Stevens, Ghalib trusts the intelligence of his readers and makes demands on it. And he demands patience. He expects that you will read all his couplets together, that you will let these couplets sink into your consciousness, and will let them reveal themselves to you gradually, over the years. He expects that you will read these couplets as impressions of a man who sought wholeness at a time when wholeness was difficult—as it always is, but more so. Also, a man who needed love, knew it, knew its failures, yet sought for it always—in himself, and in his loveless times. Ghalib was a man who wrote poetry because poetry was necessary; the times were inauspicious and poetry alone had the power to save whatever could be saved in a portrait of man that was fast disappearing. Ghalib's poetry is a work of restoration on that portrait. (pp. xxi-xxv)

> *Aijaz Ahmad, in an introduction to* Ghazals of Ghalib: Versions from the Urdu *by Aijaz Ahmand and others, edited by Aijaz Ahmad, Columbia University Press, 1971, pp. vii-xxx.*

## Yusuf Husain   (essay date 1977)

[*Husain is an acknowledged authority on Ghalib. Below, he explores Ghalib's philosophical tenets and poetic devices, praising his originality and "marriage of dynamic thought with aesthetic sensibility."*]

In religious matters Ghalib was a free thinker, tolerant to believers of every religion. All his life he remained above sectarian considerations. He rejected dogma on the basis of his own intellectual and aesthetic experience. He had friends and disciples among both Hindus and Muslims. It is true that the great religions of the world differ in fundamental respect, but they are not so far from one another as they appear. Ghalib was inclined to believe in the unity of religions. He believed that real existence belonged to God alone and that He alone has actual independent being. Although sometimes he has asserted the illusory nature of all existence and showed a penchant towards the doctrine of the "unity of being" (wahdat al wujud) it is

more by way of following a convention of ghazal writers than anything else. He was not the man to undergo any mystical discipline. He believed in enjoying the good things of life and was averse to self renunciation. It seems that Tasawwuf or mysticism was used by him to embellish his art as a matter of poetic tradition and symbolism. Most probably he was a believer in Shaikh 'Ali Hazin's dictum that 'tasawwuf was good for writing poetry.' It seems he was conscious of the inadequacy of the doctrine of "unity of being". In one ghazal he challenges the validity of the view that external phenomena are imaginary. To him the external world is real and has contingent existence which is the manifestation of ultimate Reality and cannot be ignored. He wonders at it and also enjoys it to the point of satiation.

> When nothing exists in the world without Thee,
> Then O God what is all this tumult for?
> Who are these fairy faces? And what are all
> These amorous winkings, these blandishments
>     and coquetry?
>
> Why these ambergris-perfumed, curling tresses?
> What is this antimony-anointed glance?
> From whence comes this verdure and all these
>     flowers?
> What is the cloud, and what the air?

Ghalib was an individualist par excellence. The nineteenth century was a century of liberal individualism all the world over. One of the well-marked characteristics of liberalism was its individualistic approach to life. In Ghalib individualism was allied with romanticism, aiming at vigorous and passionate feelings. This is why even when talking of the doctrine of "unity of being", it was not possible for him to surrender his intellectual individualism and become absorbed in the world of the spirit. The ideal of the Sufi was the tranquillity of annihilation, while Ghalib cherished passionate excitement all his life. To him tranquillity was so dead, so rigid, so hostile to all vigorous life that only inactive and unambitious people could endure it. (pp. 7-8)

Ghalib was the last representative of the intellectual and aesthetic achievements of Mughal culture in India. The quality and tone of literature is always related to the culture of which the author is a part, and the aesthetic situation is largely a recreation of the pattern of emotions experienced in life. Ghalib's poetry, sophisticated and sometimes obscure and oblique, expresses the cumulative experience of a very sensitive soul who was avid for knowledge in all its forms, in order to enrich the highly-strung imaginativeness of his personality.

Ghalib's early poetry shows the strong influence of [Mirza Abdul Qadir] Bedil, a poet who specialised in intellectual speculation, curiously intermingled with nostalgic love for the infinite, his assertion of self and a hopeless sense of futility. Ghalib in his youth was much attracted by the sophisticated style of this poet, and his often quaint images which reverberated in the memory through their indefinable emotional effect. Ghalib followed in his footsteps in that instead of the limpid diction employed by such masters of the ghazal as Mir Taqi Mir and Khwaja Mir Dard, he freely used a vocabulary loaded with obscure, wild and extravagant symbols and imagery. Despite his claims to the contrary, Bedil's influence persisted in Ghalib's poetry till the end, both in his Persian and in his Urdu verse. Curiously enough, Bedil's influence is more marked in his Urdu than in his Persian poetry, which is more indebted to Naziri and 'Urfi, great masters of Persian ghazal in the early Mughal period.

In his early poetry, Ghalib's use of symbolism and imagery tends to be more intellectual than emotional. He had to wait for maturity to give full expression to the wisdom gathered from his own experience. The artist, capable of gaining knowledge and experience from all the sources that life offers, finds himself in a different world in every decade of his life, or rather, he sees the same world with different eyes. Therefore the material of his art, and the manner of its presentation is continually renewed. A great poet must have other interests in life besides poetry, in order to nourish his creative imagination. The poetry of the ivory tower is without vitality. A poet is a poet because he has the capacity to turn his dominant interests, including his thought processes, into poetry.

The creative output of Ghalib warrants full and elaborate examination by our generation. His use of symbol and imagery give to his poetry a modern air. Even his ambiguities and obliquity are modern in the sense that they give us insight into something we know and recognise as contemporary reality. It seems as if he were addressing this present generation when he ruefully exclaimed:—

> My songs are prompted by delight
> In the heat of my ideas;
> I am the nightingale
> Of the flower-garden of the future.

He clearly implies that his words are the means through which his feelings are made conscious, even if they were not properly understood and appreciated by his contemporaries. The value of his words is in their contribution to the understanding and ordering of his own emotional conflicts.

Poetic experience is expressed in a form which is subject to the stress of words, and the words are ordered in a design which is part of the texture of the poet's thought and feeling. Contemplation of Ghalib's style then becomes contemplation of what is expressed by him—the integration of ideas and expression in a subtle manner. The reader becomes vividly aware of the inner experience evoked by his words. His poetry is not discursive; it does not describe, but reveals: it is obscure in the same way that one's feelings are obscure. His creative imagination clothes the emotion with life. Sensation and emotion fuse, and ideas become concentrated. Ghalib's poetry is primarily perceptive, not logical thought. His seemingly intellectual and analytical argument is in reality a subtle form of imaginative reasoning, transmuting thought into feeling.

In Ghalib feeling precedes understanding. For him, life is an emotional experience, which is only subsequently explained by reason. His heightened awareness leads him to use the condensed suggestiveness of metaphor, and with power and vividness to stretch the meaning of his words. But his metaphors do not indicate an arbitrary flight of imagination—they are always in touch with the actual world.

> O Asad, my shadow
> Runs from me like smoke;
> Who can stay near
> To such a fiery soul as I?

Sometimes Ghalib's meaning is implicit, and condensed to such an extent that words needed to complete the construction or sense are purposely omitted. The reader has to fill in the gap, as it were, from his own imagination. In a letter addressed to his favourite disciple, Har Gopal Tafta, he says that ellipsis is one of the characteristics of his poetry. For this he uses the word "Muqaddar", meaning that which is implied. [Charles] Baudelaire asserted that in all the arts there is a lacuna which is completed by the imagination of the audience. This lacuna is not a deficiency on the part of the artist, but a merit, and it is filled when the objectified feeling is received into the soul of the reader or listener. In Ghalib, the implicit is bound by definite links with his inner experience, without which it would lose its raison d'etre. Even trite images become instruments of inner awareness; the poet reendows them with their original significance:—

> Ask not about the waves of the mirage
> In the desert of loyalty:
> There each particle of sand
> Had the sharp quality of a sword.

Here the words derive their force and value not from what they say so much as from the weight of experience which lies behind them.

Poetic creation needs the height of awareness on the part of the poet, but this is not to be equated with analytical intelligence. As [Paul] Claudel stressed, "It can only watch us create". And again, "By the image the poet is like a man who ascended to higher ground and who sees all around him a vaster horizon, where relations are seen to establish themselves, relations which are not determined by logic or by the law of causality".

The poet's imaginative appreciation of beauty, and sensitive reaction to it, produce the vision of "glorious manifestation". The beautiful object, in spite of being external to the beholder, is always soaked in subjectivity. It is in the very nature of beauty to manifest itself in order to attract the attention of the lover.

> Nonchalant beauty is a buyer
> Of the waves of glorious appearance;
> The mirror on her lap shows her anxiety
> To create fresh methods of manifestation.

There seems to be a subtle equation between beauty, which is the subjective experience of value, and love, which gives rise to its enjoyment. Without this equation, aesthetic experience degenerates into sensation. In the contemplation of beauty, consciousness liberates itself from the conditioning of material life, and affirms the freedom of the human spirit. In the aesthetic experience the poet cultivates the capacity to see with the eye of the imagination, and to identify himself with the representation of the object both in its particular and universal aspect. The artist endeavours to penetrate the depth of the object of beauty as well as the depth of his own consciousness, in order to awaken the spiritual sense which is the greatest of poetic attributes.

> Before the reflection of her moon-faced beauty,
> The mirror's essence flutters for flight;
> Like particles of dust that fly up
> Through the window towards the sun.

Ghalib lays stress on the mystery of the heart, which is the receiver of the vision of beauty. While intellect may easily slip into concern with what is merely useful and factual, the heart corresponds to the inner state of the soul, and of which the poet tells the story in his richly concentrated style incarnating the charm of sound and sense. This charm is impossible to define exactly, since it is of infinite variety, covering the complete play of the poetic imagination. It embraces the source of beauty as well as the emotive power of the artist.

In Ghalib's poetry beauty and love are considered together, since the concept of beauty embraces the power to stir the heart, the centre of all emotion. It is in the heart that the feeling for beauty is generated. The permanent fixation of the lover on the beloved can only be produced through an inflow of the lover's personality into that of the beloved. A great love always presupposes a vigorous ego which the lover exteriorises in the person of the beloved by the transforming action of creative imagination. In Ghalib the identification of the lover and the beloved is so complete that he does not even want to have further longing for her:—

> We cannot even tolerate
> Envy of ourselves;
> We may die, but we do not want
> To have further longing for her.

Ghalib has identified the contemplation of beauty with the thought of good action. Unlike [John] Keats, who had identified beauty with truth, Ghalib treats beauty and goodness as identical.

> The thought of beauty merits virtue
> As much as pious action;
> For this, upon my grave
> The window of paradise is thrown wide open.

In fact the whole sphere of art lies in the ambiguous word 'good' whose meaning extends upwards towards the highest idea of perfection. Art aligns itself with ethics, because the aesthetic sensibility very much resembles the ethical susceptibility. Ethics aim at social harmony, while the poet chisels the words to perfect shape in order to harmonize them with his inner emotional reality. Both have profound human significance because they aim at harmony, the basic principle both in life and art. The indivisibility of the problems of humanity includes within itself all spheres of life. The aesthetic and the ethical are really one in the imagination of the artist.

In Ghalib, human and erotic love sometimes evokes the longing for transcendental beauty, as is expressed in the following verses imbued with spiritual and mystical imagery.

> Who can tell

> Whose is this glorious revelation?
> He has let down a veil
> Such as none can lift

> The universe is kept in motion
> By its inherent yearning for Thy grace;
> In the light of the sun
> Every particle throbs with life.

In some of his verses, Ghalib appears to take a pessimistic view of life, but on the whole his philosophy is optimistic. He is not unaware of the tragic elements in human life, but he successfully transmutes awareness of this into creative energy, making his poetry all the richer for it. His reaction to the tragic, which he calls "grief" (ghamm) is that it is inherent in life, from which there is no escape, except through creative activity.

> The affliction of eternal despair
> Must be endured;
> Happy am I that my lament breathes not
> The shame of striving for effect.

It is not pessimism, compelled by a basic mood of emptiness and dread. On the contrary, Ghalib's reaction to the tragic is wholly affirmative. His creative energy rises triumphantly above the challenges of life that seek to submerge it. It is very significant that in him even the tragic elements of life evoke a positive and dynamic reaction.

> The free feel sorrow
> No more than a moment;
> In our house of lamentation
> We light the candle from the lightning.

> O heart, even the notes of sadness
> Should be considered blessed;
> The instrument of existence
> Will be still and soundless, one day.

It would be correct to say that the tragic is a great driving force in Ghalib's poetry, imparting to it dynamic energy. Being a supreme individualist he had full confidence in whatever life had to offer. For him there could be no waiting for a world to come but a preferring of this world here and now, even to the hope of paradise. Although he is conscious of the transitoriness of human existence, yet his faith in the power of life remains unshaken. In creative action the consciousness liberates itself from the conditioning of physical laws and affirms the freedom of the human spirit. Ghalib mingles the sweet and bitter in life, recording his varying moods, now of joy and exaltation, and now of utter gloom and despair. Then he attempts to combine his contradictory feelings into a single psychologically organic whole. He even strives to blend the symbols of heaven and hell into a new entity.

> O God, why should we not
> Join paradise to hell?
> Very well, this way then let there be
> More space for sight-seeing

> (*Urdu-i-M'ualla*)

Ghalib's deepest and most original interpretations of reality come by way of imagination which is a mighty power in the world of poetry. His power of expression depends on the genuineness of his poetic experience. In fact, poetic creation is also a way of action. The creative act from its very nature is an overflow of energy which cannot be contained by the essentially utilitarian ends of life. This emotional energy cannot be communicated by mere information. This can only be done by the artist when he confronts a situation identical to those in real life which excite his emotion, but of course more idealised and far more sensitively organised. In the case of the erotic sentiment, woman is the basic stimulus and the spring season and the flower-garden act as the enhancing incentives. Ghalib has used the symbols of spring-flower even for the scars of his heart.

> I do not display my heart to you
> Because of its spring-flower scars;
> What use is this illumination
> When the master of the show is burnt?

In every work of art there is an implicit dynamism which compels the artist to seek the most appropriate method of self-expression. In the words of Paul Claudel, "the work of art is the result of the collaboration of imagination with desire. It is necessary that our sensibility should confront the object in a state of desire, that our activity should be provoked by a thousand scattered touches, and kept mobilised, so to speak, to respond to impression with expression."

The aesthetic significance of the myriad forms of creation is determined by the dynamism of desire. In fact man's freedom consists in making himself actively the principle of his desire for self-realization. In Ghalib there is no ascetic distrust of desire nor is there any distrust of the joy of life. It is rather strange that although born into a static and decadent social milieu, his approach to art and life should have been dynamic, a characteristic not shared by any of his contemporaries. It is this vitality that makes his poetry great. He is never afraid of his feelings, nor afraid of revealing them. His responses are robust and at the same time, delicate. Everything in his verses throbs with life. Even beauty is portrayed as dynamic, and not coldly devoid of movement.

> I cannot disgrace myself by my own efforts,
> But if the friend is also a lover of tumult,
> Thus shall I get my share of infamy.

Ghalib's concept of beauty is inclusive of its transformation into the active self. He is very conscious of the high status of the human self in the scheme of the universe. It is into the self that external nature passes in transformation. In the following lines he recalls the primeval state of man, referring to the refusal of Satan to prostrate himself before Adam, as described in Semitic mythology and in the *Qur'an*.

> Why have we become so contemptible
> Today, when till yesterday
> Our honour did not tolerate
> The impudence of the Angel.

Every road in the universe leads back to man, whose inner being is sufficient unto itself, having limitless freedom of choice and action.

> Man himself is a tumultuous
> Riot of ideas; even when alone
> We consider ourselves

> In very fine company.

Life is desire and strife. Its attendant tension cannot be avoided, nor does Ghalib show any wish that it should be eliminated. On the contrary, he cherishes it and gives it poetic form. The radiating light of being shines on the world of becoming and change.

The audacity of Ghalib's thought, and the stream of his powerful ideas seem to flow as naturally as water gushes from a spring. The tumult of his ideas is reflected in his choice of imagery. He imparts his own dynamism to conventional symbols and transforms the often-used mythology of Laila and Majnun, Farhad and Shirin, Khizr, and Jacob and Joseph. He is fond of such images as wild madness, whirlwind, storm, flood, waves, birds in flight, captives struggling to free themselves, dancing atoms of dust, and lightning. The metaphor of lightning is one that he frequently employs; it seems to appeal to him for its speed, its flash of diffused brightness, and its striking power of destruction:

> My heart is in search
> Of a minstrel with fiery breath,
> The splendour of whose notes
> Would be the glory of the annihilating lightning.

Ghalib made even such normally static things as doors and walls to tumble and dance for joy in welcoming the destructive force of the flood. Another image much used by the poet is that of waves. He uses the idea of the ebb and flow, the constant movement of the wave as a symbol of the pulsating of the life-force. He speaks of waves of wine, waves of existence, waves of the breeze, waves of twilight, waves of rose, wave of graceful walk, wave of breath, waves of pearl, waves of blood, wave of spring etc.

> It is said that the blood of mankind
> Lies on the neck of the wine flask;
> But the wave of wine trembles
> When it sees thy intoxicated gait.

A work of art understood dynamically, is the process of arranging images and symbols and finding affinities in disparate objects. In Ghalib's poetry the juxtaposition of unlikely words evokes in the perception of the reader the most complete image and imparts glimpses of wider horizons imaginatively conceived.

The metaphors of travelling and continuously searching occur time and again. For Ghalib, man's whole life is a restless journey, wherein he is impelled from one stage to the next, bearing all the hardships and privations of travel in this never ending search. He personifies this idea, with all its different shades of meaning in the symbol of the blister:

> O blister, be generous—
> Endure the pain of one step more;
> O light of the eye of the wilderness,
> O souvenir of the desert waste.

The greatness of Ghalib lies in his marriage of dynamic thought with aesthetic sensibility. In this regard he is unique in the history of Urdu poetry. Ghalib's message of humanism is universal in that it advocates the freedom of the human spirit. For him love or "yearning desire" is the main stay of personality, the only spiritual force capable of transfiguring human relationship. He is not content with social and religious formulas to achieve perfectibility of Man with all his inherent possibilities. The motivating fact in his ethics has as its emotional basis, human love and sympathy. Salvation to all humanity can come only through love. This ideal is worth striving for. If it cannot be achieved in the present, one should wait for the future:—

> O Lord, who has breathed,
> Into the ear of love
> The magic of expectation,
> Which is called desire.

Then again he says—

> From love itself
> Nature has found life's savour
> Found the cure for pain,
> Found the pain without a remedy.

Ghalib's thinking and feeling are mainly for himself, but because of the integrity with which they are expressed they become universal in appeal. He explores his own inner experience, yet his appeal does not lie solely in a literary or historical context, but in the undying concern of man with his destiny.

> Nothing is left except desire
> To soar higher in the search for beauty;
> The Resurrection will be a swift wind,
> Blowing away the dust of martyrs.

(pp. 13-24)

*Yusuf Husain, in an introduction to* Urdu Ghazals of Ghalib, *translated by Yusuf Husain, Ghalib Institute, 1977, pp. 1-24.*

## Annemarie Schimmel   (essay date 1987)

[*Schimmel is a German scholar of Islamic civilization. Here, she comments on Ghalib's importance for Urdu culture and on the difficulties of translating his works.*]

Mirzā Asadullāh Ghālib is, no doubt, the greatest Muslim Indian poet of the 19th century. His verses, written either in Persian or in Urdu, appeal to almost every taste. What is more important is that his verses related to each and every state of life—happiness and despair, jolly drinking and solemn praise, surprise and nostalgia, longing for death and eternal restlessness. They have become, to a large extent, proverbial, and are often quoted without a moment's hesitation. How often friends in Pakistan would bid us farewell with Ghalib's line:

> Go a thousand times, and come
> A hundred thousand times.

How often a fiery orator would be admonished for telling his thoughts too openly, with the advice of Ghālib:

> The secret which is in your heart is not fitting for
> a sermon.
> You can say it on the gallows, but not on the pulpit.

Thus, the story of Mansūr al-Hallāj, the Muslim martyr-mystic, is often told. Mansūr al-Hallāj was put to death in 922 because he had "unveiled" the secret of loving union between man and God. Nowadays when progressive writers of India and Pakistan speak of their willingness to endure *dār u rasan,* "gallows and rope," for the realization of their ideals, again the Ghālibian expression is recited referring to Hallāj's fate at the hands of the legalists or "the establishment." How often modern novels and collections of poems have derived their titles from lines of Ghālib's *Dīvān.* And so numerous are the attempts to interpret his poetry in the light of different modern currents, or to re-create his thoughts in "modern" language!

However, Ghālib defies "re-creation" in a foreign milieu. There are few poets in the history of Persian and Urdu literature whose verses and prose are as deeply filled with the whole heritage of Muslim culture as his. Behind his lines lie the wisdom, the charm, and the imagery of nearly a thousand years of Persian poetry and 800 years of Muslim rule in the northwest of the Subcontinent. It is, therefore, impossible to know Ghālib without a thorough knowledge of Persian poetical imagery, the strict rules of meter and rhyme, the numberless rhetorical devices and, of course, the religious background of a mystically tinged Islam as it has lived in the hearts of millions of people since the Middle Ages.

Ghālib's poetry can be traced back, in many cases, to the classical period of Persian poetry. The mode of expressing one's thoughts and feelings in this inherited style was common to all educated Muslims of India during the last few centuries. Ghālib studied the Persian language intensely and consequently knew Persian literature better than most of his contemporaries. He was likewise deeply steeped in the Urdu tradition which had developed in Delhi and, slightly later, in Lucknow since the early 18th century. He knew the mystical traditions of the different fraternities located in and around Delhi as well as the typical literary expression of the Shī'a persuasion of Islam. By adding to the strength and beauty of the classical Persian style the complicated, broken, and often amazingly modern images of the later Mughal poetical style, Ghālib created a very complicated web of associations and forms which has to be sorted out by the patient reader.

But if Ghālib had been only a perfect poet who applied classical models to his Urdu and Persian style, he would not have gained that much fame and would not have captured the hearts of a large part of the Urdu speaking population of India and Pakistan. His verses, despite their immense technical difficulties, lend themselves very easily to quotation since he had the gift of inserting expressions from the spoken language into the metrical scheme. In this respect he is surprisingly modern. His Urdu poetry becomes often conversational playing with the everyday language of the people around the Great Mosque in Delhi. This peculiarity also makes a perfect translation into any other idiom impossible.

The conversationalism in Ghālib's poetical creations is similar to the style of his letters which are put before the Western reader in this publication. But here, too, we are confronted with the same problem as in his poetry: even the lightest and apparently superficial talk is interspersed with the vocabulary of classical Indo-Muslim culture; even more, his most casual remarks reflect this heritage in all its different shades and moods. The perfect ease with which he enjoys the possibility to use an Arabic, sometimes a Persian, and sometimes a proper Urdu word for one and the same object reflects the integration of his personality within a highly composite culture.

As a true son of his culture he is adept at playing back and forth between honorific and familiar forms of addressing his friends of different social ranks. An English translation will naturally have to grope for some devices of capturing the drama of the author's play of interchanging pronouns.

Ghālib has joked about himself in an Urdu verse that he is "not completely crazy but not completely normal either," and has often alluded to his difficult character. For example, when he put his horoscope in poetical form he stressed the fact that it was "a combination of contrasting elements." This polarity in his character is well reflected in his Urdu writings, both in poetry and in prose. At one time his writings show absolute hopelessness and then suddenly flash up in a joke sometimes revealing a black humor. The style is high-flown and majestic, and one moment later again it is easy-going and casual. If ever a poet has lived up to [Gotthold Ephraim] Lessing's advice: "Write as if you were speaking," it is Ghālib.

It must be said that one should not be deceived by the ease and casualness that these letters seem to reveal at first sight. The reader may be reminded of the famous story of the Chinese painter who was ordered to paint a rooster, and for years nothing was heard from him. Eventually the emperor entered his study and asked for the picture. The artist took his brush, and in a few strokes he painted the most perfect rooster possible. Only then did he show the amazed emperor the thousands of sketches that were required to paint the drawing with such ease. Similar is this case to that of Ghālib and it is not in vain that he has often alluded in his poetry to the difficulty of achieving some-

thing that looks easy. The hardest work is necessary to achieve a truly artistic result. Did he not say:

> It is very difficult for anything to become easy. Even man has not yet attained the state of humanity.

The reader should think of this problem while reading Ghālib's letters. (pp. x-xiii)

*Annemarie Schimmel, in a foreword to* Urdu Letters of Mirzā Asadu'llāh Khān Ghālib, *translated by Daud Rahbar, State University of New York Press, 1987, pp. x-xv.*

---

## FURTHER READING.

Husaini, M. A., Zaidi, A. J., and Abidi, A. H. *Ghalib: Life and Work.* New Delhi, India: Ministry of Information and Broadcasting, Government of India, 1969, 42 p.

    Discusses Ghalib's career and its place in the Urdu and Persian literary traditions.

Misra, Satya Deo. *Ghalib's Passion Flower—Consuming, Flower-Fresh, Heady.* New Delhi, India: S. D. Misra, 1969, 177 p.

    A Hindu mystic's appreciation and evaluation of Ghalib's Islamic poetry, with translations.

Sud, K. N. "Mirza Ghalib: Omar Khayyam of India." *Indian and Foreign Review* XVII, No. 9 (15-29 February 1980): 20-21.

    Compares Ghalib's poetry and prose with the work of other writers from world literature.

# Nathaniel Hawthorne

## 1804-1864

(Born Nathaniel Hathorne) American novelist, short story writer, and essayist.

The following entry presents criticism of Hawthorne's novel *The House of the Seven Gables* (1851). For information on Hawthorne's complete career, as well as for additional commentary on *The House of the Seven Gables,* see *NCLC,* Vol. 2; for criticism devoted to his novels *The Scarlet Letter, The Blithedale Romance,* and *The Marble Faun,* see *NCLC,* Vol. 10, *NCLC,* Vol. 17, and *NCLC,* Vol. 23, respectively.

## INTRODUCTION

Ostensibly a tale of the effects of sin and guilt as manifested through successive generations of a New England family, Hawthorne's *The House of the Seven Gables* is a richly detailed novel with multiple levels of meaning and ambiguities that have prompted a wide array of critical interpretations. Hawthorne considered *The House of the Seven Gables* to be his greatest work—"more characteristic" of his mind and "more proper and natural" for him to write than his first novel, *The Scarlet Letter.*

Hawthorne began writing *The House of the Seven Gables* within six months after the publication of *The Scarlet Letter* in April, 1850. At the urging of his wife, Sophia, Hawthorne intended to produce a second novel more cheerful in tone than his first. However, this was more difficult for him than he had anticipated; in a letter to his publisher, James T. Fields, Hawthorne wrote that *The House of the Seven Gables* "darkens damnably towards the close, but I shall try hard to pour some setting sunshine over it." In another letter, composed while the novel was still unfinished, he wrote: "There are points where a writer gets bewildered, and cannot form any judgment of what he has done, nor tell what to do next." Finally, having completed the story, he read its conclusion to Sophia, who had complained that the ending of *The Scarlet Letter* had left her with a headache. She approved of the ending to *House of the Seven Gables,* writing in her diary of what she considered the "unspeakable grace and beauty in the conclusion." The novel, well-received by critics, also proved a popular success, outselling *The Scarlet Letter* during Hawthorne's lifetime.

The events of *The House of the Seven Gables* center on the Pyncheon House, sited on a parcel of land obtained more than one hundred-fifty years earlier by Colonel Pyncheon after he had played a role in having the land's owner, Matthew Maule, hanged as a wizard. According to legend, Maule placed a curse on the Colonel. This curse became the source of many misfortunes suffered by his descendants, including a tendency on the part of male heads of the family toward sudden death by apoplexy. As the story opens, Hepzibah Pyncheon, the aged and isolated spinster who occupies the house, is joined by her young cousin Phoebe and Hepzibah's brother Clifford, newly released from a long prison sentence after being unjustly accused of murdering his uncle. An unused gable of the house is rented to Holgrave, a young jack-of-all-trades with radical political ideas; on one occasion, he speaks out against the idea of founding a family and passing on an inheritance to one's heirs. Judge Jaffrey Pyncheon, a materially successful and publicly respected relative, plans to have Clifford returned to prison unless he reveals information Jaffrey presumes him to have regarding a source of family wealth hidden within the house. A series of fortuitous events brings the novel to a close: the Judge's sudden death, coupled with the announcement of the death of his only living heir, means that his estate is left in the hands of Phoebe and Holgrave, who have declared their love for each other. When Holgrave announces that he is actually a descendant of Matthew Maule, the long-standing animosity between the two families would seem to be ended. Holgrave claims to have discarded his radical principles and expresses a willingness to settle down and raise a family. The foursome leave the Pyncheon House to move into the late Judge's country home.

Many commentators have noted that certain events and characters in the novel have autobiographical significance for Hawthorne, whose Puritan ancestor John Hathorne participated in the persecution of alleged witches. One of his victims, Sarah Good, reportedly cursed a colleague of John Hathorne much as Maule curses Colonel Pyncheon. Other details of the plot, including a missing deed to Eastern land holdings and the marriage that resolves the ancient feud between the families, also have parallels in Hawthorne's family history. Critics generally agree that Phoebe was inspired by Hawthorne's wife.

Critical discussion of *The House of the Seven Gables* can be divided into four main areas: the characters and their function in the story; the narrative structure, or lack thereof; the significance of the conclusion; and the primary theme of the novel. Some critics have claimed that the characters are not well-drawn, believable figures and have interpreted them as allegorical representations of character traits, social classes, or aspects of the human mind. Others, however, have defended Hawthorne's characterizations as carefully detailed and entirely believable. Because the novel lacks a clearly identifiable central character, some commentators have suggested that the house itself occupies this role, citing Hawthorne's frequent personifications of the structure.

Some critics have also credited the house with providing the structural unity of the novel; Richard Gray has described it as "a kind of emblematic frame in which all the metaphors of the narrative are implicated." Other critics have found no structure to the novel at all, arguing that the narrative frequently digresses into long descriptions of scene and character that do not advance the action of the story. In this view, the narrative is at best a collection of loosely related scenes. Still others, however, have discerned an underlying structure but have disagreed on its nature. Newton Arvin and Richard H. Fogle claimed that the novel is organized around a pictorial sense of aesthetic composition; Edwin P. Whipple saw in the narrative a unity of spiritual law; and, more recently, Darrel Abel has described the novel's structure as a "prose symphony" having five distinct movements.

The apparently happy ending of the novel has long been a source of critical dissatisfaction with the work. Holgrave's declaration of love for Phoebe and his backing away from the radical sentiments he expresses earlier in the novel have seemed to some readers too unexpected to be credible. In addition, the timely announcement of the death of the Judge's only surviving heir, which leaves his fortune in the hands of the young couple, has struck some commentators as a contrived solution. Abel has called the novel's conclusion an "arbitrary and inept" wrap-up of the "realistic level" of the novel, and Newton Arvin considered the ending "far too little organic" given the prevailing gloom of the rest of the narrative. Other commentators cite Hawthorne's correspondence with his publisher as evidence that the happy conclusion was "forced" by the author, suggesting that he was more concerned with meeting the expectations of his wife or of the reading public than with preserving the integrity of the narrative. Hawthorne's method of concluding his story does have its sup-

porters, however, some of whom believe that it is intended ironically—a deliberately comic ending to mask the bitterness of the fact that the new family being created is still relying on ill-gotten inherited wealth. In Austin Warren's interpretation, the ending is not a happy one, since only Phoebe and Holgrave can look forward to any possibility of happiness. For Hepzibah and Clifford, whom he considers the main characters of the novel, there is "no real hope."

The novel's theme has provoked as much critical debate as its conclusion. Hawthorne stated in the preface to *The House of the Seven Gables* that the novel has a moral: in short, "that the wrong-doing of one generation lives into the successive ones." Many critics, however, have interpreted this overt admission of a moral as ironic. Compounding the difficulty is Hawthorne's statement later in the preface that "when romances do really teach anything . . . it is usually through a far more subtle process than the ostensible one. The author has considered it hardly worth his while, therefore, relentlessly to impale the story with its moral as with an iron rod." As Sheldon W. Liebman has pointed out, "It could not be more obvious that the story *is* 'relentlessly' impaled with the theme of ill-gotten wealth and hereditary sin." Many critics have therefore looked elsewhere in the novel for secondary levels of meaning. Several commentators have interpreted the novel as a statement of the superiority of American democracy to the Old World aristocratic social system. Michael T. Gilmore has argued that the tension Hawthorne apparently felt between his artistic impulses and the realities of the marketplace is represented in the events of the narrative. Gray and Liebman have both suggested that ambiguities in the novel are a deliberate strategy by Hawthorne to force the reader to interpret its events actively. Others, notably Hyatt H. Waggoner, have traced the roots of the work to Hawthorne's Christian faith, describing the work as an allegorical depiction of the redemptive power of love.

Though frequently faulted for its narrative structure or other perceived flaws, *The House of the Seven Gables* is generally ranked second in importance to only *The Scarlet Letter* among Hawthorne's works. Exploring the complexities and ambiguities of the novel, critics continue to acknowledge the subtlety of the work, which Waggoner judges "one of the least adequately appreciated novels in American literature."

---

### Edwin Percy Whipple   (essay date 1851)

[*Whipple was an American critic who helped to establish the reputation of his friend Hawthorne. In the following review of* The House of the Seven Gables, *he praises Hawthorne's accomplishment in the novel, citing especially the characterizations of Hepzibah and Phoebe.*]

"The wrong-doing of one generation lives into the successive ones, and, divesting itself of every temporary advantage, becomes a pure and uncontrollable mischief;" this is the leading idea of Hawthorne's new romance, and it is developed with even more than his usual power. The error in *The Scarlet Letter,* proceeded from the divorce of its humor from its pathos—the introduction being as genial as Goldsmith or Lamb, and the story which followed being tragic even to ghastliness. In *The House of the Seven Gables,* the humor and the pathos are combined, and the whole work is stamped with the individuality of the author's genius, in all its variety of power. The first hundred pages of the volume are masterly in conception and execution, and can challenge comparison, in the singular depth and sweetness of their imaginative humor, with the best writing of the kind in literature. The other portions of the book have not the same force, precision, and certainty of handling, and the insight into character especially, seems at times to follow the processes of clairvoyance more than those of the waking imagination. The consequence is that the movement of the author's mind betrays a slight fitfulness toward the conclusion, and, splendid as is the supernaturally grotesque element which this ideal impatience introduces, it still somewhat departs from the integrity of the original conception, and interferes with the strict unity of the work. The mental nerve which characterizes the first part, slips occasionally into mental nervousness as the author proceeds.

We have been particular in indicating this fault, because the work is of so high a character that it demands, as a right, to be judged by the most exacting requirements of art. Taken as a whole, it is Hawthorne's greatest work, and is equally sure of immediate popularity and permanent fame. Considered as a romance, it does not so much interest as fasten and fascinate attention; and this attractiveness in the story is the result of the rare mental powers and moods out of which the story creatively proceeds. Every chapter proves the author to be, not only a master of narrative, a creator of character, an observer of life, and richly gifted with the powers of vital conception and combination, but it also exhibits him as a profound thinker and skillful metaphysician. We do not know but that his eye is more certain in detecting remote spiritual laws and their relations, than in the sure grasp of individual character; and if he ever loses his hold upon persons it is owing to that intensely meditative cast of his mind by which he views persons in their relations to the general laws whose action they illustrate. There is some discord in the present work in the development of character and sequence of events; the dramatic unity is therefore not perfectly preserved; but this cannot be affirmed of the unity of the law. That is always sustained, and if it had been thoroughly embodied, identified, and harmonized with the concrete events and characters, we have little hesitation in asserting that the present volume would be the deepest work of imagination ever produced on the American continent.

Before venturing upon any comments on the characters, we cannot resist the temptation to call the attention of our readers to the striking thoughts profusely scattered over the volume. These are generally quietly introduced, and spring so naturally out of the narrative of incidents, that their depth may not be at first appreciated. Expediency is the god whom most men really worship and obey, and few realize the pernicious consequences and poisonous vitality of bad deeds performed to meet an immediate difficulty. Hawthorne hits the law itself in this remark: "The act of the present generation is the germ which may and must produce good or evil fruit, in a far distant time; for, together with the seed of the merely temporary crop, which mortals term expediency, they inevitably sow the acorns of a more enduring growth, which may darkly overshadow their posterity." In speaking of the legal murder of old Matthew Maule for witchcraft, he says that Matthew "was one of the martyrs to that terrible delusion, which should teach us, among its other morals, that the influential classes, and those who take upon themselves to be leaders of the people, are fully liable to all the passionate error that has ever characterized the maddest mob." In reference to the hereditary transmission of individual qualities, it is said of Colonel Pyncheon's descendants, that "his character might be traced all the way down, as distinctly *as if the colonel himself, a little diluted, had been gifted with a sort of intermittent immortality on earth.*" In a deeper vein is the account of the working of the popular imagination on the occasion of Col. Pyncheon's death. This afflicting event was ascribed by physicians to apoplexy; by the people to strangulation. The colonel had caused the death of a reputed wizard; and the fable ran that the lieutenant-governor, as he advanced into the room where the colonel sat dead in his chair, *saw a skeleton hand* at the colonel's throat, which vanished away as he came near him. Such touches as these are visible all over the volume, and few romances have more quotable felicities of thought and description.

The characters of the romance are among the best of Hawthorne's individualizations, and Miss Hepzibah and Phœbe are perhaps his masterpieces of characterization, in the felicity of their conception, their contrast, and their inter-action. Miss Hepzibah Pyncheon, the inhabitant of the gabled house, is compelled at the age of sixty to stoop from her aristocratic isolation from the world, and open a little cent shop, in order that she may provide for the subsistence of an unfortunate brother. The chapters entitled "The Little Shop-Window," "The First Customer," and a "Day Behind the Counter," in which her ludicrous humiliations are described, may be placed beside the best works of the most genial humorists, for their rapid alternations of smiles and tears, and the perfect April weather they make in the heart. The description of the little articles at the shop-window, the bars of soap, the leaden dragoons, the split peas, and the fantastic Jim Crow, "executing his world-renowned dance in gingerbread;" the attempts of the elderly maiden to arrange her articles aright, and the sad destruction she makes among them, crowned by upsetting that tumbler of marbles, "all of which roll different ways, and each individual marble, devil-directed, into the most difficult obscurity it can find;" the nervous irritation of her deportment as she puts her shop in order, the twitches of pride which agonize her breast, as stealing on tiptoe to the window, "as cautiously as if she conceived some bloody-minded villain to be watching behind the elm-tree, with intent to take her life," she stretches out her long, lank arm to put a paper of pearl-buttons, a Jew's harp, or what not, in its destined place, and then straitway vanishing back into the dusk, "as if the world need never hope for another glimpse of her;" the "ugly and spiteful little din" of the door-bell, announcing her first penny customer; all these, and many more minute details, are instinct with the life of humor, and cheerily illustrate that "entanglement of something mean and trivial with whatever is noblest in joy and sorrow," which it is the office of the humorist to represent and idealize.

The character of Phœbe makes the sunshine of the book, and by connecting her so intimately with Miss Hepzibah, a quaint sweetness is added to the native graces of her mind and disposition. The "homely witchcraft" with which she brings out the hidden capabilities of every thing, is exquisitely exhibited, and poor Uncle Venner's praise of her touches the real secret of her fascination. "I've seen," says that cheery mendicant, "a great deal of the world, not only in people's kitchens and back-yards, but at the street corners, and on the wharves, and in other places where my business calls me; but I'm free to say that I never knew a human creature do her work so much like one of God's angels as this child Phœbe does!" Holgrave, the young gentleman who carries off this pearl of womanhood, appears to us a failure. It is impossible for the reader to like him, and one finds it difficult to conceive how Phœbe herself can like him. The love scenes accordingly lack love, and a kind of magnetic influence is substituted for affection. The character of Clifford is elaborately drawn, and sustained with much subtle skill, but he occupies perhaps too much space, and lures the author too much into metaphysical analysis and didactic disquisition. Judge Pyncheon is powerfully delineated, and the account of his death is a masterpiece of fantastic description. It is needless, perhaps, to say that the characters of the book have, like those in *The Scarlet Letter,* a vital relation to each other, and are developed not successively and separately, but mutually, each implying the other by a kind of artistic necessity.

The imagination in *The House of Seven Gables,* is perhaps most strikingly exhibited in the power with which the house itself is pervaded with thought, so that every room and gable has a sort of human interest communicated to it, and seems to symbolize the whole life of the Pyncheon family, from the grim colonel, who built it, to that delicate Alice, "the fragrance of whose rich and delightful character lingered about the place where she lived, as a dried rose-bud scents the drawer where it has withered and perished."

In conclusion, we hope to have the pleasure of reviewing a new romance by Hawthorne twice a year at least. We could also hope that if Holgrave continues his contributions to the magazines, that he would send Graham some such a story as "Alice Pyncheon," which he tells so charmingly to Phœbe. *The Scarlet Letter,* and *The House of Seven Gables,* contain mental qualities which insensibly lead some readers to compare the author to other cherished literary names. Thus we have seen Hawthorne likened for this quality to Goldsmith, and for that to Irving, and for still another to Dickens; and some critics have given him the preference over all whom he seems to resemble. But the real cause for congratulation in the appearance of an original genius like Hawthorne, is not that he dethrones any established prince in literature, but that he founds a new principality of his own. (pp. 467-68)

*Edwin Percy Whipple, in an originally unsigned review titled "The House of Seven Gables," in* Graham's Magazine, *Vol. XXXVIII, No. 6, June, 1851, pp. 467-68.*

### Henry T. Tuckerman    (essay date 1851)

[*Tuckerman was a highly regarded romantic, idealistic American critic during the mid-nineteenth century. The following excerpt is from an essay that first appeared in 1851. It was later reprinted in the June 11, 1864 issue of* Littell's Living Age, *along with the text of a letter Hawthorne wrote in response to its original publication. In the letter, Hawthorne stated that Tuckerman "saw into my books and understood what I meant." In the excerpt, Tuckerman praises Hawthorne's description of both physical and psychological detail in* The House of the Seven Gables.]

The scenery, tone, and personages of [*The House of the Seven Gables*] are imbued with a local authenticity which is not, for an instant, impaired by the imaginative charm of romance. We seem to breathe, as we read, the air, and be surrounded by the familiar objects, of a New England town. The interior of the House, each article described within it,—from the quaint table to the miniature by Malbone,—every product of the old garden, the street-scenes that beguile the eyes of poor Clifford, as he looks out of the arched window, the noble elm and the gingerbread figures at the little shop-window,—all have the significance that belong to reality when seized upon by art. In these details we have the truth, simplicity, and exact imitation of the Flemish painters. So life-like in the minutiæ and so picturesque in general effect are these sketches of still-life, that they are daguerreotyped in the reader's mind, and form a distinct and changeless background, the light and shade of which give admirable effect to the action of the story; occasional touches of humor, introduced with exquisite tact, relieve the grave undertone of the narrative, and form vivacious and quaint images which might readily be transferred to canvas—so effectively are they drawn in words; take, for instance, the street-musician and the Pyncheon fowls, the Judge balked of his kiss over the counter, Phœbe reading to Clifford in the garden, or the old maid in her lonely chamber, gazing on the sweet lineaments of her unfortunate brother.

Nor is Hawthorne less successful in those pictures that are drawn exclusively for the mind's eye, and are obvious to sensation rather than the actual vision. Were a New England Sunday, breakfast, old mansion, easterly storm, or the morning after it clears, ever so well described? The skill in atmosphere we have noted in his lighter sketches is also as apparent: around and within the principal scene of this romance, there hovers an alternating melancholy and brightness which is born of genuine moral life; no contrasts can be imagined of this kind, more eloquent to a sympathetic mind than that between the inward consciousness and external appearance of Hepzibah, or Phœbe and Clifford, or the Judge. They respectively symbolize the poles of human existence, and are fine studies for the psychologist. Yet this attraction is subservient to fidelity to local characteristics. Clifford represents, though in its most tragic imaginable phase, the man of fine organization and true sentiment environed by the material realities of New England life; his plausible uncle is the type of New England selfishness, glorified by respectable conformity and wealth; Phœbe is the ideal of genuine, efficient, yet loving female character in the same latitude; Uncle Venner we regard as one of the most fresh yet familiar portraits in the book; all denizens of our eastern provincial towns must have known such a philosopher; and Holgrave embodies Yankee acuteness and hardihood redeemed by integrity and enthusiasm. The contact of these most judiciously selected and highly characteristic elements brings out, not only many beautiful revelations of nature, but elucidates interesting truth; magnetism and socialism are admirably introduced; family tyranny in its most revolting form is powerfully exemplified; the distinction between a mental and a heartfelt interest in another, clearly unfolded; and the tenacious and hereditary nature of moral evil, impressively shadowed forth. The natural refinements of the human heart, the holiness of a ministry of disinterested affection, the gracefulness of the homeliest services when irradiated by cheerfulness and benevolence, are illustrated with singular beauty. "He," says our author, speaking of Clifford,

> had no right to be a martyr; and, beholding him so fit to be happy, and so feeble for all other purposes, a generous, strong, and noble spirit would, methinks, have been ready to sacrifice what little enjoyment it might have planned for itself,—*it would have flung down the hopes so paltry in its regard—if thereby the wintry blasts of our rude sphere might come tempered to such a man:*

and elsewhere:

> Phœbe's presence made a home about her,— that very sphere which the outcast, the prisoner, the potentate, the wretch beneath mankind, the wretch aside from it, or the wretch above it, instinctively pines after,—a home. She was real! Holding her hand, you felt something; a tender something; a substance and a warm one; *and so long as you could feel its grasp, soft as it was, you might be certain that your place was good in the whole sympathetic chain of human nature.* The world was no longer a delusion.

Thus narrowly, yet with reverence, does Hawthorne analyze the delicate traits of human sentiment and character; and opens vistas into that beautiful and unexplored world of love and thought that exists in every human being, though overshadowed by maternal circumstance and technical duty. This, as we have before said, is his great service; digressing every now and then, from the main drift of his story, he takes evident delight in expatiating on phases of character and general traits of life, or in bringing into strong relief the more latent facts of consciousness. Perhaps the union of the philosophic tendency with the poetic instinct is the great charm of his genius. It is common for American critics to estimate the interest of all writings by their comparative glow, vivacity, and rapidity of action: somewhat of the restless temperament

and enterprising life of the nation infects its taste: such terms as "quiet," "gentle," and "tasteful," are equivocal, when applied in this country to a book; and yet they may envelop the rarest energy of thought and depth of insight as well as earnestness of feeling: these qualities, in reflective minds, are too real to find melodramatic development; they move as calmly as summer waves, or glow as noiselessly as the firmament; but not the less grand and mighty is their essence; to realize it, the spirit of contemplation, and the recipient mood of sympathy must be evoked; for it is not external but moral excitement that is proposed; and we deem one of Hawthorne's most felicitous merits, that of so patiently educing artistic beauty and moral interest from life and nature, without the least sacrifice of intellectual dignity.

The healthy spring of life is typified in Phœbe so freshly as to magnetize the feelings as well as engage the perceptions of the reader; its intellectual phase finds expression in Holgrave, while the state of Clifford, when relieved of the nightmare that oppressed his sensitive temperament, the author justly compares to an Indian summer of the soul. Across the path of these beings of genuine flesh and blood, who constantly appeal to our most humane sympathies, or rather around their consciousness and history, flits the pale, mystic figure of Alice, whose invisible music and legendary fate overflow with a graceful and attractive superstition, yielding an Ariel-like melody to the more solemn and cheery strains of the whole composition. Among the apt though incidental touches of the picture, the idea

---

**H. P. Lovecraft on *The House of the Seven Gables:***

The overshadowing malevolence of the ancient house— almost as alive as Poe's House of Usher, though in a subtler way—pervades the tale as a recurrent motif pervades an operatic tragedy; and when the main story is reached, we behold the modern Pyncheons in a pitiable state of decay. . . . It was almost a pity to supply a fairly happy ending, with a union of sprightly Phoebe, cousin and last scion of the Pyncheons, to the prepossessing young man who turns out to be the last of the Maules. This union, presumably, ends the curse. Hawthorne avoids all violence of diction or movement, and keeps his implications of terror well in the background; but occasional glimpses amply serve to sustain the mood and redeem the work from pure allegorical aridity. Incidents like the bewitching of Alice Pyncheon in the early eighteenth century, and the spectral music of her harpsichord which precedes a death in the family—the latter a variant of an immemorial type of Aryan myth—link the action directly with the supernatural; whilst the dead nocturnal vigil of old Judge Pyncheon in the ancient parlour, with his frightfully ticking watch, is stark horror of the most poignant and genuine sort. The way in which the Judge's death is first adumbrated by the motions and sniffing of a strange cat outside the window, long before the fact is suspected by the reader or by any of the characters, is a stroke of genius which Poe could not have surpassed.

*H. P. Lovecraft, in his* Supernatural Horror in Literature, *Ben Abramson, 1945.*

of making the music-grinder's monkey an epitome of avarice, the daguerreotype a test of latent character, and the love of the reformer Holgrave for the genially practical Phœbe win him to conservatism, strike us as remarkably natural, yet quite as ingenious and charming as philosophical. We may add that the same pure, even, unexaggerated and perspicuous style of diction that we have recognized in his previous writing is maintained in this. (pp. 522-24)

*Henry T. Tuckerman, "Nathaniel Hawthorne," in* Littell's Living Age, *Vol. LXXXI, No. 1045, June 11, 1864, pp. 518-24.*

## F. O. Matthiessen   (essay date 1941)

[*Matthiessen was an American educator, critic, and historian who was chiefly interested in the concept of cultural and literary tradition. He is considered one of the foremost critics of American literature. In the following excerpt, he discusses the themes, characters, and conclusion of* The House of the Seven Gables.]

The seventeenth-century house, grown black in the prevailing east wind, itself took on the status of a major theme [of ***The House of the Seven Gables***]. Hawthorne wrote to [his publisher, James T.] Fields that 'many passages of this book ought to be finished with the minuteness of a Dutch picture, in order to give them their proper effect'; and that aim can be read in his careful drawing of the thick central chimney, the gigantic elm at the door, the long-since exhausted garden, the monotony of occurrences in the by-street in which the mansion now fronts, the faint stir of the outside world as heard in the church bells or the far whistle of a train. As he dwelt on this example of 'the best and stateliest architecture' in a town whose houses, unaccountably to our eyes, generally struck him as having little pretense to varied beauty, he could feel that it had been 'the scene of events more full of human interest, perhaps, than those of a gray feudal castle.' This is worth noting since he seems to have forgotten it by the time he was writing the preface to ***The Marble Faun,*** where, developing the thought that romance needs ruin to make it grow, he took the conventional attitude about the thinness of material for the artist in America. Since this, in turn, gave the lead to James' famous enumeration of all 'the items of high civilization,' all the complexity of customs and manners that were left out of Hawthorne's scene, it is important that the Hawthorne of ***The Seven Gables*** believed that no matter how familiar and humble its incidents, 'they had the earth-smell in them.' He believed far more than that, for within the oak frame of the house, 'so much of mankind's varied experience had passed . . . so much had been suffered, and something, too, enjoyed, that . . . it was itself like a great human heart, with a life of its own, and full of rich and sombre reminiscences.'

These furnished him with several other themes that were central to American history. The old spinster Hepzibah Pyncheon, at the opening of the book the sole possessor of the dark recesses of the mansion, is the embodiment of decayed gentility, sustained only by her delusion of family importance, lacking any revivifying touch with outward existence. Hawthorne knew how fully her predicament

corresponded to the movement of the age, since 'in this republican country, amid the fluctuating waves of our social life, somebody is always at the drowning-point.' He made the young reformer Holgrave confront her with the unreality of her existence by declaring that the names of gentleman and lady, though they had once had a meaning and had conferred a value on their owners, 'in the present—and still more in the future condition of society—they imply, not privilege, but restriction!' Indeed, by imprisoning herself so long in one place and in the unvarying round of a single chain of ideas, Hepzibah had grown to be a kind of lunatic, pathetic in her efforts to merge with human sympathies, since no longer capable of doing so. Hawthorne posed her genteel helplessness against the demurely charming self-reliance of her niece Phoebe. By pointing out that it was owing to her father's having married beneath his rank that Phoebe possessed such plebeian capabilities as being able to manage a kitchen or conduct a school, Hawthorne deliberately etched a contrast between the Pyncheon family and the rising democracy. This contrast is sustained even down to the inbred hens in the garden, who have a 'rusty, withered aspect, and a gouty kind of movement,' in consequence of too strict a watchfulness to maintain their purity of race. This accords again with Holgrave's statement to Phoebe that 'once in every half-century, at longest, a family should be merged into the great, obscure mass of humanity, and forget all about its ancestors. Human blood, in order to keep its freshness, should run in hidden streams.'

But there is more substance to Hawthorne's contrast than the tenuous if accurate notation of the gradual waning of the aristocracy, as against the solidly based energy of common life. He had observed in one of his early sketches of Salem that the influence of wealth and the sway of class 'had held firmer dominion here than in any other New England town'; and he now traced those abuses to their source. The original power of the Pyncheons had been founded on a great wrong: the very land on which the house was built had first been occupied by the thatched hut of Matthew Maule, who had settled there because of the spring of fresh water, 'a rare treasure on the sea-girt peninsula.' But as the town expanded during its first generation, this treasure took on the aspect of a desired asset in real estate to the eyes of Colonel Pyncheon. A man of iron energy of purpose in obtaining whatever he had set his mind upon, he asserted a plausible claim to Maule's lot and a large adjacent tract of land, on the strength of a prior grant.

Hawthorne's treatment of this material is characteristic of his effort to suggest social complexity. He stated that since no written record of the dispute remained in existence, he could merely enter the doubt as to whether the Colonel's claim had not been unduly stretched. What strengthened that suspicion was the fact that notwithstanding the inequality of the two antagonists, in a period when well-to-do personal influence had great hereditary weight, the dispute remained unsettled for years and came to a close only with the death of Maule, who had clung stubbornly to what he considered his right. Moreover, the manner of his death affected the mind differently than it had at the time, since he was executed as one of the obscure 'martyrs to that terrible delusion, which should teach us, among its other morals, that the influential classes, and those who take upon themselves to be leaders of the people, are fully liable to all the passionate error that has ever characterized the maddest mob.' In the general frenzy it was hardly noted that Colonel Pyncheon had applied his whole bitter force to the persecution of Maule, though by stressing this origin of the condemned man's curse upon his enemy— 'God will give him blood to drink'—Hawthorne recognized how economic motives could enter even into the charge of witchcraft.

By the time the justification for that curse began to be whispered around, the mansion was built, and 'there is something so massive, stable, and almost irresistibly imposing in the exterior presentment of established rank and great possessions, that their very existence seems to give them a right to exist; at least, so excellent a counterfeit of right, that few poor and humble men have moral force enough to question it.' The Maules, at any rate, kept their resentment to themselves; and as the generations went on, they were usually poverty-stricken, always plebeian. They worked with 'unsuccessful diligence' at handicrafts, labored on the wharves, or went to sea before the mast. They lived here and there about the town in tenements, and went to the almshouse 'as the natural home of their old age.' Finally they had taken 'the downright plunge' that awaits all families; and for the past thirty years no one of their name had appeared in the local directory.

The main theme that Hawthorne evolved from this history of the Pyncheons and the Maules was not the original curse on the house, but the curse that the Pyncheons have continued to bring upon themselves. Clifford may phrase it wildly in his sense of release at the Judge's death: 'What we call real estate—the solid ground to build a house on—is the broad foundation on which nearly all the guilt of this world rests. A man will commit almost any wrong,—he will heap up an immense pile of wickedness, as hard as granite, and which will weigh as heavily upon his soul, to eternal ages,—only to build a great gloomy, dark-chambered mansion, for himself to die in, and for his posterity to be miserable in.' But this also corresponds to Hawthorne's view in his preface, a view from which the dominating forces of his country had just begun to diverge most widely with the opening of California: 'the folly of tumbling down an avalanche of ill-gotten gold, or real estate, on the heads of an unfortunate posterity, thereby to maim and crush them, until the accumulated mass shall be scattered abroad in its original atoms.' Hawthorne's objections to the incumbrance of property often ran close to Thoreau's.

What Hawthorne set himself to analyze is this 'energy of disease,' this lust for wealth that has held the dominating Pyncheons in its inflexible grasp. After their original victory, their drive for power had long since shifted its ground, but had retained its form of oppressing the poor, for the present Judge steps forward to seize the property of his feeble cousins Hepzibah and Clifford, with the same cold unscrupulousness that had actuated the original Colonel in his dealings with the Maules. The only variation is that, 'as is customary with the rich, when they aim at the hon-

ors of a republic,' he had learned the expediency, which had not been forced upon his freer ancestor, of masking his relentless will beneath a veneer of 'paternal benevolence.' Thus what Hawthorne saw handed down from one generation to another were not—and this paradoxical phrase was marked by Melville—'the big, heavy, solid unrealities' such as gold and hereditary position, but inescapable traits of character.

He did not, however, make the mistake of simplifying, by casting all his Pyncheons into one monotonous image. If the Judge typified the dominant strain in the family, Clifford, the most complex character in the book, could stand for the recessive. His gently sensuous, almost feminine face had received years ago its perfect recording in a Malbone miniature, since as a young man he had loved just such delicate charm. Hawthorne suggested the helplessness of his aesthetic temperament before the ruthless energy of the Judge, by saying that any conflict between them would be 'like flinging a porcelain vase, with already a crack in it, against a granite column.' By using that symbolic, almost Jamesian image, he gave further embodiment to the kind of contrast he had drawn between Owen Warland and his hostile environment. His implications also extended beyond the Pyncheon family, for the hard competitive drives that had crushed many potentialities of richer, less aggressive living, had been a distorting factor throughout the length of American experience.

But Hawthorne made no effort to idealize Clifford. Holgrave calls him an 'abortive lover of the beautiful,' and it is true that the fragile mainspring of his life has been shattered by his long imprisonment for the supposed murder of his uncle. This punishment had been especially cruel since the old man had actually died of an apoplectic seizure, the traditional Pyncheon disease, but under such suspicious circumstances that his other nephew Jaffrey, who coveted the whole inheritance, could cause it to appear an act of violence. As a result he had gained the fortune on which he was to build the career that led to the eminent respectability of a judgeship; and Hepzibah was left with only the life occupancy of the house. And to the house she clung tenaciously, though its proper maintenance was far beyond her impoverished means, in the hope that is finally realized, of welcoming home her brother after his belated release. But the man who returns no longer possesses any intellectual or moral fibre to control his sensibility. His tastes express themselves only in a selfish demand for luxuries and in an animal delight in food, an exaggeration of the defects that Hawthorne always felt to lie as a danger for the artistic temperament, whose too exclusive fondness for beauty might end by wearing away all human affections. Clifford has retrogressed until he is hardly more than an idiot, a spoiled child who takes a childish pleasure in any passing attraction that can divert him from the confused memories of his terrible years of gloom. But, occasionally, deeper forces stir within him, as one day when he is watching, from the arched window at the head of the stairs, a political procession of marching men with fifes and drums. With a sudden, irrepressible gesture, from which he is restrained just in time by Hepzibah and Phoebe, he starts forward as though to jump down into the street, in a kind of desperate effort at renewed contact with life outside himself, 'but whether impelled by the species of terror that sometimes urges its victim over the very precipice which he shrinks from, or by a natural magnetism, tending towards the great centre of humanity,' Hawthorne found it not easy to decide.

Melville considered this one of the two most impressive scenes in the book; and the currents that are stirring here rise to their climax in the chapter in which Hawthorne's imagination moves most freely, 'The Flight of Two Owls,' the poignant account of how Hepzibah is swept away by her brother's strange exhilaration at finding the Judge, who had come to threaten him, dead of a seizure. Clifford is now determined to leave the whole past behind, and impels Hepzibah to start off at once with him crazily in the rain. With no definite goal, his attention is suddenly attracted by a feature of the Salem scene unknown at the time of his imprisonment, a train at the depot. Before Hepzibah can protest, they are aboard and are started on a local towards Portsmouth. The fact that Hawthorne had made a record in his notebook, just the year before, of this very trip, seems to have helped him to catch the rhythm of kaleidoscopic impressions into which the two old people are caught up. With a giddy sense that he has finally merged with life, Clifford's excitement mounts in ever more reckless talk with a man across the aisle, in which Hawthorne ironically makes him develop the transcendental doctrine that evil is bound to disappear in the ascending spiral of human improvement. But just as the hard-eyed stranger's suspicions of his insanity are crystalizing into certitude, Clifford is seized by the impulse that he has now gone far enough. Taking advantage of the fact that the train has stopped for a moment, he again draws the bewildered Hepzibah after him and both get off. Another moment and they are alone on the open platform of a deserted way-station, under a sullen rain-swept sky. Clifford's unreal courage deserts him all at once, and he is once more helplessly dependent on his sister to get him home. The impression that Hawthorne has thus created of their solitude, of their decrepit inexperience in an uncomprehending and hostile world, may well have been part of the stimulus for the most effectively intense chapter in [Melville's] *Pierre,* where the adolescent couple arrive in New York at night, for the luridly brutal first impact of corruption upon innocence.

Still another theme is introduced through the role that is played by Holgrave. At the start of the book Hepzibah has taken him as her sole lodger, though she has become increasingly startled by his strange companions, 'men with long beards, and dressed in linen blouses, and other such new-fangled and ill-fitting garments; reformers, temperance lecturers, and all manner of cross-looking philanthropists; community-men, and come-outers, as Hepzibah believed, who acknowledged no law, and ate no solid food.' Moreover, she has read a paragraph in a paper accusing him of delivering a speech 'full of wild and disorganizing matter.' But though this has made her have misgivings whether she ought not send him away, she has to admit from her own contact with him that even by her formal standards he is a quiet and orderly young man. His first effect on Phoebe, after she has come to visit her aunt and really to take over the burden of running the house,

is more disquieting, for his conversation seemed 'to unsettle everything around her, by his lack of reverence for what was fixed.'

In unrolling Holgrave's past history, which is made up in part from the histories of various characters whom Hawthorne had picked up in his country rambles, the novelist made clear that he believed he was tapping one of the richest sources of native material. He said at more explicit length than was customary to him: 'A romance on the plan of Gil Blas, adapted to American society and manners, would cease to be a romance. The experience of many individuals among us, who think it hardly worth the telling, would equal the vicissitudes of the Spaniard's earlier life; while their ultimate success, or the point whither they tend, may be incomparably higher than any that a novelist would imagine for his hero.' Holgrave himself told Phoebe somewhat proudly that he

> . . . could not boast of his origin, unless as being exceedingly humble, nor of his education, except that it had been the scantiest possible, and obtained by a few winter-months' attendance at a district school. Left early to his own guidance, he had begun to be self-dependent while yet a boy; and it was a condition aptly suited to his natural force of will. Though now but twenty-two years old (lacking some months, which are years in such a life), he had already been, first, a country schoolmaster; next, a salesman in a country store; and either at the same time or afterwards, the political editor of a country newspaper. He had subsequently travelled New England and the Middle States, as a pedlar, in the employment of a Connecticut manufactory of cologne-water and other essences. In an episodical way he had studied and practiced dentistry, and with very flattering success, especially in many of the factory-towns along our inland streams. As a supernumerary official, of some kind or other, aboard a packet-ship, he had visited Europe, and found means, before his return, to see Italy, and part of France and Germany. At a later period he had spent some months in a community of Fourierists. Still more recently he had been a public lecturer on Mesmerism.

His present phase, as a daguerreotypist, was no more likely to be permanent than any of the preceding ones. He had taken it up 'with the careless alacrity of an adventurer, who had his bread to earn.'

Yet homeless as he had been, and continually changing his whereabouts, 'and, therefore, responsible neither to public opinion nor to individuals,' he had never violated his inner integrity of conscience, as Phoebe soon came to recognize. His hatred of the dead burden of the past was as thoroughgoing as possible; but he had read very little, and though he considered himself a thinker, with his own path to discover, he 'had perhaps hardly yet reached the point where an educated man begins to think.' 'Altogether in his culture and want of culture'—as Hawthorne summed him up, somewhat laboriously, but with telling accuracy—'in his crude, wild, and misty philosophy, and the practical experience that counteracted some of its tendencies; in his magnanimous zeal for man's welfare, and his recklessness of whatever the ages had established in man's behalf; in his faith, and in his infidelity; in what he had and in what he lacked,—the artist might fitly enough stand forth as the representative of many compeers in his native land.' His saving grace was the absence of arrogance in his ideas, which could otherwise have become those of a crank. He had learned enough of the world to be perplexed by it, and to begin to suspect 'that a man's bewilderment is the measure of his wisdom.' Melville checked that, as he did also the reflection that it would be hard to prefigure Holgrave's future, since in this country we are always meeting such jacks-of-all-trades, 'for whom we anticipate wonderful things, but of whom, even after much and careful inquiry, we never happen to hear another word.' In short, Hawthorne has presented a detailed portrait of one of Emerson's promising Young Americans.

The course that is actually foreshadowed for him is devastating in its limitations. In consequence of the awakening of his love for Phoebe and her acceptance of him, society no longer looks hostile. When Phoebe is afraid that he will lead her out of her own quiet path, he already knows that the influence is likely to be all the other way. As he says, 'the world owes all its onward impulses to men ill at ease,' and he has a presentiment that it will hereafter be his lot to set out trees and to make fences, and to build a house for another generation. Thus he admits, with a half-melancholy laugh, that he feels the traditional values already asserting their power over him, even while he and Phoebe are still standing under the gaze of the portrait of Colonel Pyncheon, whom Holgrave recognizes as 'a model conservative, who, in that very character, rendered himself so long the evil destiny of his race.'

The conclusion of this book has satisfied very few. Although Phoebe's marriage with Holgrave, who discloses himself at length as a descendant of the Maules, is meant finally to transcend the old brutal separation of classes that has hardened the poor family against its oppressors, the reconciliation is somewhat too lightly made. It is quite out of keeping with Hawthorne's seemingly deliberate answer in his preface to the new thought's doctrine of Compensation, of the way good arises out of evil. For Hawthorne said there that his book might illustrate the truth 'that the wrong-doing of one generation lives into the successive ones, and, divesting itself of every temporary advantage, becomes a pure and uncontrollable mischief.' That unrelenting strain was still at the fore in his final reflections about Clifford. Although his feeble spirits revived once the Judge's death had removed him from the sphere of that malevolent influence, 'after such wrong as he had suffered, there is no reparation . . . No great mistake, whether acted or endured, in our mortal sphere, is ever really set right. Time, the continual vicissitude of circumstances, and the invariable inopportunity of death, render it impossible. If, after long lapse of years, the right seems to be in our power, we find no niche to set it in.'

In contrast to that tragic thought, Hawthorne's comparatively flimsy interpretation of the young lovers derives from the fact that he has not visualized their future with any precision. Trollope objected to this on the basic level of plot: 'the hurrying up of the marriage, and all the dol-

lars which they inherit from the wicked Judge, and the "handsome dark-green barouche" prepared for their departure, which is altogether unfitted to the ideas which the reader has formed respecting them, are quite unlike Hawthorne, and would seem almost to have been added by some every-day, beef-and-ale, realistic novelist, into whose hands the unfinished story had unfortunately fallen.' As they leave for the new country house that has tumbled into their hands, they seem to have made the successful gesture of renouncing the worst of the past. The tone of the last page could hardly be more different from that of the end of *The Cherry Orchard,* where Chekhov dwells not on what lies ahead, but on the mingled happiness and despair that have been interwoven with the old house. But the Russian was aware of the frustration and impending breakdown of a whole social class, whereas Hawthorne assumed with confidence the continuance of democratic opportunity. Yet in the poetic justice of bestowing opulence on all those who had previously been deprived of it by the Judge, Hawthorne overlooked the fact that he was sowing all over again the same seeds of evil. (pp. 323-32)

> *F. O. Matthiessen, "A Dark Necessity: Hawthorne's Politics, with the Economic Structure of 'The Seven Gables',"  in his* American Renaissance: Art and Expression in the Age of Emerson and Whitman, *Oxford University Press, 1941, pp. 316-37.*

## Lawrence Sargent Hall   (essay date 1944)

[*Hall is an American educator and critic. In the following excerpt, he explores the social ethic in* The House of the Seven Gables.]

*The House of the Seven Gables* constitutes Hawthorne's most forthright use of American democratic philosophy as a basis for a social ethic. The theme of this romance has to do with inherited sin, the sin of aristocratic pretensions against a moral order which, in the judgment of an equalitarian like Hawthorne, calls for a truer and higher evaluation of man. For the inheritance of the Pyncheon family proves to be no more than the antagonism of the old Colonel and his world toward things democratic.

Hawthorne was a shrewd enough student of history to be aware that the Puritan society of New England had been as aristocratic in its way as the feudal society of Europe, with which he was later to have a first hand acquaintance. He saw clearly the sharp cleavage that existed then between the various members of the social group. The servants who stood inside the entrance to the House of the Seven Gables directing one class of people to the parlor and the other to the kitchen preside likewise over the social distinctions of the whole story, separating the Pyncheons from the Maules and gentility from democracy until the very end. It is Hawthorne's symbolism at its best.

In the days of the theocracy, Hawthorne is willing to admit, there may have been some "temporary advantage" to the division between high and low and the suppression of the one by the other. Though such suppression was wrong-doing regardless of extenuating circumstances, it was a type of evil that was less apparent in the days of the Colonel than it had since become.

> There is something so massive, stable, and almost irresistibly imposing in the exterior presentment of established rank and great possessions, that their very existence seems to give them a right to exist; at least, so excellent a counterfeit of right, that few poor and humble men have moral force enough to question it, even in their secret minds. Such is the case now, after so many ancient prejudices have been overthrown; and it was far more so in ante-Revolutionary days, when the aristocracy could venture to be proud, and the low were content to be abased.

The Colonel who perpetrated the original wickedness belonged to a world whose social ethic was imperfectly developed. This fact makes his sin more normal than that of his heirs, yet no less culpable in the eyes of Holgrave or Hawthorne, both of whom measure it by an ethical absolute without reference to temporal variants. Meanwhile, each heir who accepts the Colonel's ill-gotten gain is an accessory after the fact. In times of growing social enlightenment when the heir cannot help knowing that his ancestor violated the rights of the commoner Maule, he is the wilful recipient of stolen goods. If he would share the spoils he must share the guilt.

> For various reasons, however, and from impressions often too vaguely founded to be put on paper, the writer cherishes the belief that many, if not most, of the successive proprietors of this estate were troubled with doubts as to their moral right to hold it. Of their legal tenure there could be no question; but old Matthew Maule, it is to be feared, trode downward from his own age to a far later one, planting a heavy footstep, all the way, on the conscience of a Pyncheon. If so, we are left to dispose of the awful query, whether each inheritor of the property—conscious of wrong, and failing to rectify it—did not commit anew the great guilt of his ancestor, and incur all its original responsibilities.

It was to a consciousness of similar sin against the democratic morality, which he felt was the only true social ethic, that Hawthorne later tried to arouse the British upper classes. Democracy, like Maule, should plant "a heavy footstep" on the conscience of any aristocracy.

The social sinfulness of aristocracy became specific, took on symbolic expression for the purposes of art in the crime which the arrogant old Colonel committed in usurping the home of the commoner Maule. It became more explicit still in the Colonel's effort to appropriate for himself and his heirs a tract of land somewhere in Maine. The fate of this abortive estate is especially significant. It reveals the natural destruction by democracy of the artificial, unethical arrangements of feudalism.

> But, in course of time, the territory was partly regranted to more favored individuals, and partly cleared and occupied by actual settlers. These last, if they ever heard of the Pyncheon title, would have laughed at the idea of any man's asserting a right—on the strength of mouldy parchments, signed with the faded autographs of

governors and legislators long dead and forgotten—to the lands which they or their fathers had wrested from the wild hand of nature by their own sturdy toil.

The family ambition to possess such an estate is so persistent that it even haunts the ascetic daydreams of poor Hepzibah, who clings wistfully to the hope that some sort of deed may yet appear to establish arbitrarily the claim of one family in default of the rights of all those common folk who have broken, cultivated, and inhabited the land for their livelihood. There is likelihood that Hawthorne was influenced here by Rousseau, whose works he had read extensively during June, July, and August of 1848. The following passage from *The Social Contract* can conceivably have had a strong conditioning effect on his thinking in connection with the land in Waldo County, Maine.

> In general, to authorize the right of the first occupant upon any territory, the following conditions are necessary: first, that the land shall never have been occupied; second, that only such a quantity be occupied as will be necessary for subsistence; third, that it be taken possession of not by an empty ceremony but by labor and cultivation, for this is the only sign of ownership which, in default of legal title, should be respected by others.

By rendering the Pyncheon claim to such territory a snare and a delusion, Hawthorne signified the baselessness of the pretensions of gentility and its gradual absorption in the morally inevitable progress of society toward democracy.

But the Pyncheon family itself (like the illusion of property upon which still depended much of the pride that was the mainstay of their spirit) gradually became more and more attenuated as the falseness of their position was made clearer by the great movement of society toward the equalitarian ideal. In fact, by the time the story proper opens, the process by which their proudly accumulated mass of possessions (spiritual and material) "shall be scattered abroad in its original atoms" is nearly complete. Their coveted estate is occupied by common people who wrest a living from it with manual labor. One of their scions has married "a young woman of no family or property," died and left as only heir to the Pyncheon prejudices and delusions a daughter of democracy.

There are but two developments left before the final absorption of the family can be achieved; the working out of each of these is the schedule for the story. By marrying Holgrave, Phoebe must merge, under the healthy and joyous auspices of equalitarianism, the blood of the old Colonel with the blood of the commoner whom he wronged. Thus she will expiate the old social guilt by dissipating the false distinctions that underlay it. Simultaneously the grim pride of the Pyncheons, which has erected as its monument the House of the Seven Gables and maintained the house as a token of inviolateness and aloofness for generations, must be punctured and all its vital juices drawn off until there remains only a monstrous emptiness.

The undemocratic pride of the Pyncheons first manifested itself as a sin against society when the Colonel usurped the land of Matthew Maule, the commoner, on which to build a mansion to house his ill-founded pretensions. A self-destructive element in his behavior is implicit in the legend, which attributes his death to the fact that by his conduct he drew on his own head the curse of old Maule. Allegorically considered, Maule's curse is the moral sentence of society which a man inevitably brings on himself in sinning against his fellow. If we read from the legend, then, the sin of pride may be seen to contain the germ of its own annihilation. And if we translate from the legend to the fact in terms of the action of the romance, we shall further see that it is the factor of isolation in the pride of the Pyncheons which automatically effects their ruin.

Like the chickens in the yard who pointedly resemble them, the Pyncheons had "existed too long in their distinct variety." In this parable is contained all the significance of an overweening self-interest operative within the carefully prescribed limits of one family for generation after generation. Deterioration is obvious in the blighted spinster who, with her hens and her brother, still clings to the last shreds of gentility.

Uncle Venner, the commoner, once remarked to Hepzibah that her family "never had the name of being an easy and agreeable set of folks. There was no getting close to them," he said. In the absence of a claim to anything more tangible except the house itself, this is the only inheritance of the last two inhabitants of Colonel Pyncheon's mansion. " 'Miss Hepzibah,' " observed Holgrave, " 'by secluding herself from society has lost all true relation with it, and is, in fact, dead . . . ' " "She had dwelt too much alone,—too long in the Pyncheon House—until her very brain was impregnated with the dry-rot of its timbers." "In her grief and wounded pride, Hepzibah had spent her life in divesting herself of friends; she had wilfully cast off the support which God has ordained his creatures to need from one another . . . " Over against her gaunt and decadent individualism is set the contrasting figure of lively Phoebe, "a fair parallel between new Plebeianism and old Gentility." It is she who brings life into the dark house and hearts of Clifford and Hepzibah, and takes it away with her when she leaves.

But it is impossible in the present state of society even for the dark old sanctuary of Pyncheon gentility to preserve its insularity intact.

> Let us behold, in poor Hepzibah, the immemorial lady,—two hundred years old, on this side of the water, and thrice as many on the other,—with her antique portraits, pedigrees, coats of arms, records and traditions, in Pyncheon Street, under the Pyncheon Elm, and the Pyncheon House, where she has spent all her days,—reduced now, in that very house, to be the huckstress of a cent-shop.

The opening of the cent-shop to let the outside world into the stifling interior of the secluded house is a symbol of the salutary virtues of the Maule forces, or the forces of democracy, in contrast to the moribund condition of the Pyncheons. "In this republican country, amid the fluctuating waves of our social life," wrote Hawthorne, "somebody is always at the drowning point." The Pyncheons were drowning in their own separateness, unable to draw the breath of life because they had so entirely shut themselves away from it. The cent-shop is a kind of pulmonary connection from humanity to the almost strangled existence of the House of the Seven Gables.

> Hitherto, the life blood has been gradually chilling in your veins as you sat aloof, within your circle of gentility, while the rest of the world was fighting out its battle with one kind of necessity or another. Henceforth, you will at least have the sense of healthy and natural effort for a purpose, and of lending your strength—be it great or small—to the united struggle of mankind. This is success,—all the success that anybody meets with!

Holgrave was right; Hepzibah did undergo "the invigorating breath of a fresh outward atmosphere, after the long torpor and monotonous seclusion of her life." But the experience was transitory. She retained her aristocratic arrogance, and inwardly despised the people by whose pennies she hoped to be sustained. The democracy she still repudiated failed to provide for her because she tried to take it in on her own conditions, to pervert it to her own undemocratic ends. Hepzibah, "the recluse of half a lifetime," proved pathetically incapable of merging with humanity in the common struggle for existence. It is Phoebe who takes over the cent-shop.

The childish, ineffectual Clifford exemplifies if possible a worse maladjustment than his sister. He has what remains of the exquisite nature that Hawthorne describes as "always selfish in its essence." A person of his stamp "can always be pricked more acutely through his sense of the beautiful and harmonious than through his heart." Had his character been allowed an opportunity for full natural development his taste or aesthetic temper might have been so perfectly cultivated as to have "completely eaten out or filed away his affections," thus making even more complete his isolation from the human heart by which men live.

But Clifford too had moments in which he felt the regenerative urge to burst from the inner prison of himself into the stream of life. "With a shivering repugnance at the idea of personal contact with the world, a powerful impulse still seized on Clifford, whenever the rush and roar of the human tide grew strongly audible to him." On one such occasion he was watching from a window of the House of the Seven Gables when a political parade went by in the street below. It seemed "one broad mass of existence,—one great life,—one collected body of mankind, with a vast, homogeneous spirit animating it—a mighty river of life, massive in its tide, and black with mystery, and, out of its depths, calling to the kindred depth within him." So strong was the influence upon him to join in the march of his fellow men that it affected him as a sort of primal madness, and he could "hardly be restrained from plunging into the surging stream of human sympathies." He was impelled, Hawthorne suggests, by "a natural magnetism, tending towards the great centre of humanity." Breathlessly he remarked to the terrified Hepzibah that had he taken the plunge and survived it, it would have made him another man. Hawthorne interpolates again by saying that he "required to take a deep, deep plunge into the ocean of human life, and to sink down and be covered by its profoundness, and then to emerge, sobered, invigorated, restored to the world and to himself." In his desire shortly after this incident to join the villagers going to church on Sunday, he displayed a "similar yearning to renew the broken links of brotherhood with his kind." Yet he and Hepzibah were unable to go through with it once they stood on the front step in plain sight of the whole town and all its citizens. They retreated into the gloom of the house which was the historical and material symbol of the isolation of their hearts. "For, what other dungeon is so dark as one's own heart! What jailer so inexorable as one's self!"

Living arrangements like those of the later Pyncheons, as Hawthorne noted [in his sketch "Main Street," 1849], "assumed the form both of hypocrisy and exaggeration, by being inherited from the example and precept of other human beings, and not from an original and spiritual source." The point Hawthorne is trying to make is the same one which Thoreau attempted to demonstrate by his life, and Emerson by his philosophy: namely, the moral necessity for all men to establish—as Emerson put it in *Nature*—"an original relation to the universe."

In one form or another this idea had dogged the subtler American democratic thinkers since Jefferson and Tom Paine insisted that each generation not only should be able but should be made to set up its own laws and contracts. Paine thought that to escape the infelicitous prejudices of the past it was necessary for men to think as though they were the first men who thought. We have already seen from the English romance that Hawthorne felt about his own generation as Holgrave feels about his. They must slough off the second-hand arrangements of the defunct past and work out their own relation to the world. This was their responsibility according to the best theories of democratic individualism. To fail in it as the Pyncheon progeny had was "sinister to the intellect, and sinister to the heart." It inevitably brought about "miserable distortions of the moral nature."

Thus the selfish individualism of a family so jealously guarding its interests through successive epochs, in defiance of newer trends and mores to which men at large are susceptible, is shown to be self-destructive. By preserving Colonel Pyncheon's proud egocentricity, the heirs cherished the very corrosive evil which eventually ate away their humanity. " 'The truth is,' " says Hawthorne's spokesman Holgrave, " 'that, once in every half-century, at longest, a family should be merged into the great, obscure mass of humanity, and forget all about its ancestors.' " Only in this way is it possible to avoid the arrogance which represents a sin against society, morally punishable by a fearful and hopeless ostracism.

This ostracism is the real legacy which Colonel Pyncheon left to his redoubtable progeny. "A man will commit almost any wrong," said Clifford, "—he will heap up an immense pile of wickedness, as hard as granite, and which will weigh as heavily upon his soul, to eternal ages,—only to build a great gloomy, dark chambered mansion, for himself to die in, and for his posterity to be miserable in."

The dark chambered mansion is the human heart in isolation.

Maule's curse—the moral sentence passed by society—is that the Pyncheons shall be destroyed by their sin of selfishness against him and his class. But they shall meet destruction under the special and significant circumstances which are the consequences of their sin against the commoner. They shall ultimately be destroyed by the solitude which they built for themselves at Maule's expense in the shape of the House of the Seven Gables, where the Colonel died alone at the beginning of the story and where (reincarnated in the character of the Judge) he returns to die alone at the end.

A few hours earlier while impotent, friendless old Hepzibah cast futilely about, like someone in a nightmare, for succor from the wicked Judge, it seemed "as if the house stood in a desert, or, by some spell, was made invisible to those who dwelt around, or passed beside it." Here is the tragic crux of the story. This is the bitter atonement which the family has made for the guilt which it wilfully assumed for so many generations. And a few hours later—"The gloomy and desolate old house, deserted of life, and with awful Death sitting sternly in its solitude, was *the emblem of many a human heart,* which, nevertheless, is compelled to hear the thrill and echo of the world's gayety around it" [emphasis added]. The House is Hawthorne's master symbol of isolation. It stands for the spiritual condition of those who by their hostility to democracy sin against what he believed to be the true moral order, and as a result become evanescent through their utter separateness from mankind. (pp. 160-67)

> *Lawrence Sargent Hall, in his* Hawthorne: Critic of Society, *1944. Reprint by Peter Smith, 1966, 200 p.*

### Austin Warren   (essay date 1948)

[*Warren was an American educator and critic. In the following excerpt, he points out defects in the plot, structure, and characterizations of* The House of the Seven Gables *and claims that the experiences of Hepzibah and Clifford are the central focus of the novel.*]

[With] *The House of the Seven Gables* we have an instance of Hawthorne at almost his best—at what he indeed thought to be work more characteristic of him than *The Scarlet Letter.* This is a book which gains from rereadings, though the defects more clearly differentiate themselves as well.

Hawthorne's strength lies in his central myth—the situation of a declining aristocratic family contrasted with youthful vigor and adaptation—and in its psychological realism; its weakness is in its plot and in its narrative method.

His method is almost that of a succession of tableaux. The characters do not really develop or change; and we do not find it easy to remember their speech, for Hawthorne has no considered notion of what parts of his story to put into dialogue, what not. Nor does he show us the characters acting on each other, as [Henry] James does in *The Golden*

*Bowl.* Here, as elsewhere, Hawthorne arranges scenes of conversation, ordinarily between two persons, but they are expository, do not advance the action. James says of Hepzibah that "she is a picture as her companions are pictures." A few of the characters have their symbolic attitudes—the Scowl and the Sultry Smile; there is a sense of the blondness of Phoebe and the somber brunetteness of Hepzibah. Hepzibah, dimly related to [other Hawthorne characters] Hester, Zenobia, Miriam, and Sibyl Darcy, is a tragedy queen in faded silhouette.

The point of view is clumsily managed, for the novel professes to be narrated by an "I" who presently passes into a "we," a narrator whose relation to the characters in the story and whose sources of information are never elucidated—indeed, an "I" or "we" so shadowy as ordinarily to be forgotten and certainly irrelevant. The mind of no character is consistently used, though Hepzibah and Holgrave are probably the predominant reflectors; Hawthorne makes no attempt to tell his outer story of three centuries through the consciousness of Hepzibah and Clifford. Yet he never really gains by his liberties of omniscient commentator. His own moral reflections on the fable, for example, are substantially uttered in the speeches of Holgrave and, for the last chapters, of Clifford; or, more accurately, they are divided between all the principal characters excepting Hepzibah, a consciousness felt by Hawthorne too dim to afford any general illumination. It is, in point of fact, Hepzibah who suffers most from the narrator's underlining and expostulations. Without his showman's pointing and nudgings, Hawthorne has 'realized' her character; and in chapter ii he is as superfluous as tasteless and heavily humorous: "Far from us be the indecorum of assisting, even in imagination at a maiden lady's toilet . . . . The maiden lady's devotions are concluded. Will she now issue forth over the threshold of our story: Not yet, by many minutes." This chapter is a kind of preparation for the yet more melodramatic technique of the chapter, "Governor Pyncheon," in which the Judge is rhetorically interrogated as, dead from apoplexy, he sits in his chair.

The 'plot' of the novel has to do with the warfare between the ancient families of Pyncheon and Maule, the dying curse of Maule that God may give the Pyncheons blood to drink, the mesmeric power of Maules over Pyncheons, illustrated by Matthew's power over Alice and Holgrave's over Phoebe, the mysterious land claim and the mysterious portrait, and the plot of Judge Pyncheon against his cousin Clifford. But Hawthorne is not really much interested in this initial mechanism. As *The Scarlet Letter* starts after the guilty act is over and is concerned with the effects of sin, not with its perpetration, so all this plot is but to set in action something else which is Hawthorne's real plot—the effect of pride, poverty, and suffering upon two old aristocrats.

The 'plot' is viewed as an unavoidable nuisance. It is certainly managed with great awkwardness. In *The Marble Faun* two endings were still unequal to the rescue of the plot from its surrounding and overpowering art commentary, character analysis, and philosophical discussion. In the leisurely *Blithedale Romance,* the melodramatic plot—which concerns the villain Westervelt and Old Moodie (*alias* Fauntleroy) and the identity of his daughters, Zenobia and Priscilla—is crowded into a pair of hasty chapters late in the book, as difficult to recall as Hawthorne found embarrassing to manage.

The *House* properly begins with chapter ii, "The Little Shop Window." But Hawthorne fumbles through a first chapter somewhat after the fashion of a Scott opening; he hurriedly sketches Pyncheon history and mystery, inserting an episode from the eighteenth-century history of the family as a tale allegedly composed by Holgrave. James has offered the suggestive comment that the *House* seems less a great novel than the prologue to a great novel; perhaps he should have said epilogue. One can imagine Hawthorne's scenario as expanded to the dimensions of such a family saga as *Buddenbrooks.* But what we actually have is an expanded novelette covering some three months, which could take still further retrenchment and which represents the past only by implication and dramatic utterance.

Though the *House* is partly 'romance,' partly 'novel,' its strength lies in its delicate realism. With impunity and by aid of a critically subtracting memory, we can extract its Gothic plot: we can remove the theatric controversy with the Maules; disengage the inserted tale of Alice Pyncheon, the proud lady with the prouder father, who are humiliated by their contemporary Maules; forget the portrait and the mysterious and death-portending music of Alice's harpsichord, and the mesmeric phenomena. The story then reduces itself to something like this: A New England aristocrat is so reduced in means that, having already been forced to take in a talented but radical young lodger, she must now resort to the more blatant expedient of shopkeeping. On the same day a wholesome and cheerful young relative arrives; on the following day there returns, after thirty years in prison, the old lady's sensitive brother. A rich and harsh relative calls one day to intimidate the brother into showing him the location of a missing document; thwarted in his wish, he dies of apoplexy. In their terror at the sight, the old brother and sister run away, though happily they return—concurrently with the young lodger and the young relative—before the body is discovered by the world.

The central characters are Hepzibah and Clifford, both admirably keyed though treated with somewhat repetitious exposition. And the relationship between the two is perceptively defined: the reversal of roles which makes the woman the less aesthetic of the two; the adjustment of the woman to the distaste her grotesqueness occasions her brother. Both are types of aristocratic decline, too ineffectual in a hurrying world to make insistent their claims to aristocratic status. Clifford's aestheticism is passive, appreciative, and even perhaps limited largely to foods and wines and flowers and fragrances. Hepzibah lacks all aristocratic equipage except pride; in ability she is inferior to her inferiors, cannot even manage. The Fall of the House of Pyncheon is not a tragic but a pathetic fall: the house is about to end, not with a bang but with a whimper. Actually it ends, less dramatically, with a 'happy ending' which does not seem false—since it is really happy only for the young people, who, renew, with plebeian blood, the decayed stock; while for the elderly celibates there is no real hope. To the central characters, Phoebe and Holgrave offer foil and contrast; and the hens in the garden tender their mildly comic parody.

The most effective chapters in the book are those which concern Clifford, a characterization singled out for praise by Pater, a successful Clifford, in his essay on Coleridge, a Clifford of genius: the chapters called "The Guest," "The Arched Window," and "The Flight of the Owls." Though Hawthorne approaches Clifford more lightly than he does Hepzibah and the Judge, one could yet spare his commentary. His romance would gain much in artistic precision and purity—and, through purity, power—if it were pruned severely of Hawthorne's underlinings and pointings.

The book is damaged by the presence—or the handling—of Judge Pyncheon. Hawthorne's villains, from Butler in *Fanshawe* on, are the really manufactured characters. As Randall Stewart has remarked, they are "nearly all persecutors of women or of men of feminine weakness." They are lovers of cruelty to whom the weak are both repellent and at the same time fascinating objects. If we ask why these sadists are not made convincing, we must say that Hawthorne presents them in a mode alien to his general mode of characterization. He either ought to render them exclusively from the point of view of their victims—Dimmesdale's view of Chillingworth, Clifford's of the Judge—or ought to give, from within, the sadist's views. In the *House,* everyone is successively seen from inside, seen with some sympathy, except Pyncheon. He is given, that is, an exterior with no interior; he thus seems out of scale, out of key, with the other characters. (pp. 97-102)

*Austin Warren, "Nathaniel Hawthorne," in his* Rage for Order: Essays in Criticism, *1948. Reprint by The University of Michigan Press, 1959, pp. 84-103.*

## Darrel Abel   (essay date 1953)

[*In the following essay, Abel examines the structure of* The House of the Seven Gables.]

Admirers of *The House of the Seven Gables* have always been hard pressed to justify their admiration. Those who read it less as a work of literary art than as a social or moral treatise readily find in it a unity of theme which meets their slight demand for aesthetic design. They read it to trace the "moral" with which Hawthorne said he had "provided himself" in order to conform to the current fashion; but he himself deprecated the supposition that this "moral" expressed, or could express, the essential significance of a work of fiction, which could only be brought out "gradually," "deepening at every step." The moral Hawthorne stated (and, be it observed, a moral is not, after all, a theme—the moral being a retrospective abstraction, the theme an anticipative and directive judgment which controls the author's representation of life) was that "the wrongdoing of one generation lives into successive ones, and divesting itself of every temporary advantage, becomes a pure and uncontrollable mischief." Bi-

ased interpreters who follow the clue define this "wrongdoing" in the light of their own preoccupations and show how it evoked the nemesis of the Pyncheons. A recently published Yale doctoral dissertation elaborates the theory that the wrongdoing of the Pyncheons was "a sin against democracy." Although such a thesis can be plausibly maintained and contributes to our understanding of the book, it reduces it from a work of art to a rambling and awkwardly handled exemplification of truisms.

Readers of greater artistic sophistication, who make stricter aesthetic demands of the work, are likely to be more severe in their criticism. Of course they can point to the charm of its atmosphere, which, as Henry James said, "renders, to an initiated reader, the impression of a summer afternoon in an elm-shadowed New England town." But fiction of book length must have design as well as "impression" if it is to endure as a classic, and even Hawthorne's best-intentioned critics have been puzzled to make out any organizing principle in *The House of the Seven Gables:* they are unable to polarize its elements. It apparently lacks a single consecutive action and a constant set of characters. The narrative leaps over whole generations with apparent arbitrariness. The characters appear to have been prodded from repose, not into life and action, but merely into momentary and aimless liveliness; they appear to be posturing and gesturing rather than acting out the inner necessities of their individual natures according to the exigencies and opportunities of an actual environment. The story appears to progress casually, even haphazardly, rather than to advance toward a crisis determined by factors inherent in the given situation.

Situation is what normally gives a novel its unity. The unity of a long work of fiction usually derives from its being a sustained attempt to trace the release in action of the potential energies in some interesting and typical human situation which involves the fates of various persons. The situation may be local and trivial, involving the petty though piquant vanities and ambitions of a few persons, as in *Barchester Towers;* or it may be vast and momentous, involving the lives and fortunes of whole populations, as in *War and Peace;* but in any case it treats of a crisis in the relationship of a particular set of persons in a specific place at a definite time. Clear distinction of this crisis provides a center of interest in reference to which all the characters and events of the story are seen to belong to one significant configuration of life.

Critics have looked vainly in *The House of the Seven Gables* for such a dynamic situation culminating in a crisis. They find instead a series of minor, quite static, situations, a discursive rather than a plotted development. They decide either that the book has no unifying principle, no *ensemble,* or that one of its several situations is significant and that the others are extrinsic. Adopting the first of these opinions, George Woodberry, Hawthorne's first disinterested critic, pronounced *The House of the Seven Gables* not a single story but "a succession of stories bound together" by a common motif. Preferring the alternative, Austin Warren, one of the most perceptive of present-day critics of Hawthorne, calls the book "actually an expanded novelette" and proposes drastic "retrenchment" in order to get at the "real plot," which he ascertains to be a demonstration of "the effect of pride, poverty and suffering upon two old aristocrats," Hepzibah and Clifford, "the central characters."

Hawthorne himself, in his first enthusiasm for the finished book, thought it had "more merit than *The Scarlet Letter*" and was "more characteristic" of his powers. It is strange that Hawthorne, one of the best self-critics among American writers, should have thought so highly of a work allegedly so defective. Shall we trust his judgment (with due allowance for the mood of relief with which an author views a fresh accomplishment) or that of his critics? In this dilemma we may well recall Coleridge's "golden rule" of criticism: "*Until you understand a writer's ignorance, presume yourself ignorant of his understanding.*" Coleridge was admonishing a baffled reader to look further—not to assume that a book must yield his sense, but to search patiently for its sense.

Critical reprehension of *The House of the Seven Gables* evidently proceeds from fixed ideas about the substance and form proper to a long work of prose fiction. From the period when the novel first showed signs of emerging as a distinct literary genre, its usual subject has been "real life" and its technique "realism." Since the seventeenth century the trend of Western thought has been away from idealisms of whatever sort and toward materialism. Literature, especially prose fiction, while it has gradually perfected its techniques for giving adequate account of the various impressions made by the visible world upon man's senses, has correspondingly lost its techniques for giving the semblance of reality to imaginations of the ideal. During the last two centuries the novel has become a respectable and popular literary form because it is well suited to exhaustive reporting of the tangibilities of ordinary life. A modern reader's assumption about a novel is that it is primarily a more or less realistic though imaginary history of persons. Such histories may vary in scope from the introspective minutiae of *Ulysses* to the coarser and more conspicuous events in a more extended and overt range of life in *The Old Wives' Tale*. Despite striking differences of material, most novels still support Henry James's dictum in *The Art of Fiction*: "The novel is history."

Hawthorne's distinction between the novel and the romance, which Henry James dismissed as "not answering to any reality," was an attempt to admonish readers that his books were not histories: they were less concerned with facts than with ideas, with persons than with human nature, with present circumstances than with the timeless influences which animate them. As he later wrote in *Our Old Home*:

> Facts, as we really find them, whatever poetry they may involve, are covered with a stony excrescence of prose, resembling the crust on a beautiful sea-shell, and they never show their most delicate and divinest colors until we shall have dissolved away their grosser actualities in a powerful menstruum of thought.

This reminds us of Coleridge's dictum that "to remove the disturbing forces of accident is the business of ideal art." In fact, Hawthorne's distinction between the novel and the romance was a diffident transcendentalist manifesto, declaring that he would write not realistic but transcendental fictions:

> When a writer wishes to call his work a romance, . . . he wishes to claim a certain latitude, both as to its fashion and material, which he would not have felt himself entitled to assume had he professed to be writing a novel.
>
> The novel is presumed to aim at a very minute fidelity, not merely to the possible, but to the probable and ordinary course of man's experience.

Hawthorne was anxious to avoid exposing *The House of the Seven Gables* "to that inflexible and exceedingly dangerous species of criticism" which insists upon "bringing his fancy-pictures almost into positive contact with the realities of the moment."

A modern critic would say that Hawthorne was protesting the application of canons of realism to his work. One of the ambiguities of the overworked word *realism* is that it means both a mode of expression and an assumption about the nature of ultimate reality. Indicating a mode of expression, it means concrete and circumstantial rendering of sensible things. Hawthorne aimed at this sort of realism in his fiction, although in an eclectic and subdued way. Indicating the nature of reality, realism means acceptance of the world of appearance as the "real" world. Hawthorne was not a realist in this sense. Although his notebooks are full of wonderfully vivid and precise delineations of actual persons, places, and events, in his fiction, as Henry James complained, "he never attempted to render exactly or closely the actual facts of the society that surrounded him."

His whole endeavor, like that of his Artist of the Beautiful, was "to spiritualize matter"—to interpret what he called "the grand hieroglyphic" of the visible world not as the sociologist does, by drawing from it abstractions which would have their whole truth grounded in the tangibilities from which they are derived, but as a transient projection of an ideal world beyond, as merely phenomenal. Nevertheless, he was not quite a transcendentalist, for he conceded more importance to the visible world than the Alcotts and Emersons seemed to; he mistrusted their tendency to abstract ideal truth from the body of fact which gave it life. To him, transcendentalists were "young visionaries" and "gray-headed theorists." The literature of American transcendentalism characteristically took aphoristic forms, because truths fished from the sky by intuition are too fragmentary and illusive to furnish materials for a substantial edifice of narrative: a transcendental novel is almost a contradiction in terms.

Persistent reading of his romances as novels despite his repeated insistence that they should not be so read has made it difficult to clear the ground for unprepossessed examination of the actual sense and form of his work. *The House of the Seven Gables* cannot be understood as a history of particular persons in a specific place at a definite time; it is, instead, a series of *tableaux vivants et parlants* showing phases and types of humanity embodied in different generations of two families which live in significantly revelatory relationship with each other within an ancient but changing tradition. In the explication which follows, the book is considered not as a narrative organized by strict concatenation of events, but as a kind of prose symphony organized in five stages or movements. Its devices will be taken as expedients to evade present and palpable circumstance and to reveal what lies beyond it. One of these devices is *eloignment,* an attempt to transport the reader into a province of the imagination midway between the historical and the ideal, where tests of realism are not too stringently applied. In *The Blithedale Romance* he called this "an available foothold between fiction and reality," acknowledging, however, the unlikeliness of his attaining this in a society "where actualities are so terribly insisted upon as they are in America." Similarly in the Preface to *The House of the Seven Gables,* he expressed a wish that "the book may be read strictly as a Romance, having a great deal more to do with the clouds overhead than with any portion of the actual soil of the County of Essex." To quote *Blithedale* again: "His present concern is merely to establish a theatre, a little removed from the highway of ordinary travel, where the creatures of his brain may play their phantasmagorical antics, without exposing them to too close a comparison with the actual events of real lives."

A second major device of Hawthorne's is his use of a kind of magic of agencies which have the power of opening a sensitive person's vision and imagination in rare moments, so that, in Wordsworthian phrase, he "sees into the life of things." Such talismanic power is in certain objects—the well in the garden, the Malbone miniature, and the portrait of the first Pyncheon. But Hawthorne's chief device of magic is an effect of certain conditions of light, especially of moonlight. In the Preface to *The Scarlet Letter* he wrote:

> Moonlight, in a familiar room, . . . is a medium the most suitable for a romance-writer to get acquainted with his illusive guests. . . . Details . . . are so spiritualized by the unusual light, that they seem to lose their actual substance, and become things of intellect. . . . Thus, the floor of our familiar room has become a neutral territory, somewhere between the real world and fairy-land, where the Actual and the Imaginary may meet, and each imbue itself with the nature of the other.

In **"Alice Doane's Appeal,"** a disjointed and undeveloped outline for a tale, Hawthorne wrote that he "intended to throw a ghostly glimmer around the reader, so that his imagination might view the town through a medium that should take off its every-day aspect." This is the very device which Coleridge had proposed to himself as plausible for presenting the visions of a romantic imagination: to make use of "the sudden charm, which accidents of light and shade, which moonlight or sun-set diffused over a known and familiar landscape." Hawthorne had used the "moonlight of romance" as an agency of imaginative vision throughout his earlier work in such tales as **"Young Goodman Brown"** and **"My Kinsman, Major Molineux,"** and in *The Scarlet Letter.* He spoke in **"Major Molineux"** of "the moon, creating, like the imaginative power, a beautiful strangeness in familiar objects, [giving] something of

romance to a scene that might not have possessed it in the light of day." This transforming power of moonlight, which opens to the imagination the ideal truth that lies behind everyday reality, is his principal device in the climactic scene of *The House of the Seven Gables.*

A third major device of Hawthorne's is his use of parallel repetitions which suggest that supposedly distinct realities are in fact recurrent assertions of an identical ideal life which continually manifests itself in changing forms. The Pyncheon portraits remind us that this is true of members of the Pyncheon family. The Pyncheon poultry echo this motif. The Pyncheon garden is identified with the garden of Eden. Various generations of Maules and Pyncheons re-enact the same roles. As Hawthorne puts it, "the future is but the reverberation of the past."

The fourth of Hawthorne's major devices is by far the most important: his establishment and continuous development of the symbolic aspects of all the objects in the romance—the central symbol of the Pyncheon house; the symbolism of environing things, garden, well, weeds, and flowers; the symbolism of articles, portraits, poultry, clothing, music, and photography.

The first "movement" in *The House of the Seven Gables* (especially, the indispensable first chapter, which Austin Warren says should be discarded) establishes the key symbolism of the House—announces the dominant theme of the book. Although the House is necessarily first looked at at a particular time and under a particular aspect (specifically, in an ancient phase of its physical existence), it is, as any house philosophically considered must be, a projection of human ideas, an expression of tradition. As a physical fabric, Hawthorne points out that it is merely one of "the solid unrealities" that "we call real estate." But the physical edifice "seemed to constitute the least and meanest part of its reality." It exists more significantly to the moral consciousness as a projection of human character: the character of the persons who in building it expressed their own human natures, and of successive generations who have lived in it and have had their human development largely determined by it. "So much of mankind's varied experience had passed there . . . that the very timbers were oozy, as with the moisture of a heart. It was itself like a great human heart, with a life of its own, and full of rich and sombre reminiscences."

Hawthorne alters his simile to express a more extrinsic aspect of the symbol:

> The aspect of the venerable mansion has always affected me like a human countenance, bearing the traces not merely of outward storm and sunshine, but expressive, also, of the long lapse of mortal life, and accompanying vicissitudes that have passed within. Were these to be worthily recounted, they would form a narrative of no small interest and instruction, and possessing, moreover, a certain remarkable unity.

The last sentence in this quotation suggests that Hawthorne saw in the events of his narrative a unity which his critics have overlooked. The House's long continuance in the world symbolizes the remarkable unity of events during "the long lapse of mortal life," not, of course, the life of an individual, but a larger pattern of human life which includes individual lives. These events, "if adequately translated to the reader, would serve to illustrate how much of old material goes to make up the freshest novelty of human life." The House, visible and enduring, images the sameness of life during many generations. Man forms tradition, and tradition forms man. Although human institutions "grow out of the heart of man," as Hawthorne wrote in **"The Old Manse,"** they are a matrix as well as a mirror of human character; in creating traditions, man fixes his own character by making a mold for himself to grow in.

Forming traditions is essentially a process of accommodating man's ideas to natural phenomena. Nature, including human nature, is somewhat plastic. Man has imposed his ideas on his own yielding nature and has given them a corresponding external form in his created objects and institutions. Mankind might show little continuity of character over a span of generations if it had not thus embodied its ideas in things external to itself and if it did not dwell so intimately within this external embodiment that its development is thereby determined. The natural objects long associated with the House symbolize the friendliness of Nature to tradition:

> In front grew the Pyncheon elm, which, in reference to such trees as one usually meets with, might well be termed gigantic. It had been planted by a great-grandson of the first Pyncheon, and although now fourscore years of age, or perhaps nearer a hundred, was still in its strong and broad maturity, throwing its shadow from side to side of the street, overtopping the seven gables, and sweeping the whole black roof with its pendent foliage. It gave a beauty to the old edifice, and seemed to make it a part of nature.

This passage suggests three things: Nature is friendly to tradition, which becomes a kind of natural fact itself through long continuance; tradition is nevertheless artificial and subordinate—Nature overtops it; Nature appears to have perennial youth, while the traditions which it harbors visibly fall into decay and need renovation.

There were also uglier growths on the Pyncheon property. In close proximity to the House flourished "an immense fertility of burdocks." "Such rank weeds (symbolic of the transmitted vices of society) . . . are always prone to root themselves about human dwellings." Other vegetation symbolized the beauty of human character transmitted through many generations:

> A crop, not of weeds, but flower-shrubs, . . . were growing aloft in the air, not a great way from the chimney, in the nook between two of the gables. They were called Alice's Posies. The tradition was, that a certain Alice Pyncheon had flung up the seeds, in sport, and that the dust of the street and the decay of the roof gradually formed a kind of soil for them, out of which they grew, when Alice had long been in her grave.

Thus, just as vegetable nature produces both weeds and flowers, human nature puts forth its flowers of good and evil in the humus of tradition. In this passage we see the elaborateness and thoroughness of Hawthorne's symbolism. The flowers grow in the air; the burdocks on the ground. The soil in which the flowers grow is formed partly of the dust from the street, partly of the decay from the roof—that is, partly from nature and partly from man.

The second movement of *The House of the Seven Gables* concerns the building of the House (establishment of tradition) and the defining of human relationships involved in its building. A tradition is fashioned by all the human beings whose existence it takes into account and belongs to all of them, even though it affords positions of privilege to some and deprives others. The House, then, although as a piece of "real estate" it is the legal property of the Pyncheons, belongs in a larger sense to both Pyncheons and Maules; as a tradition, it is oriented toward both the aristocratic and plebeian elements of humanity and indicates their relative status as members of one body.

Even as property, the moral right of the Pyncheons to exclusive possession of the House is more cloudy than their legal right. Morally, the story tells of a heinous violation of the Mosaic law forbidding murder and of the Christian law enjoining love. It is a modern version of the story of Naboth's vineyard, the contrived murder of a worthy poor man by his rich and great neighbor who coveted his small property. More specifically, the story illustrates certain utilitarian assumptions (variously expressed by Locke, Rousseau, Franklin, and Mill) about the just tenure of property. The small plot of ground which Pyncheon obtained through the contrived murder of Maule was the latter's by triple right: (1) first occupancy: the land had belonged to no one before Maule occupied it, it was "primeval forest"; (2) improvement by labor of the occupant: "With his own toil, he had hewn out" his holding, "to be his garden ground and homestead"; (3) use: Maule had appropriated only what satisfied his legitimate need—"an acre or two of earth," "small metes and bounds." Pyncheon's claim to this property was as specious as his means of getting it was iniquitous. He not only dispossessed the first occupant and deprived him of the fruit of his labor but seized in addition "a large adjacent tract of land" and vigorously pressed a claim "to a vast and as yet unexplored and unmeasured tract of Eastern lands." Such inordinate appropriation of what Rousseau would have called "undivided property" belonging to all men in common was an ominous introduction into a new world of an inequitable way of life conveyed from a foreign tradition already moribund.

The traits of the Pyncheon family in this generation are all combined in the character of the Pyncheon founder, who was guilty of pride, covetousness, and luxury in their grossest forms. Colonel Pyncheon should not, however, be regarded as an incarnation of evil. Though not amiable, he was a strong and respectable character in terms of the tradition then valid. In private life he was capable of tenderness, as is indicated by mention of his feeling toward his young grandson; in public life, he was a respected embodiment of strict authority. The House of the Seven Gables, a House of tradition unfairly appropriated by Pyncheons to the deprivation of Maules, does not, as M. L. Étienne in a contemporary review fantastically suggested, represent the Seven Deadly Sins; it represents the whole nature of man at a given time. In Hawthorne's view the forms of society were not good or evil according to the degree of their conformity to some contemplated ideal social pattern such as democracy, "the true moral order" for Hawthorne, as one critic opines; social forms and traditions were good and evil because of the good and evil of the human nature expressed in them. Hawthorne, haunted by a sentence from Bunyan's *Mr. Badman* ("From within, out of the heart of man proceedeth sin"), held that the heart of man is "the little yet boundless sphere wherein existed the original wrong of which the crime and misery of this outward world were merely types." Although the tradition embodied in the House expressed at the period of its first planting in the New World more of the evil of the human heart than of its good, it was a strong, full, and sufficient projection of the whole social nature of man at that time.

The third movement of *The House of the Seven Gables* represents the House in apparent prosperity still, but actually in incipient decay. The exclusiveness of the Pyncheons is having fatal effect. The tradition which they have appropriated too much to their own uses and accommodated too much to their special character is disintegrating. It no longer has the vitality of humanity, but merely projects the isolated Pyncheon character. The Pyncheons, like the House in which they dwell, are undergoing a disintegration of character; specifically, the Pyncheon traits are becoming dissociated and intensified in individual members of the family. Gervayse Pyncheon possesses two traits of the old Colonel, his covetousness and his luxury. These traits have an appearance of refinement which is really a proof of their loss of vitality. The covetousness of the Colonel, a mere grasping for property, still persisted, but Gervayse looked upon property as the means of purchasing aristocratic position. The gross carnality of the Colonel was refined sybaritism in Gervayse. Such developments would be expected in a family that had inherited wealth and privilege through many generations. Alice Pyncheon embodies the arrogant pride of the Pyncheon founder, although in a more elegant form. Alice is an amiable but pathetic character because she combines with this pride a natural tenderness and sympathy which we are to understand that she has by right of feminine, not her Pyncheon, nature. Although her arrogance and her sympathy are not harmonious traits, her behavior is consistent, for her Pyncheon pride is stronger than her womanly sympathy.

All these significances are symbolically expressed in a little scene in which the current representative of the Maules, the carpenter Matthew, approaches the House and enters it on what he supposes is to be an errand of repair, and proffers during his stay a symbolic offer of reunion, which is rejected by the Pyncheons. He ponders: "Does the House need any repair? Well it may, by this time; and no blame to my father who built it." But no sign of dilapidation was evident, "though its style might be getting a little out of fashion"; it looked, "in the October sun, as if it had been new only a week ago." Its sound exterior was matched by activity within: "The house had that pleasant aspect of life which is like the cheery expression of comfortable activity in the human countenance." Servants and slaves were energetically and cheerfully plying their tasks,

and the more favored inmates of the mansion were diverting themselves pleasantly:

> At an open window of a room in the second story, hanging over some pots of beautiful and delicate flowers, exotics, . . . was the figure of a young lady, an exotic, like the flowers, and beautiful and delicate as they. Her presence imparted an indescribable grace and faint witchery to the whole edifice.

When she was not tending her flowers, beautiful and exotic Alice stirred the listeners in the House with "the sad and sweet music of her harpsichord, and the airier melancholy of her accompanying voice." Her father, Gervayse, was occupied with equally elegant affairs. Magnificently dressed, he sat "sipping coffee, which had grown to be a favorite beverage with him in France." The pretentious splendor of the apartment could not disguise that it expressed the taste of the old Colonel: "Through all this variety of decoration, however, the room showed its original characteristics." In this House built by his father, Maule is rudely reminded by Gervayse that his democratic assumption of equality is intolerable, but Maule's encounter with Alice is more significant. Although "set apart from the world's vulgar mass by a certain gentle and cold stateliness," there was "the womanly mixture" in her of "tender capabilities." All the carpenter "required was simply the acknowledgment that he was indeed a man, and a fellow-being, moulded of the same elements as she." When this acknowledgment was withheld, he asserted through his mesmeric power over Alice the fact that Maule and Pyncheon were indeed formed of the same human clay.

The tradition at this stage still has beauty in it, though not much strength. It is still no more an embodiment of evil than when it expressed primarily the character of Colonel Pyncheon. It has lost vitality, but has gained grace, the characteristic of an old but not yet thoroughly disintegrated tradition. Hawthorne was later to offer a similar judgment of the somewhat attractive decline of English tradition, in *English Notebooks:* there must have been "something very good" in such forms, "good for all classes—while the world was in a state out of which these forms naturally grew." The bad was not inherent in the tradition, but in the fact that the tradition was getting out of adjustment with the current needs of humanity.

The fourth movement of *The House of the Seven Gables* represents tradition in a dangerously advanced stage of dilapidation. Servants and masters, industry and gaiety, have all died out of it. This phase of the House, when it must either be repaired or collapse, Hawthorne chose to designate as the present time, thus giving to his narrative something like the focus and proportion which an epic achieves by beginning *in medias res.* The latent decay in both House and Pyncheon family, threatening entire disintegration, has become open and perilous. In effect, the Maules have been thrust entirely into obscurity and out of the tradition. The House is ready to fall to pieces and shelters in its rickety vastness only two human wrecks. The Pyncheon character has undergone a further disintegration. The rapacity of Gervayse has passed to Judge Pyncheon and is intensified into mania; his sybaritism has passed to Clifford, enfeebled to imbecility. The aristocratic pride of Alice has descended to Hepzibah, impoverished to absurdity; her womanly feeling has found new expression in Phoebe and is in fact Phoebe's whole and sufficient principle of life. Pride and luxury are forms of inertia; the embodiments of these still inhabit the disintegrating House. Greed and love are energetic; the embodiments of these have both left the House to find the life which the House has lost. Judge Pyncheon retains his Pyncheon name and identity and still asserts his claim of ownership to the House, because he thinks it still holds deeds which will enable him to aggrandize himself further; he intends still to exploit it selfishly. Phoebe has lost both her Pyncheon name and family character; she significantly reminds Hepzibah: "I have not been brought up a Pyncheon."

The fifth movement of *The House of the Seven Gables* is the climactic continuation of the fourth. It sees the assembling within the House once more of all the elements of life associated in its founding, which have been through generations undergoing a fatal dissociation. Maule has returned, having lost his Maule identity under the name of Holgrave, and is admitted to the House as a lodger by Hepzibah, who feels humanly drawn to him and fairly abandons her pretensions of superiority in his company. Phoebe has returned, and her love vitalizes the old House. The climax of the romance is the courtship of Phoebe by Holgrave, a symbolic repetition of Matthew Maule's overtures to Alice Pyncheon. The renovation of tradition is symbolized in a wonderfully delicate scene in the Pyncheon garden. Comment on this scene calls for notice of some of the passages which bring out the symbolic role of Phoebe as a reconciler and renovator. The contrast between Phoebe and Hepzibah is explicit.

> As to Phoebe's not being a lady, or whether she were a lady or no, it was a point, perhaps, difficult to decide, but which could hardly come up for judgment at all in any fair and healthy mind. . . . She shocked no canon of taste; she was admirably in keeping with herself, and never jarred against surrounding circumstances. . . . Instead of discussing her claim to rank among ladies, it would be preferable to regard Phoebe as the example of feminine grace and availability combined, in a state of society, if there were any such, where ladies did not exist. There it should be woman's office to move in the midst of practical affairs, and to gild them all . . . with an atmosphere of loveliness and joy.

This concept of perfect womanhood is specifically contrasted with the aristocratic concept of the lady:

> To find the born and educated lady, on the other hand, we need look no farther than Hepzibah, . . . in her rustling and rusty silks, with her deeply cherished and ridiculous consciousness of long descent. . . . It was a fair parallel between new Plebeianism and old Gentility.

But this contrast does not constitute censure of aristocracy and absolute acceptance of democracy as "the true moral order." It is the contrast of new plebeianism with old gentility; the gentility of Hepzibah is a grotesque shadow of that of Alice Pyncheon. Hawthorne favored the vital over the moribund tradition.

Instead of Pyncheon hauteur, Phoebe diffused love. "Holding her hand, . . . you might be certain that your place was good in the whole sympathetic chain of human nature." When she became the pulse of the machine in the House, it was transformed by her presence, although "no longer ago than the night before, it had resembled nothing so much as the old maid's heart." "The grime and sordidness of the House of the Seven Gables seemed to have vanished since her appearance there . . . [through] the purifying influence scattered through the atmosphere of the household by the presence of one youthful, fresh, and thoroughly wholesome heart." Nature in the vicinity of the House was reanimated by her presence. On the morning after her arrival, she discovered a rosebush in the garden, planted long before by Alice, which, though long afflicted with blight and mildew, was now so profusely covered with white blossoms that it "looked as if it had been brought from Eden that very summer," although the bush was growing in a soil "now unctuous with nearly two hundred years of vegetable decay." The fragrance of character of both Alice and Phoebe is compared to rose-scent, and Phoebe symbolically assumes the care of these roses, which stand for the continuing sense of beauty in her family. Music is also used to link the characters of Phoebe and Alice and to establish a repeated motif. Although Phoebe could not produce strains of beauty on Alice's harpsichord, that antique, exotic and genteel instrument, "she possessed the gift of song," which Hawthorne emphasizes was a gift of nature, not an effect of art and cultivation.

In effect, Phoebe was the perfection of modern womanhood, as Alice had been of ladyhood. Alice, Hepzibah, and Phoebe were distinct notes of a human melody which threaded with sweetness the darker strain of the Pyncheon fortunes. Through the feminine characters in *The House of the Seven Gables* Hawthorne shows that the qualities of a human type are not apparent in the span of a single life, but must be studied in a succession of human existences.

Phoebe as woman, then, not as Pyncheon, and Holgrave as man, not as Maule, are reconciled in the moonlight in the garden. In the course of the summer, they have been working "in this black old earth" together. On this fateful eve their working together in the garden, so reminiscent of Milton's picture of Adam and Eve's joint labors before the Fall, is in the nature of a farewell meeting. In the course of their talk, Holgrave declaims against the House, as expressive of "the odious and abominable Past," and says that it ought to be purified by fire. Later, as they are seated beneath an arbor, he reads to her his story of the disdain of Alice for Matthew and of Matthew's cruel revenge. As he reads, the family history repeats itself; his reading mesmerizes Phoebe, as his ancestor Maule had mesmerized Alice. But just as Phoebe had failed to show Pyncheon disdain for Holgrave, so does Holgrave refrain from showing Maule vindictiveness toward Phoebe. At this moment the world is magically transformed for Holgrave by the love within and the magic moonlight around him. He looks with new vision at the old House. As the moon shines out "broad and oval, in its middle pathway," its illumination of the old House is a revelation to his awakened sensibility:

> Those silvery beams were already powerful enough to change the character of the lingering daylight. They softened and embellished the aspect of the old house. . . . The commonplace characteristics—which, at noon tide, it seemed to have taken a century of sordid life to accumulate—were now transformed by a charm of romance. . . . The artist chanced to be one on whom the reviving influence fell. . . .

The daguerreotypist, who had first introduced himself to Phoebe as one who made "pictures out of sunshine," declaring "there is wonderful insight in Heaven's broad and simple sunshine," has had a revelation of spiritual truth more real to him than daylight reality:

> "It seems to me," he observed, "that I never watched the coming of so beautiful an eve. . . . After all, what a good world we live in! How good, and beautiful! How young it is, too, with nothing really rotten or age-worn in it! This old house, for example, which sometimes has positively oppressed my breath with its smell of decaying timber! And this garden, where the black mould always clings to my spade, as if I were a sexton delving in a graveyard! Could I keep the feeling that now possesses me, the garden would every day be virgin soil, with the earth's first freshness in the flavor of its beans and squashes; and the house!—it would be like a bower in Eden, blossoming with the earliest roses that God ever made. Moonlight, and the sentiment in man's heart responsive to it, are the greatest of renovators and reformers."

This sentiment, so much an echo of Hawthorne's own feeling that the Old Manse had been for him an Eden, expresses the reality of tradition for Holgrave after he acquired "the deep intelligence of love." When, later on, he proposes marriage to Phoebe the transforming power of love is again emphasized: "The bliss which makes all things true, beautiful, and holy shone around this youth and maiden. They were conscious of nothing sad nor old. They transfigured the earth, and made it Eden again."

With this Hawthorne's poem essentially ends, but in concluding chapters he ties up loose ends of the realistic level of his narrative in his usual arbitrary and inept fashion. Judge Pyncheon is disposed of by a providential stroke of apoplexy, and the Pyncheon evil is extinguished in him, for it had all been concentrated finally in his character. The survivors are left in comfortable enjoyment of his ill-gotten wealth.

*The House of the Seven Gables* is not a study of "the effect of pride, poverty, and suffering upon two old aristocrats"; that study is an incident in a much larger design. Neither is it a symbolic study of some particular sin, such as offense against "the true moral order" of democracy. Nor is it chiefly meaningful as a realistic "impression" of New England life. It is, and was intended to be, all of these things, but it is much more. It is an allegory of love versus self-love, of human tradition versus personal ambition and family pride, of imagination versus preoccupation with present fact. In each of these contrasts the faculty named in the first term of the pair is shown to embrace a larger and more valuable reality than the second. Above all, Hawthorne expressed in *The House of the Seven Gables* a conviction that the character of any distinct stream of human existence cannot be adequately scrutinized in individual lives—which, to him, were not distinct, separate, self-controlled manifestations of human reality: human character must be examined in larger configurations in which a succession of lives exhibits the prolonged development of human tendencies. Most men have a mistaken sense that each personal life can be appraised as an entity, but Hawthorne says, not so: though the individual tries to make life firmly his own, it is not a part of him; he is a part of it. (pp. 561-78)

> *Darrel Abel, "Hawthorne's House of Tradition," in* South Atlantic Quarterly, *Vol. LII, No. 4, October, 1953, pp. 561-78.*

### Rudolph Von Abele   (essay date 1955)

[*Von Abele was an American educator and critic. In the following excerpt, he discusses irony in the conclusion of* The House of the Seven Gables, *hypothesizing that the novel's characters represent "different sides of Hawthorne's nature."*]

*The House of the Seven Gables* is the only one of Hawthorne's major writings of which it *might* be said that is is "comic," in that the conflict it encloses between the Pyncheon family and the world *appears* susceptible of resolution. Whether this is actually so or not makes a neat problem in interpretation. On the surface the last scene is nothing but comedy: the ogre Jaffrey Pyncheon is dead, the houses of Maule and Pyncheon,—unlike those of Montague and Capulet—are finally cemented by the power of love, a great and ancient wrong is "righted," and everybody rolls off in a green barouche to the late Judge's country acres, while the chorus, to an accompaniment given out *andante affetuoso* by the wraith of Alice Pyncheon upon her harpsichord, makes the comment, "Pretty good business, pretty good business!" The tableau is in spirit if in nothing else not unlike that of the close of Artemus Ward's version of the "Osawatomie Brown" shows:

> Tabloo—Old Brown on a platform, pintin upards, the staige lited up with red fire. Goddiss of Liberty also on, platform, pintin upards. A dutchman in the orkestry warbles on a base drum. Curtin falls. Moosic by the band.

And Sophia Hawthorne, to whom he read the manuscript of the romance, wrote of it, "There is unspeakable grace and beauty in the conclusion, throwing back upon the sterner tragedy of the commencement an ethereal light, and a dear home-loveliness and satisfaction." Whether she interpreted the conclusion—or the book, for that matter, as a whole—properly, is certainly open to question; but there is no doubt that superficially taken the last pages do sound like this.

The pivot of this final scene is the abrupt "conversion" of Holgrave, the last surviving Maule, from a bearded, peripatetic and enthusiastic reformer to a settled and weary conservative—in part through the yeasty work of his love for Phoebe Pyncheon, but also, one imagines, in part through the influence of the fortune into most of which he is destined to come if he marries her. But one finds it impossible to accept this "conversion" at face value: it comes much too neatly, and is scarcely prepared for in the body of the book. And as a matter of fact, this is no trivial affair, inasmuch as the significance of the entire book hangs on how this "transformation" is regarded.

This is hinted at, though not very plainly, by a trivial detail in Hawthorne's description of the Pyncheon elm on the morning succeeding the equinoctial storms. A branch of this elm has been by the weather turned to "bright gold," and resembles, Hawthorne says, "the golden branch that gained Aeneas and the Sibyl admittance into Hades." Aeneas, wanderer and planter of cities, is not Clifford Pyncheon but Holgrave, and the Sibyl would appear then to be Phoebe, through whom he is led into membership in the Pyncheon family, that is, the "house" of which the House itself is but the symbol. Reformism, for Holgrave, is like wandering for Aeneas, an expression of youthful energy preceding his discovery of his "true self." Now as for the golden branch: the figure associated with gold throughout the book is of course Jaffrey Pyncheon, who carries a gold-headed cane, wears gold-bowed spectacles, and is respectably well off. Early in the romance he has been seen in all his glory standing at the threshold of the house, "as if you had seen him touching the twigs of the Pyncheon-elm, and, Midas-like, transmuting them to gold." As it happens, the Judge's death *does* transmute the elm, and everything else about the dingy old house, to gold; but it is that kind of gold, commercially amassed material wealth, to possess which is indeed to enter hell, the very hell in which the Judge has himself been living all his days. But in accepting this wealth, Holgrave and Phoebe commit the identical fault: and they too enter hell. Holgrave may have recovered what his forebears lost; he may have achieved justice; but wealth in the nineteenth century of industrial capitalism is not wealth in the seventeenth-century sense of primitive accumulation. If it were not an impropriety to pursue one's hero out of the book in which he appears, one would have to nourish the fear that Holgrave will use Jaffrey's money to underwrite a Lowell cotton mill that sweats its operatives and runs on the fourteen-hour day.

If it were not an impropriety—but a line of thought resembling this does inhabit the book, in the image of "wise Uncle Venner" (venerable), that "miscellaneous old gentleman," who battens on other people's garbage: he is intended to figure a contrast in pastoral terms to the lures of wealth. Hawthorne, it is true, chaffs him a good deal, but he chaffs everybody in this book, for some odd reason—perhaps merely the one that since people complained of the gloominess of *The Scarlet Letter,* he is going to make this work funny come hell or high water. At the end the "venerable uncle" is gathered up and taken off to the country estate also, where he will be court jester and still the happiest person in the book.

There is, moreover, the "germ" phrase in the notebooks

from whence the romance is supposed to derive: "To inherit a great fortune. To inherit a great misfortune." This is true not only of all the original Pyncheons, but of Jaffrey as well, and through him of Holgrave and Phoebe. And the departure from the House of the Seven Gables, which might be taken as a symbolic shift of scene, a break with the past of which the house has been the chiefest emblem, is in fact no such thing. The break is only nominal; as Emerson remarked of the mania for travel, "I carry my giant with me wherever I go." For the old House is exchanged a new House, but the difference between them is only the difference between the rough individualism of old Colonel Pyncheon and the suave foxiness of Jaffrey, in whom, as Hawthorne remarks, can be seen a distinct physical decline over his ancestor as well.

So the conclusion can be read ironically, and, as the chorus says, it *is* all "good business." *Revanche* is attained with the sacrifice of neither love nor money—not only for old Colonel Pyncheon's dispossession and persecution of Matthew Maule, but for young Matthew Maule's failure to win Alice Pyncheon honestly too. Holgrave (a point I wish to return to later) refrains from practicing mesmerism to win Phoebe, and gains her love in a natural way; but Matthew Maule, scorned by Alice Pyncheon, "violated" her by practicing black arts upon her. Hence the ghostly harpsichord on the very last page: for that instrument has not been played on since Alice's death, and now that a later Pyncheon is to lose her virginity in a proper way, it becomes possible for it to "sound" again.

How much credence are we to put in Hawthorne's dismissal of an economic interpretation of the romance in his preface to it on the ground that "When romances do really teach anything . . . it is usually through a far more subtle process than the ostensible one?" Which might also mean that what they teach is far more "subtle" than what they seem to teach. Yet had he not intended to stress the economic interpretation he would hardly have mentioned it. One wonders what other notion Hawthorne might have had of the book, not only beyond this but beyond the burden of satire, in the figure of Jaffrey, of Charles Upham, the Salem clergyman who helped to get him fired from his customs post, and of the satire on the Hawthorne family saga of lands in Maine. A possible reading, not necessarily Hawthorne's own, can be made to focus on Holgrave as an aesthetic rather than an economic symbol. One merit of such a view is that it brings, without doing it violence, the *Seven Gables* into line with the other three finished romances, in each of which is the same concern with the problem of the artist.

Let us make the preliminary hypothesis . . . that not merely one, but all the protagonists of this book are to be regarded as projections of different sides of Hawthorne's nature; in this case a definition of the contrasts between Maules and Pyncheons is obviously required. Holgrave is the last surviving representative of a family whose line has long been supposed extinct; a family whose characteristics, while it was known, consisted mainly in much personal reserve and a reputation for occult power over others. The surviving Pyncheons are representatives of the family responsible for the low ebb of the Maules—a family whose dominant characteristics are a certain venality and hardness of temper, coupled with a fitful practical energy. Whenever, as occasionally happens, a Pyncheon appears who is less Pyncheon than something else, perhaps Maule, he is suppressed, as Clifford Pyncheon was by Jaffrey.

Now as for Holgrave: He is an artist of sorts when we first see him (though, given his polymorphous history, there is no guarantee that he will remain one), a daguerrotypist whose art, presumably because it operates with the assistance of the sun, that is, of Nature—of which Phoebe, bringing her "sunshine" and her country butter and her ways with chickens and vegetables, is the symbol—whose art represents reality as the best portraiture cannot. His two pictures of Jaffrey, one made while the subject was alive, the other after he was dead, are revelations of the "man beneath the mask," as the sensitive Phoebe notices at once. Moreover, he is also a writer, whose name has figured "on the covers of Graham and Godey," and who reads to Phoebe one afternoon from manuscript a story about his and her common ancestors, cast in the mold of many of Hawthorne's own Twice-Told Tales. It is well-known that his angry outburst against the past—"Shall we never, never get rid of this Past! . . . It lies upon the Present like a giant's dead body!" etc.—is an almost exact transcription of a passage from the Hawthorne notebooks, a passage which, whether or not he believed it when he put it into Holgrave's mouth, Hawthorne assuredly *once* believed. Like Hawthorne himself, and others of his surrogates, Holgrave figures largely as a "spectator" of the "drama" being "enacted" around him: Phoebe accuses him on this ground of being "coldhearted," of treating the house as merely a "theatre," and Clifford and Hepzibah as actors in a "tragedy . . . played exclusively for (his) amusement." Elsewhere she thinks him "too calm and cool an observer," as he goes about his business of watching, like the lens of one of his own cameras, a drama into which he steps at the end as chief protagonist upon the Judge's death. It is also worth noting that, like Hawthorne himself, and like several other of Hawthorne's fictive surrogates, Holgrave is a handsome young man with a swarthy complexion.

Now the arts of this young man, daguerrotypy and literature, are connected by Hawthorne with his gift of mesmeric power, a naturalist version of the occult powers said to have been owned by his forebears, and for the possession of which Matthew Maule the elder was hanged, and Matthew Maule the younger obliged to fall into an obscure poverty. And as in the case of the younger Matthew, whose career is the theme of Holgrave's short story, delivered one afternoon in the Pyncheon garden to Phoebe as audience, the exercise of occult powers is related to the sexual impulse,—quite as if, by the by, a "gift" for some sort of "magic" were either adjunct to, or symbolic of, virility. Holgrave's recitation of his legend almost mesmerises Phoebe, almost puts her into an extremely suggestible state, where she may become amenable to Holgrave's amorous overtures. It is true that Hawthorne obliquely satirizes this "gift" of the young reformer's by showing him in the act, somewhat earlier, of hypnotizing one of the Pyncheon chickens; but this may be because Holgrave is never really going to use his powers, which therefore do not represent a real peril; the seriousness of Hawthorne's use of mesmerism as a symbol of unlawful influence (like art?) is generally evident. Holgrave has, we must assume, the power to do to Phoebe what the younger Matthew Maule did to Alice Pyncheon—which is what Westervelt, in *The Blithedale Romance,* does to Priscilla. His abstention from doing it is therefore crucial to the book.

So, two centuries before, was hanged for witchcraft, at Colonel Pyncheon's instigation, old Matthew Maule: and for "Colonel Pyncheon" we are, by autobiographical authority, to read "John Hathorne." This Maule's son built the House of the Seven Gables, and his son in turn, the younger Matthew, was also a carpenter, which is to say, an artisan, in a day in which to be a carpenter was to be an architect as well. Is it too much to hazard that Hawthorne is promulgating, in the Maule and Pyncheon family lines, images of the artist and the anti-artist in himself? in which case, first, Holgrave would represent something of a decadence from the social usefulness of his ancestors' calling, much as Owen Warland's interest in artificial insects, and Dimmesdale's adulterous passion, represent fallings-off from their respective proper occupations and, second, Jaffrey Pyncheon (and hence Judge John Hathorne) would become the "type" of all influences in Hawthorne's personality that strove so hard to overthrow the Maule in him. Now it is true that Hawthorne's attitude toward the Salem witchcraft trials, in which Judge Hathorne played a prominent role, was critical; that he even imputed to old Colonel Pyncheon in this romance a motive more economic than sectarian. Yet it is also true that the power witches represented, the power to control the souls of others, impressed him as dangerous, and dangerous because it was undemocratic. This is made very plain in the extraordinary early fragment, **"Alice Doane's Appeal,"** written as far back as 1825. Mesmerism is simply a nineteenth-century version of witchcraft; and Hawthorne's attitude, toward the Maules as well as the Pyncheons, is really, I think, one of even-handed condemnation. This is so at least on the plane of this discussion.

Holgrave as artist, possessing quasi-magical powers which he may use to further his own ends, and artistic power that enable him to "see through" appearances and, like the painter in **"The Prophetic Portraits,"** reveal the essence of a personality, abjures these endowments to become a wealthy bourgeois. He does so even though he has been Hawthorne's ideal artist: one who has had much experience of life, one who despite all fortune's tumblings has never lost his identity, and one who can work the highest miracle of which art is capable. And Jaffrey Pyncheon, who actually, and ironically, succeeds by dying in corrupting the Maule power for good, is the typical Victorian *paterfamilias,* like old Mr Osborne in *Vanity Fair:* a localized image of the terrifying father, Zeus, with his "rough beard," his "cold, hard, immitigable" face that resembles the "brow of a precipitous mountain," and his emblem of power, the gold-headed cane. And if he is Zeus, he is an old, lascivious Zeus, become a "great beast" at table, emitting an odor of venery when he leans over the counter to kiss Phoebe: "the man . . . the sex, was entirely too prominent in (his) demonstration . . . " There is, moreover,

*A house in Salem that Horace Conolly claims was the model for the House of the Seven Gables.*

his maltreatment of his wife, in the best Victorian tradition:

> We must not talk, but whisper low,
> Mother wants to work we know,
> That, when father comes to tea,
> All may neat and cheerful be . . .

And if Jaffrey is Zeus (therefore also Jehovah), Clifford, the epicene childman, is what Hawthorne calls him: "a thundersmitten Adam," who for his innocence and his epicureanism was tricked by his cousin Jaffrey to prison, in which place both his artistic gifts and his sexual potency were totally destroyed. Had he been allowed to "live," he might have become an artist; but imprisonment has kept him a child who indulges tantrums, notices women's clothes, likes to blow soapbubbles, eats with refined voracity, is terrified of steam-engines, and is completely virgin. Having never "quaffed the cup of passionate love," he knows "that it (is) now too late." Holgrave the swarthy worldling is not the only surrogate for Hawthorne's artistry: in the pitiful figure of Clifford it seems to me that we can read a symbolic accusation by his creator against the world that, at least in his own opinion, forced him into isolation in order to write. After all, the clergyman Charles Upham, in seeing to it that Hawthorne was replaced in his

job with the customs after the change in administrations from Democratic to Whig in 1848, was in a sense condemning him to go back to the prison of the artist's study from which he had, since 1846, been seeking to liberate himself.

The upshot of the book's organization, then, is that the Pyncheon, or bourgeois, power, epitomized in Jaffrey, indelibly corrupts, even though extinguishing itself in the process, the Maule power, as represented by the artist Holgrave. The catastrophe, as in *The Scarlet Letter,* is general, is suicidal. Holgrave's capitulation to Jaffrey's money is, however, nonetheless abrupt, surprising, dishonorable, for all that; and the way it is huddled up into the last pages, with a sweetening of pastoralism and sentimentalism leads me to suspect Hawthorne of being both confused and uncomfortable while he wrote it. The confusion and embarrassment follow, too, I think, not only from his abstract recognition of a bad situation, that in a democratic society not only the aristocratic but the artistic tempers must become corrupted by the power of economics, but also from his recognition of something else, more deeply personal.

Phoebe plays an interesting role in this romance: among

these weary towndwellers, living in the dry-rot of civilization, she is the apostle of Nature, a "country cousin" who brings life and light to a "decaying" and "weather-beaten" house She is as "pleasant about the house as a gleam of sunshine falling on the floor." When she arrives she is wearing a yellow straw hat; she comes bringing country butter in gift; the windows of her room open on the east; she presides over the weekly gathering in the garden, which occurs on Sundays; the Indian cakes she prepares for Clifford are yellower than those made by Hepzibah. She dissipates "the shadows of gloomy events," and to Holgrave she confides that she dislikes moonlight, mystery, riddles. As in *The Blithedale Romance* Zenobia's departure brings on equinoctial weather, so when Phoebe goes September gales begin, nor does the sun return till the morning she returns. In fine, she is continually linked with that life-giving thing, the sun, which is also responsible for the "truthfulness" of Holgrave's daguerrotypes. Her name itself is the feminine form of *Phoebus*. And as such she is being offered through the body of the book as an implicit alternative to Jaffrey, whose power, not of the sun, not "natural," is derived from the opposite of it, usury. He is a speculator; his life is sterile; after his death comes that of his only son, by cholera; as Phoebe comes and goes with the sun, so he is a sun unto himself—a light of a "sultry," "dog-day" quality is said to "dry up," or sterilize, the streets. As it is her role to bring and foster life, it is his to unman others, as he does his cousin.

It is in a sense neat that Holgrave, who has been "living by the sun," should at the end of the book turn to its sun-goddess for succor. The only trouble is the irony which, like presented bayonets of palace guards, confronts us no matter where we try to enter this romance: when he turns to her it is within a week of her falling heiress to Jaffrey's estate, or a large portion of it; and "Love's web," so busily being spun in the anteroom to where the Judge sits stiffly dead, is a deception at last, that only betrays Holgrave into the green barouche. The "comic" resolution of the book is, in this as in other perspectives, most unsatisfying. We may take it, of course, to read as though Holgrave's turning conservative may be only the impulse of a moment (but the consequences of impulses cannot be so easily shrugged off as the impulses can be felt), or, with F. O. Matthiessen [in his *American Renaissance,* 1941], as if Hawthorne were being in deadly earnest in writing the conclusion, which is then expressive of his inability to see the evil potentialities of American capitalism. Neither view accounts, however, for the machinery by which Hawthorne pushes this legacy into the laps of his two protagonists: the death of Jaffrey's only son, which is quite baldly an auctorial device for forcing a certain kind of conclusion, but one so at variance with the rest of his book that it must be intended as an irony.

Of course, as has been said [by Lawrence Hall in his *Hawthorne: Critic of Society,* 1944], there is a question of "poetic justice" involved here, inasmuch as the Pyncheon name, to atone for its aristocratic exclusiveness and unapproachability, must disappear: which makes it imperative that Jaffrey's son should die and leave behind only the epicene Clifford, the virgin Hepzibah, and the female Phoebe. But first, the manner of this son's death smells loudly of

the *deus ex machina* (it is a clumsy device that fails to be convincing), and second, Phoebe does not have to marry Holgrave since her name will go in the act of marriage with no matter whom. The retort to this is that she must marry Holgrave because history must come full circle. But must Holgrave be damned in order to achieve the justice that is, on this view, his right?

*The House of the Seven Gables* appears to be Hawthorne's major recording of his social egalitarianism; the warped conclusion of the book may, I think, stem out of his complicating of the theme of egalitarianism with that of art, and so producing the kind of muddle in the book that Hawthorne's mind was always in about his respective loyalties to art and to his politics. That isolation and misunderstanding was an almost necessary role for the serious artist in his America can hardly be doubted. It is not for nothing that his great sinners were men and women isolated from their fellows, and in many instances guilty of detached, instead of *at*tached, analysis. Having made Holgrave, not only a defrauded heir, but also an artist, and having endowed him with certain of his own features, he could not make and keep him a radical democrat, without being unfaithful to his inner ambivalences, for the simple reason that books must have resolutions, whereas lives have none save the resolution of death, which is by definition uncognizable. So long as he was in public service Hawthorne found it impossible to work creatively; he fell back on sketches and notebook-keeping; and the latter of these may be regarded as the making of promises to the self to come back to creative effort *mañana,* later. At the Old Manse, or later at Lenox, where he consorted with almost the only intelligentsia America could show, it was another story: but whereas Hawthorne could, in an awkward way, live two lives in one body, one or the other of Holgrave's roles must go. Hawthorne solved this problem by trundling out his machine and eliminating both roles together.

It might be pointed out that when Holgrave comes to the House of the Seven Gables he has no intention of staying there, or of mingling his fortunes with those of the Pyncheons: though he may know the whole situation as they do not, his aim, so long as he is a radical, must be to avoid it. This is much as if Hawthorne were looking back to his own early years in Salem and saying, "My intentions also were to use this only as a way-station." But the House is contagious; and having once entered it, Holgrave cannot get out without surrendering utterly—just as once incarcerated in his "prison," Clifford can never escape it either, especially not once he has been released. In his "dismal chamber" Hawthorne also fell a victim to the power of the past—the New England past which was his heritage; nor was he able afterward to get out of it, and if he could, it would be only at the cost of surrendering his artistic soul. This amounts almost to saying that for Hawthorne it was worse to be Holgrave than it was to be Jaffrey Pyncheon; which may be pursuing the thread somewhat too rigorously, but despite its Humpty-Dumpty aspects strikes me as more faithful to the book than the customary interpretations. In one respect Hawthorne may be said to be trying to "save" Holgrave, but even this goes sour: if we look at his marriage with Phoebe as that of an intellectual to a non-intellectual, we may think we are witnessing Hawthorne bestowing on his hero a pastoral benediction. For Phoebe is not only a sun-goddess, she is also a child, in the penumbra of maturity, but still a child, innocent, simple, happy. But there is still the irony of her being drowned in stocks and bonds, and being forced to abandon her naive rural scene for a grand country estate, where the garden, instead of running wild, is ordered on the best principles of Andrew Jackson Downing. Always there is the irony, which, really not confined to the end of the book merely, suffices to turn its whole face from one of pretended comedy to one of bitterness.

A word in conclusion about the romance's structure: by comparison with that of *The Scarlet Letter* it is loose and atomistic. In neither book is there any strong narrative line, but whereas in the earlier romance Hawthorne imposed control by constructing the book in terms of a series of antitheses and balances all revolving round the pivotal twelfth chapter, in which Dimmesdale stands on the scaffold at midnight, there is here no such symmetry. Things simply "happen:" Phoebe comes, Clifford comes, Jaffrey grows importunate, Jaffrey dies, Clifford and Hepzibah flee, Holgrave and Phoebe fall in love; aside from the entries these characters make, there is nothing in their relations that would forbid the dénouement from occurring all at once. No temporal, no motivational reason exists for the lapse of several months that separates Jaffrey's initial foray on Clifford from the final one which brings about his death. The only justification that can be made is that of the desirability of a certain "suspense;" but this for its own sake merely produces only padding. What the book then shows in the way of structure is an initial gathering-together and a resolution, lacking a middle, and having in its stead a number of lyric flights about Clifford's, Hepzibah's and Holgrave's personalities, which take up fully a third of the book (between the seventh and fifteenth chapters) without contributing anything but a kind of irrelevant whimsicality for the most part. Hawthorne's attack upon the sustained piece of prose fiction, that is, begins to go wrong at the outset; which is not due entirely to his wish to produce something that will please many people by its "sunniness" and "optimism," but also to his inherent inability to conceive in terms of anything larger than the *nouvelle*. (pp. 58-69)

> *Rudolph Von Abele, in his* The Death of the Artist: A Study of Hawthorne's Disintegration, *Martinus Nijhoff, 1955, 111 p.*

## Marcus Cunliffe    (essay date 1964)

[*Cunliffe is an American educator and critic. In the following essay, he explores conflicting themes in* The House of the Seven Gables *and comments on the alternative explanations that the novel offers for its events, concluding that despite its strengths, it is a "flawed book."*]

Hawthorne is said to have preferred *The House of the Seven Gables* to its immediate predecessor, *The Scarlet Letter.* Though not many would agree with him, his satisfaction is understandable. *The Scarlet Letter* was a "hell-

fired" story with a crushing sense of fatality; it was, as Hawthorne said in the novel's final words, a somber legend, relieved like the escutcheon on Hester Prynne's tomb "only by one everglowing point of light gloomier than the shadow." *The Seven Gables* has a similar initial effect of grimness. Yet Hawthorne was able to bring the book to "a prosperous close"—to cross the gap he had established in his writing, and yet was always seeking to bridge, between the imaginary and the actual, the haunted gray New England past and "our own broad daylight."

He was entitled to feel that he had accomplished this and more in *The Seven Gables.* While the detail and the implications of the plot are complex, the essential outline is simple. It is a "powerful" story, originating in the wrong done to Matthew Maule by Colonel Pyncheon, somewhere near the end of the seventeenth century, in having him hanged for witchcraft. The consequences reverberate down through the decades. The Pyncheon family, persisting in pride and greed, is persistently punished. Moral and physical heredity march together. The Pyncheons whose conduct and appearance resemble those of Colonel Pyncheon die in the same hideous manner, as if under the same curse as that pronounced on the Colonel by the condemned "wizard"—"God will give him blood to drink!" The scheme likewise enables Hawthorne to trace the decline of the Pyncheons; for those members of the family who are not hard and covetous become increasingly ineffectual and impoverished. The curse is dissipated when Holgrave and Phoebe, the youngest representatives of the Maule and Pyncheon families, fall in love and marry. One other subsidiary problem is solved: Holgrave reveals to the Pyncheons the secret hiding-place of title deeds to an immense tract of land secured long ago by Colonel Pyncheon—papers missing ever since his death. They are quite worthless, and have been for at least a century. But it is important for the symmetry of the story that the family—as represented by the dreamy Clifford Pyncheon and his crabbed but harmless sister Hepzibah—should face this fact. All is now reconciled. Evil plans, vain illusions are dispelled; the past is past.

The drama of the Maules and Pyncheons allows Hawthorne to develop three wider ideas about family and heredity, which can be summarized as follows:

1. An evil deed may have far-reaching consequences.

2. Family pride and acquisitiveness are deplorable, whether or not they involve wrongdoing.

3. Family pride, even where not actively harmful, is absurdly out of place in the American context of rapid social change.

These notions, which for convenience may be labeled Evil, Lineage, and Impermanence, matter a good deal to Hawthorne. In *The Seven Gables* each is stated more than once, as for instance in the following quotations (taken respectively from the Preface, from comments by Holgrave, and from an interpolated observation by the author):

1. Evil: ". . . The wrongdoing of one generation lives into the successive ones, and . . . be-

comes a pure and uncontrollable mischief. . . ."

2. Lineage: "To plant a family! The idea is at the
bottom of most of the wrong and mischief
which men do."

3. Impermanence: "In this republican country,
amid the fluctuating waves of our social life,
somebody is always at the drowning point.
The tragedy is enacted with as continual a
repetition as that of a popular drama on a hol-
iday."

It is not surprising that such *dicta* should figure in Hawthorne's work since they were aspects of the history of his
own family. "The Fall of the House of Pyncheon," says
Austin Warren [in his *Rage for Order,* 1948], "was the
Hawthornes' fall." The first of Hawthorne's Salem ancestors, William Hathorne, and his son, John Hathorne, were
dynasts of dubious renown. As magistrates, they had
handed out harsh justice against the Quakers. A fellow
judge of John Hathorne, indeed, had sentenced a Quaker
named Thomas Maule to imprisonment in 1695. Three
years earlier, Judge Hathorne had played an active part
in the Salem witch trials. According to tradition, he had
been cursed by one of the victims, though in fact the curse
had been aimed at his colleague Nicholas Noyes, to whom
the accused woman said, "I am no more a witch, than you
are a wizard;—and if you take away my life, God will give
you blood to drink." In the introductory section of *The
Scarlet Letter,* Hawthorne wrote of John Hathorne:

> [He] made himself so conspicuous in the martyr-
> dom of the witches, that their blood may fairly
> be said to have left a stain upon him. . . . I
> know not whether these ancestors of mine be-
> thought themselves to repent, and ask pardon of
> Heaven for their cruelties; or whether they are
> now groaning under the heavy consequences of
> them, in another state of being. At all events, I,
> the present writer, as their representative, here-
> by take shame upon myself for their sakes, and
> pray that any curse incurred by them—as I have
> heard, and as the dreary and unprosperous con-
> dition of the race, for many a long year back,
> would argue to exist—may be now and hence-
> forth removed.

During the trials of 1692, John Hathorne and another
judge had arrested John English and his wife on charges
of witchcraft. The bad feeling that resulted between the
two families was patched over many years later through
the marriage of a grandson of Judge Hathorne with a
great-granddaughter of John English. The English house,
one of several substantial old homes in Salem that may
have served as a model for the House of the Seven Gables,
passed into the possession of a Hathorne. Grand but decaying, it stood empty in Hawthorne's youth, and was finally pulled down in 1833.

Other elements in the novel lie close to Hawthorne's heritage. The Pyncheon claim to the huge Indian tract in
Waldo County, Maine, had its counterpart in Hawthorne
family legend. From his great-uncle Ebenezer Hathorne,
the novelist heard a curiously mixed stock of anecdotes
and theories: a combination of pride in family genealogy

and of "the most arrant democracy." Like the reformer
Thomas Skidmore, Ebenezer believed that "nobody ought
to possess wealth longer than his own lifetime, and that
it should return to the people." Hawthorne himself,
though skeptical of radical proposals, was equivocally involved in them. "Brook Farmer," brother-in-law of the
transcendentalist bluestocking Elizabeth Peabody, contributor to the *Democratic Review,* avowed Democrat who
owed his appointment as "locofoco Surveyor" of the Port
of Salem to party favor—Hawthorne was well versed in
all the current arguments about privilege and egalitarianism. Great-uncle Hathorne's "arrant" views, and to some
extent those of Nathaniel himself, appear in Holgrave's
outburst to Phoebe Pyncheon:

> "Shall we never, never get rid of this Past? . . .
> It lies upon the Present like a giant's dead body!
> In fact, the case is just as if a young giant were
> compelled to waste all his strength in carrying
> about the corpse of the old giant, his grandfa-
> ther, who died a long while ago, and only needs
> to be decently buried. . . .

> "The truth is, that, once in every half century,
> at longest, a family should be merged into the
> great, obscure mass of humanity, and forget all
> about its ancestors. . . . "

Events in family history probably account for some of the
details in **"Peter Goldthwaite's Treasure"** (1838), the
short story in which Hawthorne lightly anticipates *The
Seven Gables* and, in particular, the novel's third theme,
Impermanence, i.e., the absurdity of delusions of grandeur. As for Phoebe, she is a version of the purity, femin-
ity, and cheerfulness that Hawthorne found in his own
bride, Sophia Peabody, whom he had nicknamed "Phoebe" in the early years of their marriage.

*The Seven Gables,* then, was an exercise in the arrangement of a cluster of conceptions which had an intimate significance for Hawthorne. Some critics have found it—in
comparison with *The Scarlet Letter*—a rather straggling,
episodic novel. Hawthorne himself might properly have
shared the view of more enthusiastic students that the
book is economical, ingenious, and structurally sound.
Though a far longer span of time is covered than in *The
Scarlet Letter,* the historical preliminaries are swiftly des-
patched. True, the tale of Alice Pyncheon, which is supposed to have been written by Holgrave, takes the narrative back again into the past. But unlike many of the plots
within plots casually inserted in the novels of Hawthorne's
day, this one can be defended as a deliberate device: it reveals the intensity of Holgrave's interest in the Maule-
Pyncheon history and points the contrast between Holgrave's magnanimity and the wickedness, under a similar
temptation, of his necromantic ancestor, Maule the carpenter. If it is hard to say who is the main character of the
novel, at any rate Hawthorne makes do with a very small
cast. Each character, except perhaps for Holgrave,
"stands" for something distinct. Apart from the brief railroad excursion of Clifford and Hepzibah, the whole action
is confined to the central setting: the House of the Seven
Gables built by Colonel Pyncheon on the land he has
wrested from the Maules. Here the Colonel dies, seated in
his high-backed chair in the parlor, under his own por-

trait. The scene is re-enacted near the end of the novel, in the almost identical death of Judge Jaffrey Pyncheon. Battered, fading, increasingly irrelevant to and estranged from the life of the street outside, the House symbolizes the fate of its owners. It nicely accommodates various subordinate symbols: Alice Pyncheon's harpsichord, unused and out of tune; Alice's exotic flowers, surviving in a neglected crevice; the ruined garden; the ludicrous inbred fowls that wander there; the brackish well that was once pure.

Yet though the House is a witness of terrible events, Hawthorne does not avail himself of the opportunity to endow it with sinister properties. There are no ghosts, or none whose presence is intrusive. Despite the wild words of Holgrave and Clifford—on the need to tear down, to cleanse by fire, and so on—Hawthorne avoids the melodramatic and lurid finale he could have contrived. There is no collapse, no conflagration. The House remains. It matters to the story, as the Mississippi matters in Twain's *Huckleberry Finn.* But like the Mississippi, it is ultimately no more than a witness, a physical fact. Human beings are the determinant. Holgrave and Phoebe can bring brightness to the House; Alice Pyncheon's flowers can still come to bloom. In the logic of the story, we must assume that the House will no longer be lived in. It can be left to disintegrate, slowly and naturally, like the actual Salem house of the English family.

This is Hawthorne's "prosperous close." Some critics think the last chapter of *The Seven Gables* as inappropriately jolly as the closing section of *Huckleberry Finn.* The denouement reminds one exasperated commentator [Rudolph Von Abele, in his *Death of the Artist,* 1955] of Artemus Ward's account of the "Osowatomie Brown" show:

> Tabloo—Old Brown on a platform, pintin upards, the staige lited up with red fire. Goddiss of Liberty also on platform, pintin upards. A dutchman in the orkestry warbles on a base drum. Curtin falls. Moosic by the band.

Hawthorne's final chapter may indeed be considered too "stagey." But whatever one's reservations about his last few pages, we may agree that the general effect was intended. Twain—to continue with the comparison, now that it has been introduced—interrupted the composition of *Huckleberry Finn* for a period of several years: Hawthorne wrote *The Seven Gables* in a single undistracted five-month spell. Twain often improvised from one sequence to the next: Hawthorne traced the ramifications of his germinal idea with scrupulous care. We never feel that he has taken himself by surprise, any more than he expects or attempts to surprise the reader. Where everything is so contrived, so fore-known, we do not even ask that the characters should express astonishment. Nor do they: when Holgrave discloses to Phoebe, his betrothed, that he is really named Maule, she reacts as though she has known this all along. In Henry James's phrase [in his *Hawthorne,* 1879], "Hawthorne always knew perfectly what he was about."

True, there is the famous Hawthorne ambiguity, or what Yvor Winters has called [in his *In Defense of Reason,* 1947] his "formula of alternative possibilities." This may lead him into, or help to conceal, certain dilemmas; I will deal with these later. But in intent and in effect, the formula does not lead to mystification. On the contrary, it codifies and clarifies. Broadly speaking, Hawthorne's method is to provide two main sets of explanations, a natural and a supernatural. Thus, in *The House of the Seven Gables,* the supernatural explanation is that Maule's curse accounts for the death of no less than four Pyncheons, from the Colonel down to the Judge, and brings about subsidiary phenomena such as the tainting of Maule's well. The alternative, "natural" possibility is that the Pyncheons have a hereditary tendency to death by apoplexy, heightened, perhaps, by fits of guilty conscience: a belief in the validity of the legendary curse may reinforce their congenital weakness. Affairs *seem* to be shrouded in mystery; statements are qualified by a host of "perhapses" and "possiblys." Yet the main alternatives are clear. Hawthorne is at pains to supply each set with adequate supporting evidence, so that each is self-contained and self-consistent. The reader may, of course, complain that the result is irritating if not bewildering. Each alternative is alluded to often enough to acquire status. If one must be discarded, is this not a wasteful technique? The answer, I think, is that Hawthorne wishes us to entertain both sets of explanations, so far as we can. They are meant to support rather than clash with one another. They are not so much alternative as complementary possibilities.

In Hawthorne's eyes, *The House of the Seven Gables* would meet such a test: indeed, would be admirably suited to his characteristic formula. Fact and fancy overlap. As Holgrave tells Phoebe, he shares Hepzibah's conviction that all the calamities of the Pyncheons began with the quarrel with the "wizard" Matthew Maule. He believes it "not as a superstition, however, but as proved by unquestionable facts." Holgrave and Phoebe represent modernity. They are almost free from the operations of the curse. Perhaps Phoebe is entirely free; she asks Holgrave how he can believe "what is so very absurd." But though he lives in a more rational and optimistic moral climate than his forebears, Holgrave is linked to them by possessing a mesmeric gift akin to their talent for necromancy. Mesmerism is both a new discovery (described by Clifford, in his hectic conversation with the old gentleman in the train, as one of the "harbingers of a better era") and an ancient potency. A neat double explanation, then, for Hawthorne; and with the additional advantage of enabling him to introduce one of his favorite parallels—that of the artist and the necromancer. Art, Hawthorne likes to hint, frequently has a tinge of the black art; there is something wicked, or at the very least something deficient, in the cold scrutinizing detachment of the artist-intellectual. It is a quality which mars Holgrave: a quality for which Hawthorne supplies a genealogy, so to speak, in Holgrave's Maule ancestry. In becoming a normal, happy, married man, thanks to Phoebe, he can leave behind a heritage of chilly separateness.

The framework of *The Seven Gables* allows Hawthorne to explore two human types that held a particular fascination for him. They might be called the impotent and the overweening. For the one, typified by Clifford and Hepzibah Pyncheon, he expresses a remarkably sensitive sympathy. For the other, typified by Jaffrey Pyncheon, he conveys an almost ferocious scorn. In these character-studies, Hawthorne ranges far beyond the mechanisms of the plot. He is a connoisseur of the broken spirit, the vain regret, the self-indulgence, and all the other subterfuges of failure. It has often been pointed out that he is more interested in adversity than in prosperity. The metaphor he employs to describe social change is of *drowning*. Its effect is to exclude those who are rising in the social scale; for in water, the best one can hope for is merely to stay afloat. A robuster sense of the beneficent features of change invades his argument. He is whimsical, even jocular, in depicting Hepzibah's transformation from patrician lady to plebian woman. The situation is, he suggests, somewhat ludicrous. Nevertheless it is a "tragedy" of the everyday. We are much more sorry for Hepzibah than amused by her; and there is a genuine pathos in poor, bemused, ineffectual Clifford. The shock of their exposure to the outside world is beautifully conveyed in their railroad excursion—half flight, half liberation, and hopeless in either case.

Jaffrey Pyncheon is a more solid, more memorable portrait, belonging firmly to the province of the novelist, where Clifford and Hepzibah suggest the essayist side of Hawthorne. Pyncheon is a classic type. He is the kind of man we are warned against in the Bible (Luke 20:46):

> Beware of the scribes, which desire to walk in long robes, and love greetings in the markets, and the highest seats in the synagogues, and chief rooms at feasts.

Hawthorne may feel uncertain whether to lament or to welcome the American social flux: he is quite certain that the busy, pompous, carnal, office-seeking Pyncheons are detestable, like all such persons, whether or not they have been actively wicked. Note the animus in Hawthorne's assessments of the Judge:

> He had built himself a country seat within a few miles of his native town, and there spent such portions of his time as could be spared from public service in the display of every grace and virtue—as a newspaper phrased it, on the eve of an election-befitting the Christian, the good citizen, the horticulturist, and the gentleman.

> As is customary with the rich, when they aim at the honors of a republic, he apologized, as it were, to the people, for his wealth, prosperity, and elevated station, by a free and hearty manner towards those who knew him; putting off the more of his dignity in due proportion with the humbleness of the man whom he saluted; and thereby proving a haughty consciousness of his advantages as irrefragably as if he had marched forth preceded by a troop of lackeys to clear the way.

> The sudden death of so prominent a member of the social world as the Honorable Judge Jaffrey Pyncheon created a sensation (at least, in the circles more immediately connected with the deceased), which had hardly quite subsided in a fortnight.

These comments reveal a passion of distaste and a choleric mocking precision which are unusual in Hawthorne. No doubt they owe something to his own painful experience in being ousted from the surveyorship of Salem through the unsavory maneuvers of the Whig politician Charles Upham; and perhaps they throw light upon Hawthorne's complicated private defenses against worldly success. Whatever the origins of his feeling, he establishes and then destroys Judge Pyncheon with an expert relish. Villainous, vainglorious, and ultimately unimportant, Jaffrey Pyncheon embodies Hawthorne's three principal themes—Evil, Lineage, Impermanence—associated with family and heredity. There is a glittering, sardonic eloquence in the justly celebrated chapter which enumerates the various engagements that are being missed by Jaffrey, struck dead in the parlor of the old House. It is the revenge of the impotent against the overweening.

*The House of the Seven Gables* is remarkable, too, for a group of insights relating to the ideas of time and reality. Hawthorne endeavors to bring his story out into the daylight of the present day—or "an epoch not very remote from the present day": the era of railroads, daguerreotypes, "temperance lecturers," and "community men." Ned Higgins, the child with the passion for gingerbread, and Old Uncle Venner are firmly located in the *now* of Hawthorne's narrative, at the most commonplace level. The contemporariness of Holgrave and Phoebe is insisted upon (though it is a little hard to imagine this unaffected country girl obeying "the impulse of Nature," as Hawthorne drily says she does, "by attending a metaphysical or philosophical lecture"; here she sounds more like Sophia Peabody). Yet the character whose responses to *now* are most acutely analyzed is Clifford; and Clifford, like Rip Van Winkle or some victim of a time machine, is a person from another generation. Unjustly imprisoned for a crime he did not commit, Clifford has been in jail so long that he has missed half a lifetime. Returned to living after thirty years, he sees the world with the eyes of a boy: "his life seemed to be standing still at a period little in advance of childhood"; and in his dreams "he invariably played the part of a child, or a very young man." When he gazes from the arched window of the House of the Seven Gables, everything that has changed in the thirty-year interval startles him. Each time he hears the train approach and catches a glimpse of it, "flashing a brief transit across the extremity of the street," he is taken by surprise. The "terrible energy" it implies—so novel, and in such contrast to his own passivity—alarms and defeats him. Clifford cannot cope with the present. For Hawthorne, too, in this novel, despite the jolly emphasis upon nowness, the present is either rather gross and cruel—witness the callous gossip of the street—or else, and above all, unreal. Hawthorne is wonderfully perceptive in his handling of Clifford, and brilliant in suggesting what the railroad signifies, not merely to Clifford. It symbolizes velocity, disturbance, dislocation. Other contemporaries were struck by the oddity of the new mode of travel: they could hardly fail to be. Emerson noted in his journal:

> Dreamlike travelling on the railroad. The towns through which I pass . . . make no distinct impression. They are like pictures on a wall. The more, that you can read all the way in the car a French novel.

Hawthorne makes a train journey serve as a more astonishing confrontation with the present; for Clifford and Hepzibah:

> Everything was unfixed from its agelong rest, and moving at whirlwind speed in a direction opposite to their own.

The journey stimulates Clifford to a wild flight of fancy: a glimpse of a future in which life has become completely nomadic. This is an extreme revulsion from the past-haunted torpor of the House of the Seven Gables. It is only a momentary vision. The future is blank to him. But the present is equally unreal. To Clifford—and to the rest of us, Hawthorne seems to say—"this visionary and impalpable Now, . . . if you look closely at it, is nothing."

In other words, *The House of the Seven Gables* is a rich and closely textured epitome of themes that preoccupied Hawthorne. Even if one does not care for the general texture of Hawthorne's prose, or for some of the elaborate figures and set-piece passages, one should add that there are many incidental remarks which remind us how acute his novelist's intelligence could be. Here is an example:

> A recluse, like Hepzibah, usually displays remarkable frankness, and at least temporary affability, on being absolutely cornered, and brought to the point of personal intercourse; like the angel whom Jacob wrestled with, she is ready to bless you when once overcome.

*The Seven Gables,* then, is a work of high interest, of which Hawthorne might justifiably have been proud.

But it raises questions that deserve a closer investigation. The qualities that have been listed are formidable. The crucial question is this: do they form a satisfactory whole? Or do they weaken one another? Does Hawthorne's formula provide an essential structure, or does it lead him into absurdities? Do we, in the final analysis, admire him for partial or oblique perceptions which, though no doubt envisaged in his structural scheme, remain somewhat extraneous, or which could better have been stated by other means? In his interweaving of natural and supernatural, environment and heredity, present and past, does he display a wise refusal to commit himself, or a rather sluggish reluctance to think clearly?

Let us consider the interior logic of Maule's curse. Colonel Pyncheon's motives are certainly mixed: he covets the property of the alleged wizard. But there is no indication that he feels he has sent an innocent man to his death. At the moment of being cursed, Pyncheon's countenance is "undismayed." [Daniel Hoffman, in his *Form and Fable in American Fiction,* 1961] contends that Matthew Maule was entirely innocent of the charge of witchcraft: it is his *ghost* and his posterity who become witches. This is a way round an awkwardness in the plot. But even if conceivable, the theory accepts the existence of sinister forces: forces quite as evil as those typified by the covetous Colonel Pyncheon. If so, the Pyncheon descendants are as much victims as aggressors; and their sins begin to seem correspondingly less black. Is it not plausible to assume, though, that the first Maule did have temperamental oddities which, in the fevered atmosphere of the time, laid him open to the accusation of wizardry? And that Pyncheon,

not the only one to suspect him, may have believed the accusation? Or that, indeed, Maule *was* a witch, who reveals his diabolical gift by encompassing Pyncheon's death in the manner prophesied? Hawthorne mentions the remote possibility that Pyncheon might have been strangled. If so, presumably by Matthew Maule's son? But whether by family vengeance or by necromancy, was Colonel Pyncheon's death not enough to end the curse, which as spoken by Matthew Maule seems directed only at the Colonel—God will give *him* blood to drink—on the principle of a life for a life? No: we learn later from the tale of Alice Pyncheon, which Holgrave has written, that the curse will not be lifted until the claim to the House of the Seven Gables has been surrendered by the Pyncheons, even if the malediction has to last a thousand years. We learn also from Holgrave that the Maules have developed quite unmistakable necromantic powers. The grandson and namesake of the "wizard" casts a spell of "sinister or evil potency" upon the blameless Alice Pyncheon and brings about her death through his own malevolence. The wizard's carpenter son, whom Colonel Pyncheon has engaged to build the new House of the Seven Gables upon Maule's plot of ground, exacts another revenge. He manages to get hold of and conceal within the House the parchment deed entitling the Pyncheons to their huge tract of Indian land. Whether or not the title was honestly secured, they are deprived of it by the Maules. Old Matthew's vengeance would seem dreadfully complete—indeed, excessively so.

What of the complementary, "natural" set of explanations? Suppose that Hawthorne claims nothing more than the hereditary transmission of certain characteristics, notably a hypnotic talent among the Maules and an apoplectic tendency among the Pyncheons (possibly intensified, as we have said, by accumulated superstitious anxieties). This view is offered near the end of the novel by Holgrave in reassuring Phoebe that Jaffrey Pyncheon has died a "natural" death:

> "This mode of death has been an idiosyncrasy with his family, for generations past; not often occurring, indeed, but, when it does occur, usually attacking individuals about the Judge's time of life, and generally in the tension of some mental crisis, or, perhaps, in an access of wrath. Old Maule's prophecy was probably founded on a knowledge of this physical predisposition in the Pyncheon race."

It represents an ingenious interpretative modulation. And, as Daniel Hoffman points out, we may fall back upon the theory that the Maules have ceased to count: the curse has turned inward, so that the Pyncheons destroy themselves. Even so, some doubts linger, at any rate for me. It does not matter much whether aptitudes such as those of the Maules and disabilities such as those of the Pyncheons are in fact transmissible, or whether hypnotists can actually exercise so formidable an influence over their subjects. In Hawthorne's day these were plausible suppositions; and some years later, the "medicated" novels of Oliver Wendell Holmes were to place quite as great a strain upon the reader's credulity. But Holmes's aim is to raise an issue that Hawthorne passes over: namely, whether people ought to be held responsible for traits they have inherited.

In what "natural" sense can the repeated deaths of the Pyncheons be regarded as a proof of their iniquity? And if Holgrave's final explanation is acceptable to him as well as to us, ought he and Phoebe not to consider the chance that their children may inherit the Pyncheon weakness?

One may answer that such conjectures make heavy going of Hawthorne's romance, with its deprecating, half-sober, half-magical mood; and that it was against just this sort of quibbling that he claimed immunity in designating his story as a romance, not a novel. But then, his alternatives are so carefully documented that he positively invites inspection, with something of the candor of a stage magician anxious that there be no deception. His elaborate scheme seems to raise as many difficulties as it solves, and to raise them unavoidably even if one would like to dismiss them. To me, the alternatives weaken instead of reinforcing one another.

This is partly a consequence of the interfusion of the three themes—Evil, Lineage, and Impermanence. The trouble is that the first two conflict with the third. Nor do the first two, Evil and Lineage, co-exist altogether comfortably. Evil, for Hawthorne, is an abstract force, working "inevitably," wreaking "uncontrollable" mischief. It is stylized, impersonal: something asserted, to be received without demonstration as a "truth." Abstractness is not necessarily an inappropriate mode for a certain kind of fiction; and indeed Hawthorne's story seeks to demonstrate its operation circumstantially. But he proceeds as if not wholly sure what to do with it. One clue is provided by Holgrave's statement, halfway through the story, that in the House of the Seven Gables, "through a portion of three centuries, there has been perpetual remorse of conscience, a constantly defeated hope, strife amongst kindred, various misery, a strange form of death, dark suspicion, unspeakable disgrace. . . ." A *portion of three centuries*. What this means, strictly, is that the woes of the Pyncheons embrace a few years of the seventeenth century, the whole of the eighteenth, and about half of the nineteenth. If Holgrave spoke of this span as "a century and a half," it would have a less awesome effect. Hawthorne is anxious to dwell upon the enormity of the Pyncheons' iniquities and misfortunes: they must entail prolonged duration—more prolonged, ideally, than the evidence of his own plot allows, and much more prolonged and catastrophic than the actual family history upon which he draws. The notion of Evil is meant to confer solemnity upon the less abstract notion of Lineage. To some extent it does, as when Hepzibah implores Jaffrey Pyncheon not to torment her enfeebled brother:

> "Then, why, should you do this cruel, cruel thing? So mad a thing, that I know not whether to call it wicked! Alas, Cousin Jaffrey, this hard and grasping spirit has run in our blood these two hundred years [*note again the slight stretching of duration*]. You are but doing over again, in another shape, what your ancestor before you did, and sending down to your posterity the curse inherited from him!"

Here we are ready to believe that Hepzibah, at any rate, believes in the curse; just as we see nothing odd in Clifford's allusion, when he and his sister are running away from their hateful kinsman, to Christian and Hopeful escaping from Giant Despair. Such attributions grow out of the fiber of the story. Too often, however, Evil operates as a didactic distortion. Hawthorne then is in danger of lapsing into copybook morality.

He is also in danger of bringing in too much solemnity, too much direness. Lineage itself tends to become an abstract notion, a subject for sermonizing language. We are assured in the Preface, for example, of "the folly of tumbling down an avalanche of ill-gotten gold, or real estate, on the heads of an unfortunate posterity, thereby to maim and crush them, until the accumulated mass shall be scattered abroad in its original atoms." Pulpit talk of this kind denies us the understanding we need of *why* men strive to plant a family, and of the mixture of good with bad in their motives. In harping upon the past, posterity is left out of the picture. The future may be blank: men nevertheless try to chart it, if only in narrow and self-regarding ways by ensuring the perpetuation of their own name through the prosperity of their family. In emphasizing the harm done by Lineage, Hawthorne fails to make any distinction between reasonable and inordinate family pride. He writes lyrically of the redeeming power of love; and though there is no mention of a marriage ceremony between Holgrave and Phoebe, we must presume that they do marry and are likely to produce children.

This brings us again to the problem of the conclusion of **The House of the Seven Gables,** which critics have fastened upon as the book's chief weakness. Holgrave, the despiser of Lineage, becomes wealthy along with the surviving Pyncheons. The Judge's handsome fortune passes to Clifford, Hepzibah, and Phoebe (and thence to Holgrave) through the sudden death, at almost the same moment as his father, of the Judge's son, who has been traveling abroad. None of the heirs expresses dismay at the tainted inheritance. Even before it comes their way, Holgrave, in declaring his love for Phoebe, tells her:

> "I have a presentiment that, hereafter, it will be my lot to set out trees, to make fences—perhaps, even, in due time, to build a house for another generation. . . ."

Shortly afterward, when the inhabitants of the House of the Seven Gables are discussing their new-found happiness and wealth and are about to remove to the Judge's "elegant country seat," Holgrave speaks so much like a propertied conservative that Phoebe teases him for so sudden a change of face.

In defense of Hawthorne, it can be said that he too is teasing Holgrave. He has already indicated that Holgrave's radical opinions, though generous in impulse, are unsound. Holgrave now makes the discovery for himself. Moreover, he does so not because his bride has come into money but simply because he has fallen in love. Love laughs at doctrinaires no less than locksmiths. The situation has a wry quality reminiscent of the ending of Henry James's *The Bostonians*. Holgrave's explanation for his presentiment that he will build a house for another generation is: "The world owes all its onward impulses to men ill at ease. The happy man inevitably confines himself within ancient limits."

The defense is inadequate. It forces us to reconsider the total picture of Holgrave and to see that he is a mere Identi-Kit of Hawthornian types. Their disparate aspects—artist-necromancer, transcendentalist come-outer, resilient Yankee—are shrewdly observed but do not merge into a recognizable human being. His retreat into conservatism follows the dictates of a particular Hawthorne theorem (and perhaps corresponds to Hawthorne's own experience in love), but at the expense of the whole movement of the book, which should run successively through Evil to Lineage to Impermanence, like the movement of American history itself. Instead, Impermanence is discarded in favor of a revised, sunny version of Lineage for which we have not been prepared.

Much of the damage could have been avoided if Hawthorne had made the daylight of the final chapter less broad and bland. He provides prizes for everybody, including "the prettiest little yellowish-brown cottage you ever saw" for Uncle Venner and a lavish tip for little Ned Higgins. One senses the author's desire to polish the story off. The pace quickens to a trot. Previous indications that Hawthorne might have been toying with the idea of exposing poor Clifford to further indignities—because of his fugitive dash at the time of his cousin's death—come to nothing. There are signs of carelessness. Thus, in this chapter, the son of Judge Pyncheon who dies so conveniently is described as his only child. In Chapter XV, however, there is a brief reference to "an expensive and dissipated son," disinherited by the Judge, who has died some years before. Hawthorne may have meant "only *surviving* child." The suspicion though is that he had forgotten the previous reference in his haste to finish; and that it would not have lodged in his memory because he was not interested in the Judge's lineal posterity, except to arrange that there would be none. Lineage for Hawthorne is confined to the past until, abruptly, he has to say what will happen to those who are still alive. His answer is not bizarrely at variance with certain ingredients of the story; but it evades rather than resolves. The irony of Holgrave's reversal, unlike James's climax in *The Bostonians,* is fatigued and inconclusive.

As for the third theme, Impermanence, this might seem to be perfectly expressed in the closing scene of *The Seven Gables.* Clifford and Hepzibah have suffered much; the past can never be entirely obliterated for them. Yet when a coach arrives to take them away from the House of the Seven Gables, "as often proves to be the case, at moments when we ought to palpitate with sensibility—Clifford and Hepzibah bade a final farewell to the abode of their forefathers with hardly more emotion than if they had made it their arrangement to return thither at tea-time." If the theme were handled with such subtlety throughout, the result would be beyond criticism. One facet, the vanity of human wishes, has a genuine solemnity. Death mocks ambition: the Judge is remembered by his associates for only a couple of weeks.

But the main feature of Impermanence in Hawthorne's scheme of things is less bleak. What strikes him, and us, is the past-denying briskness of American life. Old wrongs fade into oblivion. Old pretensions turn into absurdity.

The travelers on the train symbolize a social order in which nothing stays put. Like Peter Goldthwaite's treasure, the Pyncheon land-claim is a comical anachronism and has long been so. The actual settlers "would have laughed at the idea of any man's asserting a right . . . to the lands which they or their fathers had wrested from the wild hand of nature by their own sturdy toil." Morality becomes blurred. In some actual situations of Hawthorne's era, such as the Anti-Rent War of the 1840's in New York, each side can believe it is in the right and passionately says so. But one feels that landlord and tenant alike also have a slightly bad conscience. Indignation and buffoonery are curiously commingled in the controversy.

Hawthorne knows this, and has as much difficulty as other Americans in making sense of the national development. He knows that, however fascinating the old legend of the Hawthorne curse, it is a picturesque and rather thrilling *excuse* for the seediness which has overtaken one family among others in a declining town. Why, then, all the bother about Evil and Lineage? Why alternate between the portentous and the playful—for this, surely, is what baffles the reader of *The Seven Gables,* not the alternation between supernatural and natural details of the plot? Why pretend to a seriousness that has to be imposed? Perhaps because otherwise Hawthorne would have no way of reducing the social flux to coherent order: because, like William Faulkner, he sought meaning in a tenuous heritage he could neither wholly admire nor wholly deplore. Each added a letter to his name (Hathorne : Hawthorne; Falkner : Faulkner) to differentiate himself from his ancestry. Each liked to think of himself as an ordinary citizen; each suspected his own introspective activity. Each grappled nobly with the problem of relating an unsatisfactory past to an unsatisfactory, yet fantastically altered, present. Each denied discontinuity in a search for significance. Each resorted to a wide and sometimes incompatible range of literary modes, Hawthorne with more diffidence but with an equal and almost staggering ambition.

To me, *The Seven Gables* is a flawed book, whose strengths are somewhat incidental to its plot. They lie in Hawthorne's acute response to the victims of social change—Hepzibah and Clifford—and to the complacent bullies—Jaffrey Pyncheon and his kind—who come close to committing the Unpardonable Sin but who do not know there is such a thing. Pyncheon is perhaps the most fully realized of all Hawthorne's characters. He is more substantial, for instance, than Chillingworth in *The Scarlet Letter.* He would have regarded the legend of Maule's curse as a piece of nonsense, to be left to more miscellaneous and divided characters such as Holgrave. And that, indeed, is what Hawthorne has done. Holgrave is left with the necromancy, and with sundry other components of the author's heroic, hesitant effort to make literature out of the proposition that happy families, in common with happy countries, have no history, backward or forward. (pp. 79-101)

*Marcus Cunliffe, " 'The House of the Seven Gables'," in* Hawthorne Centenary Essays, *edited by Roy Harvey Pearce, Ohio State University Press, 1964, pp. 79-101.*

## Frederick Crews   (essay date 1966)

[*Crews is an American educator and critic known for his psychoanalytical approach to literature. In the following excerpt, he provides a Freudian analysis of* The House of the Seven Gables, *asserting that Judge Pyncheon represents a hated and feared father figure at the center of the plot. He also finds autobiographical implications in Hawthorne's resolution of the story.*]

[*The House of the Seven Gables*] can engage the reader successfully either in its love story, its picturesque Salem history, its Yankee humor, its romantic legend, its modern realism, its melodrama, or even its few moments of Gothic terror. Only when he tries to find aesthetic order in these motley effects does the critic begin to see that there is something fundamentally contradictory in Hawthorne's romance. Why does the announced moral purpose of showing that "the wrong-doing of one generation lives into the successive ones, and . . . becomes a pure and uncontrollable mischief" get dissolved in the "dear home-loveliness and satisfaction" that Sophia Hawthorne discerned in the final pages? Is it because Hawthorne's true intention was comic and sentimental all along? But if so, how do we account for the primitive intensity with which both Hawthorne and his "good" characters seem to despise and fear the villain of the story, Judge Jaffrey Pyncheon? Why is Holgrave, the daguerreotypist, author, and social radical, represented as being both self-sufficient and in desperate need of marriage to the busy little conformist, Phoebe Pyncheon? Why does the mere death of Jaffrey Pyncheon, rather than any conscious moral penance, free the modern Pyncheons from the real or metaphorical curse that has dogged their family for two centuries? Why does Hawthorne feel obliged to dwell whimsically, but at disconcerting length, on a number of largely trivial symbols—a house, an elm, a well, a spring, a mirror, some posies, a garden, some hens, some bees? Why must he apologize over and over for being tedious or inconsistent in tone? Why does he use his plot for an extensive yet partly covert review of all the scandals and weaknesses in his own family history? And why, in his avowed attempt at writing a popular romance, does he give such prominence to two characters, Hepzibah and Clifford Pyncheon, for whom nearly all the possibilities of life are already exhausted?

In order to take a sufficiently inclusive view of *The House of the Seven Gables* we must both examine and look beyond Hawthorne's surface emphasis. The book is not a diabolical exercise in deceit; Hawthorne means, or would like to mean, what he says about his characters and their doings. But his deeper hints of characterization, his imagery, and the direction of his plot all bespeak an overriding concern with an unstated theme. The ending, which strikes the modern reader as morally complacent, is in fact psychologically urgent, an ingeniously ambiguous gesture of expiation for a dominant idea that has been warping the book's direction. When the obsessed Holgrave, the character who most nearly resembles Hawthorne-as-artist, swears to Phoebe that he has already turned conservative for her sake, he is making a declaration on behalf of the entire romance. *The House of the Seven Gables* "turns conservative" as a way of evading its deepest implications. . . . (pp. 172-73)

In one respect it is generally agreed that this romance has an autobiographical significance. The Pyncheon forebears, whose history opens the plot and is resumed at several points, are unmistakable representatives of the Hathornes; hence the mixture of nostalgia and resentment in their portrayal. Hawthorne's customary charges against his ancestors—of religious hypocrisy, social tyranny, and moral abuse—are leveled against the Pyncheons, and specific family shames such as the Salem witch hangings are exploited for the announced theme of inherited guilt. The decline of the Pyncheons is half-seriously attributed to a curse which is closely modeled on one that the accused witch Sarah Good supposedly laid upon John Hathorne (really upon Nicholas Noyes). And the disinherited modern Pyncheons resemble Hawthorne in regretting the gradual loss of the authority under which their family's historic crimes were perpetrated. In this light it is significant that the plot works toward a symbolic expiation and a reversal of bad fortune for the sympathetic Pyncheons. Hawthorne can laugh at the worthless "eastern claims" of the Pyncheon-Hathornes, but his satire is blunted by the fact that Hepzibah and Clifford come into easy circumstances, while the "guilty" remnant of Puritan days, the arch-villain Jaffrey Pyncheon, is conveniently and mysteriously put to death. The providential ending, in other words, amounts to a wishful settling of old scores on Hawthorne's part.

The very fact that Jaffrey Pyncheon *is* a villain—one who is treated even less generously than Roger Chillingworth [in *The Scarlet Letter*]—deserves pondering in view of the meaning of ancestral tyrants throughout Hawthorne's fiction. Jaffrey is a slightly attenuated reincarnation of the original Colonel Pyncheon, the family's father; and the entire romance prior to his death is oppressed with a sense of fierce authority and inhibition. Jaffrey's effect on his cousins is exactly that of Colonel Pyncheon's portrait, which, with its "stern, immitigable features," acts as "the Evil Genius of his family," ensuring that "no good thoughts or purposes could ever spring up and blossom" under his gaze. By now we might feel entitled to surmise from such phrases that Jaffrey's role in *The House of the Seven Gables* is paternal, and that the two sets of characters who survive him are symbolically his children. There is in fact more than sufficient evidence for this reading. At present, however, let us rest content with the observation that Jaffrey's death is the central event of the plot, enabling one couple to have a euphoric escape and another couple to marry and become rich. Nor should we omit the effect of Jaffrey's death on Hawthorne himself. Whether or not Jaffrey is recognized as a father figure, the reader must surely acknowledge the clogged passion, the vindictive pleasure, expressed in that extraordinary chapter (18) which is given over to a fearful taunting of Jaffrey's corpse.

A mixture of awe and hatred is discernible through the entire rendering of Judge Pyncheon. His villainy is separated from his conscience by layers of self-esteem and public honor which seem to impress Hawthorne despite his moral disapproval of them. For Hawthorne as for Clifford and Hepzibah, Jaffrey is an imminent presence, an unspecified threat, rather than an active criminal. While he is alive his specific guilt can only be suggested in an elaborate, highly tentative metaphor. In some forgotten nook of the "stately edifice" of an important man's character, says Hawthorne,

> may lie a corpse, half decayed, and still decaying, and diffusing its death-scent all through the palace! The inhabitant will not be conscious of it, for it has long been his daily breath! Neither will the visitors, for they smell only the rich odors which the master sedulously scatters through the palace . . . Now and then, perchance, comes in a seer, before whose sadly gifted eye the whole structure melts into thin air, leaving only the hidden nook, the bolted closet, . . . or the deadly hole under the pavement, and the decaying corpse within. Here, then, we are to seek the true emblem of the man's character, and of the deed which gives whatever reality it possesses to his life. And, beneath the show of a marble palace, that pool of stagnant water, foul with many impurities, and, perhaps, tinged with blood,—that secret abomination, above which, possibly, he may say his prayers, without remembering it,—is this man's miserable soul!

Hawthorne makes it sufficiently clear that Jaffrey's case is being described here, yet the deviousness and Gothic gruesomeness of the accusation show a reluctance to approach the matter very closely. The metaphor, in declaring that only the sadly gifted eye of the seer can perceive Jaffrey's real nature, encourages us to look for repressed guilt or be left with specious appearances; yet Hawthorne himself is less willing than formerly to explain the nature and operation of that guilt. Even in death Jaffrey remains inscrutable and terrifying, resistant to the autopsy of motives that Hawthorne does not yet feel ready to undertake.

We do, of course, finally learn the exact circumstances that make Hawthorne "almost venture to say . . . that a daily guilt might have been acted by [Jaffrey], continually renewed . . . without his necessarily and at every moment being aware of it." Jaffrey has robbed his uncle, named Clifford; his uncle, witnessing the deed, has consequently died of shock; and Jaffrey has framed his cousin, young Clifford Pyncheon, for this supposed murder. Thus the ex-convict Clifford is, in the sense of Hawthorne's metaphor, Jaffrey's "corpse"—or, to use another word that is much emphasized, his "ghost." In this light the manner of Jaffrey's own death becomes ironically appropriate. As Alfred H. Marks persuasively argues [in his "Who Killed Judge Pyncheon?" *PMLA,* LXXI (June 1956)], Hawthorne implies that Jaffrey's mysterious death is caused by the unexpected sight of the "ghost" Clifford Pyncheon. It is likely that Jaffrey dies in the same way as his uncle. A Clifford, in this event, has caused the death of Jaffrey after Jaffrey has caused the death of a Clifford—a symmetry of justice reminiscent of **"Roger Malvin's Burial."**

To mention **"Roger Malvin's Burial,"** however, is to measure the distance Hawthorne has traveled from the early 1830's. Jaffrey's guilt, unlike Reuben Bourne's, is never rendered in terms of observable behavior; at the moment

of his death he is as imposing and impenetrable as ever. It would seem that Hawthorne is more anxious to avoid him than to understand him. Surely it is meaningful that Jaffrey dies offstage through no one's intention, and is only gingerly approached in death by the morbidly scornful narrator. We are nearing the strange world of the unfinished romances, where figures of authority receive sudden outbursts of unexplained authorial hatred and are savagely killed, not by their antagonists, but by "innocent" mischances of plotting. Filial obsession, in other words, is beginning to destroy objective characterization and moral interest. [The critic adds in a footnote: "The privacy of Hawthorne's filial concern may be gauged from another piece of veiled family biography. Jaffrey's death is immediately, we might almost say causally, followed by the death by cholera, in a foreign port, of his last direct heir. Hawthorne's own father died of a fever (first reported to be cholera) in Surinam—a fact that could hardly have been generally known to readers of *The House of the Seven Gables.* Thus Hawthorne stamps a paternal significance on Judge Pyncheon not for any instructive purpose, but because that is what secret fantasy demands."]

Yet in a cryptic way *The House of the Seven Gables* deals extensively with moral and psychological affairs. Its "necromancies," we are told, may one day find their true meaning within "modern psychology." In various ways Hawthorne allows us to see the entire historical, social, and symbolic framework of the romance as pertaining to the question of individual guilt. The focal symbol of the House is endowed from the opening page with "a human countenance," and the struggle for possession of it follows familiar Hawthornian lines. The falsely accused wizard Matthew Maule has not been simply executed by his enemy, Colonel Pyncheon; he has been incorporated into the subsequent life of the House. The new structure "would include the home of the dead and buried wizard, and would thus afford the ghost of the latter a kind of privilege to haunt its new apartments. . . ." Like the more strictly figurative "ruined wall" of *The Scarlet Letter,* the Pyncheon estate embodies a mental condition in which an uneasy re-enactment of guilt will be made necessary by the effort to avoid responsibility for that guilt. For all its political and social ramifications, the Maule-Pyncheon antagonism is chiefly a metaphor of imperfect repression.

This imperfect repression is the agent of all the ironic justice in *The House of the Seven Gables.* Every tyrant is psychologically at the mercy of his victim; or, as Hawthorne puts it in his notebook, "All slavery is reciprocal." The rule is first applied to the original Colonel Pyncheon, who dies while inaugurating the House he has built on the executed Matthew Maule's property. It is clear that the Colonel's "curse" of susceptibility to sudden death is nothing other than his guilt toward Maule. The pattern is repeated for Gervayse Pyncheon in the story told by Holgrave; this Pyncheon's greed makes him tacitly co-operate when the second Matthew Maule, supposedly in exchange for a valuable document, takes mesmeric control over his daughter and subsequently causes her death. And if Marks's theory is correct, Jaffrey Pyncheon is similarly enslaved to the oppressed Clifford, who is able to cause Jaffrey's death merely by entering his field of vision. In all these cases it is bad conscience, rather than arbitrary plotting on Hawthorne's part, that has exacted punishment for abuses of power.

It is not possible, however, to say that perfect justice is done. If the authoritarian characters suffer from a secret *malaise* and eventually come to grief, they nevertheless have their full stomachs and public dignity for compensation; revenge is sudden and therefore incomplete. The meek victims, by contrast, are in continual misery (if they survive at all) until the reversal occurs, and even then they retain their internalized sense of persecution. Hepzibah and Clifford, who are presented as figures of infantile innocence, are more pathetic in trying to enjoy their freedom after Jaffrey's death than in their former state of intimidation. "For, what other dungeon is so dark as one's own heart! What jailer so inexorable as one's self!" These sentences, applied to two characters who have done nothing wrong and indeed have been virtually incapable of feeling temptation, may remind us that Hawthorne's focus is not on moral guilt but on a broader phenomenon of psychological tyranny. The very prominence of Hepzibah and Clifford in the plot, along with the somewhat ponderous emphasis on the wasting-away of the Pyncheon energies from generation to generation, suggests that impotence rather than guilt may be Hawthorne's true theme.

I mean the term *impotence* in both a social and sexual sense. It is implied that in some way the Pyncheons have become effete by continuing to deny the claims of the vigorous and plebeian Maules. We could say that a failure of adaptation to modern democratic conditions has left the Pyncheons socially and economically powerless. Clearly, however, this failure has a sexual dimension. Not the least of the Maules' secret privileges is to "haunt . . . the chambers into which future bridegrooms were to lead their brides"—a fairly direct reference to some interference with normal sexuality. Just as denial of the earthy Maule element in society leads eventually to a loss of social power, so the same denial in emotional nature—symbolized by refusal to intermarry with the Maule line—leads to a loss of sexual power. Hepzibah and Clifford are the embodied result of these denials, as we shall see.

The conjunction of the sexual and social themes is best illustrated in Holgrave's legend of Alice Pyncheon. The aristocratic Alice, who "deemed herself conscious of a power—combined of beauty, high, unsullied purity, and the preservative force of womanhood—that could make her sphere impenetrable," is in effect seduced by the second Matthew Maule. The language of the entire episode is transparently sexual, and Alice is drawn not merely by mesmeric prowess but by "the remarkable comeliness, strength, and energy of Maule's figure." The outcome of this seduction, however, is not a union of any sort. Having been socially insulted by Alice's arrogant father, Maule uses his sexual mastery only to demonstrate sadistic control over Alice. "A power that she little dreamed of had laid its grasp upon her maiden soul. A will, most unlike her own, constrained her to do its grotesque and fantastic bidding."

This is to say that Maule is perversely toying with Alice's unladylike susceptibility to his erotic appeal, much as the other Maules exploit the Pyncheons' unpaid debt to them. The purpose is exactly opposite to healthy fulfillment, as the final event of Alice's life makes especially clear. The still-virginal Alice, who "would have deemed it sin to marry" because she is "so lost from self-control," is hypnotically summoned to attend Matthew Maule's wedding to a laborer's daughter. Alice's former "purity" and her class-consciousness—they are really a single fastidiousness—are thus successfully flouted; she is spurned and mocked by a man who supposedly had no claim on her interest. Significantly, the only "penetration" of Alice's "sphere" occurs on the way home from this wedding, when a fatal dose of consumption makes its entry into "her thinly sheltered bosom." Alice becomes a romantic prototype of the later, more realistically inhibited Pyncheons who find themselves removed from the possibility of sexual fulfillment. The warfare between repression and the repressed will end only with the marriage of a Pyncheon to a Maule, and this will occur only after the chief impediment to both social and sexual democracy is removed.

What is that impediment? In Alice Pyncheon's case it is a father who imposes his elite pretensions on her, prevents her from considering marriage to a workingman, and half-willingly barters her away for a greedy purpose of his own. Each detail recalls the peculiarly unhealthy situation of Beatrice Rappaccini [in Hawthorne's **"Rappaccini's Daughter"**]. When we turn to the modern Pyncheon "children," Hepzibah and Clifford, we find that the role of Gervayse Pyncheon or Dr. Rappaccini is played by cousin Jaffrey. Jaffrey is after the very same document that Gervayse Pyncheon was, and he too has made a "child"—the childlike Clifford—pay for his own criminality. Most strikingly, Jaffrey has hoarded to himself the dwindling sum of Pyncheon eroticism. Though he is not completely immune to the family enervation, Jaffrey is still characterized by "a kind of fleshly effulgence" and by "brutish . . . animal instincts." In his hypocritical gesture of family affection toward Phoebe, "the man, the sex, somehow or other, was entirely too prominent . . . ." And it is suggested more than once that Jaffrey, like his first Puritan ancestor, "had fallen into certain transgressions to which men of his great animal development, whatever their faith or principles, must continue liable. . . ." We begin to understand that the theory of Pyncheon decline—a decline that seems to apply only to real or metaphorical children—is inseparable from the recurrence in each generation of a licentious and selfish male Pyncheon—a caricature of the Freudian child's imagined father.

Two lines of a familiar triangle are thus discernible as an underlying configuration in *The House of the Seven Gables:* an overbearing, terrifying, and guilty "father" is matched against innocent but emotionally withered "children." The third line, which we could infer equally well from Hawthorne's previous work or from psychoanalytic doctrine, should be incest fear—the fantasy-terror which goes into the very idea of an all-forbidding and self-indulging Jaffrey Pyncheon. The Oedipal villain, in other words, is an embodied idea of paternal punishment for thoughts of incest, and the form actually taken by such punishment is impotence.

As it happens, *The House of the Seven Gables* abounds in ambiguous innuendo about both incest and impotence. Thus, for example, Holgrave uses the Pyncheons to illustrate a caution against too prolonged a family dynasty: "in their brief New England pedigree, there has been time enough to infect them all with one kind of lunacy or another!" What cannot quite be uttered about human inbreeding can be said of the family chickens, who are explicit emblems of their owners: "It was evident that the race had degenerated, like many a noble race besides, in consequence of too strict a watchfulness to keep it pure." Whether incest has been literally committed is as open a question for the Pyncheons as it was for the Mannings [ancestral relatives of Hawthorne who were accused of incest in 1680]; the real significance of the incest hints lies in their connection to the other Oedipal features of the total work. Those features do not encourage us to look for evidence of actual incest, but on the contrary for the emotional starvation that ensues from a morbid dread of incest. And this is exactly what we find in the decrepit siblings, Hepzibah and Clifford.

Hepzibah is of course a classic old maid, and Hawthorne keeps the sexual implications of her state before our minds. He introduces her in mock-erotic terms ("Far from us be the indecorum of assisting, even in imagination, at a maiden lady's toilet!"), and he repeatedly characterizes her feelings as those of an aged virgin. He also supplies us with what might be an etiological suggestion as to why Hepzibah has remained virginal. Unlike the other modern Pyncheons, she willingly submits herself to the imposing portrait of the first Colonel Pyncheon: "She, in fact, felt a reverence for the pictured visage, of which only a far-descended and time-stricken virgin could be susceptible." The father of the Pyncheon dynasty has acquired some of the affection that would normally be reserved for a husband. And this admittedly dim suggestion of incestuous feeling is greatly heightened by Hepzibah's secret and tender absorption in another portrait, whose subject might well have been "an early lover of Miss Hepzibah"—but is in truth her brother Clifford as a young man!

Clifford in turn is effeminate and attached to the image of his mother. His physical traits alone are emphatically revealing: "full, tender lips, and beautiful eyes," a face "almost too soft and gentle for a man's," "thin delicate fingers," and so on. His portrait not only shows "feminine traits, moulded inseparably with those of the other sex"; it also makes one think inevitably "of the original as resembling his mother, and she a lovely and lovable woman, with perhaps some beautiful infirmity of character. . . ." And later we hear of Clifford's dreams, "in which he invariably played the part of a child, or a very young man. So vivid were they . . . that he once held a dispute with his sister as to the particular figure or print of a chintz morning-dress, which he had seen their mother wear, in the dream of the preceding night." Clifford's dream-memory turns out to be exact.

If Clifford's mother is his dream, I find it significant that Jaffrey, who is blamed for his passage directly "from a boy into an old and broken man," is called his "nightmare." Here again the strictest Freudian expectations are ful-

filled. The melodramatic villainy of the "father" is blamed for a failure of manhood whose sources are clearly temperamental, and which antedates that villainy. The power of intimidation which Jaffrey has come to symbolize is explained by the manner of Clifford's brief release from it at Jaffrey's death. In a wild exhilaration that contrasts sharply with Hepzibah's more anxious response, Clifford simultaneously tosses off Oedipal rivalry, the Puritan past, and moral restraint; they are all revealed to be emotionally identical. Rocketing to an unknown modern destination on a railroad train that is leaving Jaffrey's corpse ever farther behind, the timid eunuch Clifford suddenly becomes a universal Eros. By means of the telegraph, he predicts excitedly, "Lovers, day by day,—hour by hour, if so often moved to do it,—might send their heart-throbs from Maine to Florida, with some such words as these, 'I love you forever!'—'My heart runs over with love!'—'I love you more than I can!' and, again, at the next message, 'I have lived an hour longer, and love you twice as much!' " This is the Clifford who feared to venture outside his home while Jaffrey lived.

Clifford is perhaps the supreme example in Hawthorne's fiction of a man whose feelings have become polarized between an exquisite aestheticism and frustrated sensuality. His worship of the beautiful and his hypersensitivity are matched by his huge appetite for food and his rather prurient titillation in the company of the developing virgin, Phoebe. Though his interest in her is described as chaste, Hawthorne adds that

> He was a man, it is true, and recognized her as a woman. . . . He took unfailing note of every charm that appertained to her sex, and saw the ripeness of her lips, and the virginal development of her bosom. All her little womanly ways, budding out of her like blossoms on a young fruit-tree, had their effect on him, and sometimes caused his very heart to tingle with the keenest thrills of pleasure. At such moments,—for the effect was seldom more than momentary,—the half-torpid man would be full of harmonious life, just as a long-silent harp is full of sound, when the musician's fingers sweep across it.

Significantly, Phoebe's company enables Clifford to retreat more easily into a state of childhood—one in which his "gentle and voluptuous emotion" need meet no challenges from mature sexual reality.

To understand why Phoebe produces just this effect on Clifford, it is now necessary to consider her general symbolic role in the romance. It is, of course, a redemptive role, though by no means a theological one. To the social and psychological decadence of the House she brings one supreme virtue that has thus far been lacking: "There was no morbidity in Phoebe." Her function is to dispense symbolic sunshine (note her name) where hereditary gloom prevailed before. This is very obvious; but as always in Hawthorne's serious work, the banal theme is rooted in psychological relationships of considerable subtlety.

On the patent level Phoebe represents a kind of innocent energy and prettiness, a domestic competence unhindered by any brooding over the meaning of things. Her Pyncheon blood endows her marriage to Holgrave-Maule with familial symbolism, but in fact she is antithetical to most of the Pyncheon traits, and her effect on the ancestral property is to cancel or reverse many of its dark implications. Thus in the Pyncheon garden, "unctuous with nearly two hundred years of vegetable decay," she discovers a perfect rose, with "not a speck of blight or mildew in it." This "nice girl" and "cheerful little body" aligns herself with all the symbols of persisting purity amid the general collapse—with the singing birds and above all with the unpolluted fountain in the garden. She is even able to neutralize the suggestive implications of her very bedroom, where "the joy of bridal nights had throbbed itself away." Hawthorne assures us that "a person of delicate instinct would have known at once that it was now a maiden's bedchamber, and had been purified of all former evil and sorrow by her sweet breath and happy thoughts. Her dreams of the past night, being such cheerful ones, had exorcised the gloom, and now haunted the chamber in its stead."

Now, this passage shows us Phoebe's chief part in the romance, which is not simply to stand for innocence but to refute or "exorcise" sexual cynicism. Hepzibah and Clifford, after all, are innocent enough; but Phoebe's purity has thematic weight because she is seen at the brink of womanhood. Hawthorne deliberately puts her within a sexual perspective in order to declare her exempt from erotic inclinations. She dreams, but cheerfully; she has "brisk impulses," but they urge her to hike in the countryside; her "ordinary little toils," unlike Hester Prynne's [in *The Scarlet Letter*], do not register unfulfilled desire but merely "perfect health." She is even observed by Clifford at the moment of recognizing the existence of her emergent sexual appeal, yet she pays for this recognition with nothing more than a maidenly blush and a slight modification of her forthrightness.

Phoebe's role is epitomized at one point in a striking oxymoron. In neutralizing the morbidity of her surroundings she is said to wield a "homely witchcraft"—that is, a marriage of spiritual power and tidy domesticity. In Hawthorne's usual world this is unthinkable; one can be either a conventional nobody or a moral outlaw with a special potency of spirit. The "limit-loving" Phoebe, in contrast, derives her power of exorcism precisely from her ignorant conventionality—indeed, from her unwillingness to face unpleasant truths. This is especially apparent in her relations with Clifford: "whatever was morbid in his mind and experience she ignored; and thereby kept their intercourse healthy. . . ." So, too, she innocently evades the lecherous Jaffrey's kiss and fails to confirm Hepzibah's original fears that she will be a rival for Clifford's love. When she finally confesses that her sentiments toward Hepzibah and Clifford have been maternal, this exemption from sexuality takes on an Oedipal significance. Despite her youth Phoebe stands in the place of an ideal parent, a selfless breadwinner and moral guide who can replace the tyrannical parent of guilty fantasy.

The real test of this role is provided by Holgrave, whose interest in Phoebe is necessarily amorous. Like Jaffrey, he is both haunting and haunted. As a Maule he owns the mesmeric power which seduces and destroys, yet this power leaves him prone to self-destructive monomania.

By marrying Phoebe after virtually hypnotizing her and then allowing her to go free after all, he offers a model of self-restraint from the morbid "experimentation" upon womankind that is so tempting for Hawthornian males generally. He and Phoebe together—he having renounced his unconscious, she scarcely having noticed hers—finally embody a contradictory but necessary vision of mature love combined with indefinitely protracted childhood.

It is noteworthy that Hawthorne strains verisimilitude in order to work Holgrave into his concern for fathers and sons. Without any apparent reason the resourceful and independent daguerreotypist is oppressed by the figure of Jaffrey Pyncheon in death. As he tells Phoebe,

> "The presence of yonder dead man threw a great black shadow over everything; he made the universe, so far as my perception could reach, a scene of guilt and of retribution more dreadful than the guilt. The sense of it took away my youth. I never hoped to feel young again! The world looked strange, wild, evil, hostile; my past life, so lonesome and dreary; my future, a shapeless gloom, which I must mould into gloomy shapes! But, Phoebe, you crossed the threshold; and hope, warmth, and joy came in with you!"

Here the theme of patricidal guilt, again as in **"Roger Malvin's Burial,"** is being stretched to include a wholly symbolic father who has not been murdered at all. Holgrave's fear of "retribution" has no basis in stated motives, yet it reminds us that his view of society and history has been metaphorically Oedipal. The cruel world in his estimate is "that gray-bearded and wrinkled profligate, decrepit, without being venerable"; and the tyranny of the past is "just as if a young giant were compelled to waste all his strength in carrying about the corpse of the old giant, his grandfather, who died a long while ago, and only needs to be decently buried." Jaffrey's death thus satisfies a patricidal strain in Holgrave's nature—a fact which is corroborated by his "unmotivated" anxiety before Jaffrey's corpse.

The best indication that the "happy" outcome of *The House of the Seven Gables* was not cathartic for its contriver is an omnipresent uneasiness about the propriety, the honesty, and the quality of fictive art. From the defensively humble Preface onward Hawthorne seems to despair of sustaining the picturesque effects which he simultaneously equates with artistic value and denigrates as trickery. The ending to his plot confirms his pessimism: modern ordinariness triumphs over a compulsive and romantic addiction to the past. To a certain extent this pattern is put to good comic use; in the world of homely witchcraft the only ghosts are "the ghosts of departed cook-maids," and Maule's well is no more bewitched than "an old lady's cup of tea." Especially in his treatment of Hepzibah, who resembles him in trying to sell to "a different set of customers" such traditional wares as "sugar figures, with no strong resemblance to the humanity of any epoch . . . ," Hawthorne manages to take a whimsical view of his artistic plight. Like her creator in his postcollege years, Hepzibah, "by secluding herself from society, has lost all true relation with it" and must now try to "flash forth on the world's astonished gaze at once." And yet her failure to do so—her bondage to an anachronistic stock-in-trade—has a desperate autobiographical meaning for Hawthorne. He as well as Hepzibah, if they are to stay in business at all, must follow the cynical advice on modern salesmanship offered by the earthbound Yankee, Uncle Venner: "Put on a bright face for your customers, and smile pleasantly as you hand them what they ask for! A stale article, if you dip it in a good, warm, sunny smile, will go off better than a fresh one that you've scowled upon."

If Hepzibah illustrates the futility of Hawthornian art in the nineteenth century, Clifford and Holgrave may be said to illustrate the flaws and dangers of the artistic temperament. Clifford, the artist *manqué,* is both squeamish and vicariously sensual, both "ideal" and secretly voracious. At times he is merely irritable and dull, but occasionally his fantasy is given symbolic rein, as when he blows artistic bubbles to be pricked by unappreciative passers-by. In either capacity, however, he remains enveloped in a robe of moonshine, "which he hugged about his person, and seldom let realities pierce through." Thus he is an extreme version of the withdrawn Hawthornian artist, and it is not difficult to see what he has withdrawn from. His "images of women," says Hawthorne, "had more and more lost their warmth and substance, and been frozen, like the pictures of secluded artists, into the chillest ideality." As usual, ideality and coldness toward women are the same thing, and are associated with "secluded artists." Only Phoebe, the embodied negation of all unpleasant fantasies about women, can persuade Clifford that "the world was no longer a delusion."

Similarly, Phoebe aids Holgrave in restraining his tendency to be an "all-observant" peeper. His interest in his companions has essentially been an author's overview of his characters, and at one point he actually makes a literary work out of Pyncheon history. Alice Pyncheon's legend and the circumstances of its narration sum up everything Hawthorne has to say about the secret meaning of art. The legend itself, says Holgrave, "has taken hold of my mind with the strangest tenacity of clutch . . ." and he is telling it "as one method of throwing it off." Authorship, including the intention to publish the work in a magazine, is presented as a way of mastering obsession. Yet Holgrave has a more immediate purpose as well, to impress Phoebe with his talent. The covert eroticism of the story is evidently communicated to its listener, for at the end she "leaned slightly towards [Holgrave], and seemed almost to regulate her breath by his":

> A veil was beginning to be muffled about her, in which she could behold only him, and live only in his thoughts and emotions. His glance, as he fastened it on the young girl, grew involuntarily more concentrated; in his attitude there was the consciousness of power, investing his hardly mature figure with a dignity that did not belong to its physical manifestation. It was evident that, with but one wave of his hand and a corresponding effort of his will, he could complete his mastery over Phoebe's yet free and virgin spirit: he could establish an influence over this good, pure, and simple child, as dangerous, and perhaps as disastrous, as that which the carpenter of his leg-

end had acquired and exercised over the ill-fated Alice.

The thinly euphemistic nature of this scene presumably enabled its first readers to ignore, or at least to perceive indistinctly, the implication that cheery little Phoebe is endowed with sexual desire. She unconsciously welcomes her seducer, and he "involuntarily" tightens his hold on her. This hold has been won through the mesmeric power of art, and motivated not simply by desire but by the prying and rapacious tendency which in Hawthorne's harsh view constitutes the artistic character. That tendency must be "cured," at least in symbolism, if a satisfactory resolution is to be reached. And thus Holgrave obligingly steps out of his Maule identity and reforms both himself and the spirit of the romance. He relaxes his spell over Phoebe and allows her deliberate obtuseness to have the final say: "But for this short life of ours, one would like a house and a moderate garden-spot of one's own." At the end, though the revitalized Pyncheon chickens have begun "an indefatigable process of egg-laying," art has been tacitly set aside and forgotten.

The logic of this conclusion is impeccable. If the image of Jaffrey Pyncheon in death makes Holgrave's future appear to be "a shapeless gloom, which I must mould into gloomy shapes," and if Phoebe alone can erase that image from his mind, then marriage to Phoebe obviates the need for moulding further "gloomy shapes." To become free of anxiety is to lose all reason for creativity. For Holgrave it cannot matter that Phoebe is in fact a tissue of symbolic contradictions: motherly child, sisterly bride, fertile and prolific virgin. It is Hawthorne for whom this subtle compromise is finally meaningful. And in a broader sense the incongruities of his plot—the yoking together of ancestral

---

**Klaus Lubbers on the conclusion of *The House of the Seven Gables*:**

Is this close the proper resolution of a tragedy that had been steering so long toward its due catastrophe? The Judge's timely exit? An avowal of love that makes the earth Eden again? The timely establishment of Clifford's innocence? The opportune news of the decease of the Judge's only son (by cholera!)? The absurd removal of the dramatis personae to the Judge's elegant country seat (if only for the present)? Clifford's partial recovery? Holgrave's astounding about face? Hepzibah's unscrupulous acceptance of a fortune that has come her way from a dead enemy? And, to crown it all, the indefatigable process of egg-laying suddenly started by the hens? The end is contrived and specious. . . . At the level of metaphor at least, Hepzibah and Clifford are not so easily liberated and redeemed as Hawthorne and some defenders of the novel's ending would like to have us believe, and the image of life represented by the organ grinder's mechanical people may well have been the intended final truth which the author retracted after it had become too late to do so without affecting the credibility of the story.

*Klaus Lubbers, in* Literatur und Sprache der Vereinigten Staaten, *ed. by Hans Helmcke and others, Carl Winter, 1969.*

guilt, of maladaptation to modern reality, and of a villain's death which produces unholy erotic glee and a therapeutic marriage—find their rationale in Hawthorne's struggle to disbelieve that the world is indeed "a scene of guilt and of retribution more dreadful than the guilt." Not Holgrave but Hawthorne, who called his wife Phoebe, has set Phoebe-ism as the steep ransom from obsession. And it is Hawthorne, ultimately, who with secret and wistful irony measures the consequence of this surrender for his own later career. "The world owes all its onward impulses to men ill at ease," he has Holgrave tell Phoebe with great truthfulness; and shortly thereafter Holgrave adds, "If we love one another, the moment has room for nothing more." (pp. 174-93)

> *Frederick Crews, in his* The Sins of the Fathers: Hawthorne's Psychological Themes, *Oxford University Press, Inc., 1966, 279 p.*

### Francis Joseph Battaglia   (essay date 1967)

[*In the following essay, Battaglia argues that critical complaints concerning the plot, conclusion, and theme of* The House of the Seven Gables *can be resolved by a modified reading of the novel that recognizes the gradual development of its characters.*]

Many twentieth-century commentators on Hawthorne's *The House of the Seven Gables*—probably the majority of them—have found it necessary to note serious failings in the work. The censures are in a sense as different as the men who registered them, but I think they can be fairly summarized as: (1) objection to the plot as lacking coherent action and to the narrative method as partial cause of this difficulty; (2) objection to the conclusion as being artificial or forced; and (3) objection to the short-sightedness of the author in saying in his Preface and as comment within the story something which the story itself confutes. Structure, conclusion, and theme have all proved problematical.

These charges are quite considerable in range and weight, and the study which resulted in this paper was originally concerned with only the second of them. The evidence, however, which has suggested to me that the ending of Hawthorne's novel is neither artificial nor forced, in turn suggests that the plot of the novel has been in a very important particular generally misread. The whole structure of the novel is thus implicated in a discussion of its ending. In addition, an explanation of the conclusion of a novel can hardly be valid if it cannot account for the narrator's own statements. Hawthorne has told us both in the Preface and in the novel proper what *The House of the Seven Gables* is about; his statements have to be dealt with. I wish to suggest that the conclusion of Hawthorne's novel is fitting; doing so will entail consideration of the first and third objections as well. The task would be even larger were not objections one and two different sides of the same coin.

Austin Warren wrote of *The House of the Seven Gables* in 1948 [in his *Rage for Order*]: "[Hawthorne's] method is almost that of a succession of tableaux. The characters do not really develop or change. . . . Nor does he show us the characters acting on each other. . . . Scenes of conversation . . . are expository, and do not advance the action." F. O. Matthiessen and Newton Arvin are probably the most notable among the Hawthorne scholars who hold similar views of the plot of *The House of the Seven Gables.* The action of the novel has generally been found episodic rather than cumulative; characterization seems to compound the difficulty, for the persons of the novel neither develop nor interact; Hawthorne's narrative penchant is responsible for the *stasis* of his characters, for he would rather describe them than have them reveal themselves in action: even in dialogue they do not affect each other. The general objection to the novel's plot includes an ancillary concern for character development and the use of dialogue.

Hawthorne's ending to the novel has likewise, to quote Matthiessen [in his *American Renaissance,* 1941], "satisfied very few. Although Phoebe's marriage with Holgrave . . . is meant finally to transcend the old brutal separation of classes . . . the reconciliation is somewhat too lightly made." Phoebe and Holgrave emerge as lovers in the closing chapters and allow Hawthorne to arrange a happy finish to his book. But this resolution seems contrived; the final chapters are too late a point for a character to *begin* to undergo his basic change. Arvin [in his *Hawthorne,* 1961] has called Holgrave's love for Phoebe "factitious dramatically."

These objections could be further documented with quotations from the work of Henry James, George Woodberry, Herbert Gorman, Mark Van Doren, and other more recent writers, but I hope to have established at least that they are customary charges against Hawthorne's work. Insofar as there is one, they represent a consensus of opinion about the plot and conclusion of *The House of the Seven Gables.* They are not discrete points, of course. Both objections deal with a different facet of the same novel; the first overlaps the second; and characterization figures prominently in each. Even more than is intimated in this statement of their similarity, however, the charges have a common basis.

The novel has been found slow-moving, and lacking a "strong narrative line"; very little seems to happen. Rudolph Van Abele [in his *Death of the Artist,* 1955] considers a third of the book ("between the seventh and fifteenth chapters") to be "irrelevant." On the other hand, the denouement is said to unravel much too fast, with insufficient preparation for the changes which take place there. These difficulties admit the possibility of common solution: if the characters of the novel did gradually change and develop, but for some reason their alterations had not been recognized, students of the novel would understandably have remarked both that its plot was weak and that its denouement was abrupt. If the novel depends for its narrative line on progressive shifts in the attitudes of its characters, and these shifts are not discerned, the reader is very apt to find the work more like tableaux than genuine narrative. W. B. Dillingham began his article on "Structure and Theme in *The House of the Seven Gables*" [in *NCF,* June 1959] disagreeing with those who see no structural pattern in the work, but in closing he conceded a "basic weakness in plot."

Although it entails the suggestion—which anyone aware of the extent and value of existing Hawthorne scholarship would not make lightly—that most writers of *The House of the Seven Gables* have failed to discern an essential feature of the novel, I will maintain here that the solution just broached in hypothetical form is the accurate one, i.e., the novel has been in a very important particular generally misread. A modified reading of the middle events of the novel comprises my main reason for thinking the conclusion appropriate; it also provides cause for a revision of critical opinion on the novel's narrative structure. The question of theme and the author's statements about it will be taken up after these matters.

> The conclusion is unspeakably awkward. For thematic reasons Hawthorne was absolutely forced to marry Phoebe and Holgrave—but with so little interest in the business that he could not bother to prepare for the event by showing them developing so much as a real interest in each other.

Thus Philip Young restated [in his introduction to the Holt, Rinehart edition of the novel] the customary objection to the ending of *The House of the Seven Gables* in 1957. The appraisal is, however, unfair to the novel, because Hawthorne's preparations for the final union of Holgrave and Phoebe have been quite elaborate. Love between them is explicitly suggested as early as Chapter xii; their romance is fully under way in Chapter xiv, and Hawthorne in the same chapter is at pains to see that the reader is aware of it.

Chapter xii, "The Daguerreotypist," recounts a conversation between Phoebe and Holgrave in the Pyncheon Garden. In light of the fact that Hawthorne's conversations have been said not to advance the plot and they characterize individuals rather than show them interacting, it is notable that the author specifies this conversation as unique instead of typical. Having devoted several pages to a general account of the daguerreotypist and his views, the narrator says: "But our business is with Holgrave, as we find him on this particular afternoon, and in the arbor of the Pyncheon garden." Hawthorne goes on to distinguish further the conversation from others that have occurred, and he is already beginning to mark the signs of romantic feeling in Holgrave. A few pages earlier the author had noted that Phoebe "scarcely thought him affectionate in his nature. He was too calm and cool an observer. . . . He seemed to be in quest of mental food; not heartsustenance." On this particular afternoon, however, Holgrave's demeanor could not be so described: "Her thought had scarcely done him justice, when it pronounced him cold; or if so, he had grown warmer, now." Having called Holgrave "warmer," Hawthorne uses other terms suggestive of romantic affection in preparing us for the conversation which will continue for two chapters: "the artist . . . was beguiled, by some silent charm of hers, to talk freely of what he dreamed of doing in the world. He poured himself out as to another self." Holgrave's customary detachment might lead us to think that his interest in Phoebe was

"Platonic" rather than romantic, but Hawthorne playfully suggests it would not have struck an observer that way:

> Very possibly, he forgot Phoebe while he talked to her, and was moved only by the inevitable tendency of thought, when rendered sympathetic by enthusiasm and emotion, to flow into the first safe reservoir which it finds. But, had you peeped at them through the chinks of the garden fence, the young man's earnestness and heightened color might have led you to suppose that he was making love to the young girl!

"Love" is alluded to, I think for the first time in connection with the pair.

All of this, though revealing, is but preparation, for Holgrave and Phoebe do not emerge definitely as lovers until Chapter xiv. Hawthorne, however, has at this point already rather clearly admitted romantic love to his plot.

To be ready for Chapter xiv, we need note one further thing about the conversation at its outset. Not answering Phoebe's query as to why he chose to live in the old Pyncheon house, Holgrave begins his famous radical discourse against things antique. "Shall we never, never get rid of this Past?" he cries. "It lies upon the Present like a giant's dead body!" Expounding on his theme, he proposes that each generation should build its own houses; public buildings should be constructed of such materials that they would crumble to ruin once in twenty years to remind men of the need for reform in the institutions they represent. At this point he returns to the subject of the House of Seven Gables, and recommends its fiery purgation:

> Now this old Pyncheon-house! Is it a wholesome place to live in, with its black shingles, and the green moss that shows how damp they are?—its dark, low-studded rooms?—its grime and sordidness, which are the crystallization on its walls of the human breath, that has been drawn and exhaled here, in discontent and anguish? The house ought to be purified with fire—purified till only its ashes remain!"

The House of Seven Gables will again be Holgrave's topic in Chapter xiv.

The daguerreotypist has written a story detailing alleged events of Pyncheon family history. With a little encouragement from Phoebe, he is soon reading it aloud. In the tale Alice Pyncheon falls prey to the hypnotic arts of Matthew Maule, and recounting the incident, complete with gestures, Holgrave inadvertently brings Phoebe to the verge of a trance which would give him power over her similar to that gained over young Alice by the mesmerist of his story. Maurice Beebe has aptly observed [in *NCF,* June 1956] that Holgrave's refusal to exercise hypnotic power over Phoebe is an important step in his regeneration: "He ceases to be the detached observer and becomes a participator, not merely 'using' life but living it." Immediately after he takes this step, his love and Phoebe's kindle.

Chapter xiv, "Phoebe's Good-By," begins with Holgrave's refusal to complete Phoebe's spell; instead he joshes her back to her normal state, chiding her for falling asleep at his dull story. Seemingly abruptly, and quite atypically, Hawthorne turns to a description of the sun going down and the moon rising. Even more uncommonly, he has an apparently nonhuman, non-moral, non-spiritual force intervene directly in his story. Moonbeams, "chang[ing] the character of the lingering daylight," "transfigured" what they fell on "by a charm of romance." "They softened and embellished the aspect of the old house." The "reviving influence" also fell on the artist and "made him feel—what he sometimes almost forgot, thrust so early, as he had been, into the rude struggle of man with man—how youthful he still was."

In this unusual passage Hawthorne seems to be invoking moon-power, or the power of a moon-goddess, as an operative force in his story. The moon has some of the faculties of Artemis, the benign Hellenic and pre-Hellenic deity who had particular care for youth and growth, the paradoxical Woman-goddess of childbirth and chastity whom the moon represented. Even if this connection is pertinent, however, what does, or at least should, an Artemis-moon have to do with *The House of the Seven Gables?* Mythological machinery seems out of character for Hawthorne.

The agent at work is probably not mythological, though the connection with Artemis seems worth making because one of the other names of the goddess was "Phoebe." Without suggesting any relevance for Chapter xiv, Hyatt Waggoner thought the Phoebe-Artemis congruence significant enough to devote half a paragraph to it in his introduction to a recent edition of *The House of the Seven Gables* [Houghton Mifflin, 1964]. It is an engaging possibility that the "reviving influence" of moonlight on Holgrave stands for the influence of Phoebe; but this gloss is ultimately unsatisfactory, for Phoebe herself changes under the moon's beams:

> "I am sensible of a great charm in this brightening moonlight. . . . I never cared much about moonlight before. What is there, I wonder, so beautiful in it, tonight?"
>
> "And you have never felt it before?" inquired the artist . . .
>
> "Never," answered Phoebe; "and life does not look the same, now that I have felt it so."

Rather than Phoebe's power, the moon-scene is, I think, Hawthorne's allegorical rendering of the coming of love to the pair. Holgrave, who has been made to feel "how youthful he still was," offers Phoebe this very explanation, though he hardly realizes yet what his words mean:

> "Sometimes—always, I suspect, unless one is exceedingly unfortunate—there comes a sense of second youth, gushing out of the heart's *joy at being in love;* or, possibly, it may come to crown some other grand festival in life, if any other such there be" [italics mine] . . .
>
> "I hardly think I understand you," said Phoebe.
>
> "No wonder," replied Holgrave, smiling; "for I have told you a secret which I hardly began to know, before I found myself giving it utterance. Remember it, however; and when the truth be-

comes clear to you, then think of this moonlight scene!"

When the truth does become clear to her—as we shall see—she blushes.

Holgrave's first reaction to love's moonlit influence—which he feels immediately after willing not to take advantage of Phoebe—indicates the extent of the change love will have on him. F. O. Matthiessen has found Hawthorne's handling of the artist later in Chapter xx, "devastating in its limitations. . . . Society no longer looks hostile. When Phoebe is afraid that he will lead her out of her own quiet path, he already knows that the influence is likely to be all the other way." The whole development comes too abruptly, and it is hardly credible that Holgrave would know already at the point of falling in love what effects it will have on him. Chapter xxi bears out his fore-reckoning that love will mollify his social views, for there he voices the wish that Judge Pyncheon had built in stone instead of in wood. The artist, however, falls in love not in the next to last (twentieth) chapter of the book, but in the fourteenth. Moreover, Chapter xiv shows strikingly that Holgrave's radical views are even then being altered. When he "already knows" in Chapter xx that Phoebe will change him more than he will her, Holgrave is exercising hindsight, not precognition.

In Chapter xii, where love was just starting to stir in him, the artist inveighed against the Past and thought incineration the best cure for the ills of the House of Seven Gables. In Chapter xiv after he refuses to gain power over Phoebe's soul, their love burgeons, and the resultant alteration in his perspective is remarkable:

> "After all, what a good world we live in! How good, and beautiful! How young it is, too, with nothing really rotten or age-worn in it! This old house, for example, which sometimes has positively oppressed my breath with its smell of decaying timber! And this garden, where the black mould always clings to my spade, as if I were a sexton, delving in a graveyard! Could I keep the feeling that now possesses me, the garden would every day be virgin soil, with the earth's first freshness in the flavor of its beans and squashes; and the house!—it would be like a bower in Eden blossoming with the earliest roses that God ever made."

Rather than wishing to burn the Pyncheon house, Holgrave is now possessed by a feeling which makes the garden an Eden of "first freshness" and the House of Seven Gables a bower there. Holgrave's language will be echoed in Hawthorne's description of the couple in Chapter xx, "The Flower of Eden," after they have declared their love: "The bliss, which makes all things true, beautiful, and holy, shone around this youth and maiden. They were conscious of nothing sad or old. They transfigured the earth, and made it Eden again, and themselves the two first dwellers in it." The loving couple will "transfigure" the earth; moonbeams had "transfigured" all in the garden. By Chapter xiv love has already mellowed Holgrave's radical humanitarianism of Chapter xii. This "early" change in the daguerreotypist's social views has to my knowledge received attention from only three twentieth-century writers on Hawthorne. [The critic adds in a foot-note that he is referring to Darrel Abel (*SAQ*, October 1953), Clark Griffith (*MP*, February 1954), and Hubert H. Hoeltje (in his *Inward Sky*, 1962).] It is important that the change be heeded, however, for otherwise Holgrave's later preference for stone houses, like his love for Phoebe, will seem contrived.

Hawthorne's love story takes one further turn in "Phoe-be's Good-By." Chapter xiv brought Holgrave to the test of whether he would be a second Maule to cast a spell over a Pyncheon daughter. He refused, and felt with Phoebe the moonlight power of love. The artist had an inkling of what influence was affecting them, though he hardly antic-ipated his own words in telling it to Phoebe. She was not sure she understood. Later in the chapter, Hawthorne nar-rates for us the scene of her realization, and he uses the same technique employed in Chapter vi.

In that chapter Hawthorne describes Phoebe's entering the house to find Hepzibah acting strangely. Clifford has returned, though Phoebe does not know it, and Haw-thorne does not tell his readers either until the next chap-ter. Instead he recounts the scene in such a way as to make the reader aware that information is being withheld from him—Phoebe, for example, hears the footsteps of a person walking with Hepzibah, but does not know who it is. Puz-zling over the problem that the author has posed him, the reader may piece together previous hints and foreshadow-ings to realize that Clifford has come home. But whether the reader realizes or not, Hawthorne has brought height-ened attention to the fact that something new has devel-oped in the story.

The same technique draws heightened awareness in Chap-ter xiv. Two days after the garden scene with Holgrave in which she felt, but did not understand, the influence of love, Phoebe is taking leave of Clifford and Hepzibah when Clifford cries for her to come "Close!—closer!—and look me in the face!" Under his gaze she realizes what Hol-grave's self-discovering explanation had tried to tell her:

> Phoebe soon felt that, if not the profound insight of a seer, yet a more than feminine delicacy of appreciation was making her heart the subject of its regard. A moment before, she had known nothing which she would have sought to hide. Now, as if some secret were hinted to her own consciousness through the medium of another's perception, she was fain to let her eyelids droop beneath Clifford's gaze. A blush, too—the red-der, because she strove hard to keep it down— ascended higher and higher, in a tide of fitful progress, until even her brow was all suffused with it.

"It is enough" Clifford tells her. "Girlhood has passed into womanhood; the bud is a bloom!" Love has turned the girl Phoebe into a woman. She will also have occasion at another point in the novel to remember the explanation of "joy at being in love" which Holgrave ended: "when the truth becomes clear to you, then think of this moonlight scene." Later, when the artist has declared his love for her and asks "Do you love me, Phoebe?" she—again "letting her eyes droop"—will answer "You look into my heart . . . You know I love you!"

In Chapter xiv of Hawthorne's novel love kindled between Holgrave and Phoebe. Though Holgrave had the first in-kling of what was happening, Phoebe is soon acknowledg-ing their love with a blush at its realization. Holgrave, more deliberate, will require a final impetus to move him to full commitment. Just before the artist declares his love to Phoebe in Chapter xx, Hawthorne tells us: "These in-fluences [a result of their secret union in the knowledge of Judge Pyncheon's death] hastened the development of emotions, that might not otherwise have flowered so soon. Possibly, indeed, it had been Holgrave's purpose to let them die in their undeveloped germs." The daguerreotyp-ist, however, rejects this possibility as he had refused the opportunity to entrance Phoebe. As he spoke then of the "joy at being in love" he speaks now of a "joy . . . that has made this the only point of life worth living for." [The critic adds in a footnote, "The 1883 Riverside edition, the standard text for over eighty years before the appearance of the Centenary edition, originated a very important vari-ant which probably obscured for commentators on the novel the significance of the earlier garden scenes between Phoebe and Holgrave. The Riverside text elided 'soon' and thus read: 'These influences hastened the development of emotions, that might not otherwise have flowered so.' This sentence allows the possibility that at the time (Ch. xx) it was still possible for Holgrave not to love Phoebe at all, though the statement which follows it mitigates this somewhat. By contrast, with 'soon' restored to the text, we recognize a very exact allusion on Hawthorne's part. The 'germs' of love already existed in Holgrave, and further-more (as I argued from Ch. xiv) he *knew* it—for the author says it might have been the artist's 'purpose' to let them die without further development. What his closeness to Phoebe in the knowledge of Judge Pyncheon's death ('These influences') did was to cause the 'germs' (seeds) to 'flower' *sooner* than they would have otherwise."]

As Chapter xiv ends, Hawthorne's love story is ready for his last step—the mutual declaration of love—and this takes place at the very next meeting of the pair. But Phoe-be becomes aware of her state during leave-taking; before she returns the darker side of Hawthorne's plot will have brought Judge Pyncheon to the House of Seven Gables for a famous sit-in.

In meeting the second objection cited at the beginning of this paper I have sought to demonstrate that Hawthorne's conclusion to *The House of the Seven Gables* follows as a natural consequence from the forces he set in motion earlier in the novel. The couple's love and its mollifying effect on Holgrave is not a *deux ex machina*, an artificial close gratuitously provided by the author. The light and allusive handling of a disarmingly straightforward love in-terest, coupled with an unfortunate omission in the former standard text, has kept scholars from recognizing the rele-vance of the middle events of the story; but Hawthorne's ending has manifestly been working itself out since the twelfth chapter.

The examination so far given Hawthorne's love story has important implications for the first objection tendered against *The House of the Seven Gables.* For one thing, the action is not episodic, not a succession of tableaux; rather, it is cumulative: Chapter xiv carries forward the possibilities which Chapter xii has established; because of the decision to respect the freedom of her soul which precipitates his love for Phoebe, Holgrave can later, in Chapter xx, be committed by circumstances to declaring his affection for her. The failure of Hawthorne's characters to develop or interact has been the source of judgments that the plot is wooden. But both Holgrave and Phoebe develop, and each affects the other deeply. Clifford, as we have seen, also "interacts" with Phoebe; and she has a brightening effect on him. There has been the further charge that Hawthorne's conversations are expository and not dramatic. But Phoebe and Holgrave fall in love in a conversation scene: the moonlight incident is not represented solely by their talk, but the artist's change of mind on the value of the past is, his realization that love moves them is, and almost all of his effect on Phoebe is. Likewise, in Phoebe's scene with Clifford, his words do not tell us she has fallen in love— Hawthorne himself avoids saying so—but she does change in the course of the conversation. Conversations advance the action, and characters affect each other by them.

The plot will also be considered in my discussion of the theme of the novel and how the ending constitutes a working out of it, but one other matter merits attention here while character development is at issue. Of the five principal persons of the book—Phoebe, Hepzibah, Holgrave, Clifford, and Judge Pyncheon—all but the Judge develop in the course of the story and all but Clifford change substantially. I have already suggested the nature of Phoebe's and Holgrave's transformations. Hepzibah, however, is generally considered a static figure. Waggoner has argued quite plausibly that Hawthorne in writing the novel made her less of a type, more of a person, than was his original plan; though Waggoner does not propose that Hepzibah herself changes. He says instead that it is Hawthorne's "treatment of her" that becomes "more and more sympathetic as the story proceeds." Hepzibah does change, however; she is not "unbending," "inadaptive," and "indomitable" as Roy Male would have it [in his *Hawthorne's Tragic Vision,* 1957]. She not only changes, she grows.

Development of true faith in God is what Hawthorne tells us brings about her transformation. Hepzibah's development is gradual. When we first meet Hepzibah, in the very first paragraph of Chapter ii, we watch her kneel to say her prayers. Later on the day we meet her, she twice offers briefer pleas to the Almighty. Because of these facts, Male's important observation about an event later in the novel has probably been misleading. He writes: "their trip [flight from the House] has not been a total failure, for here on the isolated platform, lifting her hands to the dull, gray sky, Hepzibah is able to pray—something she has been unable to do in the house." But Hepzibah has prayed, and prayed in the House.

One Sabbath morning after Phoebe has come to the Pyncheon house, her leaving for church leads Clifford to implore Hepzibah that they go too. Looking into Clifford's face Hepzibah is moved by the desire to go and kneel down among the people. Hawthorne designates this as an important point of realization for her: "she *now* recognized" [italics mine] that she was "scarcely friends with Him

above." She is moved to go "kneel down among the people, and be reconciled to God and man at once." Her determination is short-lived, however, for when she and Clifford step across the threshold, "the eye of their Father seemed to be withdrawn." She has come to recognize the haughtiness of her spirit, but, failing to act on this realization, she turns back to find "the whole interior of the house tenfold more dismal."

Later, under the pressure of the Judge's threatened undoing of Clifford, Hepzibah will again try to pray: "and [she] strove hard to send up a prayer through the dense, gray pavement of clouds. Those mists had gathered, as if to symbolize a great, brooding mass of human trouble, doubt, confusion, and chill indifference, between earth and the better regions. *Her faith was too weak; the prayer too heavy to be thus uplifted. It fell back, a lump of lead, upon her heart*" (italics mine). She tries to pray, but her trust in God is not enough to overcome her doubts—doubts, perhaps, about the very possibility of a solution.

Not until after Judge Pyncheon's death is she able to pray. Befuddled, she at first follows Clifford without a will of her own. At the end of "The Flight of Two Owls," however, Clifford is no longer able to guide them: "You must take the lead now, Hepzibah!" Again she has nowhere to turn, again she tries to pray, and this time her faith is enough:

> She knelt down upon the platform where they were standing, and lifted her clasped hands to the sky. *The dull, gray weight of clouds made it invisible; but it was no hour for disbelief;*—no juncture this, to question that there was a sky above, and an Almighty Father looking down from it!

> "Oh, God!"—ejaculated poor, gaunt Hepzibah—then paused for a moment, to consider what her prayer should be—"Oh, God—our Father—are we not thy children? Have mercy on us!"

> (italics mine)

Despite the clouds of doubt, it is no time for "disbelief." Hepzibah can trust God enough to pray to him despite her fears and with knowledge of her unworthiness. This time her prayer is heard: Hepzibah and Clifford return to a House of Seven Gables where two lovers have just resolved a hereditary enmity.

Like Holgrave, Phoebe, and even Clifford, Hepzibah changes for the better in *The House of the Seven Gables.* When we first meet her brother he has been demented by thirty years imprisonment; but Hawthorne tells us that had Clifford's exquisite taste been able to develop unhampered, it might have "completely eaten out . . . his affections." For this reason Clifford's "black calamity may . . . have had a redeeming drop of mercy, at the bottom." Jaffrey's death brightened Clifford's wits enough to make him leader of "The Flight of Two Owls." In the closing chapter we find that despite a subsiding of his exhilaration, the good effect will be lasting: "The Shock of Judge Pyncheon's death had a permanently invigorating and ultimately beneficial effect on Clifford." The novel's main characters are not static.

The conclusion of Hawthorne's novel may naturally follow from the characters and their actions, but what of the author-narrator's comments on the action? The author at several points appears to belie his own plot. Matthiessen has said: "[The conclusion] is quite out of keeping with Hawthorne's seemingly deliberate answer in his preface. . . . For Hawthorne said there that his book might illustrate the truth 'that the wrong-doing of one generation lives into the successive ones, and, divesting itself of every temporary advantage, becomes a pure and uncontrollable mischief.' That unrelenting strain was still at the fore in his final reflections." Hawthorne has told us the moral of his story in the Preface, but it does not seem to fit. According to the author's theme, wrong-doing lives on through consecutive generations, deepening as it goes. If this is the theme of *The House of the Seven Gables,* how can Phoebe and Holgrave, Pyncheon and Maule be reconciled to each other? If this be the moral, how can the progeny of the original Pyncheon malefactor escape his curse?

These knotty questions have generally yielded answers fully satisfactory to no one. It has been maintained, for example, that Hawthorne overlooked disparities of this sort in concluding the novel. When these questions seemed to necessitate considering either the apparent moral or the outcome of the novel spurious, the book's conclusion has usually suffered by the choice. Hoeltje's position, however, is an interesting exception on both counts. He suggests that one would "be gullible to accept seriously the supposed moral." Hawthorne proffered that moral "facetiously." Hoeltje maintains instead that "More than anything else . . . *The House of the Seven Gables* depicts the assuaging and recreative power of love." Phoebe and Holgrave represent Sophia and Nathaniel Hawthorne's own love story. Hoeltje's proposals are genuinely helpful for a reading of the novel; but I believe Hawthorne meant his moral to be taken seriously. Hawthorne's theme, however, is wholly reconcilable with the denouement of his plot.

Hawthorne's moral is not incompatible with his plot, primarily because the moral itself admits the possibility of escape from hereditary evils. Almost without exception, when Hawthorne's announced theme is quoted, only the first part of the sentence is cited. But the latter half of the sentence entails a rephrasing of the theme by way of amplification:

> Not to be deficient, in this particular, the Author has provided himself with a moral;—the truth, namely, that the wrong-doing of one generation lives into the successive ones, and, divesting itself of every temporary advantage, becomes a pure and uncontrollable mischief;—and he would feel it a singular gratification, if this romance might effectually convince mankind (or, indeed, any one man) of the folly of tumbling down an avalanche of ill-gotten gold, or real estate, on the heads of an unfortunate posterity, thereby to maim and crush them, until the accumulated mass shall be scattered abroad in its original atoms.

The construction and sense of the sentence equates

> tumbling down an avalanche of ill-gotten gold, or real estate, on the heads of an unfortunate

posterity, thereby to maim and crush them, until the accumulated mass shall be scattered abroad in its original atoms

with "wrong-doing." With no injury to the meaning, the sentence could read: the moral is that wrong-doing lives on; the author would be gratified if his romance convinced even one man that wrong-doing lives on. Conversely, the moral is that tumbling down ill-gotten gold to posterity is folly; the author would be gratified if his romance convinced even one man that tumbling down ill-gotten gains to posterity is folly.

This fact about Hawthorne's expression of his theme is crucial, because the explication of the moral which the latter half of the sentence provides suggests that the evil a malefactor drew down on his children's heads would *not* be inexorable. The ill-gotten gold or real estate would maim and crush those who inherited it, *"until the accumulated mass shall be scattered abroad in its original atoms."* The inference is quite definite that when the pilfered wealth shall have gotten back to its original owners, the evil of its acquisition will cease to vex those who had been inheriting it. In terms of Hawthorne's plot, when the House of Seven Gables, dishonestly wrested from the Maules, shall have been returned to them, the curse acquired with its illicit possession will cease to plague the Pyncheons. This possibility afforded by Hawthorne's moral is realized in the novel's outcome.

On the other hand, the first facet of the moral was that the original wrong-doing would become "pure and uncontrollable mischief," and this facet too is borne out in Hawthorne's story. In *The House of the Seven Gables,* the

*An 1840 portrait of Hawthorne by Charles Osgood.*

original act of Pyncheon stealing from Maule would become Pyncheon allowing ill to befall Pyncheon—when Gervayse ignored his daughter Alice's call for help in hopes of recovering the title to Maine territory. The next step would be Pyncheon injuring Pyncheon by his own agency—first with some inadvertence when Jaffrey allowed Clifford to be blamed for murder (Jaffrey would become heir), and later with full deliberateness when for the sake of alleged riches (useless to him) Judge Jaffrey will have Clifford committed to a mental institution unless Clifford surrenders a secret. Wrong-doing grows into a "pure and uncontrollable mischief," and the offending family wreaks retribution on its own head.

Hawthorne bears out this reading of his moral by several kinds of statements within the novel. The first type of statement reiterates the *possibility* allowed by the moral: the evil *can be* escaped. Matthew Maule, after an unsuccessful attempt to elicit the secret of the Maine land title from the spirit world says:

> "It will never be allowed . . . The custody of this secret, that would so enrich his heirs, makes part of your grandfather's *retribution*. He must choke with it, until it is no longer of any value. And keep you the House of the Seven Gables! It is too dear bought an inheritance, and too heavy, with the curse upon it, to be shifted *yet awhile* from the Colonel's posterity" (italics mine).

The curse is too heavy now for the House to pass from Pyncheon hands, but apparently the curse may be lighter "awhile" in the future, when the Pyncheons will be able to give up the House. Presumably their "retribution" is helping them to atone.

The older Matthew Maule of Holgrave's story was said to haunt the House of Seven Gables offering the alternative that ground-rent be paid or the House given up, "else he, the ghostly creditor, would have his finger in all the affairs of the Pyncheons, and make everything go wrong with them, though it should be a thousand years after his death." *If* he does *not* get ground-rent or the House, he will haunt the Pyncheons. As we have seen, he was not willing to accept the House in exchange just yet, for he preferred to keep the title to the Pyncheon territories hidden until it would be no longer valuable to them. However, he, his grandson, and Holgrave telling the story indicate that the curse was not ineluctable. Their method for putting an end to the ill fortune that haunts the Pyncheons agrees exactly with Hawthorne's moral: the evil will cease to be inherited when the dishonest wealth is returned to the family from which it was originally taken. Gervayse Pyncheon's willingness to give up the House was ineffectual both because he would do so only as part of a bargain extremely profitable to himself, and because for the sake of this bargain he violated his own daughter in breaking a promise to halt the proceedings with Matthew Maule at her "slightest wish."

One other example of this type of statement—suggesting possibilities for escaping an inheritance of "wrong-doing"—is worth noting. Hawthorne himself, closing the chapter which introduced Hepzibah, calls his tale not a story of the inevitable consequences of sin, but a "history

of *retribution* for the sin of long ago" (italics mine). The author himself, very early in the novel, makes it clear that some kind of atonement is possible.

If atonement is possible, the heritage of evil will have an end. Besides providing references which corroborate the *possibility* of atonement, Hawthorne works into his novel predictions, as well as a description of a landscape, which adumbrate and identify the curse's *termination*. Holgrave explains to Phoebe in Chapter xiv his "conviction . . . that the end draws nigh" in "the drama which, for almost two hundred years, has been dragging its slow length over the ground, where you and I now tread." Later Holgrave will say that he made his way into the part of the House where the Judge sat dead because of "an indefinite sense of some catastrophe, or *consummation*" (italics mine). Hawthorne had already used the same word to describe Alice's posies on the morning after the Judge's death: they "seemed, as it were, a mystic expression that something within the house was consummated." Pyncheon retribution reached its peak when the family became its own victim. Judge Jaffrey died while carrying out an action that would have been the "utter ruin" or death of Clifford.

Hawthorne has pointed up the possibility of escaping the curse and confronted us with the fact of consummation in the two-century-old drama, but he goes further. He depicts the House of Seven Gables the morning after the Judge's death as a renewed world. Alice's posies "were flaunting in rich beauty and full bloom," but, more extraordinary, "Every object was agreeable, whether to be gazed at in the breadth, or examined more minutely." The House itself was altered: "there was really an inviting aspect over the venerable edifice, conveying an idea that its history must be a decorous and happy one." Though in one sense explicable—they assure us that the consummation has been beneficial—these changes are in another sense a puzzle. They follow the Judge's death in pursuit of Clifford and are evidence that retribution has been effected. But the results seem disproportionate to the cause; the intended victimizing of Clifford was culpable, and Clifford's actions were not especially meritorious. The family turning against itself may somehow have allowed the curse to pass, but it does not seem to have provided any reason for the House and its environs to be restored to pristine freshness. The gloom might have left the House, but why would it look happy? The love of Phoebe and Holgrave would have been a plausible agent of transformation earlier and would be later, but is not at this point. How are the changes to be accounted for?

The answer, I think, lies not with the Judge's death, except insofar as that may have weakened or helped eliminate the curse. The agency behind the transformations is the mercy of God. Hawthorne playfully allows the inference that God is the agent when he says the House "really" looked as if it had a happy history. For that description seems feasible only in light of his earlier statement that "God is the sole worker of realities." Such evidence is hardly conclusive of course; much more to the point is Hawthorne's description of dawn in the room where the Judge's dead body sat:

> Blessed, blessed radiance! The day-beam—even

what little of it finds its way into this always dusky parlour—seems part of the universal benediction, annulling evil, and rendering all goodness possible, and happiness attainable. . . . This new day . . . God has smiled upon, and blessed, and given to mankind.

Why has God chosen to extend "universal benediction" now? The mercy of God can always be explained as inexplicable, but Hawthorne has given us a better account of its workings within his story. The Judge's death brought to a close the Pyncheon retribution, but Hepzibah had gone on to reach a consummation in personal development. At the end of her flight with Clifford, kneeling on a platform, with hands raised to the sky she had asked "Oh, God—our Father . . . Have mercy on us!" Her prayer had been heard.

Hawthorne indicates that the hand of God is working in other matters of his story; the Almighty, for example, prevented the *renewal* of the Pyncheon evil. When the Judge forced Hepzibah to admit him to the House so he could question Clifford, she accused him of sacrificing Clifford for his own material gain just as an earlier Pyncheon had sacrificed a Maule. Several of her words echo Hawthorne's statement of the moral of the story in his Preface: "You are but doing over again, in another shape, what your ancestor before you did, and sending down to your posterity the curse inherited from him!" Jaffrey thinks the notion preposterous (though his reply—"Talk sense, Hepzibah, for Heaven's sake"—turns out to be ironic), and Hepzibah, still trying to penetrate his imperviousness, predicts "God will not let you do the thing you meditate!" Left by the Judge's terms with no choice but to let him see her brother, Hepzibah warns: "Be merciful in your dealings with him!—be far more merciful than your heart bids you be!—for God is looking at you, Jaffrey Pyncheon!" At this point it is evident that Hepzibah believes a watchful heaven is mindful of Clifford's plight.

As the old woman leaves to fetch Clifford, however, she is brooding on her family's "dreary past" and comes to feel with foreboding that her cousin, her brother, and she are on the verge of the grimmest event in the House's history, not just a redoing of old wrong, something worse. "Hepzibah now felt as if the Judge, and Clifford, and herself—they three together—were on the point of adding another incident to the annals of the house, with a bolder relief of wrong and sorrow, which would cause it to stand out from all the rest." This, presumably, because the family was turned against itself. Hawthorne does say at this point that "grief of the passing moment" has "a character of climax, which it is destined to lose"; however, he adds, "But Hepzibah could not rid herself of the sense of something unprecedented, at that instant passing, and soon to be accomplished." So her feeling is perhaps not to be considered merely an effect of "the passing moment."

She tries to divert her own attention from its cause of despondency, and eventually seeks the help of the daguerreotypist, who is not in his rooms. Hepzibah sees herself as justifiably friendless, and, lifting her eyes, she tries to pray. As we have already seen, her prayer was not successful this time. But the full explanation of its failure and Hawthorne's dissenting comment are especially worth noting. Hepzibah's prayer

> fell back, a lump of lead, upon her heart. It smote her with the wretched conviction, that Providence intermeddled not in these petty wrongs of one individual to his fellow, nor had any balm for these little agonies of a solitary soul, but shed its justice, and its mercy, in a broad, sunlike sweep, over half the universe at once. Its vastness made it nothing.

Moments before, Hepzibah had thought that God would not let the Judge renew the curse on the heads of the Pyncheons, that Providence was watching over Clifford. Now, however, she feels that, exactly because He is all mighty, God would not interfere in the daily affairs of individual men.

Hawthorne in no uncertain terms disagrees: "But Hepzibah did not see, that, just as there comes a warm sunbeam into every cottage-window, so comes a love-beam of God's care and pity for every separate need." This is, I believe, the point in *The House of the Seven Gables* where Hawthorne most explicitly connects Providence with his plot. Here, also, God's love-beam is likened to a sunbeam; later the sunbeam is called "Blessed, blessed radiance! The day-beam . . . part of the universal benediction, annulling evil, and rendering all goodness possible, and happiness attainable." By name as well as by action, Phoebe is a sunchild. Holgrave has told her "Providence sent you hither to help."

Hepzibah had warned the Judge "God will not let you do the thing you meditate." Because the Judge was unrelenting, it did take an act of Providence, grim and merciful both, to keep him from a new low in Pyncheon malfeasance. To Holgrave later, Jaffrey's death "so like that former one, yet attended by none of those suspicious circumstances, seems the stroke of God upon him, at once a punishment for his wickedness, and making plain the innocence of Clifford." Judge Pyncheon, the man of affairs, had ignored his old maid cousin's unwittingly prophetical warning.

In the person of Phoebe, the regenerative power of love and the redeeming force of God's mercy minister together. But Hawthorne also speaks in broad terms about the power of love to change things for the better. Chapter xi offers by itself strong evidence that Hawthorne did not mean in his Preface to propose that the wages of sin are both inheritable and ineluctable. When an organ-grinder takes up his stand before the arched window where Phoebe and Clifford watch, they see a show in which "at the same turning of a crank" various figures engage in their appropriate activity. A cobbler works on a shoe, a miser counts his gold, a scholar opens a book and reads. "Yes; and moved by the self-same impulse, a lover saluted his mistress on her lips!" However,

> the most remarkable aspect of the affair was, that, at the cessation of the music, everybody was petrified at once . . . into a dead torpor. . . . All were precisely in the same condition as before they made themselves so ridicu-

lous by their haste to toil, to enjoy, to accumulate gold, and to become wise.

Hawthorne conjectures as to the meaning of such a show: Perhaps it is meant to signify "that we mortals . . . in spite of our ridiculous activity, bring nothing finally to pass." Examining this "moral," the author considers that the lover would therefore have been "none the happier for the maiden's granted kiss!" But "rather than swallow this last too acrid ingredient," Hawthorne "reject[s] the whole moral of the show." The idea that even love "bring[s] nothing finally to pass" is enough for him to reject the supposed theme. Extended, this means he rejects the thought that even love is helpless when a family is racked by the long possession of ill-gotten gain.

In the final chapter of his romance, Hawthorne utters a statement which, while not so often quoted as the moral of his Preface, has likewise seemed to confute the movement of his story. He is explaining what will be the circumstances of Clifford's life after the Judge's death: "It was now far too late in Clifford's life for the good opinion of society to be worth the trouble and anguish of a formal vindication." The "calm of forgetfulness" will be a greater kindness to Clifford than the exoneration which his townspeople would have been "ready enough" to extend him. "After such wrong as he had suffered, there is no reparation," Hawthorne tells us, and continues with the sentence that has proved almost as troubling as the one in the Preface: "It is a truth (and it would be a very sad one, but for the higher hopes which it suggests) that no great mistake, whether acted or endured, in our mortal sphere, is ever really set right."

Matthiessen has called this the "unrelenting strain . . . still at the fore in [Hawthorne's] final reflections." The novelist seems to have summoned forth again the spectre of inescapable consequences to sin. However, this authorial observation no more runs counter to the movement of Hawthorne's plot than did the sentence in his Preface. The present passage does not mean that the chain of evil consequences to sin is irrefragable, does not mean, in other words, that Phoebe and Holgrave inherit necessarily tainted money and their subsequent years together will be ones of moral decay. In fact, the topic of sin is not raised by the passage in question at all. Hawthorne makes the statement in reference to Clifford's condition: the townspeople who had wrongly sentenced him to prison, though they might exculpate him, could never restore what they had taken from him—thirty years of his life. Hawthorne had not previously suggested and does not here propose that the townsmen sinned in sentencing Clifford, or even that they are culpable. It was Jaffrey's withholding of evidence that produced the mistrial. Thus, in its immediate context, Hawthorne's maxim does not purport to be a reflection on the consequences of an evil act.

"No great mistake, whether acted or endured, in our mortal sphere, is ever really set right." The statement refers *primarily* to the *victim* of a great mistake, rather than to its perpetrators. Hawthorne does say "whether *acted* or *endured*," but he means, I think, to indicate that the persons responsible for some great injustice have as little power to undo it as the one who suffered from it. The focus is still on the victim and the peculiar difficulties of making restitution to him. Hawthorne's meaning is that no one who suffers great wrong can receive full recompense in this world, either from those who wronged him, or by his own efforts.

Subsequent sentences bear out this reading, for Hawthorne refines and clarifies his generalization in the remarks which follow it. The next sentence is: "Time, the continual vicissitude of circumstances, and the invariable inopportunity of death, render it [really setting great mistakes right] impossible." If the preceding sentence had meant that a misdeed has an irreparable effect on its doer and his progeny as well as on the person who sustained the injury, different agents of continuation would have been named. A world in which one could not escape the effects of the sins of his father would, morally, be timeless. Hawthorne in saying that time, change, and death prevent the undoing of a great mistake is saying that all time is not one time. A person is not inextricably bound by what his foregenitors did. Holgrave did not take the opportunity to gain control over Phoebe even though his ancestor Matthew Maule had attained influence over Alice Pyncheon's soul.

The next sentences are likewise intelligible as statements about undoing harm wrongly afflicted rather than as cautions about the hopelessness of avoiding hereditary effects of sin: "If, after long lapse of years, the right seems to be in our power, we find no niche to set it in. The better remedy is for the sufferer to pass on, and leave what he once thought his irreparable ruin far behind him." The first of these sentences discusses an alternative for those who had "acted" a great mistake, the second offers advice to those who have "endured" one. The first sentence is not applicable to a person seeking to remove the guilt for sin—*that* right never seems to be in our power—though it does apply to a person trying to make up for an injury he once did. Moreover, the second statement advocates something like forgetfulness—strange advice to a person worried about the taint his own or his ancestors' wrongs have left him; humane advice, however, to someone whose reputation and position may be irretrievably and unjustly lost. Hawthorne has just recommended the "calm of forgetfulness" for Clifford.

The statement we have been examining from the last chapter does not conflict with Hawthorne's story; it is a more general amplification of a remark which preceded it: "After such wrong as he had suffered, there is no reparation." Clifford would never be fully restored, but the jury that imprisoned him, and the children of the men who served on it, were not blighted because of their action. A world in which the wrong deliberately or inadvertently done by one's ancestors leaves bleaker hope for oneself would be a constantly darkening world. The world of *The House of the Seven Gables* is optimistic, though Hawthorne's is a careful optimism. Describing "The Daguerreotypist" he had said: "He had that sense, or inward prophecy—which a young man had better never have been born, than not to have, and a mature man had better die at once, than utterly to relinquish—that we are not doomed to creep on forever in the old, bad way, but that, this very now, there are the harbingers abroad of a golden era, to be accomplished in his own lifetime." Hawthorne's thinking a prophetic sense of this kind so necessary suggests what his own view may be. He does not leave us with mere conjecture, however, for in further describing the artist Holgrave he makes his own view explicit. The daguerreotypist, he tells us, was wrong

> in supposing that this age, more than any past or future one, is destined to see the tattered garments of Antiquity exchanged for a new suit, instead of gradually renewing themselves by patchwork; in applying his own little lifespan as the measure of an interminable achievement; and, more than all, in fancying that it mattered anything to the great end in view, whether he himself should contend for it or against it.

Holgrave might overestimate his own place in the brightening history of mankind, but that human history is brightening, Hawthorne fully agrees: "As to the main point—may we never live to doubt it!—as to the better centuries that are coming, the artist was surely right." (pp. 579-90)

> *Francis Joseph Battaglia, " 'The House of the Seven Gables': New Light on Old Problems," in* PMLA, *Vol. LXXXII, No. 7, December, 1967, pp. 579-90.*

## Richard Harter Fogle    (essay date 1969)

[*Fogle is an American educator and critic. In the following essay, he discusses Hawthorne's conception of* The House of the Seven Gables *as a picture, or design. He also explores the author's use of light and shadow imagery to create a harmonious aesthetic effect.*]

Nathaniel Hawthorne's **The House of the Seven Gables** was published in 1851. Like its predecessor, **The Scarlet Letter,** its origin is in the history of the Puritans of Massachusetts; in this later book there is Hawthorne family history as well, in the story of the Pyncheon family over some two hundred years in Salem. The time is Hawthorne's day, overshadowed by the past. The story is, in the words of the Preface, "a legend prolonging itself, from an epoch now gray in the distance, down into our own broad daylight, and bringing along with it some of its legendary mist. . . . " The actual House is the material symbol of the Pyncheon fortunes, an old mansion now in decline, built upon property usurped from the original owner, Matthew Maule, by the original Pyncheon, a hard, stern Puritan. This act of Colonel Pyncheon, the "founder of the house," still grips the Pyncheons of today: Judge Pyncheon, a reincarnation of the Colonel; Hepzibah, a melancholy relic of the past, and the unfortunate Clifford, her brother. Significantly, Phoebe, the Pyncheon who redeems the family, has not been reared within the shadow of the ancient House. One other person, Holgrave, dwells in the House as a lodger. We eventually discover that he is the last survivor of the injured Maules. His life, too, has been darkened, but he has a freedom not permitted to the Pyncheons.

Posterity has not agreed with him, but Hawthorne preferred this second novel to **The Scarlet Letter.** He thought the **House** better balanced, more various, more representative of his whole mind, which contained humor and delicate sentiment as well as tragic gloom. He considered it, in fact, more fully harmonious; it possessed more colors, completely blended into a satisfying aesthetic whole.

Anyone who has considered Hawthorne's theory of composition, especially his theory of the prose romance, has undoubtedly noticed his pictorial analogies for his verbal art. Perhaps, indeed, they are so numerous and obvious that we tend to overlook them as not requiring discussion. At first glance, too, they are commonplace and traditional. They call to mind both the Horatian *ut pictura poesis* of neoclassicism and the "picturesque" of the English Romantics. But, as is also true of his symbols, which are also apparently conventional, the difference with Hawthorne is that he *means* his figure of picture. He uses it consistently and responsibly. It is assimilated in his critical discourse, and fully operative in his fiction.

This contention has an important relation to a crux of Hawthorne, criticism, his treatment of character. Looked at individually, Hawthorne's people do not satisfy us. They seem too abstract, too allegorical; they are all imperfect, mutilated, incomplete. They pretend to life, and like most nineteenth-century novelists Hawthorne wants to be conceded his *donnée* of reality. Conscious of a certain thinness, he nevertheless rather wistfully aspires to the illusion of verisimilitude. Thus if we go wrong, and we generally do on this point, our author himself is considerably to blame. He is trying to deceive us, and he is covering his weakness instead of playing from his strength.

His strength lies in his total conception of the art of fiction as picture, in which individual characters function not as individuals, but in relation to each other and to his total design. Thus Hawthorne's people should not be studied in isolation. Of themselves the characters of **The House of the Seven Gables** are all inadequate. Phoebe is too sweet, Hepzibah and Clifford Pyncheon are nearly ludicrous, and a little contemptible in their defenselessness. The formidable Judge is too melodramatic, too openly hateful, and the young photographer Holgrave too lightly drawn. Taken together, however, as parts or colors of the picture, as shading and contrast, they make up a design.

There are doubtless other reasons for the nature of Hawthorne's characterization. His view of life does not ordinarily permit of the dominant hero and heroine, or the dominant villian either. He believes in good and evil, but these are states not permanently identified with people; there is always the possibility that different circumstances would have produced different results. Even Judge Pyncheon, that iron-hearted hypocrite, is victim as well as tyrant. Again, Hawthorne does not believe in success, nor in lasting significance in objective action. In his major romances his principal characters appear in groups of four or five.

Further, **The House of the Seven Gables** is thoroughly relevant to the social, the psychological, and the religious history of colonial America and the young republic. It is family history as well, since the successful Pyncheons and the defeated Maules are simply two faces of the Hawthorne generations in Salem, Massachusetts. Issues arise: the Judge is the American materialist; and in the fortunes and the aspirations of the Pyncheons we see the principles of aristocracy and democracy in conflict in a young and growing society. Out of the American scene and problem we see emerging, too, more universal themes. The history of the Pyncheons repeats the Original Sin and the Fall of Man in indigenous Yankee terms; it issues from the crime of the original Pyncheon against the original Maule. One discerns in it, also, the immemorial tragedy of a house, like Aeschylus' *Oresteia,* or the Oedipus trilogy, or in modern American terms Eugene O'Neill's *Mourning Becomes Electra* or Faulkner's tales of the Sutpens and Compsons of Mississippi.

In their setting of time and place the characters of the book are recognizable social, historical, and moral types. The Judge is the modern reincarnation of the Original Puritan, and in himself the modern financial magnate, town father, and politician. Hepzibah is the aristocratic spinster with pathetic pretensions to gentility, in a relatively democratic society which is also strongly materialistic. She is slow to realize that without money her values are impotent, and at the beginning of the story we see her learning a cruel lesson in reality—she is forced to keep a "cent-shop," the equivalent of the twentieth-century corner confectionery. Clifford Pyncheon is the paradoxical but inevitable product of material success, the refined dilettante, who at a later date would have resorted to Henry Jamesian expatriation. Phoebe is the flower of New England provincial democracy, a new and hopeful type for the American future. She is "ladylike" without being a "lady." The more ambiguous Holgrave is, with perhaps an ironic glance at the doctrines of the Fall and Redemption, the "new man" American style, a sort of New England Mark Twain, rootless, free, mobile, and versatile; and like the others, a product of a particular society.

In *The House of the Seven Gables* Hawthorne's Preface announces the theme. The romancer may, if he think fit, "so manage his atmospherical medium as to bring out or mellow the lights and enrich the shadows of the picture." The story "is a legend prolonging itself, from an epoch now gray in the distance, down into our own broad daylight, and bringing along with it some of its legendary mist, which the reader, according to his pleasure, may either disregard, or allow it to float almost imperceptibly about the characters and events for the sake of a picturesque effect." Here is of course a fourth dimension of time, and it is well to remind ourselves of the limitations of analogy. A novel is not literally a picture, though it may profitably be compared to one. Nevertheless, time merges with the pictorial: the distant past is "gray," the present is "broad daylight," and the "legendary mist" is an imaginative atmosphere, itself a sort of total lighting or aerial perspective.

The author, as he says, does not choose to mar the harmonies of his picturesque story by didacticism. He will not impale it "with its moral as with an iron rod,—or, rather, as by sticking a pin through a butterfly,—thus at once depriving it of life, and causing it to stiffen in an ungainly

and unnatural attitude." The moral, however, may itself become an element of the harmony of the picturesque, by the gradations of its light. "A high truth, indeed, fairly, finely, and skillfully wrought out, brightening at every step, and crowning the final development of a work of fiction, may add an artistic glory. . . . "

Hawthorne asks of his reader and critic that he place himself at the proper distance for viewing his picture. Consequently he regrets the closeness of his work to "an actual locality." "Not to speak of other objections, it exposes the romance to an inflexible and exceedingly dangerous species of criticism, by bringing his fancy-pictures almost into positive contact with the realities of the moment." These realities would constitute, that is, an overstrong and generally inappropriate light for viewing. In his sketch **"Main Street,"** in which a showman exhibits more than two centuries of Salem history in a "shifting panorama," a spectator damns the exhibition. The showman defends his art: " 'But, sir, you have not the proper point of view. . . . You sit altogether too near to get the best effect of my pictorial exhibition. Pray, oblige me by removing to this other bench; and, I venture to assure you, the proper light and shadow will transform the spectacle into quite another thing.' "

With "the proper point of view," then, Hawthorne trusts that "the proper light and shadow" will appear. Seen thus, the too-simple and sunny Phoebe becomes a study in harmony; and, as good, the fullest contrast with Judge Pyncheon, the embodiment of Pyncheon evil, who is a study in disharmony and excess. Phoebe

> shocked no canon of taste; she was admirably in keeping with herself, and never jarred against surrounding circumstances. . . . She was very pretty; as graceful as a bird, and graceful much in the same way; as pleasant about the house as a gleam of sunshine falling on the floor through a shadow of twinkling leaves, or as a ray of firelight that dances on the wall while evening is drawing nigh.

Her primary image is sunshine, pleasantly tempered, a golden mean. Though delicately tanned, she is never fully exposed to the heat of the sun and everyday experience: on one occasion we find her using a sunshade. The key to her character, as to Hawthorne's moral and aesthetic values, is moderation. When the unfortunate Clifford almost involuntarily tries to throw himself out of a window into the street, "Phoebe, to whom all extravagance was a horror, burst into sobs and tears."

Judge Pyncheon's falsity, on the other hand, is manifested in excess and extremity. He is basically discordant. At his first introduction (in terms of portraiture, incidentally) he is a counterfeit of decorum and "keeping," always a little awry because he has no corresponding inner sense:

> It was the portly, and had it possessed the advantage of a little more height, would have been the stately figure of a man considerably in the decline of life, dressed in a black suit of some thin stuff, resembling broadcloth as closely as possible. A gold-headed cane, of rare Oriental wood, added materially to the high respectability of his

aspect, as did also a neckcloth of the utmost snowy purity, and the conscientious polish of his boots. His dark, square countenance, with its almost shaggy depth of eyebrows, was naturally impressive, and would, perhaps, have been rather stern, had not the gentleman considerately taken upon himself to mitigate the harsh effect by a look of exceeding good humor and benevolence. Owing, however, to a somewhat massive accumulation of animal substance about the lower region of the face, the look was, perhaps, unctuous, rather than spiritual, and had, so to speak, a kind of fleshly effulgence, not altogether so satisfactory as he doubtless intended it to be. A susceptible observer, at any rate, might have regarded it as affording very little evidence of the general benignity of soul whereof it purported to be the outward reflection. And if the observer chanced to be ill-natured, as well as acute and susceptible, he would probably suspect that the smile on the gentleman's face was a good deal akin to the shine on his boots, and that each must have cost him and his bootblack, respectively, a good deal of hard labor to bring out and preserve them.

The Judge, then, like a bad portrait is compact of harsh and glaring disharmonies. His height is not quite proportionate to his build, his suit not quite broadcloth, his linen too white, his boots too well polished. His look of benevolence is *exceeding,* and clashes with his natural sternness. He is *unctuous,* with a *fleshly effulgence,* where he intends to express spirituality.

The harmonious Phoebe, intuitively sensing his aesthetic and moral wrongness, draws back from the Judge's cousinly kiss on their first meeting. For a moment the true Judge appears, at the opposite extreme, hard and deadly cold. "It was quite as striking, allowing for the difference in scale, as that betwixt a landscape under a broad sunshine and just before a thunderstorm; not that it had the passionate intensity of the latter aspect, but was cold, hard, immitigable, like a day-long brooding cloud." In an effort to right the balance, the Judge shortly turns upon Hepzibah "a smile, so broad and sultry, that, had it been only half as warm as it looked, a trellis of grapes might at once have turned purple under its summer-like exposure."

The Judge and Hepzibah are mirror-images of each other, with attributes reversed. Hepzibah is dark, and even in her voice is a thread of blackness. Her habitual expression is a scowl, an echo of the dark-browed house of the seven gables in whose shadow she lives. But within is light, for she has a soft and loving heart. Her darkness has been impressed upon her, while it is the reality of the outward-smiling Judge. There is no blackness in the delicate hedonist Clifford, but with a difference in shading he also is the obverse of the Judge, with a certain resemblance on the other hand to Phoebe.

> Clifford readily showed how capable of imbibing pleasant tints and gleams of cheerful light from all quarters his nature must originally have been. He grew youthful while she sat by him. A beauty—not precisely real, even in its utmost manifestation, and which a painter would have watched long to seize and fix upon his canvas,

and after all, in vain—beauty, nevertheless, that was not a mere dream would sometimes play upon and illuminate his face.

One notes again the portrait motif. But Clifford's hold on reality is so precarious, his connection so tenuous, that he can hardly be pictured at all.

It is remarkable, however, that the characters of **The House of the Seven Gables** have been conceived very largely as pictures. Critics have often mentioned the role of the actual portraits in the House, and the more subtle function of its mirrors. Most central is the Colonel, the original Pyncheon and "founder of the house":

> In one sense, this picture had almost faded out into the canvas, and hidden itself behind the duskiness of age; in another . . . it had been growing more prominent, and strikingly expressive. . . . For, while the physical outline and substance were darkening away from the beholder's eye, the bold, hard, and, at the same time, indirect character of the man seemed to be brought out in a kind of spiritual relief.

Hawthorne reflects that "In such cases the painter's deep conception of his subject's inward traits has wrought itself into the essence of the picture, and is seen after the superficial coloring has been rubbed off by time."

This picture includes and focuses a good deal. It is the dark aura of the House, the mystic center of its evil. It contains within it the dimension of time. Most important, it interplays with and is a commentary upon the Judge, the Pyncheon of today. The Judge, as we have seen, is himself a portrait, but his essence is obscured by external detail. At his first introduction it is said of him that "He would have made a good and massive portrait; better now, perhaps, than at any previous period of his life, although his look might grow positively harsh in the process of being fixed upon the canvas."

There is likewise a portrait of Clifford as a young man, a Malbone miniature.

> It is a likeness of a young man, in a silken dressing gown of an old fashion, the soft richness of which is well adapted to the countenance of reverie, with its full, tender lips, and beautiful eyes, that seem to indicate not so much capacity of thought as gentle and voluptuous emotion. Of the possessor of such features we shall have a right to ask nothing, except that he would take the rude world easily, and make himself happy in it.

We see this picture again, but idealized by the loving mind of Hepzibah as she awaits the actual Clifford, many years older and just released from prison. It is "painted with more daring flattery than any artist would have ventured upon, but yet so delicately touched that the likeness remained perfect. Malbone's miniature, though from the same original, was far inferior to Hepzibah's air-drawn picture, at which affection and sorrowful remembrance wrought together." Finally, Clifford appears himself, but sadly changed. He is wearing the same dressing gown as in the Malbone miniature, but it has changed correspondingly. "At first glance, Phoebe saw an elderly personage, in an old-fashioned dressing gown of faded damask, and wearing his gray or almost white hair of an unusual length."

Two pictures more comprehensive than these illustrate Hawthorne's characteristic sense of composition and unity. The first is a kind of genre painting, Vermeer with Rembrandt shadows. The scene is a breakfast table, awaiting the first appearance of the long-banished Clifford:

> Phoebe's Indian cakes were the sweetest offering of all—in their hue befitting the rustic altars of the innocent and golden age—or, so brightly yellow were they, resembling some of the bread which was changed to glistening gold when Midas tried to eat it. The butter must not be forgotten—butter which Phoebe herself had churned, in her own rural home, and brought it to her cousin as a propitiating gift—smelling of clover blossoms, and diffusing the charm of pastoral scenery through the dark-paneled parlor. All this, with the quaint gorgeousness of the old china cups and saucers, and the crested spoons, and a silver cream jug . . . set out a board at which the stateliest of old Colonel Pyncheon's guests need not have scorned to take his place. But the Puritan's face scowled down out of the picture, as if nothing on the table pleased his appetite.

> By way of contributing what grace she could, Phoebe gathered some roses and a few other flowers, possessing either scent or beauty, and arranged them in a glass pitcher, which, having long ago lost its handle, was so much the fitter for a flower vase. The early sunshine—as fresh as that which peeped into Eve's bower while she and Adam sat at breakfast there—came twinkling through the branches of the pear tree, and fell quite across the table.

This quaint and mellow scene is carefully shaded, from the bright gold of the Indian cakes and the butter and the paler gold of morning sun to the dark-paneled walls and the scowling portrait of the Colonel. It is a chiaroscuro effect, but unobtrusive, gently lighted with the dominant gold, and given motion by the gentle stir of the pear-tree branches. As elsewhere, the gray mist of time plays its part in the portrait and the battered glass pitcher, and merges with the sense of poor, misty, time-battered Clifford, who is on the verge of appearing.

Finally, there is the Pyncheon garden by moonlight, Hawthorne's symbol for the light of imagination. It is at this moment that the sunny Phoebe falls in love, becoming a woman:

> By this time the sun had gone down, and was tinting the clouds towards the zenith with those bright hues which are not seen there until some time after sunset, and when the horizon has quite lost its richer brilliancy. The moon, too, which had long been climbing overhead, and unobtrusively melting its disk into the azure . . . now began to shine out, broad and oval, in its middle pathway. These silvery beams were already powerful enough to change the character of the lingering daylight. They softened and embellished the aspect of the old house; although

the shadows fell deeper into the angles of its many gables, and lay brooding under the projecting story, and within the half-open door. With the lapse of every moment, the garden grew more picturesque; the fruit trees, shrubbery, and flower bushes had a dark obscurity among them. The commonplace characteristics—which at noontide, it seemed to have taken a century of sordid life to accumulate—were now transfigured by a charm of romance. A hundred mysterious years were whispering among the leaves, whenever the slight sea breeze found its way thither and stirred them. Through the foliage that roofed the little summer house, the moonlight flickered to and fro, and fell silvery white on the dark floor, the table, and the circular bench, with a continual shift and play, according as the chinks and wayward crevices among the twigs admitted or shut out the glimmer.

The picture presents Hawthorne's most complex harmonies of light, color, shading, blending, and motion, along with his gift of unobtrusive but significant emphasis. The moonlight deepens Phoebe's perceptions, and adds a new tone to her character. It represents the essential truth of Hawthorne's favorite art, and illuminates his definition of his own romance, managing, as he says, "his atmospherical medium [so] as to bring out or mellow the lights and

---

**Newton Arvin on *The House of the Seven Gables*:**

The scene is set elaborately . . . the lines are drawn and the colors disposed with the last subtlety; all the properties are in exquisite keeping, and the lights are adjusted and readjusted with marvelous atmospheric skill; but the action, in the midst of this impeccable "atmosphere", is halting, torpid, and badly emphasized. Not that there are not wonderful feats of narration; no one can forget the relation of Clifford Pyncheon's uncanny homecoming, or the Judge's nightlong vigil in the parlor of the deserted mansion. But what happens momentously is painfully out of proportion to what is so copiously told. The sudden death of an avaricious hypocrite, the return from prison of a wronged man, a happy love affair between the last of the Pyncheons and the last of the Maules—these are the substance of the drama, but they are too small a portion of the substance of the book. There are plenty of "scenes", to be sure: but the curtain rises and falls upon them too abruptly, and the principle of coherence among them is less dramatic than pictorial. The story of the cent-shop takes up three deliberate chapters; a Sunday afternoon in the Pyncheon garden is described in leisurely detail; young Holgrave . . . holds up the course of the narrative with a tale of his own, which just falls short of the jejune; the Italian boy with the barrel organ is an agent of tedium, not of speed; and, at a luckless moment for the narrator, Hepzibah and Clifford escape from the old mansion to set off on a railway journey that comes close to undoing the book. All this is delightful in its way—it is even beguiling—but it is not dramatically arresting. . . .

*Newton Arvin, in his* Hawthorne, Russell & Russell, 1961.

---

enrich the shadows of the picture." It represents the aesthetic theory of *The House of the Seven Gables,* and, rightly observed, it goes far toward explaining the nature, the interrelations, and the functions of his characters. (pp. 111-20)

> Richard Harter Fogle, "Nathaniel Hawthorne: 'The House of the Seven Gables'," in Landmarks of American Writing, *edited by Hennig Cohen, Basic Books, Inc., Publishers, 1969, pp. 111-20.*

## Sheldon W. Liebman (essay date 1973)

[*In the following essay, Liebman notes the discrepancy throughout* The House of the Seven Gables *between public and private accounts of the Pyncheon-Maule dispute and asserts that Hawthorne intended his readers to choose between these conflicting points-of-view.*]

In the preface to *The House of the Seven Gables* Hawthorne calls his story a Romance: "The point of view in which this tale comes under the Romantic definition, lies," he explains, "in the attempt to connect a by-gone time with the very Present that is flitting away from us." Although the story begins with the recent past, "there will be a connection with the long past . . . which, if adequately translated to the reader, would serve to illustrate how much of the old material goes to make up the freshest novelty of human life." Hawthorne asks his readers to translate this "connection," but he warns implicitly that the task is not an easy one, for the tale "is a Legend prolonging itself, from an epoch now gray in the distance, down into our own broad daylight," which brings "along with it some of its legendary mist." Choosing to write a Romance rather than a Novel, the writer "may so manage his atmospherical medium as to bring out or mellow the lights and deepen and enrich the shadows of the picture."

As these comments suggest, a Romance is a special kind of story, told in a special way. Because Hawthorne's subject is the relationship between past and present, he must deal with the legends and traditions by which the past has been preserved and by which it has come down to the present. Yet to Hawthorne this aspect of the story is merely "atmospherical" or ornamental: "the reader, according to his pleasure, may either disregard" the information which has passed down from generation to generation by word of mouth, "or allow it to float almost imperceptibly about the characters and events, for the sake of a picturesque effect." The writer of Romances must, after all, "make a very moderate use of the privileges" of his craft, "and, especially, to mingle the Marvellous rather as a slight, delicate, and evanescent flavor, than as any portion of the actual substance of the dish offered to the Public." For this reason Hawthorne intends "to make short work with most of the traditionary lore of which the old Pyncheon house . . . has been the theme."

Thus, one of Hawthorne's contemporary reviewers, Henry Fothergill Chorley [in a review reprinted in the Norton Critical Edition of *The House of the Seven Gables,* 1967], complained that the ambiguity of the story, "that delight in playing with an idea and placing it in every

chameleon light of the prism," derived from hawthorne's "affluence of fancy." More recent critics have treated the book in the same way. Though almost all of them have recognized the ambiguity of Hawthorne's narration, few have regarded the legends in the story as anything more than picturesque.

Unlike Chorley, many critics have praised Hawthorne for his fashionably "modern" technique, but no one has entertained the possibility that this aspect of the story may be functional, and therefore central to the problem of interpretation. Yet even in the preface Hawthorne's attitude toward the legendary material is ambivalent. He "would be glad . . . if . . . the book may be read strictly as a Romance, having a great deal more to do with the clouds overhead, than with any portion of the actual soil of the County of Essex." Furthermore, "when Romances do really teach anything, or produce any effective operation, it is usually through a far more subtle process than the ostensible one."

As these remarks suggest and despite Hawthorne's disclaimers elsewhere in the preface, the legends in *The House of the Seven Gables* must be taken very seriously. For all the important events in the story and the characters who participate in them are treated in terms of two kinds of information, one based on "legends," the other based on "history," both of which interpret the connection between past and present. And throughout the book Hawthorne entertains two points of view toward these interpretations. At times he speaks favorably of chimney-corner tradition and local gossip; at times he rejects them. The same is true, of course, of his treatment of official reports and public records. One must conclude, I think, with Leo B. Levy [in his essay "Picturesque Style in *The House of the Seven Gables,*" *NEQ* 39 (1956)], that *The House of the Seven Gables* is "complicated by a deep-rooted ambivalence that enters into every aspect of the book," an ambivalence that derives from Hawthorne's shifting point of view.

In *The House of the Seven Gables* Hawthorne focuses upon every aspect of the problem of history, the relationship between past and present; specifically, history as event, as theory, and as method. For the issue inevitably raised by his narrative method is the question: What happened? Only when this question is answered can one begin to theorize about "meaning"; only then can one discern the pattern of events, their relationship to each other, and the consequences for man, as Hawthorne sees them. In pursuit of this answer Hawthorne and his characters comment extensively on heredity and history. And this is the real subject of the story. One can discover "what happened," however, only by examining the book in terms of Hawthorne's narrative points of view, for "what happened" is recorded in folk-history as well as in official history, and the reader must determine which of these versions of the past is true.

As I intend to show in this essay, Hawthorne is primarily concerned with the conflict between appearance and reality as it affects the problem of judgment for his characters and as it affects the problem of interpretation for his reader. Hawthorne's intention seems to be to make the reader become his own historian, to force the observer to discount even the narrator's interpretation of events and to reconstruct his own analysis. In this way Hawthorne engages the reader in the very dilemma his characters invariably find themselves in—the problem of moral choice. Hawthorne's narrator is a kind of confidence man, tempting the reader to come to easy conclusions by avoiding the ambiguities which are so much more the subject of the book than the narrator's *dicta,* which threaten at every point to obscure the essential action of the story and obfuscate its meaning.

Though some of the stories connected with the Pyncheon House and the Pyncheon family have only a picturesque effect, most of the legends and traditions deal with the central events and characters in **The Seven Gables.** Both the Pyncheons and the Maules are presented from both the "legendary" and the "historical" points of view, and it is necessary to come to grips with the conflict between so-called "fact" and so-called "fiction" in order to come to conclusions about the members of the two feuding families.

First, Colonel Pyncheon is treated from both legendary and historical points of view. Of the dispute over the Maule's land, for example, "no written record . . . is known to be in existence. Our acquaintance with the whole subject is derived chiefly from tradition. It would be bold, therefore," Hawthorne contends, "and possibly unjust, to venture a decisive opinion as to its merits." As Gervayse Pyncheon claims, "The matter was settled at the time, and by the competent authorities—equitably, it is to be presumed—and, at all events, irrevocably." The question at issue is whether or not the old Colonel's claim "were not unduly stretched" and Maule's rights violated. To believe "the competent authorities" is to take the view that the Pyncheon progenitor was what he *seemed* to be, a willful, perhaps, but honest man about whom the town gossips then and now have spread unjust rumors.

Yet it appears to have been at least a matter of doubt that the Colonel acted reasonably in this instance, and the "suspicion" is strengthened by the fact that the conflict lasted much longer than would have been necessary, considering the Colonel's political influence, had his claim been just. Thus, "there was much shaking of the head among the village-gossips. Without absolutely expressing a doubt whether the stalwart Puritan had acted as a man of conscience and integrity throughout the proceedings which have been sketched, they nevertheless hinted that he was about to build his house over an unquiet grave." "In after days . . . it was remembered" how zealously and bitterly old Pyncheon pursued his victim, and Maule himself complained that his enemy's objectives were material rather than spiritual. Considering the inadequacies of retrospective analysis, however, the only point in the dispute which remains indisputable is the story of Maule's curse, delivered from the scaffold, for both "history" and "fireside tradition" have "preserved the very words" of the prophecy.

Later in the novel, Hawthorne supports the legendary view less equivocally. The Colonel, "so at least says chimney-corner tradition, which *often preserves traits of character with marvellous fidelity*—was bold, imperious, relentless, crafty; laying his purposes deep, and following them out with an inveteracy of pursuit that knew neither rest nor conscience; trampling on the weak, and, when essential to his ends, doing his utmost to beat down the strong" (my emphasis). The clergyman's discourse at the Colonel's funeral "absolutely canonized" the old Puritan, and the inscription of his tombstone is "highly eulogistic; nor does history, so far as he holds a place upon its page, assail the consistency and uprightness of his character." Yet, "It is often instructive to take the woman's, the private and domestic view, of a public man; nor can anything be more curious than the vast discrepancy between portraits intended for engraving and the pencil-sketches that pass from hand to hand, behind the original's back."

The same inconsistency appears in the public and private views of Judge Pyncheon, for "neither clergyman, nor legal critic, nor inscriber of tombstones, nor historian of general or local politics, would venture a word against this eminent person's sincerity as a christian, or respectability as a man, or integrity as a judge, or courage and faithfulness as the often-tried representative of his political party"; yet, just as "tradition affirmed that the Puritan had been greedy of wealth [,] the Judge, too . . . was said to be as close-fisted as if his gripe were of iron." Indeed, at the appearance of those of the Colonel's descendants who displayed the same "hereditary qualities," "the traditionary gossips of the town" whispered "among themselves:— 'Here is the old Pyncheon come again!' " Thus, just as there are "singular stories" about his ancestors, there are "scandal[s]" and "fable[s]" about the Pyncheon of today. Besides the "cold, formal, and empty words of the chisel that inscribes, the voice that speaks, and the pen that writes for the public eye and for distant time—and which inevitably lose much of their truth and freedom by the fatal consciousness of so doing—there were traditions about the ancestor, and private diurnal gossip about the Judge, remarkably accordant in their testimony."

The Maules, too, are subjected to the same double treatment, and Hawthorne toys with the idea that the prophecy of Matthew Maule is but one of a number of strange ties between the two families. In his story of Alice Pyncheon, Holgrave mentions that "the popular belief pointed to some mysterious connection and dependence, existing between the family of the Maules, and these vast, unrealized possessions of the Pyncheons." Though one part of the story is "an ordinary saying" and another is "a byword," "these fables" have been passed on in "the fireside talk" of aged women, and "a portion of these popular rumors could be traced, though rather doubtfully and indistinctly, to chance words and obscure hints of the executed wizard's son"—not very reliable sources, after all. Yet Gervayse Pyncheon, according to Holgrave's testimony, "either fancied or remembered that Matthew's father had had some job to perform, on the day before, or possibly the very morning, of the Colonel's decease, in the private room where he and the carpenter were at this moment talking." Of course, as the reader eventually discovers, this legend is true, for Holgrave reveals the hiding place of the deed behind the Colonel's portrait, a secret apparently passed on in the Maule family from father to son.

On other "mysterious connections" between the Pyncheons and the Maules, Hawthorne is somewhat less conclusive. The Maules are rumored, for example, to have a power over the Pyncheons in their sleeping hours:

> Among other good-for-nothing properties and privileges one was especially assigned them, of exercising an influence over people's dreams. The Pyncheons, *if all stories were true,* haughtily as they bore themselves in the noonday streets of their native town, were no better than bond-servants to these plebeian Maules, on entering the topsyturvy commonwealth of sleep. (my emphasis)

Holgrave reports that young Matthew Maule "was popularly supposed to have inherited some of his ancestor's questionable traits. . . . He was fabled, for example, to have a strange power of getting into people's dreams, and regulating matters there according to his own fancy." The gossips say that "he could look into people's minds" or draw them "into his own mind." Gervayse, in fact, relies on these very powers when he asks young Matthew to find the deed, for "his mind was haunted with the many and strange tales" of the Maules' "supernatural endowments." Holgrave dismisses these legends connected with his ancestors—"It is wonderful how many absurdities were promulgated in reference to the young man"—but Hawthorne suggests that "modern psychology, it may be, will endeavor to reduce these alleged necromancies within a system, instead of rejecting them as altogether fabulous." Again, as we see at the end of Holgrave's narrative, the Maules actually do possess this power which "modern psychology" knew even in Hawthorne's day as mesmerism. Thus, while the Maules may not have the Evil Eye and "the faculty of blighting corn, and drying children into mummies with the heartburn," they can (and do, if Holgrave's story of Alice is true) get into the Pyncheons' dreams and influence their actions.

Not so susceptible of verification, however, is the legend of the looking-glass, "fabled to contain within its depths all the shapes that had ever been reflected there"; Hawthorne mentions a story,

> for which it is difficult to conceive any foundation, that the posterity of Matthew Maule had some connection with the mystery of the looking-glass and that—by what appears to have been a sort of mesmeric process—they could make its inner region all alive with the departed Pyncheons; not as they had shown themselves to the world, nor in their better and happier hours, but as doing over again some deed of sin, or in the crisis of life's bitterest sorrow.

And later in the book, at Judge Pyncheon's death, he introduces the subject again, with the same skepticism: "In fact, these tales are too absurd to bristle even childhood's hair. What sense, meaning, or moral, for example, such as even ghost-stories should be susceptible of, can be traced in the ridiculous legend that, at midnight, all the dead Pyncheons are bound to assemble in this parlor!" Yet Hawthorne is "tempted to make a little sport with the idea," and goes on to display the ancient Pyncheons and those of more recent years who have died but now parade

about the parlor before the Judge's vacant eyes. After describing the scene he apologizes for "indulging our fancy in this freak" and losing "the power of restraint and guidance": "The fantastic scene, just hinted at, must by no means be considered as forming an actual portion of our story."

One may conclude, I think, that though *some* "ghost-stories are hardly to be treated seriously, any longer," many of "the family traditions, which lingered, like cobwebs and incrustations of smoke, about the rooms and chimney-corners of the House of the Seven Gables," must be considered true. Hawthorne seems to reject only the preternatural aspects of the legendary material: the tradition of the looking glass, the ghostly presence of Alice Pyncheon, the shifting frowns and scowls of Colonel Pyncheon's portrait, the power of the Maules to call forth the dead, and much of the rest of the Gothic paraphernalia. He does *not* reject the legends of the Pyncheons' greed and the rumors of the Maules' mysterious powers.

The significance of this point can be seen in the matter of the Pyncheon deaths; for just as the Pyncheons are implicated in the sins of ill-gotten wealth, so the Maules are implicated in the crime of retribution. Indeed, the ambiguity of the novel centers upon the deaths of the Pyncheons: the Colonel's, Uncle Jaffrey's, and the Judge's. History and publicly expressed opinion consider the deaths accidental, or at worst the consequence of Maule's curse. In either case, apoplexy is the immediate cause. Legend (or privately expressed opinion) considers the deaths to be murders, perpetrated by the Maules, generation after generation. The descriptions of the dying man in each instance are identical: an unnatural distortion of the face and a bloody ruff and beard. It seems reasonable to assume, therefore, that these three men either *all* died of apoplexy, as history says, or *all* died at the hands of a murderer, as chimney-corner tradition suggests.

The circumstances of Colonel Pyncheon's death gave rise to a number of rumors: there were signs of violence and indications that someone was in the Colonel's room at the time of his death. Though the coroner's jury, Dr. Swinnerton, and the Rev. Mr. Higginson concluded that the Colonel had suffered an attack of apoplexy, other physicians, "each for himself, adopted various hypotheses, more or less plausible, but all dressed out in a perplexing mystery of phrase, which, if it do not show a bewilderment of mind in these erudite physicians, certainly causes it in the unlearned peruser of their opinions." And though Mr. Higginson pointed out the timeliness of the Colonel's death, "he unquestionably died too soon," in Hawthorne's words. With his death and the mysterious disappearance of the deed to the Maine lands, the Colonel and his heirs were unable to justify their claim. Thus, though Hawthorne rejects the possibility of murder—"It is indeed difficult to imagine that there could have been a serious suspicion of murder, or the slightest grounds for implicating any particular individual as the perpetrator"—he gives the reader every reason to conclude otherwise. Thomas Maule was in the Pyncheon House on the day of the Colonel's death, according to Gervayse Pyncheon, and Thomas apparently hid the deed behind the Colonel's portrait, as Holgrave's later "discovery" of the deed suggests.

The circumstances of Uncle Jaffrey's death are equally mysterious. In this instance, the authorities "adjudged" it a "violent death" and accused Clifford Pyncheon of the crime. By the time of the Judge's own demise, however, "the medical opinion had almost entirely obviated the idea that a murder was committed, in the former case."

Finally, at Judge Pyncheon's death, although the public reaction is short-lived, there is at least a momentary stir: "it seemed probable, at first blush, that the mode of his final departure might give him a larger and longer posthumous vogue, than ordinarily attends the memory of a distinguished man." But only "a bubble or two" ascended "out of the black depth" and burst at the surface. Again "the highest professional authority" determined "that the event was a natural, and—except for some unimportant particulars, denoting a slight idiosyncrasy—by no means an unusual form of death." As Alfred H. Marks comments [in "Who Killed Judge Pyncheon?" *PMLA* 71, 1956], "The author reports few rumors on the death of Judge Pyncheon, although it is at least as mysterious as the other two deaths. Clearly, therefore, the reader must assemble his own explanation."

Part of the explanation lies, I think, in the logic of the story. To put it simply, the reader must *choose* between the two points of view Hawthorne offers; he cannot have it both ways. He must decide to trust either legend or history and abide by that choice on all the important issues of the book: either Colonel Pyncheon did or he did not cheat Matthew Maule, and either some of the Colonel's heirs have repeated his crime of greed or they have not; either the Pyncheon descendants have died of apoplexy or they have been murdered, and either the Maules are implicated in these crimes or they are not. Furthermore, if the Pyncheons are presumed guilty of going to almost any lengths to preserve and increase their fortune, as rumors and legends suggest, then the Maules must be presumed guilty of the crimes attributed to them by the town gossips and folk-historians who help to perpetuate the traditions which implicate both Pyncheons and Maules in the age-old drama of sin and retribution. Of course, if only the official historical view is correct, there is no basis at all for the story.

To the contrary, most readers of **The Seven Gables** have ignored the need for logical consistency in their interpretations. Though F. O. Matthiessen [in his *American Renaissance,* 1941] praises Hawthorne's "device of multiple choice" and realizes that "Hawthorne leaves his reader to choose among these theories," he takes the legendary view of the Pyncheons, who have "continued to bring [the curse] upon themselves," but takes the historical view of the Maules, who have "kept their resentment to themselves." Similarly, though R. H. Fogle speaks [in his *Hawthorne's Fiction: The Light and the Dark,* 1964] of Hawthorne's ambiguity as the central feature of the book, he sees the Pyncheons as greedy sinners but the Maules as "guiltless victims": "Compared to the Pyncheons they are thus . . . closer to the great mass of humanity, yet never presuming to lay a claim to any such symbol of possession

as the house of the seven gables." Such conclusions are invalid simply because there is no basis on which to distinguish the true from the false among the nonpreternatural legends. One must either accept or reject them all.

It must be acknowledged, of course, that Hawthorne does everything he can to lead his reader astray. For one thing, he seems to condemn the Pyncheons and their sins quite unequivocally in the preface:

> Many writers lay very great stress upon some definite moral purpose, at which they profess to aim their work. Not to be deficient, in this particular, the Author has provided himself with a moral;—the truth, namely, that the wrong-doing of one generation lives into the successive ones, and, divesting itself of every temporary advantage, becomes a pure and uncontrollable mischief;—and he would feel it a singular gratification, if this Romance might effectually convince mankind (or, indeed, any one man) of the folly of tumbling down an avalanche of ill-gotten gold, or real estate, on the heads of an unfortunate posterity, thereby to maim and crush them, until the accumulated mass shall be scattered abroad in its original atoms.

And most readers have taken this "moral" to be the theme of the book. For Lawrence S. Hall [in his *Hawthorne: Critic of Society,* 1944], "The theme of the romance has to do with inherited sin, the sin of aristocratic pretensions against a moral order, which . . . calls for a truer and higher evaluation of man." Similarly, Matthiessen believes that the moral is expressed in "the curse that the Pyncheons have continued to bring upon themselves."

Furthermore, in order to make sure that the reader will remember the "moral," Hawthorne repeats it throughout the book. A great lesson may be learned, he says, "from the little regarded truth, that the act of the passing generation is the germ which may and must produce good or evil fruit, in a far distant time." The point applies specifically to the Pyncheons, for it is possible that each member of the family may have committed "anew the great guilt of his ancestor, and incur[red] all its original responsibilities." Of course the idea is offered throughout the story by Holgrave, but even Hepzibah and Clifford repeat it. And even Uncle Venner comments, "It does seem to me that men make a wonderful mistake in trying to heap property upon property."

These examples are worth noting, however, not because they prove that Hawthorne's theme is based upon the original Pyncheon crime and the inherited evils of the Pyncheon descendants, but because they prove the opposite. Hawthorne says in the preface,

> When romances do really teach anything, or produce any effective operation, it is usually through a far more subtle process than the ostensible one. The Author has considered it hardly worth his while, therefore, relentlessly to impale the story with its moral, as with an iron rod—or rather, as by sticking a pin through a butterfly—thus at once depriving it of life, and causing it to stiffen in an ungainly and unnatural attitude.

It could not be more obvious that the story *is* "relentlessly" impaled with the theme of ill-gotten wealth and hereditary sin. It seems reasonable to consider the possibility, then, that this is not Hawthorne's "moral," for though the story has a great deal to do with this particular theme, the author points his readers in an entirely different direction.

One finds in re-examining Hawthorne's professed moral in the preface that he suggests two morals: one, "the folly of tumbling down . . . ill-gotten gold, or real estate, on the heads of an unfortunate posterity," and the other, "the truth, namely, that the wrong-doing of one generation lives into the successive ones, and, divesting itself of every temporary advantage, becomes a pure and uncontrollable mischief." It should be noted that one sin is expedient—"tumbling down ill-gotten gold"—and that the other divests itself "of every temporary advantage." It is clear, at least, that the *manifest* "wrong" in *The Seven Gables* is the crime of the Pyncheon clan which lives on into successive generations. It is difficult, however, to see in Gervayse Pyncheon's compromise with Matthew Maule and in Judge Pyncheon's intimidation of Clifford—both attempts to retrieve the lost land in Maine—a wrong-doing which, "*divesting itself of every temporary advantage,* becomes a pure and uncontrollable mischief." The result of these acts must be, in the view of the perpetrators, *every* temporary advantage: for one, the inestimable wealth of the original Pyncheon. The other crime is inexpedient, and Hawthorne emphasizes its "truth" in his moral statement.

Holgrave speaks of the Pyncheon family history as a "long drama of wrong and retribution," and of the Judge's "universe" as "a scene of guilt, and of retribution more dreadful than the guilt." If what is suggested in legend and tradition is true, it is apparent that the crime of murder, the sin of retribution, is that inexpedient and "mischievous" act to which Hawthorne refers in his preface. The "wrong," committed by the old Puritan and committed again by his heirs, and the "retribution," which history attributes to the work of Providence but which folk-history assigns to the Maules, constitute the two-sided moral problem which the book dramatizes. Yet Hawthorne's emphasis in his preface is on the latent rather than the manifest, the hidden rather than the obvious. Thus, for him, *The Seven Gables* is not a history of wrong, that is, of the Pyncheon sins, but a "history of *retribution* for the sin of long ago" (my emphasis). Even Holgrave is inadvertently correct, for the retribution *is*, as he says, "more dreadful than the guilt."

The greed of the Pyncheons, like the spiritual greed of Hawthorne's Puritans and the material greed of his other New England aristocrats, is the sin of men living in a fallen world. What is important to Hawthorne, invariably, is not *this* sin but the *reaction* to it. Thus, his story focuses on the reaction of his characters to the Pyncheon past, of Hepzibah and Clifford, skepticism and withdrawal, respectively, and of Holgrave-Maule in particular, revenge and retribution. "The better remedy," Hawthorne says, "is for the sufferer to pass on, and leave what he once thought his irreparable ruin far behind him," for "it is a truth (and it would be a very sad one, but for the higher hopes which it suggests) that no great mistake, whether acted or endured, in our mortal sphere, is ever really set right"; it is sad, because those crimes of expediency are the habit of men, and it is suggestive of "higher hopes" because man's recognition of his liability to sin is the precondition for his moral salvation.

> Thus it is, that the grief of the passing moment takes upon itself an individuality, and a character of climax, which it is destined to lose, after a while, and to fade into the dark gray tissue, common to the grave or glad events of many years ago. It is but for a moment, comparatively, that anything looks strange or startling;—a truth, that has the bitter and the sweet in it!

This may be the "high truth" in the story that is not "any truer, and seldom any more evident, at the last page than the first": "how much of the old material goes to make up the freshest novelty of human life."

One is tempted to believe that "the old material" is the crime of the Pyncheons, and that it is the central event in the cycle of history, unchanging and unalterable except by the slow attenuation of evil and its final dissolution—the attrition of Pyncheon power and the demise of the last Pyncheon progenitor. What *is* central, however, is the crime of the Maules. And if this is so, then it is clear that the focus of attention in the foreground of *The Seven Gables* is Holgrave's role in the conflict between Pyncheons and Maules. And though Holgrave *seems* to forswear the habitual revenge of his ancestors, the logic of the story suggests that he does not, for if all the Pyncheon deaths are the same then the last is as likely the result of murder as the first.

The most telling evidence of Holgrave's complicity in the death of Judge Pyncheon is his consistent adoption of the historical view of his own family but the legendary view of the Pyncheons. More than any other character, he moralizes about the Pyncheon sins, but at the same time he contends that the Pyncheons have suffered at the hands of either fate or a just providence. He says to Phoebe, "Old Maule's prophecy was probably founded on a knowledge of this physical predisposition in the Pyncheon race." Yet Matthew Maule could hardly have known of any racial tendencies in the Pyncheons, for apparently his only encounter with the family was with the Colonel. Holgrave also tells Phoebe that Judge Pyncheon was responsible for his Uncle Jaffrey's death, but, Hawthorne cautions, "whether on authority available in a court of justice, we do not pretend to have investigated." In fact, as "many persons affirmed," the "facts" so presented "had been obtained by the Daguerrotypist, from one of those mesmerical seers, who now-a-days, so strangely perplex the aspect of human affairs, and put everybody's natural vision to the blush, by the marvels which they see with their eyes shut." *All* of the information on the Judge's own death comes from Holgrave. And it is he who insists on the similarities between this event and its predecessors: "there is a minute and almost exact similarity in the appearances, connected with the death that occurred yesterday, and those recorded of the death of Clifford's uncle, thirty years ago."

Evidently, the reader sees much of the story through Holgrave's eyes and depends on him for information on the most important events in the story. And significantly, though Holgrave's point of view is to many readers the same as Hawthorne's, it actually contradicts the author's on the fundamental issues of the book. One must therefore ask the usually unasked questions about Holgrave: the cause of his family's absence from Salem for thirty years (since Jaffrey Pyncheon's death), his reason for returning to the Pyncheon House, his purpose in remaining, and the causes and extent of his metamorphosis at the end of his brief stay with the Pyncheon family. In short, after the other ambiguities of the story have been cleared away, one must deal with the central ambiguity of *The House of the Seven Gables:* Holgrave's reaction to the Pyncheons. That the book has traditionally been regarded as inconsistent with itself or with the characteristically pessimistic tone of Hawthorne's other tales should suggest that its depths have not been sounded and that its complexities have not been adequately dealt with. In my view Holgrave is the Chillingworth of this story. That readers have concluded otherwise is the result, I think, of their failure to examine the confrontation between Holgrave and his family enemies in the context of Hawthorne's narrative point of view and against the background of the Maule-Pyncheon feud of earlier days. (pp. 203-11)

*Sheldon W. Liebman, "Point of View in 'The House of the Seven Gables',"* in ESQ: A Journal of the American Renaissance, *Vol. 19, No. 4, 1973, pp. 203-12.*

## Nina Baym    (essay date 1976)

[*Baym is an American educator and critic. In the following excerpt, she describes* The House of the Seven Gables *as a depiction of the struggle, both within the individual and in society, between the forces of passionate creativity and civilized control.*]

Ostensibly, [in attempting to write a novel more cheerful than *The Scarlet Letter*] Hawthorne's concern was wholly for his audience; but a letter of July 22, 1851, to [Horatio] Bridge suggests something different: "I think it a work more characteristic of my mind," he says of *The House of the Seven Gables,* "and more proper and natural for me to write, than *The Scarlet Letter;* but for that very reason, less likely to interest the public." Here Hawthorne is apparently less concerned with the audience than with fidelity to his own temperament. Yet in November 1850, while at work on *The House of the Seven Gables,* he had written to [his publisher, James T.] Fields: "It darkens damnably towards the close, but I shall try hard to pour some setting sunshine over it." Here Hawthorne is guided not by what is natural to him, but by what he wishes were natural to him. A conflict emerges thus between the writer Hawthorne wants to be and the writer he has discovered himself to be.

Attempting in *The House of the Seven Gables* to blend the different types of writing he had set side by side in previous volumes, Hawthorne interspersed with the gothic mode of the romance sketchlike and moralistic interludes and comic and sentimental touches. After he had done so he had second thoughts that anticipate what many modern readers feel about the book: "I should not wonder . . . if the romance of the book should be found somewhat at odds with the humble and familiar scenery in which I invest it." The difficulty today seems to be more than a clash of effects. The comic surface appears untrue to the gloomy import of the romance, and looks like Hawthorne's effort to conceal his own meaning.

Yet in some ways the disjunction corresponds to the meaning. For the romance assumes that behind or beneath the actual world is an unseen world of motive and meaning, which actually controls the shape of the visible. When one limits oneself entirely to observation of the actual world, it appears comic, pathetic, charming, or sentimental, and the invisible world makes itself known only by an aura of the uncanny. But this same actual world breaks down into a series of discrete items, because it lacks the coherence of a meaningful action. The unseen world manifests itself in action, which erupts into the actual world like a gothic plot. In *The House of the Seven Gables* the visible world exists in the romance's present time and is controlled by the invisible world which is the past. As it becomes increasingly clear that the seen present is controlled by the unseen past, the mood of the book darkens. The sense of the present changes; its lack of freedom becomes clear. The feeling of confinement, exemplified in the imprisoning power of the house itself, eclipses the series of pleasantries that comprises the novelistic surface of *The House of the Seven Gables.*

The action of this romance pursues the theme Hawthorne had enunciated in *The Scarlet Letter*—that of the romantic conflict, at once social and private, between forces of passion, spontaneity, and creativity and counterforces of regulation and control. In *The House of the Seven Gables* these forces are embodied respectively in Maule and Pyncheon and are represented emblematically in Maule's fountain and Pyncheon's house. The fundamental action of the novel revolves around a struggle for possession of land first occupied by Maule and then appropriated by Pyncheon, and possession in various senses is the book's major metaphor. The antagonism between Pyncheon and Maule implies many social and ideological struggles—aristocrat versus democrat, conservative versus radical, institutionalist versus transcendentalist, for example—and these have been duly noted by critics. These readings all depend, however, upon the romance's psychological core, where the struggle occurs within the single self, with authority trying to suppress passion and passion to depose authority. The apparent stability of the situation as it exists in the novel's present time is clearly unhealthy, for Maule's fountain has turned brackish and Pyncheon's house become a prison, a dead shell expressing no one's nature and deforming the lives trapped within it.

Moreover, the stability is illusory. The Maules still retain and exercise strange forms of control over the Pyncheons, who, "haughtily as they bore themselves in the noonday streets of their native town, were no better than bond-servants to these plebeian Maules, on entering the topsy-turvy commonwealth of sleep." Though they may be repressed and distorted, the energies represented by Maule cannot die until the self dies, for they are original energies.

Observe Hawthorne's myth of the beginnings of the conflict between Maule and Pyncheon. Maule was the first and the only rightful owner of the land at issue in their dispute. He brought it from a state of nature into the Edenic garden state with the labor of his own hands. Both settler and cultivator, he made the land express his being, and entered into a useful relationship with it. His symbol, appropriately, is the pure fountain, emblem of the sources and energies of life. In contrast, Pyncheon is a formalist, a man of writs, deeds, and documents, having no true relationship with the land he desires to own. He arrives on the scene after Maule, with the expansion of the village boundaries, and he claims the land not from nature but from the legislature. In every crisis, Pyncheon resorts to the law, which supports his claims.

Thus, Pyncheon represents the advent of civilization, and civilization replaces a creative and expressive relation to nature with one wholly materialistic. Land is now desired as a material possession rather than an expressive medium. Apparently, the whole apparatus of law exists to further and protect the aims of materialistic greed; it is created by men like Pyncheon and serves their interests. Pyncheon's criminal acquisition of Maule's land, by having him dispossessed and executed as a witch, is legal. Jaffrey Pyncheon has Clifford legally imprisoned for a term of years and, when it appears that Clifford will not reveal the location of the deed to the Maine lands, threatens to commit him legally to a mental asylum.

In brief, Hawthorne's myth of the origins of civilization founds it on a crime. The fact and nature of that crime irrevocably determine the character of the civilization. Maule and the qualities he represents are officially driven out of civilization and seem to disappear. The remaining civilized beings are oppressed, distorted, and incomplete. Moreover, the structure itself begins immediately to decay, because, by refusing to permit the open existence of energy and creativity, the civilization cuts its own lifelines. Because societies are composed of people and not things, the Pyncheon civilization, based on a hard materialism and formalism that are destructive to people, must eventually destroy itself. As *The House of the Seven Gables* opens, that destruction is at hand.

The social and psychological strands of the romance are closely entwined, so that any event may be referred either to the individual psyche or to the structure of the civilization. And the story is different for those imprisoned within the structure—the house, commissioned by Pyncheon but built naturally enough by Maule since all creative and constructive powers belong to him—and those who are dispossessed outside it. Psychologically speaking, Maule has lost his identity and is in some existential sense outside himself, forced to hover on the periphery of his own personality—ghostlike, sinister, misunderstood: an underground man. The Pyncheons, on the other hand, are locked into rigid identities with no opportunity for innovation, spontaneity, or refreshment. Hepzibah, who occupies so much of the foreground of the romance, is the embodiment of social forms that have lost their capacity for change or growth. Change and growth are not possible

without Maule; but for Maule nothing is possible unless he can take a rightful place above ground.

The story, then, poses two interrelated questions: can Maule make a place for himself in the social structure without destroying it? Alternatively, can he join society without destroying himself? Ultimately, this romance asks the same question that *The Scarlet Letter* asks: is civilization necessarily the tombstone of the spirit? These are transcendental queries, but *The House of the Seven Gables* does not offer transcendental answers. The foreground of the romance concerns itself with the victims within the social structure; this focus is designed to create reader approval of Maule, or Holgrave, who, in the present time of the narrative, has returned to claim what is rightfully his. His spectatorship, which Phoebe (and many critics, following her lead) mistakes for intellectual coldness, is in fact his pose. The returned exile waits for the right moment to make himself known. The right moment occurs after Pyncheon's death, and not only as a matter of strategy: Holgrave cannot really resume his identity as Maule until the obstacle to his selfhood has been removed.

It is a commonplace of interpretation that Hawthorne disapproves of radical reformers, and for this reason Holgrave's is generally read as a critical portrait. But in reading it thus, the critics must ignore Hawthorne's unambiguous praise for his young protagonist and the implicit approval of his radical ideas. Holgrave's radicalism is defined as a sense of human possibility, "which a young man had better never been born, than not to have, and a mature man had better die at once, than utterly to relinquish." Perhaps he is naive, but his errors are noble. To Hawthorne's generally weak male protagonists Holgrave is an exception, in his courage, high principles, ideals, kindheartedness, self-reliance, and sensitivity. He has "never violated the inmost man," has "carried his conscience along with him," combines inward strength with enthusiasm and warmth. He conveys a total "appearance of admirable powers."

At his entrance into the novel he is made to contrast with Hepzibah, who, as I have said, is the symbol of Pyncheon strength become withered and impotent: "Coming freshly, as he did, out of the morning light, he appeared to have brought some of its cheery influences into the shop along with him." He continues throughout the romance to diffuse vigor and joy into the pervasive atmosphere of gloom and fatigue. Tending and planting the Pyncheon garden, he recalls the original Maule, and he is associated with metaphors of fertility and sexuality, especially in the remarkable image of the bean poles vivid with scarlet blossoms and attracting to them multitudes of vibrating hummingbirds. In other, less sensuously charged scenes he diverts and enspirits the melancholy inhabitants of the house; on occasion he is so stimulating that even Clifford's somnolent soul awakens and gives off winged thoughts.

Holgrave does lack one quality that many critics, applying to *The House of the Seven Gables* an inappropriate scheme derived from Hawthorne's earlier fictions, have identified as his ruling characteristic: intellectuality. True, "he considered himself a thinker, and was certainly of a thoughtful turn," but he "had perhaps hardly yet reached the point where an educated man begins to think." The narrator does not consider this a serious shortcoming, in view of Holgrave's youth, but he does have one doubt about this otherwise admirable character. He wonders whether Holgrave will fulfill his promise or, "like certain chintzes, calicoes, and ginghams," will "assume a very sober aspect after washing-day." It is possible that his powers will not survive their first serious testing.

Because Holgrave represents creative energy he is also a type of the artist. Through him Hawthorne returns to some of the questions suggested in *The Scarlet Letter* and **"The Custom-House"** about the nature of art and the problems of the artist in a repressive society. Holgrave is a kind of archetypal artist, for he has mastered a variety of media and is unattached to his productions. Hawthorne often refers to him as "the artist." He is presented as a contrast, in his artistry, to previous Maules, in whom artistic energies were perverted; he is also contrasted with Clifford, who appears to be an artist (and unfortunately is too often taken for one in the criticism on this romance) but is in reality a travesty of one, a castrated artist such as society will allow to exist.

Hawthorne illustrates Holgrave's superiority to earlier Maules—and incidentally explains a good deal about the equation between art and wizardry (the black art)—in the scene where Holgrave reads his narrative about Alice Pyncheon to Phoebe. As he reads, the present-day characters assume the identities of those in the fiction. Holgrave becomes the wizard Maule, and Phoebe becomes Alice. Phoebe shows the same susceptibility to Holgrave that Alice felt for Maule and gives Holgrave the opportunity to repeat Maule's abuse of them. In Holgrave's narrative, Alice Pyncheon feels and unconsciously manifests a physical attraction to Maule, which he inflames into a violent physical passion. Alice, as in all cases of demonic possession, is in fact controlled by internal, invisible forces—invisible because denied. She refuses to recognize her sexual nature, and Maule takes advantage of that refusal. "This fair girl deemed herself conscious of a power—combined of beauty, high, unsullied purity, and the preservative force of womanhood—that could make her sphere impenetrable, unless betrayed by treachery within." Her inability to conceive of internal treachery delivers her to Maule.

Like all Pyncheons, she rejects, suppresses, or denies the passions that underlie human nature, with sex primary among them. Her later torments, too, result from the continued frustration of this inadmissible and yet obvious passion, for "so lost from self-control, she would have deemed it sin to marry"; and she is killed, aptly enough, by the irrevocable loss of her passion's object when Maule marries, and by Maule's astounding sadism in forcing her to attend the bride on his wedding night.

Alice is partly victimized by her self and partly by her father. His greed for possessions (like all the Pyncheons after the first, he is forever trying to find the lost deed to the Maine lands) and the Pyncheon habit of regarding people as things have induced him to permit Maule to use Alice in an experiment that promises knowledge of the deed's whereabouts. The Maule guilt in her degradation

is nevertheless obvious and terrible. His behavior is of the meanest, at once arousing and denying Alice. This nastiness figures his own degradation into a destructive Eros, which expresses itself in malicious acts, subversive thrusts that produce no release. Denied free and open expression, the fountain becomes a source of self-pollution.

Holgrave's reading re-creates Alice's erotic response in Phoebe; so Hawthorne demonstrates the sexual power of art and its near relation to witchcraft. Art and sex are both expressions of the creative energy which, ideally, they should celebrate. The common origin of art and sex in the Eros of the personality makes possible a kind of interchange of artistic and sexual metaphors, as we have already seen in *The Scarlet Letter* and **"The Custom-House."** Great works of art in Hawthorne's fictions are often unabashedly sensuous representations of beautiful women—one can think back to the figurehead in **"Drowne's Wooden Image"** and ahead to the Cleopatra of *The Marble Faun.* And as Hawthorne preaches so he practices—witness Hester, Zenobia, and Miriam.

But in a repressive society, art and sex are both inhibited and go underground. Denied legitimate expression, they erupt not only in actions that are deemed criminal by the society, but in acts that are deliberately perverse. In *The Scarlet Letter* the governor's mansion itself is the abode of Mistress Hibbens; witchcraft is a debased, perverse creativity, and it is debased because—as we recall from Hester's dialogue with Mistress Hibbens—the witch and wizard have accepted the idea that they are evil. Wizardry destroys rather than creates, controls rather than liberates, degrades instead of celebrating the life force. The self-mocking and yet deadly serious wizard, seeking to "possess" through misuse of the powers of art, is a parodist of the tyrant. He betrays his own nature by aping repressive forms. He destroys art by using it to oppress. And ultimately he reinforces the social power he defies because he offers only another version of it.

The optimist Holgrave, while recognizing that he operates in a repressive society, refuses to twist his art. He believes that the world is striding toward a Utopia where Eros will be free to express itself. He imagines art in the interim to have a certain liberating and constructive effect through its power to expose the truth. His daguerreotypes, taken with the help of the sunlight that is his friend and ally, show Pyncheon's true nature, illuminating his villainy and identifying him with his persecuting ancestor. His tale of Alice Pyncheon, developed with the help of the moonlight, which for Hawthorne always accompanies romance, exposes the depravity of the Maules and shows Holgrave's awareness of his own situation. His refusal to take advantage of the opportunity given him by Phoebe's response demonstrates his moral worth. He withstands temptation, and not only Phoebe but art as well is saved by his forbearance.

> Let us, therefore—whatever his defects of nature and education, and in spite of his scorn for creeds and institutions—concede to the Daguerreotypist the rare and high quality of reverence for another's individuality. Let us allow him integrity, also, forever after to be confided in; since he forbade himself to twine that one link more,

which might have rendered his spell over Phoebe indissoluble.

The cleansed vitality that Holgrave brings to the old conflict seems attributable to his mobility. He has severed ties with the house, abandoned the place, and refused to commit himself to any fixed form of life. He has made the particularly American response to the past—left it behind, even to the extent of creating a new identity by taking on a new name. He has escaped history by avoiding the forms through which it is preserved and transmitted. Distance has given him objectivity toward his origins. But can he maintain this vitality and objectivity if he comes back? He must now discover if freedom is possible on any terms other than perpetual rootlessness and flight. He hopes to reattach himself to his sources without forfeiting any of his spiritual independence and flexibility, to be, like the fountain, at once fixed and fluid.

Therefore he must return to Salem and confront the figure who has forced the Maules into their long exile. He is serene at the prospect of his ordeal, because he trusts himself. He does not doubt that he will triumph in this confrontation; he has no inkling of internal weakness, of "treachery within." Establishing himself in an attic gable, tending the garden—taking possession, so to speak, of the house's peripheries—he calmly bides his time, waiting, we must assume, for Maule's curse to claim its last victim. Pyncheon is naturally unaware of the other's presence and has no sense of impending doom. His attention is focused on the returned Clifford, and the possibility of wresting from him, at last, the secret of the deed to the Maine lands.

For his more practical-minded readers, Hawthorne supplies (as is customary in a gothic plot) a natural explanation for Pyncheon's death: a hereditary disposition to apoplexy. But the truth of the matter in the invisible world is that the Pyncheons are killed by Maule's curse. Through the curse, the power of the suppressed Eros is communicated to the oppressor. In any of three readings of the story—that every generation of Pyncheons and Maules repeats the story; that there is really only one Pyncheon and one Maule; or that both Pyncheon and Maule are parts of a single personality—Holgrave, as Maule, must assume some responsibility for Jaffrey Pyncheon's death. Holgrave's serenity implies that he is prepared to face that death and accept that responsibility.

Holgrave is especially interested in Clifford, in whom Hawthorne depicts the alternative—for an artistic personality—to exile. Many critics have understood Clifford as one of Hawthorne's most complete, and critical, analyses of the artist. But such an approach misses Hawthorne's point, which is that Clifford is not an artist because he has not been permitted to become one. In Clifford he shows the degradation of the artistic impulse when it is not permitted creative expression but is forced into a lifelong attitude of passive receptivity. Although physically and chronologically an old man, Clifford has the psyche of an infant. His cousin's tyranny has kept him passive, dependent, absorbed in immediate sensual (but non-sexual) gratifications, uncontrollably moody, permanently impotent, a mental somnambulist. Exile has enabled the Maules to attain some sort of warped manhood, but Clifford has been kept a child. Not allowed to grow, he atrophies.

From Clifford's first appearance we see that he has no inner resources and, apparently, no expressive needs. He achieves satisfaction through a sort of absorption of the world into himself, for which eating is the best metaphor: Hawthorne dwells much on his voracious and indelicate appetite. Such appetites imply an incompleteness which is precisely the opposite of the artist's creative urge to overflow. Clifford loves beauty, but in the manner of Owen Warland [in Hawthorne's "The Artist of the Beautiful"] he fears energy. He approaches beauty as a materialist, wishing to possess and seeing no further than the surface. The spiritual beauty of his sister goes unseen by him, because she is outwardly an ugly, aging woman. Here, much more clearly than in "The Artist of the Beautiful," and in contradistinction to the theme of "The Snow-Image," Hawthorne rejects the equation of artistry with childishness. There is no art until childhood has been left behind.

At some point in its development, the child moves from a fascination with and dependence on forms to the desire to create them; after this, forms become dependent on him. If this point is not reached, the artist remains unborn. Art is thus associated with the adult personality, as a progressive force that confronts reality rather than a regressive activity that tries to evade it. The child, as Clifford demonstrates, presents no threat to the social structure; he is easily pacified, diverted, and controlled. The artist, on the other hand, driven from within, cannot be easily placated. He threatens the stability and permanence of institutions by his continual indifference to them in the creation of his own forms. Even if he were not a deliberate rebel, the artist would quickly become one inadvertently—witness Hester.

Though he lacks the force to make art, and is terrified of raw energy, Clifford is also greatly attracted to it. Perhaps this attraction is the seed from which artistry normally matures. As soon as he escapes from the house of the seven gables Clifford runs to the railroad that has always frightened him, recognizing on this occasion, as he does sporadically, that his salvation can come only by embracing what he fears. His sympathy with the force behind the form led him, in the past, to the secret hiding place of the deed to the Maine lands (hidden by Maule when he built the house for Colonel Pyncheon). Of course, he has also forgotten his knowledge, for his insights are weak and intermittent—it is not for *him* to tumble Colonel Pyncheon's portrait from the wall. But sign of such sympathy is the signal for Jaffrey Pyncheon's oppression. Jaffrey's death means Clifford's liberation, and his essentially lightweight nature, relieved of the pressures that have constricted it for so long, achieves some fraction of the pleasing development originally possible to it. But his crushed soul can never expand into true art.

In theory the death of Jaffrey Pyncheon should liberate all the characters in the romance from their long oppression. And so it does, except in one case. For Holgrave that death is the beginning of oppression. Between the evening that he enters the parlor, prepared to face the judge, and the morning of Phoebe's return, Holgrave changes strikingly. His social radicalism disappears; he is ready to give up art and adopt the life of a country landowner. Instead of finding himself in the dark parlor, he loses himself, reclaiming the name of Maule but taking on the form of Pyncheon. We see this change at once in his new behavior toward Phoebe.

The love that he declares for her is a barely disguised plea for solace and protection:

> Could you but know, Phoebe, how it was with me, the hour before you came! A dark, cold, miserable hour. . . . I never hoped to feel young again! . . . But, Phoebe, you crossed the threshold; and hope, warmth, and joy, came in with you! The black moment became at once a blissful one. It must not pass without the spoken word. I love you!"

His betrothal to Phoebe, entered into in such a frame of mind, is the appropriate means by which he becomes the owner of the Pyncheon estate, for it expresses a wish to be limited by, and supported within, social responsibilities.

Phoebe, with all her appealing freshness and softness, is a law-abiding and limit-loving Pyncheon. She is a great comfort to Hepzibah and Clifford, but in the manner of one making prison life more tolerable rather than as an agent of release. Indeed, confined to the house, she too has been fading and drooping. At the same time she feels, like Clifford, attracted to what she fears. She loves Holgrave. Even as she tells him she is afraid to marry him, she shrinks toward him, asking him without words to help her move beyond her own limits. But Holgrave is no longer a liberator. This relationship does not signal the beginning of a new era between men and women; the two exchange their vows in the presence of a corpse. They drive off later to Pyncheon's country estate loaded with goods and dependents. Clifford, Hepzibah, Uncle Venner, and all the neighbors rejoice, but Holgrave has become a brooding, melancholy man. Would it have been a better symbol of his victory if he had built his own house or, remaining in the house of the seven gables, had made it truly his own? He abandons, however, the precious ground for which he has struggled—the ground of his own self—and goes to live in the Judge's country mansion, astonishing everyone by his lament that the wooden structure is not built of more durable material. Moving into this house, Holgrave identifies himself with all those parts of the personality he had previously been trying to overcome.

Many critics argue that Holgrave's conversion from radical to conservative opinions has been effected by love. His relationship with Phoebe ties him for the first time to the human world and gives him a new appreciation of how much is worth preserving. But behind this argument is a critical conviction that Holgrave's conversion is a good thing, and this conviction can be maintained only by ignoring the character of Pyncheon as Hawthorne created it. Moreover, the plot shows Holgrave's love as subsequent to, and indeed caused by, his change to conservatism. Love is not the agent, but the expression, of a change. The critical argument also assumes that Holgrave finds a new happiness in his love and his set of complex, stable rela-

tions to the social order; Holgrave himself appears to concur when he says that he will no longer be radical because "the world owes all its onward impulse to men ill at ease. The happy man inevitably confines himself within ancient limits." But Holgrave's words are belied by the facts. He was happy before the Judge's death; he is not happy afterward. In the opening sequence of the romance he brought the sunlight indoors with him; now he has been permanently darkened by the shadows of the house. He turns to Phoebe for comfort, as we have seen. Later, with a "half-melancholy laugh," he will pass judgment on himself for this conversion, which he calls "especially unpardonable in this dwelling of so much hereditary misfortune, and under the eye of yonder portrait of a model-conservative, who, in that very character, rendered himself so long the Evil Destiny of his race." The point could not be more clearly stated.

But the dynamics of Holgrave's conversion remain mysterious. Instead of following Holgrave's mental processes during the night he spends with the corpse, Hawthorne writes one of his nightmare-procession sequences, having troops of phantoms pass by the dead man in his chair. Are these fantasies meant to be those of the distraught Holgrave, in the manner of **"The Haunted Mind"**? One is left to guess at the connection between these images and the state of mind of the protagonist. Readers thinking ahead to the preoccupations of **The Blithedale Romance** and **The Marble Faun** might explain Holgrave's change as the result of guilt feelings incurred by the Judge's death. The first Maule, who antedated society, was the only Maule who did not have to commit a crime in order to gain his own independence. All subsequent Maules have found an authority figure blocking the path to selfhood. If, in even the slightest degree, they accept the validity of that figure, they must necessarily feel guilt for the act that deposes it. Feeling guilty, they lose the sense of their own rightness; implicated in the guilt-ridden structures of society, they acquiesce in them. Feelings of guilt are assuaged by accepting the values of the system one has overthrown; energies that were to have been expended in self-expression are diverted to atonement. The system survives the overthrow of any particular person who symbolizes authority within it; the revolutionary becomes an oppressor in his turn.

As Holgrave attempts to reattach himself to the past, he finds that he can do so only by accepting the past's whole burden. Having committed the fatal deed, he cannot return to his earlier free state. His new vision sees the whole world under the shadow of the guilt he feels: "The presence of yonder dead man threw a great black shadow over everything; he made the universe, so far as my perception could reach, a scene of guilt, and of retribution more dreadful than the guilt." Is it not death itself that has changed Holgrave? Knowing the present only, and impelled by transcendental idealism, Holgrave imagined himself to exist through an infinity of present moments. In effect, he thought himself immortal. In his impassioned speeches he used death as a trope, as though he did not feel its reality: "The case is just as if a young giant were compelled to waste all his strength in carrying about the corpse of the old giant, his grandfather, who died a long while ago, and only needs to be decently buried. Just think, a moment; and it will startle you to see what slaves we are to by-gone times—to Death, if we give the matter the right word!" But of course we are slaves to death; only the very young could be startled by that perception.

Implicit in Holgrave's language is the certainty that once we remember the past is dead, we will throw off our bondage to it with an incredulous laugh at our own stupidity. But precisely because the past has given the present its shape, it continues to exist; just as death, by giving life its shape, is in this sense also a part of life. The real existence of death parallels the real existence of the past. Dying, Judge Pyncheon becomes Death itself, the ultimate, unconquerable, tyrannizing force.

But if Pyncheon is ineluctable, he is no less hateful. Holgrave can hardly be said to embrace his destiny; he accepts it with weary melancholy. At the end of the romance he is a sad man. In him Hawthorne depicts the life of the individual as a journey away from the illusion of freedom. As the self awakens to its personal history, it becomes implicated in that history. Still, if the story is sad from the private point of view, it is perhaps less so for society. Though Maule has turned conservative, he will not be an evil tyrant like Jaffrey Pyncheon. Certainly Hepzibah, Clifford, and Phoebe are all better off living in his house than in Judge Pyncheon's. Perhaps we see here a qualified meliorism like that represented in the conclusion to *The Scarlet Letter,* the hope not of a sudden overthrow of powerful repressive institutions, but of their gradual relaxation—a relaxation evidently brought about by much human suffering and sacrifice.

The plot of *The House of the Seven Gables,* opposing passion to authority, is certainly meant to embody a universal drama in particular terms; yet since it is set in the American present and linked to the American past, some social commentary must be intended as well. Jaffrey Pyncheon is a modern representative of the Puritan character, which is now simplified—in comparison to Hawthorne's earlier treatments of the Puritans—into a dominant materialism. This type is centered on ownership, on things, and does not believe in the existence of Spirit. This is the type that naturally builds for permanence and that, if it does not create new forms, makes sure that the old ones last. By definition, this is the type that builds a civilization, and thus the American nation has been built not by lovers of freedom but by lovers of form. Hawthorne's own criticism of this materialism receives strong expression in the preface (whose import is generally ignored by his critics, *because* it is so radical), where he says that "he would feel it a singular gratification, if this Romance might effectually convince mankind (or indeed, any one man) of the folly of tumbling down an avalanche of ill-gotten gold, or real estate, on the heads of an unfortunate posterity, thereby to maim and crush them, until the accumulated mass shall be scattered abroad in its original atoms." If this is the author's view, then he cannot but see the story of his hero as a defeat.

Of course, Hawthorne is much too skeptical to imagine that reading *The House of the Seven Gables* will reform anybody, but he does make his reformist sympathies clear. But, oddly enough—and to the surely inadvertent end of

generating dozens of critical articles about his intentions—he is at pains in the conclusion to present that story, by means of its floridly happy ending, as a triumph. As I have suggested, there is no way to interpret the conclusion as triumphant within the logic of the story. Holgrave did not get what he wanted, and what he got was much inferior to what he desired. Why, then, does Hawthorne manipulate the rhetoric of the last chapter to give the impression of a happy ending? One's first thought might be that he intended to conceal his radicalism. But, then, the preface would not have expressed his radicalism so strongly. And too, his radical hopes are so confined by his sense of the unlikeliness of their being realized that they hardly require concealment.

In all probability the explanation for the strategy of the finale involves a kind of concealment different from the hiding of radical political views. Political and social radicalism was probably more acceptable in the 1840s and 1850s than at any other time in American history, before and after. It was not his radical opinions that he wished to hide, but his apparent temperamental pessimism. It is one thing to see society as full of evils, but quite another to see absolutely no hope of their ever being corrected. Those who were conservative and those who were radical in these decades publicly shared the one quality of optimism. Hawthorne did not like his inability to participate in the hopeful temperament. He wanted to be a writer of happy books. He had struggled, unsuccessfully, to lighten the gloom of *The Scarlet Letter.* He felt sure that his readers would not like so dark a tale. When they liked it, he persisted in his discomfort, asserting that so unrelieved a dark story was not healthy or natural. As *The House of the Seven Gables* began to darken toward the close, he became uneasy. Writing closer to himself as he now was doing, he was uncomfortable with the sort of writer he was finding himself to be. But why? More than reader response was involved, evidently, since *The Scarlet Letter* had succeeded. Apparently, some inner censor, rather than a wish to please his audience, directed him to be a writer of happy stories, and judged him lacking when he failed to do so. (pp. 153-72)

*Nina Baym, in her* The Shape of Hawthorne's Career, *Cornell University Press, 1976, 283 p.*

## Hyatt H. Waggoner　(essay date 1979)

[*Waggoner was an American educator and critic and an authority on the works of Hawthorne. In the following excerpt, he praises Hawthorne's imaginative characterizations in* The House of the Seven Gables *and discusses his use of biblical and classical myths, calling the novel an allegorical depiction of the redemptive power of love.*]

*The House of the Seven Gables* is Hawthorne's fictional expression of his greatly desired belief in the possibility of redemption from evil. Not surprisingly, he preferred it to *The Scarlet Letter,* precisely because it was more hopeful than that dark and ambiguous tale of sin, suffering, and alienation. The new novel, he thought, was more "representative" of him. However difficult the questions this judgment raises—for there were several creative Hawthornes, and he wrote sometimes from one level of his mind, sometimes from another—it is certainly true, on the level of consciously held belief, that Hepzibah's thought, as she and Clifford decide to go to church as a way of breaking out of their long alienation, is Hawthorne's own, expressive of an important aspect of the central meaning the new novel was to have: "She yearned . . . to kneel down among the people, and be reconciled to God and man at once." Hawthorne never knelt, but he too yearned to be reconciled.

The effort Hepzibah and Clifford make at this time to break out of the compulsive patterns of the past that have produced their alienation is ineffectual, but the novel moves steadily toward its eventual achievement. They need help to achieve the desired liberation. Simply to decide to leave the house that represents their past is not enough, as we see climactically in their attempted flight after the Judge's death. As they speed through the countryside on the train, Clifford believes at first that this movement through space will effect their escape from time, but when they get off the train the illusion quickly evaporates. What they see at the end of their abortive flight is Hawthorne's way of saying in images what he had said earlier through Hepzibah. They see a ruined and deserted church and a deserted farmhouse:

> They gazed drearily about them. At a little distance stood a wooden church, black with age, and in a dismal state of ruin and decay, with broken windows, a great rift through the main body of the edifice, and a rafter dangling from the top of the square tower. Farther off was a farmhouse, in the old style, as venerably black as the church, with a roof slooping downward from the three-story peak to within a man's height of the ground. It seemed uninhabited. There were the relics of a wood-pile, indeed, near the door, but with grass sprouting up among the chips and scattered logs. The small rain-drops came down aslant; the wind was not turbulent, but sullen, and full of chilly moisture.

All that they have learned about the world and about themselves in their flight persuades them that there is nothing for them to do but return to the house that has become a moral prison for them. But they are to be freed from it sooner than they realize. The title Hawthorne gives his last chapter, "The Departure," points to the theme he has been developing as well as to the final action toward which his plot has been moving all along. When they all leave the old house for the last time, they are not running away from a past they cannot escape but genuinely moving onward toward newness of life. Hepzibah, who "had spent her life in divesting herself of friends;—she [who] had wilfully cast off the support which God has ordained his creatures to need from one another," has many friends now. In the end she forgives even her cousin the Judge. The enmity and mutual wrong of many generations of Pyncheons and Maules have been replaced by love in the marriage of Phoebe and Holgrave.

When these two declare their love in "The Flower of Eden," the effects of the Fall are undone and an unfallen Eden restored, as much at least as it ever can be, sufficiently at least to give freedom and hope to all concerned. "And it was in this hour, so full of doubt and awe, that the one miracle was wrought, without which every human existence is a blank." Hawthorne is speaking here as interpreter of the action he has been narrating, expressing a thought that was for him a central conviction expressed over and over again throughout his career, in his fiction and outside it. The purgation effected by suffering endured and accepted, and the redemptive power of love, have at last made possible a real movement beyond the compulsions of the past. No wonder Holgrave thinks once that the old house ought to be burned. Its destruction by fire would be symbolically appropriate.

The whole course of the novel has implied that the image of life represented by the organ-grinder's mechanical puppets is only the apparent, not the real or final truth. A "cynic" might think so, Hawthorne reminds us at this point—and sometimes Hawthorne found himself almost thinking so, or at least feeling so—but the eye of faith can see that the organ grinder's "automatic community" whose "people" are moved by a crank is not an adequate symbol of life just because it contains no suggestion of the possibility of escape from compulsion. We too are puppets, Hawthorne felt, mechanically moved by an unseen crank, insofar as "the one miracle" love, is absent from our lives. Like the organ grinder's little people, we "all dance to one identical tune, and, in spite of our ridiculous activity, bring nothing finally to pass." To the extent to which we remain "unreconciled" to God and man, the cynic is justified in his interpretation of the image.

Compulsion and a sense of unreality go hand in hand in Hawthorne. Without belief in freedom and hope for the future, life is a "blank," an ultimate unreality of empty appearances, like puppets, who are very "lifelike" but not "real." Hepzibah and Clifford too, we are reminded many times, have so lost their hold on outside reality, on other people and nature, that they themselves have been emptied of reality. In their first attempt at reunion by going to church, Hepzibah realizes that their effort will have no effect because they have become "ghosts." Their ties with others have all been broken, and love has not yet mended them. Unreal themselves, they inhabit a ghostly world. "Indeed, we are but shadows," Hawthorne had written years before to Sophia when he was courting her, "We are but shadows till the heart is touched."

Beneath the work's graceful, charming, sometimes fanciful, sometimes sentimental surface and the problematic happy ending lie concerns that are ethical, psychological, and religious. Questions of justice, injustice, and retribution, of head and heart and alienation and reunion, even of what Hawthorne's ancestors would have called sin and grace are never far below the surface. If the last pair of terms seems unfitting, as suggesting that Hawthorne was closer to his Puritan forebears in belief than he actually was, an acquaintance with all of his work will suggest that in his reinterpretation of the inherited faith, he saw no such dichotomy between human and divine as his ancestors had seen. For him, the "second great commandment," love of neighbor, is the basis and necessary condition of the first, love of God, as Paul had implied in the Epistle containing what has been called his "hymn to love": "Faith, hope, and love, and the greatest of these is love." As a man of the nineteenth century with both conservative inclinations and a great desire to face life honestly, Hawthorne followed the religious liberals of his time in defining God as love, without supposing that the reverse is also true, that love is God. Though he humanized and "psychologized" the faith, he did so no more, perhaps, than many theologians who propose to save the faith by putting it in terms that are meaningful to their age. Hawthorne's terms were certainly meaningful to readers in his own century and ought to need only a little translation to be meaningful today, in a culture that has lost its sense of the sacred more than his had.

Readers in Hawthorne's own time may well have responded to the work's ethical and religious meanings without feeling any need to spell out what seemed to them obvious. But we are likely to find it a little surprising today that so many ordinarily perceptive critics appear to have missed, or been uninterested in, so much of the meaning, in the later decades of the last century and the first half of ours. Why did Henry James, for example, in his book on Hawthorne, declare the novel a mere "prologue" rather than a finished work of art? Why, after acknowledging that the work is "full of all sorts of deep intentions, interwoven threads of suggestion," did he give no indication at all of what he found some of these "deep intentions" to be, but instead chose to concentrate on the work's "charm" as an evocation of old New England, on its atmosphere, on the "local color" aspects in short? Why did he finally patronize it as a "magnificent fragment"?

The answer to these questions would have to involve several factors—including James's necessity to belittle Hawthorne at this early date in his career, when his debt to the older writer was so great and his own reputation not yet established, and including also the changes in literary fashion—that made it genuinely difficult to explain the values he found in Hawthorne's old-fashioned work. His *Hawthorne* betrays these embarrassments of his at every point. But there is another reason too why James had to underestimate Hawthorne to a degree that makes parts of his book conspicuous failures of his usual critical intelligence, a reason that comes closer to touching his own genuine achievement in surpassing the older writer. James thought that Hawthorne's characters, though often very interesting *ideas* for a novelist, had not been really *created* as fictional "persons." At best they were triumphs, as he said, of purely "descriptive" writing, intelligently conceived but inadequately dramatic.

Granted that Hawthorne's characters never, in this work or elsewhere, seem as dramatically created as James's, I can see no reason for describing them as mere ideas, abstractions in an allegory, impossible to apprehend as "persons." True, the kinds of symbolic pointers we associate with allegory are more prominent here than in *The Scarlet Letter,* presumably because Hawthorne wanted to make his meanings in this "happier" work as convincing as possible. Still, it seems to me that the characters have been fully enough imagined to make it possible both to accept them as "real" and to approach Hawthorne's intended meanings through them.

The best characters in the novel have both surface and depth. By "surface" I do not mean to praise Hawthorne for being sufficiently "realistic" in his way of presenting them, whatever such a statement would mean, and I am not sure we know. Nor by "depth" do I mean that they are "emblems," as Hawthorne might say, of intrinsically "deep" ideas. Rather, I mean that Hawthorne's imagination was working as powerfully, when he created these characters, as it ever did, except perhaps when he created Hester in *The Scarlet Letter.* By an inspired selection of details of appearance, manner, and habitual action, aided by interpretive analyses of the depths of personality that produce and are revealed by these surfaces, Hawthorne has created not allegorical types and not what James calls them, "pictures" only, but people we as readers may come to know. Hawthorne created these people out of his experience (the Pyncheons, for example, may owe much to the Hawthornes, several of whom still had wealth and position in Hawthorne's youth, though his own immediate branch of the family had become the wards of the Mannings), but his knowledge of and contacts with actual people made up only a part of his experience. His characters are at once like people he had known and, as he rightly insisted in his preface, pure creations. If the reader's own experiences and imagination are adequate to the demand Hawthorne makes that he be mature and imaginative, there is no reason why he should not find these characters both believable and illuminating.

The least "real" in the sense of most closely approaching caricature seems to me to be Judge Pyncheon. But if there is a failure here it is not so much a failure of "realism" as a failure of sympathy, an inability to suspend moral judgment. Hawthorne seldom fails in this way, but when he does, he produces his "villains," of whom the Judge is at once one of the most believable (compare, for instance, Westervelt in *Blithedale*) and one of the most unqualifiedly villainous. The Judge is no Ethan Brand, becoming demonic because his search for truth led him to become a man of pure intellect whose heart had ceased to throb with human sympathy. Rather, the Judge is a man who has no interest outside himself, recognizes no goals other than material ones, has no ability to conceive of the reality either of other people or of nonmaterial values. As Hawthorne delightfully expresses it, he is a man of "substance"—in several senses—a man of property. Unlike the destructive scientists, whose values are topsy-turvy and whose understanding of life is defective, Judge Pyncheon is a creature of darkness. The light seemingly shed by his sunny smile never deceives us for a moment.

But it deceives the society in which he conspicuously "stands in honor." This creature for whom Hawthorne cannot muster any sympathy at all, whom he treats always (unfortunately for the effectiveness of his art at this point) with hatred and contempt is thoroughly respected and "eminently successful." The truly radical implications for society have been too little noted by Hawthorne's critics. Perhaps this is because they are so sure that Hawthorne was a "conservative" that they are unprepared to recognize his implications. When he makes his villain a successful "conservative" and "capitalist" (Hawthorne's words) dedicated to maintaining the status quo of the society that has honored him and of which he seems the perfect representative, and makes the villain's antagonist a radical, a "sworn foe of wealth and all manner of conservatism—the wild reformer—Holgrave," what Hawthorne is doing ought to have been clear before this. It will not do to deny these implications on the ground that Hawthorne, speaking as intrusive author, offers a criticism of some, but not all, of Holgrave's ideas, or that he shows him being transformed into a kind of conservative himself at the end by his love of Phoebe. The point of the gentle and much-qualified criticism is that Hawthorne takes Holgrave's ideas seriously enough to wish to point out what he considers the errors in them; and the transformation after the marriage he treats with gentle amusement. No one could suppose that Hawthorne was a utopian, but it is perfectly clear that he both likes and respects Holgrave. Insofar as the book has a hero (chiefly, it has a heroine, Phoebe), the young reformer fills the role.

The way Hawthorne describes the Judge and insists upon the adequacy of his description thus has implications that constitute just as radical a rejection of what he considered the materialism of the society of his day as any that Emerson or Thoreau ever made. Emerson said that "things are in the saddle and ride mankind," and Hawthorne here illustrates the philosopher's general truth. Thoreau criticized the factory system in the light of its human cost and predicted that those who had been run over in the building of the railroad might some day rise up and overturn it. Hawthorne gives us a concrete instance of what it would be like to be more concerned with property rights than with human rights, to be a man of "things" whose ultimate concern—whose effective religion—was status and material success. The prophetic and biblical "radicalism" implicit in the portrait is dangerous to a social order that promotes injustice in any age—Old Testment, Hawthorne's, ours. Its basis is ethical, not political, but it is no less "subversive" of worldly standards for that reason. There are implications in the fact that literally no one in the story recognizes the Judge for the creature of darkness he is except Hepzibah, Clifford, and Holgrave, who are not worldly successes, who are not respected or honored, who have no status in their society.

Hawthorne's treatment of the Judge's "good works" is one of the finest things in a fine novel. The Judge teaches a Sunday school class, says grace before meals, and is well known for his many benevolences. In short, people respect him not just for his wealth, but for the soundness of his judgment, for his piety, for his public charity, for his democratic manners toward the humble, for his unfailing good humor and his automatic smile. He belongs to the right party and is a buttress of all official ideology. If Hawthorne were writing the book today, he would have to make the Judge a suburban Republican active in the Chamber of Commerce, opposed to fair housing laws because they endanger the rights of property, a member of a country club that excludes almost everyone, willing chairman of the United Fund or Community Chest drive, a trustee of a hospital and of a college, a man who despite all his good works is known as a realist with his feet on the ground who can be trusted never to be taken in by baseless idealism, or any other "isms," a staunch defender of the American way of life, and a senior warden, perhaps, of a wealthy Episcopal parish.

Once, playing with the idea of the Judge's public life as a house, Hawthorne imagines an imposing mansion with everything right and attractive about it above the ground but with a noisome pool of water and a rotting corpse in the cellar. If the odor of decay at times drifted up to the part of the house where the Judge lived, he could easily dismiss it by entering upon another charitable activity or designing another deal. Hawthorne's meaning here, in part, is that the Judge's constant activity is a way of avoiding self-knowledge. But there is another meaning, too, suggested particularly by the rotting corpse. The body is not only the Judge's past, it is his future as well. The Judge is too secular to acknowledge, and live in terms of, his own death. He acts and thinks as if he were immortal, though he carries his corpse around with him all the time. "Death," as Hawthorne had written in another context, "is an idea that cannot easily be dispensed with in any condition between the primal innocence and that other purity and perfection which perchance we are destined to attain after travelling round the full circle."

All this revelation of the Judge's public and private nature prepares us for Hawthorne's otherwise too long description of the dead Judge sitting alone in the house that pride built and that death took possession of on the day of the housewarming. Both Judge and house have not only contained but been dedicated to death from the beginning. Living by standards that spring, some psychiatrists tell us, from the fear of death in the first place, and that certainly foster death, not life, the Judge was already dead morally and spiritually when he appeared most alive. The darkness that finally hides even the whiteness of his face has always, in a moral sense, been hidden behind that too sunny smile for which he is famous. The deepest irony of the "Governor Pyncheon" chapter is that the ambitious Judge has finally come into his own.

If the Judge is a fine satirical portrait, Hepzibah and Clifford are likely to seem to the modern reader more fully realized characters in James's sense. In creating them, Hawthorne's moral and religious beliefs were not so much in control. To be sure, Hepzibah may first have taken shape in his mind as an image of decayed gentility, a living reminder of the folly of expecting that a house would continue forever, a reminder that a powerful and honored family could come to an end at once feeble, sterile, and ridiculous in the new democratic age—in an old maid, at once grotesque, deluded, and pitiable. As he pictures her getting up and preparing to face the day she has dreaded, he remarks that she deserves our pity but that we shall have to control our laughter to give it. At this stage of the writing, Hepzibah is still an idea in Hawthorne's mind, as James said all the characters are. But as he went on writing, she came to take on qualities of character he had not conceived of originally. As other writers of fiction sometimes describe similar experiences with their own characters, so Hepzibah achieved independence of her creator's control, or at least of his "ideas," and grew quite beyond his initial understanding of her. She ceased being a "type" and became a fully imagined "person."

As he wrote on, Hawthorne found himself assigning to Hepzibah ideas he himself held, feelings he himself had often felt. Her sensations when she and Clifford go out into the storm in their attempted flight were, as Hawthorne explicitly acknowledges, just such as any sensitive person might feel—not just an old maid. (Hawthorne himself had pondered long on the storminess of the world, as his **"Night Sketches,"** for just one example, makes perfectly clear.) When she prays at the end of the journey on the train, the prayer is just such a one as we can imagine her creator praying: "Oh, God,—our Father,—are we not thy children? Have mercy on us!" The treatment of her is more and more sympathetic as the story proceeds. When Hawthorne came to the stage of preparing final copy for the printer, the corrections in the manuscript show that he changed the way he had referred to her originally from "the Old Maid," which insisted on her absurdity, to neutral or sympathetic appellations. In almost every reference to her after the opening pages of the second chapter, she became "our poor Hepzibah" or "his sister," "his cousin," or just plain "Hepzibah." She had ceased to be a half-comic, half-grotesque abstraction and had come alive for him as a person whom he could both pity and respect. She seemed to him, as she should to the reader, still pitiable and grotesque, of course, but also generous, loving, and even heroic.

Hawthorne was sympathetic to Clifford from the beginning. Here his imagination works freely before Clifford even appears on the scene, when only his portrait is known to the reader. The remarkable thing about Hawthorne's achievement with Clifford is the way he makes this ruined, almost imbecilic man speak and feel and even think for Hawthorne himself—and for us—without greatly weakening the credibility of his character. Hawthorne created this character from deep parts of his own experience. He too had thought of himself as having been in a prison to which the key had been lost. He too was a "lover of the beautiful" with a tremendous distaste for the practical and the ugly. He too thought that pain was so normal a part of life that with Clifford he might have called for the prick of a rose as a test of whether he were awake. When he assigns to Clifford, during the train ride, the idea that the proper image of history is that of an ascending spiral curve, he is giving him an idea that he himself hoped might be true. Just before this in the same wild monologue, however, Clifford has been incoherently jumbling together ideas of even wilder reformers than Holgrave with ideas that sound like parodies of Emerson. Clifford has no judgment but he has a great deal of sensibility, and like his creator he is capable of entertaining almost any sort of idea, for a time at least. He is one of the fine simpletons of literature.

Holgrave seems more a creature of Hawthorne's ideas than Clifford, perhaps because Hawthorne's attitude toward him was more ambivalent. But Holgrave is neither caricatured nor rejected. Holgrave is full of ideas, but some of his ideas are those Hawthorne himself sometimes entertained, rejecting them only after giving them sympathetic consideration. In England, a few years later, encountering the rigidities and injustices of a caste society, Hawthorne several times confided to his notebooks ideas very much like Holgrave's. Once, noting what he considered typical upper-class unconcern for the poor, he predicted revolution without expressing any horror of the idea. But now, having little confidence in man's ability to design and bring into being a better society without changing the hearts of individuals, he explains Holgrave's errors by referring to his youth and inexperience. Though he considers the reformer's faith in the future both natural and desirable, and though he finds the young man's zeal for reform admirable in its way, he tells us that Holgrave's error lies partly in supposing that the Utopia he dreams of can be built in a day, partly in thinking that it will come out just as he has planned it, but especially in the notion that the present age, more than any other, is the age that will realize it by totally casting off the past. (Hawthorne did not picture history in linear terms. Though he was capable of entertaining, imagining himself as believing, almost any sort of idea, it is impossible to imagine his ever describing himself as Emerson once described himself, as "an endless seeker with no past at my back." He found the past was not so much behind him as around him and within him. To cast it off would be to deny existence to an essential part of himself.) But most of all he seems to feel that the reformer's mistake lies in supposing "that it mattered anything to the great end in view, whether he himself should contend for it or against it."

Holgrave has fallen victim to two of his age's characteristic ideas, voluntarism and the idea of automatic progress, and fallen victim also to a sin as old as man, pride—in his case not personal pride, but the pride of the modern liberal who conceives of himself and his contemporaries as standing on the pinnacle of history. Holgrave is a new American Adam in an unspoiled Garden, or so he thinks. Hawthorne hopes that when Holgrave is older he may exchange his "haughty faith" for a humbler and truer one.

The unstated assumption behind Hawthorne's criticisms of Holgrave is of course the belief he had expressed earlier in **"Earth's Holocaust,"** that all reform that leaves the heart unchanged is superficial. He was soon to write of the failure of such reform in *The Blithedale Romance.* Here he expresses an attitude like Emerson's in "Man the Reformer." "We cannot," Emerson wrote, "ever construct that heavenly society you prate of out of foolish, sick, selfish men and women, such as we know them to be." Hawthorne hopes that eventually Holgrave will come to realize "that man's best-directed effort accomplishes a kind of dream, while God is the sole worker of realities"—which sounds like a contextually inspired overstatement of an idea he would soon express with greater care for the necessary qualifications in his *Life of Pierce:* "There is no instance, in all history, of the human will and intellect having perfected any great moral reform by methods which it adapted to that end; but the progress of the world, at every step, leaves some evil or wrong on the path behind it, which the wisest of mankind, of their own set purpose, could never have found the way to rectify."

But the Holgrave Hawthorne has imagined is finally a better man than his ideas. He is very young and very intelligent, and Hawthorne leads us to expect him to learn from experience what he has not yet had time to learn. Though Holgrave defines his role to Phoebe as that of a detached observer of the inhabitants of the house, living with them in order the better to study them—as though he might become another Ethan Brand—in the end his lively intellect does not destroy his connection with "the magnetic chain of humanity." When the influence of his love for Phoebe turns him suddenly into a premature conservative dreaming of building stone houses and planting fruit trees for future generations, Hawthorne treats the change in his point of view as a delicious joke—at the expense of all radicals. Still, he seems to like this young man, and he makes us like him too. Despite the errors Hawthorne finds mixed in with the basic truth of the central article of his faith, Holgrave passes every practical test put to him in the novel. He respects and tries to help Hepzibah, when others in the town consider her a joke, he senses the evil behind the benign surface of the Judge; most significantly, he refuses to repeat his ancestor's sin against Alice Pyncheon by completing his hypnosis of Phoebe. It could be argued that because of this decision not to exercise his power it is he, and not Phoebe, who really initiates the redemptive action. I rather doubt that Hawthorne looked at it this way, but he certainly made "the artist," as he calls him, a young man to be trusted. Hawthorne's creation of Holgrave would be a sufficient reminder, if any were needed, that Hawthorne had a good deal of Keats's "negative capability," so that as an observer of the contemporary scene he could sometimes be led by what he saw to conclusions very similar to Emerson's—for Holgrave's traits and experiences are much like those described in Emerson's essay "The Young American."

Phoebe strikes the modern reader as a much less impressive achievement in character creation than any of the other major figures in the novel. She is at once Hawthorne's tribute to his wife and his acknowledgment of man's need for God's Grace. As Hawthorne believed Sophia could, Phoebe can transform the appearance of a room with a few seemingly magical touches. Though she is not notable for her ideas, her taste is admirable and her emotions sure guides. At once pious and practical like Sophia, conventional and confident, she gives those around her a sense of "reality," a firmer grip on life. She performs the meanest task as though there were joy and profit to be had from it. She handles *things* as though they were significant; she "spiritualizes," Hawthorne says, everything she touches. Most of this Hawthorne had said about his wife, at one time or another, just as he had written that she had "saved" him the way Phoebe saves Hepzibah and Clifford, bringing him out of his isolation and giving him a sense of reality. For Hawthorne there was no conflict between seeing Phoebe as rather like Sophia and seeing her as a symbol of the possibility of receiving Grace by being receptive to the sacred latent within the commonplace. Phoebe is not just religious; there is a sense, Hawthorne tells us, in which she is Religion itself.

Some of the religious implications of the treatment of Phoebe Hawthorne had [been] made clear much earlier in

**"Sunday at Home,"** in which he pictures himself as not going to church but worshipping just the same, as, through his imagination, he is able to see God in his handiwork, in nature and the very atmosphere. Phoebe's natural piety, which enables her to handle common things as though they are rare and precious, is what makes her for Hawthorne an embodiment of the very essence of religion. She appears to live effortlessly in terms of the three theological virtues, faith, hope, and love, though just what it is she has faith in is not clarified. Hawthorne's religion of the heart allowed him to agree with Paul—on a certain level of generality—that these three were essential if life were to have meaning, and to agree also that the greatest of these is love, though he would not be pressed to further clarification. He knew that, unlike Phoebe's, his own attempts to achieve these virtues were far from effortless. He saw himself as falling short by the standard they presented, particularly as regards hope. No wonder he treats Phoebe as essential to his hopeful ending.

Hawthorne calls upon every resource at his command to strengthen the implications of the way he presents his characters, weaving an intricate pattern of image, symbol, and myth. Angular and circular images begin and end the work, the decaying angular house and the spherical, cyclical elm, with the elm dominant at the end as the house is left for good. Images of light and dark too play an important part in defining for us the story behind the story. He perhaps calls attention to his flower and weed images too insistently. The modern reader becomes uneasy when Hawthorne feels it necessary to point too often to the flowers growing from the rotting roof.

*Hawthorne's wife Sophia in 1847.*

The implications of the symbolic images are supported and extended by the use that Hawthorne makes of the Bible. It seems to me very likely that he was remembering Psalm 49 while he wrote and reading into it Christian meanings presumably not intended by the Psalmist, for not only does the Psalmist's description of the wealthy unjust landowners fit Hawthorne's treatment of the Pyncheons, but several verses in the Psalm appear to be directly reflected in Hawthorne's work, particularly those containing images of seeing and of darkness and light. In the Psalm, the rich "trust in their wealth," forgetting that they are "like the beasts that perish." They are perfectly confident that "their houses shall continue for ever" and so "call their lands after their own names." Yet "death shall feed on them," like the fly on Judge Pyncheon's sightless eyes, and "the upright shall have dominion over them in the morning"—as Phoebe and Holgrave "have dominion" over the dead Judge Pyncheon in the morning after the storm. After they perish, they join their ancestors in darkness, and "they shall never see the light," as the Judge cannot despite his open eyes.

If Hawthorne had this Psalm in mind, it would explain why in his opening paragraph he repeats the name Pyncheon four times in three continuous sentences—"Pyncheon-street," "Pyncheon-house," "Pyncheon-elm," then "Pyncheon-street" again; why he felt he had to apologize for "harping" on the fading of the light and the coming of the darkness, then of light again, so insistently; why he put so much stress on the Judge's open eyes, and why the dead ancestors seem to join the dead Judge in the room. "Governor Pyncheon" has seemed unnecessarily elaborated to some readers, but a reading of Psalm 49 suggests that its images are not merely fanciful but functional.

Hawthorne apparently felt that nothing would be gained by calling attention to the Psalm, but he often reminds us of the parallels between his story and the story of the Fall in Genesis, sometimes explicitly, sometimes implicitly. When Phoebe returns from her visit to the country the day after the storm, she walks around to the back of the house, trying to get in, and enters the garden. She finds it in complete disarray from the effects of the storm. Weeds have taken over where there had been flowers and vegetables, and the whole place looks deserted, littered, and dismal. "Our first parents" have been driven out, and vegetal nature has been blasted along with human nature. Sin and death have entered the scene. No wonder innocent Phoebe, less familiar with Genesis than Hawthorne is, is puzzled by the appearance of the garden and by finding it deserted. Not until *The Marble Faun* did Hawthorne develop "the story of the fall of man" explicitly, but here in *The House* he had it much in his mind.

He draws upon classical myth too, more frequently and significantly than has usually been noted. Several examples seem to work for him especially well. First, Phoebe's name. It means "shining" in Greek, and so refers to that which emanates light, the sun in particular. Phoebus Apollo was the god of the sun, and Phoebe is one of the names of his twin sister and feminine counterpart. The sun, with its light and warmth, fosters, or is the source of, life. And Phoebe was also one of the names of Artemis,

the virgin goddess of the hunt, protectress of wild animals, particularly of the young. Her protectiveness, her cherishing and fostering of life, was not limited to animals, however, but extended to human young. Hence she was also a goddess of childbirth and of women. No wonder Phoebe seems, as Hawthorne presents her, positively to bring light and life into the house and to make possible new life in a situation where otherwise death rules. Her name *means* that—as Hawthorne, with his thorough knowledge of classical mythology, undoubtedly knew.

Even more suggestive is Hawthorne's single reference to the story of the golden bough. When Uncle Venner, the morning after the storm, approaches the house where the dead Judge still sits undiscovered in the ancestral armchair, he notes that though the elm seems not to have been damaged by the storm, "a single branch . . . had been transmuted to bright gold." Then, making his allusion explicit, Hawthorne writes: "It was like the golden branch, that gained Aeneas and the Sybil admittance into Hades. This one mystic branch hung down before the main entrance of the seven gables, so nigh the ground, that any passerby might have stood on tiptoe and plucked it off. Presented at the door, it would have been a symbol of his right to enter, and be made acquainted with all the secrets of the house."

When Aeneas and the Sybil gained admittance to the underworld by the power of the talismanic branch, Aeneas learned both the secrets of the dead and prophecies concerning the living. Reference to the myth works therefore on several levels for Hawthorne. First, it is still a secret that Judge Pyncheon is dead inside the house; anyone entering would learn that secret. But the bough is not just a sort of key to the house, it is a "mystic" branch, capable of unlocking secrets more arcane than the Judge's physical presence within. Reference to it transforms the house into an underworld, a realm where death is all-powerful and sits on the throne.

Finally, this single branch is only a small part of the tree. All the rest was "in perfect verdure," a symbol of life, not death. "Throughout its great circumference," the tree that has come to symbolize nature and nature's annual resurrection—that has been said to overshadow the house where there has been from the beginning only death, not resurrection—"was all alive, and full of the morning sun and a sweetly tempered little breeze, which lingered within this verdant sphere, and set a thousand leafy tongues a-whispering all at once." The leafy tongues are whispering the secrets of the living, not the dead. At the end of the novel, in the concluding sentences, Hawthorne makes this aspect of his allusion more explicit by telling us that the elm "whispered unintelligible prophecies." All the features of the myth have now been utilized, and each of them has reinforced some aspect of the meaning that Hawthorne has already suggested in other ways.

*The House of the Seven Gables* has come to seem to me one of the least adequately appreciated novels in American literature. I say "novel" rather than "romance" in accordance with normal contemporary usage and because Hawthorne's rather defensive distinction seems less and less necessary as the years go by and it becomes ever more apparent that he wrote in the main stream of the most lasting American fiction. If we still feel, with Lionel Trilling and Richard Chase, that the English "novel"—with its realistic intention and its implicit assumption that the manners and ways of the society it pictures are somehow absolute, the sources of the novel's own standards of value—is the normative standard for fiction, then of course we shall either not like Hawthorne's work, or, if we do like it, we shall feel it necessary to apologize for him, seeing him perhaps as handicapped by being forced by the fashions of his time and place to write in an inferior form, the allegorical "romance." The romance, from this point of view, is not a real novel.

But this is ultimately at least in part a philosophical judgment, not a purely aesthetic one. The best American writers have seldom or never taken society as an absolute. Our society has been new and raw enough, and fluid enough, and dynamic enough to discourage this particular form of idolatry. Typically American writers, both poets and writers of fiction, have seen man not within the drawing room, but, to use the words of the title of Robinson's poem, against the sky. Hawthorne anticipated James in complaining that the lack of an old and stable society in America made his job as a writer harder. Perhaps so, though I doubt it, given his natural talents and interests and his outlook; but if so he surmounted the difficulty to produce great works for which no apology of any kind is needed. And how likely is it anyway that a society most of whose greatest artists have been as antinomian and rebellious against society itself as ours have been will ever evolve into a fixed, stable, hierarchical social order, an order in which a novelist can tell who a gentleman is by how he acts and speaks and dresses, and thus economically make it clear to a reader that another character is not a gentleman, or not quite? What major American novelist has ever cared very much who a gentleman is, for that matter? Even James is only an apparent exception; ultimately he cares more about morals than manners. What major American writer of any sort has ever accepted uncritically the standards and values of his society, making them his own? Or cared enough about social customs and institutions to describe them in detail, except for the purposes of attack, unless they were in the past and so could be idealized?

The greatest American writers have generally been supramundane in the basic values that have shaped their work. If this fact is related to the nature of our society as effect, it may also, I think, be related as cause. The direction in which a society moves is influenced, in the long run, by its best and most creative minds. The Judge Pyncheons of the world may have, ultimately, less influence in determining the future than the Hawthornes and the Emersons and the Whitmans. The error of the recent deterministic past was to suppose that society not only influences but produces literature—in which case, the Judge Pyncheons will always have the last word, and Hawthorne was simply mistaken in the meanings he expressed in his novel. But it may well be that the complex truth is at least as well expressed the other way round, by saying that literature and other creations of the imagination play an important part in shaping society. If so, then the traditional distinction between the romance and the novel will have to be reformulated.

***The House of the Seven Gables*** is a very romantic and allegorical novel, but also a very protestant and a radically democratic one, subversive in its attitude toward much of society as Hawthorne found it, antinomian in its suggestion that true reality and real values are to be found only in the personal relations of the individual to other individuals and to God. The basis of its subversion of society is not an ideology but a commitment to moral and religious values derived ultimately from the Old and New Testaments. It judges society by a standard derived from a position independent of any society, radically above the actual state of any society. A more mundane standard Hawthorne would have called "worldly," and ultimately evil. At this point he is one with Mark Twain—though Twain turned to nature and not to God for his standard—and with Emerson, Thoreau, and Whitman; despite many differences, with Melville and Faulkner too. Both his idealism and the nonrealistic technique through which he expresses it are in the major American tradition in fiction.

Hawthorne's novel is alive today, relevant to us, and it demands our full attention. Its persistent presentness may be illustrated, quite arbitrarily, by comparing it with Faulkner's *Absalom, Absalom!* Formally, both largely ignore the conventions of realism. Thematically, both concern a "design" to found a family (both authors use the word *design*) that will be secure in its social eminence; both make a house a symbol of this design; both see the effort as doomed, partly because life cannot be "designed" this way, partly because of the methods used to accomplish the end that has been designed—methods in both cases involving denial of love and justice. Both the Pyncheons and Sutpen become rich and powerful, the Pyncheons also achieving eminent respectability and Sutpen hoping to; but both families end in decay and degeneracy, until in Hawthorne's story, the "miracle" of love reverses the trend. Faulkner burns his house, while Hawthorne has one of his characters suggest that his *ought* to be burned. Faulkner takes his title and ultimately the standards by which he judges both Sutpen and his society from the story of King David and his son Absalom in the Bible, and also uses classical myth; Hawthorne likewise turns to the Bible, certainly to Genesis and probably also to Psalm 49, and to classical myth for the underpinnings of his story.

If *Absalom, Absalom!* is a greater novel than ***The House,*** as it seems to most of us to be, it is not because it is more truly what has traditionally been called a "novel" than Hawthorne's is, or because it takes a more respectful attitude toward society, but because Faulkner's imaginative creation of a fictional world in *Absalom* is even deeper and richer in its evocations and its manifold meanings than is Hawthorne's in ***The House.*** Perhaps the difference between the two that finally comes to seem most important is the difference in the amount of hope offered for redemption from evils of the past. Faulkner's novel ends in anguished ambiguity, Hawthorne's in relative clarity. Hawthorne never again achieved so much clarity and light as he did in this hopeful novel. (pp. 76-97)

*Hyatt H. Waggoner, in his* The Presence of

Hawthorne, *Louisiana State University Press,*
*1979, 166 p.*

## Michael T. Gilmore   (essay date 1981)

[*In the following essay, Gilmore presents* The House of
the Seven Gables *as an embodiment of the conflict be-*
*tween Hawthorne's desire to write a novel true to his own*
*vision and his need to produce a popular work that*
*would sell.* ]

The fairy-tale ending of *The House of the Seven Gables*
has not satisfied the novel's modern readers, most of
whom have agreed with F. O. Matthiessen [in his *Ameri-*
*can Renaissance,* 1941] that "the reconciliation [of Maule
and Pyncheon] is somewhat too lightly made" and that in
bestowing the Judge's ill-gotten wealth upon the surviving
characters, Hawthorne evidently overlooked his own
warnings about the evils of inheritance. William Charvat
has suggested [in his introduction to the Centenary Edition of *The House of the Seven Gables,* 1965] that the ending's weakness may stem less from authorial oversight
than from the requirements of the marketplace. While
noting that Hawthorne himself seems to have shared the
popular preference for fiction combining "sunshine and
shadow," Charvat points out that he was also alert to "the
professional or commercial aspects of his project." Despite the moderate success of *The Scarlet Letter,* he was
still hard pressed financially and knew only too well that
his reputation for "blackness" (as Melville termed it) was
an obstacle to acceptance by the wider public. "We cannot
ignore the possibility," adds Charvat, "that Hawthorne,
in concluding his book as he did, was yielding to the
world's wish that in stories everything should turn out
well."

In fact, it seems considerably more than a possibility. The
text itself reveals a Hawthorne deeply concerned with his
relation to the public and with his priorities as a writer
who both craved fame and money and aspired—again in
Melville's words—to be a master of "the great Art of Telling the Truth." Melville's famous review of *Mosses from*
*an Old Manse* appeared just as Hawthorne began work on
*The House of the Seven Gables.* "In this world of lies,"
Melville had argued, profound authors had no choice but
to become deceivers, to hoodwink the general reader by
concealing their meanings. But Hawthorne could not
share Melville's apparent equanimity about adopting this
strategy. He reacted with pain and dismay when he found
himself obliged to employ it in his work-in-progress, and
he was unable to suppress his misgivings that in bowing
to the marketplace he was compromising his artistic independence and integrity.

Hawthorne states in the preface to *The House of the*
*Seven Gables* that the romantic character of his tale consists in its being "a Legend, prolonging itself, from an
epoch now gray in the distance, down into our own broad
daylight, and bringing along with it some of its legendary
mist. . . . " He proceeds in the opening chapter to speak
of hereditary curses and ghostly powers, but his conception of the legendary is not confined to the paraphernalia
of gothic romance. He is also referring to that body of

knowledge and speculation which is excluded from the officially sanctioned view of things. The legendary encompasses the "rumors," "traditions," and "fables" that necessarily remain clandestine and underground because they
express truths too controversial for public utterance. In
discussing Colonel Pyncheon's designs on the Maule
homestead, Hawthorne observes that "No written record
of this dispute is known to be in existence. Our acquaintance with the whole subject is derived chiefly from tradition." Tradition is also his sole authority for intimating a
connection between the executed wizard's curse—"God
will give him blood to drink"—and the mysterious manner of the Colonel's death. The Colonel's laudatory funeral sermon, "which was printed and is still extant," contains no hint of guilt and retribution. "Tradition—which
sometimes brings down truth that history has let slip, but
is oftener the wild babble of the time, such as was formerly
spoken at the fireside, and now congeals in newspapers—
tradition is responsible for all contrary averments." The
imputation of troubled consciences to the Colonel's descendants is similarly laid to the town's "traditionary gossips" and to "impressions too vaguely founded to be put
on paper."

Despite this last remark, the distinction being made here
is not primarily between speech and writing. Hawthorne
contrasts spoken words and written ones only insofar as
they lend support to the more fundamental distinction between private and public discourse. Criticism of the Pyncheons is more likely to be expressed orally than on paper
because the "written record," historical or otherwise, is
addressed to the world and dare not impeach the characters of eminent men whom all the world agrees in honor-
ing. The awareness of a potentially unsympathetic audience can be inhibiting to the artist and work against truthfulness in any medium of expression.

This notion is implicit in Hawthorne's discussion of Judge
Pyncheon. After noting that no one—neither inscriber of
tombstones, nor public speaker, nor writer of history—
would venture a word of censure against the Judge, he
continues:

> But besides these cold, formal, and empty words
> of the chisel that inscribes, the voice that speaks,
> and the pen that writes for the public eye and for
> distant time—and which inevitably lose much of
> their truth and freedom by the fatal conscious-
> ness of so doing—there were traditions about the
> ancestor, and private diurnal gossip about the
> Judge, remarkably accordant in their testimony.
> It is often instructive to take the woman's, the
> private and domestic view, of a public man; nor
> can anything be more curious than the vast dis-
> crepancy between portraits intended for engrav-
> ing, and the pencil-sketches that pass from hand
> to hand, behind the original's back.

The reference in this passage to loss of truth and freedom
has obvious relevance for an author who claims in his preface "a certain latitude" as a writer of romance and who
takes as his subject "the truth of the human heart." By extending his observations to the difference between engrav-
ings and pencil sketches, moreover, Hawthorne suggests
that a major reason for circumspection in addressing the

public is the fear of offending potential customers. The inference that the wisdom associated with the legendary is not only guarded and private but unsalable emerges clearly from his description of the Colonel's portrait hanging in the house of the seven gables. With the passage of time, the portrait's superficial coloring has faded and the inward traits of its subject have grown more prominent and striking. Such an effect, Hawthorne notes, is not uncommon in antique paintings: "They acquire a look which an artist (if he have anything like the complaisancy of artists, now-a-days) would never dream of presenting to a patron as his own characteristic expression, but which, nevertheless, we at once recognize as reflecting the unlovely truth of a human soul." In other words, the artist who is determined to express the truth openly in the present will find it impossible to sell his creations.

Perhaps the key word in Hawthorne's description of the contemporary artist is "complaisancy." Whether the prospective buyer is an individual patron or the general public, the artist has to appear accommodating if he wishes to succeed in the marketplace. He cannot afford to be honest because his truth-telling may alienate his audience and deprive him of his livelihood. Although Hawthorne is speaking here of the portrait painter in particular, his analysis applies to anyone involved in the process of exchange. In *The House of the Seven Gables* he comments most directly on the exchange process and the relation of buyer and seller in the chapters devoted to Hepzibah's opening of her cent-shop.

Finding herself practically destitute after a lifetime of patrician indolence, Hepzibah has decided to try her hand at business when the narrative proper opens in contemporary Salem. Although she herself cares little for material comforts, she expects the imminent return of her brother Clifford from jail and refuses to apply for financial assistance to their cousin the Judge, the man she holds responsible for Clifford's long imprisonment. With no other recourse but to support Clifford by her own exertions, she has mustered her courage to re-open the little shop built into the house by a penurious ancestor and long regarded as an embarrassment by the family. Hawthorne, in his capacity as "a disembodied listener," follows her protracted preparations for the first day behind the counter with a mixture of sympathy and satire. She is introduced sighing at her toilet as she struggles to overcome her reluctance about facing the world. At least twice she pauses before her toilet glass in a pathetic attempt to make herself look attractive. Stepping at last into the passageway, she slowly makes her way through the house to the shop's entrance and with a sudden effort thrusts herself across the threshold. Her hesitation returns inside the shop and she nervously sets about rearranging the goods in the window. Still she hangs back from "the public eye," as if, writes Hawthorne, she expected to come before the community "like a disembodied divinity, or enchantress, holding forth her bargains to the reverential and awe-striken purchaser, in an invisible hand." Unlike Hawthorne himself, however, she is not permitted the luxury of invisibility: "She was well aware that she must ultimately come forward, and stand revealed in her proper individuality; but, like other sensitive persons, she could not bear to be observed in the

gradual process, and chose rather to flash forth on the world's astonished gaze, at once."

Hepzibah strikingly recalls Hester Prynne standing on the scaffold with her badge of shame. Hawthorne's Puritan adulteress, who first appears before the reader in the chapter entitled "The Market-Place," is said to stagger "under the heavy weight of a thousand unrelenting eyes." As Hepzibah takes her place behind the counter, she too is tortured "with a sense of overwhelming shame, that strange and unloving eyes should have the privilege of gazing" at her. In recounting her tribulations, Hawthorne dwells on the importance of being seen in trade and making a favorable impression. Hepzibah herself feels continued uneasiness over the appearance of the window: "It seemed as if the whole fortune or failure of her shop might depend on the display of a different set of articles, or substituting a fairer apple for one which appeared to be specked." Repeatedly Hawthorne calls attention to the handicap of her scowl, which results from nearsightedness but has unfortunately given her the reputation of being ill tempered. When that shrewd Yankee Dixey passes by the shop, he loudly predicts that Hepzibah's frown will be her financial undoing. "Make it go!" he exclaims. "Not a bit of it! Why her face—I've seen it . . . her face is enough to frighten Old Nick himself, if he had ever so great a mind to trade with her." Overhearing these words, Hepzibah has a painful vision that seems to underscore the futility of her venture. On one side of the street stands her antiquated shop, over which she presides with an offending scowl, and on the other rises a magnificent bazaar, "with a multitude of perfumed and glossy salesmen, smirking, smiling, bowing, and measuring out the goods!" Even the simple-minded Uncle Venner, who offers Hepzibah encouragement along with Benjamin Franklin-like maxims, advocates a beaming countenance as "all-important" to success in business: "Put on a bright face for your customers, and smile pleasantly as you hand them what they ask for! A stale article, if you dip it in a good, warm, sunny smile, will go off better than a fresh one that you've scowled upon!"

As such passages suggest, Hawthorne is using Hepzibah to explore his own ambivalence about courting the public in order to make money. Although she herself is not an artist figure, she resembles her creator both in her history of isolation and her need to earn a living. One thinks immediately of Hawthorne's seclusion for thirteen years after graduating from Bowdoin and his self-designation as "the obscurest man of letters in America." It is no wonder that he gives Hepzibah a Puritan progenitor who was involved in the witchcraft trials like his own ancestor John Hathorne, and who appears in his portrait much as William Hathorne is described in **"The Custom-House,"** clutching a Bible and a sword. As an author who always insisted upon preserving "the inmost Me behind its veil," Hawthorne would not have found it difficult to appreciate Hepzibah's misgivings about encountering "the public gaze." He would have understood her resentment at the familiar tone adopted by her customers, who "evidently considered themselves not merely her equals but her patrons and superiors." Indeed, he draws an implicit parallel between his writing and the commodities she hopes to sell.

Her stock consists primarily of items of food like apples, Indian meal, and gingerbread men, and in the preface he speaks of his book as an object to be eaten, calling it a "dish offered to the Public." And he seems almost as hesitant about getting his narrative under way as she does about opening for business. Just as she pauses apprehensively on the threshold of her shop, so "we are loitering faint-heartedly," says Hawthorne, "on the threshold of our story."

Despite his sympathy for her discomfort, Hawthorne is far from identifying with Hepzibah uncritically. A part of him yearned "to open an intercourse with the world" [according to his preface to his *Twice-Told Tales*] and was not above advising his publisher [in a letter reprinted by Charvat] on how to entrap that "great gull," the general reader. This part finds her more comical than tragic and strongly disapproves of her reluctance to seek her own fortune. Although Hawthorne himself had difficulty supporting his family by his writing, and lobbied actively for government appointments, in print he commends the marketplace for fostering self-reliance and expresses detached amusement at Hepzibah's dreams of being rescued from trade by a sudden bequest. Too much of a democrat to endorse her aristocratic pretensions, he agrees with Holgrave that she will discover satisfaction in contributing her mite "to the united struggle of mankind." Her first sale does in fact bring her an unexpected sense of accomplishment and dispells many of her fears about commerce with the world. But she lacks both the skill and the temperament to prosper as a saleswoman, and at the end of the day she has as little to show for "all her painful traffic" as Hawthorne did after his long apprenticeship as a writer of tales and sketches.

It is through Phoebe rather than Hepzibah herself that Hawthorne expresses his conviction—or more precisely his hope—that it is possible to be engaged in market relations without suffering a sense of violation. Phoebe, who has "had a table at a fancy-fair, and made better sales than anybody," is able to drive a shrewd bargain relying only on her "native truth and sagacity." Her practical mind abounds with schemes "whereby the influx of trade might be increased, and rendered profitable, without a hazardous outlay of capital." Her smile is unconscious of itself, and therefore honest and spontaneous; for her it is a simple matter, in Uncle Venner's phrase, to "put on a bright face for [her] customers." As Hawthorne often states, she has a naturally sunny disposition, and her presence is like "a gleam of sunshine" in the gloomy old house. Hepzibah is quick to acknowledge her superiority as a shopkeeper, and the public shows its agreement by flocking to the store during the hours when she takes her turn behind the counter.

No doubt Hawthorne wished for comparable good fortune in his dealings with the public. But he seems to have suspected that his own sunny smile was not nearly so ready as Phoebe's. And he was aware of the possibilities for deception in exchange relations, being based as they are so largely on appearance. There is one character in particular in *The House of the Seven Gables* who thoroughly appreciates the marketability of a genial countenance, and who

incurs the censure that Hawthorne feels toward his own worldly ambition. Although his natural expression is anything but cheerful, Judge Jaffrey Pyncheon has worked up an extraordinary smile for public consumption. The passages describing his sham joviality are remarkable in Hawthorne's writing for their unrelieved hostility and exaggerated irony. In chapter 7, "The Pyncheon of To-day," where he first tries to gain an interview with Clifford, he puts on an especially dazzling face to win the confidence of Hepzibah and Phoebe. As he enters the house, "his smile grew as intense as if he had set his heart on counteracting the whole gloom of the atmosphere . . . by the unassisted light of his countenance." Advancing to greet Hepzibah, he wears a smile "so broad and sultry, that had it been only half as warm as it looked, a trellis of grapes might at once have turned purple under its summer-like exposure." Of course the Judge's sunshiny exterior only masks his darker purposes, and his smile changes to a frown like a thunder cloud when his wishes are opposed. But Jaffrey is too practiced a hypocrite to allow himself to be caught off guard for very long. Hawthorne devotes an entire paragraph to the ingratiating manner with which he covers his departure:

> With a bow to Hepzibah, and a degree of paternal benevolence in his parting nod to Phoebe, the Judge left the shop, and went smiling along the street. As is customary with the rich, when they aim at the honors of a republic, he apologized, as it were, to the people, for his wealth, prosperity, and elevated station, by a free and hearty manner towards those who knew him; putting off the more of his dignity, in due proportion with the humbleness of the man whom he saluted; and thereby proving a haughty consciousness of his advantages, as irrefragably as if he had marched forth, preceded by a troop of lackeys to clear the way. On this particular forenoon, so excessive was the warmth of Judge Pyncheon's kindly aspect, that (such, at least, was the rumor about town) an extra passage of water-carts was found essential, in order to lay the dust occasioned by so much extra sunshine!

The Judge clearly has much in common with the oily, grinning salesmen of Hepzibah's vision. He also bears a marked resemblance to the Italian organ-grinder's monkey, who performs "a bow and scrape" while holding out his palm to receive the public's money.

The Judge has been well rewarded for his assiduous cultivation of the public. Whereas Hepzibah's scowl threatens to ruin her, his smile has brought him every imaginable success. He is very rich, enjoys the reputation of a model citizen, and has been showered with public honors, including election to Congress. "Beyond all question," states Hawthorne, he "was a man of eminent respectability. The church acknowledged it; the state acknowledged it. It was denied by nobody." This assessment occurs in chapter 15, "The Scowl and the Smile," where Hawthorne also hints of perceptions more discerning than the world's. In an elaborate metaphor, he compares Jaffrey's public personality to a glittering and sunbathed palace, "which, in the view of other people, and ultimately in his own view, is no other than the man's character, or the man himself." But in some concealed nook of this splendid edifice, inaccessible to public view,

> may lie a corpse, half-decayed, and still decaying, and diffusing its death-scent through the palace! The inhabitant will not be conscious of it, for it has long been his daily breath! Neither will the visitors, for they smell only the rich odors which the master sedulously scatters through the palace. . . . Now and then, perchance, comes in a seer, before whose sadly gifted eye the whole structure melts into thin air, leaving only the hidden nook, the bolted closet, with the cobwebs festooned over its forgotten door, or the deadly hole under the pavement, and the decaying corpse within. Here, then, we are to seek the true emblem of the man's character, and of the deed which gives whatever reality it possesses to his life. And, beneath the show of a marble palace, that pool of stagnant water, foul with many impurities, and, perhaps, tinged with blood,—that secret abomination, above which, possibly, he may say his prayers, without remembering it,—is this man's miserable soul!

In this passage Hawthorne implicitly repudiates any connection between his own art and Jaffrey's manipulation of appearances. Jaffrey is an "artist" of the public, but Hawthorne's seer is an artist of the private, of the legendary. His unflattering vision of the human soul is no more marketable than the antique portrait of the Colonel; he could never hope to present it either to the public or the builder of the palace. Insofar as Hawthorne seeks to portray "the truth of the human heart," he himself is such an artist.

The figure in *The House of the Seven Gables* who most closely approximates this kind of artist is Holgrave, the daguerreotypist and descendant of the wizard. From the moment of their dispossession the Maules have been associated with ghostly powers, poverty, and secrecy. They are said to have outwardly cherished "no malice against individuals or the public, for the wrong which had been done them." Any grievances they may have felt were transmitted "at their own fireside" and "never acted upon, nor openly expressed." Down through the generations they have been marked off from other men by their "character of reserve" and by a self-imposed isolation which has kept them from prospering. Holgrave, who appears in the text under the veil of an assumed name, has carried the family traditions into the present. Suspected of practicing the Black Art, he holds views subversive of established authority and generally remains aloof from the society of others. As he tells Phoebe, his impulse is not to bare his heart in public but "to look on, to analyze, to explain matters to myself." Even more so than Hepzibah, he suggests the side of Hawthorne that dominates the prefaces—the Hawthorne who insists on veiling his countenance from the reader's gaze and claims [in his preface to his *The Snow Image*] that his seeming intimacies "hide the man, instead of displaying him." He further resembles his creator, who spent a year at Brook Farm, in his association with reformers and "community-men." And he writes stories which he supposedly contributes to periodicals where Hawthorne's own tales have appeared, such as *Graham's Magazine* and Godey's *Magazine and Lady's Book.*

Holgrave, in other words, is like Hawthorne before he wrote *The Scarlet Letter* and became known to the wider public. He obviously has earned little money from his periodical writing, and when Phoebe professes ignorance of his efforts, he exclaims much as the younger Hawthorne might have, "Well; such is literary fame!" The sample of his work reprinted in *The House of the Seven Gables,* "Alice Pyncheon," helps to explain his lack of success with the average reader. Like the larger text of which it forms a part, it tells a story of conflict between the Maules and Pyncheons, but it goes beyond Hawthorne's own narrative in its incautious use of the half-spoken and the legendary. The tale has Matthew Maule openly assert both his right to the house and his power over Alice, thus giving centrality to the very themes of class resentment and psychic mastery that Hawthorne tends to treat with circumspection. In writing it, as Holgrave says, he has essentially followed "wild, chimney-corner legend," and in general he shows neither aptitude nor inclination for an art that will be popular. His daguerreotypes, to borrow the distinction made by Hawthorne, are more like pencil sketches that have to be passed behind the subject's back than portraits suitable for engraving. Holgrave, who realizes this himself, explains to Phoebe that his photographic images bring out "the secret character with a truth that no painter would ever venture upon, even could he detect it. There is at least no flattery in my humble line of art." He then shows her a daguerreotype miniature of the Judge that in the manner of the Colonel's portrait reveals "the unlovely truth of a human soul." Remarkably enough, according to Holgrave, "the original wears, to the world's eye . . . an exceedingly pleasant countenance, indicative of benevolence, openness of heart, sunny good humor, and other praiseworthy qualities of that cast." The face in the daguerreotype, however, is "sly, subtle, hard, imperious, and withal, cold as ice." The picture's very truthfulness, of course, will make it impossible to sell; as Holgrave observes, "It is so much the more unfortunate, as [the original] is a public character of some eminence, and the likeness was intended to be engraved."

While Hawthorne clearly put much of himself into the daguerreotypist, it would be a mistake to exaggerate their similarities. Rather, as the preface to *The Snow-Image* suggests, one must "look through the whole range of his fictitious characters, good and evil, in order to detect any of his essential traits. . . ." The author of *The House of the Seven Gables* had too much need of money to identify completely with Holgrave's indifference to popularity. With only his writing to support himself and his family, he could not afford to despise the commercial advantage of a pleasing exterior. And while he might sympathize with Hepzibah, it is her cousin the Judge whom "the world's laudatory voice" has acclaimed and enriched. The conflict between Maule and Pyncheon, Holgrave and Jaffrey, is accordingly a conflict in Hawthorne's own mind. It reflects the division in his view of the artist as "a man of society" who appeals to the general reader [as he states in his preface to *Twice-Told Tales*] and as a private teller of truth whose revelations are unsalable. To gain acceptance with the public, is it necessary to become a hypocrite like the Judge? Is it possible to depict the truth of the heart like Holgrave without sacrificing commercial success?

Who is the rightful owner of the house of the seven gables? Of *The House of the Seven Gables?* What kind of artist is Hawthorne finally to be?

Hawthorne attempts to resolve this dilemma by reconciling Maule and Pyncheon and writing a book of truth that will attract a popular audience. He proposes to bring the legendary mist into "our own broad daylight" and to prove that Holgrave's insights are compatible with Phoebe's smile. Along with many of his readers, he had been troubled by the lack of "cheering light" in *The Scarlet Letter* and attributed its popularity primarily to the introductory sketch. The story of Hester and the minister, he had written in **"The Custom-House,"** "wears, to my eye, a stern and sombre aspect; too much ungladdened by genial sunshine; too little relieved by the tender and familiar influences which soften almost every scene of nature and real life, and, undoubtedly, should soften every picture of them." Reviewers, including Hawthorne's favorite critic, E. P. Whipple, agreed. The book was too uniformly gloomy to please the general public. In his second novel, Hawthorne was determined to remedy this commercial failing by alleviating his customary blackness with a liberal use of "genial sunshine."

The finished work does in fact avoid the relentlessly tragic tone of *The Scarlet Letter.* Although the narrative voice sometimes sounds as radical as Holgrave, many passages reveal a penchant for sentiment and fancy. Like the daguerreotypist, Hawthorne questions the integrity of great men and the political system that promotes them. In speaking of Jaffrey's gubernatorial ambitions, for example, he refers to the backroom politicians who "steal from the people, without its knowledge, the power of choosing its own rulers . . . This little knot of subtle schemers will control the convention, and, through it, dictate to the party." But these cynical reflections tend to alternate with heart-warming affirmations worthy of Phoebe. The Hawthorne who writes of the bees sent by God "to gladden our poor Clifford," or who gushes over his young heroine's domesticity, seems less an artist of the legendary than a "pen-and-ink" man addressing "the intellect and sympathies of the multitude" [as he states in his short story, **"Rappaccini's Daughter"**]. And of course the clearest indication of Hawthorne's wish to effect a compromise between Maule and Pyncheon is the romance of Holgrave and Phoebe. Both characters give up some of their family traits and move toward a common ground. Admitting that his "legend" will never do for a popular audience, the daguerreotypist refrains from exercising the psychic power of the Maules and discovers a new respect for institutions. Phoebe, who has shed some of her sunshine as a result of living in the house, becomes "more womanly, and deep-eyed, in token of a heart that had begun to suspect its depths." Hawthorne's art comes to rest at the dead center of their marriage; in contrast to "Alice Pyncheon," which ends unhappily, the novel itself finds a way to combine salability with knowledge of the heart.

Or does it? If, as Hawthorne insisted, the book was "more proper and natural" for him to write than *The Scarlet Letter,* why did he experience difficulty in completing it? According to Charvat, he probably began work in the late summer of 1850, made steady progress, and hoped to finish by November. His publishers, Ticknor, Reed, and Fields, began to advertise "A new Romance by the author of *The Scarlet Letter*" in the October *Literary World,* and looked forward to having the completed manuscript in their hands by December 1. But Hawthorne slowed down unexpectedly after his rapid start and confessed to James T. Fields on November 29 that the conclusion was giving him particular problems: "It darkens damnably towards the close, but I shall try hard to pour some setting sunshine over it." The effort proved more troublesome and disturbing than Hawthorne anticipated, as is evident from a letter dated ten days later: "My desire and prayer is, to get through with the business already in hand . . . I have been in a Slough of Despond, for some days past—having written so fiercely that I came to a stand still. There are points where a writer gets bewildered, and cannot form any judgment of what he has done, nor tell what to do next." As late as January 12, only two weeks before the completion date given in the preface, he wrote to Fields that he was still "hammering away a little on the roof, and doing up a few odd jobs that were left incomplete." The tinkering continued, Charvat believes, until Hawthorne sent the book to the printers.

There is no way of knowing precisely what changes Hawthorne made to lighten the novel's mood and bring it to "a prosperous close." But hints scattered throughout the final pages support the notion that he was unhappy with his happy ending. At one point he writes that the house continued to diffuse a gloom "which no brightness of the sunshine could dispel"; and elsewhere he compares his story to "an owl, bewildered in the daylight." The owl suggests Hepzibah, squinting and frowning in the glare of the public gaze; and Hawthorne used the same word, "bewildered," when he complained of his difficulties with the ending. The comic resolution demanded by his readers, he clearly felt, was violating the logic of his tale and covering up its scowl with an inappropriate smile.

This supposition is also suggested by Hawthorne's treatment of Holgrave in the book's concluding chapters. In chapter 20, "The Flower of Eden," the daguerreotypist declares his love for Phoebe and renounces his radicalism. Henceforth he will confine himself "within ancient limits" and even "build a house for another generation." His sudden reversal of character has left most readers unconvinced. But in reality Holgrave shows great reluctance, as Hawthorne notes, "to betake himself within the precincts of common life." He is particularly loath to publicize "the awful secret" of the Judge's death, and the reasons he gives for his hesitation are not very consistent. Supposedly he fears that Clifford's flight will be construed as an admission of guilt, yet he also says that Jaffrey's death, being "attended by none of those suspicious circumstances" which surrounded the uncle's death, will clear Clifford of the earlier crime. Phoebe is at a loss to comprehend his indecision. While he keeps putting off the moment of disclosure, she pleads with him not "to hide this thing . . . It is dreadful to keep it so closely in our hearts. Clifford is innocent. God will make it manifest! Let us throw open the doors, and call all the neighborhood to see the truth!" The "truth" in question is the knowledge of the heart, and herein lies the deeper reason for Holgrave's unwillingness to make it known. Jaffrey's body in the house of the seven gables recalls the stately palace with its hidden secret, and the daguerreotypist, who takes a picture of the scene, corresponds to the seer whose "sadly gifted eye" detects the corpse within, "the true emblem" of the man's soul. But this truth, which is also the truth of Hawthorne's art, has been characterized throughout the book as private and unsalable; in revealing it to the public, Holgrave is "inevitably" corrupted "by the fatal consciousness of so doing." His action betrays his calling as an artist of the legendary and is precisely analogous to Hawthorne's contrivance of a happy ending at the expense of narrative consistency. Though the result in both cases may be "Pretty good business," as Dixey puts it, Holgrave's reluctance to capitulate is also his creator's.

Hawthorne, to be sure, might have been masking his deeper intentions and inviting an ironic reading that emphasizes the discrepancy between appearance and reality. Melville, it will be remembered, recommended this strategy for the author "too deserving of popularity to be popular," and in the final chapters Hawthorne tries to make a virtue of necessity by implying that his story's surface is at odds with its inner meaning. When the summer storm subsides the morning after the Judge's death, he points out that the sunshine creates a false impression of the house. "So little faith is due to external appearance, that there was really an inviting aspect over the venerable edifice, conveying an idea that its history must be a decorous and happy one . . . . " Several pages later, when the organ-grinder stops to play on Pyncheon street, he continues: "to us, who know the inner heart of the seven gables, as well as its exterior face, there is a ghastly effect in this representation of light popular tunes at its door-step."

Hawthorne's insistence on the disjunction between the house's outward face and its interior is echoed by Holgrave in the book's concluding chapter. As the triumphant party of survivors prepares to take possession of the Judge's country mansion, the daguerreotypist wonders why the dead man did not see fit to embody

> so excellent a piece of domestic architecture in stone, rather than in wood. Then, every generation of the family might have altered the interior, to suit its own taste and convenience; while the exterior, through the lapse of years, might have been adding venerableness to its original beauty, thus giving that impression of permanence, which I consider essential to the happiness of any one moment.

In one sense this statement represents a compromise between reform and conservatism. Equally important, it advocates a policy of deception with regard to houses, and as such it is also a statement about Hawthorne's art. In the preface he likened the writing of his tale to "building a house, of materials long in use for constructing castles in the air," and of course the title of his novel is *The House of the Seven Gables.*

Hawthorne, then, appears to have agreed with Melville's view of the artist as a con-man; certainly he *wanted* to accept it in order to justify his surrender to the marketplace.

But the narrative itself repudiates this strategy as morally reprehensible, and Hawthorne stands condemned for employing it by the value system of his own art. Though appearances may be unreliable in the novel, only one character makes a practice of deliberate deception. Hepzibah's heart is often said to smile while her face is frowning, but she cannot help herself. Hawthorne does the opposite: he smiles while his heart is frowning. In contrast to Phoebe's "natural sunshine," the "warm, sunny smile" he presents to the reader is contrived and artificial. He had to try hard, as he admitted to Fields, to pour sunshine over the tale's darkening close, and in doing so he follows the example of Judge Pyncheon manufacturing a sunny exterior to win the favor of the public. Passages that denounce the villain for hypocrisy became ironically self-accusing when considered in relation to the novel's ending. Indeed, it is as much a struggle for Hawthorne to dispel the gloom of his narrative as it is for the Judge to disguise the "black" and "brooding" thunder cloud of his temperament. The acute observer who probably suspected "that the smile on the gentleman's face was a good deal akin to the shine on his boots, and that each must have cost him and his boot-black, respectively, a good deal of hard labor to bring out and preserve them," might have said the same thing about the Judge's creator.

Perhaps even more ironic in this connection is Holgrave's—and Hawthorne's—volte-face on houses. When the daguerreotypist expresses a wish that the exterior of a house might differ from its interior, he unwittingly endorses a scheme of domestic architecture that has been practiced metaphorically by Jaffrey Pyncheon. It seems fitting, therefore, that he should take up residence in the Judge's elegant country-seat rather than in the dwelling built by his ancestor, the house of the seven gables. Moreover, Hawthorne's house of fiction parallels the deceptive edifice of the Judge's being. Since a "devilish scowl would frighten away customers," as Dixey keeps insisting, he imposes a sunbathed conclusion on his narrative to cover up "the fearful secret, hidden within the house." Little wonder that the angry taunting of Jaffrey's corpse in chapter 18, "Governor Pyncheon," has struck many readers as excessive and slightly hysterical. It is not difficult to detect the self-reproach in Hawthorne's outbursts at the dead Judge for seeking profit and worldly honor and for wearing an "odious grin of feigned benignity, insolent in its pretense, and loathsome in its falsehood." Compelled by the pressures of the literary marketplace to "put on a bright face" for his readers, Hawthorne had become like the character whom he hated most in all his fiction.

When Holgrave reads Phoebe his story "Alice Pyncheon," and she is overcome by drowsiness, he remarks sarcastically on her "falling asleep at what I hoped the newspaper critics would pronounce a most brilliant, powerful, imaginative, pathetic, and original winding up!" With better reason, Hawthorne entertained a similar hope for the ending of his own story, and the newspaper critics responded by pronouncing *The House of the Seven Gables* a brilliant success, a book, as Whipple put it [in *Graham's Magazine* 38 (June 1851)], in which "the humor and the pathos are combined." "Taken as a whole," Whipple added, "it is Hawthorne's greatest work, and is equally sure of immediate popularity and permanent fame." Although in the long run sales lagged behind **The Scarlet Letter,** the new romance outsold its predecessor in the first year of publication and seemed to justify Hawthorne's decision (as he wrote of Hepzibah) to use "the House of the Seven Gables as the scene of his commercial speculations." But that decision also seems to have intensified his negative feelings about the marketplace and its corrupting effect both on the writer as a producer and on the work of literature as a commodity. He wrote in the text that "a person of imaginative temperament," happening to pass the house of the seven gables on the morning after the summer storm, "would conceive the mansion to have been the residence of the stubborn old Puritan, Integrity, who, dying in some forgotten generation, had left a blessing in all its rooms and chambers, the efficacy of which was to be seen in the religion, honesty, moderate competence, or upright poverty, and solid happiness, of his descendants, to this day." In an effort to obtain financial security from his writing—what he calls here a "moderate competence"—Hawthorne himself had built a literary mansion very different indeed from that inhabited by "Integrity." When he discovered soon enough that even his concession to the reader would not enable him to support his family, he may have come to feel as Hepzibah did after her first few hours behind the counter: that the enterprise "would prove [his] ruin, in a moral and religious point of view, without contributing very essentially towards even [his] temporal welfare." And while there were no doubt many causes for Hawthorne's "disintegration" as an artist, **The House of the Seven Gables** suggests that his flagging energies may well have been related to his growing alienation from the process of exchange. (pp. 172-88)

> *Michael T. Gilmore, "The Artist and the Marketplace in 'The House of the Seven Gables',"* in ELH, *Vol. 48, No. 1, Spring, 1981, pp. 172-89.*

## Richard Gray   (essay date 1982)

[*In the following essay, Gray examines ambiguity in* The House of the Seven Gables, *focusing on the novel's structure, theme, and tone.*]

Shortly after **The House of the Seven Gables** was published, Herman Melville, who had received one of the complimentary copies, wrote to congratulate its author. 'The contents of this book,' he declared enthusiastically,

> do not belie its rich, clustering, romantic title. With great enjoyment we spent almost an hour in each separate gable. This book is like a fine old chamber, abundantly, but still judiciously, furnished . . . There are rich hangings, wherein are braided scenes from tragedies! There is old china with rare devices . . . , there are long and indolent lounges to throw yourself upon; there is an admirable sideboard, plentifully stocked with good viands; . . . and, finally, in one corner, there is a dark black-letter volume in golden clasps, entitled 'Hawthorne: A Problem.' [Quoted in Julian Hawthorne's *Hawthorne and His Wife,* 1884.]

Melville then went on to praise the book both for its 'genialities' and for its representation of what he called 'a certain tragic phase in humanity', but in a sense he had already said all that was necessary. For there seems little doubt that he was at once excited and puzzled by his friend's second novel, and that his way of expressing this was to adopt its dominant image—fleshing this image out with references to abundance and inclusiveness, and falling back eventually on that enigmatic figure of a 'dark black-letter volume'. 'Hawthorne: A Problem': that phrase could perhaps be applied to any one of the novels, with their mixture of daring and evasiveness, their pervasive irony, their play with opposites, and their various attempts to conceal or neutralize what one critic [Frederick C. Crews, in his *Sins of the Fathers: Hawthorne's Psychological Themes,* 1966] has called 'the dangerous knowledge that lies at the bottom of (their) plots'. It seems, though, a particularly appropriate way of summing up the story of the Pyncheons and the Maules—not because that story is, as James claimed, 'a magnificent fragment' or, as others have argued, totally incoherent, but because it raises so many issues, of varying degrees of seriousness, not all of which the author seems willing to pursue.

'Hawthorne: A Problem': the most immediate problem, really, is one of tone and attitude. What exactly *are* Hawthorne's feelings about, say, Holgrave's conversion to conservatism? How dry *is* the author's humour when he says that Phoebe, his little sun-goddess, was obeying 'the impulse of Nature, in New England girls by attending a metaphysical or philosophical lecture or viewing a seven-mile panorama'? And what, most obviously, are we to make of that extraordinary ending in which, it appears, even the Pyncheon hens are redeemed and begin 'an indefatigable process of egg-laying'? In one respect, it is easy to say what Hawthorne's relationship to his story is; for **The House of the Seven Gables** is probably his most personal novel, in that it draws most heavily and immediately on his own experience and family memories. Maule's curse, for example, derived from a family tradition that Judge John Hathorne—Hawthorne's ancestor and a judge at the Salem witchcraft trials—had been cursed by one of his victims. 'I am no more a witch than you are a wizard,' the accused was supposed to have declared, 'and if you take away my life, God will give you blood to drink.' In fact the curse, whatever its precise wording, had been directed at a colleague of Judge Hathorne's, Nicholas Noyes: but that did not inhibit the family legend. Nor did it prevent Hawthorne from attributing the subsequent decline of the family, more than half seriously, to this chilling event. Again, another victim of harsh Puritan justice meted out by one of John Hathorne's fellow-judges was actually named Maule. A family dream of lost opportunity, just like the Pyncheons', had actually grown up over some deeds to a large tract in Maine, acquired in the seventeenth century and then unaccountably lost. And the conflict between Judge Hathorne and another person he had helped to persecute, named Philip English, was laid to rest in almost exactly the same way the Maule-Pyncheon feud is: a great grand-daughter of Philip English, apparently, married a grandson of the Judge, and the old English house, the largest and most imposing in Salem, then passed into the hands of the united families.

By the time young Nathaniel was born, the house had been abandoned and its furniture disposed of, but it was still standing during his boyhood, grand, empty, decaying—an ironic reminder of former wealth.

So the legends of the Hathorne family provide one strand of personal involvement, giving a measure of historical anchorage to the Gothic paraphernalia of missing deeds, inherited curses, dark mansions, and internecine violence. Another strand is provided by Hawthorne's own immediate experience, the various friends and acquaintances on whom the major characters of the novel are partially modelled. Judge Pyncheon, for example, is based on a Reverend Charles W. Upham, whom Hawthorne described as 'the most satisfactory villain that ever was', after Upham had been instrumental in depriving the author of his post in the Salem Custom House. Hepzibah, a ghost feeding upon memories, is a distorted reflection of Hawthorne's mother, who became something of a recluse after her husband died. Clifford and Holgrave are, as [Hubert Hoeltje puts it in his *Inward Sky: The Mind and Heart of Nathaniel Hawthorne,* (1962)], 'manifestly expressions of two aspects of Hawthorne's own character . . . the man of action and the man of beauty.' Phoebe, in turn, recalls Sophia Hawthorne, the author's wife, in her diminutive size, her practicality, her cheerfulness and apparent redemptive power—and in her name; for Hawthorne gave Sophia the pet name of Phoebe during the early years of their marriage.

This reliance on personal material does have one clear result: at times, Hawthorne assumes an extraordinary intimacy of approach with his characters. He speaks to them directly, in love or hatred, almost as if he were one of them. Indeed, apostrophe, a vivid and often exclamatory form of address, is one of the characteristic devices of the novel: whether the author is chaffing Hepzibah, arguing with Holgrave, or revealing an almost embarrassingly personal sympathy for Clifford. The heavy sarcasm that Hawthorne directs at the Judge, or the hymns of affection he sings to Phoebe: these are really only extensions of the same mode he uses in, say, his little essay on the pleasures of breakfast that begins Chapter VII; the sketches that punctuate the narrative (sometimes drawn from his own Notebooks); or in his references to his own childish memories of the old Pyncheon house. Of course, *The House of the Seven Gables* is by no means unique in this respect; a similar tone is adopted in many of the tales and sketches and in **"The Custom-House"** chapter of *The Scarlet Letter.* But nowhere in Hawthorne's novels is this personal note so obviously and pervasively present.

Almost immediately, however, a qualification is necessary. Hawthorne did draw heavily on personal experience and family legend, when writing **The House of the Seven Gables,** and this often seems to abridge the gap between tale and teller. But it would be wrong to claim that his attitude towards his second novel was unambiguous, unaffected by doubts and a characteristic lack of certainty about his aims. For a great writer, Hawthorne was unusually lacking in self-confidence—something that is especially noticeable when one looks at why and how the Pyncheon story came to be written. *The Scarlet Letter* had

been well received. Sales, however, had not been overwhelming; and more than one critic had complained about its lack of 'geniality', expressing the hope [as E. P. Whipple wrote in *Graham's Magazine,* May 1850] that his next book would be relieved by 'touches of that beautiful and peculiar humour', in which (it was claimed) Hawthorne excelled 'almost all living writers'. This, as it happened, corresponded with Hawthorne's own doubts about his first novel, and with his general feeling that an author could hedge his bets with his public by offering variety, something for everyone—or, as he put it, firing buckshot at them rather than one lump of lead. So he set about accommodating himself to this criticism, with its implicit ideal of Shakespearean abundance, and as a result found himself falling into all manner of difficulties, trapped (to use his own figure) in a sort of Slough of Despond where he could find neither firm ground nor direction. Admittedly, he could be simple and positive about his new book. For instance, in an often quoted letter to Horatio Bridge, Hawthorne avowed that *The House of the Seven Gables* was 'more proper and natural' for him to write than *The Scarlet Letter,* 'more characteristic of my mind . . . and, I think, more sure of retaining the ground it acquires.' Yet only three months earlier he had written to Bridge, "I should not wonder . . . if the romance of the book should be found somewhat at odds with the humble and familiar scenery in which I invest it.' And earlier still he had confessed, in a series of letters to his publisher, James T. Fields, that his second full-length novel required more thought than his first, that time and again it teetered 'on the utmost verge of precipitous absurdity', and that he had to work hard to 'pour some setting sunshine' over the final chapter because the logic of the narrative was leading him where he did not wish to go. As he admitted ruefully to Fields, 'it darkens damnably towards the close.'

'A man living a wicked life in one place, and simultaneously a virtuous and religious life in another.' Nobody who could jot that down as an idea for a story, or who could declare to his wife that he had led 'two . . . different lives simultaneously', can ever be easily explained. But it would seem that in writing *The House of the Seven Gables* Hawthorne was guided by what he believed his public and critics wanted, and what, to be fair, a part of him wanted as well. As far as public and critics are concerned, he appears to have been wrong: the book was never even as popular as *The Scarlet Letter,* and the reviews were more or less evenly divided when it came to comparing the second novel with the first. And as for the author himself: his mixed feelings about the work while it was still in progress find their issue in its shifting and equivocal idiom.

This, in fact, is all that can be said about the book's general tone: that it shifts, changes emphatically, while remaining qualified by an irony which is itself constantly varying in degree. To an extent, Charles Dickens acts as an influence here; Hawthorne was, we know, reading Dickens while he was writing *The House of the Seven Gables* and he seems to have been deeply affected by the sheer variability as well as the idiosyncrasies of the English writer's voice. The famous opening description of the old Pyncheon house, for example, a choice example of what might be termed urban

Gothic, seems to echo this passage from Chapter I of *Barnaby Rudge:*

> With its overhanging stories, drowsy little panes of glass, and front bulging out and projecting over the pathway, the old house looked as if it were nodding in its sleep. Indeed, it needed no very great stretch of fancy to detect in it other resemblances to humanity. The bricks of which it was built . . . had grown yellow and discoloured like an old man's skin; the sturdy timbers had decayed like teeth; and here and there the ivy, like a warm garment to comfort it in its age, wrapped its green leaves closely round the time-worn walls.

At some remove from this, there are the street scenes, where Hawthorne was aiming at what he called 'the minuteness of a Dutch picture', or the elaborately mock-heroic humour which envelopes figures like Ned Higgins or Jaffrey Pyncheon. Here, again, Dickens hovers in the background. One thinks, for example, of Mr. Pecksniff, standing by the fire, warming his hands 'as benevolently as if they were somebody else's' and his back 'as if it were a widow's back, or an orphan's back', when reading a passage like the following:

> With a bow to Hepzibah, and a degree of paternal benevolence in his parting nod to Phoebe, the Judge left the shop, and went smiling along the street. As is customary with the rich, when they aim at the honors of a republic, he apologised, as it were, to the people, for his wealth, prosperity, and elevated station, by a free and hearty manner towards those who knew him; putting off the more of his dignity in due proportion with the humbleness of the man he saluted . . .

The book accommodates other modes besides the Dickensian, however. Thus, in many ways, the anthropomorphism of the house recalls *The Fall of the House of Usher* rather than *Barnaby Rudge.* Inextricably involved with the fate of its owners, the Seven Gables, like Poe's House of Usher, is a peculiarly centripetal figure, almost forcing us to draw comparisons between outer and inner, the structures of architecture and the structures of the mind or self. One illustration of this is provided by the description of the dead Judge. Sitting alone in an inner chamber, as Hawthorne presents him he cannot help but recall this earlier portrait of a guilty conscience—which occurs in an analysis of the Judge himself and yet obviously has a more general application:

> . . . an individual . . . builds up . . . a tall and stately edifice, which, in the view of other people, and ultimately in his own view, is no other than the man's character, or the man himself. Behold, therefore, a palace! . . . With what fairer and nobler emblem could any man desire to shadow forth his character? Ah, but in some low and obscure nook . . . may lie a corpse, half decayed, and still decaying, and diffusing its death scent all through!

At another moment, Hawthorne can draw away from this sort of portentousness to a sardonic humour worthy of Mark Twain—as when he suggests that 'of all events which constitute a person's biography, there is scarcely one . . . to which the world so easily reconciles itself as to his death'; while, at others, he can resort to coy humour (as in his descriptions of Hepzibah), or a rather uneasy and equivocal kind of romanticism (as in his account of the evening when Phoebe and Holgrave pledge their love for each other). Always, Hawthorne is careful to avoid limiting himself. His main fear seems to have been of finding himself caught at one particular pitch, which would then, as he put it, 'go on interminably'; hence his difficulties, apparently, while writing the book, and hence our difficulties if and when we try to characterize the narrative voice.

Before leaving this problem of tone or voice, there are two things perhaps worth mentioning. In the first place, it seems fair to say that it is the sheer fluidity of this voice which makes **The House of the Seven Gables** seem all of a piece and yet such a puzzle—rather, that is, than the famous device of 'alternative possibilities' [as Yvor Winters puts it in his *In Defense of Reason,* 1960] whereby every major occurrence is provided with both a natural and a supernatural explanation. And, in the second, it is this again which makes it just about impossible to tell how the author felt about his admittedly disappointing conclusion. A great deal of often elephantine fun has been had at the expense of the final chapter. Critics have fallen over each other in their attempts to deal ironically with the abrupt death of the younger Jaffrey Pyncheon and the departure to a bright new house on the other side of town. The point to be made, though, is that in all this they have been anticipated by the author himself. The death of the Judge's son, for example, is announced in as cheeky and cavalier a fashion as, say, the death of Antigonus in *The Winter's Tale*—or, for that matter, the conversion of the wicked Duke Frederick in *As You Like It.* Alice Pyncheon floats heavenward as easily as any *deus ex machina.* And, along with the reader, one minor character is left scratching his head as 'Old Maid Pyncheon' and her relatives depart, declaring with mock naïveté, 'it is all very well; but if we are to take it as the will of Providence, why I can't exactly fathom it.' The aplomb is evident, the author's tongue is evidently in his cheek. The only question to be asked—and it is one that, in the end, cannot be answered—is just how firmly it is planted there.

Further discussion of the final chapter must be postponed for a while, though. For the moment, it is worth examining the second major problem that **The House of the Seven Gables** raises, which has to do with its structure, its centre of consciousness or organising principle. 'I should not wonder,' Hawthorne wrote to Fields his publisher, 'if I had not refined upon the principal character a little too much for popular appreciation.' Unfortunately, he did not go on to say who he, at least, thought this principal character was. Ever since then critics have simply added to the confusion. Phoebe, says one, is Hawthorne's spokesman; Clifford Pyncheon, declares another, is the character Hawthorne is referring to; while still others have plumped for Holgrave, Hepzibah, or Judge Pyncheon. No one, as yet, has had the temerity to propose Uncle Venner or Ned Higgins as a centre of consciousness. But there have been attempts to solve the problem, or at least shelve it, by suggesting that all the major characters are simply reflections of Hawthorne himself or, more generally, that they represent conflicting aspects of the same single mind.

Another comment by Hawthorne, however, suggests a further possibility. It occurs in a letter he wrote to Fields just before *The House of the Seven Gables* was completed. 'I am hammering away a little on the roof,' he said, 'and doing up a few odd jobs that were left incomplete. Then I must read it to my wife.' This is the figure of the house that Melville found so convenient, whereby building a dwelling and building a narrative become interchangeable activities, and the Pyncheon house provides the organising principle of the book. The author, this figure suggests, is like an architect or builder, taking fragments from his surroundings and constructing a shelter out of them, something which mediates between what Hawthorne himself termed 'cool solitude' and 'the sultry heat of society'. Part of this was suspected by at least one contemporary critic, Evert Duyckinck, who asserted in his review of the novel [in *Literary World,* April 26, 1851], 'The chief, perhaps, of the dramatis personae is the house itself.' But even Duyckinck did not seem to realize quite how far this idea could be taken, or just how intimate the relationship is between architectural and fictional structures—the habitation of the major characters and the space inhabited by author and reader for the duration of the tale.

To some extent, the importance of the house can be gauged from the opening description. Within the space of a few pages, the 'venerable mansion', the aspect of which, the narrator tells us, has always affected him 'like a human countenance', is established as a living presence, an organism which somehow incorporates within itself the entire story of the Pyncheon family. The organic metaphor, [as Richard E. Fogle has pointed out in his *Hawthorne's Fiction: The Light & the Dark,* 1952], is then developed over the entire narrative: the hearth, apparently, is the house's heart, its timbers are as 'oozy' as any human skin, the windows are the eyes looking out on the 'mighty river of life'. And so on. What the reader will hardly guess from the opening pages, however, is that the house is not just a symbol, or, more accurately, a comprehensively developed emblem, but a kind of emblematic frame in which all the metaphors of the narrative are implicated. To use another analogy: in this respect, it functions rather like one of the author's own imaginary mirrors, reflecting the various images that Hawthorne devises and uniting them, making them part of one vital design. So, it is at once heart and head, 'a part of nature' thanks to its association with the Pyncheon elm and Alice's posies and an artifact of culture. With its principal entrance like a church door it describes all that is good in inherited beliefs, while its Gothic ornamentation, of course, and its situation—withdrawn in pride from the rest of the street—project all that is corrupt and evil. With 'storm and sunshine' playing over it, its frowning exterior reminds us of the outward appearance of most of the Pyncheons, while its interior, as a passage already quoted amply suggests, commemorates their guilt-ridden consciences. Within its walls are contained some of the principal emblems: the portrait of the old Colonel, the chair in which both the Colonel and the Judge die, and the mirror which reflects the history of the Pyncheon fam-

ily. While the other emblems in the book are defined ultimately in terms of their relationship to it: the street with its small 'portion of the world's great movement' passing along outside, the garden, an Eden as full of sunshine and shade as the house itself, and the train which Clifford in a moment of ill-founded optimism sees as the human habitation of the future.

Nor is it only the metaphors which are placed in this way; the major characters are as well. Hepzibah, for example, is introduced to us on the morning when she has decided, somewhat reluctantly, to reopen the shop that one of her ancestors set up under the front gable 'about a century ago'; and her timid, equivocal attitude towards the world around her is ultimately defined by that activity. Needing the sort of involvement she has never had, yet at the same time fearing it and slightly despising those to whom such involvements come easily, reaching out hesitantly and then drawing back in a mingled gesture of self-defence and pride: what she does at the entrance to her shop is what she does, essentially, throughout the book. Similarly, the dangers implicit in what Hawthorne calls Holgrave's 'speculative and active' temperament, his desire as he himself puts it 'to look on, to analyze' people as if he were an uninvolved spectator: all this is located for us by his habitual position within the house, 'in a remote gable—quite a house by itself, indeed—with locks, bolts, and oaken bars on all the intervening doors' between himself and others. The parlour containing the chair in which 'many a . . . Pyncheon had found repose' belongs, without a doubt, to the Judge: his image is there from the beginning, in the portrait of his 'iron' predecessor, and eventually, inexorably, that image takes him over. Phoebe belongs to the garden, just as surely as the flowers with which she is associated. And Clifford will probably always remain, in the reader's mind, by the arched window: watching the Italian organ-grinder, perhaps, blowing soap bubbles ('little impalpable worlds,' Hawthorne calls them, 'with the big world depicted, in hues bright as imagination, on the nothing of their surface'), or trying desperately to leap down into the street and join in. The portraits of him there, in his different moods, capture nicely his remoteness, his pathetic love of beauty and his pursuit of imaginative release—as well as his longing to recover, somehow, the years and pleasures he has lost.

Image, character—and also plot: the narrative, as it emerges, is an elaboration of the house, a dramatization of its different aspects. Hawthorne's strategy is to lead us, as it were, through the house and its surrounds, sketching their appearance and figurative implications. This is suggested by, among other things, the headings to several of the chapters: 'The Little Shopwindow', 'Maule's Well', 'The Pyncheon Garden', 'The Arched Window', 'Clifford's Chamber', 'Alice's Posies'. Far more important than this, though, is the essentially static character of the narrative, which the characters enter by entering the house. At the very beginning of *The House of the Seven Gables,* the author and reader anticipate this movement, when together they cross what Hawthorne calls—introducing a word that reappears again and again—'the threshold of our story'. From then on, different members of the Maule and Pyncheon families are continually crossing thresholds, coming to our attention—to adopt another image used remorselessly by Hawthorne—by coming on stage. Hepzibah, for example, emerges before our eyes at the threshold of her chamber and then, having been treated to a suitably mock-heroic introduction, crosses the threshold into her shop. Clifford appears in a similar way, though with an added touch of melodrama: we hear steps in the passageway, which pause at the head of the staircase and then 'twice or thrice in the descent', the doorknob turns slowly, there is a final pause at the threshold of the parlour, and then in he comes. Phoebe arrives at the threshold of the mansion like a visitor from another world but, as it turns out, a welcome one. Judge Pyncheon, on the other hand, is always an unwelcome arrival and has to force his way over the threshold. Figuratively, in doing this he crosses the threshold from life to death; while later, we are led to believe, all the other major characters cross the threshold in another direction, towards 'hope, warmth, . . . joy' and a new life. Even the minor characters are not excluded in this respect—nor, indeed, can they be, given that they *are* a part of the story: little Ned Higgins is constantly crossing the threshold of the shop, in search of new culinary delights, while Uncle Venner's position, just on the periphery of the action, is nicely caught in a childhood memory—of the times he used to sit, as a child, at the threshold of the mansion.

The shape of the house precedes all the action, then. The characters belong to it, in the sense that they and the emblems accompanying them are defined by it, and to the extent that what happens to them is literally or figuratively a product of their being there in that particular place. Very rarely does the action move away from the mansion and its immediate environment, and when it does the movement is invariably abortive. Hepzibah and Clifford try to go to church, which is not that far away, but they only get as far as their own front door. Even when they do get further, in their memorable flight on the train, Clifford's mind is still held captive by the house, and, inevitably, following a familiar pattern in Hawthorne's writing, the escape is followed by a return. Characters, like Clifford again, may dream of a world elsewhere, departure 'to the South of France—to Italy—Paris, Naples, Venice, Rome'. But they cannot, because it is the house that gives them identity, imaginative shape and the scope for action: which, of course, is just another way of saying that the house is an analogue of the book.

Until the final chapter: what happens here, really, is that Hawthorne tries to continue the story after it is finished. The Judge is dead, the house is defunct, and with these events the novel has reached its imaginative conclusion. But at least one part of Hawthorne wants a 'prosperous close', some setting sunshine; so he cannot resist tacking on a happy ending. Admittedly, as I have suggested, that ending is hedged about with ironies, as is the ending to *The Adventures of Huckleberry Finn:* but, like the final chapter of Twain's book, Chapter XXI of *The House of the Seven Gables* constitutes a kind of betrayal. For Hawthorne has made his characters live on after the framework which gave them their being has ceased to exist. 'The dead man . . . was forgotten', the narrator declares; Clifford and Hepzibah bid farewell 'to the abode of their forefa-thers with hardly more emotion than if they had made it their arrangement to return thither at teatime'; and they and their friends set off for a new life which requires little definition because it has nothing to recommend it, either to characters or author, beyond the promise it offers of sudden escape. On a biographical level, it is as if Hawthorne is commemorating his own earlier departure from what he called the 'haunted chamber' of his youth—or trying, by a process of sympathetic magic, to engineer his release from that feeling of self-imprisonment which he tended to associate with the figure of the house. Formally, he is withdrawing from the world of the book while still continuing to write—as James sensed, starting a completely new story and not a very good one at that. And, on yet another level, he is retreating from the issues raised by the tale, that sense of history and temporal interdependence which characterizes the earlier chapters, into an historical world where past, present, and future remain dissociated.

Which brings us to the third problem raised by *The House of the Seven Gables,* the problem of what is commonly called its theme or subject. What is the book about? What issues does it explore and what conclusions, if any, does it reach concerning them? It is easy enough to see that certain things come in for close scrutiny during the course of the narrative, such as the battle between old and new, aristocratic Pyncheons and plebeian Maules; the consequences of pride and the possibility of redemption; and the conflicting claims of solitude and society. But do these constitute the real stuff, the conceptual core of the novel? In his Preface Hawthorne offers one possible answer, an apparent reading of his own story, when he suggests that the history of the Pyncheons illustrates how 'the wrongdoing of one generation lives into the successive ones, and, divesting itself of every temporary advantage, becomes a pure and uncontrollable mischief.' But this reading is presented in a typically ironic and equivocal way. Many writers, he tells us with mock naïveté, 'lay very great stress upon some definite moral purpose, at which they profess to aim in their works.' He does not wish to be thought 'deficient in this particular', and so he is offering his 'moral', for those who want one, at the very beginning. In any case, he declares, adding a strong cautionary note,

> When romances do really teach anything, or produce any effective operation, it is usually through a far more subtle process than the ostensible one.

This, surely, is a clue; and, acting upon it, perhaps it would be best to accept Hawthorne's 'moral' provisionally, while placing it in the context of the entire narrative. The idea that 'the wrongdoing of one generation lives into successive ones' presupposes a fairly specific notion of history, the relationship between past and present. Looking at the actual story of the Pyncheons and Maules, however, it becomes clear that there is more than one notion at work in it, that past and present are entangled in often contradictory ways, and that these entanglements seem to preoccupy the narrator. One way of putting it would be to say that the moral itself seems to be the subject of a 'subtle process' of investigation and, in a manner characteristic of Hawthorne, generates far more questions and hypotheses than it does answers.

Of course, there *is* a great deal in the story which reinforces the assumptions implicit in the 'moral', suggesting a somewhat static idea of history. According to this idea, the present simply repeats or mirrors the past; and Hawthorne suggests as much himself, in the opening chapter, when he declares, 'we are left to dispose of the awful query, whether each inheritor of the property—conscious of wrong, and failing to rectify it—did not commit anew the great guilt of his ancestor'. This sense of repetition is registered in things both large and small—in the Original Sin of the Pyncheons, for instance, and in the sound of blood apparently gurgling in their throats. And it receives appropriately emblematic expression in the mirror which dominates one of the rooms of the mansion, in which, so we are told, 'the departed Pyncheons' can be seen 'doing over again some deed of sin'. Even the 'freshest novelty of human life', Hawthorne remarks caustically at one point, is made up out of 'old material'; even Holgrave's rejection of the past has been repeated by 'the hopeful of every century since the epoch of Adam's grandchildren'. There is nothing new. History is a series of echoes and reflections: which is perhaps why Hawthorne often allows us to see the image or reflection of a character before we see the character himself. Certainly, it is one reason why incidents and character-types recur throughout the novel, producing a peculiar sense of *déjà vu*.

Over against this notion of history, though, is another, essentially dynamic and progressive, which seems to deny Hawthorne's 'moral'. This is most clearly articulated in the story of Holgrave and Phoebe. Holgrave reads Phoebe his account of one of her ancestors, Alice Pyncheon, who was apparently hypnotized by Matthew Maule (a carpenter and grandson of the supposed wizard), humiliated and then destroyed. When he finishes reading, Holgrave, who is, of course, a Maule himself, discovers that in imitating Matthew's gestures while telling his tale he has inadvertently hypnotized Phoebe and now has her potentially under his control. The narrator underlines the parallel, just in case the reader should miss it: Holgrave, he tells us,

> could establish an influence over this . . . child as dangerous, and perhaps as disastrous, as that which the carpenter of his legend had acquired and exercised over the ill-fated Alice.

But it is underlined only to be erased. Holgrave refuses the opportunity, because he respects Phoebe's individuality, and, instead of a symbolic rape, there is eventually a marriage. So the past can apparently be denied; the destructive consequences of earlier crimes may, as a matter of moral choice, be evaded; in sum, progress would seem to be possible.

Other things reinforce the possibility of progress: Holgrave's gardening, for instance, which involves the uprooting of 'rank weeds (symbolic of the transmitted vices of society)'. And that progress, it is clear, can be down as well as up: the Pyncheon breed of hens illustrates this—a race that has degenerated, we are told, 'like many a noble race besides, in consequence of too strict a watchfulness to keep it pure'. But quite as important in this respect is the double-edged character of much of the narrative, clues which point equivocally towards both repetition and

change. The analogy drawn between the aestheticism of Clifford and earlier Pyncheons is one example of this: is the point here their difference or their similarity? Or take the comparison between Judge Pyncheon and his ancestor the Colonel. The Judge is certainly like the Colonel, as the portraits of the two indicate: they have the same features, in some ways, the same lust for power, and the same ability to switch between public and private faces. And yet there are also differences, Hawthorne tells us: there is 'less beef' on the Judge, he has lost 'the ruddy English hue' and acquired 'a certain quality of nervousness, . . . a quicker mobility . . ., and keener vivacity'. 'In compliance', as the author puts it, 'with the requirements of a nicer age' there is a difference in moral texture too: the Judge is much smoother than the Colonel, a suave hypocrite rather than simply and roughly two-faced. The differences, which to some extent correspond with Hawthorne's general notion of what distinguishes the American race from the English, are summed up in a way that is not entirely unserious:

> This process . . . may belong to the great system of human progress, which, with every ascending footstep, as it diminishes the necessity for animal force, may be destined gradually to spiritualize us, by refining away our grosser attributes of body.

One is left wondering again, just what is the relationship between past and present? Is this a significant change or merely a change of costume?

In a sense, Hawthorne forces us to ask such questions because he is constantly raising the issue of time and historical relationships himself. The meditation on time which accompanies Clifford and Hepzibah's flight on the train is well known; so, too, is the contrast between time as duration and time as a system of measurement which frames the portrait of the dead Judge. Less well known, but more important perhaps, are those moments when the author seems to be trying to achieve some sort of resolution between his two versions of history. Holgrave, for instance, appears to offer one possible solution, when he explains how he feels now, in his newly redeemed state, about houses and the past. 'I wonder', he says (referring to the Judge's house to which they are about to move),

> that the late Judge . . . should not have felt the propriety of embodying so excellent a piece of domestic architecture in stone, rather than in wood. Then, every generation . . . might have altered the interior, to suit its own taste and convenience; while the exterior . . . might have been adding venerableness and permanence which I consider essential to the happiness of any one moment.

Essentially, this is a compromise position. The notion of recurrence, previous generations shadowing and structuring the present one, is still there, certainly: but it is qualified by a recognition of the need for, and indeed the inevitability of, gradual, specific change.

It is tempting to see this as Hawthorne's final word on the matter, reinforced as it is by other remarks. Clifford's declaration on the train, for instance, that 'all human progress is . . . in an ascending spiral curve' implies the same, basically melioristic position, and so do the narrator's own gently critical comments on Holgrave's earlier radicalism. A case could be made, too, for saying that the form of the book illustrates this idea. Everything in *The House of the Seven Gables* invites our active collusion. That fluidity of tone mentioned earlier, the Gothic paraphernalia, the emblems and characters that seem to melt into one another and then into the ambivalent figure of the house, the equivocations and the pervasive irony: all these things represent, as Frank Kermode puts it [in his *The Classic*, 1975], 'evasions of narrative authority, and imply that each man must make his own reading'. But make it, one must add surely, within certain fairly clear limits which are laid down by the house/book. The House of the Seven Gables, dwelling and narrative, is in this sense Holgrave's 'piece of domestic architecture', structuring our perceptions, leading us along specific lines of imaginative inquiry, but allowing us at the same time a good deal of freedom of interpretation according to our 'taste and convenience'. Our individual versions of the story, and our personal visions of the mansion, consequently re-enact that compromise between recurrence and change which Hawthorne and his young daguerreotypist seem to be seeking.

And yet, there is still that final chapter. Suddenly, we are back with an optimistic, progressive notion of things. The Judge is dead and quickly forgotten; the house is abandoned; Clifford, Hepzibah and company all change for the better. Nearly everyone, including the narrator, seems to wash his hands of the past. Holgrave's remark about houses, when placed in its proper context here, only tempers our disappointment; it looks to be little more than a tattered flag held aloft while the author sounds the retreat. One comes away, in fact, with the feeling that Hawthorne was finally unwilling either to remain comfortable in his unbelief or, alternatively, to articulate a possible resolution. As far as the possibility of a resolution is concerned, an interesting comparison could be made with one of Hawthorne's own favourite novelists, Sir Walter Scott, who resolved a similar conflict between two different ways of looking backward with the help of the speculative school of Scottish historians; Hawthorne was notoriously distrustful of all speculative schools and apparently reluctant, on this occasion as on others, to plunge himself into what he once referred to, in one of his sketches, as the dangerous current of a theory. Perhaps of more relevance here, though, is the dilemma explored in some of the later works, which offer a revealing parallel with *The House of the Seven Gables*. I am thinking, in particular, of the material relating to England: *Our Old Home, The English Notebooks,* and the **'American Claimant'** manuscripts. In all of this work, the leading figure—who is either Hawthorne himself or a fictional surrogate—is faced with the problem of defining his relationship, as an American, with his English past. Quite frequently, the Hawthorne figure feels as detached from his ancestors as Holgrave does at first; this finds expression in a continual harping on the differences between old world and new, aristocracy and democracy, and an almost neurotic obsession with American superiority. But then again, the author tells us, he is often conscious of 'an unspeakable yearning towards England'—and a sense of *déjà vu* so powerful that he feels he has *become* his own ancestor. There is no attempt made

to reconcile these two responses. They simply alternate with each other. The present is sometimes an echo or repetition of the past, and sometimes a separate world 'disjoined by time and the ocean'. As a result, in the abortive versions of the novel, Hawthorne seems unable to bring together what he terms 'the two ends of the story'. We never know, quite simply, whether the American claimant will accept his rightful inheritance or feel compelled to reject it.

In one sense, then, the final chapter is unclear because little attempt is made by the author to bring together and resolve earlier positions. In another sense, however, it is far too clear, too obvious and straightforward, because this avoidance of a resolution seems to issue, not from Hawthorne's innate scepticism and subtlety of imagination, but from a simple desire to leave us with a 'moral'. Admittedly, that moral is not the one offered, in such a benign and disingenuous manner, in the preface to the story, but it is a moral all the same. Admittedly, too, touches of irony and equivocation are still there. But the irony no longer feeds into the substance of the narrative, helping to shape our responses; it floats on the surface, as it were, never really impeding the basic impulse of escape. And the equivocations do not require us to participate any more, to rebuild and recreate meaning as we read; they simply qualify, in a modest way, what are essentially a series of ready-made answers—and, perhaps, help to alleviate Hawthorne's embarrassment. Whatever reservations one may make, however much the author may poke fun at his dénouement, the plain fact is that he is withdrawing—and withdrawing in a fashion that is oddly reminiscent of that other observer and writer, the young daguerreotypist: who, as we have seen, after weaving *his* spell out of a series of nicely edged comparisons between past and present, suddenly dissolves it, breaks the enchantment and releases Phoebe from his power. Abjuring his rough magic, the author of *The House of the Seven Gables* ends effectively as the author of 'Alice Pyncheon' does, by returning both himself and his audience to a more prosaic world where certain crudely specific and rather simple-minded choices are to be made.

Still, there is no point in dwelling upon this, Hawthorne's eventual reluctance either to reside amidst doubts or to resolve them. The final chapter may be a disappointment, there may be other weaknesses, but *The House of the Seven Gables* remains a remarkable and puzzling novel— and remarkable, perhaps in part, because it is so puzzling. Its incidental pleasures are numerous: the style, with its beautifully equivocal mixture of the colloquial and the elevated, the narrative easing itself backwards and forwards in time, and that peculiar blend of domestic detail and Gothic melodrama about which Hawthorne was, at times, so nervous. Then there are the greater achievements of the book: a narrator playing cunningly with different masks and creating a consistent identity out of them, the complicated series of figurative references which is given coherence and a sense of meaning by the dominating presence of the house. And, above all perhaps, Hawthorne's agnosticism: his willingness to ask questions, and offer different sets of possibilities, in a way that is at once sportive and deeply serious. At his best, indeed, which means in this novel most of the time, Hawthorne makes a positive virtue out of what he sees as necessity and turns uncertainty itself into an art; suspecting that any human category is arbitrary and conjectural, he offers us a conflict between different categories, various idioms and systems, which is only resolved, if at all, by each reader. What it comes down to, in the end, is something very simple: if the book strikes us as a problem then, quite probably, it was meant to. If the old Pyncheon house seems at once intimate and mysterious, a home and a place of imprisonment, then that perhaps is because the man who built it, Nathaniel Hawthorne, saw the world in precisely that way. (pp. 88-107)

> *Richard Gray, "Hawthorne, a Problem: 'The House of the Seven Gables',"* in Nathaniel Hawthorne: New Critical Essays, *edited by A. Robert Lee, London: Vision Press, 1982, pp. 88-109.*

### Peter Buitenhuis   (essay date 1991)

[*Buitenhuis is an English-born Canadian educator and critic. In the following excerpt, he discusses characterization in* The House of the Seven Gables.]

The characters of *Seven Gables* have sparked a lot of critical interest because they are so interesting, but also, in my view, because they are very original. It is possible to trace the influence of Charles Dickens on the characterization—for example, we can note the sentimental Em'ly and Sophy of *David Copperfield* in Phoebe—but there is little question that the major components of Hawthorne's characters came out of his own observation of his New England neighbors and his fertile imagination. For that reason, I cannot subscribe to the views . . . that the characters represent merely psychological functions or aspects of a whole personality. Eccentric, even weird, as some of these characters are, they have about them the unmistakable ring of observed life.

Hepzibah is the most memorable of the characters—the incarnation of decayed gentility and eccentric spinsterhood, she is at once absurd, comic, and pathetic. Hawthorne uses elements of caricature to portray her, in her old turban and perpetual scowl. He repeatedly uses the adjective "rusty" to describe her appearance and movements. Caricature gives way, however, to characterization as the novel proceeds from portrait painting to interaction with others. A large part of Hepzibah's problem is that she has lived for many years in almost total isolation, which Holgrave calls "aloof, within your circle of gentility," or what Hawthorne often calls "the dungeon of the heart"—which is the source of most of the problems his characters encounter. When she is forced to open up commerce with the world, quite literally, in reopening the shop that her ancestor had opened a century before in the old house, she is also forced to unbolt the locks on her heart. This fall from gentility to commerce has its tragicomic aspects, as Hawthorne indicates by his ironic references to the ghost of Hamlet's father at the beginning of chapter 3 and Lady Macbeth's bloodstained hands, but this change marks the

beginning of her return to psychic and even physical well-being.

Hawthorne also uses this incident to develop his thoughts about democracy. He had read the work of the French Utopian, socialist thinker, Charles Fourier, which indeed had influenced his decision to enter the Brook Farm community. That experience soured him on communal living, but it did not necessarily disillusion him about all of the principles of equality and the distribution of wealth implicit in Fourier's work. He had also read the work of another radical French thinker, Pierre Proudhon, who believed that property was theft—an idea that is the starting point of *Seven Gables.* Proudhon wanted to replace capitalism with a system that would organize society into groups that would bargain with each other over essential economic and political issues within the framework of consensus about fundamental egalitarian principles.

In the chapter "Behind the Counter" Hawthorne demonstrates how far American society is from these ideals. Hepzibah's first customer is an urchin, Ned Higgins, who is given a free gingerbread man and immediately comes back for another. He wants, in fact, to exploit an individual who out of generosity—and out of aristocratic reluctance to go into trade—ignores the laws of a free market economy and gives instead of barters. It is no accident, surely, that the gingerbread man is Jim Crow, the colloquial, demeaning name for blacks. (This name was applied to the infamous laws of some southern states, which, after the Civil War, disregarded the Fourteenth Amendment and denied blacks the same rights as whites.) The urchin unceremoniously swallows both Jim Crow gingerbread men. This is probably a comic but telling image of an oppressive caste and class society.

The gingerbread incident leads Hepzibah to change her mind about the class system, and she comes "to very disagreeable conclusions as to the temper and manners of what she termed the lower classes, whom, heretofore, she had looked down upon with a gentle and pitying complacence, as herself occupying a sphere of unquestionable superiority." At the same time she finds herself fiercely resentful of the idle aristocracy to which she has herself recently belonged. Seeing an expensively dressed lady floating along the street, she wonders: "Must the whole world toil, that the palms of her hands may be kept white and delicate?" Now in trade as well as desperately poor, she has a new, sour, view of the oppressive and discriminatory social system that keeps some idle while many toil and suffer.

It takes some time, therefore, for her to realize the truth in Holgrave's remark to her that in working for a living "you will at least have the sense of healthy and natural effort for a purpose, and of lending your strength—be it great or small—to the united struggle of mankind. This is success—all the success that anybody meets with!"

She needs to make an effort to overcome her aversion to trade to gain the confidence to minister to the needs of her brother, who is broken physically and psychologically after thirty years in prison. She needs confidence particularly to resist the force and oppression of Judge Pyncheon who returns to haunt the House of the Seven Gables. She becomes almost heroic in her devotion to her brother's welfare. Hawthorne does not, however, dwell on these heroic qualities; he instead continually undercuts them by his mockery. Even in her most heroic gesture, her attempt to prevent Jaffrey Pyncheon from seeing Clifford, she is defeated. Despairing, she has to give way to the superior strength and determination of the Judge in his effort to wrest from Clifford what he believes to be the secret to the hidden wealth of the Pyncheons. In the end, however, her weakness defeats the Judge's apparent strength and justifies the meaning of her Hebraic name: "My delight is in her."

The characterization of Clifford is as remarkable in its different way as that of Hepzibah. He is, until the end of the novel, the child-man, reduced to impotence by hereditary weakness that has been exacerbated by his long prison term, all of which is compounded by the savage oppression and injustice visited upon him by his cousin Judge Pyncheon. He has been reduced to almost a ghost in the "ruinous mansion" of his body, and of course in the house itself.

Seldom has the pathos of mental instability and incompetence been so well reproduced as in this portrait of Clifford. And yet, as with Hepzibah, Clifford's reentry into the world of humanity, his freedom from the literal dungeon, and then from the dungeon of the heart, signals the beginning of his painful rebirth. There is a material and sensual aspect to this reentry as when he gorges himself on the breakfast his sister prepares for him and drinks cup after cup of the fragrant coffee. He also casts more than an appreciative and avuncular eye on Phoebe's sexual attractions.

There is also a spiritual aspect to his rebirth, which is nourished by the aesthetic appeal of Phoebe's charms and by beautiful objects, especially flowers. Ugliness is mortifying to him, as Hepzibah discovers to her chagrin. In spite of all the loving care and attention she lavishes on him, her brother can scarcely bear to look at her.

Modern psychology has called Clifford's condition schizophrenia: a radical disjunction of personality. He alternates between frenzied activity and utter torpor. Sometimes he masochistically begs for pain so that he can feel that he is alive, as when he asks Phoebe for a rose so that he may press its thorns into his flesh; at another time he has to be forcibly restrained from throwing himself over the edge of the balcony of the arched window from which he is watching a parade. "He needed a shock," Hawthorne comments, "or perhaps he required to take a deep, deep plunge into the ocean of human life, and to sink down and be covered by its profoundness, and then to emerge, sobered, invigorated, restored to the world and to himself."

Such a shock is provided after Clifford discovers the body of Jaffrey Pyncheon and flees the house with Hepzibah. The escape arouses all of Clifford's dormant energies into a kind of fever of activity. He and his sister are drawn at last "into the great current of human life" when, for the first time, they board a train. Hepzibah's imagination is still stuck fast in the House of the Seven Gables where she has spent so much of her life, but Clifford is transported

literally and metaphorically. To a testy fellow traveler he launches into an encomium of trains as an emblem of a future state of happiness—an escape from "these heaps of bricks and stones" that men call house and home. His lyrical eulogy of modern scientific thought, including mesmerism and electricity, is, however, quickly deflated when the testy traveler reminds him that the telegraph can convey not only thoughts of love from Maine to Florida, but also news of fleeing murderers.

Reminded of the body in the old house, Clifford grabs Hepzibah and they leave the train at the next stop. Their return to grim reality is symbolized by a ruined church and farmhouse close to the wayside station. Dragged down to torpidity once again, Clifford can only beg Hepzibah to take the lead. All she can do is pray for God's mercy.

The leavening agent in this heavy tale is Phoebe, who has been the subject of much critical discussion. The biographical source for her is obvious: Hawthorne's wife, Sophia, had been instrumental in rescuing him from his spiritual and physical isolation and opening up for him a commerce with the world. She was of a sunny disposition, incurably optimistic, an admirable housekeeper and flower arranger and, like Phoebe, small in body. Moreover, she had urged him to write a brighter book after he had completed the dark and terrible *The Scarlet Letter.* His pet name for her was Phoebe, the small, darting, singing bird common to New England.

The literary origins of Phoebe are also clear. Her prototype is the fair lady of romance tradition, domesticated and sentimentalized by nineteenth-century melodrama. For Hawthorne she is also a symbol of that democratic renewal and energy of the common people that he saw as the transforming agent of the ancestral, aristocratic, and decaying past. She is no thinker, but an active busy housewife who has the knack, like the good fairy, of transforming her surroundings by her presence and disposition. In the novel, she is associated strongly with nature, "as graceful as a bird," Hawthorne writes, "as pleasant, about the house, as a gleam of sunshine falling on the floor through a shadow of twinkling leaves, or as a ray of firelight that dances on the wall, while evening is drawing nigh."

These qualities transform the atmosphere of the House of the Seven Gables: the grime vanishes, the dry rot is stayed, the shadows and the scent of death are banished. Phoebe is the unfallen Eve who restores to Clifford the possibility of life and even happiness. He gazes on her beauty, listens to the sweet sound of her voice, and takes sustenance from her reality. For her part, she is sometimes oppressed by the heavy atmosphere of the house and by Clifford's temperament, but she is loath to explore the riddle of his spiritual and physical enervation and refuses to reflect on it. She is content to tend him and the house and garden so that he can avoid the harsh thoughts of his past, and live in the pleasures of the present.

Phoebe is too good to be true, and Hawthorne is aware that he is sometimes stretching the credulity of his reader in his way of representing her. To justify this minute and sentimental treatment of the minutiae of household life and domestic attentions, he falls back on biblical story and allegory to justify his method. "It was the Eden of a thunder-smitten Adam," he continues, "who had fled for refuge thither out of the same dreary and perilous wilderness, into which the original Adam was expelled." Only when Phoebe returns to her parents' home for a visit is the Edenic blessing suspended, and sin and death can again enter the House of the Seven Gables in the person of Jaffrey Pyncheon.

Although he lives in one of the seven gables, Holgrave is a strangely peripheral figure for most of the action of the novel. He is mentioned early on as the first customer to visit Hepzibah's cent-shop, and he reappears again briefly in chapter 6, "Maule's Well," as indeed he should, being a Maule. His identity as such, however, is kept concealed—a Gothic secret—until almost the end of the novel. In effect, he does not make a full appearance until more than halfway through the novel, in chapter 12, "The Daguerreotypist." There Hawthorne gives him a history as well as a name, and a kind of symbolic identity as Young America. Born of poor parents, with little education, he has knocked about the world and practiced almost a dozen occupations. He is the reincarnation of Benjamin Franklin's Poor Richard. His further symbolic identity is established by his having been a Yankee pedlar, a legendary figure whose origins are in the satirical sketches of Sam Slick, a pedlar created by the nineteenth-century Canadian author T. C. Haliburton.

Holgrave is a child of the nineteenth century, having been a member of a socialist community (the hippie communes of the period), and a practicer of mesmerism, a form of hypnosis. Jack-of-all-trades, wanderer, incipient anarchist, he is in a sense outside of society, which is probably why Hawthorne kept him essentially off the scene until late in the book. Holgrave stands for youth, spiritual inexperience, impatience. This is why there is a good deal of wistful irony in Hawthorne's reflection that Holgrave is "the representative of many compeers in his native land." The phrase is reminiscent of Emerson's essay "Representative Men," and, as F. O. Matthiessen has asserted [in his *American Renaissance,* 1941] Holgrave is an ironic commentary on Emersonian optimism. Holgrave, too, at least until he encounters the dead body of the Judge, is Emerson's self-reliant man, confident of the future and scornful of the past. Holgrave's soliloquy about the past could be taken as a commentary on Emerson's address, "The American Scholar." He utters this condemnation of the past in his harangue to Phoebe in chapter 12. It is perhaps the eternal cry of the young against the authority of their elders and against the weight of the past, and it is uttered with deep emotion:

> We read in Dead Men's books! We laugh at Dead Men's jokes, and cry at Dead Men's pathos! We are sick of Dead Men's diseases, physical and moral, and die of the same remedies with which dead doctors killed their patients! We worship the living Deity, according to Dead Men's forms and creeds! Whatever we seek to do, of our own free motion, a Dead Man's icy hand obstructs us! Turn our eyes to what point

we may, a Dead Man's white, immitigable face encounters them, and freezes our very heart! And we must be dead ourselves, before we can begin to have our proper influence on our own world, which will then be no longer of our world, but the world of another generation, with which we shall have no shadow of a right to interfere. I ought to have said, too, that we live in Dead Men's houses; as, for instance, in this of the seven gables!

This sentiment is surely at the root of most revolutions and other profound social changes—a radical impatience with things as they are, which seem merely to be things as they always have been. There is a reflection of this philosophy even in the story he tells Phoebe, in "Alice Pyncheon." Holgrave's ancestor, Matthew Maule, will have nothing to do with the expected forms of the hierarchical society of the time, which is the mid-eighteenth century. As a tradesman, he is expected to go to the back door, "where servants and work-people were usually admitted." The black slave, Scipio (the Jim Crow of the period), who admits him mumbles, "Lord-a-Mercy, what a great man he be, this carpenter fellow! . . . Anybody think he beat on the door with his biggest hammer!" Even in a period that allowed the most blatant expression of the class system and slavery—which was not abolished in New England until 1779, after the American Revolution—Maule is not prepared to acknowledge rank in his behavior toward "the worshipful" Gervase Pyncheon. Pyncheon, on the other hand, takes care to address Maule by the title "Goodman," which indicates Maule's low social status. There is a strong class resentment, as well as a hereditary quarrel, in Maule's revenge on Pyncheon.

Holgrave goes beyond attacking the reign of the dead and the class system: he also attacks the root ideas of a conservative, capitalist society—tradition, succession, and property. He wants to destroy not only houses with each generation but also all public buildings—state houses, city halls, and churches—for they symbolize the permanence of ideas as well as institutions. Further, he wants to change the institution of the family, the central form and tradition of society. "To plant a family!" he exclaims. "This idea is at the bottom of most of the wrong and mischief which men do. The truth is, that, once in every half-century, at longest, a family should be merged into the great, obscure mass of humanity, and forget all about its ancestors." He holds up the various lunacies of the Pyncheon family as examples of the truth of his argument.

Phoebe takes an eminently commonsense view of these heresies. To his proposal that we should not live in Dead Men's houses, she simply replies, "And why not . . . so long as we can be comfortable in them?" She adds later that it makes her dizzy to think of living in the shifting world that would result if Holgrave's radical views were carried out.

Hawthorne is more ambivalent about Holgrave than he is about any of the other characters in the novel; and it is an ambivalence that goes to the root of the democratic, capitalistic system of the United States. "There appeared to be qualities in Holgrave," the Author comments, "such as, in a country where everything is free to the hand that can grasp it, could hardly fail to put some of the world's prizes within his reach. But these matters are delightfully uncertain." In a democracy like this, freedom to rise has to be accompanied by the freedom to fail; and promise is by no means a guarantee of achievement. The author continues his generalizations:

> At almost every step in life, we meet with young men of just about Holgrave's age, for whom we anticipate wonderful things, but of whom, even after much and careful inquiry, we never happen to hear another word. The effervescence of youth and passion, and the fresh gloss of the intellect and imagination, endow them with a false brilliancy, which makes fools of themselves and other people. Like certain chintzes, calicoes, and ginghams, they show finely in their first newness, but cannot stand the sun and rain, and assume a very sober aspect after washing-day.

This is a highly unflattering portrait of his hero, the metaphors of which are revealing. They relate to the manufacture of cheap and shoddy industrial soft goods, made for show and not for durability. They are in fact products of what used to be called "the five and dime store." A consumer society, which the United States was in the process of becoming, depends on such products to keep the economy going. Hawthorne is making an analogy between this consumer process and Holgrave's rootlessness and constantly changing occupations. Holgrave's situation reflects the complete opposite of the condition of a stable, aristocratic society, in which occupation and status are fairly well fixed and objects are produced with art and craftsmanship, for durability not mere consumption.

Holgrave's present occupation as a daguerreotypist is a perfect metaphor for his identity. It puts him at the forefront of the contemporary technology of taking photographic portraits—as opposed to the previous painstaking method of oil painting. The photograph rapidly became another consumer good and an emblem of the transience it captures so well. Daguerreotype is used skillfully by Hawthorne not only to define Holgrave's occupation and nature but to define other characters as well.

Daguerreotype photographs were made by taking a specially treated silver-surfaced plate and exposing it to the subject and developing it with the fumes from mercury. After five minutes or more, depending upon the intensity of the light, an image formed upon the plate. As Holgrave himself says to Phoebe, "I make pictures out of sunshine." He adds, "There is a wonderful insight in heaven's broad and simple sunshine. While we give it credit only for depicting the merest surface, it actually brings out the secret character with a truth no painter would ever venture upon, even could he detect it." The daguerreotype portrait could be said to reveal truth because the length of the exposure made it imperative for the subject's head to be held still in a clamp for many minutes; and it is difficult to maintain a posed and artificial expression for that length of time. Holgrave shows Phoebe a photograph that she first mistakes for her ancestor in the picture on the wall, but Holgrave assures her that it is the image of her living cousin, the Judge. He points out that although the Judge wears in the world's eye a pleasant, sunny, benevolent countenance, the sun has brought out in the daguerreotype the real man: "sly, subtle, hard, imperious, and, withal, cold as ice." Holgrave, like his photographic method, is a truth teller; and one of his roles in the novel is to reveal hidden knowledge to other characters.

Hawthorne as Author also comments on Holgrave's philosophy and indicates how far he himself has moved from his earlier days of communitarian idealism. Noting that Holgrave's ideas would inevitably be modified by advancing years, he adds that "the haughty faith, with which [Holgrave] began life, would be well bartered for a far humbler one, at its close, in discerning that man's best-directed effort accomplishes a kind of dream, while God is the sole worker of realities." This is an expression of Christian quietism that is getting perilously close to an attitude of complacency, or even apathy.

Later on, Phoebe gets to the heart of what Hawthorne seems to consider Holgrave's fallacies by pointing out his lack of bonds to the human community. Holgrave has lost touch with the rub, trouble, and joy of family life. Phoebe is right when she accuses him of looking on the drama of the House of Pyncheon as the spectator of a tragedy and on the old house itself as a theater. This isolation has its benefits artistically since it makes Holgrave analogous to the choric figure in Greek drama.

Holgrave is also that familiar figure in Hawthorne's early stories and *The Scarlet Letter,* the thinker, the scientist, the cold-hearted speculator. This aspect of his character is reflected in his name, which means "son of the grave"—a name that also prefigures his resurrection after his encounter with the body of the Judge. He has some of the Maule traits that have made them vulnerable to accusations of witchcraft. Even his photography is a means of using the Maule gifts of second sight. By photographing the Judge unawares, for example, Holgrave can penetrate his hypocritical mask and reveal the true evil beneath. In a conversation with Phoebe about Clifford he tells her that had he her opportunities for observation, "no scruples would prevent me from fathoming Clifford to the full extent of my plummet-line!" When he tells the tale of Alice Pyncheon to Phoebe, he induces in her a trancelike state and perceives that it would be easy to establish domination over her spirit. Unlike his ancestor Matthew Maule, however, he resists the temptation and releases her from the spell. He renounces his visionary powers when he realizes that they are simply too dangerous. He has, too, amid all his changes of occupation, retained his integrity; and he is learning, through his growing affection for Phoebe, to leave his cold, isolated position and participate more sympathetically in the affairs of society. His union with Phoebe starts him on the road to the conservative attitude that he articulates at the end of the novel.

Integrity and affection are not qualities possessed by Judge Pyncheon, who is the Pyncheon inheritance incarnate. As Holgrave says, "the original perpetrator and father of this mischief appears to have perpetuated himself, and still walks the street . . . with the fairest prospect of transmitting to posterity as rich, and as wretched, an inheritance as he has received!" The Judge is the emblem of prosperous hypocrisy. With his rich clothes, his gold-headed cane, and his dignified bearing, he apparently represents the father figure: respectable, responsible, authoritative; but he is actually the false father, a father of evil, a Satanic figure.

Hawthorne spends a good deal of time editorially discussing what he calls "the solid unrealities" of Pyncheon's life, for Hawthorne was fascinated by the problem of power and authority. Pyncheon to him was typical of a whole class of men who treasure form over substance and spend their lives in building up hoards of gold and quantities of real estate. From this base they seek political office and public honors. For the Judge the idea of family takes second place to the dream of wealth. He apparently achieves the release of Clifford, whom he had framed and then convicted for killing their uncle Jaffrey, not out of any sense of guilt but because Clifford would then be more accessible and more easily forced to reveal the whereabouts of the fabled riches of the Pyncheons.

When he confronts Hepzibah in chapter 15, "The Scowl and the Smile," the Judge lays it on the line when he tells her that it was one of Uncle Jaffrey's eccentricities to conceal his great wealth by making foreign investments, perhaps under assumed names, "and by various means, familiar enough to capitalists, but unnecessary here to be specified." These foreign investments were undoubtedly the nineteenth-century versions of numbered Swiss bank accounts.

Judge Pyncheon is not only the emblem of grasping, selfish capitalism, he is also unable to believe that any way of looking at life other than his own has any value. "I do not belong to the dreaming class of men," he tells Hepzibah, and yet his life is lived in dreaming of wealth that is more illusory than even the shadowy lives of Hepzibah and Clifford. He has, as the narrator remarks, the Midas touch, a gift with consequences that prove fatal, as the myth tells us.

When all is said and done, the House of the Seven Gables is the chief character in the book, as well as its structural and thematic center. On the first page of the book the Author tells us that "the venerable mansion has always affected me like a human countenance, bearing the traces not merely of outward storm and sunshine, but expressive also of the long lapse of mortal life, and accompanying vicissitudes, that have passed within." The house has a heart as well as a face: "So much of mankind's various experience had passed there . . . that the very timbers were oozy, as with the moisture of a heart. It was itself like a great human heart, with a life of its own, and full of rich and sombre reminiscences." Whenever Hawthorne mentions the human heart, he intends moral ambiguities. The heart is the seat of not only the emotion of love, but also all the other less admirable emotions too; it is therefore not surprising that Hawthorne often called the heart the dungeon: it can, by harboring the emotions of pride and envy lock the possessor into isolation. Moreover, these emotions released in passion from the dungeon could wreak terrible havoc on others.

The heart of the house is at least temporarily lightened by the advent of Phoebe. The window-eyes show this change: "It really seemed as if the battered visage of the

House . . . , black and heavy-browed as it still certainly looked, must have shown a kind of cheerfulness glimmering through its dusky windows, as Phoebe passed to-and-fro in the interior." But the heaviness of the house takes its toll even on the lightsome Phoebe. Her experience there becomes more important to her than anything she had experienced before. Every object in the house "responded to her consciousness, as if a moist human heart were in it." The house predictably has an even greater effect on its long-time denizen, Hepzibah, who incarnates it more than any of the other characters. Even when she leaves it to take the train ride with Clifford, she cannot escape it. Varied scenes rush past the train window, but she can see only "the seven old gable-peaks. . . . This one old house was everywhere!"

When Judge Pyncheon dies, the house comes alive as never before. It wrestles with the wind of the storm and bellows with its sooty throat—its wide chimney. It sings and sighs and sobs and shrieks—"A rumbling kind of a bluster roars behind the fire-board." All in all, the House of the Seven Gables is an emblem of the unregenerate heart of man, full of envy, wrath, pride, lust, and the other deadly sins; this is why the other characters are so happy to escape from it at the end of the tale.

Each character has an organic, historic connection with the house; the destinies of each, in different ways, have been shaped, or distorted, by it. Hawthorne obviously intends some kind of analogical tie, which is at least as much historical as it is psychological. Each of us is a product of our past, hereditarily and historically. Some people become dominated by their past, as are Hepzibah and Clifford. They are examples and victims of the colonial and aristocratic views of life outmoded in the nineteenth century.

The novel is making the point that unless we escape from the past and accept our common, democratic, yet independent lot, we remain shackled to it. Unless we escape from the past, both historical and parental, we remain in a state, as it were, of perpetual infancy; we can never become fully individuated or fully mature, free human beings. (pp. 91-105)

> *Peter Buitenhuis, in his* The House of the Seven Gables: Severing Family and Colonial Ties, *Twayne Publishers, 1991, 137 p.*

---

## FURTHER READING

Arac, Jonathan. "The House and the Railroad: *Dombey and Son* and *The House of the Seven Gables*." *The New England Quarterly* LI, No. 1 (March 1978): 3-22.
　　Compares *The House of the Seven Gables* with Dickens's *Dombey and Son,* focusing especially on the influence of Gothic fiction on each.

Battaglia, Frank. "*The* (Unmeritricious) *House of the Seven Gables*." *Studies in the Novel* II, No. 4 (Winter 1970): 468-73.

Cites letters from Hawthorne to support Battaglia's contention that Hawthorne was not unduly influenced by a desire to please the reading public in writing *The House of the Seven Gables.*

Beebe, Maurice. "The Fall of the House of Pyncheon." *Nineteenth Century Fiction* 11, No. 1 (June 1956): 1-17.
Considers parallels between two works, *The House of the Seven Gables* and Edgar Allan Poe's "The Fall of the House of Usher," in a discussion of the thematic and structural unity of Hawthorne's novel.

Caldwell, Wayne Troy. "The Emblem Tradition and the Symbolic Mode: Clothing Imagery in *The House of the Seven Gables.*" *Emerson Society Quarterly* 19, No. 1 (1973): 34-42.
Examines clothing imagery in *The House of the Seven Gables* as it reflects the emblem tradition popularized in Renaissance literature.

Chorley, Henry Fothergill. Review of *The House of the Seven Gables,* by Nathaniel Hawthorne. *The Athenaeum,* No. 1230 (24 May 1851): 545-47.
Asserts that *The House of the Seven Gables* establishes Hawthorne as one of "the most original and complete novelists that have appeared in modern times."

Cox, Clara B. " 'Who Killed Judge Pyncheon?' The Scene of the Crime Revisited." *Studies in American Fiction* 16, No. 1 (April 1988): 99-103.
Suggests, in response to a related article by Alfred H. Marks, that Holgrave is implicated in the death of Judge Pyncheon.

Curran, Ronald T. " 'Yankee Gothic': Hawthorne's 'Castle of Pyncheon'." *Studies in the Novel* VIII, No. 1 (April 1976): 69-80.
Identifies and discusses Gothic elements in *The House of the Seven Gables.*

Dauber, Kenneth. *"The House of the Seven Gables."* In his *Rediscovering Hawthorne,* pp. 118-48. Princeton: Princeton University Press, 1977.
Places *The House of the Seven Gables* within the context of a theory of fiction drawn from Hawthorne's prefatory remarks to his novels.

Dillingham, William B. "Structure and Theme in *The House of the Seven Gables.*" *Nineteenth Century Fiction* 14, No. 1 (June 1959): 59-70.
Argues that the apparent plot digressions of the novel contribute to the unity of its theme: the need for participation in "the united struggle of mankind."

Dryden, Edgar A. "Hawthorne's Castle in the Air: Form and Theme in *The House of the Seven Gables.*" *ELH* 38, No. 2 (June 1971): 294-317.
Traces the themes of homelessness and the desire for a "dream house" in *The House of the Seven Gables.*

Duyckinck, Evert Augustus. Review of *The House of the Seven Gables,* by Nathaniel Hawthorne. *The Literary World* 8, No. 221 (26 April 1851): 334-36.
Compliments Hawthorne on his ability to bring out the "spiritualities" of his story through subtle characterizations and vivid descriptions of scene.

Fogle, Richard Harter. "The House of the Seven Gables." In his *Hawthorne's Fiction: The Light & the Dark,* pp. 122-39. Norman: University of Oklahoma Press, 1952.

Discusses the novel as a "study in the continuity of guilt" in which the house symbolizes the Pyncheon family's sins of false pride and materialism.

Gallagher, Susan Van Zanten. "A Domestic Reading of *The House of the Seven Gables.*" *Studies in the Novel* XXI, No. 1 (Spring 1989): 1-13.
Asserts that a reading of *The House of the Seven Gables* as an embodiment of the norms of the nineteenth-century "cult of domesticity" resolves its problems of plot, characterization, and conclusion.

Gatta, John, Jr. "Progress and Providence in *The House of the Seven Gables.*" *American Literature* 50, No. 1 (March 1978): 37-48.
Describes *The House of the Seven Gables* as an essentially optimistic story in which personal and social progress are guided by Providence.

Goddu, Teresa. "The Circulation of Women in *The House of the Seven Gables.*" *Studies in the Novel* XXIII, No. 1 (Spring 1991): 119-27.
Examines the sexual politics implicit in *The House of the Seven Gables.*

Harris, Kenneth Marc. " 'Judge Pyncheon's Brotherhood': Puritan Theories of Hypocrisy and *The House of the Seven Gables.*" *Nineteenth Century Fiction* 39, No. 2 (September 1984): 144-62.
Analyzes the nature of Judge Pyncheon's hypocrisy from the point of view of Puritan theology.

Junkins, Donald. "Hawthorne's House of Seven Gables: A Prototype of the Human Mind." *Literature and Psychology* XVII, No. 4 (1967): 193-210.
Provides a Jungian psychological analysis of the characters of the novel as representing four aspects of the mind: feeling, sensation, intuition, and thinking.

Klinkowitz, Jerome F. "In Defense of Holgrave." *Emerson Society Quarterly* 62, No. 1 (Winter 1971): 4-8.
Asserts that Holgrave's transformation in *The House of the Seven Gables* is a gradual one and ought not to be the source of critical dissatisfaction with the novel's conclusion.

Levy, Alfred J. *"The House of the Seven Gables:* The Religion of Love." *Nineteenth Century Fiction* 16, No. 3 (December 1961): 189-203.
Contends that the structural and thematic unity of *The House of the Seven Gables* is provided by its characters—particularly Phoebe, whose "simple ethic of love" revives and transforms the others.

Levy, Leo B. "Picturesque Style in *The House of the Seven Gables.*" *The New England Quarterly* XXXIX, No. 2 (June 1966): 147-60.
Analyzes Hawthorne's use of picturesque imagery in *The House of the Seven Gables* to dramatize "the crisis of a decaying, aristocratic society."

Male, Roy R. "Evolution and Regeneration: *The House of the Seven Gables.*" In his *Hawthorne's Tragic Vision,* pp. 119-38. New York: W. W. Norton & Co., 1964.
Discusses *The House of the Seven Gables* and its theme of "the interpenetration of the past and the present" as it relates to mid-nineteenth-century views of evolution and genetics.

Marks, Alfred H. "Who Killed Judge Pyncheon? The Role of the Imagination in *The House of the Seven Gables.*" *PMLA* LXXI, No. 3 (June 1956): 355-69.

Argues that Judge Pyncheon's death may have been caused by shock at the sudden appearance of Clifford. Marks interprets this as a symbolic triumph of imagination over materialism.

———. "Hawthorne's Daguerreotypist: Scientist, Artist, Reformer." *Ball State Teachers College Forum* III, No. 1 (Spring 1962): 61-74.

Provides background information on daguerreotyping in an examination of the social and philosophical implications of Holgrave's profession.

Mathews, James W. "The House of Atreus and *The House of the Seven Gables.*" *Emerson Society Quarterly* 63 (Spring 1971): 31-6.

Discusses the structure and conclusion of *The House of the Seven Gables,* identifying the *Oresteia* of Aeschylus as Hawthorne's likely source of inspiration for the novel.

McPherson, Hugo. "*The House of the Seven Gables.*" In his *Hawthorne as Myth-Maker,* pp. 131-45. Toronto: University of Toronto Press, 1969.

Discusses *The House of the Seven Gables* in a larger study of how Hawthorne's interest in Greek mythology, exemplified in his *A Wonder-Book for Girls and Boys* and *Tanglewood Tales,* informs his other fiction.

Michelson, Bruce. "Hawthorne's House of Three Stories." *The New England Quarterly* LVII, No. 2 (June 1984): 163-83.

Contends that in *The House of the Seven Gables* Hawthorne achieved a balance between popular romance, moral observation, and self-reflexive inquiry into the nature of fiction.

Monteiro, George. "Hawthorne's Fable of the Reformable Man." *Dutch Quarterly Review of Anglo-American Letters* 14, No. 1 (1984): 18-29.

Examines the narrative voice and controlling metaphors of *The House of the Seven Gables.*

Ragan, J. F. "Social Criticism in *The House of the Seven Gables.*" In *Literature and Society,* edited by Bernice Slote, pp. 112-20. Lincoln: University of Nebraska Press, 1964.

Examines *The House of the Seven Gables* as allegorical social criticism depicting the conflict between beauty, exemplified by the Old World gentility of Hepzibah, and utility, exemplified by the New World practicality of Phoebe.

Schoen, Carol. "The House of the Seven Deadly Sins." *Emerson Society Quarterly* 19, No. 1 (1973): 26-33.

Offers a structural analysis of *The House of the Seven Gables* based on the Seven Deadly Sins.

Swanson, Donald R. "On Building *The House of the Seven Gables.*" *Ball State University Forum* X, No. 1 (Winter 1969): 43-50.

Considers possible historical counterparts for the characters in *The House of the Seven Gables.*

Thomas, Brook. "*The House of the Seven Gables:* Reading the Romance of America." *Publications of the Modern Language Association* 97, No. 2 (March 1982): 195-211.

Explores the social and political implications of the distinction made by Hawthorne in his preface to *The House of the Seven Gables* between the novel and the romance.

Whelan, Robert Emmett, Jr. "*The House of the Seven Gables:* Allegory of the Heart." *Renascence* XXXI, No. 2 (Winter 1979): 67-82.

Describes the novel as an allegorical depiction of a spiritual journey from selfishness to love.

Yoder, R. A. "Transcendental Conservatism and *The House of the Seven Gables.*" *The Georgia Review* XXVIII, No. 1 (Spring 1974): 33-51.

Explores links between *The House of the Seven Gables* and the Transcendental Conservatism of Ralph Waldo Emerson.

# Jean Ingelow

## 1820-1897

(Also wrote under pseudonym Orris) English poet, novelist, and short story writer.

### INTRODUCTION

Ingelow was one of the most popular writers of the Victorian era. Best known as an author of children's stories, she is also remembered for her novels and lyric poetry celebrating nature and romance. Although her verse is not widely read today, its popular appeal in England and the United States was second only to that of Lord Tennyson during the latter half of the nineteenth century.

The eldest of nine children, Ingelow was born in the coastal town of Boston in Lincolnshire. Her father was a banker, and her mother took responsibility for the children's education, teaching them herself and occasionally employing tutors. At home Ingelow learned several languages in addition to studying literature, history, and geography. She began writing while still a child, composing songs and verses reflecting her appreciation of nature. When she was fourteen, she relocated with her family to Ipswich and eventually moved with them to London in 1850. That year Ingelow's first poetry collection, *A Rhyming Chronicle of Incidents and Feelings,* was published anonymously. Although the *Chronicle* was dismissed by many readers as overly sentimental, it drew praise from Tennyson, who, in a letter to a mutual friend, indicated that the work showed promise.

Extremely reserved and shy, Ingelow was encouraged to continue writing by her family, who provided both financial and moral support for her career. Over the next decade she published *Allerton and Dreux,* a novel about religious controversy and tolerance, as well as several children's stories, under the name of Orris, in *The Youth's Magazine.* In 1863 she published the collection *Poems,* which critics hailed as the work of a talented new poet. Its popularity prompted more than twenty-five editions over the next several years, and Ingelow soon became one of the most famous poets in England and the United States. During this time Ingelow moved with her mother and two of her brothers to Kensington. She rented a flat near the family's home to use as a studio and began to earn a living through her literary career, publishing the children's novel *Mopsa the Fairy,* adult novels including *Off the Skelligs* and *Sarah de Berenger,* and a second and third series of poetry collections. Ingelow ceased writing in 1886, and although she continued to published some of her remaining manuscripts, her works gradually declined in popularity. She died in Kensington in 1897.

Influenced by the works of William Wordsworth and Tennyson, most of Ingelow's poetry centers on nature, romantic love, and childhood. Many of her poems evoke the seascape of her childhood in Lincolnshire; "The High Tide on the Coast of Lincolnshire," perhaps her most famous poem, describes in ballad form the events surrounding a tidal wave which inundated her native village in the sixteenth century. The poem celebrates the beauty of nature while expressing awe at its destructive potential. In "Divided," an allegorical poem, two lovers walk on either side of a stream that gradually swells into a river and divides them. Ingelow's verse has been praised for its clear and simple language as well as for its musical rhythms. Her novels generally center on family life and the emotional and imaginative lives of children. *Sarah de Berenger* depicts a young mother's struggles to provide her children with a stable and loving home despite the fact that their father is a criminal. *Off the Skelligs* traces the moral development of two intellectually precocious children who are cared for by tutors and a nurse while the mother pursues a literary career.

Despite the wide readership she enjoyed during her lifetime and the admiring letters she received from such literary celebrities as Elizabeth Barrett Browning, John Ruskin, and Henry Wadsworth Longfellow, Ingelow's work was largely ignored in the years following her death. Many critics attribute this decline to the fact that her works generally endorse religious faith, emotional self-restraint, and obedience to authority, Victorian values that were questioned at the close of the nineteenth century. As Edith Hamilton has observed, "Ingelow lived when art was conceived of as lightening the weight of this unintelligible world," and her work, despite the lasting appeal of such themes as love and death, came to be viewed as simplistic. Studies in the twentieth century have cited Ingelow as the first female poet in English history to earn a living by writing. Such critics, while generally considering her a minor poet, acknowledge her achievement as a skilled and popular writer.

---

## PRINCIPAL WORKS

*A Rhyming Chronicle of Incidents and Feelings*   (poetry) 1850
*Allerton and Dreux; or, the War of Opinion*   (novel) 1851
*Tales of Orris*   (short stories)   1860
*Poems*   (poetry)   1863
*Studies for Stories*   (short stories)   1864
*A Story of Doom, and Other Poems*   (poetry)   1867; also published as *Poems: Second Series,*   1874
*Mopsa the Fairy*   (novel)   1869
*Off the Skelligs*   (novel)   1872
*Fated to be Free*   (novel)   1875
*Sarah de Berenger*   (novel)   1879
*Don John*   (novel)   1881
*Poems,* third series   (poetry)   1885
*Poems of the Old Days and the New*   (poetry)   1885
*John Jerome: His Thoughts and Ways*   (novel)   1886
*A Motto Changed*   (novel)   1894

### H. Buxton Forman   (essay date 1871)

[*In the following excerpt, Forman provides an unfavorable assessment of Ingelow's poetry.*]

We do not know—we have not the slightest idea—why matters of commerce and finance in the City are shuffled by a panic every ten years; but we observe that it is so. And similarly we do not at all fathom the mystery of the public bestowing periodical worship on some of the rushlights of literature mistaken for stars. Curiously enough too, equally-worthless productions of this class frequently meet with strikingly-unequal treatment;—a fact which seems to support some vague and unpromulgated theory of periodicity in the misdirection of public favour. It is a fact worthy of observation, that the 'poems' of Lord Houghton, for instance, are scarcely mentioned at present—never were very much; while those of Miss Ingelow, which are certainly not many shades better, went through fourteen editions in five years. If the lady's poetry is a shade or two better than the lord's, it is not because there is more originality in it, or more individual merit. Whatever superiority of quality there may seem to be is due simply

to the more successful assimilation of some of the fine elements of other greater poetry. In Tennyson's *Enoch Arden* volume, it will be remembered, was a little poem headed "The Flower," aimed at the Laureate's numerous imitators and their patrons. The great master is never less great than when he attempts this sort of thing, as witness the lines "On a spiteful Letter." However, the fable of "The Flower" is considerably better than those lines: it has meaning; and, such as it is, the meaning is true, though rather small and personal for the utterance of a great man. We all know how he tells us of his flower, once called a weed, but afterwards crowned as a true flower; how thieves stole the seed, and 'sowed it far and wide'; and how

> Most can raise the flowers now,
>   For all have got the seed.
>
> And some are pretty enough,
>   And some are poor indeed;
> And now again the people
>   Call it but a weed.

Whether he would pronounce Miss Ingelow's flowers 'pretty enough' or 'poor indeed,' one cannot guess; but some of them certainly do seem pretty enough, though at the same time poor indeed because of their unoriginality; and hence it seems a little unjust on the part of Fate that, while writers of equal merit or demerit fail to attract much attention, this writer should be receiving a good deal of that very substantial attention paid in purchasing one's books.

Miss Ingelow is one of those numerous writers who, not having as a rule anything really worth saying, somehow manage to make up parcels of vacuity with enough of external mistiness to lead superficial readers to the supposition that there is something very *recherché* in the way of a kernel to this shell of expression. To such superficial readers the idea that a rich thought, easily appreciated by acute minds, lies within an impenetrable garment of rhymes, acts as a stimulant to praise. Many a silly person, who has not the slightest idea of the meaning of anything but the most superficial trash, will, for the sake of appearing wise, praise any misty nonsense in the way of 'poetry'; and thus it is, probably, that among a certain class (and that a good large class) an idea has been circulated that Miss Ingelow is a poetess of exceptional thoughtfulness. In truth she frequently takes up some image or set of images, and works through such a maze of variations that it is not quite easy to follow her; and, while this method of procedure induces many to 'give it up,' owning inwardly their own stupidity, but outwardly descanting on the deep thought of the poetess,—while the enigma remains insoluble to some, other some solve it, and find the answer to be not worth the search.

We all know the story of the emperor's new clothes, told by that wonderful Dane, Hans Christian Andersen—how certain impostors sent the emperor out naked, under the assurance that they had provided him with the most exquisite garments, which however could not be seen by any man who was either a fool or unfit for his office. Of course the emperor could not admit either proposition in regard to his own august majesty, so forth he went. Of course no one of the spectators could admit himself a fool or unfit for the position he held in life; so every one joined in the chorus of 'O, how magnificent are the emperor's new clothes!' till at last an innocent child, with that peculiarly awkward unguardedness which childhood still exhibits at times, 'let loose his opinion' that the emperor was devoid of raiment; and at last this fact became universally recognised. So we trust may the imagined depth of Miss Ingelow's significances be eventually recognised by every one as fictitious, when some unsophisticated voice shall have sufficiently spoiled of its terrors the idea of confessing that one sees nothing in the verses in which one's neighbours profess to see stupendous merit and next-to-unfathomable depth.

But the poetess does not always put on these misty coverings to her verses. Very often they are sent forth as 'utterly naked and bare' as rhymes can possibly be, without an attempt at anything beyond mere prose presentation of bald shallow matter. Take, for instance, the dialogue passages of which **"Supper at the Mill"** is mainly composed. Here is the opening:

> *Mother.* Well, Frances.
> *Frances.*    Well, good mother, how are you?
> *M.* I'm hearty, lass, but warm; the weather's warm:
> I think 'tis mostly warm on market days.
> I met with George behind the mill: said he,
> "Mother, go in and rest awhile."
> *F.*                               Aye, do,
> And stay to supper; put your basket down.
> *M.* Why, now, it is not heavy?
> *F.*                               Willie, man,
> Get up and kiss your Granny. Heavy, no!
> Some call good churning luck; but, luck or skill,
> Your butter mostly comes as firm and sweet
> As if 'twas Christmas. So you sold it all?

And so on.

Nothing could well be much more unlike poetry than this. In some other pieces of this sort there is the same attempted imitation of the most simple style adopted by the Laureate in his idyllic pieces; but as for the freshness, the vigour, the gem-like clearness of cut which we get in Tennyson at his utmost simplicity, what shadow of them is there here?

Miss Ingelow has written some pieces which would have enraptured Wordsworth in his vulgarest mood—when, that is to say, he had descended to the deepest depths of that bathos he so often stooped to, notwithstanding the soaring flights for which he was adequately winged. In **"Scholar and Carpenter,"** a good deal of which is mere imitation of Tennyson, we find this verse, of which Wordsworth might have been proud had it occurred to him in some unhappy moment:

> "For here," said he, "are bread and beer,
> And meat enough to make good cheer;
> Sir, eat with me, and have no fear,
>    For none upon my work depend,
> Saving this child; and I may say
> That I am rich, for every day
> I put by somewhat; therefore stay,
>    And to such eating condescend."

For such a solemn piece of commonplace as this it is not easy to find a fitting *pendant* beyond the lowly circuit of Wordsworth's lowest art, of which he was, alas, too fond.

But Miss Ingelow is not entirely dependent on Wordsworth for her successes in bathos. On the contrary, some of her greatest achievements in that line are peculiarly her own in a certain sense. In **"Honours"** we get passages such as we should vainly look for elsewhere. **"Honours"** is a poem in which the 'little differences' between science and revelation are brought in for trial and discussion. Science, as might be expected, is pooh-poohed as an upstart, and bantered in slightly inelegant terms, such as these three verses:

> Then all goes wrong: the old foundations rock;
>    One scorns at him of old who gazed unshod;
> One striking with a pickaxe thinks the shock
>    Shall move the seat of God.
> A little way, a very little way
>    (Life is so short), they dig into the rind,
> And they are very sorry, so they say,—
>    Sorry for what they find.
>
> But truth is sacred—aye, and must be told:
>    There is a story long beloved of man;
> We must forego it, for it will not hold—
>    Nature had no such plan.

Science can of course well afford to treat such writing as a joke, and would not fall out with Miss Ingelow if she pleases to amuse herself by writing verses on a subject concerning which she seems to have heard a piece of one side of the discussion; but would it be too hard to suggest that it might have been safer to defer the treatment of a polemical subject till she had thoroughly mastered the grammar of her language? The two lines,

> Is there, O is there aught that *such* as Thou
>    *Would'st* take from such as I?

afford a sample of false concord, which the merest friendliness would not hesitate to point out. It is moreover just possible that some representative of what Miss Ingelow grandiloquently sneers at as 'the baby science, born but yesterday,' might find a flaw in facts as here stated. Who ever heard of geologists or other men of science displaying the miserable spirit implied in the words,

> 'They are very sorry, so they say,—
>    Sorry for what they find'?

On the contrary, men of science are usually very *glad* of whatever new truth they find. Science has no object so much in view as the ascertainment of the truth, be it what it may; and, far from indulging in such hysterical stuff as Miss Ingelow credits her with, rejoices more over one false opinion exploded than over ninety-and-nine just opinions that need no explosion. Science too could teach Miss Ingelow a little of that reverence which is so largely deficient in such writing as the verses last quoted and these following:

> The garden, O the garden, must it go,
>    Source of our hope and our most dear regret?
> The ancient story, must it no more show
>    How man may win it yet?

And all upon the Titan child's decree,
  The baby science, born but yesterday,
That in its rash unlearnèd infancy
  With shells and stones at play,

And delving in the outworks of this world,
  And little crevices that it could reach,
Discovered certain bones laid up, and furled
  Under an ancient beach,

And other waifs that lay to its young mind
  Some fathoms lower than they ought to
lie . . .

The large features of Science would never condescend to a wrinkle of disturbance at this kind of intrusion: it is only the critical outsider who must claim from those who hold 'strictly orthodox' opinions the same reverential indulgence for honest labourers who unearth unpalatable truths, as Science herself, through her highest exponents, shows to the opinions and creeds of men, not only when they are doubtful, but when they are known to be false. Such reverence we find thoroughly developed in every great poetic mind; and this is peculiarly the case in Tennyson, who frequently introduces scientific ideas with rectitude of thought, as well as grandeur and delicacy of expression; but to such of his partial imitators as have, like Miss Ingelow, failed to qualify themselves by deep thought, as he has evidently done, Science is a mere bugbear. Such writers would do well to leave subjects of this sort altogether untouched; for to the weak and flabby order of mind fear of contamination must always render the book of science a 'sealed book.'

Miss Ingelow's partisans doubtless flatter themselves and her that she has 'dropped down heavily' on geology in this poem of **"Honours"**; but it only requires a very limited amount of acuteness to detect the dropping as of the baked-apple order, followed only by pulpy collapse; and they and she might find an instructive lesson on the treatment of scientific themes by unscientific poets in Miss Smedley's beautiful **"Plea for Beauty."**

The same irreverence which we have just mentioned as exhibited towards the scientific spirit of the age undergoes a very different manifestation in Miss Ingelow's most pretentious production, **"A Story of Doom"**, in which the simple old record of the preaching of Noah before the Deluge is made the foundation of a terribly tedious romance, in nine books of the driest blank-verse that it ever entered into the heart of man (or woman either) to conceive. There is no reason at all why subjects coeval with this should not be treated in modern verse; and Mrs. Browning has shown us, in her "Drama of Exile", how much true magnificence of poetry may be introduced into such a subject. Some of the speeches of Adam and Satan in the "Drama of Exile" may stand beside Milton without fear; for though they do not quite rival the state of Milton as regards the technical quality of the blank-verse, they often surpass him in fire and fury of thought, and in true humanity of feeling; and the Eve of the drama is perhaps a more exquisite creation than the Eve of the epic. But there is a huge gulf between Mrs. Browning and Miss Ingelow: where the one lays on touches of exquisite colour, and revivifies the fading tones of an antique subject, the other paints but to smutch, and

resuscitates but to exhibit an ugly monstrosity instead of a grand vital frame. Conceive the wife of Noah, when informed by her lord of the probability of a seafaring life, answering thus:

'Sir, I am much afraid: I would not hear
  Of riding on the waters'!

Note too the lack of artistic propriety in painting Methuselah as a peevish old man vowing implacable enmity to his God on account of the loss of certain talking and blaspheming Saurians which he was used to yoke to a car when he drove in state, and which God commissioned his angels to pound the heads of with stones! Conceive farther the hopeless state of imagination which would depict Noah and his wife as holding a discussion on the rectitude of a prevalent practice of obtaining a race of pigmies by selective breeding! Such a discussion we get among the grotesque improprieties apparently meant as decorations to the **"Story of Doom"**; and the practice is deprecated by two 'grave old angels,' who were 'plain'—something, no doubt, very different in all respects from the image we are accustomed to associate with the word 'angel.' The Satan too of this work is a poor production. Instead of the fine conception of a subtle but perverted intellectuality, we have a cringing, cowering, weakly-plaintive dragon, without a vestige of the resistent energy involved in the very notion of a Satan, so splendidly developed both by Milton and by Mrs. Browning.

But when all has been said that can be said against the taste and style of this popular writer, there still remains an amount of undiscussed work that cannot fairly be passed by without a few words in the reverse sense. That the author has shown here and there a good lyric faculty of the literary or uninspired order is unquestionable; nor can it be denied that she exhibited in her popular book a noteworthy share of those affinities with external nature that never fail to enrich tenfold poetry that is wealthy in other respects. In dealing with the more simple and obvious sentiments and emotions she showed a farther aptitude; and these three features seemed promising when first brought before the public. But later work does not bear out the promise; and the features in question have no sufficient prominence to support a high literary standing. That they all exist may be seen without going beyond the three poems selected for censure. The lyric faculty is perhaps best shown in the charming song, 'When sparrows build, and leaves break forth' (in **"Supper at the Mill"**); and it is traceable in **"Honours,"** though the best verses of that poem show no more than a fair capacity to reproduce the metre and style of Tennyson's "Dream of Fair Women." The first part of **"Scholar and Carpenter"** is full of little tender thoughts on nature and things living, and the last part has an admirably simple pathos in the Carpenter's story of his life: were it not for the faults already named and the conscious presence of **"The Two Voices"** in the preamble of intended subtleties, the poem might be valuable. Again, in a poem called **"Light and Shade,"** the beautiful legend of Persephone is treated at once with firmness of hand and nicety of lyric expression: these qualities, indeed, are exceedingly remarkable in the piece, considering that it is evidently a study written on a set subject (that given in the title); and the ruin of so good a poem by the anti-classic vulgarity of the opening verse is subject for more regret than the vulgarest passages of Miss Ingelow's verse usually inspire in the critical bosom. The wide disparity between Miss Ingelow and Miss Smedley as followers of Tennyson is striking: Miss Smedley has exquisite taste, whether she be writing in an imitative or in an original vein; and it is just the lack of that indispensable quality that has gone farthest to ruin Miss Ingelow's productions in both veins. (pp. 90-102)

> *H. Buxton Forman, "Jean Ingelow," in his* Our Living Poets: An Essay in Criticism, *Tinsley Brothers, 1871, pp. 87-102.*

## James Ashcroft Noble (essay date 1885)

[*In the excerpt below, Noble surveys Ingelow's career and considers the strengths and weaknesses of her third series of* Poems.]

Twenty-two years have passed since Miss Ingelow gave to the world her first volume of poems; and those of us who are crossing or have crossed the nearer frontier of middle age are old enough to remember the vivid interest it excited, and the warm welcome it received. The new singer caught at once the ear not only of the critical, but of the general non-critical public—the very public which is generally the last to come under the spell of a new poetic magician; and in a month Miss Ingelow took rank as a popular poet. The time was certainly favourable to such a success. The laureate was really the only singer who had a public audience, for Mr. Browning and Mr. Matthew Arnold were then the poets of a coterie, Mr. Swinburne's day of fame had not dawned, and the younger men who have since made their voices heard in the land were in the nursery or the schoolroom. It happened, too, that Miss Ingelow's *Poems,* published in 1863, came just in the quiet of one of Mr. Tennyson's longest silences—the silence, unbroken save by a few single utterances, between the first series of the *Idylls of the King* (1859) and *Enoch Arden* (1864)—so that the new poet had a fair field, which in the book-world counts for much. But it does not count for everything, because no literary success can be altogether explained by the theory of lucky accident. Even now, when we have become familiar with Miss Ingelow's "peculiar quality," and it has no longer the charm of novelty, we can still recognise its other charms, and can understand how it was that the work of a new poet unhelped by puffery, preliminary or other, won such an immediate welcome. In the first place, it was clear that the new poet possessed the true lyrical gift, and there is no maxim of the critics which finds more favour with the general public than this—that the poet must be, before all other things, a singer. Then, too, Miss Ingelow's singing had a recognisable spontaneity which could hardly fail to be attractive to those who, in reading Mr. Tennyson's lyrical work, instinctively perceived in it a certain self-consciousness, a premeditated adaptation of means to ends which prevented it from taking entire possession of them. His art might be only the *ars celare artem;* but it was art of *some* kind, and Miss Ingelow's verse seemed a return to nature, which to many readers was preferable to art of *any* kind. In the very first stanza in the new volume—

> An empty sky, a world of heather,
> Purple of foxglove, yellow of broom,
> We two among them wading together,
> Shaking out honey, treading perfume

there was a certain note of lyrical abandonment which had hardly been heard in English verse since Shelley, a feeling of possessing and being possessed by Nature, and by Nature not in her exceptional revelations of might, or terror, or mystery, but in her simpler and homelier moods—moods which might be studied any fine summer day on Wimbledon Common or Hampstead Heath. Of course, no reader will suppose that I mean to be guilty of such a *jugement saugrenu* as that of placing Miss Ingelow by the side of Shelley; but I do certainly mean to say that in the poem called **"Divided,"** from which I have just quoted, and in some of the other pieces in her first volume, there was the same *kind* of lyrical utterance that we have in "The Skylark," which is not only one of the most popular, but also one of the most characteristic, of Shelley's poems. In addition to this buoyant lyricism (to use an awkward but convenient word) Miss Ingelow showed herself happy in what may be called musical meditations, which, if of no great value, are pleasantly attractive; and the **"High Tide on the Coast of Lincolnshire"** proved that she possessed something which is always of value—the power to write a genuine ballad as distinguished from an ordinary narrative poem artificially cast in ballad form. It need hardly be said in the columns of the *Academy* that the archaisms of **"The High Tide"** are artificial enough; but, leaving them out of the question, the poem is still one of the best of modern ballads, and the volume in which it appeared was not a mere *succès d'estime,* but a collection of really noteworthy work.

A second volume following a successful first seems destined to disappoint the majority of readers who expect very unreasonably a repetition of the pleasure in which a sense of newness is a large constituent; and accordingly *A Story of Doom, and Other Poems,* fell somewhat flat. Perhaps it did not contain any single poem so striking as one or two of the old ones, but the average of conception and workmanship was as high as before; though neither the critics nor the public could see it, because they were all alike in an essentially uncritical mood. Now, after ceasing from verse and addicting herself to prose fiction for some eighteen years, Miss Ingelow presents us with a third series of *Poems;* and by this time it ought to be, and surely is, possible to appraise the absolute and comparative value of her work with some approach to final justice. It is with a view to such appraisement that I have dwelt at what may seem disproportionate length on some of the most obvious characteristics of the author's previous performances.

This plan of procedure is all the more justifiable because there are in this volume no surprises—hardly even any enlargements of our view. The critic, anxious to make a study of Miss Ingelow's work, which should be done quickly, and yet not be glaringly inadequate, might safely confine his studies to such early poems as **"Divided," "Honours," "The High Tide," "Brothers, and a Sermon,"** and **"Songs of Seven,"** for these, and these alone, would suffice to make him acquainted with the writer's *cachet*—with her possibilities and limitations. Still, though these new poems do not render necessary any structural revision of the old verdict, they do help us to render it more accurately discriminating by nice adjustment of emphasis. We could say before that the poet was strong here, weak there; we can now differentiate a little more finely between varying degrees of strength and weakness.

And first of the weakness. In poems of direct narrative or of simple reflection or description, Miss Ingelow has always had her pen well in hand; and all her best work belongs to one of these classes. From the first, however, she has displayed an unfortunate taste for a kind of poem made up of a skeleton of narrative, the structure of which is all but concealed by a body of description of reflection. When I say unfortunate, I use the word with a distinct personal reference, for as we all know some of the finest poems in the English language may be thus described; but the form does not suit Miss Ingelow, because in leaving the narrative, and then working back to it, she is tempted to the besetting sin of all "natural" poets—the sin of diffuse and formless expatiation. There is in this volume an Australian poem, called **"The Bell Bird,"** which is full of beautiful lines and stanzas, and yet is, as a whole, almost irritating by reason of its deficiency in organisation, and, therefore, in apprehensible outline. Such a work resembles an ill-composed picture, which has no concentration of pictorial interest, but leaves the eye to wander restlessly here and there; and, while these poems are probably written with a fatal facility, they only provide another illustration of the saying that easy writing is hard reading.

Something might be said of Miss Ingelow's infatuation for a certain forced and artificial simplicity, represented in this volume by **"Preludes to a Penny Reading,"** which is not only childish, but affectedly childish, which is still worse; but Miss Ingelow's strong points are so much more numerous and also more characteristic than her weak ones, that desultory fault-finding is rather a waste of time. In one respect the poet in this new volume has made a decided advance. She has worked through the Tennysonian imitativeness of her earlier blank verse into a really strong individuality of metrical handling. This can be best seen in **"Rosamund,"** the first poem in the book, which, though less ambitious than some of its companions, is more satisfying, because freer from disappointing lapses. The story is told by Rosamund's father, a farmer dwelling "where England narrows running north," to whom, as to his neighbours,

> Came rumours up
> Humming and swarming round our heads like
>    bees:
> 'Drake from the bay of Cadiz hath come home
> And they are forth, the Spaniards, with a force
> Invincible.'

The story is a very simple one of the love of Rosamund for a Spanish captain who has been cast ashore half dead near her father's farm; but the centre of gravity is in the earlier portion of the poem, which is devoted to a description—full of life and stir and colour—of the state of England during these days of alarm when the long line of the great Armada filled with fear, but steeled with courage, the hearts of the watchers on the coast. Rosamund's father

joins the ranks of the hastily summoned army of defence, and watches the ships of Howard and Drake and Raleigh as they sail into the sunset and at last sink "hull down, e'en with the sun." When he sees the ships again they are engaged in a harassing chase of the mighty armament.

> And while I spoke, their topsails, friend and foe,
> Glittered—and there was noise of guns; pale
>    smoke
> Lagged after, curdling on the sun-fleck'd main.
> And after that? What after that, my soul?
> Who ever saw weakling white butterflies
> Chasing of gallant swans and charging them,
> And spitting at them long red streaks of flame?
> We saw the ships of England even so
> As in my vaunting wish that mocked itself
> With 'Fool, O fool, to brag at the edge of loss.'
> We saw the ships of England even so
> Run at the Spaniards on a wind, lay to,
> Bespatter them with hail of battle, then
> Take their prerogative of nimble steerage,
> Fly off, and ere the enemy, heavy in hand,
> Delivered his reply to the wasteful wave
> That made its grave of foam, race out of range,
> Then tack and crowd all sail, and after them
> Again.
>    So harass'd they that mighty foe,
> Moving in all its bravery to the east.
> And some were fine with pictures of the saints,
> Angels with flying hair and peaked wings,
> And high red crosses wrought upon their sails;
> From every mast brave flag or ensign flew,
> And their long silken pennons serpented
> Loose to the morning. And the galley-slaves,
> Albeit their chains did clink, sang at the oar.

There is a cumulative momentum in the first part of this passage, and a certain dignified sumptuousness in the later lines which are new to Miss Ingelow's blank verse; and the whole poem shows a freedom and flexibility of handling which means mastery. Of its vigour and picturesqueness nothing need be said.

**"The Sleep of Sigismund"** is the story of a king who sold his nights to a witch in return for unbroken triumph and happiness during the hours of day, and who at last repudiating his unhallowed compact is driven from his throne into obscurity and poverty. In both subject and treatment it recalls Miss Rossetti's *Goblin Market,* but it is not, I think, equal to it either in simplicity or imaginative realisation. **"The Maid Martyr,"** the tale of a girl burnt to death for heresy, told by her lover, who is awaiting his own doom, is more powerful in passages than as a whole; and, with the exception of **"Rosamund,"** the best things in the volume are not the longer narrative poems, but are to be found among the slighter sketches and simple lyrics. **"Dora"** is a daintily pathetic portrait; in **"Kismet"** an unhackneyed *motif*—the inborn instinct of wandering in the children of those whom the sea has taken—is very skilfully and winningly treated; and the three stanzas which we quote by way of conclusion from **"Speranza,"** show that Miss Ingelow's treatment of nature has the old charm, the old spontaneity and inspiration:

> The world is stirring, many voices blend,
>    The English are at work in field and way;
> All the good finches on their wives attend,

And linnets their new towns lay out in clay;
Only the cuckoo-bird only doth say
Her beautiful name, and float at large all day.

Everywhere ring sweet clamours, chirruping,
  Chirping, that comes before the grasshopper;
The wide woods, flurried with the pulse of
    spring,
    Shake out their wrinkled buds with tremor
    and stir;
Small noises, little cries, the ear receives
Light as a rustling foot on last year's leaves.

All in deep dew the satisfied deep grass
  Looking straight upward stars itself with
    white,
Like ships in heaven full-sailed do long clouds
    pass
    Slowly o'er this great peace, and wide sweet
    light,
While through moist meads draws down yon
    rushy mere
Influent waters, sobbing, shining, clear.

I will only make the remark that the habit of repeating words—see "only" in the first of these stanzas, and "deep" in the third—is growing upon Miss Ingelow, and threatens to become an irritating trick. (pp. 396-97)

> *James Ashcroft Noble, in a review of "Poems,"* in The Academy, No. 685, June 6, 1885, pp. 396-97.

## Harriet Waters Preston   (essay date 1885)

[*Below, Preston offers an overview of Ingelow's novels, commenting on the development of her abilities in that genre.*]

Miss Ingelow has always seemed to us to suffer, as a novelist, from the obstinate reluctance of the world to accord to any individual the possession of more than one kind of ability. Do we not all naturally take it as a sort of impertinence or affront,—at the least, as evidence of a very grasping disposition,—when one who has fairly established his claim to the honors of a certain specialty asks for our suffrages in a new direction? Miss Ingelow was a poet,—a minor poet to be sure, but extremely popular as such. Perhaps none but minor poets are ever largely popular in their own day. It must be secretly grievous to a man of the highest poetic aims and sensibilities to have produced poems as widely read and universally admired as *Hiawatha* or *The Light of Asia!* Miss Ingelow, however, had opened a slender vein of poesy which was all her own. She had written a few ballads and lyrics which had instantly found their place, and will probably always retain it, in all standard collections of the gems of English song. She had developed a certain originality of rhyme and rhythm, and had shown a graceful command of a quaint, sometimes a trifle too quaint, English vocabulary. It was this which secured her the honor of poor *Fly-Leaf* Calverley's most delightful raillery, but she shared that honor with the Laureate and Mr. Browning, which might, one would think, have contented anybody.

But Miss Ingelow was not content. She tried her hand at children's tales, and produced, in **Mopsa the Fairy,** a really charming fantasy, where many of the best qualities of her poetry were found allied to a certain artless charm of transparent and direct prose diction,—where indeed some of her most exquisite poetical bits first appeared, as captions to the chapters, or songs sung by the characters. Her first attempts at the portrayal of actual English life were less successful. They may be found in a small volume characteristically entitled **Studies for Stories,** curious and interesting chiefly as revealing the serious and systematic manner in which Miss Ingelow went to work to win her laurels in prose fiction. These little sketches are exactly what they profess to be,—studies: conscientious efforts at the delineation of separate figures; attentive observation of salient characteristics, with usually an effort, a little too pronounced and palpable, at deducing a moral from their interaction. The lady was evidently bent on mastering an untried art, and was not in the least shy about letting the public perceive the humility of her first attempts. Several years—as many as seven or eight at the least—must have elapsed between the publication of these preliminary sketches and the appearance of Miss Ingelow's first novel proper, **Off the Skelligs.** It was immediately evident that her studies had borne fruit. The opening chapters of **Off the Skelligs** possess an entirely fresh and quite extraordinary charm. The childhood of Tom and Dorothea Graham is less profoundly studied, no doubt, than that of Tom and Maggie Tulliver, but it is in a wholly different *genre,* and what with the quaintness of the juvenile types portrayed, and the exceptional character of their surroundings, it is hardly less fascinating in its way than that immortal chronicle. The picture of those two precocious but perfectly simple, babyish, and unconscious mites of humanity—Snap and Missy, the boy of eight and the girl of six—declaiming scenes from Shakespeare in their nursery, and wrangling over the rules of a universal language of their own invention, is altogether captivating. They had a literary mother, poor things, who was endeavoring to make money by her pen, shut up in the solemn and inviolable privacy of a remote chamber; and we feel a lively sympathy with the superstitious emotions of the nurse, who found "something awful in their play-acting," and with the consternation of the successive tutors who were engaged to superintend this untimely intellectual development, and of whom the varying degrees of dismay are most amusingly described—. (pp. 232-33)

Miss Ingelow's poetic and dramatic powers find scope in the really thrilling description of the wreck off the rocks from which the novel takes its name; and properly enough, since its true love-story begins then and there; but it is in depicting the daily life at Wigfield that she first fully makes good her claim to be reckoned among the vivid and successful delineators of English domesticity. Affluent without ostentation; pure, healthful, and humane; pious without austerity or pretension; courteous and generous and gay; monotonous, yet always mildly amusing,—this is that life of sweet decorum, of sobriety rather than of dullness, in which we do so well to take what seems by moments, even to ourselves, an inexplicable delight. This is that true beatitude of blameless Philistinism, equally removed from the exotic vices and the barbaric expensiveness, chronicled with so much gusto by Lord Beaconsfield and Ouida, and the fantastic tricks played before high heaven by certain small but highly conscious *coteries,* important chiefly through their impertinence, and conspicuous by their absurdity.

Miss Ingelow lingers too long over the pleasant life at Wigfield for the symmetry of her tale. There is too much about the elder brother's philanthropies and there are too many of the younger brother's jokes; yet we speak for ourselves in averring that she never positively fatigues her reader, who is glad when the course of the story returns to that quiet place, after the somewhat forced episode of the heroine's attempted labors in the London slums. The weak part of *Off the Skelligs* is its plot. That a person— even a very small and self-distrustful person—of Dorothea's delightful common sense should have engaged herself to the volatile and insignificant, though amusing Valentine, when she had really given her heart to the staid and slightly magnificent Giles is hardly to be credited, and the manner in which the true lovers of the story are involved in the misunderstanding which delays their bliss implies even more than the elaborate imbecility usually displayed in such cases.

Miss Ingelow appears clearly to have perceived that her first novel had no proper *intrigue,* and to have resolved, come what might, to remedy this defect in her subsequent efforts. But first, she could not resist the temptation to de-

velop a little further the fortunes of her first-born characters, for whom she had naturally conceived a lively affection, and whose existence had probably assumed for her a sort of importunate objectivity. The experiment is always a doubtful one. It cannot be said either to have failed or to have succeeded completely, in the by no means commonplace story entitled *Fated to be Free.* Once more the author's lively imagination supplies her with a novel and highly picturesque opening to her tale. She introduces a strange set of characters, living in antiquated fashion in an out-of-the-world nook, who prove, however, to have relations of the most important kind with some whom we have already seen in *Off the Skelligs,* moving in the broad daylight of every-day life. She devises a secret, which she is so anxious not to reveal prematurely that she can hardly be said ever to reveal it satisfactorily, and with the proper dramatic effect. She broaches a moral; and of all gravest questions, the one here involved is the everlastingly staggering question of the relations between necessity and freewill. This is the way in which our author looks at it, and thus offers her suggestion for the reconcilement of the irreconcilable. An unalterable destiny gives us liberty of moral choice. We are subject to fate, but to a fate which makes us to a certain extent free. Valentine, the light, sparkling, incorrigible Valentine, who would so gladly have yielded himself wholly to the swaying of circumstance, Valentine was forced to take the responsibility of his own

*Ingelow House in Boston, England, from a sketch made in 1810.*

course, to say with a categorical *yes* or *no* whether he would enter upon his tempting but tainted and virtually forbidden inheritance; and clearly to perceive at the last, just as his vain young life was slipping from him, that it had been so, and that his fate had been to have his fate in his own hands. The story is a short and rather sad one, though brightened by much unforced light talk, and lively nonsense of young and happy people, but the author's genuine artistic instinct suffices to make it consistent and shapely, and, in fine, it has its charm.

By the time, however, that *Fated to be Free* was concluded, Miss Ingelow had become possessed, or so we divine, by certain definite theories about novel-making which she was impatient more fully to develop. First of all, the truism that truth is stranger than fiction seems to have impressed itself upon her mind with new and extraordinary force. She is struck, as most of us have been, at one time or another, by the notion that if we would but remember what we hear, and dared tell what we actually know, it would become apparent that strange coincidences and grotesque combinations do frequently occur even in the most ordinary and conventional lives. The most probable defect of the novel of comfortable English life is, naturally, a lack of incident; but it is possible to conceive, even within these highly proper bounds, of a situation so strange that incidents in abundance would inevitably grow out of it. Accordingly, still with the same happy and engaging carelessness about making her experiments in public, Miss Ingelow set herself resolutely, as it would seem, to conjure up situations of this kind, and did actually contrive two, which, so far as we know, had never been thought of before, and proceeded to work them out, like problems, in *Sarah de Berenger* and *Don John.*

The conception of the former is the more entirely novel. A poor woman, of extraordinary character, the wife of a convict just transported for fourteen years, unexpectedly falls heir to a modest competence; and in order to secure it, for the benefit of her two baby girls, from the possible future claims of their worthless father, she assumes different names for herself and for them, takes the position of their servant, and brings them up as little orphan gentlefolk, of whose income, slender for their false position, although amounting to wealth for their true one, she passes for the scrupulously honest trustee. A great deal of skill is shown in the contrivance of slight chances, whereby the self-devoted author of this pious fraud is continually enabled to escape detection; and it was clever to conceive of her as aided above all, however unwittingly, by the inveterate folly and freakishness, the long pampered eccentricities, of the wealthy and addle-pated spinster who finally leaves her money to the convict's children. The drawback is that the thing was, after all, so outrageous a fraud that our gratification at its success is felt to be uncomfortably immoral. Moreover the *bizarre* central figure of Sarah de Berenger, though happily enough imagined, is not well developed. She just fails of being an entirely credible, and therefore legitimately amusing character. The latter part of the story, from the time when the mother is forced finally to sever herself from her children and go back to her rehabilitated convict, is very painful, but, to our thinking, very powerful also; especially in the way in which we are

forced to share both the poor wife's dispassionate conviction of the reality of her wretched husband's repentance, and her invincible repugnance for his person.

The *motif* of *Don John* seems, at first sight, to be more hackneyed; but it is not so, for here we have the time-honored expedient of changing children at nurse treated in an entirely unprecedented, and yet perfectly plausible fashion. The irresponsible young wet-nurse, whose imagination has been fired, and her light head turned, by an immense consumption of the fiction furnished by a cheap circulating library, makes, in the first instance, in mere wantonness, the experiment of substituting her own child for the one which had been confided—somewhat too unquestioningly—to her care, while a severe epidemic of scarlatina took its long course through the nursery of her employers, the Johnstones. Again a chain of curious and very creditably devised chances favor—almost necessitate—the maintenance of the deception; and at length it comes about, through the sudden death, by accident, of her accomplice in the dangerous game she had been playing, that the nurse herself is not entirely certain whether it is the Johnstone baby or her own which the family reclaim, while she is herself prostrated by severe illness. The frightened woman keeps her guilty and yet rather absurd secret for a little while, but then the miserable confession will out, and the unhappy parents who have been the victims of this enraging trick find that they can do no better than pack the unprincipled nurse off to Australia, adopt the other child, and bring up the twin boys exactly alike. The history of the growth of their characters, and the development of their fates, is a singular and affecting one. It is the best told of all Miss Ingelow's tales,—the most direct and dramatic and symmetrical; and, in short, *Don John* is, to our mind, an exceedingly beautiful little story; a finished and charming specimen of that minor English fiction which is often as good, from a literary point of view, as the best produced elsewhere.

As in *Fated to be Free* the author had hovered about the eternally burning questions of fate, free-will, and foreknowledge absolute, so in the obviously *recherchés* plots of *Sarah de Berenger* and *Don John,* she finds scope for some curious speculations on the potency of education and the mysteries of heredity. It is a little difficult to make out her exact position; perhaps she has never fully defined it even to herself. Upon the whole, however, she would seem to make light of ancestral influences, and to intimate that the individual himself and his guardians and teachers in early years are alone responsible for his spiritual development and mundane destiny; thus reiterating her protest against those necessitarian doctrines which are commonly held so dangerously to benumb the moral sense.

It is to be observed, however, that the novelist who is born, not made, is not apt greatly to preoccupy himself with the illustration of points like these, or, other than incidentally, with any points whatever. Nor are we wont to perceive with him, as plainly as we cannot help doing in Miss Ingelow's case, the growth of the design and the machinery of construction. (pp. 235-238)

*Harriet Waters Preston, "Miss Ingelow and*

*Mrs. Walford," in* The Atlantic Monthly, *Vol. LVI, No. CCCXXXIV, July, 1885, pp. 230-42.*

## Arthur Symons    (essay date 1897)

[*Symons was an English critic, poet, dramatist, short story writer, and editor who established himself as one of the most important critics of the modern era. Symons provided his contemporaries with a definition of the aesthetic of symbolism in his book* The Symbolist Movement in Literature; *furthermore, he laid the foundation for much of modern poetic theory by discerning the importance of the symbol as a vehicle by which a "hitherto unknown reality was suddenly revealed." Here, he discusses the limitations of Ingelow's technique.*]

[Jean Ingelow's] work, though in date it belongs mainly to the years between 1860 and 1870, is typically Early Victorian. She is a Mrs. Hemans who has read Tennyson, an L. E. L. who has read Mrs. Browning. Like those writers, she is definitely a poetess, not a poet. In this, at the outset, we see her complete distinction from her less popular contemporary, Christina Rossetti, who is a poet among poets, womanly but not feminine. It is because she is rather feminine than womanly—feminine in the broadest and most honourable sense certainly—that Jean Ingelow has always appealed so widely to women and to that part of the reading public whose judgment in literature is similar to the literary judgment of women. Her work is always an improvisation; it has feeling and sentiment which are genuine, though not profound, it is almost entirely without affectation and entirely without insincerity; it is, for good and evil, very English, admirably so in the sense it conveys of the coast, the fisher's sea, the English hedgeside and meadow; she is religious, evangelical rather than lyrical, and thus again English; she has a singing voice, very limited, somewhat unpractised, but with a few clear, slightly pathetic notes; and her poems always tell stories. Here is a combination of qualities which, though they do not all go to the making of a distinguished, certainly go to the making of an attractive writer of verse. But her main success, her main failure, is that, while she never writes without emotion, she never expresses anything but generalized emotions. Take, for instance, her most popular poem, **"Divided,"** a poem which might almost have been written by Longfellow, so exactly does it repeat his methods. The poem is an obvious allegory, it has an obvious pathos, it is told very prettily; the meaning can be followed by every reader, the music heard by every ear, and this music is so general, this meaning so generalized, that every reader can indulge in the gratifying feeling that he might almost have written, certainly might have thought, it himself. Looking into it carefully, you will see that the image has not really been made as precise as it appears to be; that it has after all only been sketched out, the symbol after all only used as a peg, not as a root. Looking at another very popular poem, **"The High Tide on the Coast of Lincolnshire"** (which has one of her few affectations in an entirely meaningless use of "old spelling"), you will find even less precision of thought, emotion or structure. The poem is merely a good description of a flood: it has no further meaning. It is an anecdote, telling us how a husband was saved and his wife and children drowned: that is all. The situation,

if you will, is pathetic; but without something more than a pathetic situation, without some profound inner meaning, some link with the eternity of nature, a mere situation, no matter how pathetic, does not become art. Again, take the realistic sketches in blank verse, done after Tennyson's unfortunate model; take, for instance, **"Supper at the Mill."** How excellent all that would be—for it is done with a really personal touch in details—if it were a means to an end! But no, it is an end in itself; we get the anecdote, and no more. In Tennyson, if we find the false theory, we find, at all events, workmanship so finished, and so ingenious a hint (it is but a hint) of a meaning somewhere behind, that we are not unapt to overlook the essential weakness of a root which has produced so graceful a flower. Here the barrenness of the method is forced upon us, as the similarly Tennysonian manner of placing a situation is exposed, almost cruelly, by such a stanza as this:—

> Two silent girls, a thoughtful man,
>   We sunned ourselves in open light,
> And felt such April airs as fan
>   The Isle of Wight.

In her realism, as in her emotion, she still always generalizes; her very descriptions, so true in outline, of English scenes and landscapes, are for the most part lacking in precision; she is vague even among flowers, to which she refers not without a certain felicity; the exact word rarely comes, flashing the exact image. She seems, indeed, almost to seek the ready-made in language, as a visible sign of that spontaneity which she is feminine enough to think the origin and not the result of the "art which conceals art." Thus she writes, in a favourite poem, of raindrops in "genial showers," of trees "wherewith the dell was decked"; she begins a stanza, "While swam the unshed tear." Certainly she has the virtues of the improvisatore; but at what a cost!

Verse, if it is to be poetry, the poetry which lasts, must have that energy of the mind which is imagination, that energy of the soul which is ecstasy. Ecstasy, at all events, did not enter into Jean Ingelow's scheme of things. She wished to be true to nature, but she conceived nature to be a sort of "golden mean," which nature never was; nature, in her lower manifestations a splendid excess, at her highest that purified flame which has at last burned clear of smoke. Imagination she seems to have realized in the abstract, without a suspicion that it means a faculty of vision, that is, of seeing, so far-reaching that it sees precisely, without obliteration of the smallest object. There is much fancy, much thoughtful invention, in **"A Story of Doom,"** her longest poem, which tells the story of the world before the flood; but is even this more than an anecdote related; is it a thing seen? Where she is nearest to success, in her lyrics, there are moments when she seems to be about to say something quite fresh, whose saying would be poetry; some ingenuous word which she often came so near to saying. But the word is never said, only something is said about it. Let her be honoured for sincerity, for a gracious talent used graciously; but it would be idle to affect to forget that if in the pleasing writer who has just died we have lost an English poetess, we have not lost an English poet. (pp. 80-1)

*Arthur Symons, in a review of "Jean Ingelow,"
in* The Saturday Review, *London, Vol. 84, No.
2178, July 24, 1897, pp. 80-1.*

## Mackenzie Bell　(essay date 1907)

[*In the following excerpt, Bell surveys some of the
themes and techniques in Ingelow's poetry and novels.*]

Among the small group of eminent English women-poets
that the [nineteenth] century has produced, Jean Ingelow
holds a conspicuous place. She is greater than Felicia Hemans or Lætitia Landon, for she avoids sentimentality—
the characteristic weakness of both these poets. It is true
that she did not possess in an equal degree with Elizabeth
Barrett Browning that breadth of thought, that strength
of passion—that imaginative fervour, and that vigour of
execution—which give to the latter the first place among
English women-poets, nor had she that peculiarly exalted
spirituality tinctured with asceticism which distinguishes
the best work of Christina Rossetti. Nevertheless her
poems exhibit high qualities of their own. First among
these qualities is lyrical charm. Hence it is that her poems
have gained such widespread popular acceptance, for, as
Mr. Ashcroft Noble has pointed out with true critical discernment, "there is no maxim of the critics which finds
more favour with the general public than this—that the
poet must be, before all other things, a singer." Jean Ingelow's verse is always distinguished by graceful fancy, and
often by imagination of the more lofty kind. Though it
cannot be said that her range is wide, her pictures within
this range are vivid, and her verse displays a tender wom-
anliness, a reverent simplicity of religious faith, and a deep
touch of sympathy with the pain inherent in human life
which are very fascinating.

She had also the rare quality of depicting faithfully, and
sometimes with minute accuracy, the aspects of nature in
purely lyrical measures of anapæstic movement. The best
example of this is seen in **"Divided,"** where the colour of
the landscape is rendered in an exquisitely lyrical measure
with as much faithfulness as if the poem had been written
in iambic lines. And, remembering how seldom the great
English poets have succeeded in such efforts, Jean Ingelow's success in this respect may, indeed, be regarded as
a worthy achievement.

Born at Boston, in Lincolnshire, in 1820, Jean Ingelow's
first book, *A Rhyming Chronicle of Incidents and Feelings,* appeared in 1850. This was followed in 1851 by a
novel, entitled *Allerton and Dreux; or, The War of Opinion,* and in 1860 by *Tales of Orris.* But it was not until the
publication in November 1863 of the first series of her
*Poems* that she gained any important recognition. This
volume, however, was received with warm praise by the
critics, and their praise was immediately echoed and confirmed by the general public. But we need feel no surprise
at this somewhat unusual occurrence when we remember
some of the poems the volume contained. The very first
poem, **"Divided,"** was well fitted to attract both the critic
and the general reader. For while the critic would observe
its distinctive lyrical qualities, and a certain touch of sadness which is often a characteristic of its author's best

moods, the general reader, whatever the extent of his culture, could at least understand and enjoy its directness and
its simplicity, together with its lovely descriptions of some
of Nature's more familiar aspects. Perhaps none of Jean
Ingelow's other poems quite equals this in perfection of
music and lyrical freedom, though **"The High Tide on the
Coast of Lincolnshire, 1571,"** has other notable qualities.
Cast in an archaic mould, and full of deep and passionate
human feeling, the pathetic motive of the latter poem is
handled with an earnestness which is absolutely convincing. This, even more than its high technical excellence,
makes it one of the finest of modern ballads. But, perhaps,
the exquisite poem **"Requiescat in Pace"** is, in many respects, the highest effort of Jean Ingelow's poetical genius.
In it there is a touch of the supernatural which we find
elsewhere in some of her best work, though in a less intense degree. Moreover it is full of that concentrated fervour which comes only to the poet when the creative
imagination is fully alive. The manner in which the tender
mournfulness—almost the despair—of the concluding
stanzas is handled makes the poem irresistible in its appeal
to our sympathies. **"Strife and Peace,"** another beautiful
lyric, calls also for mention.

**"Supper at the Mill," "Brothers and a Sermon,"** and **"Afternoon at a Parsonage,"** all in blank verse, with interspersed songs, belong to a different class of poems—a class
for which Jean Ingelow had evidently a marked predilection—poems of mingled narrative and reflection. In the
extreme simplicity of the poems just named we see the influence of Wordsworth; while in their mingling of narrative and reflection with snatches of song we see the influence of Tennyson. It would be a mistake, however, to suppose that these remarkable poems are imitative. On the
contrary they display dramatic insight and originality
both of thought and treatment. All three poems contain
striking examples of Jean Ingelow's gift in delineating
character. In the first-named poem the middle-aged farmer's wife, as she chats at her son's house on a market day,
is as real to us as if she had been sketched by Crabbe, although, in Jean Ingelow's verse, there is nothing of that
hardness of touch which sometimes detracts from the effect of Crabbe's marvellous fidelity. Indeed, the character
painting throughout Jean Ingelow's poems is frequently
very good. But, as with the similar work of Tennyson, we
often feel it to be the character-painting of the writer of
prose fiction rather than of the poet. **"Brothers and a Sermon"** with its true vein of devotional feeling, exhibits a
certain idiosyncrasy of conception peculiar to its author.
The pretty song beginning, "Goldilocks sat on the grass,"
which occurs in this poem, is one of her most simple, and,
at the same time, one of her most finished efforts. The two
last stanzas, beginning, "As a gloriole sign o' grace," bring
before the mind of the reader, in a few delicate touches full
of subtle beauty, the change, the almost unconscious sympathy, which, to the eye of the beholder, comes over the
aspect of external nature after the first dawn of love.

**"Persephone"** is interesting as being a rendering of that
favourite theme of the poets—the story of Demeter and
her daughter. The brevity of Jean Ingelow's ballad does
not admit of the elaboration observable in the poem of
Tennyson, nor in that of Mr. Aubrey de Vere on the same

subject. But her version has a certain beauty of its own. **"The Letter L,"** fine as it is in part, is injured by that diffuseness into which Jean Ingelow's facility, both in verse and prose, not unfrequently betrayed her. It is unnecessary to dwell at any length on so widely popular and so admirable a series of poems as **"Songs of Seven."** Several of these lyrics are almost perfect of their kind. Where all is so good it is difficult to give adequate reasons for the awarding of especial praise. I may remark, however, that the first lyric, entitled **"Exultation,"** has pre-eminent merit from the fact that in it Jean Ingelow shows a rare dramatic gift—a gift of interpreting faithfully a child's emotions.

*A Story of Doom and other Poems* appeared in 1867. The title poem in this collection, the longest of Jean Ingelow's poetical efforts, tells in flowing blank verse the Biblical narrative of Noah. The theme is handled with no little skill, and many of the individual pictures are effective. Still the poem in its entirety shows that the subject she has here chosen is not so well suited to her powers as some others which she has elsewhere treated. She is a lyrist above all else, and although (as I have already remarked) she shows dramatic instinct in some of her shorter narrative poems, such as **"Supper at the Mill"** and **"Afternoon at a Parsonage,"** she does not show that consummate degree of dramatic power required by the writer who would cope effectively with the great difficulties inherent in such a theme. Much better work is to be found in **"Songs of the Voices of Birds,"** particularly in one of these called **"A Raven in a White Chine,"** and in the series of poems entitled **"Songs of the Night Watches."** The opening lyric **"Apprenticed"** and **"A Morn of May,"** the lyric which closes the sequence, are probably the most beautiful. **"Songs with Preludes,"** and **"Contrasted Songs,"** ought also to be mentioned. Of the last-named poems **"Sailing Beyond Seas"** and **"A Lily and a Lute"** are fine examples of Jean Ingelow's work.

As a novelist, as well as a poet, Jean Ingelow gives token of very considerable power in the delineation of character, especially as seen in childlife. But her work in fiction is sometimes disfigured by deficiency in construction, and by occasional prolixity in narrative. *Studies for Stories* (1864), a series of brief tales, contains some of Jean Ingelow's best work in this department of literature. There is often a quaint realism about these *Studies* which is very delightful. *Off the Skelligs* (1872) is, perhaps, the most successful of Jean Ingelow's full-length novels. Her exceptional faculty of delineating child life is shown here, and again in *Don John* (1881), where more attention is paid to the strict lines of plot than is usual with this writer. The *dénouement* is cleverly conceived and unexpected, so unexpected, indeed, that possibly some readers might be inclined to resent a conclusion so different from that which they had been disposed to look for. Among her other novels are *Fated to be Free* (1873); *Sarah de Berenger* (1879); *John Jerome: His Thoughts and Ways* (1886); and *Very Young and Quite Another Story* (1890). Jean Ingelow has long been favourably known as a writer of stories avowedly for children—stories, however, which have an appeal to readers of all ages. Indeed some of the most fascinating of all her prose work belongs to this class. *Stories told to*

*a Child* (1865) must here be named. This was followed in 1869 by *Mopsa the Fairy.* Some episodes in the last-mentioned tale are very fine of their kind: as, for example, Jack's voyage from the enchanted bay where lie the ships of bygone ages which had been sent on voyages of evil purpose. Doubtless some of Jean Ingelow's prose fiction will live by reason of the real imaginative power displayed in it.

Jean Ingelow's third series of *Poems* was published in 1885. If it cannot with candour be said that this volume is altogether free from the faults discernible in her earlier verse, and if it cannot be said that it shows a wider range, it may be said emphatically that it possesses the same great qualities which originally gained for her and still maintain her wide popularity. We see the same mingled sweetness and simplicity, the same rare lyrical gift, the same remarkable power in the description of nature, and the same profound knowledge of child-life. Her lyrical faculty, her power of depicting nature, and her subtle knowledge of the heart of a child are all revealed in the lovely poem called **"Echo and the Ferry"**. **"Rosamund,"** a narrative poem in blank verse, is of some considerable length. The scene is laid in the time of the Spanish Armada. The story is well planned and told throughout with much imaginative ardour. Jean Ingelow here exhibits even more than her accustomed ability in handling blank verse. Many excellent descriptive passages and felicitous phrases occur, and, occasionally, comes a note of true passion. **"Preludes to a Penny Reading"** belongs to the same class as **"Supper at the Mill."** Some of the interspersed songs, such as **"For Exmoor,"** are full of the lyrical beauty which we expect from Jean Ingelow. *Lyrical and other Poems, selected from the Writings of Jean Ingelow* was published in 1886. (pp. 385-92)

*Mackenzie Bell, "Jean Ingelow, 1820-1897,"*
*in* The Poets and the Poetry of the Nineteenth
Century, *edited by Alfred H. Miles, 1905-07.*
*Reprint by AMS Press, 1967, pp. 385-92.*

## Gladys Singers-Bigger (essay date 1940)

[*Below, Singers-Bigger discusses imagery in Ingelow's poetry, particularly as it relates to events in the poet's life.*]

When Jean Ingelow was fourteen her mother discovered the white shutters of her bedroom written over with verses in pencil. It was a double-windowed room looking on a garden in Ipswich, and her choice of tablets is significant. For in one sense she wrote with the shutters of life closed upon her and in the twilight, and in another they were thrown wide to beauty and the far expanse of the soul's country. As one finishes the simple record of Jean Ingelow's life, one's main impression is of gardens and clergymen—but there were birds in her gardens, and some of the clergymen had children.

She had an aunt who worked birds in wool, a quite celebrated artist in that medium; and she had a father who imitated the notes of birds, whistling them with his children raptly and rapturously listening at his knees. But Jean herself had the song of a bird at her heart, pure and nature-taught, and like the 'fair and fond dove' in her poem, she asked only to be 'left alone, for her dream was her own and her heart was full of rest'. Bird notes to her were like perfume in that they gave rise to reveries of environment appropriate to their song, whose language she had no difficulty in interpreting. She voyaged on their wings and had her own theory to account for the wonders of migration, a theory of angelic beings who have permission to take the form of birds, 'to fly and draw with them the sweet obedient flocking things'.

> How should they know their way, forsooth
>     alone?
> Men say they fly alone:
> Yet some have set on record, and averred
> That they, among the flocks had duly marked
> A leader.

Thus were the fairy fancies of her childhood hallowed into religious mysteries, and the babyhood hours at her father's knee inspired the **"Songs on the Voices of Birds"** which were the work of her maturity.

Over her gardens also, in memory if not always in reality, after the first years, there blew salt breezes from the sea, and many of her birds were sea-gulls. Like her own **"Margaret in the Xebec,"** 'when to frame a forest scene she tried, the ever-present sea would yet intrude, and all her towns were by the water's side'. Through her mind there sailed the great ships as they had once sailed past her nursery window, up and down the Boston River in Lincolnshire, where she was born in 1820. Was it only coincidence, we may ask, that one who was destined to influence the American people in much the same way as their own poet Longfellow has influenced us should also have had for her earliest impressions

> The beauty and mystery of the ships
> And the magic of the sea?

Or that in her verse the chimes from Boston Stump should answer across the Fens the carillon from the Belfry at Bruges, 'Till all the air bin full of floating bells', 'Changing like a poet's rhymes', interchanging and interweaving the thought of the old world with that of the new?

When Jean Ingelow's third collection of Poems was published the American civil war had just ceased, and a reviewer likened the voice of the new singer to that of one of the birds she loved, rising poignantly sweet after a great storm, comforting, consoling, and prophetic. Jean paid her own tribute to her brother poet in **"Gladys and Her Island,"** a delicate homage:

> Soon there came by, arrayed in Norman cap
> And kirtle, an Arcadian villager,
> Who said, 'I pray you, have you chanced to meet
> One Gabriel?' and she sighed; but Gladys took
> And kissed her hand: she could not answer her,
> Because she guessed the end.

Much as the Victorian gentlewoman shrank from any suggestion of masculinity, the fact remains that the finest women of the period were characterized by a delicate manliness, far enough removed in appearance from its modern development, but which, nevertheless, laid its foundations in moral courage and self-restraint. Those

who like Jean Ingelow sat up straightly at their desk or their needlework; who with a peculiarly sensitive reserve abjured extravagant sympathy in sorrow, and endured the narrow confines of their existence with cheerfulness rather than trespass against what they conceived to be their feminine duty, were yet paradoxically being borne onward by the wings of events more imperatively than they knew— great wings which were to materialize in a way they dreamed not of, and to sweep across oceans and continents, driven by a woman's will, the resultant outcome of those controlled and balanced intelligences which had held even a rebellious imagination in check.

Jean Ingelow had the advantage of having brothers. It was this masculine companionship which perhaps enabled her to write with sympathy and understanding of the sailors and farmers about her home, to catch the rough idiom of their speech; or to enter into the more refined rivalry and scholarship of the young men, clergymen and others, whose ambitions and contemplations she transferred to her poems and novels. In these last the vacillating Valentine and more Teutonic Brandon witness to a trenchant observation in their creator. Sometimes her character-sketches take a semi-dramatic form; they are cameos of dialogue interspersed by songs, as in **"Supper at the Mill"** and **"Afternoon at a Parsonage."** Singularly devoid of drama as her own life was, it was natural that she should dramatize her fancies, and just as natural that the call of some household duty should interrupt and leave the little scene poised, as it were (or rather should we say hastily concluded), too slight and too homely to be deemed real drama, but also so unforced as to claim our admiration for its truth to life.

We are told that it was long before Jean realized her appeal to a wider audience than her home circle. The charity of her poetic gifts certainly began at home and overflowed almost imperceptibly into the world, but we should be wrong if we denied ambition to this modest and retiring writer.

Often as she paced the 'dry smooth-shaven green' we may think of her in solitude swept by an inward storm of enthusiasm and kindled by a secret flame of emulation for the work of one whose organ-voice inspired her with intellectual hero-worship and 'a humble sense of kinship'. This was Milton; as far removed from the milder poets with whom she has been compared as the 'wandering moon' is separate from a 'student's lamp'. Milton as a Puritan spoke to the Evangelical side of her nature; as one whose fancy teemed with archangels and resounded to the choirs of heaven he provided her with just that ritual of the mind which lack of outward beauty in life reacts to and demands in contemplation; as blind and afflicted he appealed to her womanly pity.

Her metaphor, applied to one who suffered blindness in her **"Afternoon at a Parsonage,"** is Miltonic in grandeur and too majestic to be adapted to the somewhat insignificant hero of that playlet, but explicable if a mightier shadow hovered in the background of her thoughts.

> O misery and mourning! I have felt,
> Yea, I have felt like some deserted world
> That God had done with, and had cast aside

To rock and stagger through the gulfs of space,
He never looking on it any more.
Untilled, no use, no pleasure, not desired,
Nor lighted on by angels in their flight
From heaven to happier planets, and the race
That once had dwelt on it withdrawn or dead.
Could such a world have hope that some blest
   day
God would remember her and fashion her anew?

Her **"Song for the Night of Christ's Resurrection"** is avowedly written 'in humble imitation' of Milton's *"Hymn on the Morning of Christ's Nativity."* She follows the Miltonic example of mingling mythology with Christianity, though only in so far as to confirm the defeat of the ancient gods and to provide us with a memorable picture of the three Fates alone surviving the years of Ministry. Atropos, in that timeless pause of dread suspense before Easter dawns, is withheld from cutting the thread of that sacred Life, which is metamorphosed as we read from the thread of a single existence to the thread on which depends the eternal life of all creation. Implicit in that inhibition is man's whole destiny of immortality.

But it was in **"A Story of Doom,"** first published in 1867, that Jean Ingelow's ambition reached its culmination. Milton's shadow still brooded above her genius, and in courageous obedience to that urge she cast about her for a subject which should be in a direct line of descent from the *Paradise Lost*. She found in it the Biblical Legend of the Flood. The poem, which is nine books, is a noble effort of the imagination. One questions why a poem such as this should be so little known and how a jewel of language that is at once tender and sincere should be hidden under slighter and more commonly appreciated works.

Here is the prayer of Noah prior to his entrance into the Ark—could many have pleaded more passionately?

God, God! Thy billows and Thy waves
Have swallowed up my soul. Where is my God?
For I have somewhat yet to plead with Thee;
For I have walked the strands of Thy great deep,
Heard the dull thunder of its rage afar,
And its dread moaning. O the field is sweet,
Spare it. The delicate woods make white their
   trees
With blossom,—spare them. Life is sweet; be-
   hold
There is much cattle and the wild and tame,
Father, do feed in quiet,—spare them. God,
Where is my God? The long wave doth not rear
Her ghostly crest to lick the forest up,
And like a chief in battle fall,—not yet—
The lightnings pour not down, from ragged
   holes
In heaven, the torment of their forked tongues,
And like fell serpents, dart and sting—not yet.
The winds awake not, with their awful wings
To winnow, even as chaff, from out their track
All that withstandeth, and bring down the pride
Of all things strong and all things high—not yet,
O let it not be yet. Where is my God?

If we compare this agonized and repudiating prayer with the author's description of the Boston Flood of 1571, in her best-known poem, **"High Tide on the Coast of Lin-**colnshire,"** we shall discover a curious similarity of vision. The idea of an inundation seems to have been familiar to her and to have haunted her mind.

In *Mopsa the Fairy* we have the same idea rendered in prose, of the 'wonderful river' which flowed inland to the fairy countries rather than outward to the sea. Of rain there seems but little thought; it is the 'stolen tyde' in the first poem as in the last; and it may be because of the localization of the scene in her mind, as it were, that Jean Ingelow chose to leave the Covenant of the Rainbow unrecorded.

From her exposition of the age-long conflict between matter and spirit on the battleground of man's reason in one of the passages of *Doom* and from the opening lines of **"Dominion"** we may conclude that she was well read in philosophy.

But clearly hers was a philosophy of the negative—one which grew out of renunciation, the consistent crushing down in herself of the will to live.

Jean was happy in her home-life, none more so, but we have the whole witness of her dramatic poetry to confirm us in the belief that there were inward denials through which alone the even tenor of her surface way was preserved.

When I reflect how little I have done,
And add to that how little I have seen,
Then furthermore how little I have won
Of joy, or good, how little known, or been:
I long for other life more full, more keen,
And yearn to change with such as well have run,
Yet reason mocks me—nay, the soul, I ween,
Granted her choice, would dare to change with
   none.

From these denials there springs the courageous doubt-facing nobility of certain of her sonnets.

How long she wrestled with her angel before his blessing fell upon her in stark and arid counsel, leaving her exhausted but still spiritually strong, we may not guess, but it seems to me that her greatest sonnet, titled only by its first line, should accompany Emily Brontë's last utterance, for truly it may be said that 'no coward soul' was hers who wrote it. Light and darkness, the positive and the negative sides of Faith, find expression in these poems, and together they beat upon the eternal gates for admittance.

Though all great deeds were proved but fables
   fine,
Though earth's old story could be told anew,
Though the sweet fashions loved of them that
   sue
Were empty as the ruined Delphian Shrine;
Though God did never man, in words benign,
With sense of His great Fatherhood endue;
Though life immortal were a dream untrue
And He that promised it were not Divine;
Though soul, though spirit were not, and all
   hope
Reaching beyond the bourn, melted away;
Though virtue had no goal and good no scope,
But both were doomed to end with this our clay;

> Though all these were not,—to the ungraced
>     heir
> Would this remain,—to live as though they
>     were.

More tenderly in **"Failure,"** more devotionally in **"Compensation,"** we have the same trend of thought suggested; never abortive, never ending in the sterility of mere complaint, her discontents are glorified by a wideness of vision which justifies and envelops their being, rendering them beneficent and fruitful. Instinctively, in the phrase of Lord Haldane, she knew that 'the negative must be the negative pregnant'. It is curious to come across the sonnet **"Failure"** in a book for children.

Indeed, the majority of the lyrics in *Mopsa the Fairy* are palpably above the heads of children. One wonders why they were included, almost wholly irrelevant to the story as most of them appear, until we look deeper into the writer's intention, until we remember the higher perception which, undeveloped, floated alongside our own childish appreciation of the beautiful. She would infuse the young minds of her readers with music and the strange unaccountable magic of words, and this, her spell, has its part not inappropriately in the inspired inconsequence of her tale.

Who could remain insensible to the spontaneous melody of her song with its haunting repetitions?

> One morning, oh! so early, my beloved, my be-
>     loved,
> All the birds were singing blithely, as if never
>     they would cease;
> 'Twas a thrush sang in my garden, 'Hear the
>     story, hear the story!'
> And the lark sang, 'Give us glory!'
> And the dove said, 'Give us peace!'

She herself was moved by it—we know she was because immediately it is finished she smiles through her tears, disavowing the stirred feelings of an adult and poking fun at herself to show that she is once more on a level with her childish audience.

> "A very good song too," said the Dame, at the
> other end of the table, "only you made a mistake
> in the first verse. What the dove really said was,
> no doubt, 'Give us peas'. All kinds of doves and
> pigeons are very fond of peas."

Her predilection for 'doves, milking-pails, daisies and weather (with its few rhymes)' is noted by Mrs. Meynell in a brief introduction to the Red Letter Library edition of her poems, published in 1908, 'as the fashion of a day that is long over-past'.

I cannot recall any undue insistence on milking-pails or daisies, but if Jean Ingelow was preoccupied with doves and stars and children, it was because they were the colours wherewith she painted her own personal rainbow of hope. When the floods entered her soul, threatening to overbear her cheerful disposition with the loss of lover, of mother, and of brother, she had but to look up and there outspread were the tranquillizing wings of God's Paraclete.

Mrs. Meynell discovers in 'the picturesqueness of her lyri-

cal stories' a kind of popularizing of the Pre-Raphaelite movement; an observation justified by the medievalism that informs certain of the poems and by her fancy for archaic words such as 'wonned' and 'brede'.

The consolation offered to the bereaved mother in **"The Mariner's Cave"** is the traditional dream-consolation of the Middle Ages; but the correspondence between the central teaching of **"The Monitions of the Unseen"** and that of Dante Gabriel Rossetti's little prose work **"Hand and Soul"** is yet more arresting.

What governs such correspondences, involuntary as we needs must believe them? If we attribute them simply to the *Zeitgeist,* how is it that so often the moods they express are applicable also to the peculiar circumstances of the writer?

When Holman Hunt painted his picture *The Light of the World,* the figure with Christina's luminous eyes and Christina's brow knocked not only at the portals of the world but at the heart's door of each individual besides, and in poetry that insistent gentle sound was repeated. Jean Ingelow chose for the text of her seaman's sermon, finding fresh marvel in the words, 'Behold! Behold! saith He, I stand at the door and knock', and applied them with unerring perspicacity to the circumstances of her lowly fishermen, those to whom in her visits to Filey Brig her love had gone forth, finding perhaps in their environment the sea both spiritual and material towards which her life's river most unreservedly flowed.

So when, on that July morning in the Diamond Jubilee year of the great Queen whose reign her life and work had graced, the end came quietly, we have no difficulty in believing that

> (She) only saw the stars—she could not see
> The river—and they seemed to lie
> As far below as the other stars were high.

If we accept the spiritualistic hypothesis of Arthur Findlay, who maintains that the next world is composed of matter at a higher rate of vibration than this one, interpenetrating and surrounding what is here visible, then indeed Jean was uttering a more comprehensive truth than she knew when she held that 'he who has his own world has many worlds more'.

Something of Christian Science teaching is reflected in this paragraph from a letter:

> The more we know that we are spirit, that the
> body is a mere nothing, and the spirit great, and
> might be wise and holy and happy in the life of
> God, the better the body will, so to speak, be-
> have itself.

It is maybe for the sake of such mental interweaving that Jeremiah exhorts us:

> Thus saith the Lord, Stand ye in the ways, and
> see and ask for the old paths, where is the good
> way, and walk therein, and ye shall find rest for
> your souls.

So shall our pride of discovery be chastened and our knowledge widened. And so I suggest that we cannot do better than stroll awhile with Jean Ingelow through her gardens, forgetting in the quietness of her secluded life the clamours that surround us in our present world, listening only to the croon of her favourite bird,

> An emblem meet for her, the tender dove,
> Her heavenly peace, her duteous earthly love.

(pp. 78-84)

*Gladys Singers-Bigger, "Jean Ingelow," in* English, *Vol. III, No. 14, Summer, 1940, pp. 78-84.*

## Naomi Lewis    (essay date 1972)

[*In the excerpt below, Lewis comments on Ingelow's place in literary history.*]

Why do so few of Jean Ingelow's poems survive today? The fact that she was considered as Laureate in 1892 is not of importance. It was the thinnest possible time; the great old masters were dead; the new ones had not arrived. Who was awarded the prize after all but Alfred Austin? Much more to the point is that an Oxford collected edition of her poems was published in 1913, sixteen years after her death—the real trough-period, one would have thought. It is worth remembering, too, that Fitzgerald was struck by her first volume of poems; that, Tennyson liked her work enough to wish to meet her; that Christina Rossetti thought her a greater writer than herself.

But no one today, however partisan, could call her other than minor. It is no disfavour to say that like many ballads, most of Kipling and certain poems like "Love in a Valley" and "My Dark Rosaleen", her writing, even or especially at its best, seems to be apprehended with some other organ than the head. But she wrote, one suspects, too easily. What can also be said, however, is that in most of her poems, with all the evident influences, the Ingelow *sound* is unmistakable. It reflects, as the movement of words and sentences generally does, something at the core of the writer's vitality, her essential style of thought. (Anyone wishing to test this out might think, say, of Emily Dickinson, Browning, Hardy, Wilde, Henry James.)

**"High Tide on the Coast of Lincolnshire"** shows this note at its best, intense, reverberating, balladlike, but it can be felt in many less familiar pieces. Most often, it is linked with a sea theme, intensifying the effect. Here, an apprentice sings:

> Come out and hear the waters shoot, the
> owlet hoot, the owlet hoot;
> Yon crescent moon, a golden boat, hangs
> dim behind the tree, O!
> The dropping thorn makes white the grass,
> O sweetest lass, and sweetest lass;
> Come out and smell the ricks of hay adown
> the croft with me, O!

A waited ship sails in:

> The moon is bleached as white as wool,
> And just dropping under;
> Every star is gone but three,
> And they hang far asunder—
> There's a sea-ghost all in grey,

A tall shape of wonder!

One hears it in the poem **"Divided"**, with striking image of lovers walking together on opposite sides of a stream:

> The beck grows wider, the hands must sever,
> On either margin, our songs all done . . .
> He prays, "Come over"—I may not follow;
> I cry, "Return"—but he will not come;
> We speak, we laugh, but with voices hollow;
> Our hands are hanging, our hearts are
> numb . . .

This is as personal a poem as we shall find. Unlike Christina Rossetti, she chose to avoid the personal statement. She had learnt from Tennyson the trick of inserting lyrics as songs into longer narrative pieces, never mind the irrelevance. Thus, a blank verse cottage tableau, **"Supper at the Mill"**, contains, as an infant's lullaby, one of her most poignant poems of loss—**"When the Sea Gives up its Dead"**. A parrot in *Mopsa* screeches out another of her enigmatic little conversation dramas. It was one of the many Pre-Raphaelite forms that she used with some success. The poets she most resembles belong to a later date. One thinks now and then of Mary Coleridge, but Mary Coleridge was more piercing and more condensed. One thinks, too, of Charlotte Mew—especially of her haunting sea-poem that Hardy copied and kept—but Charlotte Mew, a greater poet, had a more tormented intensity. A conversation poem, **"Child and Boatman"**, has, even, a curious air of Robert Graves. Whatever it is that these poets fleetingly share, suggests, perhaps, her timbre. (p. 1487)

*Naomi Lewis, "A Lost Pre-Raphaelite," in* The Times Literary Supplement, *No. 3671, December 8, 1972, pp. 1487-88.*

---

## FURTHER READING

Birchenough, Mabel C. "Jean Ingelow." *The Fortnightly Review* LXV, No. 287 (1 March 1899): 487-499.
> Discusses the strengths and weaknesses of Ingelow's poetic style.

Calverley, Charles Stuart. *Fly Leaves.* New York: Holt & Williams, 1872, 233 p.
> Includes a parody of Ingelow's poetic style.

Hamilton, Edith. "Words, Words, Words." In her *The Ever-Present Past*, pp. 151-58. New York: W. W. Norton, 1964.
> Compares Ingelow's use of language with that of twentieth-century Welsh poet Dylan Thomas.

"Miss Ingelow's Poems." *The Saturday Review* (London) 85, No. 2211 (12 March 1898): 362-63.
> Places Ingelow in the context of Victorian culture in a review of *The Poetical Works of Jean Ingelow.*

Peters, Maureen. *Jean Ingelow: Victorian Poetess.* Totowa, N. J.: Rowman and Littlefield, 1972, 112 p.
> Biography of Ingelow. Peters observes: "Had Jean Ingelow died young, she would have been remembered as a

promising lyric writer who might have achieved great things. But she lived too long, until her work was out of fashion and her simple moral standards were scorned."

*Some Recollections of Jean Ingelow and Her Early Friends.* 1901. Reprint. Port Washington, N. Y.: Kennikat Press, 1972, 167 p.
    Memoirs of Ingelow.

Street, Jennette Atwater. "Jean Ingelow." *The Citizen* III, No. 10 (December 1897) 224-25.
    Overview of Ingelow's career, finding that her popularity "is most due to the clear pathetic notes in which she voices the moan of the sea, or the gentle sliding of the river seen far across dappled meadows."

# Guilbert de Pixerécourt

## 1773-1844

(Full name René-Charles Guilbert de Pixerécourt) French dramatist and essayist.

### INTRODUCTION

Pixerécourt was the dominant figure in the creation and popularizing of French melodrama. Taking some of his inspiration from the varied milieu of popular entertainment—music, pantomime, dance, and spectacle—Pixerécourt recognized the dramatic possibilities of incorporating colorful elements of the performing arts into the traditional theater of spoken dialogue, and he did so with an inventiveness that earned him the title "the prince of melodrama" from the critical press.

Pixerécourt was born to an aristocratic family in Nancy and was educated there by Catholic clerics. Beginning at age fourteen, he studied drawing with Lingry, an eminent painter of Nancy, demonstrating considerable artistic talent. In 1789 he began to study law at the Faculté de Nancy, but the upheavals of the French Revolution interrupted his education. On the orders of his father, the young Pixerécourt fled to Coblenz, Germany, to escape persecution by the anti-aristocratic Committee of Public Safety. He returned to France and settled in Paris in 1793, where he lived in straitened circumstances since his parents had lost most of their property during the Revolution. He married in 1795 and was forced to take odd jobs, including, for a time, painting fans, to support his family. Pixerécourt also began to adapt plays from popular novels and had sixteen plays in circulation by 1797, though none had been produced. His earliest work to be staged was *Les petits auvergnats,* presented at the Théâtre de l'Ambigue-Comique in 1797; his real fame began with the performance in 1798 of *Victor; ou, L'enfant du forêt* (*Victor; or, The Child of the Forest* ), a great popular success. Pixerécourt wrote nearly 120 plays—all of them in verse—during the next thirty-five years. Most of them were produced under his own direction. Though he is best known for his melodramas, which comprise approximately half his works, he also wrote many comedies, lyric dramas, comic operas, and vaudeville pieces. By 1822 Pixerécourt had attained such stature that he was invited to manage the floundering Opèra-Comique, one of the classical theaters run by the powerful societies of actors who had excluded Pixerécourt's own plays from their repertory. After restoring the Opèra-Comique to profitability, he resigned in 1827 to take on the directorship of the Théâtre de la Gaîté. In 1835 the Gaîté was destroyed by fire; Pixerécourt was financially ruined by the loss, and he retired from the theater. He died in Nancy in 1844, following a prolonged illness.

Critics commonly divide Pixerécourt's melodramas into

two categories: domestic melodramas dealing with themes of family relations, romance, and bourgeois morality, and historical or epic melodramas, set on a larger political stage. The influential writer and critic Charles Nodier, commenting in 1835 on the plays of Pixerécourt, dated the birth of melodrama to the production in 1800 of Pixerécourt's *Coelina; ou, L'enfant du mystère* (*Coelina, or A Tale of Mystery*). Most critics have not sought to pinpoint the invention of melodrama so absolutely, yet there is broad agreement that, if Pixerécourt did not precisely create the new dramatic form, he defined it through his use of plotting, emotional expressivity, and visual spectacle. In his brief essay "Dernières reflexions de l'auteur sur le mélodrama" ("Last Reflections of the Author on Melodrama"), Pixerécourt wrote that his formula for success in the theater involved a dramatic and moral subject, natural dialogue, a simple and true style, delicate sentiments, probity, heart, the fortunate amalgam of gaiety united to interest, sensibility, the just recompense of virtue, and the punishment of crime. To these he added the spirit of order, taste, and severity, as well as his conviction that melodrama should serve a moralizing end. The plot of *Coelina* established the formula of virtue triumphing over evil and oppression that would dominate the stages of the Boulevard Theaters (theaters of the second rank) for the next thirty years. The stereotypical characters in the formula popularized by Pixerécourt included a courageous and indomitable hero, a vulnerable but steadfast heroine, a villain with an unlimited capacity for evil behavior, and, usually, a comic character (most often a servant).

For the bourgeois and working class throngs who frequented the Boulevard Theaters, the melodramas of Pixerécourt offered an alternative to the classical eighteenth-century dramas that monopolized the Opèra-Comique and the other national theaters of the first rank in Paris. One of the outstanding characteristics of Pixerécourt's plays, as attested by critics and audiences, was their breathless pace, usually brought about by rapid situational changes, unexpected plot twists, and surprising revelations. He also made effective and innovative use of music, song, ballet, and other dance and musical components to advance the plot or to amplify the emotional tenor of specific scenes or situations. For example, elaborate masked ballets or musical pantomimes were staged as means to distract the antagonists at important junctures, or they were skillfully introduced to enable the protagonists to escape, or to communicate in disguise. In his determination to make melodrama a total theatrical experience, Pixerécourt not only wrote the scripts for his plays but directed the production, choreographed the dance sequences, coached the players, devised the scenery, and invented much of the machinery and props for special effects. These effects, intended to add both realism and excitement, were a specialty of Pixerécourt's productions and included such spectacles as the eruption of a volcano, a burning cabin, and the flooding of the entire stage, followed by the heroine's escape by clinging to a floating plank.

In his introduction to Pixerécourt's collected plays, Nodier enumerates in systematic fashion the qualities that distinguish Pixerécourt's melodramas from those of his contemporaries: clarity of exposition, competency of the direction, marvelous skill in the employment of the special effects, progressive and well-managed unfolding of events, bold but rational novelty in staging, and general appropriateness of the style, "capable," in Nodier's words, "of leaving profound traces in the spirit." The popular tragicomedies of the day were frequently chaotic in plot and incoherent, with elements of dance and music introduced seemingly at whim to add spectacle and variety. As Nodier points out, Pixerécourt clarified the plot elements of the melodrama and its unfolding of events—to the point of creating a formula for the introduction and resolution of conflict in the situations of the key characters. Critics agree that, once he defined a recognizable new genre and saw it win popular audiences, Pixerécourt's artistry lay in the continued invention of ingenious variations on this successful formula. However, the simple moral truths and the triumph of the innocent and guileless portrayed by melodrama were eventually replaced in the favor of Parisian audiences by the more emotionally tangled soul-searching of the Romantic drama. Although Pixerécourt's plays were eclipsed by this new kind of drama, they are unanimously judged by critics to have exerted a significant influence on the next generation of popular theater and on

the works of such major French writers as Victor Hugo, Alexandre Dumas the elder, and Alfred de Vigny.

## PRINCIPAL WORKS

*Les petits auvergnats* (comedy) 1797
*Victor; ou, L'enfant de la forêt* (lyric drama) 1798
 [*Victor; or, The Child of the Forest*, 1803]
*Coelina; ou, L'enfant du mystère* (melodrama) 1800
 [*Coelina; or, A Tale of Mystery*, 1802]
*L'homme à trois visages; ou, Le proscrit de Venise* (melodrama) 1801
 [*The Venetian Outlaw, His Country's Friend*, 1805]
*Le pèlerin blanc; ou, Les orphelins du hameau* (melodrama) 1801
 [*The Wandering Boys*, 1830]
*La femme à deux maris* (melodrama) 1802
 [*The Wife of Two Husbands*, 1803]
*Raymond de Toulouse; ou, Le retour de la Terre-Sainte* (lyric drama) 1802
*Les mines de Pologne* (melodrama) 1803
*Tékéli; ou, Le siège de Montgatz* (historical melodrama) 1803
 [*Tékéli; or, The Siege of Mongatz*, 1806]
*Les maures d'espagne; ou, Le pouvoir de l'enfance* (historical melodrama) 1804
*Robinson Crusoë* (melodrama) 1805
*L'ange tutélaire; ou, Le démon femelle* (melodrama) 1808
*La citerne* (melodrama) 1809
*Marguerite d'Anjou* (melodrama) 1810
 [*Margaret (of Anjou), Queen Consort of Henry VI, King of England*, 1826]
*Les ruines de Babylone; ou, Le massacre des barmécides* (historical melodrama) 1810
*Charles-le-téméraire; ou, Le siège de Nancy* (heroic drama) 1814
*Le chien de Montargis; ou, La forêt de Bondy* (historical melodrama) 1814
 [*The Forest of Bondy; or, The Dog of Montargis*, 1815]
*Christophe Colomb; ou, La découverte du nouveau monde* (historical drama) 1815
*Le belvéder; ou, La vallée de l'Etna* (melodrama) 1818
*La fille de l'exilé; ou, Huit mois en deux heures* (historical melodrama) 1819
*Valentine; ou, Le séduction* (melodrama) 1821
 [*Adeline; or, The Victim of Seduction*, 1822]
*Le chateau de Loch-Leven; ou, L'évasion de Marie Stuart* (historical melodrama) 1822
*L'abbaye aux bois; ou, La femme de chambre* (melodrama) 1832
*Théâtre choisi*. 4 vols. (dramas and essays) 1841-43

---

**Alexander Lacey (essay date 1928)**

[*In the following excerpt, Lacey examines Pixerécourt's plays, praising their elements of pathos and sentiment but finding them artistically wanting in comparison to classical tragedy.*]

The plot of Pixerécourt's *L'Homme à trois Visages* is an example of a very complex intrigue, cleverly and palpably arranged by the ingenuity of the author, entangled and disentangled by means that are quite artificial and extraordinary. Disguises, ruses, letters, pretences, discoveries, rumours, refutations of rumours, arrests, escapes—such are the means used to create an atmosphere of suspense and excitement, a series of thrills. The outcome of the play does not in the least depend on character, or on the logic of circumstances, but merely on accident, on the clever and frequent use of external means.

The following, therefore, are the chief characteristics of the melodrama of Pixerécourt in respect of dramatic values: (1) a sharp conflict of wills (the good *vs.* the bad) leading inevitably to an outward show of violence; (2) physical action for its own sake; (3) complexity of intrigue; (4) suspense and excitement produced by arbitrary means. (pp. 10-11)

• • • • •

Both Fate and mistaken identity are made use of extensively by Pixerécourt. A good example of the irony of fate may be taken from *Cœlina*. The criminal Truguelin is continually being brought face to face with the fact of his crime, committed eight years before the play is supposed to begin. It is made to appear throughout the whole play that Destiny (or, to use a modern term, Providence) is here playing the part of avenger, making use of the very victims of the crime for the purpose of ruining the criminal. There is the same irony of fate in *L'Homme à trois Visages,* where Providence, in the person of Vivaldi, works to bring about the downfall of the traitor Orsano. The same use of the irony of fate is seen in *La Femme à deux Maris,* in *La Citerne,* in almost any of the plays of Pixerécourt. (pp. 12-13)

Hegel . . . maintains that:

> tragedy depends primarily on the collision of spiritual forces in individuals whose action has an aspect both of rightness and of wrongness. These forces, especially in ancient tragedy, cannot be detached from the individual's personality, and involve, in the issue by which the conflict restores unity to the spiritual world, the destruction of the persons who represent them. This identification of the entire personalities with their substantial aims or rights is the secret of the unhappy ending. If the connection between character and issues is lost, and the story becomes one of pure innocence oppressed by the chances of a hostile world, then the tragic element is destroyed, and the effect is no longer tragic, but an idle or futile melancholy or horror.

This lack of connection between character and issues is the weak point in the construction of melodrama, and is clearly exemplified in the works of Pixerécourt. There is no attempt to identify personality with any "substantial aims or rights", no "collision of spiritual forces in individuals", no co-existence of rightness and wrongness in the actions or the character of either hero or villain.

Horror, not tragedy, is universally present in the melodrama of Pixerécourt. There may or may not be an unhappy ending, but there is bound to be plenty of the horrible. Usually the horror lies merely in the sensation of extreme danger, which passes away as quickly as it arose. There is an approach to tragedy, but not its complete attainment. The emotions of pity and terror are indeed aroused, but only to be at once alleviated. Often, however, the element of horror is heightened by the violent death of the villain, or by the sudden overwhelming of all those fighting on the side of wrong.

This inordinate cult of the horrible explains why melodrama has so often been defined as "popular tragedy". It seeks to arouse, in a clumsy and illogical way, and by the easiest means possible, the same emotions as are aroused in true tragedy. But to counterbalance this intention there is also the desire for a "satisfactory" ending, so that the audience may leave the theatre with a sense of justice done, a stronger belief in the universal triumph of good. The horrible in melodrama is usually of momentary duration only, an excitement of the nerves which soon passes away. Even in such plays as *Valentine* and *La Tête de Mort,* both of which end unhappily, the lack of logical consequence, the insistence on a moral purpose, the failure to identify character and issues, the exaggerated use of external and arbitrary means, all tend to lessen whatever tragic value might exist.

Further, the nobler emotions aroused by true tragedy are lacking in the plays of Pixerécourt. There is nothing of that sense of awe in the presence of something heroic and grand, of something in human nature that conquers death, which we are conscious of in real tragedy. The hero or heroine represents nothing universal or profound in human nature. We are not, even in the case of Valentine, stirred to wonder at the nobility of her character or the fundamental inevitability of her final act, we are simply moved (if at all) to pity the plight of one so unfortunate. It is by means of such evocations of pathos that Pixerécourt seeks to create a sort of emotional response replacing the more profound and lasting emotions of tragedy.

Just as it is necessary to distinguish carefully between the idea of the dramatic and that of the tragic, so must we separate the tragic from the pathetic. The tragic is always more or less pathetic but the pathetic is not always tragic. An event or a situation is pathetic if it inspires pity, but, as Hegel says, "pity for mere misfortune, like fear of it, is not *tragic* pity or fear". The latter "appeals not only to our sensibilities and instinct of self-preservation, but also to our deeper mind or spirit". Tragedy begets pity, but there must accompany that feeling the realization of the inevitableness of the calamity, as well as the sense of awe in the presence of noble human character. The spectacle of suffering in itself is pathetic, without reference to the how or why of the suffering. But such pathos is not *tragic* pathos since it does not appeal to the "deeper mind or spirit". To feel pity is in the power of everyone human, but to experience tragic pathos one must be able to trace the lines of action, to determine issues, to calculate the effect of circumstances upon character, to decide as to what is or is not inevitable. It is true that the spectator must do this "après coup", and not beforehand like the dramatist, yet one must be something of a dramatist oneself in order to enter fully into the spirit and emotion of a really tragic situation.

Pity itself, though not tragic pity, is easy to inspire. It is also easily felt, especially by the unsophisticated, in whom the power of the emotions is greater than that of the reason. Hence a type of drama that is confessedly popular (such as melodrama) will be sure to harp rather loudly on the pathetic string. The author of melodrama is a failure if he cannot move his audience, or a large part of it, to tears—"Vive le mélodrame, où Margot a pleuré!" Yet there is absolutely no "appeal to the deeper mind or spirit".

The pathetic element plays an important part indeed in the melodrama of Pixérécourt. It accounts for his constant use of certain stock characters, such as the oppressed orphan, the persecuted heroine, the helpless old man. It accounts also for the continual harping on family affections, the filial duties, the respect due to the aged and the infirm. Yet this sort of pathetic effect, too frequently sought and too easily obtained, is far removed from that nobler pathos aroused in the spectator by the contemplation of an awful, but inevitable, tragic dénouement.

Examples of Pixérécourt's use of the pathetic as a means of obtaining a cheap emotional effect are not difficult to find. In *Victor ou l'Enfant de la Forêt* there is the pathetic situation of the lovers, who are in danger of separation from no fault of their own, there is the pleading of Victor with his father that the latter might turn away from a bandit's life and thus make happiness possible for all concerned, there is finally the death of the bandit-father, his confession of a wasted life, his belated exhibition of parental affection—all calculated to bring tears into the eyes of the unsophisticated spectators. In *L'Homme à trois Visages* we have the oft-repeated pleadings of Rosemonde on behalf of her lover Vivaldi. In *La Femme à deux Maris* there is the spectacle of a pure, innocent woman persecuted by a worthless husband whom she has long thought dead. In the same play we have the sight of an injured daughter begging for a restored place in the affection of her afflicted father, who scorns her because he thinks her unworthy of his love. Again and again in Pixérécourt we have a pathetic situation arising from the separation of members of the same family. The grief of a mother whose children are torn from her to be offered as hostages to a cruel enemy is the subject of *Les Maures d'Espagne.* The condemnation of an innocent man for a crime committed by someone else is the central event in the plot of *Le Chien de Montargis.* One might easily multiply examples of this kind, but sufficient have been given to show that this type of play relies for its main effects on its power of arousing the sentiment of pathos in the hearts of simple-minded spectators. (pp. 13-16)

This brings us to the necessity of distinguishing between the "pathetic" and the "sentimental". The latter term is much broader in meaning, and often includes the former. . . . When we apply the term "sentimental" to a work of art, we mean to express that such a work of art portrays in a touching manner the softer feelings of the heart, ranging from simple humanity, gratitude, fidelity, to love in its various forms. Pity is naturally included among these emotions. The "sentimental" in art is always more or less self-conscious; the "pathetic", on the other hand, is often involuntary. When a writer causes his characters to descant upon their misfortunes, to complain of the hardness of their fate, to protest unduly their generosity, their gratitude, their affection, he is guilty of sentimentality. There is in the "sentimental" an element of exaggeration, a "dwelling-upon" the emotions. Sentimentality, therefore, naturally belongs to the realm of melodrama, which makes its appeal to audiences that delight in strong emotional stimuli. Most people prefer the mere tickling of the emotions to that more profound stirring in which feeling, intellect and will are all concerned. But this tickling of the emotions is beneath the dignity of true art. "Not the presentation of a passion for itself, but of a passion which leads to action is the business of dramatic art", says Freytag.

But the sentimentality which we find in the melodrama of Pixérécourt is not entirely due to the author's desire for a "popular" appeal. It is part of the legacy bequeathed by the eighteenth century. It is largely the continuation into the nineteenth century of the "sensibilité" that marks so much of the literary and dramatic work of the preceding age. In this way, indeed, the melodrama is the offspring of the "drame bourgeois". Pixérécourt continues Diderot, Sedaine and Mercier. (p. 17)

The "sensibilité" of the melodrama is visible in almost every scene and every speech. To it is due the artificiality of the style of language employed by Pixérécourt. The use of the "sentimental epithet" is a noted characteristic of that style: père *tendre,* ami *généreux,* amant *fidèle,* époux *sensible, faible* vieillard, nouvelle *affreuse,* etc. One is reminded of Alfred de Musset's sarcasm on the "abus des adjectifs" in one of the famous "*Lettres de Dupuis et Colonet*".

The morality of the melodrama of Pixérécourt is also part and parcel of its sentimentalism. It is the morality of a Jean-Jacques Rousseau, a type of morality whose source is supposed to be found in the "inherent goodness of human nature". The good characters in Pixérécourt are always "sensible". The bad ones have no feeling at all.

To this exaggerated love of sentiment is also to be attributed the use of a very common melodramatic convention, viz., the voice of the blood. This absurdity, says M. Gaiffe, was not invented by the authors of melodrama, but is found in many works of reputed importance in the eighteenth century. It occurs occasionally, though not very frequently, in Pixérécourt. Cœlina, for example, is conscious of a strange feeling of affection for Francisque long before she knows that he is her father.

It appears to be true, therefore, that the melodrama as constituted by Pixérécourt preserves and continues that "sensibilité" which is one of the chief features of "le drame bourgeois". From the beginning of the Revolution, indeed, the "drame bourgeois" itself was doomed. Driven almost entirely from the stage during the years following the fall of the Bastille, it lost most of its prestige and popularity. It still lingered on for a few years, however, in spite of the opposition of Napoleon, but it no longer held a place of importance on the stage. The melodrama, on the other hand, became more and more prominent and popular after 1800, and to a large extent took the place of "le drame". It also took on many of the characteristics of "le drame". In fact, one may say that the Revolution forced "le drame bourgeois" to find refuge on the boulevards, there to surrender itself to a process of transfusion, as it were, by means of which it yielded up its life-blood to its more plebeian descendant, the melodrama.

We must not forget, however, that while sentiment plays a very great rôle in melodrama yet the predominant interest is that supplied by the intrigue. The plot is after all the most important thing in the play. Sentiment runs a very close second. (pp. 18-19)

The sensational is the strongest element in the melodrama of Pixerécourt.

We may distinguish in the sensational, as far as drama is concerned, two separate species: (1) that which, by means of stage devices, makes a strong appeal to the senses, chiefly those of sight and hearing; (2) that which, by means of unexpected developments in the plot, produces nervous excitement and surprise in the spectator. Appreciation of the latter type of the sensational requires some slight amount of intellectual effort, which is by no means necessary in the case of the former. The one is slightly dramatic, the other merely theatrical.

No dramatist of the age understood the value of scenic effect better than did Pixerécourt. None did so much as he to introduce and maintain it on the stage, and to this fact he owed much of his success; to this fact also the boulevard theatres (La Gaieté and L'Ambigu-Comique) owed their popularity. (p. 19)

The dénouement of *La Citerne* is [an] example of sensational stage effect. . . . (pp. 19-20)

Other typical examples of the art of the decorator and stage mechanic that are found in Pixerécourt are: an eruption of Mt. Etna (in *Le Belvéder*), a flood (*Charles-le-Téméraire*), a river overflowing its banks (*La Fille de l'Exilé*). Lengthy and exact descriptions of the mechanical means used to obtain these effects are given with the text of some of these plays. Music and dancing, tableaux, the firing of guns, the clash of swords occur in almost every play. It is well-nigh impossible to exhaust the fertility of melodramatic invention in matters of mere spectacle.

The second kind of sensational effect is that which depends on sudden and unexpected developments in the plot, by means of which the audience is kept in a constant state of excitement, never knowing what is coming next. Unexpected appearances, chance meetings of long-separated relatives, narrow escapes from death, providential accidents, revelation of important secrets, clever ruses, disguises, mystifications—these are a few of the many methods adopted to keep the nerves of the spectators always on edge. (p. 20)

The stock characters of melodrama are so well known that it is quite unnecessary to consider them at any great length here. One general feature characterizes each and all of them, viz., they exist not as life-like personages but as parts of a machine for carrying on the plot. No noticeable difference in character separates a Cœlina from an Eliza or a Floreska, there is only a difference in situation. The same is true of an Edwinski and a Vivaldi, of an Orsano and a Zamoski. Strictly speaking, there are no characters in melodrama, there are only types, easily recognized and constantly recurring, such as the villain, the hero, the "persecuted innocent" and the clown or "niais". There are also, besides these four principals, two other prevailing types, the "accomplice" and the "faithful friend". But these two are to be considered as mere understudies of their respective principals, the villain and the hero.

The villain possesses nearly all the defects of character known to man, with courage as the only redeeming quality—though often he proves to be a coward at heart. His chief defect, however, is his lack of "sensibilité". He sometimes repents of his crimes, but only when his doom is near, and we doubt the sincerity of his repentance. He is often of high rank, since the greater his power and influence the greater his downfall.

The hero is in most respects the exact opposite of the villain. He is sympathetic, generous, humane, faithful, unselfish, brave, clever (like the villain, only more so), incapable of crime. He is the tool of Providence, and his functions are to protect the innocent, rescue the victim, defeat the wicked schemes of the villain. At times he himself is the persecuted one, as in *L'Homme à trois Visages*. Occasionally the part of hero is taken by a woman, as in *L'Ange Tutélaire*.

The "innocent persécuté" is usually a woman. Like the hero, she is "sensible" and possesses all the good qualities. She can sometimes defend herself (as in *Tékéli*), is often bold enough to defy the villain, is ready to suffer rather than yield to his power, but feminine weakness often gets the better of her, and she faints at the sight of blood.

The clown or "niais" provides comic relief in tense situations. He is usually on the side of the hero, though occasionally he assists the villain (*Tékéli, L'Homme à trois Visages*). In that case he is a coward (Bras-de-Fer, Calcagno). He generally speaks in dialect, uses slang and strange oaths. He is not necessarily stupid, but some times by his cleverness saves the hero from danger or death. The clown was a necessary part of melodrama as far as the audience was concerned. Those plays which had no comic character (such as *Les Maures d'Espagne*) were much less popular and had far shorter runs than the plays which did have such a character. (pp. 20-1)

Pixerécourt often tried to give an illusion of reality to his plays by generous use of "local colour". Thus, in a play of which the setting is in Venice, we have canals, gondolas, grottoes, Venetian palaces and costumes; if savages appear on the stage, we learn what their music, dancing, costumes, dwellings are like; we even hear samples of their speech. In the so-called "historical" melodramas a great number of historical personages are introduced. In some cases the very words used by certain persons are incorporated in the text of the play. In *Charles-le-Téméraire* the stage represents a portion of the city of Nancy as it appeared at the time of the events recorded in the play, the author having taken care to render all details as exact as possible. The same play as printed is preceded by a preface describing the battle of Nancy of 1477, also by several diagrams and a "note historique" in which the author enumerates at length the many documents consulted by him in order to arrive at historical accuracy.

Contrary to what one might expect, the melodrama, at least until about 1815, showed itself fairly respectful of the classical rule regarding the three unities. It is true that there was change of place from one act to another, but the change in most cases was not a great one, while change of place within an act was very rare. In 1814, however, there is a remarkable instance of change of place within an act in the case of *Charles-le-Téméraire* (Act III). But Pixerécourt has the following footnote: "C'est la première fois que je me permets cette violation des règles dramatiques, et j'en demande pardon à mes juges." The unity of time is also largely respected, in that the events of a play all happen within at most twenty-four hours. But in 1818 Pixerécourt set a precedent with his *La Fille de l'Exilé ou huit mois en deux heures.* As in the case of *Charles-le-Téméraire* he excuses himself to public and critics on the ground that "la nature du sujet m'a paru l'exiger". M. Amable Tastu, in the "Notice" to *La Fille de l'Exilé* declares that in the reign of Napoleon ("ce génie de l'autorité") Pixerécourt would not have permitted himself this violation of the rules. Pixerécourt, however, did not suffer for his boldness. The public showed itself ready to admit (at least in a melodrama) what Napoleon would have frowned upon. By 1827 what was, in 1818, considered as a remarkable thing had become quite common on the boulevard, so that nobody wondered at Ducange's *Trente ans ou la Vie d'un Joueur.*

To sum up what has been set forth in this [essay] will be to describe the melodrama of Pixerécourt partly from the negative standpoint and partly from the positive. Taking the negative first we have seen that: (1) the melodrama of Pixerécourt is not dramatic in the fullest sense of the word, but only superficially so. Physical violence for its own sake takes the place of that internal conflict which is essential in drama. The power to produce "emotional response", also essential, is indeed present, but the emotions aroused are of the crudest kind, being merely a succession of exciting thrills mingled with touches of pathos, while the means taken to evoke such feelings are unnatural and arbitrary; (2) melodrama (that of Pixerécourt at least) is not tragedy, in spite of the large place it gives to the "irony of fate" and to the depicting of the horrible. There is, indeed, the possibility of tragedy, but this possibility rarely becomes an actuality. True tragic effect is supplanted by a coarse imitation of tragedy, consisting of isolated, fragmentary outbursts of "futile melancholy and horror". The use of accidental means instead of logical development of the plot; the optimism which always provides a "moral" ending; the failure to identify character with issues—such things as these tend to destroy the germ of tragedy that exists in the melodrama of Pixerécourt.

From the positive point of view the plays of Pixerécourt

abound in pathos, a sort of pathos which is sentimental and not tragic, a pathos which exists for its own sake rather than because of any inevitable association with the issues of a play, a pathos which is often episodic and nearly always exaggerated, which is created for the evident purpose of arousing a cheap emotional response, finally, a sort of pathos which concerns the weak and not the strong, and which therefore falls far short of the nobler pathos of true tragedy.

Finally, we are forced to the conclusion that Pixerécourt relies chiefly upon sentimental, sensational and spectacular effects to win success on the stage. These are the elements that have the strongest "popular" appeal, the elements that require the least amount of intellectual effort on the part of the spectator. Victor Hugo, in the preface to *Ruy Blas,* says that in the public there are three classes: the women, the thinkers and the "crowd". The "crowd" demands action, sensation, the pleasure of the eyes; the women demand passion, emotion, the pleasure of the heart; the thinkers demand character-study, the pleasure of the mind. The melodrama of Pixerécourt, like its successor, the Romantic drama, seeks to satisfy the demand of the first two classes—the third is left to shift for itself. (pp. 22-4)

> *Alexander Lacey, in his* Pixerécourt and the French Romantic Drama, *1928. Reprint by The University of Toronto Press, 1969, 88 p.*

## O. G. Brockett (essay date 1959)

[*An American scholar, Brockett had a distinguished academic career that included endowed chairs in theater and drama. In the following excerpt, he analyzes the uses of ballet and pantomime in the melodramas of Pixerécourt.*]

> Soir et matin l'on danse
>   Le rigadon.
> Zig, zag, don, don;
> Rien n'echauff' la cadence
> Comme un' bonne action.

To this reassuring refrain, according to the stage directions, "tout le monde danse," and the curtain falls on *Coelina, ou l'enfant du mystère,* one of the earliest melodramas of the prolific Guilbert de Pixerécourt. First produced at the Théâtre Ambigu-Comique on September 2, 1800, the play is considered by some authorities to have supplied a definitive formula for the genre which was to dominate the boulevard theaters of Paris during the first thirty years of the nineteenth century. One of the features of *Coelina* which was to be repeated by Pixerécourt and other playwrights until it became an almost universal characteristic of the early French melodrama was the use of dance, illustrated in *Coelina* both in the final scene of dancing and singing and in the more elaborate ballet of Act II. So typical was the presence of dancing in the early French melodrama that Ginisty, attempting a generic definition of *le mélodrame,* lists the presence of ballet as one of the "laws" of the genre.

The practice of including one or more ballets within the dramatic framework was a feature which the French melodrama probably inherited from two of its ancestors, the hybrid *pantomime dialoguée* of the eighteenth-century popular theater and the more elevated *drame lyrique,* in both of which dancing was a traditional feature. [The critic adds in a footnote that "Pixerécourt's *Victor, ou l'enfant de la forêt* (1797), which is often cited as the first French melodrama, was originally written as a *drame lyrique,* a form of opera containing extensive spoken dialogue."] Moreover, during the years just preceding the emergence of melodrama as a distinguishable form, the popular taste for ballet had rapidly expanded, and the secondary theaters had begun to bring this type of entertainment, formerly reserved for aristocratic spectators, to the lower-class audiences of the boulevard theaters; the lavishly mounted "grand ballets" of the Théâtre Porte Saint-Martin, for example, rivaled those of the celebrated Académie de Danse. Thus there were obvious reasons why Pixerécourt and other early writers of melodrama should have chosen to preserve this popular feature of boulevard entertainment.

The importance assigned to the ballet by contemporary audiences and critics is indicated by the fact that when, toward the end of the eighteenth century, Paris newspapers began to take notice of the boulevard productions, their reviews almost invariably referred to the ballet, and, as melodramas grew in popularity and commanded more attention from the press, criticism of the dancing grew progressively more detailed and explicit. The name of the ballet master, who trained the *corps de ballet,* designed the dances, and supervised their execution, usually appeared in the newspaper reviews and on the playbills (along with the names of the author and the composer of the music) and in most cases was also recorded in published editions of Pixerécourt's plays. A sizable permanent ballet company was maintained at each of the three Paris theaters where most of Pixerécourt's melodramas were produced (the Gaîté, the Ambigu-Comique, and the Porte Saint-Martin), and the finish with which the ballets were designed and executed is indicated by contemporary references comparing them with the ballets of the Paris opera.

Celebrated in his own day as the "roi du mélodrame," Pixerécourt was among the most influential and successful playwrights in France during the period of approximately thirty years that he furnished melodramas to the secondary theaters. Although his plays seem naïve, strained, and conventional today, it is not difficult to discover in them the source of Pixerécourt's reputation, for, with all their weaknesses of style, thought, and characterization, they nevertheless demonstrate an impressive mastery of theatrical effects. Pixerécourt's competency in this respect is nowhere seen more clearly than in his utilization of the ballet, inherited from earlier theatrical forms, to serve other purposes in addition to its traditional function of providing a stage spectacle.

The obvious and primary purpose of the ballet was, of course, to enhance the visual appeal of the play. Like the lavish and spectacular scenery, which grew progressively more elaborate during the period 1800-1830, the ballet of the melodrama was designed, above all, to furnish a colorful and breath-taking display for audiences relatively in-

different to subtleties of style or characterization but avidly responsive to stage spectacle. Pixerécourt's stage directions for one of the ballets of *Les Ruines de Babylone,* for example, illustrate the type of effect he sought:

> Au son d'une musique bruyante et guerrière, on voit l'armée traverser le pont couvert dans un direction oblique. Elle disparait un moment, puis elle défile derrière la grille du sérail. Giafar, environné de nombreux trophées de sa victoire, est porté sur un magnifique palanquin. Le peuple le précède et le suit en dansant et en lui jetant des fleurs. . . . Au signal de Raymond, on exécute une fête des plus brillantes, dans laquelle se trouve réuni tout ce que le goût et la volupté ont de plus séduisant et de plus enchanteur.

Similar stage directions, emphasizing the color, movement, and visual splendor of the ballet, occur in many of the melodramas. That Pixerécourt succeeded in utilizing the dance as a means of brilliant stage spectacle is clearly indicated by the contemporary reviews, such as the following description of the production of *Les Ruines de Babylone:*

> Jamais, peut-être, on, n'a vu au théâtre des Boulevards des décorations aussi fraîches, des costumes aussi riches, des ballets aussi gracieux. . . . Une sèche analyse ne pourrait jamais, d'ailleurs, donner qu'une bien faible idée de l'intérêt, du mouvement, de la pompe répandus dans cet ouvrage, et les plus belles phrases du monde ne pourraient remplacer cette danse originale d'esclaves noirs, ou ce pas brillant de deux guerriers combattant et dansant tout à la fois.

The dances in many other melodramas were similarly praised for their spectacular appeal. The noted critic Geoffroy, reviewing *L'Ange tutélaire, ou le démon femelle,* expressed particular admiration for the "ingénieuse et originale" masquerade dance, calling it "un des grands charmes de ce spectacle," and another critic declared that this ballet was so appealing that it alone would arouse the interest of the public. Parisian audiences undoubtedly enjoyed the melodrama ballet for its own sake, simply as a diverting display of movement and color, lavish and often exotic in its setting and costuming and filled with impressive feats of dexterity and grace.

While it never ceased to fulfil its primary function as a source of colorful spectacle, the ballet was also used by Pixerécourt in certain plays as a means of forwarding the plot. In a number of his melodramas the dancing is successfully integrated into the story; often the occasion of the dance makes possible or plausible some important twist in the plot. In *Marguerite d'Anjou,* for example, the brigand who has befriended Marguerite leads a troupe of wood-cutters in some rustic dances which enable Marguerite and her son to escape from the villainous Glocester, a device which won praise from Geoffroy for its ingenuity and originality. In *Les Ruines de Babylone* the comic character, Raymond, performs a "boufonne" dance to distract the attention of Haroun-al-Raschid, whose sister has received a visit from Giafar, to whom she is secretly wed. In *L'Homme à trois visages* a masked ball in the gardens of the Doge of Venice provides the hero's confidant the opportunity to enter the garden in disguise and secure an interview with the Doge.

In other plays the use of dance to further the development of the plot is more complex and extensive. The heroine of *La Forteresse du Danube*, an example of the popular role of the *femme travestie*, appears in the disguise of "un Savoyard" at the castle where her father is held prisoner. By entertaining the company with her songs and dances, she gains access to the prison and finally secures her father's escape. Here the crucial events of the plot are dependent upon the characterization of the heroine as a singer and dancer. Still more complex is the use of dance in *L'Ange tutélaire*, in which a masked ball serves as the setting of the third act. The masquerade furnishes the occasion for an intricate plot to assassinate the Duke and an equally elaborate counterplot to save him which involves interchanging a set of disguises. Perhaps the most extensive use of dance to forward the plot occurs in *L'Évasion de Marie Stuart*. In Act II, a peasant dance in a village square gives Catherine Seyton, the queen's goddaughter, and Roland, a young page, the opportunity to meet in disguise and later enables Roland to escape from the villain, Randal, by losing himself in a group of dancing villagers. At the end of the same act a quadrille is proposed as a part of the village festivities, and, since it is a court dance, each peasant participating in it is jokingly assigned the name of one of the Scottish lords who are secretly plotting the rescue of Marie Stuart. By means of calling out directions for the quadrille, Lord Douglass is able to communicate the plan for the queen's escape without exciting the suspicion of her enemies. Contemporary newspaper reviews praised Pixerécourt's inventiveness and ingenuity in adding this touch to the story, which he had taken from Sir Walter Scott.

In other plays the ballet is less essential to the action but still has definite story-telling value because it contains extensive pantomine, another feature which the melodrama owed to its ancestor of the popular boulevard theaters. Many plays contain scenes similar to that in *Le Chien de Montargis*, in which a company of archers enters to martial music, preceded by peasants who dance around them "et leur donnent tous les signes d'admiration que des vainqueurs doivent inspirer." In *Le Belvéder, ou la vallée de l'Etna* villagers convey their felicitations to their Duchess, whose engagement has been announced, in a combination of dance and pantomime: "Dans leur joie qui ne peut plus se contenir, les villageois sautent, s'embrassent et forment des danses trèsanimées." In *Valentine, ou la séduction* winners at a "joûte" are permitted "de manifester leur joie, ce qu'ils font par des danses grotesques." In the ballet of Act III of *La Forteresse du Danube* the heroine, dancing with the *corps de ballet*, pantomimes anxious listening for sounds that will tell her that her father has made his escape.

The stage directions of *Christophe Colombe* call for more extensive ballet-pantomime. The inhabitants of the island on which Columbus has landed, upon receiving gifts from the Spaniards, express their joy through "gambades et des contorsions plaisantes." This ballet includes elaborate pantomime in which the savage Kérébek, jealous of the attentions being paid by a native girl to a young Spaniard, separates the couple and shuts the girl in a hut, despite the disapproval of the ruler of the island, all of which is conveyed during a scene of general dancing. When the savages and Spaniards have concluded their dances, "les sauvages frottent leur nez contre celui des Européens," thus conveying their friendship. In several melodramas a complicated ballet containing much pantomime occurs at the end of the play and is combined with an elaborate final tableau. The stage directions for the ending of *Les Maures d'Espagne*, for example, suggest the amount of action which sometimes occurred after the last line of dialogue had been spoken:

> Réunion des deux tribus. Tout se confond, on s'embrasse, tout respire le bonheur et la joie. Fête militaire, danses et evolutions, dans lesquelles doivent figurer les enfants, s'il est possible de les employer, soit à danser, soit à des exercices militaires; les enfants d'Abular entourent Almanzor; Ali est dans les bras de Zima et d'Abular. La fête se termine par un tableau général, dans lequel les enfants sont élevés sur des boucliers. La toile tombe.

Similarly, *Tékeli* closes with a lavish *fête militaire*, including "jeux, combats simulés, danses et évolutions," at the end of which the victorious Tékeli is enthroned. In *Le Pêlerin blanc, ou les orphelins du hameau* the inhabitants of a village celebrate the return of the Count de Castelli by a dance in which each participates and "chacun imagine quelque moyen de lui témoigner particulièrement le plaisir qu'il a de le revoir."

Although his plots abound in improbabilities and startling *coups de théâtre* which could hardly be called realistic, Pixerécourt obviously took care to motivate the presence of the *corps de ballet* and to provide an occasion in which dancing would appear natural and appropriate. [The critic adds in a footnote that "in providing for the ballet, Pixerécourt was helped by the type of setting which had been created by the demands of his plots. The situations treated in early French melodramas required that the action should take place in a public place or in a place to which many people had access. In such a setting the group dances could occur with greater probability than in the private rooms which served as settings for the domestic melodramas of other countries and periods."] If the setting is a village square, the dancers are costumed as villagers; if a country exterior, as peasants of the region; in other settings the dancers are supposed to be servants, friends, or guests of the principal characters. Pixerécourt's favorite device for motivating the ballet was to introduce a fête of some kind. In *Coelina, La Tête du mort,* and *Le Belvéder* the fête is held in honor of an engagement. The *fête militaire*, or celebration of a victory at war, provides the pretext for a ballet in *Les Maures d'Espagne, Les Ruines de Babylone,* and *Tékeli*. A ball serves as the occasion for a ballet in *Valentine, L'Ange tutélaire,* and *L'Homme à trois visages*. Scenes of village merriment or rustic holidays provide the excuses for dancing in *L'Évasion de Marie Stuart, La Citerne, La Forteresse du Danube,* and *Les Mines de Pologne,* and many plays end with dances motivated by the characters' joy at the happy outcome of events. Although these devices become conventionalized and predictable over the thirty-year span during which Pixerécourt wrote for the boulevard theaters, they nevertheless indicate competency in the technical problems of motivation and preparation.

More indicative of Pixerécourt's mastery of theatrical effects is his use of the ballet as a means of creating or heightening dramatic contrast. The device of placing a scene of gaiety and merriment immediately before a somber or threatening passage was repeatedly exploited by Pixerécourt; often such alterations in mood are achieved by the use of dance. In *Coelina,* for example, the dancing in celebration of the heroine's engagement is interrupted by the delivery of a letter announcing that Coelina is not really the niece of M. Dufour, but "l'enfant du crime et de l'adultère," a piece of news which produces "stupéfaction générale." In *Les Maures d'Espagne* an elaborate fête celebrating a recent victory of the Abencerrages is immediately followed by the discovery that these forces have suffered an unexpected and crushing defeat. Similarly, in *La Femme à deux maris* a scene of animated dancing and merrymaking is suddenly interrupted by an ominous knock on the door and the arrival of the menacing villain. In *La Citerne* the revels of fisherfolk picnicking at the seashore are interrupted by a frightful tempest in which the heroine narrowly escapes drowning. The fête celebrating the betrothal in *La Tête du mort* is dramatically interrupted by a bandit, disguised as a beggar, who leaps from a balcony and attacks the young hero, while the heroine of *Valentine,* who has been betrayed by the son of the Count de Noralberg, throws herself into a river during an elegant party in the Count's garden. Similar examples of the alteration of a gay scene of dancing with a somber passage appear in other plays; in thus using the ballet to secure dramatic contrast, Pixerécourt demonstrated his skill in creating effects of great theatricality.

---

**Pixerécourt's is a theatre of grandiose and absolute moral entities put within the reach of the people, a moral universe made available. That melodrama should have been born during the Revolution, and come of age with *Coelina* in 1800, is far from an accident: in both its audience and its profound subject, it is essentially democratic.**

**—Peter Brooks, in The Melodramatic Imagination, 1976.**

---

It is widely recognized that well before the manifestoes of French Romanticism many of the innovations preached by Hugo and others had already made their appearance in the boulevard theaters. Among the characteristics associated with Romantic drama which had already developed in the humbler *mélodrame* was the exploitation of local color and the related attempt at historical reconstruction. Although the melodramas of Pixerécourt gave very imperfect reproductions of earlier periods and remote places, nevertheless they were the first conscientious attempts in this direction and were the more significant as innovations because the boulevard theaters had hitherto dealt almost exclusively with fabulous adventures. In his preface to *Christophe Colombe,* Pixerécourt drew attention to his realistic rendering of the details of shipboard life and the characteristics of the Caribbean natives, declaring that "tout y est strictement conforme à la vérité" and citing as an authority for the language he had given to the "Caraïbes" ("l'idiome des Antilles") a *Dictionnaire Caraïbe.* For this and other melodramas his stage directions provide detailed descriptions of costumes, settings, and pantomime. For plays such as *Charles-le-Téméraire, ou le siège de Nancy* and *Latude, ou trente-cinq ans de captivité,* both of which were based upon historical events, Pixerécourt consulted many sources, some of which he reproduced in their entirety in the published edition of his plays, calling attention to the authenticity of his material. Throughout the *Théâtre choisi* the reader encounters footnotes verifying the accuracy of details of action, setting, or dialogue.

Pixerécourt's interest in local color found typical expression in the ballets. His stage directions for the dances of such plays as *Robinson Crusoë* and *Christophe Colombe,* with their Caribbean settings, specify movements which were intended to be not only diverting but also authentic—"suivant l'usage de leur pays," in Pixerécourt's words. Describing the dances of the savages of *Robinson Crusoë,* who pantomime their delight at the prospect of devouring a captive, Pixerécourt stipulates that their movements should be "toujours à la file l'un de l'autre et jamais en rang," and cites as his authority for these and similar details "l'ouvrage de P. *Lafittau,* intitulé: *Mœurs des sauvages Américains.*" The dances of *Christophe Colombe* are also designed to present novel details for which Pixerécourt again claims authenticity. The ballet which opens the third act of *La Fille de l'exilé,* set at Moscow in front of the Kremlin, features a variety of Russian folk dances obviously selected to enhance "la couleur locale":

> Au lever du rideau, des feux sont allumés sur différents points de la ville; à la lueur de ces feux et de branches de sapins qu'ils tiennent à la main, on voit des Kamtchadals, des Samoïdes, des Kourils, des Kouriaques et des Tartares de tout âge et de tout sexe, qui s'abandonnent à l'effervesence de leur joie. Ils exécutent des danses originales usitées dans le pays.

Pixerécourt's awareness of the value of dancing for local color effects is also illustrated by his stage directions for a ballet in *La Tête du mort,* set in Naples:

> Ballet très-gai, qui se composera des danses du pays, exécutées par des paysans et des paysannes des îles de Caprée et d'Ischia, dont le costume est si pittoresque.

In *Les Mines de Pologne* Polish peasants "exécutent différentes danses du pays," while *Le Monastère abandoné* opens with a scene of dancing by peasants of the French Alps.

In other plays dancing is combined with other types of spectacle in such a way as to enrich the local color effect. Act II of *L'Évasion de Marie Stuart,* set in a public square of "le Bourg de Kinross" with the lake and chateau of Loch Leven visible in the background, opens with extraordinary movement on stage: "la scène présente un tableau varié, piquant et surtout très-animé." The villagers are entertained simultaneously by a Scottish Highlander with a dancing bear, an Indian juggler who tosses balls into the air "avec une prodigieuse dextérité," and a shooting gallery in which a villager shoots a parrot and then is led in triumph in a noisy cortege, preceded by a bagpiper and drummer. Meanwhile, there is dancing and music of a type which is supposed to be characteristically Scottish:

> Tout ce qui se passe en avant n'empêche pas les danses qui ont lieu au fond et qui dureront pendant tout l'acte, en observant que, quand l'intérêt de la scène ne permet pas que l'on voie les danseurs, on entend dans le lointain des airs de gigue, danse favorite des montagnards écossais.

A similar scene of unusual variety and movement in which the details have been selected to enhance the local color effect occurs in Act II of *La Femme à deux maris,* set in the countryside near Antwerp, in which the scenery and action are supposed to re-create on stage a painting of village dancing by the seventeenth-century Flemish painter Téniers. Other examples of the use of ballet to secure local color effects occur in *Les Ruines de Babylone* (Arabian dances), *Les Maures d'Espagne* (Moorish dances), *Le Belvéder* (Sicilian dances), *L'Homme à trois visages* (Venetian masked ball), *Tékeli* (Hungarian dances), *L'Ange tutélaire* (Italian court dances), and *Pizarro, ou la conquête de Peru* (ceremonial dances of ancient Peru). Other plays feature peasant dances of the countries in which the action takes place. Since very few of Pixerécourt's melodramas are set in France, and those which are (*Le Chien de Montargis* and *Coelina,* for example) have been removed from the contemporary scene either by placing them in an earlier period or in an area remote from Paris, practically all the dances of Pixerécourt's plays may be said to have contributed to the creation of local color.

In addition to the use of different settings for the ballet, Pixerécourt has found other means of achieving variety from play to play, for, although the presence of dancing might be a convention of the melodrama, the type of dancing was not conventionalized. For some plays Pixerécourt's stage directions specify a particular dance: in *Coelina,* the *rigaudon;* in *L'Évasion de Marie Stuart,* the *gigue* and the *quadrille;* in *La Citerne,* the *fandango;* in *Les Mines de Pologne,* the *valse.* In addition to these and the regional folk dances and dance-pantomimes described earlier, the stage directions and contemporary reviews refer to two special kinds of dancing: the "danse grotesque" and the "danse armée," both of which may well have been traditional features in the repertoires of the boulevard troupes. In *Les Ruines de Babylone* mute slaves of the seraglio dance "d'une manière grotesque," as do the savages of *Robinson Crusoë* and *Christophe Colombe,* while the winners of the joust in *Valentine* perform "danses grotesques" to express their joy. Judging from the

stage directions and from contemporary reviews, the grotesque dance resembled or perhaps included acrobatics, tumbling, and various feats of strength and dexterity. In this respect the appeal of the melodrama ballet would seem to have differed little from the exhibitions of tumbling, tight-rope walking, and sword-swallowing which had delighted audiences at the early boulevard theaters and, before that, at the booths of the ancient fairs. The other special dance which receives frequent mention in Pixerécourt's stage directions is that of the *fêtes militaires,* in which dancing was combined with sword-play, saber-fights, or precision marching. Typical of this kind of dance are the ballet with which *Tékeli* ends, which includes "jeux, combats simulés, danses et évolutions," and a saber dance performed by the Tartar bandits of *La Fille d'exilé.* In *Les Maures d'Espagne,* following a passage performed by the women of the *corps de ballet,* the male dancers perform as follows:

> . . . les guerriers s'avancent et exécutent d'abord une course de bagues, ensuite le jeu de cannes, qui consiste à frapper les boucliers en cadence avec de légers roseaux qu'on jette en l'air pour les ressaisir adroitement et recommencer le même exercice.

Novelty was also obtained by the occasional use of children to perform the dances, as in *Les Maures d'Espagne* and *L'Ange tutélaire;* at the Gaîté, where the latter was produced, the ballet company included approximately ten children, some, if not all, of whom were the offspring of the famous ballet master Hullin, who designed the dances for many of Pixerécourt's plays.

Further variety was achieved by varying the number of dancers executing the ballet. Although the great majority of the ballets are group dances executed by the *corps de ballet,* some solo dances are also indicated. In *Les Mines de Pologne* a six-year-old girl is supposed to perform a solo dance with pantomime. Young women disguised as men (the popular *femmes travesties*) perform solo dances in *La Forteresse du Danube* and *La Citerne.* The male comic role is given one or more solo dances in several plays, among them *Robinson Crusoë, Les Ruines de Babylone,* and *La Forteresse du Danube.* In other plays leading characters participate in group dances, as in *L'Évasion de Marie Stuart* and *La Tête du Mort.* In some plays Pixerécourt considered the dancing of the leading characters so important that he selected and trained dancers to play these roles. He cast a dancer, Mlle Caroline Soissons, who had had little experience in spoken drama, in the role of Clara in *La Citerne,* and he selected the well-known *première danseuse,* Mlle Queriau, to play the leading role in *La Forteresse du Danube.*

An examination of the function of ballet in the work of Pixerécourt thus reveals that he skillfully exploited dance to serve various dramatic or theatrical purposes. The melodrama ballet was, as Ginisty remarked, "un hors-d'œuvre dont on ne pouvait se passer," and Pixerécourt's practice was such as to increase rather than decrease its popularity. But the advent of Romantic drama brought new tastes to the boulevards, as a result of which the melodrama was to undergo a period of transformation from which it would emerge shorn of the ballets which had once figured so prominently in the genre. (pp. 154-61)

> O. G. Brockett, "The Function of Dance in the Melodramas of Guilbert de Pixerécourt," in Modern Philology, *Vol. 56, No. 3, February, 1959, pp. 154-61.*

## O. G. Brockett  (essay date 1959)

[*In the following excerpt, Brockett discusses how Pixeré-court realized his philosophy of unified theater by personally serving as director, stage manager, choreographer, and scene designer for his own plays.*]

> A theatre piece can only be well conceived, well constructed, well written, well rehearsed, and well played under the auspices and care of one man alone, having one taste, one judgment, one mind, one heart, and one opinion.

This rather extreme statement of the concept of "unity of production" was not written by a follower of Gordon Craig; it is a pronouncement of René Charles Guilbert de Pixerécourt, "le roi du mélodrame," concerning his own practice during the period 1800-1830. Today Pixerécourt is remembered primarily as one of the creators of melodrama as a separate genre, but the success of his melodramas undoubtedly owed much to his skill as director and regisseur.

Pixerécourt was a prolific playwright, turning out approximately 120 plays, which according to his own estimate were given a total of 30,000 performances. Although the number of performances might be questioned, there is little doubt that between 1800 and 1830 Pixerécourt was the most prosperous of French dramatists and the acknowledged leader in the field of popular entertainment. Even in his own day, however, it was widely recognized that Pixerécourt's plays were full of improbabilities, and since the late nineteenth century his works have been treated with little more than condescension. No one familiar with Pixerécourt's career, on the other hand, has ever attempted to dismiss his achievement as a "man of the theatre." The attitude of his own time is succinctly summarized in a contemporary review of one of his plays:

> Everyone, including his rivals, is united in according him the palm in a genre which requires much imagination and especially a great facility and knowledge of the theatre: it is in this that the talent of M. de Pixerécourt consists. . . . He excells in those little details of scene which create the greatest effect; he accumulates them to such a degree in each play that the spectator hasn't time to notice their improbability. . . . The interest of the play comes from an infinity of details which the pantomime and acting render effective and which only appear cold and bizarre in reading.
>
> [*Petites Affiches,* June 3, 1808]

Modern critical opinion is well illustrated by Emile Faguet's estimate: "Pixerécourt was ignorant of style and perhaps even of spelling, but he knew *the* theatre and he created *a* theatre."

Pixerécourt himself recognized that much of his success came from the polished productions given his plays rather than from the writing alone.

> Undoubtedly I have been indebted for part of my success to the detailed and exacting care with which I have constantly presided over rehearsals.
>
> ["**Dernières Reflexions**"]

And one of his most steadfast beliefs, reinforced by continued success, was that "it is necessary for the dramatic author to know how to put his play on the stage himself." It was in this practice, that of acting as director and regisseur for his own plays, that Pixerécourt's procedures perhaps differed most from those of his contemporaries and especially from those of the major theatres.

The major theatres were controlled by the actors (the *societaires*) who determined the repertory, conducted the rehearsals, and attended to all details of the theatre. Dramatic authors were entirely at their mercy; plays were sometimes accepted and never performed, or frequently under-rehearsed and thus poorly played; the actors were jealous of their authority and convinced of their own artistic superiority. At first Pixerécourt attempted to write for the major theatres and had a few plays accepted by them, but his experiences with these companies were generally unpleasant. In later years he gave the following explanation of why he had chosen to work in the secondary theatres:

> The actors [*societaires*] are too insolent, too sure of the power of devouring at their ease the product of their receipts. Thanks to the way they manage their affairs, no author can be sure of seeing his play produced, even if he lived twenty-five years (at least it was so in the past century and even during the Empire). Since I wished to be played for sure and not to put myself at the mercy of these fellows, I therefore adopted a preference for the secondary theatres. There I found among the artists a great docility and flexible talent, which contributed to my success.
>
> ["Souvenirs du Jeune Age, et Détails sur ma Vie" *Théâtre Choisi,* I, xl]

Although prior to 1822 Pixerécourt was never the manager of a theatre, he was accorded what today would be the powers of producer and director when his plays were presented, and, as he put it, he reigned "as an absolute king." That Pixerécourt did act as a regisseur is indicated by the testimony of Alexandre Piccini [in a letter dated October, 1840], who composed the music for a number of Pixerécourt's plays.

> He presided at this fine ensemble, for he not only was the author of his plays but he also designed the costumes, gave the painters the plan of his decorations, explained to the machinist the means of executing the movements. Scene by scene he gave the actors the intentions of their roles. His works would have gained a great deal if he had been able to play all the parts himself.

In his relations with actors he was, it would appear, a director in the modern sense of that word. This contention is borne out by Piccini's statements as well as by other sources. Dalayrac, a contemporary composer whose works were in the repertory of the Opéra-Comique, wrote to Pixerécourt in 1805:

> How fortunate you are. . . . Your wishes never encounter the slightest obstacle, the actors submit to all your desires. I have never seen a *mise en scène* more adroit and better worked out. The carpentry of your plays is perfect, but one must give much credit to the way in which you direct the rehearsals. You bestow talent and harmony upon persons who were never aware of it before you. . . . What a difference from our *societaires,* so cold, so demanding, and especially so ungrateful . . . .
>
> Never attach yourself to the great theatres; the *societaires* are incapable of the least gratitude.

The better actors of the day were, of course, attached to the primary theatres; consequently, as Dalayrac's letter indicates, it was often necessary for Pixerécourt to train his actors. Charles Nodier, a leading writer of the period and a member of the French Academy, stated that Pixerécourt, especially in the early years, had to work without any of the outstanding actors of the time, in addition to other handicaps.

> Independently of his play, he had to create the setting, the *mise en scène,* the execution, actors to play it, and even a public to be moved by it. The rehearsal was, for M. de Pixerécourt, the education of the actor. The performance was, for M. de Pixerécourt, the education of the audience. All this was done, moreover, and it was M. de Pixerécourt who did it; and, if no one has said it before, there is no one at least who can contest it.
>
> [*Théâtre Choisi,* I, xiv]

Pixerécourt was notoriously painstaking and, it would seem, unfeeling toward his actors, from whom he demanded absolute obedience and perfection. One of his colleagues has left a description of his relationship with the actors.

> He had a twisted figure, the energetic glance of a bad-humored lord of the manor who had slept poorly and who had the gout. . . . When he came to his rehearsals in the morning, he was a tiger of severity. The actors trembled like slaves before the whip of their master; he did not pardon the slightest negligence, the least delay in duty, without imposing severe fines, and when an actor was distinguished in a role, he was not the man to compliment him, but he invariably reproached him for not having been good enough, polished enough.
> [Claude Louis Marie de Rochefort, *Memoires d'un Vaudevilliste,* 1863]

This evidence is confirmed by one of Pixerécourt's friends.

> Doubtless your excessive severity is sometimes tiring for the actors, but in any case you are acting in the best interest of everyone.
> [letter from Dalayrac, *Théâtre Choisi,* II]

Pixerécourt's own statements indicate that he considered strict discipline, enforced by one person, to be the primary requisite for success in the production of plays.

> To those essential qualities [of good plays] I should add the spirit of order so necessary in any business, next the taste and discipline which ought to reign in rehearsals and which have become a means of almost certain success when one knows how to make good use of them. . . . It is necessary that the dramatic author know how to put his play on the stage himself. . . . It is the only opportune way . . . to render the actors as good as it is possible to obtain from their capabilities and, especially, from their obedience. Now this is a difficult point. The first thing to demand of these actors is to require them to know their roles perfectly, and, since time is short, this is nearly impossible, for today there are very few directors and stage managers who know their craft. . . . To know the theatre, one must be able to govern the actors, the artists, to study the mind and the material of an undertaking of this type. It is a very long study of which very few men are capable. . . . It is necessary that one and the same mind compose, prepare, and entirely execute a work of the theatre.
> [**"Dernières Reflexions"**]

It seems clear, then, that Pixerécourt selected his actors with some care and that he coached and rehearsed them strenuously and autocratically. Perhaps this accounts for the fact that his productions were almost invariably praised for their ensemble quality and occasionally even for what today would be called their blocking. A typical comment from contemporary criticism is that "the play was performed with *beaucoup d'ensemble.*" The reviewer of **Le Chien de Montargis** remarked that "the ensemble with which the work was played must have astonished the habitual attendants of premieres." A review of **La Forteresse du Danube** called special attention to elements of acting and directing.

> Moreover the play had the merit of being well acted; all those who were in it were placed in a way that made their talent shine. Actors, dancers, mimes, all contributed to the success of the production. This art of studying talents and employing them suitably is one of the greatest means of success in the theatre.
> [*Courrier des Spectacles,* January 14, 1805]

The same periodical had earlier written of **Les Maures d'Espagne** that "the groups [were] always knowingly disposed without appearing to have been otherwise than the result of the situations." Piccini, in his remarks on **Robinson Crusoe,** touched upon the effect of Pixerécourt's directing.

> Three acts of gaiety, sentiment, a dazzling *mise en scène,* costumes severely exact, magnificent decorations, varied dances, masses who moved about without disorder—all that is owing to M. de Pixerécourt.
> [letter from Piccini, **Théâtre Choisi,** II]

The same care which Pixerécourt took in coaching actors and directing the play to achieve a pleasing ensemble was duplicated in his attention to scenery, costumes, and special effects. In regard to the mounting of plays, Ginisty has written of Pixerécourt's role in the French theatre of the period:

> Pixerécourt was a reformer and an innovator. From the beginning he ruled minutely the details of the *mise en scène,* he broke with monotony and cleared new ground. . . . His predecessors had contented themselves with curtains and side lights. He set out to change the theatre, and he principally used set pieces; his passion for the practicable became almost an abuse. . . . He was a master of the *mise en scène* for his time.
> [*Le Mélodrame,* 1910]

Ginisty has also recorded that Pixerécourt made sketches for the scenery of his plays on sheets of paper and on the corner of manuscripts. Virely, Pixerécourt's great grandson and the owner of his play manuscripts, has written that there exist detailed scenic plans made by Pixerécourt for a number of his plays.

Contemporary reviews record, almost without exception, that Pixerécourt's plays were painstakingly and lavishly furnished with scenery, machines, and costumes. Although there is evidence to indicate that he enjoyed overseeing these details, the plays were such that they would have demanded care in mounting had Pixerécourt not been interested personally in this aspect of the theatre. The action of the melodramas was complicated, requiring many practical units for climbing, hiding, unusual effects, split-second timing of action, and startling *coups de théâtre,* all of which necessitated a careful planning of the scenic elements and their arrangement on the stage. Moreover, Pixerécourt prided himself upon the historical accuracy of his settings and costumes and was an early exponent of the idea of "local color," and these interests reinforced his demand for care in the mounting of the plays.

The description of the setting for the second act of *La Fille de l'Exilé* provides a good example of the type of effect demanded by Pixerécourt's melodramas:

> The stage represents a savage place on the banks of the Kama, which crosses the stage diagonally; at the right . . . a cabin constructed of fir logs. In front of the cabin, a thick plank in the form of a gravestone, at the end of which is placed a cross, indicating the grave of Ivan's daughter. At the back . . . one sees the Poyas mountains, which separate Europe and Asia. The only trees one can distinguish are firs and birches; everything is covered with snow. The ground from the water to the front of the stage is uneven and rough. Ruggedness everywhere.
> [*Théâtre Choisi,* IV]

During the course of this act, several persons cross the river by boat, wild Tartars dance a saber dance and menace the principal characters, a storm arises, followed by a flood which inundates the entire stage and from which the heroine escapes by floating away on the plank which covered the grave. Of this scene the *Journal des Débats* reported [in March 16, 1819]:

> The scenery of the second act must be considered a marvel of perspective and mechanics. The progressive heightening of the waves, the falling

of snow and of rocks, the uprooting of trees, the balancing of the plank on the surface of the waters, all is a striking and realistic imitation.

To this account *Le Drapeau Blanc* added [on March 16, 1819]:

> This spectacle which closed the second act is so marvelously executed, the representation of it so terribly lifelike, that it excited cries of admiration intermingled with fright.

Neither the scenic demands nor the audience reactions reported here are untypical of Pixerécourt's melodramas. It is evident that to obtain the desired effects and to integrate them with the action of the play demanded careful planning.

Although the visual details of the setting were never neglected, Pixerécourt concerned himself most with the special effects. His plays frequently called for spectacular happenings not previously seen on the French stage, and "machines" had to be invented to meet these new demands. Pixerécourt prided himself almost as much on his invention of these effects, at which he excelled, as upon the writing of the plays and the printed versions of his works contain numerous descriptions of how certain effects were accomplished. For example, Pixerécourt supplied a detailed account of how the complex ending of Act II of *La Fille de l'Exilé,* summarized above, was executed. Similarly, he told how a fall of forty feet from a balcony had been accomplished in the production of *Charles le Téméraire.* Although many of these explanations were designed to help the provincial theatres (he usually suggested ways of accomplishing the effects in less well-equipped theatres), there is always a note of pride and complacency in the accounts.

While Pixerécourt did not concern himself personally as much with the pictorial aspects of the setting as with the stage effects, his plays are always set in clearly specified places, most of them picturesque, and he prided himself that they were rendered with accuracy. *Le Belvéder* shows Mount Aetna in the background; Act III of *La Fille de l'Exilé* is set in front of the Kremlin; for *La Femme à deux Maris,* a play set near Antwerp, he suggests that a scene should be "in the genre of Téniers," the seventeenth century Flemish painter. It would appear that Pixerécourt personally specified the arrangement of the set and its general appearance, but left the visualization and execution of the set to scenic artists, some of whom are named in the programs and in the printed versions of the plays.

Pixerécourt was also much concerned with historical accuracy, although from a modern viewpoint some of his demands seem both unhistorical and bizarre. In connection with the production of his historical plays he sometimes arranged displays in the lobby of the theatre of articles associated with the characters, or of models of buildings or battle fields. In the published version of the plays he frequently reprinted historical documents to show his sources and he used footnotes to cite his authorities. In his *Christophe Colombe* and *Robinson Crusoë,* both set in the Caribbean, he listed the books he had consulted for the manners, speech, and dress of the natives. For *Charles le*

*Téméraire* he included a preface written by General Jomini, who gave a detailed account and plan of the battle of Nancy, with which the play deals. According to a newspaper review, the costumes for *Tékéli,* a "mélodrame historique" about a Hungarian rebel, were "faithful copies from the portraits of the personages." A stage direction in *La Tête du Mort* would seem to indicate that Pixerécourt meant the costumes to be accurate copies of those worn by Italian peasants.

> A very gay ballet, composed of dances of the country, executed by male and female peasants of the isles of Capri and Ischia, where the costumes are so picturesque.

Local color and historical accuracy in costumes and settings and precision of stage effects were Pixerécourt's ideals for the *mise en scène.* He "took in equally well the ensemble and the details," and was praised by one journal [*Journal d'Indications,* October 4, 1805] for refusing to cede his rights to the decorator and ballet master but for knowing how to use their talents to contribute to the overall harmony of effect. His practices as an authoritarian regisseur led to one success after another; the reviews of his plays refer to him variously as "le roi du mélodrame," "le Shakespeare du Boulevard," and "le Corneille du Boulevard."

The boulevard, or secondary, theatres in the last years of the eighteenth century, when Pixerécourt began his career, were places of entertainment almost exclusively for the lower and middle classes, while the primary theatres were patronized by the upper classes. During the first quarter of the nineteenth century, however, as the quality and novelty of the offerings of the melodrama theatres increased, many members of the upper classes shifted their patronage from the primary to the secondary theatres.

> It has begun to be fashionable to frequent the spectacles of the boulevards. . . . They profit from the fact that the others [the major theatres] are stricken with sterility. . . . It is above all the Ambigu-Comique that distinguishes itself by the variety of its repertory, by the good order of its management, and above all by the taste it nearly always exercises in the choice of its plays and the talent of its actors, for it seems that there everyone works the better to please the public.
> [*Gazette de France,* December 30, 1803]

This statement, which appeared in a review of one of Pixerécourt's plays, is indicative of the prosperity of the boulevard theatres and the decline of the primary theatres.

Eventually Pixerécourt's reputation as a producer of plays became so celebrated and the plight of the Opéra-Comique so precarious that, in 1822, he was asked to take over the management of this once-mighty primary theatre, which specialized in light opera. The *societaires,* for whom Pixerécourt had always had such an aversion, offered to abandon all administrative rights. Pellissier, who worked with Pixerécourt during this period, later wrote of the results:

> I was able to observe all the marvels brought forth by the administrative genius with which Pixerécourt is endowed to such a supreme de-

gree. It was, as he himself said with justifiable pride, miracle upon miracle.
>                   ["Notice sur *Le Monastère Abandonné,*"
>                         **Théâtre Choisi,** III]

In a short time Pixerécourt established order and prosperity as the public returned. The repertory of the company did not change in any significant way; the change lay in Pixerécourt's administration and methods of production. The return to success, added to Pixerécourt's rather harsh rehearsal techniques, soon excited the resentment of the *societaires.* One newspaper, taking the side of the actors, reported that "the father of tyrants" punished them so dreadfully that he scarcely allowed them to breathe the putrid exhalations of the footlights. Although Charles II offered to confer on him even greater powers over the theatre, Pixerécourt decided to content himself with having restored the company to its former place of prosperity and prominence and resigned his position. Shortly after the return of the Opéra-Comique to the *societaires* in 1827, the theatre was in such financial straits that it was liquidated by the government. This series of events leaves little doubt as to Pixerécourt's ability as an administrator and director, although it may cast some doubt on his ability in human relations.

Pixerécourt turned his attention to the production of plays at the Gaiété, where he continued with his previous success until the combination of ill health and a disastrous fire in the theatre forced him to retire in 1835. By this time many innovations that he had introduced into the French theatre had been absorbed into the new Romantic drama. After Pixerécourt's retirement the great popularity of French melodrama subsided.

Although Pixerécourt is remembered today primarily as one of the founders of melodrama, it is likely that it was Pixerécourt the regisseur who made possible the great popular success of the new genre. Not only was Pixerécourt a pioneer in melodrama, but he also deserves recognition as an early theatre regisseur and as a pioneer of the concept of unity of production. (pp. 181-87)

> *O. G. Brockett, "Pixerécourt and Unified Production," in* Educational Theatre Journal, *Vol. 11, No. 3, October, 1959, pp. 181-87.*

### Frank Rahill    (essay date 1967)

[*In the following excerpt, Rahill distinguishes between Pixerécourt's historical and domestic melodramas, pointing out the influence of the German playwright Kotzebue on both dramatic types.*]

*Cœlina,* first produced at the Ambigu during September, 1800, marked the ripening of Pixerécourt's talents and the beginning of his reign as "king of melodrama." A career of success scarcely paralleled in all previous theatrical history lay ahead of him. Fifty-nine melodramas, twenty-one of them in collaboration with other writers, were to come from his pen in the thirty-seven years of his activity as a playwright, in addition to sixty-one plays of other types. They were to set such a high standard of popularity that when, as in the case of *Christophe Columb* (1815), a play did not survive one hundred and fifty performances, it was adjudged a failure. Five hundred was average. The staggering total of thirty thousand performances is recorded of his works between 1797 and 1834 in Paris and the provinces; *L'Homme à trois visages* was given 1,022 times, *Le Chien de Montargis,* 1,158, *Tékéli,* 1,334, *Le Pèlerin blanc,* 1,533, and *La Femme à deux maris,* 1,346. At times, Pixerécourt's name could have been seen on the billboards of as many as three Parisian theatres simultaneously.

Foreign productions were frequent. At least seventeen of the plays were given in England. From there they made their way to the United States, where one, *Le Pèlerin blanc* (in the version of the Englishman Theodore Hook, *The Wandering Boys*) was given fifteen hundred times. *Valentine* was printed twice in the U.S.A. prior to 1820. There were numerous German, Italian, Dutch, and Portuguese adaptations, and even a few in Russian and Polish. It was thanks largely to Pixerécourt that melodrama swept the Western world in the early decades of the nineteenth century; he fixed the form that remained an international standard for generations and furnished the models which two continents copied.

With success came fame; "I know nothing comparable to the popularity of the illustrious author of *Babylon,*" wrote Jules Janin, famous *Débats* critic [in *Histoire de la littérature dramatique,* Vol. IV], "men, women, children, young girls, the aged, followed him at a distance . . . when he deigned to promenade on the Boulevard du Temple, enveloped in his velvet cloak, decorated with the Cross of the Legion of Honor. He was followed in silence, he was pointed out with an impassioned gesture. 'It is he—there he is, the great punisher of all crimes, the exalted judge who reads in perverted hearts . . . ' "

Pixerécourt's success may be attributed partly to conditions prevailing in the France of his day. The passion for the theatre which manifested itself at the outbreak of the Revolution continued unabated through the Directory, the Consulate, the Empire, and the Restoration. There were twenty-three theatres in the city in 1789 (Holcroft noticed the posters of as many as eighteen open at one time), and this number had increased to thirty-two when the Napoleonic decree of 1807—in effect for a comparatively short period—reduced it to seven. A quarter of a century later when Pixerécourt was still writing, he commented that Parisians were able to choose from among no fewer than forty-four in their quest for entertainment. Between 1815 and 1830, hundreds of melodramas had their premieres in the city.

Audiences were for the most part naïve, ignorant, and uncritical, being of that unschooled generation which passed its minority in the chaotic years of the Revolution. They entered the theatres of the Boulevard desiring simply to be amused; their response to a spectacle was not complicated by aesthetic prejudices or intellectual preconceptions. Nevertheless, diverting these people called for special knowledge, a special gift; and these Pixerécourt possessed to a degree unique in his time and profession. No contemporary equalled him in number or magnitude of hits, because none approached him in insight into popular psychology or in knowledge of his trade.

He knew the value of surprise, but surprise that is led up to and prepared for; of rapidly changing and executed incident that never permits the vagrant interest of the untrained mind to wander or lag; of the regular alternation of comic and pathetic, and of the sharp contrast of black villainy and spotless innocence personified in the appealing form of women, children, the poor, and the afflicted; of the glamor of resounding names from history and legend; of the heroic attitude, the flamboyant word, the striking gesture; of regal majesty on the one hand, and simple, familiar things on the other. Giving his Boulevard public all this in strong doses, he knew that they would not strain at the improbable or even the preposterous. He realized that they looked for that sort of thing, demanded it—that they saw in those chance meetings, those last-minute rescues and reprieves, those providential acts of God and retributory accidents—collapsing bridges, thunderbolts, volcanic eruptions, floods, earthquakes—the obscure workings of a higher order, a more perfect economy, a more rigid justice than prevailed in the unsatisfactory world where they suffered, struggled, and failed.

A factor in his success was his sincerity; Pixerécourt never wrote with his tongue in his cheek. He believed in his work and took it quite seriously, defending the dignity and usefulness of melodrama with all the force at his command in more than one pamphlet on the subject. (pp. 40-2)

Pixerécourt had the acuteness to perceive that fully half the success of a play is made on the stage, and he became a close student of the theatre and an active participant in production. Two, or at the most, three weeks sufficed him for the mere writing of a piece; the more important business of translating a script into a show, however, was a labor of months. Every detail of the mounting of a play was arranged, rehearsed, and perfected under his sharp, exacting eye—casting, music, scenery, properties, acting, direction. Like Boucicault and Sardou after him he became a martinet behind the scenes, the terror of actors, scene painters, machinists, carpenters, and musicians. The results were revolutionary; this now forgotten melodramatist added a new dimension to the theatre. He made plays live on the stage as plays had never lived before his time.

Each of his plays offered at least one spectacular scenic effect: *Tékéli,* a *fête militaire; Charles le Téméraire,* a flood and an assault; *Marguerite d'Anjou,* a forest fire; *La Citerne,* an explosion; *Robinson Crusoë* and *Christophe Colomb,* full-rigged ships; *La Fille de l'exilé,* an inundation with the heroine borne across the stage clinging to a floating log, a mechanical effect which the playwright invented; *Les Chefs écossais,* the storming of Stirling castle and "a ballet of citizens of Edinburgh" at an audience with King Edward. All were woven into the dramatic action and managed with great skill. The success of the various plays owed a great deal to these embellishments, and Pixerécourt felt that many of his works did not prosper as they might have in the provinces because the staging was neglected.

Pixerécourt got his material from a wide variety of sources: Goethe, Schiller, Kotzebue, Werner, Prévost, Florian, Ducray-Duminil, La Harpe, the poet Bernard, Nodier, Chateaubriand, De Kock, Mme Cottin, Mrs.

Radcliffe, George Sand, Defoe, Jane Porter, Godwin, Walter Scott, and Shakespeare were drawn upon for subjects, plots, situations, characters, devices; and in addition to these he used *The Thousand and One Nights,* chronicles of exploration, and the newspapers. Like Shakespeare, he seldom borrowed without rehandling and transforming and always with the special requirements of the stage in mind. He took little or much as suited his purpose, often drawing upon several sources for one play. In his adaptations of novels and dramas characters disappear or are combined with others, episodes are suppressed or added with a free hand, the order of events is changed, denouements are rewritten.

The use he made of his various English sources illustrates his methods, and at the same time reveals his constructive talents. In *L'Évasion de Marie Stuart ou le Château de Loch-Leven* (1822) only the second half of Walter Scott's novel, *The Abbot,* is used. Mary's escape, which it narrates, forms a single dramatic action. There is further simplification in the compression of time and the combination of characters—Lindsay with Ruthven, Dryfesdale with Randal, and Lady Fleming with Catherine Seton. Details are changed; incidents invented. The Queen refuses to sign the papers for her abdication, and Douglas gives his life to assure her escape—improvements on the novel from the melodramatic point of view. As in so many of his adaptations, Pixerécourt here availed himself freely of the novelist's dialogue. Niceties of language do not count for much

*Théâtre de l'Ambigu-Comique, Paris, where many of Pixerécourt's melodramas were presented.*

in melodrama; dramatic situations, mimed action, striking stage effects—these are what made a play successful on the "Boulevard du Crime."

Several such effects are introduced in *L'Évasion de Marie Stuart.* The faithful Catherine Seton thrusts her arm through the staples of a door in place of a missing bolt in order to hold off the pursuers of her royal mistress, Lord Lindsay pinches the Queen's arm with his mailed gauntlet (as the Duke of Guise will pinch the arm of Catherine of Cleves in Dumas' *Henri III et sa cour*); Lady Loch Leven herself places the lamp in the loophole of the tower, not suspecting that she is thereby signalling Mary's friends that the hour of the planned escape has arrived. This last was partially at least the adaptor's invention. An even better example of theatrical imagination at work is entirely's Pixerécourt's own. It occurs in the second act. Two of Mary's friends meet at the Kinloss Fair. Not daring to speak openly lest they betray themselves, they convey to each other by means of the various figures of a quadrille the names of the men who can be trusted and the hour of the Queen's escape attempt.

Whether he borrowed or originated them, Pixerécourt in his fifty-nine melodramas managed to make use of virtually every one of the effects of this kind which became classic in the genre: the transfer of poison cups, striking clocks which set conspiracies in motion, casks in which troops are smuggled into besieged cities, telltale scars and identifying birthmarks, rings and lockets, papers that clear up mysteries, pretended invalids exposed by a discreet application of fire or the like, disguised heroes or heroines participating in councils which plot their doom, fellow criminals killing each other in mistake for their intended victims.

Charles Nodier called Pixerécourt the inventor of a new genre [in "Du Mouvement intellectuel et littéraire sous le Directoire et le Consulat," *Revue de Paris,* XIX (1835)], dismissing melodrama as it had been written previously on the Boulevard as a "misshapen, abortive, monstrous concoction." Marsan maintained that it was thanks to Pixerécourt alone that melodrama established itself in its full character. This is magnifying the shortcomings of the pioneers perhaps, but the judgment is essentially just. Certainly it is indisputable that Pixerécourt was the first master melodramatist of the Boulevard. (pp. 42-5)

· · · · ·

*Cœlina* was a domestic melodrama, to employ a term invented by early nineteenth-century reporters of the drama to distinguish pieces in which fireside interest prevailed over larger matters like the travail of Mary Stuart and the iniquities of Charles the Bold; these latter were lumped under the general head of historical. Gaiffe justly observes that domestic and historical are no more than "classifications of convenience." The adventures which take place in domestic melodrama can be quite as harrowing and fantastic as those of the historical pieces, and the characters are the same wooden puppets whether they appear in the Bagdad of Haroun al Raschid's reign; the Venice of the Renaissance; the Spain of the Moors; primitive Africa; or nineteenth-century France, Scotland, or Italy. The language scarcely ever varies from one classification to another. Pixerécourt invented an astonishing gibberish for his aborigines in **Christophe Colomb,** employed provincial dialects for many of his comics as Molière and the Italian comedy had done before him, and sprinkled archaic expressions through some of his period plays; otherwise his dialogue relied upon the pedestrian and the pretentious.

The affinities of domestic melodrama are with *drame.* This mixed form, a sentimental, moral, middle-class tragicomedy in prose deriving from the theories of Diderot, Beaumarchais and Mercier, had lost caste as a distinct dramatic genre at the Français before the Revolution. It survived in a modified form at the Opéra Comique, but it never had been received with any enduring enthusiasm on the Boulevard. (p. 46)

Pixerécourt must have seen one or both of the Paris productions of [Kotzebue's *Menschenhass und Reue*]. Certainly he knew of it and in the original, since he translated Kotzebue's entire works and borrowed from the German's store for at least three of his plays. To *Menschenhass and Reue* may be attributed some of the qualities which appear in **La Femme à deux maris** (1802), though the outline of the plot is taken from a novel by Ducray-Duminil. (p. 47)

**La Femme à deux maris** is the usual shrewdly compounded mélange. There is a ballet introduced as part of a fête to welcome the "good man" upon his return from a journey. Comedy is introduced, and domestic tenderness and sentimentality generally are played up throughout. One scene, was particularly appealing: the innocently bigamous wife Eliza pleading with her blind father for forgiveness using the third person.

The play ran 451 times in Paris and was a hit in various foreign capitals including London and St. Petersburg. The skeleton of the plot was to be used over and over again in melodrama—in *Hunted Down, The Parson's Bride, My Pal and My Partner Joe, Nuits de la Seine,* and *Fairfax.*

Another play of Pixerécourt's with a similar appeal, **Le Chien de Montargis,** was one of the most popular dramas of the century throughout Europe and America. The plot is based on a medieval legend which was treated in a twelfth-century *chanson de geste.* The action occurs at and near a country inn where a company of archers is billeted for the night as the play begins. It deals with a blind boy, Eloi, falsely accused of a murder and saved from execution at the last moment by an extraordinary dog detective who had been at the scene of the crime, but was tied to a tree by the villains while they committed it. As Eloi is being conducted to the scaffold in the last act, the dog, joining the crowd, sees the murderer, flies at his throat, and justice is done.

Count de Fersen, the "good man," had uttered the customary moralizing tag at the conclusion of **La Femme à deux maris**—"an offended father who pardons is the most perfect image of the divinity"; in **Le Chien de Montargis** it is the crushed villain who performs this office. "Heaven is just," he cries; "it saves the innocent and strikes down the guilty at one and the same time." This is the essence of melodrama.

*Sensible,* lovable characters like Eloi, Eliza, and Cœlina suffer in all the plays Pixerécourt wrote; he never neglected that pathetic interest which had proved so potent with Mercier and Florian. This element, however, usually takes second place to the breathless hurry of the plot from one exciting situation to another. Dynamic conduct of the fable is the supreme virtue of this playwright and was the most important factor in his success. Suffering heroines not infrequently accommodate themselves to it, stepping out of their characteristically passive roles to fight back at their persecutors and thus in some measure usurping the role of the hero. There is a distressed maiden, Seraphine, in **La Citerne** (1809), but her energetic sister Clara steals the show with various ingenious and audacious moves to check the villain. In **La Forteresse du Danube** (1805), Celestine supplies the excitement and suspense by gaining entrance, in the disguise of a male Savoyard entertainer, to a stronghold where her father is held prisoner and distracting the guards with her singing and dancing while the old man makes his escape. The heroic, resourceful female is a mother in **Charles le Téméraire** (1814), Léontine, daughter of the Governor of Nancy. She penetrates the camp of the Burgundians who are besieging the city, learns their plans, retrieves her child who has been taken as a hostage, fends off the sack of the city by a stratagem, and finally opens the dikes to inundate the area where the troops of the enemy are encamped; then, vizor down— borrowing from Schiller's *Die Jungfrau von Orleans*— slays the evil Duke himself in single combat.

It is in **L'Ange tutélaire ou le démon femelle** (1808), however, that the intrepid woman reaches the heights. The Flora of this Renaissance drama is a veritable female demon in her fierce energy, her bold courage, and her subtle craft exercised on behalf of her lover, the Duke of Ferrara, whose guardian angel she becomes, crushing a conspiracy hatched by his faithless brother. Among the disguises assumed by this busy amazon are those of a gypsy, a page boy, an old man, a court dame, and a magician.

Such plays are definitely in the zone of historical melodrama. Here as in domestic melodrama Kotzebue must be considered an influence. *Rollas Tod,* written by the German on the basis of an adventure tale by Marmontel, was given at the Porte Saint-Martin when that theatre was reopened in 1802, and Pixerécourt himself did an adaptation produced in the same year, **Pizarre ou la conquête du Pérou.** Kotzebue's play . . . ends unhappily, but its battles and pursuits, its pathos and its preaching are all in the melodramatic style. There were, of course, other influences which led Pixerécourt and his French contemporaries to seek stirring themes in history: *Richard Coeur-de-Lion* and other *opéras comiques,* tragedies such as Chenier's *Charles IX,* Goethe's *Goetz von Berlichingen,* Schiller's dramas, Shakespeare's chronicle plays, and the heroic pantomime. And, of course, his early exemplar, Mercier.

Pixerécourt's historical melodramas stand apart from these works, German, English and French, most obviously in that quality of headlong speed which has been noted above, that frenetic press of episode upon episode which was to be his most valuable legacy to the genre and to which Hugo and Dumas were indebted. **L'Homme à trois** *visages* (1801), the earliest of them, has this quality in a superlative degree. (pp. 48-50)

It is in the energetic hero's lightning-like changes from one to another of his *trois visages*, or three faces, and in the dangers he thereby exposes himself to, that the breathless interest of the piece resides. The climax comes in a grand session of the Council of State at which the traitors [led by Vivaldi's enemy, Orsini, a band of conspirators plotting to overthrow the Republic of Venice] have agreed to act. After skillfully decoying them into showing their hand, the hero tosses off his disguise (which includes a bandit's stock red beard) and reveals himself as Vivaldi, come to save Venice from a disaster he himself has been unjustly convicted of plotting. At his signal his troops swarm into the chamber and overpower the conspirators. The Republic is preserved, the Doge is saved, and husband and wife [Vivaldi and Rosamonde] are reunited.

*Tékéli ou le siège de Mongatz* (1803), which Pixerécourt thought of most highly among all his plays, gets into more definitely historical matters: the Prince from whom the title derives was a seventeenth-century Hungarian patriot who led his people in revolt against their Austrian oppressors. The play was something of a tour de force in that it made a romantic hero of a character who for the greater part of an act remained hidden in a barrel while his foes searched for him. Melodramatic heroes as a rule disdain such undignified shifts preferring to fight it out in the open be the odds what they may.

Contemporary history was another field wherein Pixerécourt opened up new paths for melodrama. His *Le Suicide ou le vieux sergeant* (1816) was the first of that vast library of shockers based upon recent crimes. It dealt with the attempt of a provincial family of some eminence to place blame upon an old servant for a murder committed by one of its own members. Another of Pixerécourt's dramas of this kind was *La Chapelle des bois ou le témoin invisible* (1818), an arrangement of the notorious Fualdès case, one of the strangest crimes in police annals. H. B. Irving has retold the story of this fantastic murder in his *Occasional Papers*. Gericault used it as the subject of a famous painting shown in the exhibition of 1824. (pp. 51-2)

> *Frank Rahill, "The Art of Pixerécourt" and "The Plays of Pixerécourt," in his* The World of Melodrama, *The Pennsylvania State University Press, 1967, pp. 40-5, 46-52.*

## W. D. Howarth    (essay date 1980)

[*An English scholar and critic, Howarth has published extensively on French literature and drama, notably on Molière and the Romantics. In the following excerpt, he examines the relationship between spoken dialogue and visual effects in the melodramas of Pixerécourt.*]

What importance should we give to Pixerécourt's well-known statement, 'I am writing for those who cannot read'? How literally should it be taken, and what are its implications for anyone inquiring into the nature of popular drama in early-nineteenth-century France? It could reasonably be argued that the degree of literacy of a theatre audience is irrelevant to the production of a spectacle designed to be seen and heard; and no doubt those who approve of the gradual emancipation of European drama from what they regard as excessively literary influences would applaud Pixerécourt's statement as heralding a move away from text towards spectacle. On the other hand, it is possible to interpret the 'popular' character of his melodramas in a different light, and to see this genre, for all its visual spectacle and despite its apparent anti-literary tendency, as one still dependent on literary traditions, one in which the spoken word is still used in a recognisably 'literary' manner, even if this manner is generally simplified and often debased. I propose in this [essay] to examine the relationship between spoken word and visual image in a number of representative plays; and I shall attempt to justify the phrase 'the dramaturgy of the strip-cartoon'.

The emergence of melodrama in the years around 1800 is best explained by the fusion of two developments, one popular and one literary, in the drama of the preceding generation. The importance of the *pantomime,* or musical mime-play, to which enterprising directors of independent theatres resorted in order to circumvent the monopoly of spoken and sung drama held by the official houses, has been stressed by Pitou and others. However, the formula of *pantomime* did not remain stable for very long, and the fact that it soon evolved into a bizarre hybrid with the contradictory label of 'pantomime dialoguée' seems to indicate the inadequacy of pure mime to express the range of thoughts and emotions that melodrama was later to attempt. It would in any case be wrong to give too much prominence to these affinities with popular antecedents; and Geoffroy, the contemporary critic, for one had no doubt that the new melodrama represented a degenerate form of the literary drama of the previous century: 'a kind of tragedy fit for the lower classes'. Others since Geoffroy have taken a similar view, seeing the principal sources of melodrama either in Voltaire's tragedy or in Diderot's domestic drama; and however important the links, through *pantomime,* with the popular traditions of the fairground theatres, it is clear that such links do not of themselves fully account for the peculiar characteristics of Pixerécourt's melodrama.

The literary drama of the previous generation was by no means a static recitative lacking all visual appeal. On the one hand, in tragedy, 'melodramatic' features of plot, as well as a tendency towards spectacle on a grand scale, were already well established; on the other hand, in sentimental domestic drama, the use of *pantomime* and *tableaux* compensated to some extent for the acknowledged inadequacy of the spoken word. However, both of these genres obviously remained forms of drama in which speech was paramount; and the prose of *drame bourgeois,* no less than the verse of tragedy, was a highly stylised medium, with its own specialised form of literary rhetoric.

But whereas verse tragedy catered for the traditionalist spectators of the Comédie-Française, and Diderot's *drame* appealed to less conservative members of the same culture-group—and whereas such novelties as the *pantomime* also attracted cultured patrons looking for lighter entertainment—melodramas of the 1800s were written for a quite different kind of spectator. The new genre came into being at the end of a decade in which the old monopoly had been broken, the prestige of the Comédie-Française had seemingly been irrevocably shattered by the repeated closure of the theatre and the imprisonment of half the company, and Parisian theatres generally, now more numerous, had become much more responsive to political and social changes. The theatre-going public was no longer confined to those with a certain level of education and culture: Grimod de la Reynière, writing in 1797, speaks of a new mania for the theatre that had spread through all ranks of society. There was now a new kind of audience, who had lived through the revolution and had a well-developed taste for violent sensations: 'soldiers; adolescents who would be better suited to the classroom than to the theatre; the lowest grades of the working class; finally, a few clerks, a class which used to have some education, but is now semi-illiterate'. Such audience says La Reynière, 'are so ignorant of the most basic elements of grammar and versification that they don't know verse from prose; they can't tell comedy from farce, bombast from sublimity, pathos from cheap sentimentality . . . And these are the judges in whose hands the future of the French theatre rests!' [Quoted by W. G. Hartog in *Guilbert de Pixérécourt*, 1913].

This is a graphic portrait of Pixerécourt's audience, the 'illiterate' for whom he claimed to be writing. And at first sight, when we look at the spectacular effects of his finales, the crude sentimentality of his dramatic climaxes, and the lack of sophistication of his comic scenes, we might be forgiven for assuming that the purpose of such plays was simply to exploit the naivety of these uncultured audiences by offering them a totally undemanding form of entertainment. Pixerécourt was no mere entertainer, however; still less was he a cynic, prepared to exploit for his own benefit the naivety or gullibility of others. 'Unlike the Roman crowd who called for bread and circuses', says La Reynière, 'the people of Paris want only circuses'—but Pixerécourt, who had an unshakeable conviction in the didactic force of the theatre, was determined to give them moral sustenance as well, and his melodramas were all conceived with that end in view.

Charles Nodier, in his flattering introduction to the four-volume *Théâtre choisi* of Pixerécourt (1841-3), explicitly links the playwright's moral purpose and his prose style. Drawing attention to the sudden interruption of the church's moral role in the revolutionary decade, he suggests that melodrama 'took the place of the silent pulpit'; Pixerécourt, he says, was conscious of his lofty mission, as of a veritable apostolate, 'and the most important condition of any apostolate is a knowledge of the language proper to the country in which one is going to exercise one's mission'. Contemporary French usage, Nodier maintains, was marked by a taste for extravagant, bombastic rhetoric, a debased form of revolutionary oratory, perpetuated in the political clubs, the law courts and the press; and it was only by adopting the same hollow verbiage that a popular dramatist could capture the imagination of his audiences.

It is impossible to say how far Pixerécourt's turgid manner in fact derives from a conscious attempt to speak the language of his spectators, and how far it reflects earlier literary influences—for after all, the characters of Diderot and Mercier had often spoken in a similar declamatory style. But whatever its source, there is no difficulty in recognising the diction of Pixerécourt's characters as speech inflated well above the level of normal colloquial usage. The following highly literary examples of hyperbole, apostrophe, balance and repetition are typical of the 'Corneille of the boulevards':

> —Ah! Sir, one would need to be totally lacking in delicacy of feeling not to cherish the most worthy, the most generous of men!
>
> —Humble dwelling where for twenty years I knew naught but innocence and peace, would to heaven I had never left you!
>
> —The wretched Eliza, once more destined to shame, again the object of calumny, will see herself hated, despised, abandoned by everyone. . . .

Pixerécourt's characters are ever ready to resort to the moral maxim, a prose equivalent of the *sententiae* familiar from the tragedy and the *haute comédie* of a century and a half:

> —A wronged father who forgives his child is the most perfect representation of the deity.
>
> —The virtuous man punishes, but he does not kill.
>
> —If only men knew what it costs to stop being virtuous, there would be hardly any villains left on earth. . . .

Finally, nothing betrays the literary ancestry of this new genre so much as the soliloquies in which sinners acknowledge the voice of conscience. Here are the closing lines from a long soliloquy by Macaire, the villain of *Le Chien de Montargis:*

> A source of horror to myself, consumed by remorse, bathed in the blood of my fellow-man, I hasten towards the scaffold that awaits me, and which can alone put an end to the frightful torments that I undergo; for that is where unbridled passions drive whoever is weak and cowardly enough to give himself up without a struggle to their fatal dominion.

*Mutatis mutandis,* these are the self-incriminating accents of a whole series of tragic characters stretching back to Racine's Phèdre.

The passages of extremely economical writing, on the other hand—those sequences, for instance, in which characters converse in a crude approximation to the stichomythia of classical verse drama:

> —Your name?
>
> —Polina. (*Aside*) What hope . . . ! (*Aloud*) Your own?
>
> —Polaski.

—You are . . . ?

—Polish.

—The Cossacks . . . ?

—Beaten.

—Edwinski . . . ?

—Safe.

—Zamoski . . . ?

—Dead.

—O Providence!

—Someone is coming . . . !

may well suggest a more obvious analogy with the cartoonist's reductive techniques. There are also, of course, episodes in which essential dramatic action is accompanied by no verbal commentary at all. To take just one example, in *Le Pèlerin blanc,* when the Count, disguised as an elderly retainer in his own castle, saves his young sons who are in the power of Roland, the evil *intendant,* by switching bottles so that the latter drinks the poison he has prepared for the boys, this vital sequence, on which the dénouement will depend, takes place without a word being uttered—not even one of the asides by which Pixerécourt's good, as well as his evil, characters habitually keep the less perceptive spectators informed of what is going on. But very few sustained dramatic sequences in Pixerécourt depend entirely on visual rather than on spoken communication; and in many cases where this might be expected, the visual is pointedly translated into the medium of speech. For instance, the sign-language of the dumb characters, Francisque in *Coelina* and Eloi in *Le Chien de Montargis,* is accompanied at the most crucial points by an explicit commentary spoken by their interpreters; while in the latter work in the case of the dog itself, that representative of divine justice whose action in 'accusing' his master's murderer provided the anecdotal source of the play, Pixerécourt seems deliberately to have avoided the challenge to let visual action speak for itself: Dragon's inspired intervention takes place offstage and has to be reported, and his only appearance on stage also needs to be interpreted by a spoken commentary.

However, if the visual spectacle is seldom allowed any genuinely autonomous standing—if generally speaking not only the moral values, but also most of the actions are generated by dialogue of very conventional style—it can also be shown that Pixerécourt's dialogue too lacks the self-sufficient, autonomous quality of the classical text. The speech of Pixerécourt's characters depends on visual reinforcement to a degree that is difficult to imagine when one has nothing but the text to rely on. There can be no doubt about the literary ancestry of the rhetoric of melodrama, but to read the dialogue on the printed page certainly tends to give a disproportionate emphasis to its conventional literary qualities. It is abundantly clear that in the theatre it was not an intellectual appeal to the minds of his spectators that the dramatist was seeking, but an affective appeal to their sensibility; and in that affective ap-

peal the interrelationship between the spoken word and the accompanying image was absolutely vital.

In this regard, Pixerécourt's grandiose operatic finales may seem to be examples of spectacle for the sake of spectacle, pure visual entertainment for simple-minded spectators. Yet if we look at what is surely the most sensational of these spectacular scenes, the eruption of Vesuvius at the end of *La Tête de mort,* it can be seen that the physical setting of the play—the ruins of Pompeii, with the volcano brooding ominously in the background—is by no means an arbitrary adjunct to the human action. There is an evident affinity between the forces of nature and the divine justice that Réginald and his accomplices have offended; human notions of right and wrong are powerfully reinforced by the intervention of the natural order, and this primitive form of the pathetic fallacy is certainly implicit in the final stage direction as the volcano erupts, covering the body of Réginald (who has just died of remorse) and killing the other evil-doers:

> . . . The red glow in which all these objects are bathed, the terrifying noise of the volcano, the cries, the commotion and the universal despair, all combine to make this dreadful upheaval of nature a picture of utter horror, worthy to be compared with the Nether Regions.

Here, the natural setting is no mere picturesque backcloth: the volcano becomes an active participant in a cosmic drama. We may compare the stage direction at the beginning of Act III of *Coelina,* where the disruption of the moral order, with the temporary triumph of Truguelin and the banishment of the heroine and her father, is symbolised by the violent storm that accompanies the action: 'au lever du rideau toute la nature paraît en désordre; les éclairs brillent de toutes parts, le torrent roule avec fureur, les vents mugissent, la pluie tombe avec fracas, et des coups de tonnerre multipliés qui se répètent cent fois, par l'écho des montagnes, portent l'épouvante et la terreur dans l'âme'. No wonder that Truguelin comments: 'Il me semble que tout dans la nature se réunit pour m'accuser'. . . . (pp. 17-23)

It would be no exaggeration to regard Pixerécourt's whole *oeuvre* as a vast metaphysical drama portraying a Manichaean conflict on a cosmic scale. Nevertheless, the individual episodes of this struggle are normally acted out in a less spectacular setting, and the visual illustrations of the ways of Providence are seldom as striking as in *La Tête de mort,* or even as in certain parts of *Coelina* or *Le Monastère abandonné;* so that as regards the relationship between the spoken and the visual in his plays taken as a whole, the domesticated dumb-show deriving from the *drame bourgeois* tradition is much more significant than the occasional spectacular *tour de force.* In the more mundane settings of the domestic melodramas, Providence may not show its hand quite so openly—but its workings can nevertheless be seen as well as heard. As in the gothic novel, occult correspondences are taken for granted; the place where a crime has been committed, the weapon with which it was committed, as well as the hour at which the deed was done: all of these are capable of operating powerfully on the mind of the wrongdoer. Thus, in the same way that Truguelin is affected when he revisits the scene of his crime—'Ciel! . . . que vois-je? . . . ce pont . . . ces rochers . . . ce torrent . . . c'est là . . . là . . . que ma main criminelle versa le sang d'un infortuné . . . O terre! entr'ouvre-toi! . . . abîme dans ton sein un monstre indigne dela vie . . . '—Piétro in *Le Monastère abandonné* also suffers at the tangible reminder of the crime he thinks he has committed:

> *The big monastery clock strikes nine. Its prolonged, reverberating strokes are truly terrifying. Piétro stops and counts under his breath; at eight, he cries out, as if to bring time to a halt:* 'Stop! 'tis enough . . . That is the hour at which I was accursed.'

In these and similar ways, the playwright underlines his somewhat simplistic message: the eventual punishment of the evildoer is forecast by a system of signs and portents, by which Providence uses the material world to work on an uneasy conscience. Moreover, the uneasy conscience constantly betrays itself by physical signs. The comforting message—that the unscrupulous characters who exploit their fellow-men never enjoy the real happiness that only virtue can bring—is expressed, as we have seen, in the form of soliloquies or conventional asides to the audience; it is also frequently reinforced by reference to visual indicators. Carlo, the righter of wrongs in *La Tête de mort,* speaks of Réginald as follows:

> 'Everything helps to justify the suspicion which led me to this place. Always sombre and solitary, I have never known him to smile. His stern, composed expression, his cold reserve, his melancholy, sorrowful manner: all this denotes a tormented heart, a conscience ill at ease. He is afraid of being found out.'

Characters blush, or go livid, as a sign of guilt:

> —Are you aware, Sir, that before accusing a man of so serious a crime, you need to have proof ?
>
> —I have an irrefutable proof.
>
> —And that is . . . ?
>
> —Your pallor.

They start apprehensively, recoil in fear, and continually betray their guilty conscience: at the appearance of the mute Francisque, his victim of eight years earlier, Truguelin 'recule de quelques pas, et paraît frappé de terreur'; Macaire, returning after the murder of Aubry, enters 'avec l'air égaré d'un hómme qui vient de commettre un crime'; and the same Macaire, perhaps the most obviously conscience stricken of all Pixerécourt's criminals, has constantly to be reproved by his accomplice, Landry, because the visible signs of his remorse threaten to give the guilty pair away.

The aside to the audience is, of all the features of the dialogue of melodrama, the one with the most obvious counterpart in the cartoonist's art. The comments at first hand by participants in the action—'Fâcheux contretemps!', 'Quel supplice!', 'D'où vient que le coeur me bat avec tant de force!' and countless similar interjections—are the nearest equivalent of the 'balloons' representing unspoken thoughts; and it would surely be right to imagine these asides being delivered with the accompaniment of appropriately theatrical gestures providing a stylised show of annoyance, anguish, or apprehension. There are sequences in which a dialogue is punctuated throughout by this kind of comment; for instance, every encounter between Raymond and Isouf, in *Les Ruines de Babylone,* where each is trying to deceive the other, is built up on this basis:

> —You are right. (*Aside*) I think he is deceiving me.
>
> —(*Aside*) Let's find out if he knows the truth. (*Aloud*) What progress have you made in the meantime? What have you learned?

These scenes have a likely source in the verbal duel between Figaro and Count Almaviva in Act III of *Le Mariage de Figaro*—though it may well be felt that contrived, patterned dialogue of this sort remains more appropriate to comedy than to would-be serious drama.

Another use of the aside is to provide a comment at second hand, as it were, by a bystander. At its simplest, this is illustrated by the scene in which Coelina overhears Truguelin and his accomplice plotting the death of Francisque:

> TRUGUELIN:—At midnight, then, if he resists . . .
>
> GERMAIN:—He's a dead man.
>
> TRUGUELIN:—Let us withdraw.
>
> COELINA:—(*aside*) The monsters!
>
> TRUGUELIN:—I hear a sound.
>
> GERMAIN:—Someone is coming . . . It is he.
>
> TRUGUELIN:—He! why delay?
>
> GERMAIN:—It is not yet time.
>
> TRUGUELIN:—You'll keep a look-out.
>
> GERMAIN:—You'll do the deed.
>
> COELINA:—(*aside*) The villains!

Although in the passages just quoted there are no stage directions to indicate any visual accompaniment to the verbal expression of emotion or sentiment, Pixerécourt's plays do contain a wealth of stage directions which show how speech was intended to be reinforced by such means. The following examples, all taken from *Coelina,* suggest a repertory of conventional facial and gestural expressions that would be readily understood by the audience:

> *In a forced manner, and showing an assumed interest.*
>
> *Endeavouring to recover his composure.*
>
> *With complete composure.*
>
> *In a brusque manner, after glancing scornfully at Truguelin.*

More obviously, at moments of emotional crisis characters raise their hands towards heaven, throw themselves at each other's knees, embrace one another and swoon; while in addition to such cases in which dialogue is supplemented by the conventional language of gestures, there is of course abundant gestural by-play involving disguise, letters, weapons, and all the other material objects which are given so prominent a place in the dramaturgy of melodrama (the passage referred to above from **Le Pèlerin blanc** is a good example of this). Such a technique once again suggests that of the cartoonist, in its reliance on a stereotyped language of signs designed to produce the desired affective appeal to an unsophisticated audience. (pp. 23-6)

When Artaud called for 'a new physical language, based no longer on *words* but on *signs*'; when he specified that 'it is not a question of doing away with conventional speech, but of endowing language with the sort of meaning that it possesses in our dreams'; and when he then went on to say that the only form of Western theatre to have succeeded in breaking down the 'descriptive' theatre of the neo-classical age had been the Romantic melodrama of the early nineteenth century, one cannot help thinking that this was an example of wishful thinking. For surely the mixture of the spoken and the visual in Pixerécourt's melodrama is not significantly different from the mixture in Voltaire's tragedy or in Diderot's *drame bourgeois:* what is different is the level on which the whole operates. Pixerécourt's is essentially still a *descriptive* form of drama, to use Artaud's term: the language of signs and gestures is a closed one, with clear-cut correspondences between the visual and the spoken, not the sort of open system whose interpretation depends on the free exercise of the spectator's imagination.

Similarly, when the author of an excellent recent study of melodrama [*The Melodramatic Imagination*], Peter Brooks, writes: 'The gestures that we see on stage, the visible movements, can perhaps best be considered . . . the vehicle of a metaphor whose tenor is a vaguely defined yet grandiose emotional or spiritual force that gesture seeks to make present without directly naming it, by pointing toward it', this would appear to be valid only insofar as the role of gesture in melodrama can be considered to be independent of the spoken word. It is true that the gestures of Pixerécourt's characters are almost always hyperbolic—but so is their language; and as I have attempted to show, the nature of this hyperbole is essentially reductive: the polarisation of motives into extremes of good and evil, expressed in the most explicit terms, the use of gesture as a schematised representation of equally explicit responses, renders the emotional effects crude and unsubtle. (p. 27)

It may seem unduly dismissive to talk of the 'dramaturgy of the strip-cartoon'. Pixerécourt's dialogue does not descend to the 'Aaargh' and 'Ouch!' of the present-day practitioners . . . Nevertheless, in the mutual dependence of word and image; in the polarisation of characters into elementary stereotypes of good and evil; in the abuse of the aside to guide the audience's reactions; in the over-simplified function of the soliloquy; in the undemanding explicitness of both speech and gesture; in the fondness for static tableaux representing emotional states in a highly stylised manner: in all of these ways, Pixerécourt's practice involves an impoverishment of dramatic art for the

benefit of naive and uncultured spectators; and the analogy with the cartoonist presenting a simple story in palatable form for the relatively unlettered is perhaps not too wide of the mark. (p. 28)

> W. D. Howarth, "Word and Image in Pixeré-court's Melodramas: The Dramaturgy of the Strip-Cartoon," in Performance and Politics in Popular Drama: Aspects in Popular Entertainment in Theatre, Film and Television, 1800-1976, David Bradby, Louis James and Bernard Sharratt, eds., Cambridge University Press, 1980, pp. 17-32.

## Gabrielle Hyslop (essay date 1985)

[*In the following excerpt, Hyslop focuses on the importance of women's roles in the plays of Pixerécourt, interpreting in social terms the distinction between his active, independent heroines and his more conventional female leads—the embodiments of domestic virtue and morality.*]

René-Charles Guilbert de Pixerécourt was arguably *the* playwright who, more than any other, established the conventions of melodrama, the most popular form of theatre in the nineteenth century. Although Pixerécourt was a phenomenally successful writer and theatre craftsman during his day, his plays are no longer performed or even calling for revival. His works deserve attention, however, because melodrama was one of the earliest and most powerful forms of mass media, and it has continued to dominate popular drama right up until the present. The sensationalism, plot structures, character types and value system which Pixerécourt helped to codify at the very beginning of the nineteenth century remain with us in the works of Pixerécourt's direct descendants, the producers of block buster movies and television soap operas. In order to understand better these *contemporary* forms of popular entertainment, which fulfill for our society the same function that melodrama fulfilled when it first emerged, we need to examine Pixerécourt's value system and the theatrical techniques he employed to inculcate it.

In the value system presented by Pixerécourt's melodramas, the role of women is crucial. I will begin with some general remarks about Pixerécourt's aims as a playwright and go on to explain the central position occupied by women in his melodramas. While I intend to draw general conclusions about the role of women in melodrama, I shall be focusing my attention on the heroine in Pixerécourt's plays. This is partly because the values she represents are, for the most part, reflected by the secondary female characters, and also, more importantly, because she is the most interesting and complex female character in melodrama. Michael Booth describes the heroine as "a fitting symbol of all melodrama" ["The Acting of Melodrama," *University of Toronto Quarterly*, XXXIV (October 1964)]. She clearly deserves our close attention. I will examine first the 'normal' type of melodrama heroine and then proceed to discuss those heroines who do not conform to the normal pattern but who exhibit deviant and dangerous behaviour.

Pixerécourt began writing and staging melodramas in the

1790s during the final turbulent years of the French Revolution. His declared aim was to entertain and instruct the uneducated, and throughout Pixerécourt's long career of nearly forty years, many critics acknowledged his significance as a playwright whose spectacular and highly entertaining productions, based on conservative moral values, helped to re-establish and maintain law and order in postrevolutionary France.

In his introduction to the four volume edition of Pixerécourt's selected works, Charles Nodier, an important Romantic novelist, playwright and critic, wrote enthusiastically about melodrama's dual function, entertainment and instruction. . . . [He also] spelt out melodrama's socially corrective value: . . .

> As to (melodrama's) effect on public morality, do I have to repeat that the long period of time spanned by M. de Pixerécourt's plays is that most free from crime of any period cited in our legal records. Do I have to say yet again that crime has never been more rare, especially among the lower classes? That's because the lower classes sought at the theatre emotions which were never dangerous, which were often salutary; melodrama was a carefully highlighted picture in which crime appeared in all its repulsive ugliness, in which virtue was clothed in all the grace which makes it appealing, in which the role of providence in human affairs was revealed through the most realistic and striking situations; everyone always left, a better person, and this is no foolish exaggeration.

It is clear from these comments, as well as from Pixerécourt's plays themselves, that melodrama is popular in the sense of being *for* the common people. What is also clear from the writings of critics like Nodier, creative expression *of* the people themselves. It is not proletarian art. Like other forms of mass media, Pixerécourt's melodramas were presented in order to impose the values of the dominant social class on the common people. Melodrama expresses the conservative patriarchal ideas of the middle class who aim to control the opinions and life-styles of the men and women they regard as their inferiors.

I should point out here that I am using 'middle class' very loosely in this [essay]. Historians are divided about the use of this term in relation to early nineteenth-century French history. It can be argued that 'the middle class' did not emerge until the coming of the Industrial Revolution, which occurred much later in France than it did in England. It is evident however that the value system based on concepts such as patriotism, piety, courage, self-sacrifice, the rights and duties of parents and of children, values that we associate with the middle class, were already manifest in Pixerécourt's melodramas, and even in the 'drama bourgeois' of the eighteenth century.

I am focusing my attention in this [essay] on the heroines in Pixerécourt's melodramas because he continually tried to show that the essential moral purity of women is vital in ensuring the survival of the value system he approved of. Women's role in society is presented in melodrama as primarily domestic, and whether the heroine appears on stage safe and happy with her husband and children at home, or endangered and distraught, fleeing from the villain across rugged mountains, it is as a member of the family—mother, wife, daughter—that Pixerécourt's heroines interact with others.

The "beautiful Floreska, ornament of Poland" ("La belle Floreska, l'ornament de la Pologne" I,1) is a typical melodrama heroine. In *The Polish Mines (Les Mines de Pologne)*, 1803, she and her little daughter Angéla have been kidnapped by Zamoski, the villain, who imprisons his victims in the impenetrable Minski castle up in the Krapack mountains. Even Zamoski who, like many melodrama villains, is motivated by lust, acknowledges the heroine's devotion and loyalty to her family, saying: "Tender mother, faithful wife, all her affections are focused on her husband Edwinski and her daughter. . . . Nothing can equal the horror that my presence inspires in her". When *The Polish Mines* opens, the virtuous heroine is already in the villain's clutches. The first time the audience sees Floreska, her fragile vulnerability is emphasized: she is carried onto the stage in a dead faint from which she soon emerges in a state of panic and frenzy, which subsides into despair. This behaviour is typical of the heroine-victim, powerless to overcome the persecutions of the villain in any way apart from the unwavering denial of her favours. She combines physical weakness and overt emotionalism with moral courage and strength.

Pixerécourt extols the moral purity and family loyalty of women both by demonstrating their admirable behaviour in adverse situations and by celebrating women's domestic role in picturesque scenes of family happiness. During the opening scenes of *Rosa,* 1800, for example, an adoring husband and child prepare a spectacle to celebrate the wife/mother heroine. Garlands decorate the garden in front of their cottage and Rosa's name is written in roses above the door. She makes her entrance beneath an arch of flowers and her son strews flowers before her as he leads her to the central position on the stage where bouquets of flowers are placed at her feet. Beauty and happiness are always indicative of virtue in Pixerécourt's plays and this joyful spectacle centered upon Rosa is a typical celebration of the virtuous wife and mother.

Values in Pixerécourt's melodramas are transmitted to the audience through verbal and visual signals. Before Rosa enters, the audience has received a considerable amount of information about her from the words and actions of her husband and son, and from a conversation between the villain and his accomplice. Rosa's virtue, like Floreska's, is so powerful that even the villain recognises her as worthy of respect. He spells out for the audience the characteristics of the ideal woman: "As virtuous as she is beautiful, the happiness of her family is her sole preoccupation. . . . Everyone loves her". It is significant that the happiness of her family is described as Rosa's 'sole' preoccupation. This is not simply to emphasize the high degree of the heroine's devotion, but has the more important effect of excluding all other aspects of life, notably those beyond the home, from her world. The action of the rest of the play, in fact, demonstrates that life in the outside world is not safe for women and children. Threatened by the villain and his accomplice, Rosa and her son have to

*The actress and dancer Caroline Soisson in the role of Clara in* La Citerne *by Pixerécourt.*

flee from their cottage. In Act II they find themselves in the wilderness ("un lieu sauvage") and in Act III they are imprisoned in a castle which threatens their lives when it burns down. Without the intervention of vice, Rosa would have remained safe and happy at home, where Pixerécourt believed she belonged.

The reason women in Pixerécourt's melodramas appear to belong in predominantly domestic situations is that he wished to reinforce for his public the idea that women have a vital role to play as the moral adhesive binding the family together. Since virtue in the family has traditionally been regarded by the middle class as essential for the survival of a virtuous, stable society, it is hardly surprising that middle class Pixerécourt stresses domestic virtues in his plays, the virtues associated with the 'wife' and 'mother'. Pixerécourt, in common with writers such as Rousseau, saw this family-centered role of women as natural and therefore unquestionable. In **The Spanish Moors (Les Maures d'Espagne)**, 1804, a play which celebrates motherhood in a variety of sentimental and sensational scenes, the wife-mother heroine refers to "the instinct nature gives to all mothers" ("l'instinct que la nature donne à toutes

les mères" II, 7). Throughout Pixerécourt's long career his melodramas repeatedly invited the audience to admire the image of the woman who would suffer anything to protect her children and remain loyal to her husband. For Pixerécourt, as for Rousseau, then, normal women have a vast influence for good which is primarily exerted through their role as chaste and devoted wives and mothers.

Pixerécourt also shared with Rousseau a peculiar attitude to sexual love. Both writers regarded love between a man and a woman as potentially destructive. Pixerécourt's plays present the ideal relationship between husband and wife as one of affection and respect. Love scenes in Pixerécourt's melodramas are relatively rare and when they do occur they are very restrained. It is significant, moreover, that many melodrama villains are motivated by an uncontrollable passion. Pixerécourt's female characters are never seen forcing their attentions on an unwilling man. The main problem their love for a man creates for the heroine is conflict with their fathers over the choice of a husband. The role of 'daughter', like that of 'wife' and 'mother', is a third equally important family role played by melodrama heroines.

The conflict between fathers and daughters which occurs in a large number of Pixerécourt's melodramas is usually the result of the father's failure to recognise the virtue of the hero whom his daughter loves. Again we find evidence of Pixerécourt's faith in the essential moral superiority of women over men. Not only do Pixerécourt's 'daughters' recognise the virtue of the hero, so too do their mothers. Indeed, the heroine has frequently received her mother's blessing for her relationship with the falsely accused hero. These morally perceptive female parents however are a potential source of marital discord because their judgment conflicts with the opinions of their husbands. In order to avoid showing the audience the disturbing image of a wife with right on her side challenging her husband, Pixerécourt usually kills off these wise mothers before the play begins. This does not stop the daughter from invoking her mother's name at moments when her own moral perspicacity is questioned. The heroine confronting her morally blind father in **The Man with Three Faces (L'Homme à trois visages)**, 1801, and declaring that her deceased mother gave her consent to the secret marriage of her daughter, cries "Ah! would that she were still alive. Her feeble voice would be raised in defence of innocence". This remark gives the audience infallible proof that the heroine and the hero are indeed virtuous. A dead mother is never wrong.

The image of women in melodrama is then clearly one of excessive virtue. They may lack physical strength but they are morally invincible. In the fifty melodramas we have that Pixerécourt wrote between 1798 and 1835, only four female characters are evil. Interestingly, a number of other heroines, particularly in plays written in the 1820s, are fallen women. Almost all of these evil or tainted women, however, are the victims of wicked or foolish *men*. Women almost never initiate wrong. Even as companions of vice they are more virtuous than men are.

To recapitulate, a typical, normal melodrama heroine is excessively virtuous, naturally domestic and as physically weak as she is morally strong.

Despite the impression given by many critics, however, not all Pixerécourt's heroines are restricted to the role of passive victim, persecuted by villains and rescued by heroes. Especially during the first half of his career, Pixerécourt introduced a number of energetic heroines who function successfully amidst spectacular settings beyond the peaceful realm of domesticity. These active heroines exhibit deviant and dangerous behaviour, in marked contrast to their weaker sisters who constitute the *normal* melodrama heroine. We need to ask whether or not Pixerécourt reveals a radical attitude to the role of women by presenting in a number of his most popular melodramas, heroines who subvert the norm.

Almost all of Pixerécourt's strong heroines move beyond the family circle and become involved in public, political situations which are normally the prerogative of men. In one of Pixerécourt's earliest and most successful plays, *The Man with Three Faces,* the heroine disobeys her father, the Doge of Venice, and appears before the entire governing body to defend her wrongly accused husband, Vivaldi. Rosemonde declares "with extreme intensity" ("avec la plus grande énergie") that she will die rather than leave without a reprieve for the hero (III, 8). During the debate concerning her husband's fate, Rosemonde is described in the stage directions as having "a steady expression" ("sa contenance est ferme") and she speaks "with nobility and steadfastness" ("avec noblesse et fermeté") in defence of Vivaldi (III, 9). Her proud bearing and her courageous confrontation with the men who rule Venice distinguish Rosemonde from Pixerécourt's usual model of the submissive heroine.

Another more striking example of an unusual female who has an excessive amount of physical courage, even when compared with that shown by the melodrama hero, is Elisabeth in *The Exile's Daughter (La Fille de l'exilé),* 1819. This heroine is only sixteen years old but she walks, for the most part alone, right across Russia from Siberia to Moscow, to beg the Tsar to restore her falsely condemned father and his family to their rightful position in Russian aristocratic society. At the beginning of the play Elisabeth's mother, blinded by sixteen years of misery in exile, fears for her daughter's safety, but her companions remind each other that "this young person knows absolutely no fear of danger" ("cette jeune personne ne connait aucun danger" I, 1). They go on to describe Elisabeth as combining courage and energy with constant sweetness, infinite patience, a loving, sensitive soul and the candour of an angel. This heroine possesses the best qualities of melodrama's heroes and heroines. When Elisabeth first talks about her plan to go to the Tsar she is warned, and the audience thus made explicitly aware of, the physical difficulties she will face: "Torrents and rivers to ford, immense forests and deserts to cross; in a word, dangers of all kinds and way beyond your strength to endure". Elisabeth replies, "No one has ever managed to calculate the strength of a child who wishes to restore honour and life to the creators of her being". This intrepid heroine plans her departure, confronts and subdues a series of tough male adversaries including a band of forbidding Tartars who are armed to the teeth, and finally lays her suit at the feet of the Tsar.

Rosemonde and Elisabeth resemble the typical melodrama heroine by displaying an extreme form of virtue, but their behaviour transcends that of the normal heroine in Pixerécourt's plays because they combine this 'feminine' moral strength with an almost 'masculine' physical courage and strength. Heroines like Rosemonde and to a greater degree, Elisabeth would appear to challenge the natural superiority of men which is a basic assumption underlying almost all melodramas. A number of factors, however, ensure that male dominance is upheld in *The Man with Three Faces* and *The Exile's Daughter.* First, both heroines are pursuing justice on behalf of a man's cause. They are therefore playing a supportive, albeit highly energetic and demanding role, rather than an independent one. They serve others. It is also significant that both of the men for whom these two heroines risk their lives are close members of their family, Rosemonde's husband and Elisabeth's father. This again reminds the audience of the essentially domestic role of women, despite their forays into public life. Male dominance is also ensured by a second factor: both plays show that political power, as Pixerécourt's audiences would have expected, is in the hands of men. Despite the heroics of Rosemonde and Elisabeth, it is ultimately men who enable them to achieve their noble aims. Both have to appeal to male judge figures, the Doge and the Tsar, and rely on the ability of these men to recognise virtue. Rosemonde's husband eventually persuades the Doge that he is innocent, and a series of men including a government courtier, a former courtier and a reformed Tartar all play vital roles in restoring Elisabeth's family's honour. The third and final reason why these two heroines pose little threat to the dominant societal image of women as weaker than men which Pixerécourt aimed to project, is that they are viewed by the other characters in the plays as extraordinary and in that sense abnormal. Exceptional circumstances have led to their exceptional behaviour but the final view spectators have of Rosemonde and Elisabeth shows them restored to the safety of their families. Elisabeth is united with her parents, the perfect daughter, and Rosemonde is pressed to the hero's breast, the perfect wife. Pixerécourt's ideal world of domestic harmony and tranquility has bee. restored.

Although Pixerécourt's heroines rarely venture into public life or exercise political power, two of his melodramas include a heroine with public status: they are both queens who, moreover, have no king beside them. Marguerite d'Anjou, in the play of the same name 1810, is a widow and Marie Stuart in *The Castle of Loch-Leuven,* 1882, is unmarried. Here is an ideal opportunity for Pixerécourt to present a woman with real power. Her lack of physical strength is no disadvantage when it comes to exercising political authority. What does Pixerécourt do? While Marguerite and Marie both have the right to exercise political power, they are the victims of evil plots which challenge their positions as queen and they do *not* therefore actually govern during the play. Each of these heroines is given regal dignity, courage and wisdom, but no real power. Their enemies have prevented them from ruling and they need the assistance of heroes, soldiers and male peasants to protect not only their political positions but even their lives. Their political and physical vulnerability means that these queens basically conform to the 'weak female' sex role Pixerécourt presents throughout his works.

A very few of the heroines in Pixerécourt's plays actually do challenge his dominant image of women as passive, gentle creatures. Among the heroines who do not conform to the usual submissive model, more than half wear men's clothes at some time during the play. All melodrama character types resort to disguise in order to outwit their enemies, and heroines are no exception. Pixerécourt's male characters in disguise always remain men. Pixerécourt's heroines sometimes disguise themselves as peasant girls or old women, but also, significantly, they sometimes disguise themselves as men. This latter group of transvestite women constitute the most interesting group of heroines in Pixerécourt's melodramas. (pp. 65-72)

*Why* do some of Pixerécourt's heroines resort to transvestism?

The first and most obvious explanation, of course, has to do with fashion and sex appeal. Women dressed as men in the nineteenth century offered the audience a rare opportunity to see the female figure, in particular the legs, which were normally covered all the way down to the ankle in skirts and petticoats.

The second explanation has to do with the nineteenth-century view of the changing role of women in society. In her recent mongoraph, *Understudies, Theatre and Sexual Politics,* Michelene Wandor makes the following general point about transvestism that is relevant to the theme of my [essay]:

> It is interesting to note that transvestite theatre has flourished at times of changing attitudes to women in the theatre and to sexuality in society—the Restoration, the industrial revolution, the suffrage agitation and now, in the second half of the twentieth century. At such times clearly there is a tension between the surface appearance of how men and women are supposed to 'be' and the changing reality.

The early period of Pixerécourt's career, especially, was a time of radically changing attitudes to women in France. Feminist ideas were being discussed in Paris at the turn of the nineteenth century by Condorcet, Odette de Mourges, Mary Wolstonecraft and others, a fact that disturbed conservatives who regarded women's role as naturally intended to be only that of wife and mother. The family was also seen by many to be under threat during the Empire because of Napoleon's new legislation allowing divorce and because of the high number of illegitimacies resulting from social dislocation caused by the Napoleonic wars. For conservatives like Pixerécourt, these threats must have been alarming, and not surprisingly, many of his plays embody attempts to shore up institutions like marriage and the family which he thought were in danger of collapse.

One would expect that transvestism in melodrama would operate as a perfect image of a collapsing society since the clear sex role demarcation is apparently challenged. Michelene Wandor argues, however, that not only does transvestism challenge the established roles, but it may

also paradoxically reinforce them. She claims that: "The function of transvestite theatre thus becomes twofold; on the one hand, it is an effort to contain rebellion by ridiculing any departure from the 'norm' and on the other, it becomes an expression of a rebellion against the status quo". The situation is, I believe, even more complex than Michelene Wandor suggests. Because women's status is inferior to men's, and this is certainly true in the world of Pixerécourt's melodramas, it is regarded as ridiculous for men to appear in feminine curls and skirts because this demeans them, whereas women dressed in trousers or tights are seen as attractive and powerful. Masculine attire enhances women's status. Furthermore, in nineteenth-century melodrama men's clothes enable the heroine to operate successfully in a male world. When there is no hero to offer her the assistance of his brave and brawny arm, the heroine, by adopting the external appearance of a hero, is granted the physical strength and courage normally confined to men. (pp. 72-3)

Pixerécourt's most powerful heroine who wears men's clothes and challenges the typical image of women, is Léontine in *Charles the Bold (Charles-le-Téméraire),* 1814. I shall therefore examine the role of Léontine in some detail.

Even when not disguised as a man, Léontine is an impressive figure. In Act I, disguised this time as a wood-cutter's wife, she helps to rescue her son from the enemy camp. In Act II and early in Act III, she saves her father and her son from disaster several times. Her physical courage is spectacularly demonstrated in Act II, scene 12 when *she* is the one who rushes into a burning house to snatch her child from the flames. This scene is highly reminiscent of a scene in *Rosa,* one of Pixerécourt's very first plays. In that early play, just as the audience would have expected, it is the father-hero who manages to reach safety with the child just as the burning building collapses. Pixerécourt was probably intending to increase the suspense of the situation in *Charles the Bold* by having a woman instead of a man perform this feat of physical daring. At this stage, when she is displaying supreme *maternal* devotion, Léontine is dressed as a woman.

It is not until Act III, scene 12 that this heroine appears disguised as a man, a knight in full and need I say whining armour. In Act II, scene 9, when exhorting the women of her beseiged city of Nancy to fight and even to die in the city's defence, Léontine reminds them that they live in Joan of Arc country. With this explicit reference to the celebrated military heroine of French history, Pixerécourt prepared his audience to admire his own military heroine. Her actions soon prove admirable. First she demonstrates military acumen, normally associated with men, when she manages to flood a marsh and drown a large number of enemy soldiers. Léontine then proceeds to exhibit even more deviant and dangerous behaviour in the penultimate scene of the play. Visor lowered, she challenges, fights, defeats and kills the villain, Charles the Bold. He has already been established as a courageous but fearsome opponent, a daunting prospect for anyone, much less a female fighter. But Léontine has strong and complex motives for attacking Charles. He is not only the leader of the enemies of her people, but he has also shown himself to be a harsh, cruel ruler. As far as Léontine is personally concerned, the main reason Charles deserves to die is that he captured and ignobly hanged her soldier husband. In fighting and killing Charles, Léontine is spurred on by the thought that she is both obliterating a political enemy and obtaining vengeance for the dishonourable death her husband received at the villain's hands.

Although Léontine has assistance from men at various points in the play, the most sensational and dangerous feats she is involved in, rescuing her son, defeating enemy soldiers and killing the villain, are all accomplished by her alone. How did Pixerécourt's public react to this dashing and dauntless heroine? To judge first from the large number of performances **Charles the Bold** received (more than 400 between 1814 and 1844, an impressive score for that period), and second from the enthusiasm shown in reviews for the play in general and for Léontine in particular, she was a popular character in a popular play. Critics commented specifically on her heroism: "However, there is no love interest; the author has managed to do without it, he has substituted heroism for love, and a woman is the bearer of this virtue." Another reviewer praised the actress playing Léontine for having lots of energy and for fighting "with surprising skill" ("avec une addresse surprenante"). Clearly the predominant note in these reviews is one of admiration for an unusual heroine.

It seems to me likely that Pixerécourt's audiences enjoyed Léontine's impressive behaviour precisely because she was a woman. As a female she was not expected to have the masculine characteristics of physical courage and military shrewdness required to overcome a series of dangerous threats. Pixerécourt constantly sought to provide his public with the new forms of sensationalism and the deviant and dangerous behaviour of the heroine in **Charles the Bold** proved to be a successful twist to the basic, established conventions of melodrama. The fact that Pixerécourt created so few heroines along the dashing, masculine lines of Léontine, despite her popularity, indicates that he wished to maintain her status as that of an atypical heroine who did not seriously challenge the predominant image found in Pixerécourt's melodramas of the gentle, vulnerable heroine, epitome of femininity.

Half of Pixerécourt's heroines who wear men's clothes, like Léontine, are involved in situations where they are compelled to use a weapon to defend themselves against the forces of evil. The male clothes they wear miraculously endow them with fighting skills normally possessed by males only. An equal number of Pixerécourt's transvestite heroines, although not obliged to fight, are required to protect and even rescue virtue in distress, a role normally associated with the actions of the hero. It is often said that clothes make the man—in these cases, men's clothes make the woman.

Beneath the apparently radical surface of the plays we have been examining, we find that the heroine's deviant and dangerous behaviour is far from subverting the dominant patriarchal structures of Pixerécourt's society, in fact merely supply the audience with a *frisson* of change. For Pixerécourt, woman's place is definitely in the home, where she plays a fundamentally dependent role. Although Pixerécourt gives his heroines the invaluable capacity to hold society together through their virtue, this capacity is insufficient on its own to uphold the structure of society. When the home or the state collapses, men almost always have to come to the rescue. The moral adhesive power given to women by Pixerécourt is a means by which the male-dominanted society aims to keep women happy in an oppressed position. Like Aldous Huxley's lesser characters in *Brave New World,* Pixerécourt's heroines can be glad they are gammas. (pp. 73-5)

*Gabrielle Hyslop, "Deviant and Dangerous Behavior: Women in Melodrama," in* Journal of Popular Culture, *Vol. 19, No. 3, Winter, 1985, pp. 65-77.*

---

## FURTHER READING

Brooks, Peter. *The Melodramatic Imagination: Balzac, Henry James, Melodrama, and the Mode of Excess.* New Haven and London: Yale University Press, 1976, 235 p.

Analytical study of the meaning and development of melodrama. Brooks uses psychoanalytic method to explicate recurring themes and images in Pixerécourt's plays.

# Friedrich Schiller

## 1759-1805

(Born Johann Cristoph Friedrich von Schiller) German dramatist, poet, historian, philosopher, and essayist.

### INTRODUCTION

One of the preeminent German authors of the nineteenth century, Schiller is esteemed as an adept lyricist and theoretician whose works are informed by his conviction that the writer should strive not only to entertain, but also to instruct and improve his audience. He was an immensely popular poet during his life, but is best remembered for his dramas. Of these, his early plays reflect his affinity with the *Sturm und Drang* movement, which championed the passionate expression of emotional and spiritual struggle, and emphasize both his idealism and his concern for human freedom; his later plays are characterized by more realistic, moral, and Classical subjects and forms.

The son of an army captain, Schiller was born in Marbach, a town in the southwestern state of Würtemberg. Aspiring to become a clergyman, he began his studies in 1766 at the Latin School in Ludwigsburg. However, in 1773, against the wishes of his parents, Schiller was drafted into the elite Karlsschule in Stuttgart, a rigidly disciplined military academy established to train the sons of German army officers for public service. Schiller entered the academy's medical department two years later. During this time he developed an interest in literature—secretly studying the works of William Shakespeare and the contraband works of the revolutionary author Friedrich Gottlieb Klopstock—and began to write, composing part of his first drama, *Die Räuber* (*The Robbers*). In 1780, Schiller was released from the academy and assigned to a regiment in Stuttgart as a surgeon; he completed *The Robbers* the following year. Unable to find a publisher, he printed the play anonymously at his own expense, and it soon attracted the attention of Wolfgang von Dalberg, director of the Mannheim National Theater, who staged *The Robbers* in 1781. The drama was both popular and controversial. Reviewers debated the morality of its characters, and Schiller, jailed for two weeks, was forbidden to publish further due to the revolutionary fervor the play allegedly inspired. The following year, Schiller deserted the army and fled to Mannheim, where he entered into a contract to provide Dalberg with three more plays. The first of these, *Die Verschwörung des Fiesko zu Genua* (*Fiesco; or, The Genoese Conspiracy*), met with mixed reviews, but *Kabale und Liebe* (*Intrigue and Love*) was tremendously popular, establishing Schiller as a master of drama. In 1785, Schiller moved to Leipzig and then Dresden, editing the literary journal *Die rheinische Thalia* and publishing several poems—including his most famous piece, "An die Freude" ("To Joy"). By 1787 he had completed the third

drama contracted by Dalberg, the successful *Don Karlos, Infant von Spanien* (*Don Carlos, Infant of Spain*).

Over the next ten years, Schiller ceased composing drama in favor of other intellectual pursuits. He accepted a position as a history professor at the University of Jena and wrote several historical treatises while devoting much time to studying philosophy, particularly that of Immanuel Kant. In 1794 he became acquainted with Johann Wolfgang von Goethe, who shared his growing interest in Classical art and literature. After years of correspondence on a variety of philosophical and aesthetic issues, Schiller joined Goethe in Germany's cultural capital of Weimar. During the course of their friendship they exercised a great influence on each other's work and collaborated on several literary projects, including the popular collection of epic ballads entitled *Musen-Almanach fur das Jahr 1789*. In 1799 Schiller completed the dramatic trilogy *Wallenstein*, a work often cited among the greatest German tragedies, and Goethe staged the play in its entirety the following year. Although Schiller's final years were marked by failing health, probably due to tuberculosis, he continued to write for the theater, composing *Maria Stuart, Die Jungfrau von Orleans* (*The Maid of Orleans*), *Die*

*Braut von Messina (The Bride of Messina)*, and *Wilhelm Tell (William Tell)*. *Demetrius*, a play which according to many critics promised to be Schiller's finest achievement, was left unfinished upon his death in 1805.

Critics generally trace the development of Schiller's dramas from the end of the Sturm und Drang movement to the height of German Classicism. His early plays feature the passionate struggles of heroes who pursue freedom and justice in hypocritical societies. *The Robbers*, for example, is an imaginative and often violent glorification of a rebel who, along with a band of thieves, attempts to overthrow a corrupt political order. Similarly *Fiesco* and *Intrigue and Love* feature criminals and idealistic reformers in plots involving class discrimination and greed. *Don Carlos*, Schiller's first play written in verse, is generally cited as a transitional drama in his career, resembling the earlier efforts in its plea for political freedom but also anticipating the style of his later Classical works.

*Wallenstein* signals a shift in Schiller's philosophical and aesthetic tenets. No longer convinced of the individual's ability to achieve freedom through revolution, Schiller conceived of a more personal and spiritual freedom developed through moral responsibility, maintaining that humankind may rise above corrupt conditions and attain dignity without violence. The *Wallenstein* trilogy, comprising *Wallenstein's Camp*, *The Piccolomini*, and *The Death of Wallenstein*, is generally regarded as the peak of Schiller's classical phase and, like all of his later works, is written in blank verse. Chronicling a brief period of political events during the Thirty Years War, the trilogy focuses on the downfall of the Catholic commander General Albrecht von Wallenstein, who is suspected of treason and tragically assassinated. Historical events also inform *Maria Stuart* and *The Maid of Orleans*, in which Schiller depicted the lives of Mary, Queen of Scots and Joan of Arc. For Schiller, each of these heroines achieves freedom, despite her tragic circumstances and eventual death, by rising above the corruption of church and government and fulfilling her own sense of moral obligation. In *The Bride of Messina*, which recalls Sophocles's *Oedipus Tyrannus*, Schiller used a chorus reminiscent of the ancient Greek tragedies in a drama of two brothers fated to fall in love with a woman who turns out to be their sister. *William Tell*, on the other hand, is based on a folk drama in which the eponymous hero, a skilled marksman, incurs the disfavor of the regional despot and is charged with testing his skill by shooting an apple off his son's head. The plot also centers on the events surrounding a rebellion planned by the Swiss against the Austrians. Critics note that although the theme of revolution in *William Tell* recalls Schiller's early plays, the achievement of national liberation through moral autonomy aptly reflects his later concerns.

Schiller's development as a poet is generally divided into three periods. While the poems of his youth are grandiloquent and emotional, covering a wide range of subjects from idyllic love to despotic brutality, the poems he wrote between 1785 and 1789 mark the maturation of Schiller's skills, featuring a more refined style and philosophical themes. "To Joy," perhaps his best known poem, is an enthusiastic tribute to brotherhood and peace, and "Die

Kunstler" ("The Artist") suggests that art is the motivating force behind social revolution, an idea Schiller explored further in his essays on aesthetics. Critics generally consider the poems Schiller wrote after 1795 his greatest. Primarily philosophical—focusing particularly on the idea of art allowing humanity to transcend everyday life—these poems also reflect Schiller's growing interest in Greek antiquity in both content and style. The popular ballads of this period in the *Musen-Almanach fur das Jahr 1798* draw from a wide range of literary, historical, mythological, and philosophical subjects.

Criticism of Schiller's works centers on his dramas. Scholars have regarded Schiller's early plays as thematically inconsistent and melodramatic, and most praise the later works for their poetic diction, vivid characterizations, and coherent plots. Recent criticism debates the philosophical perspective advanced in Schiller's works. Hermann Weigand has referred to Schiller as a "poet of general ideas," rather than of a specific philosophical position, and Ilse Appelbaum–Graham has found that his characters reflect "the starry heavens above them and the moral law within them." Wilhelm Emrich has suggested that Schiller struck a classical balance between idealism and realism by demonstrating the triumph of both the spiritual and natural sides of humanity. Nevertheless, Erich Heller has written that Schiller "is a striking instance of a European catastrophe of the spirit: the invasion and partial disruption of the aesthetic faculty by unemployed religious impulses." While many scholars agree that Schiller's dramas are less accessible to the modern reader due to their Baroque language, many have also detected in them modern complexities. For example, Helmut Rehder has suggested that Schiller's works feature certain images of humanity, emptiness, and space that anticipate the modern tendency towards nihilism and abstraction.

In Germany Schiller's work is regarded as a national legacy; his poem "To Joy" was set to music by Ludwig von Beethoven in the Ninth Symphony, and his philosophical writings have influenced the work of Friedrich Wilhelm Nietzsche, G. W. F. Hegel, and Karl Marx. Schiller has also exerted a profound impact on world literature, prompting the critic Josiah Royce to assert that he was a classical poet who belonged to no school or nation but "to the history of the human mind as a whole, and to the literature of the world at large."

## PRINCIPAL WORKS

*Die Räuber: Ein Schauspiel* (drama) 1781
  [*The Robbers*, 1792]
*Anthologie auf das Jahr 1782* (poetry) 1782
*Die Verschwörung des Fiesko zu Genua: Ein republicanisches Trauerspiel* (drama) 1783
  [*Fiesco; or, The Genoese Conspiracy*, 1796]
*Kabale und Liebe: Ein bürgerliches Trauerspiel in fünf Aufzügen* (drama) 1784
  [*The Minister: A Tragedy in Five Acts*, 1797; also translated as *Intrigue and Love*, 1953]

---

### Friedrich Schiller   (essay date 1781)

[*In the following preface from his first edition of* The Robbers, *Schiller outlines his intentions for the play and defends it from claims that its content is immoral, asserting that "it is the course of mortal things that the good should be shadowed by the bad, and virtue shine the brightest when contrasted with vice."*]

[*The Robbers*] is to be regarded merely as a *dramatic* narrative, in which, for the purpose of tracing out the innermost workings of the soul, advantage has been taken of the *dramatic* method, without otherwise conforming to the stringent rules of theatrical composition, or seeking the dubious advantage of stage adaptation. It must be admitted as somewhat inconsistent that three very remarkable people, whose acts are dependent on perhaps a thousand contingencies, should be completely developed within three hours, considering that it would scarcely be possible, in the ordinary course of events, that three such remarkable people should, even in twenty-four hours, fully reveal their characters to the most penetrating inquirer. A greater amount of incident is here crowded together than it was possible for me to confine within the narrow limits prescribed by Aristotle and Batteux.

It is, however, not so much the bulk of my play as its contents which banish it from the stage. Its scheme and economy require that several characters should appear, who would offend the finer feelings of virtue, and shock the delicacy of our manners. Every delineator of human character is placed in the same dilemma, if he proposes to give a faithful picture of the world as it really is, and not an ideal phantasy, a mere creation of his own. It is the course of mortal things that the good should be shadowed by the bad, and virtue shine the brightest when contrasted with vice. Whoever proposes to discourage vice, and to vindicate religion, morality, and social order, against their adversaries, must unveil crime in all its deformity, and place it before the eyes of men in its colossal magnitude. He must diligently explore its dark mazes, and make himself familiar with sentiments at the wickedness of which his soul revolts.

Vice is here exposed in its innermost workings. In Francis it resolves all the confused terrors of conscience into wild abstractions, destroys virtuous sentiments by dissecting them, and holds up the earnest voice of religion to mockery and scorn. He who has gone so far (a distinction by no means enviable) as to quicken his understanding at the expense of his soul—to him the holiest things are no longer holy—to him God and man are alike indifferent, and both worlds are as nothing. Of such a monster I have endeavoured to sketch a striking and lifelike portrait, to hold up to abhorrence all the machinery of his scheme of vice, and to test its strength by contrasting it with truth. How far my narrative is successful in accomplishing these objects, the reader is left to judge. My conviction is, that I have painted nature to the life.

Next to this man (Francis) stands another, who would perhaps puzzle not a few of my readers. A mind for which the greatest crimes have only charms through the glory which attaches to them, the energy which their perpetration requires, and the dangers which attend them. A remarkable and important personage, abundantly endowed with the power of becoming either a Brutus or a Catiline, according as that power is directed. An unhappy conjunction of circumstances determines him to choose the latter for his example, and it is only after a fearful straying that he is recalled to emulate the former. Erroneous notions of activity and power, an exuberance of strength which bursts through all the barriers of law, must of necessity conflict with the rules of social life. To these enthusiast dreams of greatness and efficiency, it needed but a sarcastic bitterness against the unpoetic spirit of the age, to complete the strange Don Quixote, whom, in the Robber Moor, we at once detest and love, admire and pity. It is, I hope, unnecessary to remark, that I no more hold up this picture as a warning exclusively to robbers, than the greatest Spanish satire was levelled exclusively at knight-errants.

It is now-a-days so much the fashion to be witty at the expense of religion, that a man will hardly pass for a genius if he does not allow his impious satire to run a-tilt at its most sacred truths. The noble simplicity of holy writ must needs be abused and turned into ridicule at the daily assemblies of the so-called wits; for what is there so holy and serious that will not raise a laugh if a false sense be attached to it? Let me hope that I shall have rendered no inconsiderable service to the cause of true religion and morality in holding up these wanton misbelievers to the detestation of society, under the form of the most despicable robbers.

But still more. I have made these said immoral characters to stand out favourably in particular points, and even in some measure to compensate by qualities of the head for what they are deficient in those of the heart. Herein I have done no more than literally copy nature. Every man, even the most depraved, bears in some degree the impress of the Almighty's image, and perhaps the greatest villain is not farther removed from the most upright man, than the petty offender; for the moral forces keep even pace with the powers of the mind, and the greater the capacity bestowed on man, the greater and more enormous becomes his misapplication of it, the more responsible is he for his errors.

The "Adramelech" of Klopstock (in his Messiah) awakens in us a feeling in which admiration is blended with detestation. We follow Milton's Satan with shuddering wonder through the pathless realms of chaos. The Medea of the old dramatists is, in spite of all her crimes, a great and wondrous woman, and Shakespeare's Richard the Third is sure to excite the admiration of the reader, much as he would hate the reality. If it is to be my task to portray men as they are, I must at the same time include their good qualities, of which even the most vicious are never totally destitute. If I would warn mankind against the tiger, I must not omit to describe his glossy, beautifully marked skin, lest, owing to this omission, the ferocious animal should not be recognised till too late. Besides this, a man who is so utterly depraved as to be without a single redeeming point, is no meet subject for art, and would disgust rather than excite the interest of the reader; who would turn over with impatience the pages which concern him. A noble soul can no more endure a succession of moral discords, than the musical ear the grating of knives upon glass.

And for this reason I should have been ill advised in attempting to bring my drama on the stage. A certain strength of mind is required both on the part of the poet and the reader; in the former that he may not disguise vice, in the latter that he may not suffer brilliant qualities to beguile him into admiration of what is essentially detestable. Whether the author has fulfilled his duty, he leaves others to judge, that his readers will perform theirs he by no means feels assured. The vulgar—among whom I would not be understood to mean merely the rabble—the vulgar, I say (between ourselves) extend their influence far around, and unfortunately—set the fashion. Too short-sighted to reach my full meaning, too narrow-minded to comprehend the largeness of my views, too disingenuous

to admit my moral aim—they will, I fear, almost frustrate my good intentions, and pretend to discover in my work an apology for the very vice which it has been my object to condemn, and will perhaps make the poor poet, to whom anything rather than justice is usually accorded, responsible for his simplicity.

Thus we have a *Da capo* of the old story of Democritus and the Abderitans, and our worthy Hippocrates would needs exhaust whole plantations of hellebore, were it proposed to remedy this mischief by a healing decoction. Let as many friends of truth as you will, instruct their fellow-citizens in the pulpit and on the stage, the vulgar will never cease to be vulgar, though the sun and moon may change their course, and "heaven and earth wax old as a garment." Perhaps, in order to please tender-hearted people, I might have been less true to nature; but if a certain beetle, of whom we have all heard, could extract filth even from pearls, if we have examples that fire has destroyed and water deluged, shall therefore pearls, fire, and water be condemned? In consequence of the remarkable catastrophe which ends my play, I may justly claim for it a place among books of morality, for crime meets at last with the punishment it deserves; the lost one enters again within the pale of the law, and virtue is triumphant. Whoever will but be courteous enough towards me to read my work through with a desire to understand it, from him I may expect—not that he will admire the poet, but that he will esteem the honest man. (pp. xiii-xvii)

*Friedrich Schiller, in a preface to his* The Works of Frederick Schiller, *translated by Henry G. Bohn, George Bell & Sons, 1873, pp. xiii-xvii.*

### Friedrich Schiller  (lecture date 1784)

[*In the following essay, delivered as a lecture in 1784, Schiller discusses the merits of the theater.*]

Theater was born out of a universal, irresistible attraction to the new and extraordinary, a desire to feel oneself put into a state of passion, to use Sulzer's expression. Exhausted by higher mental exertions, worn down by the monotonous, often oppressive affairs of daily life, and bombarded by sensuality, man necessarily felt an inner emptiness which clashed with his eternal desire for activity. Our nature, equally incapable of remaining forever in a bestial condition or of continuously carrying on the intricate work of the Understanding, required an intermediate condition that would unite these two contradictory extremes, resolving their harsh tension into gentle harmony and facilitating the alternating passage from one state into the other. This service is performed by the Aesthetic Sense, or the Sense of the Beautiful. But since the wise legislator's chief object must be to select the superior of two possible courses of action, he will not acquiesce in merely neutralizing popular sentiments, but will, whenever possible, use those sentiments as means to accomplish higher ends, endeavoring to transform them into a source of general happiness. And that is why he chose theater above all else, since it opens up infinite horizons to the spirit thirsting for activity, providing nourishment to the soul's every power without overtaxing any single one, and uniting the acculturation of mind and heart with the noblest sort of entertainment.

Whoever first observed that *religion* is the mightiest pillar of the state, and that laws themselves lose their power once religion is removed, has perhaps given us—without knowing or intending it—our best defense of the theater on behalf of its noblest side. This inadequacy, this unstable character of political laws, which makes religion indispensable to the State, also conditions the moral influence exerted by the state. Laws, he was trying to say, revolve around duties of denial; religion extends its demands to true action. Laws restrict only those activities which tend to weaken society's cohesion; religion ordains those which deepen it. Laws rule only over the outward expressions of the will, and deeds are their only subjects; religion extends its jurisdiction into the heart's most hidden recesses, and pursues thoughts to their most inward source. Laws are slippery and malleable, as changeable as mood and passion; religion forms strong and eternal bonds. Now, if we were to assume something which is not the case—if we conceded that religion possessed this tremendous power over every human heart, then will it, or can it completely develop our character? Religion (and here I am dealing solely with its divine, and not its political aspects) generally acts more upon the sensuous side of the population—indeed, it is probably because of this effect on the sensuous that its influence is so sure. Deprived of this, religion's power vanishes—and whence the influence of the stage? Religion ceases to exist for the greater part of humankind, the moment we destroy its symbols and mysteries, the moment we efface its renderings of Heaven and Hell. And yet, these are merely fantastic portraits, riddles without solution, terror-figures, and distant enticements. Consider now, how religion and law are strengthened as they enter into alliance with the theater, where virtue and vice, happiness and misery, wisdom and folly are accurately and palpably led out before man in a thousand images; where Providence solves its riddles, untangles its knots before his eyes; where the human heart confesses its subtlest stirrings while tortured on the rack of passion; where all masks fall away, the makeup is removed, and truth sits in judgment, incorruptible as Rhadamanthus.

The jurisdiction of the stage begins where the domain of secular law leaves off. Whenever justice is dazzled by gold and gloats in the pay of infamy; when the crimes of the mighty mock their own impotence, and mortal fear stays the ruler's arm—then theater takes up the sword and scales, and hauls infamy before the dreadful tribune of justice. The entire realm of fantasy and history, past and present, stand at its beck and call. Monstrous criminals, long rotted to dust, are summoned by poesy's omnipotent call, to relive their shameful lives for the grim edification of later generations. Unconsciously, like empty shadows, the horrors of their own age pass before our eyes while we, horrified yet fascinated, curse their memory. Someday, when morality is no longer taught, when religion is no longer met with mere faith, when laws become superfluous, we shall still tremble as Medea totters down the palace steps, fresh from the murder of her child. Mankind shall still be seized with healthy terror, and all will silently rejoice over their own clear conscience, as Lady Macbeth, the dreadful sleepwalker, washes her hands and summons all the perfumes of Arabia to extinguish the hateful odor of murder. As surely as visual representation is more compelling than the mute word or cold exposition, it is equally certain that the theater wields a more profound, more lasting influence than either morality or laws.

In doing so, it is merely *assisting* human justice; but yet another, broader field is open to it as well. The theater has the power to punish the thousand vices which justice must patiently tolerate; the thousand virtues which the latter must let pass without comment, on the stage are held up for general admiration. And here, at its side, are wisdom and religion. From their pure fountain it draws its lessons and examples, and clothes stern duty in charming and alluring robes. How it swells our soul with great emotions, resolves, passions—what a divine ideal it sets up for us to emulate! When good-hearted Augustus extends his hand to the traitor Cinna, who could already read the death sentence on his lips, and Augustus, great as his gods, says: "Cinna, let us be friends"—who among the audience, at *that* moment, would not also like to be shaking the hand of his own mortal enemy, in imitation of this god-like Roman? When Franz von Sickingen, on his way to punish a prince and wage war for others' rights, inadvertently turns his head and sees the smoke rising from his fortress, where his helpless wife and children have remained behind, and he—*moves onward* to keep his sacred word—how great does man become for me at that moment, how small and contemptible his dreaded, invincible fate!

In the theater's fearsome mirror, the vices are shown to be as loathsome as virtue is lovely. When, in night and tempest, old Lear knocks in vain at his daughter's door; when, his white hair streaming in the wind, he tells the raging elements of his Regan's unnatural conduct; when his agony finally bursts from his lips with those awful words: "I have given you all!"—how despicable does ingratitude seem to us then! How solemnly we vow to practice filial love and respect!

But the stage extends its sphere of influence further still. Even in those regions where religion and law deem it beneath their dignity to accompany human sentiment, the theater is still at work for our cultural weal. Human folly can disturb social harmony just as easily as can crime and vice. A lesson as old as history itself teaches that in the fabric of human events, the greatest weights are often suspended by the most slender and delicate threads, and, if we follow actions back to their sources, we will have to laugh ten times before we draw back once in horror. With each day I grow older, my catalogue of villains grows shorter, and my index of fools longer and more complete. If the entire moral guilt of the one species of person stems from one and the same source; if all the monstrous extremes of vice which have ever branded him, are merely altered forms, higher grades of a quality which, in the end, we can all laugh about and love—why, then, would nature have taken some different route with the other species? I know of only *one* secret for guarding man against depravity, and that is: to arm his heart against weaknesses.

We can expect a great share of this work to fall to the

stage. The stage holds up a mirror to that most populous class, the fools, and exposes their thousand varieties to relief-bringing ridicule. What in the former case it effected through emotional turmoil and horror, here it accomplishes (and, perhaps, more speedily and infallibly) through humor and satire. If we were to evaluate tragedy and comedy according to the magnitude of achieved effect, then experience would probably decide in favor of the latter. Man's pride is more deeply wounded by ridicule and contempt, than his conscience is tormented by abhorrence. Our cowardice, when confronted with terror, crawls away in fear; but this very cowardice delivers us over to the sting of satire. Laws and conscience can protect us *most of the time* from crimes and vices; the ludicrous requires a more refined discernment, and nowhere can this be presented to greater effect than on the stage's forum. We might perhaps instruct a friend to assault our morals and our heart, but we can scarcely prevail upon ourselves to forgive him a single laugh. Our transgressions might abide a monitor and judge, but we can scarcely suffer witnesses to our private perversities. Only the stage is permitted to ridicule our weaknesses, since it spares our sensibilities, and knows no such thing as a guilty fool. Without reddening with embarrassment, in its mirror we can see our own mask fall away, and thank it secretly for this gentle reproach.

But its sphere of influence is greater still. The stage is, more than any other public institution, a school of practical wisdom, a guide to our daily lives, an infallible key to the most secret accesses of the human soul. I am the first to admit that its influence is not infrequently nullified by self-love and mental obdurancy; that a thousand vices still impudently step before its glass; that a thousand fine emotions are pushed away by the cold-hearted audience. I will even venture to say that Molière's Harpagon has probably never reformed a single usurer, that the suicide Beverly has held few of his brothers back from the gambling table, that the robber Karl Moor's tragic story will scarcely make the highways any less dangerous. But, even if we so qualify this great effect of the stage, even if we are so unfair as to deny it altogether—what a wealth of influence it still retains! Although it has neither eradicated nor diminished the sum of our vices, did it not first make us familiar with them?—We will always have to live with vicious and foolish people. We must either avoid or confront them; we either seek to undermine them, or must become their victims. But no longer do they take us by surprise. Now we are prepared for their assaults. The theater has fathomed the secrets of how to root them out and render them harmless. It was the theater which drew the mask from the hypocrite's face, and revealed the traps which cabals and intrigues have laid for us. It has hauled falsehood and deception out from its twisted labyrinths, and exposed its awful face to the light of day. It may be that the dying Sara does not deter a single debauchee; that all the world's depictions of the seducer punished will not quench his own fire; and that the coquettish actress herself does her best to allay this effect—is it not reward enough, that unsuspecting innocence can now recognize its snares; that the theater has taught it to mistrust its oaths and to shrink back from its attestations of love?

The theater sheds light not only on man and his character, but also on his destiny, and teaches us the great art of facing it bravely. In the fabric of our lives, *chance* and *design* play equally important roles; the latter is directed by *us,* while we must blindly submit to the former. We have already come a long way, if the inevitable does not catch us wholly unprepared, if our courage and resourcefulness have already been tested by similar events, and our heart has been hardened for its blow. The stage brings before us a rich array of human woes. It artfully involves us in the troubles of others, and rewards us for this momentary pain with tears of delight and a splendid increase in our courage and experience. In its company, we follow the forsaken Ariadne through echoing Naxos; we descend into Ugolino's tower of starvation; we ascend the frightful scaffold, and witness the solemn hour of death. What our soul only senses as distant premonition, here we can hear audibly and incontrovertibly affirmed by the startled voice of nature. Under the tower's vault, the deceived favorite is deprived of his queen's favor; now that he must die, the intimidated Moor finally drops his treacherous sophistry. Eternity leaves its dead behind, so that they may reveal secrets which the living could never divine, and the cocksure villain is driven from his final ghastly lair, for even graves blurt out their secrets.

But, not satisfied with merely acquainting us with the fates of mankind, the stage also teaches us to be more just toward the victim of misfortune, and to judge him more leniently. For, only once we can plumb the depths of his tormented soul, are we entitled to pass judgment on him. No crime is more heinous than that of the thief; but do we not all soften our verdict with a tear of compassion, when we imagine ourselves in the same horrible predicament which compels Eduard to commit the deed?—Suicide is generally detested as sacrilege; but when Marianne, assailed by an enraged father's threatenings, assailed by love and by the thought of a dreadful convent's prison walls, drinks from her poisoned cup—who among us will be the first to condemn this pitable victim of an infamous social practice?—Humaneness and toleration are becoming the predominant spirit of our times; their rays have penetrated into the courtrooms, and further still, into the hearts of our rulers. What share of this divine labor falls to our theaters? Is it not *these* which have acquainted man with his fellow man, and have explored the hidden mechanism of his actions?

One noteworthy class of men has special grounds for giving particular thanks to the stage. Only here do the world's mighty men hear what they never or rarely hear elsewhere: Truth. And here they see what they never or rarely see: Man.

Thus is the great and varied service done to our moral culture by the better-developed stage; the full enlightenment of our intellect is no less indebted to it. Here, in this lofty sphere, the great mind, the fiery patriot first discovers how he can fully wield its powers.

Such a person lets all previous generations pass in review, weighing nation against nation, century against century, and finds how slavishly the great majority of the people are ever languishing in the chains of prejudice and opinion, which eternally foil their strivings for happiness; he finds that the pure radiance of truth illumines only a few isolated minds, who probably had to purchase that small gain at the cost of a lifetime's labors. By what means, then, can the wise legislator induce the entire nation to share in its benefits?

The theater is the common channel through which the light of wisdom streams down from the thoughtful, better part of society, spreading thence in mild beams throughout the entire state. More correct notions, more refined precepts, purer emotions flow from here into the veins of the population; the clouds of barbarism and gloomy superstition disperse; night yields to triumphant light. From among the myriad and magnificent fruits of the better-developed stage, I will select only two. Who could not notice the universal spread of toleration toward religious sects in recent years? Long before Nathan the Jew and Saladin the Saracen filled us with shame and preached to us that the divine doctrine of submission to God's Will is not irrevocably tied to whatever we might imagine His nature to be, and long before Joseph II combated the fearsome hydra of pious hatred, the theater had already emplanted humanity and gentleness into our hearts. The revolting spectacle of the priests' pagan fanaticism taught us to eschew religious hatred; within the frame of this dreadful mirror, Christianity washed out its shameful stains. From the stage's forum, we might also combat errors in *education* with equal success; we are still awaiting the piece which deals with this noteworthy theme. For, judging from its consequences, no subject has greater importance for the future of the republic, than education; and yet, no area has been more neglected, and none so completely abandoned to the individual citizen's illusions and caprice. The stage alone would be able to confront him with touching, soul-stirring scenes depicting the unfortunate victims of neglected education; here our fathers could learn to forego their foolish maxims, and our mothers to temper their love with rationality. False notions can lead even the finest heart astray; and what a disaster, when these begin to boast a *method,* and systematically spoil the tender stripling within the walls of philanthropic institutes and academic hot-houses.

No less readily—if only the chiefs and guardians of the state learned to do this—the stage could be utilized to correct the nation's opinions concerning the government and those it governs. Here, legislative power might speak to the subject through unfamiliar symbols, could respond to his complaints even before these were uttered, and could quash his doubts without seeming to do so. Even industry and inventiveness could and would be imbued with fiery emotion on the stage's forum, if our poets ever deemed it worth their while to be patriots, and if the state would ever condescend to listen to them.

I cannot possibly neglect to mention the great influence that a fine standing theater would have upon the spirit of our nation. I define a people's national spirit as the similarity and agreement of its opinions and inclinations concerning matters in which another nation thinks and feels differently. Only the stage is capable of eliciting a high degree of such agreement, because it ranges throughout the entire domain of human knowledge, exhausts all the situations of life, and pokes its rays into the heart's every cranny; because within it, it unites all classes and social strata, and can boast the most well-beaten pathway to our heart and our understanding. If *one* principle feature could characterize all our plays; if our poets could agree amongst themselves to establish a firm alliance to this end; if their works could be guided by a rigorous selection process, and they applied their brush only to subjects of national import—in short, if we could witness the birth of our own national theater, then we would truly become a nation. What bound the Greeks so firmly together? What was it that drew its people so irresistibly to its stage? Nothing other than the patriotic content of their pieces; it was the Grecian spirit, the great, overwhelming interest of the republic, and of a better humanity which lived and breathed within them.

The stage possesses another merit, one which I am all the more willing to claim, since I suspect that its legal contest with the prosecution has already been won. What we have heretofore undertaken to demonstrate—that the stage wields critical, determining influence over morality and enlightened thought—was a dubious quest. But even the theater's worst enemies concede that of all contrivances of luxury, and of all the institutions of public entertainment, it reigns supreme. But what it accomplishes in this respect, is more important than we are wont to imagine.

Human nature cannot bear the uninterrupted and eternal rack of daily business; and sensual excitement simply dies with its own gratification. Man, overwrought by animal enjoyments, fatigued from protracted labors, tormented by his eternal compulsion to remain active, thirsts for better and more select amusement—either this, or he will blindly plunge into wild revelry, accelerating his own demise and disrupting the peace of society. Bacchanalian debauchery, ruinous gambling, a thousand follies hatched from idleness—these are the inevitable consequences of the legislator's inability to rechannel these tendencies within the population. The businessman is in danger of developing stomach ulcers as his atonement for a life of selfless dedication to the state; the scholar is in danger of degenerating into a dull pedant; the common man, into a beast. The stage is the institution where instruction and pleasure, exertion and repose, culture and amusement are wed; where no one power of the soul need strain against the others, and no pleasure is enjoyed at the expense of the whole. When grief gnaws at our heart, when melancholy poisons our solitary hours; when we are revolted by the world and its affairs; when a thousand troubles weigh upon our souls, and our sensibilities are about to be snuffed out underneath our professional burdens—then the theater takes us in, and within its imaginary world we dream the real one away; we are given back to ourselves; our sensibilities are reawakened; salutary emotions agitate our slumbering nature, and set our hearts pulsating with greater vigor. Here the unfortunate, seeing another's grief, can cry out his own; the jolly will be sobered, and the secure will grow concerned. The delicate weakling becomes hardened into manhood, and here the first tender emotions are awakened within the barbarian's breast. And then, at last—O Nature! what a triumph for you!—

Nature, so frequently trodden to the ground, so frequently risen from its ashes!—when man at last, in all districts and regions and classes, with all his chains of fad and fashion cast away, and every bond of destiny rent asunder—when man becomes his brother's brother with a *single* all-embracing sympathy, resolved once again into a *single* species, forgetting himself and the world, and reapproaching his own heavenly origin. Each takes joy in others' delights, which then, magnified in beauty and strength, are reflected back to him from a hundred eyes, and now his bosom has room for a *single* sentiment, and this is: to be truly *human*. (pp. 211-19)

> *Friedrich Schiller, "Theater Considered as a Moral Institution," translated by John Sigerson and John Chambless in* Friedrich Schiller: Poet of Freedom, *New Benjamin Franklin House, 1985, pp. 211-19.*

---

**Coleridge on Schiller's *Robbers:***

'Tis past one o'clock in the morning. I sat down at twelve o'clock to read the ***The Robbers*** of Schiller. I had read, chill and trembling, when I came to the part where the Moor fixes a pistol over the robbers who are asleep. I could read no more. My God . . . who is this Schiller, this convulser of the heart? Did he write his tragedy amid the yelling of fiends? I should not like to be able to describe such characters. I tremble like an aspen leaf. Upon my soul, I write to you because I am frightened. I had better go to bed. Why have we ever called Milton sublime? that Count de Moor horrible wielder of heart-withering virtues? Satan is scarcely qualified to attend his execution as gallows chaplain.

*Samuel Taylor Coleridge, in a letter to Robert Southey, November, 1794.*

---

## George Bancroft (essay date 1823)

[*Bancroft was an American historian and critic best known for his ten-volume* History of the United States from the Discovery of the Continent *(1834-75). In the following excerpt, he surveys Schiller's minor poems, finding them moral, patriotic, and effective in their treatment of themes from nature and antiquity.*]

The genius of Schiller never appears more pleasing or more admirable, than in his minor poems. While the enthusiasm of his own character is very happily expressed in them, and the reflections of a vigorous and well educated mind are joined to the most various kinds of poetic invention, his language is uniformly pure and his style exquisitely finished. We have the elevated sentiments of a poet, conveyed with careful elegance in the most beautiful measures of which the copious German dialect admits, and his pieces are uniformly remarkable for the charm of their numbers and diction. In poetry so much depends on the choice of words, that this alone would ensure him a high reputation. But it is the least praise of Schiller. He is no less distinguished for his genius and the purity of his taste, than for the perfection of his style. In the early part of his literary career, his works were the productions of a mind, which seemed always in a state of excitement. They possess all the vehemence of passionate description, but in his moral speculations there is nothing of the tranquillity, which belongs to a mind already conversant with those subjects. They give proofs of a constant fever of imagination, of restlessness and anxiety in their author. These first fruits of his genius are rather to be taken as early indications of his extraordinary powers, than as finished specimens of them. But even while his mind was in this unsettled state, Schiller never inclined to the demoralizing principles, which distinguished many of his poetical contemporaries. He was naturally enthusiastic and noble; he believed in virtue and the excellence of human nature, and had an abhorrence of that scepticism, which represents disinterestedness as nowhere existing. He preserves the purest character throughout all his writings, and although one or two small pieces have some allusions which are not altogether free from coarseness, he is never licentious; and all his works show him to have been full of reverence for the sanctity of religion and the domestic affections.

This is no small praise in a poet, who was almost contemporary with Wieland and Voltaire, and who lived in a period, when unexampled popularity was obtained by writers who knew how to join licentiousness and profaneness to wit. But his reputation has been far from suffering from the elevated character of his style and sentiments. There is no lasting poetical fame, except where the eloquence of virtue is united to the inspiration of poetry; and it is hardly less pleasing in point of morals than of good taste to find that, while most of the corrupting writers of his time are forgotten, Schiller is becoming more and more popular; and is hardly less admired at Milan and at Paris, than at Berlin and Weimar.

Schiller belonged to that class of men, who are willing to admire wherever any distinguished virtue is exhibited; and he was far from desiring to take from the great names of antiquity the veneration, with which mankind has been accustomed to regard them. Although his works are full of passages in which he complains of the little sympathy he could find in others, he never despaired of human nature.

The character and feelings of Schiller as an individual appear throughout his poetry. Every sentiment seems to derive its peculiar cast from his own mind, just as certain plants take the color of their leaves from the soil in which they grow. In this he differs remarkably from the poet, who disputes with him the admiration of his country. Goethe reflects in his poems the feelings of others; Schiller felt deeply himself, and knew how to embody his feelings in verse. In whatever age or country Goethe places his invention, he instantly adapts himself to its manners and tone; Schiller always preserves under all changes of scene the peculiar characteristics of his own mind. The person of Goethe is never seen through his verse; that of Schiller presents itself constantly. It is the German poet in Spain, in Switzerland, in France; seizing on all opportunities of paying tribute to excellence, truth, and liberty. We may learn from Goethe what the world is; but Schiller teaches us what it should be. (pp. 268-70)

In his critical opinions on subjects connected with poetry, Schiller shares the free spirit of his literary countrymen. The rules of the French drama were insupportable to him, and when Goethe prepared the Mahomet of Voltaire for the German stage, Schiller expostulated with him, 'that he, who was already crowned as the priest of the tragic art, should sacrifice on the broken altars of a foreign muse.'—'The genius of the German has dared of itself to enter into the sanctuary of the arts, and has advanced in the footsteps of the Greeks and the English.'—'Poetic excellence can be created by no Louis; it borrows nothing from earthly majesty; it allies itself with nothing but truth.'

It is indeed one of the most distinguishing features in the history of modern German literature, that the greatest efforts have been made by persons of the inferior classes of society, and that they have received little support from their princes and little patronage from the nobles. 'No Augustan age,' says Schiller,

> bloomed for the German Muse; the kindness of no prince, like the Medici, smiled on her; she was not fostered by fame; nor did she unfold herself in the beams of royal favor. From the greatest of German heroes, from the throne of Frederic the Great, she withdrew without protection and without honor. The German may say with pride, that he has himself created his own merit. And hence the poetry of German bards rises in a bolder arch, and pours with a more copious stream.

To his national feelings Schiller unites a tinge of melancholy. He was fond of philosophy, and, though he never pursued those studies with method, he was accustomed to speculate boldly on the duties and destiny of man. He seems to have had in his own mind an image of moral and mental greatness, and he strove to realize that image in the world. He was of course disappointed; but, far from abusing his fellowmen for their want of the virtues which he believed essential to the dignity of our nature, he looks forward the more earnestly for better days. (pp. 272-73)

The personification of nature is common to all great poets. The works of Scott, and still more of Byron, abound in them. It forms one of the charms of oriental literature, and when it is not carried so far as to seem insincere, its effect is always pleasing. In Schiller it is united with depth and vigor of conception; but some of the inferior poets have almost no other inspiration. Descriptive poetry, under its best forms, is not of the highest order; it is a greater effort to unfold the passions, than to sketch a landscape, and we are soon tired of the most highly wrought pictures of natural scenery, unless there is some Rinaldo in peril, or Erminia in need of seclusion and shelter. Some have endeavored to compensate for the lifelessness of description by supposing the plants possessed of thought and language, and relating their loves and jealousies. Though this may be exceedingly pretty in a short poetical composition, yet when extended through a long poem it is necessarily dull.

The fondness of Schiller for nature is of a higher kind. He seems to have regarded her as a companion, that suited the pensive character of his mind and encouraged in him his favorite reflections. This is seen in no poem more remarkably than in the classic elegy, 'The Walk,' a piece of about two hundred lines; in which the poet gives way to the contemplative mood, occasioned by a solitary excursion. He passes through the meadows and woods, and his soul opens to the loveliness of the landscape. The tranquillity of country life is contrasted with the bustle of the distant city; the prospect of which excites reflections on social union, the progress of the arts, the prosperity, revolutions, and ruin of states, the perpetual change of the governments of men; while nature, in unchanging beauty, remains true to her ancient law, extending the same azure above, the same verdure beneath the nearest and the remotest generations, and the sun of Homer smiles now on us.

Schiller was a lover of the antique. In one of his tragedies, which is full of lyric beauties, he has attempted to revive the ancient chorus; but he is much more successful in imitating the tone and feelings of the ancients in some of his smaller poems. The nuptials of a daughter of Priam are celebrated with royal pomp; 'Cassandra' rushes from the assembly, for her prophetic eye has already had a vision of the impending ruin of her country, and all the horrors which her father's family were to undergo. In **'The Triumphal Banquet,'** after Troy had been taken, the Grecian heroes pledge each other at the board, heedless of the dangers and wretchedness, which awaited many of them on their return. This short poem possesses high tragic interest, for Schiller very ingeniously intersperses in their conversation those moral reflections, which may remind the reader of their melancholy end. There is more richness of imagination and glow of language in **'The Eleusinian Feast,'** in which the influence of the gift of Ceres on human society is magnificently described with all the life and beauty of ancient mythology; and in **'The Gods of Greece,'** he explains the influence of that mythology on the imagination, and the cheerful character of that religion, according to which, 'a kiss took away the last breath of life; a Genius inverted his torch; the child of a mortal held the balances at the entrance of Orcus, and the furies themselves relented at the pathetic complaint of the Thracian.' (pp. 274-75)

In the choice of his subjects Schiller was bold and poetical. At a time, when the maid of Orleans had become associated with licentious wit and ridicule, Schiller ventured to vindicate her character, and redeemed her name from the degradation, not to say infamy, into which it had sunk, in the hands of her countryman. There is one subject, which is, we believe, entirely of Schiller's invention; ' **"The Song of the Bell"**; vivos voco, mortuos plango, fulgura frango.' Workmen, who are casting a bell, describe all the events, which are solemnized by its voice; the morning of birth; the wedding-day; fires and funerals; the hour of vespers, when it is the signal of repose and domestic quiet; times of danger and alarm; wars and seditions. The bell which they are making they name Concordia, and raise it up, that 'high above earthly life, it may swing in the azure tent of heaven, be the neighbor of the thunder, and become a voice from above, like the bright host of the stars.' This poem addresses itself to all that is gentle and good in our natures; it is rapid, eloquent, and beautiful; it is finished with consummate care, and its measure, varying with the sentiment, is always harmonious and expressive. It has lately been translated by Lord Gower.

The Germans have ever been celebrated for their ballads. The 'Leonora' and 'Wild Huntsman' of Bürger are familiar to the lovers of translated verse; and a translation of Goethe's 'Erl king' was, we believe, one of the earliest efforts of Sir Walter Scott. The ballads of Schiller are more pleasing than those of Bürger and Goethe. They are almost always of a cheerful character; but where they are sad, they have the sadness of sentiment and not of horrors. (pp. 278-79)

Throughout the poetry of Schiller the chaste and delicate character of his mind is apparent. He was fond of purity and virtue, of studious retirement and domestic happiness. He has several little pieces, in which he elegantly expresses his admiration of woman, and his female characters are often invented with peculiar felicity. **'The Girl from Abroad,' 'The Voice of a Spirit,' 'The Maiden's Complaint,'** are three beautiful specimens of his manner in this department of poetry. He has contrasted in one of his poems [**'The Dignity of Woman'**] the character and offices of woman and man. This piece is a favorite with all lovers of the German muse; but in attempting to translate lines on a subject, in which every man is too much interested to adopt without addition the sentiments of another, a literal version has seemed impossible, and nothing has been produced but a feeble imitation. (p. 285)

Schiller was happy in private life, and he deserved to be so. He gained also what to the poet is more desirable than private ease; he gained that which is the best inspiration of the bard, and the best reward of bravery,—that which made Hector valiant, and the Lacedemonians temperate,—that which best encourages eloquence and excites to mental labour,—the Praise of Woman. He is the great favorite of his fair countrywomen. To them he seems to appeal with a modest confidence in his own merit and the purity of his works. 'In the female forum,' says he, 'the judgment of individual actions may be wrong; the judgment of character never.' 'The opinion of man,' he expresses himself in a distich, 'is founded on reason, that of woman on her feelings; when she does not feel, woman has already passed sentence.' And when he takes leave of his reader, and modestly speaks of the nature of his poems and of whom he would gain the approbation, he says,

> The echo of them will be lost, when the season is gone by; the desire of the moment gave birth to them; they fly away in the light dance of the hours; only if they deserve a crown, may it be from the virtuous, from those to whom truth is pleasing, but for whom gaudiness has no charms; from those who possess hearts to discriminate and to cherish the beautiful.
>
> (p. 287)

*G. Bancroft, "Schiller's Minor Poems," in* The North American Review, *Vol. VIII, No. 4, October, 1823, pp. 268-87.*

---

**Goethe on Schiller's dramatic motifs:**

He seized boldly on a great subject, and turned it this way and that. But he saw his object only on the outside; a quiet development from its interior was not within his province. His talent was more desultory. Thus he was never decided—could never have *done*. He often changed a part just before a rehearsal.

And, as he went so boldly to work, he did not take sufficient pains about *motifs*. I recollect what trouble I had with him, when he wanted to make Gessler, in *Tell*, abruptly break an apple from the tree, and have it shot from the boy's head. This was quite against my nature, and I urged him to give at least some motive to this barbarity, by making the boy boast to Gessler of his father's dexterity, and say that he could shoot an apple from a tree at a hundred paces. Schiller, at first, would have nothing of the sort; but at last he yielded to my arguments and intentions, and did as I advised him. I, on the other hand, by too great attention to *motifs*, kept my pieces from the theatre. My *Eugenie* is nothing but a chain of *motifs*, and this cannot succeed on the stage.

Schiller's genius was really made for the theatre. With every piece he progressed, and became more finished; but, strange to say, a certain love for the horrible adhered to him from the time of the **Robbers,** which never quite left him even in his prime.

*Johann Wolfgang von Goethe, in* Conversations with Goethe, *translated by John Oxenford, J. M. Dent and Sons, 1930.*

---

## Thomas Carlyle    (essay date 1825)

[*A noted nineteenth-century essayist, historian, critic, and social commentator, Carlyle was a central figure of the Victorian age. In his writings, Carlyle advocated a Christian work ethic and stressed the importance of order, piety, and spiritual fulfillment. Known to his contemporaries as the "Sage of Chelsea," Carlyle exerted a powerful moral influence in an era of rapidly shifting values. In the following excerpt from his highly regarded biography* The Life of Friedrich Schiller, *originally published in 1825, he examines each of Schiller's plays, pointing out their strengths and weaknesses and commenting on their popular appeal.*]

Among the writers of the concluding part of the last century there is none more deserving of our notice than Friedrich Schiller. Distinguished alike for the splendour of his intellectual faculties, and the elevation of his tastes and feelings, he has left behind him in his works a noble emblem of these great qualities: and the reputation which he thus enjoys, and has merited, excites our attention the more, on considering the circumstances under which it was acquired. Schiller had peculiar difficulties to strive with, and his success has likewise been peculiar. Much of his life was deformed by inquietude and disease, and it terminated at middle age; he composed in a language then scarcely settled into form, or admitted to a rank among the cultivated languages of Europe: yet his writings are remarkable for their extent and variety as well as their intrinsic excellence; and his own countrymen are not his only, or perhaps his principal admirers. It is difficult to collect or interpret the general voice; but the World, no less than Germany, seems already to have dignified him with the reputation of a classic; to have enrolled him among that select number whose works belong not wholly to any age or nation, but who, having instructed their own contemporaries, are claimed as instructors by the great family of mankind, and set apart for many centuries from the common oblivion which soon overtakes the mass of authors, as it does the mass of other men. (p. 1)

The publication of the **Robbers** forms an era not only in Schiller's history, but in the Literature of the World. . . . Schiller commenced it in his nineteenth year; and the circumstances under which it was composed are to be traced in all its parts. It is the production of a strong untutored spirit, consumed by an activity for which there is no outlet, indignant at the barriers which restrain it, and grappling darkly with the phantoms to which its own energy thus painfully imprisoned gives being. A rude simplicity, combined with a gloomy and overpowering force, are its chief characteristics; they remind us of the defective cultivation, as well as of the fervid and harassed feelings of its author. Above all, the latter quality is visible; the tragic interest of the **Robbers** is deep throughout, so deep that frequently it borders upon horror. A grim inexpiable Fate is made the ruling principle: it envelops and overshadows the whole; and under its louring influence, the fiercest efforts of human will appear but like flashes that illuminate the wild scene with a brief and terrible splendour, and are lost forever in the darkness. The unsearchable abysses of man's destiny are laid open before us, black and profound and appalling, as they seem to the young mind when it first attempts to explore them: the obstacles that thwart our faculties and wishes, the deceitfulness of hope, the nothingness of existence, are sketched in the sable colours so natural to the enthusiast when he first ventures upon life, and compares the world that is without him to the anticipations that were within.

Karl von Moor is a character such as young poets always delight to contemplate or delineate; to Schiller the analogy of their situations must have peculiarly recommended him. Moor is animated into action by feelings similar to those under which his author was then suffering and longing to act. Gifted with every noble quality of manhood in overflowing abundance, Moor's first expectations of life, and of the part he was to play in it, had been glorious as a poet's dream. But the minor dexterities of management were not among his endowments; in his eagerness to reach the goal, he had forgotten that the course is a labyrinthic maze, beset with difficulties, of which some may be surmounted, some can only be evaded, many can be neither. Hurried on by the headlong impetuosity of his temper, he entangles himself in these perplexities; and thinks to penetrate them, not by skill and patience, but by open force. He is baffled, deceived, and still more deeply involved; but injury and disappointment exasperate rather than instruct him. He had expected heroes, and he finds mean men; friends, and he finds smiling traitors to tempt him aside, to profit by his aberrations, and lead him onward to de-

struction: he had dreamed of magnanimity and every generous principle, he finds that prudence is the only virtue sure of its reward. Too fiery by nature, the intensity of his sufferings has now maddened him still farther: he is himself incapable of calm reflection, and there is no counsellor at hand to assist him; none, whose sympathy might assuage his miseries, whose wisdom might teach him to remedy or to endure them. He is stung by fury into action, and his activity is at once blind and tremendous. Since the world is not the abode of unmixed integrity, he looks upon it as a den of thieves; since its institutions may obstruct the advancement of worth, and screen delinquency from punishment, he regards the social union as a pestilent nuisance, the mischiefs of which it is fitting that he in his degree should do his best to repair, by means however violent. Revenge is the mainspring of his conduct; but he ennobles it in his own eyes, by giving it the colour of a disinterested concern for the maintenance of justice,—the abasement of vice from its high places, and the exaltation of suffering virtue. Single against the universe, to appeal to the primary law of the stronger, to 'grasp the scales of Providence in a mortal's hand,' is frantic and wicked; but Moor has a force of soul which makes it likewise awful. The interest lies in the conflict of this gigantic soul against the fearful odds which at length overwhelm it, and hurry it down to the darkest depths of ruin.

The original conception of such a work as this betrays the inexperience no less than the vigour of youth: its execution gives a similar testimony. The characters of the piece, though traced in glowing colours, are outlines more than pictures: the few features we discover in them are drawn with elaborate minuteness; but the rest are wanting. Everything indicates the condition of a keen and powerful intellect, which had studied men in books only; had, by self-examination and the perusal of history, detected and strongly seized some of the leading peculiarities of human nature; but was yet ignorant of all the minute and more complex principles which regulate men's conduct in actual life, and which only a knowledge of living men can unfold. If the hero of the play forms something like an exception to this remark, he is the sole exception, and for reasons alluded to above: his character resembles the author's own. Even with Karl, the success is incomplete: with the other personages it is far more so. Franz von Moor, the villain of the Piece, is an amplified copy of Iago and Richard; but the copy is distorted as well as amplified. There is no air of reality in Franz: he is a villain of theory, who studies to accomplish his object by the most diabolical expedients, and soothes his conscience by arguing with the priest in favour of atheism and materialism; not the genuine villain of Shakspeare and Nature, who employs his reasoning powers in creating new schemes and devising new means, and conquers remorse by avoiding it,—by fixing his hopes and fears on the more pressing emergencies of worldly business. So reflective a miscreant as Franz could not exist: his calculations would lead him to honesty, if merely because it was the best policy.

Amelia, the only female in the piece, is a beautiful creation; but as imaginary as her persecutor Franz. Still and exalted in her warm enthusiam, devoted in her love to Moor, she moves before us as the inhabitant of a higher and simpler world than ours. "*He* sails on troubled seas," she exclaims, with a confusion of metaphors, which it is easy to pardon,

> he sails on troubled seas, Amelia's love sails with him; he wanders in pathless deserts, Amelia's love makes the burning sand grow green beneath him, and the stunted shrubs to blossom; the south scorches his bare head, his feet are pinched by the northern snow, stormy hail beats round his temples—Amelia's love rocks him to sleep in the storm. Seas, and hills, and horizons, are between us; but souls escape from their clay prisons, and meet in the paradise of love!

She is a fair vision, the *beau idéal* of a poet's first mistress; but has few mortal lineaments.

Similar defects are visible in almost all the other characters. Moor, the father, is a weak and fond old man, who could have arrived at grey hairs in such a state of ignorance nowhere but in a work of fiction. The inferior banditti are painted with greater vigour, yet still in rugged and ill-shapen forms; their individuality is kept up by an extravagant exaggeration of their several peculiarities. Schiller himself pronounced a severe but not unfounded censure, when he said of this work, in a maturer age, that his *chief* fault was in 'presuming to delineate men two years before he had met one.'

His skill in the art of composition surpassed his knowledge of the world; but that too was far from perfection. Schiller's style in the **Robbers** is partly of a kind with the incidents and feelings which it represents; strong and astonishing, and sometimes wildly grand; but likewise inartificial, coarse, and grotesque. His sentences, in their rude emphasis, come down like the club of Hercules; the stroke is often of a crushing force, but its sweep is irregular and awkward. When Moor is involved in the deepest intricacies of the old question, necessity and free will, and has convinced himself that he is but an engine in the hands of some dark and irresistible power, he cries out: "Why has my Perillus made of me a brazen bull to roast men in my glowing belly?" The stage-direction says, 'shaken with horror': no wonder that he shook!

Schiller has admitted these faults, and explained their origin, in strong and sincere language. . . . 'A singular miscalculation of nature,' he says,

> had combined my poetical tendencies with the place of my birth. Any disposition to poetry did violence to the laws of the institution where I was educated, and contradicted the plan of its founder. For eight years my enthusiasm struggled with military discipline; but the passion for poetry is vehement and fiery as a first love. What discipline was meant to extinguish, it blew into a flame. To escape from arrangements that tortured me, my heart sought refuge in the world of ideas, when as yet I was unacquainted with the world of realities, from which iron bars excluded me. I was unacquainted with men; for the four hundred that lived with me were but repetitions of the same creature, true casts of one single mould, and of that very mould which plastic nature solemnly disclaimed. . . . Thus circum-

stanced, a stranger to human characters and human fortunes, to hit the medium line between angels and devils was an enterprise in which I necessarily failed. In attempting it, my pencil necessarily brought out a monster, for which by good fortune the world had no original, and which I would not wish to be immortal, except to perpetuate an example of the offspring which Genius in its unnatural union with Thraldom may give to the world. I allude to the **Robbers.**

Yet with all these excrescences and defects, the unbounded popularity of the **Robbers** is not difficult to account for. To every reader, the excitement of emotion must be a chief consideration; to the mass of readers it is the sole one: and the grand secret of moving others is, that the poet be himself moved. We have seen how well Schiller's temper and circumstances qualified him to fulfil this condition: treatment, not of his choosing, had raised his own mind into something like a Pythian frenzy; and his genius, untrained as it was, sufficed to communicate abundance of the feeling to others. Perhaps more than abundance; to judge from our individual impression, the perusal of the **Robbers** produces an effect powerful even to pain; we are absolutely wounded by the catastrophe; our minds are darkened and distressed, as if we had witnessed the execution of a criminal. It is in vain that we rebel against the inconsistencies and crudities of the work: its faults are redeemed by the living energy that pervades it. We may exclaim against the blind madness of the hero; but there is a towering grandeur about him, a whirlwind force of passion and of will, which catches our hearts, and puts the scruples of criticism to silence. (pp. 13-19)

The **Robbers** is a tragedy that will long find readers to astonish, and, with all its faults, to move. It stands, in our imagination, like some ancient rugged pile of a barbarous age; irregular, fantastic, useless; but grand in its height and massiveness and black frowning strength. It will long remain a singular monument of the early genius and early fortune of its author.

The publication of such a work as this naturally produced an extraordinary feeling in the literary world. Translations of the **Robbers** soon appeared in almost all the languages of Europe, and were read in all of them with a deep interest, compounded of admiration and aversion, according to the relative proportions of sensibility and judgment in the various minds which contemplated the subject. In Germany, the enthusiasm which the **Robbers** excited was extreme. The young author had burst upon the world like a meteor; and surprise, for a time, suspended the power of cool and rational criticism. In the ferment produced by the universal discussion of this single topic, the poet was magnified above his natural dimensions, great as they were: and though the general sentence was loudly in his favour, yet he found detractors as well as praisers, and both equally beyond the limits of moderation.

One charge brought against him must have damped the joy of literary glory, and stung Schiller's pure and virtuous mind more deeply than any other. He was accused of having injured the cause of morality by his work; of having set up to the impetuous and fiery temperament of youth a model of imitation which the young were too likely to pursue with eagerness, and which could only lead them from the safe and beaten tracks of duty into error and destruction. (pp. 21-2)

Nothing, at any rate, could be farther from Schiller's intention than such a consummation. In his preface, he speaks of the moral effects of the **Robbers** in terms which do honour to his heart, while they show the inexperience of his head. Ridicule, he signifies, has long been tried against the wickedness of the times, whole cargoes of hellebore have been expended,—in vain; and now, he thinks, recourse must be had to more pungent medicines. We may smile at the simplicity of this idea; and safely conclude that, like other specifics, the present one would fail to produce a perceptible effect: but Schiller's vindication rests on higher grounds than these. His work has on the whole furnished nourishment to the more exalted powers of our nature; the sentiments and images which he has shaped and uttered, tend, in spite of their alloy, to elevate the soul to a nobler pitch: and this is a sufficient defence. As to the danger of misapplying the inspiration he communicates, of forgetting the dictates of prudence in our zeal for the dictates of poetry, we have no great cause to fear it. Hitherto, at least, there has always been enough of dull reality, on every side of us, to abate such fervours in good time, and bring us back to the most sober level of prose, if not to sink us below it. We should thank the poet who performs such a service; and forbear to inquire too rigidly whether there is any 'moral' in his piece or not. The writer of a work, which interests and excites the spiritual feelings of men, has as little need to justify himself by showing how it exemplifies some wise saw or modern instance, as the doer of a generous action has to demonstrate its merit, by deducing it from the system of Shaftesbury, or Smith, or Paley, or whichever happens to be the favourite system for the age and place. The instructiveness of the one, and the virtue of the other, exist independently of all systems or saws, and in spite of all. (p. 23)

In the **Conspiracy of Fiesco** we have to admire not only the energetic animation which the author has infused into all his characters, but the distinctness with which he has discriminated, without aggravating them; and the vividness with which he has contrived to depict the scene where they act and move. The political and personal relation of the Genoese nobility; the luxurious splendour, the intrigues, the feuds, and jarring interests, which occupy them, are made visible before us: we understand and may appreciate the complexities of the conspiracy; we mingle, as among realities, in the pompous and imposing movements which lead to the catastrophe. The catastrophe itself is displayed with peculiar effect. The midnight silence of the sleeping city, interrupted only by the distant sounds of watchmen, by the low hoarse murmur of the sea, or the stealthy footsteps and disguised voice of Fiesco, is conveyed to our imagination by some brief but graphic touches; we seem to stand in the solitude and deep stillness of Genoa, awaiting the signal which is to burst so fearfully upon its slumber. At length the gun is fired; and the wild uproar which ensues is no less strikingly exhibited. The deeds and sounds of violence, astonishment and terror; the volleying cannon, the heavy toll of the alarm-bells, the acclamation of assembled thousands, 'the voice of Genoa

speaking with Fiesco,'—all is made present to us with a force and clearness, which of itself were enough to show no ordinary power of close and comprehensive conception, no ordinary skill in arranging and expressing its results.

But it is not this felicitous delineation of circumstances and visible scenes that constitutes our principal enjoyment. The faculty of penetrating through obscurity and confusion, to seize the characteristic features of an object, abstract or material; of producing a lively description in the latter case, an accurate and keen scrutiny in the former, is the essential property of intellect, and occupies in its best form a high rank in the scale of mental gifts: but the creative faculty of the poet, and especially of the dramatic poet, is something superadded to this; it is far rarer, and occupies a rank far higher. In this particular, **Fiesco,** without approaching the limits of perfection yet stands in an elevated range of excellence. The characters, on the whole, are imagined and portrayed with great impressiveness and vigour. Traces of old faults are indeed still to be discovered: there still seems a want of pliancy about the genius of the author; a stiffness and heaviness in his motions. His sublimity is not to be questioned; but it does not always disdain the aid of rude contrasts and mere theatrical effect. He paints in colours deep and glowing, but without sufficient skill to blend them delicately: he amplifies nature more than purifies it; he omits, but does not well conceal the omission. **Fiesco** has not the complete charm of a true though embellished resemblance to reality; its attraction rather lies in a kind of colossal magnitude, which requires it, if seen to advantage, to be viewed from a distance. Yet the prevailing qualities of the piece do more than make us pardon such defects. If the dramatic imitation is not always entirely successful, it is never very distant from success; and a constant flow of powerful thought and sentiment counteracts, or prevents us from noticing, the failure. We find evidence of great philosophic penetration, great resources of invention, directed by a skilful study of history and men; and everywhere a bold grandeur of feeling and imagery gives life to what study has combined. The chief incidents have a dazzling magnificence; the chief characters, an aspect of majesty and force which corresponds to it. Fervour of heart, capaciousness of intellect and imagination, present themselves on all sides: the general effect is powerful and exalting.

Fiesco himself is a personage at once probable and tragically interesting. The luxurious dissipation, in which he veils his daring projects, softens the rudeness of that strength which it half conceals. His immeasurable pride expands itself not only into a disdain of subjection, but also into the most lofty acts of magnanimity: his blind confidence in fortune seems almost warranted by the resources which he finds in his own fearlessness and imperturbable presence of mind. His ambition participates in the nobleness of his other qualities; he is less anxious that his rivals should yield to him in power than in generosity and greatness of character, attributes of which power is with him but the symbol and the fit employment. Ambition in Fiesco is indeed the common wish of every mind to diffuse its individual influence, to see its own activity reflected back from the united minds of millions: but it is the common wish acting on no common man. He does not long to rule, that he may sway other wills, as it were, by the physical exertion of his own: he would lead us captive by the superior grandeur of his qualities, once fairly manifested; and he aims at dominion, chiefly as it will enable him to manifest these. 'It is not the arena that he values, but what lies in that arena': the sovereignty is enviable, not for its adventitious splendour, not because it is the object of coarse and universal wonder; but as it offers, in the collected force of a nation, something which the loftiest mortal may find scope for all his powers in guiding. "Spread out the thunder," Fiesco exclaims, "into its single tones, and it becomes a lullaby for children: pour it forth together in *one* quick peal, and the royal sound shall move the heavens." His affections are not less vehement than his other passions: his heart can be melted into powerlessness and tenderness by the mild persuasions of his Leonora; the idea of exalting this amiable being mingles largely with the other motives to his enterprise. He is, in fact, a great, and might have been a virtuous man; and though in the pursuit of grandeur he swerves from absolute rectitude, we still respect his splendid qualities, and admit the force of the allurements which have led him astray. It is but faintly that we condemn his sentiments, when, after a night spent in struggles between a rigid and a more accommodating patriotism, he looks out of his chamber, as the sun is rising in its calm beauty, and gilding the waves and mountains, and all the innumerable palaces and domes and spires of Genoa, and exclaims with rapture: "This majestic city— mine! To flame over it like the kingly Day; to brood over it with a monarch's power; all these sleepless longings, all these never satiated wishes to be drowned in that unfathomable ocean!" We admire Fiesco, we disapprove of him, and sympathise with him: he is crushed in the ponderous machinery which himself put in motion and thought to control: we lament his fate, but confess that it was not undeserved. He is a fit 'offering of individual free-will to the force of social conventions.'

Fiesco is not the only striking character in the play which bears his name. The narrow fanatical republican virtue of Verrina, the mild and venerable wisdom of the old Doria, the unbridled profligacy of his Nephew, even the cold, contented, irreclaimable perversity of the cutthroat Moor, all dwell in our recollections: but what, next to Fiesco, chiefly attracts us, is the character of Leonora his wife. Leonora is of kindred to Amelia in the **Robbers,** but involved in more complicated relations, and brought nearer to the actual condition of humanity. She is such a heroine as Schiller most delights to draw. Meek and retiring by the softness of her nature, yet glowing with an ethereal ardour for all that is illustrious and lovely, she clings about her husband, as if her being were one with his. She dreams of remote and peaceful scenes, where Fiesco should be all to her, she all to Fiesco: her idea of love is, that '*her* name should lie in secret behind every one of his thoughts, should speak to him from every object of Nature; that for him, this bright majestic universe itself were but as the shining jewel, on which her image, only *hers,* stood engraved.' Her character seems a reflection of Fiesco's, but refined from his grosser strength, and transfigured into a celestial form of purity, and tenderness, and touching grace. Jealousy cannot move her into anger; she languish-

es in concealed sorrow, when she thinks herself forgotten. It is affection alone that can rouse her into passion; but under the influence of this, she forgets all weakness and fear. She cannot stay in her palace, on the night when Fiesco's destiny is deciding; she rushes forth, as if inspired, to share in her husband's dangers and sublime deeds, and perishes at last in the tumult.

The death of Leonora, so brought about, and at such a time, is reckoned among the blemishes of the work: that of Fiesco, in which Schiller has ventured to depart from history, is to be more favourably judged of. Fiesco is not here accidentally drowned; but plunged into the waves by the indignant Verrina, who forgets or stifles the feelings of friendship, in his rage at political apostasy. 'The nature of the Drama,' we are justly told, 'will not suffer the operation of Chance, or of an immediate Providence. Higher spirits can discern the minute fibres of an event stretching through the whole expanse of the system of the world, and hanging, it may be, on the remotest limits of the future and the past, where man discerns nothing save the action itself, hovering unconnected in space. But the artist has to paint for the short view of man, whom he wishes to instruct; not for the piercing eye of superior powers, from whom he learns.'

In the composition of **Fiesco,** Schiller derived the main part of his original materials from history; he could increase the effect by gorgeous representations, and ideas preëxisting in the mind of his reader. Enormity of incident and strangeness of situation lent him a similar assistance in the **Robbers. Kabale und Liebe** is destitute of these advantages; it is a tragedy of domestic life; its means of interesting are comprised within itself, and rest on very simple feelings, dignified by no very singular action. The name, **Court-Intriguing and Love,** correctly designates its nature; it aims at exhibiting the conflict, the victorious conflict, of political manœuvering, of cold worldly wisdom, with the pure impassioned movements of the young heart, as yet unsullied by the tarnish of every-day life, inexperienced in its calculations, sick of its empty formalities, and indignantly determined to cast-off the mean restrictions it imposes, which bind so firmly by their number, though singly so contemptible. The idea is far from original: this is a conflict which most men have figured to themselves, which many men of ardent mind are in some degree constantly waging. To make it, in this simple form, the subject of a drama, seems to be a thought of Schiller's own; but the praise, though not the merit of his undertaking, considerable rather as performed than projected, has been lessened by a multitude of worthless or noxious imitations. The same primary conception has been tortured into a thousand shapes, and tricked out with a thousand tawdry devices and meretricious ornaments, by the Kotzebues, and other 'intellectual Jacobins,' whose productions have brought what we falsely call the 'German Theatre' into such deserved contempt in England. Some portion of the gall, due only to these inflated, flimsy, and fantastic persons, appears to have acted on certain critics in estimating this play of Schiller's. August Wilhelm Schlegel speaks slightingly of the work: he says, 'it will hardly move us by its tone of overstrained sensibility, but may well afflict us by the painful impressions which it leaves.' Our own experience has been different from that of Schlegel. In the characters of Louisa and Ferdinand Walter we discovered little overstraining; their sensibility we did not reckon very criminal; seeing it united with a clearness of judgment, chastened by a purity of heart, and controlled by a force of virtuous resolution, in full proportion with itself. We rather admired the genius of the poet, which could elevate a poor music-master's daughter to the dignity of a heroine; could represent, without wounding our sense of propriety, the affection of two noble beings, created for each other by nature, and divided by rank; we sympathised in their sentiments enough to feel a proper interest in their fate, and see in them, what the author meant we should see, two pure and lofty minds involved in the meshes of vulgar cunning, and borne to destruction by the excess of their own good qualities and the crimes of others.

Ferdinand is a nobleman, but not convinced that 'his patent of nobility is more ancient or of more authority than the primeval scheme of the universe': he speaks and acts like a young man entertaining such persuasions: disposed to yield everything to reason and true honour, but scarcely anything to mere use and wont. His passion for Louisa is the sign and the nourishment rather than the cause of such a temper: he loves her without limit, as the only creature he has ever met with of a like mind with himself; and this feeling exalts into inspiration what was already the dictate of his nature. We accompany him on his straight and plain path; we rejoice to see him fling aside with a strong arm the artifices and allurements with which a worthless father and more worthless associates assail him at first in vain: there is something attractive in the spectacle of native integrity, fearless though inexperienced, at war with selfishness and craft; something mournful, because the victory will seldom go as we would have it.

Louisa is a meet partner for the generous Ferdinand: the poet has done justice to her character. She is timid and humble; a feeling and richly gifted soul is hid in her by the unkindness of her earthly lot; she is without counsellors except the innate holiness of her heart, and the dictates of her keen though untutored understanding; yet when the hour of trial comes, she can obey the commands of both, and draw from herself a genuine nobleness of conduct, which secondhand prudence, and wealth, and titles, would but render less touching. Her filial affection, her angelic attachment to her lover, her sublime and artless piety, are beautifully contrasted with the bleakness of her external circumstances: she appears before us like the '*one rose of the wilderness left on its stalk*,' and we grieve to see it crushed and trodden down so rudely.

The innocence, the enthusiasm, the exalted life and stern fate of Louisa and Ferdinand give a powerful charm to this tragedy: it is everywhere interspersed with pieces of fine eloquence, and scenes which move us by their dignity or pathos. We recollect few passages of a more overpowering nature than the conclusion, where Ferdinand, beguiled by the most diabolical machinations to disbelieve the virtue of his mistress, puts himself and her to death by poison. There is a gloomy and solemn might in his despair; though overwhelmed, he seems invincible: his enemies have blinded and imprisoned him in their deceptions; but

only that, like Samson, he may overturn his prison-house, and bury himself, and all that have wronged him, in its ruins.

The other characters of the play, though in general properly sustained, are not sufficiently remarkable to claim much of our attention. Wurm, the chief counsellor and agent of the unprincipled, calculating Father, is wicked enough; but there is no great singularity in his wickedness. He is little more than the dry, cool, and now somewhat vulgar miscreant, the villanous Attorney of modern novels. Kalb also is but a worthless subject, and what is worse, but indifferently handled. He is meant for the feather-brained thing of tags and laces, which frequently inhabits courts; but he wants the grace and agility proper to the species; he is less a fool than a blockhead, less perverted than totally inane. Schiller's strength lay not in comedy, but in something far higher. The great merit of the present work consists in the characters of the hero and heroine; and in this respect it ranks at the very head of its class. As a tragedy of common life, we know of few rivals to it, certainly of no superior.

The production of three such pieces as the **Robbers, Fiesco,** and **Kabale und Liebe,** already announced to the world that another great and original mind had appeared, from whose maturity, when such was the promise of its youth, the highest expectations might be formed. These three plays stand related to each other in regard to their nature and form, as well as date: they exhibit the progressive state of Schiller's education; show us the fiery enthusiasm of youth, exasperated into wildness, astonishing in its movements rather than sublime; and the same enthusiasm gradually yielding to the sway of reason, gradually using itself to the constraints prescribed by sound judgment and more extensive knowledge. Of the three, the **Robbers** is doubtless the most singular, and likely perhaps to be the most widely popular: but the latter two are of more real worth in the eye of taste, and will better bear a careful and rigorous study. (pp. 31-9)

The story of Don Carlos seems peculiarly adapted for dramatists. The spectacle of a royal youth condemned to death by his father, of which happily our European annals furnish but another example, is among the most tragical that can be figured: the character of that youth, the intermixture of bigotry and jealousy, and love, with the other strong passions, which brought on his fate, afford a combination of circumstances, affecting in themselves, and well calculated for the basis of deeply interesting fiction. Accordingly they have not been neglected: Carlos has often been the theme of poets; particularly since the time when his history, recorded by the Abbé St. Réal, was exposed in more brilliant colours to the inspection of every writer, and almost of every reader.

The Abbé St. Réal was a dexterous artist in that half-illicit species of composition, the historic novel: in the course of his operations, he lighted on these incidents; and, by filling-up according to his fancy, what historians had only sketched to him, by amplifying, beautifying, suppressing, and arranging, he worked the whole into a striking little narrative, distinguished by all the symmetry, the sparkling graces, the vigorous description, and keen thought, which characterise his other writings. This French Sallust, as his countrymen have named him, has been of use to many dramatists. His *Conjuraison contre Venise* furnished Otway with the outline of his best tragedy; *Epicaris* has more than once appeared upon the stage; and *Don Carlos* has been dramatised in almost all the languages of Europe. Besides Otway's *Carlos,* so famous at its first appearance, many tragedies on this subject have been written: most of them are gathered to their final rest; some are fast going thither; two bid fair to last for ages. Schiller and Alfieri have both drawn their plot from St. Réal; the former has expanded and added; the latter has compressed and abbreviated.

Schiller's **Carlos** is the first of his plays that bears the stamp of anything like full maturity. The opportunities he had enjoyed for extending his knowledge of men and things, the sedulous practice of the art of composition, the study of purer models, had not been without their full effect. Increase of years had done something for him; diligence had done much more. The ebullience of youth is now chastened into the steadfast energy of manhood; the wild enthusiast, that spurned at the errors of the world, has now become the enlightened moralist, that laments their necessity, or endeavours to find out their remedy. A corresponding alteration is visible in the external form of the work, in its plot and diction. The plot is contrived with great ingenuity, embodying the result of much study, both dramatic and historical. The language is blank verse, not prose, as in the former works; it is more careful and regular, less ambitious in its object, but more certain of attaining it. Schiller's mind had now reached its full stature: he felt and thought more justly; he could better express what he felt and thought.

The merit we noticed in **Fiesco,** the fidelity with which the scene of action is brought before us, is observable to a still greater degree in **Don Carlos.** The Spanish court in the end of the sixteenth century; its rigid, cold formalities; its cruel, bigoted, but proud-spirited grandees; its inquisitors and priests; and Philip, its head, the epitome at once of its good and its bad qualities, in all his complex interests, are exhibited with wonderful distinctness and address. Nor is it at the surface or the outward movements alone that we look; we are taught the mechanism of their characters, as well as shown it in action. The stony-hearted Despot himself must have been an object of peculiar study to the author. Narrow in his understanding, dead in his affections, from his birth the lord of Europe, Philip has existed all his days above men, not among them. Locked up within himself, a stranger to every generous and kindly emotion, his gloomy spirit has had no employment but to strengthen or increase its own elevation, no pleasure but to gratify its own self-will. Superstition, harmonising with these native tendencies, has added to their force, but scarcely to their hatefulness: it lends them a sort of sacredness in his own eyes, and even a sort of horrid dignity in ours. Philip is not without a certain greatness, the greatness of unlimited external power, and of a will relentless in its dictates, guided by principles, false, but consistent and unalterable. The scene of his existence is haggard, stern and desolate; but it is all his own, and he seems fitted for it. We hate him

and fear him; but the poet has taken care to secure him from contempt.

The contrast both of his father's fortune and character are those of Carlos. Few situations of a more affecting kind can be imagined, than the situation of this young, generous and ill-fated prince. From boyhood his heart had been bent on mighty things; he had looked upon the royal grandeur that awaited his maturer years, only as the means of realising those projects for the good of men, which his beneficent soul was ever busied with. His father's dispositions, and the temper of the court, which admitted no development of such ideas, had given the charm of concealment to his feelings; his life had been in prospect; and we are the more attached to him, that deserving to be glorious and happy, he had but expected to be either. Bright days, however, seemed approaching; shut out from the communion of the Albas and Domingos, among whom he lived a stranger, the communion of another and far dearer object was to be granted him; Elizabeth's love seemed to make him independent even of the future, which it painted with still richer hues. But in a moment she is taken from him by the most terrible of all visitations; his bride becomes his mother; and the stroke that deprives him of her, while it ruins him forever, is more deadly, because it cannot be complained of without sacrilege, and cannot be altered by the power of Fate itself. Carlos, as the poet represents him, calls forth our tenderest sympathies. His soul seems once to have been rich and glorious, like the garden of Eden; but the desert-wind has passed over it, and smitten it with perpetual blight. Despair has overshadowed all the fair visions of his youth; or if he hopes, it is but the gleam of delirium, which something sterner than even duty extinguishes in the cold darkness of death. His energy survives but to vent itself in wild gusts of reckless passion, or aimless indignation. There is a touching poignancy in his expression of the bitter melancholy that oppresses him, in the fixedness of misery with which he looks upon the faded dreams of former years, or the fierce ebullitions and dreary pauses of resolution, which now prompts him to retrieve what he has lost, now withers into powerlessness, as nature and reason tell him that it cannot, must not be retrieved.

Elizabeth, no less moving and attractive, is also depicted with masterly skill. If she returns the passion of her amiable and once betrothed lover, we but guess at the fact; for so horrible a thought has never once been whispered to her own gentle and spotless mind. Yet her heart bleeds for Carlos; and we see that did not the most sacred feelings of humanity forbid her, there is no sacrifice she would not make to restore his peace of mind. By her soothing influence she strives to calm the agony of his spirit; by her mild winning eloquence she would persuade him that for Don Carlos other objects must remain, when his hopes of personal felicity have been cut off; she would change his love for her into love for the millions of human beings whose destiny depends on his. A meek vestal, yet with the prudence of a queen, and the courage of a matron, with every graceful and generous quality of womanhood harmoniously blended in her nature, she lives in a scene that is foreign to her; the happiness she should have had is beside her, the misery she must endure is around her; yet she utters no regret, gives way to no complaint, but seeks to draw from duty itself a compensation for the cureless evil which duty has inflicted. Many tragic queens are more imposing and majestic than this Elizabeth of Schiller; but there is none who rules over us with a sway so soft and feminine, none whom we feel so much disposed to love as well as reverence.

The virtues of Elizabeth are heightened by comparison with the principles and actions of her attendant, the Princess Eboli. The character of Eboli is full of pomp and profession; magnanimity and devotedness are on her tongue, some shadow of them even floats in her imagination; but they are not rooted in her heart; pride, selfishness, unlawful passion are the only inmates there. Her lofty boastings of generosity are soon forgotten when the success of her attachment to Carlos becomes hopeless; the fervour of a selfish love once extinguished in her bosom, she regards the object of it with none but vulgar feelings. Virtue no longer according with interest, she ceases to be virtuous; from a rejected mistress the transition to a jealous spy is with her natural and easy. Yet we do not hate the Princess: there is a seductive warmth and grace about her character, which makes us lament her vices rather than condemn them. The poet has drawn her at once false and fair.

In delineating Eboli and Philip, Schiller seems as if struggling against the current of his nature; our feelings towards them are hardly so severe as he intended; their words and deeds, at least those of the latter, are wicked and repulsive enough; but we still have a kind of latent persuasion that they meant better than they spoke or acted. With the Marquis of Posa, he had a more genial task. This Posa, we can easily perceive, is the representative of Schiller himself. The ardent love of men, which forms his ruling passion, was likewise the constant feeling of his author; the glowing eloquence with which he advocates the cause of truth, and justice, and humanity, was such as Schiller too would have employed in similar circumstances. In some respects, Posa is the chief character of the piece; there is a preëminent magnificence in his object, and in the faculties and feelings with which he follows it. Of a splendid intellect, and a daring devoted heart, his powers are all combined upon a single purpose. Even his friendship for Carlos, grounded on the likeness of their minds, and faithful as it is, yet seems to merge in this paramount emotion, zeal for the universal interests of man. Aiming, with all his force of thought and action, to advance the happiness and best rights of his fellow-creatures; pursuing this noble aim with the skill and dignity which it deserves, his mind is at once unwearied, earnest and serene. He is another Carlos, but somewhat older, more experienced, and never crossed in hopeless love. There is a calm strength in Posa, which no accident of fortune can shake. Whether cheering the forlorn Carlos into new activity; whether lifting up his voice in the ear of tyrants and inquisitors, or taking leave of life amid his vast unexecuted schemes, there is the same sedate magnanimity, the same fearless composure: when the fatal bullet strikes him, he dies with the concerns of others, not his own, upon his lips. He is a reformer, the perfection of reformers; not a revolutionist, but a prudent though determined improver. His enthusiasm does not burst forth in violence, but in

manly and enlightened energy: his eloquence is not more moving to the heart than his lofty philosophy is convincing to the head. There is a majestic vastness of thought in his precepts, which recommends them to the mind independently of the beauty of their dress. Few passages of poetry are more spirit-stirring than his last message to Carlos, through the Queen. The certainty of death seems to surround his spirit with a kind of martyr glory; he is kindled into transport, and speaks with a commanding power. The pathetic wisdom of the line, 'Tell him, that when he is a man, he must reverence the dreams of his youth,' has often been admired: that scene has many such.

The interview with Philip is not less excellent. There is something so striking in the idea of confronting the cold solitary tyrant with 'the only man in all his states that does not need him'; of raising the voice of true manhood for once within the gloomy chambers of thraldom and priestcraft, that we can forgive the stretch of poetic licence by which it is effected. Philip and Posa are antipodes in all respects. Philip thinks his new instructor is a 'Protestant'; a charge which Posa rebuts with calm dignity, his object not being separation and contention, but union and peaceful gradual improvement. Posa seems to understand the character of Philip better; not attempting to awaken in his sterile heart any feeling for real glory, or the interests of his fellow-men, he attacks his selfishness and pride, represents to him the intrinsic meanness and misery of a throne, however decked with adventitious pomp, if built on servitude and isolated from the sympathies and interests of others. (pp. 61-7)

Had the character of Posa been drawn ten years later, it would have been imputed, as all things are, to the 'French Revolution'; and Schiller himself perhaps might have been called a Jacobin. Happily, as matters stand, there is room for no such imputation. It is pleasing to behold in Posa the deliberate expression of a great and good man's sentiments on these ever-agitated subjects: a noble monument, embodying the liberal ideas of his age, in a form beautified by his own genius, and lasting as its other products.

Connected with the superior excellence of Posa, critics have remarked a dramatic error, which the author himself was the first to acknowledge and account for. The magnitude of Posa throws Carlos into the shade; the hero of the first three acts is no longer the hero of the other two. The cause of this, we are informed, was that Schiller kept the work too long upon his own hands:

'In composing the piece,' he observes,

> many interruptions occurred; so that a considerable time elapsed between beginning and concluding it; and, in the mean while, much within myself had changed. The various alterations which, during this period, my way of thinking and feeling underwent, naturally told upon the work I was engaged with. What parts of it had at first attracted me, began to produce this effect in a weaker degree, and, in the end, scarcely at all. New ideas, springing up in the interim, displaced the former ones; Carlos himself had lost my favour, perhaps for no other reason than because I had become his senior; and, from the opposite cause, Posa had occupied his place. Thus

I commenced the fourth and fifth acts with quite an altered heart. But the first three were already in the hands of the public; the plan of the whole could not now be re-formed; nothing therefore remained but to suppress the piece entirely, or to fit the second half to the first the best way I could.

The imperfection alluded to is one of which the general reader will make no great account; the second half is fitted to the first with address enough for his purposes. Intent not upon applying the dramatic gauge, but on being moved and exalted, we may peruse the tragedy without noticing that any such defect exists in it. The pity and love we are first taught to feel for Carlos abide with us to the last; and though Posa rises in importance as the piece proceeds, our admiration of his transcendent virtues does not obstruct the gentler feelings with which we look upon the fate of his friend. A certain confusion and crowding together of events, about the end of the play, is the only fault in its plan that strikes us with any force. Even this is scarcely prominent enough to be offensive.

An intrinsic and weightier defect is the want of ease and lightness in the general composition of the piece; a defect which all its other excellencies will not prevent us from observing. There is action enough in the plot, energy enough in the dialogue, and abundance of individual beauties in both; but there is throughout a certain air of stiffness and effort, which abstracts from the theatrical illusion. The language, in general impressive and magnificent, is now and then inflated into bombast. The characters do not, as it were, verify their human nature, by those thousand little touches and nameless turns, which distinguish the genius essentially dramatic from the genius merely poetical; the Proteus of the stage from the philosophic observer and trained imitator of life. We have not those careless felicities, those varyings from high to low, that air of living freedom which Shakspeare has accustomed us, like spoiled children, to look for in every perfect work of this species. Schiller is too elevated, too regular and sustained in his elevation, to be altogether natural.

Yet with all this, *Carlos* is a noble tragedy. There is a stately massiveness about the structure of it; the incidents are grand and affecting; the characters powerful, vividly conceived, and impressively if not completely delineated. Of wit and its kindred graces Schiller has but a slender share: nor among great poets is he much distinguished for depth or fineness of pathos. But what gives him a place of his own, and the loftiest of its kind, is the vastness and intense vigour of his mind; the splendour of his thoughts and imagery, and the bold vehemence of his passion for the true and the sublime, under all their various forms. He does not thrill, but he exalts us. His genius is impetuous, exuberant, majestic; and a heavenly fire gleams through all his creations. He transports us into a holier and higher world than our own; everything around us breathes of force and solemn beauty. The looks of his heroes may be more staid than those of men, the movements of their minds may be slower and more calculated; but we yield to the potency of their endowments, and the loveliness of the scene which they animate. The enchantments of the poet are strong

enough to silence our scepticism; we forbear to inquire whether it is true or false. (pp. 76-8)

In *Wallenstein* he wished to embody the more enlarged notions which experience had given him of men, especially which history had given him of generals and statesmen; and while putting such characters in action, to represent whatever was, or could be made, poetical, in the stormy period of the Thirty-Years War. As he meditated on the subject, it continued to expand; in his fancy, it assumed successively a thousand forms; and after all due strictness of selection, such was still the extent of materials remaining on his hands, that he found it necessary to divide the play into three parts, distinct in their arrangements, but in truth forming a continuous drama of eleven acts. In this shape it was sent forth to the world, in 1799; a work of labour and persevering anxiety, but of anxiety and labour, as it then appeared, which had not been bestowed in vain. *Wallenstein* is by far the best performance he had yet produced; it merits a long chapter of criticism by itself; and a few hurried pages are all that we can spend on it.

As a porch to the great edifice stands Part first, entitled *Wallenstein's Camp*, a piece in one act. It paints, with much humour and graphical felicity, the manners of that rude tumultuous host which Wallenstein presided over, and had made the engine of his ambitious schemes. Schiller's early experience of a military life seems now to have stood him in good stead: his soldiers are delineated with the distinctness of actual observation; in rugged sharpness of feature, they sometimes remind us of Smollett's seamen. Here are all the wild lawless spirits of Europe assembled within the circuit of a single trench. Violent, tempestuous, unstable is the life they lead. Ishmaelites, their hands against every man, and every man's hand against them; the instruments of rapine; tarnished with almost every vice, and knowing scarcely any virtue but those of reckless bravery and uncalculating obedience to their leader, their situation still presents some aspects which affect or amuse us; and these the poet has seized with his accustomed skill. Much of the cruelty and repulsive harshness of these soldiers, we are taught to forget in contemplating their forlorn houseless wanderings, and the practical magnanimity, with which even they contrive to wring from Fortune a tolerable scantling of enjoyment. Their manner of existence Wallenstein has, at an after-period of the action, rather movingly expressed:

> Our life was but a battle and a march,
> And, like the wind's blast, never-resting, homeless,
> We storm'd across the war-convulsed Earth.

Still farther to soften the asperities of the scene, the dialogue is cast into a rude Hudibrastic metre, full of forced rhymes, and strange double-endings, with a rhythm ever changing, ever rough and lively, which might almost be compared to the hard, irregular, fluctuating sound of the regimental drum. In this ludicrous doggrel, with phrases and figures of a correspondent cast, homely, ridiculous, graphic, these men of service paint their hopes and doings. There are ranks and kinds among them; representatives of all the constituent parts of the motley multitude, which followed this prince of *Condottieri*. The solemn pedantry

*Wallenstein's Camp.*

of the ancient Wachtmeister is faithfully given; no less so are the jocund ferocity and heedless daring of Holky's Jägers, or the iron courage and stern camp-philosophy of Pappenheim's Cuirassiers. Of the Jäger the sole principle is military obedience; he does not reflect or calculate; his business is to do whatever he is ordered, and to enjoy whatever he can reach. 'Free wished I to live,' he says,

> Free wished I to live, and easy and gay,
> And see something new on each new day;
> In the joys of the moment lustily sharing,
> 'Bout the past or the future not thinking or car-
>     ing:
> To the Kaiser, therefore, I sold my bacon,
> And by him good charge of the whole is taken.
> Order me on 'mid the whistling fiery shot,
> Over the Rhine-stream rapid and roaring wide,
> A third of the troop must go to pot,—
> Without loss of time, I mount and ride;
> But farther, I beg very much, do you see,
> That in all things else you would leave me free.

The Pappenheimer is an older man, more sedate and more indomitable; he has wandered over Europe, and gathered settled maxims of soldierly principle and soldierly privilege: he is not without a *rationale* of life; the various pro-fessions of men have passed in review before him, but no coat that he has seen has pleased him like his own 'steel doublet,' cased in which, it is his wish,

> Looking down on the world's poor restless
>     scramble,
> Careless, through it, astride of his nag to ramble.

Yet at times with this military stoicism there is blended a dash of homely pathos; he admits,

> This sword of ours is no plough or spade,
> You cannot delve or reap with the iron blade;
> For us there falls no seed, no corn-field grows,
> Neither home nor kindred the soldier knows:
> Wandering over the face of the earth,
> Warming his hands at another's hearth:
> From the pomp of towns he must onward roam;
> In the village-green with its cheerful game,
> In the mirth of the vintage or harvest-home,
> No part or lot can the soldier claim.
> Tell me then, in the place of goods or pelf,
> What has he unless to honour himself?
> Leave not even *this* his own, what wonder
> The man should burn and kill and plunder?

But the camp of Wallenstein is full of bustle as well as speculation; there are gamblers, peasants, sutlers, soldiers,

315

recruits, capuchin friars, moving to and fro in restless pursuit of their several purposes. The sermon of the Capuchin is an unparalleled composition; a medley of texts, puns, nicknames, and verbal logic, conglutinated by a stupid judgment, and a fiery catholic zeal. It seems to be delivered with great unction, and to find fit audience in the camp: towards the conclusion they rush upon him, and he narrowly escapes killing or ducking, for having ventured to glance a censure at the General. The soldiers themselves are jeering, wrangling, jostling; discussing their wishes and expectations; and, at last, they combine in a profound deliberation on the state of their affairs. A vague exaggerated outline of the coming events and personages is imaged to us in their coarse conceptions. We dimly discover the precarious position of Wallenstein; the plots which threaten him, which he is meditating: we trace the leading qualities of the principal officers; and form a high estimate of the potent spirit which binds this fierce discordant mass together, and seems to be the object of universal reverence where nothing else is revered.

In the **Two Piccolomini,** the next division of the work, the generals for whom we have thus been prepared appear in person on the scene, and spread out before us their plots and counterplots; Wallenstein, through personal ambition and evil counsel, slowly resolving to revolt; and Octavio Piccolomini, in secret, undermining his influence among the leaders, and preparing for him that pit of ruin, into which, in the third Part, **Wallenstein's Death,** we see him sink with all his fortunes. The military spirit which pervades the former piece is here well sustained. The ruling motives of these captains and colonels are a little more refined, or more disguised, than those of the Cuirassiers and Jägers; but they are the same in substance; the love of present or future pleasure, of action, reputation, money, power; selfishness, but selfishness distinguished by a superficial external propriety, and gilded over with the splendour of military honour, of courage inflexible, yet light, cool and unassuming. These are not imaginary heroes, but genuine hired men of war: we do not love them; yet there is a pomp about their operations, which agreeably fills up the scene. This din of war, this clash of tumultuous conflicting interests, is felt as a suitable accompaniment to the affecting or commanding movements of the chief characters whom it envelops or obeys.

Of the individuals that figure in this world of war, Wallenstein himself, the strong Atlas which supports it all, is by far the most imposing. Wallenstein is the model of a high-souled, great, accomplished man, whose ruling passion is ambition. He is daring to the utmost pitch of manhood; he is enthusiastic and vehement; but the fire of his soul burns hid beneath a deep stratum of prudence, guiding itself by calculations which extend to the extreme limits of his most minute concerns. This prudence, sometimes almost bordering on irresolution, forms the outward rind of his character, and for a while is the only quality which we discover in it. The immense influence which his genius appears to exert on every individual of his many followers, prepares us to expect a great man; and, when Wallenstein, after long delay and much forewarning, is in fine presented to us, we at first experience something like a disappointment. We find him, indeed, possessed of a staid grandeur;

yet involved in mystery; wavering between two opinions; and, as it seems, with all his wisdom, blindly credulous in matters of the highest import. It is only when events have forced decision on him, that he rises in his native might, that his giant spirit stands unfolded in its strength before us;

Night must it be, ere Friedland's star will beam:

amid difficulties, darkness and impending ruin, at which the boldest of his followers grow pale, he himself is calm, and first in this awful crisis feels the serenity and conscious strength of his soul return. Wallenstein, in fact, though preëminent in power, both external and internal, of high intellect and commanding will, skilled in war and statesmanship beyond the best in Europe, the idol of sixty thousand fearless hearts, is not yet removed above our sympathy. We are united with him by feelings which he reckons weak, though they belong to the most generous parts of his nature. His indecision partly takes its rise in the sensibilities of his heart, as well as in the caution of his judgment: his belief in astrology, which gives force and confirmation to this tendency, originates in some soft kindly emotions, and adds a new interest to the spirit of the warrior; it humbles him, to whom the earth is subject, before those mysterious Powers which weigh the destinies of man in their balance, in whose eyes the greatest and the least of mortals scarcely differ in littleness. Wallenstein's confidence in the friendship of Octavio, his disinterested love for Max Piccolomini, his paternal and brotherly kindness, are feelings which cast an affecting lustre over the harsher, more heroic qualities wherewith they are combined. His treason to the Emperor is a crime, for which, provoked and tempted as he was, we do not greatly blame him; it is forgotten in our admiration of his nobleness, or recollected only as a venial trespass. Schiller has succeeded well with Wallenstein, where it was not easy to succeed. The truth of history has been but little violated; yet we are compelled to feel that Wallenstein, whose actions individually are trifling, unsuccessful, and unlawful, is a strong, sublime, commanding character; we look at him with interest, our concern at his fate is tinged with a shade of kindly pity.

In Octavio Piccolomini, his war-companion, we can find less fault, yet we take less pleasure. Octavio's qualities are chiefly negative: he rather walks by the letter of the moral law, than by its spirit; his conduct is externally correct, but there is no touch of generosity within. He is more of the courtier than of the soldier: his weapon is intrigue, not force. Believing firmly that 'whatever is, is best,' he distrusts all new and extraordinary things; he has no faith in human nature, and seems to be virtuous himself more by calculation than by impulse. We scarcely thank him for his loyalty; serving his Emperor, he ruins and betrays his friend: and, besides, though he does not own it, personal ambition is among his leading motives; he wishes to be general and prince, and Wallenstein is not only a traitor to his sovereign, but a bar to this advancement. It is true, Octavio does not personally tempt him towards his destruction; but neither does he warn him from it; and perhaps he knew that fresh temptation was superfluous. Wallenstein did not deserve such treatment from a man whom he had trusted as a brother, even though such confidence was blind, and guided by visions and starry omens. Octavio is a skilful, prudent, managing statesman; of the kind praised loudly, if not sincerely, by their friends, and detested deeply by their enemies. His object may be lawful or even laudable; but his ways are crooked; we dislike him but the more that we know not positively how to blame him.

Octavio Piccolomini and Wallenstein are, as it were, the two opposing forces by which this whole universe of military politics is kept in motion. The struggle of magnanimity and strength combined with treason, against cunning and apparent virtue, aided by law, gives rise to a series of great actions, which are here vividly presented to our view. We mingle in the clashing interests of these men of war; we see them at their gorgeous festivals and stormy consultations, and participate in the hopes or fears that agitate them. The subject had many capabilities; and Schiller has turned them all to profit. Our minds are kept alert by a constant succession of animating scenes of spectacle, dialogue, incident: the plot thickens and darkens as we advance; the interest deepens and deepens to the very end.

But among the tumults of this busy multitude, there are two forms of celestial beauty that solicit our attention, and whose destiny, involved with that of those around them, gives it an importance in our eyes which it could not otherwise have had. Max Piccolomini, Octavio's son, and Thekla, the daughter of Wallenstein, diffuse an ethereal radiance over all this tragedy; they call forth the finest feelings of the heart, where other feelings had already been aroused; they superadd to the stirring pomp of scenes, which had already kindled our imaginations, the enthusiasm of bright unworn humanity, 'the bloom of young desire, the purple light of love.' The history of Max and Thekla is not a rare one in poetry; but Schiller has treated it with a skill which is extremely rare. Both of them are represented as combining every excellence; their affection is instantaneous and unbounded; yet the coolest, most sceptical reader is forced to admire them, and believe in them.

Of Max we are taught from the first to form the highest expectations: the common soldiers and their captains speak of him as of a perfect hero; the Cuirassiers had, at Pappenheim's death, on the field of Lützen, appointed him their colonel by unanimous election. His appearance answers these ideas: Max is the very spirit of honour, and integrity, and young ardour, personified. Though but passing into maturer age, he has already seen and suffered much; but the experience of the man has not yet deadened or dulled the enthusiasm of the boy. He has lived, since his very childhood, constantly amid the clang of war, and with few ideas but those of camps; yet here, by a native instinct, his heart has attracted to it all that was noble and graceful in the trade of arms, rejecting all that was repulsive or ferocious. He loves Wallenstein his patron, his gallant and majestic leader: he loves his present way of life, because it is one of peril and excitement, because he knows no other, but chiefly because his young unsullied spirit can shed a resplendent beauty over even the wastest region in the destiny of man. Yet though a soldier, and the bravest

of soldiers, he is not this alone. He feels that there are fairer scenes in life, which these scenes of havoc and distress but deform or destroy; his first acquaintance with the Princess Thekla unveils to him another world, which till then he had not dreamed of; a land of peace and serene elysian felicity, the charms of which he paints with simple and unrivalled eloquence. Max is not more daring than affectionate; he is merciful and gentle, though his training has been under tents; modest and altogether unpretending, though young and universally admired. We conceive his aspect to be thoughtful but fervid, dauntless but mild: he is the very poetry of war, the essence of a youthful hero. We should have loved him anywhere; but here, amid barren scenes of strife and danger, he is doubly dear to us. (pp. 128-36)

The Princess Thekla is perhaps still dearer to us. Thekla, just entering on life, with 'timid steps,' with the brilliant visions of a cloister yet undisturbed by the contradictions of reality, beholds in Max, not merely her protector and escort to her father's camp, but the living emblem of her shapeless yet glowing dreams. She knows not deception, she trusts and is trusted: their spirits meet and mingle, and 'clasp each other firmly and forever.' All this is described by the poet with a quiet inspiration, which finds its way into our deepest sympathies. Such beautiful simplicity is irresistible. 'How long,' the Countess Terzky asks,

> How long is it since you disclosed your heart?
> MAX. This morning first I risked a word of it.
> COUN. Not till this morning during twenty days?
> MAX. 'Twas at the castle where you met us, 'twixt this
> And Nepomuk, the last stage of the journey.
> On a balcony she and I were standing, our looks
> In silence turn'd upon the vacant landscape;
> And before us the dragoons were riding,
> Whom the Duke had sent to be her escort.
> Heavy on my heart lay thoughts of parting,
> And with a faltering voice at last I said:
> All this reminds me, Fräulein, that today
> I must be parted from my happiness;
> In few hours you will find a father,
> Will see yourself encircled by new friends;
> And I shall be to you nought but a stranger,
> Forgotten in the crowd—"Speak with Aunt Terzky!"
> Quick she interrupted me; I noticed
> A quiv'ring in her voice; a glowing blush
> Spread o'er her cheeks; slow rising from the ground,
> Her eyes met mine: I could control myself
> No longer—
> [*The Princess appears at the door, and stops; the Countess, but not Piccolomini, observing her.*]
>
> —I clasp'd her wildly in my arms,
> My lips were join'd with hers. Some footsteps stirring
> I' th' next room parted us; 'twas you; what then
> Took place, you know.
> COUN.          And can you be so modest,
> Or incurious, as not once to ask me
> For *my* secret, in return?
> MAX.          Your secret?

COUN. Yes, sure! On coming in the moment
     after,
How my niece receiv'd me, what i' th' instant
Of her first surprise she—
     MAX.          Ha?
     THEKLA [*enters hastily*].          Spare yourself
The trouble, Aunt! That he can learn from me.

We rejoice in the ardent, pure and confiding affection of
these two angelic beings: but our feeling is changed and
made more poignant, when we think that the inexorable
hand of Destiny is already lifted to smite their world with
blackness and desolation. Thekla has enjoyed 'two little
hours of heavenly beauty'; but her native gaiety gives place
to serious anticipations and alarms; she feels that the camp
of Wallenstein is not a place for hope to dwell in. The in-
structions and explanations of her aunt disclose the secret:
she is not to love Max; a higher, it may be a royal, fate
awaits her; but she is to tempt him from his duty, and
make him lend his influence to her father, whose daring
projects she now for the first time discovers. From that
moment her hopes of happiness have vanished, never
more to return. Yet her own sorrows touch her less than
the ruin which she sees about to overwhelm her tender and
affectionate mother. For herself, she awaits with gloomy
patience the stroke that is to crush her. She is meek, and
soft, and maiden-like; but she is Friedland's daughter, and
does not shrink from what is unavoidable. There is often
a rectitude, and quick inflexibility of resolution about
Thekla, which contrasts beautifully with her inexperience
and timorous acuteness of feeling: on discovering her father's treason, she herself decides that Max 'shall obey his
first impulse,' and forsake her.

There are few scenes in poetry more sublimely pathetic
than this. We behold the sinking but still fiery glory of
Wallenstein, opposed to the impetuous despair of Max
Piccolomini, torn asunder by the claims of duty and of
love; the calm but broken-hearted Thekla, beside her broken-hearted mother, and surrounded by the blank faces of
Wallenstein's desponding followers. There is a physical
pomp corresponding to the moral grandeur of the action;
the successive revolt and departure of the troops is heard
without the walls of the Palace; the trumpets of the Pap-
penheimers reëcho the wild feelings of their leader. What
follows too is equally affecting. Max being forced away by
his soldiers from the side of Thekla, rides forth at their
head in a state bordering on frenzy. Next day come tidings
of his fate, which no heart is hard enough to hear unmoved. The effect it produces upon Thekla displays all the
hidden energies of her soul. The first accidental hearing of
the news had almost overwhelmed her; but she summons
up her strength: she sends for the messenger, that she may
question him more closely, and listen to his stern details
with the heroism of a Spartan virgin. (pp. 141-43)

Thekla has yet another pang to encounter; the parting
with her mother: but she persists in her determination,
and goes forth to die beside her lover's grave. The heart-
rending emotions, which this amiable creature has to undergo, are described with an almost painful effect: the fate
of Max and Thekla might draw tears from the eyes of a
stoic.

Less tender, but not less sublimely poetical, is the fate of
Wallenstein himself. We do not pity Wallenstein; even in
ruin he seems too great for pity. His daughter having vanished like a fair vision from the scene, we look forward to
Wallenstein's inevitable fate with little feeling save expec-
tant awe:

This kingly Wallenstein, whene'er he falls,
Will drag a world to ruin down with him;
And as a ship that in the midst of ocean
Catches fire, and shiv'ring springs into the air,
And in a moment scatters between sea and sky
The crew it bore, so will he hurry to destruction
Ev'ry one whose fate was join'd with his.

Yet still there is some touch of pathos in his gloomy fall;
some visitings of nature in the austere grandeur of his
slowly-coming, but inevitable and annihilating doom. The
last scene of his life is among the finest which poetry can
boast of. Thekla's death is still unknown to him; but he
thinks of Max, and almost weeps. He looks at the stars:
dim shadows of superstitious dread pass fitfully across his
spirit, as he views these fountains of light, and compares
their glorious and enduring existence with the fleeting
troubled life of man. The strong spirit of his sister is subdued by dark forebodings; omens are against him; his as-
trologer entreats, one of the relenting conspirators entreats, his own feelings call upon him, to watch and be-
ware. But he refuses to let the resolution of his mind be
over-mastered; he casts away these warnings, and goes
cheerfully to sleep, with dreams of hope about his pillow,
unconscious that the javelins are already grasped which
will send him to his long and dreamless sleep. The death
of Wallenstein does not cause tears; but it is perhaps the
most high-wrought scene of the play. A shade of horror,
of fateful dreariness, hangs over it, and gives additional effect to the fire of that brilliant poetry, which glows in every
line of it. Except in *Macbeth* or the conclusion of *Othello*,
we know not where to match it. Schiller's genius is of a
kind much narrower than Shakspeare's; but in his own peculiar province, the exciting of lofty, earnest, strong emotion, he admits of no superior. Others are finer, more
piercing, varied, thrilling, in their influence: Schiller, in his
finest mood, is overwhelming.

This tragedy of **Wallenstein,** published at the close of the
eighteenth century, may safely be rated as the greatest dramatic work of which that century can boast. . . . Germany, indeed, boasts of Goethe: and on some rare occasions,
it must be owned that Goethe has shown talents of a
higher order than are here manifested; but he has made
no equally regular or powerful exertion of them: *Faust* is
but a careless effusion compared with **Wallenstein.** The
latter is in truth a vast and magnificent work. What an assemblage of images, ideas, emotions, disposed in the most
felicitous and impressive order! We have conquerors,
statesmen, ambitious generals, marauding soldiers, heroes, and heroines, all acting and feeling as they would in
nature, all faithfully depicted, yet all embellished by the
spirit of poetry, and all made conducive to heighten one
paramount impression, our sympathy with the three chief
characters of the piece. (pp. 149-51)

[*Maria Stuart*] is upon a subject, the incidents of which
are now getting trite, and the moral of which has little that
can peculiarly recommend it. To exhibit the repentance of

a lovely but erring woman, to show us how her soul may be restored to its primitive nobleness, by sufferings, devotion and death, is the object of *Maria Stuart.* It is a tragedy of sombre and mournful feelings; with an air of melancholy and obstruction pervading it; a looking backward on objects of remorse, around on imprisonment, and forward on the grave. Its object is undoubtedly attained. We are forced to pardon and to love the heroine; she is beautiful, and miserable, and lofty-minded; and her crimes, however dark, have been expiated by long years of weeping and woe. Considering also that they were the fruit not of calculation, but of passion acting on a heart not dead, though blinded for a time, to their enormity, they seem less hateful than the cold premeditated villany of which she is the victim. Elizabeth is selfish, heartless, envious; she violates no law, but she has no virtue, and she lives triumphant: her arid, artificial character serves by contrast to heighten our sympathy with her warmhearted, forlorn, ill-fated rival. These two Queens, particularly Mary, are well delineated: their respective qualities are vividly brought out, and the feelings they were meant to excite arise within us. There is also Mortimer, a fierce, impetuous, impassioned lover; driven onward chiefly by the heat of his blood, but still interesting by his vehemence and unbounded daring. The dialogue, moreover, has many beauties; there are scenes which have merited peculiar commendation. Of this kind is the interview between the Queens; and more especially the first entrance of Mary, when, after long seclusion, she is once more permitted to behold the cheerful sky. In the joy of a momentary freedom, she forgets that she is still a captive; she addresses the clouds, the 'sailors of the air,' who 'are not subjects of Elizabeth,' and bids them carry tidings of her to the hearts that love her in other lands. Without doubt, in all that he intended, Schiller has succeeded; *Maria Stuart* is a beautiful tragedy; it would have formed the glory of a meaner man, but it cannot materially alter his. Compared with *Wallenstein,* its purpose is narrow, and its result is common. We have no manners or true historical delineation. The figure of the English court is not given; and Elizabeth is depicted more like one of the French Medici, than like our own politic, capricious, coquettish, imperious, yet on the whole truehearted, 'good Queen Bess.' With abundant proofs of genius, this tragedy produces a comparatively small effect, especially on English readers. (pp. 153-54)

[In Schiller's *The Maid of Orleans*] the Maid of Arc . . . is invested with a certain faint degree of mysterious dignity, ultimately represented as being in truth a preternatural gift; though whether preternatural, and if so, whether sent from above or from below, neither we nor she, except by faith, are absolutely sure, till the conclusion.

The propriety of this arrangement is liable to question; indeed, it has been more than questioned. But external blemishes are lost in the intrinsic grandeur of the piece: the spirit of Joanna is presented to us with an exalting and pathetic force sufficient to make us blind to far greater improprieties. Joanna is a pure creation, of half-celestial origin, combining the mild charms of female loveliness with the awful majesty of a prophetess, and a sacrifice doomed to perish for her country. She resembled, in Schiller's view, the Iphigenia of the Greeks; and as such, in some respects, he has treated her.

The woes and desolation of the land have kindled in Joanna's keen and fervent heart a fire, which the loneliness of her life, and her deep feelings of religion, have nourished and fanned into a holy flame. She sits in solitude with her flocks, beside the mountain chapel of the Virgin, under the ancient Druid oak, a wizard spot, the haunt of evil spirits as well as of good; and visions are revealed to her such as human eyes behold not. It seems the force of her own spirit, expressing its feelings in forms which react upon itself. The strength of her impulses persuades her that she is called from on high to deliver her native France; the intensity of her own faith persuades others; she goes forth on her mission; all bends to the fiery vehemence of her will; she is inspired because she thinks herself so. There is something beautiful and moving in the aspect of a noble enthusiasm, fostered in the secret soul, amid obstructions and depressions, and at length bursting forth with an overwhelming force to accomplish its appointed end: the impediments which long hid it are now become testimonies of its power; the very ignorance, and meanness, and error, which still in part adhere to it, increase our sympathy without diminishing our admiration; it seems the triumph, hardly contested, and not wholly carried, but still the triumph, of Mind over Fate, of human volition over material necessity.

All this Schiller felt, and has presented with even more than his usual skill. The secret mechanism of Joanna's mind is concealed from us in a dim religious obscurity; but its active movements are distinct; we behold the lofty heroism of her feelings; she affects us to the very heart. The quiet, devout innocence of her early years, when she lived silent, shrouded in herself, meek and kindly though not communing with others, makes us love her: the celestial splendour which illuminates her after-life adds reverence to our love. Her words and actions combine an overpowering force with a calm unpretending dignity: we seem to understand how they must have carried in their favour the universal conviction. Joanna is the most noble being in tragedy. We figure her with her slender lovely form, her mild but spirit-speaking countenance; 'beautiful and terrible'; bearing the banner of the Virgin before the hosts of her country; travelling in the strength of a rapt soul; irresistible by faith; 'the lowly herdsmaid,' greater in the grandeur of her simple spirit than the kings and queens of this world. Yet her breast is not entirely insensible to human feeling, nor her faith never liable to waver. When that inexorable vengeance, which had shut her ear against the voice of mercy to the enemies of France, is suspended at the sight of Lionel, and her heart experiences the first touch of mortal affection, a baleful cloud overspreads the serene of her mind; it seems as if Heaven had forsaken her, or from the beginning permitted demons or earthly dreams to deceive her. The agony of her spirit, involved in endless and horrid labyrinths of doubt, is powerfully portrayed. She has crowned the king at Rheims; and all is joy, and pomp, and jubilee, and almost adoration of Joanna: but Joanna's thoughts are not of joy. The sight of her poor but kind and true-hearted sisters in the crowd, moves her to the soul. Amid the tumult and magnificence of this royal pageant, she sinks into a reverie; her small native dale of Arc, between its quiet hills, rises on her mind's eye, with its straw-roofed huts, and its clear greensward; where the sun is even then shining so brightly, and the sky is so blue, and all is so calm and motherly and safe. She sighs for the peace of that sequestered home; then shudders to think that she shall never see it more. Accused of witchcraft, by her own ascetic melancholic father, she utters no word of denial to the charge; for her heart is dark, it is tarnished by earthly love, she dare not raise her thoughts to Heaven. Parted from her sisters; cast out with horror by the people she had lately saved from despair, she wanders forth, desolate, forlorn, not knowing whither. Yet she does not sink under this sore trial: as she suffers from without, and is forsaken of men, her mind grows clear and strong, her confidence returns. She is now more firmly fixed in our admiration than before; tenderness is united to our other feelings; and her faith has been proved by sharp vicissitudes. Her countrymen recognise their error; Joanna closes her career by a glorious death; we take farewell of her in a solemn mood of heroic pity.

Joanna is the animating principle of this tragedy; the scenes employed in developing her character and feelings constitute its great charm. Yet there are other personages in it, that leave a distinct and pleasing impression of themselves in our memory. Agnes Sorel, the soft, languishing, generous mistress of the Dauphin, relieves and heightens by comparison the sterner beauty of the Maid. Dunois, the Bastard of Orleans, the lover of Joanna, is a blunt, frank, sagacious soldier, and well described. And Talbot, the grey veteran, delineates his dark, unbelieving, indomitable soul, by a few slight but expressive touches: he sternly passes down to the land, as he thinks, of utter nothingness, contemptuous even of the fate that destroys him, and

> On the soil of France he sleeps, as does
> A hero on the shield he would not quit.

A few scattered extracts may in part exhibit some of these inferior personages to our readers, though they can afford us no impression of the Maid herself. Joanna's character, like every finished piece of art, to be judged of must be seen in all its bearings. It is not in parts, but as a whole, that the delineation moves us; by light and manifold touches, it works upon our hearts, till they melt before it into that mild rapture, free alike from the violence and the impurities of Nature, which it is the highest triumph of the Artist to communicate. (pp. 156-59)

The introduction of supernatural agency in this play, and the final aberration from the truth of history, have been considerably censured by the German critics: Schlegel, we recollect, calls Joanna's end a 'rosy death.' In this dramaturgic discussion, the mere reader need take no great interest. To require our belief in apparitions and miracles, things which we cannot now believe, no doubt for a moment disturbs our submission to the poet's illusions: but the miracles in this story are rare and transient, and of small account in the general result: they give our reason little trouble, and perhaps contribute to exalt the heroine in our imaginations. It is still the mere human grandeur of Joanna's spirit that we love and reverence; the lofty devotedness with which she is transported, the generous be-

nevolence, the irresistible determination. The heavenly mandate is but the means of unfolding these qualities, and furnishing them with a proper passport to the minds of her age. To have produced, without the aid of fictions like these, a Joanna so beautified and exalted, would undoubtedly have yielded greater satisfaction: but it may be questioned whether the difficulty would not have increased in a still higher ratio. The sentiments, the characters, are not only accurate, but exquisitely beautiful; the incidents, excepting the very last, are possible, or even probable: what remains is but a very slender evil.

After all objections have been urged, and this among others has certainly a little weight, the *Maid of Orleans* will remain one of the very finest of modern dramas. Perhaps, among all Schiller's plays, it is the one which evinces most of that quality denominated *genius* in the strictest meaning of the word. *Wallenstein* embodies more thought, more knowledge, more conception; but it is only in parts illuminated by that ethereal brightness, which shines over every part of this. The spirit of the romantic ages is here imaged forth; but the whole is exalted, embellished, ennobled. It is what the critics call idealised. The heart must be cold, the imagination dull, which the *Jungfrau von Orleans* will not move. (pp. 169-70)

The *Braut von Messina* was an experiment; an attempt to exhibit a modern subject and modern sentiments in an antique garb. The principle on which the interest of this play rests is the Fatalism of the ancients: the plot is of extreme simplicity; a Chorus also is introduced, an elaborate discussion of the nature and uses of that accompaniment being prefixed by way of preface. The experiment was not successful: with a multitude of individual beauties this *Bride of Messina* is found to be ineffectual as a whole: it does not move us; the great object of every tragedy is not attained. The Chorus, which Schiller, swerving from the Greek models, has divided into two contending parts, and made to enter and depart with the principals to whom they are attached, has in his hands become the medium of conveying many beautiful effusions of poetry; but it retards the progress of the plot; it dissipates and diffuses our sympathies; the interest we should take in the fate and prospects of Manuel and Cæsar, is expended on the fate and prospects of man. For beautiful and touching delineations of life; for pensive and pathetic reflections, sentiments, and images, conveyed in language simple but nervous and emphatic, this tragedy stands high in the rank of modern compositions. There is in it a breath of young tenderness and ardour, mingled impressively with the feelings of greyhaired experience, whose recollections are darkened with melancholy, whose very hopes are chequered and solemn. The implacable Destiny which consigns the brothers to mutual enmity and mutual destruction, for the guilt of a past generation, involving a Mother and a Sister in their ruin, spreads a sombre hue over all the poem; we are not unmoved by the characters of the hostile Brothers, and we pity the hapless and amiable Beatrice, the victim of their feud. Still there is too little action in the play; the incidents are too abundantly diluted with reflection; the interest pauses, flags, and fails to produce its full effect. For its specimens of lyrical poetry, tender, affecting, sometimes exquisitely beautiful, the *Bride of Messina* will long deserve a careful perusal; but as exemplifying a new form of the drama, it has found no imitators, and is likely to find none.

The slight degree of failure or miscalculation which occurred in the present instance, was next year abundantly redeemed. *Wilhelm Tell,* sent out in 1804, is one of Schiller's very finest dramas; it exhibits some of the highest triumphs which his genius, combined with his art, ever realised. The first descent of Freedom to our modern world, the first unfurling of her standard on the rocky pinnacle of Europe, is here celebrated in the style which it deserved. There is no false tinsel-decoration about *Tell,* no sickly refinement, no declamatory sentimentality. All is downright, simple, and agreeable to Nature; yet all is adorned and purified and rendered beautiful, without losing its resemblance. An air of freshness and wholesomeness breathes over it; we are among honest, inoffensive, yet fearless peasants, untainted by the vices, undazzled by the theories, of more complex and perverted conditions of society. The opening of the first scene sets us down among the Alps. It is

> a high rocky shore of the Luzern Lake opposite to Schwytz. The lake makes a little bight in the land, a hut stands at a short distance from the bank, the fisher-boy is rowing himself about in his boat. Beyond the lake, on the other side, we see the green meadows, the hamlets and farms of Schwytz, lying in the clear sunshine. On our left are observed the peaks of the Hacken surrounded with clouds: to the right, and far in the distance, appear the glaciers. We hear the *ranz des vaches* and the tinkling of cattle-bells.

This first impression never leaves us: we are in a scene where all is grand and lovely; but it is the loveliness and grandeur of unpretending, unadulterated Nature. These Switzers are not Arcadian shepherds or speculative patriots; there is not one crook or beechen bowl among them, and they never mention the Social Contract, or the Rights of Man. They are honest people, driven by oppression to assert their privileges; and they go to work like men in earnest, bent on the despatch of business, not on the display of sentiment. They are not philosophers or tribunes; but frank, stalwart landmen: even in the field of Rütli, they do not forget their common feelings; the party that arrive first indulge in a harmless little ebullition of parish vanity: "*We are first here!*" they say, "we Unterwaldeners!" They have not charters or written laws to which they can appeal; but they have the traditionary rights of their fathers, and bold hearts and strong arms to make them good. The rules by which they steer are not deduced from remote premises, by a fine process of thought; they are the accumulated result of experience, transmitted from peasant sire to peasant son. There is something singularly pleasing in this exhibition of genuine humanity; of wisdom, embodied in old adages and practical maxims of prudence; of magnanimity, displayed in the quiet unpretending discharge of the humblest every-day duties. Truth is superior to Fiction: we feel at home among these brave good people; their fortune interests us more than that of all the brawling, vapid, sentimental heroes in creation. Yet to make them interest us was the very highest problem of art; it was to copy

lowly Nature, to give us a copy of it embellished and refined by the agency of genius, yet preserving the likeness in every lineament. The highest quality of art is to conceal itself: these peasants of Schiller's are what every one imagines he could imitate successfully; yet in the hands of any but a true and strong-minded poet they dwindle into repulsive coarseness or mawkish insipidity. Among our own writers, who have tried such subjects, we remember none that has succeeded equally with Schiller. One potent but ill-fated genius has, in far different circumstances and with far other means, shown that he could have equalled him: the *Cotter's Saturday Night* of Burns is, in its own humble way, as quietly beautiful, as *simplex munditiis,* as the scenes of *Tell.* No other has even approached them; though some gifted persons have attempted it. Mr. Wordsworth is no ordinary man; nor are his pedlars, and leech-gatherers, and dalesmen, without their attractions and their moral; but they sink into whining drivellers beside *Rösselmann the Priest, Ulric the Smith, Hans of the Wall,* and the other sturdy confederates of Rütli.

The skill with which the events are concatenated in this play corresponds to the truth of its delineation of character. The incidents of the Swiss Revolution, as detailed in Tschudi or Müller, are here faithfully preserved, even to their minutest branches. The beauty of Schiller's descriptions all can relish; their fidelity is what surprises every reader who has been in Switzerland. Schiller never saw the scene of his play; but his diligence, his quickness and intensity of conception, supplied this defect. Mountain and mountaineer, conspiracy and action, are all brought before us in their true forms, all glowing in the mild sunshine of the poet's fancy. The tyranny of Gessler, and the misery to which it has reduced the land; the exasperation, yet patient courage of the people; their characters, and those of their leaders, Fürst, Stauffacher, and Melchthal; their exertions and ultimate success, described as they are here, keep up a constant interest in the piece. It abounds in action, as much as the *Bride of Messina* is defective in that point.

But the finest delineation is undoubtedly the character of Wilhelm Tell, the hero of the Swiss Revolt, and of the present drama. In Tell are combined all the attributes of a great man, without the help of education or of great occasions to develop them. His knowledge has been gathered chiefly from his own experience, and this is bounded by his native mountains: he has had no lessons or examples of splendid virtue, no wish or opportunity to earn renown: he has grown up to manhood, a simple yeoman of the Alps, among simple yeomen; and has never aimed at being more. Yet we trace in him a deep, reflective, earnest spirit, thirsting for activity, yet bound in by the wholesome dictates of prudence; a heart benevolent, generous, unconscious alike of boasting or of fear. It is this salubrious air of rustic, unpretending honesty that forms the great beauty in Tell's character: all is native, all is genuine; he does not declaim: he dislikes to talk of noble conduct, he exhibits it. He speaks little of his freedom, because he has always enjoyed it, and feels that he can always defend it. His reasons for destroying Gessler are not drawn from jurisconsults and writers on morality, but from the everlasting instincts of Nature: the Austrian Vogt must die; because if not, the wife and children of Tell will be destroyed by him. The scene, where the peaceful but indomitable archer sits waiting for Gessler in the hollow way among the rocks of Küssnacht, presents him in a striking light. Former scenes had shown us Tell under many amiable and attractive aspects; we knew that he was tender as well as brave, that he loved to haunt the mountain tops, and inhale in silent dreams the influence of their wild and magnificent beauty: we had seen him the most manly and warm-hearted of fathers and husbands; intrepid, modest, and decisive in the midst of peril, and venturing his life to bring help to the oppressed. But here his mind is exalted into stern solemnity; its principles of action come before us with greater clearness, in this its fiery contest. The name of murder strikes a damp across his frank and fearless spirit; while the recollection of his children and their mother proclaims emphatically that there is no remedy. Gessler must perish: Tell swore it darkly in his secret soul, when the monster forced him to aim at the head of his boy; and he will keep his oath. His thoughts wander to and fro, but his volition is unalterable; the free and peaceful mountaineer is to become a shedder of blood: woe to them that have made him so!

Travellers come along the pass; the unconcern of their everyday existence is strikingly contrasted with the dark and fateful purposes of Tell. The shallow innocent garrulity of Stüssi the Forester, the maternal vehemence of Armgart's Wife, the hard-hearted haughtiness of Gessler, successively presented to us, give an air of truth to the delineation, and deepen the impressiveness of the result. (pp. 172-77)

The death of Gessler, which forms the leading object of the plot, happens at the end of the fourth act; the fifth, occupied with representing the expulsion of his satellites, and the final triumph and liberation of the Swiss, though diversified with occurrences and spectacles, moves on with inferior animation. A certain want of unity is, indeed, distinctly felt throughout all the piece; the incidents do not point one way; there is no connexion, or a very slight one, between the enterprise of Tell and that of the men of Rütli. This is the principal, or rather sole, deficiency of the present work; a deficiency inseparable from the faithful display of the historical event, and far more than compensated by the deeper interest and the wider range of action and delineation, which a strict adherence to the facts allows. By the present mode of management, Alpine life in all its length and breadth is placed before us: from the feudal halls of Attinghausen to Ruodi the Fisher of the Luzern Lake, and Armgart,—

> The poor wild-hay-man of the Rigiberg,
> Whose trade is, on the brow of the abyss,
> To mow the common grass from craggy shelves
> And nooks to which the cattle dare not climb,—

we stand as if in presence of the Swiss, beholding the achievement of their freedom in its minutest circumstances, with all its simplicity and unaffected greatness. The light of the poet's genius is upon the Four Forest Cantons, at the opening of the Fourteenth Century: the whole time and scene shine as with the brightness, the truth, and more than the beauty, of reality.

The tragedy of *Tell* wants unity of interest and of action; but in spite of this, it may justly claim the high dignity of ranking with the very best of Schiller's plays. Less comprehensive and ambitious than *Wallenstein*, less ethereal than the *Jungfrau*, it has a look of nature and substantial truth, which neither of its rivals can boast of. The feelings it inculcates and appeals to are those of universal human nature, and presented in their purest, most unpretending form. There is no high-wrought sentiment, no poetic love. Tell loves his wife as honest men love their wives, and the episode of Bertha and Rudenz, though beautiful, is very brief, and without effect on the general result. It is delightful and salutary to the heart to wander among the scenes of *Tell:* all is lovely, yet all is real. Physical and moral grandeur are united; yet both are the unadorned grandeur of Nature. There are the lakes and green valleys beside us, the Schreckhorn, the Jungfrau, and their sister peaks, with their avalanches and their palaces of ice, all glowing in the southern sun; and dwelling among them are a race of manly husbandmen, heroic without ceasing to be homely, poetical without ceasing to be genuine. (pp. 186-87)

Schiller gives a fine example of the German character: he has all its good qualities in a high degree, with very few of its defects. We trace in him all that downrightness and simplicity, that sincerity of heart and mind, for which the Germans are remarked; their enthusiasm, their patient, long-continuing, earnest devotedness; their imagination, delighting in the lofty and magnificent; their intellect, rising into refined abstractions, stretching itself into comprehensive generalisations. But the excesses to which such a character is liable are, in him, prevented by a firm and watchful sense of propriety. His simplicity never degenerates into ineptitude or insipidity; his enthusiasm must be based on reason; he rarely suffers his love of the vast to betray him into toleration of the vague. The boy Schiller was extravagant; but the man admits no bombast in his style, no inflation in his thoughts or actions. He is the poet of truth; our understandings and consciences are satisfied, while our hearts and imaginations are moved. His fictions are emphatically nature copied and embellished; his sentiments are refined and touchingly beautiful, but they are likewise manly and correct; they exalt and inspire, but they do not mislead. Above all, he has no cant; in any of its thousand branches, ridiculous or hateful, none. He does not distort his character or genius into shapes, which he thinks more becoming than their natural one: he does not hang out principles which are not his, or harbour beloved persuasions which he half or wholly knows to be false. He did not often speak of wholesome prejudices; he did not 'embrace the Roman Catholic religion because it was the grandest and most comfortable.' Truth with Schiller, or what seemed such, was an indispensable requisite: if he but suspected an opinion to be false, however dear it may have been, he seems to have examined it with rigid scrutiny, and if he found it guilty, to have plucked it out, and resolutely cast it forth. The sacrifice might cause him pain, permanent pain; real damage, he imagined, it could hardly cause him. It is irksome and dangerous to travel in the dark; but better so, than with an *Ignis-fatuus* to guide us. Considering the warmth of his sensibilities, Schiller's merit on this point is greater than we might at first suppose. For a man with whom intellect is the ruling or exclusive faculty, whose sympathies, loves, hatreds, are comparatively coarse and dull, it may be easy to avoid this half-wilful entertainment of error, and this cant which is the consequence and the sign of it. But for a man of keen tastes, a large fund of innate probity is necessary to prevent his aping the excellence which he loves so much, yet is unable to attain. Among persons of the latter sort, it is extremely rare to meet with one completely unaffected. Schiller's other noble qualities would not have justice, did we neglect to notice this, the truest proof of their nobility. Honest, unpretending, manly simplicity pervades all parts of his character and genius and habits of life. We not only admire him, we trust him and love him. (pp. 197-98)

*Thomas Carlyle, in his* The Life of Friedrich Schiller: Comprehending an Examination of His Works, *second edition, 1845. Reprint by Gale Research Company, 1970, 357 p.*

## Johann Wolfgang von Goethe and Johann Peter Eckermann (conversation date 1827)

[*Eckermann was Goethe's companion and secretary between 1823 and 1832. In 1837 he published* Gespräche mit Goethe in den letzen Jahren seines Lebens (Conversations with Goethe, *1850), a transcription of his discussions with the writer. The work is prized as an important source of information on Goethe's ideas in his later years. In the following passage from that book, the two men discuss Schiller's early plays.*]

We talked of Schiller's *Fiesco,* acted last Saturday. "I saw it for the first time," said I, "and have been thinking whether those extremely rough scenes could not be softened; but I find very little could be done without spoiling the character of the whole."

"You are right—it cannot be done," replied Goethe. "Schiller often talked with me on the matter; for he himself could not endure his first plays, and would never allow them to be acted while we had the direction of the theatre. At last we were in want of pieces, and would willingly have had those three powerful firstlings for our repertoire. But we found it impossible; all the parts were too closely interwoven one with another, so that Schiller found himself constrained to give it up and leave the pieces just as they were."

"'Tis a pity," said I; "for, notwithstanding all their roughness, I love them a thousand times as well as the weak, forced, and unnatural pieces of some of the best of our later tragic poets. A grand intellect and character is felt in everything of Schiller's."

"Yes," said Goethe; "Schiller might do what he would, he could not make anything that would not come out far greater than the best things of these later people. Even when he cut his nails, he showed he was greater than these gentlemen.

"But I have known persons who could never be pleased with those first dramas of Schiller. One summer, at a bathing-place, I was walking through a very secluded narrow path which led to a mill. There Prince —— met me; and, as at the same moment some mules laden with meal-sacks came up to us, we were obliged to get out of the way and enter a small house. Here, in a narrow room, we fell into deep discussion about things divine and human; we came to Schiller's *Robbers,* and the prince expressed himself thus: 'If I had been the Deity on the point of creating the world, and had foreseen that Schiller's *Robbers* would be written in it, I would have left the world uncreated.' What do you say to that? That is a considerable dislike, scarcely comprehensible."

"There is nothing of this dislike," I observed, "in our young people, especially our students. The most excellent and matured pieces by Schiller and others may be performed, and we shall see but few young people and students in the theatre; but if Schiller's *Robbers* or Schiller's *Fiesco* is given, the house is almost filled by students alone."

"So it was," said Goethe, "fifty years ago, and so it will probably be fifty years hence. Let us not imagine that the world will so much advance in culture and good taste that young people will pass over the ruder epoch. What a young man has written is always best enjoyed by young people. Even if the world progresses generally, youth will always begin at the beginning, and the epochs of the world's cultivation will be repeated in the individual. . . ." (pp. 151-52)

*Johann Peter Eckermann, in a conversation with Johann Wolfgang von Goethe on January 17, 1827, in his* Conversations with Goethe, *edited by J. K. Moorhead, translated by John Oxenford, J. M. Dent & Sons Ltd., 1930, pp. 149-53.*

## William Cullen Bryant (essay date 1859)

[*Bryant is considered one of the most accomplished American poets of the nineteenth century, and is generally identified as one of the earliest figures in the Romantic movement in American literature. In the following address, delivered at a festival celebrating the one-hundredth anniversary of Schiller's birth, Bryant discusses Schiller's dramatic works and suggests that their predominant focus on truth and freedom lend them international appeal.*]

It might seem a presumptuous, if not an absurd, proceeding for an American to speak of the literary character of Schiller in the presence of Germans, who are familiar with all that he has written to a degree which cannot be expected of us, and by whom the spirit of his writings, to the minutest particular, must be far more easily, and, we may therefore suppose, should be more thoroughly apprehended. Yet let me be allowed to say that the name of Schiller, more than that of any other poet of his country, and for the very reason that he was a great tragic poet, belongs not to the literature of his country alone, but to the literature of the world. The Germans themselves have taught us this truth in relation to the tragic poets. In no part of the world is our Shakespeare more devoutly studied than in Germany; nowhere are his writings made the subject of profounder criticism, and the German versions of his dramas are absolute marvels of skilful translation.

We may therefore well say to the countrymen of Schiller: "Schiller is yours, but he is ours also. It was your country that gave him birth, but the people of all nations have made him their countryman by adoption. The influences of his genius have long since overflowed the limits within which his mother tongue is spoken, and have colored the dramatic literature of the whole world. In some shape or other, with abatements, doubtless, from their original splendor and beauty, but still glorious and still powerful over the minds of men, his dramas have become the common property of mankind. His personages walk our stage, and, in the familiar speech of our firesides, utter the sentiments which he puts into their mouths. We tremble alternately with fear and hope; we are moved to tears of admiration, we are melted to tears of pity; it is Schiller who touches the master chord to which our hearts answer. He compels us to a painful sympathy with his Robber Chief; he makes us parties to the grand conspiracy of Fiesco, and willing lieges of Fiesco's gentle consort Leonora; we sorrow with him for the young, magnanimous, generous, unfortunate Don Carlos, and grieve scarcely less for the guileless and angelic Elizabeth; he dazzles us with the splendid ambition and awes us with the majestic fall of Wallenstein; he forces us to weep for Mary Stuart and for the Maid of Orleans; he thrills us with wonder and delight at the glorious and successful revolt of William Tell. Suffer us, then, to take part in the honors you pay to his memory, to shower the violets of spring upon his sepulchre, and twine it with the leaves of plants that wither not in the frost of winter."

---

> Schiller perceived the great truth that old laws, if not watched, slide readily into abuses, and knew that constant revision and renovation are the necessary conditions of free political society; but he would have the revision made without forgetting that the men of the present day are of the same blood with those who lived before them.
>
> —*William Cullen Bryant*

---

We of this country, too, must honor Schiller as the poet of freedom. He was one of those who could agree with Cowper in saying that, if he could worship aught visible to the human eye or shaped by the human fancy, he would rear an altar to Liberty, and bring to it, at the beginning and close of every day, his offering of praise. Schiller began to write when our country was warring with Great Britain for its independence, and his genius attained the maturity of its strength just as we had made peace with our powerful adversary and stood upon the earth a full-grown nation. It was then that the poet was composing his noble drama of *Don Carlos,* in which the Marquis of Posa is introduced as laying down to the tyrant, Philip of Spain, the great law of freedom. In the drama of the *Robbers,* written

in Schiller's youth, we are sensible of a fiery, vehement, destructive impatience with society, on account of the abuses which it permits; an enthusiasm of reform, almost without plan or object; but in his works composed afterward we find the true philosophy of reform calmly and clearly stated. The Marquis of Posa, in an interview with Philip, tells him, at the peril of his life, truths which he never heard before; exhorts him to lay the foundations of his power in the happiness and affections of his people, by observing the democratic precept that no tie should fetter the citizen save respect for the rights of his brethren, as perfect and as sacred as his own, and prophesies the approaching advent of freedom, which, unfortunately, we are looking for still—that universal spring which should yet make young the nations of the earth.

Yet was Schiller no mad innovator. He saw that society required to be pruned, but did not desire that it should be uprooted—he would have it reformed, not laid waste. What was ancient and characteristic in its usages and ordinances, and therefore endeared to many, he would, where it was possible, improve and adapt to the present wants of mankind. I remember a passage in which his respect for those devices of form and usage, by which the men of a past age sought to curb and restrain the arbitrary power of their rulers, is beautifully illustrated. I quote it from the magnificent translation of *Wallenstein* made by Coleridge. Let me say here that I know of no English translation of a poem of any length which, a few passages excepted, so perfectly reproduces the original as this, and that, if the same hand had given us in our language the other dramas of this author, we should have had an English Schiller, worthy to be placed by the side of the German. "My son," says Octavio Piccolomini, addressing the youthful warrior Max,

> My son, of those old narrow ordinances
> Let us not hold too lightly. They are weights
> Of priceless value, which oppressed mankind
> Tied to the volatile will of the oppressor.
> For always formidable was the league
> And partnership of free power with free will.

And then, remarking that what slays and destroys goes directly to its mark, like the thunderbolt and the cannon-ball, shattering everything that lies in their way, he claims a beneficent circuitousness for those ancient ordinances which make so much of the machinery of society.

> My son, the road the human being travels,
> That on which Blessing comes and goes, doth follow
> The river's path, the valley's playful windings,
> Curves round the cornfield and the hill of vines,
> Honoring the holy bounds of property,
> And thus, secure, though late, leads to its end.

Schiller perceived the great truth that old laws, if not watched, slide readily into abuses, and knew that constant revision and renovation are the necessary conditions of free political society; but he would have the revision made without forgetting that the men of the present day are of the same blood with those who lived before them. He would have the new garments fitted to the figure that must wear them, such as nature and circumstances have made it, even to its disproportions. He would have the old pass into the new by gradations which should avoid violence, and its concomitants, confusion and misery.

The last great dramatic work of Schiller—and whether it be not the grandest production of his genius I leave to others to judge—is founded on the most remarkable and beneficent political revolution which, previous to our own, the world had seen—an event the glory of which belongs solely to the Teutonic race—that ancient vindication of the great right of nationality and independent government, the revolt of Switzerland against the domination of Austria, which gave birth to a republic now venerable with the antiquity of five hundred years. He took a silent page from history, and, animating the personages of whom it speaks with the fiery life of his own spirit, and endowing them with his own superhuman eloquence, he formed it into a living protest against foreign dominion which yet rings throughout the world. Wherever there are generous hearts, wherever there are men who hold in reverence the rights of their fellow-men, wherever the love of country and the love of mankind coexist, Schiller's drama of *William Tell* stirs the blood like the sound of a trumpet.

It is not my purpose to dwell on the eminent literary qualities which make so large a part of the greatness of Schiller, and which have been more ably set forth by others than they can be by me. It is not for me to analyze his excellences as a dramatic poet; I will not speak of his beautiful and flowing lyrics, the despair of translators; I will say nothing of his noble histories, written like his dramas, for all mankind—for it was his maxim that he who wrote for one nation only proposed to himself a poor and narrow aim. These topics would require more time than you could give me, and I should shrink with dismay from a task of such extent and magnitude. Let me close with observing that there is yet one other respect in which, as a member of the great world of letters, Schiller is entitled to the veneration of all mankind.

He was an earnest seeker after truth; a man whose moral nature revolted at every form of deceit; a noble example of what his countrymen mean when they claim the virtue of sincerity for the German race. He held with Akenside that

—Truth and Good are one,
And Beauty dwells in them;

that on the ascertainment and diffusion of truth the welfare of mankind largely depends, and that only mischief and misery can spring from delusions and prejudices, however enshrined in the respect of the world and made venerable by the lapse of years. The office of him who labored in the field of letters, he thought, was to make mankind better and happier by illustrating and enforcing the relations and duties of justice, beneficence, and brotherhood, by which men are bound to each other; and he never forgot this in anything which he wrote. Immortal honor to him whose vast powers were employed to so worthy a purpose, and may the next hundredth anniversary of his birth be celebrated with even a warmer enthusiasm than this! (pp. 215-20)

*William Cullen Bryant, "Frederick Schiller,"*

*in his* Prose Writings of William Cullen Bryant, Vol. 2, *edited by Parke Godwin, 1884. Reprint by Russell & Russell, Inc., 1964, pp. 215-20.*

### Margaret Oliphant    (essay date 1873)

[*Oliphant was a prolific nineteenth-century Scottish novelist, critic, biographer, and historian. A regular contributor to* Blackwood's Magazine, *she published nearly one hundred novels, including her best known work, the series of novels known as* Chronicles of Carlingford. *In the following excerpt from an essay published anonymously in* Blackwood's, *she offers a laudatory overview of Schiller's plays.*]

Schiller has nothing in him of the demigod; he stands firm upon mortal soil, where the motives, and wishes, and aspirations of common humanity have their full power. Even the visionary part of him is all human, Christian, natural; and when he touches upon the borders of the supernatural, as in those miraculous circumstances which surround his *Maid of Orleans,* it is still pure humanity and no fantastic archdemoniac inspiration which moves him. He is infinitely more of a man, and—paradoxical as the words may appear—infinitely less of a German, than his greater rival. The standing-point from which Goethe contemplates the world is that of a separate being, able, upon his detached point of vision, to see as it were all round the human figure which he contemplates, to behold it in relief, with a full sense of the perpetual complication of meaner with higher impulses, and the confused mixture of petty external circumstances with the wild and violent movements of unrestrained will and passion. The man who sees thus from an intellectual eminence should, it might be said, see better and more clearly than the observer on the common level. But yet it is not so; for the very gain in point of perspective has a confusing effect upon the landscape. The lines are altered by the apparently impartial distance from which he views them. There is something wanting to the human aspect of the work—a something which is made up by the keener sense of local colour, the sharper perception of all differences in atmosphere, the currents of air, the clouds and shadows, which give special character to the scene. Thus the fantastic wildness of the German imagination—the aspect, half picturesque, half grotesque, of its special temper and tendencies—works into the picture with double force from the Goethe altitude, thus making the more abstract poet at the same time the more national. We feel the apparent fallacy involved in these words: they are a paradox; yet they are true as far as our perception goes.

But Schiller stands upon no smiling grand elevation of superiority: he stands among the men and women whom he pictures, sympathising with them, sometimes wondering at them, sometimes regarding them with that beautiful enthusiasm of the maker for the thing created, by which the poet abdicates his own sovereignty, and represents himself to himself as the mere portrait-painter of something God—not he—has made. How faithfully, how nobly, without one thought of self-reflection, he follows the lines of his hero's noble but faulty figure, not sparing Wallenstein—putting his strength as well as his weakness on the canvas, yet showing ever the heroic magnitude of both! With what a swell of high and generous emotion he holds his Shepherd-maiden spotless through the stormy scenes of her brief drama! His own individuality has nothing to do with these noble pictures. He puts himself aside altogether from the stage, from the canvas, and throws his whole magnanimous force into the being whom it is his business to present to the world. **Wallenstein** is no more equal to *Hamlet* than it is to *Faust;* but in this particular at least, the art of Schiller is more Shakespearian than that of Goethe. There is much in it of the high unconscious humility, the simple putting aside of all personality, which distinguishes our greatest poet. Instinctively we find in Werter, in Meister, even in Faust, the poet himself, who lurks within the figures he has made; but we no more look for Schiller in his Wallenstein, in Max, or Carlos, or Tell, than we look for Shakespeare under the robes of Prospero or in Hamlet's inky suit. Schiller paints humankind without reference to himself, as Shakespeare did, throwing himself into characters different from his own, in which he can imagine a fashion of being perhaps greater than his own; whereas Goethe paints always a certain reflection of himself pre-eminent, and humankind only in relation to and contrast with that self, somewhat discredited and insignificant in the comparison. Such a difference is one of kind and not of degree, and may be traced through many lesser grades of power—one of those great distinctions between genius and genius which we must call moral rather than intellectual. We might say that the same distinction could be drawn between Milton and Shakespeare, were it not that this double contrast would land us in confusion inextricable. To place Schiller in the position of Milton, and Goethe in that of Shakespeare, is, we are aware, a common judgment of critics; and it is impossible to refuse to perceive how the breadth and impartiality, the ease and grandeur, of the greater German, correspond with the qualities of our supreme poet; or how the narrower and intenser feeling of Schiller, his earnest morality, and ideal elevation of the good and the true, reflect themselves in Milton. Yet notwithstanding this broad general resemblance, we feel that there is an interior and profound difference between the two, in each case, which suggests another classification. Milton is one of the egoist-poets, conscious, first of all, in the universe, of his own supreme existence, the standard of all things, throwing the rest of humanity into the shade. He is his own Satan, as Goethe is his own Faust. The highest conception of intellect and immortal spirit which either can grasp is himself. Thus, though in one phase of character Schiller resembles most the austere, learned, impassioned, and virtuous Milton, by another he takes his place on the side of Shakespeare, showing the same power of self-obliteration, if not the wonderful calm and impartiality with which that boundless intelligence represents all mankind. This moral difference is more subtle and delicate than almost any intellectual distinction. It is a difference which critics may miss, but which the common mind recognises without knowing why, and demonstrates by a warmer tenderness, a deeper personal feeling, towards the less selfish genius. The heart never hesitates in its conclusion, and we believe its judgment to be infallible. We admire with perhaps a certain

shudder the great and gloomy spirit in his fallen grandeur, the great Satan, the mysterious Faust. But the humbler and sweeter nature which forgets itself, whether conjoined as in Shakespeare's case with the higher genius, or as in Schiller's with the less, touches us beyond intellectual admiration, and makes its possessor the poet of our hearts. (pp. 185-87)

***The Robbers*** is too well known to require any lengthened description. It is the story of two brothers, one of whom, by the most primitive and unmitigated villany, drives the other from the refuge of his father's heart and house, which might have saved him from the crime to which he was driven by desperation. Karl von Moor, the injured and maligned hero, becomes the chief of a band of desperadoes, and sets himself to the work of doing wild justice in the oppressed country, robbing the rich to give to the poor, with the innocent and primitive magnanimity of a Robin Hood, though with all the wild storms of sentiment, passion, remorse, and misery which belong to an age more advanced in the representation of emotions. Every one who has read it must remember the sunset scene in which this young hero laments the innocence he has forfeited, and compares the feelings of his childhood with those which a career of crime and violence has left in his mind. This scene expresses the prevailing sentiment of the whole drama. A burning sense of wrong, and fierce disappointment with life, have driven the young man into wild action, visible rebellion against not only tyranny but law. Yet, through all, he holds fast by an imaginary intention which is noble, not criminal, and suffers agonies of remorseful misery when his followers break, as they do constantly, his own fanciful rules of mingled mercy and retribution. He is driven from crime to crime by that sequence of events which no human hand can stop, yet cannot consent to be criminal, or clear his mind from an inextinguishable longing for purity and peace.

This noble and melancholy criminal, however, is surrounded by very primitive and elementary figures—types of conventional classes of mankind, rather than men. The immense force of emotion in the drama, its fury and fervour, defraud us of the smile which rightfully attends such wild youthful demonstrations of life's impossibility; it is so deadly serious, so impressed with its own reality, that the reader is carried along as upon a boiling and foaming torrent; but on a calmer inspection, the boyish simple-minded blackness of shadow and clearness of light become very apparent. The preposterous transparent guilt of the villanous Franz, so perfectly frank and undisguised to himself, and so quickly fathomed and seen through by others; the weak old man so easily and perfectly deceived; and the angelic type of woman, faithful to the last,—are like the rude forcible figures drawn by a child, in which the rough outline of the human form is put down typically, on the simplest principles of construction. But notwithstanding this primitive treatment, and the extreme youth of the composition—notwithstanding its effervescence of lawlessness, and protest against repression—there is all the simplicity of innocence in Schiller's first drama. In all its heat of passion, in all its flow of speculation, and apparent thoughtfulness, its pretence at something like philosophy,—it is as innocent as our Robin Hood ballads. Youth is rampant in it, but youth that has known no evil. We are told that it put wicked thoughts into the heads of the German youth, and tempted them to rebellion. And no doubt the author thought himself gloriously wicked as he poured forth those thunders and lightnings of fancy, making the welkin ring again with his shout of defiance to all constituted authority, all decorum, discipline, and law. But, notwithstanding, we repeat *The Robbers* is the most innocent of all youthful efforts to be very wicked. The young poet dashes across his stage, thundering out his words, mouthing the biggest blasphemies he can invent; but the very effort is the best proof of his purity and innocence. All the ill he knows he heaps into his first tragic production, but that is so transparent, so straightforward, so frankly monstrous! It is wickedness as conceived by an innocent heart.

And what fire and vehemence are in the wild drama—what unbounded youthful energy and force! At what a pace it goes, blazing upon its way, holding the reader breathless with the rush of incident, the fierce heat of emotion! We indeed may smell only gunpowder in all those thunderings and lightnings, and feel the display to be pyrotechnic; but to the author the bolts he wielded came hot out of the hand of Jove, and the sympathetic audience whose interest he carried with him, accepted his certainty that the fire was divine, and felt it blaze and crackle with a universal thrill of emotion. Seldom has genius taken such hot and sudden vengeance on the authority which held it; and even now, at this calm distance, the reader understands and sympathises with the excitement of both author and audience, and feels the sweep of the fiery current which carries him along breathless to the end of the drama. Like a very firebrand, exciting all, frightening and scandalising many, it dropped into that iron-bound century, fettered by a hundred petty tyrannies. It ran through Germany like wildfire: students and other lawless lads were said to have taken to the woods and hills in emulation of Karl von Moor's dare-devils; and the generous Robber, who took from the rich to give to the poor, became for a time the idol of all those revolutionaries who were native to the age, but who, happily for themselves, in Germany at least, expended their revolutionary fire in *Robbers* and other literary mediums. Schiller gave, had his petty tyrant but known it, the most useful safety-valve by this means for the rising vapours of speculation. He relieved his own bosom at the same time of perilous stuff which might have wrought him greater harm in after-life. (pp. 189-90)

The master-note of conflict against the injustices and inequalities of life, which had been struck so strongly in *The Robbers,* and which had run through the historical plot of *Fiesko,* vibrated perhaps more warmly than ever in the domestic tale of *Luise Millerin,* in which a reflection of his own personal troubles is to be found. The story is that of a young noble who loves the humble daughter of a musician, and for her is ready to sacrifice everything. This youth is destined by his noble and ambitious father to build up his fortunes by marrying the mistress of the reigning highness. By the inconceivable baseness of this ambition, Schiller hurled his worst thunderbolt at the Highnesses and Wellborn Barons, who had wrought him mickle woe. There is much that is touching in the picture of the lover's despair, especially when we look upon it as inspired by the young poet's own sense of the gulf which separated from him one sweet Lotte and another, high well-born maidens, above a poet's rank, who was but the son of poor old Captain Schiller, and had as yet no scrap of nobility to wrap himself in. When his Ferdinand demands indignantly, if his "patent of nobility is more ancient or of more authority than the primeval scheme of the universe," it is clear that all Schiller's indignant young soul speaks in him. Thus, after he has struck widely at the inequalities of ordinary existence, the "spurns which patient merit from the unworthy takes," the sufferings of the poor and the tyrannies of the rich, the bitter disappointment of those who rely upon the comprehension of their fellows, in his first work; and upon the horrors of tyranny, and self-deceptions of ambition in the second; he comes to those social difficulties which give to all distinctions of class their sharpest pang, in the drama which brings this first youthful chapter of his history to a conclusion. It is in this episode that the reader will have most sympathy with the young poet; for, indeed, it is always hard upon a young man when cruel fate separates him from his Lotte—and minds which have little patience with the vague struggle of youthful rebellion against constituted authority and the force of circumstance, may yet feel the misery of the separated lovers, who can be united only by death. At the same time, Schiller never made a more tremendous assault upon the depravity of his age, that when he opposed to his fine and beautiful plebeian heroine the ambitious project of Ferdinand's father, and the shameful marriage which was to form the foundation of the young noble's fortune. *The Robbers* itself contains no such trenchant blow. (p. 193)

Schiller's Wallenstein stands between the temptations of ambition and that hard strain of unrewarded, unappreciated duty, which so often makes the weary soul faint in the midst of the way. His is the bitter mortification which makes us almost pardon the rebellion of a faithful servant wronged; for his services have never been justly recognised, nor his honour trusted. Between ambition and loyalty, and between prudence and daring—between the new, which is always attractive to genius, and the old, which is ever binding on the heart—the hero stands in the midst of the problems of middle age, not those of youth; and with a noble force and minuteness the poet follows him through his struggle. The sentiments with which we look on are not those of the ordinary dramatic spectator. The interest is deep and tragical, but we scarcely venture to pity, nor is there any tragic complication of Fate to appal us. The circumstances are dangerous and terrible, but the man is greater than the circumstances. The moment he comes before us we feel the magnitude of a being greatly formed—nay, before we see him, when the mere reflection of him even through the rude soldiers that follow his banners, betrays his imposing influence and *prestige*.

It is thus a great moral picture which is carefully, even elaborately, set forth before us, rather than the spontaneous outburst of a creative imagination. In most of the graver and more philosophical creations of Shakespeare there is a sweep of passion which produces an entirely different effect upon the reader, which breaks out, even through the hesitations of Hamlet, and which carries us on with resistless force in sympathy with the jealousy of Othello—the madness of Lear. Even in Macbeth, the tremendous force of remorse, working with and through his guilty ambition, confers upon the drama a might of tragic passion which is unknown to the German poet. Wallenstein scarcely goes the length of guilt. We have the struggle of purpose, of intention, of varying plan and uncompleted design; but even his treason is little more than theoretical. He has not yet lifted a finger against his emperor, when the toils of Fate close round him, and he falls ere ever he has completed one act to justify his doom. This austere reticence of design affects the feelings of the reader in the most curious way. The catastrophe leaves us half exultant that the hero has been saved from any outward stain of guilt. The growing darkness that encompasses him—the snare into which he thrusts his noble head with generous confidence—the terrible sense of approaching fate, which fills the very air with gloom as we accompany him to the last scene—restore to Wallenstein the support of our moral sympathy, even in his intended treason. Nobly unsuspicious, incapable of learning the very alphabet of distrust, and with a certain majestic confidence in the stars, and in his own high fortune, he marches forward to the great treason he contemplates, without believing it possible that other men can be traitors. Though he has been taught the lesson in the most forcible way, he cannot be convinced of anything so alien to his nature, although himself on the way to commit a similar crime; and so great is the skill of the poet, that we feel this curious paradox to be completely truthful, and perceive that it is impossible for Wallenstein, even when deserted by the great mass of his followers, to doubt for a moment the fidelity of those who remain. At the same time we watch all the humiliating circumstances of his downfall, the desertion of his generals, the failure even of that awe which has always encompassed his personal appearance on the scene to his soldiers—with no sense that the man is humiliated, but, on the contrary, with a growing conviction of that internal nobleness which no affront can affect. The anguish of his discovery that Piccolomini has been his enemy throughout, the blow to his affections conveyed by the defection of Max, and afterwards by the young hero's death—excite our sympathy not only for the pain he endures, but for the noble effort with which we feel him to surmount these miseries—struck to the heart, yet never yielding a step though heaven and hell combine against him. His great soul is not discouraged though his heart is torn to pieces. He dies unsubdued, falling as a great tree falls, to the confusion of his enemies no less than of his friends. Nothing can be more masterly than the delineation of Wallenstein's sentiments throughout. If he never reaches the level of the Hamlets, he is more full of power and meaning than any individual hero of Shakespeare's historical dramas; for it is not as a historical figure only that he is presented to us. History in Schiller's reading of it is no picturesque chronicle, but the deepest philosophical record of human principle and action. He selects his hero, not because his story is striking or his position nationally important, but because it permits, along with these natural advantages, much searching of a great human heart, and investigation into its problems. It is this which gives to the drama of *Wallenstein* its great and simple dignity and its greatest charm.

The story is told more after the fashion of Shakespeare's historical plays than of any other modern productions. The first part of it, which is a striking and animated picture of *Wallenstein's Camp,* is but little known in England. It has no connection with the tale, if tale it can be called, but forms a kind of introductory chapter for those who wish to acquaint themselves fully with the *mise en scène.* It is a fragment from the noisy, boisterous camp life, a panorama of rude moving figures, clink of spurs, trumpet-notes breathing across the landscape, gleams of steel and brilliant colours, loud voices, loud steps, careless jesting, rough levity and gravity, one as little seemly as the other. A rude company of soldiers from all countries tell in their various ways of the motives that have brought them thither, the noisy freedom which they purchase by absolute obedience, and all the rude delights of war and combat. It ends with a tumult and commotion produced by the bold (and most quaint) sermon of a Capuchin friar, in which the leader of the army is commented upon. They will not hear a word uttered against their chief. Wallenstein is at once their inspiration and their confidence, the only real thing they believe in. When this curious preface, so purposeless yet so full of purpose, ends, the real drama opens upon us. We are introduced to the society of Wallenstein's generals, among whom an emissary from the emperor, charged to convey the thunderbolt of the imperial displeasure, is making a cautious round; but only to find them all devoted to their spirited leader, and indifferent—when not indignant—to the messenger of their sovereign. This ambassador is accompanied by Octavio Piccolomini, Wallenstein's seeming brother and bosom friend, but in reality the secret enemy who is planning his overthrow. The other chief figure in the play is the young and ardent Max Piccolomini, a young soldier trained in camps, who has just made the blissful discovery of what peace is, in the wonderful journey through a smiling undevastated country which he has taken as escort to Wallenstein's wife and young daughter Thekla. There are few things more beautiful in poetry than the young man's enthusiastic description of this journey which has revealed so much to him—and the sudden longing for peace which breathes out of the ardent young soldier's soul. (pp. 198-200)

It is almost needless to describe the beautiful character of Thekla, proud, sweet, tender, and gentle princess, to whom out of her convent, as to Max out of the camp, that wonderful revelation has come. This brief journey has been to both the crown of life—it is all that life has to offer them. The beautiful eager girl, seeing her hero-father for the first time since her childhood, proud of him, exulting in him—yet more tenderly concerned for her mother, whose heart his ambition and danger have wellnigh broken, than for the less-known parent—is touched with the rarest and most delicate skill. She is "Friedland's daughter,"—at her weakest moment, proud, still, and strong as he, but with a melancholy in her soul which springs into foreboding strength when a sense of the dark mysteries going on around her opens to her mind. Thekla is no soft enchantress, serving the aims of an ambition which is beyond her sphere. Her judgment is unclouded even by her love: at the risk of her own heartbreak, she bids her lover obey his honourable and direct impulse to leave her father when Wallenstein throws off his allegiance; and when the news of Max's death, the only news that was to be looked for, comes, Thekla is heroic in the great calm of grief that succeeds her first desperation. Her famous song has afforded a sentimentally foolish expression of fictitious or superficial feeling to so many, that we almost fear to quote it as showing the very key-note of her noble character. There is no wail of discontent in it, but a magnificent stillness of woe. "I have had all the happiness of earth—I have lived and loved." What finer utterance was ever given to Youth's pathetic record of its own brief existence, its characteristic mingling of satisfaction and despair?—a whole world of meaning breathes through the brief simplicity of those much-abused words.

We need not go further into the drama, nor point out the somewhat stern and careless hand with which Schiller draws his group of generals—all moved by one impulse, and that the meanest motive of which humanity is capable, mere self-interest. Perhaps our interest would have been distracted from the principal figure had the poet shown us any relenting on the part of these rough soldiers, any power of judgment or lingering softness of sympathy and devotion to the chief who had dealt so generously with them. As it is, their universal exhibition of a coarser material nature, the instant response which all make to Piccolomini's whisper of danger on one side and reward on the other—with the one exception of Butler, who is moved by the sharper sting of injured self-love; and on the other hand, the equally coarse partisanship of Tertski and Illo, to the chief whom they drag on to his ruin, hoping for unparalleled success and advancement through his means,—kept in perfect relief the one great form, whom we seem to see against a pure heaven of blue, even in his wrongdoing, instead of the stormy and crowded background which is appropriate to the others. The tragedy winds up with almost as much slaughter as Hamlet, but the reader is not permitted to see the massacre. The confusion, excitement, and terror of the murder of Wallenstein, which we divine vaguely at a distance by means of the sudden tragic commotion and half-heard tumult; the pathos of Thekla's flight to the tomb of her lover, where we know her broken heart will cease to beat; and the brief tragic record of that young hero's end in the heat of battle,—come one after another, with differing degrees of pain, which gather into one sombre but fine climax. All the noble figures thus depart by separate ways into the darkness; the ignoble remain to wear out their meaner lives as fate permits; but the poet reserves one final touch of anguish, more bitter, more sharp than death, for the ambitious schemer Piccolomini, who has built his own fortunes on the ruin of his brother-in-arms. Wallenstein is dead, swept out of the world, his glory, his power, his honour, his family, all made an end of, in total and universal destruction. The other wins; but he wins by losing all that has made the struggle worth his while. When the now childless Octavio stands in the desolate lodging of his friend and victim, and has the imperial letter put into his hand addressed to the *Prince* Piccolomini, we see that success has a more desperate punishment than failure, and that there is in the victory of deceit and self-regard a more appalling blackness and anguish than in ruin itself.

Thus the high moral which Schiller loved to carry through all the realms of fancy has its most full and impressive expression.

The only other of Schiller's dramas into which our space permits us to enter, and which is to ourselves one of the most beautiful works of imagination in existence, is the *Maid of Orleans.* No being more attractive to the imagination than Joan of Arc has ever found a place in history; and in this drama the poet has poured all the glowing light of genius upon that beautiful simple figure, expanding its outlines into an angelic grandeur and sweetness, and surrounding it with an atmosphere of generous enthusiasm and visionary glory. No historical doubt or questioning interferes with Schiller's fervour of poetic admiration. His natural love of everything ideally pure and lofty finds the most genuine satisfaction in such a subject. The tender skill with which he contrives for his heroine a shadow of weakness as ideal as her strength and purity—the wavering of her virgin soul from absolute duty at the sight of the fair-faced Englishman—the soft magic which steals into her imagination alone, most sacred and stainless of visionary sins,—could only have originated in a mind as pure, and a heart as capable of understanding purity. Here genius itself would not be half so great, but for the aid of the pure soul and stainless moral temperament. This noble rendering of the Pucelle's wonderful story gives us not only one of the finest of imaginative creations, but reveals to us the purity, the simplicity, the sweetness of the poet's mind, capable, in an age so soiled and so unbelieving, in the very shadow of that vile image by which Voltaire made himself infamous, of placing so fair a vision before the world. How far the supernatural elements involved are justifiable we need not ask; for anything is justifiable which contributes to the excellence of a creation at once so lovely and so heroic.

There is no need to indicate the features of a tale so universally known. The character of Jeanne d'Arc herself is what we seek in every repetition of her story; and we know none so elevated or so beautiful as that of Schiller. A shade of musing sadness mingles at all times with the radiance of high purpose and rapt resolution which carry her through her mission. In the midst of battle and council, in the presence of the king, between the suitors who contend for her favour, and the archbishop before whom she bows in loyal humility, she is a thing apart, softly abstracted in her simplicity and straightforwardness. No complication of other emotions breaks in, except once, to weaken the single and fixed purpose which gives so much grandeur to her figure. The cloud which passes over her is absolute, like the brightness of her first appearance. Her visionary sin darkens her whole being while it lasts. She has not a word to say to answer to the accusation of witchcraft. That guilt is not hers; but other guilt is hers, of which no one knows, which shuts her mouth from all pleas of innocence. She is silent, for she has gone astray. She suffers dumbly the false blame, the ungrateful frenzy of the populace against her, who but now made the heavens ring with her name. She wanders forth alone, uncomplaining, not even breathing to her own faithful companion the fact that she is innocent. Musing she goes, as musing she came, her soul wrapt in thoughts incomprehensible to those around her; until in the silence and unresisted shame her heart is freed from her error, her divine confidence returns. Schiller has not dared to follow Joanna through the real facts of her story—he has shrunk from the stake, and that profound misapprehension of her contemporaries which even our Shakespeare was not great enough to free his kingly imagination from. He has given to his heroic maiden a death less terrible and more poetic, a change for which perhaps in the interests of humanity we may thank him, though we can conceive how those terrible facts might be so treated as to add yet a nobler drama to literature. Joanna dies gloriously after a victory in Schiller's noble poem—a fact which satisfies better the natural human craving for some sort of poetic justice, popularly so called.

We need not discuss the other dramas, which are less lofty than these two supreme productions of the poet's imagination. The *Tell,* which is one of the best known, is a fine, animated, and picturesque production, full of life and action, and with many passages of great poetical merit; but it fails in character, there being too much action, and variety of scene for any consistent study of individual mind or heart. To ourselves **Don Carlos** is more interesting than either **Tell** or **Mary Stuart;** but the reputation of Schiller, we believe, can never be more fitly justified and realised than by the two works to which we have specially referred,—the great philosophical conception of Wallenstein—the pure, noble, and glowing imagination which appears in the story of the heroic Maid. (pp. 200-03)

It is comfortable to know that the gentle poet, to whom friendship and love were as the breath of his nostrils, had fully and richly all that better part of success which is dear to the poetic soul. He was never rich, but his country set him in her heart, and wherever he went honour and tender homage surrounded him. Once after the performance of his **Maid of Orleans,** the beautiful crown of all his poetical works, the whole audience hurried out to the doors of the theatre, and made an avenue for him to pass, holding up their children to see the glory of their race. He had the warm friendship and admiration of Goethe, the greatest intellect of the time, and was surrounded by the affection of all worth caring for in Germany. A tender enthusiasm for himself—so gentle always, so friendly, tender, and true—as well as for his noble poetry, seems to have filled the country and universal heart. (p. 205)

*"A Century of Great Poets, from 1750 Downwards,"in* Blackwood's Edinburgh Magazine, *Vol. CXIV, No. DCXCIV, August, 1873, pp. 183-206.*

## William Norman Guthrie   (essay date 1909)

[*In the excerpt below, Guthrie assesses Schiller's religious poetry.*]

Ever since that centennial celebration of the poet's death, I for one have been re-reading, every little while, my Schiller, blessing (with mental reservations) Sir Edgar and Bulwer-Lytton [the translators]—shaking my head at Arnold-Forster ominously, and pondering an onslaught on them who superciliously venture to ignore the claims of Germany's darling bard.

A Burns, a Chatterton, a Keats in one; to these add Wordsworth and a suspicion of the Landorian dignity and classic aloofness; fail not to assume the "mighty line" of Marlowe, and somewhat of the youthful rebellion and melancholy of Byron—and then perhaps for him, who knows not Schiller in the original, a notion of the German adoration may gently dawn on his bewildered eye.

The ballads gave to Schiller the hearts of the plain people; the plays secured the more sophisticated; and on these two performances must rest, no doubt, his reputation. **"The Ring of Polycrates," "The Cranes of Ibycus," "The Fight with the Dragon,"** and **"The Diver"**—are, by common consent, achievements of the very first order. Even to-day **Maria Stuart** and **Wilhelm Tell** appear gracious, warm creations, that bind us with a spell of dramatic eloquence, which we are too grateful to disavow. Yet for those of us who believe in the prophetic office of the poet; who suspect that the test of life's aching needs is some warrant of moral truth in the preacher's deliverance; and that the æsthetic suasion of his form, coercing the sensitive poet, assists to chasten spiritual extravagance, to render sweet and sane the religious quest; for those who, while they would not bring ethical and dogmatic criticism to bear directly on the creations of the poet—to gyve his feet or clip his pinions—yet cannot but believe that (other things being equal) a poem gains much by its ability to feed our "moral being" and sustain our aspiration; for us, and the like of us, surely, an inventory of Schiller's lyric and epigrammatic poems of moral and religious thought, will not prove wholly valueless. For them, however, who reck nothing of such adventitious desert in things of beauty, we have no irate rebuke—only a courteous dismissal to the exquisite company of the "art for art's sake" guides into Elysian fields.

---

**Weigand on Schiller's tragedies:**

In all of [Schiller's tragedies] the action is centered around men and women of highly superior emotional range, strength, and ingrained nobility. They get involved with the dark forces of life through headlong impulse or ambition. They engage in the struggle for highest stakes, boldly, courageously, generously. They perish. But in each case the figure of the protagonist, the *Gestalt,* is enduringly stamped upon our inner eye as the incorporation of timeless human values. They are heroes, exemplars of human freedom within the framework of a higher moral law to which they pay tribute in their very transgression. The net effect of each of Schiller's tragedies is to leave us with a quickened sense of life as a proving ground of personality. Our response to the heroic struggle of the protagonists and the vindication of the moral law in their downfall is affirmative. A life that affords room for personalities of such scope to develop is good. We are impelled to emulate them in the hope of ourselves leaving a significant mark for posterity. Thus Schiller's pattern of tragedy is basically optimistic.

*Hermann J. Weigand, in* A Schiller Symposium: In Observance of the Bicentenary of Schiller's Birth, *The University of Texas, 1960.*

From the poems of Schiller's "first period" little falls within the scheme we have proposed. The afflatus of the *Robbers* is not to be denied. Lovers of the "Gothic romance," so-called, may rejoice therein. Anne Radcliffe, Monk Lewis, Bulwer-Lytton, Edgar Allan Poe and Co., should never be without literary progeny. Yet, to have survived and outlived a "Storm and Stress" period of perfervid adolescence is, for a poet, no small luck and praise.

So we note, only in passing, the manful self-assertion that expressed itself in Burns' immortal song, "A man's a man for a' that," and much less worthily, we regret to say, in Schiller's piece of verse-strutting, *Männerwürde,* and his honest rebuke to a pompous Pharisee:

> A man am I. Who's more a man?
> Who claims to be? Go, spring
> Freely under God's shining sun,
> And lustily leap and sing!
>
> . . . . .
>
> Well, if through ice of the sophistic mind
> The warm blood hath a little gladlier purled;
> What may not be achieved of human kind
> Leave thou to denizens of a better world.
>
> My earthly fellow doth the spirit immure,
> Though heaven-begotten; and behold, I can
> Nowise become a holy angel pure:
> So let me follow him, and be a man!

Far more profoundly are we moved, however, by certain poems of the second period, especially the three: **"Der Kampf " ("The Conflict")**, **"Resignation,"** and **"Die Götter Griechenlands" ("The Gods of Greece")**. The first stanza of his **"Hymn of Joy" ("An die Freude")** had the signal honor to become part of Beethoven's Choral Symphony. The Goddess of Joy makes all her votaries kin. And youth feels itself made solely to possess her forever! The moments when the human race triumphed signally we may therefore assimilate in our young enthusiasm, delighting in the personal value we assign to them as self-expression. *"Afflavit deus, et dissipati sunt"* The vessels of our foe are scattered over the vasty deep. What youthful heart does not beat high?

But, however fancy and imagination may so transport us, we return ever in due time to our own single self; and there in our life we front quite another spectacle:

> No, I will fight this giant fight no longer,—
> The fight of duty and sacrifice.
> If the heart's hot rage to soothe, thou be no
>      stronger,
> Virtue, ask not of me such cruel price.
>
> Sworn have I, yea, most bindingly have sworn
>      it,
> To wrestle with myself for mastery:
> Have back thy victor's wreath; though I have
>      worn it,
> I'll wear it never. To sin let me be free!

What biographically the immediate nature of the fight may have been is of no poetic consequence. Indeed, the last stanza profits by its very ambiguity, thereby getting reaches of significance that belong to the uttermost of man's aspiration:

> Fair and dear soul, trust not this angel-seeming,
> For crime, thy piteous kindness arms me now.
> In the infinite realms with life's fair marvels
>      teeming
> Is there another fairer prize than thou?
>
> Or than the very crime I flee from, ever?
> O fate most tyrannous;—
> The prize to crown my virtuous will's endeavor
> Doth slay my virtue—thus!

Howbeit, only on condition of ascetic self-denial may higher quests enjoy their fair fruition. Not that any mystic merit of the sacrifice secures our reward. Not that there has been providential malice in the universal order requiring our deliberate purchase with pain of the more enduring pleasure. Merely, that to no one may all at once be granted. With our inevitable, quite innocent limits of time and space and vitality, choice must be exercised as discreetly as may be, and the consequences abided by. This simple fact, when first intimately realized, causes each soul in turn acutest suffering; and hence to mankind the promises of compensation in some life-to-come have been reiterated pathetically, and cherished in sheer despair of egoism. On these Schiller will not place reliance:

> I also in Arcadia was born;
> And in my childish years,
> Nature to grant me happiness hath sworn.
> I also in Arcadia was born,
> Yet my short springtide yielded only—tears!

Enumerating his sacrifices, his illusions, and disillusionments, shrinking from the cynical onlooker who recks not of invisible treasures, disquieted, disconsolate, all but remorseful for the irrevocable worthy choice, he obtains this oracle:

> "I love with one love all my children," cried
> A genius veiled from sight.
> "Children of men, hearken; two flowers abide
> The prudent seeker, blowing side by side,—
> Hope and immediate Delight."
>
> Who hath one blossom culled of the twain,
> Let him not crave her sister-bloom.
> Who hath not faith—enjoy! This lore's refrain,
> Old as the world: whoso hath faith—abstain!
> The world's recorded life—its Day of doom.
>
> Hope hath been thine; then hast thou gained thy
>      due.
> Thy faith—the grace awarded thee!
> Thou shouldst have asked thy wise men, for they
>      knew:
> What might not of the moment's flight accrue,
> Shall be restored not of eternity!

Schiller's famous elegy on departed Hellenic polytheism—**"The Gods of Greece"**—has been fluently rendered by Mr. Arnold-Forster. That most pregnant epigram, however, which ends the poem, is not Englished with sufficient pungency:

> And Fancy, crushed by life's stern pressure,
> Lives but in poetry sublime,

is more elegant, but not so direct as Bowring's:

> All that is to live in endless song,

Must in life-time first be drowned,

although it was not Schiller who specified a watery grave!

Again our subject is the question of a definite choice. Immortal life in song (that is long continued influence through the better part of man, his imagination and craving for the ideal) must first make itself known, ay more, deliver its credentials by tragic catastrophe:

> *Wass unsterblich im Gessang soll leben,*
> *Muss im Leben untergehn.*

> All that in Poesy shall live forever
> Must perish first in actual life.

With this insight, the poet Schiller, conscious of his divine call, could himself forego pleasure, and refrain from passion, not without intimations perhaps of his own early end. He too, must accept his destiny, and serve as an incentive, and live so that the spell of his verse should be reinforced by the idealization of his personal career. Surely a fate deserving from happier men no unworthy pity!

Not that the young poet will fail at moments to regret the days of unreasonable expectations, and will hush melodious complaints which are themselves consolatory. So the elegy called **"Ideals"** makes an irresistible appeal to all who can love the palpitant life of youth in retrospect:

> Ah, cruel, must thou then depart
> And leave me joyless and alone,
> Forgetful of what joy and smart
> In close communion we have known?
> Can nothing thy departure stay,
> Thou golden stage of earthly time?
> 'Tis vain: thy billows roll away
> To the eternal sea sublime.

For eight more stanzas Schiller reviews the losses and bewails them, ending as the undefeated man, whose vocation, and the fellowship it earns for him, suffice to keep him erect, with countenance of resolute cheer, face forward:

> Of all that merry company,—
> Which stood beside me to the last?
> Which comforted my parting sigh?
> Which will abide when all is past?
> Friendship, 'tis thou, whose healing balm,
> Is lightly spread o'er every wound,
> Sharing our ills with loving calm;
> Thou whom I early sought and found.

> And Labor, thou, who, hand in hand
> With her, can exercise the soul;
> Who canst all weariness withstand;
> Whose solid tasks with time unroll,
> Although thou travail, grain by grain,
> To rear Eternity sublime;
> Years, minutes, days, thou canst detain
> From the tremendous debt of Time.

In two at least of the ballads we seem to hear echoes of that oracle that came to him, so unambiguous and not to be denied: "Whoso hath faith—abstain!"

The classical allegory of the divine envy serves to illustrate the principle that not all can be had which the heart desires; nay, what is more, all that should not be had, even

if accorded of a partial fate. Polycrates, after exhibitions of incredible good fortune is admonished by his friend:

> Wouldst thou immunity from grief?
> Then pray the Gods, in kind relief,
> To shade thy luck with sorrow's tone.
> No man true happiness has gained
> On whom the generous Gods have rained
> Untempered benefits alone.

In the **"Cranes of Ibycus,"** by the operation of an Æschylean Chorus of the Furies, two murderers of the expected winner of poetic laurels, stand self-confessed. The awe is realized with great dramatic force, and we feel that somehow this was with Schiller a very real experience. He was not cold-bloodedly constructing a ballad to illustrate Kant's conception of the "categorical imperative;" he was imparting to us, by a tale, something of his own shudder at the mystery of conscience:

> And between truth and wonderment
> Each quaking heart with doubt is rent,
> And worships the tremendous might
> Which, all unseen, protects the right;
> Unfathomable, unexplained,
> By which the threads of Fate are spun,
> Deep in the human heart contained,—
> Yet ever hiding from the sun.

But our quest of truth has ever been at the expense of conscience. Always the old was settled in rightful possession. The new appeared as rebel, as invader. The youth, therefore, who would unveil the Image of Truth at Sais was indeed to Schiller more than the hero of a legend.

> Far heavier than thou deemest
> Is this thin gauze, my son. Light to thy hand
> It may be—but most weighty to thy conscience.

He lifted the veil. He saw. And never did he publish his vision;—only lived to warn all questioners:

> "Woe—woe to him who treads through guilt to
> TRUTH."

The Truth even can be approached no otherwise than as God's law doth allow. But the poets with all other artists have their custody of more than truth:

> Ye hold in trust the honour of mankind.
> Guard it! With yours 'tis closely intertwined.
> The charm of poetry we rightly deem
> Part of creation's well-appointed scheme.
> Let it roll on and melt into the sea
> Of a divinely blended harmony . . .
> When Truth is taunted by its proper age,
> Let her appeal to the poetic page
> And seek a refuge in the Muse's choir.
> Her real claims more readily inspire
> Respect, that they are shrouded o'er with grace.
> May she in song forever find a place,
> And on her dastard enemies shall rain
> Avenging pæans in triumphal strain. . . .

> Ye freeborn scions of a mother free,
> Press onward firmly with exalted eyes;
> Perfected beauty only may ye see,
> And lesser crowns ye need not stoop to prize!
> The sister missing in this present sphere
> Clasped to her mother's bosom ye shall find;

What lofty souls as beautiful revere
Must noble be, and perfect of its kind.
Poised high above your life-appointed span,
Let your ecstatic pinions freely swell.

The dawning image in your mirror scan,
And the approaching century foretell.
By thousand paths and many devious ways
Through every varied turning ye shall glide
To welcome in the fulness of her days
Harmonious concord, your delight and guide.

With so deep a conviction, then, of his vocation, and with so exalted a faith in the divine function thus allowed him, why should the poet refuse to be deprived (by his great ministry of delight) of what the common lot offers to mankind? Having friendship and work, knowing the tragic law of higher life through death, apprehending the oracle of necessary choice,—why should not the poet be of good cheer, even though Zeus seems to have divided out the earth already, reserving for him no equitable portion? His high-priesthood was, to be sure, foreseen:

Part of creation's well-appointed scheme.

And so, it could not have been, after all, an oversight, albeit the ballad entitled **"The Partition of the World,"** so has it:

"If thou to dwell in dreamland hast elected,"
Replied the God, "lay not the blame on me.
Where wast thou when the sharing was effected?"
"I was," the Poet said, "by thee.

"Mine eye upon thy countenance was dwelling,
Thy heavenly harmony entranced mine ear;
Forgive the mind, thine influence compelling
Rendered oblivious of this sphere!"

"What can I do?" said Zeus. "For all is given;
The harvest, sport, the markets, all are seized.
But, an thou choose to live with me in heaven,
Come when thou wilt, and I shall be well pleased."

So much for the prophetic revelation Schiller had as poet; a double assurance of the worth of intelligent sacrifice of the less excellent for the more perfect; the hallowed privilege of special self-immolation when granted a place near to the gods, and an influence on the lives of his fellow men beyond the span of his own personal life. (pp. 192-200)

*William Norman Guthrie, "The Religious Poetry of Schiller," in* The Sewanee Review, *Vol. XVII, No. 2, April, 1909, pp. 190-215.*

## Benedetto Croce   (essay date 1923)

[*An Italian educator, philosopher, and author, Croce developed a highly influential theory of literary creation and a concomitant critical method that emphasized judging each work as a separate, independent entity. In the following excerpt from an essay originally published in Italian in 1923, Croce contends that Schiller's poetry is largely derivative and finds his dramas "cold and artificial." Croce concludes that Schiller's talents were better suited to philosophical inquiry.*]

Frederick Schiller is a great name, which has filled a great place and will continue to fill a great place in the history of poetry. Yet how does he come by that name and that position unless it be due entirely to the hybrid method usual in the writing of poetical history? Indeed, his case can be quoted as a clear instance of the errors in perspective due to such hybrid treatment. For it is only owing to the confusion of history of poetry with that of culture that it has been possible to create the couple Goethe-Schiller, *par nobile fratrum, lucida sidera* of poetry in general and of German poetry in particular. This equivalence or juxtaposition is due to motives really external to art, and to some extent dissimilar from those which led to the coupling of Dante and Petrarch, Ariosto and Tasso, Corneille and Racine. It was suggested and imposed, from the fact that the two men had been friends and collaborators for some years, that both had received the applause and the confidence of their compatriots at the moment of their first appearance in the literary world, from their common lot of being selected as standard bearers in Germanic literary and political conflicts. And, on the other hand, it is only owing to the confusion of the history of poetry with that of literary classes and institutions that we hear Schiller exalted as the poet who "created the German national theatre," the poet whose plays (as a recent historian of literature has declared), "whatever may be their deficiencies, and were they even greater than they are, belong always to the classical drama of Germany."

If we regard the matter, on the other hand, from the exclusive standpoint of poetry, and if we argue with the simplicity of heart which is not unsuitable to that form of history, we should come to the natural conclusion that Schiller belongs to it only as a poet of the second rank. In saying this, we go against the opinion of Horace, for whom poetry of the second rank is unacceptable to gods, men, and booksellers. From our point of view, poets of the second rank would be those ingenious and expert men of letters who avail themselves of artistic forms already discovered, employ them with judgment, and enrich them with psychological, social, and natural observations, in order to compose instructive, elevating or agreeable works. Such men are sensible and decorous writers, yet they are not poets: a fact which does not imply that their works are not sometimes most acceptable, and in their way more "useful," than those of the true poets. That Schiller was a poet of this secondary sort is a conviction which has now penetrated, although not always very clearly stated as having done so, not only the consciousness of other peoples, but also of the Germans themselves. The former, for a brief period, read, translated, and imitated Schiller, looking upon him as a sort of modernized Shakespeare, but now he is neglected, and with the change of political conditions, the recurrence of the first centenary since his death was celebrated in a very different fashion from that of the famous centenary of his birth, in 1859. German artists and critics, on being asked for their opinions, have confirmed the fall of the poetical reputation of Schiller, though expressing themselves in pious euphemisms. A certain British writer, too, who must be set down as a crank, on being also invited to express a judgment on the matter, candidly confessed that he had never read a line of Schiller, but declared, at the same time, that since he had been endowed with the gift of deducing from the sound of an author's name the quality and value of his work, this gift enabled him to infer that "Schiller" was one of those authors highly recommended in schools, who extract vast yawns from the breast. The gentleman in question was not altogether wrong in his theory of the sound of the name, because the name of a celebrated man becomes impregnated with all the impressions aroused by his work, with the judgments of admiration or of disapproval which it has received, and with the greater or lesser degree of warmth of the said judgments. For this reason, it is very often possible that one who knows nothing but the sound of a name may yet be able to gather from that, whether it be a question of a great, a little or a mediocre writer, of a genius or a pedant, of an author mysterious and profound in thought and feeling, or easy and accessible to the delight of everyone. It is true that, in reducing the glory of Schiller to modest dimensions, an attempt has also been made to change the value of its various components and by belittling the merit of his mature plays, those which used to be considered perfect, to extol that of his early plays, which are imperfect and chaotic. But I have strong reasons for suspecting that this inversion of values has been brought about by a criterion active in Germany (and also outside Germany properly so-called). This criterion came into fashion with the great value attached to the *echtdeutsch,* the *ur-Germanisch,* whereby a realism overexcited and convulsed has been taken as the mark of genuine, sublime poetry. This realism, save for its crudity, seems to me to be quite other than purely and primitively Germanic, derived from the forest of Arminius; indeed it is nothing but an indigestion of Shakespeare, blended with the generous vintage of Rousseau, which first appeared in Germany at the end of the eighteenth century and several times renewed itself, with other vinous admixtures, among which must not be forgotten powerful but perfidious draughts drawn from the Catholic—sacrilegious—incestuous *cantines* of the Vicomte de Chateaubriand.

Shakespeare is a moment of the spirit's history, and he cannot be repeated at pleasure; so that when we see his Lears, his Edmunds, his Cordelias in the costumes of the old Moor, or of Franz Moor, or of Amalia in the *Raüber,* we seem to be passing from myth and fable to a brutal realism, which violates the lofty and delicate creations of great poetry. Giannettino Doria too, in the *Fiesco,* is an evil-minded, tyrannous bully compared with Richard III, and the Moorish assassin of the same play, instead of attending to his ignoble business, engages in fool's talk like certain of the Elizabethan clowns, thereby transporting something foreign into the society where it is introduced. The imitation is strident. I am quite well aware of the effect that must have been produced in those days by the furious tirades of Charles Moor against social laws and tyrannies:

> No, I cannot think of it.—I am to constrict my body in stays and let my will be snared by the laws. The law has reduced what should have been the flight of an eagle to the crawling of a snail. The law has never yet formed a great man, but liberty breeds Colossi and extraordinary beings. . . .

And the frantic resolution which follows:

> Behold, it falls like a cataract from my eyes: how mad was I to wish to return to the cage!—My spirit thirsts for action, my every breath is liberty's.—Assassins! Robbers!—With these words was law rolled beneath my feet. Men have concealed humanity from me, when I appealed to humanity. Away from me, sympathy and pity! . . .

But this Moor, who selects the trade of brigand, yet is seized with indignation when the brigands proceed to act according to the logic of their trade, is a brigand who looks round him and wishes to retain the sympathy of the pit:

> Shame! Slaughter of children! Slaying of women! Slaying of sick people! How this deed overcomes me! It has poisoned my most beautiful works!

The structure of the play shows itself to be intellectualistic and calculated in the midst of all this din and violent action: nothing ever happens unexpectedly. Charles Moor's relinquishment of society and his repugnance for the deeds of the brigands, his sadness and return to the paternal abode that he may salute it and again depart, the death of Amalia—all this has been calculated. The composition of *Kabale und Liebe* is also intellectualistic, and this play is for the rest a literary reminiscence of middle-class French and English drama and fiction and of Lessing's dramatic work. There is little to admire in it, save here and there a trait in the personage of the old musician Müller.

Schiller was a moralist and a polemist in these dramas of which he had borrowed the literary forms, and for this reason I am unable to join recent critics in regretting his abandonment of his early style and in noting the decadence of the later work, beginning with *Don Carlos,* that is to say, *Don Carlos* in verse, which alone survives. To me it seems to be altogether natural and most praiseworthy that with the refinement of his taste and the heightening of his conception of art, he should have separated himself from his juvenile manner, which although quite suitable to a medical student, was no longer in place with the refined and thoughtful man of letters he had become. Nor do I discern any loss of his natural gifts in the course of this transition. He did not lose the gift of imaginative spontaneity, which he had never possessed, nor the moral enthusiasm and the polemical energy, which he had possessed and retained, adding to it a better knowledge of history, of philosophy and of art itself. These gifts of an apostle of morality and of a sententious psychological playwright were what acquired for him the favour of democracies, both in his own country and elsewhere, in our Italy, for instance, where Mazzini, among others, admired and preferred him to Goethe and also to Shakespeare. The reason for this is to be found in the fact that it is proper to democracies to prefer declining values in art to genuine values, which are aristocratic and anti-utilitarian. The Marquis of Posa has been defined as a "personified categoric imperative"; but such a personage as he was already present in the juvenile plays, as the old Republican conspirator who slays his friend Fiesco because he suspects him of ambitious plans for the domination of others, and the change is only in the wider ideal circle in which moves that champion of religious tolerance and of the freedom of peoples, and in the greater experience acquired by the artist. Nor has the possibly changed political attitude of Schiller, inclining him rather towards interior freedom than towards politics, as a possible result of the revolutionary events in France, any importance as regards his poetry. It may be true and it may be false that he changed his point of view, but poetry might equally well appear in either or neither of these cases.

What becomes clear, on the contrary, in the period of Schiller's maturity after the **Don Carlos** is that, when the effervescence of youth, which he himself and others mistook for poetical genius and inspiration, had calmed down, Schiller entered into that spiritual condition which is almost equally as painful for him who suffers from it as for him who contemplates the suffering. He was not carried away or guided by an interior necessity to solve a problem, developing within him as though it were an objective process, with its necessary stages and a natural passage from one to another of these, shaping itself in a natural way or determining with ever increasing accuracy its own form, but, on the contrary, he remained puzzled, uncertain which way to go, and began to argue and distinguish minutely what themes he should treat and what forms were to be considered the best adapted and the most beautiful. This is a condition (we must speak the unkind word) of impotence which is frequently to be observed. No remedy can be applied, for it is possible to correct a force which has strayed from its correct line owing to accidental circumstances, but not to inspire force when it is absent. Then the artist becomes clever and begins to conceive thoughts which seem to him and to others to be astonishingly poetical, but which have precisely the defect of being thoughts very like those deduced by critics from works already composed. These thoughts, due to an intellect seeking a possible expression in art, will never have vigour enough to generate it. Hence the lamentation, so apt to fall from the lips, when contemplating the splendour of such thoughts: "What a pity!"—just as though they were residues and remainders of magnificent works lost or destroyed. To mention one of them, let us take Mary Stewart, the beautiful yet sinful lady, who, although rendered austere by misfortune, yet arouses frantic desires and disseminates death. Or again, that *Jungfräu von Orleans,* Joan, who, no sooner does she brandish the spear and is seized with a feeling of human affection, than she is abandoned by the prodigious strength which God had conferred upon her for an ideal Cause, superior to any individual affection or inclination. Or take the sketch of that unfinished play *Die Maltheser,* where a group of Cavaliers, who should defend to the last a certain position, yet are not equal to the task, although renowned for their prowess and heroism, owing to these being of a mundane nature mingled with other motives, such as love, riches, ambition, national pride, and therefore no longer that pure ecclesiastical heroism, such as is required for the carrying out of the enterprise: they have become void "of the pure spirit of the Order." In such conceptions as these, the artist feels that, like Peter Schlemihl, he has lost his shadow, his natural form, and goes looking about him in search of an artificial one or one that he can appropriate. Thus he plans to combine Greek tragedy with Shakespearean drama, or to introduce the chorus of the ancients, or to revive the idea of fate, or to employ an altogether objective style, in which

the true inclinations of the author shall be altogether impossible to divine events and personages moving of themselves; and so on. In all these attempts, Schiller traversed a field identical with the fruitless efforts of the most modern literature; he was even a precursor of that ideal, which is the most characteristic sign of artistic impotence for everyone who understands the question—the ideal, that is to say, of drama as "pure condensed poetry," free from all traces of imitation of nature, obtaining light and air by means of the introduction of "symbolical concepts taking the place of the object in all respects where such object does not form part of the true artistic environment of poets and cannot be represented, but must be merely mentioned," thus approaching the nature of music and opera.

The plays of Schiller's maturity, constructed on such models as these, are, *kalt und gemacht,* cold and artificial, as his ballads seemed to Schopenhauer. The unexpected is even more to seek in them than in the early plays; everything is exactly as was to be expected, because everything answers to a conception, which becomes immediately known to us the moment it is uttered, with its facile inferences. In true poetry, on the other hand, there is discovery, penetration by the imagination of a world previously unknown; here the simplest expressions fill us with surprise and with joy, because they reveal to us ourselves. But the schematic William Tell of Schiller would not be Tell if he did not save the fugitive about to perish in the waters of the tempestuous lake, and if he did not reject with disdain the parricide John, who knocks at his door certain of finding a warm greeting from a colleague in political assassination. The knightly Max Piccolomini must hurl himself upon the foreign regiment which comes to the assistance of Wallenstein, and allow himself to be slain, between his love for Wallenstein's daughter and his loyalty to the Emperor. The sense of manufacture is present too in the masterly picture of Wallenstein's camp; and the Switzerland of William Tell, with its mountains and lakes, its shepherds and its fishermen, its flocks and their bells, has the appearance of a *crèche.* Instead of the poetically unexpected, we find sickly romanticism and melodrama in those plays. We read such scenes as the reconciliation of the Duke of Burgundy with King Charles I in the *Jungfräu von Orleans* with a feeling of nausea, when, for instance, the Duke says carelessly, referring to Agnes Sorel: "Why did you not send her to me? I would not have resisted her tears," or, even worse, when the King proceeds to make fatherly suggestions of matrimony to the Maid: "Now the voice of the Spirit speaks in thee, and love is silent in thy breast filled with God. But, believe me, it will not always be silent. Arms will be still, victory will bring peace. . . ."

These frequent sweetenings, whether they occur in the action or in the dialogue, and the allocutions, and they are to be found even in the melodramatic passing from recitative to the rhymed and vocal portions, are tinsel, *clinquant,* substituted for the gold of poetry.

It demands some effort, but the effort is due, to prevent the lack of sympathy aroused by this quality of art from leaving that sphere of art and attaching itself to the person of Schiller, who was a man of noble and gentle character, both as thinker and author, imbued with that austere moral feeling, that *sittliche Ernst,* which his compatriots praise in him. He was not merely the poet to please the fancy of young ladies and cause old maids to shed tears, but the educator of several generations of Germans, both in the family and in the school. And if his work must be excluded almost altogether from the history of poetry, properly so-called, I believe that a more important place should be granted to him in the history of philosophy than is usually done, even if this resolve itself into receiving there those souls who were moved to make their contribution by genuine impulse, and to restore to the history of academies and universities the greater part of those arid and tiresome makers of systems and followers of schools, who continue to encumber it to-day. What happened to Schiller was that on having recourse to philosophy, in order to strengthen the fibre of his talent as a poet instead of employing it capriciously and turning it to his own uses, as a poet of vigorous temperament would have done, he considered it attentively and became to such an extent its devotee that he was obliged to confess to its having rather injured than aided his artistic end, as a distraction leading him off the right road by splitting up his spiritual strength and depriving him of the ingenuousness required. (pp. 31-41)

> *Benedetto Croce, "Schiller," in his* European Literature in the Nineteenth Century, *translated by Douglas Ainslie, Alfred A. Knopf, 1924, pp. 30-44.*

## Ernst Rose (lecture date 1934)

[*A German-born American educator and critic, Rose wrote several studies of German literature, including* Contemporary German Literature from Sensuous to Spiritual Poetry, 1880-1930 *(1930) and* A History of German Literature *(1960). In the following excerpt from a lecture delivered in 1934, he traces the development of Schiller's concept of poetry from the passion of his early works to the objectivity and rationalism of the later works.*]

In the beginning of his poetic career, Schiller appears to be the typical representative of the Storm and Stress movement. His early dramas from *The Robbers* up to *Don Carlos* evoke the pure, unadulterated feeling of the outstanding individual against the complex, cool reasoning of statesmen and men of the world. In the same way, the poems of the youthful Schiller accentuate the intense contrast in which his independent genius found himself to the antiquated and artificial social conditions which surrounded him in the petty principality of Wuerttemberg. The poet revolts against practically everything. In the odes addressed to his early erotic ideal, Laura, Schiller soars high above reality, at once sensuous and spiritual. In other poems, he becomes ecstatic about friendship, or he dreams of the joys of Elysium. And in 1785, in his *Song to Joy,* he envisions a time when the pure emotion of love will have united all human beings. Joyous enthusiasm here is the mainspring of the universe.

But even the early Schiller can also show another face, and we do find indications that he tries to overcome the purely subjective conception of poetry characteristic of the Storm and Stress movement. In the poem **"The Size of the World"** (1781) he calls his spirit back from a futile trip into infinity, and in still other poems, he tries to confine himself to an objective presentation of the outside world. Such a poem is **"In a Battle,"** of 1781, describing wartime experiences of Schiller's father. The different style of these creations clearly shows that Schiller began to realize that the function of poetry was something more than merely to give expression to one's personal feelings regardless of the outside world.

When Schiller became fully aware of this, he at once gave up all semblance of spontaneousness and delved deeply into philosophy and aesthetic theory. Schiller never was a naive realist and so his approach to a more objective form of poetry was long and indirect.

When he first tried to define the functions of art and poetry, Schiller very significantly sided with the rationalists. The ideas of Wolff's pupil Sulzer and also of Lessing figure large in an early paper (1784) on the functions of the stage. The drama here is envisioned as aiding religion and law enforcement in elevating mankind to a higher moral plane. It could, among other things, weld the Germans into a nation, and it could bring all human beings together into one great society.

The function of the poet here is narrowly didactic and even a trifle utilitarian. In the following years, however, Schiller gradually broadens his ideas, until, in the long philosophical poem **"The Artists"** of 1789, art no longer teaches definite ideas; it aims only to make man into a cultured being.

The poem **"The Artists"** still leaves a taste of rationalism. Its last traces do not vanish until the **"Letters upon the Aesthetic Education of Man"** of 1795. Meanwhile, Schiller had become thoroughly acquainted with the philosophy of Kant, the irrationalistic aspects of which found in him a congenial interpreter.

Schiller now clearly realizes that his conception of the educational function of art and poetry stands in sharp contrast to the philosophic ideas of rationalism. For art and poetry attempt to do what rationalism has failed to do. It has, indeed, undermined the medieval state which Schiller calls the "state of nature," but it has not erected its own ideal state, the "state of reason," because it has not prepared men for it. All it has achieved, is an antagonism of one-sided individuals and of special faculties. Yet "the tension of the isolated spiritual forces may make extraordinary men; but it is only the well-tempered equilibrium of these forces that can produce happy and accomplished men." And this harmonizing function Schiller ascribes to art and poetry. In the aesthetic human being, the shortcomings of the natural individual are momentarily overcome. There is no longer a one-sided desire for reality, a mere "thing-bent," neither is there a one-sided desire for personality, a mere "form-bent." No, both are united in the "play-bent," the desire to be a living personality, which is the essential basis for beauty. It is only in this state that we feel our whole humanity. Thus art and poetry carry on the education of humankind and show us the ideal to be reached. However, it is only the ideal, and we must not confuse it with reality. Schiller warns against a too narrowly didactic conception of art and poetry. The poem **"Pegasus in Harness"** of the same year (1795) describes how any attempt to harness the winged steed will fail, and in the poem **"The Partition of the Earth,"** also of 1795, heaven, and not earth, is claimed as the poet's realm.

This broad educational conception is applied to poetry alone in the important essay **"On Naive and Sentimental Poetry"** (also of 1795). Here a difference is made between two functions of poetry, though both contribute to the final aim of all art, as set forth in the **"Letters."** The one function of all poetry is to give us recreation, i.e., to bring us from a tense state of mind into an ideal state of unlimited possibilities. The other function of poetry is education; but it is to be achieved not by the boundless exaltation of the usual poetic enthusiasm, but by giving us clear, realistic examples which adhere to the golden rule.

It is from the point of view set forth in his theoretical writings, that all the poetic products of the mature Schiller must be considered. To be sure, his personal experience continued to play a great part in his poetry. But that part was an indirect one. Schiller's poetic powers now were subject to his philosophical conception of the function of the poet. His experience he uses merely as source material that he willfully shapes towards the attainment of a definite theoretical end. This is what we mean in calling Schiller a classicist. For classicism was that synthesis between the rationalistic emphasis on general poetic rules and the Storm and Stress emphasis on spontaneousness, in which the rationalistic element was the leading one. In German romanticism, the other synthesis, the irrationalistic elements were predominant.

In Schiller's mature poetry, there is very little of direct personal expression and very much of the more reflective forms of poetry.

We have, above all, a vast amount of epigrams, which in a pointed and often dialectic manner directly set forth philosophic or critical statements.

Next to the epigram, Schiller also employs other forms of poetry for an outspokenly didactic purpose. As an example, one may read the long poem **"The Ideal and Life"** of 1785, in which Schiller restates his entire philosophy in rich poetic imagery. One may discover a trace of the born dramatist in the fact that this poem deliberately works with sharp contrasts.

A third group of didactic poems proceeds in a less abstract way, by adducing concrete examples. Into this group belong **"The Walk"** of 1795, **"The Eleusinian Festival"** of 1798, and, finally, **"The Lay of the Bell"** of 1799. In this, the most popular of Schiller's didactic poems, we have a series of incidents taken from the average human life and evoked by successive stages in bell-founding. Each of them occasions some wise reflections, which, taken as a whole, give a comprehensive picture of the entire circle of civilization. As the bad example of generations of German schoolmasters has shown, such poems easily lend themselves to a narrow, utilitarian interpretation, but one

should not blame Schiller for this; the unprejudiced reader even today can enjoy **"The Lay of the Bell"** as a poem rich in philosophical reflections and picturesque details.

Already in the poems just mentioned, the purely didactic lines tend to recede behind the realistic pictures from life. In a fourth group, the poetic pictures become all important. I refer to Schiller's narrative poems, usually called ballads, which since 1797 form the most numerous single group of his poems. Here the story tells itself, without the addition of a long, separate explanation. The didactic stanzas in **"The Cranes of Ibycus"** (1797) are sung by the furies and form an integral part of the story. Similarly, **"The Glove"** (1797) teaches only by implication.

The inner form of most of these so-called ballads is clearly dramatic. **"The Cranes of Ibycus"** progresses towards a clear climax, the discovery of Ibycus' murderers. **"The Ring of Polycrates"** (1797) employs dramatic dialogue. No wonder then, that after 1800 Schiller more and more gave up his narrative poetry in favor of his dramas, and that these dramas, from *Wallenstein* to *William Tell,* are the most direct expression of his personality. Here, the poet has definitely overcome his early Storm and Stress subjectivism and has found the long sought road to objectivity. Lyric poetry, the character of which is always more subjective, in Schiller's last years clearly becomes a by-product. Some of his most purely lyrical verses form the opening songs of *William Tell* (1804) and do not portray a direct personal experience.

Thus we have followed Schiller the poet on his whole way from subjectivism to objectivity, and also from a utilitarian conception of poetry to a broadly educational conception. It may be said in conclusion that Schiller was one of the last and one of the finest representatives of the poetic ideal first established by the Renaissance movement of the early sixteenth century. For the last time, he tried to save the Renaissance conception, which wanted a *"poeta"* to be at the same time an inspiring scholar, a teacher of rhetoric, and a creative genius. By giving to this ideal the widest possible interpretation, Schiller once more let it shine in all its radiance, before it finally went down in favor of romantic subjectivism and of the aesthetic aloofness of the modern author. (pp. 72-6)

*Ernst Rose, "The Function of Poetry According to Schiller," in* Modern Language Forum, *Vol. XX, No. 3, September, 1965, pp. 71-6.*

### F. W. Kaufmann   (essay date 1942)

[*In the following excerpt, Kaufmann maintains that Schiller's early poetry is characterized by tension and disillusionment.*]

German idealism marks the climax of that secularization of Christianity which began in the late Middle Ages and the Renaissance. During the eighteenth century, rationalism completed the secularization of Christianity in the domain of philosophic theory, while poetry contributed to the secularization of emotions. Thus Klopstock combines in his odes religious feeling with an idealistic enthusiasm for the beauty of the universe and the harmony between men. Klopstock gave new expression to the tension between reality and ideality inherent in the Christian view of life. It was under his influence that the fourteen-year-old Schiller first formulated the theme whose importance for his own thinking and his later work he could not then realize.

In the hymn **"An die Sonne,"** he follows Klopstock in attempting with the immature pathos of youth to express the traditional contrast between earthly decay and heavenly bliss. Light and darkness, life and death, eternity and transitoriness are opposed to each other in irreconcilable antithesis. When the sun disappears, then

> fall into dust all thrones and the shining glory of the cities. Ah, earth itself is turned into a graveyard, but the Sun travels his heavenly course smiling at the murderer Time.

In the poem **"Der Abend,"** written about three years later, the religious theme appears only as the final climax. The poet does not dwell on the transitory aspects of life. He describes a pastoral landscape with its oaks and mountain summits, with herds and shepherds, with nightingales and cascades. Yet, reality does not satisfy his imagination even in this idealized form. The "poet's spirit" rises on "audacious wings" of enthusiasm to ethereal spheres. In a final climax his ardent song dies away in naught, overwhelmed by the thought of infinity and eternity, which he hopes will soon be his abode. The enthusiasm professed in this poem clearly reveals a genuine feeling; its flowery and pompous style and the antithesis of the finite and the infinite, however, suggest its dependence on baroque tradition.

Even more indebted to the conventions of the past are the poems which Schiller wrote in praise of the Duke of Württemberg and his mistress Franziska von Hohenheim. One can hardly imagine that Schiller should have been ignorant of the corruption of the court when he wrote these poems. The flatteries of the court poems may be partially excused because they are in keeping with an established literary tradition and because the administration of the school probably urged the young student to write them. As far as they can be considered a sincere expression of Schiller's own ideas, they reflect the general trend of his mind to flee from a disappointing reality into the sphere of idealistic imagination where true friendship and noble virtues reign. It is quite conceivable that the praise which he bestows upon the ruler and his companion is meant not only as a conventional compliment, but also as an exhortation to his fellow-students to live up to the ideals expressed in lines like these:

> Their life is the most beautiful harmony, surrounded with the splendor of thousands of virtuous deeds; behold virtue rewarded . . . We shall be more ardently inspired to follow virtue's worthy model.

Later court poems are less cautious in their wording and less flattering in their praise; they even contain hidden attacks on the despotic ruler of his state as implied by this mention of chains [in **"Ode auf die glückliche Wiederkunft unseres gnädigsten Fürsten"**]:

> Foreigners, do you not squint with jealous eyes

at Württemberg's happy huts? Republics, would you not gladly bear the chains if your ruler were—he?

The poem **"Der Eroberer"** decries in the shrillest tones the cruelties of an imaginary tyrant. Again theme and style follow a literary pattern of the past; yet the pathos reflects Schiller's own revolt against the military discipline of the Academy. As in *Die Räuber* Schiller combines the condemnation of despotic brutality with the admiration of indomitable power. Apparently he is asking for himself the verve to shake off tyranny when his imagination raves thus about the joys of terror:

> Oh, you do not know what joy it is, what an Elysium blooms in the mind, to become the horror of frightened enemies, the terror of a trembling world.

Openly revolutionary is the poem **"Die schlimmen Monarchen"**:

> Does the veil, then, e'en on monarchs fall,
> Which enshrouds their humble flatt'rers' glance?
> And ye ask for worship in the dust,
> Since the blind jade, Fate, a world has thrust
> In your purse, perchance?
>           . . . . .
> Let your tow-ring be hid from sight
> In the garment of a sovereign's right,
> From the ambush of the throne outspring!
> Tremble, though, before the voice of song:
> Through the purple, vengeance will, ere long,
> Strike down e'en a king!

Schiller's love poetry betrays the fact that he was deprived of the natural influence of feminine society during his Academy years. He speaks of this in the **"Rheinische Thalia"** as follows:

> Since I was not acquainted with the fair sex (the gates of this institution are opened . . . to women only before they begin to attract any interest and after they have passed this stage) . . . my painter's brush necessarily missed the middle line between the angel and the devil.

Laura, the idol of Schiller's love poems, was in reality the widow of an army captain, mother of six children, and a woman of questionable character. Again reality is mainly the spark which inflames his imagination, and not an occasion for a profoundly stirring emotional experience. Love, in these poems, is not an enhancing community of kindred souls; it is either sensual passion or it is idealized to an extent that transcends all natural bounds. Actual experience vanishes in sublime symbols in a poem like **"Phantasie an Laura"**:

> (Love) teaches yonder roving planets,
> Round the sun to fly in endless race;
> And as children play round their mother,
> Checkered circles round the orb to trace.

When Laura plays the piano, the poet describes himself as enraptured by the harmony of melodies. They conjure up for him the storm of creation, the silvery rustling of the brook, the gentle whisper of the wind:

> I dream, I quaff ethereal dew,

When my own form I mirrored view
In those blue eyes divine!
["Rapture—To Laura"]

The pathos with which Schiller depicts his love causes us to doubt the depth of his emotions. In fact, he prefers to think about love's ennobling effects on humanity: how it raises the barbarian to the dignity of man and gives him belief in God and immortality, and how it humanizes man by restraining his ambition. Even in the most sensual moments, love resolves itself into sublime, metaphysical thoughts. When Schiller contemplates the beauty of his Laura, "his thoughts whirl beyond the bounds of reason." The lovers' souls were one in God and in the union of their love; God's oneness, lost in creation, is restored:

Weep for the godlike life we lost afar—
Weep!—thou and I its scattered fragments are;
And still the unconquered yearning we retain—
Sigh to restore the rapture and the reign,
And grow divine again;
And therefore came to me the wish to woo
thee—
Still, lip to lip, to cling for aye unto thee;
This made thy glances to my soul the link—
This made me burn thy very breath to drink—
My life in thine to sink.
["The Mystery of Reminiscence"]

Sensuality and metaphysics, instinctual drive and moral freedom plainly clash in these poems, barely concealing the ardent desire for a harmonious relation between the two sides of human nature.

Idealization indicates Schiller's struggle against the debasing effects of his own sensual nature. It has its counterpart in the condemnation and brutal exposition of sensual desires, as in the poem **"Männerwürde"** or of woman's impudence and man's lasciviousness in **"Der Venuswagen."**

The language of Schiller's love poems corresponds to the forced and unbalanced treatment of the theme. They abound in antitheses and paradoxes, monstrous word combinations, hyperboles, and awkward rhymes. The pathos is often exaggerated to the point of hollowness. Yet, Schiller's pathos, too, reveals an honest desire to harmonize the sensual and the spiritual, and to avoid the brutality of naturalism and the barrenness of dry abstraction:

Leave it to the denizens of higher spheres
To accomplish that which mortal ne'er achieves.
And yet my earthly counsellor delights
My heaven-begotten spirit to enchain.
He will not let me rise to Angel heights,
Let me as man, then, follow in his train.
["To a Moralist"]

A similar tension prevails in Schiller's philosophical poems. On the one hand, he professes an enthusiastic optimism inspired by Shaftesbury's philosophy and Klopstock's odes. On the other hand, he is deeply impressed by the pessimism of a materialistic and deterministic interpretation of life. Praise of cosmic beauty and harmony, and despair over the brutality of a mechanistic world stand side by side without any attempt at reconciliation in the *Anthologie auf das Jahr 1782.*

An almost mystic longing is expressed in the poem **"Der**

**Abend"** and the **"Oden an Laura."** In **"Die Hymne an den Unendlichen"** and the fantastic poem **"Die Herrlichkeit der Schöpfung,"** the young poet praises God's might and glory as they manifest themselves in nature. He worships in God the creator of the laws which rule both the physical and the spiritual world. As the "rivers press to the ocean-tide" so do the spirits "press toward the great master-spirit." It is this same cosmic law which unites men in love and friendship:

And was it not this influence divine
Which knit our hearts for ever-thine and mine—
In exultant fellowship of love?
. . . . .
Even if Chaos split the world in twain,
Yet kindred atoms will unite again;
Happen what may, our spirits will combine.
["Elegy on the Death of a Young Man"]

By establishing the cosmic order the Creator satisfied his desire for the happiness of self-contemplation:

Friendless was the Mighty Lord of Earth,
Felt a Want—so gave the Spirit birth,
Mirror blest where His own glories shine!

But the more man desires harmony with the infinite, the more he must realize how vain and transient are all human endeavors. Thus despair over the limitation of everything great and beautiful on earth accompanies his lofty expectations:

Ah! thrice unhappy who essay
To strike the spark divine from clay.
Before the bold harmonious note
The trembling harp-strings leap and burst,
And Genius' rays in space which float
On life's poor flame alone are nursed.
["To Laura, Melancholy"]

Yet, for Schiller the imperfections and disappointments of reality are not sufficient reason for despair and the abandonment of all striving; on the contrary, they are a challenge to concentrate all energies on the realization of the highest ideals:

Maiden, thy poet, sturdy as an oak,
Stands; on his hardy youth descends in vain
The piercing shaft, the death-compelling stroke.

Despite all cosmic optimism expressed in his poems, Schiller's belief in a future life is not so firm that he might face death with equanimity. His moral conviction has not yet matured enough to make conscientious fulfillment of duty seem in itself a sufficient reward. For him, there still is a cruelty in death which makes him despair of the value of life, God's goodness, and the beauty of the world. Men may calmly sacrifice their lives on the battlefield and forget the inhumanity of war, as long as they are convinced of the goodness of their cause and of a better life to come. But no belief in God's wisdom and goodness comforts the mother who dies under the axe of the executioner because a faithless lover drove her to despair. Since she murdered her illegitimate child to save it from disgrace, she can hardly accept death as an atonement for her own guilt. If she prays for her lover, this very prayer is a desperate indictment of a cruel world order in which the innocent is punished and the criminal goes unscathed.

In the **"Elegie auf den Tod eines Jünglings"** [**"Elegy on the Death of a Young Man"**], Schiller doubts the sense of a universe where lives are brutally destroyed and all hopes are crushed by early death:

> Let once the canker worm the bud assail,
> And who but fools will battle with decay?
> Above and here below what can avail
> When Death in such a stripling finds a prey?

Such experience must undermine man's faith in Providence and immortality:

> Can it be true that, as the Pilgrim said,
> Beyond the tomb there still is room for thought?
> That virtue o'er the grave and bridge can
>     spread?
> Or are there fancies which must count for
>     naught?

If there is an almighty God, he is not only responsible for the happiness in this world, but also for the brutal destruction in nature and the senseless horrors of human suffering:

> Plague's contagious murderous breath
> God's strong might with terror reveals,
> As through the dreary valley of death
> When its brotherhood fell it steals!
> . . . . .
> Funeral silence—churchyard calm,
> Rapture change to dread alarm.—
> Thus the plague God wildly praises!
>
> [**"The Plague"**]

On the whole, these early poems give the impression that Schiller gradually realizes the gap between man's desires and the limitations of his will power, between moral idealism and sensual determinism. He is torn between a desperate scepticism and an ardent belief in God, immortality,

---

**"To the Author of 'The Robbers'"** by Samuel Taylor Coleridge:

> Schiller! that hour I would have wished to die,
> If thro' the shuddering midnight I had sent
> From the dark dungeon of the tower time-rent
> That fearful voice, a famished Father's cry—
> Lest in some after moment aught more mean
> Might stamp me mortal! A triumphant shout
> Black Horror screamed, and all her goblin rout
> Diminished shrunk from the more withering
>     scene!
> Ah! Bard tremendous in sublimity!
> Could I behold thee in thy loftier mood
> Wandering at eve with finely-frenzied eye
> Beneath some vast old tempest-swinging wood!
> Awhile with mute awe gazing I would brood:
> Then weep aloud in a wild ecstasy!

*Samuel Taylor Coleridge,* The Complete Poetical Works of Samuel Taylor Coleridge, *The Clarendon Press, 1974.*

---

and cosmic harmony. There still is no hope of reconciling the two extremes of man's potential infinity and actual finiteness. The struggle which circumstances forced upon Schiller from his childhood on, is responsible for the extraordinary intensity of his disillusionment. He approached the world with ideal expectations, but he was brutally thrown back upon his inner self whenever he "embraced the world with his glowing ardor." The experience of trust and disappointment, of belief and despair, the tension between All and Nothing, thus, becomes the keynote of his early works. (pp. 7-13)

*F. W. Kaufmann, in his* Schiller: Poet of Philosophical Idealism, *The Academy Press, 1942, 192 p.*

## R. Marleyn  (essay date 1957)

[*In the following essay, Marleyn compares Schiller's* Wallenstein *to his other dramas, suggesting that the unity and realism in* Wallenstein *makes it Schiller's greatest play.*]

Criticism of Schiller's works has in the past twenty-five years moved a long way from the classification of his tragedies into four early glorifications of social and political freedom and four later glorifications of transcendental idealism, a classification which has been associated with the indiscriminate worship of Schiller by the German Nationalists of 1850 and the indiscriminate contempt of the German aestheticists of 1900. There is now general recognition that Schiller's dramatic spirit moves between two poles—the idealistic and the realistic—the realistic pole exercising a stronger attraction on the later dramas than on the earlier ones.

This recognition emerged from a discussion of the "genuineness" of the tragic element in Schiller's dramas. Gerhard Fricke [in his *Der religiöse Sinn der Klassik Schillers zum Verhältnis von Idealismus und Christentum,* 1927] found the essence of Schiller's spirit to lie in an idealistic religiosity, rooted in German Protestantism, which excluded authentic tragedy, but traced in the dramas also a secondary strain which represented a truly tragic element. Walter Rehm [in "Schiller und Barockdrama," *Deutsche Vierteljahresschrift,* Vol. XIX, 1941], thinking exclusively of the theme of "sublime suffering," showed an affinity between Schiller's dramas and the non-tragic *Trauerspiel* (not *Tragödie*) of the German Barock and the dramas of Calderon. But Kurt May [in his *Friedrich Schiller,* 1948], giving equal weight to both elements in Schiller's plays, raised the question: Why should the realistic type of tragedy be considered more "genuinely" tragic merely because it is more "radically" tragic, i.e. because the sphere within which the tragic conflict is resolved is more restricted? Idealistic tragedy, he maintained, is different from, but not necessarily inferior to realistic tragedy.

The unexpectedness of this question and the fact that it seems unanswerable illustrate the weaknesses of a literary criticism which proceeds from a consideration of the relations between human attitudes and works of art to value-judgments about those works of art. The only escape from the impasse created by Kurt May's question lies in reversing this procedure. The function of literary criticism of this sort is, by reference to general human attitudes, to illumine aesthetic judgments, not to engender them.

Criticism of Schiller's works must proceed, not from a contrast between the earlier and later dramas, whether based on an antithesis of "freedoms" or on a general discussion of what is tragic and what is not tragic, but from the judgment that of Schiller's dramas only *Wallenstein* achieves true greatness as a whole, that is, in Goethe's words, "so groß, daß in seiner Art zum zweiten Mal nicht etwas Ähnliches vorhanden ist"—and also from the judgment that his other dramas are good in so far as they share the virtues of *Wallenstein* and bad in so far as they do not.

*Wallenstein* is a more "realistic" tragedy than the preceding dramas in the important sense that for the first time Schiller presents a protagonist who is not an idealist. All Schiller's heroes have "greatness" and in the fact that their greatness is undiminished by tragedy lies the element of reconciliation in his dramas. But before *Wallenstein* the great protagonist was the great idealist. Wallenstein, on the other hand, owes his central position in the drama not to idealism, but to his being a great leader of men, a magnetic personality and a soldier of genius. Such idealism as he possesses is "embedded" in the rest of his character, blended with his ambition, with his urge to action and leadership. The element of reconciliation is accordingly reduced in *Wallenstein,* at least as far as the protagonist is concerned, to the indestructability of stark human greatness, signifying no ideal beyond itself.

Is there any connection between this "realism" in *Wallenstein* and the superior quality of the drama? Some critics who have been primarily concerned with a contrast between the earlier and the later works have pointed to particular technical merits of the latter, associated with their greater degree of "realism." Thus Storz [in his *Das Drama Friedrich Schillers,* 1938] speaks of Schiller's new-found joy in the depiction of characters and situations for their own sake, and Karl Schmid [in his *Schillers Gestaltungsweise,* 1935] of the improvement in psychological consistency in the individual scenes of the later plays, their overall conception still being dominated by an "idea." These indications are useful, because they direct attention to the fact that an answer to questions about the relative "genuineness" of the one or other form of the "tragic" in Schiller can be found only within the wider field of the dramatic. "The tragic" is met with in abundance outside the drama, in lyric poetry, in epic literature and in life, but a "tragedy" stands or falls as a drama.

The present article, however, seeks to show that the outstanding quality of *Wallenstein* rests on a more fundamental and comprehensive advance in Schiller's dramatic art than those suggested by Storz or Schmid, an advance of which such things as "living" characters and consistency of psychological detail are partial symptoms. This advance is the achievement by Schiller for the first time of a unity of the dramatic world, that is, of an inner form in the drama which molds the sayings and doing of all the characters into a single process.

It is no accident that the demand for unity has been voiced more frequently and more insistently in connection with the drama than in connection with any other art-form. The fact that the dramatic medium of expression is primarily a centrifugal one, being dispersed among a multiplicity of characters, none of whom speaks for the drama as a whole (apart from such occasional devices as chorus, narrator, prologue, epilogue), requires that the centripetal force of the inner form should be correspondingly powerful. The "classical" unities of time, place, and action, in so far as they did more than register particular conditions of performance, represented an attempt to formulate in terms of externals the indispensable unity of the dramatic world, and the centuries of controversy about these unities has been useful only when it has related them to this deeper unity, as, for instance, when Lessing replaced their binding authority by the concept of dramatic structure as a microcosm, a "Schatterneiß von dem Ganzen des ewigen Schöpfers."

In a tragedy the unity of the dramatic world is ensured by causing that world to be enveloped in its totality by the tragic conflict. For a tragic conflict is at its deepest level a unifying force, differing as it does from other conflicts precisely in the ultimate identity of the two sides, on which the tragic inevitability rests. This total envelopment of the dramatic world by the unifying force of the tragic conflict is what Schiller achieves in *Wallenstein.* The dramatic world is here an army which is presented in such a way that it stands adequately for an Empire. It is the Kaiser's army, but it is in an equally vital sense Wallenstein's army. Only the almost magical force of his military genius and personality has been able to bring together and hold together this motley horde drawn from every corner of a multi-national Empire. But it becomes increasingly evident from *Wallenstein's Lager* onwards that even his magnetism can achieve this only because and so long as he is the Kaiser's general. The army owes its very existence to the co-incidence of a unique personal force with the universal significance of established authority.

But the relation between these two pre-conditions of the army's existence is one of irreconcilable conflict. Wallenstein's genius is inseparable from a determination to hold fast to the power which gives him scope for action and influence: "Wenn ich nicht wirke mehr, bin ich vernichtet." But this very determination, together with his indispensability to the army, makes him potentially a mortal danger to the established authority of the Empire. The inevitability of his conflict is, in this most "analytic" of all Schiller's dramatic structures, guaranteed by the "Vorgeschichte"—the earlier deposition of Wallenstein, after a series of brilliant victories, at the Diet of Regensburg and his subsequent re-appointment as supreme general. At the beginning of the drama it is already beyond question that the Kaiser can neither tolerate Wallenstein nor do without him, and that Wallenstein can neither act effectively without the Kaiser nor continue to act without challenging the Kaiser's authority. The forces loyal to the Kaiser and those supporting Wallenstein form a tragic unity of will and interest which is bodied forth in the dramatic world of the army. Thus the betrayal of the Hapsburg Emperor by Wallenstein in the third part of the trilogy is seen as the work as much of the Emperor himself as of Wallenstein, and the fall of Wallenstein must entail the fall of the Hapsburg power (the actual historical outcome is, of course, irrelevant to the dramatic situation). Just as *Die Piccolomini* ends with Max's trenchant prophecy:

> Denn dieser Königliche, wenn er fällt,
> Wird eine Welt im Sturze mit sich reißen,

so Oktavio's upward glance at the very end of the drama is far more significant even than is commonly recognized,—it conveys not only shame at the methods he has had to employ and the thought of the loss of his son, but above all the knowledge that after this second, irrevocable removal of Wallenstein there can be no recalling the man by whose military leadership the Empire stands or falls.

Essential to the appreciation of this tragic unity of *Wallenstein* is the realization that the sole causes of Wallenstein's fall are the fact that his nature makes it impossible for him to relinquish power and the fact that his army is the Kaiser's army. The assumption so often made that the catastrophe follows from Wallenstein's hesitation, that it might have been avoided if he had acted earlier, is untenable. It is made abundantly clear that at whatever time Wallenstein had made his treasonable "decision," his intention would have become known to Oktavio immediately, both through his spies and from Wallenstein himself and that, with or without the Imperial decree, Oktavio would have conveyed this intention to the army, which would have refused to go over to the enemy.

In particular, the notion must be rejected that Wallenstein's hesitation is due to a moral conflict within him and that the catastrophe is a personal nemesis provoked by his moral uncertainty or by a wrong moral decision. In reality, Wallenstein's inner conflict is an extremely complex one, waged between no fewer than four distinct forces—his inclination to act "freely," his increasing awareness of the immensity of the dangers confronting him, his eventual recognition that he is compelled to act even in defiance of those dangers, and his faith in his ultimate success. Conscience in the moral sense, in so far as it is present at all, is subordinate to "conscience" in the Shakespearian sense (awareness) and this "conscience" for a time "makes a coward" of Wallenstein. At the same time the prominence of this awareness-element in the inner conflict is one of the close links between that conflict and the dramatic world as a whole.

The interpretation of the role of the stars as astrological symbols in the play is closely connected with this question of the relation between the inner conflict and the dramatic world. Kurt May shares with many other commentators the view that the stars symbolize a divine power which imposes a nemesis upon Wallenstein. He perceives, however, that this divine power cuts a sorry figure and that the drama issues in a contrast between the unworthiness of its human instruments and the greatness of Wallenstein's bearing in misfortune. It would be more natural to conclude that the stars do *not* symbolize a divine power and that there is no nemesis of this kind in *Wallenstein.*

The astrological symbolism has here, in fact, two distinct referents, the one objective and the other subjective. Objectively the stars, as a law-bound system, signify that unity of the dramatic world which is at the same time the tragic object of Wallenstein's awareness. In this aspect they point to fateful phenomenal connections without reference to weal or woe. That Wallenstein and Oktavio were born under the same stars means that their lives are interlinked—for good or ill. At the turning-point of the action the stars indicate that Wallenstein must act—for good or ill, and they announce the hour of his death as a point in the nexus of events, not as a nemesis. Subjectively, as an object of Wallenstein's *faith,* they proclaim a hierarchy of values culminating in the supreme worth of Jupiter = Wallenstein. The two aspects are linked in Wallenstein's mind in so far as he believes—at those moments when his faith is uppermost—that any action he may undertake in obedience to total necessity of character and circumstances will contribute to his ultimate triumph. The nature of things will not betray its own system of values.

The psychological state from which springs this elaboration of Wallenstein's faith dates, like the essential structure of the whole drama, from the time of the Diet of Regensburg. Robbed of his position and power after rendering unique services to the Emperor, Wallenstein begins to recognize his tragic destiny, the slow approach of a terrifying necessity, and to hold in reserve the faith that will enable him to press onward in the grip of that necessity, the faith that dies only at the last moment:

> Die Weisung hätte früher kommen sollen,
> Jetzt brauch' ich keine Sterne mehr dazu.

Thus in *Wallenstein* the external conflict, the inner conflict and the star-symbolism form an organic dramatic unity.

In the earlier dramas the tragic conflict does not envelop the dramatic world as it does in *Wallenstein.* It appears as a monodrama of inner tension. The greatness of Schiller's idealist-heroes is always heavily charged with megalomania and the inner conflict occurs between the forces of idealism and megalomania within the protagonist. In *Die Räuber* Karl Moor believes in heroism, honesty, and justice, but he also feels, even before he is maddened by Franz's deception, that his own superior nature constitutes a vocation to force these ideals on the whole of society by means of a violent onslaught. The fanaticism of Verrina, the austere Republican, makes him a tyrant in his home and the murderer of Fiesco in the name of a "Weltgericht." Ferdinand, in *Kabale und Liebe,* is ready to sacrifice his aristocratic position for his love, but assumes from the outset a quasi-divine role in relation to Luise—"Mir vertraue dich! Du brauchst keinen Engel mehr!" (I, iv). Marquis Posa holds that human beings should always be treated as free agents, but omnisciently trusts himself to guide dangerous passions to good ends in accordance with secret plans of his own.

This monodrama proceeds through a climax in which idealism is overpowered by megalomania—Karl Moor's life as leader of the robber-band, Verrina's cynical use of Fiesco as a tool with the intention of murdering him when he has served his purpose, Ferdinand's jealous frenzy, Posa's assumption of his hazardous role between the King and Carlos—to a harmony of the two elements which accompanies the catastrophe. In this harmony the self-aggrandizing imagination of the hero is fully preserved, though it is at the last brought into consonance with his idealism. Karl Moor's final: "zwei Menschen wie ich den ganzen Bau der sittlichen Welt zu Grund richten würden" is no less megalomaniac than his initial: "Stelle mich vor ein Heer Kerls wie ich, und aus Deutschland soll eine Republik werden, gegen die Rom und Sparta Nonnenklöster sein sollen." (I, ii), just as in a later drama Maria Stuart, having striven in vain to humiliate herself before Elizabeth,—"Fahr' hin, ohnmächt'ger Stolz der edeln Seele!"—(III, iv), assures her attendants in her final phase of inner harmony: (V, vi)

> Die Krone fühl' ich wieder auf dem Haupt,
> Den würd'gen Stolz in meiner edeln Seele.

But in what relation does the rest of the dramatic world stand to this monodrama of inner tension and resolution? It does not grow as a unity out of the tragic conflict itself, but is constructed unit by unit in order to subserve the elements of the inner conflict.

In relation to the hero's idealism the dramatic world is an object of interpretation. The radical idealist has started from the assumption that society ought to be perfect; he has found that the society of his own day is far from perfect and therefore interprets it as the embodiment of evil. Out of this interpretation by the protagonist is constructed the "character" of his antagonist, the "villain"—Franz, Gianettino, Wurm and the President, Alba and Domingo. These figures, though they may in turn be endowed with a certain greatness, cannot be allowed to develop the slightest human complexity, for their *raison d'être* is to exemplify by their unrelieved viciousness the protagonist's interpretation of his society. Moreover, in the very act of interpreting his society in this way, the idealist hero places himself outside it and dissociates himself entirely from it, so that any possibility of an ultimate tragic unity between himself and his antagonist, who symbolizes the evil essence of that society, is unthinkable.

In *Die Räuber* and *Don Carlos* the final establishment of inner harmony in the protagonist is accompanied by a second act of interpretation on his part, by which he comes to see the forces opposed to him as an instrument of self-punishment. Karl Moor decides to use the legal machinery of an evil society for his self-immolation and Posa turns the brutal methods of a despotic government to similar account. This is the element of "sublime suffering," the aesthetic status of which Schiller was to investigate in his Kantian period and which is so prominent in the tragedies written after *Wallenstein.* By this sublime reinterpretation the dissociation of protagonist from antagonist is even further intensified. When Oedipus the King puts out his eyes and asks Creon to banish him, there is genuine self-humiliation before his supreme value, namely the good of the city which he has sought throughout to serve, and his involvement in the dramatic world is drawn tighter, not broken. But when Karl Moor "humbles" himself he uses the society he still despises as an instrument for his individual reconciliation with God, as a means to constitute himself the lone proclaimer of the majesty of God's law to which that society is an utter stranger, and

his isolation from the dramatic world thereby reaches its climax.

In relation to the hero's megalomania the "villains" are allotted the function of *provocateurs* who goad the self-asserting side of his nature to a point at which, for the time being, it overpowers his idealism. Thus although they are by nature mere objects of interpretation, they have to serve as prime movers in the action and because of the gulf which separates them from the protagonist, this primary stratum of the plot can consist only of intrigue and misunderstanding. The assault by intrigue reaches the hero through the medium of passive "bridge-figures"—Vater Moor, Luise, Princess Eboli—who therefore also stand in an entirely extrinsic relation to the tragic conflict. Even the "tragic" aspect of King Philip in *Don Carlos* amounts in reality to no more than his becoming a passive instrument of the intrigues first of Alba and Domingo, then of Posa, the transition being motivated by a mood of despair in the King.

Thus the three main character-units—protagonist, antagonists, and passive "bridge-figures"—are bound together by no tragic unity whatsoever. There may appear a further rift in the dramatic world—a duality of contrasting idealisms. Thus the emotional Arcadianism of Ferdinand and Carlos is confronted in the one case with the religious quietism of Luise and in the other with the political utopianism of Posa. Here the secondary idealist-figure is isolated not only from the dramatic world as a whole, but also from the protagonist. Between divergent, but equally radical faiths, no relation is possible except misunderstanding resting on contrast, not tragic conflict.

Only once in these earlier dramas does Schiller give promise of his ability to mold a tragic world—in that aspect of *Die Räuber* in which Karl Moor appears not only as idealist and megalomaniac, but also, to that extent anticipating Wallenstein, as a leader of men. His band of robbers is held together dramatically somewhat as the army in Wallenstein, though at a more primitive level of presentation. A basically similar conflict between the imperative necessity for unity (the *Böhmische Wälder* scene) and the inevitable threat of disintegration (Spiegelberg's treachery) envelops them all, and Schiller succeeds in involving Karl in this conflict on the one hand by means of the impression created that he is the only possible leader, and on the other hand by virtue of his solemn oath of loyalty. But since there is no possibility of integrating this little world into the structure of the drama as a whole, the effect of disunity is only reinforced by its presence. Fiesco, too, is presented as a born leader of men, but the structural possibilities this opens up come to nothing because, in spite of the weight given to Fiesco's personality, the tragic conflict is confined to the Verrina monodrama. The frequent assumption of an inner conflict in Fiesco rests exclusively on a brief monologue (II, xix) which amounts to no more than one of the operatic gestures in which the play abounds. Fiesco, in fact, for all the room he takes up in the drama, is merely an extrapolation of the megalomaniac force in Verrina and, with the latter as the real protagonist, the play shares with the other early dramas the structural weaknesses of the tragedy of idealism.

*The Robbers.*

Only, therefore, when Schiller turned away from his idealist heroes was it possible for him to achieve the dramatic unity of *Wallenstein.* He learned his new conception of the protagonist from history. The enthusiasm with which he first set about serious historical studies had been evoked by a French history of the Thirty Years' War with an examination of Wallenstein's character added by way of preface by the German translator [Guillaume H. Bougeant; *Historie des Dreißigjährigen Krieges und des darauf folgenden Westfälischen Friedens,* 1758]. There follows some years later Schiller's own history of the Thirty Years' War with its wavering assessments of Wallenstein's moral character and then the creation of that highly ambivalent figure in his drama which, in Schiller's own judgment, defies and makes irrelevant all moral valuation:

> Besonders bin ich froh, eine Situation hinter mir
> zu haben, wo die Aufgabe war, das ganz gemeine
> moralische Urteil über das Wallensteinische
> Verbrechen auszusprechen und eine solche an
> sich triviale und unpoetische Materie poetisch
> und geistreich zu behandeln . . . Bei dieser
> Gelegenheit habe ich aber recht gefühlt, wie leer
> das eigentlich Moralische ist . . . (to Goethe
> (Feb 27, 1798)).

So Schiller arrived at a protagonist commensurate with the tragic complexity of a genuine dramatic world, in place of the fanatic on whose behalf a pseudo-world had to be artificially constructed unit by unit. Wallenstein's antagonist is, accordingly, not a symbol of evil, but a figure as ambivalent in his smaller way as the hero himself and in the plot of *Wallenstein* intrigue determines not the nature of events, but only the pace at which they shall move.

The introduction of radical idealist characters in the persons of Max and Thekla does not disrupt the structure of this drama. They do, indeed, like the heroes of the earlier dramas, dissociate themselves from the rest of human society and again that dissociation reaches a climax with their sublime deaths, but since the dramatic world is self-sufficient without them, the presence of these contrasting figures even enhances its unity, somewhat as the detached judgements of the chorus heighten the sense of unity in Greek tragedy. That there remains something unsatisfactory about Max's position in relation to the drama as a whole is due to the fact that he combines with the role of radical idealist which he shares with Thekla another role, in which he is fully involved in the tragic process, that of the inexperienced, helpless youth who is bound by intense feeling to both sides in the conflict, without being able to integrate these feelings into a realisation of the tragic inevitability of the whole process. In the presence of his father he shows his emotional sense of the daemonic element in Wallenstein's nature—"*Der* Geist ist nicht zu fassen wie ein andrer"—but believes all would be well if only Oktavio would deal frankly with Wallenstein. In the presence of Wallenstein he proclaims the simple, inescapable truth that Wallenstein's army is the Kaiser's army, but can find no other way out of the dilemma than to urge Wallenstein to obliterate himself as an active force—Geh! vom Schauplatz!—a step so inherently impossible that the Countess Terzky had just before been able to use the mere thought of it as her decisive argument for the necessity of treacherous action on Wallenstein's part!

Thus Max stands both within the drama and outside it and this single weakness in its structure foreshadows the major problem in the making of the three tragedies which follow Wallenstein—the difficulty of integrating the glorification of a "sublime" character with the conception of a dramatic world totally enveloped by a tragic conflict.

Many remarks in Schiller's letters in the years 1791 to 1798 bear witness to the vast and exhausting effort which the achievement of the new dramatic form of *Wallenstein* had cost him, and when the trilogy had been completed he wrote to Goethe (Mar. 3, 1799): "zugleich ist es mir, als wenn es absolut unmöglich wäre, daß ich wieder etwas hervorbringen könnte." Yet he began almost immediately the composition of *Maria Stuart* and the last six years of his life represents a continuous process of dramatic creation. It is one of the most interesting problems of Schiller-criticism, which can be only briefly touched upon in concluding the present article, to examine how, on the one hand, Schiller strives in these later dramas to reproduce the structural technique of *Wallenstein* and how, on the other hand, a deeply-rooted tendency of his nature drove him not merely to retain the element of "sublime" idealism, but even to re-endow it with such a degree of prominence as to frustrate the potentialities of an organic dramatic world and to force a return to the artificial constructions of the earlier dramas.

The key to the new inner form in *Wallenstein* had been the replacement of the idealist-hero by the figure of a leader of men whose tragedy was one with the tragedy of an Empire. The Mary Stuart episode in British history contains the germ of a tragic theme basically similar to that of *Wallenstein,* for it is known that one of the principal reasons for Elizabeth's uneasiness and vacillation with regard to the treatment of Mary Queen of Scots was her fear that, at a time when the Divine Right of Kings was the subject of hot debate, to place a queen before a tribunal on a criminal charge might undermine the prestige of monarchy in general. This unifying motif is not entirely absent from *Maria Stuart.* The Scottish queen exhorts Elizabeth:

> entweihet, schändet nicht
> Das Blut der Tudor, das in meinen Adern
> Wie in den euern fließt—.

But far more prominent is the tragic issue which this drama shares with *Die Jungfrau von Orleans:* the potential contradictions between a woman's nature and the position of ruler or leader. Maria, like Wallenstein, appears as a magnetic personality. Even during her long imprisonment she unwittingly and invisibly inspires the Catholic cause throughout Western Europe. But her power rests too largely on sensual femininity and it is this flaw which has cost her the Scottish throne. Mortimer's zeal, too, beginning with the sight of her picture and passing through the sublimated phase of his aesthetic conversion to the Catholic religion, reverts to its sensual origins at his second encounter with Maria. Elizabeth is a victim of the same contradiction in a different form. Her rule has brought England unprecedented happiness—"So schöne Tage hat dies Eiland nie / Gesehn,"—and she has won the devotion of her people to such an extent that rioting breaks out at the mere rumor of her assassination, but this has been achieved at the price of a distortion of her emotional life which in turn infects her political conduct with bitterness, jealousy, vanity, and fear. She alienates her trusted councillors and her lover and suffers in one brief final scene that process of total desertion which in *Wallenstein's Tod* occupies two whole acts.

If this tragic link between the fates of the two queens had been allowed to determine the structure of the drama, it could have engendered a single dramatic world of Renaissance statecraft blended with Renaissance sensuality which would have corresponded structurally to the army in *Wallenstein.* But such a *Maria Stuart* never came into being, because the resurgence of Schiller's innate interest in "sublimity" made him shape the main structure of the play from the catastrophe backwards. The execution of Maria is conceived as a "sublime" death and, in consequence, an idealist character is superimposed on the heroine's tragic weakness. Once such a character stands at the center of the drama, the familiar characteristics of Schiller's idealist-tragedies ensue. A monodrama, the self-sufficiency of which is enhanced by its prison locale, follows the progress of Maria's soul towards a total renunciation of the world. Elizabeth becomes largely an object of Maria's interpretation, a "villainess." The tragic unity linking the predicaments of the two queens is so far dissipated that in the central scene of their meeting they seem barely capable of listening to one another. So entirely has Maria shed her political existence and Elizabeth suppressed her humanity that the two can no more speak a common language than can Ferdinand and Luise. Then the protagonist's final re-interpretation of the forces opposed to her as an instrument of self-punishment is made more explicit in this play than elsewhere with the famous lines:

> Gott würdigt mich durch diesen unverdienten
> Tod
> Die frühe schwere Blutschuld abzubüßen

and the extent to which such an act of re-interpretation marks a climax in the isolation of the heroine from the rest of the dramatic world is underlined here by the fact that the only character who knows anything of this crucial development is a new figure—Melvil—introduced solely for this purpose in the last act of the drama.

The tragic contradiction in the character of Elizabeth—

leadership resting on the suppression of the feminine in woman—lies also at the heart of Schiller's Joan of Arc tragedy. But at this point it is as though Schiller had recognized his failure to unify the dramatic world in *Maria Stuart.* For both in *Die Jungfrau von Orleans* and in his last completed tragedy, *Die Braut von Messina,* he uses an entirely new structural technique—the construction of a mythological framework intended, as in the Greek drama, to belong to the life of the dramatic world regarded as a community and so to unify it, and at the same time to symbolize the tragic conflict itself. To this end Schiller creates a mythology of Nature in the widest sense in which the juxtaposition of divergent religious symbols stands for a profound contradiction in the operation of natural forces, and the pattern of human tragedy is seen as exemplifying that contradiction.

The very forces in Nature which make for unity and stability may at the same time be forces of violence and destruction and humanity is not exempt from this inherent duality—that is the shadow which lies across human life in these two tragedies (and it is also the basic theme of the *Schauspiel* which follows them, *Wilhelm Tell.* In *Die Jungfrau von Orleans* Johanna, the defender of a patriarchal order rooted in nature, must become a ruthless slaughterer and the contradiction is eventually reflected in the heroine's inner conflict. In *Die Braut von Messina* Isabella, striving to preserve the unity of her family, which is itself, as the ruling house, responsible for the cohesion of the Sicilian community with its idyllic nature-background, derives her authority from invasion and usurpation, and the frustration of her efforts is preordained.

This tragic self-contradiction in Nature is reflected in a duality of mythological forms. Medieval Christian symbols stand in both tragedies for the forces of preservation and stability. In *Die Jungfrau von Orleans* the violent aspect of Johanna's mission is expressed by pagan or magical symbols—the sacred oak, the Black Knight, the thunderclaps. Most significant is the stage-setting of the Prologue, with a Christian chapel on the right and the sacred oak on the left, anticipating by a few years that of Goethe's *Pandora,* in which again a sharp contrast between the two sides of the stage corresponds to a mythological dualism. In *Die Braut von Messina* the Christian prophecy of unification in love is countered by the Arab prophecy of destruction.

Thus the introduction of the mythological background means that the tragic conflict has assumed a form in which it is eminently capable of enveloping and unifying the dramatic world. Yet the achievement of *Wallenstein* is repeated in neither of these dramas. In the case of *Die Jungfrau von Orleans* even the new integrating force cannot prevail against the overwhelming temptation to make of Johanna a "sublime" character. In the first half of the drama the heroine's pure idealism reduces her father's sense of the tragic ambivalence of her mission and the echoes of this awareness in the archbishop and Dunois to the rank of deluded unbelief. In the second half, after Johanna herself has been assailed by inner conflict, the other characters become mere uninvolved appendages of a monodra-

ma. Once more the protagonist's re-interpretation of the forces opposed to her idealism (the accusation of witchcraft) as an instrument of self-punishment marks a climax in her isolation from the dramatic world. Even the minor figure, Raimond, who is permitted a glimpse of her moral regeneration, learns nothing of the cause or nature of her conflict.

"Sublimity" plays a far more restricted part in *Die Braut von Messina,* making a somewhat abrupt appearance in the expiatory suicide of Don Cesar at the end of the play. Unhappily, however, it coincides in the structure of this tragedy with another weakness. Throughout the main body of the drama Schiller is concerned to such an extent with the unifying mythological framework of the dramatic world that he neglects to people that world with characters. The Fate Tragedy requires, of course, that the victims of Fate should be unaware of the precise implications of their individual actions, but it does not require that they should be oblivious of the underlying tragic issues. This is shown clearly enough not only by Greek tragedy, but also by the impressive tragic figure of the mother in Schiller's play. But Isabella's sons are mere puppets, absent-minded lovers obsessed with off-stage passions, who have no time for their mother's tragedy and it is upon one of these puppets that the aura of sublimity descends in the final scene. Thus the disintegrating effect of the "sublime" ending is here particularly drastic, involving as it does the sudden transference of the center of interest from the tragic character of Isabella to the untragic figure of Don Cesar.

The greatness of Wallenstein appears, then, to be indeed inseparable from its "realism," but not because "realist" tragedy necessarily expresses "the tragic" in a more genuine form, but because for Schiller it involved the elimination of "sublime" idealism at the heart of the dramatic structure. Idealism is itself for Schiller a profoundly tragic theme, but a tragic theme does not suffice to make a tragedy. Again and again in the dramas written before and after *Wallenstein* the idealist theme shows its inherent tendency to break up the dramatic world into discrete elements subserving a central monodrama. Only in *Wallenstein* does a fully "realist" conflict achieve that total envelopment of the dramatic world which is indispensable to a great tragedy. (pp. 186-99)

*R. Marleyn, " 'Wallenstein' and the Structure of Schiller's Tragedies," in* The Germanic Review, *Vol. XXXII, No. 1, February, 1957, pp. 186-99.*

## Helmut Rehder    (essay date 1959)

[*Rehder was a German-born American educator and critic who produced several studies of German language and literature. In the following excerpt, he examines Schiller's works in the context of the Classical belief that drama should strive to improve and enlighten humanity.*]

Among the minds of Europe that have left their lasting imprint upon the pages of the past two hundred years the genius of Friedrich Schiller is one of the most commanding and enigmatic. Commanding—because like no other poet of his day he has become a part of of the living memory of his people and, almost against his will, has shaped the categories of their thinking. Enigmatic—because, despite our extensive knowledge of his life and writings, we are not fully certain about the sources that fed his imagination nor the forces that determined the forms and directions of his creative mind. In stature, he rises like a huge windowless tower above the horizon of his day; with its interior hidden from our view, it is difficult to say whether this immense structure is a silo holding the intellectual harvest of many centuries or a transformer adapting the tensions of the past to modern voltage. To some it may appear like a lofty memorial of the kind the German nation has been accustomed to erect in celebration of historical grandeur; to others it may merely be a ruin that is left standing from a time for which we no longer possess genuine understanding.

Perhaps it is altogether unwarranted to search for mystery in Schiller's work. The surprising absence of themes reflecting personal experience, the clarity of style and composition governing even the smallest detail, and the consistency of ethical drive and conviction out of which his dramatic characters are conceived reveal a degree of conscious planning that left little to the chance of momentary inspiration. Occasionally Schiller's writings convey impressions of barrenness and artificiality; but these are effectively balanced by sweeps of monumental design and bursts of enthusiasm which, at times, can be truly disarming. We have long been appraising Schiller with the eyes of the nineteenth century to which the lure of the heroic, the glitter of the rhetorical, and the pathos of moralizing commonplaces may have been rather appealing. But we feel that these are not the features revealing Schiller's deeper and lasting human significance. Proximity often gives rise to distortion. If we could make ourselves view Schiller as we are accustomed to view the masters of ancient tragedy—through the medium of more than two thousand rather than only two hundred years—then we might comprehend him within the range of which he is a part, a significant peak thrust upward by the pressure of centuries of the cumulative emotional and spiritual experience of man and shaped by the forces that at all times have signified limitation, obliteration, or survival of human endeavor.

To comprehend Schiller's enduring contribution, we must not let ourselves be misled by his choice of subject matter nor by the peculiarities of his stylistic expression, no matter how essential these features may be for the understanding of his unique historical position. As we shall see, the one was the result of little more than fruitful chance and poetic whim, the other an indication of Schiller's indebtedness to his own temperament and a tribute to the taste of his times. More significant, it seems, is the literary configuration he gave to the problem of human existence itself, his interpretation of the purpose and function of man, and the manner he considered necessary in order to realize that purpose.

In Schiller's writings we witness at work the maker of a peculiarly modern mythology, if by mythology we mean to cast into a timeless, unhistorical, fresco-like image the age-old story of human aspiration, frustration, and renewed enterprise. Just as Aeschylus or Euripides dramatized for their time the myth of antiquity, Schiller dramatized a significant aspect of the myth of Western, occidental civilization in that he substituted Wilhelm Tell for Prometheus, Maria Stuart for Helen of Troy, and the archetype of modern diplomacy, Wallenstein, for the patriarchal ruler of the Hellenic tribes, Agamemnon. But where the ancients stopped to render humble and somewhat hesitant homage to the power of a limiting, inexorable fate, Schiller went beyond them to give voice to freedom—the one and indeed the central concept and ideal that distinguishes Western civilization from all others. For Schiller, the struggle for the intellectual liberation of man that has filled the annals of universal history is the fundamental theme of all poetic endeavor. It is this insistence on freedom that renders Schiller's work so compelling; it is the hazy and equivocal meaning of freedom that makes it so enigmatic.

In his *plays,* Schiller presented the pursuit of freedom in all its inspiring and often dubious grandeur, only to demonstrate, in the moment of its failure, the action of an impenetrable, transcendental power which man had neglected to include in his hopes and calculations. In his *ballads,* he became more specific in that he depicted, within the narrower confines of a single situation, human beings who, believing themselves secure, are threatened by an unexpected stroke of fate that rouses them, shakes them into consciousness, and annihilates them. In his *philosophical poems,* the only works approaching lyrical temper and symbolic atmosphere, he showed the human race on its upward course from the dullness of savagery to the enjoyment of civilization and order, happiness and freedom. And in his *essays in prose and verse,* perhaps the most genuine mirror of his personality, he assigned to the artist, more especially to the poet, the mission of leading mankind precisely along the course to freedom, making it quite clear and explicit that neither the technological mastery over nature nor the philosophical recognition of truth, neither moral nor intellectual perfection, would alone suffice to attain the promised goal. For Schiller this achievement is left only to the aesthetic powers of man, for the sense of beauty is the one faculty which, utilizing and surpassing the others, will bring about at least a semblance of the perfect fusion of nature and spirit, of the human and the divine—in one word, the image of freedom.

Seen within the perspective of the philosophy of time and history that has governed occidental ideologies from Hesiod to Toynbee, Schiller's work appears to be just one more variation on a familiar theme—the concept of the four ages of mankind which have succeeded one another in a consistent trend toward progress or decline—depending on which end of the binoculars one is looking through. The works which have contributed most to Schiller's fame, because they supplied an exciting formulation for a succinct and memorable insight or event—his **"Lied von der Glocke,"** for example, or his *Wilhelm Tell,* or his prudent essay **"Ueber naive und sentimentalische Dichtung"**—are all touched off by a latent juxtaposition of "ancient" and "modern" and by the supposition that in all forms of human life, no matter how complex, diffuse, or degenerate, there are still present the seeds of its inception which will determine the quality of its fruit. Schiller's merit consists in the fact that he converted a question which had been the domain of scholarly "querelles" into a problem of fundamental human concern. Himself the child of an age fully familiar with the possibilities of scepticism and nihilism, he confessed his faith in the continued progress of the human race in a manner so unconditional, so uncompromising and absolute that it permitted no alternative.

This faith is the fundamental element determining Schiller's literary stature. It even eclipsed those factors which we generally consider essential in the make-up of a creative artist—the appreciation of subject matter, feeling, experience. It is surprising to find that Schiller's poetic production, in contrast to that of many "modern" writers, is singularly free from reflections of personal experience. There is scarcely a dramatic character, a poetic figure, a lyrical line that might suggest the intensity of intimate suffering or personal elation—no Werther or Egmont, no Gretchen, no Mignon or Iphigenie. An Eichendorff was able to transfigure the woods of his childhood into an intimate symbol of the German landscape; a Mörike projected the innermost doubts and desires of his student days into his conception of Mozart; even Hölderlin, who most closely resembled Schiller in artistic intent and structure, filled Diotima, his paragon of human insight and conduct, with the heartbeat of his own exaltations and disappointments. Schiller remains aloof from his creations, not mysterious but enigmatic. His experience was that of the abstract, the spiritual, the timeless structure of man which he sought to inject into or read out of the figures of history—or his own imagination. Reality—and experience—he viewed with reservation, considerable contempt, and a little envy. We know of the agonizing difficulties he encountered whenever he attempted to suit the unwieldy subject matter—and any subject matter appeared "unwieldy"—to fit his ideal purpose. Nor was he motivated by any sentimental or particularly patriotic considerations. That is why he could skip around on the European scene and select materials now from Spanish or French, now British or Italian, now Dutch or Russian history as topics for dramatic or essayistic treatment,—and had he lived long enough and been imbued with the facts and fancies of the proper chronicles, he might have given Finland or Chile their national festival plays. But he died before he could execute the grandiose plan of his "sea dramas" in which he wanted to portray the whole of mankind in an ideal, exotic, insular situation.

He was filled with the greatest scepticism in regard to the modern age of mankind, the age that had attained the highest achievements in the realm of the arts and the sciences and yet permitted barbarities to be perpetrated in the service of this or that ideology. But he was too much removed from the pulse of realities in his day to transform his disapproval into genuine satire, as Wieland had done, with the perfect refinement and wit of a gentleman of the world, or as the young Goethe, with the intuitive assurance of genius. Nor did he become idyllic, like most of the romanticists of the time. His indebtedness to antiquity which, to a large extent, was promoted by the educational standards of his age made him find an authentic expression of his creed in the elegy, a form that came closest to his own intellectual needs and that he cultivated to perfection in many of his poems. But in his innermost nature he was didactic by temper; and he felt his purpose fulfilled when, according to his own words, he was able to speak *into* his public—"ins Publikum hineinzusprechen"—carried by the intensity of his vision and the truth of his creed. Whenever, like a mediaeval painter, he did permit his humble self to appear on his canvasses, then it was in the subordinate role of a preacher—Pastor Moser in his *Räuber* or the Capuchin friar in *Wallensteins Lager*—significantly, not without a shade of irony and self-ridicule. Such signs of self-restraint and gentle humor disappear, however, whenever Schiller could step before his public with the full authority of his office and in direct and undisguised pronouncement of his views—in his critical essays dealing with the advancement of human nature. On the other hand, if the stage, according to Schiller's early view, was but a moral institution, could it be that his calling as a poet was merely of secondary importance?

We read that at one time Schiller requested his publisher, Goeschen, that he secure for him some cameos as possible models for the fashioning of a signet. If a duke or king could exhibit on his seal the eminence of his station, why not a poet as well who, by his very calling, moved on the heights of mankind, kept company with Zeus and, in the authentic meaning of the word, lived and labored by the grace of God? But as long as everybody was cultivating the habit of projecting his real or imagined self into the delicate emblem of a carved stone, what image was there left for a poet who took his mission seriously, striving "den tiefen Grund der Menschheit aufzuregen"—to stir up the deepest ground of human nature—and who was yet so much absorbed in himself that at every turn of the road he was painfully reminded of his own shortcomings and ignorance in matters of the world? Perhaps the image of a *genius* was an appropriate symbol, a symbol of that spirit of flaming youth which had hurled defiance at men and manners by ignoring the social conventions and by conjuring up the rebellious pride of Prometheus and the melancholy phantom of Shakespeare. But then, even the message of *Storm and Stress* had turned out to be but a passing fashion that had excited some artistic minds without moving the people, mankind itself, any closer to genuine liberation. Besides, the symbol of genius was not wholly free from the vestiges of subjectivity, and the poet who would proclaim himself a seer of truth might prove to be a whining minstrel magnifying his own feelings.

Perhaps the image of Orpheus would fit the intended purpose for it patently suggested the mysterious forces of poetry—"die im Herzen wunderbar schliefen"—that had turned savages into human beings and made nature into cities and gardens of harmony. But the image of Orpheus would likely be an empty convention, as it had been appropriated for centuries by the guild of poets who had possibly furthered the cause of poetics without furthering that of human progress. Schoolboys and academicians might be able to recite Orpheus' achievements while princes and politicians would be oblivious of him except at ballets and evenings at the opera. Moreover, the myth of Orpheus suggested a tragic union of poetry with love and death, an undercurrent of lawlessness and erotic confusion which was essentially alien to Schiller's reasoning mind and moral convictions. More appealing were the rites of immortality woven around the legends of Orpheus' death and transfiguration, the story of his lyre and his oracular head that outlasted the immolation of his body—both reminders of Apollo himself, the progenitor of the immortal bard. As an emblem, what could be simpler and more eloquent than the concept of the muted Orphic strings and the countenance of Apollo, the Delphic god, who could be as mysterious, terrifying, and vengeful as he was serene and beneficial. But was one to ignore the fascination of the Eleusinian mysteries which testified to the unconscious will of man to extricate himself from the sleep of the senses and permit a higher pattern of order to direct human conduct? After all, even as enlightened a writer as Wieland had not hesitated to dwell at length on these aberrations of the human mind and thereby himself fallen victim to the temptations of lower sensualities.

However intriguing such reflections on the mythical lore of poetry might have been to the student of classical tradition, the disciple of Winckelmann and author of the *"Götter Griechenlands,"* they were lacking in substance without the consideration of the human element from which poetry proceeds and for which it is intended. What was this "human element"—this mankind, Schiller's ideal and object of affection—but an abyss filled with contrasts without resolution? And how could it be made visible to the imagining mind? Was it the host of the many who had peopled this earth from the caves of the troglodytes to the fanciful courts of modern Europe? the thousands who battled during the Thirty Years' War as they had battled on the plains of Ilium? the hapless beings who are suspended between the heights of joy and the depths of desperation, between heaven and hell, between freedom of the will and the necessities of nature? Or was it just the one, the most gentle being imaginable, the butterfly of the human soul, suspended between time and eternity? And if a clear, transparent emblem were possible for this concept of mankind, what would be the function of the poet and how could it be transmitted to the mind of men who are constantly harassed by haste and a multitude of purposes and diversions? It was impossible to resolve these problems in one image. Schiller asked Goeschen to send him four cameos representing a lyre, psyche—the soul—a head of Apollo, and an image of Homer.

In keeping with Schiller's singular desire for clarity and organization, the four seals indicate four areas of the human mind with which Schiller was exceptionally familiar by talent and training and in which he was accustomed to deploy his forces and map out his strategy for something like a cultural crusade. For in spite of his protestations of a generally artistic purpose, his works reveal the energies of a reformer and the dynamics of a conqueror. He felt the urge to change—not merely the current artistic style and taste, not the outward social and economic conditions, not the face of the earth, but the very nature of man himself which history had shown to be such an unfelicitous mixture of exaltation and gravity. It is only through the improvement and refinement of character and disposi-

tion, he wrote in his letters on the aesthetic education of man, that there can be progress toward a liberation and spiritual justification of human existence. The four areas, therefore, in which he proposed to undertake his humanistic operation—art, psychology, religion, and politics—represent but four different aspects of the one total entity that he considered to be man. All of them overlap one another and are to some extent interrelated; but each is determined by the characteristic and fundamental position of Schiller himself—his attitude toward transcendence, his view on the relationship between God and man. "Gottgleichheit ist die Bestimmung des Menschen," he wrote in the idiom of his time, the century of the Enlightenment: "Likeness with God is the destiny and determination of man." Schiller's writings abound with variations of this thought. "The mere will elevates man above animality; moral will elevates him toward the deity." The purpose of the tragedy, we read, is to make us sense "the nearness of the godhead." "The ultimate purpose of art is the representation of the supramundane; tragic art in particular achieves this by rendering visible our moral independence from the laws of nature," he wrote in his essay **"On Pathos."**

Apollo and Homer—they are, as it were, the symbols of the extreme boundaries circumscribing the possibilities of the poetic vocation: the one, fiery and supreme, emanating radiance too glaring for human eyes; the other, humble and blinded, with his glance turned inward and his mind absorbed in the contemplation on the abundance of his vision. Apollo erect and victorious, with the pride of intuition and youth; Homer stooped with experience and old age and with the mark of apprehension on his forehead. For it is the poet's lot to be engaged in a constant struggle with the material world—the price he has to pay for having been selected as bearer of the spirit on earth. It is worthy of notice that, like the writers of the Renaissance, Schiller frequently formulated an apology of poetry; as if his plays and his ballads were not sufficient to justify his existence. It almost looks as if, by assuring others, he was seeking himself assurance on the continued validity of the divine gift of poetry, the highest of all arts. "All tracks of the human mind," he wrote to one of his patrons, "end up in poetry—the highest philosophy, the highest morality, the highest politics, all terminate in a poetic idea. It is the spirit of poetry that assigns to all three their own purpose; to verify this ideal is their highest accomplishment." A few years later this conviction found laconic expression in a formula capable of ever new variations: "The human element is but the beginning of the poetic," or: "Only the poet is the true human being," or: "Only the perfect poet expresses the whole of mankind."

It is not surprising, then, that with the consistent reduction of the complex meaning of poetry to ever simpler rationalizations, the symbol of the lyre itself assumed a renewed meaning, becoming synonymous with the spirit of lightness, chastity and joy, beauty and grace. Ibycus, the "pious" poet, was its master as was Orpheus when he moved Hades to release the beloved shade of Eurydice from the dead. Somehow the unaffected, simple strains of the lyre, the very prototype of lyrical poetry, must have appeared analogous to harmony and form in Schiller's reasoning, for he specifically pointed out that the horror-provoking and electrifying chant of the Eumenides in **"Die Kraniche des Ibykus"** does not tolerate the serene tune of the lyre. In its paralyzing impact this chant is essentially artless because it is formless and generates fear, and thereby arrests man within the barriers of the senses. Art, on the other hand, is the activity in which man subjugates and dissolves the material reality of sensation, bestowing on it the form presented by the mind. In such a creative moment, the experience of existence has quieted all desires, and time has dissolved in the illusion of an everlasting moment. Here art no longer seeks to "idealize" the things of reality; but it apprehends the "Gestalt," the timeless structures themselves which represent and logically precede the existence of things; and man—creative man—becomes a reflection of the supreme Creator.

The secret of "form" represents the arcanum of Schiller's poetic thinking. Its origins reach so far down into the realms of abstraction that any attempt at sounding their depth is beset by the danger of dogmatism and the risk of mere generalization. Historically, Schiller's theory of form is as much indebted to the upsurge of studies in mathematical theory characterizing the eighteenth century as it is to the rise of transcendentalism in philosophy. Both disciplines discovered the function of the infinite and successfully employed it in the definition of the finite. Recognizing the perennial "structures" underlying *things* is like calculating an event from an uncertain number of probabilities; understanding the fate of an individual presupposes complete knowledge of everything past, present, and future—in other words, an infinite mind in which will and causality have become one. Schiller precisely visualized such a concept of an infinite mind when he conceived his theory of art as a supreme play with matter and form—a play in which man is free and, at the same time, subject to the voluntarily accepted rules of the game. In the play of art, therefore, man can rise to a state of divine equilibrium. Then he is able to throw off "die Angst des Irdischen"—the anxiety of the earthly—and enter into the realm of ideas. Aesthetic man, who has received the deity in his will—"Nehmt die Gottheit auf in euren Willen"—is able to elevate himself above reality without relinquishing it. Thus the artist assumes the rôle of a mediator whose function it is to deliver man in a state of freedom through the grace of beauty. In the last analysis, the process of forming and the discovery of the "Gestalt" is the mystery and the "martyrdom" of art. It is significant that Schiller makes the attainment of this state of supreme "play" contingent upon an intense and incessant inward effort, resembling the process of spiritual purification. Repeatedly he warned of the dangers of mellowness and relaxation; again and again he demanded complete surrender to the ideal. In a letter to a friend he described both the intellectual effort and the artistic satisfaction he experienced in his endeavor to "individualize objectively" the ideal of beauty. About his projected hymn on the union of the earthly and the divine—the marriage of Hercules and Hebe—he wrote as follows:

> Beyond this subject matter there is none left for a poet; for the latter must not relinquish human

nature, and it is precisely this transcending of man into God that my poem is to deal with.

> Just imagine the delight, when in a poetic design you see all mortality wiped out, nothing but light, simply freedom, simply potentiality,—no shadow, no barrier, nothing of all that.—I am virtually dizzy when I think of this task—of the possibility of its solution.

> I am not really disheartened, if only my mind were wholly free and washed clean of all the grime of reality; then I'll gather together all at once my whole power and the whole ethereal part of my nature—even though it might simply be used up on this occasion.—

Although the temper of tragedy must have amply familiarized Schiller with the motif of readiness for self-sacrifice and transcending—as it is expressed in these lines—he portrayed a similar readiness on only one other occasion—in his play on Joan of Arc. To be sure, self-sacrifice as evidence of supreme heroism or moral virtue is not unusual in Schiller's writings, nor is suicide as evidence of ultimate despair. But in the *Jungfrau von Orleans* it assumes a unique meaning. To begin with, Johanna is distinguished—to use Schiller's words—by the "ethereal part of her nature." Her tragedy is that, in spite of her devotion to the reality that has produced her, she does not fit into this world which is shown to be by no means all harsh, all wicked, insensitive, or unjust. Her function is to inject into the world a sensitivity for transcendence, which she does by acting according to the law of her nature, thereby performing the act of transcending in a fusion of necessity and will. Johanna is more than merely a poetic symbolization of the human soul; at least, she is an indication of all the freedom, will, and triumph over the self of which Schiller desired the human soul to be capable. The very image in which he visualized her transfiguration, the tableau of her soaring aloft—

> Der schwere Panzer wird zum Flügelkleide.
> Hinauf—hinauf—die Erde flieht zurück—
> Kurz ist der Schmerz und ewig ist die Freude—

turns into a picture of ecstasy, serenity, and freedom of which Schiller remarked, on another occasion, "that the ability to defeat gravity [by means of wings] is often used as a symbol of freedom."

Even though the idealistic and austere style of the *Jungfrau von Orleans* differs sharply from the shadowy prose world suggested by *Die Räuber* and *Kabale und Liebe,* this tragedy could never have been written without the achievements of the psychological perspective that precipitated those early plays. It is not that the *Jungfrau von Orleans* is a model of psychological observation and analysis. That was not its intent. Rather it focuses our attention on all those tender vibrations and sensitivities which are comprised in our concept of the human soul, or the self which, as we have seen, formed one of the four fundamental aspects of Schiller's poetic theory. Like the image of the lyre, it reflects Schiller's devotion to the ideal of simplicity and purity, youth and grace, in which he sought comfort after every severe encounter with the "common matter" of this world. Serenity, "Heiterkeit," was its natural form of existence. "Mein Gemüt ist wieder ganz heiter," he would write when he had passed through a particularly disturbing experience or a paroxysm of his illness. Philosophically, this was the principle of identity which is ultimately responsible for the creation of "form," the innermost unity of the "Ich denke" that Kant had couched in the elusive term of transcendental synthesis of apperception. It signified the original act of self-realization beyond which nothing could be conceived. In a variation of Descartes' more celebrated maxim on the primacy of cogitation, "fingo ergo sum" could have been Schiller's device; except for the reservation that the melody which is heard in the moment of lyrical figuration no longer expresses the meaning for which it stands:

> Spricht die Seele, so spricht, ach, schon die Seele
> nicht mehr.

Among Schiller's poetic conceits the image of the human soul is one of the most intriguing since it conveys the notion of extreme solitude. This is true of the figure of Christopher Columbus who braves the silent seas against all better counsel, as it is of Maria Stuart who in the garden of her prison yearns for the freedom of the sailing clouds. It applies to the vision of the solitary pilgrim who travels through the wastes of outer space as it does to the courageous diver who defies the monsters of the deep. Extreme heights, distances, and depths become the customary dimensions in Schiller's visions. Often his characters appear isolated, as if they were surrounded by a layer of empty space, and distinguished by lack of genuine communication. Philipp II of Spain, Wallenstein, Queen Elizabeth—all of them suffer the same fate of loneliness which is not merely the solitude of the peak but a fundamental feeling of forsakenness in the face of transcendence from which they are in vain expecting an echo, a faint response, a sign of comfort or reassurance. Even Wilhelm Tell, despite his loving attachment to his family, is perhaps more at home near the icy altitudes from which he must gather his livelihood and glean his decisions. Schiller's favorite image of soaring through space, the "higher regions of pure forms," contains a peculiar ambiguity. On the one hand, it denotes the exaltation of freedom and the joy of hovering far above terrestrial imperfections; on the other, it signifies the stillness of non-existence. With their lofty purposes, Schiller's characters carry the seeds of death within them. The genius of Apollonian serenity is balanced by the specter of barrenness, the void, and non-existence.

The Aristotelian rules of tragedy forbid the representation of complete evil in a dramatic character. As an experienced practitioner of the theater, Schiller observed this advice, however reluctantly, as the conception of his characters shows. None of them is intrinsically deficient or wholly immaculate, and even the most warped being is granted some form of vindication. Schiller even defended the "sublime criminal," Wallenstein, despite his basic immorality, against too narrow-minded criticism. It may be argued that the Hellenic pantheon which furnished Schiller with the pattern and standards of evaluation did not possess the proper gauge for absolute evil. It is surprising, to say the least, that in his discussions with Goethe on *Faust* we find little more than casual remarks on Mephistopheles, although we might suspect that this demon of negation

would have elicited Schiller's intense interest and excitement. Are we to assume, then, that the optimism of his vision had dazzled Schiller to such a degree that the problem of absolute evil, as an artistic concern, did not trouble him particularly?

Such a conclusion would be misleading. We must remember that in his early dramas Schiller quite plainly identified evil with certain of his characters, that equally plainly he placed the stage in the service of moral improvement, and that he considered the history of the world a tribunal before which the justice of God is to be demonstrated. We must also remember that there were moments in which the figure of Lucifer would win the fascination of the young author who would go to any extreme when it came to expressing his profound contempt for the deficiencies of the age. The peculiar thing is that inflexible moralism vanished from Schiller's mature works only to make room for the compelling enthusiasm of an aesthetic idealism which permits different levels of moral perfection without singling out a particular principle of evil. In other words, the view of moral rigidity was melted down to a more sophisticated form of relativism.

The reason for this change lay in Schiller's enigmatic concept of freedom itself which had meanwhile expanded from the moral, social, and political fields into those of artistic creativeness and metaphysical thinking. Now he no longer considered freedom the mere ability to choose between good and evil, the mere emancipation from social pressures or natural needs, the vague urge to aspire to higher forms of existence. Now the very principle—the drive toward freedom on whose realization Schiller had bent his "whole power and the whole ethereal part" of his nature—had come to contain the alternative between true autonomy through self-limitation and shipwreck in the face of transcendence. For freedom is meaningful only in relation to a—higher—whole. But the whole as totality is transcendence, ever receding before the grasp of human comprehension; and any being that arrogates to itself participation in totality faces the risk of possible non-existence. The principle of form, a symbol of totality, can be both a sign of animation and life—and a sign of rigidity and lifelessness. Maria and Elizabeth appear side by side; the genius of Apollonian serenity is balanced by the specter of barrenness, the void, and non-existence.

Wherever Schiller set his course on the idealism of freedom, he touched upon the possibility of nihilism; for in every form of idealism there is a trace of something not quite true, not quite authentic or genuine. It is here that the image of Homer as a symbol of human endeavor becomes significant. For Homer exemplified that supreme gift of balanced playfulness which permitted the fusion of time and timelessness. He portrayed gods as men and showed men as if they were gods. He knew how to apprehend the fleeting structures of the "Gestalt" in the objective calm of things and of people. Above all he signified that realistic world of human action without which Schiller's esoteric musings on the poetic vocation, the human mind, and the ultimate meaning of form had to remain on the level of pure abstraction. Besides, Homer seemed to have solved the secret that had teased creative minds of all times: the secret of forming a living totality in which the individual recedes into the mass and the mass becomes apparent in the life of the individual. Homer's lines suggested the ideal of politics: he pictured mankind as the manifestation of a totality. This view explains why all of Schiller's plays are essentially conceived as political in nature; why in his **Wallenstein,** in particular, he was concerned with the various possible aspects of human freedom rather than the intrigues and operations of a power-thirsty generalissimo; and why, in his **"Aesthetic Education of Man,"** he chose to write about the perfection of art when actually he meant to point the way to the perfection of the state. In art, the ideal of freedom and totality can be demonstrated in the beauty of form; in the political world, however, the ideal of freedom can never be completely realized for, like the horizon, it always recedes before the eyes of advancing man.

The mythological manner of his thinking made Schiller see the world of Homer as a sort of lost paradise from which all latecomers seemed forever excluded. Why was the modern writer condemned to melancholy yearning for the lost ideal of simplicity and grace, and to the painful effort of "bearing again an ideal Greece from within himself"? Was it because modern man had lost the ability to perceive transcendence and therefore turned into a shapeless multitude, unorganized and insensitive to the meaning of form? Like his ideal of freedom, Schiller's image of man is marked by an inner contradiction indicative of his bent toward abstraction. On the one side, he harbored for man a feeling of reverence; on the other, a feeling of scorn. Humans, he wrote, are not worth an intelligent person's losing his mind over them. "Fervor for the ideal of humanity, sympathy for individual people, and indifference toward the multitude as it really exists—that is my maxim." Would the spirit of aesthetic education, the sensitivity for freedom and form ever succeed in converting the multitude into an ideal humanity? There was an abyss to be filled. There is no answer in Schiller's works other than his unshakable faith—the faith in the unlimited progress of man.

Friedrich Schlegel, during Schiller's lifetime possibly his most violent adversary, once wrote a statement revealing his keen perception of, and possibly a deep-seated kinship with, Schiller's mode of thinking. "Only he is human," he wrote, "who can rise above mankind, that is to say, who can judge life and earth from the point of view of sun and death." A similar absoluteness of judgment prevails in Schiller's thinking. While it is impossible to fathom the origins of Schiller's thought, we may perhaps be able to circumscribe the boundaries of his poetic style and define the points of contact he had in common with his own and preceding centuries. The probe of his relations to the philosophy of transcendentalism, the movement of the Enlightenment, to sentimentalism, Swabian Protestantism, and to the baroque world of seventeenth-century letters has brought to light many new aspects of Schiller's complex and almost inscrutable literary personality. That the core of his thinking reaches far deeper than the veneer of his Hellenic idealism seems to indicate, and that it actually extends into the very substance of the Christian tradition has long been suspected. It is in regard to the *age* of this tradi-

tion that our knowledge fails us. Connecting him with the views and practices of eighteenth-century Pietism would be like assigning to a gigantic superstructure surprisingly shallow foundations. However significantly it may have molded Schiller's views on conscience and the will, the leanness of Pietism does not account for the magnitude of the artistic expression which he felt compelled to give his spiritual and psychological experience. Schiller's fundamentally ecstatic nature shows far greater kinship to the masters of the Christian Middle Ages who had erected towering cathedrals and fashioned haunting images of human suffering, inspired by their faith in the redemption of man. Nowhere except in the Gothic art of the Middle Ages had the human mind associated more eloquently its anxiety of the earthly and its hope for ultimate deliverance with the dimensions of profound depth and soaring height; nowhere had it shown a more genuine concern for the sufferance of human imperfection and guilt, and a greater reliance on transcendence and its manifestation. Schiller's enigmatic concept of freedom, if interpreted as the desire to inject aspects of transcendence into even the most insignificant practical action, appears like a variation of that mediaeval ideal of "Seligkeit" and perfect inner equilibrium in which necessity has turned into a serene play and the commandments of morality have become the objects of inclination.

And then, there are the visions of emptiness and universal space which give Schiller's lyrics that peculiarly abstract, functional, modern complexion epitomized in the problem of individual consciousness and responsibility. No ancient space concept, whether embodied in temple or theater or in the Arcadian landscape, ever conveyed the impression of utmost solitude that is suggested by the mysterious vaults of Gothic cathedrals, the very realization of man's abandonment in the face of transcendence. Even Schiller's most emphatic confession to Hellenism, his elegiac ode to the gods of Greece, which brought him the accusation of pantheism and disbelief, is inspired by this yearning for "Seligkeit" which demands the transcending of life for the sake of—freedom:

> Was unsterblich im Gesang soll leben,
> Muss im Leben untergehn.

For freedom is the possibility of existence in relation to the whole.

If, according to Toynbee, the temper of Hellenism was expressed in the unreserved worship of man, Schiller's use of the Hellenic symbol represents a significant departure from the ancient idiom. For him, the poet, as the bearer of the spirit on earth, has the twofold function of alerting man to the image of freedom through the creation of form. Form may prove lifeless and sterile—or productive, stimulating, inspiring. And freedom may prove a commodity to be traded or enjoyed—or an act by which man ventures existence in relation to the whole, or the risk of nothingness. Schiller's belief in the progress of man is tempered by his faith in transcendence.

It is difficult, if not impossible, to demonstrate in detail Schiller's indebtedness to the Christian Middle Ages. The belief in the salvation of the soul would have to pass through manifold transformations before it could emerge in such doctrines as the undeniable claim of human freedom and the liberating function of art. It would even have to probe its very opposite—the possibility of nonexistence—in order to test the qualifications of man as his own liberator. In Schiller's writings there are not traces left of the hierarchic structure of mediaeval cosmology; the perspective of chiliastic gloom has given way to a totally different atmosphere of all-pervading serenity. And still at the root of his thinking we find the earnestness of a prophet raising his voice to inquire whether man will endure before the timelessness of transcendence. In the imposing structure of his work, itself the product of barely twenty-five years, he furnished an enduring answer under the placid signs of the poet and the soul, the god and the man—the lyre, Psyche, Apollo and Homer—ancient symbols that are as remote from the spirit of the Middle Ages as a Gothic cathedral is from the spirit of the ancients. (pp. 11-27)

> *Helmut Rehder, "The Four Seals of Schiller,"* in A Schiller Symposium: In Observance of the Bicentenary of Schiller's Birth, *edited by A. Leslie Willson, The University of Texas, 1960, pp. 11-27.*

## Hermann J. Weigand   (essay date 1959)

[*Weigand was an American educator and critic specializing in German and medieval literature. In the following excerpt, he discusses Schiller's early works, charging them with melodramatizing but extolling their structure and artistic experimentation with sexual, scientific, and religious themes.*]

Poetic language was to Schiller only so much decorative drapery, never bearing too close an examination. A touch of the figurative was his way of giving a graceful turn to a sentiment, and the same conventional imagery could as often as not be given a twist to make it equally applicable to a contrary sentiment. (We could trace the ever-recurring image of "picking flowers," now with a negative, now with a positive connotation, to illustrate the arbitrary mobility of Schiller's conventional imagery.) That is the weakness of Schiller's flowery language. He had come early to think of poetic language as an embellishment superimposed on a reality that needed the embellishing touch to make it bearable. Poetic language was an attractive façade to cover up the sober prose of "truth," to conceal the distasteful tissue of material existence, which his study of medicine had taught him to see in terms of organic decay and nauseous odor. To put it crassly, the function of poetry was for Schiller, among other things, that of the Hollywood master mortician, who decks out the corpse to give a deceptive semblance of smiling prettiness and cheer. Schiller, the student of medicine, the "Regimentsarzt," did not have to fall back merely on the baroque tradition of *memento mori* for this view: he knew the stench of disease, death and decomposition from the anatomical laboratory and the hospital. One of his poems to Laura anticipates Baudelaire's "Une Charogne" in projecting a view of his beloved, a few years hence, as a rotting carrion. Life, tending inevitably to hideous dissolution, must not be viewed at too close a range. The poet who covers it with a flowery mantle is a benefactor of mankind.

This view of poetry came to young Schiller as a matter of firsthand experience. Coupled with it was the theoretical idea, presented in the science course of the *Akademie,* that Nature, taken in its largest aspect, the stellar universe, is a dead, soulless aggregate of mechanical processes. Likewise, except for man, all the teeming life on earth, the trees and the flowers, the tiger, the maggot and the microbe, are soulless phenomena, products of the interaction of physical and chemical law. It is the function of the poet to endow all these with human desires and emotions on a strictly make-believe basis in order to comfort man with a deceptive sense of intimacy. The more effectively the poet succeeds in deceiving us into accepting this false, humanized, soul-endowed picture of nature in place of the monstrously ticking mechanical clock of the universe, the more he deserves the gratitude of mankind. This profoundly pessimistic view of life and this view of poetry as an opiate and intoxicant determines, to a large extent, Schiller's outlook, his *Lebensgefühl,* during the whole of his short span of life. They become modified and blended with optimistic crosscurrents as Schiller's faith in man's inalienable metaphysical freedom emerges; but his optimism is reserved for man's innermost drive and for a realm of absolute values beyond space and time.

As a type, Schiller is the poet of general ideas. His imagination never dwells on particulars. Schiller has no eyes, but his eye has a commanding sweep. Intimate personal experience contributes a minimal share to the tissue of his poetry. It is always in bold fresco style that he conjures up his pictures of nature. He knew a lily from a rose, but it is to be doubted whether he could tell a violet from a pansy, an oak from a beech. In the animal world, it is always the tiger and the worm that turn up as his stock examples. When one reads the body of Schiller's poetry in chronological sequence, from his juvenilia to the great philosophical poems of his maturity, one keeps constantly asking: What does Schiller believe in? How does Schiller view man's place in the cosmos? What is the meaning of human life? Schiller started out in his youth with the ready-made values of Christian tradition. They were quickly discarded in favor of a scientific, mechanistic view of the universe; but the temper of the Enlightenment, religiously oriented despite its rejection of revealed religion, exposed Schiller to a great variety of mutually contradictory philosophies on which his imagination seized and with which it experimented. During the turbulent years of his storm and stress, Schiller felt free to play with all manner of extravagant hypotheses. After his life had taken a more settled turn, he was constrained by circumstances to adopt the preceptorial pose of an apostle of the Enlightenment and to pretend to serene assurance of insight regarding the course of human history and the providential plan unfolded in its stages. But while he entered into his rôle with gusto and flattered himself with the elegance of his performance, he did so with a bad conscience. He was well aware of the fact, if his readers were not, that he was trafficking in glittering phrases for the edification of simple minds; that his pretended insight was just another phase of poetic make-believe, offering a colorful imaginative show that masqueraded as truth. It was only when he came into contact with the philosophy of Kant (in the early 1790's) and sank his teeth into it that he found a platform on which he could henceforth stand with assurance. He had saved his soul at last, and the words he henceforth uttered had the ring of conviction.

Let us attempt a brief survey of Schiller's development up to the point of his encounter with Kant's abstract critical doctrine.

There is first the traditional Protestant outlook implanted in the boy by family and teachers. The chill of shrinking fear and the warmth of expanding love appear blended in this austere faith reared on a base of unquestioning submission to paternal and political authority. The uneasy symbiosis of these ingredients is vividly exhibited in the career of his father, a remarkable man who left us a straightforward and highly revealing account of his life. His talents, his practical mind, and his tenacity won out over his limited education and made him rise from very humble beginnings to honestly earned middle-class prosperity in the service of Duke Karl Eugen of Württemberg. An apprentice barber and field surgeon in his teens, he was repeatedly taken prisoner in local wars and forced to don the uniform of his captors. He saw his share of engagements, he fought, killed, and took booty. Later he managed the tree nurseries of his Duke. He has to his credit the planting of tens of thousands of fruit trees on the Duke's estates, and he published a treatise on his specialty. The fact that his son's spectacular insubordination and flight did not cause him to lose the favor of the Duke speaks for his integrity and his close-mouthed caution. His character suggests the hardy stamina of the best of the American pioneers. In his son we see the same unflagging energy, ambition, and capacity for self-discipline; also, in his later years, a sense of diplomatic tact and a skill in negotiating practical matters which come as a surprise in the idealistic poet. The female side of the family stayed within the bounds of mediocrity. Schiller's sister Christophine, the poet's elder by two years, who lived to a ripe old age, is largely responsible by her sentimental anecdotes for the legendary image of the gentle poet that made him the idol of the German middle class in the nineteenth century. She exhibits the limitations of her matter-of-fact endowment rather cruelly in her account of her own unromantic marriage. It was, as she puts it, the presence of so many cavalry officers at the court, and all their horses and the indelicacy of the stables that prevailed on her sensitivity to cast her lot with the hunchbacked Meiningen librarian Reinwald, twenty years her senior, who befriended Schiller during the months he spent in hiding after his flight.

The first stage of naïvely innocent acceptance of traditional piety came to an end when the adolescent Friedrich was assigned a place in the Duke's *Akademie.* This was an honor, but it came as a keen disappointment to the boy that he had to renounce his wish to become a preacher, as the school did not provide for a theological education. First enrolled as a student of law, he was later permitted to switch to medicine. Whether his awakening from innocence took a gradual or an abrupt course is rather obscure. We know that he conformed to the strict discipline of the

Academy. For years he was in great personal favor with the middle-aged Duke who, after a dissolute youth, had one day surprised the country with the announcement, read from all the pulpits, that he had resolved henceforth to be a real father to his people. Education became his particular hobby, and he loved to attend class exercises and other functions in the company of his young, pretty, and popular mistress. The Duke was not slow to discover Schiller's oratorical talent, and he fostered it by competitive assignments for orations on set topics dealing with moot aspects of virtue—performances in which young Schiller starred. Some of Schiller's exercises, presenting a glittering show of empty dialectics, have been preserved for us. They abound in passages lavishing the most extravagantly fulsome praise on the Duke, his foster-father, to whom, as he puts it, he owes an infinitely greater debt of gratitude and reverence than to his physical father, and whom he adores as the incarnation of true virtue. This was the tone prescribed for such occasions, and Schiller no doubt took it up with gusto at first, giving rein to his faculty of polishing phrases, and ending up his elaborate periods with effective flourishes. Was he sincere in any of this? Most likely the question of sincerity did not enter the adolescent mind at all for some time: he simply gloried in the opportunity to show off his gifts. But as his critical maturity developed he took a cynical joy in mouthing these phrases tongue in cheek. Later, when the seething revolt of his heart made this tone of flattery nauseous to him, he branded this false cult of virtue as "lächerliche Tugend, die—Hanswurst erfand." He came to regard the moral training aimed at by the school and its ducal preceptor as a systematic corruption of youth. He resented bitterly not only what it had done to the whole academic community, but what it had done to him personally. The passage of the years after he had escaped from this atmosphere did not still his rancor. As far as public utterance was concerned he kept a dignified silence: after all, the Duke had ignored his flight instead of sending his henchmen to trap him, and the Duke had generously ignored the Jena professor's nine months' visit to his native land. But after the Duke's death in 1793, nine years after the poet's rebelliousness had burst into open flame, Schiller vented his rancor in a letter by referring to the late Duke as "der alte Herodes." The moral slaughter of the innocents still preyed on his mind. (We are reminded of Rilke's vehemently denunciatory reaction to a friendly letter addressed to him in later years by one of his one-time teachers at the military academy at St. Pölten.)

Once kindled, the spirit of inner revolt against the prevailing atmosphere of sycophantic subservience festered in young Schiller the more violently, the more carefully it had to be concealed at first from his mentors. At this time Schiller was experiencing an enormous upsurge of his oratorical and poetic powers. His clandestine preoccupation with literature produced his first drama **Die Räuber,** and spawned the poems of the **Anthologie.** They inaugurated his phase of titanism, which carried over from his last years before graduation into his term of service as "Regimentsarzt," through his flight from the Duke's territory, and through three succeeding years which began with fantastic hopes and brought crushing disillusionment, insecurity, acute want, starvation, a mountain of debts and a radically disordered existence in their wake. What we call his titanism is a sense of intoxication with his creative power, an overwhelming inflation of his ego. He, the individual, feels himself cut adrift from society and perceives all its values as mere conventions. He, the titan, is the measure of all things. His creative urge disports itself among a welter of ideas; his imagination plays with all the philosophical attitudes that come into his ken. During this stage of his titanism Schiller has no point of view that can be called his own; he experiments with them all.

Schiller's titanism is a sustained exhibitionistic pose. In a literary way it was a late wave of the tide of the Storm and Stress movement that swept across Germany in the 1770's. But the personal experience that touched it off in Schiller was the physical maturing of his sex. The male sex drive, now naked, now cerebrally masked, exhibits itself to full view in the most characteristic poems of this period. Actual contact with the opposite sex played a minimal part in this intoxicating expansion of his ego. The counterpart, the opposite pole of what he felt surging within him, was, on the one hand, the image of woman in general, and, on the other, nothing less than the physical universe. As could not but be the case in a youth reared in the Christian tradition, this drive manifested itself as a welter of desires and taboos. It raised him up to heaven, it plunged him into hell. It was the forbidden fruit of Paradise that now put him on a par with the gods and now made him tremble as at the perpetration of sacrilege. In the experience of sex the moral dichotomy of duty and impulse confronted Schiller in the core of his personality. The poems of Schiller's youth, though crude and raw as poems, are, psychologically considered, the most interesting product of Schiller's career. In a sense, their turbulent dynamics and crass antitheses anticipate everything that the later Schiller formed with more conventional restraint. Desire stalks through all of the later Schiller's poems and essays as the contaminating drive to be renounced in favor of disinterested contemplation. It is always referred to in general terms and embroidered with mythological allusions, because direct reference to the facts of life violates the code of prissy gentility insisted on by his wife; but whenever the concept of desire is evoked the sex drive is meant.

When we approach the poems of Schiller's youth with the question, what did he believe, we get a great variety of contradictory answers from them. His mind, stored with a host of half-assimilated literary and philosophical ideas, is in a state of flux and experiment. A great many of the early poems operate on a base of traditional Christian belief. Poems like **"Der Abend," "An die Sonne,"** sing the praise of the Creator by glorifying His works. They display a theatrical panorama of nature in which the poet manipulates the show, with its lights and shadows, with the roll of thunder, the roar of the waterfall, the ripple of the brook, the myriad tiny voices of the insect world. The poet prostrates himself before the Almighty, but it is his own self-conscious touch that really makes creation arise out of chaos. The piety of these poems, unlike that of their model, Klopstock, is a matter of showmanship. There is a very revealing passage where the poet, overwhelmed by the spectacle of sunset, apostrophizes the Lord in the lines:

> Vater der Heil'gen vergib.
> O vergib mir, dass ich auf mein Angesicht falle
> Und anbete dein Werk!

He transgresses against the Lord's command to worship the Creator and not His creation, but is not his confessing to his transgression a gesture of flattery no different in kind from those that his Duke would have graciously acknowledged? He may surely be pardoned for letting his theologically trained reason be overcome by the magnificence of the spectacle. The lines quoted, moreover, have been the subject of an unresolved controversy: Is a printer's oversight responsible for the omission of a "nicht" in the middle line?

> Vergib mir, dass ich *nicht* auf mein Angesicht falle
> Und anbete dein Werk!

Such a reading would certainly enhance the subtle dialectics of flattery with the poet saying: Forgive me, father, for remembering your injunction in the face of such rapture.

There are funeral odes, occasional pieces, some of them done to order, in which Schiller, after the manner of an accomplished pulpit orator, plucks the heartstrings of the bereaved survivors, now making them sob and groan over their loss, now inducing a flood of sparkling tears at the thought that the departed has entered upon the bliss of Paradise. There is a stanza in which Schiller does not shrink from having the bereaved father rail in blasphemous fury against a "barbarous" deity that has blasted his hopes—to return, of course, from this paroxysm to humble acceptance of the dictates of an all-wise Providence. But when it is General Rieger, one of Karl Eugen's top officers, who is carried to the grave, Schiller exploits his privilege of religious oratory to deliver a blow below the belt. First he employs all his transfiguring rhetoric to paint the deceased in the guise of an angel. Then, shifting the scene to the bar of divine judgment where man is stripped of all earthly accessories, he exclaims: What are all Karl's decorations now but trash and tinsel! As a general reflection this was unexceptionable, but the personal twist made it highly offensive, the more so as Schiller had been foxy enough to introduce the Duke's name early in the poem by addressing the mourners as "Krieger Karls." He could play the innocent, then, in reverting to the personal note at the end as in keeping with the rest of the poem. But we can be sure that Karl Eugen was not fooled. It is safe to assume that he resolved not to let his stripling creature's insolence go unpunished.

The scales of judgment, so prominently displayed in Klopstock's odes, Schiller learned to employ as the heaviest brass of his lyric orchestra. He uses them with telling effect in **"Der Eroberer."** This is among the most interesting of Schiller's youthful poems by virtue of the extreme involvement of its dynamic build-up and the bizarre emotionalism of its climax. The Conqueror is pictured as a fiend of colossal stature who has trodden humanity into the dust. Then Schiller imagines the sounding of the trumpet of Judgment Day to bring the enemy of mankind to book. There, suspended between heaven and earth is the scale in which the Conqueror's deeds are to be weighed. This scale is empty while the Conqueror sits enthroned in his purple in the other. First, the host of the Conqueror's victims, an endless throng, file past and hurl their cry of vengeance into the empty scale. Then the sun, the moon, and all the spheres throw their weight into the scale. They are followed by all the celestial hosts who do the same. Weighted with all these curses, the scale begins to sink and the other scale slowly rises to bring the malefactor into the presence of God. And now comes the climactic gesture to complete his doom: a thundering curse issuing from the poet's lungs contributes the deciding weight to make the scale of the Conqueror's crimes plunge to the abyss of hell. The final scene shows the poet rolling in the dust with convulsive joy and chanting through all eternity his praise of the beautiful Day of Judgment. This is juvenile titanism foaming at the mouth. But in the middle of the poem he came so close to identifying with the Conqueror's dreams of grandeur as to all but confess: If I cannot be God I would be Lucifer. The Conqueror is Milton's Satan thinly disguised. It is pointless to ask what human figure he had in mind, an Alexander, an Attila, a Ghengis Khan. His own age supplied no model for the colossus. A generation later there was a real conqueror, Napoleon, whom the frenzied hatred of a Kleist execrated as "ein der Hölle entstiegener Vatermördergeist." But young Schiller had to spend his anathema on a straw man of the imagination, just as he, like Klopstock before him and Hölderlin a little later, had to glory in the posture of dying for the fatherland without there being anything on the contemporary map to warrant that exalted name. The fatherland Schiller longed to die for was the brainchild of the German humanists of the sixteenth century, and it was the Roman legionaries of Varus in whose blood he longed to bathe.

In a piece cautiously entitled **"Die *schlimmen* Monarchen"** (italics mine), Schiller directs his fire against potentates and princes whose mad orgy of power, pomp, and lust has come to a halt in the silent stench of the tomb. His lips curl with a sneer as he repeatedly apostrophizes the fallen mighty as "Erdengötter." (How different the temper of Goethe in his *Tasso* where, eight years later, the princes of the Renaissance are still referred to as "Erdengötter" without any satiric overtone!) Schiller wallows in offensive imagery, he inflates his nostrils to savor the pus of decomposition. He pulls all the registers of pointed insult, and the last line of each stanza rhetorically cracks the whip over his silent victims. No vindictive proletarian has ever gloated with more ghoulish glee over his reduced exploiters. There is the difference, of course, that Schiller's sadistic resentment vents itself within a framework of holy religious zeal. He poses as the mouthpiece of divine wrath annihilating the perverters of true virtue.

There is a poem on Rousseau apotheosizing the saintly martyr who fought against the three monsters of the age: religious fanaticism, prejudice, and egotism. Schiller couples his fate with that of Socrates as he lashes out against the Christian world in the poem's most pointed stanza:

> Wann wird doch die alte Wunde narben?
> Einst war's finster—und die Weisen starben,
>   Nun ist's lichter—und der Weise stirbt.
> Sokrates ging unter durch Sophisten,
> Rousseau leidet—Rousseau fällt durch Christen,

Rousseau—der aus Christen Menschen wirbt.

In this poem there is an undercurrent of high hopes in the dawn of the Enlightenment, which Schiller, a few years later, so eloquently hails as the new era that has achieved the enthronement of the dignity of man. But for the time being Schiller's imagination is involved in other topics.

I have already remarked on the dominant rôle of sex during Schiller's phase of titanism. We must now turn to the working out of this theme in the poems. In its simplest aspect we see it in a piece called **"Kastraten und Männer,"** an exuberant panegyric on raw, ithyphallic masculinity. "Ich bin ein Mann," he shouts. He exults in being able to show in his male organs "den Stempel zu Gottes Ebenbild." He boasts of being able by virtue of this to put to flight even the emperor's daughter should he meet her alone. He pours scorn upon castrates. He sums up the glory of his status in the lines:

> Wer keinen Menschen machen kann,
> Der kann auch keinen lieben.

Except for its allusions to figures of Roman history this piece sounds like the blatant exhibitionism of a young savage, and the crudity of its versification is in keeping with this posture:

> Ich bin ein Mann, das könnt ihr schon
>   An meiner Leier riechen,
> Sie donnert wie im Sturm davon,
>   Sonst müsste sie ja kriechen.

But this jubilant, uncomplicated proclamation of male potency becomes involved with philosophic speculation in a long series of poems addressed to the idea of woman under the name of Laura. In the Laura poems sex is the central mystery of life. A number of these culminate in the depiction of the physiological orgasm. But it is scarcely a man and a woman, it is rather a pair of cosmic forces that we see celebrating the mating act in the lines:

> Wenn dann, wie gehoben aus den Achsen
> Zwei Gestirn', in Körper Körper wachsen,
>   Mund an Mund gewurzelt brennt,
> Wollustfunken aus den Augen regnen,
> Seelen wie entbunden sich begegnen
>   In des Atems Flammenwind—

Quite literally, they whirl through space as companions and coequals of suns:

> Aus den Angeln drehten wir Planeten.

The earth is left behind. They soar among stars. The scene of their orgies is always the stellar universe—and not just a poet's but a scientist's universe, a universe governed by the inviolable laws of celestial mechanics as evidenced by the repeated invocation of Newton's name. Gravitation is the spring that keeps the wheels of the universe turning.

So far science; but philosophy enters into the picture by contributing the idea that the prime law of attraction and repulsion also governs the universe of spirit. What operates as gravitation in the physical world is experienced in the world of spirit as *Sympathie*. Schiller takes over this favorite term of Wieland's as the name of the binding universal force, and he still uses it to conjure with in **"An die Freude"**:

> Was den grossen Ring bewohnet
> Huldige der Sympathie!

Thus Schiller tries to bridge the dualism of matter and mind by a monistic synthesis. We should refer to this as mystical (and at moments it is mystical!) if the imagined unity were not so patently cerebral. Leaving aside passages where labored allegory stamps it as a mere exercise of abstract reflection, the best example to reveal this monism as essentially cerebral is the first strophe of **"Die Freundschaft."** The poem exhibits some of Schiller's finest *Schwung* and enthusiasm, but the comprehension of the first strophe hinges on the impossible stressing of a dative plural ending:

> Freund, genügsam ist der Weltenlenker—
> Schämen sich kleinmeisterliche Denker,
> Die so ängstlich nach Gesetzen spähn—
> Geisterreich und Körperweltgewühle
> Wälzet Eines Rades Schwung zum Ziele,
> *Hier* sah es mein Newton gehn.

Turned into prose, this says: Friend, Economy is the Creator's maxim. Shame on petty thinkers who try to discover a plurality of fundamental laws. It is the momentum of but one single wheel that governs both the realm of spirits and the whirl of the world of matter. It was in this latter area that the great Newton observed its workings.

Crosscurrents of dualism and monism that fail to integrate play across the most ambitious, artful, and psychologically revealing of the Laura poems. **"Das Geheimnis der Reminiszenz"** begins with a subconscious wish fantasy for an erection of eternal duration:

> Ewig starr an deinem Mund zu hangen,
> Wer enträtselt mir dies Wutverlangen?

But the psychological core of the brilliant imagery of the next two stanzas is a sense of being rendered impotent when confronted with the physical presence of the object of his desire. He experiences a desperate sense of frustration and inner conflict: the unity of the self is reduced to a battleground of conflicting forces. Soul and senses are at loggerheads. The mastering will of the soul is betrayed and deserted by a host of treacherous vassals and recreant slaves. Brooding on this dualism, his overheated fancy takes a flight into pre-existence to picture himself and his Laura whirling through space as a single entity of free spirit. Plato had started Schiller on his flight, but Archimedes and Milton help to sustain it; for that free spirit-force glories in "heaving planets out of their hinges" and shattering worlds (the answering rhyme to "dein Dichter" is "ein Weltzernichter"!). No wonder that it becomes the victim of the Deity's jealous wrath. It is fissioned into a male and a female half and both are imprisoned in bodies. Henceforth their existence exhausts itself in fruitless tormented desire to recapture the primal state of union. This is the sex drive, but it is checked by a sense of taboo, taint, and sin. The final scene of the poem drops the cosmic stage to revert to the myth of Genesis. It pictures the glee of the devils as they see the *innocently* whirling creatures trapped by the toils of lust.

In another of these poems Schiller holds out to his Laura the prospect of an enduring nuptial night. This will come about when Time and Eternity are locked in embrace as the world is consumed by fire.

All these poems are the product of a superheated brain feeding on cosmic and apocalyptic imagery. Sex in search of an object exhausts itself in gigantic dynamics. As poems they are monstrous. Most of them are much too long. They cannot sustain the fire of their initial *élan*. The white-hot rhetoric of their turgid blocks of phrases forbids any intimate identification. Yet close analysis is rewarding. What at first reading seems nothing but a foaming, disordered orgy turns out, more often than not, to follow an ingenious structural plan. Despite their bombast they are not formless effusions but works of calculated art. If they do not appeal as music, this is because the melodic theme is drowned out by an excess of orchestration.

Leafing through the poems of the **Anthologie** and trying to extract from them the outline of a *Weltanschauung,* the positive yield is very limited. The twenty-three-year-old poet believed in his own powers, in his freedom, and he believed in the facts of natural science. Everything else, all the notions derived from religion and philosophy were so many theatrical properties for him to set up at will and rearrange and discard, as it suited his fancy. But perhaps the most important observation regarding the cerebral display is this: He not only puts on a spectacular show but he reserves for himself the star part in the performance. In the love poems, he does all the whirling and the talking, Laura is only a dummy. In the religious poems, it is the flame of his voice that sears the culprit. In a poem about the vastness of the starry universe, **"Die Grösse der Welt,"** it is he who shoots through cosmic space with the speed of light. It does not occur to him that the grandiose effect aimed at may boomerang. It is no small feat of course to exchange a word with a wanderer coming from the opposite direction and bent on the same errand. And whereas the poet is awed by the report of the limitless spaces left behind, are we not more likely to remark in the face of such a meeting: What a small world it is, after all! Or, returning to the poem about the Conqueror, where Schiller wants us to feel that the weight of *his* curse matches that of the victims, the sun, moon and stars, and the heavenly hosts combined, we may be tempted to think of it rather as the straw that breaks the camel's back.

Before leaving the lyric theater of Schiller's titanism, let us dwell upon one of his grandiose built-in pieces of imagery to illustrate the intoxicating pomp and glitter of his youthful style. There is a superlative purple passage in **"Vorwurf an Laura,"** a poem that develops the theme of a feigned reproach but is really an extravagant gesture of homage to Laura. The first three stanzas have stated in general terms (involving the imagery of piled-up mountains, pyramids and the river of Hades) that he is no longer the giant he was before he succumbed to Laura's spell. Now he begins to develop by more specific examples the change she has wrought in him. The first of these, rendered in sober prose, would say: Formerly, when the sun rose, I leapt to greet it, but what of me now! Schiller uses a whole six-line strophe to introduce the idea of sunrise as a build-up before asking the fatal question. He begins with a dazzling image in which the thunderous clash of lances arouses victorious warriors from the embrace of beautiful courtesans. He suggests the glint of steel armor reflecting the rosy glow of female nudity—all this as an elaborate simile for the mythological image of the Sun-god leaving the rosy bed of Dawn to bring joy to an awakening world:

> Siegern gleich, die wach von Donnerlanzen
> In des Ruhmes Eisenfluren tanzen
>     Losgerissen von der Phrynen Brust,
> Wallet aus Auroras Rosenbette
> Gottes Sonne über Fürstenstädte,
>     Lacht die junge Welt in Lust.

This grand preamble is followed by the question:

> Hüpft der Heldin noch dies Herz entgegen?

"Die Heldin" is the sun, not Laura, as Schiller would have made abundantly clear in oral recital by an outstretched arm and an eye focused on a point of the horizon. But the reader is likely to miss this all-important point without a footnote to unmask the baroque eroticism of the passage as an allusion to Schiller's favorite verse from the nineteenth psalm, reading in Luther's translation: "Die Sonne gehet hervor wie ein Bräutigam aus seiner Kammer und freuet sich wie ein *Held* zu laufen den Weg." Schiller's transformation of the bridegroom and hero of the original into a "Heldin" conforms to the sun's grammatical gender, but it is motivated also by the erotic ardor of his context. In *Die Räuber* the allusion to the same Biblical passage retains the masculine gender. "So stirbt ein Held," says Karl Moor, his gaze lost in the splendors of the sunset. And it recurs in masculine form, a few years later, in one of the really fine passages of *An die Freude:*

> Froh, wie seine Sonnen fliegen
> Durch des Himmels prächtgen Plan,
> Wandelt, Brüder, eure Bahn,
> Freudig wie ein Held zum Siegen.

It is fitting to conclude this sketchy survey of Schiller's poetry of titanism with the **"Reproach to Laura."** The poem builds up to a highly effective climax when the poet throws off the transparent mask of reproach in order to fling himself at Laura's feet and proclaim that he owes his all to her love. Without her he would have been just a superman, but thanks to her he has become something higher, a lover of mankind:

> Über Menschen hätt ich mich geschwungen.
> Itzo lieb ich sie.

In its context, this seems no more than a glittering phrase uttered for dramatic effect. But this sentiment, here voiced for the first time (unless the logic of "Männerwürde": Wer keinen Menschen machen kann, der kann auch keinen lieben, be taken in this spirit!), is destined to become the keynote of Schiller's next phase. The titan, the iconoclast, the scourge of society blossoms into an ecstatic lover of humanity in general. When he is in his cups, he flings his arms around mankind:

> Seid umschlungen, Millionen,
> Diesen Kuss der ganzen Welt!

And when he is sober, his heart beats for the human race

in the lyrical eloquence of Marquis Posa that all but moves the hardened tool of the Spanish Inquisition to turn the grim prison of his empire into an earthly paradise. (pp. 88-103)

> *Hermann J. Weigand, "Schiller: Transfiguration of a Titan," in* A Schiller Symposium: In Observance of the Bicentenary of Schiller's Birth, *edited by A. Leslie Willson, The University of Texas, 1960, pp. 85-132.*

### Ilse Appelbaum-Graham    (essay date 1961)

[*Appelbaum-Graham was a German essayist and critic who established herself as an authority on nineteenth-century German literature, writing a series of books on the subject in both German and English that included* Goethe and Lessing: The Wellsprings of Creation *(1973), and* Schiller: A Master of the Tragic Form *(1975). In the essay below, she argues that, in dismissing Schiller's early poetry as excessively abstract, critics have failed to recognize the young poet's stylistic innovations.*]

Myths proverbially die hard. One which still lingers on in the popular imagination and is proving exceedingly hard to eradicate is the myth of Friedrich Schiller as a perennial youth, permanently attired, as it were, in a 'Schillerkragen', that symbol of adolescent storm and stress everywhere. This is the Schiller of countless schoolboys and girls, of as many teachers, of popular monographs, and, I suspect, the image which many of us have of him on an emotional level that has not been informed by our own better knowledge and by learned books. Most importantly, this is the Schiller of Beethoven, of Theodor Körner, of the 'Freiheitskriege' and 1848, of Dostoyevski, of Verdi and of Nietzsche (who detested him).

The trouble with this Schiller is that he is both too far and too near. Too far, in that his poetic vision seems to be focused on eternal values and verities of such a degree of abstractness and generality that we often feel our individual self with its tentative perceptions to be left out of such unquestioned sublimity. He does not often appear to speak to us in our intimate reality with the personal voice of a Goethe or a Mörike or Rilke. What shudders of mortality touch Max Piccolomini or Don Cesar as they prepare to die? How deeply is the experience of loving a man of flesh and blood permitted to invade Johanna's consciousness, and through her, ours? Even in their most feeling moments Schiller's characters appear to be more urgently related to the starry heavens above them and the moral law within them than to the intricacies of their immediate situation. And at times we react impatiently to such remoteness and feel his poetic conceptions to be lacking in that complexity which is a mark of maturity.

And then again this self-same Schiller seems to come too close. Who has not on occasion felt him to be uncomfortably direct in his love scenes—perhaps the very love scenes which at the same time vex us by their remoteness—in the moral sentiments he voices and in his philosophical reflections? His poetic utterances often seem to lack that indefinable quality of 'otherness' which marks great poetry, for all the intensity of its communication, as belonging to a world apart from the world of common cares and passions and convictions; a quality which makes it remain within invisible bounds however much it reaches out to us, and makes us remain within ourselves, inviolate, however much we go out to its appeal. Schiller's poetry often seems to lack that distance. It touches us on the raw, as it were, invading our practical self and leaving us defenceless; an appeal to which some respond by making him into a 'cause' and others by recoiling. And again we resent this strident directness and feel it to be adolescent, just like his remoteness. The extravagances of the Laura odes, of Karl Moor's last encounter with Amalie or of Fiesco at the sight of the dead body of his wife come to mind as examples, but other instances could easily be found from his later works as well. One need only think of Don Cesar's love-making to Beatrice, of Mortimer's passionate protestations, or, for that matter, of the poet's readiness to lapse into strongly rhythmical and rhyming verse forms to mark points of heightened emotion, however different the specific emotion may be: witness the formal similarity of Johanna's and Maria's lyrical outbursts, the one at having lost her integrity and the other at having gained her freedom!

At such points embarrassment lurks just around the corner, not because the poet gets too deep beneath the skin of his subject (this is the kind of embarrassment some feel with, say, Rilke) but because such passages tend to arouse in us a curiously inverted and divided response, which is impersonal and yet violent where it should be personal and yet distanced; a response, in short, in which mediacy and immediacy are placed on the wrong side of the scales, as it were, and which for that reason fails to fuse into a unified experience.

This type of aesthetic experience has been admirably described by Edward Bullough [in *Aesthetics,* edited by E. M. Wilkinson, 1957] in a passage which may well help us towards a better understanding of our mixed reaction by making us aware of its cause.

In speaking of idealistic art, which he defines as 'Art springing from abstract conceptions, expressing allegorical meanings, or illustrating general truths', Bullough makes the following observation:

> Generalizations and abstractions suffer under this disadvantage that they have too much general applicability to invite a personal interest in them, and too little individual concreteness to prevent them applying to us in all their force . . . General conceptions like Patriotism, Friendship, Love, Hope, Life, Death, concern as much Dick, Tom and Harry as myself, and I, therefore, either feel unable to get any personal kind of relation to them, or, if I do so, they become at once, emphatically and concretely, *my* Patriotism, *my* Friendship, *my* Love, *my* Hope, *my* Life and Death. By mere force of generalization, a general truth or a universal idea is so far distanced from myself that I fail to realize it concretely at all, or, when I do so, I can realize it only as part of my practical actual being, i.e. it falls below the Distance-limit altogether. 'Idealistic Art' suffers consequently under the peculiar difficulty that its excess of Distance turns gener-

ally into an under-distanced appeal—all the more easily, as it is the usual failing of the subject to *under-* rather than to *over-* distance.

According to Bullough, then, the principal cause of the unsatisfactory response to what he calls 'Idealistic Art' lies in the generality of its poetic conceptions. From this follows that uneasy blend of stridency and impersonality which many of us, at least on occasion, associate with Schiller's poetry. But are Schiller's poetic conceptions in truth as generalized as we are in the habit of assuming? This, I suggest, is the point where the myth has obscured the man and where the legend of the starry-eyed idealist in the 'Schillerkragen' has robbed us of a very real poetic legacy. It would be idle to deny, of course, that the art of this poet-philosopher is characterized by an unusually strong intellectual and moral component. But that this element should have been isolated out of the aesthetic organism in which it functions is due, I contend, not principally to a lack of concretion and complexity on the part of his poetic conceptions but to a peculiarly unfortunate historical configuration: it is due to the fact that this highly intellectual artist was born into an incorrigibly philosophizing country, in an age when total philosophical doctrines were springing up thick and fast and when the critical tradition, too—contrary to the trend, say, in France—was to become ever more dominated by the concern for the ideological 'content' of his poetry. It is Schiller's bad luck that he lends himself to this kind of reading, but it is not his fault. It is we, inured as we are to a tradition of 'Geistesgeschichte' and a heroically hollow image of Schiller, who approach his poetic conceptions with an impatient insistence on general meanings and messages, and we can hardly be surprised at the ensuing emptiness of our response.

If this be so, the remedy for this state of affairs must surely lie in a concerted effort to counteract the force of historical habit and to accord to Schiller's verbal structures the kind of patient and unprejudiced attention which all poetry demands (and which other types of poetry receive much more readily and liberally) in order to reveal the fullness of its intention. As soon as we do so, we discover that the integrity of Schiller's poetry is restored and the balance of our response righted. We discover complex and individual conceptions, which, by their degree of concretization and by other highly original means, command a nice balance of distance and intensity, safeguarding us as they move us. Schiller *is* both close and far, but he is both of these things in the proper place and in the right proportion; indeed, to achieve this double end he considered to be the most important task of the poet in general and the tragic poet in particular and to its accomplishment he gave all his strength as an artist and thinker. In short, I suggest that when we bring the tools of modern critical methods to bear upon this poet we shall restore his picture and reveal, beneath the crude likeness of the youthful idealist in the 'Schillerkragen', a portrait of the mature artist in unexceptional modern dress.

Look at Fiesco for instance, hero of Schiller's second drama, which is rarely read nowadays because of its linguistic crudeness. What a complicated fellow he really is—a brilliant political adventurer, plotting with the republican party of his native Genoa and yet secretly siding with the enemy in the hour of decision: play-acting his way through life, never committing himself to any cause or person, but committed to one thing only: the maintenance of his own playful equipoise, of his virtuosity *vis-à-vis* life itself. A pose? Yes, but a very sophisticated one, surely, this insistence on an aesthetic distance. It springs from a terror which many will recognize and which is subtly indicated in the play: the terror of being caught and crushed by the elemental forces within and without and of being lost in the rough and tumble of life. The flight from immediacy of experience into the careful uncommittedness of a 'l'art pour l'art' attitude—this is surely not all a simple-souled situation for the poet to have picked on: it is, moreover, a startlingly modern one. As we recall the various dramas, the predicament envisaged in them remains the same. Look at Marquis Posa in ***Don Carlos,*** at Wallenstein or at Demetrius, hero of Schiller's last unfinished tragedy: characters of dazzling brilliance all of these, as charming as they are ambitious, and rising to great heights by reason of their extraordinary gifts: and withal indecisive, vacillating, uncommitted, remaining just a little unreal, and falling into a frenzy of anxiety when finally they are trapped by consequences of their own making. And everywhere we discern, unobtrusively yet carefully articulated, the same psychological motivation of the desire to stay aloof from the turbulence of life: a deep sense of inferiority and insecurity ineradicably stamped on the hero's mind by some traumatic experience which has to be surmounted at all cost: witness the ugliness of Franz Moor, young Wallenstein's fall from the window at Burgau, Demetrius's flight from fire as a child, the stigma of Elisabeth's plainness, of her illegitimate birth and her upbringing in the Tower of London, Marquis Posa's gnawing sense of a common birth, etc. etc. Every time some early hurt has left the Schillerian hero profoundly vulnerable and has imbued him with a distrust of life on its deepest levels, of the body, the senses, of nature, of the heart, of the unconscious, or however we choose to describe what Schiller himself has called by many names and enshrined in many poetic symbols. The answer of his characters to this mistrust (which may remain entirely unconscious, as in the case of Demetrius, where it is only communicated to us by means of the poetic imagery) is always the same: it is an attempt to control a life that cannot be trusted, by a variety of means: by the force of sheer goodness, through astrology, through prophetic foresight, through clever calculation or, if need be, through naked power—but always through a dominant attitude of contemplative aloofness and a refusal to be unconditionally committed to the immediate situation. Such a pattern of a basic anxiety that is unendurable and a consequent retreat into an unassailable aesthetic distance from life comes as something of a surprise. It seems to bear little or no resemblance to the conventional clichés we connect with Schillerian characters, such as 'Sinnenglück' and 'Seelenfrieden'; instead, it seems a highly perceptive account of a basic human response to the rigours of reality, and one which makes good sense to us of the post-Freudian era.

Indeed, it would be difficult to find a more complete portrait gallery of 'neurotics' than that which Schiller has created in his tragedies! A work like his ***Jungfrau von Orle-*** ***ans*** is breath-taking in its psychological insight into unconscious processes. In Schiller's reading, the Johanna who at first obeys the call of the spirit is what we would now call a split personality. If there is no conflict in her it is because that part of her psyche which does not assent to her spiritual mission—her vital instinctual drives—is totally dissociated from her consciousness and merely manifests itself in the irrational excess that characterizes her behaviour. Impelled by secret drives that she neither admits nor controls, she is perpetually carried beyond her proper goal and her actions take on a demoniacal and automatic quality which is frightening to herself as well as others. The most palpable symbol of these alienated forces of her psyche is her sword, the live tool that moves at will in her powerless hands, striking and finding its mark by magic. The moment that secret estranged self is aroused and becomes incorporated in her consciousness, the sword loses its power and magic ceases. Johanna is vanquished. The split of her personality now gives way to a conflict *within* her personality in which all her psychic energies are engaged. In one sense, the onset of her conflict marks the turning point of the drama and brings about her crisis and catastrophe. In another, and deeper, sense, it is the beginning of health. For conflict is a necessary stage on the way to that psychic reintegration which in the end she must and does achieve. This is a remarkably searching and balanced analysis of religious genius; Johanna's spiritual experience is critically scrutinized and counted valuable and valid only when, in the end, it flows from and is supported by the total personality, the unconscious as well as the conscious part of her being.

Such unexpected depth of psychological insight may be encountered on every page of Schiller's poetry, but—it must be repeated—one finds it only when one reads him as every poet deserves to be read—two-dimensionally, attending to the verbal surface of the work and letting the texture itself create its own perspective and depth: a paradox which is nowhere more striking than in criticism of Schiller.

The presence of such sophisticated and interesting thematic material may be surprising to those of us who have been reared on the myth of the man. Far more surprising is the *raison d'être* of these recurring materials. We are altogether mistaken if we surmise that the poet created a portrait gallery of neurotics because he was a neurotic himself. He may well have been, but if he was, he was neurotic in a qualitatively different sense from the characters he created, because by the very act of articulating and objectifying their sickness he proved and ensured his own mental health. However that may be, the fact is that he created such characters for a reason that fits the customary picture of Schiller even less than do the characters themselves. He created them because these characters, and they alone, would, in his view, support the sort of aesthetic structure he knew a tragedy to be. For throughout his poetic career the starry-eyed young man in the open shirt collar reflected very sharply and soberly on the nature of his craft and on the special requirements of his chosen medium—the genre of tragedy. In Schiller's view, the trouble with tragedy is that it suffers from an excessive immediacy and therefore constantly threatens the aesthetic distance of the percipient. His tragic heroes, uncommitted, playful, responding to suffering by seeking to remain in contemplative aloofness above the pull and thrust of the action rather than accelerating it, furnish the poet's answer to this artistic problem. By their own aesthetic defence they arrest the tempestuous rush of the action. Thus they save the spectators from being lost in the welter of events and from losing the aesthetic distance without which no experience of art is possible. That aesthetic distance is steadily prefigured, as it were, in the distanced response of the principal character itself. How paradoxical! Schiller, the earnest propounder of sublime generalities, pulling a deep and truly felt human predicament out of his hat and using it as a sort of trick to make his art form function the more efficiently; handling the experience he articulates, in fact, as mere material in the service of something that seems to preoccupy him more passionately than any given 'content'—the artistic form he is creating. It is that sovereign freedom with which he handles all matter whatsoever, not just his psychological material, but in equal measure his moral, metaphysical, religious, emotional material, it is, in fact, that quality of artistic irony which is the least familiar quality in Schiller and the one which places him most clearly in the great European tradition of literature. How superbly he could articulate this indifference of the artist to all but his art as early as *Fiesco,* that most underrated of all his dramas. For Fiesco is an artist, not in stone or oils, to be sure, but in life, and in handling life situations he permits himself to be ruled by considerations of form with the same indifference to the practical interests or moral values involved which the sculptor evinces towards the market value of his materials or even their intrinsic beauty. Whether at the disclosure of his conspiratorial activities he freezes the dumbfounded republicans into a living tableau or whether, at the height of battle, he goes to warn his adversary of his plans, his actions always evince the same disregard of any end outside themselves, of any end apart from the virtuosity of their performance and the significance of the situation he creates. It is Schiller's subtle insight into the artist's psychology and into the tragic shortcomings of an exclusively aesthetic response to life which makes this early work such fascinating and—let it be repeated—essentially modern reading.

Schiller himself evinces the same quality of artistic indifference *vis-à-vis* his own materials which he portrays in Fiesco, not, to be sure, as long as they remain stuff of his immediate human experience, but as soon as they become raw material of his art waiting to be organized. In his letters to Goethe he calls the moral verdict on Wallenstein's crime which is to emerge from the tragedy 'eine an sich triviale und unpoetische Materie', adding that his work on this portion of his drama has made him realize—'wie leer das eigentlich Moralische ist'; of the heroic in Corneille he speaks disparagingly as 'dieses an sich nicht sehr reichhaltige Ingrediens'. It is a mind of aristocratic cast that judges, with unerring certainty, 'dass dem Ästhetischen, so wenig es auch die Leerheit vertragen kann, die Frivolität doch weit weniger widerspricht als die Ernsthaftigkeit'. And with the same sovereign irony with which he handles his other materials, the emotional ingredient is held in place in his tragedies. At the outset of his labours on *Wallenstein* he is aware of the personal nature of his involve-

ment in the love idyll between Wallenstein's daughter and young Piccolomini. A year later its function has become clarified, as is evident both from the play itself and his utterances about it. Love, being an unpurposive response that brings into play and releases the total personality, is for that reason akin to the aesthetic mode and productive of it. Thus the love-element, like the quasi-aesthetic response of the tragic hero, became yet another means of creating an aesthetic area within the turbulent rush of the tragic action and of inducing an aesthetic response in the spectator. Schiller was to use both devices with transparent clarity and consciousness in his last tragedy, *Die Braut von Messina.* This tragedy reads like a poet's soliloquy on the redeeming power of form, in which we are privileged to share because his very theme has come to reflect his secret formal preoccupation.

Thus poetic raw materials provided by experience are transmuted by form and in turn formative processes themselves are reflected in the theme. Here is the constant forward and backward flow between inspiration and medium, matter and technique which is the secret of the transmuting power of art. And how freely his materials develop under the forming impulse—with what disregard of the laws of common reality he explores their formal potentialities! How his heroes' speeches swell and spread and flower into a different time-dimension which momentarily transcends the time-dimension of the plot! How fleeting and contracted, by comparison with their contemplations, are their moments of anguished action! Such elongations and foreshortenings are deliberate distortions, as unmistakable in their intention as the expressionistic distortions of an El Greco or the surrealist shapes of a Picasso. Only I think that we are slower to recognize the abstract handling of human forms in drama, partly because of the representational character of language *per se* and partly because our imagination is conditioned by the inevitable realism of the enactment of drama on the stage, by real persons. We even expect one personality to be contained within one skin! Nothing could be further from the truth, since Schiller, like Shakespeare before him, readily externalizes some aspect of one character in the separate being of another, who is 'other' and at the same time 'himself'. The truth of the matter being that words have no skin. It is not for nothing that Schiller and Goethe prized opera so highly as an art form, and that all Schiller's later plays—*Die Jungfrau von Orleans, Die Braut von Messina* and *Wilhelm Tell* in different ways introduced operatic elements. For opera is the dramatic form *par excellence* in which his anti-naturalistic and anti-realistic tendencies could have come to full fruition. In the world of fairy tale and musical forms the claims of common reality recede, the boundaries of personality become fluid and representation ceases. One thing is itself and another. How Schiller would have relished a work like *Die Frau ohne Schatten!*

It is, then, such mature poetic conceptions and such sovereign artistry which entitle Schiller to be regarded as an essentially contemporary poet of European stature. In the measure in which we cease to approach his poetry with preconceived notions and permit it to reveal its riches, it yields us a differentiated aesthetic experience which is both personal and distanced and affords us an aesthetic delight of an unusually pure and conscious quality.

But what about the man himself? Even if we concede the aesthetic temper of his art and his reflections about art, can we discern this strain in his make-up as a person? The young man with the ascetic look, it is true, may have started by being a rather unsubtle puritanical figure, living in a crude black and white universe of sensual temptation and moral conquest. But under the discipline of forms his mind soon became refined. And the precise aesthetic colouring of his mature references to freedom and necessity, to disinterestedness and compulsion, has only too often been missed. He was a conqueror, but not a stoic one. His was the light, ironical victory of an aesthetic temper over the seriousness and ponderousness of all matter *per se*. He was free, supremely free. But this freedom was not based on the denial of personal bonds and interests; it was a subtler one in which the most varied bonds, balanced and tempered by the constant discipline of forms, became transparent and left him uncompelled and serene. Goethe's wonderful portrayal of his friend, in the poem *Epilog zu Schillers Glocke*, is informed with this refined aesthetic freedom. It is expressed in words which come from the very heart of Schiller's own aesthetic thinking:

> Denn hinter ihm, in *wesenlosem Scheine*,
> lag was uns alle bändigt, das Gemeine.

It is in keeping with the temper of the artist and the man that he should have bequeathed to us as his most cherished philosophical legacy his essay **'Über die *ästhetische* Erziehung des Menschen'** and that he should have counted play—that untrammelled, harmonious and deeply useless activity of the whole person—to be the most serious business of humanity. 'Der Mensch spielt nur, wo er in voller Bedeutung des Worts Mensch ist, und *er ist nur da ganz Mensch, wo er spielt'*, we read in the XVth letter, and again: 'Mit dem Angenehmen, mit dem Guten, mit dem Vollkommenen ist es dem Menschen *nur* ernst; aber mit

der Schönheit spielt er.' '*Nur* ernst'; *merely* in earnest: never has so little a word been used so devastatingly, so audaciously and so maturely. For all the quietness with which it is spoken, it signifies a profound spiritual revolution, a revaluation of all values. Like a beacon from receding shores, the rich maturity of Schiller's 'nur ernst' shines across two centuries into our own world of totalitarian dogmas and frenzied specialization and shows up the cracks in its spiritual foundations, for us to see and to mend. (pp. 151-59)

> *Ilse Appelbaum-Graham, "Friedrich Von Schiller: A Portrait of Maturity," in* German Life & Letters, *Vol. XIV, No. 3, April, 1961, pp. 151-59.*

### Donald E. Allison   (essay date 1964)

[*In the following essay, Allison considers the relevance of Schiller's works to modern society.*]

The works of an author who has become an official classic may well lose in timeliness whatever they gain in timelessness. This has been in one respect the predicament of the German dramatist Friedrich Schiller (1759-1805). In being venerated, he has been stereotyped as an idealist who, indifferent to reality, would seemingly lack an understanding of the problems of our age. On the other hand, no German writer has remained more popular with the general public. Political factions of the most divergent sort have recognized this and have enlisted his name in promoting their causes; he has been described as a champion of the liberal democratic movement, a comrade-at-arms by the Nazis, an advocate of revolution by the Communists. Is Schiller any of these? Can the ideals for which he stood be reduced to those of a narrowly political movement? Is his idealism remote from the complexities of life in his day or in ours? To answer these questions let us reconsider what freedom, which he stressed above everything else, meant to him.

A little less than two months before the storming of the Bastille, Schiller had been officially installed at the University of Jena as professor of history. In this capacity he might be expected to take more than a casual interest in this political upheaval. That he could subscribe to the aims of the French Revolution as proclaimed in its motto is not in doubt, and in 1792 he was awarded honorary citizenship by the French. But Karl Reinhard, who did much to popularize Schiller's dramas in France, received no answer to a request for a statement endorsing the uprising.

Reinhard would have been less surprised at Schiller's silence if he had been as familiar with the dramatist's approach to history, or with *Don Carlos,* as he apparently was with the earlier plays. In *Carlos,* Posa's entreaty for freedom of thought envisions nothing so radical as abolition of the monarchy. Rather, this basic freedom is to become the foundation for a truly enlightened state. The violent course taken by the French Revolution horrified Schiller, and he realized that such outbreaks imperil rather than promote the cause of freedom. Among the *Xenien,* on which he collaborated with Goethe, we read: "Priests of freedom, you have never seen the goddess and never

---

**Miller on the importance of freedom in Schiller's works:**

The idea of freedom is so fundamental in Schiller that all other ideas must be related to it, if they are to be properly understood. Freedom lies behind Schiller's conception of human reason; it also underlies his view of nature and of the naïve. Freedom explains human 'dignity'; it is also the hallmark of beauty and grace. It is the very principle of tragedy; in a different form it is also the life-breath of comedy. It explains Schiller's appreciation of the ancient Greeks; it is the guiding principle in his conception of the ideal modern State. Such ideas as god and immortality, though they are not always directly related to freedom, nevertheless illustrate freedom indirectly. Without the fundamental idea of freedom, such ideas as 'contemplation' and 'imagination' jostle each other meaninglessly in Schiller's aesthetic theory; with it, they fall into place in a meaningful whole.

*R. D. Miller, in his* Schiller and the Ideal of Freedom: A Study of Schiller's Philosophical Works With Chapters on Kant, *Clarendon Press, 1970.*

---

will, for this divine being is never revealed in brute force." And again: "Do you think the Germans are so stupid, you apostles of freedom? Everyone sees that your only concern is to seize power for yourselves!" Moreover, Schiller feared that even those reformers who were not prompted by selfish motives might be misguided in their zeal to establish a new order and would distort the proper relationship between the citizen and the state. In a letter to his future sister-in-law he explains:

> every single human soul which is developing its full powers is far more than the greatest human society when I survey the latter as a whole. The greatest state is a work of men; man is the work of unattainable, great nature. The state is a creation of chance, but man is a necessary being; and how does the state reach greatness but through the strengths of its citizens? The state is only one effect of human ability, only a work of thought; but man is the source of this strength and the creator of the thought.

A little more than a year after writing this letter, he continues in the same vein in an essay entitled **"The Legal Codes of Lycurgus and Solon"**: "If the constitution of a state prevents men from developing all their innate powers and inhibits the progressive growth of the spirit, it is reprehensible and harmful, no matter how perfect it may otherwise be."

In both of these statements the emphasis is on the individual, and underlying it is the recognition that freedom is a property of the spirit. As such, it is not something that can be conferred from without or fully achieved on a merely political level. Freedom was for the poet an ever deepening concept, which Goethe once pointed out in a reminiscence to Eckermann: "The idea of freedom is present in all of Schiller's works, and this idea underwent change just as Schiller himself changed and progressed in his development. In his youth it was physical freedom that motivated him and which carried over into his writings; later in his life it was an ideal freedom. . . ." What was this transition which Goethe detected and what does it mean?

The essay *On the Sublime* begins with a quotation from Lessing's *Nathan:* "No man has to do anything." And Schiller adds these significant words: "Man is the creature with a will of his own." Inherent in this will is the freedom to exercise it, and only by doing so can man achieve full realization of self. In practice, this means that we are obliged to oppose all forces that are inimical to our will, and we are told that this is possible in two ways: realistically or idealistically. The former refers quite simply to physical resistance. But the limits here are obvious, and Schiller offers the following alternative: "If man can no longer effectively oppose physical forces with similar faculties, he has no choice but to abandon a competition in which he is at a disadvantage and from which he can only suffer and to destroy a force conceptually that he must endure in actuality. To destroy a force conceptually means to submit to it voluntarily." This is achieved, Schiller asserts, through what he terms a "moral discipline." He now gives us his definition of the man who is truly free: "The morally disciplined man, he alone is completely free. Either he is superior to nature as a force or he is in accord

with her. Then nothing she does to him is force since before it happens to him it has already become his own act. . . ." Stated otherwise, freedom consists in submitting to that which is inevitable, not with resignation, but voluntarily. Thus man makes of necessity an act of his own will.

Of Kant, Schiller once wrote: "No mortal man has uttered a greater word than 'act of your own will. . . .' " That this imperative as a challenge of potentially heroic proportions would in itself have appealed to Schiller is readily understandable, but he recognized it for more than that. In this call for the individual to assume absolute responsibility for his actions—not responsibility in any passive sense, but the attainment of full control over his actions, thoughts, and feelings—Schiller perceived the ultimate goal of man's development. The principle of self-determination is in his view the mark and the measure of all human dignity, the essence and the consecration of mankind. For man to behave as a creature of impulse, to heed mandates imposed by any authority without himself being able to sanction them, to let his actions be determined by any source other than his innermost being, this would be to forfeit his freedom, to desecrate the human condition. To act out of expediency or conformity would be the very antithesis of the autonomy on which Schiller insists and which implies a faith in that which *should be* rather than acceptance of that which *is*. It is an unshakable conviction that existence can and should be shaped by something that is higher.

There are those who claim that Schiller turned to the study of philosophy to seek refuge from reality. Nothing could be farther from the truth. There is no discrepancy between life and his thinking; his philosophy grew out of intense preoccupation with reality. In fact, he came to recognize the limits of speculative thinking and would have concurred in the opinion of a later thinker who held that life may teach us how to think, but mere thinking can never teach us how to live. Had Schiller given us only theoretical formulations, we might well be suspicious; but in his dramas he has left us the demonstration of his thought.

What, after all, is taught in his later tragedies? It is quite simply that the dignity of man consists in the preservation of his freedom, in not becoming inwardly the captive of fate or circumstance. In maintaining this principle, Wallenstein, Maria Stuart, Joan of Arc—whatever their guilt may have been—attain sublimity. Thus Wallenstein, confronted on all sides by disaster, speaks with a conviction that is a greater gain than any of his victories on the field of battle had ever been: "Are you already in port, old man? Not I. My undaunted courage still drives me gloriously along the crest of life. I still call hope my goddess. The spirit is ever young. . . ." The same confidence is to be heard in the words of Maria Stuart, whose nobility of spirit as she goes to her execution is at last commensurate with her regal rank: "Why do you lament? Why do you weep? You should rejoice with me that the goal of my suffering is finally at hand. My bonds fall away, the prison opens, and my soul in joy soars on angelic wings to eternal freedom." Likewise, Joan reassures her faithful and despairing companion: "I am not as miserable as you think. I suffer want, but that is no misfortune for my situation. . . . You see only the outer aspect of things, for earthly limitations obscure your vision." In these dramas Schiller portrays characters who attain freedom of spirit, which in terms of tragedy he called sublimity. The heroic is their substance, and this quality could hardly be presented more strikingly. These plays are a tribute to man's effort to oppose suffering and hardship. Just a few weeks before his death Schiller wrote in much the same vein to Wilhelm von Humboldt: "In the final analysis, we are both idealists and would be ashamed to have it said of us that things formed us rather than that we formed things."

But how did Schiller come to attach such great importance to the attainment of freedom? In all of this there is a profound sense of urgency.

Along with many of his contemporaries, Schiller realized even as a young man that he had been born into an age that was spiritually depleted. An echo of this is to be heard in his first drama in the outcry of Karl Moor against this "ink-splashing age" as he reads in his Plutarch of great men. While protests against sophistry and the artificiality of society were in part Schiller's inheritance from the Storm and Stress, he felt more and more keenly as the years passed that civilization was not only failing to hold its own but that it was rapidly deteriorating. In the Prologue to **Wallenstein** he warns of the "narrow sphere" of middle class existence and assigns to art the role of enlarging it: "For only a lofty subject can stir the unfathomable depths of humanity. The mind becomes narrow in a narrow sphere, and man grows with greater causes." The enfeeblement of life becomes an ever recurrent theme in his writing, and his dramas are remarkably uniform in that they display almost no departure from this preoccupation. His heroes and heroines are generally frustrated or corrupted by degenerate civilized society: they become rebels and conspirators, they succumb to the lure of power, or they are outsiders impelled by a mission.

In a more personal sense Schiller explained how these conditions had affected his own life: "Now I saw everything I brought into the world as immature and far below the ideal that was alive within me; with a sense of the perfection that was possible I had to hurry before the eyes of the public with my immature fruit and establish myself so needy of instruction against my will as a teacher of mankind." Elsewhere he observes that the poet must be increasingly on guard against lowering his standards in such times. There could be no compromise, for he earnestly believed, although he had no illusions about the magnitude of the task, that men could be elevated through art. Thus he wrote to Goethe about the function of poetry: "There is something in everyone that speaks in favor of the poet. Even though you may be an unbelieving realist, you must admit that this something is the seed of idealism and that it is this alone which prevents real life with its crass materialism from destroying all receptivity to the poetic . . . and much is already gained in that an outlet from this materialism is opened." Such quotations offer only the briefest statement of Schiller's anxiety about an age engulfed by material interests. He concludes that modern civilization has deprived man of wholeness of being, and the alter-

native he advocates is the idealism embodied in his dramas and elaborated in his philosophical and aesthetic writings.

Today Schiller's concern seems even more timely. He would most certainly have concurred in the views of those who still speak in the name of humanity. Whitehead has warned us that "the values of life are ebbing." Albert Schweitzer tells us: "My own impression was that in our intellectual and spiritual life we were not only below the level of past generations, but were in many respects only living on their achievements, and that not a little of this heritage was beginning to melt away in our hands. . . . Our spiritual life is rotten throughout. . . ." And we may add the words of Gandhi: "I wholeheartedly detest this mad desire . . . to increase animal appetites and go the ends of the earth in search of satisfaction. If modern civilization stands for this, and I have understood it to do so, I call it Satanic. . . . Modern civilization as represented by the West of today has given matter a place which by right belongs to the spirit." Certainly Schiller deserves a place in the vanguard of such spokesmen. In his opinion nothing short of spiritual regeneration would do, and he made it emphatically clear that this must begin in the tradition of the humanistic injunctions: "Know thyself " and "Physician, heal thyself." Of all the threats to which mankind is exposed, whether in his time or ours, he feared none so greatly as a catastrophe of the spirit, the inner deterioration of the individual.

Goethe, Mozart, Wilhelm von Humboldt, Beethoven, and Kant are only a few of the contemporaries with whom Schiller shared an acute awareness of the fundamental weakness of the age in which they lived. The achievements of all of these men are remarkable in themselves, but nothing about them is more impressive than their profound dedication to humanity. Theirs was not merely an interest in man for what he is and has been in terms of history, sociology, psychology or theology; theirs was a comprehensive vision of what man could and should become. It is such a belief in an ideal humanity which is professed by the priest Sarastro in a magnificent aria in *The Magic Flute:* "Within these sacred walls where man loves man no traitor shall hide, for the enemy will find forgiveness. Those who do not like such thoughts do not deserve to be human beings."

Inseparable from this ideal, to which Schiller's contribution was by no means small, was the question of how it could be attained. This gave rise to much discussion of education, although not in the more restricted sense in which we are likely to understand that word today. The German term *Bildung,* which has much broader implications, would be more appropriate. This idea of education had its roots in antiquity and in the attitude of Schiller and his contemporaries toward Greek civilization. The latter was held in high esteem not only because of its surpassing achievements in many fields; it stood as a way of life that had produced the highest type of individual. What had impressed Schiller more than anything else about the ancient Greeks was their wholeness—a perfectly integrated development of all elements of human character, the oneness of man with himself and with the world about him. In contrast to this Golden Age was the plight of modern man.

The latter, no longer possessing such integrity of being, was painfully conscious of the loss. With faith in the perfectibility of modern man Schiller sought to overcome this deficiency. He proclaimed an ideal of freedom according to which the individual should at all times attempt to shape his life. It is this striving, this unremitting endeavor that *Bildung* signifies: the training of one's whole being to the highest possible degree. The aim is not development in a self-centered sense, but cultivation of the values that ennoble mankind. As Goethe once observed, Schiller's own life was the exemplification of the *Bildung* in which he so devoutly believed: "One hardly knew him after a week had gone by; he was a different person and a more perfect one."

Schiller had both a sense of direction and faith in the dignity of man. Is it necessary to ask further whether he still has any meaning for us? (pp. 140-47)

Donald E. Allison, "Schiller Today," in Prairie Schooner, *Vol. XXXVIII, No. 2, Summer, 1964, pp. 140-47.*

## Erich Heller   (essay date 1965)

[*In the following excerpt, Heller analyzes the evolution of idealism in Schiller's dramas.*]

Friedrich Schiller is the name of a poetical disaster in the history of German literature, a disaster, however, of great splendor. His work—a lifework of considerable genius, moving single-mindedness, and great moral integrity—is a striking instance of a European catastrophe of the spirit: the invasion and partial disruption of the aesthetic faculty by unemployed religious impulses. He is one of the most conspicuous and most impressive figures among the host of theologically displaced persons who found a precarious refuge in the emergency camp of Art.

His place of origin is situated on the crossroads of all philosophies which constitute, or result from, German Idealism. Partly instructed by contemporary philosophers, partly anticipating thoughts to come, Schiller's mind is perpetually torn between the many conflicting ideas and attitudes suggested by the Idealist philosophers and their successors as alternatives to the traditional, but apparently no longer acceptable, systems of theology. Fichte's omnipotent Ego as well as Hegel's *Weltgeist* which gradually realizes itself with an enormous display of dialectical noise, struggle, and fury as the final state of harmony on earth; Schopenhauer's pure aesthetic contemplation as well as Nietzsche's celebration of the Will, have their uneasy rendezvous in Schiller's philosophy. His poetical output is something in the nature of an oversized hymn book compiled for all denominations of Idealism.

Like all Idealist thinkers, Schiller was first baptized into the philosophy of Immanuel Kant. It is a neat coincidence that **The Robbers,** his first drama, and Kant's *Critique of Pure Reason* appeared in the same year, 1781. The question, so often raised by literary critics, whether the study of Kant did Schiller any good, merely shows a misapprehension of the nature of intellectual experience. At least with minds of distinction, what is called "influence"

*Title page to the second edition of Schiller's* The Robbers.

works with the inevitability of the chemical law of elective affinity. Fundamentally, a man is no more free to choose his intellectual parents than he is to select his physical ancestors. Schiller was a Kantian before he had read a line of Kant, and remained one even after he had learned, through his contact with Goethe, theoretically to appreciate the dangers to which that philosophy exposes the artistic imagination. Indeed, to what degree he had come to appreciate Goethe's aversion to transcendental speculations, is shown in a letter written about two years before his death. Hurt as he was by an annoying "abstract" critique a disciple of Schelling's had published about **The Maid of Orleans,** he complained to Goethe (January 20, 1802) about the helplessness of transcendental philosophers in dealing with a particular work of art. "There is no bridge yet," he said (and he did say "yet"), "that leads from transcendental philosophy to the real fact: the philosopher's principles cut a very strange figure when applied to the reality of a given case; they either destroy it or are being destroyed by it." It is a case of "Telling Goethe!" But as Schiller continued to lament "the absence of an organon capable of mediating between philosophy and art," Goethe could hardly have sorrowed with him. He never shared either the implied expectation (and a very Romantic expectation it was!) of a future merger, profitable to both disciplines, between philosophy and art, or the hope that the construction of a "bridge" between the two would do away with the poverty oppressing the land on both sides. But to Schiller, the Kantian poet, it still appeared to be due to the missing link that "everything that now is said in general cannot but sound hollow and empty, and everything that [in literature] is produced in particular be shallow and insignificant."

On August 23, 1794, Schiller wrote his first personal letter to Goethe. It finally convinced the reluctant Goethe that at last he had met with an understanding friend who could relieve the strain of intellectual isolation from which he suffered after his return from Italy. In that letter Schiller attempted to give a diagnosis of the greater poet's difficulties: to be a poet in a climate of the spirit unwarmed by the "sun of Homer" and unmellowed by any genuine tradition of poetry; and to have to provide everything out of one's own sovereign mind and imagination—subject matter, form, and poetic atmosphere. Would not the dire compulsion of having to design, plant, and cultivate in a desert the very gardens of the spirit which the poet desired to contemplate, overtax the aesthetic sensibility? What a predicament that he must begin with an idea rather than with a real experience of a world of poetry, and must support the tender growth of intuition with the coarse props of reflection! "The logical discipline," Schiller wrote,

> which the human mind must adopt for its reflective activities is ill–matched with the aesthetic impulse through which alone it can become creative. This imposes upon you a double task: for as you first proceeded from intuition to abstraction, so now you must translate ideas back into intuitions, and thoughts into feelings, for it is only in these that the productions of genius have their roots.

It may be doubted whether this is a correct description of Goethe's poetic difficulty; but it is certainly a precise analysis of Schiller's own approach to poetry. Soon afterward he realized this *quid pro quo,* and in his greatest essay in aesthetic philosophy, **"On Naïve and Sentimental Poetry"** (1795), the passage quoted became the very center of his definition of the "sentimental" poet, that is, of his own poetic nature, as opposed to the type of "naïve" poet represented by Goethe.

The world of the mind as it emerges from Kant's philosophy is the legitimate home for the modern natural scientist, but the artist lives in it as an enemy alien, spied upon and constantly suspected of being a dangerous agent in the service of a foreign power; for he may be in communication with the incommunicable, and may even undermine the Kantian defenses of pure immanence by maintaining within the sealed-off realm of the senses clandestine relations with that which is transcendent. But by order of Kant all transcendence, except that aspect of it which is accessible to the moral sense, had been decreed out of bounds.

This was an icy blast for the artistic imagination; for if the phenomenal world was no longer the visible symbol of an infinitely creative power, it was, for the artist, reduced to a state of sterile petrifaction. The real poet—for instance, Goethe—was bound to find this imprisonment of vision within the restrictive categories of human understanding either meaningless or a tiresome nuisance. He could not be party to this profoundly intelligent plot—so profound, indeed, that sober reason rose in its execution to the grandeur of genius—which, in the long run, had to make revealed mysteries convertible into intellectual problems, and the debt of tragedy and sin payable in moral currency. It was a philosophy upon which Goethe—in spite of occasional compliments—uneasily frowned, and which drove Kleist to distraction. Kant, in his time, made perfectly articulate the predicament of religion as well as of art in the modern world.

Had poetry been Schiller's native territory—in the "naïve" sense in which he himself believed that it was Goethe's—he might never have become entangled in Kant's philosophy. True, there are issues on which he does not see eye to eye with Kant, but the very manner of his disagreeing is Kantian. The stumbling blocks for Schiller are, significantly enough, Kant's conception of the nature of Beauty and of the Moral Will. Might it not be possible, Schiller asks, to rescue the Beautiful from the spider web of pure immanence and from the arbitrariness of subjective judgment? In the winter of 1792 Schiller announced to his friend Gottfried Körner that he thought he had discovered the objective standard for beauty and thus the "objective principle of taste"—the search for which had been "the despair of Kant." The work (it was to be called "Kallias," or "On Beauty") in which Schiller planned to develop this philosophical discovery remained unwritten. Its sketch, however, is contained in a series of letters to Körner. So far as can be gathered from these letters, the "objective criterion" would, in the last analysis, still have been a subjectively psychological one, even though Schiller had promised to raise it above the sphere of mere "experience" where, according to Kant, it "unavoidably" had to be left. In the end Schiller too, it seems, would have been constrained to define Beauty as that which evokes in the beholder the *illusion* of freedom, because what is beautiful *seems* to be free of determining causes and not dependent either on the materials of which it has been made or on the subjective personality who made it.

In one of the so-called "Kallias" letters, Schiller quotes a sentence from Kant's *Critique of Judgment,* a sentence which, he claims, can finally be vindicated only by his own emergent theory of Beauty: *Nature,* wrote Kant, *is beautiful when it looks like Art; Art is beautiful when it looks like Nature.* Inspired by this Kantian pronouncement, Schiller hopes to allow Nature—that is, Kant's *phenomenal* world, laboring in the bondage of causality—to share, by virtue of what is beautiful in it, in the *noumenal* freedom of the Absolute which lies beyond the rational mechanism of cause and effect. And what is beautiful in Nature? For instance, the poplar tree which, at this point, Schiller plants in the soil of the Absolute. How it loves—*apparently* free from the encumbrance of massiveness—to fulfill its Idea by growing, upright and slender, toward the sky, and how, bent by the wind, it yet asserts its freedom in the rhythm of its resilient swaying! And as Schiller thus allots to the beauty of Nature a little freehold on the land of Kant's noumenal freedom, so he arranges for the *free* creations of human art to be *bound,* without detriment to their freedom, by their obedience to laws and rules. Thus Beauty, for Schiller, becomes inescapably linked to the one and only transcendental faculty which Kant acknowledged in human beings: the moral sense. Consistently enough, the work "Kallias," which was to be about the problem of Beauty by itself, never progressed beyond the preparatory stage. But the following years (1793-5) saw a spate of finished essays (**"The Graceful and the Exalted," "On Pathos," "On the Sublime," "On the Aesthetic Education of Man"**) in which the aesthetic question is inseparable from the moral problem.

If, however, Beauty was to be even moderately successful in its struggles to bypass the fortifications which Kant had built along the frontier of transcendence, the belligerent nature of his ethics had to be slightly pacified first. And, indeed, nothing can better convey Kant's seriousness in separating Nature from the Absolute than the obstacles he put in the way of his only legitimate messenger from the one to the other: the *moral* man had to produce a score of victories over "natural inclination" before he would be allowed to pass the demarcation line. But was not this morality with clenched fists an insult to the idea of Beauty? Schiller felt it was: "A moral deed can never be beautiful," he wrote to Körner (February 19, 1793), "when we have to watch the operation through which it is forced out of our intimidated sensuous nature." Hence Schiller's attempt at a reconciliation of duty and inclination in the Beautiful Soul whose impulses have become so purified that, without having to rely upon moral reflection for guidance, they effortlessly will be good. Theologically speaking, the Beautiful Soul is a soul in the state of grace.

The question has often been asked how much Schiller's Beautiful Soul owes to Shaftesbury's moral "virtuoso," and how it is related to the Renaissance ideal of aesthetic civility as expounded in Castiglione's *Il Cortegiano.* All such speculations and researches, however, are beside the point. For Schiller's grand essays in aesthetic theory, insofar as they express his missionary zeal to make peace between the aesthetic and the moral experience, are unsupported by his spiritual nature. He is unable to believe that the two are equal in spiritual rank. Even less is he ever prompted, as Castiglione and Shaftesbury were, by any spontaneous faith in the superiority of aesthetic experience. On the contrary, he always aims at winning the sanction of the moralist in him for his aesthetic activities. Even in the essay **"The Graceful and the Exalted,"** the enthusiasm of his thought and style is at its highest when the inner harmony of the Beautiful Soul is once more upset, the peace between aesthetics and morals is broken again, and man has to win his ultimate moral freedom and dignity from Fate and Necessity by freely accepting his own tragic defeat. This is Schiller's theodicy, his Book of Job. It was the essay which so infuriated Goethe that he determined to avoid any contact with its author. Even in the creator of the Beautiful Soul he sensed the austerity of the moralist who seemed to him barred from any intimate knowledge of the nature of artistic creation.

How then is one to account for his later friendship with

Schiller, and for the great inspiration he drew from it? This was mainly due to Schiller's "integrity and rare seriousness," on which Goethe complimented him in one of his earliest letters (August 27, 1794); to the subtlety and intelligence of his critical faculties; to his sense of quality, so rare among their contemporaries; and above all to his readiness to acknowledge Goethe's superior *poetic* nature. So strong was the effect of this friendship upon Schiller that at one point he succeeded in writing a play which is almost free from the flaws marring his other dramas, and which has done more toward justifying his claim to greatness as a dramatic writer than all the rest of his productions: **Wallenstein.** It is with ironical surprise that one reads what he writes to Goethe about his new manner of working: he has adopted a "coldly artistic" approach to his subject—the manner which he believed was Goethe's and which had, before their friendship, filled him with moral indignation. "You will probably be pleased about the spirit that animates me in my labors," he says on November 28, 1796. "I succeed quite well in keeping myself at a distance from the subject matter and in rendering it quite objectively. I am even tempted to say that I am not at all interested in the *sujet,* and never before have I combined within myself so much coldness concerning the subject with so much warmth concerning my work. The main character and most of the minor characters I treat with the pure love of the artist. . . . "

In the correspondence between the two men, one can follow step by step the slow changes which Schiller's aesthetic ideas underwent through his intimate contact with Goethe. And yet there are still signs of Goethe's old impatience with the theorizing of his friend—that impatience which Goethe well remembered even many years after Schiller's death. On March 23, 1829, he said to Eckermann:

> Schiller was like all people who start from preconceived ideas. He knew no peace, nor did he ever feel that anything could be brought to its natural conclusion, as you can see from his letters about my *Wilhelm Meister* which he wished me to change now this way, and now again that way. I had to be perpetually on my guard to protect my own work, and his, from such influence.

There is an exchange of letters (March 27-April 6, 1801) in which Schiller, in a manner almost indistinguishable from Goethe's, speaks of the process of poetic creation. It begins, he says, with "an obscure, but powerful and comprehensive idea" that precedes the technical execution of the poem; the poetry has to communicate this dark and hardly conscious notion by finding an object that can express it clearly. "In recent years," Schiller continues, "the concept of poetry has become blurred through attempts to raise it to a higher rank." This, indeed, is the precise formula for Schiller's own aesthetic sins. And the irony in Goethe's reply is unmistakable:

> As for the high demands which nowadays are made upon poetry, it is my conviction too that they are not likely to produce a single poet. If a man is to write poetry, he must have a certain good-natured love for the Real, a simplicity of mind behind which the Absolute lies hidden.

The higher demands, imposed from above, only destroy this creative state of innocence. For the sake of nothing but poetry, they put in the place of poetry something which is, once and for all, not poetry at all. Do we not, to our dismay, see this happen all around us? . . . This is, without any further pretensions, my poetic creed.

There can be no more penetrating and satisfying summing up of Schiller's failings as a poet, but it does seem a little unfair of a father confessor to hurl back on the sinner what he himself had confessed a few years before. On August 31, 1794, Schiller had written to Goethe:

Your intention must be to simplify the vast diversity of the world of your imagination, whereas my aim is to bring some variety into my little possessions. You have to rule a kingdom, I merely a modestly large family of ideas which I sincerely hope to expand into a little universe . . . In past years . . . the poet in me used to overtake me when I should have been thinking philosophically, and the spirit of philosophy when I wished to write poetry. . . . And even now it happens often enough that my imagination interferes with my abstractions, and cold reason with my poetry.

How did Schiller, who was by the very cast of his mind the least "naturally" poetic writer among those of high poetic reputation, come to be a poet? The answer may be simple enough: because he was not allowed to become a minister of the Church. Had the then Duke of Württemberg not had his own self-willed ideas about education, and had he left it to Schiller's humble parents to make their own provisions for the professional training of their son, Schiller would, in accordance with his own wish, have been sent to a theological seminary. As it was, he grew up to make the stage his pulpit, and aesthetic theory his theology. The young boy, with the black apron of his sister for a surplice, used to preach to her from a chair; or he would stand on a hillside, blessing, "with an unforgettable expression on his face," some houses in the village beneath, cursing others. Soon his curses and blessings were to fall on creatures of his imagination. Art became the vehicle of the young man's prophetic zeal. Hiding the manuscript from the executants of a petty school-discipline, he wrote his first drama, *The Robbers.* His hero was goodness itself, tricked by a wicked society into sin, crime, and punishment.

The themes were set and were never abandoned. Whether in "Shakespearean" prose (the sometimes comic, sometimes pathetic, and only rarely fruitful misunderstanding of Shakespeare's genius which characterizes the literary productions of the German *Storm and Stress*) or in the iambic plaster casts of ancient marble images (the adaptation of Greek antiquity by a monumental freemason), almost all of Schiller's dramas hinge on rebellion, intrigue, conspiracy, the fascinating and corrupting lure of power, a sense of mission gone awry, and, issuing from it, the moral ambiguity of action. It is through such excitements, rather than through the rigid verse which hardly lends itself to rendering undertones or subtler shades, that Schiller's dramas come to life on the stage.

It has been repeated time and again that Schiller's great virtue as a dramatist is his "objectivity," the absence in his works of biographical or confessional elements. But if this is so, it is due to the fact that, to an unusual extent, Schiller's real biography is written within his soul, a soul that has hardly any "objective correlative" in the external events of his life. It is the biography of a great moralist. He achieves the powerful sentimental effects of his dramas, in spite of the impersonal and rhetorical character of his verse, by transferring to the stage, with blatant directness, the most biographical, most intimate concerns, wounds, delights, and fascinations of his soul: the conflict within himself between the moralist who dreams of saintliness, and the psychologist who sneers at the mirage of holiness, suspicious as he is of the frustrated thirst for power seeking compensatory satisfaction in moral goodness. We can see it in *Fiesco,* in *Wallenstein,* in *Maria Stuart;* even in *Wilhelm Tell* with its excessive pleading for the moral justification of an assassination; in the fragment **"Perkin Warbeck"**; and above all in what might have been, had Schiller lived to finish it, his greatest drama: *Demetrius.* In the sketch for this play, a kind of Russian Richmond, with his claim to the throne almost realized, comes to see that he is a usurper after all, and kills the man who has revealed to him the sinister secret of his illegitimacy. He is driven to murder not so much by the fear that the catastrophic news may spread as by the perverse impulse to annihilate the lie by which he has lived. "You have robbed me of my faith in myself," the notes to the play say. "I and Truth are separated forever!" It almost sounds like the outcry, dramatically heightened, of the Kantian turned poet, of the radical moralist who has tasted the forbidden fruit of the theater's glamour and power.

Schiller, in his sketches for *Demetrius,* describes the character of the hero as "the hybrid nature of a person brought up as a monk, being at the same time of knightly disposition . . . half scholar and half adventurer, in brief, a baroque, mysterious, uncanny creature." This person, it seems, would have much resembled the recent self-portraits Germany has painted of her historical personality. To imagine such a character crowned with the halo of Schiller's rhetorical brilliance means to understand the dramatist's immense popularity among nineteenth-century Germans. The German bourgeois used the fire of Schiller's moral enthusiasm to light with it the lantern which was to illumine the dimness of his own aspirations to power and self-assertion. Certainly, Schiller would not have consented; and yet he bears some faint responsibility for the illicit transaction. It was Jean Paul who described this great and noble rhetorician, this untiring moral guardian of the German stage and "aesthetic educator of man," as a "cherub with the impending Fall inscribed in his features." Schiller's "opinions"—so different from Nietzsche's in their democratic liberalism and humanitarian idealism—are "safe" enough; the menace of the "Fall" comes from his confused sensibility: the sensibility of one who is "half monk and half adventurer." And no amount of moral determination on the part of such a poet can prevent his poetry from having confusing effects.

Thus it happened that, despite his "cherubic" intentions, Schiller was destined to provide the heroic *vade mecum* for the German schoolmaster and his pupils. It was not his ideas, it was his very verse that instructed the mediocre in dramatic elocution, and taught the spiritually shallow the gestures of greatness. There is tragic irony in the fact that this high-minded idealist was posthumously accused of having perverted the moral sense of his nation. This is what Otto Ludwig wrote in the second half of the nineteenth century: "How are we Germans to attain to morality and to a proper understanding of history if our favourite poet chose to confuse our moral feeling by dressing up and sentimentalizing history with so much false idealism?" But it was more the verse than the idealism that did it.

Nietzsche too, calling Schiller the *"Moral-Trompeter von Säckingen,"* the moral trumpeter of Säckingen, and naming him among those figures whom he found "impossible," recognized the fatal role which the legacy of Schiller has played in the German body politic. "Goethe," he said, "lived and is alive for very few; for the majority he is nothing but a fanfare of vanity which from time to time is blown across the German frontier. Goethe, not only a great and good man, but a whole civilization—Goethe is in German history an accident without consequences. Who could show the slightest trace of Goethe's spirit in German politics during the last seventy years? But a great deal of Schiller has been in it. . . . "

There was only one period in which Germany had some power over English literary affairs and it is possible to say that it began one night in November 1794 when the young Coleridge sat in his room at Jesus College, Cambridge, reading a translation of Schiller's first drama, *The Robbers.* In the middle of the play he broke off and wrote to his friend Southey: "My God, Southey, who is this Schiller, this convulser of the heart? . . . I tremble like an aspen leaf. Upon my soul, I write to you because I am frightened . . . Why have we ever called Milton sublime?"

"Who is this Schiller?" German archivists have since done their best to answer Coleridge's question: Schiller's life lies as open to inspection as any that has ever been buried in immortality and scholarship. His interpreters too have expressed themselves upon their subject with a most generous neglect of economy, and have taken their cue, it would seem, from the ingenuous confession he once made to Goethe: "I allow my characters to express themselves rather profusely, even where it is undeniable that fewer words would do." And yet "Who is this Schiller?" is as unanswered now as it was on that November night at Jesus College. When Schiller died at the age of forty-six, this *medicus,* poet, dramatist, aesthetic philosopher, historian, left behind a lifework of imposing dimensions. There has been no scarcity of communication and self-expression, and yet we do not know him.

Much can be said about the difficulty of knowing other minds, and much more than can be said has in fact been said about the impossibility of knowing the nature of genius. In the case of Goethe, for instance, it is a measure of the fineness of our perception whether or not in the end we come to see and respect the intangible barrier which protects the core of his person from our intrigued curiosity. Compared with him, Schiller hardly withholds a secret from us. Strange, very strange, that we are nonetheless on

more intimate terms with Goethe's mysteriousness, or with Kleist's distraught imagination, or even with Hölderlin's luminous obscurity, than we are with Schiller's blatant articulateness. We seem to have become such accomplished readers of the perplexities of the spirit, the intricacies of the mind, the ambiguities of poetic diction, the symbolic smoulderings of the unconscious, that we are shocked into incomprehension by the plainly comprehensible—or, rather, by what would be plainly comprehensible if our minds were still able to respond with loyal seriousness to our idealist-humanist tradition and its lucid declarations of meanings, virtues, and vices. Schiller is an embarrassment to us because he is singularly unembarrassed by this tradition. He is its truest poetic genius: the genius of literalness. For him everything is what our language suggests it is. He takes the world at its word. Hence he is often confused but never ambiguous; and when he writes for the theater, he is unscrupulously theatrical; when he has something to teach, he is unashamedly didactic; and when a speech is called for in a scene, he indulges in rhetoric without inhibition. Clearly, he is not a "modern" poet. His poetry reflects the belief (and among his contemporaries he is one of the very few in whom this belief is still amazingly intact) that rhyme and reason are attributes possessed by the world itself, and not something that has to be conquered in ever renewed expeditions into yet untried regions below the threshold of human consciousness or above the common intimations of language. Indeed, he is a "classic" if ever there was one.

This immensely intelligent man, who endlessly reflected upon his poetic creations and who all his life envied Goethe his creative spontaneity—a gift which, in his justly most celebrated essay, he called "naïveté"—this man was yet in a sense incomparably more "naïve" than the older friend. For he believed, unsmilingly and instinctively, in a universe made to support the big, clean, resounding nouns of our intellectual and moral history: Freedom, Bondage; Truth, Untruth; Goodness, Evil; Beauty, Ugliness. He was more *literally* an idealist than any writer writing in the age of German Idealism, and was more *literally* great—greater, not better—than any great poet. Goethe sensed this when he said that Schiller was great in whatever he did—"at the tea-table as much as he would have been in the Council of State." And once, in the last year of his life, Goethe harshly rebuked Ottilie, his beloved daughter-in-law, for finding Schiller sometimes boring: "You are all far too small for him," he said, "too much of this earth."

But this is misleading. It might suggest that Schiller was the owner of an undisturbed seraphic vision. No, he *was* of this earth; very much so. His *Wallenstein* is the only drama written after Shakespeare that shows a profound *political* imagination. Also, he knew with clinical precision how to "convulse the heart" and how to administer dramatic intoxicants to even the most stubbornly sober audiences. Goethe, somewhat unproudly but not unwisely, once left it to him to adapt his *Egmont* for the stage, and then found it extremely difficult to prevent Schiller from perpetrating the most violent acts of theatrical demagogy. And how adept he was, this master of sublimity, in the manufacture of homely platitudes! He had no equal in producing proverbs, all of them as practical as, say, that of the stitch in time which will save nine. Not of this earth? And yet Goethe was true and just when, in his Epilogue to Schiller's **"Song of the Bell"**—that grandly resounding structure of metallic banalities—he celebrated the memory of his dead friend by saying of him:

> *Denn hinter ihm, in wesenlosem Scheine,*
> *Lag, was uns alle bändigt, das Gemeine.*

It means that Schiller had freed himself from the base and common world which binds us all. Indeed, it is hard to know him.

Schiller was sixteen when he was first deeply wounded by not being known and understood. It happened in that austere academy where only three years later he produced **The Robbers**—the fulfillment of his young ambition to write a work "which absolutely must be burnt by the hangman." He was devoted to a fellow-pupil, the hero of some of his earliest poems. But the passionate friendship came to an end: the friend gave notice. He found he could not believe any more in Schiller. His whole being, he said, was "merely a poem"; all his sentiments, whether they concerned God, religion, or friendship, were "only theater," dramatizations of imagined feelings, feelings not truly felt by a Christian or by a friend, but conceived by a poet for the sake of poetry. Schiller was desperate; and as if to show his incomprehension of his friend's distrust, he protested the genuineness of his heart in a letter aglow with poetic frenzy and dramatic indignation.

Was he genuine? Overpoweringly so; and sixteen. And the other boy—was he a little philistine, unable, even at so naturally romantic an age, to have mercy upon the finer affections? Not necessarily; he may have been merely estranged by what is strange, and puzzled by our puzzle: that someone should *feel* ideally and *live* by the truths of poetry, and yet *know* that the ideal and the poetic are not the truths of life. And Schiller must have loved him truly and knowingly: in retrospect at least it seems as if his own mind had become indissolubly married there and then to the friend's suspicious mind. For what, if not this early falling-out, this youthful sad encounter between the aspirations of the soul and the rebuffs of disbelief, between **"Das Ideal und das Leben,"** the ideal and life (to name one of his most celebrated philosophical poems)—what if not this is the dominant theme of that endless debate which Schiller conducts in his dramas as well as in his philosophical speculations?

He knew two things with absolute certainty—a certainty which time and again exasperated Goethe, and time and again Goethe admired. Schiller knew what man *ought* to be, and he knew that man *was not* what he ought to be; and he believed that in the dialogue between this "ought" and this "was not" lay the only significant drama of human life; that it was the dramatist's business to voice this drama and no other; and that no knowledge of what man "really" was could produce poetry—save the knowledge which above everything else comprehended what man was really *meant* to be. And for Schiller the only repository of such knowledge was the mind of poetry. But— was the indisputably most poetic mind of the epoch, was Goethe's mind cast in this mold? Most decidedly not. In-

deed, it seems that Schiller had to win Goethe's friendship in order not to be crushed by his superior "otherness." We need only read what they said about each other before they became friends: Goethe was aloof and hostile. He regarded Schiller's early success in the theater as one of the deplorable symptoms of Germany's lack of natural culture, and looked upon Schiller as a restless agitator, abstract speculator, and enemy of Nature. Schiller, on the other hand, admired *and* hated Goethe. Less than five years before their friendship began, he confessed that he felt about Goethe as Brutus and Cassius felt about Caesar: "I could murder his spirit and yet love it again with all my heart. I am most anxious to know what he thinks of me . . . and as I shall never ask him myself, I shall surround him with eavesdroppers." (A very Schillerian remark. Had he been a lesser artist, he would have inaugurated the genre of detective fiction.) To be with Goethe for any length of time would surely make him unhappy; for Goethe, he thought, was cold, egotistical, elusive; he had no beliefs, no convictions, and dismissed all philosophical ideas as necessarily "subjective." In short, Goethe was ironical and "artistic," and he would never have any spontaneous sympathy with Schiller's transcendent faith in art.

Goethe never had. How could he? His own "poetic creed" he once defined in a manner that could not but have hurt Schiller. It was in the letter in which, as we have seen, he spoke of "a certain good-natured love for the Real" as the condition *sine qua non* of poetic genius, and of the "higher demands, imposed from above" as destructive of the creative state of innocence. And this he wrote at the height of their friendship. The pronouncement merely enlarged upon a point that Schiller himself had made, but the eagerness and finality with which Goethe uttered it must have struck home a little too forcibly. "Good-natured love for the Real," "creative innocence"—Goethe could hardly have done better if he had wished to define poetry as something unattainable by Schiller.

It was an intriguing friendship: noble and yet rich in tension. They certainly respected and admired each other, but Goethe did so with his eyebrows often raised and with an occasional shaking of his head at Schiller's incessant "higher demands"; and on Schiller's part there was a considerable measure of diplomacy, just as if he had aimed at insuring the balance of power in the realm of German literature. True, in his essay on **"Naïve and Sentimental Poetry"** he pays homage to Goethe's surpassing genius; but his very praise is tinged with an element of power-politics. For the "creative state of innocence," or the "naïveté"—in fact, Goethe's genius—emerges at the end of the essay as an all but outdated blessing, a kind of prelapsarian regression and a splendid whim of history, almost freakish in its uniqueness. On the other hand, the "sentimental poet"— and his name is Schiller—is awarded ample damages for the loss of his poetic spontaneity and the pains of self-consciousness: he is to inherit the future. Here and now he may have to tread more warily: for he sees before his eyes the gulf that time and consciousness have fixed between the "higher demands" of the poetic ideal and the spontaneous flow of poetry on earth. Yet in the end he will be the begetter of a new and higher "naïveté": an Adam Hercules who will outwit the serpent, uproot the tree of knowledge, and replant it in the safer ground of *knowing* innocence. The break between the ideal and life, poetry and truth, sentiment and consciousness, will be healed through him, the wounded, the "sentimental" poet. Let then the naïve bury the naïve; and that boy from the academy will at last believe in his consciously conceived poetic feelings. It is a scheme of heroic grandeur—with an element in it of sublime roguery.

For the time being, the "sentimental" poet has the harder life. "What I am," Schiller once wrote, "I am through the often unnatural exertion of all my strength"; and he suffered no more grievous affliction, he said, than the knowledge that he was not what he desired to be. This is spoken with that young unbelieving voice from the past—and with the voice of the dramatist who was irresistibly drawn toward that tragic consummation which occurs when a man comes to know that he was not what he believed he was—that he was not what he ought to have been. This is as much as to say that Schiller was the tragic poet of Idealism. For it is the potential tragedy of Idealism that in the last resolve it cannot be absolutely certain of its certitudes: it lacks the ultimate sanction of a theological faith. Hence the question arises: how real is the Idealist's idea of man? Is it lodged in the mind of a Creator who possesses perfect Reality? Or is it merely a creation of man's own creative imagination, a projection of his need to think well of himself? Is it true—or "merely poetry?" Must it come to grief when all of the illusions are gone and man is forced by tragic circumstance at last to know—to know himself? Or will he prove the truth of the ideal by dying into its sublimity? The soul suspended between these two extremes—this makes for the dramatic suspense of many dramas by Friedrich Schiller. And if he but rarely convinces us with his sublime solutions, and if he is nowhere more poetic than in his heroes' disillusionments—well, he was an idealist, but also an artist and an honest man.

In *Don Carlos,* for instance, it is not the prince's somewhat confused innocence that most deeply engages our sympathy; nor is it Marquis de Posa's liberal manifestos; and it is not this noble and single-minded plotter's final (and rather forced) bid for sublimity. No, the tragic climax of the drama is the destruction of King Philip's faith in man, in the one man he had trusted: Marquis de Posa. And where is tragedy to be found in *Wallenstein,* where did Schiller himself find it, after much searching in this, as he thought, "truly unthankful," "unpoetic," and utterly "unmalleable material"? In the young Piccolomini's discovery that the ideal is not true, that man is mean, that Wallenstein is a traitor. In his last years, Schiller's choice of subject matters was guided more and more by his ambition to enact this drama, this conspiracy of the real against the ideal, not through a clash between two characters but within a single soul. For none of his plays did he show as much affection as for his *Maid of Orleans.* Time and again he said that it came "straight from the heart"; and the more it came from the heart, the less it came from history. For the tragedy of his Joan is not consummated in the fire of the Inquisition. She burns in her own Hell: she comes to know that she is not what she believed she was, not what she was meant to be. She thought that God had raised her above all womankind to love only Him, His

Saints, and France; but she had remained a woman and fell in love with a man, an enemy of God and her country. She was defeated not by her adversaries; her self-discovery was her undoing.

How right, poetically, and yet how uncomprehending were the most distinguished critics of *The Maid of Orleans!* Goethe, who had congratulated Schiller on this "incomparably good and beautiful play," observed later in his diary that the drama was decisively flawed: Joan, he said, should have been taught by some ensuing catastrophe that by falling in love with Lionel she had betrayed her mission and thus become guilty; it was a mistake that she should be conscious of it at the time. And Hebbel too noted in his diary: "In no circumstances should Joan have reflected about herself. She should have fulfilled her destiny with her eyes closed, like a sleep-walker." *The Maid of Orleans* might be a better drama if it were what Goethe and Hebbel wished it to be; but it would not be Schiller's drama. In Schiller's drama there had to be this fall from grace into articulate self-consciousness. Had Schiller lived to finish his last drama *Demetrius,* he would most probably have written a greater play than *The Maid of Orleans,* a tragedy still more his own. Radiant with faith in himself, and heroic in his idealist zeal against the usurper, Demetrius was to discover, as we have seen, that he too had no legitimate claim to the throne, that he too was a usurper; and he was to kill the only witness of the truth. That sentence from *Demetrius,* "I and Truth are separated forever," comprises all the fear and terror of Schiller's tragic inspiration. And its hope? He once described to Wilhelm von Humboldt his vision of a final apotheosis of the ideal:

> Everything that is mortal is dissolved, nothing but light, nothing but freedom . . . no shadow, no barrier . . . It makes me feel giddy to think of this task: . . . to compose a scene on Olympus . . . I am not quite despondent. I may do it one day when my mind is wholly free and cleansed from the pollution of the real world. Then I shall gather once again all my strength and all that is ethereal in my nature even if I have to exhaust it all in writing this work.

It is surprising that even a first contact with Schiller's *Robbers* made Coleridge doubt whether Milton had a right to be called sublime; but in the undergraduate ebullience of his judgment, he yet grasped something of Schiller's distinction. What is it that makes it hard for us to know him? Is it his idealist manner of aspiring to sublimity? Or is it simply the distance that separates the sublime from *"das Gemeine,"* from "the base and common"? The latter is more likely: for little has happened to reduce this distance since Goethe wrote that valediction to his friend. (pp. 47-72)

> *Erich Heller, "In Two Minds About Schiller,"
> in his* The Artist's Journey into the Interior
> and Other Essays, *Random House, 1965, pp.
> 47-72.*

## Wilhelm Emrich   (essay date 1968)

[*In the following essay, originally published in German in 1968, Emrich explores contradictions in Schiller's thought and works, finding that Schiller was "neither an idealist nor a realist, but both together."*]

At the Schiller celebrations in 1859 the whole nation was at one in paying the poet a unique tribute that far outshone even the posthumous fame of his friend Goethe. But an examination of literary developments since then shows that Schiller's writing and thought have suffered a progressive devaluation. The critical attack has been directed at the very heart and substance of his poetry. Roughly speaking, the contention is that what Schiller wrote was not poetry, but rhetoric. He is held to have known nothing of the hidden side of poetry, of the element of the unspoken, the unbidden, in poetic expression. He is considered to lack the lyric charm of Goethe's poetry, the mysterious depth of Goethe's characters. His work is said to be all intent and purpose, loud grandiloquence, obvious and deliberate intellectual manipulation, and planned construction. The emotionalism of his language is felt to be unconvincing, his characters to be unnatural, mere fantasies of the mind, exaggeratedly idealistic or satanic, and his images and similes artificial and unorganic. And even his supreme mastery of dramatic technique and stage effects is said to have overreached itself in the invention of the most improbable plots and elaborate complications.

Intimately related to all this is the criticism of the spiritual content of his poetry, of what is known as Schiller's "idealism." Just as Schiller's language sacrificed everything individual to the universal and transformed the voice of the personal soul into a didactic general maxim, so, it is felt, did his idealism preclude any genuine tragic conflict without issue, since it sheltered the catastrophes of his heroes under a saving heaven of transcendental ideas, destroyed the tragedy of individual human life which a dramatist like, say, Heinrich von Kleist carried through to its utmost limit and inevitable end. Thus Schiller was, in the last resort, not a tragic poet. He had never penetrated to the very depths of the "concrete situation of human existence," either in suffering or in expression. His poetry was made of human ideas instead of human life. Hence it is not surprising that, with the ascendancy of vitalism and later of existentialism in the present century, Schiller's star has sunk more and more; in his place Goethe, seemingly closer to life and nature, or Kleist and Hölderlin, interpreted in existentialist terms, increasingly came to the fore and indeed were often played off against Schiller.

At the same time there has been no lack of attempts at rescue operations. Efforts have been made to demonstrate a so-called realistically tragic turn in Schiller's later period, in **Wallenstein** and above all in the **Demetrius** fragment, which relates him to Kleist; but clearly this argument completely misses the point about Schiller's own individual approach and, in reality, discredits it.

The fundamental cause of all these misconceptions and futile rescue operations is to be found not in Schiller, but in ourselves—that is to say, in the conceptions and lines of thought that have evolved during the past century or so and have come to determine our present-day consciousness and feeling. Let us set aside our prejudices and ask ourselves whether we, for our own part, measure up to the greatness of Schiller's thought and poetry; such self-criticism will suddenly reveal Schiller not only as a classical poet "who pleased the greatest masters of his time," but as one belonging to "all times"—and more especially to our own time with its spiritual, moral, and political crises, for which Schiller has a store of answers and interpretations pointing far beyond anything now usually proffered by the exalters of ineluctable tragedy or masochistic doomsday attitudes.

It is true that Schiller is the poet of the universal, and not, like Goethe, of man as an individual developing organically into typical forms in accordance with his own inner law. But for Schiller it is the universal that is our destiny; it is society, the state, history, our reality itself. To withstand it, know it, master it, and translate it into a reality of humane living was Schiller's most pressing concern in all his works, from the social criticism of his early dramas through his great historical works to the late history plays, **Wallenstein, Mary Stuart, The Maid of Orleans, William Tell,** and the **Demetrius** fragment. At stake are the great themes of mankind, not merely the tragedies of individual life:

> For only some grand theme will have the force
> To stir the deeper reaches of mankind.
> Man's thought is shrunken by a narrow round,
> But as his aims are greater, so he grows.
> Now to its solemn end the century draws,
> When poetry finds matter in the real,
> When we behold the clash of mighty souls
> Over a worthy goal, when struggles rage
> For what is greatest among human themes,
> Freedom and domination. And now art
> Upon its shadow stage may set itself
> To reach for higher flights—indeed it must,
> Or else be put to shame by life's own stage.

Art, then, is to be measured against reality itself; it has to prove itself in the face of the conflicts of its time. But historical reality is seen in a perspective entirely different from that to which we are now accustomed. The aim is not, as in the great masterpieces of historism, to describe the separate forces and personalities of history, to define their own evolution and, as it were, explain them from within, nor to understand each epoch and phenomenon as a unique, individual event. In terms of his naive-sentimental syzygy, Schiller would have considered such an objective, fact-oriented view of history as naive thinking, as a naive surrender to facts that deprives the observer of any point of view of his own and leads to the relativization of historical reality, to a neutral acceptance of man's historical deeds and misdeeds without reference to their value, and thus to the neglect and ultimate abolition of every absolute human value, of every moral judgment in the course of history. For to understand everything is to forgive everything.

However, Schiller was not a critical moralist in the narrow sense in which Nietzsche defined and attacked him. Unlike the pragmatic historians of the eighteenth century and present-day public opinion, he did not evaluate history from a one-sided moralizing or ideological standpoint, which in its turn is historically conditioned. Rather was he concerned with the fundamental "critical" definition of the a priori conditions of human history and reality themselves. He wanted to bring to light the a priori contradictions that are necessary constituents of human existence and the reconciliation of which is the origin both of the course and the unity of human life and history. Schiller's purpose in his philosophical writings was to gain insight into the general, antinomic unity of human and historical reality common to all epochs.

What, actually, is man? What, actually, is historical reality? How can man achieve his own integration? How is historical reality to be shaped to make possible a life worthy of man? These are the crucial questions in Schiller's work. In the passage quoted above from the prologue to *Wallenstein,* he says that the struggle for domination and freedom is the great theme of poetry; this struggle, which he treated in all his plays, is likewise concerned with the fundamental "critical" problem of what are the human conditions that necessarily lead to forms of domination and demands for freedom, and what the anthropological and social conditions by which these conflicts may again and again be overcome and reconciled.

---

[Schiller's] aim is to bring into consciousness the universal truth of our social and political reality, a truth unknown because it is concealed and distorted by our individual feelings, experiences, and destinies; in consequence, his language is passionately rhetorical, it elevates to a level of principle every personal particular, and with its very passion summons mankind to liberation— to concrete, real liberation, not a mere dream.

—*Wilhelm Emrich*

---

In his **"On the Aesthetic Education of Man"** (in a series of letters) Schiller analyzed these basic conditions as follows: Man, being possessed of the power to know, to investigate, to control nature, carries within himself the conditions for attaining the highest degree of freedom and self-determination, and also for falling prey to the basest slavery and self-disintegration. For the more man advances in the direction of understanding—knowing and freely creating his world—the more does this world of his become multifarious, fragmented, manifold, and the more does he become dependent upon his own creation and lose his unity and freedom.

> This antagonism of forces is the great instrument of civilization. . . . Civilization, far from setting us free, merely creates a new need with every force it develops in us. . . . The inner bond of human nature was broken and the harmony of its forces disrupted by a pernicious conflict as soon as, on the one hand, a sharper distinction among the sciences was made necessary by wider experience and more precise thinking, and on the other a stricter separation of the estates and trades by the more intricate mechanism of states. [Individual, independent life] now gave way to an ingenious clockwork where a mechanical, collective life is generated by the assemblage of innumerable, but lifeless parts. State and Church were torn asunder, so too the law and morality; pleasure was divorced from work, means from ends, effort from reward. Bound eternally to a single, minute fragment of the whole, man himself became a mere fragment; with nothing in his ears but the eternal monotonous rumbling of the wheel he trod, man never developed his natural harmony, and instead of minting the likeness of humanity in himself, he turned into a mere cast of his trade or science. But even the scant, fragmentary association by which the separate units are still linked to the whole does not depend on forms of their own choice and making, but is rigorously prescribed for them by a schedule in which their free judgment is confined. The dead letter replaces the living intelligence, and a practiced memory is a safer guide than genius and sensibility. . . . Thus, gradually, individual concrete life is exterminated to provide a scant subsistence for the abstract whole, and the state remains forever alien to its citizens, because their heart finds no way to it. The governing fraction, obliged as it is to make the variety of citizens more manageable by classification, and to deal with people only at one remove through their representatives, at last loses sight of them completely by confounding them with a mere intellectual construction. In their turn, the subjects can feel nothing but indifference for laws which take so little account of them.

This description might well have been written today. It is an inimitably striking anticipation of the whole problem of modern technology, division of labor, bureaucracy, and the machinery of government. For this problem is an inevitable consequence of man's own nature and of the necessities of life. "The compulsion of needs" and man's attempts to master these needs through wider knowledge lead to the situation described, to that "antagonism of forces," in every civilization, even though it is true that in the twentieth century the antagonism has been intensified to a degree unimaginable in the past. Thus, according to Schiller, the forms of state and society, ancient and modern alike, stem from man's physical necessities, from the attempt to ensure his survival amid external nature. For this reason, Schiller gave the collective name of "natural state" or "need-conditioned state" to all these historical forms of state and society. "But man, as a moral being, could not and cannot be satisfied with the need-conditioned state which is the result of man's place in nature and devised for that alone—and woe to him if he could!" Man as a moral being demands a higher form of state and society, one in which he can freely and completely develop the fullness of his powers, and which, as it were, allows the perfect realization of what is essentially human in man's nature. It is true that this higher form of state and society, or, for that matter, this human perfection, this higher "natural condition" of man, does not actually exist anywhere in the real world, but it is an aim and purpose set to man, an idea originating of necessity in man's rational disposition, demanded by his reason. The consciousness of such a higher aim is the source of all mankind's great movements for political and social freedom. "This," said Schiller, with an obvious allusion to the French Revolution, "is the genesis and justification of the attempt of a nation come of age to convert its natural state into a moral one."

At the same time, however, Schiller elaborates on the unavoidable difficulties, the fatal outcome, of all revolutionary liberation movements.

> Whereas physical man is *real,* moral man is merely *problematical.* When reason abolishes the natural state, as it necessarily must if it is to replace it by its own, then it risks physical, real man for the sake of a problematical moral man, it risks the existence of society for the sake of a merely potential (even if morally necessary) ideal of society. It takes from man something he really possesses, and proposes to him instead something he could or should possess. Thus the great difficulty is that the continuity in time of physical society must not for a moment be interrupted while moral society is forming as an idea, that man's existence must not be endangered for the sake of his dignity. When a craftsman has to mend a clock he lets the wheels run down to a stop, but the living clockwork of the state has to be mended while it strikes the hour, and the task is to replace the moving wheel as it revolves.

Here Schiller states with the utmost clarity the contradictions between revolution and concrete society, between idea and reality, indeed the basic tragedy of human history. Schiller has no intention of sacrificing reality to idea, but neither does he mean to betray the idea for the sake of reality. He is neither an idealist nor a realist, but both together. Physical man, pursuing only his needs, instincts, purposes, and immediate advantages, is for Schiller a "savage" who just lets things drift and who uncritically puts up with the existing order of the natural, need-conditioned state and thereby obstructs any kind of "higher humanity." But the man of abstract reason, the idealist who tries to subjugate reality to his ideas, to sacrifice the natural state to the ideal state, is for Schiller a "barbarian" who meddles destructively with nature and society, suppresses them with the tyrannical law of his idea and his moral demands, and thus uses moral man to annihilate natural man. In short, the idea of freedom becomes the source of servitude, and the ideal state a tyranny.

The savage and the barbarian—these are precisely the constantly recurring manifestations of modern civilized man. In state and society the one finds expression in unbridled, irresponsible decadence and in the exploitations of *laissez-faire, laissez-aller,* and the other in the rigid, revolutionary suppression of the individual and of actual society.

Both alternatives, the physical urge to live and the pursuit of the ideal, are intrinsic to man, who is at once nature and spirit. Each excludes the other, yet man is not complete without both. It follows that each must be both negated

and affirmed. On the one hand, reason must abolish the historically real, natural, and need-conditioned state, physical society as such; it must take from man what he really is, for the sake of the problematical, ideal ultimate aim. On the other hand, reason must affirm and uphold precisely the existence of physical society, so as not to destroy it, and hence destroy man as well.

To master this paradoxical situation is the essential problem of Schiller's tragedies and thought. It runs through his discussion of the concepts of the naive and the sentimental, of grace and dignity, ancient and modern, and it appears in the problem of guilt in his tragedies, in which moral man enforcing his moral demands sins against natural man and his real physical society, just as, conversely, natural realistic man sins against the ideal. The profundity of this conception of guilt lies in its arising of necessity from man's nature and his historical reality, with the result that in Schiller's late works this guilt took on the characteristics of invincible fate.

Schiller's classicism lies in his mastery of this paradox without sacrificing either idea or reality, without betraying man's freedom and yet without any Utopian transgression of his natural conditions and limits. His classical balance, his model classicism, consists in the maintenance of tragic tension, of the eternal antagonism in man and society, that is to say in an uncompromising critical protest against every fixed, unambiguous position that might threaten and abolish the wholeness of man and his very humanity.

This becomes clear in Schiller's solutions. The problem he set himself was how to mend the living mechanism of the state while it is running, how to replace the moving wheel while it revolves, how to make the idea alter human society without endangering its very existence. According to Schiller, this can be done neither by the natural nor the moral quality of man, but only by a third quality "which is related to both" and mediates between them. If state and society are dominated by ideas and principles, the result is intolerance, party strife, ideological conflict, blindness to the essential nature of one's fellow men and to the actual circumstances of life in its ever changing reality. If state and society are dominated solely by considerations of material ends and utility, by the pursuit of physical, material gain and personal advantage, the result is chaos and brute irresponsibility. Both situations, which in modern life govern public and private affairs alike to an unimaginable extent, are, for Schiller, an expression of extreme inhumanity, of savagery and barbarism. Both can be overcome only by being negated and simultaneously affirmed, each in its respective antithesis. Principles must no longer be seen in isolation to be faced, as it were, as something other than man, as a law, a commandment, a transcendental idea, but must instead become manifest in their antithesis, in the sensual nature of man itself, that is, they must be lived, must find direct expression in man's nature and actions and in his whole attitude, as though they were his second nature. Conversely, man's sensual nature attains its own fullness only in its antithesis, when it is integrated into consciousness and thereby acquires intellectual and spiritual significance. Only that makes humanity possible, enables people to live together, to respect their fellow men's different opinions and indeed their being different, and to understand each other's nature. For when spiritual principles are actually lived, when we really encounter them in an individual and find them expressed in his very nature, they inspire respect, regard, and love, just as man's sensual nature can be understood and loved only when it is a manifest characteristic of his spiritual and intellectual personality. This means that the gulf between moral demands and nature is bridged, and there is hope, too, for the successful transformation of the natural, need-conditioned state into a moral state. The revolutionary's moral demands will continually readjust themselves in the light of the actual nature and potentialities of society, and in turn the irresponsibility of sensual man, who uncritically follows his nature or submits to things as they are, will readjust itself in the light of an idea of humanity which, like a tacit challenge, marks every human encounter and alone makes it possible. This third quality, in which man's moral and sensual qualities interpenetrate each other, is called by Schiller "aesthetic," because the aesthetic form confers on everything sensual a spiritual significance and on everything spiritual a natural appearance.

But it would be a complete misunderstanding of the aesthetic education of man to suppose that Schiller wanted all people to be brought up as artists or even as aesthetes. Rather, what is required is something much deeper and sterner. What is required of moral, spiritual man is ceaseless criticism and self-criticism of his own ideas, lest for lack of the breath of life they become fixed and rigid and thereby vitiate or even imperil the wholeness of man and his society. And what is required of physical man is the transformation of his natural instincts into spiritual, free self-determination, for only then can he enter into the estate of man in the true sense of the word.

Since, in practice, people always have both a natural and a spiritual side, man himself and his society are faced with both requirements simultaneously; that is, natural, sensual man must not be sacrificed to an idea, nor spiritual and moral man to nature. The road to humanity, which was the final aim of all Schiller's exertions, resembles a path along a mountain crest, where every step into a comfortable, unambiguous position has to be paid for by a fall into inhumanity. When freedom seeks to prevail in its pure, exclusive form, it turns into serfdom. When nature is left entirely to itself and rejects every spiritual and moral refinement, it turns into chaos.

Schiller's tragedies are above all demonstrations of such continual inner alternations. They show to what perils a truly humane way of life is exposed, but also show that it is possible. This is true as much of his first work, *Die Räuber,* in which human law and order are destroyed by the rational, coldly calculating Franz Moor no less than by the impulsive Karl Moor, who spontaneously obeys his natural urge for freedom, as of Schiller's last work, the *Demetrius* fragment, in which Demetrius, inspired by faith in his higher destiny and historical mission, is appalled when he suddenly realizes that his birth and nature by no means make him the direct incarnation of this mission, and thereupon tries to force his idea upon his nature. Another example is the narrow path which Fiesco treads between a humane desire for freedom and a personal desire for power—so much so that Schiller wrote several versions of the drama, in which first one aspect and then the other predominated. It will be recalled, too, how in *Mary Stuart* the two opponents, Mary and Elizabeth, are torn by the conflict between instinct and morality, between humanity and the interests of the state. In general, the mature Schiller, from *Wallenstein* on, was more and more at pains to develop the double nature in his main heroes; thus, his idealized Piccolomini is overshadowed by the complex central character of Wallenstein, whereas in the early works the writer's sympathies still clearly lie with Karl Moor, Ferdinand, or Don Carlos and their idealistic passion for freedom, even though he was consistent enough to condemn these heroes to failure in their conflict with the actual order of society. It may be said of Schiller's plays that they are exceedingly elaborate symbols and changing constellations of the ever unchanging conflict within man and his history. Likewise, the language and construction of Schiller's plays can be understood only by accepting them as exemplary, paradigmatic symbols, rather than naively as mere representations of the real world. The seemingly artificial construction of these plays, the improbable web of intrigue in, say, *Fiesco, Love and Intrigue,* or *Don Carlos,* and the confrontation of this web of intrigue with his doomed heroes' ideal passion for freedom and love are precisely the expression, the symbols, of the irreconcilable contrasts that occur every day in our political and social life, of the machinery in which humanity is destroyed, of the purposeful calculations on which freedom and love founder. But Schiller does the reverse as well, lets the machinery come to grief on itself—witness the despair and human desolation which are the lot of his coldly calculating plotters; and thus, in the annihilation of both protagonists, Schiller invokes the quest for a possible reconciliation of the conflict that determines man's nature and history, and in which we are locked just as much as Schiller's contemporaries.

It follows that the emotionalism of Schiller's plays—the seemingly artificial construction and inorganic quality not only of his plots, but also of his language—arises from an unsparing revelation of the truth of our historical reality itself. The poet's aim is to bring into consciousness the universal truth of our social and political reality, a truth unknown because it is concealed and distorted by our individual feelings, experiences, and destinies; in consequence, his language is passionately rhetorical, it elevates to a level of principle every personal particular, and with its very passion summons mankind to liberation—to concrete, real liberation, not a mere dream. Wrote Schiller in his foreword to *The Bride of Messina:*

> The purpose of genuine art is not a mere passing show; it seeks in earnest not just to give man a momentary dream of freedom, but to set him truly and really free. And for the very reason that genuine art is concerned with something real and objective, it cannot rest content with the semblance of truth; its ideal edifice is built upon truth itself, upon the firm, deep foundations of nature. Thus art is simultaneously both wholly ideal and in the most profound sense real.

Therefore the less today's generation allows itself to be blinded by delusions in coming to terms with the hidden causes of the crisis in contemporary political and social life, and the more resolutely youth cares about the realization of human freedom—not just blaming our cultural crisis on this or that so-called historical factor, nor retreating with lamentations into personal concerns or "existential insecurity"—the more will Schiller's significance again grow in stature. For the antinomies that Schiller dramatized in his plays are those of our own society. (pp. 79-95)

> *Wilhelm Emrich, "Schiller and the Antinomies of Human Society," in his* The Literary Revolution and Modern Society and Other Essays, *translated by Alexander Henderson and Elizabeth Henderson, Frederick Ungar Publishing Co., 1971, pp. 79-95.*

### Alan Menhennet   (essay date 1973)

[*In the following excerpt, Menhennet discusses Schiller's later dramas.*]

After **Don Carlos** (1787), there followed a more than ten-year gap in Schiller's serious dramatic production, until **Wallenstein.** In the interim, he was going through the period of self-training and self-discipline which finally put him into a position to realize the Classical ideal, which he had meanwhile consolidated in himself in theoretical form, in terms of practical drama. **Carlos,** the product of a long period of gestation, had, admittedly, begun to show the signs of a firmer approach in the change to blank verse and in greater objectivity in the treatment of issues and characters. But it is still predominantly a subjective play and the elements of order (e.g. the objective portrait of the king, the self-discipline of the queen) are not by any means an equal counterweight to the rampant idealism and passion of Posa and Carlos, to the impulse towards freedom in general. The extreme degree of self-identification with his hero which led Schiller in the initial stages to refer to him as 'to a certain extent, taking the place of a sweetheart' was certainly modified, but not to the extent of providing a sufficient counterweight to the—to our taste—excessive warmth of his emotions. True, Posa shows him a less self-indulgent outlet for these, but the heat of passion is not abated. In the scene (Act II, scene 2) in which the young and passionate Carlos confronts the old and chilly king, there is nothing to indicate that Schiller disapproves of the extravagance of his hero's feelings. Goethe, in the exchange between the subjective idealist Tasso and the objective realist Antonio maintains a much better balance, though his sympathies are largely on Tasso's side. In the period that elapsed between **Don Carlos** and **Wallenstein,** Schiller achieved much greater objectivity. In the confrontation between Wallenstein and Max in Act II scene 2 of **Wallensteins Tod,** he even allows the former to administer a chastening rebuke to Max, the apple of his eye:

> Schnell fertig ist die Jugend mit dem Wort,
> Das schwer sich handhabt, wie des Messers Schneide,
> Aus ihrem heissen Kopfe nimmt sie keck
> Der Dinge Mass, die nur sich selber richten.

Schiller's ability to see Wallenstein objectively and with understanding is the best symbol of the advance he has made since **Don Carlos.** There, the king, even if he was given some measure of humanity, remained in the last analysis a tyrant, seen from the outside, and without deep sympathy. That the new objectivity was not entirely easy to achieve or maintain is certainly true and we shall look, together with **Wallenstein,** at the play in which the Classical balance was most seriously threatened by the by no means extinct volcano within, namely **Die Jungfrau von Orleans.**

Throughout his Classical period, Schiller worked on his subjects with great conscientiousness, using historical sources wherever appropriate, seeking to build up his plays with solidity and individual life while at the same time serving the other master, the ideal. He was never a realist in the proper sense of the word, not even in **Wallenstein,** which was written in the consciousness that 'the poet, like the artist in general, must distance himself in a public and honest way from actuality', but he did not wish altogether to lose contact with 'nature' and with the sense of objective reality. Thus he took considerable trouble to maintain the 'objective and definite' quality which attracted him to historical material in the first place. He sought works on astrology from Körner to help him with the figure of Seni in **Wallenstein** and read the seventeenth-century preacher Abraham a Sancta Clara in order to find the right tone for the Capuchin's harangue in **Wallensteins Lager,** the prelude to the tragedy. Plays like **Maria Stuart** have more of a sense of locality about them than had **Die Räuber,** even though the locality in question was much further removed from Schiller in space and time.

In addition, characters of what Schiller would have called an 'unpoetic' type and function, like Burleigh in **Maria Stuart** or Illo and Terzky in **Wallenstein,** are given a degree of independent life and colour that they would never have had in the 'Sturm und Drang' plays, where the dominance of the central figures is much more marked. The 'poetic' quality here, i.e. the quality which conforms to the higher, ideal demands of art, would have to come from the 'form', the manner in which the material was presented. The main characters and action of the latter play had never had an appeal for him in themselves: it was, as he wrote to Goethe (1 December 1797), a 'prosaic' material. The tug-of-war between this and his own innate idealizing tendency may have been what led here to the best example in all his dramatic work of synthesis between freedom and order, or, to use his own formulation in a letter to Körner, power and control.

The situation was very different with **Die Jungfrau von Orleans.** While the play still demanded long and hard work from him, it was not, in this case, because of any lack of spiritual sustenance in the material. This was, as he put it to Körner, 'poetic to a very high degree', and it buoyed him up through the donkey-work of his historical researches. In his poem '**Das Mädchen von Orleans**', Schiller addresses Joan: 'The world loves to blacken that which shines and to drag the sublime in the dust; but have no fear! There are still hearts of unsullied spiritual beauty ('schöne Herzen') which are fired with love for what is high and glorious.' Schiller's was such a heart, and in this play he wrote more directly from the heart than in any other Classical drama. As a result we find that, if the Classical balance is upset anywhere, it is here, in favour of freedom. Figures like Countess Terzky and Buttler in **Wallenstein** have their grandeur and 'beauty', but this has nothing to do with their moral characters. In the **Jungfrau,** the figure most nearly corresponding to the Countess, Queen Isabeau, is allowed a moment of self-justification (Act II scene 2), but is mainly a negative contrast-figure. Talbot has one speech, his dying lament for reason (as *he* conceives it), in which he expresses a philosophy with which Schiller disagreed in a way which gives it dramatic dignity and conviction, but in general, he is prevented from achieving real dramatic stature. We shall be discussing these two plays in more detail later as examples of the two main trends in the Classical Schiller, but before that, it is necessary to look at the underlying principles of his Classical drama as a whole.

Man is the measure of all Classical German literature. Schiller's natural tendency towards the idealistic leads him to see his subject in general terms, rather than the individual ones of Goethe. Even if he had not been already inclined in that direction by temperament, this alone would have impelled him to seek a wider stage than that inhabited by Goethe's characters, to go for the heroic atmosphere, the 'great' issue. As the prologue to **Wallenstein** has it: 'only the great object is capable of arousing the furthest depths of humanity'. What particularly interested Schiller the dramatist was, in the words of 'Shakespeares Schatten', 'that great, gigantic Fate which elevates man when it crushes him'. All that is not 'human', then, is alien to Schiller's drama—which distinguishes him from the Romantics—but his concept of what is human is considerably wider than that of the 'Aufklärer'. It has at least one foot in the camp of metaphysics, in rather the same way that Kant's philosophy has, and its root, as with Kant's moral philosophy, is the concept of freedom. Only as a vehicle for demonstrating the essential moral freedom of man is history of real intrinsic interest for Schiller.

Schiller's dramatic characters realize the ideal of freedom either in the state of moral 'beauty' (complete harmony of their desires with the moral law) or 'sublimity' (when they rise, by virtue of their moral freedom, above the compulsion of outside forces to which, as physical beings, they are inevitably subject). No one character is shown as being constantly in one or other of these states, nor is any one shown to be totally incapable of them, as Franz Moor, for example, had been. Schiller was more objective now, and he was also more clearly aware of the difference between the aesthetic and the purely philosophical, as he showed in **'Uber das Pathetische'.** At the same time, some characters are so much inclined to the morally beautiful as to deserve the title of 'schöne Seelen' (e.g. Max and Thekla in **Wallenstein**) and others, even if not painted entirely black, are flawed in such a way that it is hard to conceive of their achieving sublimity in adversity as is the case with Wallenstein himself.

Schiller's Classical dramas show considerable variation of form, and on the more general level, they all reflect the in-

terplay between freedom and control. After some hesitation, Schiller decided to use verse for **Wallenstein** and then, finding that it corresponded to the spiritual qualities he wished to cultivate, retained it for all his other plays. Its formality helps to temper the variegated and often turbulent nature of his plots. Schiller's verse is, broadly speaking, firm and regular, with occasional interludes in lyric metre. The language shows the same balance of orderly homogeneity and individual freedom. Illo, Wallenstein and Countess Terzky speak in styles graded according to their natures, and all fall short of the somewhat exalted language in which Max, the 'poetic' character, expresses himself. In **Wallensteins Lager,** there is even some colloquial speech, again distributed in degrees relating to the standing of the character. But when one looks more closely at them, one sees that the range of the colloquial usages employed is not really wide: omissions, elisions, familiar use of the definite article with proper names, idiomatic use of 'tun' and so on. By comparison with the raciness and richness of idiom to be found in Grimmelshausen's *Courasche* or Brecht's *Mutter Courage,* the equivalent here, the 'Marketenderin' of Scene 5, is a rather pale figure:

> Der Spitzbub! der hat mich schön betrogen.
> Fort ist er! Mit allem davon gefahren,
> Was ich mir tät am Leibe ersparen.
> Liess mir nichts als den Schlingel da!

Schiller wants a certain amount of the sap and colour of colloquial speech, but not enough to disturb the ordered regularity of his whole concept.

Dramatic form and construction show broadly the same picture. Schiller paints on a wide canvas, with a large and socially differentiated cast, but his technique is still broadly classicistic. He infringes the unities of time and place in their strict definition, but handles these elements with firm control. The sequence of scenes is never so rapid as to confuse, or so disjointed as to produce the dynamic, kaleidoscopic effect of a 'Sturm und Drang' play. And while there is action, action tends to speak less loudly than words. The drama is carried by verbal exchanges, often in long, set-piece speeches.

As has been said, the Classical Schiller works on wide canvases, but he always maintains unity and order. These canvases are not chosen for themselves alone. They are normally demanded by the central theme, which in turn gives the play integrity. In **Wilhelm Tell,** for example, the theme of justifiable revolution demanded a portrait of a whole people. In the case of **Wallenstein,** Schiller realized that the understanding of his hero's actions demanded full knowledge of the whole range of factors which conditioned them, and accordingly embarked on a unique expansion of the traditional five-act tragedy. Certainly the action and the detail interested him, but by comparison with Arnim's practice in a typical Romantic historical work like *Die Kronenwächter,* Schiller's background remains very much *subordinate* background.

It was the powerful and enigmatic figure of the historical Wallenstein which first fascinated Schiller, as it has many another historian of the Thirty Years War. Schiller was never entirely at home with the character, but during the composition of his *History* he came gradually to feel less absolute hostility towards him. Among other factors, one feels here the growing appreciation of the point of view of the realist, so that while he still could not condone treachery, he arrived at the more understanding formulation: 'Wallenstein did not fall because he rebelled, but he rebelled because he was falling.'

Wallenstein is conceived in the image of the realist, the man whose horizon is bounded by the world of nature. Universal abstract ideals are alien to his way of thought, and moral imperatives having their origin in pure reason would be meaningless to him. This does not necessarily shut him off from all contact with law and morality, however, since these things can be seen as present in nature, taken as a whole. Further, Schiller believes that the realist is capable of feeling the justice of the ideal and the beauty of morality, even if it may be at the expense of a logical inconsistency in his outlook: he will claim that he knows these things from nature, but they are ideals. Wallenstein is only partially aware of the deeper roots of his way of acting, but his conscious belief in Fate as the agency which shapes our ends is a reflection of his general tendency.

The belief in astrology, which Schiller handles with detachment, does reflect something positive: the feeling that the world is not without law, and the desire to be in harmony with what law exists. Illo sees only the argument of practical personal interest, which he has in mind in the phrase 'the stars that govern your fate are in your breast'. The astrological view of life which Wallenstein develops in reply to this view of the man who can only 'grub, gloomy and blind, in the earth' is superior for Schiller, for it reflects, however distortedly, a recognition of considerations above everyday practicality. Even when the capture of his secret messenger seems to have forced his hand, Wallenstein needs a great deal of persuading. He *can* act decisively, as he later proves, when he is convinced that he is doing so in accordance with the ruling principle of nature, necessity. But this necessity is not 'blindly commanding chance', which seeks to propel him like a will-less piece of driftwood.

Wallenstein's revolt against such a demeaning state is expressed in the monologue of *Wallensteins Tod,* Act I, Scene 4. Even after he has at last agreed terms with the Swedish emissary, he still feels that fidelity is a factor of real importance and is inclined to step back from treason (Scene 6). Not until Countess Terzky has articulated the realist's belief in necessity on the highest level, appealing to Nature herself, can he see the way forward. He is still taking a wrong path, certainly, but Schiller makes him do this in a way which is clearly distinct from that of the opportunist who can see no further than material gain or self-preservation, and with a higher degree of freedom.

Similarly, his heart is open to the beautiful to some extent. The key is the character of Max Piccolomini. Himself a person of great beauty of soul, he is an indicator both of Wallenstein's imperfection (in his refusal to stay with him) and of the fact that there is good in him, in that he clearly prefers the general to his own father, Octavio. Wallenstein's reaction to his loss is stronger evidence still. Quite apart from the importance that his standing among the soldiers gives him, Max is of great value to Wallenstein for the very moral qualities which in fact part them. On hearing of Max's death, he expresses clearly for the first time the side of his character which distinguishes him from 'common' realists of the type of Terzky and Illo. Max was the 'flower' of his life and wove beauty round 'the common ('gemein') clarity of things'. To his own astonishment, he had found 'the flat everyday shapes of life' exalted by the fire of Max's feeling. Max and Thekla are crushed by Fate, but their freedom is never in doubt, even if they are not spared the pain and in Max's case (since the crucial decision is his) even confusion of violently opposed inclinations. By the light which they cast and which it is their primary function to cast, we see that all the other characters are flawed to a greater or lesser extent, and to that extent not free. No one is painted as black as was Franz Moor, who, we recall, had emancipated himself to such a degree that he was completely a prisoner. Wallenstein and Gräfin Terzky achieve echoes of sublimity, Buttler, the murderer, assumes a degree of grandeur in his role of Nemesis; even Illo dies fighting bravely.

Freedom, then, in the context of man's ability to remain man even in the face of the overpowering force of Fate, is a key concept in *Wallenstein.* Schiller's outlook and mood show a greater stability and balance than was observable in the hectic 'Sturm und Drang' works. The primacy of the ideal is maintained, but the claims of practical reality, when they conflict with it, are not simply swept aside, nor are they felt as an entirely negative, crushing weight. In a Germany which has not changed radically from what it was in the first half of the century as far as social structure and conditions are concerned, and in which injustice, restriction and the other material and psychological pressures are still present, there is a feeling that one can preserve spiritual integrity without adopting a totally negative attitude to the real world.

But there is something of the precariousness of compromise about the Classical balance, however well it is worked out in Goethe and Schiller, which makes us hesitate to think of it as a true and final solution. The fact that they are the only two writers who can be called Classical in a really full sense is itself significant. And there is an element of stress and strain observable even in them. It is easier to see in the case of Schiller, who, for all his more rationalistically coloured and generalized approach to art, was probably temperamentally and emotionally closer to the Romantics than Goethe. Our last example, *Die Jungfrau von Orleans,* is chosen with this in mind.

Deep personal involvement is both a strength and a weakness of Schiller as a dramatist. The warmth of his heart gave his works a strong impetus, but it was in need of discipline. He had sought and achieved this discipline in large measure, and *Wallenstein* and *Maria Stuart,* his best completed Classical plays, are fine monuments to it. A certain amount of the spirit of discipline had gone over into his inner nature; even *Die Jungfrau von Orleans* is careful to cultivate the sense of the historical period as far as possible in the scheme, to characterize secondary figures in the round, and so on. But all the time one senses a force which is putting considerable strain on the balanced and objective form in which he still wishes to work. We are asked to see this as drama in the real human world and its problems as human problems. Yet there is an undercurrent of the operatic which comes to the surface strongly at times, as in the Prologue, the long and metrically varied first scene of Act IV, or the ending. The verse often has great beauty, but as often, it seems to be there as much to create beauty as to carry dramatic import. The characters surrounding the heroine are nothing like as solid and rounded as, say Elizabeth, Leicester, Mortimer, Burleigh, Paulet and the others in *Maria Stuart*. The play has great movement, light and colour, but it lacks the elements of stillness, and containment and management of this ubiquitous light and colour, which would give the Classical balance.

Schiller has *attempted* to anchor it in this way, for example by avoiding a true sense of the mysterious. His wonders are not the 'sweet wonders' of which a Romantic like Brentano speaks and which are incompatible with the clear daylight of rationalism: quite the contrary. He uses the Christian framework, but in a spirit much more in tune with the Greek culture. The very echoes of the New and Old Testament which are sprinkled quite liberally through the text in fact enhance this impression. They tend to be generalized and human-ized in the form in which they appear, just as the vision of the Virgin described by Johanna in Act I, Scene 10 (lines 1072 ff.) is numinous only in so far as that is compatible with a Classical mood. There is too much distinctness, both visually and in the language spoken. It is all reduced to the level of what the eye can see and the reason comprehend. The ascent of the Virgin into Heaven has none of the real wonder of a Transfiguration or Ascension:

> Und also sprechend liess sie das Gewand
> Der Hirtin fallen und als Königin
> Der Himmel stand sie da im Glanz der Sonnen,
> Und goldne Wolken trugen sie hinauf
> Langsam verschwindend in das Land der Won-
> nen

The root of the trouble seems to be that this play is in large measure a superior kind of escape-literature. The idealist can maintain his faith in the higher reality while living in the imperfect actual world, he can even show it triumphant within corrupted human nature. The Classical Schiller, as Melitta Gerhard says, had 'matured in the acceptance and the overcoming of the inevitable'. And as we have seen, he still desires an anchorage in reality even in this play. But the strain of his position was severe. Not only was he physically, and perhaps to some extent even economically under strain, his temperament was less able to adapt and take a cool or humorous view than was Goethe's. His Classical balance contains much more deliberate restraint than Goethe's and he must have felt the need to relax it at times, to let his heart have its way.

In *Die Jungfrau von Orleans,* Schiller indulges his desire for the light to the extent that he causes it to flood more or less unchecked by what he once called, in a letter to Wilhelm von Humboldt of 30 November 1795, 'the filth of actuality'. He was speaking there of the idea of a 'sentimental idyll': 'All that is mortal' was to be 'extinguished', there was to be 'nothing but light, nothing but freedom,

nothing but capacity—no shadow, no limitation, nothing more of all that to be seen.' All who have experienced the exaltation of the ending of Beethoven's Choral Symphony will recognize this mood and accept its genuineness, even perhaps the possibility that Schiller might have been able to express it in literary form. But it could hardly have been in conventional dramatic form, certainly not in one which will not detach itself from the motivation of real life on the one hand, or a secularized humanist view on the other.

Schiller went some way towards the operatic in this play, as he also did towards the wondrousness of the fairy-tale. He felt the attraction of both these genres, no doubt because, at the expense of the solidity and credibility of the more realistic genres, they have freed themselves from the shackles which reality places on the ideal. Schiller is even reported to have exclaimed, when close to death: 'Give me fairy-tales and tales of chivalry: that is where the stuff of all goodness and greatness lies.' In these circumstances, one can sympathize with Schiller's desire to relax the controls. It is less easy to do so in the case of *Die Jungfrau von Orleans.*

Here, Schiller uses a real historical personage in a real setting, to write what is primarily a hymn of praise to pure spirit. Johanna's actual mission is less important than the fact and the conditions of mission: the special relationship in which she stands to the 'Geisterreich' and the need for unsullied purity in her spirituality. Johanna must be human; Schiller insists on this at all times, not only in her fall from grace. The theme of love and her relationship with men form the symbolic vehicle of her ordinary humanity, as the mission is a symbol of her participation in the highest, ideal humanity. In the case of both love and mission, we feel that these things are of no real validity in themselves, but are simply being used. This gives them an emptiness which does not adhere to Maria Stuart's religious faith or to the love of Max and Thekla. But the objective control is not strong enough to enable Schiller to make Johanna human in the straightforward sense. She is given no hint of sensuality, of quickness of temper or pride; indeed, no hint of a clear individuality. Thekla may be a 'schöne Seele', but she is also 'Friedland's daughter', and can hold her own with Countess Terzky when the latter cross-examines her. Well before the great glory of the ending, Johanna has the flawless and unvarying light, the complete freedom, of the idyllic state. The formula is that she is the human vehicle for the divine power and glory, a kind of Samson-figure, perhaps. But the Samson of the Bible, for all his superhuman exploits, is much more convincing as a human, and therefore corruptible being. We can distinguish between what he is of himself, and what God works in him.

Schiller lacks the religious feeling to make the spiritual factor in his play truly superhuman and this means that he is also unable to make his heroine ordinarily human. Her reply to Karl in Act III, Scene 4, in which she rejects the idea of marriage, remains the best indication of what she is:

> Dauphin! Bist du der göttlichen Erscheinung
> Schon müde, dass du ihr Gefäss zerstören,
> Die reine Jungfrau, die dir Gott gesendet,

Herab willst ziehn in den gemeinen Staub?

The one word 'gemein' is enough to show us where we are. Schiller allows Johanna to 'fall', so that she shall rise again in sublime glory, but there is no suggestion that she has involved herself in 'das Gemeine'. Indeed, in the scene (Act IV, Scene 1) in which Johanna analyses her 'crime' to herself, he is not at all explicit about what she actually felt when she saw Lionel. That it was love we must assume, but there is no suggestion of a parallel to what Samson felt for Delilah.

The triumph of free spirit over the reality which seems to imprison it could well be the best formulation of Schiller's intention in the play as it stands. But to attain that triumph, one needs to feel the resistance of reality, one needs flesh and blood, and all the ties and conditions of actual, practical life. Schiller was able to portray these, and preserve his faith in the ideal and the beautiful. He can show its moral superiority, but also its destruction, sometimes in ugly circumstances, as in the death of Max Piccolomini, who is trampled to death beneath horses' hooves. 'That,' as Thekla says, 'is the lot of the beautiful on this earth.' As a citizen of this earth, Schiller recognized that. But he could not entirely reconcile himself to life's imperfections and needed at times to compensate himself for the strains it imposed on him. ***Die Jungfrau von Orleans*** is a play in which he does this more openly and more obviously than in any other, with the possible exception of ***Don Carlos,*** in which he indulges himself in the portrait of Posa, who describes himself as a citizen, not of his own age, but of 'the centuries which are to come'. But Posa, after all, lived in the present and strove to realize his ideals within it. So it was with Schiller in general, and the play on which he was working at his death, ***Demetrius,*** would have been much closer to ***Wallenstein*** than to ***Die Jungfrau von Orleans*** in character. In the latter play, he had placed himself in danger of the mistake against which he had warned the 'sentimental' poet, i.e. of 'leaving human nature completely behind' and thereby becoming 'überspannt'.

'Nature', the concept which links the material and spiritual and the individual and general, is probably the one in which the balance of freedom and order in the outlook of the major Classicists is best expressed. Modern society is not in harmony with it, as that of the Greeks had been. The impulses of modern man towards freedom for reason and desire lead, as Schiller puts it in **'Der Spaziergang'**, to unhappiness and confusion. Here, as elsewhere, the Classicist rejects the path of revolution. But there is no need to flee into some kind of restrictive stockade, or to despair of all harmony. The greater order of nature still exists and offers to the individual at least (and for the Schiller of the ***Ästhetische Erziehung,*** to society as well) a path to true harmony and fulfilment within reality:

Und die Sonne Homers, siehe! sie lächelt auch uns. (pp. 221-32)

*Alan Menhennet, "Synthesis in Literature (II): Schiller," in his* Order and Freedom: Literature and Society in Germany from 1720 to 1805, *Weidenfeld and Nicolson, 1973, pp. 220-32.*

## Ellis Finger    (essay date 1980)

[*In the essay below, Finger describes Schiller's concept of the sublime, as it is evident in his dramas* Don Carlos *and* Mary Stuart.]

Schiller prefaced the central arguments of his essay, **"Über das Erhabene,"** with the following proposition: confronted by forces which threaten to destroy us, we are able to maintain our dignity and independence only by willfully subjugating ourselves to these forces. He argues the paradox that man can attain moral superiority over annihilating circumstance by making the annihilation an act of his own will:

> Kann er also den physischen Kräften keine verhältnismäßige physische Kraft mehr entgegensetzen, so bleibt ihm, um keine Gewalt zu erleiden, nichts anders übrig, als: *ein Verhältnis,* welches ihm so nachteilig ist, *ganz und gar aufzuheben* und eine Gewalt, die er der Tat nach erleiden muß, *dem Begriff nach zu vernichten.* Eine Gewalt dem Begriffe nach vernichten, heißt aber nichts anders, als sich derselben freiwillig unterwerfen.

The closeness of this paradox to the kind of triumphant death celebrated in a number of Schiller's tragedies has made this passage a favorite citation in judging characters as diverse as Posa, Maria Stuart, Johanna, and Max Piccolomini. And indeed the formula seems tailormade for the kind of moral ennoblement which Schiller imparted to many of the tragic struggles in his dramas. But because of this closeness, applications of this essay have tended to become predictable. The concepts explored here lend themselves so easily to the dynamics of his tragedies that this one section is often lifted from context and used alone to explicate characterizations. Certain critics have even been charged, somewhat facetiously, with believing that "the hero or heroine of Schiller's later plays were aware of a duty to attain a state of 'Erhabenheit' which he or she can know only from a perusal of **"Über das Erhabene."** [G. W. McKay, "Three Scenes from *Wilhelm Tell*," in *The Discontinuous Tradition,* 1971.] Such narrow dependence is unfortunate, for the elaboration of these ideas elsewhere in the essay offers the most trenchant commentary to the major questions of tragedy as developed by Schiller. By working outward from this initial statement to the full context of the elaborations, two features of Schiller's work come sharply into focus: a surprisingly distrusting view of two crucial concepts (beauty and nature), a view which clashes with the presuppositions of his major essays of the mid 1790's; and an understanding of tragic conflict which moves us beyond those characters usually revered for moral integrity and begs consideration of certain figures whose flawed and compromised actions also bear sublime features. In pursuing these two related matters, we shall first explore the position of Schiller's essay within the body of his theoretical writings, and then apply the findings to the major characterizations in **Don Carlos** and **Maria Stuart,** with emphasis on how the crucial roles of each drama are marked by sublimity.

**"Über das Erhabene"** was published in 1801. Scholars look to the years 1792-94 as a likely date of origin. Terminology and argumentation agree closely with other essays of the Kantian period in Schiller's life. The familiar tensions between the intellect and the senses common at this time set the tone also for the essay. It is not so important to fix an exact time of composition, but it is crucial to note the discrepancies between certain basic assumptions of this essay and presuppositions of other writings which tend to dominate discussion of Schiller's aesthetic values. Specifically, Schiller takes a view of nature in his essay which deviates sharply from the underlying premise of **"Über naive und sentimentalische Dichtung"**; and **"Ästhetische Erziehung"** projects a trust in beauty which runs totally counter to the central arguments of his treatise on the sublime.

These are not outright contradictions; concepts and terms remain fairly consistent from one essay to the next. Nevertheless, differences exist in the tone of argumentation and the intended results of analysis. **"Über naive and sentimentalische Dichtung"** depends on a beneficent, trusting view of nature. Separation from nature is acknowledged as the fate of modern man, but the implicit hope throughout the essay is reintegration into the purity of the natural state. Among Schiller's finest tributes to the "perfectness" of nature is his discussion of the idyll:

> Aber wenn du über das verlorene Glück der Natur getröstet bist, so laß ihre *Vollkommenheit* deinem Herzen zum Muster dienen. Trittst du heraus zu ihr aus deinem künstlichen Kreis, steht sie vor dir in ihrer großen Ruhe, in ihrer naiven Schönheit, in ihrer kindlichen Unschuld und Einfalt; dann verweile bei diesem Bilde, pflege diesem Gefühl, es ist deiner herrlichsten Menschheit würdig.
>
> (v. 708-9)

When we turn to **"Über das Erhabene"** we find Schiller in a very different posture; here he regards nature with suspicion and distrust, and stresses the adversary relationship between its destructive powers and the individual's struggle to maintain moral autonomy. The kind of harmonious unity aimed for in the other document, though briefly mentioned, is kept in the background; emphasis is on physical superiority. The vocabulary itself reflects this bias: words of compromise are almost totally eclipsed by the language of forceful collision and domination. A sampling of imagery early in the essay includes "Gewalt erleiden," "überlegen sein," "den Meister spielen," "Herr werden," "beherrschen," and "Kräfte abwehren" (v. 792-93). Nature's influence over man is not at all perceived as a beneficent guide. Quite the opposite, nature poses a danger to man's well-being which must be counteracted either by transforming it to his own use or by seeking refuge from its destructive powers:

> Der Mensch bildet seinen Verstand und seine sinnlichen Kräfte aus, um die Naturkräfte nach ihren eigenen Gesetzen entweder zu Werkzeugen seines Willens zu machen, oder sich vor ihren Wirkungen, die er nicht lenken kann, in Sicherheit zu setzen.
>
> (v. 793)

An even stronger hostility governs his attitude toward sensual beauty. By way of comparison, the great synthesis of opposites in **"Ästhetische Erziehung"** draws equally upon the rival sides of man's being—intellect and sense perception, form and content, necessity and freedom—to create a cooperative whole, which gains strength from both halves of this new partnership. The central feature of this partnership is man's aesthetic sense, the "play" of his imagination, which is capable of achieving the final link between the realm of perception and that of ideas: "Die Schönheit ist allerdings das Werk der freien Betrachtung, und wir treten mit ihr in die Welt der Ideen—aber was wohl zu bemerken ist, ohne darum die sinnliche Welt zu verlassen. . . ." (v. 653). Once again, as we move from these finely-argued conclusions, rich in synthesis and compromise, to the presuppositions of **"Über das Erhabene,"** differences are immediately apparent. Most important, the powers of sensuous beauty that figure so prominently in **"Ästhetische Erziehung"** are regarded here as seductive, even debilitating. Instead of liberating us from the duality of human existence, beauty holds us captive and bars us from the moral freedom which only the sublime can offer:

> Die Schönheit unter der Gestalt der Göttin Kalypso hat den tapfern Sohn des Ulysses bezaubert, und durch die Macht ihrer Reizungen hält sie ihn lange Zeit auf ihrer Insel gefangen. Lange glaubt er einer unsterblichen Gottheit zu huldigen, da er doch nur in den Armen der Wollust liegt—aber ein erhabener Eindruck ergreift ihn plötzlich unter Mentors Gestalt, erinnert sich seiner bessern Bestimmung, wirft sich in die Wellen und ist frei.
>
> (v. 800)

Schiller maintains this "escapist" attitude throughout the essay, not simply discounting the creative powers of physical beauty, but arguing the urgent need to turn inward upon the resources of mind and will, seeking through this sublime disposition "einen Ausgang aus der sinnlichen Welt" (v. 799).

The full implications of these contrasts are too large to measure here. But from this brief overview, two major matters do emerge to guide further considerations. First, Schiller's fascination with the sublime led him toward assumptions about human nature that are different from those expressed in his most famous essays; though he does not refute the more harmonious view of man projected elsewhere, he in effect acknowledges another vantage point from which the idealized solutions are deemed unattainable. Second, the view of man from this new vantage point is overwhelmingly tragic in its sense of anguish and terror. Physical suffering and relentless struggle are pictured as the environment of man's actions and moral choices. Conflict is inevitable, with human frailty being no match for the physical superiority of outside forces. The only way to maintain moral autonomy and to exert control over such challenges is the earlier-mentioned paradox of making annihilation an act of one's own will. By willfully submitting to the brutality and blindness of death, man exalts himself above the mean conditions of his defeat and attains what Schiller views as an undisputed triumph of the sublime.

Many of the concerns raised by Schiller in connection with the sublime come into play in ***Don Carlos.*** Even though this drama predates his essay, several of the central ideas later developed under the influence of Kant's writings are already present in embryo form in the character portraits of Carlos, Posa, and Philipp.

A coincidence in phraseology leads first to Carlos, himself. In an early scene with Elisabeth, he states his desires in words that prefigure almost verbatim the argument upon which Schiller later bases his definition of the sublime. Working at the outset of the essay with the contrast between necessity and free will—"müssen-wollen"—he seals his position with the well-known phrase: "Alle andere Dinge müssen, der Mensch ist das Wesen, welches will" (v. 792). Carlos uses this identical contrast in his insistence not to relinquish claim to Elisabeth's heart, stressing "Daß Carlos nicht gesonnen ist, zu müssen, / Wo er zu wollen hat." The common wording, in this case at least, is not a sign of continuity, however, but rather an accentuation of changes in Schiller's temperament. Carlos' defiance of necessity and trust in the will aim clearly at the overthrow of all barriers that block his desires. In his own words, he seeks "den Umsturz der Gesetze" (l. 727) and shuns all accommodation or compromise to interests different from his own. By the time the concept of sublimity later took shape, his attitude had undergone an almost total reversal: although the will remains the cornerstone of Schiller's position, it now concedes the superior might of outside circumstance and seeks only to control the individual's submission in a manner consistent with the dictates of moral freedom.

More directly pertinent to the themes of the essay are the resentment and scorn that Carlos feels toward those who constrict his freedom. This is seen most clearly when Posa cautions him against delighting in his role as "der Beleidigte," and explains that sensitive souls often take pleasure in suffering injustice: "Unrecht leiden schmeichelt großen Seelen" (l. 2434). Again, the resentment felt by Carlos—a destructive and debilitating self-pity—is far removed from the rechanneling of this kind of harm into a weapon of strength and self-elevation in the later theory of the sublime.

The character whose situation, temperament, and conduct seem closest to the terms of the essay is Posa. The similarity between his self-sacrifice for political freedoms and the willful submission which Schiller associated with the sublime has caused commentators to group him with other "erhabene Seelen" of later dramas. In many respects Posa seems to exemplify these qualities. From his first appearance, he is shown to be in conflict with the ruling social order; he speaks often of his spiritual and historical dislocation and weighs the failures of the present regime against dreams of a future political system that favors the highest aspirations of mankind. His vision of free thought and expression, furthermore, seems certain of defeat when confronted by the authorities of Church and State. This inevitable collision of wills, finally, is colored by the kind of voluntary submission and sacrifice that Schiller was later to define as "sublimity": Posa willfully subjects himself to forces he cannot overcome, but does so with the belief that his death will bring to fruition the ideals he has nurtured.

In crucial sections of the drama, however, Posa's role strays from the guidelines of this concept. Indeed, the two scenes that should be closest in mood and content to the theory of the sublime actually unfold in ways far different from those described in the essay. In Posa's conference with Philipp (Act III), he comes face to face with the man responsible for the injustices he decries. Instead of a battle of wills, with Posa pre-empting his vulnerability to Philipp's power, however, Schiller molds the scene into a delicate study of character and situation. Posa, on the one hand, shows no signs of bowing to Philipp's authority and argues fearlessly the principles upon which he grounds his vision of a perfect state. Philipp, on the other hand, makes no move to silence this rebellious voice. He prefers to overlook the content of Posa's words in order to embrace the candor and courage with which they are spoken. What at first seemed to be an inevitable clash of ideologies is thus defused and converted into a joining of human needs.

A similar difficulty is a deterrent to labeling as sublime Posa's later submission to death. Though his sacrifice is a willful and self-exalting act, it is made necessary by conditions largely of his own making. Having dirtied his hands in the kind of intrigue he earlier resisted, Posa falls victim to the very machinations he had once rebuked before Philipp and Carlos. When he finally is driven to accept death, his gesture, sadly, is not so much a purely heroic act as a desperate attempt to extricate his friend (and their political vision) from entrapment brought on by his own miscalculations.

The character study that actually lies closest to the themes of the essay is that of Philipp. To recognize the somewhat twisted connections between his role and the conditions of the sublime, we first need to consider that facet of Schiller's theory in which awesome, frightful circumstances are discussed as objects of aesthetic and moral ennoblement. In his reasoning, man requires constant exposure to Nature's dreadful, destructive might in order to value his moral invulnerability: "in eben dieser wilden Ungebundenheit der Natur [findet die Vernunft] ihre eigene Unabhängigkeit von Naturbedingungen dargestellt" (v. 803). From this angle, the deep anguish suffered by Philipp can be viewed as the ordeal of one driven to the limits of sublime struggle. To be sure, much of this crisis stems from Philipp's own errors: his early rebuff of Carlos, his mistrust of Elisabeth, and his overestimation of Alba and Domingo. Schiller isolates other severities that spring rather from inherent conflicts of Philipp's position as monarch and family head.

This inner divisiveness is displayed most clearly in the crucial scene with Posa discussed earlier. Here Philipp grapples with the paradoxes of statesmanship, conscience, and personal need. He listens as Posa recites political values that undermine the very foundation of his regime, but instead of silencing the speaker, he takes him into his confidence. So desperate is Philipp's need for courage and honesty among his followers that he places trust in one whose beliefs and ideals call into question even his reason for being. Yet at the same time, he stands too insecure in his rule to consider granting the reforms Posa recommends, no matter how sympathetically he may respond to the idealized vision put forward.

The struggle is felt even more forcefully in Philipp's family relationships. Schiller's skill at intertwining the private and public strands of Philipp's life yields numerous examples of domestic strife mirroring failures in political stewardship. As his grasp of government weakens almost to the point of impotence, equivalent changes are noted within the family circle. Ties to wife and son become further strained. Suspicion and fear gnaw at these fundamental human bonds. The precarious state of his marriage and administration, in turn, leads to a severe crisis of identity. Schiller suggests the awesome burden of the sublime in Philipp's soliloquy before his infant daughter (Act IV). Holding an image of Carlos in one hand and a mirror in the other, he struggles to determine whose features predominate in the child's face. Finally, he is driven to doubt his own fatherhood, and is drawn by this despair to loss of faith in all social and ethical values: "Ich kenne / Mich nicht mehr—" he cries, "ich ehre keine Sitte / Und keine Stimme der Natur und keinen / Vertrag der Nationen mehr—" (ll. 3786-89). When he later learns that Posa has betrayed his trust by giving to Carlos the ultimate love he had coveted for himself, his despair becomes even more acute. His brief surrender of authority and his ensuing threats of terror and vengeance evoke the strongest feelings of awe and dread—those elements of our fascination with the sublime which Kant defined as "eine negative Lust."

Philipp's sublimity, however, is not limited to his experience of anguish; as he acts in the final scenes to restore order to his rule, Schiller overlays his gestures with a somewhat distorted version of the qualities of character that later become the axis of his theory of the sublime. His meeting with the Grand Inquisitor, in particular, is conceived as a ritualistic submission to authority and a self-willed sacrifice of his own flesh and blood. Having borne the Inquisitor's rebuke, Philipp asks, "Sind wir versöhnt?" The response, "Wenn Philipp sich in Demut beugt," accents the forced subjugation of self (ll. 5259-60). Philipp then confirms his volition by offering up his scepter: "Ich lege / Mein Richteramt in deine Hände" (ll. 5273-74). This symbolic submission is then followed by the move to deliver up his son for execution. In his bidding that the Inquisitor follow him, "Aus meiner Hand das Opfer zu empfangen" (l. 5279), lies the total suffering of a father and king forced to sacrifice that life which could have given continuation to his reign. The questionable morality of Philipp's conduct prevents us from drawing parallels between these final measures and the sublime triumph of true moral courage. But the outer gestures of submission and self-sacrifice, together with the abundance of anguish and horror in this character struggle, speak directly to the conditions and motives from which this crowning segment of the essay is later to be developed.

A similar situation can be found in *Maria Stuart*. Like Posa, the heroine passes through a crisis of the spirit only to arrive at a final impasse. Certain of suffering a demeaning death, she seizes control of her fate by manipulating the terms of her execution to satisfy her sense of moral rec-

titude. She is able ultimately to assert the dignity of her position and thereby nullifies the degradation imposed on her by the unjust conviction. But is it correct to view her triumph in terms of sublime anguish, as Schiller described it in his essay? As we examine different sections of this drama, aspects of Maria's character will present themselves that cannot be reconciled with the spirit or the letter of the essay. Even as we find this one role moving beyond the scope of this concept, the adversary role of Elisabeth is seen to be marked in some measure by the struggle and anguish that Schiller associated with the sublime.

There is no doubt that elements of the sublime are potentially present in Maria's role. She is held captive by a monarch whose authority she does not accept and she faces execution for a crime she has not committed. In short, she stands powerless before an immovable adversary at whose hands she is certain to suffer as the victim of an unjust exercise of power. In the famous third-act meeting between Maria and Elisabeth, the conditions point toward the kind of submission that distinguishes the sublime hero. In his essay, Schiller prescribed the paradoxical act of asserting one's superiority over threatening forces by willfully surrendering to their claims: defiant self-exaltation fused with voluntary submission. At the beginning of the scene, Schiller seems to be moving toward this solution. Maria struggles to overcome "den heftigsten Kampf" and throws herself at Elisabeth's feet; twice her words concern the important theme of forced submission, each time with the modal verb, "wollen": "Ich will mich . . . unterwerfen" (l. 2245) and "ich will vor ihr mich niederwerfen" (l. 2248). She then completes the symbolic gesture and requests of the queen: "Eure Hand / Streckt aus . . . Mich zu erheben" (ll. 2254-56). But the continuation of the scene fails to lead Maria to what could be judged a sublime bearing. Instead of maintaining moral superiority, she allows herself to be humiliated by Elisabeth's goading insults. After seeing her request for justice rejected in such demeaning fashion, she loses all self-control. Driven from humiliation to anger and finally to her impassioned assault on Elisabeth's character, she conveys the severity of her struggle, but without grounding her anguish in sublime dignity. Far more evident is the image of a broken spirit, maligned and utterly degraded. Maria's own words reveal how remote this ideal remains: "Ach, meines Geistes Schwingen sind gelähmt . . . Gebrochen ist . . . Der edle Mut—" (ll. 2380, 2383-84).

A more satisfying view of Maria's exalted spirit is her scene with Burleigh at the end of Act I. Upon learning that she will likely be convicted and sentenced to death, she lashes out against the foundations of Elisabeth's legal claims and fully overturns the balance of guilt and innocence, criminality and rectitude. Unmasking her adversary's "Gaukelspiel" (l. 970) and exposing her "heiligen Schein der Tugend" (l. 973), she stands resolute before Elisabeth's power, while asserting her own reliance on higher codes of justice: "Doch sie gestehe dann, daß sie die Macht / Allein, nicht die Gerechtigkeit geübt" (ll. 964-65). Her performance is surely a tour de force and would come close to the desired blend of defiance and submission were it not for the fact that she had just learned of Mortimer's plan to secure her release. The self-assurance and exalted courage that she displays, therefore, should probably not be ascribed to the inescapable necessity that attends the sublime; in fact, she may simply be relishing the foretaste of a liberation that she now believes is imminent.

Another scene often cited as proof of Maria's sublime spirit is her acceptance of the death sentence in Act V. In Maria's speeches, the many oxymorons on the themes of victory-submission, freedom-captivity, and innocence-guilt recall phrases in the essay, particularly the central concept of willfully subjecting oneself to forces that strike counter to the noblest ideals of one's spirit. Her view of death as a "Triumph" (l. 3497) and a liberation "zur ewgen Freiheit" (l. 3484) points still closer to the mental state described in the essay. The religious context of these statements, and indeed of her entire disposition in these final scenes, however, places a barrier between the kind of triumph she enjoys and the conditions of sublime struggle that Schiller reserved for the ultimate test of human suffering. By making Maria's final appearance an absolution before a priest, Schiller drained her submission of all torment and made it less awesome, less terrible, less fearful. On two crucial points, her conduct differs from the prescribed elements of the sublime: first, by attributing her punishment to an earlier crime, she moderates the hateful travesty of her sentence and converts her fate into a reasonable and proper enactment of justice; and second, in emptying her heart of malice and resentment, she forfeits the sense of superiority that the sublime hero bears toward his oppressor. Though she stands as a triumphant spirit, she no longer regards her victory as a defiant mastery over Elisabeth, as in Act III. She deliberately asks Burleigh to convey forgiveness to Elisabeth and to apologize for her angry outburst of the previous day. She is now a transfigured, purified spirit, and the resentment and defiance which earlier led her close to a sublime state have been transformed into Christian humility. In unburdening herself of scorn toward Elisabeth and in reconciling herself to her fate, she also eases the gravity of her struggle. Indeed, she moves toward her death freed of anguish and inner conflict, at peace with herself and the world. She is so completely a transfigured spirit, "ein schon verklärter Geist" (l. 3845), that the pendulum seems to have swung away from "Würde," the dominant tone throughout most of the drama, to "Anmut," that rare aura that Schiller reserves for the exceptional "schöne Seele."

This change in temperament places in question not only the sublimity of her final moments, but also the entire tragic sense of her death. Addressing himself to a similar situation in his *Hamburgische Dramaturgie,* Lessing observed that the emotional appeals of tragedy precluded Christian themes and characterizations. To mitigate suffering and catastrophe with overtones of grace, humility, and transcendence defuses the cathartic powers of tragedy and creates a different kind of theatrical effect:

> Ist ein solches Stück aber auch wohl möglich? Ist der Charakter des wahren Christen nicht etwa ganz untheatralisch? Streiten nicht etwa die Gelassenheit, die unveränderliche Sanftmut, die seine wesentlichsten Züge sind, mit dem ganzen Geschäfte der Tragödie, welches Leiden-

> schaften zu reinigen sucht? Widerspricht nicht etwa seine Erwartung einer belohnenden Glückseligkeit nach diesem Leben der Uneigennützigkeit, mit welcher wir alle grosse und gute Handlungen auf der Bühne unternommen und vollzogen zu sehen wünschen?

Maria's altered bearing in the closing scenes also brings to mind Schiller's reaction more than a decade earlier to the ending of Goethe's *Egmont.* In his 1788 review, he questioned Goethe's decision to deflect the tragic potential of his play by providing for the visionary peacefulness at the close: "Kurz, mitten aus der wahrsten und rührendsten Situation werden wir durch ein Salto mortale in eine Opernwelt versetzt. . . ."

In *Maria Stuart,* therefore, Schiller once again produced a potentially sublime characterization, but developed it into something quite different by accentuating other qualities than those described in the essay. Yet he retained many aspects of the sublime in his drama, again by imparting to the adversary role a somewhat distorted version of these qualities.

Although Elisabeth's character is compromised by many flaws, she shows signs of suffering a personal crisis no less severe than Maria's. Admittedly, Schiller portrayed her in harsh, unflattering tones, but he supplied her struggle with a fascinating backdrop upon which important moral issues are projected. The conflicting facets of her role—the grandeur of her position and the meanness with which she discharges her office—are reflected in the divergent judgments of recent criticism. On the one hand, she has been called "the richest and most complete portrait of man as a political being" "[Oscar Seidlin, "The Poet of Politics," in *A Schiller Symposium,* 1960]. On the other hand, the view has been expressed that Schiller badly weakened the historical complexities of her reign, reducing the role to what Jeffrey Sammons [in "Mortimer's Conversion and Schiller's Allegiances," *JEGP,* Vol. 72, 1973] has termed "a missed opportunity of major dimensions." Despite this appearance, Schiller certainly did not undervalue the intricacies of her characterization. In preparing an early production of the work, he showed more concern for the difficult performance of Elisabeth's role than for Maria's. . . . (pp. 166-76)

The themes central to Elisabeth's dilemma are announced in her first appearance. Responding to questions about her willingness to marry, she tells how difficult it is to reconcile personal desires with the will of her people. Her view of her office is clearly rooted in the familiar dualism of Schiller's essays. In weighing the conflicts of inclination and duty, private happiness and public welfare, freedom and necessity, she shows herself to be cut from the same fabric as many of Schiller's other characters. Typical of the contradictions to which she feels subjected is the following: "Die Könige sind nur Sklaven ihres Standes / Dem eignen Herzen dürfen sie nicht folgen" (ll. 1155-56).

The elements of this conflict reappear, with sharpened intensity, when Elisabeth must decide how to handle the court's conviction of Maria. Uncertain of how to proceed, she imagines herself torn between popular insistence on Maria's execution and her own hesitancy before this extreme act. Critical among her worries is the threat she sees to her freedom of choice. Her monologue in the Fourth Act opens appropriately with the cry, "O Sklaverei des Volksdiensts!" (l. 3190). The irony of a ruling monarch bereft of power recurs frequently in her speech. She completely inverts the privileges of authority by regarding political dealings as "Die allgewaltige / Notwendigkeit, die auch das freie Wollen / Der Könige zwingt" (ll. 3209-11). Under the burden of her decision, she sees herself assaulted from all sides: "Mich zu vernichten streben alle Mächte" (l. 3214). This sense of utter powerlessness, described at one point as "Ohnmacht" (l. 3165), agrees almost completely with the forced subjugation of the human will described in **"Über das Erhabene."** Of course, the connection is distorted by the irony of a powerful ruler pleading impotence. Yet the closeness of Elisabeth's struggle to the conditions of the sublime is unmistakable. In part, this results from Schiller's counterpointing of the two roles, with much of the anguish and turmoil of Maria's struggle being transferred to Elisabeth as the drama progresses. In part, her crisis is marked by sublime qualities that stem directly from her own position as monarch and her grasp of its limitations.

As with Philipp, Elisabeth's case is made complete by a kind of desperate submission—a surrender which in some ways resembles that described in the essay. In confessing her "Ohnmacht," she admits that she is ready to submit her decision to the people's will: "Mein Volk mag wählen, / Ich geb ihm seine Majestät zurück" (ll. 3149-50). The submission she considers here becomes fact in her dealings with Davison: in dispatching the signed death sentence while refusing responsibility for its enactment, she in effect renounces her position of authority. The fact that her submission results from weakness of character rather than moral strength places her defeat in direct contrast to the exalted triumph enjoyed by the sublime heroine. Yet by viewing her case from the standpoint of a sublime struggle, the conditions of her tragedy define themselves in sharper tones.

For Schiller as for Kant, the sublime is understood on two levels. It can first apply to an immediate personal experience and the moral ennoblement attained through struggle; but it can also result from the contemplation of awesomeness, removed from the threat of physical harm. In this latter respect, furthermore, it is possible for actions that we view as morally reprehensible to exert an edifying influence on us. Here Schiller even cites moral anarchy as one of the most forceful instances of the sublime. As Thomas Weiskel explains [in his *The Romantic Sublime*, 1976]: "*confusion* is the preeminent occasion of the sublime. And by 'confusion' he [Schiller] means not merely 'the spiritual disorder of a natural landscape' but also 'the uncertain anarchy of the moral world,' including the amoral chaos of human history in which all best things are confused to ill." From this perspective, the closeness of Philipp and Elisabeth to Schiller's grasp of the sublime presents itself convincingly. We need not hesitate, therefore, to respond to the emotional content of their dilemmas, however much the fruits of their struggles may offend our sense of rectitude. (pp. 177-78)

*Ellis Finger, "Schiller's Concept of the Sublime and Its Pertinence to 'Don Carlos' and 'Maria Stuart',"* in The Journal of English and Germanic Philology, *Vol. LXXIX, No. 2, April, 1980, pp. 166-78.*

---

**George Henry Lewes on Schiller's *The Robbers*:**

What mischief **The Robbers** effected must be laid to the account of the age itself, with its deep disquiet, its revolutionary instincts, its volcanic vehemence against effete corrupt forms of social life. This daring play could only have been written by a boy of genius; a man of genius would have pruned the extravagances, and thereby have destroyed its effect. Less absurd, it would have been less successful, because less startling. For I must frankly confess that, with all my admiration for Schiller, directly I quit the *historical* for the *critical* point of view—directly I cease to regard it as a fiery product of a volcanic period, and view it purely as a work of art—it appears to me an intolerable absurdity, and mainly, perhaps, from the cause so candidly stated by Schiller himself: "I attempted to delineate men two years before I had seen one." Hence it is that character, motive, passion,—all that makes the substance of a dramatic work— are of all vague, false, rhetorical nature, which we see in the writings of boys (and most men never quit their teens in this respect). But this, which prevents **The Robbers** from ranking as a work of art, in no way interfered with its vehemence as an assault upon social conventions. Therefore its success was prodigious; Schiller soon learned to feel ashamed of his first-born, and nothing can be more unlike it than **Wallenstein** or **William Tell**.

*George Henry Lewes, in his* Dramatic Essays, *Walter Scott, Limited, 1851.*

---

**Margaret T. Peischl   (essay date 1982)**

[*In the following essay, Peischl examines the theme of power in Schiller's poetry.*]

Consistent with the traditional image of Friedrich Schiller as Germany's idealistic poet of freedom, scholars have concentrated on that positive aspect of his work rather than on his treatment of forces interfering with or opposing freedom. Abusers of power, however, stand flagrantly in the foreground of Schiller's dramas; his persistent concern with the misappropriation of power is conspicuous throughout his entire dramatic production, from the motto *in tyrannos* in **Die Räuber** to his **Demetrius** fragment, in which the protagonist is seduced by the possibility of a despotic reign. To a less consistent and less blatant degree, but nonetheless discernibly, Schiller deals with the theme of power in his philosophical essays; particularly in his treatise **"Über das Erhabene"** he emphasizes that the forceful domination of others and the dignity of man are irreconcilable concepts. The question thus remains as to the role and delineation of power in Schiller's poetry, a topic Schiller scholars have not dealt with in a complete or systematic fashion. The intent of this article is consequently to elucidate the theme of power in Schiller's lyrical works and to demonstrate how the destructive force of misappropriated political rule in his early poems gradually yields priority in the later ones to a loftier and mightier authority, namely that of the spirit as manifested in song, that is, poetry. This discussion has been prompted by two considerations: the question of to what extent Schiller dealt with the deprivation of freedom through worldly power in his poetry and an interest in investigating how Schiller's own very antithetical cast of mind is reflected in his treatment of power in his lyrics.

The title of one of Schiller's very earliest poems, **"Der Eroberer"** (1777), immediately announces the young poet's concern with unjustly administered political power. Although there is a preponderance of examples of the misuse of power by unjust or unenlightened rulers in Schiller's early poems, such poems as **"Elegie auf den Tod eines Jünglings,"** **"Totenfeier,"** and **"Trauerode"** indicate that the young poet was also struggling with the irrefutable power of death. There is indication, however, even at this early stage of Schiller's life and career, that the appalling omnipotence of death also serves a positive purpose, for, as these poems demonstrate, the great equalizer Death strikes down all men and exempts no one, not even the mighty and merciless despot. Death thus becomes less horrendous and terrifying for Schiller; years later with the writing of his essay **"Über das Erhabene"** (1794-96) he proposes a moral victory over death through acknowledgment and acceptance of its supremacy and a readiness to relinquish all earthly attachments.

A third ingredient of Schiller's early poetry is the power of love. In the Laura poems he frequently uses vocabulary dealing with struggle, resistance, and imprisonment, and constantly reminds readers of the indomitable strength of love. If these poems are interpreted not as the expressions of a personal experience and of a strong attraction to a specific woman, but rather as an indication of Schiller's theoretical interest in the phenomenon of love, then love is construed chiefly as a counterforce to negative power such as that of the unjust tyrant or that of death. Suprapersonal love is that positive power, which, in the thinking of the older and increasingly theory-oriented Schiller, no longer has a direct connection to particular human beings, but instead becomes the general power of the spirit and of song. Since the dualist Schiller intuitively separated the physical and the spiritual world, as his doctoral dissertation, "Versuch über den Zusammenhang der tierischen Natur des Menschen mit seiner geistigen," already indicated, it can be expected that Schiller's preoccupation with the idea of power emphasized either its physical or spiritual aspects, according to the particular stage or circumstances of his life at the time of the writing of a given poem.

In his earliest poems Schiller thus acknowledges three varieties of power: the destructive physical and political force that one individual can exert over others; the power of death to which every human being is ultimately subject, but which, according to the more mature Schiller, has validity essentially only in the physical realm; and finally that power superior to both of these, i.e., "des Geistes tapf'rer Gegenwehr." Although Schiller was only later to expand upon his idea of the mightiest of these powers in both his poetry and his expository writings, he alludes to

it as early as 1781 in the poem **"Der Triumf der Liebe"** when he states: "durch die Liebe Menschen Göttern gleich." The progression from Schiller's portrayal of despotic potentates to his concentration on the invincible human spirit of enlightened individuals as expressed in song will be illustrated through a chronological investigation of his poetry.

In **"Der Eroberer,"** which appears in the *Nationalausgabe* of Schiller's works as his second poem, the poet expresses not only his overpowering hatred for the tyrant but also a certain identification—one could almost call it admiration—and ultimately also the gratifying feeling of revenge when the despot is judged by God and thrown into hell. We see here the conqueror's unrestrained celebration of victory ("Stolz auf türmt er sich nun, dampfendes Heldenblut / Trieft am Schwerd hin . . . ") which the poet condemns as execrable, despite the fact that he both glorifies and envies the evildoer: "Oh, ihr wißt es noch nicht, welch ein Gefühl es ist, / Welch Elysium schon in dem Gedanken blüht, / Bleicher Feinde Entsetzen, / Schrecken zitternder Welt zu sein." The moralist Schiller is, however, fully satisfied only when the scales of justice send the tyrant into the abyss of hell; he enjoys that "mit voller Wonn, mit allen Entzückungen," and one notes that the poet's desire for revenge and the fascination that power holds for him are perhaps almost as demonic as the hunger for power that the described conqueror exhibits. In any case, this is Schiller's first and most terse expression of the unjustified use of power.

Joachim Müller correctly assesses the revolutionary aspect of Schiller's anonymously published collection *Anthologie auf das Jahr 1782* when he maintains: "Die Anthologie greift rücksichtslos an und packt zu: ihr Objekt ist die Welt des fürstlichen Despoten und der höfischen Korruption." In **"Die schlimmen Monarchen"** the true order of things is reinstated only when "mit Rudersklaven / Könige auf einem Polster schlafen." Here Schiller deals in an especially sarcastic and scornful manner with the powerlessness of once omnipotent rulers, whom not even debauchery can awaken. That the grave permits no concealment of the inner worthlessness of monarchs is felt to be appropriate, and here again the poet exposes his own vengefulness: "Berget immer die erhabne Schande / Mit des Majestätsrechts Nachtgewande! . . . Aber zittert für des Liedes Sprache, / Kühnlich durch den Purpur bohrt der Pfeil der Rache / Fürstenherzen kalt." The opposing positive power, the power of song, which is here mentioned, comes to play an increasingly important role in Schiller's writings.

The poem **"Kastraten und Männer"** in the same anthology is less an attack on royalty as such than an acknowledgment of healthy masculine joy in life. Corrupt court life serves as a symbol for unnatural and ineffectual asexuality. The poet makes a potent criticism of those responsible for such a situation: "Tyrannen haßt mein Talisman / Und schmettert sie zu Boden, / Und kann er's nicht, führt er die Bahn / Freiwillig zu den Todten."

Schiller's ambivalent attitude toward the "edlen Verbrecher" is illustrated in **"Monument Moors des Räubers."** "Der Eroberer" is envied for his greatness; here one perceives something similar, for the "majestätischer Sünder" Moor is viewed in a positive manner despite his crimes. The poem begins with "Hail to you" and is followed by the lines: "Einst wird unter dir auch die Schande zerstieben, / Und dich reicht die Bewunderung." Although this is again a case of the misappropriation of power: "Zu den Sternen des Ruhms / Klimmst du auf den Schultern der Schande," Moor is no actual tyrant and Schiller does not communicate the same unbridled abhorrence for the powerful as he does in his earlier poems. Criticism takes the form of a warning: the moralistic poet wants to teach ambitious youths a lesson through the hubris of the reckless Moor as well as through the example of the mythical Phaethon.

Although the *Schiller-Nationalausgabe* questions the authenticity of two poems it nonetheless includes, attention might be drawn to them as possible exceptions to the young Schiller's virulent attacks against men of noble rank. **"Ode auf die glückliche Wiederkunft unseres gnädigen Fürsten"** was reportedly written on the occasion of the successful return of Herzog Karl Eugen from a trip to the north on March 6, 1781. Surprisingly, only apparently positive things are said about the reigning sovereign, at least on the surface. Even if the poem is to be designated as a *Gelegenheitsgedicht* and thus as a necessarily flattering, if actually sarcastic, tribute to Karl Eugen, it is nonetheless remarkable if the same poet who wrote **"Der Eroberer"** only four years earlier is now even feigning deference toward the very magnate for whom he avowedly felt so much hostility. If we are to assume that this poem is indeed by Schiller, we need not assume that it is a sincere expression on his part; nonetheless the apparent enthusiasm it contains offers a marked contrast to **"Die schlimmen Monarchen,"** in which the loathing felt for sovereigns is believed to be a direct reference to Schiller's feelings toward the same Herzog Karl Eugen. **"Auf die Ankunft des Grafen von Falkenstein"** is likewise a laudatory treatment of a personage with political status. When the poet explicitly states that the visitor has come to Stuttgart "Nicht als Monarch; als Menschenfreund," he gives clear indication that authoritarianism and goodwill toward one's fellow men are to his way of thinking mutually exclusive concepts.

**"Graf Eberhard der Greiner von Wirtemberg"** (1781), a poem definitely attributed to Schiller and contained in the *Anthologie,* does, however, make a positive judgment of an aristocrat. Schiller altered the historical facts in this war poem so as to make the warrior a revered hero. The compassion of the count is underscored through his shedding of tears at the death of his son; the weeping King Philipp in **Don Carlos** and the even more humane Graf von Habsburg in the ballad with the same title are anticipated here. Perhaps Schiller grants the count in this poem more positive recognition because he is a war hero and thus has a different commission from that of a ruler who even in peacetime exercises his power over his subjects arbitrarily. The use of power by a soldier apparently serves a different purpose in Schiller's eyes from that of sheer egotism, and even the young Schiller does not condemn all powerful men as evil overlords.

After the poetry of his youth Schiller becomes more and more inclined toward abstract philosophical themes. The outer, empirical world is of less interest to him than the presentation of his philosophical concerns. As a *sentimentaler Dichter,* he did not long occupy himself with the plastic delineation of power-hungry tyrants, but moved on to the presentation of his intellectual perceptions of and reflections on tyranny as a phenomenon. Even the wielders of power that he created as a young poet indicate that Schiller was not so much concerned with them and their actions as such as he was with the actual fact of their existence. The figure of the conqueror represents a cosmic power rather than a politically powerful human being; the evil monarchs were of interest to Schiller for reasons of the principle of justice that they violate and through which they go to ruin. In the poem about the robber Moor, as in **"Der Eroberer,"** it is the danger of hubris that intrigues Schiller. The development of the theme of power and its misuse in Schiller's works demonstrates his gradually acquired insight that power in day-to-day, practical life could not be assaulted directly by him, but was to be destroyed in concept. Already in his early poems he began to attack the unbridled use of power with his poetic gifts and "des Geistes tapf'rer Gegenwehr." As his own intellectual powers and verbal creativity developed, he sensed the power of his own eloquence and gradually came to envy the might of the worldly conqueror less. With words alone he began to exert a more impressive and often a more potent influence than did the ruler with mere physical power.

This tendency in Schiller can be shown by a comparison of two poems from the year 1784, **"Freigeisterei der Leidenschaft"** and **"Resignation."** The first poem and its later title **"Kampf"** are still expressions of Schiller's youthful revolutionary spirit. The defiance against convention and "tyrannisches Geschick" is unequivocally stated. The conclusion of the poem anticipates **"Die Götter Griechenlands,"** for in both poems the highest being is identified as an unmerciful, treacherous god, almost a tyrant in the manner of **"Der Eroberer."** The title of **"Resignation,"** on the other hand, already discloses the substance of the poem's content. The poet relinquishes claim to sensual happiness in this life as well as hope for a reward for his virtue in the next. He acknowledges a spiritual life for himself, although he can also still respond emotionally to his physical nature. While both of these poems are still subjective expressions of emotional states, considered together they demonstrate something of the poet's growing capacity for philosophical distance. The first poem still illustrates the spiteful resistance of the rebel; the second adumbrates Schiller's movement toward the spiritual life and his interest in philosophical speculation, which was the actual impetus for his virtual abandonment of the theme of misappropriation of power during the late eighties and the nineties. The philosophical poetry and the theoretical essays of this period do treat the problem of power, but rather from a theoretical standpoint and in reference to the higher authority of the spirit and of song. Schiller had already written his first four plays at this time, and for more than a decade after **Don Carlos** (1787) he produced no dramatic work. Interest in philosophy took precedence over his interest in drama and lyric poetry, as his *Gedankenlyrik* of the period testifies.

Any mention of rulers in the poetry of this period also includes mention of their positive characteristics, or at least of the possibility of such, as in the poems **"Die Priesterinnen der Sonne"** (1788) and **"Die Flüsse"** (1796). The poet's orientation toward political rule thus becomes less negative and pessimistic, and the maturing Schiller actually conceives an ideal kind of rule: in the poem *An die Freude* (1786) he speaks of brotherhood among all men. In **"Die unüberwindliche Flotte"** (1786) he praises the English Magna Carta. In **"Deutschland und seine Fürsten"** (1795) he gives his own country an important commission: "Aber versuch' es, O Deutschland, und mach' es deinen Beherrschern, / Schwerer als Könige groß, leichter nur Menschen zu seyn." The rise to power in Schiller's early poems means a definite loss of humanity, but here he is occupied with a reversal of the idea and deals more frequently with humanity and brotherliness and less frequently with the misuse of power.

**"Die Macht des Gesanges"** (1795) is prominent among the poems of the nineties for its treatment of a unique kind of authority. Here Schiller speaks unequivocally about the might that he considers the only valid kind, the supremacy of the spirit: "Und jede andere Macht muß schweigen . . . / Solang des Liedes Zauber walten." Earthly tyrants do not concern him anymore; he recognizes that as an artist he has a claim to the highest and ultimate authority. Physical force and political might are of no consequence. The poem **"Macht des Weibes"** (1796) is of interest since the words "Macht" and "herrschen" have a meaning different from that in earlier poems and have nothing to do with tyrannical despots. The line "Aber durch Anmuth allein herrschet und herrsche das Weib" emphasizes the nobility and passive dignity of which the individual human being is capable. In **"Die Worte des Glaubens"** (1797) we have a spirited expression of Schiller's optimism and his belief that an individual is subject only to himself: "Der Mensch ist frei geschaffen, ist frei / Und würd' er in Ketten geboren. / Laßt euch nicht irren des Pöbels Geschrei, / Nicht den Mißbrauch rasender Toren."

Schiller criticism has illustrated how the poet's developing impulse toward objectivity led him from philosophical poetry to ballads and then back again to drama, and has demonstrated how his creativity took a new direction toward the tangible and the graphically concrete. At first glance this might appear to be an unnatural development for the speculatively oriented Schiller, but not when one remembers the dualistic stance he had assumed with his doctoral dissertation. The writer functioned as a dramatist as well as a philosopher; he was a physician who dealt with the external, physical side of life, as well as an observer of the life of the soul. The two aspects of his personality and his penchant for dichotomy can already be seen in the Baroque characteristics of his early lyrics. After years of philosophical activity during which his speculative side concentrated on the inner life, Schiller returned, with the objective vision of a dramatist, to dealing with the external aspects of life. In the year 1797 he worked on the drama

*Wallenstein* and also wrote several ballads in which—not surprisingly—wielders of power again appear.

The ballad that is most strikingly reminiscent of the young poet is **"Der Taucher."** Here Schiller presents an arrogant king who commits the gross crime of using another human being for his own selfish purposes. The tyrant exploits not only his subject, but also his own daughter, whose request he ignores and whose dignity he debases when he promises her as a bride to the servant, should the latter be successful in retrieving the goblet. The most interesting feature of this poem and a new development for Schiller is the fact that the crime goes unpunished. The king himself does not suffer; the youth drowns, and the kindhearted daughter must observe how her vindictive father causes the senseless death. The conclusion of the poem is entirely unjust, quite the contrary from the case in **"Der Eroberer"** and **"Die schlimmen Monarchen."** If the moralist Schiller in this exceptional case wants to move the reader to compassion rather than to teach an ethical lesson, that is not the case in the ballad **"Der Handschuh."** Here the vain Kunigunde, whose overweening opinion of herself supersedes regard for human life, receives an appropriate recompense. She defiles the knight's love; like the king in **"Der Taucher,"** she exhibits an especially severe abuse of power, for the highest and noblest of human sentiments and potentially of human power, namely love, is destroyed by basest ambition and arrogance.

**"Der Ring des Polykrates"** seems at first glance to deal with neither an unjust despot nor an inhuman exploitation of power. It appears as though quite the contrary were the case and as though the sovereign Polykrates, who is not shown as a despicable tyrant, is granted boundless good fortune and will remain unaffected by the unfounded warnings of the Egyptian king. Perhaps Polykrates is cursed in a paradoxical way, however, since his excessive success has isolated him from other men and also from his humaneness: he has in the final analysis only his material possessions and, as Schiller sees it, he is lacking the most vital of all possessions, human dignity. If this is the case, it might have been Schiller's intent to leave the tragic conclusion of the poem open but to hint at the defeat of the historical Polykrates. Such an interpretation stresses not the blatant fall of a bloodthirsty potentate, but the fact that monarchical rule per se signifies an imbalance, an indefensible inequality among men, and for that reason itself should be impermissible. On the other hand, the demonstrable guilt of Polykrates might be seen as the consequence of his habit of thinking only of himself.

The Graf von Savern in **"Der Gang nach dem Eisenhammer"** is likewise no extremely odious ruler: he is simply a weak individual who lets himself be persuaded by the devious hunter Robert that the servant Fridolin is a threat to his honor and must therefore be eliminated. Fridolin's own virtue saves him, however, and the conclusion of the ballad adumbrates **"Die Bürgschaft,"** for the count also becomes a better man: "Und gütig, wie er nie gepflegt, / Nimmt er des Dieners Hand, . . . "

The ballad **"Die Bürgschaft,"** written in the year 1798, gives the first instance in Schiller's work of an evil tyrant who undergoes an inner transformation; he does so through the example of the humanity and trust of his servant, who declares himself prepared to die out of loyalty to his friend. The heretofore ruthless tyrant is visibly moved by such devotion, grants each of them, the servant and the friend, his life, and desires to be included in their bond of friendship.

The emperor in **"Der Graf von Habsburg"** (1803) is in all respects the antithesis of the conqueror in the poet's early poem of that title. An essential characteristic of this monarch is illustrated when he calls for the singer and acknowledges his worth. In Schillerian fashion the emperor expresses his awe at the power of song: in his behavior toward the singer he demonstrates the same high regard for art and artists that Schiller articulates in the poem **"Die Künstler"** when he speaks of the artist as providing his fellow men with the first step into the higher world of the spirit. One is again reminded of Schiller's assertion: "Und jede andre Macht muß schweigen, . . . " in the presence of the power of song. In the minstrel's song one learns of the humility of the count who hands over his own horse to the priest for his pastoral service, and after the song one also witnesses the emperor's diffidence before the singer, in whom he recognizes the priest. Here we see a charitable ruler who knows how to preserve the dignity of man.

One does not always encounter such an unequivocal situation in Schiller: one learns to expect also the opposite state of affairs from one so given to antipodal thinking. This is actually the case in the poem **"an Goethe,"** which appeared only three years earlier than **"Der Graf von Habsburg"** and in which Schiller reminds us: "Denn dort, wo Sklaven knien, Despoten walten, / Wo sich die eitle Aftergröße bläht, / Da kann die Kunst das Edle nicht gestalten." The pessimist and the combatant who knows that ideals must always be won anew speaks here. Nonetheless there are fewer and fewer examples of the abuse of power in the older Schiller and more and more frequent cases of generous potentates who place greater value on humaneness than on political might. The mature poet who valued the artist and "des Geistes tapf'rer Gegenwehr" in himself came to be concerned chiefly with a superior kind of humanity that paradoxically lays claim to its lofty position and power both in spite and because of the baser forms of worldly power to which it is opposed. (pp. 155-64)

> *Margaret T. Peischl, "The Faces of Power in the Poetry of Friedrich Schiller," in* The Journal of English and Germanic Philology, *Vol. 86, No. 2, April, 1982, pp. 155-64.*

## Gordon A. Craig    (essay date 1983)

[*Craig is a Scottish-born American historian who specializes in German history, politics, and modern culture. In the following excerpt, Craig comments on the relationship between power and freedom in Schiller's* Intrigue and Love *and* Don Carlos.]

It is true that, unlike some of his contemporaries, Schiller was not induced by the tumultuous political events of his time—the coming of the French Revolution and its ultimately shattering effects in his own country—to become an activist. If his first plays reflected the revolutionary aspirations of his age, he was not tempted, like Georg Forster for example, to try by his own efforts to realize them. When the Bastille fell, he was intent upon his duties as professor of history and philosophy at the University of Jena; during the Terror, he was composing his **Letters on the Aesthetic Education of Mankind;** and when the French legions began their systematic conquest of his country he devoted himself to literary production. Even so, his interest in contemporary politics never flagged; no member of his generation reflected more deeply upon the tendencies of his time, on the great struggle of men and nations for what he once called "mankind's mighty objects, power and freedom," and no one had such chillingly accurate perceptions of the seductiveness of the former and the deep ambiguity of man's devotion to the latter.

Schiller's thinking about the relationship between power and freedom is most explicit in his plays, and this is not accidental. The poet regarded the theater as a moral institution, "the common channel," he once said, "through which the glow of wisdom flows from the intelligent superior part of society and spreads itself in gentle streams through the whole state." He believed that the dramatist should be the preceptor of his people, and this is what he set out to become himself, by means of plays that would not only excite and entertain audiences but also instruct them and possibly help lay the foundations for a better and freer society.

This is nowhere more apparent than in [**Intrigue and Love** and **Don Carlos**]. Written within three years of each other in the decade before the outbreak of the French Revolution, both are, on one level, plays about parental authority and filial rebellion. But it would be a very obtuse reader who failed to perceive the political passion that informs them. **Intrigue and Love,** one of the first social dramas in German literature, is a powerful attack upon the evils of absolutism in the petty German states of the eighteenth century, whose rulers disposed of the lives of their subjects as if they were their own property. **Don Carlos** is a more balanced and sophisticated treatment of the same theme in the world of the Great Powers; based upon a story by the Abbé de Saint-Réal about the tragic fate of the son of Philipp II of Spain, it was undertaken, Schiller wrote in a letter, to correct "the lack of German plays that deal with great persons of state."

In both dramas, freedom from arbitrary authority, the right of the individual to live his life as he chooses, is a major theme, and the passages that deal with it have an eloquence that explains why the triumphant revolutionaries in France in 1789 made Schiller an honorary citizen of the Republic. But it cannot be said that they provide any evidence that their author believed that there was much hope of such freedom being realized in his own time. The political world that he describes in these plays has such endurance and resilience that even a cataclysm like the fall of the power-brokers Wurm and Walther in **Intrigue and Love** cannot be expected to make it change its ways. The structures of authority are too strong to be toppled easily (even momentary deviations from their norms by the ruler himself are quickly corrected, as the intervention of the Grand Inquisitor in **Don Carlos** proves), and they are able to defeat the rebelliousness of ordinary subjects either by brutal suppression or by the corruptive powers in their possession.

In *Intrigue and Love,* the only person who is truly free is Luise, who is realistic enough to see that her lover's defiance of court society will be ineffective and courageous enough to accept death as the means of self-liberation. All of the others have, consciously or unconsciously, made concessions to the system that have compromised their independence. One suspects, after the scene with the purse of gold, that Miller's self-reliance is less perfect than he claims; Ferdinand's ties with the court are too close to make either his love for Luise, which is sustained more by childish defiance and jealousy than by any other emotions, or his plans for flight credible; and Lady Milford's illusion of freedom is the result as much of her own vanity and self-indulgence as it is of her lover's deceit. In *Don Carlos,* even the Marquis of Posa, who speaks of freedom with such fervor, has been corrupted by the political world in which he lives. In the pursuit of his political objectives, he has no scruple about betraying his friends, and in his advice to the King there is what seems to modern ears to be a suggestion of proneness to authoritarian behavior, for he is clearly just as willing to be ruthless in his choice of means to achieve his ends as the Grand Inquisitor is in his determination to defeat them.

Schiller was too discriminating a political observer to see power only in its negative aspects. He was fully aware that it was the indispensable factor in the political process, a force for good as well as for evil; and in *Don Carlos* he has presented an incisive analysis of the problem of the responsibility of power. The tragedy of the King is that he feels that he cannot permit in himself the weaknesses of ordinary human beings and that his private feelings must be subordinate to his duties as ruler. There is no doubt that he has allowed this conviction to turn him into a monster, whose relations with his wife and son have hardened into rigid formality, any violation of which, however trivial, arouses in him groundless suspicions and fears for the welfare of the State. It is a tribute to Schiller's great force as an artist that he can make us see the human face behind the ceremonial mask and sense the burden of responsibility that weighs Philipp down. The anguish of the man who must sustain the system alone, since most of his associates are bound to him only by fear or ambition, is palpable in the great soliloquy in which the King betrays his own vulnerability.

> I need the truth—to dig its silent source
> Out from the gloomy rubble of what's false
> Is not the lot of kings. But give me just
> That one unusual man . . .
> . . . who can help me find it— . . .

Heinrich Heine once wrote of *Don Carlos* that in it "love of the future . . . shines forth like a forest of flowers." If that is true, it is also true that Schiller's hope that his fellow Germans might progress toward a juster and more equitable form of society was accompanied by the conviction that this would be possible only if they learned to understand the realities and ambiguities of the political process. Because he contributed so much to that understanding by

his dramas of intrigue, ambition, and the manipulation of power, Benno von Wiese is perhaps justified in calling him "the only example of a great political writer among the Germans." (pp. vii-x)

> *Gordon A. Craig, in a foreword to* Plays: 'Intrigue and Love' and 'Don Carlos' *by Friedrich Schiller, edited by Walter Hinderer, Continuum, 1983, pp. vii-x.*

### F. J. Lamport    (essay date 1990)

[*Lamport is an English educator and critic. In the following excerpt, he surveys Schiller's early prose plays, concluding that he achieved greater dramatic expression in his poetry than in his prose.*]

In 1827, in conversation with Johann Peter Eckermann, the principal companion and literary assistant of his last years, Goethe observed that the ideal of freedom runs through all Schiller's works, but that in the earlier ones he is concerned with 'physical', in the later with 'ideal' freedom. The distinction is a useful one. Whereas Schiller's early heroes seek to achieve freedom in the real world, freedom to be themselves and to live their own lives, his later plays tend increasingly to be concerned with the realisation that this goal is an illusory one and that true freedom is to be found in the acceptance of necessity and of moral responsibility. But this realisation is present from the very beginning; and all Schiller's plays do indeed 'turn upon that secret point' which Goethe had identified as the key to Shakespeare's, 'where the vaunted freedom of our will collides with the inexorable course of the whole'. The young Schiller naturally shared his forerunners' enthusiasm for Shakespeare, and many echoes of Shakespeare—of *Hamlet* and the Roman plays, of *Macbeth*, of *Richard III* and *King Lear*—can be heard in his work, as well as the more direct influence of his immediate predecessors in the 'Sturm and Drang' and of Lessing, especially *Emilia Galotti*. But he is also from the beginning a writer of powerful originality, with an unmistakable voice of his own.

Schiller's first three plays were all completed within the space of two or three years. The first, *Die Räuber* (*The Robbers,* or *Brigands*) was written while he was still a pupil (or prisoner) in the Karlsschule, and smuggled out to a publisher in Mannheim, capital of the Pfalz or Rhenish Palatinate. Here it appeared in print in 1781, and in the following year it was performed, albeit in a drastically revised version, at the Palatine court theatre, designated 'Nationaltheater' in 1778 (it still retains this name today). Baron Dalberg, the director of the theatre, had seen Schiller's manuscript and had realised that here was a work of real theatrical genius; one reviewer of the production declared that here at last was the long-awaited German Shakespeare.

Like *Götz von Berlichingen, Die Räuber* is a huge, sprawling work which flagrantly, indeed flamboyantly defies all the rules of neo-classic drama. The unities of time and place are swept away, violent action takes place on the stage, and the dialogue, especially in the scenes featuring the hero Karl Moor's band of libertine-turned-brigand friends, is spiced with obscenities far more colourful than the homely earthiness of a Götz; in much of this the young Schiller is plainly and simply out to shock. And again as in *Götz,* the classical unity of action is abandoned in favour of a loose, episodic chronicle of events, held together by a unity of theme—the desire for freedom and self-realisation—and of character. Or rather we should speak of a duality of character, for this is the most striking and original formal feature of *Die Räuber.* The play is ostensibly a story of fraternal hatred like *Die Zwillinge,* with the contrast between the brothers even more stridently marked. The evil, ugly and vindictive Franz Moor persuades his father, through slander and treachery, to disinherit his noble, handsome and forthright brother Karl. Karl becomes an outcast, leader of a band of robbers, like Robin Hood (the English outlaw-hero is actually mentioned in the play) a friend of the oppressed and an enemy of the rich and powerful, while Franz shuts his father up in a subterranean dungeon to starve to death and rules as Count in his stead, a sadistic tyrant supplanting a benevolent patriarch. (The plot is, as will be seen, a complex of familiar 'Sturm und Drang' themes and motifs.) Karl returns to exact revenge, but Franz evades capture by killing himself, and Karl, realising that his violent rebellion has caused more evil than good, gives himself up to justice. But the rivalry between the brothers which motivates the plot is only a mechanism which enables Schiller to present to us a pair of character portraits, parallel and ultimately, for all the contrasts, profoundly similar. In terminology borrowed from Schiller's later essay **"Über naive und sentimentalische Dichtung"** (**"On Naive and Reflective Poetry"**), Karl is often described as an idealist and Franz his opponent as a realist. But although it is true that Karl is spontaneous where Franz is calculating, and that Karl's ends, if not the means he employs to achieve them, are good where Franz's are evil, it is probably more accurate to describe both as perverted idealists. The characteristic theme of Schiller's early plays is not so much the conflict of realism and idealism as the pitfalls of idealism itself. Both Karl and Franz desire, above all else, freedom—freedom to be their own masters, to live their own lives, to spread their wings and fly like eagles far above the snail's pace of ordinary life—the contrasted images of 'Adlerflug' and 'Schneckengang' are invoked by each of them in turn. Both are rebels: Karl a rebel against society and the perversions of man-made institutions, Franz against nature itself and the deepest ties of blood and kinship. And both are brought to despair (the very word, 'Verzweifelung', sounds like a knell throughout the play) as they realise the failure of their rebellion, though Karl conquers his despair in his final act of submission and atonement, while Franz is left in his despair to die. Each of the brothers has, so to speak, his own half of the play, each his own location or series of locations. Franz remains at home in the family castle, while Karl roams about central and southern Germany, from Saxony to the Bohemian forest and the banks of the Danube, with his robber band, before returning home in Act IV to meet again his childhood sweetheart Amalia, his faithful old servant Daniel and at last his father, whom he releases from his prison on the point of death—but never actually encountering Franz, the true author of all his miseries. He sends his men to capture Franz and bring him to be judged, but they find only his corpse. So, in what is perhaps the most remarkable technical feature of the play, the two brothers never actually meet on stage.

*Die Räuber* is thus a kind of double tragedy, with a 'hero' and a 'villain' of almost equal tragic status, martyrs both to the elusive ideal of human autonomy and freedom. Karl and Franz both cast themselves in roles of power and greatness; and the motif of role-playing is another that will recur throughout Schiller's dramatic work. Franz dreams of the triumph of mind over matter, believing himself—but himself only—superior to the 'Schnekkengang der Materie', the 'snail's pace of material existence' (II, i), and to the filthy 'morass' of human life (IV, ii), which he describes with eloquent loathing in his lengthy monologues, strongly reminiscent (like much of his role) of Shakespeare's Richard III. Karl's first words in the play, 'This ink-splashing century disgusts me, when I read in my Plutarch of great men', his lament that the 'bright spark of Promethean fire is burnt out', his wish 'that the spirit of Hermann still glowed in the ashes' (I, ii), reveal a longing for a lost ideal of heroic greatness that recalls Goethe's nostalgia in *Götz* or *Egmont;* but here the nostalgia is Karl's and not Schiller's, for Schiller shows it to be deeply problematic. Despite the social concerns which Karl voices, and despite the grandiose denunciation of corruption which reaches its peak in the great harangue which he delivers to the priest sent to demand his surrender in Act II (again very different from Götz's brief and earthy dismissal of the Imperial officer!), his attempt to put his ideals into practice leads to crimes scarcely less horrendous in nature, and on a far larger scale, then those which Franz in his cynicism openly embraces. Within Karl's band this cynicism finds an advocate in Spiegelberg, Karl's brutal, boastful rival for the leadership; and even Spiegelberg is a kind of grotesque caricature of the idealist in his desire for freedom, a goal which he of course interprets with crude materialism as freedom from all restraints whether physical or moral. The world of Schiller's vision is not, it seems, the perfect creation of a benevolent Providence, as Lessing had argued, but the idealist who seeks to right its imperfections may himself be just as deeply flawed in his own character, and may thus bring upon himself and others evils as great as those he seeks to eradicate.

In *Die Räuber,* as in *Götz von Berlichingen,* and in full accord with the dramatic theory of the early 'Stürmer und Dränger', the articulation of a plot, the 'imitation of an action' in the Aristotelian sense, takes second place to the unfolding of character and the expression of a central idea or theme by the use of parallel and contrast and the deployment of secondary characters and episodes. In his preface, Schiller describes the work as a 'dramatised history' (the phrase recalls Goethe's designation of the original version of *Götz,* which Schiller, however, can hardly have known) in which the dramatic method is used to 'catch the secret operations of the soul'. The plot is arbitrarily constructed and the play is full of inconsistencies, improbabilities and crudely melodramatic devices, but this is of little consequence, for its real substance lies in its evocation of character, theme and mood. Here too there are crudities and excesses. Many of the scenes and speeches are too long; Schiller's prose style is uneven, the mixture of registers often dissonant and less convincing than in *Götz;* sentimentality rears its head in the portrayal of old Count Moor, the brothers' father, and of Amalia, the only woman in a large and otherwise all-male cast. Schiller himself soon realised these faults, and in his two subsequent prose plays he is plainly trying, in different ways, to discipline his exuberant imagination. But *Die Räuber* is nevertheless a work of unmistakable genius, an extraordinary first achievement by a young man of twenty-two. For all its complexities it has a powerful basic simplicity; its principal characters, Karl, Franz and Spiegelberg, are striking and memorable; and its language has at its best a blazing intensity, notably in the evocation of that key emotion of despair—in Karl's great speech to the setting sun by the Danube in (III, ii) or in Franz's night of terror leading to his suicide (V, i). We can already see in it not only its author's characteristic themes and preoccupations, but also clear intimations of his talent for poetic drama.

It is also a superbly theatrical work and achieved a tremendous success at Mannheim in 1782, even if in what we must regard as a travestied version. Not only had Schiller mutilated his text at Dalberg's insistence, but the Mannheim 'house style' was in general much more restrained than that which *Die Räuber* called for. Schiller's taste was for the flamboyant gesture, often carried to excess: in a production of Goethe's *Clavigo* by the students at the Karlsschule in 1780 Schiller, playing the title role, had reduced the audience to helpless laughter by his convulsively exaggerated performance, and in *Die Räuber* Old Moor tears his face and hair, Franz writhes in his chair in torment, and Karl in his despair charges into an oak-tree. In Mannheim the part of Franz was played by Iffland, who was much acclaimed for his performance, but he was much concerned to tone down Franz's daemonic will to evil, his radical egocentricity and his nihilism in favour of a characterisation more humanly comprehensible, 'more in keeping with the conduct of a son and a gentleman'— roles which Schiller's Franz explicitly repudiates. But the compromises which Schiller was forced to make, however reluctantly, with Dalberg led to a period of fruitful collaboration between Schiller and the Mannheim theatre, even if it was inevitably accompanied by a good deal of continuing friction; and Schiller remained for the rest of his life on good terms with Iffland, who as director of the Prussian court theatre in Berlin from 1796 was to be responsible for memorable productions of Schiller's later plays.

In his second play, *Die Verschwörung des Fiesko zu Genua* (*The Conspiracy of Fiesco at Genoa*), Schiller turned for the first time to history, which was to furnish the characteristic themes and subject-matter of the plays of his maturity. *Fiesco* is not, however, a play about history in the sense that *Götz* or *Egmont* is: it is a character drama, the portrait of a great man, and the history of sixteenth-century Italy serves only as a colourful background against which the protagonist can be exhibited. But neither is Fiesco a great man like Götz or Egmont as Goethe saw them, assured and self-confident in their greatness; he is rather a man obsessed, like Karl or Franz Moor, with the ideal of achieving greatness, and hesitating in his

choice of means to this end. He poses as the champion of political liberty, plotting with fellow-republicans to overthrow the despot Andreas Doria, but all the time contemplating seizing despotic power for himself. What matters to Schiller is not so much Fiesco's actual choice between republican idealism and despotic ambition as the hesitation which reveals both as no more than alternative forms of self-aggrandisement; the decision itself is not as important as the grand histrionic gesture with which it is made. 'To win a diadem is noble, to throw it away is godlike', reflects Fiesco at the end of Act II; but then, when we next see him, in Act III, ii, 'It is contemptible to empty a purse, it is impudent to embezzle a million, but it is noble beyond telling to steal a crown' (III, ii). Schiller himself was almost as undecided as his hero, for he wrote two endings to the play, though again it was Dalberg who was principally responsible for the change. In the original, published version Fiesco dons the ducal purple, but is assassinated by the fanatical republican Verrina for his betrayal of the ideal; but in the version performed at Mannheim in 1784 Fiesco renounces power, liberty is restored and he lives on as an ordinary citizen. (Neither ending is historically accurate, for the historical Fiesco, at the moment of his triumph over Andreas Doria in 1547, fell into the harbour and drowned by accident.) The outcome of the plot is relatively unimportant: what matters is the portrayal of Fiesco's character, the ambiguity of the hero's aspiration to greatness.

Very like Goethe in his progression from *Götz* to *Egmont,* Schiller in *Fiesco* moves from the dynamic style of *Die Räuber* to a more static manner of presentation—from life-story, as it were, to portrait. But whereas in Goethe's case this meant a change from the rapid movement of many short scenes to a greater breadth and a more leisurely pace, here Schiller takes the opposite course. In *Die Räuber* the individual scenes are long and often somewhat static and slow; in *Fiesco* this is replaced by busy movement and rapid comings and goings—emphasised on the printed page by the adoption of the French convention of scene-division, numbering a new scene ('Auftritt') for each entry or exit, which had been used by Lessing and his predecessors, whereas the original version of *Die Räuber* marks a new scene ('Szene') only at a change of décor. (The 'Trauerspiel' version already adopts the French convention, perhaps like the subtitle itself a sign of compromise with more traditional dramatic and theatrical practice.) As in *Götz,* however, all this surface activity does not necessarily add up to a coherent plot. Rather, the portrait of the hero is rounded out through the depiction of his relations with, and the reactions he produces in, a variety of other characters, often sharply contrasted among themselves. These include the austere Verrina and the other conspirators, many of them pursuing selfish ends of their own; the dignified patriarch Andreas Doria and his vicious, depraved nephew and heir-apparent Gianettino; Fiesco's gentle wife Leonore and the imperious Countess Julia, Gianettino's sister, to whom he pays half-pretended court; and, perhaps most interesting of all, his henchman the Moor Muley Hassan, one of Schiller's few comic characters, who makes one regret that he did not essay the vein more often. The Moor does most of Fiesco's dirty work for him, while Fiesco stands by making the grand gestures;

*The Conspiracy of Fiesco at Genoa.*

at the end, he is hanged for his pains. 'The Moor has done his work, the Moor can go' (III, iv) is probably the play's most often-quoted line.

*Fiesco* has generally been assigned a minor place in Schiller's dramatic output, but it marks a further stage in his treatment of the theme of individual autonomy, and though it lacks the elemental forcefulness of *Die Räuber* it represents in some ways a stylistic advance. Its prose is generally more restrained and homogeneous, though it rises to heights of considerable rhetorical power, notably in Fiesco's two great monologues in Acts II and III. In recent years it has enjoyed more favour with both critics and producers, its searching portrayal of political intrigue and corruption seeming perhaps more in accord with modern taste than the supposed 'idealism' of the later Schiller. It develops further the themes of political freedom and of charismatic political leadership, which Goethe had broached in *Götz* and *Egmont,* and to which after 1789 the events of history were to give a new and urgent topicality.

The ringing denunciation of political abuses in Schiller's third play, *Kabale und Liebe* (*Intrigue and Love*), has no doubt also played its part in ensuring this work's continuing popularity. Originally entitled *Luise Millerin* after its

heroine, it was renamed at Iffland's suggestion, as 'double' titles of this kind were coming into theatrical fashion (Verdi's operatic version reverts to Schiller's original title, but retains little else of his play in recognisable form). It is a 'bürgerliches Trauerspiel' with a highly realistic contemporary German setting which, though no real names are named, transparently represents Schiller's own native Württemberg, just as the Prince who looms so large in the background (very unlike the ultimately benign Frederick the Great of *Minna von Barnhelm*) strongly suggests Schiller's own Duke Karl Eugen. (In a famous Berlin production of the 1960s, the stage was dominated by the legs of a colossal figure representing the Duke, so that the whole action was literally played out by 'petty men' walking 'under his huge legs' and scurrying between his feet.) The play was completed in 1783 and followed its predecessors on the Mannheim stage in April 1784, by which time Schiller had fled from Württemberg and taken up residence in Mannheim as official playwright to the National Theatre. The Palatinate was, of course, foreign territory from which the Duke of Württemberg could not extradite him: for Schiller, as for Gottsched before him, the political divisions of eighteenth-century Germany did have their advantages.

Quite apart from the obvious specific references to Württemberg, the play attacks the abuses of contemporary absolutism much more directly than Lessing or even Lenz had done. Lessing had, or so he claimed, deliberately depoliticised the story of *Emilia Galotti* in order to concentrate on its purely human content. Lenz had attacked peripheral manifestations of class conflict rather than the heart of the political system itself. Schiller shows us the corruption and oppression upon which that system rests: the criminal intrigues by which a minister overthrows his rival and keeps himself in power, and the financing of princely extravagance by the exploitation of the people, as young men are forcibly recruited and sold off to fight in America to pay for jewels for the Prince's mistress. The hero, Baron Ferdinand von Walter, son of the corrupt President (chief minister), falls in love with Luise Miller, daughter of a humble professional musician ('Millerin' is an archaic feminine form of the name). Inspired by his love, he rebels against his father and against the whole vicious system which he represents: 'I will pierce the fabric of his intrigues—tear asunder all these iron fetters of prejudice—free as a man I will make my choice, and these insect souls shall reel before the towering edifice of my love' (II, vi). But Ferdinand's rebellion is broken, and he is destroyed. He succumbs to the intrigues of the 'insect souls', the President and his appropriately named henchman Wurm (the German means not only 'worm' but also 'serpent'), to the 'fetters of prejudice' and not least to the fatal weakness of his own character, the egocentricity of the idealist which his own extravagant rhetoric all too plainly betrays. With breathtaking ease the President and Wurm persuade him of Luise's infidelity, for as Wurm observes, 'Either I have no skill in reading the barometer of the soul, or milord the Baron is as fearsome in his jealousy as in his love' (III, i). Ferdinand denounces her as a whore and poisons her, then drinks the rest of the poison himself and dies, but with his last breath he forgives his father, who is brought to justice for his crimes.

*Kabale und Liebe* is a highly effective piece of stage writing, much better constructed in a traditional sense than either *Die Räuber* or *Fiesco,* with its principals clearly drawn and its minor characters and episodes much more successfully integrated with the plot than are some of their equivalents in the earlier works. Its continuing success is not undeserved. But . . . it does have a strong streak of melodrama about it. This seems, paradoxically enough, to be underscored by Schiller's realism and by the forcefulness of his social criticism. In a well-known study [*Mimesis: The Representation of Reality in Western Literature,* 1953], the critic Erich Auerbach speaks of the 'hair-raising rhetorical pathos' of Schiller's portrayal of the contemporary world, and of the failure of *Kabale und Liebe* (and of the 'bürgerliches Trauerspiel' in general) to achieve a convincingly realistic style. There is certainly a disparity of style in the work, between the traditional elements of tragedy—individual passion and emotion, and the suggestion of an inevitable fate awaiting the 'star-cross'd lovers'—and the more modern elements of critical realism and social satire. Yet essentially it is not the realistic but the tragic side of Schiller's play which is melodramatic, and for 'hair-raising rhetorical pathos' we should look not at the denunciations of princely extravagance

such as the famous scene between the Prince's mistress Lady Milford and the lackey in Act II, in which the fate of the conscripts is revealed, but rather at the expressions of Ferdinand's heaven-storming egoism, such as that already quoted, 'Free as a man I will make my choice . . . ', or his later declaration of his decision to kill Luise and die with her, 'An eternity bound with her upon a wheel of damnation—eye rooted in eye—hair standing against hair on end in terror—even our hollow moaning melted in one together—And now to repeat my endearments, and now to recite to her again her oaths of fidelity—God! God! the betrothal is fearful—but eternal!' (IV, iv).

Yet this, in the violence and extravagance of its imagery and its disruptions of normal prose syntax, is the authentic voice of the young Schiller, his own personal version of 'Sturm und Drang'. With *Kabale und Liebe* Schiller's dramatic writing reached a crisis. In his own, anonymously published, review of *Die Räuber* he had identified as one of that work's principal deficiencies its failure to achieve a consistent style: 'The language and the dialogue ought to be more harmonious', he had written, 'and on the whole less poetic.' In *Fiesco* and *Kabale und Liebe* he had tried on the whole, and with a good deal of success, to curb the 'poetic' excesses and to achieve a more generally realistic manner. But the rhetoric and the melodrama remain, and it is they—no mere pose as in Klinger—which seem to express the authentic Schillerian sensibility. The three prose plays are also 'poetic' in their use of pervading patterns of imagery which underline their unifying themes. Animal imagery runs through all three: Schiller had concluded his medical studies at the Karlsschule with a dissertation entitled *Über den Zusammenhang der tierischen Natur des Menschen mit seiner geistigen* (*On the Connection between the Animal and the Spiritual Nature of Man*), and the theme continued to preoccupy him. Wild beasts and bestiality are repeatedly invoked in the imagery of *Die Räuber.* In *Fiesco* the hero himself tells the citizens of Genoa a parable of the animal kingdom, in which he appears, naturally, as the lion (II, viii), but the language of the play would furnish a whole menagerie, from the elephant to the worm. In *Kabale und Liebe* we move generally on a lower level, amidst vermin, insects, scorpions and treacherous serpents; much of this, of course, has biblical associations too, and there is much talk of death and judgement, of heaven and hell, of angels and devils. *Kabale und Liebe* is also rich in imagery relating to money, appropriate enough in the realistic setting, and constantly intimating that this is a world in which human beings are accounted mere chattels to be bought and sold. Despite the stylistic uncertainties, language and imagery constitute one of the most important unifying factors in these plays. The real answer to Schiller's perceived stylistic problem lay therefore in making his language not on the whole less poetic but more so: that is, in aiming for the higher degree of uniformity of register which goes with poetic stylisation, rather than for a greater degree of realism, which if it does not bring variety can only lead to flatness. The prose plays constitute a series of stylistic explorations whose true if unconscious goal is the creation not of a realistic but of a poetic form of drama.

Schiller's early development can thus be seen to parallel

Goethe's. Each of them, in his next dramatic work, was to take the decisive step from the rebellious exuberance of 'Sturm und Drang' to the discipline of a classical style, most conspicuously in the adoption of verse instead of prose. But this does not mean that they had abandoned the ideals of their youth. On a higher level of dramatic expression, those ideals, the highest ideals of the age, could be given a form appropriate to their seriousness and dignity. Others too had felt the inadequacy of prose for this purpose. Perhaps most surprisingly, Lessing himself, the pioneer of realism, had himself chosen to give final and definitive expression to his own enlightened humanitarianism in the form of a 'dramatic poem'. (pp. 53-64)

> F. J. Lamport, "The Revolt of Prometheus (ii): Schiller's Prose Plays," in his German Classical Drama: Theatre, Humanity and Nation, 1750-1870, *Cambridge University Press, 1990, pp. 52-64.*

## FURTHER READING

Appelbaum-Graham, Ilse. *Schiller's Drama: Talent and Integrity.* London: Methuen & Co., 1974, 406 p.
  Outlines the "thematic, artistic, and aesthetic idiosyncrasies" of Schiller's plays.

———. *Schiller: A Master of the Tragic Form, His Theory in His Practice.* Pittsburgh: Duquesne University Press, 1975, 185 p.
  Seeks to "define the precise mode of interrelation between Schiller's tragedies themselves, his theory of tragedy, and his more wide–ranging aesthetic-philosophical pronouncements as a whole."

Benn, Sheila Margaret. *Pre-Romantic Attitudes to Landscape in the Writings of Friedrich Schiller.* Berlin: Walter de Gruyter, 1991, 242 p.
  Dismisses the traditional estimation of Schiller as hostile towards nature, asserting that the pre-Romantic affinity for nature, especially the natural sublime, exercised a profound influence on his literary works.

Bennett, Benjamin. "Schiller's Theoretical Impasse and *Maria Stuart.*" In his *Modern Drama and German Classicism: Renaissance from Lessing to Brecht,* pp. 188-228. Ithaca, N.Y.: Cornell University Press, 1979.
  Examines Schiller's aesthetic theory, focusing particularly on the ways in which it is manifest in *Mary Stuart,* which Bennett regards as Schiller's "crowning achievement."

DeQuincey, Thomas. "Schiller." In his *Biographical Essays,* pp. 263-86. Boston: Ticknor and Fields, 1861.
  Overview of Schiller's life which includes a general discussion of German literary history.

Ewen, Frederic. *The Prestige of Schiller in England: 1788-1859.* New York: Columbia University Press, 1932, 287 p.
  Traces the course of Schiller's literary reputation in England between 1788 and 1859.

Garland, H. B. *Schiller.* London: George G. Harrap & Co., 1949, 273 p.
  Detailed assessment of Schiller's life and works.

———. *Schiller, the Dramatic Writer: A Study of Style in the Plays.* London: Oxford at the Clarendon Press, 1969, 301 p.
  Focuses on language and its function in each of Schiller's plays, maintaining that "the fascination of Schiller derives . . . from his singular power to manipulate words, making the commonplace unique and the dingy luminous."

Hudson, William Henry. *Schiller and His Poetry.* London: Ballantyne Press, 1914, 191 p.
  Biographical and critical overview of Schiller's life and works.

Kaufmann, F. W. *Schiller: Poet of Philosophical Idealism.* Oberlin, Ohio: The Academy Press, 1942, 192 p.
  Explores idealism in Schiller's poetry, historical essays, ballads, and dramas.

Kontje, Todd Curtis. *Constructing Reality: A Rhetorical Analysis of Friedrich Schiller's Letters on the Aesthetic Education of Man.* New York: Peter Lang, 1987, 162 p.
  Introductory overview of Schiller's aesthetic theory including a formal study of its structure, content, and historical significance.

Mainland, W. F. "Schiller and Shakespeare—Some Points of Contact." In *Affinities: Essays in German and English Literature,* edited by R. W. Last, pp. 19-33. London: Oswald Wolff, 1971.
  Compares Schiller's plays with those of William Shakespeare, finding similarities in characterization, theme, and plot.

Mann, Thomas. "On Schiller." In his *Last Essays,* pp. 3-95, translated by Richard Winston and others. New York: Alfred A. Knopf, 1958.
  Laudatory overview of Schiller's works, focusing especially on his later dramas.

Metzger, Lore. "The Call for a Modern Pastoral." In *One Foot in Eden: Modes of Pastoral in Romantic Poetry,* pp. 3-42. Chapel Hill: University of North Carolina Press, 1986.
  Includes discussion of Schiller's poetry and aesthetic theory as helping to shape the tradition of the Romantic pastoral.

Miller, R. D. *Interpreting Schiller: A Study of Four Plays.* Harrogate, England: Duchy Press, 1986, 146 p.
  Provides analyses of Schiller's *William Tell, The Maid of Orleans, Don Carlos,* and *Wallenstein.*

Passage, Charles E. *Friedrich Schiller.* New York: Frederick Ungar, 1975, 205 p.
  Introductory biographical and critical evaluation of Schiller's career, featuring individual discussions of his dramas.

Phelps, William Lyon. "Schiller's Personality and Influence." In his *Essays on Books,* pp. 295-313. New York: Macmillan Co., 1922.
  Overview of Schiller's life, including a discussion of his influence on English and American literature.

Prudhoe, John. *The Theatre of Goethe and Schiller.* Totowa, N. J.: Rowman and Littlefield, 1973, 218 p.
  Includes chapters on "Schiller's *Strum und Drang* Dra-

mas" and "Schiller's Major Plays: His Theory and Practice" in a study of the contributions of Schiller and Johann Wolfgang von Goethe to German theater.

Reed, T. J. *Schiller.* Oxford: Oxford University Press, 1991, 120 p.

Assesses the impact of Schiller's personal life on his writings, maintaining that "Schiller, though a moralist, is not a moralizer."

Royce, Josiah. "Schiller's Ethical Studies." In *Fugitive Essays by Josiah Royce,* pp. 41-65. Cambridge: Harvard University Press, 1920.

Outlines the ethical conflicts in Schiller's works, tracing the influence of philosopher Immanuel Kant's ethical doctrines on his thought.

Sharpe, Lesley. *Schiller and the Historical Character: Presentation and Interpretation in the Historiographical Works and in the Historical Dramas.* Oxford: Oxford University Press, 1982, 211 p.

Analyzes the "impact of historical study on Schiller's dramatic practice," and demonstrates his "continued interest as a dramatist in the relation of the individual to the movement of history."

————. *Friedrich Schiller: Drama, Thought, and Politics.* Cambridge: Cambridge University Press, 1991, 389 p.

Traces Schiller's development as a poet, dramatist, and thinker, and provides detailed discussions of his major works, including his essays on aesthetics.

Simons, John D. *Friedrich Schiller.* Boston: Twayne Publishers, 1981, 163 p.

Focuses on the fundamentals of Schiller's aesthetics, poetry, and dramas.

Stahl, E. L. "The Genesis of Schiller's Theory of Tragedy." In *German Studies: Presented to Professor H. G. Fiedler, M. V. O.,* pp. 403-23. London: Oxford at the Clarendon Press, 1938.

Outlines Schiller's theory of tragedy by comparing his early and classical dramas, concluding that Schiller "does not develop towards a denial of an earlier idealism, but progresses from subjective to objective idealism."

————. *Friedrich Schiller's Drama: Theory and Practice.* London: Oxford at the Clarendon Press, 1954, 172 p.

Examines the affinities between Schiller's philosophical theories and his literary practice as evident in his plays.

Thomas, Calvin. *The Life and Works of Friedrich Schiller.* New York: Henry Holt and Co., 1906, 481 p.

Biography.

Triebel, L. A. "Germany's Greatest Dramatist—Schiller: Outdated or Ahead of His Time?" *The Canadian Modern Language Review* XII, No. 3 (Fall 1955): 7-10.

Comments on Schiller's dramatic achievements, concluding that he "fought all his life for virtue as the highest good and never divorced his art from moral values."

Ungar, Frederick. "An Account of Schiller's Life and Work." In *Friedrich Schiller: An Anthology for Our Time,* pp. 15-192. New York: Frederick Ungar Publishing Co., 1959.

Provides an overview of Schiller's career, suggesting that the moral and political content of his works remain significant for modern society.

Waldeck, Marie-Luise. *The Theme of Freedom in Schiller's Plays.* Akademischer Verlag Stuttgart: Hans-Dieter Heinz, 1986, 96 p.

Argues that "in the course of his dramas Schiller subjects the theme of freedom to a penetrating analysis, exhibiting it in its immense richness and complexity."

Wells, G. A. "Poetry and Politics: An Aspect of Schiller's Diction." *German Life and Letters* XVIII, No. 2 (January 1965): 101-10.

Examines language in Schiller's later plays, concentrating on speeches that address legal and political issues.

————. "Villainy and Guilt in Schiller's *Wallenstein* and *Maria Stuart*." In *Deutung and Bedeutung: Studies in German and Comparative Literature Presented to Karl-Werner Maurer,* edited by Brigitte Schludermann and others, pp. 100-17. The Hague: Mouton, 1973.

Assesses the relationship between individual culpability and tragic destiny in Schiller's plays, finding that "from *Wallenstein* through *Maria Stuart* to *Die Jüngfrau von Orleans* the link between the hero's character and his death becomes progressively weaker."

Witte, William. *Schiller.* Oxford: Basil Blackwell, 1949, 211 p.

Studies Schiller's creative efforts as letter-writer, poet, and playwright and includes discussion of his less popular works.

# Nineteenth-Century Literature Criticism

*Cumulative Indexes*
*Volumes 1-39*

# How to Use This Index

## The main references

> **Calvino, Italo**
> 1923-1985.....CLC 5, 8, 11, 22, 33, 39,
> 73; SSC 3

list all author entries in the following Gale Literary Criticism series:

*CLC* = *Contemporary Literary Criticism*
*CLR* = *Children's Literature Review*
*CMLC* = *Classical and Medieval Literature Criticism*
*DC* = *Drama Criticism*
*LC* = *Literature Criticism from 1400 to 1800*
*NCLC* = *Nineteenth-Century Literature Criticism*
*PC* = *Poetry Criticism*
*SSC* = *Short Story Criticism*
*TCLC* = *Twentieth-Century Literary Criticism*

## The cross-references

> See also CANR 23; CA 85-88;
> obituary CA 116

list all author entries in the following Gale biographical and literary sources:

*AAYA* = *Authors & Artists for Young Adults*
*AITN* = *Authors in the News*
*BLC* = *Black Literature Criticism*
*BW* = *Black Writers*
*CA* = *Contemporary Authors*
*CAAS* = *Contemporary Authors Autobiography Series*
*CABS* = *Contemporary Authors Bibliographical Series*
*CANR* = *Contemporary Authors New Revision Series*
*CAP* = *Contemporary Authors Permanent Series*
*CDALB* = *Concise Dictionary of American Literary Biography*
*CDBLB* = *Concise Dictionary of British Literary Biography*
*DLB* = *Dictionary of Literary Biography*
*DLBD* = *Dictionary of Literary Biography Documentary Series*
*DLBY* = *Dictionary of Literary Biography Yearbook*
*HW* = *Hispanic Writers*
*MAICYA* = *Major Authors and Illustrators for Children and Young Adults*
*MTCW* = *Major 20th-Century Writers*
*SAAS* = *Something about the Author Autobiography Series*
*SATA* = *Something about the Author*
*WLC* = *World Literature Criticism, 1500 to the Present*
*YABC* = *Yesterday's Authors of Books for Children*

**Appleton, Lawrence**
See Lovecraft, H(oward) P(hillips)

**Apuleius, (Lucius Madaurensis)**
125(?)-175(?) . . . . . . . . . . . . . . . **CMLC 1**

**Aquin, Hubert** 1929-1977 . . . . . . . . . **CLC 15**
See also CA 105; DLB 53

**Aragon, Louis** 1897-1982 . . . . . . . . **CLC 3, 22**
See also CA 69-72; 108; CANR 28;
DLB 72; MTCW

**Arany, Janos** 1817-1882 . . . . . . . . **NCLC 34**

**Arbuthnot, John** 1667-1735 . . . . . . . . . **LC 1**
See also DLB 101

**Archer, Herbert Winslow**
See Mencken, H(enry) L(ouis)

**Archer, Jeffrey (Howard)** 1940- . . . . **CLC 28**
See also BEST 89:3; CA 77-80; CANR 22

**Archer, Jules** 1915- . . . . . . . . . . . . . **CLC 12**
See also CA 9-12R; CANR 6; SAAS 5;
SATA 4

**Archer, Lee**
See Ellison, Harlan

**Arden, John** 1930- . . . . . . . . . **CLC 6, 13, 15**
See also CA 13-16R; CAAS 4; CANR 31;
DLB 13; MTCW

**Arenas, Reinaldo** 1943-1990 . . . . . . . **CLC 41**
See also CA 124; 128; 133; HW

**Arendt, Hannah** 1906-1975 . . . . . . . . **CLC 66**
See also CA 17-20R; 61-64; CANR 26;
MTCW

**Aretino, Pietro** 1492-1556 . . . . . . . . . **LC 12**

**Arguedas, Jose Maria**
1911-1969 . . . . . . . . . . . . . . . **CLC 10, 18**
See also CA 89-92; DLB 113; HW

**Argueta, Manlio** 1936- . . . . . . . . . . **CLC 31**
See also CA 131; HW

**Ariosto, Ludovico** 1474-1533 . . . . . . . . **LC 6**

**Aristides**
See Epstein, Joseph

**Aristophanes**
450B.C.-385B.C. . . . . . . . **CMLC 4; DC 2**

**Arlt, Roberto (Godofredo Christophersen)**
1900-1942 . . . . . . . . . . . . . . . **TCLC 29**
See also CA 123; 131; HW

**Armah, Ayi Kwei** 1939- . . . . . . . . **CLC 5, 33**
See also BLC 1; BW; CA 61-64; CANR 21;
DLB 117; MTCW

**Armatrading, Joan** 1950- . . . . . . . . . **CLC 17**
See also CA 114

**Arnette, Robert**
See Silverberg, Robert

**Arnim, Achim von (Ludwig Joachim von**
**Arnim)** 1781-1831 . . . . . . . . . **NCLC 5**
See also DLB 90

**Arnim, Bettina von** 1785-1859 . . . . **NCLC 38**
See also DLB 90

**Arnold, Matthew**
1822-1888 . . . . . . . . . **NCLC 6, 29; PC 5**
See also CDBLB 1832-1890; DLB 32, 57;
WLC

**Arnold, Thomas** 1795-1842 . . . . . . **NCLC 18**
See also DLB 55

**Arnow, Harriette (Louisa) Simpson**
1908-1986 . . . . . . . . . . . . . . **CLC 2, 7, 18**
See also CA 9-12R; 118; CANR 14; DLB 6;
MTCW; SATA 42, 47

**Arp, Hans**
See Arp, Jean

**Arp, Jean** 1887-1966 . . . . . . . . . . . . . . **CLC 5**
See also CA 81-84; 25-28R

**Arrabal**
See Arrabal, Fernando

**Arrabal, Fernando**
1932- . . . . . . . . . . . **CLC 2, 9, 18, 58, 73**
See also CA 9-12R; CANR 15

**Arrick, Fran** . . . . . . . . . . . . . . . . . . **CLC 30**

**Artaud, Antonin** 1896-1948 . . . . . **TCLC 3, 36**
See also CA 104

**Arthur, Ruth M(abel)** 1905-1979 . . . . **CLC 12**
See also CA 9-12R; 85-88; CANR 4;
SATA 7, 26

**Artsybashev, Mikhail (Petrovich)**
1878-1927 . . . . . . . . . . . . . . . . **TCLC 31**

**Arundel, Honor (Morfydd)**
1919-1973 . . . . . . . . . . . . . . . . . **CLC 17**
See also CA 21-22; 41-44R; CAP 2;
SATA 4, 24

**Asch, Sholem** 1880-1957 . . . . . . . . . **TCLC 3**
See also CA 105

**Ash, Shalom**
See Asch, Sholem

**Ashbery, John (Lawrence)**
1927- . . . **CLC 2, 3, 4, 6, 9, 13, 15, 25, 41**
See also CA 5-8R; CANR 9, 37; DLB 5;
DLBY 81; MTCW

**Ashdown, Clifford**
See Freeman, R(ichard) Austin

**Ashe, Gordon**
See Creasey, John

**Ashton-Warner, Sylvia (Constance)**
1908-1984 . . . . . . . . . . . . . . . . . **CLC 19**
See also CA 69-72; 112; CANR 29; MTCW

**Asimov, Isaac**
1920-1992 . . . . . . . . **CLC 1, 3, 9, 19, 26**
See also BEST 90:2; CA 1-4R; 137;
CANR 2, 19, 36; CLR 12; DLB 8;
MAICYA; MTCW; SATA 1, 26

**Astley, Thea (Beatrice May)**
1925- . . . . . . . . . . . . . . . . . . . . . **CLC 41**
See also CA 65-68; CANR 11

**Aston, James**
See White, T(erence) H(anbury)

**Asturias, Miguel Angel**
1899-1974 . . . . . . . . . . . . . . **CLC 3, 8, 13**
See also CA 25-28; 49-52; CANR 32;
CAP 2; DLB 113; HW; MTCW

**Atares, Carlos Saura**
See Saura (Atares), Carlos

**Atheling, William**
See Pound, Ezra (Weston Loomis)

**Atheling, William Jr.**
See Blish, James (Benjamin)

**Atherton, Gertrude (Franklin Horn)**
1857-1948 . . . . . . . . . . . . . . . . . **TCLC 2**
See also CA 104; DLB 9, 78

**Atherton, Lucius**
See Masters, Edgar Lee

**Atkins, Jack**
See Harris, Mark

**Atticus**
See Fleming, Ian (Lancaster)

**Atwood, Margaret (Eleanor)**
1939- . . . . **CLC 2, 3, 4, 8, 13, 15, 25, 44;**
**SSC 2**
See also BEST 89:2; CA 49-52; CANR 3,
24, 33; DLB 53; MTCW; SATA 50; WLC

**Aubigny, Pierre d'**
See Mencken, H(enry) L(ouis)

**Aubin, Penelope** 1685-1731(?) . . . . . . . **LC 9**
See also DLB 39

**Auchincloss, Louis (Stanton)**
1917- . . . . . . . . . . . . . **CLC 4, 6, 9, 18, 45**
See also CA 1-4R; CANR 6, 29; DLB 2;
DLBY 80; MTCW

**Auden, W(ystan) H(ugh)**
1907-1973 . . . . . **CLC 1, 2, 3, 4, 6, 9, 11,**
**14, 43; PC 1**
See also CA 9-12R; 45-48; CANR 5;
CDBLB 1914-1945; DLB 10, 20; MTCW;
WLC

**Audiberti, Jacques** 1900-1965 . . . . . . **CLC 38**
See also CA 25-28R

**Auel, Jean M(arie)** 1936- . . . . . . . . . **CLC 31**
See also AAYA 7; BEST 90:4; CA 103;
CANR 21

**Auerbach, Erich** 1892-1957 . . . . . . . **TCLC 43**
See also CA 118

**Augier, Emile** 1820-1889 . . . . . . . . **NCLC 31**

**August, John**
See De Voto, Bernard (Augustine)

**Augustine, St.** 354-430 . . . . . . . . . . **CMLC 6**

**Aurelius**
See Bourne, Randolph S(illiman)

**Austen, Jane**
1775-1817 . . . . . . . . **NCLC 1, 13, 19, 33**
See also CDBLB 1789-1832; DLB 116;
WLC

**Auster, Paul** 1947- . . . . . . . . . . . . . . **CLC 47**
See also CA 69-72; CANR 23

**Austin, Mary (Hunter)**
1868-1934 . . . . . . . . . . . . . . . . . **TCLC 25**
See also CA 109; DLB 9, 78

**Autran Dourado, Waldomiro**
See Dourado, (Waldomiro Freitas) Autran

**Averroes** 1126-1198 . . . . . . . . . . . . . **CMLC 7**
See also DLB 115

**Avison, Margaret** 1918- . . . . . . . . . . **CLC 2, 4**
See also CA 17-20R; DLB 53; MTCW

**Ayckbourn, Alan**
1939- . . . . . . . . . . **CLC 5, 8, 18, 33, 74**
See also CA 21-24R; CANR 31; DLB 13;
MTCW

**Aydy, Catherine**
See Tennant, Emma (Christina)

**Ayme, Marcel (Andre)** 1902-1967 . . . **CLC 11**
See also CA 89-92; CLR 25; DLB 72

**Ayrton, Michael** 1921-1975 . . . . . . . . . **CLC 7**
See also CA 5-8R; 61-64; CANR 9, 21

Azorin............................ CLC 11
See also Martinez Ruiz, Jose

Azuela, Mariano 1873-1952........ TCLC 3
See also CA 104; 131; HW; MTCW

Baastad, Babbis Friis
See Friis-Baastad, Babbis Ellinor

Bab
See Gilbert, W(illiam) S(chwenck)

Babbis, Eleanor
See Friis-Baastad, Babbis Ellinor

Babel, Isaak (Emmanuilovich)
1894-1941(?) ................. CLC 73
See also CA 104; TCLC 2, 13

Babits, Mihaly 1883-1941 ........ TCLC 14
See also CA 114

Babur 1483-1530.................. LC 18

Bacchelli, Riccardo 1891-1985 ..... CLC 19
See also CA 29-32R; 117

Bach, Richard (David) 1936-....... CLC 14
See also AITN 1; BEST 89:2; CA 9-12R;
CANR 18; MTCW; SATA 13

Bachman, Richard
See King, Stephen (Edwin)

Bachmann, Ingeborg 1926-1973..... CLC 69
See also CA 93-96; 45-48; DLB 85

Bacon, Francis 1561-1626 .......... LC 18
See also CDBLB Before 1660

Bacovia, George................. TCLC 24
See also Vasiliu, Gheorghe

Badanes, Jerome 1937-............ CLC 59

Bagehot, Walter 1826-1877 ...... NCLC 10
See also DLB 55

Bagnold, Enid 1889-1981.......... CLC 25
See also CA 5-8R; 103; CANR 5; DLB 13;
MAICYA; SATA 1, 25

Bagrjana, Elisaveta
See Belcheva, Elisaveta

Bagryana, Elisaveta
See Belcheva, Elisaveta

Bailey, Paul 1937- .............. CLC 45
See also CA 21-24R; CANR 16; DLB 14

Baillie, Joanna 1762-1851 ........ NCLC 2
See also DLB 93

Bainbridge, Beryl (Margaret)
1933- .... CLC 4, 5, 8, 10, 14, 18, 22, 62
See also CA 21-24R; CANR 24; DLB 14;
MTCW

Baker, Elliott 1922- .............. CLC 8
See also CA 45-48; CANR 2

Baker, Nicholson 1957-........... CLC 61
See also CA 135

Baker, Ray Stannard 1870-1946... TCLC 47
See also CA 118

Baker, Russell (Wayne) 1925-...... CLC 31
See also BEST 89:4; CA 57-60; CANR 11;
MTCW

Bakshi, Ralph 1938(?)-........... CLC 26
See also CA 112; 138

Bakunin, Mikhail (Alexandrovich)
1814-1876 ................. NCLC 25

Baldwin, James (Arthur)
1924-1987 ..... CLC 1, 2, 3, 4, 5, 8, 13,
15, 17, 42, 50, 67; DC 1; SSC 10
See also AAYA 4; BLC 1; BW; CA 1-4R;
124; CABS 1; CANR 3, 24;
CDALB 1941-1968; DLB 2, 7, 33;
DLBY 87; MTCW; SATA 9, 54; WLC

Ballard, J(ames) G(raham)
1930- ........ CLC 3, 6, 14, 36; SSC 1
See also AAYA 3; CA 5-8R; CANR 15, 39;
DLB 14; MTCW

Balmont, Konstantin (Dmitriyevich)
1867-1943 ................. TCLC 11
See also CA 109

Balzac, Honore de
1799-1850 ........ NCLC 5, 35; SSC 5
See also DLB 119; WLC

Bambara, Toni Cade 1939- ........ CLC 19
See also AAYA 5; BLC 1; BW; CA 29-32R;
CANR 24; DLB 38; MTCW

Bamdad, A.
See Shamlu, Ahmad

Banat, D. R.
See Bradbury, Ray (Douglas)

Bancroft, Laura
See Baum, L(yman) Frank

Banim, John 1798-1842 ......... NCLC 13
See also DLB 116

Banim, Michael 1796-1874 ...... NCLC 13

Banks, Iain
See Banks, Iain M(enzies)

Banks, Iain M(enzies) 1954-....... CLC 34
See also CA 123; 128

Banks, Lynne Reid ................ CLC 23
See also Reid Banks, Lynne
See also AAYA 6

Banks, Russell 1940- .......... CLC 37, 72
See also CA 65-68; CAAS 15; CANR 19

Banville, John 1945-.............. CLC 46
See also CA 117; 128; DLB 14

Banville, Theodore (Faullain) de
1832-1891 ................. NCLC 9

Baraka, Amiri
1934- ... CLC 1, 2, 3, 5, 10, 14, 33; PC 4
See also Jones, LeRoi
See also BLC 1; BW; CA 21-24R; CABS 3;
CANR 27, 38; CDALB 1941-1968;
DLB 5, 7, 16, 38; DLBD 8; MTCW

Barbellion, W. N. P............... TCLC 24
See also Cummings, Bruce F(rederick)

Barbera, Jack 1945-.............. CLC 44
See also CA 110

Barbey d'Aurevilly, Jules Amedee
1808-1889 ................. NCLC 1
See also DLB 119

Barbusse, Henri 1873-1935 ........ TCLC 5
See also CA 105; DLB 65

Barclay, Bill
See Moorcock, Michael (John)

Barclay, William Ewert
See Moorcock, Michael (John)

Barea, Arturo 1897-1957 ........ TCLC 14
See also CA 111

Barfoot, Joan 1946-............. CLC 18
See also CA 105

Baring, Maurice 1874-1945 ....... TCLC 8
See also CA 105; DLB 34

Barker, Clive 1952- ............. CLC 52
See also BEST 90:3; CA 121; 129; MTCW

Barker, George Granville
1913-1991 ................. CLC 8, 48
See also CA 9-12R; 135; CANR 7, 38;
DLB 20; MTCW

Barker, Harley Granville
See Granville-Barker, Harley
See also DLB 10

Barker, Howard 1946-........... CLC 37
See also CA 102; DLB 13

Barker, Pat 1943-............... CLC 32
See also CA 117; 122

Barlow, Joel 1754-1812 ......... NCLC 23
See also DLB 37

Barnard, Mary (Ethel) 1909-...... CLC 48
See also CA 21-22; CAP 2

Barnes, Djuna
1892-1982 ... CLC 3, 4, 8, 11, 29; SSC 3
See also CA 9-12R; 107; CANR 16; DLB 4,
9, 45; MTCW

Barnes, Julian 1946-............. CLC 42
See also CA 102; CANR 19

Barnes, Peter 1931- ............ CLC 5, 56
See also CA 65-68; CAAS 12; CANR 33,
34; DLB 13; MTCW

Baroja (y Nessi), Pio 1872-1956 .... TCLC 8
See also CA 104

Baron, David
See Pinter, Harold

Baron Corvo
See Rolfe, Frederick (William Serafino
Austin Lewis Mary)

Barondess, Sue K(aufman)
1926-1977 .................... CLC 8
See also Kaufman, Sue
See also CA 1-4R; 69-72; CANR 1

Baron de Teive
See Pessoa, Fernando (Antonio Nogueira)

Barres, Maurice 1862-1923 ....... TCLC 47
See also DLB 123

Barreto, Afonso Henrique de Lima
See Lima Barreto, Afonso Henrique de

Barrett, (Roger) Syd 1946- ........ CLC 35
See also Pink Floyd

Barrett, William (Christopher)
1913- ........................ CLC 27
See also CA 13-16R; CANR 11

Barrie, J(ames) M(atthew)
1860-1937 .................... TCLC 2
See also CA 104; 136; CDBLB 1890-1914;
CLR 16; DLB 10; MAICYA; YABC 1

Barrington, Michael
See Moorcock, Michael (John)

Barrol, Grady
See Bograd, Larry

Barry, Mike
See Malzberg, Barry N(athaniel)

Barry, Philip 1896-1949......... TCLC 11
See also CA 109; DLB 7

**Bart, Andre Schwarz**
See Schwarz-Bart, Andre

**Barth, John (Simmons)**
1930- ...... **CLC 1, 2, 3, 5, 7, 9, 10, 14, 27, 51; SSC 10**
See also AITN 1, 2; CA 1-4R; CABS 1; CANR 5, 23; DLB 2; MTCW

**Barthelme, Donald**
1931-1989 ..... **CLC 1, 2, 3, 5, 6, 8, 13, 23, 46, 59; SSC 2**
See also CA 21-24R; 129; CANR 20; DLB 2; DLBY 80, 89; MTCW; SATA 7, 62

**Barthelme, Frederick** 1943-........ **CLC 36**
See also CA 114; 122; DLBY 85

**Barthes, Roland (Gerard)**
1915-1980 ................. **CLC 24**
See also CA 130; 97-100; MTCW

**Barzun, Jacques (Martin)** 1907- .... **CLC 51**
See also CA 61-64; CANR 22

**Bashevis, Isaac**
See Singer, Isaac Bashevis

**Bashkirtseff, Marie** 1859-1884 ... **NCLC 27**

**Basho**
See Matsuo Basho

**Bass, Kingsley B. Jr.**
See Bullins, Ed

**Bassani, Giorgio** 1916-............. **CLC 9**
See also CA 65-68; CANR 33; MTCW

**Bastos, Augusto (Antonio) Roa**
See Roa Bastos, Augusto (Antonio)

**Bataille, Georges** 1897-1962 ....... **CLC 29**
See also CA 101; 89-92

**Bates, H(erbert) E(rnest)**
1905-1974 .......... **CLC 46; SSC 10**
See also CA 93-96; 45-48; CANR 34; MTCW

**Bauchart**
See Camus, Albert

**Baudelaire, Charles**
1821-1867 .......... **NCLC 6, 29; PC 1**
See also WLC

**Baudrillard, Jean** 1929- ........... **CLC 60**

**Baum, L(yman) Frank** 1856-1919 ... **TCLC 7**
See also CA 108; 133; CLR 15; DLB 22; MAICYA; MTCW; SATA 18

**Baum, Louis F.**
See Baum, L(yman) Frank

**Baumbach, Jonathan** 1933- ...... **CLC 6, 23**
See also CA 13-16R; CAAS 5; CANR 12; DLBY 80; MTCW

**Bausch, Richard (Carl)** 1945- ...... **CLC 51**
See also CA 101; CAAS 14

**Baxter, Charles** 1947-............ **CLC 45**
See also CA 57-60

**Baxter, James K(eir)** 1926-1972 .... **CLC 14**
See also CA 77-80

**Baxter, John**
See Hunt, E(verette) Howard Jr.

**Bayer, Sylvia**
See Glassco, John

**Beagle, Peter S(oyer)** 1939-........ **CLC 7**
See also CA 9-12R; CANR 4; DLBY 80; SATA 60

**Bean, Normal**
See Burroughs, Edgar Rice

**Beard, Charles A(ustin)**
1874-1948 ................. **TCLC 15**
See also CA 115; DLB 17; SATA 18

**Beardsley, Aubrey** 1872-1898 ..... **NCLC 6**

**Beattie, Ann**
1947- .... **CLC 8, 13, 18, 40, 63; SSC 11**
See also BEST 90:2; CA 81-84; DLBY 82; MTCW

**Beattie, James** 1735-1803 ....... **NCLC 25**
See also DLB 109

**Beauchamp, Kathleen Mansfield** 1888-1923
See Mansfield, Katherine
See also CA 104; 134

**Beauvoir, Simone (Lucie Ernestine Marie Bertrand) de**
1908-1986 ... **CLC 1, 2, 4, 8, 14, 31, 44, 50, 71**
See also CA 9-12R; 118; CANR 28; DLB 72; DLBY 86; MTCW; WLC

**Becker, Jurek** 1937-............ **CLC 7, 19**
See also CA 85-88; DLB 75

**Becker, Walter** 1950-............. **CLC 26**

**Beckett, Samuel (Barclay)**
1906-1989 ..... **CLC 1, 2, 3, 4, 6, 9, 10, 11, 14, 18, 29, 57, 59**
See also CA 5-8R; 130; CANR 33; CDBLB 1945-1960; DLB 13, 15; DLBY 90; MTCW; WLC

**Beckford, William** 1760-1844 .... **NCLC 16**
See also DLB 39

**Beckman, Gunnel** 1910-........... **CLC 26**
See also CA 33-36R; CANR 15; CLR 25; MAICYA; SAAS 9; SATA 6

**Becque, Henri** 1837-1899........ **NCLC 3**

**Beddoes, Thomas Lovell**
1803-1849 ................. **NCLC 3**
See also DLB 96

**Bedford, Donald F.**
See Fearing, Kenneth (Flexner)

**Beecher, Catharine Esther**
1800-1878 ................. **NCLC 30**
See also DLB 1

**Beecher, John** 1904-1980........... **CLC 6**
See also AITN 1; CA 5-8R; 105; CANR 8

**Beer, Johann** 1655-1700............ **LC 5**

**Beer, Patricia** 1924-.............. **CLC 58**
See also CA 61-64; CANR 13; DLB 40

**Beerbohm, Henry Maximilian**
1872-1956 ................. **TCLC 1, 24**
See also CA 104; DLB 34, 100

**Begiebing, Robert J(ohn)** 1946-..... **CLC 70**
See also CA 122

**Behan, Brendan**
1923-1964 ............ **CLC 1, 8, 11, 15**
See also CA 73-76; CANR 33; CDBLB 1945-1960; DLB 13; MTCW

**Behn, Aphra** 1640(?)-1689 ........... **LC 1**
See also DLB 39, 80; WLC

**Behrman, S(amuel) N(athaniel)**
1893-1973 ................. **CLC 40**
See also CA 13-16; 45-48; CAP 1; DLB 7, 44

**Belasco, David** 1853-1931 ........ **TCLC 3**
See also CA 104; DLB 7

**Belcheva, Elisaveta** 1893- ........ **CLC 10**

**Beldone, Phil "Cheech"**
See Ellison, Harlan

**Beleno**
See Azuela, Mariano

**Belinski, Vissarion Grigoryevich**
1811-1848 ................. **NCLC 5**

**Belitt, Ben** 1911-................. **CLC 22**
See also CA 13-16R; CAAS 4; CANR 7; DLB 5

**Bell, James Madison** 1826-1902 ... **TCLC 43**
See also BLC 1; BW; CA 122; 124; DLB 50

**Bell, Madison (Smartt)** 1957- ...... **CLC 41**
See also CA 111; CANR 28

**Bell, Marvin (Hartley)** 1937-..... **CLC 8, 31**
See also CA 21-24R; CAAS 14; DLB 5; MTCW

**Bell, W. L. D.**
See Mencken, H(enry) L(ouis)

**Bellamy, Atwood C.**
See Mencken, H(enry) L(ouis)

**Bellamy, Edward** 1850-1898 ...... **NCLC 4**
See also DLB 12

**Bellin, Edward J.**
See Kuttner, Henry

**Belloc, (Joseph) Hilaire (Pierre)**
1870-1953 ............... **TCLC 7, 18**
See also CA 106; DLB 19, 100; YABC 1

**Belloc, Joseph Peter Rene Hilaire**
See Belloc, (Joseph) Hilaire (Pierre)

**Belloc, Joseph Pierre Hilaire**
See Belloc, (Joseph) Hilaire (Pierre)

**Belloc, M. A.**
See Lowndes, Marie Adelaide (Belloc)

**Bellow, Saul**
1915- ..... **CLC 1, 2, 3, 6, 8, 10, 13, 15, 25, 33, 34, 63**
See also AITN 2; BEST 89:3; CA 5-8R; CABS 1; CANR 29; CDALB 1941-1968; DLB 2, 28; DLBD 3; DLBY 82; MTCW; WLC

**Belser, Reimond Karel Maria de**
1929-..................... **CLC 14**

**Bely, Andrey** ..................... **TCLC 7**
See also Bugayev, Boris Nikolayevich

**Benary, Margot**
See Benary-Isbert, Margot

**Benary-Isbert, Margot** 1889-1979... **CLC 12**
See also CA 5-8R; 89-92; CANR 4; CLR 12; MAICYA; SATA 2, 21

**Benavente (y Martinez), Jacinto**
1866-1954 ................. **TCLC 3**
See also CA 106; 131; HW; MTCW

**Benchley, Peter (Bradford)**
1940-..................... **CLC 4, 8**
See also AITN 2; CA 17-20R; CANR 12, 35; MTCW; SATA 3

**Benchley, Robert (Charles)**
1889-1945 ................. **TCLC 1**
See also CA 105; DLB 11

**Benedikt, Michael** 1935- ........ **CLC 4, 14**
See also CA 13-16R; CANR 7; DLB 5

Benet, Juan 1927-............... **CLC 28**

Benet, Stephen Vincent
1898-1943 ........... **TCLC 7; SSC 10**
See also CA 104; DLB 4, 48, 102; YABC 1

Benet, William Rose 1886-1950 ... **TCLC 28**
See also CA 118; DLB 45

Benford, Gregory (Albert) 1941-.... **CLC 52**
See also CA 69-72; CANR 12, 24;
DLBY 82

Bengtsson, Frans (Gunnar)
1894-1954 .................. **TCLC 48**

Benjamin, Lois
See Gould, Lois

Benjamin, Walter 1892-1940...... **TCLC 39**

Benn, Gottfried 1886-1956......... **TCLC 3**
See also CA 106; DLB 56

Bennett, Alan 1934-.............. **CLC 45**
See also CA 103; CANR 35; MTCW

Bennett, (Enoch) Arnold
1867-1931 ............. **TCLC 5, 20**
See also CA 106; CDBLB 1890-1914;
DLB 10, 34, 98

Bennett, Elizabeth
See Mitchell, Margaret (Munnerlyn)

Bennett, George Harold 1930-
See Bennett, Hal
See also BW; CA 97-100

Bennett, Hal ..................... **CLC 5**
See also Bennett, George Harold
See also DLB 33

Bennett, Jay 1912-............... **CLC 35**
See also CA 69-72; CANR 11; SAAS 4;
SATA 27, 41

Bennett, Louise (Simone) 1919-..... **CLC 28**
See also BLC 1; DLB 117

Benson, E(dward) F(rederic)
1867-1940 .................. **TCLC 27**
See also CA 114

Benson, Jackson J. 1930-.......... **CLC 34**
See also CA 25-28R; DLB 111

Benson, Sally 1900-1972 .......... **CLC 17**
See also CA 19-20; 37-40R; CAP 1;
SATA 1, 27, 35

Benson, Stella 1892-1933......... **TCLC 17**
See also CA 117; DLB 36

Bentham, Jeremy 1748-1832 ..... **NCLC 38**
See also DLB 107

Bentley, E(dmund) C(lerihew)
1875-1956 .................. **TCLC 12**
See also CA 108; DLB 70

Bentley, Eric (Russell) 1916-....... **CLC 24**
See also CA 5-8R; CANR 6

Beranger, Pierre Jean de
1780-1857 ................. **NCLC 34**

Berger, Colonel
See Malraux, (Georges-)Andre

Berger, John (Peter) 1926- ...... **CLC 2, 19**
See also CA 81-84; DLB 14

Berger, Melvin H. 1927-.......... **CLC 12**
See also CA 5-8R; CANR 4; SAAS 2;
SATA 5

Berger, Thomas (Louis)
1924-......... **CLC 3, 5, 8, 11, 18, 38**
See also CA 1-4R; CANR 5, 28; DLB 2;
DLBY 80; MTCW

Bergman, (Ernst) Ingmar
1918-.................... **CLC 16, 72**
See also CA 81-84; CANR 33

Bergson, Henri 1859-1941....... **TCLC 32**

Bergstein, Eleanor 1938-........... **CLC 4**
See also CA 53-56; CANR 5

Berkoff, Steven 1937-............. **CLC 56**
See also CA 104

Bermant, Chaim (Icyk) 1929- ...... **CLC 40**
See also CA 57-60; CANR 6, 31

Bernanos, (Paul Louis) Georges
1888-1948 ................... **TCLC 3**
See also CA 104; 130; DLB 72

Bernard, April 1956- ............. **CLC 59**
See also CA 131

Bernhard, Thomas
1931-1989 ............. **CLC 3, 32, 61**
See also CA 85-88; 127; CANR 32;
DLB 85; MTCW

Berrigan, Daniel 1921-............ **CLC 4**
See also CA 33-36R; CAAS 1; CANR 11;
DLB 5

Berrigan, Edmund Joseph Michael Jr.
1934-1983
See Berrigan, Ted
See also CA 61-64; 110; CANR 14

Berrigan, Ted.................... **CLC 37**
See also Berrigan, Edmund Joseph Michael
Jr.
See also DLB 5

Berry, Charles Edward Anderson 1931-
See Berry, Chuck
See also CA 115

Berry, Chuck.................... **CLC 17**
See also Berry, Charles Edward Anderson

Berry, Jonas
See Ashbery, John (Lawrence)

Berry, Wendell (Erdman)
1934-............. **CLC 4, 6, 8, 27, 46**
See also AITN 1; CA 73-76; DLB 5, 6

Berryman, John
1914-1972 ..... **CLC 1, 2, 3, 4, 6, 8, 10,
13, 25, 62**
See also CA 13-16; 33-36R; CABS 2;
CANR 35; CAP 1; CDALB 1941-1968;
DLB 48; MTCW

Bertolucci, Bernardo 1940- ........ **CLC 16**
See also CA 106

Bertrand, Aloysius 1807-1841 .... **NCLC 31**

Bertran de Born c. 1140-1215 ..... **CMLC 5**

Besant, Annie (Wood) 1847-1933 ... **TCLC 9**
See also CA 105

Bessie, Alvah 1904-1985.......... **CLC 23**
See also CA 5-8R; 116; CANR 2; DLB 26

Bethlen, T. D.
See Silverberg, Robert

Beti, Mongo..................... **CLC 27**
See also Biyidi, Alexandre
See also BLC 1

Betjeman, John
1906-1984 ....... **CLC 2, 6, 10, 34, 43**
See also CA 9-12R; 112; CANR 33;
CDBLB 1945-1960; DLB 20; DLBY 84;
MTCW

Betti, Ugo 1892-1953 ............. **TCLC 5**
See also CA 104

Betts, Doris (Waugh) 1932-.... **CLC 3, 6, 28**
See also CA 13-16R; CANR 9; DLBY 82

Bevan, Alistair
See Roberts, Keith (John Kingston)

Beynon, John
See Harris, John (Wyndham Parkes Lucas)
Beynon

Bialik, Chaim Nachman
1873-1934 .................. **TCLC 25**

Bickerstaff, Isaac
See Swift, Jonathan

Bidart, Frank 19(?)-............. **CLC 33**

Bienek, Horst 1930-............ **CLC 7, 11**
See also CA 73-76; DLB 75

Bierce, Ambrose (Gwinett)
1842-1914(?) ..... **TCLC 1, 7, 44; SSC 9**
See also CA 104; CDALB 1865-1917;
DLB 11, 12, 23, 71, 74; WLC

Billings, Josh
See Shaw, Henry Wheeler

Billington, Rachel 1942-.......... **CLC 43**
See also AITN 2; CA 33-36R

Binyon, T(imothy) J(ohn) 1936- .... **CLC 34**
See also CA 111; CANR 28

Bioy Casares, Adolfo 1914-.... **CLC 4, 8, 13**
See also CA 29-32R; CANR 19; DLB 113;
HW; MTCW

Bird, C.
See Ellison, Harlan

Bird, Cordwainer
See Ellison, Harlan

Bird, Robert Montgomery
1806-1854 .................. **NCLC 1**

Birney, (Alfred) Earle
1904-.................. **CLC 1, 4, 6, 11**
See also CA 1-4R; CANR 5, 20; DLB 88;
MTCW

Bishop, Elizabeth
1911-1979 ..... **CLC 1, 4, 9, 13, 15, 32;
PC 3**
See also CA 5-8R; 89-92; CABS 2;
CANR 26; CDALB 1968-1988; DLB 5;
MTCW; SATA 24

Bishop, John 1935-............... **CLC 10**
See also CA 105

Bissett, Bill 1939-................ **CLC 18**
See also CA 69-72; CANR 15; DLB 53;
MTCW

Bitov, Andrei (Georgievich) 1937-... **CLC 57**

Biyidi, Alexandre 1932-
See Beti, Mongo
See also BW; CA 114; 124; MTCW

Bjarme, Brynjolf
See Ibsen, Henrik (Johan)

Bjornson, Bjornstjerne (Martinius)
1832-1910 ............... **TCLC 7, 37**
See also CA 104

**Black, Robert**
See Holdstock, Robert P.

**Blackburn, Paul** 1926-1971 ...... **CLC 9, 43**
See also CA 81-84; 33-36R; CANR 34;
DLB 16; DLBY 81

**Black Elk** 1863-1950 ........... **TCLC 33**

**Black Hobart**
See Sanders, (James) Ed(ward)

**Blacklin, Malcolm**
See Chambers, Aidan

**Blackmore, R(ichard) D(oddridge)**
1825-1900 .................. **TCLC 27**
See also CA 120; DLB 18

**Blackmur, R(ichard) P(almer)**
1904-1965 ................. **CLC 2, 24**
See also CA 11-12; 25-28R; CAP 1; DLB 63

**Black Tarantula, The**
See Acker, Kathy

**Blackwood, Algernon (Henry)**
1869-1951 .................. **TCLC 5**
See also CA 105

**Blackwood, Caroline** 1931- ....... **CLC 6, 9**
See also CA 85-88; CANR 32; DLB 14;
MTCW

**Blade, Alexander**
See Hamilton, Edmond; Silverberg, Robert

**Blaga, Lucian** 1895-1961 ......... **CLC 75**

**Blair, Eric (Arthur)** 1903-1950
See Orwell, George
See also CA 104; 132; MTCW; SATA 29

**Blais, Marie-Claire**
1939- ............. **CLC 2, 4, 6, 13, 22**
See also CA 21-24R; CAAS 4; CANR 38;
DLB 53; MTCW

**Blaise, Clark** 1940- .............. **CLC 29**
See also AITN 2; CA 53-56; CAAS 3;
CANR 5; DLB 53

**Blake, Nicholas**
See Day Lewis, C(ecil)
See also DLB 77

**Blake, William** 1757-1827 ....... **NCLC 13**
See also CDBLB 1789-1832; DLB 93;
MAICYA; SATA 30; WLC

**Blasco Ibanez, Vicente**
1867-1928 .................. **TCLC 12**
See also CA 110; 131; HW; MTCW

**Blatty, William Peter** 1928- ........ **CLC 2**
See also CA 5-8R; CANR 9

**Bleeck, Oliver**
See Thomas, Ross (Elmore)

**Blessing, Lee** 1949- ............... **CLC 54**

**Blish, James (Benjamin)**
1921-1975 .................. **CLC 14**
See also CA 1-4R; 57-60; CANR 3; DLB 8;
MTCW; SATA 66

**Bliss, Reginald**
See Wells, H(erbert) G(eorge)

**Blixen, Karen (Christentze Dinesen)**
1885-1962
See Dinesen, Isak
See also CA 25-28; CANR 22; CAP 2;
MTCW; SATA 44

**Bloch, Robert (Albert)** 1917- ...... **CLC 33**
See also CA 5-8R; CANR 5; DLB 44;
SATA 12

**Blok, Alexander (Alexandrovich)**
1880-1921 .................. **TCLC 5**
See also CA 104

**Blom, Jan**
See Breytenbach, Breyten

**Bloom, Harold** 1930- ............. **CLC 24**
See also CA 13-16R; CANR 39; DLB 67

**Bloomfield, Aurelius**
See Bourne, Randolph S(illiman)

**Blount, Roy (Alton) Jr.** 1941- ...... **CLC 38**
See also CA 53-56; CANR 10, 28; MTCW

**Bloy, Leon** 1846-1917 ........... **TCLC 22**
See also CA 121; DLB 123

**Blume, Judy (Sussman)** 1938- ... **CLC 12, 30**
See also AAYA 3; CA 29-32R; CANR 13,
37; CLR 2, 15; DLB 52; MAICYA;
MTCW; SATA 2, 31

**Blunden, Edmund (Charles)**
1896-1974 ................. **CLC 2, 56**
See also CA 17-18; 45-48; CAP 2; DLB 20,
100; MTCW

**Bly, Robert (Elwood)**
1926- .......... **CLC 1, 2, 5, 10, 15, 38**
See also CA 5-8R; DLB 5; MTCW

**Bobette**
See Simenon, Georges (Jacques Christian)

**Boccaccio, Giovanni** 1313-1375
See also SSC 10

**Bochco, Steven** 1943- ............. **CLC 35**
See also CA 124; 138

**Bodenheim, Maxwell** 1892-1954 ... **TCLC 44**
See also CA 110; DLB 9, 45

**Bodker, Cecil** 1927- ............. **CLC 21**
See also CA 73-76; CANR 13; CLR 23;
MAICYA; SATA 14

**Boell, Heinrich (Theodor)** 1917-1985
See Boll, Heinrich (Theodor)
See also CA 21-24R; 116; CANR 24;
DLB 69; DLBY 85; MTCW

**Bogan, Louise** 1897-1970 ..... **CLC 4, 39, 46**
See also CA 73-76; 25-28R; CANR 33;
DLB 45; MTCW

**Bogarde, Dirk** ................... **CLC 19**
See also Van Den Bogarde, Derek Jules
Gaspard Ulric Niven
See also DLB 14

**Bogosian, Eric** 1953- ............. **CLC 45**
See also CA 138

**Bograd, Larry** 1953- ............. **CLC 35**
See also CA 93-96; SATA 33

**Boiardo, Matteo Maria** 1441-1494 .... **LC 6**

**Boileau-Despreaux, Nicolas**
1636-1711 ................... **LC 3**

**Boland, Eavan** 1944- ........... **CLC 40, 67**
See also DLB 40

**Boll, Heinrich (Theodor)**
1917-1985 ... **CLC 2, 3, 6, 9, 11, 15, 27,
39, 72**
See also Boell, Heinrich (Theodor)
See also DLB 69; DLBY 85; WLC

**Bolt, Robert (Oxton)** 1924- ........ **CLC 14**
See also CA 17-20R; CANR 35; DLB 13;
MTCW

**Bomkauf**
See Kaufman, Bob (Garnell)

**Bonaventura** .................... **NCLC 35**
See also DLB 90

**Bond, Edward** 1934- ....... **CLC 4, 6, 13, 23**
See also CA 25-28R; CANR 38; DLB 13;
MTCW

**Bonham, Frank** 1914-1989 ........ **CLC 12**
See also AAYA 1; CA 9-12R; CANR 4, 36;
MAICYA; SAAS 3; SATA 1, 49, 62

**Bonnefoy, Yves** 1923- ........ **CLC 9, 15, 58**
See also CA 85-88; CANR 33; MTCW

**Bontemps, Arna(ud Wendell)**
1902-1973 ................. **CLC 1, 18**
See also BLC 1; BW; CA 1-4R; 41-44R;
CANR 4, 35; CLR 6; DLB 48, 51;
MAICYA; MTCW; SATA 2, 24, 44

**Booth, Martin** 1944- .............. **CLC 13**
See also CA 93-96; CAAS 2

**Booth, Philip** 1925- .............. **CLC 23**
See also CA 5-8R; CANR 5; DLBY 82

**Booth, Wayne C(layson)** 1921- ..... **CLC 24**
See also CA 1-4R; CAAS 5; CANR 3;
DLB 67

**Borchert, Wolfgang** 1921-1947 ..... **TCLC 5**
See also CA 104; DLB 69

**Borges, Jorge Luis**
1899-1986 ... **CLC 1, 2, 3, 4, 6, 8, 9, 10,
13, 19, 44, 48; SSC 4**
See also CA 21-24R; CANR 19, 33;
DLB 113; DLBY 86; HW; MTCW; WLC

**Borowski, Tadeusz** 1922-1951 ...... **TCLC 9**
See also CA 106

**Borrow, George (Henry)**
1803-1881 .................. **NCLC 9**
See also DLB 21, 55

**Bosschere, Jean de** 1878(?)-1953 ... **TCLC 19**
See also CA 115

**Boswell, James** 1740-1795 .......... **LC 4**
See also CDBLB 1660-1789; DLB 104;
WLC

**Bottoms, David** 1949- ............. **CLC 53**
See also CA 105; CANR 22; DLB 120;
DLBY 83

**Boucolon, Maryse** 1937-
See Conde, Maryse
See also CA 110; CANR 30

**Bourget, Paul (Charles Joseph)**
1852-1935 .................. **TCLC 12**
See also CA 107; DLB 123

**Bourjaily, Vance (Nye)** 1922- .... **CLC 8, 62**
See also CA 1-4R; CAAS 1; CANR 2;
DLB 2

**Bourne, Randolph S(illiman)**
1886-1918 .................. **TCLC 16**
See also CA 117; DLB 63

**Bova, Ben(jamin William)** 1932- .... **CLC 45**
See also CA 5-8R; CANR 11; CLR 3;
DLBY 81; MAICYA; MTCW; SATA 6,
68

Bowen, Elizabeth (Dorothea Cole)
1899-1973 . . . . . **CLC 1, 3, 6, 11, 15, 22;**
**SSC 3**
See also CA 17-18; 41-44R; CANR 35;
CAP 2; CDBLB 1945-1960; DLB 15;
MTCW

Bowering, George 1935- . . . . . . . **CLC 15, 47**
See also CA 21-24R; CAAS 16; CANR 10;
DLB 53

Bowering, Marilyn R(uthe) 1949- . . . **CLC 32**
See also CA 101

Bowers, Edgar 1924- . . . . . . . . . . . . . **CLC 9**
See also CA 5-8R; CANR 24; DLB 5

Bowie, David . . . . . . . . . . . . . . . . . . . . **CLC 17**
See also Jones, David Robert

Bowles, Jane (Sydney)
1917-1973 . . . . . . . . . . . . . . . . **CLC 3, 68**
See also CA 19-20; 41-44R; CAP 2

Bowles, Paul (Frederick)
1910- . . . . . . . **CLC 1, 2, 19, 53; SSC 3**
See also CA 1-4R; CAAS 1; CANR 1, 19;
DLB 5, 6; MTCW

Box, Edgar
See Vidal, Gore

Boyd, Nancy
See Millay, Edna St. Vincent

Boyd, William 1952- . . . . . . . **CLC 28, 53, 70**
See also CA 114; 120

Boyle, Kay 1902- . . **CLC 1, 5, 19, 58; SSC 5**
See also CA 13-16R; CAAS 1; CANR 29;
DLB 4, 9, 48, 86; MTCW

Boyle, Mark
See Kienzle, William X(avier)

Boyle, Patrick 1905-1982 . . . . . . . . . **CLC 19**
See also CA 127

Boyle, T. Coraghessan 1948- . . . . **CLC 36, 55**
See also BEST 90:4; CA 120; DLBY 86

Brackenridge, Hugh Henry
1748-1816 . . . . . . . . . . . . . . . . . . **NCLC 7**
See also DLB 11, 37

Bradbury, Edward P.
See Moorcock, Michael (John)

Bradbury, Malcolm (Stanley)
1932- . . . . . . . . . . . . . . . . . . . **CLC 32, 61**
See also CA 1-4R; CANR 1, 33; DLB 14;
MTCW

Bradbury, Ray (Douglas)
1920- . . . . . . . . . . **CLC 1, 3, 10, 15, 42**
See also AITN 1, 2; CA 1-4R; CANR 2, 30;
CDALB 1968-1988; DLB 2, 8; MTCW;
SATA 11, 64; WLC

Bradford, Gamaliel 1863-1932 . . . . . **TCLC 36**
See also DLB 17

Bradley, David (Henry Jr.) 1950- . . . **CLC 23**
See also BLC 1; BW; CA 104; CANR 26;
DLB 33

Bradley, John Ed 1959- . . . . . . . . . . . **CLC 55**

Bradley, Marion Zimmer 1930- . . . . . **CLC 30**
See also AAYA 9; CA 57-60; CAAS 10;
CANR 7, 31; DLB 8; MTCW

Bradstreet, Anne 1612(?)-1672 . . . . . . . **LC 4**
See also CDALB 1640-1865; DLB 24

Bragg, Melvyn 1939- . . . . . . . . . . . . . **CLC 10**
See also BEST 89:3; CA 57-60; CANR 10;
DLB 14

Braine, John (Gerard)
1922-1986 . . . . . . . . . . . . . . **CLC 1, 3, 41**
See also CA 1-4R; 120; CANR 1, 33;
CDBLB 1945-1960; DLB 15; DLBY 86;
MTCW

Brammer, William 1930(?)-1978 . . . . **CLC 31**
See also CA 77-80

Brancati, Vitaliano 1907-1954 . . . . . **TCLC 12**
See also CA 109

Brancato, Robin F(idler) 1936- . . . . . **CLC 35**
See also AAYA 9; CA 69-72; CANR 11;
SAAS 9; SATA 23

Brand, Millen 1906-1980 . . . . . . . . . . **CLC 7**
See also CA 21-24R; 97-100

Branden, Barbara . . . . . . . . . . . . . . . . **CLC 44**

Brandes, Georg (Morris Cohen)
1842-1927 . . . . . . . . . . . . . . . . . **TCLC 10**
See also CA 105

Brandys, Kazimierz 1916- . . . . . . . . . **CLC 62**

Branley, Franklyn M(ansfield)
1915- . . . . . . . . . . . . . . . . . . . . . **CLC 21**
See also CA 33-36R; CANR 14, 39;
CLR 13; MAICYA; SATA 4, 68

Brathwaite, Edward (Kamau)
1930- . . . . . . . . . . . . . . . . . . . . . **CLC 11**
See also BW; CA 25-28R; CANR 11, 26

Brautigan, Richard (Gary)
1935-1984 . . . . **CLC 1, 3, 5, 9, 12, 34, 42**
See also CA 53-56; 113; CANR 34; DLB 2,
5; DLBY 80, 84; MTCW; SATA 56

Braverman, Kate 1950- . . . . . . . . . . . **CLC 67**
See also CA 89-92

Brecht, Bertolt
1898-1956 . . . . . **TCLC 1, 6, 13, 35; DC 3**
See also CA 104; 133; DLB 56; MTCW;
WLC

Brecht, Eugen Berthold Friedrich
See Brecht, Bertolt

Bremer, Fredrika 1801-1865 . . . . . **NCLC 11**

Brennan, Christopher John
1870-1932 . . . . . . . . . . . . . . . . . **TCLC 17**
See also CA 117

Brennan, Maeve 1917- . . . . . . . . . . . . **CLC 5**
See also CA 81-84

Brentano, Clemens (Maria)
1778-1842 . . . . . . . . . . . . . . . . . . **NCLC 1**

Brent of Bin Bin
See Franklin, (Stella Maraia Sarah) Miles

Brenton, Howard 1942- . . . . . . . . . . . **CLC 31**
See also CA 69-72; CANR 33; DLB 13;
MTCW

Breslin, James 1930-
See Breslin, Jimmy
See also CA 73-76; CANR 31; MTCW

Breslin, Jimmy . . . . . . . . . . . . . . . . **CLC 4, 43**
See also Breslin, James
See also AITN 1

Bresson, Robert 1907- . . . . . . . . . . . . **CLC 16**
See also CA 110

Breton, Andre 1896-1966 . . . **CLC 2, 9, 15, 54**
See also CA 19-20; 25-28R; CAP 2;
DLB 65; MTCW

Breytenbach, Breyten 1939(?)- . . **CLC 23, 37**
See also CA 113; 129

Bridgers, Sue Ellen 1942- . . . . . . . . . **CLC 26**
See also AAYA 8; CA 65-68; CANR 11,
36; CLR 18; DLB 52; MAICYA;
SAAS 1; SATA 22

Bridges, Robert (Seymour)
1844-1930 . . . . . . . . . . . . . . . . . **TCLC 1**
See also CA 104; CDBLB 1890-1914;
DLB 19, 98

Bridie, James . . . . . . . . . . . . . . . . . . . **TCLC 3**
See also Mavor, Osborne Henry
See also DLB 10

Brin, David 1950- . . . . . . . . . . . . . . . **CLC 34**
See also CA 102; CANR 24; SATA 65

Brink, Andre (Philippus)
1935- . . . . . . . . . . . . . . . . . . . **CLC 18, 36**
See also CA 104; CANR 39; MTCW

Brinsmead, H(esba) F(ay) 1922- . . . . **CLC 21**
See also CA 21-24R; CANR 10; MAICYA;
SAAS 5; SATA 18

Brittain, Vera (Mary)
1893(?)-1970 . . . . . . . . . . . . . . . **CLC 23**
See also CA 13-16; 25-28R; CAP 1; MTCW

Broch, Hermann 1886-1951 . . . . . . . **TCLC 20**
See also CA 117; DLB 85

Brock, Rose
See Hansen, Joseph

Brodkey, Harold 1930- . . . . . . . . . . . **CLC 56**
See also CA 111

Brodsky, Iosif Alexandrovich 1940-
See Brodsky, Joseph
See also AITN 1; CA 41-44R; CANR 37;
MTCW

Brodsky, Joseph . . . . . . . **CLC 4, 6, 13, 36, 50**
See also Brodsky, Iosif Alexandrovich

Brodsky, Michael Mark 1948- . . . . . **CLC 19**
See also CA 102; CANR 18

Bromell, Henry 1947- . . . . . . . . . . . . . **CLC 5**
See also CA 53-56; CANR 9

Bromfield, Louis (Brucker)
1896-1956 . . . . . . . . . . . . . . . . . **TCLC 11**
See also CA 107; DLB 4, 9, 86

Broner, E(sther) M(asserman)
1930- . . . . . . . . . . . . . . . . . . . . . **CLC 19**
See also CA 17-20R; CANR 8, 25; DLB 28

Bronk, William 1918- . . . . . . . . . . . . **CLC 10**
See also CA 89-92; CANR 23

Bronstein, Lev Davidovich
See Trotsky, Leon

Bronte, Anne 1820-1849 . . . . . . . . . . **NCLC 4**
See also DLB 21

Bronte, Charlotte
1816-1855 . . . . . . . . . . . . . **NCLC 3, 8, 33**
See also CDBLB 1832-1890; DLB 21; WLC

Bronte, (Jane) Emily
1818-1848 . . . . . . . . . . . . . . **NCLC 16, 35**
See also CDBLB 1832-1890; DLB 21, 32;
WLC

Brooke, Frances 1724-1789 . . . . . . . . . **LC 6**
See also DLB 39, 99

Brooke, Henry 1703(?)-1783 . . . . . . . . **LC 1**
See also DLB 39

Brooke, Rupert (Chawner)
1887-1915 . . . . . . . . . . . . . . . . **TCLC 2, 7**
See also CA 104; 132; CDBLB 1914-1945;
DLB 19; MTCW; WLC

**Brooke-Haven, P.**
See Wodehouse, P(elham) G(renville)

**Brooke-Rose, Christine** 1926- ...... **CLC 40**
See also CA 13-16R; DLB 14

**Brookner, Anita** 1928- ...... **CLC 32, 34, 51**
See also CA 114; 120; CANR 37; DLBY 87;
MTCW

**Brooks, Cleanth** 1906- ............ **CLC 24**
See also CA 17-20R; CANR 33, 35;
DLB 63; MTCW

**Brooks, George**
See Baum, L(yman) Frank

**Brooks, Gwendolyn**
1917- ........... **CLC 1, 2, 4, 5, 15, 49**
See also AITN 1; BLC 1; BW; CA 1-4R;
CANR 1, 27; CDALB 1941-1968;
CLR 27; DLB 5, 76; MTCW; SATA 6;
WLC

**Brooks, Mel**..................... **CLC 12**
See also Kaminsky, Melvin
See also DLB 26

**Brooks, Peter** 1938- .............. **CLC 34**
See also CA 45-48; CANR 1

**Brooks, Van Wyck** 1886-1963...... **CLC 29**
See also CA 1-4R; CANR 6; DLB 45, 63,
103

**Brophy, Brigid (Antonia)**
1929- .................. **CLC 6, 11, 29**
See also CA 5-8R; CAAS 4; CANR 25;
DLB 14; MTCW

**Brosman, Catharine Savage** 1934-.... **CLC 9**
See also CA 61-64; CANR 21

**Brother Antoninus**
See Everson, William (Oliver)

**Broughton, T(homas) Alan** 1936- ... **CLC 19**
See also CA 45-48; CANR 2, 23

**Broumas, Olga** 1949- ......... **CLC 10, 73**
See also CA 85-88; CANR 20

**Brown, Charles Brockden**
1771-1810 ................ **NCLC 22**
See also CDALB 1640-1865; DLB 37, 59,
73

**Brown, Christy** 1932-1981........ **CLC 63**
See also CA 105; 104; DLB 14

**Brown, Claude** 1937- ............ **CLC 30**
See also AAYA 7; BLC 1; BW; CA 73-76

**Brown, Dee (Alexander)** 1908- .. **CLC 18, 47**
See also CA 13-16R; CAAS 6; CANR 11;
DLBY 80; MTCW; SATA 5

**Brown, George**
See Wertmueller, Lina

**Brown, George Douglas**
1869-1902 ................. **TCLC 28**

**Brown, George Mackay** 1921-.... **CLC 5, 48**
See also CA 21-24R; CAAS 6; CANR 12,
37; DLB 14, 27; MTCW; SATA 35

**Brown, (William) Larry** 1951-...... **CLC 73**
See also CA 130; 134

**Brown, Moses**
See Barrett, William (Christopher)

**Brown, Rita Mae** 1944-........ **CLC 18, 43**
See also CA 45-48; CANR 2, 11, 35;
MTCW

**Brown, Roderick (Langmere) Haig-**
See Haig-Brown, Roderick (Langmere)

**Brown, Rosellen** 1939-............ **CLC 32**
See also CA 77-80; CAAS 10; CANR 14

**Brown, Sterling Allen**
1901-1989 ............. **CLC 1, 23, 59**
See also BLC 1; BW; CA 85-88; 127;
CANR 26; DLB 48, 51, 63; MTCW

**Brown, Will**
See Ainsworth, William Harrison

**Brown, William Wells**
1813-1884 ............. **NCLC 2; DC 1**
See also BLC 1; DLB 3, 50

**Browne, (Clyde) Jackson** 1948(?)-... **CLC 21**
See also CA 120

**Browning, Elizabeth Barrett**
1806-1861 ......... **NCLC 1, 16; PC 6**
See also CDBLB 1832-1890; DLB 32; WLC

**Browning, Robert**
1812-1889 ............ **NCLC 19; PC 2**
See also CDBLB 1832-1890; DLB 32;
YABC 1

**Browning, Tod** 1882-1962 ......... **CLC 16**
See also CA 117

**Bruccoli, Matthew J(oseph)** 1931- .. **CLC 34**
See also CA 9-12R; CANR 7; DLB 103

**Bruce, Lenny**.................... **CLC 21**
See also Schneider, Leonard Alfred

**Bruin, John**
See Brutus, Dennis

**Brulls, Christian**
See Simenon, Georges (Jacques Christian)

**Brunner, John (Kilian Houston)**
1934- ..................... **CLC 8, 10**
See also CA 1-4R; CAAS 8; CANR 2, 37;
MTCW

**Brutus, Dennis** 1924- .............. **CLC 43**
See also BLC 1; BW; CA 49-52; CAAS 14;
CANR 2, 27; DLB 117

**Bryan, C(ourtlandt) D(ixon) B(arnes)**
1936- ...................... **CLC 29**
See also CA 73-76; CANR 13

**Bryan, Michael**
See Moore, Brian

**Bryant, William Cullen**
1794-1878 .................. **NCLC 6**
See also CDALB 1640-1865; DLB 3, 43, 59

**Bryusov, Valery Yakovlevich**
1873-1924 .................. **TCLC 10**
See also CA 107

**Buchan, John** 1875-1940 ........ **TCLC 41**
See also CA 108; DLB 34, 70; YABC 2

**Buchanan, George** 1506-1582 ........ **LC 4**

**Buchheim, Lothar-Guenther** 1918- ... **CLC 6**
See also CA 85-88

**Buchner, (Karl) Georg**
1813-1837 ................ **NCLC 26**

**Buchwald, Art(hur)** 1925-......... **CLC 33**
See also AITN 1; CA 5-8R; CANR 21;
MTCW; SATA 10

**Buck, Pearl S(ydenstricker)**
1892-1973 .............. **CLC 7, 11, 18**
See also AITN 1; CA 1-4R; 41-44R;
CANR 1, 34; DLB 9, 102; MTCW;
SATA 1, 25

**Buckler, Ernest** 1908-1984........ **CLC 13**
See also CA 11-12; 114; CAP 1; DLB 68;
SATA 47

**Buckley, Vincent (Thomas)**
1925-1988 ................. **CLC 57**
See also CA 101

**Buckley, William F(rank) Jr.**
1925- .................. **CLC 7, 18, 37**
See also AITN 1; CA 1-4R; CANR 1, 24;
DLBY 80; MTCW

**Buechner, (Carl) Frederick**
1926- ................... **CLC 2, 4, 6, 9**
See also CA 13-16R; CANR 11, 39;
DLBY 80; MTCW

**Buell, John (Edward)** 1927-........ **CLC 10**
See also CA 1-4R; DLB 53

**Buero Vallejo, Antonio** 1916- ... **CLC 15, 46**
See also CA 106; CANR 24; HW; MTCW

**Bufalino, Gesualdo** 1920(?)-........ **CLC 74**

**Bugayev, Boris Nikolayevich** 1880-1934
See Bely, Andrey
See also CA 104

**Bukowski, Charles** 1920-.... **CLC 2, 5, 9, 41**
See also CA 17-20R; DLB 5; MTCW

**Bulgakov, Mikhail (Afanas'evich)**
1891-1940 ............. **TCLC 2, 16**
See also CA 105

**Bullins, Ed** 1935- ............. **CLC 1, 5, 7**
See also BLC 1; BW; CA 49-52; CAAS 16;
CANR 24; DLB 7, 38; MTCW

**Bulwer-Lytton, Edward (George Earle Lytton)**
1803-1873 ................. **NCLC 1**
See also DLB 21

**Bunin, Ivan Alexeyevich**
1870-1953 ............ **TCLC 6; SSC 5**
See also CA 104

**Bunting, Basil** 1900-1985.... **CLC 10, 39, 47**
See also CA 53-56; 115; CANR 7; DLB 20

**Bunuel, Luis** 1900-1983 .......... **CLC 16**
See also CA 101; 110; CANR 32; HW

**Bunyan, John** 1628-1688 ............ **LC 4**
See also CDBLB 1660-1789; DLB 39; WLC

**Burford, Eleanor**
See Hibbert, Eleanor Burford

**Burgess, Anthony**
1917- ..... **CLC 1, 2, 4, 5, 8, 10, 13, 15,
22, 40, 62**
See also Wilson, John (Anthony) Burgess
See also AITN 1; CDBLB 1960 to Present;
DLB 14

**Burke, Edmund** 1729(?)-1797........ **LC 7**
See also DLB 104; WLC

**Burke, Kenneth (Duva)** 1897- .... **CLC 2, 24**
See also CA 5-8R; CANR 39; DLB 45, 63;
MTCW

**Burke, Leda**
See Garnett, David

**Burke, Ralph**
See Silverberg, Robert

Carlyle, Thomas 1795-1881 . . . . . **NCLC 22**
See also CDBLB 1789-1832; DLB 55

Carman, (William) Bliss
1861-1929 . . . . . . . . . . . . . . **TCLC 7**
See also CA 104; DLB 92

Carossa, Hans 1878-1956. . . . . . . . **TCLC 48**
See also DLB 66

Carpenter, Don(ald Richard)
1931- . . . . . . . . . . . . . . . . . . . **CLC 41**
See also CA 45-48; CANR 1

Carpentier (y Valmont), Alejo
1904-1980 . . . . . . . . . . . . . **CLC 8, 11, 38**
See also CA 65-68; 97-100; CANR 11;
DLB 113; HW

Carr, Emily 1871-1945 . . . . . . . . . . **TCLC 32**
See also DLB 68

Carr, John Dickson 1906-1977 . . . . . . **CLC 3**
See also CA 49-52; 69-72; CANR 3, 33;
MTCW

Carr, Philippa
See Hibbert, Eleanor Burford

Carr, Virginia Spencer 1929-. . . . . . . **CLC 34**
See also CA 61-64; DLB 111

Carrier, Roch 1937- . . . . . . . . . . . . . **CLC 13**
See also CA 130; DLB 53

Carroll, James P. 1943(?)- . . . . . . . . **CLC 38**
See also CA 81-84

Carroll, Jim 1951- . . . . . . . . . . . . . **CLC 35**
See also CA 45-48

Carroll, Lewis . . . . . . . . . . . . . . . . . **NCLC 2**
See also Dodgson, Charles Lutwidge
See also CDBLB 1832-1890; CLR 2, 18;
DLB 18; WLC

Carroll, Paul Vincent 1900-1968. . . . **CLC 10**
See also CA 9-12R; 25-28R; DLB 10

Carruth, Hayden 1921- . . . . **CLC 4, 7, 10, 18**
See also CA 9-12R; CANR 4, 38; DLB 5;
MTCW; SATA 47

Carson, Rachel Louise 1907-1964. . . **CLC 71**
See also CA 77-80; CANR 35; MTCW;
SATA 23

Carter, Angela (Olive)
1940-1991 . . . . . . . . . . . . . . **CLC 5, 41**
See also CA 53-56; 136; CANR 12, 36;
DLB 14; MTCW; SATA 66; SATO 70

Carter, Nick
See Smith, Martin Cruz

Carver, Raymond
1938-1988 . . . **CLC 22, 36, 53, 55; SSC 8**
See also CA 33-36R; 126; CANR 17, 34;
DLBY 84, 88; MTCW

Cary, (Arthur) Joyce (Lunel)
1888-1957 . . . . . . . . . . . . . . **TCLC 1, 29**
See also CA 104; CDBLB 1914-1945;
DLB 15, 100

Casanova de Seingalt, Giovanni Jacopo
1725-1798 . . . . . . . . . . . . . . . . . . **LC 13**

Casares, Adolfo Bioy
See Bioy Casares, Adolfo

Casely-Hayford, J(oseph) E(phraim)
1866-1930 . . . . . . . . . . . . . . . **TCLC 24**
See also BLC 1; CA 123

Casey, John (Dudley) 1939-. . . . . . . **CLC 59**
See also BEST 90:2; CA 69-72; CANR 23

Casey, Michael 1947- . . . . . . . . . . . . . **CLC 2**
See also CA 65-68; DLB 5

Casey, Patrick
See Thurman, Wallace (Henry)

Casey, Warren (Peter) 1935-1988 . . . **CLC 12**
See also CA 101; 127

Casona, Alejandro. . . . . . . . . . . . . . . **CLC 49**
See also Alvarez, Alejandro Rodriguez

Cassavetes, John 1929-1989. . . . . . . **CLC 20**
See also CA 85-88; 127

Cassill, R(onald) V(erlin) 1919-. . . **CLC 4, 23**
See also CA 9-12R; CAAS 1; CANR 7;
DLB 6

Cassity, (Allen) Turner 1929- . . . . **CLC 6, 42**
See also CA 17-20R; CAAS 8; CANR 11;
DLB 105

Castaneda, Carlos 1931(?)-. . . . . . . . **CLC 12**
See also CA 25-28R; CANR 32; HW;
MTCW

Castedo, Elena 1937- . . . . . . . . . . . . **CLC 65**
See also CA 132

Castedo-Ellerman, Elena
See Castedo, Elena

Castellanos, Rosario 1925-1974. . . . . **CLC 66**
See also CA 131; 53-56; DLB 113; HW

Castelvetro, Lodovico 1505-1571. . . . . **LC 12**

Castiglione, Baldassare 1478-1529 . . . **LC 12**

Castle, Robert
See Hamilton, Edmond

Castro, Guillen de 1569-1631. . . . . . . **LC 19**

Castro, Rosalia de 1837-1885 . . . . . **NCLC 3**

Cather, Willa
See Cather, Willa Sibert

Cather, Willa Sibert
1873-1947 . . . . . . **TCLC 1, 11, 31; SSC 2**
See also CA 104; 128; CDALB 1865-1917;
DLB 9, 54, 78; DLBD 1; MTCW;
SATA 30; WLC

Catton, (Charles) Bruce
1899-1978 . . . . . . . . . . . . . . . . . **CLC 35**
See also AITN 1; CA 5-8R; 81-84;
CANR 7; DLB 17; SATA 2, 24

Cauldwell, Frank
See King, Francis (Henry)

Caunitz, William J. 1933- . . . . . . . **CLC 34**
See also BEST 89:3; CA 125; 130

Causley, Charles (Stanley) 1917-. . . . . **CLC 7**
See also CA 9-12R; CANR 5, 35; DLB 27;
MTCW; SATA 3, 66

Caute, David 1936-. . . . . . . . . . . . . . **CLC 29**
See also CA 1-4R; CAAS 4; CANR 1, 33;
DLB 14

Cavafy, C(onstantine) P(eter). . . . . . **TCLC 2, 7**
See also Kavafis, Konstantinos Petrou

Cavallo, Evelyn
See Spark, Muriel (Sarah)

Cavanna, Betty . . . . . . . . . . . . . . . . **CLC 12**
See also Harrison, Elizabeth Cavanna
See also MAICYA; SAAS 4; SATA 1, 30

Caxton, William 1421(?)-1491(?). . . . . **LC 17**

Cayrol, Jean 1911- . . . . . . . . . . . . . . **CLC 11**
See also CA 89-92; DLB 83

Cela, Camilo Jose 1916-. . . . . . **CLC 4, 13, 59**
See also BEST 90:2; CA 21-24R; CAAS 10;
CANR 21, 32; DLBY 89; HW; MTCW

Celan, Paul . . . . . . . . . . . . . . . . . . . **CLC 53**
See also Antschel, Paul
See also DLB 69

Celine, Louis-Ferdinand
. . . . . . . . . . . . . **CLC 1, 3, 4, 7, 9, 15, 47**
See also Destouches, Louis-Ferdinand
See also DLB 72

Cellini, Benvenuto 1500-1571 . . . . . . . **LC 7**

Cendrars, Blaise
See Sauser-Hall, Frederic

Cernuda (y Bidon), Luis
1902-1963 . . . . . . . . . . . . . . . . . **CLC 54**
See also CA 131; 89-92; HW

Cervantes (Saavedra), Miguel de
1547-1616 . . . . . . . . . . . . . . . . . . . **LC 6**
See also WLC

Cesaire, Aime (Fernand) 1913-. . **CLC 19, 32**
See also BLC 1; BW; CA 65-68; CANR 24;
MTCW

Chabon, Michael 1965(?)- . . . . . . . . **CLC 55**

Chabrol, Claude 1930- . . . . . . . . . . . **CLC 16**
See also CA 110

Challans, Mary 1905-1983
See Renault, Mary
See also CA 81-84; 111; SATA 23, 36

Chambers, Aidan 1934- . . . . . . . . . . **CLC 35**
See also CA 25-28R; CANR 12, 31;
MAICYA; SAAS 12; SATA 1, 69

Chambers, James 1948-
See Cliff, Jimmy
See also CA 124

Chambers, Jessie
See Lawrence, D(avid) H(erbert Richards)

Chambers, Robert W. 1865-1933. . . **TCLC 41**

Chandler, Raymond (Thornton)
1888-1959 . . . . . . . . . . . . . . . **TCLC 1, 7**
See also CA 104; 129; CDALB 1929-1941;
DLBD 6; MTCW

Chang, Jung 1952- . . . . . . . . . . . . . **CLC 71**

Channing, William Ellery
1780-1842 . . . . . . . . . . . . . . . . **NCLC 17**
See also DLB 1, 59

Chaplin, Charles Spencer
1889-1977 . . . . . . . . . . . . . . . . . **CLC 16**
See also Chaplin, Charlie
See also CA 81-84; 73-76

Chaplin, Charlie
See Chaplin, Charles Spencer
See also DLB 44

Chapman, Graham 1941-1989 . . . . . . **CLC 21**
See also Monty Python
See also CA 116; 129; CANR 35

Chapman, John Jay 1862-1933 . . . . . **TCLC 7**
See also CA 104

Chapman, Walker
See Silverberg, Robert

Chappell, Fred (Davis) 1936-. . . . . . . **CLC 40**
See also CA 5-8R; CAAS 4; CANR 8, 33;
DLB 6, 105

**Clarke, Austin** 1896-1974......... **CLC 6, 9**
See also CA 29-32; 49-52; CAP 2; DLB 10,
20

**Clarke, Gillian** 1937-............. **CLC 61**
See also CA 106; DLB 40

**Clarke, Marcus (Andrew Hislop)**
1846-1881 ................ **NCLC 19**

**Clarke, Shirley** 1925-............. **CLC 16**
................................. **CLC 30**
See also Headon, (Nicky) Topper; Jones,
Mick; Simonon, Paul; Strummer, Joe

**Claudel, Paul (Louis Charles Marie)**
1868-1955 ............... **TCLC 2, 10**
See also CA 104

**Clavell, James (duMaresq)**
1925-.................... **CLC 6, 25**
See also CA 25-28R; CANR 26; MTCW

**Cleaver, (Leroy) Eldridge** 1935-.... **CLC 30**
See also BLC 1; BW; CA 21-24R;
CANR 16

**Cleese, John (Marwood)** 1939-..... **CLC 21**
See also Monty Python
See also CA 112; 116; CANR 35; MTCW

**Cleishbotham, Jebediah**
See Scott, Walter

**Cleland, John** 1710-1789 ........... **LC 2**
See also DLB 39

**Clemens, Samuel Langhorne** 1835-1910
See Twain, Mark
See also CA 104; 135; CDALB 1865-1917;
DLB 11, 12, 23, 64, 74; MAICYA;
YABC 2

**Clerihew, E.**
See Bentley, E(dmund) C(lerihew)

**Clerk, N. W.**
See Lewis, C(live) S(taples)

**Cliff, Jimmy**..................... **CLC 21**
See also Chambers, James

**Clifton, (Thelma) Lucille**
1936-.................... **CLC 19, 66**
See also BLC 1; BW; CA 49-52; CANR 2,
24; CLR 5; DLB 5, 41; MAICYA;
MTCW; SATA 20, 69

**Clinton, Dirk**
See Silverberg, Robert

**Clough, Arthur Hugh** 1819-1861.. **NCLC 27**
See also DLB 32

**Clutha, Janet Paterson Frame** 1924-
See Frame, Janet
See also CA 1-4R; CANR 2, 36; MTCW

**Clyne, Terence**
See Blatty, William Peter

**Cobalt, Martin**
See Mayne, William (James Carter)

**Coburn, D(onald) L(ee)** 1938-...... **CLC 10**
See also CA 89-92

**Cocteau, Jean (Maurice Eugene Clement)**
1889-1963 ........ **CLC 1, 8, 15, 16, 43**
See also CA 25-28; CAP 2; DLB 65;
MTCW; WLC

**Codrescu, Andrei** 1946-........... **CLC 46**
See also CA 33-36R; CANR 13, 34

**Coe, Max**
See Bourne, Randolph S(illiman)

**Coe, Tucker**
See Westlake, Donald E(dwin)

**Coetzee, J(ohn) M(ichael)**
1940-................. **CLC 23, 33, 66**
See also CA 77-80; MTCW

**Cohen, Arthur A(llen)**
1928-1986 ................. **CLC 7, 31**
See also CA 1-4R; 120; CANR 1, 17;
DLB 28

**Cohen, Leonard (Norman)**
1934-.................... **CLC 3, 38**
See also CA 21-24R; CANR 14; DLB 53;
MTCW

**Cohen, Matt** 1942-............... **CLC 19**
See also CA 61-64; DLB 53

**Cohen-Solal, Annie** 19(?)- ......... **CLC 50**

**Colegate, Isabel** 1931-.......... **CLC 36**
See also CA 17-20R; CANR 8, 22; DLB 14;
MTCW

**Coleman, Emmett**
See Reed, Ishmael

**Coleridge, Samuel Taylor**
1772-1834 ................ **NCLC 9**
See also CDBLB 1789-1832; DLB 93, 107;
WLC

**Coleridge, Sara** 1802-1852....... **NCLC 31**

**Coles, Don** 1928- ................ **CLC 46**
See also CA 115; CANR 38

**Colette, (Sidonie-Gabrielle)**
1873-1954 ...... **TCLC 1, 5, 16; SSC 10**
See also CA 104; 131; DLB 65; MTCW

**Collett, (Jacobine) Camilla (Wergeland)**
1813-1895 ................ **NCLC 22**

**Collier, Christopher** 1930-........ **CLC 30**
See also CA 33-36R; CANR 13, 33;
MAICYA; SATA 16, 70

**Collier, James L(incoln)** 1928-..... **CLC 30**
See also CA 9-12R; CANR 4, 33;
MAICYA; SATA 8, 70

**Collier, Jeremy** 1650-1726.......... **LC 6**

**Collins, Hunt**
See Hunter, Evan

**Collins, Linda** 1931-.............. **CLC 44**
See also CA 125

**Collins, (William) Wilkie**
1824-1889 .............. **NCLC 1, 18**
See also CDBLB 1832-1890; DLB 18, 70

**Collins, William** 1721-1759 ......... **LC 4**
See also DLB 109

**Colman, George**
See Glassco, John

**Colt, Winchester Remington**
See Hubbard, L(afayette) Ron(ald)

**Colter, Cyrus** 1910- .............. **CLC 58**
See also BW; CA 65-68; CANR 10; DLB 33

**Colton, James**
See Hansen, Joseph

**Colum, Padraic** 1881-1972........ **CLC 28**
See also CA 73-76; 33-36R; CANR 35;
MAICYA; MTCW; SATA 15

**Colvin, James**
See Moorcock, Michael (John)

**Colwin, Laurie (E.)**
1944-1992 ............. **CLC 5, 13, 23**
See also CA 89-92; CANR 20; DLBY 80;
MTCW

**Comfort, Alex(ander)** 1920-........ **CLC 7**
See also CA 1-4R; CANR 1

**Comfort, Montgomery**
See Campbell, (John) Ramsey

**Compton-Burnett, I(vy)**
1884(?)-1969 ..... **CLC 1, 3, 10, 15, 34**
See also CA 1-4R; 25-28R; CANR 4;
DLB 36; MTCW

**Comstock, Anthony** 1844-1915 .... **TCLC 13**
See also CA 110

**Conan Doyle, Arthur**
See Doyle, Arthur Conan

**Conde, Maryse** .................. **CLC 52**
See also Boucolon, Maryse

**Condon, Richard (Thomas)**
1915- ............. **CLC 4, 6, 8, 10, 45**
See also BEST 90:3; CA 1-4R; CAAS 1;
CANR 2, 23; MTCW

**Congreve, William**
1670-1729 ............. **LC 5, 21; DC 2**
See also CDBLB 1660-1789; DLB 39, 84;
WLC

**Connell, Evan S(helby) Jr.**
1924-................. **CLC 4, 6, 45**
See also AAYA 7; CA 1-4R; CAAS 2;
CANR 2, 39; DLB 2; DLBY 81; MTCW

**Connelly, Marc(us Cook)**
1890-1980 .................... **CLC 7**
See also CA 85-88; 102; CANR 30; DLB 7;
DLBY 80; SATA 25

**Connor, Ralph** .................... **TCLC 31**
See also Gordon, Charles William
See also DLB 92

**Conrad, Joseph**
1857-1924 ...... **TCLC 1, 6, 13, 25, 43;**
**SSC 9**
See also CA 104; 131; CDBLB 1890-1914;
DLB 10, 34, 98; MTCW; SATA 27; WLC

**Conrad, Robert Arnold**
See Hart, Moss

**Conroy, Pat** 1945-............. **CLC 30, 74**
See also AAYA 8; AITN 1; CA 85-88;
CANR 24; DLB 6; MTCW

**Constant (de Rebecque), (Henri) Benjamin**
1767-1830 ................ **NCLC 6**
See also DLB 119

**Conybeare, Charles Augustus**
See Eliot, T(homas) S(tearns)

**Cook, Michael** 1933- ............. **CLC 58**
See also CA 93-96; DLB 53

**Cook, Robin** 1940-............... **CLC 14**
See also BEST 90:2; CA 108; 111

**Cook, Roy**
See Silverberg, Robert

**Cooke, Elizabeth** 1948-........... **CLC 55**
See also CA 129

**Cooke, John Esten** 1830-1886..... **NCLC 5**
See also DLB 3

**Cooke, John Estes**
See Baum, L(yman) Frank

**Crumarums**
See Crumb, R(obert)

**Crumb, R(obert)** 1943- . . . . . . . . . . . **CLC 17**
See also CA 106

**Crumbum**
See Crumb, R(obert)

**Crumski**
See Crumb, R(obert)

**Crum the Bum**
See Crumb, R(obert)

**Crunk**
See Crumb, R(obert)

**Crustt**
See Crumb, R(obert)

**Cryer, Gretchen (Kiger)** 1935- . . . . . . **CLC 21**
See also CA 114; 123

**Csath, Geza** 1887-1919 . . . . . . . . . . **TCLC 13**
See also CA 111

**Cudlip, David** 1933- . . . . . . . . . . . . . **CLC 34**

**Cullen, Countee** 1903-1946 . . . . . **TCLC 4, 37**
See also BLC 1; BW; CA 108; 124;
CDALB 1917-1929; DLB 4, 48, 51;
MTCW; SATA 18

**Cum, R.**
See Crumb, R(obert)

**Cummings, Bruce F(rederick)** 1889-1919
See Barbellion, W. N. P.
See also CA 123

**Cummings, E(dward) E(stlin)**
1894-1962 . . . . . **CLC 1, 3, 8, 12, 15, 68;**
**PC 5**
See also CA 73-76; CANR 31;
CDALB 1929-1941; DLB 4, 48; MTCW;
WLC 2

**Cunha, Euclides (Rodrigues Pimenta) da**
1866-1909 . . . . . . . . . . . . . . . . . **TCLC 24**
See also CA 123

**Cunningham, E. V.**
See Fast, Howard (Melvin)

**Cunningham, J(ames) V(incent)**
1911-1985 . . . . . . . . . . . . . . . **CLC 3, 31**
See also CA 1-4R; 115; CANR 1; DLB 5

**Cunningham, Julia (Woolfolk)**
1916- . . . . . . . . . . . . . . . . . . . . **CLC 12**
See also CA 9-12R; CANR 4, 19, 36;
MAICYA; SAAS 2; SATA 1, 26

**Cunningham, Michael** 1952- . . . . . . . **CLC 34**
See also CA 136

**Cunninghame Graham, R(obert) B(ontine)**
1852-1936 . . . . . . . . . . . . . . . . **TCLC 19**
See also Graham, R(obert) B(ontine)
Cunninghame
See also CA 119; DLB 98

**Currie, Ellen** 19(?)- . . . . . . . . . . . . . **CLC 44**

**Curtin, Philip**
See Lowndes, Marie Adelaide (Belloc)

**Curtis, Price**
See Ellison, Harlan

**Czaczkes, Shmuel Yosef**
See Agnon, S(hmuel) Y(osef Halevi)

**D. P.**
See Wells, H(erbert) G(eorge)

**Dabrowska, Maria (Szumska)**
1889-1965 . . . . . . . . . . . . . . . . . **CLC 15**
See also CA 106

**Dabydeen, David** 1955- . . . . . . . . . . **CLC 34**
See also BW; CA 125

**Dacey, Philip** 1939- . . . . . . . . . . . . . **CLC 51**
See also CA 37-40R; CANR 14, 32;
DLB 105

**Dagerman, Stig (Halvard)**
1923-1954 . . . . . . . . . . . . . . . . . **TCLC 17**
See also CA 117

**Dahl, Roald** 1916-1990 . . . . . . . **CLC 1, 6, 18**
See also CA 1-4R; 133; CANR 6, 32, 37;
CLR 1, 7; MAICYA; MTCW; SATA 1,
26; SATO 65

**Dahlberg, Edward** 1900-1977 . . . **CLC 1, 7, 14**
See also CA 9-12R; 69-72; CANR 31;
DLB 48; MTCW

**Dale, Colin** . . . . . . . . . . . . . . . . . . . **TCLC 18**
See also Lawrence, T(homas) E(dward)

**Dale, George E.**
See Asimov, Isaac

**Daly, Elizabeth** 1878-1967 . . . . . . . . **CLC 52**
See also CA 23-24; 25-28R; CAP 2

**Daly, Maureen** 1921- . . . . . . . . . . . . **CLC 17**
See also AAYA 5; CANR 37; MAICYA;
SAAS 1; SATA 2

**Daniels, Brett**
See Adler, Renata

**Dannay, Frederic** 1905-1982 . . . . . . . **CLC 11**
See also Queen, Ellery
See also CA 1-4R; 107; CANR 1, 39;
MTCW

**D'Annunzio, Gabriele**
1863-1938 . . . . . . . . . . . . . . . **TCLC 6, 40**
See also CA 104

**d'Antibes, Germain**
See Simenon, Georges (Jacques Christian)

**Danvers, Dennis** 1947- . . . . . . . . . . . **CLC 70**

**Danziger, Paula** 1944- . . . . . . . . . . . **CLC 21**
See also AAYA 4; CA 112; 115; CANR 37;
CLR 20; MAICYA; SATA 30, 36, 63

**Dario, Ruben** . . . . . . . . . . . . . . . . . . **TCLC 4**
See also Sarmiento, Felix Ruben Garcia

**Darley, George** 1795-1846 . . . . . . . **NCLC 2**
See also DLB 96

**Daryush, Elizabeth** 1887-1977 . . . . **CLC 6, 19**
See also CA 49-52; CANR 3; DLB 20

**Daudet, (Louis Marie) Alphonse**
1840-1897 . . . . . . . . . . . . . . . . . **NCLC 1**
See also DLB 123

**Daumal, Rene** 1908-1944 . . . . . . . . **TCLC 14**
See also CA 114

**Davenport, Guy (Mattison Jr.)**
1927- . . . . . . . . . . . . . . . . **CLC 6, 14, 38**
See also CA 33-36R; CANR 23

**Davidson, Avram** 1923-
See Queen, Ellery
See also CA 101; CANR 26; DLB 8

**Davidson, Donald (Grady)**
1893-1968 . . . . . . . . . . . . . **CLC 2, 13, 19**
See also CA 5-8R; 25-28R; CANR 4;
DLB 45

**Davidson, Hugh**
See Hamilton, Edmond

**Davidson, John** 1857-1909 . . . . . . . **TCLC 24**
See also CA 118; DLB 19

**Davidson, Sara** 1943- . . . . . . . . . . . . **CLC 9**
See also CA 81-84

**Davie, Donald (Alfred)**
1922- . . . . . . . . . . . . . **CLC 5, 8, 10, 31**
See also CA 1-4R; CAAS 3; CANR 1;
DLB 27; MTCW

**Davies, Ray(mond Douglas)** 1944- . . **CLC 21**
See also CA 116

**Davies, Rhys** 1903-1978 . . . . . . . . . . **CLC 23**
See also CA 9-12R; 81-84; CANR 4

**Davies, (William) Robertson**
1913- . . . . . . . . **CLC 2, 7, 13, 25, 42, 75**
See also BEST 89:2; CA 33-36R; CANR 17;
DLB 68; MTCW; WLC

**Davies, W(illiam) H(enry)**
1871-1940 . . . . . . . . . . . . . . . . . **TCLC 5**
See also CA 104; DLB 19

**Davies, Walter C.**
See Kornbluth, C(yril) M.

**Davis, B. Lynch**
See Bioy Casares, Adolfo; Borges, Jorge
Luis

**Davis, Gordon**
See Hunt, E(verette) Howard Jr.

**Davis, Harold Lenoir** 1896-1960 . . . . **CLC 49**
See also CA 89-92; DLB 9

**Davis, Rebecca (Blaine) Harding**
1831-1910 . . . . . . . . . . . . . . . . . **TCLC 6**
See also CA 104; DLB 74

**Davis, Richard Harding**
1864-1916 . . . . . . . . . . . . . . . . **TCLC 24**
See also CA 114; DLB 12, 23, 78, 79

**Davison, Frank Dalby** 1893-1970 . . . **CLC 15**
See also CA 116

**Davison, Lawrence H.**
See Lawrence, D(avid) H(erbert Richards)

**Davison, Peter** 1928- . . . . . . . . . . . . **CLC 28**
See also CA 9-12R; CAAS 4; CANR 3;
DLB 5

**Davys, Mary** 1674-1732 . . . . . . . . . . . . **LC 1**
See also DLB 39

**Dawson, Fielding** 1930- . . . . . . . . . . . **CLC 6**
See also CA 85-88

**Day, Clarence (Shepard Jr.)**
1874-1935 . . . . . . . . . . . . . . . . **TCLC 25**
See also CA 108; DLB 11

**Day, Thomas** 1748-1789 . . . . . . . . . . . . **LC 1**
See also DLB 39; YABC 1

**Day Lewis, C(ecil)**
1904-1972 . . . . . . . . . . . . . **CLC 1, 6, 10**
See also Blake, Nicholas
See also CA 13-16; 33-36R; CANR 34;
CAP 1; DLB 15, 20; MTCW

**Dazai, Osamu** . . . . . . . . . . . . . . . . . **TCLC 11**
See also Tsushima, Shuji

**de Andrade, Carlos Drummond**
See Drummond de Andrade, Carlos

**Deane, Norman**
See Creasey, John

**Dickinson, Peter (Malcolm)**
1927- . . . . . . . . . . . . . . . . . . . . **CLC 12, 35**
See also AAYA 9; CA 41-44R; CANR 31;
DLB 87; MAICYA; SATA 5, 62

**Dickson, Carr**
See Carr, John Dickson

**Dickson, Carter**
See Carr, John Dickson

**Didion, Joan** 1934- . . . . . **CLC 1, 3, 8, 14, 32**
See also AITN 1; CA 5-8R; CANR 14;
CDALB 1968-1988; DLB 2; DLBY 81,
86; MTCW

**Dietrich, Robert**
See Hunt, E(verette) Howard Jr.

**Dillard, Annie** 1945- . . . . . . . . . . . **CLC 9, 60**
See also AAYA 6; CA 49-52; CANR 3;
DLBY 80; MTCW; SATA 10

**Dillard, R(ichard) H(enry) W(ilde)**
1937- . . . . . . . . . . . . . . . . . . . . . . . **CLC 5**
See also CA 21-24R; CAAS 7; CANR 10;
DLB 5

**Dillon, Eilis** 1920- . . . . . . . . . . . . . . **CLC 17**
See also CA 9-12R; CAAS 3; CANR 4, 38;
CLR 26; MAICYA; SATA 2

**Dimont, Penelope**
See Mortimer, Penelope (Ruth)

**Dinesen, Isak** . . . . . . . . . . **CLC 10, 29; SSC 7**
See also Blixen, Karen (Christentze
Dinesen)

**Ding Ling** . . . . . . . . . . . . . . . . . . . . . . **CLC 68**
See also Chiang Pin-chin

**Disch, Thomas M(ichael)** 1940- . . . **CLC 7, 36**
See also CA 21-24R; CAAS 4; CANR 17,
36; CLR 18; DLB 8; MAICYA; MTCW;
SAAS 15; SATA 54

**Disch, Tom**
See Disch, Thomas M(ichael)

**d'Isly, Georges**
See Simenon, Georges (Jacques Christian)

**Disraeli, Benjamin** 1804-1881 . . **NCLC 2, 39**
See also DLB 21, 55

**Ditcum, Steve**
See Crumb, R(obert)

**Dixon, Paige**
See Corcoran, Barbara

**Dixon, Stephen** 1936- . . . . . . . . . . . . **CLC 52**
See also CA 89-92; CANR 17

**Doblin, Alfred** . . . . . . . . . . . . . . . . **TCLC 13**
See also Doeblin, Alfred

**Dobrolyubov, Nikolai Alexandrovich**
1836-1861 . . . . . . . . . . . . . . . . . **NCLC 5**

**Dobyns, Stephen** 1941- . . . . . . . . . . . **CLC 37**
See also CA 45-48; CANR 2, 18

**Doctorow, E(dgar) L(aurence)**
1931- . . . . . **CLC 6, 11, 15, 18, 37, 44, 65**
See also AITN 2; BEST 89:3; CA 45-48;
CANR 2, 33; CDALB 1968-1988; DLB 2,
28; DLBY 80; MTCW

**Dodgson, Charles Lutwidge** 1832-1898
See Carroll, Lewis
See also CLR 2; MAICYA; YABC 2

**Doeblin, Alfred** 1878-1957 . . . . . . . **TCLC 13**
See also Doblin, Alfred
See also CA 110; DLB 66

**Doerr, Harriet** 1910- . . . . . . . . . . . . . **CLC 34**
See also CA 117; 122

**Domecq, H(onorio) Bustos**
See Bioy Casares, Adolfo; Borges, Jorge
Luis

**Domini, Rey**
See Lorde, Audre (Geraldine)

**Dominique**
See Proust,
(Valentin-Louis-George-Eugene-)Marcel

**Don, A**
See Stephen, Leslie

**Donaldson, Stephen R.** 1947- . . . . . . . **CLC 46**
See also CA 89-92; CANR 13

**Donleavy, J(ames) P(atrick)**
1926- . . . . . . . . . . . . . **CLC 1, 4, 6, 10, 45**
See also AITN 2; CA 9-12R; CANR 24;
DLB 6; MTCW

**Donne, John** 1572-1631 . . . . . . . **LC 10; PC 1**
See also CDBLB Before 1660; DLB 121;
WLC

**Donnell, David** 1939(?)- . . . . . . . . . . . **CLC 34**

**Donoso (Yanez), Jose**
1924- . . . . . . . . . . . . . . . **CLC 4, 8, 11, 32**
See also CA 81-84; CANR 32; DLB 113;
HW; MTCW

**Donovan, John** 1928-1992 . . . . . . . . **CLC 35**
See also CA 97-100; 137; CLR 3;
MAICYA; SATA 29

**Don Roberto**
See Cunninghame Graham, R(obert)
B(ontine)

**Doolittle, Hilda**
1886-1961 . . . . **CLC 3, 8, 14, 31, 34, 73;
PC 5**
See also H. D.
See also CA 97-100; CANR 35; DLB 4, 45;
MTCW; WLC

**Dorfman, Ariel** 1942- . . . . . . . . . . . . **CLC 48**
See also CA 124; 130; HW

**Dorn, Edward (Merton)** 1929- . . . **CLC 10, 18**
See also CA 93-96; DLB 5

**Dorsan, Luc**
See Simenon, Georges (Jacques Christian)

**Dorsange, Jean**
See Simenon, Georges (Jacques Christian)

**Dos Passos, John (Roderigo)**
1896-1970 . . . **CLC 1, 4, 8, 11, 15, 25, 34**
See also CA 1-4R; 29-32R; CANR 3;
CDALB 1929-1941; DLB 4, 9; DLBD 1;
MTCW; WLC

**Dossage, Jean**
See Simenon, Georges (Jacques Christian)

**Dostoevsky, Fedor Mikhailovich**
1821-1881 . . . . **NCLC 2, 7, 21, 33; SSC 2**
See also WLC

**Doughty, Charles M(ontagu)**
1843-1926 . . . . . . . . . . . . . . . . . **TCLC 27**
See also CA 115; DLB 19, 57

**Douglas, Ellen**
See Haxton, Josephine Ayres

**Douglas, Gavin** 1475(?)-1522 . . . . . . . **LC 20**

**Douglas, Keith** 1920-1944 . . . . . . . . **TCLC 40**
See also DLB 27

**Douglas, Leonard**
See Bradbury, Ray (Douglas)

**Douglas, Michael**
See Crichton, (John) Michael

**Douglass, Frederick** 1817(?)-1895 . . **NCLC 7**
See also BLC 1; CDALB 1640-1865;
DLB 1, 43, 50, 79; SATA 29; WLC

**Dourado, (Waldomiro Freitas) Autran**
1926- . . . . . . . . . . . . . . . . . . . . **CLC 23, 60**
See also CA 25-28R; CANR 34

**Dourado, Waldomiro Autran**
See Dourado, (Waldomiro Freitas) Autran

**Dove, Rita (Frances)** 1952- . . . **CLC 50; PC 6**
See also BW; CA 109; CANR 27; DLB 120

**Dowell, Coleman** 1925-1985 . . . . . . . **CLC 60**
See also CA 25-28R; 117; CANR 10

**Dowson, Ernest Christopher**
1867-1900 . . . . . . . . . . . . . . . . . . **TCLC 4**
See also CA 105; DLB 19

**Doyle, A. Conan**
See Doyle, Arthur Conan

**Doyle, Arthur Conan** 1859-1930 . . . . **TCLC 7**
See also CA 104; 122; CDBLB 1890-1914;
DLB 18, 70; MTCW; SATA 24; WLC

**Doyle, Conan**
See Doyle, Arthur Conan

**Doyle, John**
See Graves, Robert (von Ranke)

**Doyle, Sir A. Conan**
See Doyle, Arthur Conan

**Doyle, Sir Arthur Conan**
See Doyle, Arthur Conan

**Dr. A**
See Asimov, Isaac; Silverstein, Alvin

**Drabble, Margaret**
1939- . . . . . . . . . **CLC 2, 3, 5, 8, 10, 22, 53**
See also CA 13-16R; CANR 18, 35;
CDBLB 1960 to Present; DLB 14;
MTCW; SATA 48

**Drapier, M. B.**
See Swift, Jonathan

**Drayham, James**
See Mencken, H(enry) L(ouis)

**Drayton, Michael** 1563-1631 . . . . . . . . . **LC 8**

**Dreadstone, Carl**
See Campbell, (John) Ramsey

**Dreiser, Theodore (Herman Albert)**
1871-1945 . . . . . . . . . . **TCLC 10, 18, 35**
See also CA 106; 132; CDALB 1865-1917;
DLB 9, 12, 102; DLBD 1; MTCW; WLC

**Drexler, Rosalyn** 1926- . . . . . . . . . . **CLC 2, 6**
See also CA 81-84

**Dreyer, Carl Theodor** 1889-1968 . . . . **CLC 16**
See also CA 116

**Drieu la Rochelle, Pierre(-Eugene)**
1893-1945 . . . . . . . . . . . . . . . . . **TCLC 21**
See also CA 117; DLB 72

**Drop Shot**
See Cable, George Washington

**Droste-Hulshoff, Annette Freiin von**
1797-1848 . . . . . . . . . . . . . . . . . **NCLC 3**

**Drummond, Walter**
See Silverberg, Robert

Esenin, Sergei (Alexandrovich)
1895-1925 ................. **TCLC 4**
See also CA 104

Eshleman, Clayton 1935- ........... **CLC 7**
See also CA 33-36R; CAAS 6; DLB 5

Espriella, Don Manuel Alvarez
See Southey, Robert

Espriu, Salvador 1913-1985 ........ **CLC 9**
See also CA 115

Espronceda, Jose de 1808-1842 ... **NCLC 39**

Esse, James
See Stephens, James

Esterbrook, Tom
See Hubbard, L(afayette) Ron(ald)

Estleman, Loren D. 1952- ......... **CLC 48**
See also CA 85-88; CANR 27; MTCW

Evans, Mary Ann
See Eliot, George

Evarts, Esther
See Benson, Sally

Everett, Percival
See Everett, Percival L.

Everett, Percival L. 1956- ......... **CLC 57**
See also CA 129

Everson, R(onald) G(ilmour)
1903- ...................... **CLC 27**
See also CA 17-20R; DLB 88

Everson, William (Oliver)
1912- ................... **CLC 1, 5, 14**
See also CA 9-12R; CANR 20; DLB 5, 16;
MTCW

Evtushenko, Evgenii Aleksandrovich
See Yevtushenko, Yevgeny (Alexandrovich)

Ewart, Gavin (Buchanan)
1916- ................... **CLC 13, 46**
See also CA 89-92; CANR 17; DLB 40;
MTCW

Ewers, Hanns Heinz 1871-1943 ... **TCLC 12**
See also CA 109

Ewing, Frederick R.
See Sturgeon, Theodore (Hamilton)

Exley, Frederick (Earl) 1929- .... **CLC 6, 11**
See also AITN 2; CA 81-84; 138; DLBY 81

Eynhardt, Guillermo
See Quiroga, Horacio (Sylvestre)

Ezekiel, Nissim 1924- ............ **CLC 61**
See also CA 61-64

Ezekiel, Tish O'Dowd 1943- ....... **CLC 34**
See also CA 129

Fagen, Donald 1948- ............. **CLC 26**

Fainzilberg, Ilya Arnoldovich 1897-1937
See Ilf, Ilya
See also CA 120

Fair, Ronald L. 1932- ............. **CLC 18**
See also BW; CA 69-72; CANR 25; DLB 33

Fairbairns, Zoe (Ann) 1948- ....... **CLC 32**
See also CA 103; CANR 21

Falco, Gian
See Papini, Giovanni

Falconer, James
See Kirkup, James

Falconer, Kenneth
See Kornbluth, C(yril) M.

Falkland, Samuel
See Heijermans, Herman

Fallaci, Oriana 1930- ............ **CLC 11**
See also CA 77-80; CANR 15; MTCW

Faludy, George 1913- ............ **CLC 42**
See also CA 21-24R

Faludy, Gyoergy
See Faludy, George

Fanon, Frantz 1925-1961 ......... **CLC 74**
See also BLC 2; BW; CA 116; 89-92

Fanshawe, Ann ................... **LC 11**

Fante, John (Thomas) 1911-1983 ... **CLC 60**
See also CA 69-72; 109; CANR 23;
DLBY 83

Farah, Nuruddin 1945- ............ **CLC 53**
See also BLC 2; CA 106

Fargue, Leon-Paul 1876(?)-1947 ... **TCLC 11**
See also CA 109

Farigoule, Louis
See Romains, Jules

Farina, Richard 1936(?)-1966 ...... **CLC 9**
See also CA 81-84; 25-28R

Farley, Walter (Lorimer)
1915-1989 ................. **CLC 17**
See also CA 17-20R; CANR 8, 29; DLB 22;
MAICYA; SATA 2, 43

Farmer, Philip Jose 1918- ....... **CLC 1, 19**
See also CA 1-4R; CANR 4, 35; DLB 8;
MTCW

Farquhar, George 1677-1707 ....... **LC 21**
See also DLB 84

Farrell, J(ames) G(ordon)
1935-1979 ................... **CLC 6**
See also CA 73-76; 89-92; CANR 36;
DLB 14; MTCW

Farrell, James T(homas)
1904-1979 ........ **CLC 1, 4, 8, 11, 66**
See also CA 5-8R; 89-92; CANR 9; DLB 4,
9, 86; DLBD 2; MTCW

Farren, Richard J.
See Betjeman, John

Farren, Richard M.
See Betjeman, John

Fassbinder, Rainer Werner
1946-1982 ................... **CLC 20**
See also CA 93-96; 106; CANR 31

Fast, Howard (Melvin) 1914- ...... **CLC 23**
See also CA 1-4R; CANR 1, 33; DLB 9;
SATA 7

Faulcon, Robert
See Holdstock, Robert P.

Faulkner, William (Cuthbert)
1897-1962 .... **CLC 1, 3, 6, 8, 9, 11, 14,
18, 28, 52, 68; SSC 1**
See also AAYA 7; CA 81-84; CANR 33;
CDALB 1929-1941; DLB 9, 11, 44, 102;
DLBD 2; DLBY 86; MTCW; WLC

Fauset, Jessie Redmon
1884(?)-1961 .............. **CLC 19, 54**
See also BLC 2; BW; CA 109; DLB 51

Faust, Irvin 1924- ................ **CLC 8**
See also CA 33-36R; CANR 28; DLB 2, 28;
DLBY 80

Fawkes, Guy
See Benchley, Robert (Charles)

Fearing, Kenneth (Flexner)
1902-1961 .................. **CLC 51**
See also CA 93-96; DLB 9

Fecamps, Elise
See Creasey, John

Federman, Raymond 1928- ...... **CLC 6, 47**
See also CA 17-20R; CAAS 8; CANR 10;
DLBY 80

Federspiel, J(uerg) F. 1931- ....... **CLC 42**

Feiffer, Jules (Ralph) 1929- .... **CLC 2, 8, 64**
See also AAYA 3; CA 17-20R; CANR 30;
DLB 7, 44; MTCW; SATA 8, 61

Feige, Hermann Albert Otto Maximilian
See Traven, B.

Fei-Kan, Li
See Li Fei-kan

Feinberg, David B. 1956- ......... **CLC 59**
See also CA 135

Feinstein, Elaine 1930- ............ **CLC 36**
See also CA 69-72; CAAS 1; CANR 31;
DLB 14, 40; MTCW

Feldman, Irving (Mordecai) 1928- .... **CLC 7**
See also CA 1-4R; CANR 1

Fellini, Federico 1920- ............ **CLC 16**
See also CA 65-68; CANR 33

Felsen, Henry Gregor 1916- ....... **CLC 17**
See also CA 1-4R; CANR 1; SAAS 2;
SATA 1

Fenton, James Martin 1949- ....... **CLC 32**
See also CA 102; DLB 40

Ferber, Edna 1887-1968 ........... **CLC 18**
See also AITN 1; CA 5-8R; 25-28R; DLB 9,
28, 86; MTCW; SATA 7

Ferguson, Helen
See Kavan, Anna

Ferguson, Samuel 1810-1886 ..... **NCLC 33**
See also DLB 32

Ferling, Lawrence
See Ferlinghetti, Lawrence (Monsanto)

Ferlinghetti, Lawrence (Monsanto)
1919(?)- ........ **CLC 2, 6, 10, 27; PC 1**
See also CA 5-8R; CANR 3;
CDALB 1941-1968; DLB 5, 16; MTCW

Fernandez, Vicente Garcia Huidobro
See Huidobro Fernandez, Vicente Garcia

Ferrer, Gabriel (Francisco Victor) Miro
See Miro (Ferrer), Gabriel (Francisco
Victor)

Ferrier, Susan (Edmonstone)
1782-1854 .................. **NCLC 8**
See also DLB 116

Ferrigno, Robert ................... **CLC 65**

Feuchtwanger, Lion 1884-1958 ..... **TCLC 3**
See also CA 104; DLB 66

Feydeau, Georges (Leon Jules Marie)
1862-1921 .................. **TCLC 22**
See also CA 113

Ficino, Marsilio 1433-1499 ........ **LC 12**

Fiedler, Leslie A(aron)
1917- .................. **CLC 4, 13, 24**
See also CA 9-12R; CANR 7; DLB 28, 67;
MTCW

Field, Andrew 1938-.............. **CLC 44**
See also CA 97-100; CANR 25

Field, Eugene 1850-1895 ........ **NCLC 3**
See also DLB 23, 42; MAICYA; SATA 16

Field, Gans T.
See Wellman, Manly Wade

Field, Michael ................... **TCLC 43**

Field, Peter
See Hobson, Laura Z(ametkin)

Fielding, Henry 1707-1754 .......... **LC 1**
See also CDBLB 1660-1789; DLB 39, 84,
101; WLC

Fielding, Sarah 1710-1768 ........... **LC 1**
See also DLB 39

Fierstein, Harvey (Forbes) 1954- ... **CLC 33**
See also CA 123; 129

Figes, Eva 1932-................. **CLC 31**
See also CA 53-56; CANR 4; DLB 14

Finch, Robert (Duer Claydon)
1900-...................... **CLC 18**
See also CA 57-60; CANR 9, 24; DLB 88

Findley, Timothy 1930- ........... **CLC 27**
See also CA 25-28R; CANR 12; DLB 53

Fink, William
See Mencken, H(enry) L(ouis)

Firbank, Louis 1942-
See Reed, Lou
See also CA 117

Firbank, (Arthur Annesley) Ronald
1886-1926 .................... **TCLC 1**
See also CA 104; DLB 36

Fisher, Roy 1930-................ **CLC 25**
See also CA 81-84; CAAS 10; CANR 16;
DLB 40

Fisher, Rudolph 1897-1934 ....... **TCLC 11**
See also BLC 2; BW; CA 107; 124; DLB 51,
102

Fisher, Vardis (Alvero) 1895-1968.... **CLC 7**
See also CA 5-8R; 25-28R; DLB 9

Fiske, Tarleton
See Bloch, Robert (Albert)

Fitch, Clarke
See Sinclair, Upton (Beall)

Fitch, John IV
See Cormier, Robert (Edmund)

Fitgerald, Penelope 1916- ........ **CLC 61**

Fitzgerald, Captain Hugh
See Baum, L(yman) Frank

FitzGerald, Edward 1809-1883 .... **NCLC 9**
See also DLB 32

Fitzgerald, F(rancis) Scott (Key)
1896-1940 .... **TCLC 1, 6, 14, 28; SSC 6**
See also AITN 1; CA 110; 123;
CDALB 1917-1929; DLB 4, 9, 86;
DLBD 1; DLBY 81; MTCW; WLC

Fitzgerald, Penelope 1916-...... **CLC 19, 51**
See also CA 85-88; CAAS 10; DLB 14

FitzGerald, Robert D(avid)
1902-1987 .................... **CLC 19**
See also CA 17-20R

Fitzgerald, Robert (Stuart)
1910-1985 .................... **CLC 39**
See also CA 1-4R; 114; CANR 1; DLBY 80

Flanagan, Thomas (James Bonner)
1923-.................... **CLC 25, 52**
See also CA 108; DLBY 80; MTCW

Flaubert, Gustave
1821-1880 ..... **NCLC 2, 10, 19; SSC 11**
See also DLB 119; WLC

Flecker, (Herman) James Elroy
1884-1915 ................ **TCLC 43**
See also CA 109; DLB 10, 19

Fleming, Ian (Lancaster)
1908-1964 ................ **CLC 3, 30**
See also CA 5-8R; CDBLB 1945-1960;
DLB 87; MTCW; SATA 9

Fleming, Thomas (James) 1927- .... **CLC 37**
See also CA 5-8R; CANR 10; SATA 8

Fletcher, John Gould 1886-1950 ... **TCLC 35**
See also CA 107; DLB 4, 45

Fleur, Paul
See Pohl, Frederik

Flying Officer X
See Bates, H(erbert) E(rnest)

Fo, Dario 1926-................. **CLC 32**
See also CA 116; 128; MTCW

Fogarty, Jonathan Titulescu Esq.
See Farrell, James T(homas)

Folke, Will
See Bloch, Robert (Albert)

Follett, Ken(neth Martin) 1949- .... **CLC 18**
See also AAYA 6; BEST 89:4; CA 81-84;
CANR 13, 33; DLB 87; DLBY 81;
MTCW

Fontane, Theodor 1819-1898 ..... **NCLC 26**

Foote, Horton 1916-.............. **CLC 51**
See also CA 73-76; CANR 34; DLB 26

Foote, Shelby 1916- .............. **CLC 75**
See also CA 5-8R; CANR 3; DLB 2, 17

Forbes, Esther 1891-1967........... **CLC 12**
See also CA 13-14; 25-28R; CAP 1;
CLR 27; DLB 22; MAICYA; SATA 2

Forche, Carolyn (Louise) 1950-..... **CLC 25**
See also CA 109; 117; DLB 5

Ford, Elbur
See Hibbert, Eleanor Burford

Ford, Ford Madox
1873-1939 ............ **TCLC 1, 15, 39**
See also CA 104; 132; CDBLB 1914-1945;
DLB 34, 98; MTCW

Ford, John 1895-1973............. **CLC 16**
See also CA 45-48

Ford, Richard 1944-.............. **CLC 46**
See also CA 69-72; CANR 11

Ford, Webster
See Masters, Edgar Lee

Foreman, Richard 1937-.......... **CLC 50**
See also CA 65-68; CANR 32

Forester, C(ecil) S(cott)
1899-1966 .................... **CLC 35**
See also CA 73-76; 25-28R; SATA 13

Forez
See Mauriac, Francois (Charles)

Forman, James Douglas 1932-...... **CLC 21**
See also CA 9-12R; CANR 4, 19;
MAICYA; SATA 8, 70

Fornes, Maria Irene 1930-...... **CLC 39, 61**
See also CA 25-28R; CANR 28; DLB 7;
HW; MTCW

Forrest, Leon 1937- .............. **CLC 4**
See also BW; CA 89-92; CAAS 7;
CANR 25; DLB 33

Forster, E(dward) M(organ)
1879-1970 .... **CLC 1, 2, 3, 4, 9, 10, 13,
15, 22, 45**
See also AAYA 2; CA 13-14; 25-28R;
CAP 1; CDBLB 1914-1945; DLB 34, 98;
DLBD 10; MTCW; SATA 57; WLC

Forster, John 1812-1876 ........ **NCLC 11**

Forsyth, Frederick 1938-...... **CLC 2, 5, 36**
See also BEST 89:4; CA 85-88; CANR 38;
DLB 87; MTCW

Forten, Charlotte L. .............. **TCLC 16**
See also Grimke, Charlotte L(ottie) Forten
See also BLC 2; DLB 50

Foscolo, Ugo 1778-1827.......... **NCLC 8**

Fosse, Bob ...................... **CLC 20**
See also Fosse, Robert Louis

Fosse, Robert Louis 1927-1987
See Fosse, Bob
See also CA 110; 123

Foster, Stephen Collins
1826-1864 ................ **NCLC 26**

Foucault, Michel
1926-1984 ............ **CLC 31, 34, 69**
See also CA 105; 113; CANR 34; MTCW

Fouque, Friedrich (Heinrich Karl) de la Motte
1777-1843 ................ **NCLC 2**
See also DLB 90

Fournier, Henri Alban 1886-1914
See Alain-Fournier
See also CA 104

Fournier, Pierre 1916-............ **CLC 11**
See Gascar, Pierre
See also CA 89-92; CANR 16

Fowles, John
1926- .... **CLC 1, 2, 3, 4, 6, 9, 10, 15, 33**
See also CA 5-8R; CANR 25; CDBLB 1960
to Present; DLB 14; MTCW; SATA 22

Fox, Paula 1923-................ **CLC 2, 8**
See also AAYA 3; CA 73-76; CANR 20,
36; CLR 1; DLB 52; MAICYA; MTCW;
SATA 17, 60

Fox, William Price (Jr.) 1926- ..... **CLC 22**
See also CA 17-20R; CANR 11; DLB 2;
DLBY 81

Foxe, John 1516(?)-1587 ........... **LC 14**

Frame, Janet .......... **CLC 2, 3, 6, 22, 66**
See also Clutha, Janet Paterson Frame

France, Anatole ................... **TCLC 9**
See also Thibault, Jacques Anatole Francois
See also DLB 123

Francis, Claude 19(?)- ............ **CLC 50**

Francis, Dick 1920- ......... **CLC 2, 22, 42**
See also AAYA 5; BEST 89:3; CA 5-8R;
CANR 9; CDBLB 1960 to Present;
DLB 87; MTCW

Francis, Robert (Churchill)
1901-1987 ................ **CLC 15**
See also CA 1-4R; 123; CANR 1

**Frank, Anne(lies Marie)**
1929-1945 .................. **TCLC 17**
See also CA 113; 133; MTCW; SATA 42;
WLC

**Frank, Elizabeth** 1945-........... **CLC 39**
See also CA 121; 126

**Franklin, Benjamin**
See Hasek, Jaroslav (Matej Frantisek)

**Franklin, (Stella Maraia Sarah) Miles**
1879-1954 .................. **TCLC 7**
See also CA 104

**Fraser, Antonia (Pakenham)**
1932- .................... **CLC 32**
See also CA 85-88; MTCW; SATA 32

**Fraser, George MacDonald** 1925-.... **CLC 7**
See also CA 45-48; CANR 2

**Fraser, Sylvia** 1935- .............. **CLC 64**
See also CA 45-48; CANR 1, 16

**Frayn, Michael** 1933-...... **CLC 3, 7, 31, 47**
See also CA 5-8R; CANR 30; DLB 13, 14;
MTCW

**Fraze, Candida (Merrill)** 1945-..... **CLC 50**
See also CA 126

**Frazer, J(ames) G(eorge)**
1854-1941 .................. **TCLC 32**
See also CA 118

**Frazer, Robert Caine**
See Creasey, John

**Frazer, Sir James George**
See Frazer, J(ames) G(eorge)

**Frazier, Ian** 1951-................ **CLC 46**
See also CA 130

**Frederic, Harold** 1856-1898...... **NCLC 10**
See also DLB 12, 23

**Frederick the Great** 1712-1786...... **LC 14**

**Fredro, Aleksander** 1793-1876..... **NCLC 8**

**Freeling, Nicolas** 1927- ........... **CLC 38**
See also CA 49-52; CAAS 12; CANR 1, 17;
DLB 87

**Freeman, Douglas Southall**
1886-1953 .................. **TCLC 11**
See also CA 109; DLB 17

**Freeman, Judith** 1946-........... **CLC 55**

**Freeman, Mary Eleanor Wilkins**
1852-1930 ............ **TCLC 9; SSC 1**
See also CA 106; DLB 12, 78

**Freeman, R(ichard) Austin**
1862-1943 .................. **TCLC 21**
See also CA 113; DLB 70

**French, Marilyn** 1929-...... **CLC 10, 18, 60**
See also CA 69-72; CANR 3, 31; MTCW

**French, Paul**
See Asimov, Isaac

**Freneau, Philip Morin** 1752-1832 .. **NCLC 1**
See also DLB 37, 43

**Friedan, Betty (Naomi)** 1921-...... **CLC 74**
See also CA 65-68; CANR 18; MTCW

**Friedman, B(ernard) H(arper)**
1926-........................ **CLC 7**
See also CA 1-4R; CANR 3

**Friedman, Bruce Jay** 1930-.... **CLC 3, 5, 56**
See also CA 9-12R; CANR 25; DLB 2, 28

**Friel, Brian** 1929-........... **CLC 5, 42, 59**
See also CA 21-24R; CANR 33; DLB 13;
MTCW

**Friis-Baastad, Babbis Ellinor**
1921-1970 .................... **CLC 12**
See also CA 17-20R; 134; SATA 7

**Frisch, Max (Rudolf)**
1911-1991 ..... **CLC 3, 9, 14, 18, 32, 44**
See also CA 85-88; 134; CANR 32;
DLB 69; MTCW

**Fromentin, Eugene (Samuel Auguste)**
1820-1876 ................. **NCLC 10**
See also DLB 123

**Frost, Robert (Lee)**
1874-1963 ... **CLC 1, 3, 4, 9, 10, 13, 15,
26, 34, 44; PC 1**
See also CA 89-92; CANR 33;
CDALB 1917-1929; DLB 54; DLBD 7;
MTCW; SATA 14; WLC

**Froy, Herald**
See Waterhouse, Keith (Spencer)

**Fry, Christopher** 1907-....... **CLC 2, 10, 14**
See also CA 17-20R; CANR 9, 30; DLB 13;
MTCW; SATA 66

**Frye, (Herman) Northrop**
1912-1991 ............... **CLC 24, 70**
See also CA 5-8R; 133; CANR 8, 37;
DLB 67, 68; MTCW

**Fuchs, Daniel** 1909-........... **CLC 8, 22**
See also CA 81-84; CAAS 5; DLB 9, 26, 28

**Fuchs, Daniel** 1934-.............. **CLC 34**
See also CA 37-40R; CANR 14

**Fuentes, Carlos**
1928-...... **CLC 3, 8, 10, 13, 22, 41, 60**
See also AAYA 4; AITN 2; CA 69-72;
CANR 10, 32; DLB 113; HW; MTCW;
WLC

**Fuentes, Gregorio Lopez y**
See Lopez y Fuentes, Gregorio

**Fugard, (Harold) Athol**
1932-....... **CLC 5, 9, 14, 25, 40; DC 3**
See also CA 85-88; CANR 32; MTCW

**Fugard, Sheila** 1932- .............. **CLC 48**
See also CA 125

**Fuller, Charles (H. Jr.)**
1939-................. **CLC 25; DC 1**
See also BLC 2; BW; CA 108; 112; DLB 38;
MTCW

**Fuller, John (Leopold)** 1937-....... **CLC 62**
See also CA 21-24R; CANR 9; DLB 40

**Fuller, Margaret** ................. **NCLC 5**
See also Ossoli, Sarah Margaret (Fuller
marchesa d')

**Fuller, Roy (Broadbent)**
1912-1991 ................. **CLC 4, 28**
See also CA 5-8R; 135; CAAS 10; DLB 15,
20

**Fulton, Alice** 1952-................ **CLC 52**
See also CA 116

**Furphy, Joseph** 1843-1912........ **TCLC 25**

**Fussell, Paul** 1924-.............. **CLC 74**
See also BEST 90:1; CA 17-20R; CANR 8,
21, 35; MTCW

**Futabatei, Shimei** 1864-1909...... **TCLC 44**

**Futrelle, Jacques** 1875-1912 ...... **TCLC 19**
See also CA 113

**G. B. S.**
See Shaw, George Bernard

**Gaboriau, Emile** 1835-1873...... **NCLC 14**

**Gadda, Carlo Emilio** 1893-1973 .... **CLC 11**
See also CA 89-92

**Gaddis, William**
1922-........ **CLC 1, 3, 6, 8, 10, 19, 43**
See also CA 17-20R; CANR 21; DLB 2;
MTCW

**Gaines, Ernest J(ames)**
1933-.................. **CLC 3, 11, 18**
See also AITN 1; BLC 2; BW; CA 9-12R;
CANR 6, 24; CDALB 1968-1988; DLB 2,
33; DLBY 80; MTCW

**Gaitskill, Mary** 1954-.............. **CLC 69**
See also CA 128

**Galdos, Benito Perez**
See Perez Galdos, Benito

**Gale, Zona** 1874-1938 ............ **TCLC 7**
See also CA 105; DLB 9, 78

**Galeano, Eduardo (Hughes)** 1940-... **CLC 72**
See also CA 29-32R; CANR 13, 32; HW

**Galiano, Juan Valera y Alcala**
See Valera y Alcala-Galiano, Juan

**Gallagher, Tess** 1943-......... **CLC 18, 63**
See also CA 106; DLB 120

**Gallant, Mavis**
1922-........... **CLC 7, 18, 38; SSC 5**
See also CA 69-72; CANR 29; DLB 53;
MTCW

**Gallant, Roy A(rthur)** 1924- ....... **CLC 17**
See also CA 5-8R; CANR 4, 29; MAICYA;
SATA 4, 68

**Gallico, Paul (William)** 1897-1976 ... **CLC 2**
See also AITN 1; CA 5-8R; 69-72;
CANR 23; DLB 9; MAICYA; SATA 13

**Gallup, Ralph**
See Whitemore, Hugh (John)

**Galsworthy, John** 1867-1933.... **TCLC 1, 45**
See also CA 104; CDBLB 1890-1914;
DLB 10, 34, 98; WLC 2

**Galt, John** 1779-1839........... **NCLC 1**
See also DLB 99, 116

**Galvin, James** 1951-.............. **CLC 38**
See also CA 108; CANR 26

**Gamboa, Federico** 1864-1939...... **TCLC 36**

**Gann, Ernest Kellogg** 1910-1991.... **CLC 23**
See also AITN 1; CA 1-4R; 136; CANR 1

**Garcia Lorca, Federico**
1898-1936 ..... **TCLC 1, 7; DC 2; PC 3**
See also CA 104; 131; DLB 108; HW;
MTCW; WLC

**Garcia Marquez, Gabriel (Jose)**
1928- ... **CLC 2, 3, 8, 10, 15, 27, 47, 55;
SSC 8**
See also Marquez, Gabriel (Jose) Garcia
See also AAYA 3; BEST 89:1; 90:4;
CA 33-36R; CANR 10, 28; DLB 113;
HW; MTCW; WLC

**Gard, Janice**
See Latham, Jean Lee

**Graham, Tom**
See Lewis, (Harry) Sinclair

**Graham, W(illiam) S(ydney)**
1918-1986 ............... **CLC 29**
See also CA 73-76; 118; DLB 20

**Graham, Winston (Mawdsley)**
1910- ...................... **CLC 23**
See also CA 49-52; CANR 2, 22; DLB 77

**Granville-Barker, Harley**
1877-1946 .................. **TCLC 2**
See also Barker, Harley Granville
See also CA 104

**Grass, Guenter (Wilhelm)**
1927- .. **CLC 1, 2, 4, 6, 11, 15, 22, 32, 49**
See also CA 13-16R; CANR 20; DLB 75;
MTCW; WLC

**Gratton, Thomas**
See Hulme, T(homas) E(rnest)

**Grau, Shirley Ann** 1929- ......... **CLC 4, 9**
See also CA 89-92; CANR 22; DLB 2;
MTCW

**Gravel, Fern**
See Hall, James Norman

**Graver, Elizabeth** 1964- ........... **CLC 70**
See also CA 135

**Graves, Richard Perceval** 1945- .... **CLC 44**
See also CA 65-68; CANR 9, 26

**Graves, Robert (von Ranke)**
1895-1985 ..... **CLC 1, 2, 6, 11, 39, 44,**
**45; PC 6**
See also CA 5-8R; 117; CANR 5, 36;
CDBLB 1914-1945; DLB 20, 100;
DLBY 85; MTCW; SATA 45

**Gray, Alasdair (James)** 1934- ...... **CLC 41**
See also CA 126; MTCW

**Gray, Amlin** 1946- ............... **CLC 29**
See also CA 138

**Gray, Francine du Plessix** 1930-.... **CLC 22**
See also BEST 90:3; CA 61-64; CAAS 2;
CANR 11, 33; MTCW

**Gray, John (Henry)** 1866-1934 .... **TCLC 19**
See also CA 119

**Gray, Simon (James Holliday)**
1936- .................. **CLC 9, 14, 36**
See also AITN 1; CA 21-24R; CAAS 3;
CANR 32; DLB 13; MTCW

**Gray, Spalding** 1941- ............. **CLC 49**
See also CA 128

**Gray, Thomas** 1716-1771 ...... **LC 4; PC 2**
See also CDBLB 1660-1789; DLB 109;
WLC

**Grayson, David**
See Baker, Ray Stannard

**Grayson, Richard (A.)** 1951- ....... **CLC 38**
See also CA 85-88; CANR 14, 31

**Greeley, Andrew M(oran)** 1928- .... **CLC 28**
See also CA 5-8R; CAAS 7; CANR 7;
MTCW

**Green, Brian**
See Card, Orson Scott

**Green, Hannah** ................. **CLC 3**
See also CA 73-76

**Green, Hannah**
See Greenberg, Joanne (Goldenberg)

**Green, Henry** ................. **CLC 2, 13**
See also Yorke, Henry Vincent
See also DLB 15

**Green, Julian (Hartridge)**
1900- ...................... **CLC 3, 11**
See also CA 21-24R; CANR 33; DLB 4, 72;
MTCW

**Green, Julien** 1900-
See Green, Julian (Hartridge)

**Green, Paul (Eliot)** 1894-1981 ...... **CLC 25**
See also AITN 1; CA 5-8R; 103; CANR 3;
DLB 7, 9; DLBY 81

**Greenberg, Ivan** 1908-1973
See Rahv, Philip
See also CA 85-88

**Greenberg, Joanne (Goldenberg)**
1932- .................... **CLC 7, 30**
See also CA 5-8R; CANR 14, 32; SATA 25

**Greenberg, Richard** 1959(?)- ....... **CLC 57**
See also CA 138

**Greene, Bette** 1934- .............. **CLC 30**
See also AAYA 7; CA 53-56; CANR 4;
CLR 2; MAICYA; SATA 8

**Greene, Gael** ..................... **CLC 8**
See also CA 13-16R; CANR 10

**Greene, Graham (Henry)**
1904-1991 ... **CLC 1, 3, 6, 9, 14, 18, 27,**
**37, 70, 72**
See also AITN 2; CA 13-16R; 133;
CANR 35; CDBLB 1945-1960; DLB 13,
15, 77, 100; DLBY 91; MTCW;
SATA 20; WLC

**Greer, Richard**
See Silverberg, Robert

**Greer, Richard**
See Silverberg, Robert

**Gregor, Arthur** 1923- .............. **CLC 9**
See also CA 25-28R; CAAS 10; CANR 11;
SATA 36

**Gregor, Lee**
See Pohl, Frederik

**Gregory, Isabella Augusta (Persse)**
1852-1932 ................... **TCLC 1**
See also CA 104; DLB 10

**Gregory, J. Dennis**
See Williams, John A(lfred)

**Grendon, Stephen**
See Derleth, August (William)

**Grenville, Kate** 1950- .............. **CLC 61**
See also CA 118

**Grenville, Pelham**
See Wodehouse, P(elham) G(renville)

**Greve, Felix Paul (Berthold Friedrich)**
1879-1948
See Grove, Frederick Philip
See also CA 104

**Grey, Zane** 1872-1939 ........... **TCLC 6**
See also CA 104; 132; DLB 9; MTCW

**Grieg, (Johan) Nordahl (Brun)**
1902-1943 .................. **TCLC 10**
See also CA 107

**Grieve, C(hristopher) M(urray)**
1892-1978 ............... **CLC 11, 19**
See also MacDiarmid, Hugh
See also CA 5-8R; 85-88; CANR 33;
MTCW

**Griffin, Gerald** 1803-1840 ....... **NCLC 7**

**Griffin, John Howard** 1920-1980.... **CLC 68**
See also AITN 1; CA 1-4R; 101; CANR 2

**Griffin, Peter** ..................... **CLC 39**

**Griffiths, Trevor** 1935- .......... **CLC 13, 52**
See also CA 97-100; DLB 13

**Grigson, Geoffrey (Edward Harvey)**
1905-1985 ................. **CLC 7, 39**
See also CA 25-28R; 118; CANR 20, 33;
DLB 27; MTCW

**Grillparzer, Franz** 1791-1872...... **NCLC 1**

**Grimble, Reverend Charles James**
See Eliot, T(homas) S(tearns)

**Grimke, Charlotte L(ottie) Forten**
1837(?)-1914
See Forten, Charlotte L.
See also BW; CA 117; 124

**Grimm, Jacob Ludwig Karl**
1785-1863 ................... **NCLC 3**
See also DLB 90; MAICYA; SATA 22

**Grimm, Wilhelm Karl** 1786-1859 .. **NCLC 3**
See also DLB 90; MAICYA; SATA 22

**Grimmelshausen, Johann Jakob Christoffel**
von 1621-1676 .............. **LC 6**

**Grindel, Eugene** 1895-1952
See Eluard, Paul
See also CA 104

**Grossman, David** ................. **CLC 67**
See also CA 138

**Grossman, Vasily (Semenovich)**
1905-1964 ................... **CLC 41**
See also CA 124; 130; MTCW

**Grove, Frederick Philip** ........... **TCLC 4**
See also Greve, Felix Paul (Berthold
Friedrich)
See also DLB 92

**Grubb**
See Crumb, R(obert)

**Grumbach, Doris (Isaac)**
1918- ................. **CLC 13, 22, 64**
See also CA 5-8R; CAAS 2; CANR 9

**Grundtvig, Nicolai Frederik Severin**
1783-1872 ................... **NCLC 1**

**Grunge**
See Crumb, R(obert)

**Grunwald, Lisa** 1959- ............. **CLC 44**
See also CA 120

**Guare, John** 1938- ....... **CLC 8, 14, 29, 67**
See also CA 73-76; CANR 21; DLB 7;
MTCW

**Gudjonsson, Halldor Kiljan** 1902-
See Laxness, Halldor
See also CA 103

**Guenter, Erich**
See Eich, Guenter

**Guest, Barbara** 1920- ............. **CLC 34**
See also CA 25-28R; CANR 11; DLB 5

Guest, Judith (Ann) 1936- . . . . . . . CLC 8, 30
See also AAYA 7; CA 77-80; CANR 15;
MTCW

Guild, Nicholas M. 1944- . . . . . . . . . CLC 33
See also CA 93-96

Guillemin, Jacques
See Sartre, Jean-Paul

Guillen, Jorge 1893-1984 . . . . . . . . . CLC 11
See also CA 89-92; 112; DLB 108; HW

Guillen (y Batista), Nicolas (Cristobal)
1902-1989 . . . . . . . . . . . . . . . . . . CLC 48
See also BLC 2; BW; CA 116; 125; 129;
HW

Guillevic, (Eugene) 1907- . . . . . . . . . CLC 33
See also CA 93-96

Guillois
See Desnos, Robert

Guiney, Louise Imogen
1861-1920 . . . . . . . . . . . . . . . TCLC 41
See also DLB 54

Guiraldes, Ricardo (Guillermo)
1886-1927 . . . . . . . . . . . . . . . . . TCLC 39
See also CA 131; HW; MTCW

Gunn, Bill . . . . . . . . . . . . . . . . . . . . . CLC 5
See also Gunn, William Harrison
See also DLB 38

Gunn, Thom(son William)
1929- . . . . . . . . . . . . . . . CLC 3, 6, 18, 32
See also CA 17-20R; CANR 9, 33;
CDBLB 1960 to Present; DLB 27;
MTCW

Gunn, William Harrison 1934(?)-1989
See Gunn, Bill
See also AITN 1; BW; CA 13-16R; 128;
CANR 12, 25

Gunnars, Kristjana 1948- . . . . . . . . . CLC 69
See also CA 113; DLB 60

Gurganus, Allan 1947- . . . . . . . . . . . CLC 70
See also BEST 90:1; CA 135

Gurney, A(lbert) R(amsdell) Jr.
1930- . . . . . . . . . . . . . . . CLC 32, 50, 54
See also CA 77-80; CANR 32

Gurney, Ivor (Bertie) 1890-1937 . . . TCLC 33

Gurney, Peter
See Gurney, A(lbert) R(amsdell) Jr.

Gustafson, Ralph (Barker) 1909- . . . . CLC 36
See also CA 21-24R; CANR 8; DLB 88

Gut, Gom
See Simenon, Georges (Jacques Christian)

Guthrie, A(lfred) B(ertram) Jr.
1901-1991 . . . . . . . . . . . . . . . . . CLC 23
See also CA 57-60; 134; CANR 24; DLB 6;
SATA 62; SATO 67

Guthrie, Isobel
See Grieve, C(hristopher) M(urray)

Guthrie, Woodrow Wilson 1912-1967
See Guthrie, Woody
See also CA 113; 93-96

Guthrie, Woody . . . . . . . . . . . . . . . . CLC 35
See also Guthrie, Woodrow Wilson

Guy, Rosa (Cuthbert) 1928- . . . . . . . CLC 26
See also AAYA 4; BW; CA 17-20R;
CANR 14, 34; CLR 13; DLB 33;
MAICYA; SATA 14, 62

Gwendolyn
See Bennett, (Enoch) Arnold

H. D. . . . . . . . . CLC 3, 8, 14, 31, 34, 73; PC 5
See also Doolittle, Hilda

Haavikko, Paavo Juhani
1931- . . . . . . . . . . . . . . . . . . CLC 18, 34
See also CA 106

Habbema, Koos
See Heijermans, Herman

Hacker, Marilyn 1942- . . . . CLC 5, 9, 23, 72
See also CA 77-80; DLB 120

Haggard, H(enry) Rider
1856-1925 . . . . . . . . . . . . . . . . . TCLC 11
See also CA 108; DLB 70; SATA 16

Haig, Fenil
See Ford, Ford Madox

Haig-Brown, Roderick (Langmere)
1908-1976 . . . . . . . . . . . . . . . . . CLC 21
See also CA 5-8R; 69-72; CANR 4, 38;
DLB 88; MAICYA; SATA 12

Hailey, Arthur 1920- . . . . . . . . . . . . . CLC 5
See also AITN 2; BEST 90:3; CA 1-4R;
CANR 2, 36; DLB 88; DLBY 82; MTCW

Hailey, Elizabeth Forsythe 1938- . . . CLC 40
See also CA 93-96; CAAS 1; CANR 15

Haines, John (Meade) 1924- . . . . . . . CLC 58
See also CA 17-20R; CANR 13, 34; DLB 5

Haldeman, Joe (William) 1943- . . . . . CLC 61
See also CA 53-56; CANR 6; DLB 8

Haley, Alex(ander Murray Palmer)
1921-1992 . . . . . . . . . . . . . . . . CLC 8, 12
See also BLC 2; BW; CA 77-80; 136;
DLB 38; MTCW

Haliburton, Thomas Chandler
1796-1865 . . . . . . . . . . . . . . . . . NCLC 15
See also DLB 11, 99

Hall, Donald (Andrew Jr.)
1928- . . . . . . . . . . . . . . CLC 1, 13, 37, 59
See also CA 5-8R; CAAS 7; CANR 2;
DLB 5; SATA 23

Hall, Frederic Sauser
See Sauser-Hall, Frederic

Hall, James
See Kuttner, Henry

Hall, James Norman 1887-1951 . . . TCLC 23
See also CA 123; SATA 21

Hall, (Marguerite) Radclyffe
1886(?)-1943 . . . . . . . . . . . . . . . TCLC 12
See also CA 110

Hall, Rodney 1935- . . . . . . . . . . . . . . CLC 51
See also CA 109

Halliday, Michael
See Creasey, John

Halpern, Daniel 1945- . . . . . . . . . . . CLC 14
See also CA 33-36R

Hamburger, Michael (Peter Leopold)
1924- . . . . . . . . . . . . . . . . . . . CLC 5, 14
See also CA 5-8R; CAAS 4; CANR 2;
DLB 27

Hamill, Pete 1935- . . . . . . . . . . . . . . CLC 10
See also CA 25-28R; CANR 18

Hamilton, Clive
See Lewis, C(live) S(taples)

Hamilton, Edmond 1904-1977 . . . . . . . CLC 1
See also CA 1-4R; CANR 3; DLB 8

Hamilton, Eugene (Jacob) Lee
See Lee-Hamilton, Eugene (Jacob)

Hamilton, Franklin
See Silverberg, Robert

Hamilton, Gail
See Corcoran, Barbara

Hamilton, Mollie
See Kaye, M(ary) M(argaret)

Hamilton, (Anthony Walter) Patrick
1904-1962 . . . . . . . . . . . . . . . . . CLC 51
See also CA 113; DLB 10

Hamilton, Virginia 1936- . . . . . . . . . CLC 26
See also AAYA 2; BW; CA 25-28R;
CANR 20, 37; CLR 1, 11; DLB 33, 52;
MAICYA; MTCW; SATA 4, 56

Hammett, (Samuel) Dashiell
1894-1961 . . . . . . . . CLC 3, 5, 10, 19, 47
See also AITN 1; CA 81-84;
CDALB 1929-1941; DLBD 6; MTCW

Hammon, Jupiter 1711(?)-1800(?) . . NCLC 5
See also BLC 2; DLB 31, 50

Hammond, Keith
See Kuttner, Henry

Hamner, Earl (Henry) Jr. 1923- . . . . CLC 12
See also AITN 2; CA 73-76; DLB 6

Hampton, Christopher (James)
1946- . . . . . . . . . . . . . . . . . . . . . . CLC 4
See also CA 25-28R; DLB 13; MTCW

Hamsun, Knut . . . . . . . . . . . . . . . TCLC 2, 14
See also Pedersen, Knut

Handke, Peter 1942- . . CLC 5, 8, 10, 15, 38
See also CA 77-80; CANR 33; DLB 85;
MTCW

Hanley, James 1901-1985 . . . CLC 3, 5, 8, 13
See also CA 73-76; 117; CANR 36; MTCW

Hannah, Barry 1942- . . . . . . . . . . CLC 23, 38
See also CA 108; 110; DLB 6; MTCW

Hannon, Ezra
See Hunter, Evan

Hansberry, Lorraine (Vivian)
1930-1965 . . . . . . . . . . CLC 17, 62; DC 2
See also BLC 2; BW; CA 109; 25-28R;
CABS 3; CDALB 1941-1968; DLB 7, 38;
MTCW

Hansen, Joseph 1923- . . . . . . . . . . . . CLC 38
See also CA 29-32R; CANR 16

Hansen, Martin A. 1909-1955 . . . . . TCLC 32

Hanson, Kenneth O(stlin) 1922- . . . . CLC 13
See also CA 53-56; CANR 7

Hardwick, Elizabeth 1916- . . . . . . . . CLC 13
See also CA 5-8R; CANR 3, 32; DLB 6;
MTCW

Hardy, Thomas
1840-1928 . . . . . TCLC 4, 10, 18, 32, 48;
SSC 2
See also CA 104; 123; CDBLB 1890-1914;
DLB 18, 19; MTCW; WLC

Hare, David 1947- . . . . . . . . . . . . CLC 29, 58
See also CA 97-100; CANR 39; DLB 13;
MTCW

Harford, Henry
See Hudson, W(illiam) H(enry)

Heiney, Donald (William) 1921- ..... **CLC 9**
See also CA 1-4R; CANR 3

Heinlein, Robert A(nson)
1907-1988 ...... **CLC 1, 3, 8, 14, 26, 55**
See also CA 1-4R; 125; CANR 1, 20;
DLB 8; MAICYA; MTCW; SATA 9, 56,
69

Helforth, John
See Doolittle, Hilda

Hellenhofferu, Vojtech Kapristian z
See Hasek, Jaroslav (Matej Frantisek)

Heller, Joseph
1923- ........ **CLC 1, 3, 5, 8, 11, 36, 63**
See also AITN 1; CA 5-8R; CABS 1;
CANR 8; DLB 2, 28; DLBY 80; MTCW;
WLC

Hellman, Lillian (Florence)
1906-1984 ..... **CLC 2, 4, 8, 14, 18, 34,**
**44, 52; DC 1**
See also AITN 1, 2; CA 13-16R; 112;
CANR 33; DLB 7; DLBY 84; MTCW

Helprin, Mark 1947- ..... **CLC 7, 10, 22, 32**
See also CA 81-84; DLBY 85; MTCW

Helyar, Jane Penelope Josephine 1933-
See Poole, Josephine
See also CA 21-24R; CANR 10, 26

Hemans, Felicia 1793-1835 ...... **NCLC 29**
See also DLB 96

Hemingway, Ernest (Miller)
1899-1961 ... **CLC 1, 3, 6, 8, 10, 13, 19,**
**30, 34, 39, 41, 44, 50, 61; SSC 1**
See also CA 77-80; CANR 34;
CDALB 1917-1929; DLB 4, 9, 102;
DLBD 1; DLBY 81, 87; MTCW; WLC

Hempel, Amy 1951- ............. **CLC 39**
See also CA 118; 137

Henderson, F. C.
See Mencken, H(enry) L(ouis)

Henderson, Sylvia
See Ashton-Warner, Sylvia (Constance)

Henley, Beth ..................... **CLC 23**
See also Henley, Elizabeth Becker
See also CABS 3; DLBY 86

Henley, Elizabeth Becker 1952-
See Henley, Beth
See also CA 107; CANR 32; MTCW

Henley, William Ernest
1849-1903 .................. **TCLC 8**
See also CA 105; DLB 19

Hennissart, Martha
See Lathen, Emma
See also CA 85-88

Henry, O. ........... **TCLC 1, 19; SSC 5**
See also Porter, William Sydney
See also WLC

Henryson, Robert 1430(?)-1506(?).... **LC 20**

Henry VIII 1491-1547 ............. **LC 10**

Henschke, Alfred
See Klabund

Hentoff, Nat(han Irving) 1925- ..... **CLC 26**
See also AAYA 4; CA 1-4R; CAAS 6;
CANR 5, 25; CLR 1; MAICYA;
SATA 27, 42, 69

Heppenstall, (John) Rayner
1911-1981 ................... **CLC 10**
See also CA 1-4R; 103; CANR 29

Herbert, Frank (Patrick)
1920-1986 ......... **CLC 12, 23, 35, 44**
See also CA 53-56; 118; CANR 5; DLB 8;
MTCW; SATA 9, 37, 47

Herbert, George 1593-1633 .......... **PC 4**
See also CDBLB Before 1660

Herbert, Zbigniew 1924- ........ **CLC 9, 43**
See also CA 89-92; CANR 36; MTCW

Herbst, Josephine (Frey)
1897-1969 ................... **CLC 34**
See also CA 5-8R; 25-28R; DLB 9

Hergesheimer, Joseph
1880-1954 ................. **TCLC 11**
See also CA 109; DLB 102, 9

Herlihy, James Leo 1927- .......... **CLC 6**
See also CA 1-4R; CANR 2

Hermogenes fl. c. 175- ........... **CMLC 6**

Hernandez, Jose 1834-1886 ...... **NCLC 17**

Herrick, Robert 1591-1674 ......... **LC 13**

Herriot, James ................... **CLC 12**
See Wight, James Alfred
See also AAYA 1

Herrmann, Dorothy 1941- ........ **CLC 44**
See also CA 107

Herrmann, Taffy
See Herrmann, Dorothy

Hersey, John (Richard)
1914- .............. **CLC 1, 2, 7, 9, 40**
See also CA 17-20R; CANR 33; DLB 6;
MTCW; SATA 25

Herzen, Aleksandr Ivanovich
1812-1870 ................. **NCLC 10**

Herzl, Theodor 1860-1904 ....... **TCLC 36**

Herzog, Werner 1942- ............ **CLC 16**
See also CA 89-92

Hesiod c. 8th cent. B.C.- ......... **CMLC 5**

Hesse, Hermann
1877-1962 ... **CLC 1, 2, 3, 6, 11, 17, 25,**
**69; SSC 9**
See also CA 17-18; CAP 2; DLB 66;
MTCW; SATA 50; WLC

Hewes, Cady
See De Voto, Bernard (Augustine)

Heyen, William 1940- ........ **CLC 13, 18**
See also CA 33-36R; CAAS 9; DLB 5

Heyerdahl, Thor 1914- ............ **CLC 26**
See also CA 5-8R; CANR 5, 22; MTCW;
SATA 2, 52

Heym, Georg (Theodor Franz Arthur)
1887-1912 .................. **TCLC 9**
See also CA 106

Heym, Stefan 1913- .............. **CLC 41**
See also CA 9-12R; CANR 4; DLB 69

Heyse, Paul (Johann Ludwig von)
1830-1914 ................... **TCLC 8**
See also CA 104

Hibbert, Eleanor Burford 1906- ..... **CLC 7**
See also BEST 90:4; CA 17-20R; CANR 9,
28; SATA 2

Higgins, George V(incent)
1939- ............. **CLC 4, 7, 10, 18**
See also CA 77-80; CAAS 5; CANR 17;
DLB 2; DLBY 81; MTCW

Higginson, Thomas Wentworth
1823-1911 ................. **TCLC 36**
See also DLB 1, 64

Highet, Helen
See MacInnes, Helen (Clark)

Highsmith, (Mary) Patricia
1921- ............. **CLC 2, 4, 14, 42**
See also CA 1-4R; CANR 1, 20; MTCW

Highwater, Jamake (Mamake)
1942(?)- ...................... **CLC 12**
See also AAYA 7; CA 65-68; CAAS 7;
CANR 10, 34; CLR 17; DLB 52;
DLBY 85; MAICYA; SATA 30, 32, 69

Hijuelos, Oscar 1951- ............. **CLC 65**
See also BEST 90:1; CA 123; HW

Hikmet, Nazim 1902-1963 ......... **CLC 40**
See also CA 93-96

Hildesheimer, Wolfgang
1916-1991 ................... **CLC 49**
See also CA 101; 135; DLB 69

Hill, Geoffrey (William)
1932- ................ **CLC 5, 8, 18, 45**
See also CA 81-84; CANR 21;
CDBLB 1960 to Present; DLB 40;
MTCW

Hill, George Roy 1921- ........... **CLC 26**
See also CA 110; 122

Hill, Susan (Elizabeth) 1942- ....... **CLC 4**
See also CA 33-36R; CANR 29; DLB 14;
MTCW

Hillerman, Tony 1925- ............ **CLC 62**
See also AAYA 6; BEST 89:1; CA 29-32R;
CANR 21; SATA 6

Hilliard, Noel (Harvey) 1929- ...... **CLC 15**
See also CA 9-12R; CANR 7

Hillis, Rick 1956- ................ **CLC 66**
See also CA 134

Hilton, James 1900-1954 ........ **TCLC 21**
See also CA 108; DLB 34, 77; SATA 34

Himes, Chester (Bomar)
1909-1984 ........ **CLC 2, 4, 7, 18, 58**
See also BLC 2; BW; CA 25-28R; 114;
CANR 22; DLB 2, 76; MTCW

Hinde, Thomas ................. **CLC 6, 11**
See also Chitty, Thomas Willes

Hindin, Nathan
See Bloch, Robert (Albert)

Hine, (William) Daryl 1936- ....... **CLC 15**
See also CA 1-4R; CAAS 15; CANR 1, 20;
DLB 60

Hinkson, Katharine Tynan
See Tynan, Katharine

Hinton, S(usan) E(loise) 1950- ..... **CLC 30**
See also AAYA 2; CA 81-84; CANR 32;
CLR 3, 23; MAICYA; MTCW;
SATA 19, 58

Hippius, Zinaida ................. **TCLC 9**
See also Gippius, Zinaida (Nikolayevna)

Hiraoka, Kimitake 1925-1970
See Mishima, Yukio
See also CA 97-100; 29-32R; MTCW

Ishiguro, Kazuo 1954- ...... CLC 27, 56, 59
See also BEST 90:2; CA 120; MTCW

Ishikawa Takuboku
1886(?)-1912 ............... TCLC 15
See also CA 113

Iskander, Fazil 1929- ............ CLC 47
See also CA 102

Ivan IV 1530-1584 ............... LC 17

Ivanov, Vyacheslav Ivanovich
1866-1949 ................. TCLC 33
See also CA 122

Ivask, Ivar Vidrik 1927- .......... CLC 14
See also CA 37-40R; CANR 24

Jackson, Daniel
See Wingrove, David (John)

Jackson, Jesse 1908-1983 ......... CLC 12
See also BW; CA 25-28R; 109; CANR 27;
CLR 28; MAICYA; SATA 2, 29, 48

Jackson, Laura (Riding) 1901-1991 .. CLC 7
See also Riding, Laura
See also CA 65-68; 135; CANR 28; DLB 48

Jackson, Sam
See Trumbo, Dalton

Jackson, Sara
See Wingrove, David (John)

Jackson, Shirley
1919-1965 ........ CLC 11, 60; SSC 9
See also AAYA 9; CA 1-4R; 25-28R;
CANR 4; CDALB 1941-1968; DLB 6;
SATA 2; WLC

Jacob, (Cyprien-)Max 1876-1944 ... TCLC 6
See also CA 104

Jacobs, Jim 1942- ............... CLC 12
See also CA 97-100

Jacobs, W(illiam) W(ymark)
1863-1943 ................. TCLC 22
See also CA 121

Jacobsen, Jens Peter 1847-1885 .. NCLC 34

Jacobsen, Josephine 1908- ........ CLC 48
See also CA 33-36R; CANR 23

Jacobson, Dan 1929- ......... CLC 4, 14
See also CA 1-4R; CANR 2, 25; DLB 14;
MTCW

Jacqueline
See Carpentier (y Valmont), Alejo

Jagger, Mick 1944- .............. CLC 17

Jakes, John (William) 1932- ...... CLC 29
See also BEST 89:4; CA 57-60; CANR 10;
DLBY 83; MTCW; SATA 62

James, Andrew
See Kirkup, James

James, C(yril) L(ionel) R(obert)
1901-1989 ................. CLC 33
See also BW; CA 117; 125; 128; MTCW

James, Daniel (Lewis) 1911-1988
See Santiago, Danny
See also CA 125

James, Dynely
See Mayne, William (James Carter)

James, Henry
1843-1916 ..... TCLC 2, 11, 24, 40, 47;
SSC 8
See also CA 104; 132; CDALB 1865-1917;
DLB 12, 71, 74; MTCW; WLC

James, Montague (Rhodes)
1862-1936 ................. TCLC 6
See also CA 104

James, P. D. ............... CLC 18, 46
See also White, Phyllis Dorothy James
See also BEST 90:2; CDBLB 1960 to
Present; DLB 87

James, Philip
See Moorcock, Michael (John)

James, William 1842-1910 ..... TCLC 15, 32
See also CA 109

James I 1394-1437 ............... LC 20

Jami, Nur al-Din 'Abd al-Rahman
1414-1492 ................. LC 9

Jandl, Ernst 1925- .............. CLC 34

Janowitz, Tama 1957- ........... CLC 43
See also CA 106

Jarrell, Randall
1914-1965 ...... CLC 1, 2, 6, 9, 13, 49
See also CA 5-8R; 25-28R; CABS 2;
CANR 6, 34; CDALB 1941-1968; CLR 6;
DLB 48, 52; MAICYA; MTCW; SATA 7

Jarry, Alfred 1873-1907 ....... TCLC 2, 14
See also CA 104

Jarvis, E. K.
See Bloch, Robert (Albert); Ellison, Harlan;
Silverberg, Robert

Jeake, Samuel Jr.
See Aiken, Conrad (Potter)

Jean Paul 1763-1825 ............ NCLC 7

Jeffers, (John) Robinson
1887-1962 ........ CLC 2, 3, 11, 15, 54
See also CA 85-88; CANR 35;
CDALB 1917-1929; DLB 45; MTCW;
WLC

Jefferson, Janet
See Mencken, H(enry) L(ouis)

Jefferson, Thomas 1743-1826 .... NCLC 11
See also CDALB 1640-1865; DLB 31

Jeffrey, Francis 1773-1850....... NCLC 33
See also DLB 107

Jelakowitch, Ivan
See Heijermans, Herman

Jellicoe, (Patricia) Ann 1927- ...... CLC 27
See also CA 85-88; DLB 13

Jen, Gish ........................ CLC 70
See also Jen, Lillian

Jen, Lillian 1956(?)-
See Jen, Gish
See also CA 135

Jenkins, (John) Robin 1912- ....... CLC 52
See also CA 1-4R; CANR 1; DLB 14

Jennings, Elizabeth (Joan)
1926- .................. CLC 5, 14
See also CA 61-64; CAAS 5; CANR 8, 39;
DLB 27; MTCW; SATA 66

Jennings, Waylon 1937-........... CLC 21

Jensen, Johannes V. 1873-1950.... TCLC 41

Jensen, Laura (Linnea) 1948- ...... CLC 37
See also CA 103

Jerome, Jerome K(lapka)
1859-1927 ................. TCLC 23
See also CA 119; DLB 10, 34

Jerrold, Douglas William
1803-1857 ................. NCLC 2

Jewett, (Theodora) Sarah Orne
1849-1909 ......... TCLC 1, 22; SSC 6
See also CA 108; 127; DLB 12, 74;
SATA 15

Jewsbury, Geraldine (Endsor)
1812-1880 ............... NCLC 22
See also DLB 21

Jhabvala, Ruth Prawer
1927- .............. CLC 4, 8, 29
See also CA 1-4R; CANR 2, 29; MTCW

Jiles, Paulette 1943-.......... CLC 13, 58
See also CA 101

Jimenez (Mantecon), Juan Ramon
1881-1958 ................. TCLC 4
See also CA 104; 131; HW; MTCW

Jimenez, Ramon
See Jimenez (Mantecon), Juan Ramon

Jimenez Mantecon, Juan
See Jimenez (Mantecon), Juan Ramon

Joel, Billy ...................... CLC 26
See also Joel, William Martin

Joel, William Martin 1949-
See Joel, Billy
See also CA 108

John of the Cross, St. 1542-1591 .... LC 18

Johnson, B(ryan) S(tanley William)
1933-1973 ................ CLC 6, 9
See also CA 9-12R; 53-56; CANR 9;
DLB 14, 40

Johnson, Charles (Richard)
1948- .................. CLC 7, 51, 65
See also BLC 2; BW; CA 116; DLB 33

Johnson, Denis 1949-............. CLC 52
See also CA 117; 121; DLB 120

Johnson, Diane (Lain)
1934- ................. CLC 5, 13, 48
See also CA 41-44R; CANR 17; DLBY 80;
MTCW

Johnson, Eyvind (Olof Verner)
1900-1976 .................. CLC 14
See also CA 73-76; 69-72; CANR 34

Johnson, J. R.
See James, C(yril) L(ionel) R(obert)

Johnson, James Weldon
1871-1938 ...............TCLC 3, 19
See also BLC 2; BW; CA 104; 125;
CDALB 1917-1929; DLB 51; MTCW;
SATA 31

Johnson, Joyce 1935-............. CLC 58
See also CA 125; 129

Johnson, Lionel (Pigot)
1867-1902 ................. TCLC 19
See also CA 117; DLB 19

Johnson, Mel
See Malzberg, Barry N(athaniel)

Johnson, Pamela Hansford
1912-1981 ............... CLC 1, 7, 27
See also CA 1-4R; 104; CANR 2, 28;
DLB 15; MTCW

Johnson, Samuel 1709-1784........ LC 15
See also CDBLB 1660-1789; DLB 39, 95,
104; WLC

Johnson, Uwe
1934-1984 .......... CLC 5, 10, 15, 40
See also CA 1-4R; 112; CANR 1, 39;
DLB 75; MTCW

Johnston, George (Benson) 1913- ... CLC 51
See also CA 1-4R; CANR 5, 20; DLB 88

Johnston, Jennifer 1930- ........... CLC 7
See also CA 85-88; DLB 14

Jolley, (Monica) Elizabeth 1923- ... CLC 46
See also CA 127; CAAS 13

Jones, Arthur Llewellyn 1863-1947
See Machen, Arthur
See also CA 104

Jones, D(ouglas) G(ordon) 1929-.... CLC 10
See also CA 29-32R; CANR 13; DLB 53

Jones, David (Michael)
1895-1974 ........ CLC 2, 4, 7, 13, 42
See also CA 9-12R; 53-56; CANR 28;
CDBLB 1945-1960; DLB 20, 100; MTCW

Jones, David Robert 1947-
See Bowie, David
See also CA 103

Jones, Diana Wynne 1934- ........ CLC 26
See also CA 49-52; CANR 4, 26; CLR 23;
MAICYA; SAAS 7; SATA 9, 70

Jones, Gayl 1949-................ CLC 6, 9
See also BLC 2; BW; CA 77-80; CANR 27;
DLB 33; MTCW

Jones, James 1921-1977.... CLC 1, 3, 10, 39
See also AITN 1, 2; CA 1-4R; 69-72;
CANR 6; DLB 2; MTCW

Jones, John J.
See Lovecraft, H(oward) P(hillips)

Jones, LeRoi ........ CLC 1, 2, 3, 5, 10, 14
See also Baraka, Amiri

Jones, Louis B. .................... CLC 65

Jones, Madison (Percy Jr.) 1925-.... CLC 4
See also CA 13-16R; CAAS 11; CANR 7

Jones, Mervyn 1922- .......... CLC 10, 52
See also CA 45-48; CAAS 5; CANR 1;
MTCW

Jones, Mick 1956(?)- ............. CLC 30
See also The Clash

Jones, Nettie (Pearl) 1941- ....... CLC 34
See also CA 137

Jones, Preston 1936-1979 ........ CLC 10
See also CA 73-76; 89-92; DLB 7

Jones, Robert F(rancis) 1934-....... CLC 7
See also CA 49-52; CANR 2

Jones, Rod 1953- ................ CLC 50
See also CA 128

Jones, Terence Graham Parry
1942- ...................... CLC 21
See also Jones, Terry; Monty Python
See also CA 112; 116; CANR 35; SATA 51

Jones, Terry
See Jones, Terence Graham Parry
See also SATA 67

Jong, Erica 1942-.......... CLC 4, 6, 8, 18
See also AITN 1; BEST 90:2; CA 73-76;
CANR 26; DLB 2, 5, 28; MTCW

Jonson, Ben(jamin) 1572(?)-1637...... LC 6
See also CDBLB Before 1660; DLB 62, 121;
WLC

Jordan, June 1936-......... CLC 5, 11, 23
See also AAYA 2; BW; CA 33-36R;
CANR 25; CLR 10; DLB 38; MAICYA;
MTCW; SATA 4

Jordan, Pat(rick M.) 1941- ........ CLC 37
See also CA 33-36R

Jorgensen, Ivar
See Ellison, Harlan

Jorgenson, Ivar
See Silverberg, Robert

Josipovici, Gabriel 1940-........ CLC 6, 43
See also CA 37-40R; CAAS 8; DLB 14

Joubert, Joseph 1754-1824 ....... NCLC 9

Jouve, Pierre Jean 1887-1976...... CLC 47
See also CA 65-68

Joyce, James (Augustine Aloysius)
1882-1941 .... TCLC 3, 8, 16, 35; SSC 3
See also CA 104; 126; CDBLB 1914-1945;
DLB 10, 19, 36; MTCW; WLC

Jozsef, Attila 1905-1937.......... TCLC 22
See also CA 116

Juana Ines de la Cruz 1651(?)-1695 ... LC 5

Judd, Cyril
See Kornbluth, C(yril) M.; Pohl, Frederik

Julian of Norwich 1342(?)-1416(?) .... LC 6

Just, Ward (Swift) 1935- ........ CLC 4, 27
See also CA 25-28R; CANR 32

Justice, Donald (Rodney) 1925- .. CLC 6, 19
See also CA 5-8R; CANR 26; DLBY 83

Juvenal c. 55-c. 127 ............. CMLC 8

Juvenis
See Bourne, Randolph S(illiman)

Kacew, Romain 1914-1980
See Gary, Romain
See also CA 108; 102

Kadare, Ismail 1936- ............. CLC 52

Kadohata, Cynthia................. CLC 59

Kafka, Franz
1883-1924 ...... TCLC 2, 6, 13, 29, 47;
SSC 5
See also CA 105; 126; DLB 81; MTCW;
WLC

Kahn, Roger 1927-............... CLC 30
See also CA 25-28R; SATA 37

Kain, Saul
See Sassoon, Siegfried (Lorraine)

Kaiser, Georg 1878-1945 ......... TCLC 9
See also CA 106

Kaletski, Alexander 1946-........ CLC 39
See also CA 118

Kalidasa fl. c. 400- ............. CMLC 9

Kallman, Chester (Simon)
1921-1975 ................... CLC 2
See also CA 45-48; 53-56; CANR 3

Kaminsky, Melvin 1926-
See Brooks, Mel
See also CA 65-68; CANR 16

Kaminsky, Stuart M(elvin) 1934- ... CLC 59
See also CA 73-76; CANR 29

Kane, Paul
See Simon, Paul

Kane, Wilson
See Bloch, Robert (Albert)

Kanin, Garson 1912-............. CLC 22
See also AITN 1; CA 5-8R; CANR 7;
DLB 7

Kaniuk, Yoram 1930-............. CLC 19
See also CA 134

Kant, Immanuel 1724-1804 ...... NCLC 27
See also DLB 94

Kantor, MacKinlay 1904-1977 ...... CLC 7
See also CA 61-64; 73-76; DLB 9, 102

Kaplan, David Michael 1946- ...... CLC 50

Kaplan, James 1951- ............. CLC 59
See also CA 135

Karageorge, Michael
See Anderson, Poul (William)

Karamzin, Nikolai Mikhailovich
1766-1826 ................. NCLC 3

Karapanou, Margarita 1946-....... CLC 13
See also CA 101

Karinthy, Frigyes 1887-1938...... TCLC 47

Karl, Frederick R(obert) 1927-..... CLC 34
See also CA 5-8R; CANR 3

Kastel, Warren
See Silverberg, Robert

Kataev, Evgeny Petrovich 1903-1942
See Petrov, Evgeny
See also CA 120

Kataphusin
See Ruskin, John

Katz, Steve 1935-................ CLC 47
See also CA 25-28R; CAAS 14; CANR 12;
DLBY 83

Kauffman, Janet 1945-............. CLC 42
See also CA 117; DLBY 86

Kaufman, Bob (Garnell)
1925-1986 ................... CLC 49
See also BW; CA 41-44R; 118; CANR 22;
DLB 16, 41

Kaufman, George S. 1889-1961..... CLC 38
See also CA 108; 93-96; DLB 7

Kaufman, Sue .................... CLC 3, 8
See also Barondess, Sue K(aufman)

Kavafis, Konstantinos Petrou 1863-1933
See Cavafy, C(onstantine) P(eter)
See also CA 104

Kavan, Anna 1901-1968........ CLC 5, 13
See also CA 5-8R; CANR 6; MTCW

Kavanagh, Dan
See Barnes, Julian

Kavanagh, Patrick (Joseph)
1904-1967 ................... CLC 22
See also CA 123; 25-28R; DLB 15, 20;
MTCW

Kawabata, Yasunari
1899-1972 ............ CLC 2, 5, 9, 18
See also CA 93-96; 33-36R

Kaye, M(ary) M(argaret) 1909-..... CLC 28
See also CA 89-92; CANR 24; MTCW;
SATA 62

Kaye, Mollie
See Kaye, M(ary) M(argaret)

Kaye-Smith, Sheila 1887-1956..... TCLC 20
See also CA 118; DLB 36

**Kaymor, Patrice Maguilene**
See Senghor, Leopold Sedar

**Kazan, Elia** 1909- . . . . . . . . . . **CLC 6, 16, 63**
See also CA 21-24R; CANR 32

**Kazantzakis, Nikos**
1883(?)-1957 . . . . . . . . . . **TCLC 2, 5, 33**
See also CA 105; 132; MTCW

**Kazin, Alfred** 1915- . . . . . . . . . . **CLC 34, 38**
See also CA 1-4R; CAAS 7; CANR 1;
DLB 67

**Keane, Mary Nesta (Skrine)** 1904-
See Keane, Molly
See also CA 108; 114

**Keane, Molly** . . . . . . . . . . . . . . . . . . . . **CLC 31**
See also Keane, Mary Nesta (Skrine)

**Keates, Jonathan** 19(?)- . . . . . . . . . . . **CLC 34**

**Keaton, Buster** 1895-1966 . . . . . . . . **CLC 20**

**Keats, John** 1795-1821 . . . . . . **NCLC 8; PC 1**
See also CDBLB 1789-1832; DLB 96, 110;
WLC

**Keene, Donald** 1922- . . . . . . . . . . . . . **CLC 34**
See also CA 1-4R; CANR 5

**Keillor, Garrison** . . . . . . . . . . . . . . . . . **CLC 40**
See also Keillor, Gary (Edward)
See also AAYA 2; BEST 89:3; DLBY 87;
SATA 58

**Keillor, Gary (Edward)** 1942-
See Keillor, Garrison
See also CA 111; 117; CANR 36; MTCW

**Keith, Michael**
See Hubbard, L(afayette) Ron(ald)

**Kell, Joseph**
See Wilson, John (Anthony) Burgess

**Keller, Gottfried** 1819-1890 . . . . . . **NCLC 2**

**Kellerman, Jonathan** 1949- . . . . . . . . **CLC 44**
See also BEST 90:1; CA 106; CANR 29

**Kelley, William Melvin** 1937- . . . . . . **CLC 22**
See also BW; CA 77-80; CANR 27; DLB 33

**Kellogg, Marjorie** 1922- . . . . . . . . . . . **CLC 2**
See also CA 81-84

**Kellow, Kathleen**
See Hibbert, Eleanor Burford

**Kelly, M(ilton) T(erry)** 1947- . . . . . . . **CLC 55**
See also CA 97-100; CANR 19

**Kelman, James** 1946- . . . . . . . . . . . . . **CLC 58**

**Kemal, Yashar** 1923- . . . . . . . . . . **CLC 14, 29**
See also CA 89-92

**Kemble, Fanny** 1809-1893 . . . . . . . **NCLC 18**
See also DLB 32

**Kemelman, Harry** 1908- . . . . . . . . . . . **CLC 2**
See also AITN 1; CA 9-12R; CANR 6;
DLB 28

**Kempe, Margery** 1373(?)-1440(?) . . . . . **LC 6**

**Kempis, Thomas a** 1380-1471 . . . . . . . **LC 11**

**Kendall, Henry** 1839-1882 . . . . . . . **NCLC 12**

**Keneally, Thomas (Michael)**
1935- . . . . . . **CLC 5, 8, 10, 14, 19, 27, 43**
See also CA 85-88; CANR 10; MTCW

**Kennedy, Adrienne (Lita)** 1931- . . . . **CLC 66**
See also BLC 2; BW; CA 103; CABS 3;
CANR 26; DLB 38

**Kennedy, John Pendleton**
1795-1870 . . . . . . . . . . . . . . . . **NCLC 2**
See also DLB 3

**Kennedy, Joseph Charles** 1929- . . . . . . **CLC 8**
See also Kennedy, X. J.
See also CA 1-4R; CANR 4, 30; SATA 14

**Kennedy, William** 1928- . . . **CLC 6, 28, 34, 53**
See also AAYA 1; CA 85-88; CANR 14,
31; DLBY 85; MTCW; SATA 57

**Kennedy, X. J.** . . . . . . . . . . . . . . . . . . . **CLC 42**
See also Kennedy, Joseph Charles
See also CAAS 9; CLR 27; DLB 5

**Kent, Kelvin**
See Kuttner, Henry

**Kenton, Maxwell**
See Southern, Terry

**Kenyon, Robert O.**
See Kuttner, Henry

**Kerouac, Jack** . . . . . **CLC 1, 2, 3, 5, 14, 29, 61**
See also Kerouac, Jean-Louis Lebris de
See also CDALB 1941-1968; DLB 2, 16;
DLBD 3

**Kerouac, Jean-Louis Lebris de** 1922-1969
See Kerouac, Jack
See also AITN 1; CA 5-8R; 25-28R;
CANR 26; MTCW; WLC

**Kerr, Jean** 1923- . . . . . . . . . . . . . . . . **CLC 22**
See also CA 5-8R; CANR 7

**Kerr, M. E.** . . . . . . . . . . . . . . . . . . **CLC 12, 35**
See also Meaker, Marijane (Agnes)
See also AAYA 2; SAAS 1

**Kerr, Robert** . . . . . . . . . . . . . . . . . . . . **CLC 55**

**Kerrigan, (Thomas) Anthony**
1918- . . . . . . . . . . . . . . . . . . . . **CLC 4, 6**
See also CA 49-52; CAAS 11; CANR 4

**Kerry, Lois**
See Duncan, Lois

**Kesey, Ken (Elton)**
1935- . . . . . . . . . . **CLC 1, 3, 6, 11, 46, 64**
See also CA 1-4R; CANR 22, 38;
CDALB 1968-1988; DLB 2, 16; MTCW;
SATA 66; WLC

**Kesselring, Joseph (Otto)**
1902-1967 . . . . . . . . . . . . . . . . . **CLC 45**

**Kessler, Jascha (Frederick)** 1929- . . . . **CLC 4**
See also CA 17-20R; CANR 8

**Kettelkamp, Larry (Dale)** 1933- . . . . **CLC 12**
See also CA 29-32R; CANR 16; SAAS 3;
SATA 2

**Kherdian, David** 1931- . . . . . . . . . . **CLC 6, 9**
See also CA 21-24R; CAAS 2; CANR 39;
CLR 24; MAICYA; SATA 16

**Khlebnikov, Velimir** . . . . . . . . . . . . . **TCLC 20**
See also Khlebnikov, Viktor Vladimirovich

**Khlebnikov, Viktor Vladimirovich** 1885-1922
See Khlebnikov, Velimir
See also CA 117

**Khodasevich, Vladislav (Felitsianovich)**
1886-1939 . . . . . . . . . . . . . . . . **TCLC 15**
See also CA 115

**Kielland, Alexander Lange**
1849-1906 . . . . . . . . . . . . . . . . . **TCLC 5**
See also CA 104

**Kiely, Benedict** 1919- . . . . . . . . . . **CLC 23, 43**
See also CA 1-4R; CANR 2; DLB 15

**Kienzle, William X(avier)** 1928- . . . . **CLC 25**
See also CA 93-96; CAAS 1; CANR 9, 31;
MTCW

**Kierkegaard, Soeren** 1813-1855 . . . **NCLC 34**

**Kierkegaard, Soren** 1813-1855 . . . . **NCLC 34**

**Killens, John Oliver** 1916-1987 . . . . . **CLC 10**
See also BW; CA 77-80; 123; CAAS 2;
CANR 26; DLB 33

**Killigrew, Anne** 1660-1685 . . . . . . . . . . **LC 4**

**Kim**
See Simenon, Georges (Jacques Christian)

**Kincaid, Jamaica** 1949- . . . . . . . . **CLC 43, 68**
See also BLC 2; BW; CA 125

**King, Francis (Henry)** 1923- . . . . . **CLC 8, 53**
See also CA 1-4R; CANR 1, 33; DLB 15;
MTCW

**King, Stephen (Edwin)**
1947- . . . . . . . . . . . . . . **CLC 12, 26, 37, 61**
See also AAYA 1; BEST 90:1; CA 61-64;
CANR 1, 30; DLBY 80; MTCW;
SATA 9, 55

**King, Steve**
See King, Stephen (Edwin)

**Kingman, Lee** . . . . . . . . . . . . . . . . . . . **CLC 17**
See also Natti, (Mary) Lee
See also SAAS 3; SATA 1, 67

**Kingsley, Charles** 1819-1875 . . . . . **NCLC 35**
See also DLB 21, 32; YABC 2

**Kingsley, Sidney** 1906- . . . . . . . . . . . **CLC 44**
See also CA 85-88; DLB 7

**Kingsolver, Barbara** 1955- . . . . . . . . . **CLC 55**
See also CA 129; 134

**Kingston, Maxine (Ting Ting) Hong**
1940- . . . . . . . . . . . . . . . . **CLC 12, 19, 58**
See also AAYA 8; CA 69-72; CANR 13,
38; DLBY 80; MTCW; SATA 53

**Kinnell, Galway**
1927- . . . . . . . . . . **CLC 1, 2, 3, 5, 13, 29**
See also CA 9-12R; CANR 10, 34; DLB 5;
DLBY 87; MTCW

**Kinsella, Thomas** 1928- . . . . . . . . . **CLC 4, 19**
See also CA 17-20R; CANR 15; DLB 27;
MTCW

**Kinsella, W(illiam) P(atrick)**
1935- . . . . . . . . . . . . . . . . . . . **CLC 27, 43**
See also AAYA 7; CA 97-100; CAAS 7;
CANR 21, 35; MTCW

**Kipling, (Joseph) Rudyard**
1865-1936 . . . . **TCLC 8, 17; PC 3; SSC 5**
See also CA 105; 120; CANR 33;
CDBLB 1890-1914; DLB 19, 34;
MAICYA; MTCW; WLC; YABC 2

**Kirkup, James** 1918- . . . . . . . . . . . . . . **CLC 1**
See also CA 1-4R; CAAS 4; CANR 2;
DLB 27; SATA 12

**Kirkwood, James** 1930(?)-1989 . . . . . . **CLC 9**
See also AITN 2; CA 1-4R; 128; CANR 6

**Kis, Danilo** 1935-1989 . . . . . . . . . . . . **CLC 57**
See also CA 109; 118; 129; MTCW

**Kivi, Aleksis** 1834-1872 . . . . . . . . . **NCLC 30**

**Kizer, Carolyn (Ashley)** 1925- . . . **CLC 15, 39**
See also CA 65-68; CAAS 5; CANR 24;
DLB 5

**Klabund** 1890-1928............ **TCLC 44**
See also DLB 66

**Klappert, Peter** 1942-............ **CLC 57**
See also CA 33-36R; DLB 5

**Klein, A(braham) M(oses)**
1909-1972................. **CLC 19**
See also CA 101; 37-40R; DLB 68

**Klein, Norma** 1938-1989.......... **CLC 30**
See also AAYA 2; CA 41-44R; 128;
CANR 15, 37; CLR 2, 19; MAICYA;
SAAS 1; SATA 7, 57

**Klein, T(heodore) E(ibon) D(onald)**
1947-..................... **CLC 34**
See also CA 119

**Kleist, Heinrich von** 1777-1811.... **NCLC 2**
See also DLB 90

**Klima, Ivan** 1931-............... **CLC 56**
See also CA 25-28R; CANR 17

**Klimentov, Andrei Platonovich** 1899-1951
See Platonov, Andrei
See also CA 108

**Klinger, Friedrich Maximilian von**
1752-1831................. **NCLC 1**
See also DLB 94

**Klopstock, Friedrich Gottlieb**
1724-1803................. **NCLC 11**
See also DLB 97

**Knebel, Fletcher** 1911-............ **CLC 14**
See also AITN 1; CA 1-4R; CAAS 3;
CANR 1, 36; SATA 36

**Knickerbocker, Diedrich**
See Irving, Washington

**Knight, Etheridge** 1931-1991....... **CLC 40**
See also BLC 2; BW; CA 21-24R; 133;
CANR 23; DLB 41

**Knight, Sarah Kemble** 1666-1727..... **LC 7**
See also DLB 24

**Knowles, John** 1926-...... **CLC 1, 4, 10, 26**
See also CA 17-20R; CDALB 1968-1988;
DLB 6; MTCW; SATA 8

**Knox, Calvin M.**
See Silverberg, Robert

**Knye, Cassandra**
See Disch, Thomas M(ichael)

**Koch, C(hristopher) J(ohn)** 1932-... **CLC 42**
See also CA 127

**Koch, Christopher**
See Koch, C(hristopher) J(ohn)

**Koch, Kenneth** 1925-......... **CLC 5, 8, 44**
See also CA 1-4R; CANR 6, 36; DLB 5;
SATA 65

**Kochanowski, Jan** 1530-1584........ **LC 10**

**Kock, Charles Paul de**
1794-1871................. **NCLC 16**

**Koda Shigeyuki** 1867-1947
See Rohan, Koda
See also CA 121

**Koestler, Arthur**
1905-1983....... **CLC 1, 3, 6, 8, 15, 33**
See also CA 1-4R; 109; CANR 1, 33;
CDBLB 1945-1960; DLBY 83; MTCW

**Kohout, Pavel** 1928-............... **CLC 13**
See also CA 45-48; CANR 3

**Koizumi, Yakumo**
See Hearn, (Patricio) Lafcadio (Tessima
Carlos)

**Kolmar, Gertrud** 1894-1943....... **TCLC 40**

**Konrad, George**
See Konrad, Gyoergy

**Konrad, Gyoergy** 1933-...... **CLC 4, 10, 73**
See also CA 85-88

**Konwicki, Tadeusz** 1926-..... **CLC 8, 28, 54**
See also CA 101; CAAS 9; CANR 39;
MTCW

**Kopit, Arthur (Lee)** 1937-.... **CLC 1, 18, 33**
See also AITN 1; CA 81-84; CABS 3;
DLB 7; MTCW

**Kops, Bernard** 1926-.............. **CLC 4**
See also CA 5-8R; DLB 13

**Kornbluth, C(yril) M.** 1923-1958.... **TCLC 8**
See also CA 105; DLB 8

**Korolenko, V. G.**
See Korolenko, Vladimir Galaktionovich

**Korolenko, Vladimir**
See Korolenko, Vladimir Galaktionovich

**Korolenko, Vladimir G.**
See Korolenko, Vladimir Galaktionovich

**Korolenko, Vladimir Galaktionovich**
1853-1921................. **TCLC 22**
See also CA 121

**Kosinski, Jerzy (Nikodem)**
1933-1991... **CLC 1, 2, 3, 6, 10, 15, 53,
70**
See also CA 17-20R; 134; CANR 9; DLB 2;
DLBY 82; MTCW

**Kostelanetz, Richard (Cory)** 1940-.. **CLC 28**
See also CA 13-16R; CAAS 8; CANR 38

**Kostrowitzki, Wilhelm Apollinaris de**
1880-1918
See Apollinaire, Guillaume
See also CA 104

**Kotlowitz, Robert** 1924-............ **CLC 4**
See also CA 33-36R; CANR 36

**Kotzebue, August (Friedrich Ferdinand) von**
1761-1819................. **NCLC 25**
See also DLB 94

**Kotzwinkle, William** 1938-... **CLC 5, 14, 35**
See also CA 45-48; CANR 3; CLR 6;
MAICYA; SATA 24, 70

**Kozol, Jonathan** 1936-............ **CLC 17**
See also CA 61-64; CANR 16

**Kozoll, Michael** 1940(?)-.......... **CLC 35**

**Kramer, Kathryn** 19(?)-.......... **CLC 34**

**Kramer, Larry** 1935-............. **CLC 42**
See also CA 124; 126

**Krasicki, Ignacy** 1735-1801....... **NCLC 8**

**Krasinski, Zygmunt** 1812-1859.... **NCLC 4**

**Kraus, Karl** 1874-1936........... **TCLC 5**
See also CA 104; DLB 118

**Kreve (Mickevicius), Vincas**
1882-1954................. **TCLC 27**

**Kristofferson, Kris** 1936-......... **CLC 26**
See also CA 104

**Krizanc, John** 1956-............. **CLC 57**

**Krleza, Miroslav** 1893-1981........ **CLC 8**
See also CA 97-100; 105

**Kroetsch, Robert** 1927-...... **CLC 5, 23, 57**
See also CA 17-20R; CANR 8, 38; DLB 53;
MTCW

**Kroetz, Franz**
See Kroetz, Franz Xaver

**Kroetz, Franz Xaver** 1946-........ **CLC 41**
See also CA 130

**Kroker, Arthur** 1945-............ **CLC 75**

**Kropotkin, Peter (Aleksieevich)**
1842-1921................. **TCLC 36**
See also CA 119

**Krotkov, Yuri** 1917-............. **CLC 19**
See also CA 102

**Krumb**
See Crumb, R(obert)

**Krumgold, Joseph (Quincy)**
1908-1980................. **CLC 12**
See also CA 9-12R; 101; CANR 7;
MAICYA; SATA 1, 23, 48

**Krumwitz**
See Crumb, R(obert)

**Krutch, Joseph Wood** 1893-1970.... **CLC 24**
See also CA 1-4R; 25-28R; CANR 4;
DLB 63

**Krutzch, Gus**
See Eliot, T(homas) S(tearns)

**Krylov, Ivan Andreevich**
1768(?)-1844................ **NCLC 1**

**Kubin, Alfred** 1877-1959........ **TCLC 23**
See also CA 112; DLB 81

**Kubrick, Stanley** 1928-............ **CLC 16**
See also CA 81-84; CANR 33; DLB 26

**Kumin, Maxine (Winokur)**
1925-................. **CLC 5, 13, 28**
See also AITN 2; CA 1-4R; CAAS 8;
CANR 1, 21; DLB 5; MTCW; SATA 12

**Kundera, Milan**
1929-............ **CLC 4, 9, 19, 32, 68**
See also AAYA 2; CA 85-88; CANR 19;
MTCW

**Kunitz, Stanley (Jasspon)**
1905-................. **CLC 6, 11, 14**
See also CA 41-44R; CANR 26; DLB 48;
MTCW

**Kunze, Reiner** 1933-............. **CLC 10**
See also CA 93-96; DLB 75

**Kuprin, Aleksandr Ivanovich**
1870-1938................. **TCLC 5**
See also CA 104

**Kureishi, Hanif** 1954(?)-.......... **CLC 64**

**Kurosawa, Akira** 1910-............ **CLC 16**
See also CA 101

**Kuttner, Henry** 1915-1958........ **TCLC 10**
See also CA 107; DLB 8

**Kuzma, Greg** 1944-................ **CLC 7**
See also CA 33-36R

**Kuzmin, Mikhail** 1872(?)-1936.... **TCLC 40**

**Kyd, Thomas** 1558-1594............. **DC 3**
See also DLB 62

**Kyprianos, Iossif**
See Samarakis, Antonis

**La Bruyere, Jean de** 1645-1696...... **LC 17**

Levinson, Deirdre  1931-.......... CLC 49
  See also CA 73-76

Levi-Strauss, Claude  1908- ....... CLC 38
  See also CA 1-4R; CANR 6, 32; MTCW

Levitin, Sonia (Wolff)  1934- ...... CLC 17
  See also CA 29-32R; CANR 14, 32;
  MAICYA; SAAS 2; SATA 4, 68

Levon, O. U.
  See Kesey, Ken (Elton)

Lewes, George Henry
  1817-1878 ............... NCLC 25
  See also DLB 55

Lewis, Alun  1915-1944........... TCLC 3
  See also CA 104; DLB 20

Lewis, C. Day
  See Day Lewis, C(ecil)

Lewis, C(live) S(taples)
  1898-1963 ........ CLC 1, 3, 6, 14, 27
  See also AAYA 3; CA 81-84; CANR 33;
  CDBLB 1945-1960; CLR 3, 27; DLB 15,
  100; MAICYA; MTCW; SATA 13; WLC

Lewis, Janet  1899-............. CLC 41
  See also Winters, Janet Lewis
  See also CA 9-12R; CANR 29; CAP 1;
  DLBY 87

Lewis, Matthew Gregory
  1775-1818 ............... NCLC 11
  See also DLB 39

Lewis, (Harry) Sinclair
  1885-1951 ........ TCLC 4, 13, 23, 39
  See also CA 104; 133; CDALB 1917-1929;
  DLB 9, 102; DLBD 1; MTCW; WLC

Lewis, (Percy) Wyndham
  1884(?)-1957 ........... TCLC 2, 9
  See also CA 104; DLB 15

Lewisohn, Ludwig  1883-1955...... TCLC 19
  See also CA 107; DLB 4, 9, 28, 102

Lezama Lima, Jose  1910-1976 ... CLC 4, 10
  See also CA 77-80; DLB 113; HW

L'Heureux, John (Clarke)  1934-.... CLC 52
  See also CA 13-16R; CANR 23

Liddell, C. H.
  See Kuttner, Henry

Lie, Jonas (Lauritz Idemil)
  1833-1908(?) ................. TCLC 5
  See also CA 115

Lieber, Joel  1937-1971............ CLC 6
  See also CA 73-76; 29-32R

Lieber, Stanley Martin
  See Lee, Stan

Lieberman, Laurence (James)
  1935- ................... CLC 4, 36
  See also CA 17-20R; CANR 8, 36

Lieksman, Anders
  See Haavikko, Paavo Juhani

Li Fei-kan  1904-................. CLC 18
  See also CA 105

Lifton, Robert Jay  1926-.......... CLC 67
  See also CA 17-20R; CANR 27; SATA 66

Lightfoot, Gordon  1938-.......... CLC 26
  See also CA 109

Ligotti, Thomas  1953- ........... CLC 44
  See also CA 123

Liliencron, (Friedrich Adolf Axel) Detlev von
  1844-1909 ............... TCLC 18
  See also CA 117

Lima, Jose Lezama
  See Lezama Lima, Jose

Lima Barreto, Afonso Henrique de
  1881-1922 ................. TCLC 23
  See also CA 117

Limonov, Eduard.................. CLC 67

Lin, Frank
  See Atherton, Gertrude (Franklin Horn)

Lincoln, Abraham  1809-1865..... NCLC 18

Lind, Jakov ............... CLC 1, 2, 4, 27
  See also Landwirth, Heinz
  See also CAAS 4

Lindsay, David  1878-1945 ....... TCLC 15
  See also CA 113

Lindsay, (Nicholas) Vachel
  1879-1931 ................. TCLC 17
  See also CA 114; 135; CDALB 1865-1917;
  DLB 54; SATA 40; WLC

Linke-Poot
  See Doeblin, Alfred

Linney, Romulus  1930- .......... CLC 51
  See also CA 1-4R

Li Po  701-763 .................. CMLC 2

Lipsius, Justus  1547-1606 ......... LC 16

Lipsyte, Robert (Michael)  1938-.... CLC 21
  See also AAYA 7; CA 17-20R; CANR 8;
  CLR 23; MAICYA; SATA 5, 68

Lish, Gordon (Jay)  1934-.......... CLC 45
  See also CA 113; 117

Lispector, Clarice  1925-1977...... CLC 43
  See also CA 116; DLB 113

Littell, Robert  1935(?)- ........... CLC 42
  See also CA 109; 112

Littlewit, Humphrey Gent.
  See Lovecraft, H(oward) P(hillips)

Litwos
  See Sienkiewicz, Henryk (Adam Alexander
  Pius)

Liu E  1857-1909................ TCLC 15
  See also CA 115

Lively, Penelope (Margaret)
  1933- ................... CLC 32, 50
  See also CA 41-44R; CANR 29; CLR 7;
  DLB 14; MAICYA; MTCW; SATA 7, 60

Livesay, Dorothy (Kathleen)
  1909- ................... CLC 4, 15
  See also AITN 2; CA 25-28R; CAAS 8;
  CANR 36; DLB 68; MTCW

Lizardi, Jose Joaquin Fernandez de
  1776-1827 ................. NCLC 30

Llewellyn, Richard ............... CLC 7
  See also Llewellyn Lloyd, Richard Dafydd
  Vivian
  See also DLB 15

Llewellyn Lloyd, Richard Dafydd Vivian
  1906-1983
  See Llewellyn, Richard
  See also CA 53-56; 111; CANR 7;
  SATA 11, 37

Llosa, (Jorge) Mario (Pedro) Vargas
  See Vargas Llosa, (Jorge) Mario (Pedro)

Lloyd Webber, Andrew  1948-
  See Webber, Andrew Lloyd
  See also AAYA 1; CA 116; SATA 56

Locke, Alain (Le Roy)
  1886-1954 ................. TCLC 43
  See also BW; CA 106; 124; DLB 51

Locke, John  1632-1704 ............ LC 7
  See also DLB 101

Locke-Elliott, Sumner
  See Elliott, Sumner Locke

Lockhart, John Gibson
  1794-1854 ................. NCLC 6
  See also DLB 110, 116

Lodge, David (John)  1935-........ CLC 36
  See also BEST 90:1; CA 17-20R; CANR 19;
  DLB 14; MTCW

Loennbohm, Armas Eino Leopold  1878-1926
  See Leino, Eino
  See also CA 123

Loewinsohn, Ron(ald William)
  1937- ..................... CLC 52
  See also CA 25-28R

Logan, Jake
  See Smith, Martin Cruz

Logan, John (Burton)  1923-1987..... CLC 5
  See also CA 77-80; 124; DLB 5

Lo Kuan-chung  1330(?)-1400(?)...... LC 12

Lombard, Nap
  See Johnson, Pamela Hansford

London, Jack....... TCLC 9, 15, 39; SSC 4
  See also London, John Griffith
  See also AITN 2; CDALB 1865-1917;
  DLB 8, 12, 78; SATA 18; WLC

London, John Griffith  1876-1916
  See London, Jack
  See also CA 110; 119; MAICYA; MTCW

Long, Emmett
  See Leonard, Elmore (John Jr.)

Longbaugh, Harry
  See Goldman, William (W.)

Longfellow, Henry Wadsworth
  1807-1882 ................. NCLC 2
  See also CDALB 1640-1865; DLB 1, 59;
  SATA 19

Longley, Michael  1939-.......... CLC 29
  See also CA 102; DLB 40

Longus  fl. c. 2nd cent. - .......... CMLC 7

Longway, A. Hugh
  See Lang, Andrew

Lopate, Phillip  1943-............. CLC 29
  See also CA 97-100; DLBY 80

Lopez Portillo (y Pacheco), Jose
  1920- ..................... CLC 46
  See also CA 129; HW

Lopez y Fuentes, Gregorio
  1897(?)-1966 ................. CLC 32
  See also CA 131; HW

Lorca, Federico Garcia
  See Garcia Lorca, Federico

Lord, Bette Bao  1938-............ CLC 23
  See also BEST 90:3; CA 107; SATA 58

Lord Auch
  See Bataille, Georges

**Lord Byron**
See Byron, George Gordon (Noel)

**Lord Dunsany** . . . . . . . . . . . . . . . . . . . TCLC 2
See also Dunsany, Edward John Moreton
Drax Plunkett

**Lorde, Audre (Geraldine)**
1934- . . . . . . . . . . . . . . . . . . . CLC 18, 71
See also BLC 2; BW; CA 25-28R;
CANR 16, 26; DLB 41; MTCW

**Lord Jeffrey**
See Jeffrey, Francis

**Lorenzo, Heberto Padilla**
See Padilla (Lorenzo), Heberto

**Loris**
See Hofmannsthal, Hugo von

**Loti, Pierre** . . . . . . . . . . . . . . . . . . . TCLC 11
See also Viaud, (Louis Marie) Julien
See also DLB 123

**Louie, David Wong** 1954- . . . . . . . . CLC 70

**Louis, Father M.**
See Merton, Thomas

**Lovecraft, H(oward) P(hillips)**
1890-1937 . . . . . . . . TCLC 4, 22; SSC 3
See also CA 104; 133; MTCW

**Lovelace, Earl** 1935- . . . . . . . . . . . . . CLC 51
See also CA 77-80; MTCW

**Lowell, Amy** 1874-1925 . . . . . . . . TCLC 1, 8
See also CA 104; DLB 54

**Lowell, James Russell** 1819-1891 . . NCLC 2
See also CDALB 1640-1865; DLB 1, 11, 64,
79

**Lowell, Robert (Traill Spence Jr.)**
1917-1977 . . . CLC 1, 2, 3, 4, 5, 8, 9, 11,
15, 37; PC 3
See also CA 9-12R; 73-76; CABS 2;
CANR 26; DLB 5; MTCW; WLC

**Lowndes, Marie Adelaide (Belloc)**
1868-1947 . . . . . . . . . . . . . . . . . TCLC 12
See also CA 107; DLB 70

**Lowry, (Clarence) Malcolm**
1909-1957 . . . . . . . . . . . . . TCLC 6, 40
See also CA 105; 131; CDBLB 1945-1960;
DLB 15; MTCW

**Lowry, Mina Gertrude** 1882-1966
See Loy, Mina
See also CA 113

**Loxsmith, John**
See Brunner, John (Kilian Houston)

**Loy, Mina** . . . . . . . . . . . . . . . . . . . . . . CLC 28
See also Lowry, Mina Gertrude
See also DLB 4, 54

**Loyson-Bridet**
See Schwob, (Mayer Andre) Marcel

**Lucas, Craig** 1951- . . . . . . . . . . . . . . . CLC 64
See also CA 137

**Lucas, George** 1944- . . . . . . . . . . . . . . CLC 16
See also AAYA 1; CA 77-80; CANR 30;
SATA 56

**Lucas, Hans**
See Godard, Jean-Luc

**Lucas, Victoria**
See Plath, Sylvia

**Ludlam, Charles** 1943-1987 . . . . . CLC 46, 50
See also CA 85-88; 122

**Ludlum, Robert** 1927- . . . . . . . . . CLC 22, 43
See also BEST 89:1, 90:3; CA 33-36R;
CANR 25; DLBY 82; MTCW

**Ludwig, Ken** . . . . . . . . . . . . . . . . . . . . CLC 60

**Ludwig, Otto** 1813-1865 . . . . . . . . . NCLC 4

**Lugones, Leopoldo** 1874-1938 . . . . . TCLC 15
See also CA 116; 131; HW

**Lu Hsun** 1881-1936 . . . . . . . . . . . . . TCLC 3

**Lukacs, George** . . . . . . . . . . . . . . . . . CLC 24
See also Lukacs, Gyorgy (Szegeny von)

**Lukacs, Gyorgy (Szegeny von)** 1885-1971
See Lukacs, George
See also CA 101; 29-32R

**Luke, Peter (Ambrose Cyprian)**
1919- . . . . . . . . . . . . . . . . . . . . . CLC 38
See also CA 81-84; DLB 13

**Lunar, Dennis**
See Mungo, Raymond

**Lurie, Alison** 1926- . . . . . . . CLC 4, 5, 18, 39
See also CA 1-4R; CANR 2, 17; DLB 2;
MTCW; SATA 46

**Lustig, Arnost** 1926- . . . . . . . . . . . . . CLC 56
See also AAYA 3; CA 69-72; SATA 56

**Luther, Martin** 1483-1546 . . . . . . . . . . LC 9

**Luzi, Mario** 1914- . . . . . . . . . . . . . . . CLC 13
See also CA 61-64; CANR 9

**Lynch, B. Suarez**
See Bioy Casares, Adolfo; Borges, Jorge
Luis

**Lynch, David (K.)** 1946- . . . . . . . . . . CLC 66
See also CA 124; 129

**Lynch, James**
See Andreyev, Leonid (Nikolaevich)

**Lynch Davis, B.**
See Bioy Casares, Adolfo; Borges, Jorge
Luis

**Lyndsay, Sir David** 1490-1555 . . . . . . . LC 20

**Lynn, Kenneth S(chuyler)** 1923- . . . . CLC 50
See also CA 1-4R; CANR 3, 27

**Lynx**
See West, Rebecca

**Lyons, Marcus**
See Blish, James (Benjamin)

**Lyre, Pinchbeck**
See Sassoon, Siegfried (Lorraine)

**Lytle, Andrew (Nelson)** 1902- . . . . . . CLC 22
See also CA 9-12R; DLB 6

**Lyttelton, George** 1709-1773 . . . . . . . . LC 10

**Maas, Peter** 1929- . . . . . . . . . . . . . . . CLC 29
See also CA 93-96

**Macaulay, Rose** 1881-1958 . . . . . TCLC 7, 44
See also CA 104; DLB 36

**MacBeth, George (Mann)**
1932-1992 . . . . . . . . . . . . . . . CLC 2, 5, 9
See also CA 25-28R; 136; DLB 40; MTCW;
SATA 4; SATO 70

**MacCaig, Norman (Alexander)**
1910- . . . . . . . . . . . . . . . . . . . . . CLC 36
See also CA 9-12R; CANR 3, 34; DLB 27

**MacCarthy, (Sir Charles Otto) Desmond**
1877-1952 . . . . . . . . . . . . . . . . . TCLC 36

**MacDiarmid, Hugh** . . . . . CLC 2, 4, 11, 19, 63
See also Grieve, C(hristopher) M(urray)
See also CDBLB 1945-1960; DLB 20

**MacDonald, Anson**
See Heinlein, Robert A(nson)

**Macdonald, Cynthia** 1928- . . . . . . CLC 13, 19
See also CA 49-52; CANR 4; DLB 105

**MacDonald, George** 1824-1905 . . . . . TCLC 9
See also CA 106; 137; DLB 18; MAICYA;
SATA 33

**Macdonald, John**
See Millar, Kenneth

**MacDonald, John D(ann)**
1916-1986 . . . . . . . . . . . . . CLC 3, 27, 44
See also CA 1-4R; 121; CANR 1, 19;
DLB 8; DLBY 86; MTCW

**Macdonald, John Ross**
See Millar, Kenneth

**Macdonald, Ross** . . . . . CLC 1, 2, 3, 14, 34, 41
See also Millar, Kenneth
See also DLBD 6

**MacDougal, John**
See Blish, James (Benjamin)

**MacEwen, Gwendolyn (Margaret)**
1941-1987 . . . . . . . . . . . . . . . CLC 13, 55
See also CA 9-12R; 124; CANR 7, 22;
DLB 53; SATA 50, 55

**Machado (y Ruiz), Antonio**
1875-1939 . . . . . . . . . . . . . . . . . . TCLC 3
See also CA 104; DLB 108

**Machado de Assis, Joaquim Maria**
1839-1908 . . . . . . . . . . . . . . . . . TCLC 10
See also BLC 2; CA 107

**Machen, Arthur** . . . . . . . . . . . . . . . . . TCLC 4
See also Jones, Arthur Llewellyn
See also DLB 36

**Machiavelli, Niccolo** 1469-1527 . . . . . . LC 8

**MacInnes, Colin** 1914-1976 . . . . . . CLC 4, 23
See also CA 69-72; 65-68; CANR 21;
DLB 14; MTCW

**MacInnes, Helen (Clark)**
1907-1985 . . . . . . . . . . . . . . . CLC 27, 39
See also CA 1-4R; 117; CANR 1, 28;
DLB 87; MTCW; SATA 22, 44

**Mackenzie, Compton (Edward Montague)**
1883-1972 . . . . . . . . . . . . . . . . . . CLC 18
See also CA 21-22; 37-40R; CAP 2;
DLB 34, 100

**Mackintosh, Elizabeth** 1896(?)-1952
See Tey, Josephine
See also CA 110

**MacLaren, James**
See Grieve, C(hristopher) M(urray)

**Mac Laverty, Bernard** 1942- . . . . . . . CLC 31
See also CA 116; 118

**MacLean, Alistair (Stuart)**
1922-1987 . . . . . . . . . . CLC 3, 13, 50, 63
See also CA 57-60; 121; CANR 28; MTCW;
SATA 23, 50

**MacLeish, Archibald**
1892-1982 . . . . . . . . . . . CLC 3, 8, 14, 68
See also CA 9-12R; 106; CANR 33; DLB 4,
7, 45; DLBY 82; MTCW

**MacLennan, (John) Hugh**
1907- . . . . . . . . . . . . . . . . . . . . . CLC 2, 14
See also CA 5-8R; CANR 33; DLB 68;
MTCW

**MacLeod, Alistair** 1936- . . . . . . . . . CLC 56
See also CA 123; DLB 60

**MacNeice, (Frederick) Louis**
1907-1963 . . . . . . . . . . . CLC 1, 4, 10, 53
See also CA 85-88; DLB 10, 20; MTCW

**MacNeill, Dand**
See Fraser, George MacDonald

**Macpherson, (Jean) Jay** 1931- . . . . . . CLC 14
See also CA 5-8R; DLB 53

**MacShane, Frank** 1927- . . . . . . . . . . CLC 39
See also CA 9-12R; CANR 3, 33; DLB 111

**Macumber, Mari**
See Sandoz, Mari(e Susette)

**Madach, Imre** 1823-1864 . . . . . . . NCLC 19

**Madden, (Jerry) David** 1933- . . . . CLC 5, 15
See also CA 1-4R; CAAS 3; CANR 4;
DLB 6; MTCW

**Maddern, Al(an)**
See Ellison, Harlan

**Madhubuti, Haki R.**
1942- . . . . . . . . . . . . . . CLC 6, 73; PC 5
See also Lee, Don L.
See also BLC 2; BW; CA 73-76; CANR 24;
DLB 5, 41; DLBD 8

**Madow, Pauline (Reichberg)** . . . . . . . . CLC 1
See also CA 9-12R

**Maepenn, Hugh**
See Kuttner, Henry

**Maepenn, K. H.**
See Kuttner, Henry

**Maeterlinck, Maurice** 1862-1949 . . . TCLC 3
See also CA 104; 136; SATA 66

**Maginn, William** 1794-1842 . . . . . . NCLC 8
See also DLB 110

**Mahapatra, Jayanta** 1928- . . . . . . . . CLC 33
See also CA 73-76; CAAS 9; CANR 15, 33

**Mahfouz, Naguib (Abdel Aziz Al-Sabilgi)**
1911(?)-
See Mahfuz, Najib
See also BEST 89:2; CA 128; MTCW

**Mahfuz, Najib** . . . . . . . . . . . . . . CLC 52, 55
See also Mahfouz, Naguib (Abdel Aziz
Al-Sabilgi)
See also DLBY 88

**Mahon, Derek** 1941- . . . . . . . . . . . . . CLC 27
See also CA 113; 128; DLB 40

**Mailer, Norman**
1923- . . . . . . CLC 1, 2, 3, 4, 5, 8, 11, 14,
28, 39, 74
See also AITN 2; CA 9-12R; CABS 1;
CANR 28; CDALB 1968-1988; DLB 2,
16, 28; DLBD 3; DLBY 80, 83; MTCW

**Maillet, Antonine** 1929- . . . . . . . . . . CLC 54
See also CA 115; 120; DLB 60

**Mais, Roger** 1905-1955 . . . . . . . . . . . TCLC 8
See also BW; CA 105; 124; MTCW

**Maitland, Sara (Louise)** 1950- . . . . . . CLC 49
See also CA 69-72; CANR 13

**Major, Clarence** 1936- . . . . . . . CLC 3, 19, 48
See also BLC 2; BW; CA 21-24R; CAAS 6;
CANR 13, 25; DLB 33

**Major, Kevin (Gerald)** 1949- . . . . . . . CLC 26
See also CA 97-100; CANR 21, 38;
CLR 11; DLB 60; MAICYA; SATA 32

**Maki, James**
See Ozu, Yasujiro

**Malabaila, Damiano**
See Levi, Primo

**Malamud, Bernard**
1914-1986 . . . . . CLC 1, 2, 3, 5, 8, 9, 11,
18, 27, 44
See also CA 5-8R; 118; CABS 1; CANR 28;
CDALB 1941-1968; DLB 2, 28;
DLBY 80, 86; MTCW; WLC

**Malcolm, Dan**
See Silverberg, Robert

**Malherbe, Francois de** 1555-1628 . . . . . LC 5

**Mallarme, Stephane**
1842-1898 . . . . . . . . . . . . . NCLC 4; PC 4

**Mallet-Joris, Francoise** 1930- . . . . . . CLC 11
See also CA 65-68; CANR 17; DLB 83

**Malley, Ern**
See McAuley, James Phillip

**Mallowan, Agatha Christie**
See Christie, Agatha (Mary Clarissa)

**Maloff, Saul** 1922- . . . . . . . . . . . . . . . CLC 5
See also CA 33-36R

**Malone, Louis**
See MacNeice, (Frederick) Louis

**Malone, Michael (Christopher)**
1942- . . . . . . . . . . . . . . . . . . . . . . CLC 43
See also CA 77-80; CANR 14, 32

**Malory, (Sir) Thomas**
1410(?)-1471(?) . . . . . . . . . . . . . . . LC 11
See also CDBLB Before 1660; SATA 33, 59

**Malouf, (George Joseph) David**
1934- . . . . . . . . . . . . . . . . . . . . . . CLC 28
See also CA 124

**Malraux, (Georges-)Andre**
1901-1976 . . . . . . CLC 1, 4, 9, 13, 15, 57
See also CA 21-22; 69-72; CANR 34;
CAP 2; DLB 72; MTCW

**Malzberg, Barry N(athaniel)** 1939- . . . CLC 7
See also CA 61-64; CAAS 4; CANR 16;
DLB 8

**Mamet, David (Alan)**
1947- . . . . . . . . . . . . . CLC 9, 15, 34, 46
See also AAYA 3; CA 81-84; CABS 3;
CANR 15; DLB 7; MTCW

**Mamoulian, Rouben (Zachary)**
1897-1987 . . . . . . . . . . . . . . . . . . CLC 16
See also CA 25-28R; 124

**Mandelstam, Osip (Emilievich)**
1891(?)-1938(?) . . . . . . . . . . . . TCLC 2, 6
See also CA 104

**Mander, (Mary) Jane** 1877-1949 . . . TCLC 31

**Mandiargues, Andre Pieyre de** . . . . . . CLC 41
See also Pieyre de Mandiargues, Andre
See also DLB 83

**Mandrake, Ethel Belle**
See Thurman, Wallace (Henry)

**Mangan, James Clarence**
1803-1849 . . . . . . . . . . . . . . . . NCLC 27

**Maniere, J.-E.**
See Giraudoux, (Hippolyte) Jean

**Manley, (Mary) Delariviere**
1672(?)-1724 . . . . . . . . . . . . . . . . . . LC 1
See also DLB 39, 80

**Mann, Abel**
See Creasey, John

**Mann, (Luiz) Heinrich** 1871-1950 . . . TCLC 9
See also CA 106; DLB 66

**Mann, (Paul) Thomas**
1875-1955 . . . TCLC 2, 8, 14, 21, 35, 44;
SSC 5
See also CA 104; 128; DLB 66; MTCW;
WLC

**Manning, Frederic** 1887(?)-1935 . . . TCLC 25
See also CA 124

**Manning, Olivia** 1915-1980 . . . . . . CLC 5, 19
See also CA 5-8R; 101; CANR 29; MTCW

**Mano, D. Keith** 1942- . . . . . . . . . . CLC 2, 10
See also CA 25-28R; CAAS 6; CANR 26;
DLB 6

**Mansfield, Katherine** . . . TCLC 2, 8, 39; SSC 9
See also Beauchamp, Kathleen Mansfield
See also WLC

**Manso, Peter** 1940- . . . . . . . . . . . . . CLC 39
See also CA 29-32R

**Mantecon, Juan Jimenez**
See Jimenez (Mantecon), Juan Ramon

**Manton, Peter**
See Creasey, John

**Man Without a Spleen, A**
See Chekhov, Anton (Pavlovich)

**Manzoni, Alessandro** 1785-1873 . . NCLC 29

**Mapu, Abraham (ben Jekutiel)**
1808-1867 . . . . . . . . . . . . . . . . NCLC 18

**Mara, Sally**
See Queneau, Raymond

**Marat, Jean Paul** 1743-1793 . . . . . . . LC 10

**Marcel, Gabriel Honore**
1889-1973 . . . . . . . . . . . . . . . . . . CLC 15
See also CA 102; 45-48; MTCW

**Marchbanks, Samuel**
See Davies, (William) Robertson

**Marchi, Giacomo**
See Bassani, Giorgio

**Marie de France** c. 12th cent. - . . . . . CMLC 8

**Marie de l'Incarnation** 1599-1672 . . . . LC 10

**Mariner, Scott**
See Pohl, Frederik

**Marinetti, Filippo Tommaso**
1876-1944 . . . . . . . . . . . . . . . . TCLC 10
See also CA 107; DLB 114

**Marivaux, Pierre Carlet de Chamblain de**
1688-1763 . . . . . . . . . . . . . . . . . . . LC 4

**Markandaya, Kamala** . . . . . . . . . . CLC 8, 38
See also Taylor, Kamala (Purnaiya)

**Markfield, Wallace** 1926- . . . . . . . . . . CLC 8
See also CA 69-72; CAAS 3; DLB 2, 28

**Markham, Edwin** 1852-1940 . . . . . . TCLC 47
See also DLB 54

**Markham, Robert**
See Amis, Kingsley (William)

**Marks, J**
See Highwater, Jamake (Mamake)

**Marks-Highwater, J**
See Highwater, Jamake (Mamake)

**Markson, David M(errill)** 1927- .... **CLC 67**
See also CA 49-52; CANR 1

**Marley, Bob** .................... **CLC 17**
See also Marley, Robert Nesta

**Marley, Robert Nesta** 1945-1981
See Marley, Bob
See also CA 107; 103

**Marlowe, Christopher** 1564-1593 ..... **DC 1**
See also CDBLB Before 1660; DLB 62;
WLC

**Marmontel, Jean-Francois**
1723-1799 .................... **LC 2**

**Marquand, John P(hillips)**
1893-1960 ................. **CLC 2, 10**
See also CA 85-88; DLB 9, 102

**Marquez, Gabriel (Jose) Garcia** ...... **CLC 68**
See also Garcia Marquez, Gabriel (Jose)

**Marquis, Don(ald Robert Perry)**
1878-1937 .................. **TCLC 7**
See also CA 104; DLB 11, 25

**Marric, J. J.**
See Creasey, John

**Marrow, Bernard**
See Moore, Brian

**Marryat, Frederick** 1792-1848 .... **NCLC 3**
See also DLB 21

**Marsden, James**
See Creasey, John

**Marsh, (Edith) Ngaio**
1899-1982 ................. **CLC 7, 53**
See also CA 9-12R; CANR 6; DLB 77;
MTCW

**Marshall, Garry** 1934- ........... **CLC 17**
See also AAYA 3; CA 111; SATA 60

**Marshall, Paule** 1929- .. **CLC 27, 72; SSC 3**
See also BLC 3; BW; CA 77-80; CANR 25;
DLB 33; MTCW

**Marsten, Richard**
See Hunter, Evan

**Martha, Henry**
See Harris, Mark

**Martin, Ken**
See Hubbard, L(afayette) Ron(ald)

**Martin, Richard**
See Creasey, John

**Martin, Steve** 1945- .............. **CLC 30**
See also CA 97-100; CANR 30; MTCW

**Martin, Webber**
See Silverberg, Robert

**Martin du Gard, Roger**
1881-1958 ................. **TCLC 24**
See also CA 118; DLB 65

**Martineau, Harriet** 1802-1876.... **NCLC 26**
See also DLB 21, 55; YABC 2

**Martines, Julia**
See O'Faolain, Julia

**Martinez, Jacinto Benavente y**
See Benavente (y Martinez), Jacinto

**Martinez Ruiz, Jose** 1873-1967
See Azorin; Ruiz, Jose Martinez
See also CA 93-96; HW

**Martinez Sierra, Gregorio**
1881-1947 .................. **TCLC 6**
See also CA 115

**Martinez Sierra, Maria (de la O'LeJarraga)**
1874-1974 .................. **TCLC 6**
See also CA 115

**Martinsen, Martin**
See Follett, Ken(neth Martin)

**Martinson, Harry (Edmund)**
1904-1978 .................. **CLC 14**
See also CA 77-80; CANR 34

**Marut, Ret**
See Traven, B.

**Marut, Robert**
See Traven, B.

**Marvell, Andrew** 1621-1678.......... **LC 4**
See also CDBLB 1660-1789; WLC

**Marx, Karl (Heinrich)**
1818-1883 ................. **NCLC 17**

**Masaoka Shiki** ................. **TCLC 18**
See also Masaoka Tsunenori

**Masaoka Tsunenori** 1867-1902
See Masaoka Shiki
See also CA 117

**Masefield, John (Edward)**
1878-1967 ................ **CLC 11, 47**
See also CA 19-20; 25-28R; CANR 33;
CAP 2; CDBLB 1890-1914; DLB 10;
MTCW; SATA 19

**Maso, Carole** 19(?)- .............. **CLC 44**

**Mason, Bobbie Ann**
1940- ............ **CLC 28, 43; SSC 4**
See also AAYA 5; CA 53-56; CANR 11,
31; DLBY 87; MTCW

**Mason, Ernst**
See Pohl, Frederik

**Mason, Lee W.**
See Malzberg, Barry N(athaniel)

**Mason, Nick** 1945- .............. **CLC 35**
See also Pink Floyd

**Mason, Tally**
See Derleth, August (William)

**Mass, William**
See Gibson, William

**Masters, Edgar Lee**
1868-1950 ......... **TCLC 2, 25; PC 1**
See also CA 104; 133; CDALB 1865-1917;
DLB 54; MTCW

**Masters, Hilary** 1928- ............ **CLC 48**
See also CA 25-28R; CANR 13

**Mastrosimone, William** 19(?)- ...... **CLC 36**

**Mathe, Albert**
See Camus, Albert

**Matheson, Richard Burton** 1926- ... **CLC 37**
See also CA 97-100; DLB 8, 44

**Mathews, Harry** 1930- ......... **CLC 6, 52**
See also CA 21-24R; CAAS 6; CANR 18

**Mathias, Roland (Glyn)** 1915- ...... **CLC 45**
See also CA 97-100; CANR 19; DLB 27

**Matsuo Basho** 1644-1694 ........... **PC 3**

**Mattheson, Rodney**
See Creasey, John

**Matthews, Greg** 1949- ............. **CLC 45**
See also CA 135

**Matthews, William** 1942- ......... **CLC 40**
See also CA 29-32R; CANR 12; DLB 5

**Matthias, John (Edward)** 1941- ...... **CLC 9**
See also CA 33-36R

**Matthiessen, Peter**
1927- ........... **CLC 5, 7, 11, 32, 64**
See also AAYA 6; BEST 90:4; CA 9-12R;
CANR 21; DLB 6; MTCW; SATA 27

**Maturin, Charles Robert**
1780(?)-1824 ............... **NCLC 6**

**Matute (Ausejo), Ana Maria**
1925- ...................... **CLC 11**
See also CA 89-92; MTCW

**Maugham, W. S.**
See Maugham, W(illiam) Somerset

**Maugham, W(illiam) Somerset**
1874-1965 .... **CLC 1, 11, 15, 67; SSC 8**
See also CA 5-8R; 25-28R;
CDBLB 1914-1945; DLB 10, 36, 77, 100;
MTCW; SATA 54; WLC

**Maugham, William Somerset**
See Maugham, W(illiam) Somerset

**Maupassant, (Henri Rene Albert) Guy de**
1850-1893 ............. **NCLC 1; SSC 1**
See also DLB 123; WLC

**Maurhut, Richard**
See Traven, B.

**Mauriac, Claude** 1914- ............ **CLC 9**
See also CA 89-92; DLB 83

**Mauriac, Francois (Charles)**
1885-1970 .............. **CLC 4, 9, 56**
See also CA 25-28; CAP 2; DLB 65;
MTCW

**Mavor, Osborne Henry** 1888-1951
See Bridie, James
See also CA 104

**Maxwell, William (Keepers Jr.)**
1908- ...................... **CLC 19**
See also CA 93-96; DLBY 80

**May, Elaine** 1932- ............... **CLC 16**
See also CA 124; DLB 44

**Mayakovski, Vladimir (Vladimirovich)**
1893-1930 ............... **TCLC 4, 18**
See also CA 104

**Mayhew, Henry** 1812-1887 ...... **NCLC 31**
See also DLB 18, 55

**Maynard, Joyce** 1953- ............. **CLC 23**
See also CA 111; 129

**Mayne, William (James Carter)**
1928- ...................... **CLC 12**
See also CA 9-12R; CANR 37; CLR 25;
MAICYA; SAAS 11; SATA 6, 68

**Mayo, Jim**
See L'Amour, Louis (Dearborn)

**Maysles, Albert** 1926- ............. **CLC 16**
See also CA 29-32R

**Maysles, David** 1932- ............. **CLC 16**

Mazer, Norma Fox 1931- ......... **CLC 26**
See also AAYA 5; CA 69-72; CANR 12,
32; CLR 23; MAICYA; SAAS 1;
SATA 24, 67

Mazzini, Guiseppe 1805-1872 .... **NCLC 34**

McAuley, James Phillip
1917-1976 .................. **CLC 45**
See also CA 97-100

McBain, Ed
See Hunter, Evan

McBrien, William Augustine
1930- ...................... **CLC 44**
See also CA 107

McCaffrey, Anne (Inez) 1926-...... **CLC 17**
See also AAYA 6; AITN 2; BEST 89:2;
CA 25-28R; CANR 15, 35; DLB 8;
MAICYA; MTCW; SAAS 11; SATA 8,
70

McCann, Arthur
See Campbell, John W(ood Jr.)

McCann, Edson
See Pohl, Frederik

McCarthy, Cormac 1933-........ **CLC 4, 57**
See also CA 13-16R; CANR 10; DLB 6

McCarthy, Mary (Therese)
1912-1989 ... CLC **1, 3, 5, 14, 24, 39, 59**
See also CA 5-8R; 129; CANR 16; DLB 2;
DLBY 81; MTCW

McCartney, (James) Paul
1942- .................... **CLC 12, 35**

McCauley, Stephen 19(?)-......... **CLC 50**

McClure, Michael (Thomas)
1932- ..................... **CLC 6, 10**
See also CA 21-24R; CANR 17; DLB 16

McCorkle, Jill (Collins) 1958-...... **CLC 51**
See also CA 121; DLBY 87

McCourt, James 1941-............ **CLC 5**
See also CA 57-60

McCoy, Horace (Stanley)
1897-1955 .................. **TCLC 28**
See also CA 108; DLB 9

McCrae, John 1872-1918........ **TCLC 12**
See also CA 109; DLB 92

McCreigh, James
See Pohl, Frederik

McCullers, (Lula) Carson (Smith)
1917-1967 .. CLC **1, 4, 10, 12, 48; SSC 9**
See also CA 5-8R; 25-28R; CABS 1, 3;
CANR 18; CDALB 1941-1968; DLB 2, 7;
MTCW; SATA 27; WLC

McCulloch, John Tyler
See Burroughs, Edgar Rice

McCullough, Colleen 1938(?)-...... **CLC 27**
See also CA 81-84; CANR 17; MTCW

McElroy, Joseph 1930- ......... **CLC 5, 47**
See also CA 17-20R

McEwan, Ian (Russell) 1948- ... CLC **13, 66**
See also BEST 90:4; CA 61-64; CANR 14;
DLB 14; MTCW

McFadden, David 1940-.......... **CLC 48**
See also CA 104; DLB 60

McFarland, Dennis 1950- ........ **CLC 65**

McGahern, John 1934-........ CLC **5, 9, 48**
See also CA 17-20R; CANR 29; DLB 14;
MTCW

McGinley, Patrick (Anthony)
1937- ...................... **CLC 41**
See also CA 120; 127

McGinley, Phyllis 1905-1978 ...... **CLC 14**
See also CA 9-12R; 77-80; CANR 19;
DLB 11, 48; SATA 2, 24, 44

McGinniss, Joe 1942-............. **CLC 32**
See also AITN 2; BEST 89:2; CA 25-28R;
CANR 26

McGivern, Maureen Daly
See Daly, Maureen

McGrath, Patrick 1950-.......... **CLC 55**
See also CA 136

McGrath, Thomas (Matthew)
1916-1990 ................ CLC **28, 59**
See also CA 9-12R; 132; CANR 6, 33;
MTCW; SATA 41; SATO 66

McGuane, Thomas (Francis III)
1939- ................ CLC **3, 7, 18, 45**
See also AITN 2; CA 49-52; CANR 5, 24;
DLB 2; DLBY 80; MTCW

McGuckian, Medbh 1950-......... **CLC 48**
See also DLB 40

McHale, Tom 1942(?)-1982....... CLC **3, 5**
See also AITN 1; CA 77-80; 106

McIlvanney, William 1936-........ **CLC 42**
See also CA 25-28R; DLB 14

McIlwraith, Maureen Mollie Hunter
See Hunter, Mollie
See also SATA 2

McInerney, Jay 1955- ............ **CLC 34**
See also CA 116; 123

McIntyre, Vonda N(eel) 1948- ..... **CLC 18**
See also CA 81-84; CANR 17, 34; MTCW

McKay, Claude ......... TCLC **7, 41; PC 2**
See also McKay, Festus Claudius
See also BLC 3; DLB 4, 45, 51, 117

McKay, Festus Claudius 1889-1948
See McKay, Claude
See also BW; CA 104; 124; MTCW; WLC

McKuen, Rod 1933-............. CLC **1, 3**
See also AITN 1; CA 41-44R

McLoughlin, R. B.
See Mencken, H(enry) L(ouis)

McLuhan, (Herbert) Marshall
1911-1980 .................. **CLC 37**
See also CA 9-12R; 102; CANR 12, 34;
DLB 88; MTCW

McMillan, Terry 1951- ........ CLC **50, 61**

McMurtry, Larry (Jeff)
1936- ......... CLC **2, 3, 7, 11, 27, 44**
See also AITN 2; BEST 89:2; CA 5-8R;
CANR 19; CDALB 1968-1988; DLB 2;
DLBY 80, 87; MTCW

McNally, Terrence 1939-...... CLC **4, 7, 41**
See also CA 45-48; CANR 2; DLB 7

McNamer, Deirdre 1950-........ **CLC 70**

McNeile, Herman Cyril 1888-1937
See Sapper
See also DLB 77

McPhee, John (Angus) 1931- ...... **CLC 36**
See also BEST 90:1; CA 65-68; CANR 20;
MTCW

McPherson, James Alan 1943-..... **CLC 19**
See also BW; CA 25-28R; CANR 24;
DLB 38; MTCW

McPherson, William (Alexander)
1933- ...................... **CLC 34**
See also CA 69-72; CANR 28

McSweeney, Kerry ................ **CLC 34**

Mead, Margaret 1901-1978........ **CLC 37**
See also AITN 1; CA 1-4R; 81-84;
CANR 4; MTCW; SATA 20

Meaker, Marijane (Agnes) 1927-
See Kerr, M. E.
See also CA 107; CANR 37; MAICYA;
MTCW; SATA 20, 61

Medoff, Mark (Howard) 1940- ... CLC **6, 23**
See also AITN 1; CA 53-56; CANR 5;
DLB 7

Meged, Aharon
See Megged, Aharon

Meged, Aron
See Megged, Aharon

Megged, Aharon 1920-............. **CLC 9**
See also CA 49-52; CAAS 13; CANR 1

Mehta, Ved (Parkash) 1934-....... **CLC 37**
See also CA 1-4R; CANR 2, 23; MTCW

Melanter
See Blackmore, R(ichard) D(oddridge)

Melikow, Loris
See Hofmannsthal, Hugo von

Melmoth, Sebastian
See Wilde, Oscar (Fingal O'Flahertie Wills)

Meltzer, Milton 1915-............ **CLC 26**
See also AAYA 8; CA 13-16R; CANR 38;
CLR 13; DLB 61; MAICYA; SAAS 1;
SATA 1, 50

Melville, Herman
1819-1891 ...... NCLC **3, 12, 29; SSC 1**
See also CDALB 1640-1865; DLB 3, 74;
SATA 59; WLC

Menander
c. 342B.C.-c. 292B.C.... CMLC **9; DC 3**

Mencken, H(enry) L(ouis)
1880-1956 .................. **TCLC 13**
See also CA 105; 125; CDALB 1917-1929;
DLB 11, 29, 63; MTCW

Mercer, David 1928-1980.......... **CLC 5**
See also CA 9-12R; 102; CANR 23;
DLB 13; MTCW

Merchant, Paul
See Ellison, Harlan

Meredith, George 1828-1909 ... TCLC **17, 43**
See also CA 117; CDBLB 1832-1890;
DLB 18, 35, 57

Meredith, William (Morris)
1919- .............. CLC **4, 13, 22, 55**
See also CA 9-12R; CAAS 14; CANR 6;
DLB 5

Merezhkovsky, Dmitry Sergeyevich
1865-1941 .................. **TCLC 29**

Merimee, Prosper
1803-1870 ........... NCLC **6; SSC 7**
See also DLB 119

Merkin, Daphne 1954-............ CLC 44
See also CA 123

Merlin, Arthur
See Blish, James (Benjamin)

Merrill, James (Ingram)
1926-....... CLC 2, 3, 6, 8, 13, 18, 34
See also CA 13-16R; CANR 10; DLB 5;
DLBY 85; MTCW

Merriman, Alex
See Silverberg, Robert

Merritt, E. B.
See Waddington, Miriam

Merton, Thomas
1915-1968 ........... CLC 1, 3, 11, 34
See also CA 5-8R; 25-28R; CANR 22;
DLB 48; DLBY 81; MTCW

Merwin, W(illiam) S(tanley)
1927-...... CLC 1, 2, 3, 5, 8, 13, 18, 45
See also CA 13-16R; CANR 15; DLB 5;
MTCW

Metcalf, John 1938-.............. CLC 37
See also CA 113; DLB 60

Metcalf, Suzanne
See Baum, L(yman) Frank

Mew, Charlotte (Mary)
1870-1928 .................. TCLC 8
See also CA 105; DLB 19

Mewshaw, Michael 1943-.......... CLC 9
See also CA 53-56; CANR 7; DLBY 80

Meyer, June
See Jordan, June

Meyer-Meyrink, Gustav 1868-1932
See Meyrink, Gustav
See also CA 117

Meyers, Jeffrey 1939- ........... CLC 39
See also CA 73-76; DLB 111

Meynell, Alice (Christina Gertrude Thompson)
1847-1922 .................. TCLC 6
See also CA 104; DLB 19, 98

Meyrink, Gustav ................. TCLC 21
See also Meyer-Meyrink, Gustav
See also DLB 81

Michaels, Leonard 1933-........ CLC 6, 25
See also CA 61-64; CANR 21; MTCW

Michaux, Henri 1899-1984 ...... CLC 8, 19
See also CA 85-88; 114

Michelangelo 1475-1564........... LC 12

Michelet, Jules 1798-1874....... NCLC 31

Michener, James A(lbert)
1907(?)-.......... CLC 1, 5, 11, 29, 60
See also AITN 1; BEST 90:1; CA 5-8R;
CANR 21; DLB 6; MTCW

Mickiewicz, Adam 1798-1855 ..... NCLC 3

Middleton, Christopher 1926-...... CLC 13
See also CA 13-16R; CANR 29; DLB 40

Middleton, Stanley 1919-........ CLC 7, 38
See also CA 25-28R; CANR 21; DLB 14

Migueis, Jose Rodrigues 1901-..... CLC 10

Mikszath, Kalman 1847-1910 ..... TCLC 31

Miles, Josephine
1911-1985 ........ CLC 1, 2, 14, 34, 39
See also CA 1-4R; 116; CANR 2; DLB 48

Militant
See Sandburg, Carl (August)

Mill, John Stuart 1806-1873 ..... NCLC 11
See also CDBLB 1832-1890; DLB 55

Millar, Kenneth 1915-1983 ........ CLC 14
See also Macdonald, Ross
See also CA 9-12R; 110; CANR 16; DLB 2;
DLBD 6; DLBY 83; MTCW

Millay, E. Vincent
See Millay, Edna St. Vincent

Millay, Edna St. Vincent
1892-1950 ............. TCLC 4; PC 6
See also CA 104; 130; CDALB 1917-1929;
DLB 45; MTCW

Miller, Arthur
1915-...... CLC 1, 2, 6, 10, 15, 26, 47;
DC 1
See also AITN 1; CA 1-4R; CABS 3;
CANR 2, 30; CDALB 1941-1968; DLB 7;
MTCW; WLC

Miller, Henry (Valentine)
1891-1980 ....... CLC 1, 2, 4, 9, 14, 43
See also CA 9-12R; 97-100; CANR 33;
CDALB 1929-1941; DLB 4, 9; DLBY 80;
MTCW; WLC

Miller, Jason 1939(?)-............. CLC 2
See also AITN 1; CA 73-76; DLB 7

Miller, Sue 19(?)-................ CLC 44
See also BEST 90:3

Miller, Walter M(ichael Jr.)
1923-.................... CLC 4, 30
See also CA 85-88; DLB 8

Millett, Kate 1934-.............. CLC 67
See also AITN 1; CA 73-76; CANR 32;
MTCW

Millhauser, Steven 1943-....... CLC 21, 54
See also CA 110; 111; DLB 2

Millin, Sarah Gertrude 1889-1968 .. CLC 49
See also CA 102; 93-96

Milne, A(lan) A(lexander)
1882-1956 ................... TCLC 6
See also CA 104; 133; CLR 1, 26; DLB 10,
77, 100; MAICYA; MTCW; YABC 1

Milner, Ron(ald) 1938-........... CLC 56
See also AITN 1; BLC 3; BW; CA 73-76;
CANR 24; DLB 38; MTCW

Milosz, Czeslaw
1911-.......... CLC 5, 11, 22, 31, 56
See also CA 81-84; CANR 23; MTCW

Milton, John 1608-1674............. LC 9
See also CDBLB 1660-1789; WLC

Minehaha, Cornelius
See Wedekind, (Benjamin) Frank(lin)

Miner, Valerie 1947- ............. CLC 40
See also CA 97-100

Minimo, Duca
See D'Annunzio, Gabriele

Minot, Susan 1956- .............. CLC 44
See also CA 134

Minus, Ed 1938-................. CLC 39

Miranda, Javier
See Bioy Casares, Adolfo

Miro (Ferrer), Gabriel (Francisco Victor)
1879-1930 .................. TCLC 5
See also CA 104

Mishima, Yukio
....... CLC 2, 4, 6, 9, 27; DC 1; SSC 4
See also Hiraoka, Kimitake

Mistral, Gabriela................. TCLC 2
See also Godoy Alcayaga, Lucila

Mistry, Rohinton 1952-.......... CLC 71

Mitchell, Clyde
See Ellison, Harlan; Silverberg, Robert

Mitchell, James Leslie 1901-1935
See Gibbon, Lewis Grassic
See also CA 104; DLB 15

Mitchell, Joni 1943-.............. CLC 12
See also CA 112

Mitchell, Margaret (Munnerlyn)
1900-1949 ................. TCLC 11
See also CA 109; 125; DLB 9; MTCW

Mitchell, Peggy
See Mitchell, Margaret (Munnerlyn)

Mitchell, S(ilas) Weir 1829-1914 .. TCLC 36

Mitchell, W(illiam) O(rmond)
1914-..................... CLC 25
See also CA 77-80; CANR 15; DLB 88

Mitford, Mary Russell 1787-1855.. NCLC 4
See also DLB 110, 116

Mitford, Nancy 1904-1973........ CLC 44
See also CA 9-12R

Miyamoto, Yuriko 1899-1951 ..... TCLC 37

Mo, Timothy (Peter) 1950(?)-...... CLC 46
See also CA 117; MTCW

Modarressi, Taghi (M.) 1931-...... CLC 44
See also CA 121; 134

Modiano, Patrick (Jean) 1945-..... CLC 18
See also CA 85-88; CANR 17; DLB 83

Moerck, Paal
See Roelvaag, O(le) E(dvart)

Mofolo, Thomas (Mokopu)
1875(?)-1948 ................ TCLC 22
See also BLC 3; CA 121

Mohr, Nicholasa 1935-............ CLC 12
See also AAYA 8; CA 49-52; CANR 1, 32;
CLR 22; HW; SAAS 8; SATA 8

Mojtabai, A(nn) G(race)
1938-.............. CLC 5, 9, 15, 29
See also CA 85-88

Moliere 1622-1673 ............... LC 10
See also WLC

Molin, Charles
See Mayne, William (James Carter)

Molnar, Ferenc 1878-1952........ TCLC 20
See also CA 109

Momaday, N(avarre) Scott
1934-.................... CLC 2, 19
See also CA 25-28R; CANR 14, 34;
MTCW; SATA 30, 48

Monroe, Harriet 1860-1936....... TCLC 12
See also CA 109; DLB 54, 91

Monroe, Lyle
See Heinlein, Robert A(nson)

Montagu, Elizabeth 1917-........ NCLC 7
See also CA 9-12R

Montagu, Mary (Pierrepont) Wortley
1689-1762 .................... LC 9
See also DLB 95, 101

**Montague, John (Patrick)**
1929- . . . . . . . . . . . . . . . . . . CLC 13, 46
See also CA 9-12R; CANR 9; DLB 40;
MTCW

**Montaigne, Michel (Eyquem) de**
1533-1592 . . . . . . . . . . . . . . . . . LC 8
See also WLC

**Montale, Eugenio** 1896-1981 . . . CLC 7, 9, 18
See also CA 17-20R; 104; CANR 30;
DLB 114; MTCW

**Montesquieu, Charles-Louis de Secondat**
1689-1755 . . . . . . . . . . . . . . . . . LC 7

**Montgomery, (Robert) Bruce** 1921-1978
See Crispin, Edmund
See also CA 104

**Montgomery, Marion H. Jr.** 1925- . . . CLC 7
See also AITN 1; CA 1-4R; CANR 3;
DLB 6

**Montgomery, Max**
See Davenport, Guy (Mattison Jr.)

**Montherlant, Henry (Milon) de**
1896-1972 . . . . . . . . . . . . . . . . CLC 8, 19
See also CA 85-88; 37-40R; DLB 72;
MTCW

**Monty Python** . . . . . . . . . . . . . . . . . CLC 21
See also Chapman, Graham; Cleese, John
(Marwood); Gilliam, Terry (Vance); Idle,
Eric; Jones, Terence Graham Parry; Palin,
Michael (Edward)
See also AAYA 7

**Moodie, Susanna (Strickland)**
1803-1885 . . . . . . . . . . . . . . . NCLC 14
See also DLB 99

**Mooney, Edward** 1951- . . . . . . . . . . CLC 25
See also CA 130

**Mooney, Ted**
See Mooney, Edward

**Moorcock, Michael (John)**
1939- . . . . . . . . . . . . . . . . CLC 5, 27, 58
See also CA 45-48; CAAS 5; CANR 2, 17,
38; DLB 14; MTCW

**Moore, Brian**
1921- . . . . . . . . CLC 1, 3, 5, 7, 8, 19, 32
See also CA 1-4R; CANR 1, 25; MTCW

**Moore, Edward**
See Muir, Edwin

**Moore, George Augustus**
1852-1933 . . . . . . . . . . . . . . . . . TCLC 7
See also CA 104; DLB 10, 18, 57

**Moore, Lorrie** . . . . . . . . . . . . CLC 39, 45, 68
See also Moore, Marie Lorena

**Moore, Marianne (Craig)**
1887-1972 . . . CLC 1, 2, 4, 8, 10, 13, 19,
47; PC 4
See also CA 1-4R; 33-36R; CANR 3;
CDALB 1929-1941; DLB 45; DLBD 7;
MTCW; SATA 20

**Moore, Marie Lorena** 1957-
See Moore, Lorrie
See also CA 116; CANR 39

**Moore, Thomas** 1779-1852 . . . . . . . NCLC 6
See also DLB 96

**Morand, Paul** 1888-1976 . . . . . . . . . CLC 41
See also CA 69-72; DLB 65

**Morante, Elsa** 1918-1985 . . . . . . . CLC 8, 47
See also CA 85-88; 117; CANR 35; MTCW

**Moravia, Alberto** . . . . . . CLC 2, 7, 11, 27, 46
See also Pincherle, Alberto

**More, Hannah** 1745-1833 . . . . . . . NCLC 27
See also DLB 107, 109, 116

**More, Henry** 1614-1687 . . . . . . . . . . . LC 9

**More, Sir Thomas** 1478-1535 . . . . . . LC 10

**Moreas, Jean** . . . . . . . . . . . . . . . . TCLC 18
See also Papadiamantopoulos, Johannes

**Morgan, Berry** 1919- . . . . . . . . . . . . CLC 6
See also CA 49-52; DLB 6

**Morgan, Claire**
See Highsmith, (Mary) Patricia

**Morgan, Edwin (George)** 1920- . . . . . CLC 31
See also CA 5-8R; CANR 3; DLB 27

**Morgan, (George) Frederick**
1922- . . . . . . . . . . . . . . . . . . . CLC 23
See also CA 17-20R; CANR 21

**Morgan, Harriet**
See Mencken, H(enry) L(ouis)

**Morgan, Jane**
See Cooper, James Fenimore

**Morgan, Janet** 1945- . . . . . . . . . . . . CLC 39
See also CA 65-68

**Morgan, Lady** 1776(?)-1859 . . . . . NCLC 29
See also DLB 116

**Morgan, Robin** 1941- . . . . . . . . . . . . CLC 2
See also CA 69-72; CANR 29; MTCW

**Morgan, Scott**
See Kuttner, Henry

**Morgan, Seth** 1949(?)-1990 . . . . . . . CLC 65
See also CA 132

**Morgenstern, Christian**
1871-1914 . . . . . . . . . . . . . . . . . TCLC 8
See also CA 105

**Morgenstern, S.**
See Goldman, William (W.)

**Moricz, Zsigmond** 1879-1942 . . . . . TCLC 33

**Morike, Eduard (Friedrich)**
1804-1875 . . . . . . . . . . . . . . . NCLC 10

**Mori Ogai** . . . . . . . . . . . . . . . . . . TCLC 14
See also Mori Rintaro

**Mori Rintaro** 1862-1922
See Mori Ogai
See also CA 110

**Moritz, Karl Philipp** 1756-1793 . . . . . . LC 2
See also DLB 94

**Morren, Theophil**
See Hofmannsthal, Hugo von

**Morris, Julian**
See West, Morris L(anglo)

**Morris, Steveland Judkins** 1950(?)-
See Wonder, Stevie
See also CA 111

**Morris, William** 1834-1896 . . . . . . . NCLC 4
See also CDBLB 1832-1890; DLB 18, 35, 57

**Morris, Wright** 1910- . . . CLC 1, 3, 7, 18, 37
See also CA 9-12R; CANR 21; DLB 2;
DLBY 81; MTCW

**Morrison, Chloe Anthony Wofford**
See Morrison, Toni

**Morrison, James Douglas** 1943-1971
See Morrison, Jim
See also CA 73-76

**Morrison, Jim** . . . . . . . . . . . . . . . . CLC 17
See also Morrison, James Douglas

**Morrison, Toni** 1931- . . . . . CLC 4, 10, 22, 55
See also AAYA 1; BLC 3; BW; CA 29-32R;
CANR 27; CDALB 1968-1988; DLB 6,
33; DLBY 81; MTCW; SATA 57

**Morrison, Van** 1945- . . . . . . . . . . . . CLC 21
See also CA 116

**Mortimer, John (Clifford)**
1923- . . . . . . . . . . . . . . . . . . CLC 28, 43
See also CA 13-16R; CANR 21;
CDBLB 1960 to Present; DLB 13;
MTCW

**Mortimer, Penelope (Ruth)** 1918- . . . . CLC 5
See also CA 57-60

**Morton, Anthony**
See Creasey, John

**Mosher, Howard Frank** . . . . . . . . . . CLC 62

**Mosley, Nicholas** 1923- . . . . . . . CLC 43, 70
See also CA 69-72; DLB 14

**Moss, Howard**
1922-1987 . . . . . . . . . . CLC 7, 14, 45, 50
See also CA 1-4R; 123; CANR 1; DLB 5

**Motion, Andrew** 1952- . . . . . . . . . . . CLC 47
See also DLB 40

**Motley, Willard (Francis)**
1912-1965 . . . . . . . . . . . . . . . . . CLC 18
See also BW; CA 117; 106; DLB 76

**Mott, Michael (Charles Alston)**
1930- . . . . . . . . . . . . . . . . . . CLC 15, 34
See also CA 5-8R; CAAS 7; CANR 7, 29

**Mowat, Farley (McGill)** 1921- . . . . . CLC 26
See also AAYA 1; CA 1-4R; CANR 4, 24;
CLR 20; DLB 68; MAICYA; MTCW;
SATA 3, 55

**Moyers, Bill** 1934- . . . . . . . . . . . . . . CLC 74
See also AITN 2; CA 61-64; CANR 31

**Mphahlele, Es'kia**
See Mphahlele, Ezekiel

**Mphahlele, Ezekiel** 1919- . . . . . . . . . CLC 25
See also BLC 3; BW; CA 81-84; CANR 26

**Mqhayi, S(amuel) E(dward) K(rune Loliwe)**
1875-1945 . . . . . . . . . . . . . . . . TCLC 25
See also BLC 3

**Mr. Martin**
See Burroughs, William S(eward)

**Mrozek, Slawomir** 1930- . . . . . . . . CLC 3, 13
See also CA 13-16R; CAAS 10; CANR 29;
MTCW

**Mrs. Belloc-Lowndes**
See Lowndes, Marie Adelaide (Belloc)

**Mtwa, Percy** (?)- . . . . . . . . . . . . . . CLC 47

**Mueller, Lisel** 1924- . . . . . . . . . . . CLC 13, 51
See also CA 93-96; DLB 105

**Muir, Edwin** 1887-1959 . . . . . . . . . . TCLC 2
See also CA 104; DLB 20, 100

**Muir, John** 1838-1914 . . . . . . . . . . . TCLC 28

**Mujica Lainez, Manuel**
1910-1984 . . . . . . . . . . . . . . . . . CLC 31
See also Lainez, Manuel Mujica
See also CA 81-84; 112; CANR 32; HW

**Pater, Walter (Horatio)**
1839-1894 ................. NCLC 7
See also CDBLB 1832-1890; DLB 57

**Paterson, A(ndrew) B(arton)**
1864-1941 ................. TCLC 32

**Paterson, Katherine (Womeldorf)**
1932- ................... CLC 12, 30
See also AAYA 1; CA 21-24R; CANR 28;
CLR 7; DLB 52; MAICYA; MTCW;
SATA 13, 53

**Patmore, Coventry Kersey Dighton**
1823-1896 ................. NCLC 9
See also DLB 35, 98

**Paton, Alan (Stewart)**
1903-1988 .......... CLC 4, 10, 25, 55
See also CA 13-16; 125; CANR 22; CAP 1;
MTCW; SATA 11, 56; WLC

**Paton Walsh, Gillian** 1939-
See Walsh, Jill Paton
See also CANR 38; MAICYA; SAAS 3;
SATA 4

**Paulding, James Kirke** 1778-1860.. NCLC 2
See also DLB 3, 59, 74

**Paulin, Thomas Neilson** 1949-
See Paulin, Tom
See also CA 123; 128

**Paulin, Tom** ................... CLC 37
See also Paulin, Thomas Neilson
See also DLB 40

**Paustovsky, Konstantin (Georgievich)**
1892-1968 ................. CLC 40
See also CA 93-96; 25-28R

**Pavese, Cesare** 1908-1950 ......... TCLC 3
See also CA 104

**Pavic, Milorad** 1929- ............. CLC 60
See also CA 136

**Payne, Alan**
See Jakes, John (William)

**Paz, Gil**
See Lugones, Leopoldo

**Paz, Octavio**
1914- ...... CLC 3, 4, 6, 10, 19, 51, 65;
PC 1
See also CA 73-76; CANR 32; DLBY 90;
HW; MTCW; WLC

**Peacock, Molly** 1947-............. CLC 60
See also CA 103; DLB 120

**Peacock, Thomas Love**
1785-1866 ................. NCLC 22
See also DLB 96, 116

**Peake, Mervyn** 1911-1968 ...... CLC 7, 54
See also CA 5-8R; 25-28R; CANR 3;
DLB 15; MTCW; SATA 23

**Pearce, Philippa** ................. CLC 21
See also Christie, (Ann) Philippa
See also CLR 9; MAICYA; SATA 1, 67

**Pearl, Eric**
See Elman, Richard

**Pearson, T(homas) R(eid)** 1956- .... CLC 39
See also CA 120; 130

**Peck, John** 1941- ................. CLC 3
See also CA 49-52; CANR 3

**Peck, Richard (Wayne)** 1934- ...... CLC 21
See also AAYA 1; CA 85-88; CANR 19,
38; MAICYA; SAAS 2; SATA 18, 55

**Peck, Robert Newton** 1928-........ CLC 17
See also AAYA 3; CA 81-84; CANR 31;
MAICYA; SAAS 1; SATA 21, 62

**Peckinpah, (David) Sam(uel)**
1925-1984 ................. CLC 20
See also CA 109; 114

**Pedersen, Knut** 1859-1952
See Hamsun, Knut
See also CA 104; 119; MTCW

**Peeslake, Gaffer**
See Durrell, Lawrence (George)

**Peguy, Charles Pierre**
1873-1914 ................. TCLC 10
See also CA 107

**Pena, Ramon del Valle y**
See Valle-Inclan, Ramon (Maria) del

**Pendennis, Arthur Esquir**
See Thackeray, William Makepeace

**Pepys, Samuel** 1633-1703.......... LC 11
See also CDBLB 1660-1789; DLB 101;
WLC

**Percy, Walker**
1916-1990 ... CLC 2, 3, 6, 8, 14, 18, 47,
65
See also CA 1-4R; 131; CANR 1, 23;
DLB 2; DLBY 80, 90; MTCW

**Perec, Georges** 1936-1982 ........ CLC 56
See also DLB 83

**Pereda (y Sanchez de Porrua), Jose Maria de**
1833-1906 ................. TCLC 16
See also CA 117

**Pereda y Porrua, Jose Maria de**
See Pereda (y Sanchez de Porrua), Jose
Maria de

**Peregoy, George Weems**
See Mencken, H(enry) L(ouis)

**Perelman, S(idney) J(oseph)**
1904-1979 ... CLC 3, 5, 9, 15, 23, 44, 49
See also AITN 1, 2; CA 73-76; 89-92;
CANR 18; DLB 11, 44; MTCW

**Peret, Benjamin** 1899-1959 ....... TCLC 20
See also CA 117

**Peretz, Isaac Loeb** 1851(?)-1915... TCLC 16
See also CA 109

**Peretz, Yitzhok Leibush**
See Peretz, Isaac Loeb

**Perez Galdos, Benito** 1843-1920 ... TCLC 27
See also CA 125; HW

**Perrault, Charles** 1628-1703 ......... LC 2
See also MAICYA; SATA 25

**Perry, Brighton**
See Sherwood, Robert E(mmet)

**Perse, Saint-John**
See Leger, (Marie-Rene) Alexis Saint-Leger

**Perse, St.-John** ............. CLC 4, 11, 46
See also Leger, (Marie-Rene) Alexis
Saint-Leger

**Peseenz, Tulio F.**
See Lopez y Fuentes, Gregorio

**Pesetsky, Bette** 1932-............. CLC 28
See also CA 133

**Peshkov, Alexei Maximovich** 1868-1936
See Gorky, Maxim
See also CA 105

**Pessoa, Fernando (Antonio Nogueira)**
1888-1935 ................. TCLC 27
See also CA 125

**Peterkin, Julia Mood** 1880-1961.... CLC 31
See also CA 102; DLB 9

**Peters, Joan K.** 1945-............. CLC 39

**Peters, Robert L(ouis)** 1924-........ CLC 7
See also CA 13-16R; CAAS 8; DLB 105

**Petofi, Sandor** 1823-1849........ NCLC 21

**Petrakis, Harry Mark** 1923-........ CLC 3
See also CA 9-12R; CANR 4, 30

**Petrov, Evgeny** ................... TCLC 21
See also Kataev, Evgeny Petrovich

**Petry, Ann (Lane)** 1908- ...... CLC 1, 7, 18
See also BW; CA 5-8R; CAAS 6; CANR 4;
CLR 12; DLB 76; MAICYA; MTCW;
SATA 5

**Petursson, Halligrimur** 1614-1674 .... LC 8

**Philipson, Morris H.** 1926-........ CLC 53
See also CA 1-4R; CANR 4

**Phillips, David Graham**
1867-1911 ................. TCLC 44
See also CA 108; DLB 9, 12

**Phillips, Jack**
See Sandburg, Carl (August)

**Phillips, Jayne Anne** 1952- ..... CLC 15, 33
See also CA 101; CANR 24; DLBY 80;
MTCW

**Phillips, Richard**
See Dick, Philip K(indred)

**Phillips, Robert (Schaeffer)** 1938-... CLC 28
See also CA 17-20R; CAAS 13; CANR 8;
DLB 105

**Phillips, Ward**
See Lovecraft, H(oward) P(hillips)

**Piccolo, Lucio** 1901-1969.......... CLC 13
See also CA 97-100; DLB 114

**Pickthall, Marjorie L(owry) C(hristie)**
1883-1922 ................. TCLC 21
See also CA 107; DLB 92

**Pico della Mirandola, Giovanni**
1463-1494 ................... LC 15

**Piercy, Marge**
1936- ......... CLC 3, 6, 14, 18, 27, 62
See also CA 21-24R; CAAS 1; CANR 13;
DLB 120; MTCW

**Piers, Robert**
See Anthony, Piers

**Pieyre de Mandiargues, Andre** 1909-1991
See Mandiargues, Andre Pieyre de
See also CA 103; 136; CANR 22

**Pilnyak, Boris** ................... TCLC 23
See also Vogau, Boris Andreyevich

**Pincherle, Alberto** 1907-1990 ... CLC 11, 18
See also Moravia, Alberto
See also CA 25-28R; 132; CANR 33;
MTCW

**Pineda, Cecile** 1942-............. CLC 39
See also CA 118

**Pinero, Arthur Wing** 1855-1934 ... TCLC 32
See also CA 110; DLB 10

**Pinero, Miguel (Antonio Gomez)**
1946-1988 ................. CLC 4, 55
See also CA 61-64; 125; CANR 29; HW

**Priestley, J(ohn) B(oynton)**
1894-1984 . . . . . . . . . . . **CLC 2, 5, 9, 34**
See also CA 9-12R; 113; CANR 33;
CDBLB 1914-1945; DLB 10, 34, 77, 100;
DLBY 84; MTCW

**Prince, F(rank) T(empleton)** 1912- . . **CLC 22**
See also CA 101; DLB 20

**Prince** 1958(?)- . . . . . . . . . . . . . . . . **CLC 35**

**Prince Kropotkin**
See Kropotkin, Peter (Aleksieevich)

**Prior, Matthew** 1664-1721 . . . . . . . . . . **LC 4**
See also DLB 95

**Pritchard, William H(arrison)**
1932- . . . . . . . . . . . . . . . . . . . . . . **CLC 34**
See also CA 65-68; CANR 23; DLB 111

**Pritchett, V(ictor) S(awdon)**
1900- . . . . . . . . . . . . . . . **CLC 5, 13, 15, 41**
See also CA 61-64; CANR 31; DLB 15;
MTCW

**Private 19022**
See Manning, Frederic

**Probst, Mark** 1925- . . . . . . . . . . . . . . **CLC 59**
See also CA 130

**Prokosch, Frederic** 1908-1989 . . . . **CLC 4, 48**
See also CA 73-76; 128; DLB 48

**Prophet, The**
See Dreiser, Theodore (Herman Albert)

**Prose, Francine** 1947- . . . . . . . . . . . . **CLC 45**
See also CA 109; 112

**Proudhon**
See Cunha, Euclides (Rodrigues Pimenta) da

**Proust,**
**(Valentin-Louis-George-Eugene-)Marcel**
1871-1922 . . . . . . . . . . . **TCLC 7, 13, 33**
See also CA 104; 120; DLB 65; MTCW;
WLC

**Prowler, Harley**
See Masters, Edgar Lee

**Prus, Boleslaw** . . . . . . . . . . . . . . . . . **TCLC 48**
See also Glowacki, Aleksander

**Pryor, Richard (Franklin Lenox Thomas)**
1940- . . . . . . . . . . . . . . . . . . . . . . **CLC 26**
See also CA 122

**Przybyszewski, Stanislaw**
1868-1927 . . . . . . . . . . . . . . . . **TCLC 36**
See also DLB 66

**Pteleon**
See Grieve, C(hristopher) M(urray)

**Puckett, Lute**
See Masters, Edgar Lee

**Puig, Manuel**
1932-1990 . . . . . . . . **CLC 3, 5, 10, 28, 65**
See also CA 45-48; CANR 2, 32; DLB 113;
HW; MTCW

**Purdy, A(lfred) W(ellington)**
1918- . . . . . . . . . . . . . . **CLC 3, 6, 14, 50**
See also Purdy, Al
See also CA 81-84

**Purdy, Al**
See Purdy, A(lfred) W(ellington)
See also DLB 88

**Purdy, James (Amos)**
1923- . . . . . . . . . . **CLC 2, 4, 10, 28, 52**
See also CA 33-36R; CAAS 1; CANR 19;
DLB 2; MTCW

**Pure, Simon**
See Swinnerton, Frank Arthur

**Pushkin, Alexander (Sergeyevich)**
1799-1837 . . . . . . . . . . . . . . **NCLC 3, 27**
See also SATA 61; WLC

**P'u Sung-ling** 1640-1715 . . . . . . . . . . . **LC 3**

**Putnam, Arthur Lee**
See Alger, Horatio Jr.

**Puzo, Mario** 1920- . . . . . . . . . **CLC 1, 2, 6, 36**
See also CA 65-68; CANR 4; DLB 6;
MTCW

**Pym, Barbara (Mary Crampton)**
1913-1980 . . . . . . . . . . . . . **CLC 13, 19, 37**
See also CA 13-14; 97-100; CANR 13, 34;
CAP 1; DLB 14; DLBY 87; MTCW

**Pynchon, Thomas (Ruggles Jr.)**
1937- . . **CLC 2, 3, 6, 9, 11, 18, 33, 62, 72**
See also BEST 90:2; CA 17-20R; CANR 22;
DLB 2; MTCW; WLC

**Qian Zhongshu**
See Ch'ien Chung-shu

**Qroll**
See Dagerman, Stig (Halvard)

**Quarrington, Paul (Lewis)** 1953- . . . . **CLC 65**
See also CA 129

**Quasimodo, Salvatore** 1901-1968 . . . **CLC 10**
See also CA 13-16; 25-28R; CAP 1;
DLB 114; MTCW

**Queen, Ellery** . . . . . . . . . . . . . . . . **CLC 3, 11**
See also Dannay, Frederic; Davidson,
Avram; Lee, Manfred B(ennington);
Sturgeon, Theodore (Hamilton); Vance,
John Holbrook

**Queen, Ellery Jr.**
See Dannay, Frederic; Lee, Manfred
B(ennington)

**Queneau, Raymond**
1903-1976 . . . . . . . . . . . **CLC 2, 5, 10, 42**
See also CA 77-80; 69-72; CANR 32;
DLB 72; MTCW

**Quin, Ann (Marie)** 1936-1973 . . . . . . . **CLC 6**
See also CA 9-12R; 45-48; DLB 14

**Quinn, Martin**
See Smith, Martin Cruz

**Quinn, Simon**
See Smith, Martin Cruz

**Quiroga, Horacio (Sylvestre)**
1878-1937 . . . . . . . . . . . . . . . . **TCLC 20**
See also CA 117; 131; HW; MTCW

**Quoirez, Francoise** 1935- . . . . . . . . . . . **CLC 9**
See also Sagan, Francoise
See also CA 49-52; CANR 6, 39; MTCW

**Raabe, Wilhelm** 1831-1910 . . . . . . . **TCLC 45**

**Rabe, David (William)** 1940- . . . **CLC 4, 8, 33**
See also CA 85-88; CABS 3; DLB 7

**Rabelais, Francois** 1483-1553 . . . . . . . **LC 5**
See also WLC

**Rabinovitch, Sholem** 1859-1916
See Aleichem, Sholom
See also CA 104

**Radcliffe, Ann (Ward)** 1764-1823 . . **NCLC 6**
See also DLB 39

**Radiguet, Raymond** 1903-1923 . . . . **TCLC 29**
See also DLB 65

**Radnoti, Miklos** 1909-1944 . . . . . . . **TCLC 16**
See also CA 118

**Rado, James** 1939- . . . . . . . . . . . . . . **CLC 17**
See also CA 105

**Radvanyi, Netty** 1900-1983
See Seghers, Anna
See also CA 85-88; 110

**Raeburn, John (Hay)** 1941- . . . . . . . . **CLC 34**
See also CA 57-60

**Ragni, Gerome** 1942-1991 . . . . . . . . . **CLC 17**
See also CA 105; 134

**Rahv, Philip** . . . . . . . . . . . . . . . . . . . **CLC 24**
See also Greenberg, Ivan

**Raine, Craig** 1944- . . . . . . . . . . . . . . **CLC 32**
See also CA 108; CANR 29; DLB 40

**Raine, Kathleen (Jessie)** 1908- . . . **CLC 7, 45**
See also CA 85-88; DLB 20; MTCW

**Rainis, Janis** 1865-1929 . . . . . . . . . . **TCLC 29**

**Rakosi, Carl** . . . . . . . . . . . . . . . . . . . **CLC 47**
See also Rawley, Callman
See also CAAS 5

**Raleigh, Richard**
See Lovecraft, H(oward) P(hillips)

**Rallentando, H. P.**
See Sayers, Dorothy L(eigh)

**Ramal, Walter**
See de la Mare, Walter (John)

**Ramon, Juan**
See Jimenez (Mantecon), Juan Ramon

**Ramos, Graciliano** 1892-1953 . . . . . **TCLC 32**

**Rampersad, Arnold** 1941- . . . . . . . . . **CLC 44**
See also CA 127; 133; DLB 111

**Rampling, Anne**
See Rice, Anne

**Ramuz, Charles-Ferdinand**
1878-1947 . . . . . . . . . . . . . . . . **TCLC 33**

**Rand, Ayn** 1905-1982 . . . . . . . . **CLC 3, 30, 44**
See also CA 13-16R; 105; CANR 27;
MTCW; WLC

**Randall, Dudley (Felker)** 1914- . . . . . . **CLC 1**
See also BLC 3; BW; CA 25-28R;
CANR 23; DLB 41

**Randall, Robert**
See Silverberg, Robert

**Ranger, Ken**
See Creasey, John

**Ransom, John Crowe**
1888-1974 . . . . . . . . . **CLC 2, 4, 5, 11, 24**
See also CA 5-8R; 49-52; CANR 6, 34;
DLB 45, 63; MTCW

**Rao, Raja** 1909- . . . . . . . . . . . . . **CLC 25, 56**
See also CA 73-76; MTCW

**Raphael, Frederic (Michael)**
1931- . . . . . . . . . . . . . . . . . . . **CLC 2, 14**
See also CA 1-4R; CANR 1; DLB 14

**Ratcliffe, James P.**
See Mencken, H(enry) L(ouis)

**Rathbone, Julian** 1935- . . . . . . . . . . . **CLC 41**
See also CA 101; CANR 34

**Rattigan, Terence (Mervyn)**
1911-1977 . . . . . . . . . . . . . . . . . . **CLC 7**
See also CA 85-88; 73-76;
CDBLB 1945-1960; DLB 13; MTCW

Ratushinskaya, Irina   1954- ........ **CLC 54**
See also CA 129

Raven, Simon (Arthur Noel)
   1927- ...................... **CLC 14**
See also CA 81-84

Rawley, Callman   1903-
See Rakosi, Carl
See also CA 21-24R; CANR 12, 32

Rawlings, Marjorie Kinnan
   1896-1953 .................. **TCLC 4**
See also CA 104; 137; DLB 9, 22, 102;
   MAICYA; YABC 1

Ray, Satyajit   1921-.............. **CLC 16**
See also CA 114; 137

Read, Herbert Edward   1893-1968.... **CLC 4**
See also CA 85-88; 25-28R; DLB 20

Read, Piers Paul   1941- ...... **CLC 4, 10, 25**
See also CA 21-24R; CANR 38; DLB 14;
   SATA 21

Reade, Charles   1814-1884 ........ **NCLC 2**
See also DLB 21

Reade, Hamish
See Gray, Simon (James Holliday)

Reading, Peter   1946- ............. **CLC 47**
See also CA 103; DLB 40

Reaney, James   1926- ............. **CLC 13**
See also CA 41-44R; CAAS 15; DLB 68;
   SATA 43

Rebreanu, Liviu   1885-1944 ...... **TCLC 28**

Rechy, John (Francisco)
   1934- ............. **CLC 1, 7, 14, 18**
See also CA 5-8R; CAAS 4; CANR 6, 32;
   DLB 122; DLBY 82; HW

Redcam, Tom   1870-1933 ......... **TCLC 25**

Reddin, Keith..................... **CLC 67**

Redgrove, Peter (William)
   1932- .................... **CLC 6, 41**
See also CA 1-4R; CANR 3, 39; DLB 40

Redmon, Anne................... **CLC 22**
See also Nightingale, Anne Redmon
See also DLBY 86

Reed, Eliot
See Ambler, Eric

Reed, Ishmael
   1938- ........ **CLC 2, 3, 5, 6, 13, 32, 60**
See also BLC 3; BW; CA 21-24R;
   CANR 25; DLB 2, 5, 33; DLBD 8;
   MTCW

Reed, John (Silas)   1887-1920 ...... **TCLC 9**
See also CA 106

Reed, Lou...................... **CLC 21**
See also Firbank, Louis

Reeve, Clara   1729-1807 ........ **NCLC 19**
See also DLB 39

Reid, Christopher   1949-........... **CLC 33**
See also DLB 40

Reid, Desmond
See Moorcock, Michael (John)

Reid Banks, Lynne   1929-
See Banks, Lynne Reid
See also CA 1-4R; CANR 6, 22, 38;
   CLR 24; MAICYA; SATA 22

Reilly, William K.
See Creasey, John

Reiner, Max
See Caldwell, (Janet Miriam) Taylor
   (Holland)

Reis, Ricardo
See Pessoa, Fernando (Antonio Nogueira)

Remarque, Erich Maria
   1898-1970 ................... **CLC 21**
See also CA 77-80; 29-32R; DLB 56;
   MTCW

Remizov, A.
See Remizov, Aleksei (Mikhailovich)

Remizov, A. M.
See Remizov, Aleksei (Mikhailovich)

Remizov, Aleksei (Mikhailovich)
   1877-1957 .................. **TCLC 27**
See also CA 125; 133

Renan, Joseph Ernest
   1823-1892 ................. **NCLC 26**

Renard, Jules   1864-1910 ........ **TCLC 17**
See also CA 117

Renault, Mary.............. **CLC 3, 11, 17**
See also Challans, Mary
See also DLBY 83

Rendell, Ruth (Barbara)   1930- .. **CLC 28, 48**
See also Vine, Barbara
See also CA 109; CANR 32; DLB 87;
   MTCW

Renoir, Jean   1894-1979 .......... **CLC 20**
See also CA 129; 85-88

Resnais, Alain   1922-............. **CLC 16**

Reverdy, Pierre   1889-1960 ....... **CLC 53**
See also CA 97-100; 89-92

Rexroth, Kenneth
   1905-1982 ...... **CLC 1, 2, 6, 11, 22, 49**
See also CA 5-8R; 107; CANR 14, 34;
   CDALB 1941-1968; DLB 16, 48;
   DLBY 82; MTCW

Reyes, Alfonso   1889-1959 ....... **TCLC 33**
See also CA 131; HW

Reyes y Basoalto, Ricardo Eliecer Neftali
See Neruda, Pablo

Reymont, Wladyslaw (Stanislaw)
   1868(?)-1925 ................ **TCLC 5**
See also CA 104

Reynolds, Jonathan   1942- ....... **CLC 6, 38**
See also CA 65-68; CANR 28

Reynolds, Joshua   1723-1792 ........ **LC 15**
See also DLB 104

Reynolds, Michael Shane   1937- .... **CLC 44**
See also CA 65-68; CANR 9

Reznikoff, Charles   1894-1976 ....... **CLC 9**
See also CA 33-36; 61-64; CAP 2; DLB 28,
   45

Rezzori (d'Arezzo), Gregor von
   1914- ...................... **CLC 25**
See also CA 122; 136

Rhine, Richard
See Silverstein, Alvin

Rhys, Jean
   1890(?)-1979 .... **CLC 2, 4, 6, 14, 19, 51**
See also CA 25-28R; 85-88; CANR 35;
   CDBLB 1945-1960; DLB 36, 117; MTCW

Ribeiro, Darcy   1922- ............. **CLC 34**
See also CA 33-36R

Ribeiro, Joao Ubaldo (Osorio Pimentel)
   1941- .................... **CLC 10, 67**
See also CA 81-84

Ribman, Ronald (Burt)   1932- ....... **CLC 7**
See also CA 21-24R

Ricci, Nino   1959-................ **CLC 70**
See also CA 137

Rice, Anne   1941- ................ **CLC 41**
See also AAYA 9; BEST 89:2; CA 65-68;
   CANR 12, 36

Rice, Elmer (Leopold)
   1892-1967 ................ **CLC 7, 49**
See also CA 21-22; 25-28R; CAP 2; DLB 4,
   7; MTCW

Rice, Tim   1944- ................. **CLC 21**
See also CA 103

Rich, Adrienne (Cecile)
   1929- ...... **CLC 3, 6, 7, 11, 18, 36, 73;**
                                    **PC 5**
See also CA 9-12R; CANR 20; DLB 5, 67;
   MTCW

Rich, Barbara
See Graves, Robert (von Ranke)

Rich, Robert
See Trumbo, Dalton

Richards, David Adams   1950-...... **CLC 59**
See also CA 93-96; DLB 53

Richards, I(vor) A(rmstrong)
   1893-1979 ................ **CLC 14, 24**
See also CA 41-44R; 89-92; CANR 34;
   DLB 27

Richardson, Anne
See Roiphe, Anne Richardson

Richardson, Dorothy Miller
   1873-1957 .................. **TCLC 3**
See also CA 104; DLB 36

Richardson, Ethel Florence (Lindesay)
   1870-1946
See Richardson, Henry Handel
See also CA 105

Richardson, Henry Handel......... **TCLC 4**
See also Richardson, Ethel Florence
   (Lindesay)

Richardson, Samuel   1689-1761 ....... **LC 1**
See also CDBLB 1660-1789; DLB 39; WLC

Richler, Mordecai
   1931- ........ **CLC 3, 5, 9, 13, 18, 46, 70**
See also AITN 1; CA 65-68; CANR 31;
   CLR 17; DLB 53; MAICYA; MTCW;
   SATA 27, 44

Richter, Conrad (Michael)
   1890-1968 .................. **CLC 30**
See also CA 5-8R; 25-28R; CANR 23;
   DLB 9; MTCW; SATA 3

Riddell, J. H.   1832-1906 ........ **TCLC 40**

Riding, Laura.................... **CLC 3, 7**
See also Jackson, Laura (Riding)

Riefenstahl, Berta Helene Amalia   1902-
See Riefenstahl, Leni
See also CA 108

Riefenstahl, Leni.................. **CLC 16**
See also Riefenstahl, Berta Helene Amalia

Riffe, Ernest
See Bergman, (Ernst) Ingmar

**Riley, Tex**
See Creasey, John

**Rilke, Rainer Maria**
1875-1926 ....... **TCLC 1, 6, 19; PC 2**
See also CA 104; 132; DLB 81; MTCW

**Rimbaud, (Jean Nicolas) Arthur**
1854-1891 ......... **NCLC 4, 35; PC 3**
See also WLC

**Ringmaster, The**
See Mencken, H(enry) L(ouis)

**Ringwood, Gwen(dolyn Margaret) Pharis**
1910-1984 .................. **CLC 48**
See also CA 112; DLB 88

**Rio, Michel** 19(?)- ............... **CLC 43**

**Ritsos, Giannes**
See Ritsos, Yannis

**Ritsos, Yannis** 1909-1990 ..... **CLC 6, 13, 31**
See also CA 77-80; 133; CANR 39; MTCW

**Ritter, Erika** 1948(?)- ............ **CLC 52**

**Rivera, Jose Eustasio** 1889-1928 ... **TCLC 35**
See also HW

**Rivers, Conrad Kent** 1933-1968 ...... **CLC 1**
See also BW; CA 85-88; DLB 41

**Rivers, Elfrida**
See Bradley, Marion Zimmer

**Riverside, John**
See Heinlein, Robert A(nson)

**Rizal, Jose** 1861-1896 .......... **NCLC 27**

**Roa Bastos, Augusto (Antonio)**
1917- ...................... **CLC 45**
See also CA 131; DLB 113; HW

**Robbe-Grillet, Alain**
1922- ...... **CLC 1, 2, 4, 6, 8, 10, 14, 43**
See also CA 9-12R; CANR 33; DLB 83;
MTCW

**Robbins, Harold** 1916- ............ **CLC 5**
See also CA 73-76; CANR 26; MTCW

**Robbins, Thomas Eugene** 1936-
See Robbins, Tom
See also CA 81-84; CANR 29; MTCW

**Robbins, Tom** ............... **CLC 9, 32, 64**
See also Robbins, Thomas Eugene
See also BEST 90:3; DLBY 80

**Robbins, Trina** 1938- ............ **CLC 21**
See also CA 128

**Roberts, Charles G(eorge) D(ouglas)**
1860-1943 ................. **TCLC 8**
See also CA 105; DLB 92; SATA 29

**Roberts, Kate** 1891-1985 .......... **CLC 15**
See also CA 107; 116

**Roberts, Keith (John Kingston)**
1935- ...................... **CLC 14**
See also CA 25-28R

**Roberts, Kenneth (Lewis)**
1885-1957 ................. **TCLC 23**
See also CA 109; DLB 9

**Roberts, Michele (B.)** 1949- ....... **CLC 48**
See also CA 115

**Robertson, Ellis**
See Ellison, Harlan; Silverberg, Robert

**Robertson, Thomas William**
1829-1871 ................. **NCLC 35**

**Robinson, Edwin Arlington**
1869-1935 ............. **TCLC 5; PC 1**
See also CA 104; 133; CDALB 1865-1917;
DLB 54; MTCW

**Robinson, Henry Crabb**
1775-1867 ................. **NCLC 15**
See also DLB 107

**Robinson, Jill** 1936- ............. **CLC 10**
See also CA 102

**Robinson, Kim Stanley** 1952- ...... **CLC 34**
See also CA 126

**Robinson, Lloyd**
See Silverberg, Robert

**Robinson, Marilynne** 1944- ........ **CLC 25**
See also CA 116

**Robinson, Smokey** .................. **CLC 21**
See also Robinson, William Jr.

**Robinson, William Jr.** 1940-
See Robinson, Smokey
See also CA 116

**Robison, Mary** 1949- ............. **CLC 42**
See also CA 113; 116

**Roddenberry, Eugene Wesley** 1921-1991
See Roddenberry, Gene
See also CA 110; 135; CANR 37; SATA 45

**Roddenberry, Gene** ................ **CLC 17**
See also Roddenberry, Eugene Wesley
See also AAYA 5; SATO 69

**Rodgers, Mary** 1931- ............. **CLC 12**
See also CA 49-52; CANR 8; CLR 20;
MAICYA; SATA 8

**Rodgers, W(illiam) R(obert)**
1909-1969 ................. **CLC 7**
See also CA 85-88; DLB 20

**Rodman, Eric**
See Silverberg, Robert

**Rodman, Howard** 1920(?)-1985 ..... **CLC 65**
See also CA 118

**Rodman, Maia**
See Wojciechowska, Maia (Teresa)

**Rodriguez, Claudio** 1934- ......... **CLC 10**

**Roelvaag, O(le) E(dvart)**
1876-1931 ................. **TCLC 17**
See also CA 117; DLB 9

**Roethke, Theodore (Huebner)**
1908-1963 ...... **CLC 1, 3, 8, 11, 19, 46**
See also CA 81-84; CABS 2;
CDALB 1941-1968; DLB 5; MTCW

**Rogers, Thomas Hunton** 1927- ..... **CLC 57**
See also CA 89-92

**Rogers, Will(iam Penn Adair)**
1879-1935 ................. **TCLC 8**
See also CA 105; DLB 11

**Rogin, Gilbert** 1929- ............. **CLC 18**
See also CA 65-68; CANR 15

**Rohan, Koda** ................... **TCLC 22**
See also Koda Shigeyuki

**Rohmer, Eric** .................... **CLC 16**
See also Scherer, Jean-Marie Maurice

**Rohmer, Sax** ................... **TCLC 28**
See also Ward, Arthur Henry Sarsfield
See also DLB 70

**Roiphe, Anne Richardson** 1935- ... **CLC 3, 9**
See also CA 89-92; DLBY 80

**Rolfe, Frederick (William Serafino Austin
Lewis Mary)** 1860-1913 ..... **TCLC 12**
See also CA 107; DLB 34

**Rolland, Romain** 1866-1944 ...... **TCLC 23**
See also CA 118; DLB 65

**Rolvaag, O(le) E(dvart)**
See Roelvaag, O(le) E(dvart)

**Romain Arnaud, Saint**
See Aragon, Louis

**Romains, Jules** 1885-1972 .......... **CLC 7**
See also CA 85-88; CANR 34; DLB 65;
MTCW

**Romero, Jose Ruben** 1890-1952 ... **TCLC 14**
See also CA 114; 131; HW

**Ronsard, Pierre de** 1524-1585 ........ **LC 6**

**Rooke, Leon** 1934- ............ **CLC 25, 34**
See also CA 25-28R; CANR 23

**Roper, William** 1498-1578 ......... **LC 10**

**Roquelaure, A. N.**
See Rice, Anne

**Rosa, Joao Guimaraes** 1908-1967 ... **CLC 23**
See also CA 89-92; DLB 113

**Rosen, Richard (Dean)** 1949- ....... **CLC 39**
See also CA 77-80

**Rosenberg, Isaac** 1890-1918 ...... **TCLC 12**
See also CA 107; DLB 20

**Rosenblatt, Joe** .................. **CLC 15**
See also Rosenblatt, Joseph

**Rosenblatt, Joseph** 1933-
See Rosenblatt, Joe
See also CA 89-92

**Rosenfeld, Samuel** 1896-1963
See Tzara, Tristan
See also CA 89-92

**Rosenthal, M(acha) L(ouis)** 1917- ... **CLC 28**
See also CA 1-4R; CAAS 6; CANR 4;
DLB 5; SATA 59

**Ross, Barnaby**
See Dannay, Frederic

**Ross, Bernard L.**
See Follett, Ken(neth Martin)

**Ross, J. H.**
See Lawrence, T(homas) E(dward)

**Ross, (James) Sinclair** 1908- ....... **CLC 13**
See also CA 73-76; DLB 88

**Rossetti, Christina (Georgina)**
1830-1894 ................. **NCLC 2**
See also DLB 35; MAICYA; SATA 20;
WLC

**Rossetti, Dante Gabriel**
1828-1882 ................. **NCLC 4**
See also CDBLB 1832-1890; DLB 35; WLC

**Rossner, Judith (Perelman)**
1935- .................. **CLC 6, 9, 29**
See also AITN 2; BEST 90:3; CA 17-20R;
CANR 18; DLB 6; MTCW

**Rostand, Edmond (Eugene Alexis)**
1868-1918 ............... **TCLC 6, 37**
See also CA 104; 126; MTCW

**Roth, Henry** 1906- ............ **CLC 2, 6, 11**
See also CA 11-12; CANR 38; CAP 1;
DLB 28; MTCW

**Roth, Joseph** 1894-1939 ......... **TCLC 33**
See also DLB 85

**Sanchez, Sonia** 1934- . . . . . . . . . . . . . . **CLC 5**
See also BLC 3; BW; CA 33-36R;
CANR 24; CLR 18; DLB 41; DLBD 8;
MAICYA; MTCW; SATA 22

**Sand, George** 1804-1876. . . . . . . . . **NCLC 2**
See also DLB 119; WLC

**Sandburg, Carl (August)**
1878-1967 . . . **CLC 1, 4, 10, 15, 35; PC 2**
See also CA 5-8R; 25-28R; CANR 35;
CDALB 1865-1917; DLB 17, 54;
MAICYA; MTCW; SATA 8; WLC

**Sandburg, Charles**
See Sandburg, Carl (August)

**Sandburg, Charles A.**
See Sandburg, Carl (August)

**Sanders, (James) Ed(ward)** 1939- . . . **CLC 53**
See also CA 13-16R; CANR 13; DLB 16

**Sanders, Lawrence** 1920- . . . . . . . . . **CLC 41**
See also BEST 89:4; CA 81-84; CANR 33;
MTCW

**Sanders, Noah**
See Blount, Roy (Alton) Jr.

**Sanders, Winston P.**
See Anderson, Poul (William)

**Sandoz, Mari(e Susette)**
1896-1966 . . . . . . . . . . . . . . . . . . **CLC 28**
See also CA 1-4R; 25-28R; CANR 17;
DLB 9; MTCW; SATA 5

**Saner, Reg(inald Anthony)** 1931- . . . . **CLC 9**
See also CA 65-68

**Sannazaro, Jacopo** 1456(?)-1530 . . . . . . **LC 8**

**Sansom, William** 1912-1976. . . . . . . **CLC 2, 6**
See also CA 5-8R; 65-68; MTCW

**Santayana, George** 1863-1952 . . . . . **TCLC 40**
See also CA 115; DLB 54, 71

**Santiago, Danny** . . . . . . . . . . . . . . . . . **CLC 33**
See also James, Daniel (Lewis); James,
Daniel (Lewis)
See also DLB 122

**Santmyer, Helen Hooven**
1895-1986 . . . . . . . . . . . . . . . . . . **CLC 33**
See also CA 1-4R; 118; CANR 15, 33;
DLBY 84; MTCW

**Santos, Bienvenido N(uqui)** 1911- . . . **CLC 22**
See also CA 101; CANR 19

**Sapper** . . . . . . . . . . . . . . . . . . . . . . . **TCLC 44**
See also McNeile, Herman Cyril

**Sappho** fl. 6th cent. B.C.- . . . . **CMLC 3; PC 5**

**Sarduy, Severo** 1937- . . . . . . . . . . . . . . **CLC 6**
See also CA 89-92; DLB 113; HW

**Sargeson, Frank** 1903-1982 . . . . . . . . **CLC 31**
See also CA 25-28R; 106; CANR 38

**Sarmiento, Felix Ruben Garcia** 1867-1916
See Dario, Ruben
See also CA 104

**Saroyan, William**
1908-1981 . . . . . **CLC 1, 8, 10, 29, 34, 56**
See also CA 5-8R; 103; CANR 30; DLB 7,
9, 86; DLBY 81; MTCW; SATA 23, 24;
WLC

**Sarraute, Nathalie**
1900- . . . . . . . . . . **CLC 1, 2, 4, 8, 10, 31**
See also CA 9-12R; CANR 23; DLB 83;
MTCW

**Sarton, (Eleanor) May**
1912- . . . . . . . . . . . . . . . . . **CLC 4, 14, 49**
See also CA 1-4R; CANR 1, 34; DLB 48;
DLBY 81; MTCW; SATA 36

**Sartre, Jean-Paul**
1905-1980 . . . **CLC 1, 4, 7, 9, 13, 18, 24,
44, 50, 52; DC 3**
See also CA 9-12R; 97-100; CANR 21;
DLB 72; MTCW; WLC

**Sassoon, Siegfried (Lorraine)**
1886-1967 . . . . . . . . . . . . . . . . . . **CLC 36**
See also CA 104; 25-28R; CANR 36;
DLB 20; MTCW

**Satterfield, Charles**
See Pohl, Frederik

**Saul, John (W. III)** 1942- . . . . . . . . . **CLC 46**
See also BEST 90:4; CA 81-84; CANR 16

**Saunders, Caleb**
See Heinlein, Robert A(nson)

**Saura (Atares), Carlos** 1932- . . . . . . . **CLC 20**
See also CA 114; 131; HW

**Sauser-Hall, Frederic** 1887-1961. . . . **CLC 18**
See also CA 102; 93-96; CANR 36; MTCW

**Savage, Catharine**
See Brosman, Catharine Savage

**Savage, Thomas** 1915- . . . . . . . . . . . . **CLC 40**
See also CA 126; 132; CAAS 15

**Savan, Glenn** . . . . . . . . . . . . . . . . . . . **CLC 50**

**Saven, Glenn** 19(?)- . . . . . . . . . . . . . **CLC 50**

**Sayers, Dorothy L(eigh)**
1893-1957 . . . . . . . . . . . . . . . **TCLC 2, 15**
See also CA 104; 119; CDBLB 1914-1945;
DLB 10, 36, 77, 100; MTCW

**Sayers, Valerie** 1952- . . . . . . . . . . . . . **CLC 50**
See also CA 134

**Sayles, John Thomas** 1950- . . . **CLC 7, 10, 14**
See also CA 57-60; DLB 44

**Scammell, Michael** . . . . . . . . . . . . . . . **CLC 34**

**Scannell, Vernon** 1922- . . . . . . . . . . . **CLC 49**
See also CA 5-8R; CANR 8, 24; DLB 27;
SATA 59

**Scarlett, Susan**
See Streatfeild, (Mary) Noel

**Schaeffer, Susan Fromberg**
1941- . . . . . . . . . . . . . . . . **CLC 6, 11, 22**
See also CA 49-52; CANR 18; DLB 28;
MTCW; SATA 22

**Schary, Jill**
See Robinson, Jill

**Schell, Jonathan** 1943- . . . . . . . . . . . **CLC 35**
See also CA 73-76; CANR 12

**Schelling, Friedrich Wilhelm Joseph von**
1775-1854 . . . . . . . . . . . . . . . . **NCLC 30**
See also DLB 90

**Scherer, Jean-Marie Maurice** 1920-
See Rohmer, Eric
See also CA 110

**Schevill, James (Erwin)** 1920- . . . . . . . **CLC 7**
See also CA 5-8R; CAAS 12

**Schiller, Friedrich** 1759-1805 . . . . **NCLC 39**
See also DLB 94

**Schisgal, Murray (Joseph)** 1926- . . . . . **CLC 6**
See also CA 21-24R

**Schlee, Ann** 1934- . . . . . . . . . . . . . . **CLC 35**
See also CA 101; CANR 29; SATA 36, 44

**Schlegel, August Wilhelm von**
1767-1845 . . . . . . . . . . . . . . . . **NCLC 15**
See also DLB 94

**Schlegel, Johann Elias (von)**
1719(?)-1749 . . . . . . . . . . . . . . . . . **LC 5**

**Schmidt, Arno (Otto)** 1914-1979 . . . . **CLC 56**
See also CA 128; 109; DLB 69

**Schmitz, Aron Hector** 1861-1928
See Svevo, Italo
See also CA 104; 122; MTCW

**Schnackenberg, Gjertrud** 1953- . . . . . **CLC 40**
See also CA 116; DLB 120

**Schneider, Leonard Alfred** 1925-1966
See Bruce, Lenny
See also CA 89-92

**Schnitzler, Arthur** 1862-1931 . . . . . . **TCLC 4**
See also CA 104; DLB 81, 118

**Schor, Sandra (M.)** 1932(?)-1990 . . . **CLC 65**
See also CA 132

**Schorer, Mark** 1908-1977 . . . . . . . . . . **CLC 9**
See also CA 5-8R; 73-76; CANR 7;
DLB 103

**Schrader, Paul Joseph** 1946- . . . . . . . **CLC 26**
See also CA 37-40R; DLB 44

**Schreiner, Olive (Emilie Albertina)**
1855-1920 . . . . . . . . . . . . . . . . . **TCLC 9**
See also CA 105; DLB 18

**Schulberg, Budd (Wilson)**
1914- . . . . . . . . . . . . . . . . . . . **CLC 7, 48**
See also CA 25-28R; CANR 19; DLB 6, 26,
28; DLBY 81

**Schulz, Bruno** 1892-1942 . . . . . . . . . . **TCLC 5**
See also CA 115; 123

**Schulz, Charles M(onroe)** 1922- . . . . . **CLC 12**
See also CA 9-12R; CANR 6; SATA 10

**Schuyler, James Marcus**
1923-1991 . . . . . . . . . . . . . . . **CLC 5, 23**
See also CA 101; 134; DLB 5

**Schwartz, Delmore (David)**
1913-1966 . . . . . . . . . . . **CLC 2, 4, 10, 45**
See also CA 17-18; 25-28R; CANR 35;
CAP 2; DLB 28, 48; MTCW

**Schwartz, Ernst**
See Ozu, Yasujiro

**Schwartz, John Burnham** 1965- . . . . **CLC 59**
See also CA 132

**Schwartz, Lynne Sharon** 1939- . . . . . **CLC 31**
See also CA 103

**Schwartz, Muriel A.**
See Eliot, T(homas) S(tearns)

**Schwarz-Bart, Andre** 1928- . . . . . . . **CLC 2, 4**
See also CA 89-92

**Schwarz-Bart, Simone** 1938- . . . . . . . . **CLC 7**
See also CA 97-100

**Schwob, (Mayer Andre) Marcel**
1867-1905 . . . . . . . . . . . . . . . . **TCLC 20**
See also CA 117; DLB 123

**Sciascia, Leonardo**
1921-1989 . . . . . . . . . . . . . **CLC 8, 9, 41**
See also CA 85-88; 130; CANR 35; MTCW

**Scoppettone, Sandra** 1936- . . . . . . . . **CLC 26**
See also CA 5-8R; SATA 9

**Scorsese, Martin** 1942- . . . . . . . . . . **CLC 20**
See also CA 110; 114

**Scotland, Jay**
See Jakes, John (William)

**Scott, Duncan Campbell**
1862-1947 . . . . . . . . . . . . . . . . . . **TCLC 6**
See also CA 104; DLB 92

**Scott, Evelyn** 1893-1963 . . . . . . . . . . **CLC 43**
See also CA 104; 112; DLB 9, 48

**Scott, F(rancis) R(eginald)**
1899-1985 . . . . . . . . . . . . . . . . . . **CLC 22**
See also CA 101; 114; DLB 88

**Scott, Frank**
See Scott, F(rancis) R(eginald)

**Scott, Joanna** 1960- . . . . . . . . . . . . . **CLC 50**
See also CA 126

**Scott, Paul (Mark)** 1920-1978 . . . . **CLC 9, 60**
See also CA 81-84; 77-80; CANR 33;
DLB 14; MTCW

**Scott, Walter** 1771-1832 . . . . . . . . **NCLC 15**
See also CDBLB 1789-1832; DLB 93, 107,
116; WLC; YABC 2

**Scribe, (Augustin) Eugene**
1791-1861 . . . . . . . . . . . . . . . . **NCLC 16**

**Scrum, R.**
See Crumb, R(obert)

**Scudery, Madeleine de** 1607-1701 . . . . . **LC 2**

**Scum**
See Crumb, R(obert)

**Scumbag, Little Bobby**
See Crumb, R(obert)

**Seabrook, John**
See Hubbard, L(afayette) Ron(ald)

**Sealy, I. Allan** 1951- . . . . . . . . . . . . **CLC 55**

**Search, Alexander**
See Pessoa, Fernando (Antonio Nogueira)

**Sebastian, Lee**
See Silverberg, Robert

**Sebastian Owl**
See Thompson, Hunter S(tockton)

**Sebestyen, Ouida** 1924- . . . . . . . . . . **CLC 30**
See also AAYA 8; CA 107; CLR 17;
MAICYA; SAAS 10; SATA 39

**Sedges, John**
See Buck, Pearl S(ydenstricker)

**Sedgwick, Catharine Maria**
1789-1867 . . . . . . . . . . . . . . . . **NCLC 19**
See also DLB 1, 74

**Seelye, John** 1931- . . . . . . . . . . . . . . . **CLC 7**

**Seferiades, Giorgos Stylianou** 1900-1971
See Seferis, George
See also CA 5-8R; 33-36R; CANR 5, 36;
MTCW

**Seferis, George** . . . . . . . . . . . . . . **CLC 5, 11**
See also Seferiades, Giorgos Stylianou

**Segal, Erich (Wolf)** 1937- . . . . . . . **CLC 3, 10**
See also BEST 89:1; CA 25-28R; CANR 20,
36; DLBY 86; MTCW

**Seger, Bob** 1945- . . . . . . . . . . . . . . . **CLC 35**

**Seghers, Anna** . . . . . . . . . . . . . . . . . . **CLC 7**
See also Radvanyi, Netty
See also DLB 69

**Seidel, Frederick (Lewis)** 1936- . . . . . **CLC 18**
See also CA 13-16R; CANR 8; DLBY 84

**Seifert, Jaroslav** 1901-1986 . . . . . **CLC 34, 44**
See also CA 127; MTCW

**Sei Shonagon** c. 966-1017(?) . . . . . . **CMLC 6**

**Selby, Hubert Jr.** 1928- . . . . . . **CLC 1, 2, 4, 8**
See also CA 13-16R; CANR 33; DLB 2

**Selzer, Richard** 1928- . . . . . . . . . . . . **CLC 74**
See also CA 65-68; CANR 14

**Sembene, Ousmane**
See Ousmane, Sembene

**Senancour, Etienne Pivert de**
1770-1846 . . . . . . . . . . . . . . . . **NCLC 16**
See also DLB 119

**Sender, Ramon (Jose)** 1902-1982 . . . . **CLC 8**
See also CA 5-8R; 105; CANR 8; HW;
MTCW

**Seneca, Lucius Annaeus**
4B.C.-65 . . . . . . . . . . . . . . . . . . **CMLC 6**

**Senghor, Leopold Sedar** 1906- . . . . . . **CLC 54**
See also BLC 3; BW; CA 116; 125; MTCW

**Serling, (Edward) Rod(man)**
1924-1975 . . . . . . . . . . . . . . . . . . **CLC 30**
See also AITN 1; CA 65-68; 57-60; DLB 26

**Serna, Ramon Gomez de la**
See Gomez de la Serna, Ramon

**Serpieres**
See Guillevic, (Eugene)

**Service, Robert**
See Service, Robert W(illiam)
See also DLB 92

**Service, Robert W(illiam)**
1874(?)-1958 . . . . . . . . . . . . . . . **TCLC 15**
See also Service, Robert
See also CA 115; SATA 20; WLC

**Seth, Vikram** 1952- . . . . . . . . . . . . . . **CLC 43**
See also CA 121; 127; DLB 120

**Seton, Cynthia Propper**
1926-1982 . . . . . . . . . . . . . . . . . . **CLC 27**
See also CA 5-8R; 108; CANR 7

**Seton, Ernest (Evan) Thompson**
1860-1946 . . . . . . . . . . . . . . . . . . **TCLC 31**
See also CA 109; DLB 92; SATA 18

**Seton-Thompson, Ernest**
See Seton, Ernest (Evan) Thompson

**Settle, Mary Lee** 1918- . . . . . . . . **CLC 19, 61**
See also CA 89-92; CAAS 1; DLB 6

**Seuphor, Michel**
See Arp, Jean

**Sevigne, Marie (de Rabutin-Chantal) Marquise
de** 1626-1696 . . . . . . . . . . . . . . . . **LC 11**

**Sexton, Anne (Harvey)**
1928-1974 . . . **CLC 2, 4, 6, 8, 10, 15, 53;
PC 2**
See also CA 1-4R; 53-56; CABS 2;
CANR 3, 36; CDALB 1941-1968; DLB 5;
MTCW; SATA 10; WLC

**Shaara, Michael (Joseph Jr.)**
1929-1988 . . . . . . . . . . . . . . . . . . **CLC 15**
See also AITN 1; CA 102; DLBY 83

**Shackleton, C. C.**
See Aldiss, Brian W(ilson)

**Shacochis, Bob** . . . . . . . . . . . . . . . . . **CLC 39**
See also Shacochis, Robert G.

**Shacochis, Robert G.** 1951-
See Shacochis, Bob
See also CA 119; 124

**Shaffer, Anthony (Joshua)** 1926- . . . . **CLC 19**
See also CA 110; 116; DLB 13

**Shaffer, Peter (Levin)**
1926- . . . . . . . . . . . **CLC 5, 14, 18, 37, 60**
See also CA 25-28R; CANR 25;
CDBLB 1960 to Present; DLB 13;
MTCW

**Shakey, Bernard**
See Young, Neil

**Shalamov, Varlam (Tikhonovich)**
1907(?)-1982 . . . . . . . . . . . . . . . . **CLC 18**
See also CA 129; 105

**Shamlu, Ahmad** 1925- . . . . . . . . . . . . **CLC 10**

**Shammas, Anton** 1951- . . . . . . . . . . . . **CLC 55**

**Shange, Ntozake**
1948- . . . . . . . . **CLC 8, 25, 38, 74; DC 3**
See also AAYA 9; BLC 3; BW; CA 85-88;
CABS 3; CANR 27; DLB 38; MTCW

**Shanley, John Patrick** 1950- . . . . . . . **CLC 75**
See also CA 128; 133

**Shapcott, Thomas William** 1935- . . . **CLC 38**
See also CA 69-72

**Shapiro, Karl (Jay)** 1913- . . **CLC 4, 8, 15, 53**
See also CA 1-4R; CAAS 6; CANR 1, 36;
DLB 48; MTCW

**Sharp, William** 1855-1905 . . . . . . . . **TCLC 39**

**Sharpe, Thomas Ridley** 1928-
See Sharpe, Tom
See also CA 114; 122

**Sharpe, Tom** . . . . . . . . . . . . . . . . . . . **CLC 36**
See also Sharpe, Thomas Ridley
See also DLB 14

**Shaw, Bernard** . . . . . . . . . . . . . . . . . **TCLC 45**
See also Shaw, George Bernard

**Shaw, G. Bernard**
See Shaw, George Bernard

**Shaw, George Bernard**
1856-1950 . . . . . . . . . . . . . **TCLC 3, 9, 21**
See also Shaw, Bernard
See also CA 104; 128; CDBLB 1914-1945;
DLB 10, 57; MTCW; WLC

**Shaw, Henry Wheeler**
1818-1885 . . . . . . . . . . . . . . . . **NCLC 15**
See also DLB 11

**Shaw, Irwin** 1913-1984 . . . . . . . **CLC 7, 23, 34**
See also AITN 1; CA 13-16R; 112;
CANR 21; CDALB 1941-1968; DLB 6,
102; DLBY 84; MTCW

**Shaw, Robert** 1927-1978 . . . . . . . . . . . **CLC 5**
See also AITN 1; CA 1-4R; 81-84;
CANR 4; DLB 13, 14

**Shaw, T. E.**
See Lawrence, T(homas) E(dward)

**Shawn, Wallace** 1943- . . . . . . . . . . . . **CLC 41**
See also CA 112

**Sheed, Wilfrid (John Joseph)**
1930- . . . . . . . . . . . . . . **CLC 2, 4, 10, 53**
See also CA 65-68; CANR 30; DLB 6;
MTCW

**Sheldon, Alice Hastings Bradley**
1915(?)-1987
See Tiptree, James Jr.
See also CA 108; 122; CANR 34; MTCW

**Sheldon, John**
See Bloch, Robert (Albert)

**Shelley, Mary Wollstonecraft (Godwin)**
1797-1851 ................ **NCLC 14**
See also CDBLB 1789-1832; DLB 110, 116;
SATA 29; WLC

**Shelley, Percy Bysshe**
1792-1822 ................. **NCLC 18**
See also CDBLB 1789-1832; DLB 96, 110;
WLC

**Shepard, Jim** 1956-............... **CLC 36**
See also CA 137

**Shepard, Lucius** 19(?)-............ **CLC 34**
See also CA 128

**Shepard, Sam**
1943-........ **CLC 4, 6, 17, 34, 41, 44**
See also AAYA 1; CA 69-72; CABS 3;
CANR 22; DLB 7; MTCW

**Shepherd, Michael**
See Ludlum, Robert

**Sherburne, Zoa (Morin)** 1912-...... **CLC 30**
See also CA 1-4R; CANR 3, 37; MAICYA;
SATA 3

**Sheridan, Frances** 1724-1766........ **LC 7**
See also DLB 39, 84

**Sheridan, Richard Brinsley**
1751-1816 ............ **NCLC 5; DC 1**
See also CDBLB 1660-1789; DLB 89; WLC

**Sherman, Jonathan Marc**.......... **CLC 55**

**Sherman, Martin** 1941(?)-......... **CLC 19**
See also CA 116; 123

**Sherwin, Judith Johnson** 1936-... **CLC 7, 15**
See also CA 25-28R; CANR 34

**Sherwood, Robert E(mmet)**
1896-1955 ................. **TCLC 3**
See also CA 104; DLB 7, 26

**Shiel, M(atthew) P(hipps)**
1865-1947 ................. **TCLC 8**
See also CA 106

**Shiga, Naoya** 1883-1971........... **CLC 33**
See also CA 101; 33-36R

**Shimazaki Haruki** 1872-1943
See Shimazaki Toson
See also CA 105; 134

**Shimazaki Toson**................. **TCLC 5**
See also Shimazaki Haruki

**Sholokhov, Mikhail (Aleksandrovich)**
1905-1984 ................. **CLC 7, 15**
See also CA 101; 112; MTCW; SATA 36

**Shone, Patric**
See Hanley, James

**Shreve, Susan Richards** 1939-...... **CLC 23**
See also CA 49-52; CAAS 5; CANR 5, 38;
MAICYA; SATA 41, 46

**Shue, Larry** 1946-1985........... **CLC 52**
See also CA 117

**Shu-Jen, Chou** 1881-1936
See Hsun, Lu
See also CA 104

**Shulman, Alix Kates** 1932-...... **CLC 2, 10**
See also CA 29-32R; SATA 7

**Shuster, Joe** 1914-............... **CLC 21**

**Shute, Nevil**.................... **CLC 30**
See also Norway, Nevil Shute

**Shuttle, Penelope (Diane)** 1947-..... **CLC 7**
See also CA 93-96; CANR 39; DLB 14, 40

**Sidney, Mary** 1561-1621 .......... **LC 19**

**Sidney, Sir Philip** 1554-1586....... **LC 19**
See also CDBLB Before 1660

**Siegel, Jerome** 1914-............. **CLC 21**
See also CA 116

**Siegel, Jerry**
See Siegel, Jerome

**Sienkiewicz, Henryk (Adam Alexander Pius)**
1846-1916 ................. **TCLC 3**
See also CA 104; 134

**Sierra, Gregorio Martinez**
See Martinez Sierra, Gregorio

**Sierra, Maria (de la O'LeJarraga) Martinez**
See Martinez Sierra, Maria (de la
O'LeJarraga)

**Sigal, Clancy** 1926-................ **CLC 7**
See also CA 1-4R

**Sigourney, Lydia Howard (Huntley)**
1791-1865 ................. **NCLC 21**
See also DLB 1, 42, 73

**Siguenza y Gongora, Carlos de**
1645-1700 ................... **LC 8**

**Sigurjonsson, Johann** 1880-1919... **TCLC 27**

**Sikelianos, Angelos** 1884-1951 .... **TCLC 39**

**Silkin, Jon** 1930-............ **CLC 2, 6, 43**
See also CA 5-8R; CAAS 5; DLB 27

**Silko, Leslie Marmon** 1948-.... **CLC 23, 74**
See also CA 115; 122

**Sillanpaa, Frans Eemil** 1888-1964... **CLC 19**
See also CA 129; 93-96; MTCW

**Sillitoe, Alan**
1928-.......... **CLC 1, 3, 6, 10, 19, 57**
See also AITN 1; CA 9-12R; CAAS 2;
CANR 8, 26; CDBLB 1960 to Present;
DLB 14; MTCW; SATA 61

**Silone, Ignazio** 1900-1978 ......... **CLC 4**
See also CA 25-28; 81-84; CANR 34;
CAP 2; MTCW

**Silver, Joan Micklin** 1935- ........ **CLC 20**
See also CA 114; 121

**Silverberg, Robert** 1935- .......... **CLC 7**
See also CA 1-4R; CAAS 3; CANR 1, 20,
36; DLB 8; MAICYA; MTCW; SATA 13

**Silverstein, Alvin** 1933-........... **CLC 17**
See also CA 49-52; CANR 2; CLR 25;
MAICYA; SATA 8, 69

**Silverstein, Virginia B(arbara Opshelor)**
1937-...................... **CLC 17**
See also CA 49-52; CANR 2; CLR 25;
MAICYA; SATA 8, 69

**Sim, Georges**
See Simenon, Georges (Jacques Christian)

**Simak, Clifford D(onald)**
1904-1988 ................ **CLC 1, 55**
See also CA 1-4R; 125; CANR 1, 35;
DLB 8; MTCW; SATA 56

**Simenon, Georges (Jacques Christian)**
1903-1989 ... **CLC 1, 2, 3, 8, 18, 47**
See also CA 85-88; 129; CANR 35;
DLB 72; DLBY 89; MTCW

**Simic, Charles** 1938-... **CLC 6, 9, 22, 49, 68**
See also CA 29-32R; CAAS 4; CANR 12,
33; DLB 105

**Simmons, Charles (Paul)** 1924-..... **CLC 57**
See also CA 89-92

**Simmons, Dan** 1948-.............. **CLC 44**
See also CA 138

**Simmons, James (Stewart Alexander)**
1933-...................... **CLC 43**
See also CA 105; DLB 40

**Simms, William Gilmore**
1806-1870 ................. **NCLC 3**
See also DLB 3, 30, 59, 73

**Simon, Carly** 1945-............... **CLC 26**
See also CA 105

**Simon, Claude** 1913-....... **CLC 4, 9, 15, 39**
See also CA 89-92; CANR 33; DLB 83;
MTCW

**Simon, (Marvin) Neil**
1927-.......... **CLC 6, 11, 31, 39, 70**
See also AITN 1; CA 21-24R; CANR 26;
DLB 7; MTCW

**Simon, Paul** 1942(?)-............. **CLC 17**
See also CA 116

**Simonon, Paul** 1956(?)-........... **CLC 30**
See also The Clash

**Simpson, Harriette**
See Arnow, Harriette (Louisa) Simpson

**Simpson, Louis (Aston Marantz)**
1923-................ **CLC 4, 7, 9, 32**
See also CA 1-4R; CAAS 4; CANR 1;
DLB 5; MTCW

**Simpson, Mona (Elizabeth)** 1957-... **CLC 44**
See also CA 122; 135

**Simpson, N(orman) F(rederick)**
1919-...................... **CLC 29**
See also CA 13-16R; DLB 13

**Sinclair, Andrew (Annandale)**
1935-...................... **CLC 2, 14**
See also CA 9-12R; CAAS 5; CANR 14, 38;
DLB 14; MTCW

**Sinclair, Emil**
See Hesse, Hermann

**Sinclair, Mary Amelia St. Clair** 1865(?)-1946
See Sinclair, May
See also CA 104

**Sinclair, May**.................. **TCLC 3, 11**
See also Sinclair, Mary Amelia St. Clair
See also DLB 36

**Sinclair, Upton (Beall)**
1878-1968 .......... **CLC 1, 11, 15, 63**
See also CA 5-8R; 25-28R; CANR 7;
CDALB 1929-1941; DLB 9; MTCW;
SATA 9; WLC

**Singer, Isaac**
See Singer, Isaac Bashevis

Stewart, J(ohn) I(nnes) M(ackintosh)
1906- ................. CLC **7, 14, 32**
See also CA 85-88; CAAS 3; MTCW

Stewart, Mary (Florence Elinor)
1916- .................... CLC **7, 35**
See also CA 1-4R; CANR 1; SATA 12

Stewart, Mary Rainbow
See Stewart, Mary (Florence Elinor)

Still, James 1906-................ CLC **49**
See also CA 65-68; CANR 10, 26; DLB 9;
SATA 29

Sting
See Sumner, Gordon Matthew

Stirling, Arthur
See Sinclair, Upton (Beall)

Stitt, Milan 1941-................ CLC **29**
See also CA 69-72

Stockton, Francis Richard 1834-1902
See Stockton, Frank R.
See also CA 108; 137; MAICYA; SATA 44

Stockton, Frank R. ................ TCLC **47**
See also Stockton, Francis Richard
See also DLB 42, 74; SATA 32

Stoddard, Charles
See Kuttner, Henry

Stoker, Abraham 1847-1912
See Stoker, Bram
See also CA 105; SATA 29

Stoker, Bram ..................... TCLC **8**
See also Stoker, Abraham
See also CDBLB 1890-1914; DLB 36, 70;
WLC

Stolz, Mary (Slattery) 1920-....... CLC **12**
See also AAYA 8; AITN 1; CA 5-8R;
CANR 13; MAICYA; SAAS 3;
SATA 10, 70, 71

Stone, Irving 1903-1989............ CLC **7**
See also AITN 1; CA 1-4R; 129; CAAS 3;
CANR 1, 23; MTCW; SATA 3; SATO 64

Stone, Oliver 1946-............... CLC **73**
See also CA 110

Stone, Robert (Anthony)
1937- .................. CLC **5, 23, 42**
See also CA 85-88; CANR 23; MTCW

Stone, Zachary
See Follett, Ken(neth Martin)

Stoppard, Tom
1937- ... CLC **1, 3, 4, 5, 8, 15, 29, 34, 63**
See also CA 81-84; CANR 39;
CDBLB 1960 to Present; DLB 13;
DLBY 85; MTCW; WLC

Storey, David (Malcolm)
1933- ................. CLC **2, 4, 5, 8**
See also CA 81-84; CANR 36; DLB 13, 14;
MTCW

Storm, Hyemeyohsts 1935-......... CLC **3**
See also CA 81-84

Storm, (Hans) Theodor (Woldsen)
1817-1888 ................. NCLC **1**

Storni, Alfonsina 1892-1938 ....... TCLC **5**
See also CA 104; 131; HW

Stout, Rex (Todhunter) 1886-1975 ... CLC **3**
See also AITN 2; CA 61-64

Stow, (Julian) Randolph 1935- .. CLC **23, 48**
See also CA 13-16R; CANR 33; MTCW

Stowe, Harriet (Elizabeth) Beecher
1811-1896 ................. NCLC **3**
See also CDALB 1865-1917; DLB 1, 12, 42,
74; MAICYA; WLC; YABC 1

Strachey, (Giles) Lytton
1880-1932 ................. TCLC **12**
See also CA 110; DLBD 10

Strand, Mark 1934- ...... CLC **6, 18, 41, 71**
See also CA 21-24R; DLB 5; SATA 41

Straub, Peter (Francis) 1943- ...... CLC **28**
See also BEST 89:1; CA 85-88; CANR 28;
DLBY 84; MTCW

Strauss, Botho 1944- ............. CLC **22**

Streatfeild, (Mary) Noel
1895(?)-1986 ................. CLC **21**
See also CA 81-84; 120; CANR 31;
CLR 17; MAICYA; SATA 20, 48

Stribling, T(homas) S(igismund)
1881-1965 ................. CLC **23**
See also CA 107; DLB 9

Strindberg, (Johan) August
1849-1912 .......... TCLC **1, 8, 21, 47**
See also CA 104; 135; WLC

Stringer, Arthur 1874-1950 ....... TCLC **37**
See also DLB 92

Stringer, David
See Roberts, Keith (John Kingston)

Strugatskii, Arkadii (Natanovich)
1925-1991 ................. CLC **27**
See also CA 106; 135

Strugatskii, Boris (Natanovich)
1933- ..................... CLC **27**
See also CA 106

Strummer, Joe 1953(?)- ........... CLC **30**
See also The Clash

Stuart, Don A.
See Campbell, John W(ood Jr.)

Stuart, Ian
See MacLean, Alistair (Stuart)

Stuart, Jesse (Hilton)
1906-1984 ........ CLC **1, 8, 11, 14, 34**
See also CA 5-8R; 112; CANR 31; DLB 9,
48, 102; DLBY 84; SATA 2, 36

Sturgeon, Theodore (Hamilton)
1918-1985 ................ CLC **22, 39**
See also Queen, Ellery
See also CA 81-84; 116; CANR 32; DLB 8;
DLBY 85; MTCW

Sturges, Preston 1898-1959 ....... TCLC **48**
See also CA 114; DLB 26

Styron, William
1925- .......... CLC **1, 3, 5, 11, 15, 60**
See also BEST 90:4; CA 5-8R; CANR 6, 33;
CDALB 1968-1988; DLB 2; DLBY 80;
MTCW

Suarez Lynch, B.
See Bioy Casares, Adolfo; Borges, Jorge
Luis

Suarez Lynch, B.
See Borges, Jorge Luis

Su Chien 1884-1918
See Su Man-shu
See also CA 123

Sudermann, Hermann 1857-1928 .. TCLC **15**
See also CA 107; DLB 118

Sue, Eugene 1804-1857 .......... NCLC **1**
See also DLB 119

Sueskind, Patrick 1949-.......... CLC **44**

Sukenick, Ronald 1932-..... CLC **3, 4, 6, 48**
See also CA 25-28R; CAAS 8; CANR 32;
DLBY 81

Suknaski, Andrew 1942- .......... CLC **19**
See also CA 101; DLB 53

Sullivan, Vernon
See Vian, Boris

Sully Prudhomme 1839-1907 ...... TCLC **31**

Su Man-shu .................... TCLC **24**
See also Su Chien

Summerforest, Ivy B.
See Kirkup, James

Summers, Andrew James 1942-..... CLC **26**
See also The Police

Summers, Andy
See Summers, Andrew James

Summers, Hollis (Spurgeon Jr.)
1916- ...................... CLC **10**
See also CA 5-8R; CANR 3; DLB 6

Summers, (Alphonsus Joseph-Mary Augustus)
Montague 1880-1948........ TCLC **16**
See also CA 118

Sumner, Gordon Matthew 1951-.... CLC **26**
See also The Police

Surtees, Robert Smith
1803-1864 ................. NCLC **14**
See also DLB 21

Susann, Jacqueline 1921-1974....... CLC **3**
See also AITN 1; CA 65-68; 53-56; MTCW

Suskind, Patrick
See Sueskind, Patrick

Sutcliff, Rosemary 1920-.......... CLC **26**
See also CA 5-8R; CANR 37; CLR 1;
MAICYA; SATA 6, 44

Sutro, Alfred 1863-1933........... TCLC **6**
See also CA 105; DLB 10

Sutton, Henry
See Slavitt, David R.

Svevo, Italo ................... TCLC **2, 35**
See also Schmitz, Aron Hector

Swados, Elizabeth 1951- ......... CLC **12**
See also CA 97-100

Swados, Harvey 1920-1972 ........ CLC **5**
See also CA 5-8R; 37-40R; CANR 6;
DLB 2

Swan, Gladys 1934- .............. CLC **69**
See also CA 101; CANR 17, 39

Swarthout, Glendon (Fred) 1918- ... CLC **35**
See also CA 1-4R; CANR 1; SATA 26

Sweet, Sarah C.
See Jewett, (Theodora) Sarah Orne

Swenson, May 1919-1989..... CLC **4, 14, 61**
See also CA 5-8R; 130; CANR 36; DLB 5;
MTCW; SATA 15

Swift, Augustus
See Lovecraft, H(oward) P(hillips)

Swift, Graham 1949- ............. CLC **41**
See also CA 117; 122

**Swift, Jonathan** 1667-1745 . . . . . . . . . . **LC 1**
See also CDBLB 1660-1789; DLB 39, 95,
101; SATA 19; WLC

**Swinburne, Algernon Charles**
1837-1909 . . . . . . . . . . . . . . **TCLC 8, 36**
See also CA 105; CDBLB 1832-1890;
DLB 35, 57; WLC

**Swinfen, Ann** . . . . . . . . . . . . . . . . . . . . **CLC 34**

**Swinnerton, Frank Arthur**
1884-1982 . . . . . . . . . . . . . . . . . . **CLC 31**
See also CA 108; DLB 34

**Swithen, John**
See King, Stephen (Edwin)

**Sylvia**
See Ashton-Warner, Sylvia (Constance)

**Symmes, Robert Edward**
See Duncan, Robert (Edward)

**Symonds, John Addington**
1840-1893 . . . . . . . . . . . . . . . . **NCLC 34**
See also DLB 57

**Symons, Arthur** 1865-1945 . . . . . . . **TCLC 11**
See also CA 107; DLB 19, 57

**Symons, Julian (Gustave)**
1912- . . . . . . . . . . . . . . . . . **CLC 2, 14, 32**
See also CA 49-52; CAAS 3; CANR 3, 33;
DLB 87; MTCW

**Synge, (Edmund) J(ohn) M(illington)**
1871-1909 . . . . . . . . . . **TCLC 6, 37; DC 2**
See also CA 104; CDBLB 1890-1914;
DLB 10, 19

**Syruc, J.**
See Milosz, Czeslaw

**Szirtes, George** 1948- . . . . . . . . . . . . **CLC 46**
See also CA 109; CANR 27

**Tabori, George** 1914- . . . . . . . . . . . . **CLC 19**
See also CA 49-52; CANR 4

**Tagore, Rabindranath** 1861-1941 . . . . **TCLC 3**
See also CA 104; 120; MTCW

**Taine, Hippolyte Adolphe**
1828-1893 . . . . . . . . . . . . . . . . **NCLC 15**

**Talese, Gay** 1932- . . . . . . . . . . . . . . . **CLC 37**
See also AITN 1; CA 1-4R; CANR 9;
MTCW

**Tallent, Elizabeth (Ann)** 1954- . . . . . **CLC 45**
See also CA 117

**Tally, Ted** 1952- . . . . . . . . . . . . . . . . **CLC 42**
See also CA 120; 124

**Tamayo y Baus, Manuel**
1829-1898 . . . . . . . . . . . . . . . . . **NCLC 1**

**Tammsaare, A(nton) H(ansen)**
1878-1940 . . . . . . . . . . . . . . . . **TCLC 27**

**Tan, Amy** 1952- . . . . . . . . . . . . . . . . . **CLC 59**
See also AAYA 9; BEST 89:3; CA 136

**Tandem, Felix**
See Spitteler, Carl (Friedrich Georg)

**Tanizaki, Jun'ichiro**
1886-1965 . . . . . . . . . . . . . . **CLC 8, 14, 28**
See also CA 93-96; 25-28R

**Tanner, William**
See Amis, Kingsley (William)

**Tao Lao**
See Storni, Alfonsina

**Tarassoff, Lev**
See Troyat, Henri

**Tarbell, Ida M(inerva)**
1857-1944 . . . . . . . . . . . . . . . . . **TCLC 40**
See also CA 122; DLB 47

**Tarkington, (Newton) Booth**
1869-1946 . . . . . . . . . . . . . . . . . . **TCLC 9**
See also CA 110; DLB 9, 102; SATA 17

**Tarkovsky, Andrei (Arsenyevich)**
1932-1986 . . . . . . . . . . . . . . . . . . **CLC 75**
See also CA 127

**Tasso, Torquato** 1544-1595 . . . . . . . . . . **LC 5**

**Tate, (John Orley) Allen**
1899-1979 . . . . **CLC 2, 4, 6, 9, 11, 14, 24**
See also CA 5-8R; 85-88; CANR 32;
DLB 4, 45, 63; MTCW

**Tate, Ellalice**
See Hibbert, Eleanor Burford

**Tate, James (Vincent)** 1943- . . . **CLC 2, 6, 25**
See also CA 21-24R; CANR 29; DLB 5

**Tavel, Ronald** 1940- . . . . . . . . . . . . . . . **CLC 6**
See also CA 21-24R; CANR 33

**Taylor, Cecil Philip** 1929-1981 . . . . . **CLC 27**
See also CA 25-28R; 105

**Taylor, Edward** 1642(?)-1729 . . . . . . . **LC 11**
See also DLB 24

**Taylor, Eleanor Ross** 1920- . . . . . . . . **CLC 5**
See also CA 81-84

**Taylor, Elizabeth** 1912-1975 . . . **CLC 2, 4, 29**
See also CA 13-16R; CANR 9; MTCW;
SATA 13

**Taylor, Henry (Splawn)** 1942- . . . . . . **CLC 44**
See also CA 33-36R; CAAS 7; CANR 31;
DLB 5

**Taylor, Kamala (Purnaiya)** 1924-
See Markandaya, Kamala
See also CA 77-80

**Taylor, Mildred D.** . . . . . . . . . . . . . . . **CLC 21**
See also BW; CA 85-88; CANR 25; CLR 9;
DLB 52; MAICYA; SAAS 5; SATA 15,
70

**Taylor, Peter (Hillsman)**
1917- . . . . . **CLC 1, 4, 18, 37, 44, 50, 71;**
**SSC 10**
See also CA 13-16R; CANR 9; DLBY 81;
MTCW

**Taylor, Robert Lewis** 1912- . . . . . . . . **CLC 14**
See also CA 1-4R; CANR 3; SATA 10

**Tchekhov, Anton**
See Chekhov, Anton (Pavlovich)

**Teasdale, Sara** 1884-1933 . . . . . . . . . **TCLC 4**
See also CA 104; DLB 45; SATA 32

**Tegner, Esaias** 1782-1846 . . . . . . . . **NCLC 2**

**Teilhard de Chardin, (Marie Joseph) Pierre**
1881-1955 . . . . . . . . . . . . . . . . . . **TCLC 9**
See also CA 105

**Temple, Ann**
See Mortimer, Penelope (Ruth)

**Tennant, Emma (Christina)**
1937- . . . . . . . . . . . . . . . . . **CLC 13, 52**
See also CA 65-68; CAAS 9; CANR 10, 38;
DLB 14

**Tenneshaw, S. M.**
See Silverberg, Robert

**Tennyson, Alfred**
1809-1892 . . . . . . . . . . . **NCLC 30; PC 6**
See also CDBLB 1832-1890; DLB 32; WLC

**Teran, Lisa St. Aubin de** . . . . . . . . . . **CLC 36**
See also St. Aubin de Teran, Lisa

**Teresa de Jesus, St.** 1515-1582 . . . . . . **LC 18**

**Terkel, Louis** 1912-
See Terkel, Studs
See also CA 57-60; CANR 18; MTCW

**Terkel, Studs** . . . . . . . . . . . . . . . . . . . **CLC 38**
See also Terkel, Louis
See also AITN 1

**Terry, C. V.**
See Slaughter, Frank G(ill)

**Terry, Megan** 1932- . . . . . . . . . . . . . . **CLC 19**
See also CA 77-80; CABS 3; DLB 7

**Tertz, Abram**
See Sinyavsky, Andrei (Donatevich)

**Tesich, Steve** 1943(?)- . . . . . . . . . **CLC 40, 69**
See also CA 105; DLBY 83

**Teternikov, Fyodor Kuzmich** 1863-1927
See Sologub, Fyodor
See also CA 104

**Tevis, Walter** 1928-1984 . . . . . . . . . . **CLC 42**
See also CA 113

**Tey, Josephine** . . . . . . . . . . . . . . . . . . **TCLC 14**
See also Mackintosh, Elizabeth
See also DLB 77

**Thackeray, William Makepeace**
1811-1863 . . . . . . . . . . . **NCLC 5, 14, 22**
See also CDBLB 1832-1890; DLB 21, 55;
SATA 23; WLC

**Thakura, Ravindranatha**
See Tagore, Rabindranath

**Tharoor, Shashi** 1956- . . . . . . . . . . . **CLC 70**

**Thelwell, Michael Miles** 1939- . . . . . **CLC 22**
See also CA 101

**Theobald, Lewis Jr.**
See Lovecraft, H(oward) P(hillips)

**The Prophet**
See Dreiser, Theodore (Herman Albert)

**Theroux, Alexander (Louis)**
1939- . . . . . . . . . . . . . . . . . . . . **CLC 2, 25**
See also CA 85-88; CANR 20

**Theroux, Paul (Edward)**
1941- . . . . . . . . . **CLC 5, 8, 11, 15, 28, 46**
See also BEST 89:4; CA 33-36R; CANR 20;
DLB 2; MTCW; SATA 44

**Thesen, Sharon** 1946- . . . . . . . . . . . . **CLC 56**

**Thevenin, Denis**
See Duhamel, Georges

**Thibault, Jacques Anatole Francois**
1844-1924
See France, Anatole
See also CA 106; 127; MTCW

**Thiele, Colin (Milton)** 1920- . . . . . . . **CLC 17**
See also CA 29-32R; CANR 12, 28;
CLR 27; MAICYA; SAAS 2; SATA 14

**Thomas, Audrey (Callahan)**
1935- . . . . . . . . . . . . . . . . . **CLC 7, 13, 37**
See also AITN 2; CA 21-24R; CANR 36;
DLB 60; MTCW

Thomas, D(onald) M(ichael)
1935- . . . . . . . . . . . . . . CLC 13, 22, 31
See also CA 61-64; CAAS 11; CANR 17;
CDBLB 1960 to Present; DLB 40;
MTCW

Thomas, Dylan (Marlais)
1914-1953 . . . . . . . TCLC 1, 8, 45; PC 2;
SSC 3
See also CA 104; 120; CDBLB 1945-1960;
DLB 13, 20; MTCW; SATA 60; WLC

Thomas, (Philip) Edward
1878-1917 . . . . . . . . . . . . . . . . . TCLC 10
See also CA 106; DLB 19

Thomas, Joyce Carol   1938- . . . . . . . . CLC 35
See also BW; CA 113; 116; CLR 19;
DLB 33; MAICYA; MTCW; SAAS 7;
SATA 40

Thomas, Lewis   1913- . . . . . . . . . . . . . CLC 35
See also CA 85-88; CANR 38; MTCW

Thomas, Paul
See Mann, (Paul) Thomas

Thomas, Piri   1928- . . . . . . . . . . . . . . CLC 17
See also CA 73-76; HW

Thomas, R(onald) S(tuart)
1913- . . . . . . . . . . . . . . . . CLC 6, 13, 48
See also CA 89-92; CAAS 4; CANR 30;
CDBLB 1960 to Present; DLB 27;
MTCW

Thomas, Ross (Elmore)   1926- . . . . . . CLC 39
See also CA 33-36R; CANR 22

Thompson, Francis Clegg
See Mencken, H(enry) L(ouis)

Thompson, Francis Joseph
1859-1907 . . . . . . . . . . . . . . . . . . TCLC 4
See also CA 104; CDBLB 1890-1914;
DLB 19

Thompson, Hunter S(tockton)
1939- . . . . . . . . . . . . . . . . CLC 9, 17, 40
See also BEST 89:1; CA 17-20R; CANR 23;
MTCW

Thompson, Jim   1906-1976 . . . . . . . . CLC 69

Thompson, Judith . . . . . . . . . . . . . . . CLC 39

Thomson, James   1700-1748 . . . . . . . . LC 16

Thomson, James   1834-1882 . . . . . . NCLC 18

Thoreau, Henry David
1817-1862 . . . . . . . . . . . . . . NCLC 7, 21
See also CDALB 1640-1865; DLB 1; WLC

Thornton, Hall
See Silverberg, Robert

Thurber, James (Grover)
1894-1961 . . . . . . . CLC 5, 11, 25; SSC 1
See also CA 73-76; CANR 17, 39;
CDALB 1929-1941; DLB 4, 11, 22, 102;
MAICYA; MTCW; SATA 13

Thurman, Wallace (Henry)
1902-1934 . . . . . . . . . . . . . . . . . TCLC 6
See also BLC 3; BW; CA 104; 124; DLB 51

Ticheburn, Cheviot
See Ainsworth, William Harrison

Tieck, (Johann) Ludwig
1773-1853 . . . . . . . . . . . . . . . . . NCLC 5
See also DLB 90

Tiger, Derry
See Ellison, Harlan

Tilghman, Christopher   1948(?)- . . . . . CLC 65

Tillinghast, Richard (Williford)
1940- . . . . . . . . . . . . . . . . . . . . . CLC 29
See also CA 29-32R; CANR 26

Timrod, Henry   1828-1867 . . . . . . NCLC 25
See also DLB 3

Tindall, Gillian   1938- . . . . . . . . . . . . CLC 7
See also CA 21-24R; CANR 11

Tiptree, James Jr. . . . . . . . . . . . . . CLC 48, 50
See also Sheldon, Alice Hastings Bradley
See also DLB 8

Titmarsh, Michael Angelo
See Thackeray, William Makepeace

Tocqueville, Alexis (Charles Henri Maurice
Clerel Comte)   1805-1859 . . . . . NCLC 7

Tolkien, J(ohn) R(onald) R(euel)
1892-1973 . . . . . . . CLC 1, 2, 3, 8, 12, 38
See also AITN 1; CA 17-18; 45-48;
CANR 36; CAP 2; CDBLB 1914-1945;
DLB 15; MAICYA; MTCW; SATA 2,
24, 32; WLC

Toller, Ernst   1893-1939 . . . . . . . . . TCLC 10
See also CA 107

Tolson, M. B.
See Tolson, Melvin B(eaunorus)

Tolson, Melvin B(eaunorus)
1898(?)-1966 . . . . . . . . . . . . . . . CLC 36
See also BLC 3; BW; CA 124; 89-92;
DLB 48, 76

Tolstoi, Aleksei Nikolaevich
See Tolstoy, Alexey Nikolaevich

Tolstoy, Alexey Nikolaevich
1882-1945 . . . . . . . . . . . . . . . . . TCLC 18
See also CA 107

Tolstoy, Count Leo
See Tolstoy, Leo (Nikolaevich)

Tolstoy, Leo (Nikolaevich)
1828-1910 . . . . . TCLC 4, 11, 17, 28, 44;
SSC 9
See also CA 104; 123; SATA 26; WLC

Tomasi di Lampedusa, Giuseppe   1896-1957
See Lampedusa, Giuseppe (Tomasi) di
See also CA 111

Tomlin, Lily . . . . . . . . . . . . . . . . . . . CLC 17
See also Tomlin, Mary Jean

Tomlin, Mary Jean   1939(?)-
See Tomlin, Lily
See also CA 117

Tomlinson, (Alfred) Charles
1927- . . . . . . . . . . . CLC 2, 4, 6, 13, 45
See also CA 5-8R; CANR 33; DLB 40

Tonson, Jacob
See Bennett, (Enoch) Arnold

Toole, John Kennedy
1937-1969 . . . . . . . . . . . . . . . CLC 19, 64
See also CA 104; DLBY 81

Toomer, Jean
1894-1967 . . . . . CLC 1, 4, 13, 22; SSC 1
See also BLC 3; BW; CA 85-88;
CDALB 1917-1929; DLB 45, 51; MTCW

Torley, Luke
See Blish, James (Benjamin)

Tornimparte, Alessandra
See Ginzburg, Natalia

Torre, Raoul della
See Mencken, H(enry) L(ouis)

Torrey, E(dwin) Fuller   1937- . . . . . . CLC 34
See also CA 119

Torsvan, Ben Traven
See Traven, B.

Torsvan, Benno Traven
See Traven, B.

Torsvan, Berick Traven
See Traven, B.

Torsvan, Berwick Traven
See Traven, B.

Torsvan, Bruno Traven
See Traven, B.

Torsvan, Traven
See Traven, B.

Tournier, Michel (Edouard)
1924- . . . . . . . . . . . . . . . . CLC 6, 23, 36
See also CA 49-52; CANR 3, 36; DLB 83;
MTCW; SATA 23

Tournimparte, Alessandra
See Ginzburg, Natalia

Towers, Ivar
See Kornbluth, C(yril) M.

Townsend, Sue   1946- . . . . . . . . . . . . CLC 61
See also CA 119; 127; MTCW; SATA 48,
55

Townshend, Peter (Dennis Blandford)
1945- . . . . . . . . . . . . . . . . . . . CLC 17, 42
See also CA 107

Tozzi, Federigo   1883-1920 . . . . . . . . TCLC 31

Traill, Catharine Parr
1802-1899 . . . . . . . . . . . . . . . . . NCLC 31
See also DLB 99

Trakl, Georg   1887-1914 . . . . . . . . . . TCLC 5
See also CA 104

Transtroemer, Tomas (Goesta)
1931- . . . . . . . . . . . . . . . . . . . CLC 52, 65
See also CA 117; 129

Transtromer, Tomas Gosta
See Transtroemer, Tomas (Goesta)

Traven, B.   (?)-1969 . . . . . . . . . . . . . CLC 8, 11
See also CA 19-20; 25-28R; CAP 2; DLB 9,
56; MTCW

Treitel, Jonathan   1959- . . . . . . . . . . . CLC 70

Tremain, Rose   1943- . . . . . . . . . . . . . CLC 42
See also CA 97-100; DLB 14

Tremblay, Michel   1942- . . . . . . . . . . . CLC 29
See also CA 116; 128; DLB 60; MTCW

Trevanian (a pseudonym)   1930(?)- . . . CLC 29
See also CA 108

Trevor, Glen
See Hilton, James

Trevor, William
1928- . . . . . . . . . . . CLC 7, 9, 14, 25, 71
See also Cox, William Trevor
See also DLB 14

Trifonov, Yuri (Valentinovich)
1925-1981 . . . . . . . . . . . . . . . . . CLC 45
See also CA 126; 103; MTCW

Trilling, Lionel   1905-1975 . . . . . CLC 9, 11, 24
See also CA 9-12R; 61-64; CANR 10;
DLB 28, 63; MTCW

Trimball, W. H.
See Mencken, H(enry) L(ouis)

**Tristan**
See Gomez de la Serna, Ramon

**Tristram**
See Housman, A(lfred) E(dward)

**Trogdon, William (Lewis)** 1939-
See Heat-Moon, William Least
See also CA 115; 119

**Trollope, Anthony** 1815-1882 .. **NCLC 6, 33**
See also CDBLB 1832-1890; DLB 21, 57;
SATA 22; WLC

**Trollope, Frances** 1779-1863 ..... **NCLC 30**
See also DLB 21

**Trotsky, Leon** 1879-1940 ........ **TCLC 22**
See also CA 118

**Trotter (Cockburn), Catharine**
1679-1749 ..................... **LC 8**
See also DLB 84

**Trout, Kilgore**
See Farmer, Philip Jose

**Trow, George W. S.** 1943- ........ **CLC 52**
See also CA 126

**Troyat, Henri** 1911- .............. **CLC 23**
See also CA 45-48; CANR 2, 33; MTCW

**Trudeau, G(arretson) B(eekman)** 1948-
See Trudeau, Garry B.
See also CA 81-84; CANR 31; SATA 35

**Trudeau, Garry B.** ................. **CLC 12**
See also Trudeau, G(arretson) B(eekman)
See also AITN 2

**Truffaut, Francois** 1932-1984 ...... **CLC 20**
See also CA 81-84; 113; CANR 34

**Trumbo, Dalton** 1905-1976 ........ **CLC 19**
See also CA 21-24R; 69-72; CANR 10;
DLB 26

**Trumbull, John** 1750-1831 ...... **NCLC 30**
See also DLB 31

**Trundlett, Helen B.**
See Eliot, T(homas) S(tearns)

**Tryon, Thomas** 1926-1991 ....... **CLC 3, 11**
See also AITN 1; CA 29-32R; 135;
CANR 32; MTCW

**Tryon, Tom**
See Tryon, Thomas

**Ts'ao Hsueh-ch'in** 1715(?)-1763 ...... **LC 1**

**Tsushima, Shuji** 1909-1948
See Dazai, Osamu
See also CA 107

**Tsvetaeva (Efron), Marina (Ivanovna)**
1892-1941 ................ **TCLC 7, 35**
See also CA 104; 128; MTCW

**Tuck, Lily** 1938- ................. **CLC 70**

**Tunis, John R(oberts)** 1889-1975 ... **CLC 12**
See also CA 61-64; DLB 22; MAICYA;
SATA 30, 37

**Tuohy, Frank** ..................... **CLC 37**
See also Tuohy, John Francis
See also DLB 14

**Tuohy, John Francis** 1925-
See Tuohy, Frank
See also CA 5-8R; CANR 3

**Turco, Lewis (Putnam)** 1934- ... **CLC 11, 63**
See also CA 13-16R; CANR 24; DLBY 84

**Turgenev, Ivan**
1818-1883 .......... **NCLC 21; SSC 7**
See also WLC

**Turner, Frederick** 1943- ........... **CLC 48**
See also CA 73-76; CAAS 10; CANR 12,
30; DLB 40

**Tusan, Stan** 1936- ............... **CLC 22**
See also CA 105

**Tutuola, Amos** 1920- ........ **CLC 5, 14, 29**
See also BLC 3; BW; CA 9-12R; CANR 27;
MTCW

**Twain, Mark**
............ **TCLC 6, 12, 19, 36, 48; SSC 6**
See also Clemens, Samuel Langhorne
See also DLB 11, 12, 23, 64, 74; WLC

**Tyler, Anne**
1941- ........ **CLC 7, 11, 18, 28, 44, 59**
See also BEST 89:1; CA 9-12R; CANR 11,
33; DLB 6; DLBY 82; MTCW; SATA 7

**Tyler, Royall** 1757-1826 .......... **NCLC 3**
See also DLB 37

**Tynan, Katharine** 1861-1931 ...... **TCLC 3**
See also CA 104

**Tytell, John** 1939- ............... **CLC 50**
See also CA 29-32R

**Tyutchev, Fyodor** 1803-1873 ..... **NCLC 34**

**Tzara, Tristan** ................... **CLC 47**
See also Rosenfeld, Samuel

**Uhry, Alfred** 1936- .............. **CLC 55**
See also CA 127; 133

**Ulf, Haerved**
See Strindberg, (Johan) August

**Ulf, Harved**
See Strindberg, (Johan) August

**Unamuno (y Jugo), Miguel de**
1864-1936 ......... **TCLC 2, 9; SSC 11**
See also CA 104; 131; DLB 108; HW;
MTCW

**Undercliffe, Errol**
See Campbell, (John) Ramsey

**Underwood, Miles**
See Glassco, John

**Undset, Sigrid** 1882-1949 ......... **TCLC 3**
See also CA 104; 129; MTCW; WLC

**Ungaretti, Giuseppe**
1888-1970 ............ **CLC 7, 11, 15**
See also CA 19-20; 25-28R; CAP 2;
DLB 114

**Unger, Douglas** 1952- ............ **CLC 34**
See also CA 130

**Updike, John (Hoyer)**
1932- ...... **CLC 1, 2, 3, 5, 7, 9, 13, 15,
23, 34, 43, 70**
See also CA 1-4R; CABS 1; CANR 4, 33;
CDALB 1968-1988; DLB 2, 5; DLBD 3;
DLBY 80, 82; MTCW; WLC

**Upshaw, Margaret Mitchell**
See Mitchell, Margaret (Munnerlyn)

**Upton, Mark**
See Sanders, Lawrence

**Urdang, Constance (Henriette)**
1922- ...................... **CLC 47**
See also CA 21-24R; CANR 9, 24

**Uris, Leon (Marcus)** 1924- ...... **CLC 7, 32**
See also AITN 1, 2; BEST 89:2; CA 1-4R;
CANR 1; MTCW; SATA 49

**Urmuz**
See Codrescu, Andrei

**Ustinov, Peter (Alexander)** 1921- .... **CLC 1**
See also AITN 1; CA 13-16R; CANR 25;
DLB 13

**V**
See Chekhov, Anton (Pavlovich)

**Vaculik, Ludvik** 1926- ............. **CLC 7**
See also CA 53-56

**Valenzuela, Luisa** 1938- .......... **CLC 31**
See also CA 101; CANR 32; DLB 113; HW

**Valera y Alcala-Galiano, Juan**
1824-1905 ................. **TCLC 10**
See also CA 106

**Valery, (Ambroise) Paul (Toussaint Jules)**
1871-1945 ............. **TCLC 4, 15**
See also CA 104; 122; MTCW

**Valle-Inclan, Ramon (Maria) del**
1866-1936 ................... **TCLC 5**
See also CA 106

**Vallejo, Antonio Buero**
See Buero Vallejo, Antonio

**Vallejo, Cesar (Abraham)**
1892-1938 .................. **TCLC 3**
See also CA 105; HW

**Valle Y Pena, Ramon del**
See Valle-Inclan, Ramon (Maria) del

**Van Ash, Cay** 1918- .............. **CLC 34**

**Vanbrugh, Sir John** 1664-1726 ...... **LC 21**
See also DLB 80

**Van Campen, Karl**
See Campbell, John W(ood Jr.)

**Vance, Gerald**
See Silverberg, Robert

**Vance, Jack** ..................... **CLC 35**
See also Vance, John Holbrook
See also DLB 8

**Vance, John Holbrook** 1916-
See Queen, Ellery; Vance, Jack
See also CA 29-32R; CANR 17; MTCW

**Van Den Bogarde, Derek Jules Gaspard Ulric
Niven** 1921-
See Bogarde, Dirk
See also CA 77-80

**Vandenburgh, Jane** ............... **CLC 59**

**Vanderhaeghe, Guy** 1951- ......... **CLC 41**
See also CA 113

**van der Post, Laurens (Jan)** 1906- ... **CLC 5**
See also CA 5-8R; CANR 35

**van de Wetering, Janwillem** 1931- .. **CLC 47**
See also CA 49-52; CANR 4

**Van Dine, S. S.** ................... **TCLC 23**
See also Wright, Willard Huntington

**Van Doren, Carl (Clinton)**
1885-1950 ................. **TCLC 18**
See also CA 111

**Van Doren, Mark** 1894-1972 ..... **CLC 6, 10**
See also CA 1-4R; 37-40R; CANR 3;
DLB 45; MTCW

**Wakoski, Diane**
1937-. . . . . . . . . . **CLC 2, 4, 7, 9, 11, 40**
See also CA 13-16R; CAAS 1; CANR 9;
DLB 5

**Wakoski-Sherbell, Diane**
See Wakoski, Diane

**Walcott, Derek (Alton)**
1930-. . . . . . . **CLC 2, 4, 9, 14, 25, 42, 67**
See also BLC 3; BW; CA 89-92; CANR 26;
DLB 117; DLBY 81; MTCW

**Waldman, Anne** 1945- . . . . . . . . . . . . . **CLC 7**
See also CA 37-40R; CANR 34; DLB 16

**Waldo, E. Hunter**
See Sturgeon, Theodore (Hamilton)

**Waldo, Edward Hamilton**
See Sturgeon, Theodore (Hamilton)

**Walker, Alice (Malsenior)**
1944- . . . . . . **CLC 5, 6, 9, 19, 27, 46, 58;**
**SSC 5**
See also AAYA 3; BEST 89:4; BLC 3; BW;
CA 37-40R; CANR 9, 27;
CDALB 1968-1988; DLB 6, 33; MTCW;
SATA 31

**Walker, David Harry** 1911-1992. . . . **CLC 14**
See also CA 1-4R; 137; CANR 1; SATA 8;
SATO 71

**Walker, Edward Joseph** 1934-
See Walker, Ted
See also CA 21-24R; CANR 12, 28

**Walker, George F.** 1947- . . . . . . . **CLC 44, 61**
See also CA 103; CANR 21; DLB 60

**Walker, Joseph A.** 1935- . . . . . . . . . . **CLC 19**
See also BW; CA 89-92; CANR 26; DLB 38

**Walker, Margaret (Abigail)**
1915- . . . . . . . . . . . . . . . . . . . **CLC 1, 6**
See also BLC 3; BW; CA 73-76; CANR 26;
DLB 76; MTCW

**Walker, Ted**. . . . . . . . . . . . . . . . . . **CLC 13**
See also Walker, Edward Joseph
See also DLB 40

**Wallace, David Foster** 1962- . . . . . . . **CLC 50**
See also CA 132

**Wallace, Dexter**
See Masters, Edgar Lee

**Wallace, Irving** 1916-1990. . . . . . . **CLC 7, 13**
See also AITN 1; CA 1-4R; 132; CAAS 1;
CANR 1, 27; MTCW

**Wallant, Edward Lewis**
1926-1962 . . . . . . . . . . . . . . . **CLC 5, 10**
See also CA 1-4R; CANR 22; DLB 2, 28;
MTCW

**Walpole, Horace** 1717-1797. . . . . . . . . **LC 2**
See also DLB 39, 104

**Walpole, Hugh (Seymour)**
1884-1941 . . . . . . . . . . . . . . . . . **TCLC 5**
See also CA 104; DLB 34

**Walser, Martin** 1927- . . . . . . . . . . . . **CLC 27**
See also CA 57-60; CANR 8; DLB 75

**Walser, Robert** 1878-1956. . . . . . . **TCLC 18**
See also CA 118; DLB 66

**Walsh, Jill Paton**. . . . . . . . . . . . . . . **CLC 35**
See also Paton Walsh, Gillian
See also CLR 2; SAAS 3

**Walter, Villiam Christian**
See Andersen, Hans Christian

**Wambaugh, Joseph (Aloysius Jr.)**
1937- . . . . . . . . . . . . . . . . . . **CLC 3, 18**
See also AITN 1; BEST 89:3; CA 33-36R;
DLB 6; DLBY 83; MTCW

**Ward, Arthur Henry Sarsfield** 1883-1959
See Rohmer, Sax
See also CA 108

**Ward, Douglas Turner** 1930-. . . . . . **CLC 19**
See also BW; CA 81-84; CANR 27; DLB 7,
38

**Warhol, Andy** 1928(?)-1987. . . . . . . **CLC 20**
See also BEST 89:4; CA 89-92; 121;
CANR 34

**Warner, Francis (Robert le Plastrier)**
1937- . . . . . . . . . . . . . . . . . . . . **CLC 14**
See also CA 53-56; CANR 11

**Warner, Marina** 1946-. . . . . . . . . . . **CLC 59**
See also CA 65-68; CANR 21

**Warner, Rex (Ernest)** 1905-1986. . . . **CLC 45**
See also CA 89-92; 119; DLB 15

**Warner, Susan (Bogert)**
1819-1885 . . . . . . . . . . . . . . . . **NCLC 31**
See also DLB 3, 42

**Warner, Sylvia (Constance) Ashton**
See Ashton-Warner, Sylvia (Constance)

**Warner, Sylvia Townsend**
1893-1978 . . . . . . . . . . . . . . . **CLC 7, 19**
See also CA 61-64; 77-80; CANR 16;
DLB 34; MTCW

**Warren, Mercy Otis** 1728-1814. . . **NCLC 13**
See also DLB 31

**Warren, Robert Penn**
1905-1989 . . . **CLC 1, 4, 6, 8, 10, 13, 18,**
**39, 53, 59; SSC 4**
See also AITN 1; CA 13-16R; 129;
CANR 10; CDALB 1968-1988; DLB 2,
48; DLBY 80, 89; MTCW; SATA 46, 63;
WLC

**Warshofsky, Isaac**
See Singer, Isaac Bashevis

**Warton, Thomas** 1728-1790. . . . . . . . **LC 15**
See also DLB 104, 109

**Waruk, Kona**
See Harris, (Theodore) Wilson

**Warung, Price** 1855-1911. . . . . . . . **TCLC 45**

**Warwick, Jarvis**
See Garner, Hugh

**Washington, Alex**
See Harris, Mark

**Washington, Booker T(aliaferro)**
1856-1915 . . . . . . . . . . . . . . . . **TCLC 10**
See also BLC 3; BW; CA 114; 125;
SATA 28

**Wassermann, (Karl) Jakob**
1873-1934 . . . . . . . . . . . . . . . . . **TCLC 6**
See also CA 104; DLB 66

**Wasserstein, Wendy** 1950-. . . . . . **CLC 32, 59**
See also CA 121; 129; CABS 3

**Waterhouse, Keith (Spencer)**
1929- . . . . . . . . . . . . . . . . . . . . **CLC 47**
See also CA 5-8R; CANR 38; DLB 13, 15;
MTCW

**Waters, Roger** 1944-. . . . . . . . . . . . . **CLC 35**
See also Pink Floyd

**Watkins, Frances Ellen**
See Harper, Frances Ellen Watkins

**Watkins, Gerrold**
See Malzberg, Barry N(athaniel)

**Watkins, Paul** 1964-. . . . . . . . . . . . . **CLC 55**
See also CA 132

**Watkins, Vernon Phillips**
1906-1967 . . . . . . . . . . . . . . . . **CLC 43**
See also CA 9-10; 25-28R; CAP 1; DLB 20

**Watson, Irving S.**
See Mencken, H(enry) L(ouis)

**Watson, John H.**
See Farmer, Philip Jose

**Watson, Richard F.**
See Silverberg, Robert

**Waugh, Auberon (Alexander)** 1939-. . . **CLC 7**
See also CA 45-48; CANR 6, 22; DLB 14

**Waugh, Evelyn (Arthur St. John)**
1903-1966 . . . **CLC 1, 3, 8, 13, 19, 27, 44**
See also CA 85-88; 25-28R; CANR 22;
CDBLB 1914-1945; DLB 15; MTCW;
WLC

**Waugh, Harriet** 1944- . . . . . . . . . . . . **CLC 6**
See also CA 85-88; CANR 22

**Ways, C. R.**
See Blount, Roy (Alton) Jr.

**Waystaff, Simon**
See Swift, Jonathan

**Webb, (Martha) Beatrice (Potter)**
1858-1943 . . . . . . . . . . . . . . . . **TCLC 22**
See also Potter, Beatrice
See also CA 117

**Webb, Charles (Richard)** 1939-. . . . . . **CLC 7**
See also CA 25-28R

**Webb, James H(enry) Jr.** 1946- . . . . **CLC 22**
See also CA 81-84

**Webb, Mary (Gladys Meredith)**
1881-1927 . . . . . . . . . . . . . . . . **TCLC 24**
See also CA 123; DLB 34

**Webb, Mrs. Sidney**
See Webb, (Martha) Beatrice (Potter)

**Webb, Phyllis** 1927-. . . . . . . . . . . . . **CLC 18**
See also CA 104; CANR 23; DLB 53

**Webb, Sidney (James)**
1859-1947 . . . . . . . . . . . . . . . . **TCLC 22**
See also CA 117

**Webber, Andrew Lloyd**. . . . . . . . . . . **CLC 21**
See also Lloyd Webber, Andrew

**Weber, Lenora Mattingly**
1895-1971 . . . . . . . . . . . . . . . . **CLC 12**
See also CA 19-20; 29-32R; CAP 1;
SATA 2, 26

**Webster, John** 1579(?)-1634(?) . . . . . . . **DC 2**
See also CDBLB Before 1660; DLB 58;
WLC

**Webster, Noah** 1758-1843 . . . . . . . **NCLC 30**

**Wedekind, (Benjamin) Frank(lin)**
1864-1918 . . . . . . . . . . . . . . . . . **TCLC 7**
See also CA 104; DLB 118

**Weidman, Jerome** 1913-. . . . . . . . . . . **CLC 7**
See also AITN 2; CA 1-4R; CANR 1;
DLB 28

**Wicker, Tom** . . . . . . . . . . . . . . . . . . . . . CLC 7
See also Wicker, Thomas Grey

**Wideman, John Edgar**
1941- . . . . . . . . . . . . . . CLC 5, 34, 36, 67
See also BLC 3; BW; CA 85-88; CANR 14;
DLB 33

**Wiebe, Rudy (H.)** 1934- . . . . . . CLC 6, 11, 14
See also CA 37-40R; DLB 60

**Wieland, Christoph Martin**
1733-1813 . . . . . . . . . . . . . . . . NCLC 17
See also DLB 97

**Wieners, John** 1934- . . . . . . . . . . . . . . CLC 7
See also CA 13-16R; DLB 16

**Wiesel, Elie(zer)** 1928- . . . . . CLC 3, 5, 11, 37
See also AAYA 7; AITN 1; CA 5-8R;
CAAS 4; CANR 8; DLB 83; DLBY 87;
MTCW; SATA 56

**Wiggins, Marianne** 1947- . . . . . . . . . CLC 57
See also BEST 89:3; CA 130

**Wight, James Alfred** 1916-
See Herriot, James
See also CA 77-80; SATA 44, 55

**Wilbur, Richard (Purdy)**
1921- . . . . . . . . . . . . . CLC 3, 6, 9, 14, 53
See also CA 1-4R; CABS 2; CANR 2, 29;
DLB 5; MTCW; SATA 9

**Wild, Peter** 1940- . . . . . . . . . . . . . . . CLC 14
See also CA 37-40R; DLB 5

**Wilde, Oscar (Fingal O'Flahertie Wills)**
1854(?)-1900 . . . . . . . TCLC 1, 8, 23, 41;
SSC 11
See also CA 104; 119; CDBLB 1890-1914;
DLB 10, 19, 34, 57; SATA 24; WLC

**Wilder, Billy** . . . . . . . . . . . . . . . . . . . CLC 20
See also Wilder, Samuel
See also DLB 26

**Wilder, Samuel** 1906-
See Wilder, Billy
See also CA 89-92

**Wilder, Thornton (Niven)**
1897-1975 . . . . . CLC 1, 5, 6, 10, 15, 35;
DC 1
See also AITN 2; CA 13-16R; 61-64;
DLB 4, 7, 9; MTCW; WLC

**Wilding, Michael** 1942- . . . . . . . . . . . CLC 73
See also CA 104; CANR 24

**Wiley, Richard** 1944- . . . . . . . . . . . . . CLC 44
See also CA 121; 129

**Wilhelm, Kate** . . . . . . . . . . . . . . . . . . CLC 7
See also Wilhelm, Katie Gertrude
See also CAAS 5; DLB 8

**Wilhelm, Katie Gertrude** 1928-
See Wilhelm, Kate
See also CA 37-40R; CANR 17, 36; MTCW

**Wilkins, Mary**
See Freeman, Mary Eleanor Wilkins

**Willard, Nancy** 1936- . . . . . . . . . . . CLC 7, 37
See also CA 89-92; CANR 10, 39; CLR 5;
DLB 5, 52; MAICYA; MTCW;
SATA 30, 37, 71

**Williams, C(harles) K(enneth)**
1936- . . . . . . . . . . . . . . . . . . CLC 33, 56
See also CA 37-40R; DLB 5

**Williams, Charles**
See Collier, James L(incoln)

**Williams, Charles (Walter Stansby)**
1886-1945 . . . . . . . . . . . . . . . TCLC 1, 11
See also CA 104; DLB 100

**Williams, (George) Emlyn**
1905-1987 . . . . . . . . . . . . . . . . . . CLC 15
See also CA 104; 123; CANR 36; DLB 10,
77; MTCW

**Williams, Hugo** 1942- . . . . . . . . . . . . CLC 42
See also CA 17-20R; DLB 40

**Williams, J. Walker**
See Wodehouse, P(elham) G(renville)

**Williams, John A(lfred)** 1925- . . . . CLC 5, 13
See also BLC 3; BW; CA 53-56; CAAS 3;
CANR 6, 26; DLB 2, 33

**Williams, Jonathan (Chamberlain)**
1929- . . . . . . . . . . . . . . . . . . . . . CLC 13
See also CA 9-12R; CAAS 12; CANR 8;
DLB 5

**Williams, Joy** 1944- . . . . . . . . . . . . . CLC 31
See also CA 41-44R; CANR 22

**Williams, Norman** 1952- . . . . . . . . . CLC 39
See also CA 118

**Williams, Tennessee**
1911-1983 . . . . CLC 1, 2, 5, 7, 8, 11, 15,
19, 30, 39, 45, 71
See also AITN 1, 2; CA 5-8R; 108;
CABS 3; CANR 31; CDALB 1941-1968;
DLB 7; DLBD 4; DLBY 83; MTCW;
WLC

**Williams, Thomas (Alonzo)**
1926-1990 . . . . . . . . . . . . . . . . . . CLC 14
See also CA 1-4R; 132; CANR 2

**Williams, William C.**
See Williams, William Carlos

**Williams, William Carlos**
1883-1963 . . . CLC 1, 2, 5, 9, 13, 22, 42,
67
See also CA 89-92; CANR 34;
CDALB 1917-1929; DLB 4, 16, 54, 86;
MTCW

**Williamson, David Keith** 1942- . . . . . CLC 56
See also CA 103

**Williamson, Jack** . . . . . . . . . . . . . . . CLC 29
See also Williamson, John Stewart
See also CAAS 8; DLB 8

**Williamson, John Stewart** 1908-
See Williamson, Jack
See also CA 17-20R; CANR 23

**Willie, Frederick**
See Lovecraft, H(oward) P(hillips)

**Willingham, Calder (Baynard Jr.)**
1922- . . . . . . . . . . . . . . . . . . . CLC 5, 51
See also CA 5-8R; CANR 3; DLB 2, 44;
MTCW

**Willis, Charles**
See Clarke, Arthur C(harles)

**Willy**
See Colette, (Sidonie-Gabrielle)

**Willy, Colette**
See Colette, (Sidonie-Gabrielle)

**Wilson, A(ndrew) N(orman)** 1950- . . CLC 33
See also CA 112; 122; DLB 14

**Wilson, Angus (Frank Johnstone)**
1913-1991 . . . . . . . . . CLC 2, 3, 5, 25, 34
See also CA 5-8R; 134; CANR 21; DLB 15;
MTCW

**Wilson, August**
1945- . . . . . . . . . . CLC 39, 50, 63; DC 2
See also BLC 3; BW; CA 115; 122; MTCW

**Wilson, Brian** 1942- . . . . . . . . . . . . . CLC 12

**Wilson, Colin** 1931- . . . . . . . . . . . CLC 3, 14
See also CA 1-4R; CAAS 5; CANR 1, 22,
33; DLB 14; MTCW

**Wilson, Dirk**
See Pohl, Frederik

**Wilson, Edmund**
1895-1972 . . . . . . . . . CLC 1, 2, 3, 8, 24
See also CA 1-4R; 37-40R; CANR 1;
DLB 63; MTCW

**Wilson, Ethel Davis (Bryant)**
1888(?)-1980 . . . . . . . . . . . . . . . . CLC 13
See also CA 102; DLB 68; MTCW

**Wilson, John (Anthony) Burgess**
1917- . . . . . . . . . . . . . . . . . CLC 8, 10, 13
See also Burgess, Anthony
See also CA 1-4R; CANR 2; MTCW

**Wilson, John** 1785-1854 . . . . . . . . . . NCLC 5

**Wilson, Lanford** 1937- . . . . . . . CLC 7, 14, 36
See also CA 17-20R; CABS 3; DLB 7

**Wilson, Robert M.** 1944- . . . . . . . . . CLC 7, 9
See also CA 49-52; CANR 2; MTCW

**Wilson, Robert McLiam** 1964- . . . . . CLC 59
See also CA 132

**Wilson, Sloan** 1920- . . . . . . . . . . . . . CLC 32
See also CA 1-4R; CANR 1

**Wilson, Snoo** 1948- . . . . . . . . . . . . . . CLC 33
See also CA 69-72

**Wilson, William S(mith)** 1932- . . . . . CLC 49
See also CA 81-84

**Winchilsea, Anne (Kingsmill) Finch Counte**
1661-1720 . . . . . . . . . . . . . . . . . . . . LC 3

**Windham, Basil**
See Wodehouse, P(elham) G(renville)

**Wingrove, David (John)** 1954- . . . . . . CLC 68
See also CA 133

**Winters, Janet Lewis** . . . . . . . . . . . . . CLC 41
See also Lewis, Janet
See also DLBY 87

**Winters, (Arthur) Yvor**
1900-1968 . . . . . . . . . . . . . CLC 4, 8, 32
See also CA 11-12; 25-28R; CAP 1;
DLB 48; MTCW

**Winterson, Jeanette** 1959- . . . . . . . . . CLC 64
See also CA 136

**Wiseman, Frederick** 1930- . . . . . . . . . CLC 20

**Wister, Owen** 1860-1938 . . . . . . . . . TCLC 21
See also CA 108; DLB 9, 78; SATA 62

**Witkacy**
See Witkiewicz, Stanislaw Ignacy

**Witkiewicz, Stanislaw Ignacy**
1885-1939 . . . . . . . . . . . . . . . . . . TCLC 8
See also CA 105

**Wittig, Monique** 1935(?)- . . . . . . . . . . CLC 22
See also CA 116; 135; DLB 83

**Wittlin, Jozef** 1896-1976 . . . . . . . . . CLC 25
See also CA 49-52; 65-68; CANR 3

Zangwill, Israel   1864-1926....... **TCLC 16**
  See also CA 109; DLB 10

Zappa, Francis Vincent Jr.   1940-
  See Zappa, Frank
  See also CA 108

Zappa, Frank.................... **CLC 17**
  See also Zappa, Francis Vincent Jr.

Zaturenska, Marya   1902-1982.... **CLC 6, 11**
  See also CA 13-16R; 105; CANR 22

Zelazny, Roger (Joseph)   1937- ..... **CLC 21**
  See also AAYA 7; CA 21-24R; CANR 26;
    DLB 8; MTCW; SATA 39, 57

Zhdanov, Andrei A(lexandrovich)
    1896-1948 ................. **TCLC 18**
  See also CA 117

Zhukovsky, Vasily   1783-1852 .... **NCLC 35**

Ziegenhagen, Eric ................ **CLC 55**

Zimmer, Jill Schary
  See Robinson, Jill

Zimmerman, Robert
  See Dylan, Bob

Zindel, Paul   1936- ............. **CLC 6, 26**
  See also AAYA 2; CA 73-76; CANR 31;
    CLR 3; DLB 7, 52; MAICYA; MTCW;
    SATA 16, 58

Zinov'Ev, A. A.
  See Zinoviev, Alexander (Aleksandrovich)

Zinoviev, Alexander (Aleksandrovich)
    1922- ...................... **CLC 19**
  See also CA 116; 133; CAAS 10

Zoilus
  See Lovecraft, H(oward) P(hillips)

Zola, Emile (Edouard Charles Antoine)
    1840-1902 ......... **TCLC 1, 6, 21, 41**
  See also CA 104; 138; DLB 123; WLC

Zoline, Pamela   1941- ............. **CLC 62**

Zorrilla y Moral, Jose   1817-1893.. **NCLC 6**

Zoshchenko, Mikhail (Mikhailovich)
    1895-1958 ................. **TCLC 15**
  See also CA 115

Zuckmayer, Carl   1896-1977....... **CLC 18**
  See also CA 69-72; DLB 56

Zuk, Georges
  See Skelton, Robin

Zukofsky, Louis
    1904-1978 ....... **CLC 1, 2, 4, 7, 11, 18**
  See also CA 9-12R; 77-80; CANR 39;
    DLB 5; MTCW

Zweig, Paul   1935-1984........ **CLC 34, 42**
  See also CA 85-88; 113

Zweig, Stefan   1881-1942 ........ **TCLC 17**
  See also CA 112; DLB 81, 118

# Literary Criticism Series
# Cumulative Topic Index

This index lists all topic entries in the Gale Literary Criticism Series *Contemporary Literary Criticism, Literature Criticism from 1400 to 1800, Nineteenth-Century Literature Criticism,* and *Twentieth-Century Literary Criticism.*

# *NCLC* Cumulative Nationality Index

Nationality Index